Macroeconomic Analysis
Fifth Edition

Macroeconomic Analysis
Fifth Edition

Edward Shapiro
University of Toledo

Harcourt Brace Jovanovich, Inc.
New York San Diego Chicago San Francisco Atlanta
London Sydney Toronto

To the memory of my father

Cover art by Al Held, *Inversion VIII,* 1977, from the collection of Paul and Camille Oliver Hoffmann, courtesy André Emmerich Gallery, Inc.

Printed in the United States of America

Library of Congress Catalog Card Number: 81-82171

ISBN: 0-15-551215-3

Preface

Professors who have used *Macroeconomic Analysis* in previous editions may require a second glance to recognize this latest incarnation. Several major and countless smaller changes have been made. However, one feature that remains unchanged is the book's objective of providing a treatment of macroeconomic measurement, theory, and policy designed specifically for students whose economics background is limited to the customary year of introductory survey work. Furthermore, it is not assumed that students have thoroughly absorbed all the macroeconomics to which they were exposed in their survey work. Many textbooks devote one chapter to reviewing this basic material; this text continues to give basic macroeconomics a more lengthy treatment (Chapters 4–7).

Also, unlike many others, this text does not require that students bridge the huge gap between elementary and graduate level macroeconomics in the one-quarter or one-semester course usually devoted to the subject. The theoretical analysis is sufficiently rigorous to provide students with a solid grasp of the generally recognized fundamentals of macroeconomic analysis, but it is not so advanced that the student is likely to become lost in a sea of unfathomable abstractions.

As in preceding editions, the material is presented essentially in non-algebraic form. It has been argued that there are no important ideas in economics that cannot be explained in carefully written English. Written explanations supplemented by diagrams remain the basic tool employed in this book. The effectiveness of the diagrams has been enhanced in this edition through the use of color. The contrast provided by color obviously becomes especially beneficial in complicated diagrams that require the student to grasp the relationships among three or more curves.

Organizational Changes_____

Instructors will probably agree that the details on consumption and invest-ment—for example, the various consumption hypotheses and the various theories of investment—are more appropriately covered (if they are cov-ered at all) after the development of the *IS–LM* model. Accordingly, the three chapters devoted to the development of the *IS–LM* model have been moved forward to permit an unbroken flow as the analysis proceeds from the simplest Keynesian model in Chapters 4–7 through some prerequisite material in Chapters 8–11 to the *IS–LM* model in Chapters 12–14. This reorganization has beneficial side effects. For example, we can now con-sider issues in investment theory which were precluded in preceding edi-tions by the fact that investment theory was discussed before the *IS–LM* model was in place.

Another organizational change is the postponement of the integration of aggregate supply and aggregate demand *as functions of the price level* into the analysis until the *IS–LM* framework has been developed. In the previous edition, this was done as soon as the simple Keynesian model had been constructed. It was believed that this innovation would promote student understanding; however, it does not appear to have had that sal-utary effect. Therefore, this edition returns to the customary procedure.

Also of an organizational nature is the addition of introductory overviews to each chapter. These identify the subject matter of each chapter and describe how the chapter has been structured to develop it. If students can discern the route that will be followed from the beginning to the end of a chapter, they are likely to better understand the ideas encountered along the way.

Substantive Changes_____

Three new chapters have been added to the Fifth Edition. The previous edition gave only passing mention to the process by which the money supply grows and the tools with which the Federal Reserve controls this growth. This edition's new Chapter 10 is devoted entirely to the money supply process and its control. The previous edition gave considerable attention to inflation, but probably less than this overwhelming problem warrants. Chapter 21, "Inflation: Definitions, Measures, and Effects," has been so extensively rewritten and expanded as to almost qualify as a new chapter. This edition extends the coverage from two to three chapters (21–23) by adding a new chapter (23) on "Inflation and Unemployment." The previous edition touched lightly on incomes policy; this edition devotes all of a new Chapter 24 to it. A large part of this chapter is concerned with tax-based incomes policy (TIP), which is of keen interest to those who believe that inflation can best be controlled through a judicious incomes policy. (To make room for these new chapters as well as the expansion of others, the preceding edition's chapter on "Business Cycle Theory" and the long appendix on "National Income Accounting" were dropped.)

Numerous additions of less-than-chapter length were also made. In Chapter 1, the historical record of aggregate output, employment, and inflation is integrated with a discussion of the development of macroeconomic theory from the pre-Keynesian (or old classical) theory to the new classical theory of the rational expectationists. In Chapter 15, the life-cycle hypothesis has been included so that the chapter now presents all four consumption hypotheses. In Chapter 18, a section on the derivation and implications of the upward-sloping *LM* curve has been added. Chapter 20 now provides a diagrammatic model of the popular "supply-side" economics embraced by the Reagan administration. Chapter 21 includes a section on the different measures of inflation, an examination of the case against the use of the Consumer Price Index for indexation, and a section on "who wins" and "who loses" from inflation. Chapter 22 now offers an analysis of supply-shock inflation and an explanation of how supply management might use fiscal policy to combat various kinds of supply-side inflation. In examining the issue of whether the money supply or interest rates serve as the better guide to monetary policy, Chapter 26 now employs the *IS–LM* framework to show that the answer varies with different sets of conditions. Chapter 26 also includes a section on Federal funds targeting versus reserve targeting to control the monetary aggregates. Dozens of other additions of shorter length appear throughout the book.

Suggestions for a "Short Course"————

More material has been added for this edition than has been deleted. This results in a text that contains more material than can be covered in the usual one-semester or one-quarter course. However, as stated in the preceding edition, because not all instructors assign the same importance to various topics, a longer book from which individual instructors may omit less important topics seems more useful than a shorter book that denies any such choice. The reorganized chapter sequence now allows considerable flexibility in omitting chapters or sections of chapters without producing significant breaks in continuity.

Although most instructors will probably find Chapter 1 useful for its discussion of the evolution of modern macroeconomic theory, the historical record of national output, unemployment, and inflation, it can be omitted. Chapter 2 offers a minimum introduction to national income accounting and is definitely needed for the subsequent work in theory. However, the sections of this chapter that consider special problems in national income accounting (imputations, inventory valuation adjustment, and capital consumption adjustment) as well as the final section on the relationship between national product and national welfare may be dropped. Chapter

3, "Basic Concepts," may be omitted, or perhaps assigned for self-study as it is a fairly easy chapter.

Part 2, Chapters 4–7, develops the simple Keynesian model. The material here is, of course, part of the foundation for the *IS* curve and is therefore essential. However, it is also basically an elaboration (including an algebraic formulation) of introductory course material. Those instructors who choose to exclude the international sector from their course will omit Chapter 7, "Foreign Spending," and Chapter 14, "The Extended Model: Foreign Sector Included," which combines the *BP* (balance of payments) curve with the *IS* and *LM* curves. (Chapter 7 may be included with Chapter 14 excluded, but not vice versa.)

In Part 3, Chapter 8, "The Aggregate Supply Function: Keynesian and Classical," is essential to an understanding of the *IS–LM* model developed in Chapters 12–14. Those who do not wish to work through "The Simple Classical Model" in the detail provided by Chapter 9 may limit their attention to pages 148–55 and 163–69, which are essential to an understanding of Chapter 11 (in which the development of the Keynesian theory of the demand for money assumes that the reader is familiar with the simple quantity theory of money) and Chapter 13 (in which the "classical aggregate demand curve" plays a role). Although Chapter 10, "The Money Supply Process," covers an important subject area, the last two sections of the chapter—"Deposit Expansion and Contraction: Three Complications" and "Treasury Financing and the Money Supply" may be excluded. Chapter 11, "The Supply of and Demand for Money and the Rate of Interest," is a prerequisite to the following three chapters; however, the last section, "The Demand for Money from Simple Quantity Theory to Modern Quantity Theory," may be dropped without causing later difficulties.

If there is not enough time to work through all of the *IS–LM* material in Chapters 12–14, a large portion of Chapter 13 (pages 266–77) may be omitted; this section covers the classical theory's argument that wage and price deflation will eliminate unemployment, Keynes' attack on this argument, and the Pigovian reply. Despite this omission, the last section of the chapter—"Monetary and Fiscal Policies and the Full Employment Equilibrium"—is still manageable, particularly if the instructor briefly explains how deflation shifts the *IS* curve rightward. If these pages of Chapter 13 are omitted, the only material in the following chapters that must also be omitted is the section in Chapter 14—"Wage-Price Flexibility and Full Employment"—that extends the analysis of wage-price deflation to an economy including an international sector.

Instructors who choose to exclude all or part of the body of Chapter 14 may still want to include the "Concluding Note," part of which offers a fourteen-part diagrammatic summary of the theory developed through the preceding chapters. Because this graphic system incorporates the foreign sector, it cannot be followed in its entirety without an understanding of Chapter 14. However, by ignoring Parts J, K, and L and the *BP* curve of Part D, the balance of the system should still be meaningful.

For Parts 4 and 5, Chapters 15–26, there is almost complete flexibility. If time is short, one may go directly from the *IS–LM* analysis of Chapters 12–14 to the discussions of inflation in Chapters 21–23. However, for those who want to devote some time to consumption and investment, the following notes will be of interest.

One may cover all four of Chapter 15's consumption hypotheses or any one alone may be studied by simply omitting the material under the headings of the other three. Anyone who may want to cover the nonincome influences on consumption but to omit the income influences is free to exclude Chapter 15 and include Chapter 16 (except for item 3, pages 357–59). The way that investment theory is developed in Chapters 18 and 19 makes Chapter 17 a prerequisite. In Chapter 18, the second section on the accelerator theory may be covered without the first section on the profits theory. Similarly, the second section of Chapter 19 may be covered without the first part of that chapter. Also, Chapter 19 may be considered in whole or in part without working through Chapter 18.

In Part 5, Chapter 20 is not a prerequisite to any of the material in the remaining six chapters. However, the accelerator theory section of Chapter 18 is a prerequisite to the Harrod–Domar growth theory section of Chapter 20. One may work through Chapter 20's presentation of the popular "supply-side" model of growth, yet omit the earlier sections of this chapter (although some neo-classical growth theory is included in the supply-side model). In view of the current importance of inflation, many instructors may choose to cover all three chapters devoted to this subject. However, it is not essential to work through all of Chapter 21 before moving on to Chapters 22 and 23, although the brief first section on definition seems essential. One may turn to the final section of Chapter 21 on the effects of inflation without first covering the second section on the measures of inflation. It is possible to move directly from Chapter 21 to Chapter 23 with only a moderate break in continuity, but the omission of Chapter 22 will leave untouched some basic concepts and ideas concerning inflation. Chapter 22 examines the causes of inflation within the familiar framework of aggregate supply and aggregate demand. Anyone who so chooses may skip the third section—"Supply-Side Inflation: The Problem of Control"—and still cover the final section—"Supply-Side Inflation: Its Relation to Demand-Side Inflation"—without encountering any discontinuity. Chapter 23 extends the analysis of inflation beyond the conventional aggregate supply and demand curves. The rate of inflation replaces the price level; the rate of unemployment replaces the output level. In Chapter 23, the first two major sections—"The Elements of the Model" and "The Phillips Curve: Tradeoff and Non-Tradeoff"—must be worked through in their entirety. Although the third major section takes up four of the most interesting topics in inflation, any or all of these may be omitted.

Instructors who want to concentrate the time available for policy on fiscal and monetary policy may omit Chapter 24, "Incomes Policy." Those who wish to give some attention to incomes policy but less than is provided by Chapter 24 may omit without discontinuity the section that surveys U.S. experience with incomes policy over the last twenty years. Finally, anyone who wants to cover only monetary policy (Chapter 26) may skip Chapter 25 (fiscal policy). Both Chapter 25 and Chapter 26 are divided into three major sections which, to a large degree, are independent.

Although these notes reveal what can be omitted from the book as written, they do nothing for the instructor who finds that material he or she believes should be included has been omitted. An author's choices are almost unlimited. I can only hope that what I have included provides a well-balanced coverage of what most instructors believe is appropriate for a course at this level.

I also hope that the Fifth Edition of *Macroeconomic Analysis* contains fewer of the ambiguities and inconsistencies that seem to occur in even the most carefully written text. Over the fifteen years since this book first appeared, many teachers and students have been kind enough to point out such difficulties. I am indebted to all of them, particularly to those who pointed out such difficulties in the Fourth Edition. I would also like to acknowledge the suggestions of Professors James M. Rock, University of Utah, and Robert Renshaw, Northern Illinois University. I also want to thank Jack Thomas of Harcourt Brace Jovanovich for an efficient, thorough editing of this Fifth Edition.

Edward Shapiro

Contents

PART FOUR

The Theory of Consumption and Investment Spending

Macroeconomic Analysis
Fifth Edition

Introduction:
Measurement
and Concepts

1

The Meaning of Macro-economics

OVERVIEW

Although there is actually only "one" economics, the overall field is divided into two areas which in turn are very broad: microeconomics and macroeconomics. The first part of this chapter explains the difference between the two and notes why economists concentrated their attention on the area of microeconomics before the 1930s and why over the fifty years since then they have given so much more attention to macroeconomics.

Macroeconomics, in its briefest description, is the study of the economy's total output, employment, and the price level. The reason why it has received so much attention since the 1930s becomes apparent when we examine what may be called the macroeconomic record—that is, the record of the changes in total output, unemployment, and the price level over the last six decades.

The second part of the chapter provides a brief review of this record for the U.S. economy. The best measure of total output is the economy's real gross national product or real GNP. To the degree that the economy does not make full use of its resources, its *actual* real GNP falls below its *potential* GNP, which is what the real GNP would be under full employment of its resources. The spread between these is called the GNP gap. The Great Depression of the 1930s stands out because of a gap and a rate of unemployment unprecedented in the nation's history. It was the dismal performance of the economy in the 1930s and the appearance of a bombshell of a book by John Maynard Keynes in 1936 that gave rise to the great surge of interest in macroeconomics.

The review of the macroeconomic record from the 1920s to the 1980s, especially the disaster of the 1930s, helps us understand how macroeconomic theory developed. This is the subject of the third part of the chapter. Before the 1930s, the long-accepted classical theory of how aggregate output and employment are determined had been occasionally questioned but had not been successfully challenged. Keynes successfully challenged it in the 1930s. In the "new" economics of Keynes, many economists believed they saw the way to prevent not just another disaster like the Great Depression, but to rid ourselves of the small ups and downs of economic activity. The pre-Keynesian or classical economics accepted these as unavoidable, but also maintained they were self-correcting in short order. The enthusiasm for the Keynesian medicine reached a peak in the

1960s, then subsided in the 1970s as that medicine was found to be inadequate to meet the different kinds of problems confronting us then. Economists found that something more than what they had gotten from Keynes was needed.

The fourth part of the chapter briefly examines the varieties of macroeconomic theory. After Keynes' work appeared, for a time a simple division existed between classical and Keynesian macroeconomic theory. Then, from the pre-Keynesian classical theory developed neoclassical, monetarist, and most recently rational expectations or new classical theory. From Keynes' original theory developed neo-Keynesian and post-Keynesian theories, terms which have more than one meaning. For most of the work in this book, it will not be necessary to go beyond a comparison of classical and Keynesian theory.

The final part of this chapter offers a brief description of the plan of the book as a whole.

In a field of study that changes as fast as economics, anything that persists for more than a decade qualifies as "traditional." By this criterion, the division of most topics in economics into the two branches of macroeconomics and microeconomics is now traditional, these terms having been in general use for several decades.

Although some older terms are sometimes used to identify these two branches, they have never become part of the language of economics in the way that macroeconomics and microeconomics have over the past decades. In fact, until the 1930s there was little need to distinguish between the two branches; economists concentrated their attention almost exclusively on what is now traditionally known as microeconomics. Macroeconomics was clearly the junior partner. However, a new interest in macroeconomics arose after 1936, the year John Maynard Keynes published *The General Theory of Employment, Interest, and Money.*[1] That year marked the beginning of a change so momentous that some choose to call it the "Keynesian revolution." With the ferment begun by the ideas in Keynes' book, economists' relative neglect of macroeconomics ended.

Macroeconomics and Microeconomics

What specifically is the meaning of macroeconomics? To start with, here are a few short descriptions. "The term 'macro-economics' applies to the study of relations between broad economic aggregates."[2] "Macroeconomic theory is the theory of income, employment, prices and money."[3] Macroeconomics is "that part of economics which studies the overall averages and aggregates of the system."[4] And macroeconomics is "the study of the forces or factors that determine the levels of aggregate production, employment, and prices in an economy, and their rates of change over time."[5] None of these statements, or any other short statement that could be given, satisfactorily defines the term, and each author just quoted follows his short statement with several more sentences, paragraphs, or even pages in an attempt to give the term a clear meaning. Although they differ somewhat in emphasis, all such explanations emphasize the idea that macroeconomics deals with the functioning of the economy *as a whole,* including how the econ-

---

[1] John Maynard Keynes, *The General Theory of Employment, Interest, and Money,* Harcourt Brace Jovanovich, 1936. This work will hereafter be referred to as the *General Theory.*

[2] R.G.D. Allen, *Macro-Economic Theory,* St. Martins, 1967, p. 1.

[3] J.M. Culbertson, *Macroeconomic Theory and Stabilization Policy,* McGraw-Hill, 1968, p. 7.

[4] K.E. Boulding, *Economic Analysis,* Vol. II, 4th ed., Harper & Row, 1966, p. 1.

[5] G. Ackley, *Macroeconomics: Theory and Policy,* Macmillan, 1978, p. 3.

omy's total output of goods and services, the price level of goods and services and the total employment of resources are determined and what causes these magnitudes to fluctuate. Macroeconomics seeks to explain why at some times as little as 3 percent of the labor force is unemployed and at other times as much as 9 percent or even more, and why at some times there is full utilization of the economy's productive capacity as measured by its workers, factories, equipment, and technological know-how and why at other times a good part of this capacity goes to waste. It also seeks to explain why the total of goods and services produced grows at an average rate of 4 percent per year in one decade and at an average rate of 2 percent in another, and why in some time periods the price level rises sharply, whereas in others it remains stable or even falls. In short, macroeconomics attempts to deal with the truly "big" issues of economic life—full employment or unemployment, capacity or undercapacity production, a satisfactory or unsatisfactory rate of growth, inflation or price level stability.

In contrast, microeconomics is concerned, not with total output, total employment, or total spending, but with the output of particular goods and services by single firms or industries and with the spending on particular goods and services by single households or by households in single markets. The unit of study is the part rather than the whole. For example, microeconomics seeks to explain how the single firm determines the sale price for a particular product, what amount of output will maximize its profits, and how it determines the lowest cost combination of labor, materials, capital equipment, and other inputs needed to produce this output. It is also concerned with how the individual consumer determines the distribution of his or her total spending among the many products and services available so as to maximize utility. In its approach, microeconomics essentially assumes as *given* the total output, total employment, and total spending for all goods and services; it then proceeds to examine how output and employ-

ment are allocated among various individual industries and firms within industries and how the prices of the various products of these individual firms are established. Microeconomics asks how shifts in consumer spending from the product of one industry to that of another, or from the product of one firm within an industry to that of a competitor, will cause output and employment to be reallocated among different goods and services and among different industries and firms.

What microeconomics takes as *given*—the total output for the economy as a whole—is what macroeconomics takes as the prime *variable* whose size or value is to be determined. What macroeconomics takes as *given*—the distribution of output, employment, and total spending among the particular goods and services of individual industries and firms—are all *variables* in microeconomics. In regard to prices, what microeconomics takes as given—the general price level—macroeconomics takes as a variable; and what macroeconomics takes as given—the relative prices or exchange ratios among individual goods and services—microeconomics takes as variables.

Although such a sharp distinction helps to clarify the essential differences, the preceding discussion admittedly makes a much sharper distinction than can legitimately be made. Strictly speaking, there is only one "economics." Macroeconomic theory has a foundation in microeconomic theory and microeconomic theory has a foundation in macroeconomic theory. In practice, analysis of the economy is not conducted separately in two watertight compartments. As we analyze macroeconomic variables and their relationships, we must also allow for changes in microeconomic variables that may affect the macroeconomic variables and vice versa.[6] As we analyze the economic processes that determine the nation's material well-being,

---

[6]For example, to the extent that labor's geographical immobility is such that workers fail to move from an area whose industry is declining to another whose industry is growing, total output and total employment may be less than they would be with more mobility.

we must consider both macroeconomic and microeconomic aspects. From the macroeconomic point of view, the nation's material well-being will be greater the closer the economy comes to *full utilization* of its total resources, taking as given the allocation, good to bad, of the amount of these resources that are actually employed in the production of the economy's output. From the microeconomic point of view, material well-being will be greater the closer the economy comes to *optimum allocation* of its resources, taking as given the degree of utilization, partial to full, of its total resources. Clearly, the basic goal is the same from both points of view: the maximum material well-being for the population as a whole. This goal can only be attained with both full utilization and optimum allocation of all available resources.

The distinction just drawn between macroeconomics and microeconomics helps account for the shift of emphasis from the traditional concern with microeconomics to concern with the economy as a whole, a shift of emphasis that is generally recognized as a Keynesian phenomenon. Before the 1930s, economists emphasized microeconomics as if by default, because at the time it seemed there was little more to say about macroeconomics. The accepted macroeconomic theory of the day argued that total output was not really a variable but more in the nature of a constant in any short period, because its actual amount in any such period was simply whatever the fully employed economy could produce with the state of technology then existing. If this were indeed the case, the only relevant question would be whether or not these fully employed resources were being used to the best advantage—that is, whether or not they were optimally allocated among rival lines of production. However, if it were not in fact the case, the question of whether resources were being allocated to their best uses would lose much of its relevance.

Optimal allocation of resources assumes the greatest importance when those resources are being fully utilized; then there is truly a scarcity of resources. But in an economy operating substantially below full utilization, resources are not actually scarce, at least not at that time. To produce additional output of almost any kind under these conditions does not require that resources be diverted from the production of other kinds of output. The opportunity cost of producing additional output of almost any kind is close to zero as long as such output can be obtained by making use of otherwise idle resources. Therefore, to the extent that the economy departs from full utilization, macroeconomics assumes greater relative importance and microeconomics less relative importance.

The Macroeconomic Record in Brief

A major reason for the ascendancy in importance of macroeconomics is evident from a look at the actual record of resource utilization. How close an economy has come to achieving full utilization of its resources is best measured by how close the actual gross national product has come to the economy's potential gross national product. The *actual* gross national product or GNP is a measure of the market value of the output of final goods and services that are produced by an economy's resources during a specified time period, ordinarily a year.[7] The *potential* GNP is the market value of the output that would have been produced during that time period if there had been full utilization of the economy's resources. The difference between the two amounts is known as the GNP gap.

The market value of an economy's actual output will, of course, change from year to year not only due to changes in the physical quantity of goods and services actually produced, but due

[7]This general description of the meaning of GNP is adequate for present purposes. Chapter 2 goes into the meaning more fully. The coverage of some other topics is also limited to a general statement in this introductory chapter; fuller treatment is provided elsewhere in the book.

to changes in the prices at which those goods and services are valued. To compare what happened between years in real terms, changes in the market value of output from year to year which are due to changes in prices must be excluded or, in other words, the values of output for different years must be expressed in constant prices or in dollars of constant purchasing power.

In the following discussion, all figures are given in 1972 dollars. Accordingly, a figure for actual GNP for any year is a measure of what the actual output of final goods and services produced in that year would have been worth if it had been valued at 1972 prices. In the same way, the value for each year's potential output is in 1972 dollars. With actual and potential output measured in 1972 prices, the GNP gap for any year is also measured in 1972 prices. Because 1932 prices were far below 1972 prices, the GNP gap in 1932 is much larger than it would be if it were measured in 1932 prices; because prices in 1980 were substantially above what they were in 1972, the GNP gap in 1980 is much smaller than it would be if it were measured in 1980 prices.

Given any year's figure for actual GNP, the GNP gap for that year will be larger or smaller depending on the meaning we give to the concept of "full utilization of resources." A key element in this is the determination of the unemployment rate that is deemed consistent with full employment or full utilization of the labor force. For a year in which the actual unemployment rate is 7 percent, an economist who insists that we don't have full employment unless the unemployment rate is 5 percent or less will estimate a much larger GNP than will an economist who accepts a 6 percent unemployment rate as the full employment–unemployment rate. With a U.S. labor force of about 110 million people, the difference between these two percentages amounts to over 1 million workers. The potential output of an extra 1 million plus workers is obviously significant.

Whatever percentage is accepted as the full employment–unemployment percentage at any

time, the economy's annual potential output will grow simply due to the fact that a growing labor force means a proportional growth in *potential* employment. The growth in potential employment consistent with given growth in the labor force will vary inversely with the unemployment rate identified as the full employment–unemployment rate. Beyond the growth in potential output due to growth in potential employment is the growth due to change in the length of the average workweek. However, because the length of the workweek declines over time, this factor reduces the rate of growth of potential output. The last element is the growth in the average productivity or output per man-hour of labor. Once we know the growth rate for potential employment, the growth rate (negative) of the average workweek, and the growth rate of the average productivity of labor, we can obtain the growth rate of potential GNP by adding these three figures.

As developments in the economy appear to warrant, the Council of Economic Advisers (CEA) periodically revises its estimates of these three growth rates. For example, in its 1980 Annual Report, the CEA indicated a 2½ percent estimated annual growth rate of potential GNP for 1979–81. This was made up of an estimated annual growth rate in potential employment of approximately 2 percent, an estimated growth rate of labor productivity of about 1 percent, and an estimated 0.5 percent rate of decline in hours per week. From the 2½ percent growth rate, the estimated billions-of-dollars figure for 1979 potential GNP is then obtained simply by raising the earlier estimated billions-of-dollars figure for 1978 by 2½ percent, and so forth for 1980 and 1981. The CEA notes that figures for the dollar level of potential GNP are less meaningful than figures for the growth rate of potential GNP, but a diagram that shows the level of both potential and actual GNP over time and therefore shows how the GNP gap varies over time is informative. Before we examine a diagram of this kind for the period 1952–80, we will review the record for an earlier period.

The Record before the 1950s

The record before the 1950s is of special interest because what happened then goes far toward explaining why the study of macroeconomic questions later assumed such great importance. We refer to the disastrous experience of the 1930s during which the actual output levels of the United States and other industrialized countries dropped below their potential output levels to a degree never before and never since experienced. The subject of macroeconomics would be of secondary importance in an economy that operated almost continuously with full utilization of its resources; it becomes a subject of supreme importance in an economy that operates as so many economies did during the 1930s.

How bad were the 1930s?[8] For the decade as a whole, 1930–39, actual output was just over 75 percent of potential output—that is, almost 25 percent of potential output was not produced. In the worst year, 1933, actual output was only 64 percent of potential—that is, the economy could have produced half again as much as it actually produced. To put numbers like these in perspective, consider 1975, during which the recession that began in 1973 ended. This was the worst year since the 1930s, but in that year actual output was 92 percent of potential output, a shortfall nowhere near the shortfall in any year of the 1930s. 1980 was another year of slowdown, but in that year actual output was 96 percent of potential output.

Of course, during the 1930s, observers could only look back to the 1920s and earlier to gauge how hard the economy had been struck. The

early 1920s were years of serious unemployment, but the balance of the decade saw full employment; for the full decade, 1920–29, actual output was almost 95 percent of potential output. Therefore, to compare decades, there was what can only be called a disastrous drop from producing 5 percent below potential in the 1920s to producing 25 percent below potential in the 1930s.

The problem of the 1930s was underproduction on an unprecedented scale. However, another macroeconomic problem with which we have become all too familiar in the past decade and a half is one that did not exist during the 1930s. On the contrary, instead of the problem of inflation that has long plagued us, the problem then was that of deflation. So rapid was the fall in prices during the early 1930s that the federal government introduced a program under the National Industrial Recovery Act that sought to control the decline in prices just as in recent years the federal government has resorted to programs of wage and price controls in the effort to control the rise in prices. Following a sharp spurt of prices after World War I, prices drifted downward through the 1920s, fell very rapidly during the early 1930s, and then moved up moderately during the balance of the 1930s. It was not until 1942, the first full year of U.S. participation in World War II, that prices returned to their level of twenty years earlier. Accordingly, whereas inflation has become a major macroeconomic problem over the past decade or so, it was almost a nonexistent problem during the 1920s and 1930s. Whatever its other shortcomings, the decade of the 1920s, once past the severe recession of 1921, was one of virtually full employment without inflation. We have had no such equally long period during which we enjoyed the blessings of both full employment and price stability over the fifty-plus year span since then.

The 1940s were almost the opposite of the 1930s. Full employment was realized through most of the decade. The unemployment rate was below 4 percent from 1943 to 1948, below even 2 percent during the peak war years of 1943–45, and at an all-time low of 1.2 percent in 1944. This

---

[8] The CEA has not published estimates of potential GNP for the years before 1952. The figures in the following paragraphs for earlier years are based on estimates by R.J. Gordon, *Macroeconomics,* 2nd ed., Little Brown, 1981, Appendix B, pp. xv–xvii. Gordon estimates *natural* output rather than potential output, but the two concepts are sufficiently close in meaning to permit the kind of broad comparisons that will be made here. Also, to avoid the use of two terms, we will refer to potential output in all cases.

means that for 1943–45 actual GNP exceeded potential GNP by a substantial margin. By anybody's definition of full employment, the economy had more than full employment during those years. In 1944, actual GNP was a phenomenal 22 percent above potential GNP. This prodigious rate of production was made possible with three-shift, seven-day operations in much of manufacturing, and with fifty- to sixty-hour workweeks very common. Rates of output like these in the peak war years were sustainable only for a few years, but during those years they put actual GNP well above potential GNP.

On the side of prices, the 1940s also differed drastically from the 1930s. Although the rate of price level advance was temporarily held in check during the war years by a comprehensive system of price controls with "teeth" (including jail sentences for violators), the early post-war years saw a drastic upsurge in the price level. This was inevitable as the price controls came off at the same time that the demand for durable consumer goods exploded. The production of such goods had practically been suspended during the war years so the pent-up demand for them was enormous. As industry converted from war goods production, it could not begin to satisfy all of this demand in the first couple of years. This gave us a period of double-digit inflation not again experienced until 1974 and 1979–80.

The Record since the 1950s

What happened to actual and potential GNP over the years from 1952 to 1980 is shown in Part A of Figure 1-1. The spread between the two lines for the actual and potential GNP identifies the GNP gap. It was noted in reviewing the pre-1952 period that potential GNP exceeded actual GNP during a few years of World War II; we see something similar here. The line for actual GNP lies above that for potential GNP during parts of the Korean and Vietnam war periods. War periods typically lead to the rapid growth of output that

temporarily pushes actual GNP above potential GNP. Of course, what stands out most clearly from a glance at Part A is the frequency with which actual GNP falls below potential GNP. For the years covered, the divergence is greatest during the 1973–75 recession. All of the recessions over the years covered are marked off by the shaded areas.

Part B of Figure 1-1 shows the actual unemployment rate and the full employment–unemployment rate. The actual rate shown is the estimate of the U.S. Department of Labor. There are a number of estimates of the full employment–unemployment rate, but all of these agree that this rate has been rising substantially since the 1950s. The curve for this rate in Part B of Figure 1-1 describes the general trend. The rate was about 4 percent through most of the 1950s. At the beginning of the 1980s, some estimates put it as low as 5 percent and some put it at or above 6 percent. It is shown as 5.6 percent for 1980 in the diagram.

Because the potential GNP in each year partially depends on potential employment for each year (which varies with the definition of full employment), actual GNP will tend to be most markedly below the potential GNP for the years in which the actual unemployment rate is most markedly above the full employment–unemployment rate. Accordingly, the largest GNP gap in Part A of Figure 1-1 occurs in 1975 and it is this year in which the largest discrepancy occurs between the actual unemployment rate and the full employment–unemployment rate in Part B.

The other variable we have examined in this review is the price level. Figure 1-2 shows the percentage rate of change per year in the Consumer Price Index from 1952 to 1980. With the exception of some quarters of 1954–55, during which there was a slight decline in the price level, prices have risen every year over this span. With the one exception, the line is consistently above the zero percent level. If we were to begin this diagram thirty years earlier, we would see several years, like 1921 and 1932, during which there

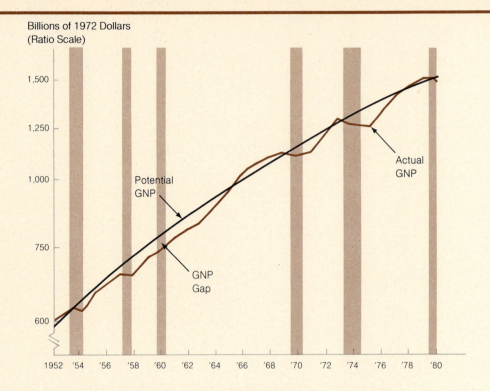

Billions of 1972 Dollars
(Ratio Scale)

Potential
GNP

Actual
GNP

GNP
Gap

1,500

1,250

1,000

750

600

1952 '54 '56 '58 '60 '62 '64 '66 '68 '70 '72 '74 '76 '78 '80

FIGURE 1-1

A   Actual and Potential GNP, 1952–80

SOURCE: Potential GNP from *Chase Econometrics Database;* real GNP from *Economic Report of the President,* January 1981.

were double-digit rates of *deflation.* However, over the period actually shown, the only double-digit rates of price change have been on the up side, specifically in 1974, 1979, and 1980. Since 1952, rates of inflation have varied between these highs and the lows of just over 1 percent per year experienced from 1958 to 1964. Whether so low a rate as this is to be called inflation is debatable. But if it is called inflation, then the record shown in Figure 1-2 is (with a single exception) one of uninterrupted inflation. It is not surprising that most people today are too young to have had personal experience with anything but rising prices. One actually must be sixty or older to have personal recollection of falling prices.

The Background of Macroeconomic Theory

Our brief review of the macroeconomic record from the 1920s to the 1980s helps us understand why macroeconomic theory developed as it did. The most dramatic development over these years was that in the 1930s. What economic theory needed during the 1930s was an explanation of the disastrous experience of those years. How could an economy plunge to a predicament in which a quarter of a nation's resources were idle? Keynes' book in 1936 provided a theory to

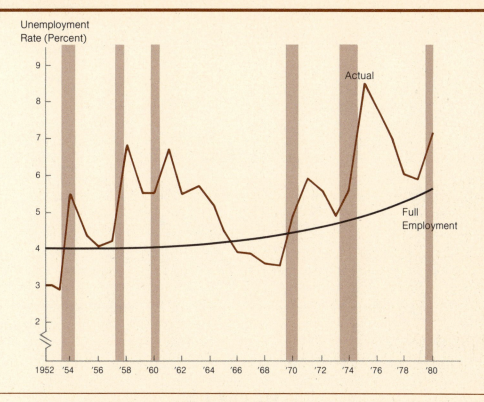

B   Actual Unemployment Rate and Full Employment—Unemployment Rate, 1952–80

SOURCE: *Economic Report of the President,* January 1981.

explain this phenomenon; it was so successful that it began a Keynesian era in macroeconomic theory that stood in sharp contrast to the theory that had prevailed over the preceding century or more.

Although the punishing plunge of the 1930s brought the issue of the underutilization of resources to the forefront in a way that had never happened before, economists had long before this recognized that departures from full utilization of resources occur from time to time. The accepted economic theory of the pre-Keynesian era did not maintain that the economy remained uninterruptedly at full utilization. However, it did argue that full utilization was the normal state of

affairs and that departures from this were strictly temporary. It argued that the automatic forces of competitive markets would carry the actual level of output back to its potential level in short order. Consequently, departures from full utilization of resources or from full employment did not generate widespread concern among economists as long as they believed that the potential level of output was the normal level to which the economy would automatically and promptly return. The fact that there were relatively few severe or prolonged depressions through at least the first half of the nineteenth century gave support to this belief. Lapses from full employment, because they were both infrequent and short-lived, could

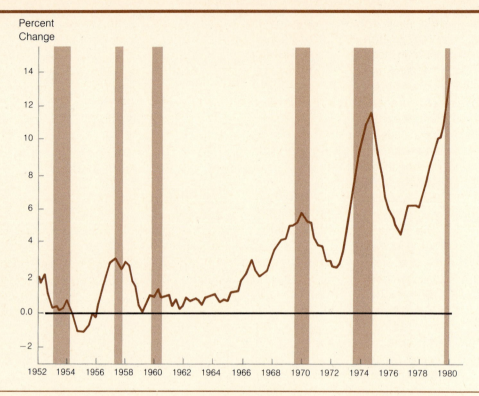

FIGURE 1-2
Percent Change of the Consumer Price Index, 1952–80

SOURCE: *Economic Report of the President,* January 1981.

be easily explained away as exceptions to the full utilization or full employment rule.

Even though viewed as exceptions to the rule, the "panics," "crises," and "depressions" of the nineteenth century were nevertheless the subject of much study. David Ricardo wrote in 1817 of "revulsions in trade," and Mill in 1848 discussed "commercial crises" at length. However, the basic tenet underlying full employment as the norm went unchallenged by Ricardo, Mill, and others. On the contrary, they staunchly defended it against the attacks of what few dissenters there were. This basic tenet was that aggregate demand for goods and services could not, other than temporarily, fall short of the aggregate supply of goods and services. As long as

this was so, there was no barrier to the production of the aggregate supply that corresponded with full employment.

The handful of dissenters who attacked the rule that the economy automatically generated sufficient demand to absorb the supply produced under conditions of full employment failed, because none was able to buttress his attack with an alternative theory capable of supplanting the orthodox theory. As James B. Conant observed, "It takes a new conceptual scheme to cause the abandonment of an old one."[9] Before Keynes' there had been no alternative theory that

[9]James B. Conant, *On Understanding Science,* Yale Univ. Press, 1947, p. 89.

could be made to stick. Thomas R. Malthus, a dissenter of the early nineteenth century, attacked the accepted theory unsuccessfully, for, in Keynes' words, "Since Malthus was unable to explain clearly (apart from an appeal to the facts of common observation) how and why effective demand could be deficient or excessive, he failed to furnish an alternative construction."[10] Although a number of other attacks were made on the classical orthodoxy during these many years, a really successful one did not come until over a hundred years after Malthus. Keynes' *General Theory* presented an alternative theory of the determination of employment and output that explained why the forces of a market economy did not assure that aggregate demand would automatically be that which was necessary for full employment. He maintained that the level of employment was a variable, with full employment simply one possible level; an unlimited number of less-than-full employment levels were also possible.

Keynes' *General Theory* offered an explanation of the economic disaster that the United States and many other countries suffered during the 1930s, something the then existing body of theory was quite incapable of doing. The *General Theory* did not depend merely on "an appeal to the facts of common observation" to show that demand could be less than that needed for full employment; it supplied a theory to explain the facts that were apparent to all in the early 1930s. A "new" theory had come forth to deal with the reality of those depressed times.

During the decade following the appearance of the *General Theory,* economists addressed themselves to refining and building on the pioneer work of Keynes, to analyzing the complex economic processes that determine the actual level of employment—a level that the new theory showed could be one of full employment, one of severe unemployment, or any other level between these extremes. Keynesian theory was also

applied during and after World War II to an analysis of inflation, a condition that was found to be closely connected with an economy at or near full employment. From such analysis came policy prescriptions designed to lift the system up to the full employment level to which automatic forces might fail to carry it and to maintain this level without inflation.

By the mid-1960s, Keynesian theory reigned supreme. There was a feeling that the major macroeconomic problems, even if not completely solved, were at least well under control. A series of earlier, less notable, policy successes had been capped with the impressive success of the large 1964 tax cut, which had been urged by some economists as a means of returning the economy to full employment and raising the lagging growth rate. This produced very much the results that these economists had forecast. With the record before them, economists were by then quite generally satisfied that the new economics of Keynes had given them the know-how to do a reasonably good job of restoring the system to full employment on the occasions when it slipped away from that position. With basic macroeconomic problems believed to be in hand, a greater share of effort could be devoted to microeconomic problems. This was reinforced by the fact that problems like pollution control, energy supplies, consumer protection, crime control, and health care had rather suddenly assumed much greater importance than before; these problems are essentially microeconomic in their economic aspects.

The self-satisfaction that the economics profession felt in its macroeconomics branch was, however, short-lived. Although the boom and inflation that began in 1965 might have been prevented if the tax increases recommended by economists at that time had been put into effect, the process of curbing a boom and checking an inflation that had been permitted to gain momentum turned out to be more difficult and subject to greater uncertainty than had been thought to be the case by economists just a few years earlier. The increase in income tax rates finally put

---

[10] *General Theory,* p. 32. See Keynes' Chapter 23 for his review of the "dissenters," or "heretics," of their time who are identified as the precursors of his own theory.

through in 1968 did not begin to have the dampening effect that economists had generally expected it to have. Moreover, the various other restrictive policy actions taken over the next several years also were unable to check the inflation, although it turned out that they were able to push the economy into a recession in 1970.

Then, a few years later bad came to worse. The recovery from the 1970 recession had by 1973 reached boom proportions, but at the end of 1973, both in the United States and other major industrialized countries, began the sharpest recession experienced since the desperate days of the 1930s. But the ultimate blow was not the severity of the recession itself; it was the fact that this grueling contraction was accompanied by one of the most rapid rates of inflation experienced since World War II. The term "double-digit inflation" became part of the language in 1974. There were, of course, special problems that are not amenable to domestic economic policy—such as the quadrupling of oil prices by the OPEC cartel in 1974—but the simultaneous occurrence of sharply declining output and employment and sharply rising prices was the source of great discomfiture to the economics profession.

Under the influence of Keynesian economics, the available tools had been designed almost exclusively to control aggregate demand. But in the 1970s we had to face this question: Can we simultaneously tackle the problems of recession and inflation by managing aggregate demand? To expand aggregate demand will raise the level of output and end the recession, but it probably will also raise the inflation rate. To contract aggregate demand will probably slow the rate of inflation, but it will also reduce the level of output and worsen the recession. Viewed in this way, what we needed were tools to change aggregate supply as well as aggregate demand when confronted simultaneously by recession and inflation. Keynesian economics had only provided tools to manage the demand side; in recent years, economists have devoted considerable effort to the development of tools to manage the long-neglected supply side.

In view of our experience beginning in the early 1970s, economists who during the 1960s had believed that the Keynesian tools then at hand were adequate to meet whatever macroeconomic problems might confront us in the future were convincingly disabused of such beliefs. Problems were being faced that had not been encountered before; and macroeconomics, which had risen during the 1940s and 1950s, was not about to return to obscurity in the 1980s for lack of basic problems with which to occupy itself.

Varieties of Macroeconomic Theory

In the early years following the appearance of Keynes' *General Theory,* macroeconomic theory could be neatly divided into two parts—classical and Keynesian. Keynes chose to contrast the ideas he presented in the *General Theory* with the prevailing ideas by labeling those prevailing ideas as classical. In economic theory, the term "classical" had been coined by Karl Marx, who used it to cover the theories of David Ricardo, James Mill, and their predecessors. Keynes extended the term to include "the followers of Ricardo, those, that is to say, who adopted and perfected the theory of the Ricardian economics, including (for example) J.S. Mill, Marshall, Edgeworth, and Prof. Pigou."[11] This is now the generally accepted meaning of "classical" in its application to macroeconomic theory.

Despite the tremendous success of Keynes' work, it did not by any means put an end to the further development of classical macroeconomics. New and different formulations or reconstructions of classical theory appeared under the heading of neoclassical, especially during the 1950s in the area of growth theory that gave us neoclassical growth models. Beginning in the 1950s and continuing to the present has been the work on another extension of classical

---

[11] *General Theory*, p. 3.

macroeconomic theory known as monetarism, so called because of the critical role it assigns to money as a determinant of what happens in the economy. Keynes' *General Theory* began what came to be called the Keynesian revolution; the work of the monetarists, especially that of Milton Friedman, during the 1960s and 1970s, gained so much influence that it may be regarded as a counter-revolution.[12] Finally, in the 1970s came the latest theoretical development with roots in classical theory: The new classical economics that builds on the old by inserting the concept of rational expectations.

As these developments were occurring on the classical side, there were also changes on the Keynesian side. To start off, one must distinguish between "the economics of John Maynard Keynes" and "Keynesian economics." Keynes himself must be singled out as the founding father, but his role, important as it is, is only this. The economics of Keynes is the foundation on which Keynesian economics has been constructed. Over the years following the publication of the *General Theory,* economists refined and extended the many insights contained in that book and gradually built an edifice known as Keynesian economics.

Part of this structure is commonly referred to as the Keynesian income–expenditure model. It is this that most economists think of when they think of the core of Keynesian economics. This kind of Keynesian economics is so widely recognized that it is commonly regarded as Keynesian orthodoxy. However, it should be noted that there are critics who maintain that what has passed as Keynesian orthodoxy for a generation or more is in fact, in the words of the distinguished British economist, Joan Robinson, a "bastard" Keynesianism that grossly distorts Keynes' own work. Members of this school, predominantly British, are sometimes described as Neo-Keynesians. Another group, predominantly

American, also maintains that the standard interpretation of Keynes is counterfeit, because it departs from some other central ideas that Keynes emphasized. These people have been distinguished from others by being called Post-Keynesians.[13]

Because the kind of Keynesianism presented in this book is not that of the Neo-Keynesians nor of the Post-Keynesians as those terms are here used, it will be referred to simply as Keynesian. Much of the material is post-Keynesian, not in the sense of our previous definition, but in the sense that it is Keynesian in origin and post-Keynesian in terms of the time that it was developed and published. Keynes' own work obviously ended with his death in 1946. In this book, all of the material on the Keynesian side will be described simply as Keynesian; that term without any prefix will suffice throughout the book. However, on the classical side, more than one term will be needed. Although in many places it will suffice to refer merely to classical theory, in other places the neoclassical, monetarist, and new classical or rational expectations expansions of the early classical theory will be brought into the analysis. The content of each of these will be covered in later chapters where they first appear.

The Plan of the Book in Brief

This introductory chapter has provided some idea of the content of macroeconomics and its development since Keynes' work began the "Keynesian revolution" a couple of generations ago. Because aggregate income and output are central elements of macroeconomics, an understanding of the meaning of these and related aggregates and the relationships among them is essential to the analysis that will follow. Chapter 2 provides the minimum of national income

---

[12]For an essay on the economics and sociology of this development, see H.G. Johnson, "The Keynesian Revolution and the Monetarist Counter-Revolution," *American Economic Review,* May 1971, pp. 1–14.

[13]For the specific differences between the different schools, see J.R. Crotty, "Post-Keynesian Economic Theory: An Overview and Evaluation," *American Economic Review,* May 1980, pp. 20–25.

accounting needed for this purpose. Chapter 3 concludes the introductory material presented in Part 1 of the book with a nontechnical review of a few of the basic concepts that run throughout macroeconomics.

Part 2 presents the simplest possible Keynesian model of income and output determination, according to which the actual level of income and output depends on aggregate spending for goods and services. Despite the oversimplifications that are made in constructing this model, the model facilitates the presentation of some basic ideas in easily understood form. For example, we can see quite clearly the basis for the Keynesian conclusion that the economy does not automatically tend to move to the full employment level of output as held by the classical theory. The Keynesian conclusion follows from the belief that aggregate spending may be too little to call forth the full employment level of output; the opposite or classical conclusion follows from the belief that aggregate spending will always be the amount needed to carry output to its full employment level.

The Keynesian model of Part 2 simplifies in one way by assigning no causal role to money and interest in the process of income determination. Part 3 brings money and interest into the analysis in a causal way and in so doing enables us to construct an extended model in contrast to the simple model of Part 2. However, before turning to the extended model that takes up Chapters 12–14 of Part 3, Chapters 8–11 work through some prerequisite material. Chapter 8 derives the aggregate supply curve that shows how the aggregate amount of goods and services supplied varies with the price level. The shape of this curve will be altogether different, depending on whether we make Keynesian or classical assumptions. Chapter 9 describes the construction of the simple classical model. As with the simple Keynesian model, the simple classical model facilitates the presentation of some basic classical ideas in easily understood form, despite the oversimplifications that are made in constructing this model. For example, we can see

quite clearly the basis for the classical conclusion that the economy tends automatically to produce at its full employment level of output.

Because Part 3 brings money into the model of income determination, we must explain the money supply process—that is, how changes in the supply of money occur. This is done in Chapter 10. The next step is the Keynesian theory of the rate of interest; Chapter 11 shows how the supply of and demand for money determine the rate of interest in that theory. After all of this preparation, the extended model of income determination is put together in three steps in three chapters: Chapter 12 assumes a closed economy (no transactions with other countries) with a stable price level; Chapter 13 assumes a closed economy with a variable price level; and Chapter 14 expands the analysis to cover the case of an open economy with a variable price level.

In the simple Keynesian model developed in Part 2, the actual level of income or output depends only on aggregate spending. What determines aggregate spending is not a simple matter; the complications faced in trying to explain the size of the various components of aggregate spending are side-stepped in Part 2. The major purpose of Part 4 is to deal with what determines the consumption and investment components of aggregate spending. Chapters 15 and 16 are concerned with the explanation of consumption spending, Chapter 17 with the relationship between investment spending and the capital stock, and Chapters 18 and 19 with the explanation of investment spending itself.

Part 5 is concerned with these major topics: growth, inflation, and economic stabilization. The analysis in Parts 2 and 3 is primarily short run. Chapter 20, which starts off Part 5, gets into the long run; other aspects of growth are considered briefly, but the bulk of this chapter is devoted to economic growth theory—that is, the theory of what determines the rate at which the economy's output increases over the long run. A set of three chapters on inflation follows. Chapter 21 covers the matters of definition, measurement, and effects of inflation; Chapter 22 turns to an explanation of inflation through an aggregate supply and demand model that permits us to see how price level changes arise on both the supply side and demand side; Chapter 23 brings in the important relationship between inflation and unemployment and constructs a model made up of the Phillips curve and an inflationary pressure curve, which together explain the determination of the inflation and unemployment rates. Finally, another set of three chapters on economic stabilization concludes Part 5. Stabilization policy takes three forms: incomes policy, fiscal policy, and monetary policy, and one chapter is devoted to each of these in the order noted.

National Income Accounting

OVERVIEW

A major task of macroeconomics is the explanation of what determines the economy's aggregate output of goods and services. In any time period that output may be equal to what can be produced with full utilization of the economy's resources or it may be something below this. What it actually is can only be ascertained by measurement. Why it is what it is can only be explained by macroeconomic theory.

The question of measurement comes under the heading of national income accounting. This chapter covers a few essentials of national income accounting that are needed for an understanding of macroeconomic theory. There are two basic approaches to the measurement of the value of the economy's total output—the expenditures approach and the income approach—and most of this chapter is devoted to setting out the way in which this aggregate may be obtained through each of these approaches. When economists refer to this kind of an aggregate without qualification, they usually mean the gross national product. But there are two other widely used aggregates of the value of the economy's output—net national product and national income. The relationships among these three aggregates are covered in this chapter. Two other aggregates will appear in our later work: personal income and

disposable personal income. Although these are not measures of the economy's output, it is important to understand what they do measure and how they are related to the gross national product, net national product, and national income.

Conceptually, the expenditures and income approaches to measurement yield the same figure for the value of the economy's final output of goods and services. Every dollar of expenditure is matched by a dollar of income. This total figure is broken down to provide a framework for use in later chapters. On the expenditures side are the amounts accounted for by the expenditures of consumers, businesses, government, and the rest of the world; on the income side are the amounts devoted to the payment of taxes, purchases of consumer goods and services, and saving. All this is expressed by a series of identities developed in this chapter.

The value of the economy's output may change from one period to the next, as a result of a change in the amount of goods and services produced, the prices of these goods and services, or both. For most purposes, we want quarter-to-quarter and year-to-year figures that indicate only changes in the amount of goods and services produced or figures for final product expressed in dollars of constant purchasing power. Figures in current dollars express both real changes and price changes. The procedure by which the constant dollar figures are estimated is briefly described in this chapter.

The chapter also provides an introduction to a few of the many special problems faced in national income accounting—imputations, the inventory valuation adjustment, and the capital consumption adjustment. The last topic considered in this chapter is of a different nature: the relationship between national product and national welfare.

Whereas ordinary business accounting summarizes a firm's performance by measuring its profit or loss over a specified period of time, national income accounting summarizes a country's economic performance by measuring its aggregate income and output of goods and services over a specified period of time. In the early 1930s, national income accounting provided little more than figures for the economy's aggregate income. It was the new interest in macroeconomic theory sparked by the publication of Keynes' *General Theory* in 1936 that was largely responsible for the development of national income accounting from its rudimentary form to the advanced form it had assumed following World War II. This development included a more elaborate framework of accounts and initiated the collection of data for many income and output measures that appeared for the first time in this expanded framework.

Long before the 1930s, economists had been interested in knowing each year's aggregate income and output as well as its composition. However, as long as the economy appeared to show no more than short-lived, moderate departures from full employment, detailed figures for its actual income and output from period to period were less important than they would be for an economy that showed greater instability. Expressed in terms of Figure 1-1 (page 10), if actual output rarely fell even moderately short of potential, interest in obtaining output estimates

would not be as great as it is. However, because the economy has experienced large and prolonged gaps between actual and potential output, output figures are of great interest; they provide a good overall measurement of how bad things were during any such episode. For this very reason, the first estimates of actual national income prepared by a U.S. government agency were produced in response to the most serious case of a gap between actual and potential output—the 1929–33 depression.

The advent of the Keynesian theory not only hastened the development of national income accounting; it also influenced the form of that development. The conceptual framework in which the accounts are presented was deliberately designed to facilitate the study of macroeconomic problems with Keynesian tools. For example, beyond simply showing the total output of the economy, one may break that total down in various ways—by industry of origin (manufacturing, agriculture, transportation, and so on), or by kind of output (durable goods, nondurable goods, services, and structures). However, Keynesian theory made aggregate demand the key to explaining aggregate output and explained aggregate demand by considering the spending of consumers, businesses, government, and foreigners. Consequently, the classification of the economy's aggregate output into the parts obtained by each of these four groups is now the core of the accounting framework.

In its entirety, this accounting framework offers a systematic picture of the economic structure and process in terms of the interrelated flows of income and product, the basic variables of the economic process. Although the quarterly accounting data for the interrelated income and product flows merely identify the changes that have occurred, a study of these changes enables economists to explain why they may have occurred and, more importantly, to forecast future changes. For example, suppose that we are given only the quarterly figures for the spending flows of the four groups, namely, personal consumption expenditures (C), private domestic investment (I)—which is broken down into fixed investment and the change in inventories—government purchases of goods and services (G), and net foreign purchases, equal to exports (X) minus imports (M) or ($X - M$). If there is a series of quarterly inventory increases the size of which seems substantially different from the increases in other flows such as consumption expenditures, an economist might forecast that a recession will occur to correct what seems to be excessive inventory accumulation. The economist could reach such a tentative judgment by studying only the data provided in one part of the overall accounting framework—the National Income and Product Account, which shows the breakdown of aggregate output into the kinds noted above.

For the macroeconomic theory in the following parts of this book, it is not essential for us to examine the accounting framework in its entirety. The complete framework is composed of a set of interconnected accounts—a Personal Income and Outlay Account, which shows the various sources of income of persons and the disposition of that income; a Government Receipts and Expenditures Account, which does the same for all governmental units; a Foreign Transactions Account, which shows receipts from foreigners for sale of goods and services to them and payments to foreigners for purchases of goods and services from them; implicitly a consolidated Business Income and Product Account, which shows output produced and income generated within all business firms consolidated; and a Gross Saving and Investment Account, which lists the amounts of gross saving of different sectors on one side and the matching amount of gross investment on the other side. Finally, the National Income and Product Account is a kind of summary account for the overall framework and is the account on which we will concentrate. For 1980, this account is shown on page 27.[1]

Income and Product

In conventional business accounting, a basic financial statement is the balance sheet. In it assets are listed on one side and liabilities and the various accounts that make up net worth are listed on the other side. In national income accounting, an equally basic statement is the National Income and Product Account. In it various income flows are listed on one side and various product flows are listed on the other side.

---

[1] For more complete treatments of national income accounting, including the complete accounting framework and the sector accounts out of which it is built, as well as the details behind the accounts, see J.W. Kendrick, *Economic Accounts and Their Uses,* McGraw-Hill, 1972; S. Rosen, *National Income and Other Social Accounts,* Holt, Rinehart and Winston, 1972; and W.I. Abraham, *National Income and Economic Accounting,* Prentice-Hall, 1969. For a comparison of the national income accounting systems of the major countries, see M. Yanovsky, *Social Accounting Systems,* Aldine, 1965, and W. Beckerman, *International Comparisons of Real Incomes,* Development Center of the Organization for Economic Cooperation and Development, Paris, 1966. For the system adopted by the United Nations for the international reporting of comparable national accounting data, see *A System of National Accounts,* Department of Economic and Social Affairs, United Nations, New York, 1975. For an excellent summary explanation of the national income and product accounts of the United States prepared by the Department of Commerce, see C.S. Carson and G. Jaszi, "The National Income and Product Accounts of the United States: An Overview," *Survey of Current Business,* February 1981, pp. 22–34. This article also presents the full set of sector accounts including data for 1980.

As in the case of the balance sheet, the two sides of the National Income and Product Account show the same total because the terms are defined to assure that outcome. A dollar of income is generated for every dollar of goods and services produced in the economy or a dollar of goods and services is produced for every dollar of income generated in the economy. Because it is customary in the accounting framework to refer to goods and services as product, we may also say that there is a dollar of product for every dollar of income.[2]

This means that once we have adopted a consistent set of definitions of income and product, we can estimate the value of the economy's output for any time period from either side by totaling the value of all goods and services that are counted as product or by totaling all the income generated in the course of producing these goods and services. Because the information on each side is useful both for the total it reveals and for other purposes, both income and product estimates are made. The estimates on the product side are based essentially on the expenditures made for product; consequently, the derivation of estimates on that side is usually called the expenditure approach. The estimates on the income side are estimates of income itself; the derivation of estimates on this side is usually called the income approach.

These two approaches to the measurement of the value of the economy's output, as well as some of the conceptual problems faced in measurement, are each examined in the following pages.

---

[2] As will be seen presently, the identity between income and product is based on a broad definition of income that includes flows like indirect taxes and depreciation charges not usually thought of as income. However, this broad definition of income is most convenient at the outset. Once the structure of the National Income and Product Account is grasped, one has no problem in switching to a narrower definition of income for which the identity is no longer income equals product but income plus certain nonincome flows equal product.

Measuring the Value of the Economy's Output of Goods and Services: The Expenditures Approach

One way to arrive at a figure for the value of the economy's aggregate product for a given time period would be to get figures on the number of units of each of millions of different goods and services produced during that time period (each different size and quality of a "good" is in effect a different good), gather thousands of price lists, and proceed with the necessary multiplication of quantities by prices and add these to obtain a total. Even assuming all these data were available, it would be virtually impossible to work a mass of data in this form into a summary figure that could be described with any accuracy as the value of the economy's output for the time period. However, a summary figure of this kind can be reached in a much more direct way and with far more accuracy by counting each unit produced at the time it is purchased and valuing it at the actual purchase price. If we add up total expenditures on goods and services, we will have (subject to a number of qualifications to which we will turn next) the total we seek, and also a total in which each unit of output is valued at what appears to be the best available indicator of the value of that unit to society—the price actually paid for it.

Exclusions from Expenditures This general approach to measuring the value of output through expenditures is perfectly proper and manageable, but obviously it must be refined. It will not be useful to simply obtain a total that includes expenditures for all goods and services without qualification. The desired total measures the amount of output produced by the economy during a specified time period; therefore, it must clearly include only expenditures on the purchase of goods and services produced during that time period. It must not include any part of the many billions of dollars spent during that time period on goods produced in *earlier* time periods. All expenditures of this kind merely reflect changes in the ownership of preexisting output; as such, they are not part of the total of expenditures that measures the value of current output.

The desired total must also exclude all expenditures for anything that is neither a good nor a service and therefore does not reflect production at all, either current or past. For example, people in each time period spend billions of dollars on stock and bonds, some of which are purchased from other people who acquired them in earlier years and some of which are newly issued by corporations during that time period. Whether currently issued or not, these billions of dollars must *not* be counted as so many billions of dollars of expenditure in the total that is being built. There is no production or output of goods and services corresponding to expenditures for mere pieces of paper.

Somewhat less obviously, but for the same basic reason, we must also exclude all expenditures by federal, state, and local government *for which the government does not receive a good or service in exchange*. The huge amount of government expenditures for social security, unemployment compensation, and veterans' benefits is not spending for a good or service; the recipients of these amounts spent by government do not provide a good or service to the government in exchange. This type of expenditure—so-called government transfer payments—must therefore be excluded, because it does not reflect output of goods and services. Its inclusion would rob the total expenditure figure of its usefulness as a measure of the value of the economy's output of goods and services.

Intermediate vs. Final Product   Even after excluding expenditures of the kinds indicated, we still cannot include all of the remaining dollar amounts spent on the purchase of every kind of good or service produced during the time period. Such a total would count some goods or services

in the total output once, others twice, still others three times, and so forth, thereby drastically overstating the economy's true total output.

The objective is to count, for example, the dollar value of the amount of bread that was produced during the period, but not to count the dollar value of the flour used to produce the bread, even though that amount of flour was produced by millers and sold to the bakers during the same time period. By the same reasoning, we should not add to the dollar value of the amount of bread the dollar value of the wheat used to produce the flour that went into the bread, even though that wheat was produced by farmers and sold to millers during the same time period. At this point, the wheat in the bread would be counted three times. Counting expenditures for the bread alone counts the wheat only once, as desired.

In order to include in the total for the time period only the output that may be viewed as so-called final product—for example, bread—we must exclude all other output that, although produced during the time period in question, is used up in the course of producing that time period's final product—for example, wheat and flour. Such excluded output is described as intermediate product.

Distinguishing Intermediate and Final Product   The rationale for excluding intermediate product is clear enough in principle, but extremely difficult in application. Unlike spending in the simple wheat–flour–bread case, large amounts of spending do not fall distinctly into one or the other of the two categories. Many government purchases of services fall into the gray area. For example, should the billions of dollars spent by state and local governments to provide police protection be classified as spending for a final product or should it be viewed as spending for an intermediate product—that is, as something "used up" in the course of producing a final product? If we view police protection merely as something without which the private sector would be unable to operate effectively, then police protection takes on the characteristic of an intermediate product that is used up in the course of producing the output of factories, offices, and stores. On the other hand, if we think of it as a service that exists apart from the goods and services produced by the factories, offices, and stores, then it is more in the nature of a final product.

The issue here is distinct from the earlier issue of government spending for goods and services versus government spending in the form of transfer payments. Here there is no question but that the recipients of the government spending—for example, police officers—render a service in exchange; there is production of a kind corresponding to the government spending. The question is whether the service or good produced is more in the nature of an intermediate product like flour that is used up in making bread or a final product like bread itself.

Questionable cases between final and intermediate product are by no means limited to government spending. For example, consumer expenditures for transportation to and from work, for medical care, and for many other purposes sometimes described as "regrettable necessities" may perhaps be more appropriately classified as spending for intermediate product. A person's spending to get to and from work may be viewed as spending for a service that is "used up" in the course of producing the good or service that comes out of the place of employment and to the production of which he or she contributes. Similarly, spending for medical care may be viewed as spending necessary to maintain health and therefore necessary to the performance of a job; as such, it is something "used up" in the course of producing the good or service.

The number of such cases is almost endless. It might seem at first that the best approach would be to classify them one by one as cases of intermediate product or final product through a careful evaluation of the "merits" of each. However, the evaluation of each, no matter how care-

fully done, is still largely subjective; equally competent people will not reach the same conclusion in each case. Although it is quite arbitrary, an alternative that avoids subjective evaluation is to treat all spending by both governmental units and individuals as spending on final product—but only, of course, if it is spending for which the governmental unit or the individual receives a currently produced good or service in exchange. Despite the fact that this alternative is less than ideal, it is used in preparing the official governmental estimates of the economy's output in the United States and in some other countries. In these estimates, both personal consumption expenditures (C) and government purchases of goods and services (G) include all expenditures on goods and services by individuals and governmental units, respectively, subject to the qualifications noted.

Final Product: $C + I + G$ To reach a total for spending on final product by consumers, businesses, and governmental units—that is, a total for $C + I + G$—we must obtain a figure for the amount of business spending on goods and services that is to be included. Of all business spending for goods and services during a given time period, how much is to be excluded as intermediate product? In other words, how much is to be included as final product?

Let us go back to the simple illustration of the production of wheat, flour, and bread. The production of flour requires more than just wheat; among other things, millers need buildings and within them specialized kinds of machinery. Over a period of time, millers as a group will, of course, buy wheat, electric power, pens and pencils, insurance coverage, and other nondurable items. In any time period, some millers will also buy newly constructed buildings and/or new milling machinery. Each miller not only uses up wheat, electric power, and the like; he also uses up plant and equipment as these durable assets gradually wear out. To find out how much of all the goods and services purchased by our millers as a group during the period is *not* used up during the period in question, it would appear that all one has to do is find out how much they spent for new plant and equipment during that period and subtract from this the amount of plant and equipment they "used up" during the course of the period's production. An approximate figure for the amount of this "wear and tear" is provided by the amount that the firms charged in their books as depreciation expense for the period. The gross amount spent for new plant and equipment is called gross fixed investment; the net amount arrived at by subtracting the figure for plant and equipment used up is called net fixed investment.

What is done for the millers is done for every other industry: Gross and net fixed investment spending are determined for each and the totals for all industries combined are the gross fixed and net fixed investment for the economy as a whole. These may be designated as I_{gf} and I_{nf} in which *gf* and *nf*, respectively, mean gross fixed and net fixed. The figure for I_{nf} then yields what appears to be a measure of the amount of total business spending for final product. If we now add to the figures for spending by persons, *C*, and spending by governmental units, *G*, the figure found for I_{nf}, we will presumably have a total for spending on final product.

However, although this total is a measure of spending on final product by the three sectors, from one period to the next it will either overstate or understate the actual final product accounted for by the three sectors. This total is obtained by counting all of the spending for final goods and services during the period; therefore, it will equal the actual total being sought only if there is an exact correspondence between the amount of final goods and services produced and the sum of *C*, *G*, and I_{nf}. The problem is that the total of these three types of expenditure need not and, as a practical matter, will not be the same as the amount of final product actually produced. For example, some goods produced during the period may remain unsold during the period, which means there is no spending or final sale to reflect their production. The difference between

what was produced and what was sold during the period will appear as an increase in business inventories. Consequently, an estimate of this amount must be added to the total derived for expenditures to reach the figure for the economy's output of final goods and services.

In the previous example, we cannot assume that all of the millers' spending for goods and services, other than the amount measured as their I_{nf}, is for goods and services used up in the course of producing flour during the period. If at the end of the period they have a larger inventory of wheat than at the beginning of the period, the value of this increase must be counted as part of final product for the period. If it had not gone into inventory but into the making of flour and then into the making of bread purchased by consumers, it would have been counted under *C*. However, it has actually gone into inventories and must be counted in that form or it will escape counting altogether and cause that much of an understatement of final product. By the same argument, if the millers show an increase in the inventory of their end product, flour, this increase too must be counted as part of final product. In general, if the millers as a group show an increase in the value of their combined inventories of raw materials (wheat), goods in process, and end product (flour), this amount must be counted as part of final product. This incidentally, brings out the frequently misunderstood fact that *final* product is not identical with *finished* product. An increase in business inventories of raw materials and goods in process must be included as part of the period's final product, although such goods plainly don't qualify as finished product by the usual meaning of that word.

Adding the change in the millers' inventories to their net fixed investment yields the correct figure for the amount of the economy's final product accounted for by investment within this industry. The figure thus obtained is called net investment (with the qualifier "fixed" dropped), I_n. It measures the sum of the amount of goods that millers purchased from other firms (such as wheat and flour-making machines) that was not used up in the course of producing other goods and the amount of goods produced (such as flour) that were not sold to other firms during the time period. An addition to inventories is therefore like an addition to plant and equipment—each represents something produced during the period, not used up in further production during the period, and consequently something found in the possession of business at the end of the period. If the change in inventories is combined with gross fixed investment, the total is, by the same reasoning, called **gross investment** (with the qualifier "fixed" dropped), I_g.

The change in the millers' inventories for a time period may, of course, also be negative. In this event, to arrive at the figure for I_n, the change in the millers' inventories must be subtracted from I_{nf}. If it also happened that the amount of plant and equipment used up by the millers during the period exceeded the amount of their spending for new plant and equipment, I_{nf} would be negative as well. The amount of the economy's final product accounted for by net investment within this industry—the sum of net fixed investment and the change in inventories—would then be negative. The amount of gross investment accounted for by this industry would be the figure obtained by combining the change in inventories and gross fixed investment. The latter figure is the millers' total spending for plant and equipment and, unlike net fixed investment, cannot be less than zero. Although a negative figure for gross investment can result from a decrease in an industry's inventories larger than its gross fixed investment spending, this would be a rarity for any single industry and does not occur at all for all industries combined.

What is done for the milling industry must be done for all industries. If for any particular time period all industries combined show an increase in inventories, the economy's final product will exceed the total of consumption spending, government spending, and business net fixed investment spending by that amount, which must accordingly be added to the total of the spending flows to obtain the total for final product. Similarly,

a decrease in inventories must be subtracted from the total of the spending flows. The total of the spending flows is commonly called **final sales.** The total for final product is equal to final sales plus the change in business inventories.

Final Product: Net Exports Added The sum of $C + I_n + G$ would be the final product for the economy as a whole only if the economy were closed. However, every economy actually imports some goods and services from the rest of the world and exports some goods and services to it. If during a time period the domestic economy on balance exports more than it imports, this difference is part of the domestic economy's final product. However, this part will not be picked up in the course of deriving the total spending of the three sectors within the economy and in working out the estimate for the change in inventories. This amount will be included only by adding it to the spending of the three domestic sectors.

For a numerical illustration, suppose that spending on final product by the three domestic sectors totals $98 (all figures in billions), the change in inventories is +$2, the economy's exports of goods and services are $6, and imports are $5. Included in the $100 billion sum for spending by the three domestic sectors and the change in inventories will be $5 spent by these three sectors on imported goods and services, so that only $95 of this total of $100 is matched by domestically produced goods and services. However, because $6 of domestically produced goods and services have been exported, this amount must be added to the $95 of domestically produced goods and services that remained within the economy. The total for the domestic economy's output is accordingly $101. Notice that this total is equal to the sum of the total spending of $98 by the three domestic sectors, the +$2 change in inventories, and the net export balance of $1 (exports of $6 minus imports of $5).

For the opposite case in which the domestic economy imports more goods and services than it exports, that difference is a part of the output of other countries. However, this output would be counted as part of the domestic economy's output, if we merely derived the total for the spending of the three sectors within the economy and added the change in inventories. To avoid this overstatement, the amount in question must be subtracted from the sum of the total spending of the three domestic sectors plus the change in inventories.

For example, assume the same figures of $98 for spending by the three domestic sectors and +$2 for the change in inventories, but assume that imports were $6 and exports $5. Now we find $6 of imported goods and services in the $100 total ($98 + $2), which means that only $94 of the $100 reflects domestically produced goods and services. To this we must add $5 of domestically produced goods and services that were exported to give us a total for the domestic economy's output of $99. Again, the total equals the sum of the total spending of $98 by the three domestic sectors, the +$2 change in inventories, and the net export balance of −$1 (exports of $5 minus imports of $6).

To sum up, inclusion of the economy's net export or import balance allows for the fact that total spending on final goods and services by the domestic sectors will not correspond with total final sales of goods and services. To estimate the value of the economy's output of final goods and services by means of the expenditures approach, we must total the spending on final product not only by the three domestic sectors but the positive or negative net spending on the domestic economy's product by the foreign sector. The sum of these four spending flows plus the change in inventories for the period will be the total sought.

Gross and Net National Product; Gross and Net Domestic Product   According to Department of Commerce estimates, the sum of the spending flows plus the change in inventories, known as gross national product (GNP), was $2,628.8 billion for 1980. As shown on the right side of Table 2-1, the four expenditure flows, C, I_g, G, and $(X - M)$, were, respectively, $1,671.1, $399.8, $534.8, and $26.1 billion, which gives a total for final sales of $2,631.8 billion. Adding to this the change in inventories of −$3.0 billion yields $2,628.8 billion for GNP. Because gross investment, I_g, is the sum of gross fixed investment and the change in inventories, GNP may be shown as the sum of the four flows, $C + I_g + G + (X - M)$ in which I_g is $396.8 billion. This conforms with the breakdown of the GNP aggregate in Table 2-1.

The GNP aggregate is the most familiar concept, but it includes some recognized "double counting" by failing to deduct from total business spending on capital goods (structures and durable equipment) the amount of such goods that were used up in the course of producing the year's output of goods and services. The total of business spending on capital goods is the I_g figure of $399.8 billion and the amount of the existing stock of such goods used up during the year is $287.5 billion as shown by the last entry on the income side of Table 2-1. If $287.5 billion is subtracted from $399.8 billion, the remainder is I_n of $112.3 billion or the amount of capital goods added to the preexisting stock during the year. Just as subtracting the figure for capital goods used up from gross fixed investment converts the latter figure into net fixed investment, it converts the total at the bottom of the right side from GNP to NNP. NNP is accordingly $2,628.8 billion minus $287.5 billion or $2,341.3 billion. The only difference between the GNP and NNP aggregates is the amount of capital consumption allowances.'

As will be explained more fully in the next section, because by definition the final amounts of the product and income sides of the account are identical, a broader definition of product like GNP is accompanied by a broader definition of income, and a narrower definition of product like the NNP is accompanied by a narrower definition of income. For every dollar of product there is a dollar of income: The exclusion from product of

TABLE 2-1
National Income and Product Account, 1980
(billions of dollars)

	Compensation of employees			1,596.7
	Wages and salaries		1,343.8	
	Supplements to wages and salaries		252.9	
	Employer contributions for social insurance	115.8		
	Other labor income	137.1		
	Proprietors' income with inventory valuation and capital consumption adjustments			130.6
	Rental income of persons with capital consumption adjustment			31.9
	Corporate profits with inventory valuation and capital consumption adjustments			182.1
	Profits before tax		242.7	
	Profits tax liability	80.8		
	Dividends	56.0		
	Undistributed profits	105.9		
	Inventory valuation adjustment		−43.3	
	Capital consumption adjustment		−17.2	
	Net interest			180.1
NI	National Income			2,121.4
	Business transfer payments			10.5
	Indirect business tax			212.2
	Less: Subsidies less current surplus of government enterprises			4.5
	Statistical discrepancy			1.7
NNP	Charges against Net National Product			2,341.3
	Capital consumption allowances with capital consumption adjustment			287.5
GNP	Charges against Gross National Product			2,628.8

C	Personal consumption expenditures			1,671.1
	Durable goods			211.6
	Nondurable goods			674.3
	Services			785.3
I_g	Gross private domestic investment			396.8
I_{gf}	Fixed investment			399.8
	Nonresidential		294.7	
	Structures	108.3		
	Producers' durable equipment	186.5		
	Residential		105.1	
	Change in business inventories		−3.0	
G	Government purchases of goods and services			534.8
	Federal		199.2	
	National defense	131.9		
	Nondefense	67.3		
	State and local		335.6	
X − M	Net exports of goods and services			26.1
X	Exports		340.6	
M	Imports		314.5	
GNP	Gross National Product			2,628.8

SOURCE: *Survey of Current Business*, U.S. Department of Commerce, February 1981.

the amount of capital goods used up during the period is accompanied by the exclusion from income of the amount otherwise set aside to replace the capital goods consumed.

In the preceding pages, we have focussed on I_{nf}, fixed investment that is a nonduplicative figure, and correspondingly on NNP, also a non-duplicative figure. However, over the years the GNP figure of Table 2-1 has been ordinarily presented to the public and used by economists as the summary figure for the economy's "final" output, despite the double counting it contains. The statisticians derive the NNP figure by subtracting the figure for capital consumption allowances from the figure for GNP. This means that the NNP figure from one year to the next will reflect any inaccuracy in the estimate of the amount of capital goods used up, but the GNP figure will not be affected at all by that error. The technical difficulties faced in estimating the amount of actual capital consumption have made this estimate one of the least reliable in the accounts. Therefore, to avoid the errors that would otherwise be introduced, the Department of Commerce has long emphasized the GNP rather than the NNP aggregate—and correspondingly, the I_{gf} rather than the I_{nf} figure. However, continuing work on the problem led to the publication in 1976 of new estimates of capital consumption that are viewed as sufficiently accurate to permit meaningful measures of I_{nf} and NNP.[3] Therefore, the concept of NNP may gradually come to be as widely recognized by the general public as is the concept of GNP.

Both GNP and NNP include the value of the goods and services produced by labor and property supplied by residents of the United States, whether that labor and property is located in the United States or in other countries. For certain purposes, it is useful to have measures that exclude the value of goods and services produced by the portion of this labor and property

located abroad. If one deducts from GNP the net inflow of income earned on labor and property supplied by U.S. residents abroad (the gross amount so earned minus the amount earned by foreign residents on their labor and property located in this country), the remainder is called **gross domestic product** or GDP.

As will be seen in the following section, the term **national income** is used in the United States accounts for the total of incomes earned by labor and various kinds of property known as factors of production; the amount deducted from GNP to obtain GDP is the portion of the economy's national income that originates in the rest of the world. In 1980 that was $49.9 billion; consequently, GDP was $2,578.9 billion ($2,628.8 billion minus $49.9 billion).

If we start with NNP instead of GNP, a figure for **net domestic product**, NDP, is obtained in the same way. In 1980 NNP was $2,341.3; therefore, NDP was $2,291.4 billion ($2,341.3 minus $49.9). So far, GNP is the more widely used of the two national measures, GNP and NNP. Similarly, GDP is the more widely used of the two domestic measures, GDP and NDP.

Measuring the Value of the Economy's Output of Goods and Services: The Income Approach

Because each dollar's worth of goods produced is matched by a dollar of income, we could arrive at the same figure for the value of the economy's output of goods and services on the income side that we reach on the product side (assuming there are no errors, deficiencies, or inconsistencies in the data or in the estimating procedures). In this section, we will examine the principal steps that must be taken and the principal problems that must be resolved in estimating the value of the economy's output from the income side. Much of what was said in the preceding section of this chapter applies here with appropriate modifications. Just as the approach on the

---

[3]The capital consumption adjustment that underlies these new estimates is described in a later part of this chapter.

expenditures side requires careful specification of what is to be included under the heading of expenditures, so the approach on the income side requires the same for what is to be included under the heading of income. In general, we may include only those particular income flows that originate with the production of the goods and services whose total we seek to estimate. Only then will the total of the income flows equal the total of goods and services.

Exclusions from Income Specifically, on the income side we cannot count the billions of dollars received by people who sell buildings, automobiles, or any other good produced in an earlier time period, because what they receive in payment is not "income" in the sense of something generated in the course of producing the output of the current period. Actually, because such transactions involve a receipt of money from a sale of *assets,* such receipts would not be counted as income in any other sense of the term.

We must also exclude from the income total anything for which neither a good nor a service is supplied in exchange (and for which there is therefore no corresponding production). For example, people who sell stocks and bonds they own receive billions of dollars. But these are simply financial transactions; what the sellers receive is not "income" either in the sense of something generated in the course of producing output during the time period or in any of the other senses usually given to this term. A less obvious example is the income received by people from government in the form of transfer payments (income for which the recipient provides no good or service in exchange). Just as government transfer payments had to be excluded on the expenditures side because they are not expenditures for a good or service, so they must be excluded on the income side because they are not income for which there is corresponding production. The same is true for income received by people from other individuals for which no productive service is rendered. These are nothing more than interpersonal transfer payments. The income total

that we seek is a measure of the value of the economy's output of final goods and services; it can only be such a measure if it excludes every dollar of income which is not matched by a dollar's worth of production of final goods and services. The flows here marked for exclusion are clearly unmatched by any production of goods and services.

What Counts as Income? It might seem at first glance that under this heading we can include all of the receipts of business firms, because each dollar of their receipts is matched by a dollar's worth of goods or services sold. However, it should be apparent that adding up all these amounts will involve the same sort of double, triple, or higher multiple counting that we had to avoid on the expenditures side. We may no more count all the receipts of the wheat farmers, the millers, and the bakers as part of the income total being sought than we could count all the spending by millers, bakers, and people as part of the expenditure total being sought. Only the spending for bread is for a final product. The baker's spending for flour used in making bread and the miller's spending for wheat used in making flour are spending for intermediate products. If a loaf of bread is purchased by a person for 60¢, that is the only spending to be counted in connection with this output.

In working on the income side, total income must equal the value of the economy's output of final goods and services. Accordingly, in the present illustration, income must be defined so that there is a total of 60¢ of income—no more and no less—generated by the production of a loaf of bread. Clearly, if the method of counting income yields a total of 60¢ income for the loaf of bread, the approach on the income side yields the same result as the approach on the spending side. We will get this same result, if from the *total receipts* of the baker, the miller, and the farmer is deducted whatever each of these paid to purchase materials from other firms that each in turn used up at his stage of production. This is the equivalent of the earlier discussed process of cancelling out intermediate product to arrive at final product, but here it is viewed as a cancelling out of part of a firm's total receipts to arrive at what may be called income in the sense here given to that term.

For a simple numerical illustration, suppose again that a consumer spends 60¢ for a loaf of bread at the bakery. As we have seen, this is spending for final product and that 60¢ enters into the total that is GNP for that period. The baker obviously shows 60¢ of receipts as a result of this transaction, but that 60¢ is not all income as the term is here defined. From it must be deducted the amount of materials purchased from other firms. Assume for simplicity that the only material needed to make bread is flour and that the purchase price of the flour that goes into a loaf of bread is 32¢. Deducting 32¢ from 60¢ leaves 28¢ to be counted as income. Assume that the miller who received the 32¢ from the baker paid 20¢ to the farmer for the wheat involved. Deducting the 20¢ from the 32¢ leaves 12¢ to be counted as income by the miller. Lastly, assuming that the wheat farmer makes no purchases from any other firms, there is no deduction from the 20¢ he receives so that it can be counted as income in its entirety. Summing up, we find that the loaf of bread is matched by 20¢ of income generated at the farmer stage, 12¢ of income generated at the miller stage, and 28¢ of income generated at the baker stage—a total of 60¢, the same amount at which this unit of output would be valued when approached from the expenditure side.

Although our purpose here is to focus on the fact that the 20¢, 12¢, and 28¢ amounts are amounts of income generated at the successive stages of production, note that these amounts are also commonly described as amounts of **value added.** Because the miller takes 20¢ of wheat and turns it into something he sells for 32¢, he is said to add 12¢ of value to the wheat. In the same way, the baker adds 28¢ of value to the flour purchased from the miller. Because the farmer did not purchase anything from any other firm, the entire 20¢ for which he sells the wheat is value added.

"Value added" may seem a more appropriate term than "income" to describe the amounts in question. Most people think of the amount of income originating in a bakery or on a farm or in any other firm as the amount of the firm's *profit.* As used here, income includes profit and much more. To turn again to our illustration, in the case of the baker we know that 32¢ of materials (assuming flour to be the only material) is used up in producing a loaf of bread that can be sold for 60¢. However, the remaining 28¢ (here called income) is not the baker's profit on this unit of production. Suppose that 20¢ is the amount of wage and salary costs incurred in producing this unit of output, that 2¢ is due the government for sales tax included in the sale price, that 1¢ is to be allowed to cover depreciation of the baker's ovens and other durable assets, and that another 1¢ is charged to meet the interest cost on the firm's debts. If anything is left, that is the amount of the baker's profit on this unit of ouput. The present illustration shows this residual to be 4¢, but it could be a larger or smaller amount, even a negative amount, depending on the total of the other costs. Although the baker is, for obvious reasons, primarily concerned with this profit residual, we are primarily concerned with finding the total amount of income that originates in each firm as a step toward deriving an estimate for the value of the economy's output as measured from the income side.

It should be clear that what was described here for the baker could in the same way be described for the miller and the farmer. In each case, there is no problem in seeing why the wage and salary costs incurred by each firm are called income, once we examine these from the viewpoint of the worker to whom they are receipts. Similarly, the firms' interest costs, indirect tax costs, and the residual called profit are all plainly income from the viewpoint of the recipient. Depreciation costs are also a part of income by the present definition, but they are retained by the firm and in effect set aside for possible future use. In this way, the 60¢ value of the loaf of bread will correspond to 60¢ of income made up of wage and salary income, interest income, profit income, government income from sales and related types of taxes known as indirect taxes, and an amount of income retained by firms in the form of additions to depreciation reserves.[4]

Having established what is to be included as income, we need not concern ourselves with the income generated by the production of any one loaf of bread or by all loaves of bread combined or even with the income generated by the whole baking industry. We may turn directly to industry as a whole. Our immediate purpose is to estimate from the income side the value of the whole economy's output of final goods and services. We may proceed straightforwardly toward this objective by preparing economy-wide estimates of the totals for wages and salaries, interest, business profits, and other income items that are to be included. Apart from a few minor items not here entered into, the total of these amounts is the total income of the economy in the present sense of the term. Once allowance is made for the items not here covered, the total so obtained will be the same as the total that was reached on the expenditures side (assuming equally good data and estimations on the two sides).

From Gross National Product to Disposable Personal Income

The approach on the expenditures side yielded two totals, GNP and NNP, which differ by the amount of capital consumption. We could identify two corresponding totals on the income side and assign corresponding names to them. Thus, some people choose to label as Gross National Income the total on the income side that is equal to GNP on the product side. Similarly, by sub-

tracting capital consumption from Gross National Income on the income side, the remainder may be called Net National Income because it equals Net National Product on the product side. However, usual practice is to use only the GNP and NNP terms when referring to these totals. As shown in Table 2-1, which in general follows the National Income and Product Account as presented by the Department of Commerce, the two totals in question are not designated income totals but Charges against GNP and Charges against NNP.

GNP and NNP are two of three principal measures of the economy's output presented in the U.S. national income accounts. National Income, NI, found on the income side of Table 2-1, is the third measure. NI values output at "factor cost" or in terms of the factor incomes earned (though not necessarily received) by the factors of production. As shown by the classification on the income side of Table 2-1, *NI* is the sum of the following: compensation of employees, which is made up of wages and salaries and supplements such as employer contributions for social insurance and private pension plans; proprietors' income, which is income of self-employed individuals; rental income, which includes rental income of persons only incidentally engaged in the real estate business and imputed rental income on owner-occupied dwellings; corporate profits, including inventory valuation and capital consumption adjustments; and net interest, which is paid to people by business units.[5] Each of these income flows is a return for the amount of a service rendered by a factor of production; the total is the amount earned by all the factors of production for all factor services rendered by

---

[4] Government will, of course, take part of wage and salary income, interest income, and profit income through direct taxes or income taxes, but that is another matter. Here we look at these income receipts before income taxes on them are paid.

[5] The imputation for rental value of owner-occupied dwellings and the inventory valuation and capital consumption adjustments under corporate profits are all explained in later sections of this chapter. (Inventory valuation and capital consumption adjustments for proprietors' income and a capital consumption adjustment for rental income of persons also exist, but are not shown separately in Table 2-1; the figures given there include these adjustments.)

them. That total is, therefore, a measure of the value of the economy's output based on factor cost. On the expenditures side, GNP and NNP are derived by adding up expenditures on goods and services, with each unit of each good and service valued at the price paid for it. This approach values goods at "market price." The market price of any good, from a loaf of bread to a jet aircraft, will typically be greater than the "factor cost" of producing that good. The market price will ordinarily include an amount to cover depreciation of the capital goods used in its production and an amount to cover any indirect taxes—sales taxes, for example—that must be paid by its seller to the government.

As we have seen, NNP for any period is a measure of a smaller amount of actual output than is GNP. NNP excludes the portion of output equal to the capital goods used up in producing that period's output. NNP and NI, however, are both measures of the same amount of goods, although they value these goods on different bases. NNP will always be greater than NI, because the market price of the amount of goods in question will always exceed the factor cost by approximately the amount of indirect taxes. As shown by Table 2-1, for 1980 the NNP of $2,341.3 billion exceeded the NI of $2,121.4 billion by $219.9 billion, which is primarily accounted for by indirect taxes of $212.2 billion and business transfer payments (gifts, prizes, and such for which business receives no good or service in exchange) of $10.5. Two minor items make up the balance of the difference between NI and NNP: subsidies less current surplus of government enterprises (a very small but rather technical item that will not be covered) and the statistical discrepancy. Statistical discrepancy is merely the difference between the estimated sum of the items on the product side and the items on the income side. If the sum on the income side exceeds that on the product side, a corresponding negative figure is entered on the income side to make the sum on that side equal the sum on the product side; in the opposite case, the appropriate positive amount is entered.

Although they are not measures of the economy's output, there are two other important income measures, Personal Income, PI, and Disposable Personal Income, DPI, the second of which is especially important for our later work on personal consumption spending. Personal income is the current income of persons from all sources. It is not a measure of output or production, because it includes some amount to which there is no corresponding production. It includes both receipts for the productive services provided by individuals and receipts, such as transfer payments, for which no productive services were provided by the recipients. DPI is derived from PI simply by deducting the amount taken by government in personal taxes. The remainder is available to people to dispose of as they see fit. Because DPI is derived from PI, which is not a measure of output, DPI in turn is not a measure of output.

The way in which PI and DPI are related to the three measures of output—GNP, NNP, and NI—and also the way in which these measures of output are related to each other is best seen by starting with the broadest aggregate, GNP, and identifying the flows that are subtracted and added in moving from one aggregate to the next. This is done in Table 2-2. As in Table 2-1, the figures are for 1980.

The steps downward from GNP to NNP and from NNP to NI in Table 2-2 are the same as the steps upward from the total at the bottom of the income side of Table 2-1 to the NI figure on that side of Table 2-1. However, whereas Table 2-1 then shows above NI the various factor income flows which add up to NI, Table 2-2 proceeds to show how another income aggregate, PI, is related to NI. First, those portions of NI that are not received by individuals are subtracted. As shown in Table 2-1, the major component of NI is compensation of employees; the figure for this component is an estimate of the amount earned for the labor services provided by all employees. However, if we want to know the amount actually received by all employees for their labor services, we must deduct from compensation of

TABLE 2-2
Relation of Gross National Product, Net National Product, National Income, Personal Income, and Disposable Personal Income, 1980
(billions of dollars)

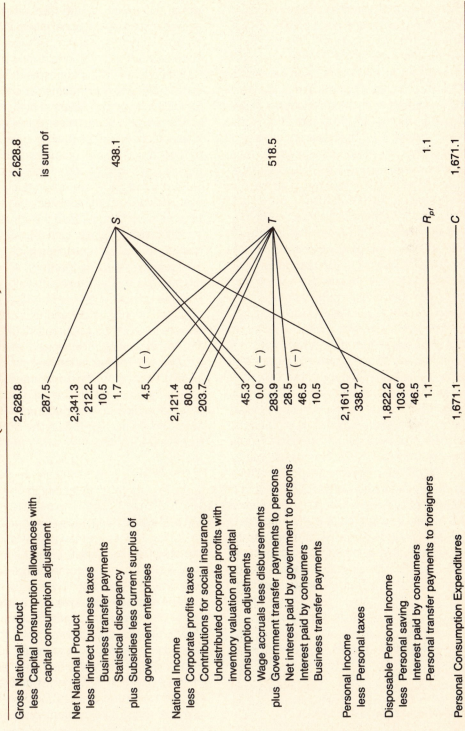

Gross National Product	2,628.8	2,628.8 — is sum of
less Capital consumption allowances with capital consumption adjustment	287.5	
Net National Product	2,341.3	
less Indirect business taxes	212.2	
Business transfer payments	10.5	
Statistical discrepancy	1.7	*S* 438.1
plus Subsidies less current surplus of government enterprises	4.5 (−)	
National Income	2,121.4	
less Corporate profits taxes	80.8	
Contributions for social insurance	203.7	
Undistributed corporate profits with inventory valuation and capital consumption adjustments	45.3	
Wage accruals less disbursements	0.0 (−)	
plus Government transfer payments to persons	283.9	*T* 518.5
Net interest paid by government to persons	28.5 (−)	
Interest paid by consumers	46.5	
Business transfer payments	10.5	
Personal Income	2,161.0	
less Personal taxes	338.7	
Disposable Personal Income	1,822.2	
less Personal saving	103.6	
Interest paid by consumers	46.5	
Personal transfer payments to foreigners	1.1	R_{pf} 1.1
Personal Consumption Expenditures	1,671.1	*C* 1,671.1

SOURCE: *Survey of Current Business*, U.S. Department of Commerce, February 1981.

employees the contributions for social insurance which is an amount diverted to the government.[6] Similarly, the total of corporate profits is factor income and therefore part of NI, but part of this total is paid to government in corporate profits taxes and part is withheld by corporations as undistributed profits. Only the remainder (dividends) is passed on to become income of people; in other words, only this part of corporate profits is included in PI. The treatment of the other components of NI—proprietors' income, rental income of individuals, and net interest—shows the full amount of each passing on to become income of individuals.

Next, to arrive at the total for PI, it is necessary to add other income of individuals that is not income received for productive services rendered to the portion of NI that becomes PI. As shown in Table 2-2, the additions are government transfer payments, interest income from government and consumers, and business transfer payments. The first of these four items is by far the largest. Remember that only government purchases of goods and services are included on the expenditure side of Table 2-1, because there is a dollar of production corresponding only to each of these dollars of government spending. Therefore, this portion of government spending is included in GNP and thus is reflected in the total at the top of Table 2-2. The balance of government spending—primarily government transfer payments—is not part of GNP, but is part of PI. Consequently, it is picked up in the PI total as shown in Table 2-2. The other major item that is not part of GNP but is part of PI is certain interest income. Briefly, the net interest component of NI in Table 2-1 is interest paid by business. This kind of interest is treated as part of NI because business uses the borrowed funds for productive purposes. Borrowing by government and by consumers is not viewed as borrowing for productive purposes; consequently, the interest paid on such borrowing is not included in NI. However, like government transfer payments, this interest is counted as part of PI and is inserted as shown to arrive at that total. Finally, there is the addition of the amount of business transfer payments. This amount is part of GNP but is subtracted in moving from GNP to NI, because such payments are not factor income to their recipients who provide no productive service in exchange. However, they are income to persons and are added back in to get from NI to PI.

After working down to PI from GNP, the step from PI to the final income aggregate, DPI, is made by subtracting personal tax payments (such as personal income taxes) from PI. DPI is then the amount available to people to dispose of as they choose, and they choose to save some amount of this total each year. Deducting from DPI the amount of personal saving and amounts for personal transfer payments to foreigners and interest payments by consumers leaves the amount of personal consumption expenditures, C, which makes up the great bulk of DPI every year. The figure found here for C is the same figure shown for that flow on the product side of Table 2-1.

Accounting Identities

The structure of Table 2-2 has permitted us to start out with a figure for the GNP or the gross income flow and to work down to find how much of it was spent on consumer goods and services. Out of the gross of $2,628.8 billion for 1980, $1,671.1 billion was spent on consumption. The structure of Table 2-2 also permits us to derive the amount of the gross income flow that was taken by government in taxes and the amount that went into private saving. Given the way that saving and taxes are defined in the accounts, the

---

[6]One might argue that a deduction should be made for the amount of income taxes withheld from paychecks because that amount of employee compensation also is not received by people. However, as this is only part of personal income taxes, the practice is to include as Personal Income all such income before the personal income taxes thereon and then deduct the total of such income taxes in one step going from PI to DPI.

difference of $957.7 billion between the gross income flow and the amount of it spent on consumption is, apart from a minor amount for personal transfer payments to foreigners, entirely accounted for by the sum of taxes, $518.5 billion, and private saving, $438.1 billion.

Bringing together the breakdown on the product side and the breakdown on the income side gives the following GNP identity:[7]

$$C + S + T + R_{pf} \equiv GNP$$
$$\$1,671.1 + 438.1 + 518.5 + 1.1 = 2,628.8$$
$$\equiv C + I + G + (X - M)$$
$$= 1,671.1 + 396.8 + 534.8 + (340.6 - 314.5)$$

Here S is the sum of personal and business saving and T is the sum of social insurance contributions or taxes, indirect taxes, corporate profits taxes, and personal taxes after an adjustment of that sum that will be noted later. The derivation of the figures in this identity may be seen by following the lines in Table 2-2 which classify various items listed on the left under C, S, and T and R_{pf} on the right.

The figure for C appears explicitly because Table 2-2 is structured to show this figure as one end product. The minor item, R_{pf}, is also explicitly identified. The figure for S is derived by adding together the amounts of the gross income flow saved by businesses and by individuals, the private domestic sectors of the economy. This total is found as the sum of the amounts given for four items. First, the amount of the gross income flow that shows up as capital consumption allowances, $287.5 billion, is a kind of business saving, a portion of the gross flow received by businesses that is set aside for replacement of capital goods. Next, the amount that is retained by busi-

nesses as undistributed profits, $45.3 billion, is quite clearly saving—a portion of corporate profits that is not paid out to anyone else.[8] The sum of these two amounts, $332.8 billion, is total business saving. The total for private saving is then obtained by adding to total business saving the amount of personal saving ($103.6 billion) and the minor amount for the statistical discrepancy, $1.7 billion (which must be put in somewhere to provide a balance and is put in here on the assumption that the discrepancy arises from errors in the estimates of the indicated saving flows). The addition of these three amounts yields S of $438.1 billion.

How much of the gross income flow is taken by government in taxes? In Table 2-2, four of the lines running to T show the four kinds of tax receipts of government into which all tax receipts are classified. These are indirect business taxes, $212.2 billion, corporate profits taxes, $80.8 billion, contributions for social insurance, $203.7 billion (a tax in effect though not in name), and personal taxes, $338.7 billion. The total is $835.4 billion. If we add this total for T to the amounts already found for C, S, and R_{pf}, the sum will be $2,945.7 billion. This amount is $316.9 billion greater than GNP or, what is the same thing, that much greater than the total for $C + I + G + (X - M)$. The discrepancy arises from the fact that we quite correctly include only government purchases of goods and services in G on the product side of the previous GNP identity and so far have included gross tax receipts on the income side of that identity. To be consistent, as all government expenditures other than those for goods and services are omitted on the product side, an equal amount of tax receipts should be omitted on the income side. To show tax receipts on such a net basis, an amount equal to government expenditures other than those for goods and services is deducted from gross tax receipts.

---

[7]To simplify, I now appears without a subscript. However, if reference is to GNP, I must be I_g, and if reference is to NNP, I must be I_n. Similarly, on the income side, if reference is to the gross concept, S must include the capital consumption allowances component of private saving, and if reference is to the net concept, S must exclude this component of saving.

---

[8]The original amount of undistributed profits, $105.9 billion, is adjusted downward by $60.5 billion, the sum of the inventory valuation adjustment and the capital consumption adjustment.

These expenditures are identified in Table 2-2 by the other three lines running to T: subsidies less current surplus of government enterprises, $4.5 billion, government transfer payments, $283.9 billion, and government interest payments to persons, $28.5 billion. Subtracting the total of these three items, $316.9 billion, from gross taxes of $835.4 billion leaves net taxes of $518.5 billion, which is the net tax concept to which T in Table 2-2 refers. With taxes on a net basis, the sum of $C + S + T + R_{pf}$ is found to be identical with GNP.

Another basic identity is obtained by dropping C from both sides of the GNP identity first stated in this section.

$$S \quad + \quad T \quad + \quad R_{pf} \equiv$$
$$\$438.1 + \ 518.5 + \ 1.1 \qquad = \$957.7$$

$$I \quad + \quad G \quad + \quad (X \quad - \quad M)$$
$$\$396.8 + \ 534.8 + \ (340.6 - 314.5) = \$957.7$$

The sum on the top is the amount of the gross income flow not devoted to consumption expenditures. The sum on the bottom is the amount of the gross output flow that does not go into the hands of consumers. Roughly, this identity reveals that during any time period there is a dollar of saving or taxes in the system for every dollar of investment, government purchases, and net exports. The full significance of this identity and the GNP identity above will become clear in Part 2. There these accounting relationships provide a framework within which we build the theory of income determination.

The GNP identity above includes all four sectors—consumers, businesses, governmental units, and the rest of the world—found in the actual economy. However, in developing the theory of income determination in Part 2, we will not start off by including all four sectors; we will therefore not start with the GNP identity for a four-sector economy. To approach the complications of the real economy by steps, we begin with a hypothetical economy limited to consumers and businesses only. In such a two-sector economy, the GNP identity is reduced to

$$C + S \equiv GNP \equiv C + I$$

The omission of government removes G and T, and the omission of the rest of the world removes $(X - M)$ and R_{pf}. On the product side, the amount of the economy's output obtained by consumers is measured by personal consumption expenditures; the amount that remains is investment for that time period. On the income side, the income flow equal to the value of output is divided between personal consumption expenditures and saving.

Another identity for the two-sector economy is derived from the first by dropping C from both sides.

$$S \equiv I$$

For the simple case of a two-sector economy, this identity reveals that there is a dollar of investment for every dollar of saving. Because there is a dollar of income for every dollar of output and because the amount of income not spent for consumer goods is equal to saving in this two-sector economy, it follows that the amount of saving is equal to the amount of investment. In other words, the amount of income that is not used to purchase consumer goods and services is equal to the amount of output that does not go into the hands of consumers.

A special property of a two-sector economy is that NNP, NI, PI, and DPI all become equal if we make a few assumptions. With government excluded, most of the items that are found between NNP and DPI in Table 2-2 simply drop out. If we assume that corporations pay out all earnings in dividends (undistributed profits are zero), and assume a zero value for the statistical discrepancy, business transfer payments, inventory valuation adjustment and capital consumption adjustment, and consumer interest payments, the result will be NNP = NI = PI = DPI. This special case—in which there is a dollar of DPI for every dollar of NNP—is employed in the analysis of Chapters 4 and 5.

The three-sector economy examined in Chapter 6 adds the government sector to the consumer and business sectors, but excludes the rest of the world. There is then a three-way split on both sides of the GNP identity:

$$C + S + T \equiv \text{GNP} \equiv C + I + G$$

As before, by dropping C from both sides, another identity, a saving and investment identity, is derived:

$$S + T \equiv I + G$$

This may also be written as

$$S + (T - G) \equiv I$$

S has been identified as private saving, the sum of consumer and business saving. Total saving is the sum of private saving and public saving, and public saving is $(T - G)$, positive for a budget surplus and negative for a budget deficit. With government included, there is still an identity between saving and investment; the sum of private and public saving is now by definition equal to investment. However, unlike the identity for the two-sector economy, private saving, S, is no longer by definition equal to I. S will equal I only if $(T - G)$ equals zero—that is, only if there is a balanced budget. With a balanced budget, there is neither public saving (a surplus) nor public dissaving (a deficit).

Finally, bringing in the rest of the world returns us to the four-sector economy with which we started and for which the GNP identity is

$$C + S + T + R_{pf} \equiv \text{GNP} \equiv C + I + G + (X - M)$$

In Chapter 7, we will work with this identity for a four-sector economy.

Chapters 4–7 are concerned with the development of what is commonly called the simple theory of income determination, and the series of identities that have emerged from the national income accounting so far covered in this chapter will be used in those chapters in the order indicated.

Final Product— Current and Constant Dollars

All references to income and product totals so far in this chapter have been to those for the year 1980. Each of these totals, of course, changes from year to year. The change in each may be due to a change in the physical quantities being measured, a change in the prices at which these quantities are valued, or both. Consequently, a total like the GNP can rise from one year to the next even though the amount of actual output measured by GNP decreases. This last happened from 1979 to 1980; the rise in prices was sufficiently large to result in a higher GNP in 1980 than in 1979, despite the fact that actual output had decreased.

Figures for GNP or other totals for different years are usually compared to determine the changes that have occurred in the underlying real amounts. However, if these yearly totals are expressed in prices current in each year, such comparisons cannot be made. The effects of price changes must be eliminated from these figures to reveal the actual volume changes over time.

One apparently easy method of accomplishing this might be to divide any year's final product, valued in that year's prices, by a price index such as the Consumer Price Index. By doing so one expresses the value of that year's final product as the dollar amount it would have been if prices had been the same as those in the base year of the index. For example, suppose that the Consumer Price Index, equal to 100 in the selected base year 1967, was 120 in the year 1971. This would indicate that consumer prices were 20 percent higher in 1971 than in 1967. Suppose further that 1967 final product valued in 1967 prices is $200 and 1971 final product valued in 1971 prices is $300. Because we know that prices have risen during these years, this increase of $100 in final product is clearly not altogether due to increased volume. How do we determine what part of the increase is attributable to higher prices and what part to higher volume? One way of solving the problem is to divide 1971 final product valued in 1971 prices by the ratio of 1971 prices to 1967 prices:

$$\frac{\$300}{120/100} = \$300 \times \frac{100}{120} = \$250$$

This reveals that half of the increase in final product of $100 measured in 1971 prices was due to an increase in volume and half to a rise in prices. In other words, 1971 final product valued in 1967 prices was $250. Final product for other years could be converted from prices current in each of those years to the prices in effect in 1967 in the same fashion. Accordingly, final product for each year would be expressed in "constant dollars of 1967 purchasing power," here measuring changes in the purchasing power of the dollar by the Consumer Price Index.[9]

In our numerical example, we may reliably conclude that the volume of final goods and services in 1971 was not 50 percent greater than

[9] Designating final product by GNP, it follows that in any given year (g), GNP is that year's volume of output (O_g) multiplied by the prices paid for each unit of that output (P_g), or $GNP_g = O_g \times P_g$. Expressing prices of any given year as a percentage of prices in the base year yields a price index in which base-year prices are equal to 100. In other words, the index number for any given year is P_g/P_b, in which b designates the base year. Finally, the GNP figure for any given year may be converted into a figure for the output of the given year valued in base-year prices by dividing it by the price index for the given year:

$$\frac{GNP_g}{P_g/P_b} = \frac{O_g \times P_g}{P_g/P_b} = O_g \times P_g\frac{P_b}{P_g} = O_g \times P_b$$

Performing this operation for each given year yields a series of final figures for GNP in which output, O_g, is valued in base-year prices, P_b. Comparison of these adjusted GNP figures will presumably show only changes in volume, the effect of changes in prices having been eliminated.

that in 1967 ($300/$200 = 1.50). Can we also reliably conclude that it was 25 percent greater than that in 1967 ($250/$200 = 1.25), as indicated by the 1971 dollar value of $300 corrected to $250 by the Consumer Price Index? No. We have merely adjusted the 1971 market value of all kinds of diverse goods and services by a single price index. This price index is at best appropriate only to that part of final product made up of the goods and services purchased by consumers. For the same reason, adjustment of 1971 final product by the Producer Price Index or any other single price index would be unreliable.

The fact that no single price index is appropriate suggests that we must break down final product as finely as possible and then adjust each part by a price index appropriate to the goods and services included in it. This is essentially the procedure followed by the Commerce Department.[10] Personal consumption expenditures are broken down into dozens of parts; for each part, a special price index is prepared if an acceptable one is not already available. A similar procedure is followed for government purchases of goods and services, gross domestic investment, and exports and imports. In each case, the dollar value of each part for the given year is divided by its price index number for that year. When totaled, the resulting dollar value is the given year's GNP valued in base-year prices.

At present, base-year prices are those of 1972. Therefore, in any year, the price-adjusted figure for each part of GNP is what the physical amount of goods and services that make up that

[10] In cases for which there are ways of measuring directly the change in volume of a final good or service over time (for example, in gross domestic investment, the number of freight cars of a given description purchased by railroads, or in government purchases of goods and services, the man-hours of labor, or the number of persons of a given class employed), the physical quantity purchased in any year multiplied by the base-year price per unit will equal the value of that final good or service for the year in base-year prices. This technique bypasses the need for a price index. If data on volume are available, the department uses this method whenever it appears that it can obtain more accurate results.

part would have been valued at if those goods and services had carried 1972 price tags rather than their actual price tags. Adding up the values expressed in 1972 prices of all the separate parts of GNP yields a total expressed in 1972 prices. For example, the 1980 GNP was $2,628.8 billion before this price adjustment; after the adjustment, it was $1,481.8 billion. This means that the physical amount of goods and services that actually made up 1980 GNP could have been purchased for $1,481.8 billion in 1972 prices.

We can follow the same steps to produce a series of figures for the years from 1929 to 1980. The GNP figure for each before price adjustment is known as *GNP in current dollars;* after price adjustment, it is known as *GNP in constant dollars.* The current dollar and constant (1972) dollar GNP figures for selected years from 1929 through 1980 are listed in columns 2 and 3 of Table 2-3 (page 40).[11] These two series are also plotted for 1973–80 in Figure 2-1. This figure shows the rate of change for each of the two series for indicated portions of the 1973–80 period.

The constant dollar figures for GNP are also commonly referred to as the "deflated" values, a term which suggests that the effect of higher prices has been taken out. This term is entirely appropriate for all of the years since 1972, the base year, because the price level in all of these years has been higher than in 1972. However, to obtain constant dollar figures for years before 1972, it is actually necessary to inflate rather than deflate the current dollar figures because the price level in each year from 1929 through 1971 was lower than it was in 1972. For example, the current dollar GNP for 1929 was $103.4 billion. But prices in 1972 were about three times what they were in 1929. Therefore, after adjusting the current dollar figure for each part of 1929 GNP with the appropriate price index, the sum of the adjusted figures adds up to $315.7 billion. Constant dollar GNP for 1929 (in 1972 dollars) is a little over three times the current dollar GNP for that year. Although the procedure amounts to "inflating" rather than "deflating" the current dollar GNP, by convention the term "deflating" is used in both cases.

Our immediate interest here is with the distinction between current dollar and constant dollar GNP and the way in which the latter is obtained. However, an important byproduct of the deflation procedure that yields the constant dollar GNP is the **GNP implicit price deflator.** The 1980 current dollar GNP was $2,628.8 billion; the 1980 constant dollar GNP was $1,481.8 billion. The ratio of the 1980 current dollar figure to the 1980 constant dollar figure is the ratio of 1980 prices to 1972 prices for all the goods and services in the GNP. In 1980, that ratio was 1.774; in other words, 1980 prices were 77.4 percent higher than 1972 prices. Expressed as an index number with 1972 = 100, the number for 1980 was 177.4. This is the GNP implicit price deflator for 1980. The GNP deflator for other years is obtained in the same way. These numbers are listed in Column 4 of Table 2-3.

Because this price index number emerges indirectly from the deflation procedure which yields the constant dollar GNP, it is referred to as *implicit.* Unlike the Consumer Price Index or the Producer Price Index, it is not directly calculated but is implicit in the current and constant dollar GNP figures. We will examine this price index further in Chapter 21, in which we examine the Consumer Price Index, the Producer Price Index, and other prices indexes widely used to measure the rate of inflation.

Imputations

In a predominantly market economy like that of the United States, the great bulk of the economy's income and output will be counted in the course of estimating the amounts of income and expenditure that are explicitly in monetary form. How-

---

[11] Although GNP in constant dollars remains the most widely used measure of real aggregate output, NNP and NI as well as other aggregates are reported in constant as well as current dollars. Data for these series as well as the implicit price deflators for each will be found in the *Survey of Current Business.*

TABLE 2-3
GNP in Current and Constant Dollars
and the GNP Implicit Price Deflator,
Selected Years, 1929–80
(billions of dollars)

(1) Year	(2) Current Dollars	(3) Constant Dollars	(4) GNP Implicit Price Deflator
1929	$ 103.4	$ 315.7	32.8
1933	55.8	222.1	25.1
1937	90.9	310.2	29.3
1939	90.9	319.8	28.4
1945	212.4	560.4	37.9
1948	259.5	489.8	53.0
1950	286.5	534.8	53.6
1954	366.8	616.1	59.6
1957	444.0	683.8	64.9
1958	449.7	680.9	66.0
1962	565.0	800.3	70.6
1965	691.1	929.3	74.4
1968	873.4	1,058.1	82.5
1969	944.0	1,087.6	86.8
1970	992.7	1,085.6	91.4
1971	1,077.6	1,122.4	96.0
1972	1,185.9	1,185.9	100.0
1973	1,326.4	1,255.0	105.7
1974	1,434.2	1,248.0	114.9
1975	1,549.2	1,233.9	125.6
1976	1,718.0	1,300.4	132.1
1977	1,918.0	1,371.7	139.8
1978	2,156.1	1,436.9	150.0
1979	2,413.9	1,483.0	162.8
1980	2,628.8	1,481.8	177.4

SOURCE: *Economic Report of the President*, January 1981, and *Survey of Current Business*, U.S. Department of Commerce, February 1981.

ever, even in an economy like ours, restricting income and product to those flows that take monetary form clearly understates the economy's actual income and output. There are nonmonetary income and product flows that would escape inclusion unless certain imputed values were added to the accounts. We can best reveal the nature of these imputations by describing some of those presently made by the U.S. Department of Commerce in the preparation of its income and product estimates.

Rental Value of Owner-Occupied Dwellings

A person who rents a home to another earns gross rental income, which becomes net rental

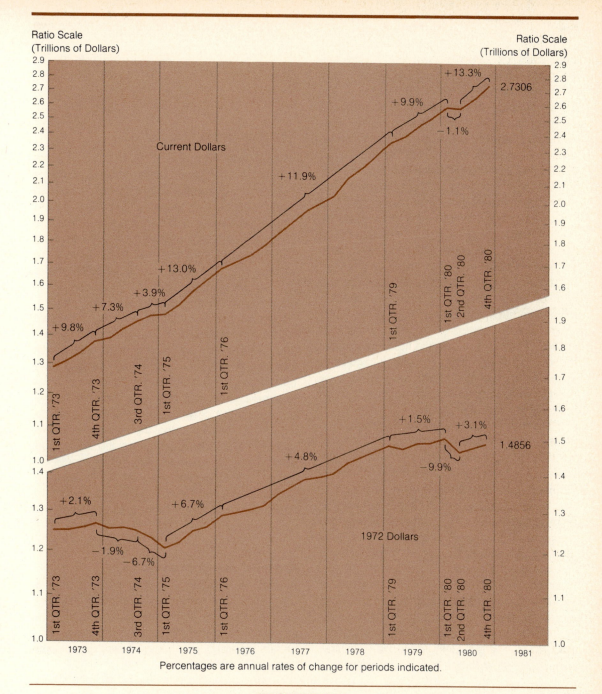

FIGURE 2-1
Gross National Product Quarterly Totals
at Annual Rates, 1973–80

SOURCE: *National Economic Trends*, Federal Reserve Bank of St. Louis, March 1981.

income after deduction of expenses.[12] To the tenant, rent paid for the dwelling is an expenditure for the purchase of the services of property. It is part of personal consumption expenditures and therefore part of GNP. For owner-occupied dwellings, however, there is in monetary terms neither net rental income as part of national income nor rent paid as part of GNP. Because the same real product is provided by a house whether it is owner or tenant occupied, an imputation is made to provide consistent treatment in the accounts. It is assumed for accounting purposes that house ownership is a business in which the owner sells the services of the house to himself as a tenant. The amount of imputed rent is estimated as the sum for which the owner-occupied dwelling could have been rented; the imputed net rental income is estimated as that portion of the sum that would have accrued to the homeowner after deduction of all expenses. As such, it somewhat resembles a profit that would be earned by a property owner whose ordinary business is the renting of residential property.

As a result of this imputation, personal consumption expenditure is increased on the product side of the National Income and Product Account by the imputed gross rental for owner-occupied dwellings. Net rental income of individuals, indirect taxes (property taxes), net interest (on mortgages), capital consumption allowances (depreciation of owner-occupied homes), plus other adjustments add an equal amount on the income side of the account.

Without this imputation, GNP would vary in response to changes toward or away from home ownership. In any given time period, the larger the fraction of total housing that was tenant occupied, the larger GNP would be. Similarly, GNP would grow larger over successive time periods with a trend away from home ownership toward home rental. By making this imputation, we avoid such distortions in GNP.

Wages and Salaries Paid in Kind

In Table 2-1, included among the supplements that are part of compensation of employees is an imputed amount for wages and salaries paid in kind. This simply acknowledges the fact that some compensation of employees takes the form of food and lodging provided by employers. No allowance for this labor income would be made in the national accounts if compensation of employees were limited only to monetary income. Accordingly, an estimate of wages and salaries paid in kind is shown as a supplement to wages and salaries on the income side and as an increase in personal consumption expenditures on the product side. In effect, this accounting treatment assumes that the employer pays employees the dollar value of the free food and lodging provided and that the employees in turn spend this amount to purchase the same food and lodging from the employer. The imputation thereby adds an equal amount to GNP in the form of personal consumption expenditures and to national income in the form of compensation of employees.

Other Imputations

Among the other imputations included in the official accounts are those made for food and fuel produced and consumed on farms, and for non-monetary income and product flows arising from certain operations of commercial banks and financial intermediaries.

There are many other possible imputations that are not included in the official accounts. One of these is production in the form of housewives' services in their own homes. Because there is no statistically sound method of estimating the value of this production, there is no way of including it

---

[12] Net rental income of persons is limited to the rental income of persons *not* primarily engaged in the real estate business. Net rental income of those so engaged appears as proprietors' income and, in the case of corporations, as corporate profits.

by imputation. We must live with the paradox that results from its omission.[13] All of the housewife's output is excluded from the national output. If, however, the housewife were to hire a woman who was previously employed in a factory to do the housework, and she took that woman's place in the factory, GNP would show a net increase equal to the amount of the salary paid to the woman hired to perform the housework. Actual output would be unchanged, but the estimate for GNP would be larger. The same paradox applies to work performed by men around the house. None of this production is included in GNP, yet all of it would be included at the full price paid if a gardener, painter, baby sitter, or cook were hired to do the same work.[14]

With recognition of imputations—both those that are made and those that are not—comes recognition of the frequently overlooked fact that GNP, as officially defined, does not purport to be a measure of the economy's output in any all-inclusive sense. By the same token, national income does not purport to be a measure of factor earnings in any all-inclusive sense. Much is excluded from both income and product that would be included under broader definitions.

Change in Inventories and the Inventory Valuation Adjustment

Part of final product for any year is whatever change in inventories occurs during that year. In 1980 the change was − $3.0 billion, which made final product that much smaller than it otherwise would have been for that year. In 1979 the change was $17.5 billion, which had a corresponding effect in the other direction.

Figures like − $3.0 or $17.5 billion are the Commerce Department's estimates of the physical volume change in inventories for the year, valued at average prices paid for goods added to inventories during the year. This change may be larger or smaller than the book value change in inventories for the year as shown by the accounting data of business firms. The difference between the department's published figure and the figure derived from business accounting data is the inventory valuation adjustment (IVA). This adjustment, on the product side of the National Income and Product Account, is designed to avoid under- or overstating the change in inventories and therefore to avoid under- or overstating gross domestic investment and gross national product; on the income side, the adjustment avoids under- or overstating corporate profits and proprietors' income and therefore national income.

Although the department's methods of estimating the amount of the adjustment are very complicated, the meaning of the adjustment itself is fairly simple. Suppose, for example, that business book values show an increase in inventories of $3 billion during the year. This figure may be accompanied by an increase, no change, or even a decrease in the physical volume of inventories, because the book value change depends not only on the change in volume but also on changes over the year in the prices paid for inventories acquired. Assume that the change in inventories valued at average prices for the year is only $1 billion. The discrepancy between the two figures then follows from book values based on prices that are higher than average prices for the year. The Commerce Department would add

---

[13]For an approach to the measurement of this production, see R. Gronau, "The Measurement of Output of the Nonmarket Sector: The Evaluation of Housewives' Time," in M. Moss, editor, *The Measurement of Economic and Social Performance,* Volume Thirty-Eight, Studies in Income and Wealth, National Bureau of Economic Research, 1973. If this production were included, it would appear as

compensation of employees on the income side and as personal consumption expenditures on the product side.

[14]Only that part of production represented by the homeowner's labor services escapes inclusion; the grass seed, paint, lumber, and other materials are included in gross national product in both cases.

an IVA of − $2 billion to the book value figure of $3 billion to derive a net change of $1 billion in inventories valued at average prices for the year.

If prices were falling during the year, the discrepancy would be positive. The change in inventories might show a book value of − $2 billion, but a value at average prices over the year of $1 billion. Accordingly, the IVA is $3 billion. Regardless of the direction of change in the physical volume of inventories, if prices have risen over the period, the IVA will necessarily be negative; if prices have fallen over the period, the IVA will necessarily be positive.[15]

The IVA does not appear explicitly on the product side of the National Income and Product Account; instead it is included in the published figure for the change in inventories. The adjustment does appear explicitly on the income side as an adjustment to corporate profits and pro-

prietors' income, because specifically these two types of income would otherwise be either over- or understated. Suppose that the IVA were − $2 billion, indicating that $2 billion of the change in the book value of inventories was merely the results of valuation at prices higher than the period's average prices. This amounts to an understatement of $2 billion in the amount of non-capital goods used up by business during the period and therefore a $2 billion overstatement of the profits of business. The opposite would, of course, be true of an adjustment of + $2 billion.

The IVA in the official accounts varies from negligible to sizable amounts, depending primarily on the change in the physical volume of inventories and the change in prices at which these inventories are valued by business. For example, as a percentage of national income, it was an extraordinarily large 3.7 in 1974, 0.7 in 1970, and a negligible 0.01 in 1961. However, whether large or small in any particular year, it is explicitly shown in the official National Income and Product Account. Some understanding of its nature is helpful to an understanding of that account.

Capital Consumption Allowances and the Capital Consumption Adjustment

As shown on the income side of Table 2-1, the difference between charges against GNP and charges against NNP or, what is the same thing, the difference between GNP and NNP, is capital consumption allowances with capital consumption adjustment (CCAdj). Prior to the introduction of the CCAdj in the 1976 revisions of the national income and product accounts, the difference between the two aggregates was capital consumption allowances only. These allowances consist of depreciation charges and accidental damage to fixed business capital; the amount of these allowances is determined primarily from the depreciation charges reported in the federal

---

[15] For any time period, the size of the inventory valuation adjustment varies with the particular methods used by business in charging inventories against cost of goods sold. Under one method [First In, First Out (FIFO)], inventories are charged against cost of goods sold in the order that inventories were acquired. Under another method [Last In, First Out (LIFO)], inventories are charged against cost of goods sold in reverse of the order that inventories were acquired. If both prices and the volume of inventories are rising, FIFO shows an inventory increase that reflects both the increase in volume and the higher prices paid for the last inventories acquired. With inventories carried in the books at original cost, FIFO includes the lower-cost inventories acquired earlier as a cost of goods sold during the period and includes the higher-cost inventories acquired later in the book value of inventories at the end of the period. The change in book values from the first to the end of the period thereby overstates the increase in volume, and a negative inventory valuation adjustment is required. If prices are falling and the volume of inventory is rising, the change in book values under FIFO understates the change in volume, and a positive inventory valuation adjustment is required. Whether prices are rising or falling, as long as volume is rising, LIFO results in neither overstatement nor understatement of the change in volume, and no inventory valuation adjustment is required. However, under LIFO, if the volume is decreasing, the decrease is then being measured not in prices paid for those inventories acquired last but in prices paid for those inventories acquired earlier, and an adjustment is required.

income tax returns of firms. The figure for capital consumption allowances is therefore essentially the amount of depreciation recorded in the books of business. Consequently, it is an acceptable measure of the amount of the business capital stock actually used up to the extent that the bookkeeping entries for depreciation correspond to the actual wear and tear on capital.

There are a number of reasons why these amounts may not closely correspond. For one, depreciation reported in tax returns is based on asset lives and depreciation formulas that may not agree very closely with the using up of plant and equipment. For example, Internal Revenue Service regulations may understate the true service life of various kinds of assets and may permit accelerated depreciation formulas that compress much of the total depreciation into the first few years of the lives of those assets. The changes in regulations during the postwar period appear to have resulted in write-offs of assets at a more rapid rate than assets have been used up. A second shortcoming is that the depreciation recorded in tax returns is based on the original or historical costs of assets; it therefore values different assets on different price bases, depending on the various years in which assets were acquired. A figure for the value of capital goods consumed by all firms in 1980 should not be influenced by the particular mixture of prices that is given by the happenstance of the years in which different assets were acquired, but this result follows from the use of depreciation charges.

To avoid the shortcomings requires an alternative that is not based on tax-return depreciation charges. In 1976, the Department of Commerce incorporated into the national income and product accounts new estimates based on an alternative method. These estimates are derived from stocks of fixed capital calculated by the perpetual inventory method. This method uses estimates of gross investment and service lives of capital goods to derive estimates of the gross stock of capital goods. The gross stock in any year is therefore the cumulative gross investment of prior years less the gross investment in fixed

assets that have completed their service lives. Capital consumption allowances are derived for any one year as a portion of the investment elements that remain in the gross stock. This amount is obtained by applying a straight-line depreciation formula to the stocks of various classes of fixed assets with the life for each class being its service life. The valuation basis for assets is not the original or historical cost, but replacement cost.

The new measure of capital consumption allowances is greater than the old in some years and less than the old in other years. *The new measure minus the old equals a new item called the* capital consumption adjustment *(CCAdj).* For example, in 1980 the new measure was $287.5 billion and the old was $224.1 billion. The CCAdj was therefore $63.4 billion. The adjustment figure reveals that the old or tax-return based measure of $224.1 billion understated the amount of capital used up by $63.4 billion.

Whatever its size, the CCAdj has no effect on GNP or gross private domestic investment. However, it changes both the amount subtracted from GNP to arrive at NNP and the amount subtracted from gross private domestic investment to arrive at net private domestic investment. It therefore does affect NNP and net private domestic investment. In Table 2-1, the CCAdj of $63.4 billion makes the figure for the capital consumption entry that much larger than it would otherwise be and thereby makes NNP that much smaller than it otherwise would be. Under the old measure, NNP would have been $2,404.7 billion instead of the $2,341.3 billion shown. The introduction of the CCAdj also changes the estimates of business income. As shown in Table 2-1, proprietors' income, rental income of individuals, and corporate profits each includes a CCAdj. The adjustment appears explicitly only for corporate profits: −$17.2 billion of the 1980 CCAdj of $63.4 billion was in this share. Part of the balance, −$8.8 billion, was in proprietors' income; another −$33.3 billion was in rental income of persons. In the case of corporate profits, the −$17.2 billion adjustment means that the $182.1 billion figure is $17.2 billion lower than it would have been under the old tax-return based measurement basis. The same kind of conclusion may be drawn for the other two income shares noted.

Note that this treatment is similar to that described for the IVA. The IVA is necessary to correct for an over- or understatement of profit-type incomes that results from the way that firms value their inventories. The CCAdj corrects for an over- or understatement of profit-type incomes that results from the failure of tax-return depreciation charges to measure the actual wear and tear on the capital stock.

National Product and National Welfare

Although those who produce the official estimates of GNP and the other measures of income and output have long told the users of these figures that they are not designed as measures of national welfare, to many of these users this very fact constitutes a major shortcoming of the national income accounts. To them, the failure of an aggregate like GNP to measure national welfare indicates a fault in the way the GNP is estimated. As they see it, after adjustment for changes in prices and population, a 5 percent increase in the figure for GNP should reflect a 5 percent increase in national welfare and vice versa. As presently constituted, it clearly does not do this.

No one criterion of national welfare is universally accepted. However, the most widely adopted criterion holds that the national welfare is enhanced by an expansion of goods and services designed to satisfy the needs of ultimate consumers today and in the future.[16] Although we did not look at them from this particular point

of view, we have already seen various illustrations of why there are differences between national welfare expressed in terms of this criterion and national output as defined by the Department of Commerce. The Department of Commerce definition now excludes from GNP some goods and services that contribute to an enhancement of national welfare and includes others that do not.

What is now excluded from GNP that should be included if changes in GNP are to reflect changes in national welfare? The major omissions are those services that do not involve market transactions and that are also not picked up by imputations. The foremost case of these is the value of housewives' services. Such services surely qualify for inclusion under the above criterion, but the difficulty is, as we saw earlier, that there is no statistically sound method of assigning them a dollar and cents value. Of course, each time a housewife cuts back her specific role as housewife to take a position in the business world, we place a value on at least part of her services and include their market value in GNP. This means a greater figure for GNP than would otherwise be the case, and, on the basis of the most reasonable approach to the question, the increase in GNP is accompanied by an increase in welfare. If we accept the argument that the individual is the best judge of what increases or decreases his or her welfare, the very fact that a housewife voluntarily takes a position in business means that to her taking a job outside the home brings with it an increase in welfare. If the other members of her family also find an increase (or at least no decrease) in their welfare as a result of this action, her outside employment involves an unambiguous increase in family welfare.

But even though this increase in welfare will be reflected in a change in GNP that is in the right direction, the change in GNP will apparently seriously overstate the increase in welfare. No dollar value at all was placed on the housewife's services in the home, whereas her services to business were counted at the full market value paid for them. Some subtraction from this latter figure is required to allow for what may be

[16]When the criterion includes the needs of consumers in the future as well as the present, the goods that qualify to meet the needs are capital goods as well as consumer goods and services. Capital goods increase the economy's capacity to produce more consumer goods and services in the future.

reduced services in the home. There is, however, no way of adjusting for this without placing a dollar and cents value on the housewife's services in the home. This, of course, is the stumbling block that prevents the inclusion of these services in GNP in the first place.

Although GNP thereby overstates the increase in welfare that presumably results from housewives' taking outside employment, the far more serious problem presented by this same stumbling block remains the one discussed earlier. The complete exclusion from GNP of all of the services performed within the home means that GNP is, as a result of this exclusion alone, a very poor measure of welfare, if our criterion is that welfare is enhanced by an expansion of consumer goods and services. The amount of these services provided within homes grows over time more or less in line with the growth in the number of families, but none of this is reflected in the changes in GNP from year to year.

What is now included in GNP that should be excluded if changes in GNP are to reflect changes in national welfare? Of the many areas in which this problem appears, the major one is government purchases. At present, GNP includes all government purchases of goods and services, whatever their nature. From the standpoint of national welfare, many of these purchases should be excluded because they do not meet our welfare criterion of adding to the output of goods and services designed to satisfy the needs of consumers today and in the future. Most notable is government expenditure for national defense, an expenditure likely to rise rapidly during the 1980s. In the view of many people, an expansion in this area of spending means a contraction of national welfare through the diversion of resources that could otherwise be used to produce goods and services that satisfy the needs of consumers. However, under present definitions, each dollar so spent appears as an additional dollar of GNP, all else being equal. As these people view the result, national welfare and national product seem to move in opposite directions in this case.

Although the unusually strong opposition to military spending during the late 1960s and early 1970s was in large part attributable to the unfortunate Vietnam experience, in other times there have been arguments that such spending should be included as part of GNP. Nobel laureate, Simon Kuznets, one of the leading students of national income measurement, during the years before World War II argued for the exclusion of government military outlays (as well as certain other classes of government purchases) because they do not meet the criterion noted earlier. However, during World War II he modified the criterion and reversed his position on the grounds that national survival becomes an end of economic activity that should be included along with the individualistic goal of satisfying consumer wants. In the view of many today, the massive Soviet military build up of recent years raises a question as to the national survival of this country in the years ahead. If one accepts this view, the large increases in U.S. expenditures for national defense during the 1980s are a matter of national survival; therefore the portion of GNP accounted for by such expenditures is matched by a corresponding contribution to national welfare.

We could go down the list of military and all other government purchases and somehow classify them into those that do or do not contribute to consumer satisfaction, and then include in GNP only those that do. Although the GNP would thereby presumably come closer to being a measure of national welfare, it would be far more influenced by personal judgments and biases than the present measure. Which government expenditures should be included or excluded might vary from time to time as conditions changed (as in the World War II illustration) and as the decision makers themselves changed. Instead of getting a measure that reflects meaningful changes in national welfare, we might get a measure that reflects nothing at all accurately. Little would be gained, and the resonably definite measure we now have would be lost.

But even if these apparently unsolvable problems were solved and the national income accountants could somehow identify and include in GNP all of those goods and services that are designed to satisfy the present and future needs of consumers and exclude all those that are not, the GNP figure so constituted would still not be a significant indicator of national welfare. It would be so only to the extent that national welfare can be measured by the amount of consumer-satisfying goods and services produced. There are numerous and serious shortcomings to this total as a measure of welfare.

An increase in the total of such goods would ordinarily indicate an increase in national welfare. However, the extent of this increase would depend very much, for one thing, on the distribution of the GNP or, as this is usually expressed, on the distribution of income. A more equal distribution of the existing level of income and output might make a greater contribution to national welfare than a sizable increase in the total with no change in its distribution. The approach to improving welfare via income redistribution as compared to income expansion has received increasing attention in recent years.

Even if there were no change in the distribution of income, we still could not conclude that welfare is accurately reflected by the output of goods. A major consideration is not only the amount of goods produced, but the "human cost" of producing that amount. A given amount will mean greater or lesser welfare depending on the human cost of its production. Mechanization of arduous and repetitive tasks, improvements in work safety, and revised production techniques that restore "pride of workmanship" are examples of things that reduce the human cost. But the largest single factor under this heading is probably the number of hours per week the average employee must work. If a given total of output can be secured through a substantially smaller number of hours of labor, it clearly would be incorrect to say that the constancy of output means a constancy of welfare. To the unchanged output of goods must now be added the additional "output" in the form of additional leisure.

Leisure, like goods, satisfies the needs of consumers; but, unlike goods, leisure is not counted in the GNP. Like housewives' services in the home, there is no reasonably determinate way of putting a dollar and cents value on leisure. The amount of this kind of "output" has greatly increased over the years; its exclusion from the GNP is one of the major reasons that GNP cannot serve as a measure of welfare.

If a dollar value could be placed on a change in the distribution of income and the output of leisure as it is on the output of goods—and if a myriad of similar problems could be solved—the resultant GNP figure would have moved a long way toward becoming a measure of welfare. However, it would still be such a measure only in terms of a criterion that makes national welfare a matter of the amount of output produced and its distribution or essentially a matter of materialism. This is, as everyone will agree, an extremely narrow criterion of national welfare. Any number of other things quite unrelated to the output of goods and services could make the nation better off: peace, improved race relations, equal educational opportunity for all, elimination of crime and violence, a greater voice for minorities, an improved system of courts and justice, and so on.

The possibility of ever being able to put a reasonable dollar value on the things discussed earlier is small enough; the possibility of doing this for hundreds of things like those just noted is far smaller. Yet this is what would have to be done to convert GNP into a meaningful measure of national welfare. And even then we would not really be in the clear. We will not pursue this aspect, but according to one school of thought (which includes economists like John Kenneth Galbraith and E.J. Mishan), the criterion that national welfare is enhanced by an expansion of goods and services designed to satisfy the present and future needs of consumers is itself unacceptable, so the whole structure built on it has no real foundation. The basic argument of this school is that the developed countries of the world have already reached a state at which all rational needs for goods and services have been or can be satisfied and that mere expansion of goods and services does not add to national welfare. The argument is also extended to hold that we have reached a situation in which the further expansion of goods may involve a decrease rather than an increase in welfare. The deterioration in environmental quality and the reduction in amenities that result from producing more and more output are costs that exceed the benefits of having that greater output. When we charge the negative amounts for ecological damage against the positive amounts represented by the goods themselves, the balance is negative—a decline in welfare stems from growth in goods. This conclusion leads some to support zero economic growth (ZEG) or a nonexpanding level of national output hereafter. There is much to be said for the arguments of this school, and the critics have much to say against them.

Directly relevant to the question before us is the following: If we reach the point at which we must question whether even an expansion of national output of goods and services increases or decreases national welfare, little doubt can remain that a measure that does no more than put a dollar value on the national output of goods and services is a far cry from a measure of national welfare. And this is essentially all that the measure called gross national product now does—and, in view of all the obstacles previously considered, all that it is likely to do in the future. There is clearly a great need to develop measures or indexes of national welfare; but it is unlikely that GNP or any other such aggregate will evolve into such a measure. It will probably continue to be what it is now and to do what it does now: It provides a reasonably good measure of the value of the output of final goods and services, where final goods and services are defined as they were earlier in this chapter.

3

Basic Concepts

OVERVIEW _____

The task of measuring an economy's income and output is distinct from that of explaining why the income and output are what they are in any time period. In a word, accounting is distinct from theory. This chapter begins with a discussion of this difference, then progresses to its principal concern—the introduction of several pairs of basic concepts that are used repeatedly in later chapters and that are essential to an understanding of the material in those chapters. Although they have been isolated in this chapter in order to develop their meaning adequately, these concepts assume their full significance as they are applied in the following chapters.

The first pair of concepts, stocks and flows, may very well be unfamiliar to some students. Although it is not difficult to grasp the idea that some variables have a time dimension and can be measured only over a period of time, whereas others have no such dimension and are accordingly measured at a point in time, the failure to recognize this difference causes faulty economic reasoning. Students should ask themselves whether each new variable encountered is a stock or a flow. Once variables are so identified, there will be no danger of such errors as equating the dollar amount of money (a stock) with the dollar volume of spending (a flow), or failing to distinguish between inventories (a stock) and a change in inventories (a flow).

The second pair of concepts, equilibrium and disequilibrium, has surely been encountered earlier. The discussion in this chapter provides a review of the basic terms and illustrates their meaning through supply and demand analysis, both microeconomic and macroeconomic. The meaning of microeconomic analysis is illustrated with supply and demand curves for a single commodity; the meaning of macroeconomic analysis is illustrated with supply and demand curves for all commodities combined or aggregate supply and aggregate demand curves. The two pairs of concepts, stocks and flows, equilibrium and disequilibrium, are next tied together in the concepts of flow equilibrium and disequilibrium and stock equilibrium and disequilibrium.

The last pair of concepts examined here, statics and dynamics, refers to the two general methods employed in economic analysis. The distinction between the two is explained simply through the use of a supply and demand model introduced earlier in the chapter. To tie concepts together, the discussion also covers the link between the static method and equilibrium models, on the one hand, and the dynamic method and disequilibrium models, on the other hand.

Perhaps the most useful and commonly employed technique of analysis is that called comparative statics. The chapter's coverage of statics and dynamics ends with an explanation of this technique and its relation to pure statics and dynamics.

The U.S. economy's actual output of goods and services in 1980 was $1,481.8 billion, but its potential output in that year was $1,548.5 billion (both figures in 1980 dollars). When an economy fails to produce actual output equal to its potential, as the U.S. economy did in 1980, we cannot begin to explain its failure unless we can first explain what determines its actual output. In other words, whether actual output reaches or falls below potential, to explain what we actually observe, we must have a theory of what determines aggregate output. To provide that theory is one of the major tasks of macroeconomics—one that will be our major concern through most of this book. The development of that theory begins in Chapter 4; this chapter is primarily devoted to an introduction of some basic concepts that run the full breadth of economic theory.[1] The coverage here is limited to the three pairs of concepts identified in the Overview to this chapter; many other concepts of narrower application may be more advantageously treated, where pertinent, in the chapters ahead.

From Macroeconomic Accounting to Macroeconomic Theory

Although it may seem otherwise at first glance, national income accounting does not provide the answer to what determines the economy's actual level of output in any period. The data provide us with estimates of the economy's output for any time period, but they do not tell us what determines that output or what determines the changes that occur from one time period to another. For example, we may compare GNP in constant dollars for two years and label the difference the change in the economy's output from the first to the second year. Thus, for the U.S. economy in 1979 and 1980 we have the following figures in billions of 1972 dollars for the product side of the GNP identity:

$$
\begin{array}{rllll}
& \text{GNP} & = & C & + & I \\
1979 & 1{,}483.0 & = & 930.9 & + & 232.6 \\
1980 & 1{,}481.8 & = & 934.2 & + & 204.5 \\
& & & + & G & + & (X - M) \\
& & & & +281.8 & + & 37.7 \\
& & & & +290.1 & + & 53.1 \\
\end{array}
$$

The figure for GNP in 1980 is simply the official estimate of the final output flow for the year, and the figures for C, I, G, and (X − M) are simply estimates of the composition of this total flow. GNP of $1,481.8 billion was necessarily identical with the sum of its component parts, because it was derived by summing these parts.[2] Although this is valuable for other purposes, it is nothing more than an identity and as such is valueless as an explanation of *why* output was actually this amount in 1980.

What then determined the economy's output in 1980 or in any other period we might choose to consider? As a first step toward any kind of an answer to this very complex question, we must discover the major variables that influence how much output the economy produces and detect the relationships among these variables that give rise to the actual results we find in any period. In other words, as a first step we need a theory of income determination, which, in full-blown form, is a detailed analytical framework or model that expresses how each variable in the model is related to the other variables that have been identified as relevant to the problem. Such relationships are functional relationships in the sense that one variable in the relationship is believed to be a function of one or more other variables in a

---

[1] For an advanced discussion of these particular concepts, see J.R. Hicks, *Capital and Growth,* Oxford Univ. Press, 1965, Chs. 1–3 and 8.

[2] GNP may be broken down in other ways without altering this conclusion. For example, by major type of product—durable goods of $279.8 billion, nondurable goods of $386.5 billion, services of $696.3 billion, and structures of $119.2 billion, all adding up to GNP of $1,481.8 billion in 1980. In no sense, however, does this alternative breakdown—or any other—tell us what actually determined GNP in 1980.

way specified by the particular theory that has been advanced. The relationship that makes aggregate consumption expenditures a function of disposable personal income is such a relationship; it expresses a theory, however simple, of the determination of aggregate consumption. It is only by devising theories, by hypothesizing functional relationships, that we can progress toward an explanation of the facts revealed, for example, by the data in the preceding identities. And devising theories, however indispensable in the process of explanation, is only a step in the process, because the theories devised may or may not be supportable. In order to decide which theories are to be at least tentatively retained and which are to be rejected, we must test them against the "facts." Furthermore, a theory that is so supported is only provisionally accepted, because such support can never "prove" a theory. Sometimes we find a number of conflicting theories that receive equal support from the available data. In such cases, the question of which is the "true" theory remains at least temporarily unresolved.

We can bypass these and other complications of actually constructing and testing a detailed model and still say something meaningful about what determines the economy's output by reverting to the simplest possible model of Keynesian theory. In that theory, the basic force determining aggregate output is aggregate demand, and the simplified model that emerges includes little more than a few functional relationships designed to explain the determination of the level of each of the major components into which aggregate demand may be divided. There is a theory for aggregate consumption expenditure (the one noted above) and an equally simple theory for the other components. Although no one who seriously sets out to explain output determination would limit himself to so crude a model, even here this simple model will help us to answer the question of what determines the economy's output.

Unlike the simplest theoretical framework, no accounting framework can in itself provide the answer we seek. Any accounting framework, however elaborate, is based on identities, but identities in themselves do not explain. Nonetheless, the accounting framework and the definitions of the items that comprise it provide an essential setting within which we may develop the theoretical framework that will give us the answer. The more detailed the theoretical framework, the more detailed must be the accounting framework that supports it. If our purpose were only to develop the theory of the determination of income and output for a hypothetical two-sector economy, all we would need would be the simple accounting framework for such an economy from which emerge the fundamental identities, $C + S$ $\equiv$ GNP $\equiv C + I$ and $S \equiv I$. If our purpose were to develop the theory for a hypothetical three-sector economy, we would need the accounting framework for such an economy from which emerge the fundamental identities, $C + S + T$ $\equiv$ GNP $\equiv C + I + G$ and $S + (T - G) \equiv I$. And if the purpose were to do the same for a hypothetical four-sector economy, we would need a corresponding accounting framework from which emerge the fundamental identities, $C + S + T$ $\equiv$ GNP $\equiv C + I + G + (X + M)$ and $S + T$ $\equiv I + G + (X - M)$. (In a hypothetical four-sector economy, one may simplify by assuming R_{pf} $= 0$). Beyond this, if our purpose were to use the developed theory as the basis for policy—and such is the ultimate purpose of theory—we would need the detail of a real-world, four-sector accounting framework such as the one provided by the U.S. Department of Commerce. Finally, if our purpose were to test the developed theory against the facts—and such is obviously desirable for any theory—we would again need a real-world accounting framework and the "facts" for the real world as provided in that framework. The relationships between the accounting framework and the theoretical framework present a question that will be answered in the later parts of this book. We will see how macroeconomic theory—especially the application of this theory to questions of policy—is intimately tied to macroeconomic accounting.

Stocks and Flows[3] _____

The twin concepts of stocks and flows are not especially difficult to understand, but they can cause great difficulty if misunderstood or misused. To begin with, stocks and flows are both variables; they are quantities that may increase or diminish over time. The distinction between them is that a stock is a quantity measurable at a specified *point* in time, whereas a flow is a quantity that can be measured only in terms of a specified *period* of time. For example, a gauge may indicate that the stock of water in a reservoir is 50 million gallons; the stock variable is 50 million gallons at this particular point in time. It would be meaningless to describe this as 50 million gallons a year, a month, a week, or a day. Another gauge may indicate that the flow of water into the reservoir amounted to 365 million gallons over the year then ended. Assuming that the flow was at a fixed rate over the year, this reading would also indicate that water had flowed in at a *rate* of 7 million gallons per week or 1 million gallons per day.

As another example, consider the total number of persons employed in the United States—this is a stock variable. In contrast, the number of persons who secure new jobs or leave employment are flow variables. The number employed is, say, 90 million at a point in time (on a particular day); it is nonsense to speak of the number employed as 90 million per year.[4] The number of persons who find employment may be, say, 100,000 for a given time period, the month of June. This is not 100,000 at a specific point in time, however.

Money is a stock, but the spending of money is a flow. To say simply that the stock of money is $375 billion has no meaning until we specify the point in time—March 31, 1980—at which this was the stock.[5] Similarly, the statement that total spending for final output amounted to $2,629 billion is meaningless until we specify the time period, the year 1980, during which this amount was spent. Here we can see the serious errors that can result from a failure to distinguish stocks from flows. Some people fail to make a distinction between the *amount* of money and the *spending* of money. They simply equate the two, perhaps because whatever money they get their hands on they promptly spend. From this error follows the more serious error of imagining an increase in the stock of money to be a certain means of producing an equal increase in the flow of spending. Far from being equal, however, the two at times do change in opposite directions to produce a combination of more money and less spending or less money and more spending. Once we realize that the variable money is a stock and the variable spending is a flow, there can be no equating of the two.

There are other illustrations of the stock/flow distinction in the national income and product account on p. 27. Every entry in that account is a dollar figure measuring a flow. Some of these figures, such as "change in business inventories," may at first glance appear to measure stocks. Notice, however, that the entry is not "inventories," which is clearly a stock, but rather "*change* in inventories," which is just as clearly a flow, because a change in any variable can only be measured over a period of time.

Some macroeconomic variables that have flow magnitudes also have direct counterpart stock variables. However, others—such as imports

---

[3] See also G. Ackley, *Macroeconomics: Theory and Policy,* Macmillan, 1978, pp. 8–10, and L.H. Meyer, *Macroeconomics,* South-Western, 1980, pp. 5–7.

[4] We can say that employment or the number of persons employed *averaged* 90 million during the year, a figure derived by estimating employment at a number of specific points in time (for example, the middle of each month during the year) and then computing the average value of these estimates. The average figure, no less than each of the twelve mid-month figures from which it was derived,

is still a stock variable. This is not to be confused with the "unemployment rate," however, which is a *ratio* of two *stock* variables, the number unemployed divided by the number in the labor force.

[5] As in the case of employment, we can say that the stock of money averaged so many billions of dollars for the year, but again this average figure is a stock variable.

and exports, wages and salaries, tax payments, social security benefits, and dividends—are only flows; none has a direct stock counterpart (it is impossible to conceive of a "stock of imports" or a "stock of wages and salaries"). Although such flows have no direct stock counterparts, they indirectly affect the sizes of other stocks. Imports may affect the size of business inventories or the stock of capital goods; wage and salary receipts devoted to the purchase of newly produced houses may affect the stock of housing. For some flows that have a direct counterpart in a stock, statistics on both the stock and the flow variable are unfortunately reported under headings that are practically the same. A woman's saving is a flow ($25 for April), but her savings are a stock ($500 accumulated as of April 30); a firm's gross investment is a flow ($50,000 for April), but the *total invested,* or the dollar value of real capital accumulated, is a stock ($1 million as of April 30); the *change* in the nation's money supply is a flow ($1 billion increase during April), but the money supply itself is a stock ($350 billion as of April 30).

For those flow variables that have a direct stock counterpart, any change in the magnitude of the stock variable between two specified points in time depends on the magnitudes of its counterpart flow variables during the period.[6] For example, the number of persons employed increases, decreases, or remains unchanged between two points in time, depending on the number of persons who secure employment and the number of persons who leave employment during the intervening period. The nation's stock of capital changes between two points in time depending on the inflow (the amount of gross investment or capital goods produced) and the outflow (the amount of capital goods consumed) during the intervening period.

Although a stock can change only as a result of flows, the magnitudes of the flows themselves may be determined in part by changes in the stock. The best example of this is the relationship between the stock of capital and the flow of investment. The stock of capital can increase only as a result of an excess of the flow of investment or of new capital goods produced over the flow of capital goods consumed. However, the flow of investment itself depends, among other things, on the size of the capital stock. In many theories of the business cycle, a critical factor in the explanation of business downturns is a decrease in the flow of investment brought on by an "excessive" stock of capital resulting from an earlier, prolonged upsurge in the flow of investment. This earlier upsurge in the flow of investment was usually brought on by a decrease in the stock of capital during the preceding depression when the flow of investment fell below that of the preceding period of prosperity. As is apparent, this process may continue ad infinitum and carry with it the endless sequence of ups and downs known as business cycles.

By definition, stocks can exert an influence on flows only if the time period is long enough to produce the required change in stocks. Where stocks are very large relative to flows, the changes in stocks resulting from flows are typically so small in the short-run period that stocks may be assumed to be constant in that period. Therefore, although flows may be influenced by changes in stocks, they will not be so influenced by changes in stocks in the short run. For example, if the net effect of the flows of gross investment and capital consumption is an increase in the stock of capital between January 1 and December 31 amounting to a fraction of 1 percent of the January 1 stock of capital, then the capital stock may be assumed to be approximately constant. Because it is approximately constant, it can have no significant effect on the flow of net investment in the following period.[7]

---

[6]Because stocks and flows in macroeconomics are usually expressed in dollars, a change in a stock may occur with no change in the real counterpart flows but simply as a result of a change in the basis of valuation for a given physical stock. Thus, the existing U.S. gold stock officially increased in value in 1972 and again in 1973 with the devaluations of the dollar in those years.

---

[7]Among other things, this illustration glosses over the question of how investment is distributed by industry. If the increase should be concentrated in a few strategic industries, aggregate investment in the next year may be

With respect to this relationship between the flow of investment and the stock of capital, we may define the short-run period as one in which changes in the stock of capital are too small to influence the flow of investment. The long-run period is one in which such changes are large enough to influence the flow of investment. In this sense, elementary macroeconomic theory is primarily short-run; it is essentially a study of relationships among flows in which the size of each flow in any time period is determined solely by the sizes of other flows. In the simplest formulation of Keynesian theory, the flow of consumer spending is determined by the flow of income, and the flow of income equals the flow of consumer spending plus the flow of investment spending. Although we are primarily concerned with elementary theory in this book, we will devote some attention to more advanced theory in which changes in such critical stocks as the stock of capital affect the all-important flows of income and product.

Equilibrium and Disequilibrium[8]

Equilibrium and its absence, disequilibrium, are concepts familiar in some degree to all students, from their study of economics or of other social or physical sciences. The definition of equilibrium in the physical sciences as a state of balance between opposing forces or actions applies without modification in the field of economic theory. Disequilibrium in turn simply becomes the absence of a state of balance—a state in which opposing forces produce imbalance.

In economics we are continuously dealing with variables whose values change over time; therefore, the state of balance that defines equilibrium may perhaps be better expressed as a state of no change over time. This is not to say that economic equilibrium is a motionless state in which no action takes place; rather, it is a state in which there is action, but action of a repetitive nature. Each time period exactly duplicates the preceding time period. This state of equilibrium is maintained, even though the forces acting on the system are in a continuous state of change, as long as the net effect of these changing forces does not disturb the established position of equilibrium.

Let us turn for a moment to microeconomic theory and consider the ordinary supply and demand analysis of price determination for a single commodity in which quantity supplied varies directly with price and quantity demanded varies inversely with price. In Figure 3-1, supply *(S)*, and demand (*D*), are in equilibrium only at a price of *OP* and a quantity of *OA*. At any price higher or lower than *OP*, there is disequilibrium: At any price above *OP* the quantity supplied will exceed the quantity demanded, and at any price below *OP* the quantity demanded will exceed the quantity supplied. In this particular model, in the event of disequilibrium, the forces are such as to move price back to the equilibrium level of *OP* and quantity back to the equilibrium level of *OA*.[9]

Supply and demand are functions that indicate the different quantities of a commodity that will be supplied and demanded at various prices *for a particular time period.* As flow variables,

---

adversely affected by a small increase in the aggregate stock of capital this year. This might be the case if these industries discovered that they had overexpanded facilities relative to final demand for their products.

[8]For more on the meaning of equilibrium, see C.A. Tisdell, *Microeconomics—The Theory of Economic Allocation,* Wiley, 1972, Ch. 4. See also F. Machlup, "Equilibrium and Disequilibrium: Misplaced Concreteness and Disguised Politics," in *Economic Journal,* March 1958, pp. 1–24, reprinted in the author's *Essays in Economic Semantics,* Norton, 1967.

[9]Throughout this discussion it is assumed for simplicity that the particular equilibrium indicated by any pair of supply and demand curves will be attained as long as those curves remain unchanged for whatever time period is required for the adjustment process to work itself out. Actually, the mere fact that such an equilibrium exists does not necessarily mean that the system will move to it even over time. What happens depends on the nature of the dynamic process by which the system adjusts to a disequilibrium, and this process is not necessarily one that carries the system to the equilibrium position. For an introduction to this complex subject, see W.J. Baumol, *Economic Dynamics,* 3rd ed., Macmillan, 1970, Ch. 7.

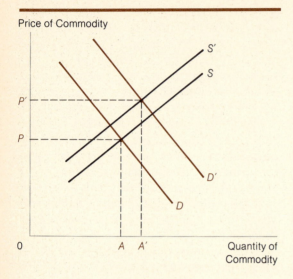

Price of Commodity

Quantity of Commodity

FIGURE 3-1
Supply of and Demand for a Commodity

supply and demand may be expressed in terms of quantity per minute, hour, day, week, or any other time period. If supply and demand in each time period are the same as in the preceding time period, the equilibrium quantity of the commodity purchased or sold will be *OA* and the equilibrium price will be *OP,* one time period after the other. The market is in balance, but it is not motionless, because sellers continually bring more of the commodity to market and buyers continually take more of it away. In other words, the market is in equilibrium; there is no change in the magnitude of the price and quantity variables.

Over time, of course, changes in supply and demand take place. Depending on the direction and the magnitude of the changes in supply or demand or both, equilibrium price and quantity may increase or decrease, with price and quantity changing in opposite directions or in the same direction. *S'* and *D'* in Figure 3-1 illustrate this last possibility. The new equilibrium price becomes *OP',* and the new equilibrium quantity becomes *OA'.* As long as a supply curve sloping

upward to the right intersects a demand curve sloping downward to the right, any possible change in supply and demand will define a new equilibrium price and a new equilibrium quantity at the point of intersection of the two curves.

In practice, the new equilibrium price and quantity are not instantaneously established. The process takes time, and during this time price and quantity are changing, and the market is by definition in disequilibrium. If the changes in supply and demand are frequent, sizable, or erratic, equilibrium may never be established. Before the market can reach that price–quantity combination that represents equilibrium for one set of supply and demand conditions, the supply and demand conditions change. In such a situation, the market is constantly moving toward equilibrium, but equilibrium always recedes before it can be reached. However, even for markets in continuous disequilibrium, the concept of equilibrium is a valuable analytic tool. If at any point in time an equilibrium position exists, this at least tells us which way the system is going to move next, even though we know that before the system gets to the equilibrium position toward which it is momentarily headed, it will be detoured by a change in the forces that change the equilibrium position.

Figure 3-1 was chosen to illustrate the concept of equilibrium because it is the simplest possible microeconomic model of a system with an equilibrium solution. This model contains only three variables—quantity of the commodity supplied, quantity of the commodity demanded, and price of the commodity—and only three relationships among these variables. Two are functional relationships: Quantity demanded is an inverse function of price, and quantity supplied is a direct function of price. The third relationship specifies the condition necessary for equilibrium: The quantity that suppliers wish to sell must be equal to the quantity that demanders wish to purchase, or, in brief, supply must equal demand. All the variables that cause shifts in the supply and demand curves—such as buyers' incomes and tastes, the prices of other commodities, and the prices of inputs used in producing the commodity—are assumed to remain temporarily unchanged in order to focus attention on the way in which the equilibrium price is determined under given conditions of supply and demand.

Although the model for a single commodity is the more familiar, there is a macroeconomic model that parallels the microeconomic one. The microeconomic model covers just one of the many thousands of different goods and services supplied and demanded in markets; the macroeconomic model covers all of these goods and services at once. Therefore, in the macroeconomic model of Figure 3-2, the amounts measured along the horizontal axis are different aggregate quantities of goods and services. Because each of the many goods and services in such an aggregate has its own price, what is measured along the vertical axis must correspondingly be the price level or an approximately weighted average of the prices of all the goods and ser-

vices whose combined quantity is measured along the horizontal axis.[10]

---

[10] The giant step from the quantity of a single good or service to the quantity of all goods and services raises difficult questions. Merely to illustrate with a brief look at one of these, consider the problem of measuring the change in the aggregate quantity of goods and services. One need go no further than two goods, say bread and cars, to see the nature of the problem. If there were only one good, bread, an increase from 100 to 200 loaves would clearly indicate a 100 percent increase in quantity. But take the case of two goods: The quantity of cars increases from 10 to 12 units and the quantity of bread increases from 100 to 200 loaves. Because both goods have increased in quantity, it is evident that aggregate quantity has increased, but one can not say specifically how large an increase has occurred unless one first assigns weights to each good to reflect the relative importance of each. This relative importance is best indicated by the prices at which the two goods sell in the market. If the price of a loaf of bread were $1 and the price of a car were $1,000 both before and after the change in quantities, weighting the original quantities by these prices and adding the two weighted quantities gives us (100 loaves × $1) + (10 cars × $1,000) = $10,100 and weighting the changed quantities by the prices gives us (200 loaves × $1) + (12 cars × $1,000) = $12,200. Because $12,200 equals 120.8 percent of $10,100, the increase in aggregate quantity is 20.8 percent. If we wanted to show the two aggregate quantities in a diagram with aggregate quantity measured along the horizontal axis, each aggregate quantity would have to be expressed in dollars (of constant purchasing power, as is assumed in our illustration). The two points along the axis would be $10,100 and $12,200 in the present case, and the difference between them would be one measure of the difference between the two aggregates of cars and bread. In the same way, the change in aggregate quantity for any other combination of quantities, including a decrease in both or an increase in one and a decrease in the other, may be calculated and the point for each located along the axis of a diagram.

As previously demonstrated, the measurement of the change in aggregate quantity presents no conceptual difficulty as long as the prices of the goods remain unchanged (or as long as all prices change by the same percentage), but this does not occur in practice. With prices of different goods changing at different rates, the measurement of the change in aggregate output is not the unambiguous matter of our simple illustration. For a discussion of the so-called "index number problem" here confronted, see G. Ackley, *Macroeconomic Theory*, Macmillan, 1961, pp. 78–88; and, in a more technical vein, W.J. Baumol, *Economic Theory and Operations Analysis*, 4th ed., Prentice-Hall, 1977, pp. 350–53.

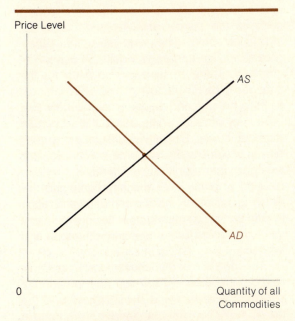

Price Level

AS

AD

0   Quantity of all
                                     Commodities

FIGURE 3-2
Aggregate Supply and Aggregate Demand

Because Figure 3-2 shows for the aggregate of goods and services what Figure 3-1 shows for any single good or service, it is appropriate to designate the curves in Figure 3-2 also as supply and demand curves, but to distinguish their much broader content from that of the curves in Figure 3-1 by affixing an adjective, *aggregate* supply *(AS)* and *aggregate* demand *(AD)*. In microeconomics, any reference to the demand for a good or service immediately suggests a curve like the colored *D* curve in Figure 3-1. However, in macroeconomics, reference to aggregate demand may suggest a curve like the colored *AD* curve in Figure 3-2 which relates the aggregate quantity of all goods and services demanded to the price level of all goods and services; or it may suggest a quite different functional relationship, namely, that between the aggregate quantity of all goods and services which all buyers seek to purchase and the *aggregate income* of all buyers. To avoid the possible confusion that results from attaching the same name to quite different relationships or curves, in this text we will use the concept of aggregate demand to describe only the kind of relationship shown in Figure 3-2; we will adopt other terminology to cover the other kind of relationship. Such a distinction has the added advantage of giving the same meaning to the concept of demand whether we are working in microeconomics or macroeconomics.

Paralleling the meaning of the intersection between the *D* and *S* curves for a single commodity in Figure 3-1, the intersection of the *AD* and *AS* curves in Figure 3-2 indicates the price level at which the aggregate quantities of goods and services supplied and demanded are equal. As in the case of a single commodity, at any price level higher or lower than that indicated by this intersection, there is disequilibrium. At a higher price level, the aggregate quantity supplied will exceed the aggregate quantity demanded and the price level will tend to fall to achieve equilibrium; at a lower price level, the opposite will be found and the price level will tend to rise to achieve equilibrium.

If the price level is higher or lower than that required for equilibrium, obviously the prices of some individual goods and services will have to change in the process of attaining aggregate equilibrium. Less obviously, the prices of some individual goods and services may also change while the equilibrium price level and quantity remain unchanged at the levels indicated by the intersection of the given aggregate supply and demand curves. That is, because shifts may occur in the individual supply and demand curves, changes may also occur in the equilibrium price, equilibrium quantity, or in both for individual goods and services without the occurrence of any shift in the aggregate supply or aggregate demand curve. In this case, the shifts in the curves for particular goods are such that the increase in the equilibrium quantity of some goods is just matched by the decrease in the equilibrium quantity of others, and the rise in the equilibrium price for some goods is just matched by the decrease in the equilibrium price for others. In other words, there may be offsetting shifts in the supply and demand curves for individual commodities that leave the aggregate supply and aggregate demand curves unchanged. There is, however, no need for the changes to be offsetting in this way. On balance, shifts in the demand curves for some individual items may produce some shift in the aggregate demand curve. Similarly, shifts in the supply curves of some items may produce some shift in the aggregate supply curve. Therefore, the combination of price level and aggregate quantity which identifies an initial macroeconomic equilibrium can be displaced by shifts in supply and demand curves for some individual goods and services.

The idea of macroeconomic equilibrium may also be illustrated in a different way, through the concepts of stocks and flows examined in the previous section. Suppose water flowed into a reservoir at a rate of 100,000 gallons per day and out of the reservoir at a rate of 90,000 gallons per day. These flows would be described as equilibrium flows as long as they did not vary in size from day to day or over the period of time considered relevant. This produces *flow* equilibrium, but it necessarily also produces a disequilibrium in the *stock* of water. If the stock of water were measured at the same point in time each day, the gauge would show that the stock was growing by 10,000 gallons each day. Because the stock is changing, there is stock disequilibrium; because the flows are constant, there is flow equilibrium. Stock disequilibrium is therefore logically consistent with flow equilibrium. Over time, however, a sufficient change in stock will begin to affect the previously constant flows. Unless the stock of water is permitted to overflow the banks of the reservoir, there must be a change in the inflow (from 100,000 to 90,000 gallons per day), in the outflow (from 90,000 to 100,000 gallons per day), or in both (to 95,000 gallons per day). If changes of this sort are made in the size of the flows, the system will be one in which both flows and stocks are in equilibrium.

An analogous situation is found in the flow of investment (capital goods produced), the flow of capital goods consumed, and the stock of capital goods. Gross investment at a constant rate of $95 billion per year and capital consumption at a constant rate of $55 billion per year define a flow equilibrium. These flows also define a stock disequilibrium in which the stock of capital increases every year by the amount of $40 billion.[11] This is one indication that this is a "growing" economy if we measure economic "growth" by the accumulation of capital. In contrast, an economy exhibiting equilibrium in both flows and

stock, with, say, gross investment of $55 billion and capital consumption of $55 billion per year, is a "stationary" economy if we define a "stationary" economy as one whose stock of capital neither increases nor decreases over time.

Flow equilibrium may therefore be described as short-run equilibrium, and both flow and stock equilibrium may be described as long-run equilibrium. Because stock equilibrium cannot exist without flow equilibrium, long-run equilibrium cannot exist without short-run equilibrium. In short-run equilibrium, we disregard the disequilibrating effects that flows produce on stocks and consider only the conditions necessary to achieve flow equilibrium. In long-run equilibrium, however, the countereffects produced on flows by disequilibrium in stocks must be recognized, and conditions for full equilibrium encompass those necessary for both flow and stock equilibrium.

An economic theory or model abstracts from the infinite complexity of the real world by establishing what are believed to be the significant relationships among a limited number of variables deemed relevant to the problem at hand. The concept of equilibrium is a valuable tool of theory because it identifies a position in which the values of the model's variables are in balance. This helps simplify the complexity of the real world, where these same variables may actually be in continuous short- and long-run disequilibrium. Disequilibrium is also a valuable tool of theory, but in a different sense: By simplifying less, it more closely approximates economic reality. In fact, it may be said that short-run equilibrium analysis is a maximum in simplification and long-run disequilibrium analysis is a minimum in simplification. The more difficult branch of macroeconomic theory is therefore that which deals with systems in long-run disequilibrium by admitting into the analysis continuing changes in both flows and stocks.

At the end of the previous section we indicated that we would be primarily concerned with elementary macroeconomic theory in which changes in flows are considered but changes in

---

[11] This conclusion of a stock disequilibrium follows from the definition of disequilibrium as an *absolute* change in the variable. If investment, capital consumption, and the stock of capital grow at such rates that the *ratio* of the stock of capital to the flow variables does not change period by period, then, even though the stock of capital is changing in absolute terms, it is not changing relative to flows. From this emerges a different and more complex definition of equilibrium as constancy in the ratio of capital stock to the relevant flows. Under this definition, then, what is disequilibrium in absolute terms may be equilibrium in relative terms. In this book, unless otherwise noted, equilibrium is a position of no change in absolute terms.

stocks are not. For the same reason, we will consider models that have, for the most part, an equilibrium solution. In other words, we will confine ourselves largely to short-run equilibrium models.

Statics and Dynamics[12]

We have noted that stocks and flows are the two types of variables found in economic models and that equilibrium and disequilibrium are the two possible positions of such models at any point in time. The actual position at any point in time is determined by the values attached to the variables that are parts of the model. Now let us examine briefly the two general methods employed in the construction and analysis of economic models—statics and dynamics.

These terms have been defined in somewhat different ways by different economists. One definition that conveys the meaning of dynamics in nontechnical language is offered by William J. Baumol: "Economic dynamics is the study of economic phenomena in relation to preceding and succeeding events."[13] Other definitions could be offered, but in each the essence of the definition is the *explicit recognition of time in the process of economic change*.

In constructing formal models, we may explicitly incorporate time by splitting it up into periods and examining how what happens in one period is related to what happened in preceding periods and to what is expected to happen in succeeding periods. In other words, the variables in dynamic models are said to be "dated." In contrast, the variables in static models all pertain to the same period of time, and there is no need to bother with dating. By dating the variables in dynamic models, we can investigate such things as how the amount of goods that business people plan to purchase for inventory in a period may depend on the amount of their sales in a previous period or on the amount of change in their sales between two previous periods. In turn, we can also investigate to what degree the sales volume in a previous period, or the change in sales between two periods, is influenced by the level of income of the economy in that previous period or by the change in the level of income between periods. In short, through this technique dynamic analysis is able to trace the changes in the values of the variables *over time*. The change in each variable from one period to the next is determined in a specified way by changes in the other variables included in the model.

Because statics ignores the passage of time, it cannot explain the *process of change* in a model. It can indicate the position of the model for a given period, but it cannot, except in a special case, reveal exactly what the position will be in any other period. In the special case where the model is not changing but simply repeating the same motion period after period, static analysis can reveal both where the system is in the present period and precisely where it will be in any future period—namely, exactly where it is in the present period. This special case is termed "stationary equilibrium," because the equilibrium position remains unchanged from one period to the next.

Pure static analysis is applicable only to a model in which a single, unshifting equilibrium position is established by the relationships among the variables. Applying statics to such a model in a period when it is in disequilibrium can only reveal for that particular period the values of the variables that are changing from that period to the next. Statics can explain *why* this is a disequilibrium, what relationship among the variables is necessary for equilibrium, and in what direction

[12]For an introduction to the concepts of statics and dynamics with special reference to Keynes's *General Theory*, see A.H. Hansen, *A Guide to Keynes*, McGraw-Hill, 1953, pp. 44–54. See also J.R. Hicks, *Value and Capital*, Oxford Univ. Press, 1939, Ch. 9; P.A. Samuelson, *Foundations of Economic Analysis*, Harvard Univ. Press, 1947, pp. 311–17; and F. Machlup, "Statics and Dynamics: Kaleidoscopic Words," in *Southern Economic Journal*, Oct. 1959, pp. 91–110, reprinted in the author's *Essays in Economic Semantics*, Norton, 1967.

[13]W.J. Baumol, *Economic Dynamics*, 3rd ed., Macmillan, 1970, p. 4.

the system will next move. Given the fact that a single, unshifting equilibrium position exists, it may describe in general terms where the system must move to reach this predetermined equilibrium position. However, statics cannot explain the *actual process,* step by step or period by period, that the system follows over time to reach that equilibrium position.

As the static method of analysis applies to models in equilibrium, the dynamic method of analysis applies to models in disequilibrium. Dynamics traces the process of change in the values of a model's variables over time, and a system in disequilibrium is, by definition, one whose variables are changing in value. Therefore, to analyze a model in disequilibrium, we must use dynamics, the method capable of following the system from one point of disequilibrium to another toward an eventual equilibrium position or through an unending succession of disequilibrium positions.

For example, let us return again to the microeconomic supply and demand model of Figure 3-1 discussed in the previous section. If, for a given period, the price–quantity combination is other than the equilibrium combination, price and quantity must change. Because we have assumed that there is an equilibrium position, the changes over time will be changes that are working toward this equilibrium price–quantity combination. Given the original supply and demand curves and assuming that the very process of working toward the indicated equilibrium of supply and demand will not cause a shift in either the supply or demand curves and therefore in the equilibrium position, static analysis can identify the equilibrium position and describe in general terms how the system will move to this position. If we were given more information about the way this market operates—much more than just the market's original supply and demand curves—dynamic analysis could be used to do what statics cannot. Dynamics could trace, period by period, the changes in the values of the variables as they moved through successive disequilibrium positions toward the single price–quantity equilibrium position.[14]

Comparative Statics

We have noted that the static method is meaningful only when applied to models with equilibrium positions. We also know that the economic forces that determine the equilibrium position for a model may be expected to change over time so as to displace the original equilibrium and, under certain conditions, to lead to the establishment of a new equilibrium. Given an initial position of equilibrium and some specified changes in underlying forces, if it is possible to determine how these forces affect the position of the new equilibrium, one can compare the two equilibrium positions and explain the change between the two in terms of the changes in forces. It is the analysis of this particular kind of change, from one equilibrium position to another, that may be handled by the method of comparative statics.

Consider once again the supply and demand model of Figure 3-1. The original equilibrium is defined by the intersection of the supply curve (S), and the demand curve (D). Suppose that changes in conditions external to the model, such as changes in income, buyers' tastes,

---

[14] As noted in footnote 11, we have assumed for simplicity that the equilibrium price *(OP)* and quantity *(OA)* will be reached. However, it is possible that in any period purchases and sales made at prices other than the equilibrium price will cause shifts in the supply and demand curves in the next period. This means that transactions in the present period at disequilibrium prices can in the next period produce a change in the equilibrium price. Statics is forced to circumvent this problem in some way. One way is to assume that the original equilibrium price is "instantaneously" reached; another is to assume that all purchases and sales are tentative rather than final until the particular price at which there is equilibrium is arrived at by all buyers and sellers. The latter process is sometimes referred to as "recontract." Without such unrealistic assumptions, which statics is forced to make, purchases and sales made at disequilibrium prices may set into motion a process that never reaches equilibrium, one disequilibrium price succeeding another. This may occur, for example, if a change in price in the present period gives rise to expectations among both buyers and sellers that there will be further price changes in the same direction during following periods. An analysis of a market such as this is possible only with the methods of dynamics.

prices of competing products, or prices of inputs used in production, cause the supply curve to shift to S' and the demand curve to shift to D'. Through the method of comparative statics, we can show the direction and the magnitude of the change in equilibrium price and quantity that follows from changes in the underlying forces that cause the shifts in the supply and demand curves. In our example, the changes in these forces are such as to raise the equilibrium price from OP to OP' and the equilibrium quantity from OA to OA'. Comparative statics can also reveal the magnitude and the direction of change in equilibrium price and quantity if the only shift that occurs is in the demand curve or in the supply curve. For example, if in our diagram a rise in consumer income were to shift the demand curve upward from D to D', we could confidently predict that, with the supply curve (S) as shown, the equilibrium price must rise. Therefore, we have the comparative statics result that, with an upward sloping supply curve, a rise in income that shifts the demand curve upward must raise the equilibrium price.

We can conduct the same sort of analysis for changes in supply or demand other than those illustrated in Figure 3-1. However, comparative statics is adequate for this task only when in each case a new equilibrium position succeeds the old. Comparative statics is inadequate for the task when, as a result of changes in underlying economic forces, a system goes into a state of continuous disequilibrium. Furthermore, even if a new equilibrium does succeed the old, comparative statics is incapable of explaining the path followed by the system over time in moving from the old position of equilibrium to the new. In other words, comparative statics bridges the gap between equilibrium positions in one instantaneous jump, but it reveals nothing about *how* we got from one position to the other. In reality, because positions of disequilibrium are more the norm than the exception, we are likely to be more interested in the path followed *between* positions of equilibrium than in the positions themselves. Only dynamic analysis can handle this task.

The relationships between statics and dynamics and the concepts examined earlier in this chapter can be summarized as follows: The variables found in an economic model are either stocks or flows. Any given model may include only flow variables or both flow and stock variables. Certain relationships are postulated among these variables, such that the value of one variable is a function of the value of one or more of the other variables in the model. If all variables are considered in the same time period, the relationships are all *static;* if they cover different time periods, the relationships are *dynamic.* Therefore, in the supply and demand models as presented, the relationships are static; all the variables in the models are considered during the same time period.

Any given set of relationships may or may not produce an equilibrium solution for a model. In the microeconomic supply and demand model, equilibrium requires that the quantity of the commodity supplied be equal to the quantity of the commodity demanded. If there is a pair of values for these two variables that will equate the two, the price at which they are equal is the equilibrium price. If no such pair of values exists, there is no equilibrium price. The resultant model is a disequilibrium model in which the relationships between quantity supplied and quantity demanded must lead to constantly changing prices and quantities as transactions are carried through period after period at prices other than an equilibrium price.

If the model has an equilibrium solution, it may be analyzed by the static method. If it has no equilibrium solution, it can only be analyzed by the dynamic method. If the model is such that one equilibrium position, if upset by a change in some variable, will tend to be succeeded by a different equilibrium position in a manner that can be calculated from the change in the disturbing variable, the change from one equilibrium position to the next may be analyzed by the method of comparative statics, but the actual path followed between equilibrium positions may not.

The Simple
Keynesian Model
of Income
Determination

OVERVIEW

This is the first of a sequence of four chapters in Part 2 concerned with how the equilibrium level of income is determined in the simple Keynesian model. This and Chapter 5 are limited to a two-sector model, that is, one that includes only households and businesses. Chapter 6 adds government spending and taxing to produce a three-sector model, and Chapter 7 adds foreign spending to produce a four-sector model.

The simple Keynesian model assumes that the aggregate supply curve is perfectly elastic up to the full employment level of output. This means that the price level in an economy operating below full employment is determined entirely by the height of the aggregate supply curve. The explanation of what determines this position is deferred until Chapter 8; for present purposes, the level of the perfectly elastic portion of this curve is simply taken as given.

With an aggregate supply curve of this kind, the equilibrium level of income is determined solely by aggregate spending. Therefore, the basic question in this simple model is what determines aggregate spending. For the two-sector economy, this is the question of what determines the total of consumption and investment spending. Consumption spending and saving are explained by the level of income; the relationships between spending–saving and the level of income are shown by the consumption function and the saving function. This chapter develops the essentials of these concepts and works through the mechanics of the average and marginal propensities to consume and to save.

Once the apparatus of the consumption and saving functions are understood, it is possible to

Consumption and Investment Spending

determine what the equilibrium level of income will be. This chapter presents only the simplest possible theory of income determination—a theory that assumes some given amount of investment spending. In other words, no theory of what determines investment spending is provided here. An aggregate spending function or curve is derived by adding this given amount of investment to the consumption function. Given the resultant aggregate spending curve, the equilibrium level of income is readily identified graphically. Alternatively, the equilibrium level of income is readily identified on another graph which plots the saving function and the given amount of investment spending. The analysis shows why any income level other than that so identified is necessarily a disequilibrium level.

The last part of the chapter examines the crucial distinction between planned and realized quantities in income theory. For the work that follows, it is essential to understand why realized saving and investment are always equal, whatever the level of income, and why planned saving and investment are equal only at the equilibrium level of income.

A basic proposition of Keynesian theory is that the equilibrium level of income and output depends on the economy's aggregate spending for output. If aggregate spending is not sufficient to call forth the level of output that requires the employment of all available workers for its production, unemployment results, and production of goods and services falls below its potential. If aggregate spending is just sufficient, full employment results, and production reaches its potential. If aggregate spending is excessive, inflation also results. However, any level of output—from that which calls for full employment of the labor force to that which imposes idleness on a large part of the labor force—is a possible equilibrium level. Given this wide range of possible equilibrium levels, the actual equilibrium level in any time period is determined by aggregate spending for that period.

In the simplest version of Keynesian theory, the level of output not only depends on aggregate spending, but varies proportionally with it. The output obtained by buyers for spending of, say, $500 billion would increase by 10 percent if total spending increased by 10 percent from $500 billion to $550 billion. This says that the increased spending would not cause any rise in the price level, because a 10 percent increase in spending must result in less than a 10 percent increase in output to the degree that the increased spending is absorbed in paying higher prices for the total of goods and services purchased. This proportional relationship between aggregate spending and output follows from the special kind of aggregate supply curve which Keynes suggested. In contrast to the one in Figure 3-2 (p. 57), this aggregate supply curve resembles the one in Figure 4-1. It has the special characteristic of being perfectly elastic up to the full employment level of output (Y_f). Once at the level of output that can be produced with full employment, the economy runs into a wall and the *AS* curve becomes vertical.

Such a special kind of *AS* curve seems reasonable enough when one recognizes the conditions under which economies were operating at the time that Keynes wrote the *General Theory*. Unemployment was at record high rates in the early thirties. In terms of Figure 4-1, economies were operating far below the output level at which the *AS* curve becomes vertical. Suppliers were

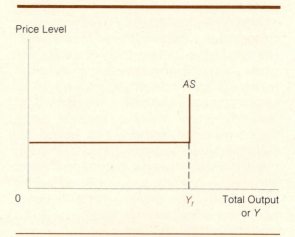

**FIGURE 4-1
Aggregate Supply**

more than willing to provide huge amounts of labor and other resources to buyers at existing prices. Under such conditions, it is not implausible to expect that increases in spending will exert no upward pressure on the prices of all kinds of goods whose output can be greatly expanded without running into higher per unit costs of production. With prices of goods remaining unchanged, increases in spending are matched by proportional increases in the amount of goods that purchasers get for their increase in spending.

In Chapters 4–7, we develop the simple Keynesian model which assumes that the aggregate supply curve resembles that in Figure 4-1 and further assumes that any change in the level at which the economy operates always leaves the actual level of output below the full employment level. As we have seen, this removes in one step the price level as a variable from the model. In effect, it also eliminates the aggregate supply curve from any active role in the analysis. For this reason, it is possible and customary to develop the simple Keynesian model with no explicit attention given to the supply side. Ordinarily, the supply curve of Figure 4-1 does not appear in the analysis. To answer the basic question of what determines the equilibrium level of output, all one needs is aggregate spending on output. With the price level known from the position of the aggregate supply curve and with that price level unchanging, the level of aggregate spending can be directly converted to a level of output; and any change in the level of aggregate spending can be directly converted to a proportional change in the level of output. Therefore, in this simple model, the problem of identifying the equilibrium level of aggregate output that will be produced is simply one of explaining aggregate spending.

In developing the simple Keynesian model of income and output determination to which this and the following three chapters are devoted, we proceed in the following steps. Chapters 4 and 5 will be limited to an economy in which there are only households and businesses. Government

and the rest of the world are assumed not to exist for the time being. Aggregate spending is therefore determined by consumption spending and private domestic investment spending. To explain what determines aggregate spending in any time period, we must first develop the essentials of the theory of consumption spending. This is done in the section that follows. Then, by at first simply assuming that investment spending is constant at some fixed dollar amount, we can proceed without further delay to find the level of aggregate spending. In Chapter 5 we trace the process by which shifts in the aggregate spending curve occur in the two-sector economy and therefore how changes in aggregate output occur in our simple model of such an economy. Chapter 6 expands this model to three sectors by adding government, and Chapter 7 brings in the rest of the world to provide the four-sector simple model.

Because the areas of consumption and investment spending receive minimum coverage in Part 2, but are nonetheless the areas that present the major theoretical questions in the field of aggregate spending, Part 4 is devoted to a detailed examination of some of the theoretical questions in the areas of consumption and investment spending.

Consumption Spending and the Consumption Function_____

What determines the aggregate amount of goods purchased by consumers in any time period? In the elementary Keynesian model, the real income of households basically provides the answer. A rise in real income will lead households to increase the amount of goods purchased and vice versa. This does not deny that there are many other less important determinants of real consumer spending, and some of these will be considered in Chapter 16. Here the assumption is that the aggregate amount of consumer goods purchased or the aggregate amount of real consumer spending is determined exclusively by the real income of consumers, that is, by real disposable personal income.

The Consumption Function

To consider how consumption expenditures are related to disposable income, we may begin by positing that consumption expenditures vary directly with disposable income. Second, we can be more specific and say something about how much such expenditures will vary as disposable income varies. Keynes did this in his "fundamental psychological law" which states that "men are disposed, as a rule and on the average, to increase their consumption as their income increases, but not by as much as the increase in their income."[1] In other words, as income increases, consumers will spend part but not all of the increase, choosing instead to save some part of it. Therefore, the total increase in income will be accounted for by the sum of the increase in consumption expenditures and the increase in personal saving, if we simplify by assuming that all consumer income goes into these two uses. Finally, can we be still more specific on the nature of this relationship? Although Keynes placed great confidence in the correctness of his "fundamental psychological law," he advanced with less confidence the argument that a smaller *proportion* of income will be consumed (or a larger *proportion* of income will be saved) as income increases. If this is true, not only will the absolute amount of saving increase with increases in income as indicated by the "fundamental psychological law," but the ratio of saving to income will become greater with increases in income. Keynes felt that this was to be expected, *as a rule*, because, despite the fact that "the satisfaction of the immediate primary needs of a man and his family is usually a stronger motive than the motives toward accumulation," the latter

"acquire effective sway when a margin of comfort has been established."[2]

This relationship between consumption and income advanced by Keynes is employed in the simple theory of income determination to be developed here.[3] We will, in other words, proceed on the assumption that the absolute level of consumption varies directly with the level of income and that the fraction of income consumed varies inversely with the level of income.

Theoretical and Empirical Consumption Functions The relationship between consumption and income that emerges from these particular assumptions is referred to as a theoretical consumption function. As a tool of theory, a consumption function is somewhat analogous to an ordinary market–demand function for a single commodity, such as that shown in Figure 3-1. Just as a theoretical demand curve usually implies that the quantity of a commodity that will be purchased varies inversely with its price, all other things (including income) being unchanged, so the theoretical consumption function here employed holds that aggregate consumption varies directly but not proportionally with consumer *income,* all other things (including prices) being unchanged. The theoretical consumption function that we shall draw, like the theoretical demand function of Figure 3-1, is not derived from actual statistical data. It is nothing more than an attempt to describe in general terms, on the basis of the previously stated assumptions, a typical functional relationship between two variables, all other things being unchanged. Actually, for this purpose, no explicit dollar amounts need be indicated; for example, they are not used in Figure 3-1.

---

[1] John Maynard Keynes, *The General Theory of Employment, Interest, and Money.* Harcourt Brace Jovanovich, 1936, p. 96.

[2] *Ibid.,* p. 97.

[3] It may be noted here that the particular relationship between consumption and income advanced by Keynes is perhaps the first statement of what later came to be known as the absolute income hypothesis. This will be examined in Chapter 15 along with the relative income, permanent income, and life-cycle hypotheses.

A distinctly different type of consumption function, the historical or empirical consumption function, will be examined in Chapter 15. Here we may note that the simplest form of an empirical consumption function describes the statistics of income and consumption for each year over a period of years. Because these are recorded quantities, nothing can be assumed to have remained unchanged over the period of years involved. As a result, the actual level of consumption that accompanies the actual level of income for any year reflects every factor that influenced consumption expenditures during that year, not just the year's disposable income. In fact, the nonincome factors may be such as to cause the actual level of consumption in any one year to rise above that of the preceding year, despite a fall in the actual level of disposable income. On the basis of income alone, a decrease in consumption would be expected between these two years, but what otherwise would have been a decrease was more than offset by these other factors that made for a net increase. We will note actual cases like this in Chapter 15 when we look into empirical consumption functions. However, for our present purpose—namely to develop the simple theory of income determination—we need only the theoretical consumption function, which abstracts from all nonincome influences on consumption and posits a relationship between consumption and disposable income that satisfies certain assumptions.

The line labeled C in Part A of Figure 4-2 is one of many possible theoretical consumption functions that satisfy the specific assumptions stated previously. The other line is a 45° guideline; any point on this line is equidistant from the vertical and horizontal axes. For example, point K on the 45° line represents a value of income, or $Y = 160$, on the horizontal axis and an equal value of consumption plus saving on the vertical axis.

Because by definition any portion of disposable income that is not consumed must be saved, given the consumption function, the guideline, and the hypothetical amounts laid off on the axes, we can tell at a glance how people plan to allocate any given level of disposable income between spending and saving. For example, at $Y = 160$ (point M), total income is given by $MK = 160$. Because consumption is $ML = 140$, saving must equal the balance of income, $MK - ML = LK$, or $160 - 140 = 20$.

The specific consumption function in Figure 4-2 is drawn on the assumption that there is some level of income at which planned consumption is exactly equal to income. This is referred to as the "break-even" level of income; here it occurs at level 80, because the consumption function cuts the guideline at this level. At any higher level of income, people collectively feel well enough off to save some part of their aggregate income. Above the break-even level, therefore, the consumption function lies below the guideline, and the vertical distance between the two lines equals the amount of saving for that level of income. At any level of income below 80, people collectively spend more than their aggregate income. In this situation, the consumption function lies above the guideline and the vertical distance between the two lines equals the amount of dissaving, or the excess of consumption over income, at that level of income. At the income level of 40, the consumption function is 10 above the guideline and the excess of consumption over income is 10.

Average Propensity to Consume   The average consumption–income relationship is defined by the ratio C/Y for different levels of Y. For the function in Figure 4-2, at Y of 40, we have C of 50, so that $C/Y = 50/40$, or 1.25. At Y of 80, we have C of 80, so that $C/Y = 80/80$, or 1, the break-even ratio. At Y of 160, we have C of 140, so that $C/Y = 140/160$, or 0.875. The C/Y ratio could be computed for any other level of Y in similar fashion. However, from what is given, it is apparent that the ratio of C to Y in this consumption function decreases steadily as income increases, and vice versa. In other words, C increases less than proportionally with increases in Y, and vice versa. The C/Y ratio is one of two basic ratios that

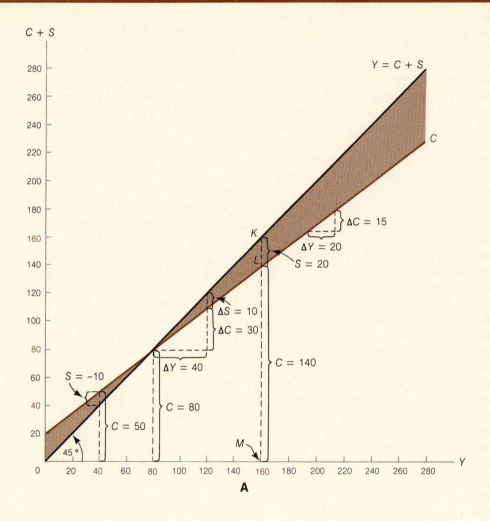

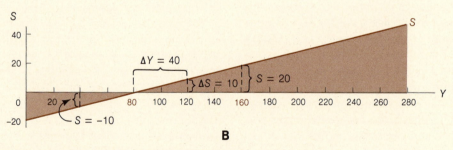

FIGURE 4-2
Consumption and Saving Functions

may be derived from the consumption function and is known as the **average propensity to consume,** or the APC.

Marginal Propensity to Consume If we know the APC at all levels of disposable income, we know how each level of disposable income will be divided between consumption and saving. Suppose, however, we also want to know how any given *change* in the level of income will be divided between a *change* in consumption and a *change* in saving. The APC will not give us the answer directly, but the slope of the consumption function will. To see this, take any two levels of disposable income and call the difference between them ΔY. Then determine the amount of consumption at each of these two levels and call the difference between these two amounts of consumption ΔC. For example, if we take Y of 200 and Y of 220, ΔY is 20. With Y of 200, C is 170; with Y of 220, C is 185; therefore, ΔC is 15. Expressed as a ratio, $\Delta C/\Delta Y = 15/20 = 3/4$. In Figure 4-2, for any selected change in income taken anywhere along the income axis, the same result will be found; for every change of 4 in Y there will be a change of 3 in C, or a constant ratio of $\Delta C/\Delta Y = 3/4$. Geometrically, it should be clear that this ratio equals the slope of the consumption function. $\Delta C/\Delta Y$ is the second basic ratio derived from the consumption function and is known as the **marginal propensity to consume,** or the MPC.

Note, however, that only if the consumption function is a straight line like the one in Figure 4-2 will the MPC be the same for any change in income. Any other straight-line consumption function with a slope different from that in Figure 4-2 will indicate an MPC that is larger or smaller than 3/4, but still the same for any change in income. The slope of the consumption function is the geometric representation of the MPC.[4]

Up to this point, we have not considered any evidence that would indicate whether a consumption function of the type given in Figure 4-2 is a realistic description of the way that people divide their income between consumption and saving at different levels of disposable income. We will turn to this question in Chapter 15, but at the moment all we have is the hypothesis that the consumption–income relationship exhibits certain properties that may be summarized as follows. The MPC is positive but less than 1, this being Keynes's "fundamental psychological law." The MPC is the same for any change in income, this following from the assumption that the consumption function is a straight line. The APC is infinity at a zero level of income and declines steadily as income rises but is always greater than the MPC, this following from the previous assumptions plus the assumption that consumption remains positive no matter how low the level of income may fall.[5]

---

with the guideline (which has a slope of 1) and the MPC becomes 1. Tilt it even more, and the MPC exceeds 1. Tilt the consumption function downward from its given position, and the MPC will become less than 3/4. Tilt it so that it becomes parallel with the horizontal axis, and the MPC becomes zero.

[5] Geometrically, at any level of income, the APC is equal to the slope of a line from the origin to the point on the consumption function corresponding to that level of income. If such lines are drawn into Figure 4-2, it will be seen that the slopes of such lines start at infinity at zero income and fall steadily as income increases. Because the MPC equals the slope of the consumption function itself, any straight-line consumption function that cuts the vertical axis above the origin as in Figure 4-2 is a line whose constant slope is at all points less than the slope of a line from the origin to that point. In other words, for such a consumption function we have the property that $C/Y > \Delta C/\Delta Y$ at all levels of income. Note, however, that any straight-line consumption function that intersects the axes at the origin will be one for which $C/Y = \Delta C/\Delta Y$ at all levels of income. Finally, any straight-line consumption function that intersects the vertical axis below the origin will be one in which $C/Y < \Delta C/\Delta Y$ at all levels of income. For nonlinear consumption functions, the relationships between C/Y and $\Delta C/\Delta Y$ are more complex.

---

[4] If this is not apparent, keep the present straight-line consumption function anchored in its given position on the vertical axis and visually tilt it upward. The MPC will become greater than 3/4. Tilt it so that it becomes parallel

The Consumption Function—Equations
Mathematically, the straight-line consumption function shown in Figure 4-2 may be described in terms of its intercept with the vertical axis and its slope with the aid of the simple equation of the straight line.[6] In the case of this consumption function, the intercept with the vertical axis indicates that C is 20 when Y is 0. For any level of income above 0, given the slope or the MPC as 3/4, C will be the 20 it would be at zero income *plus* 3/4 of the difference between zero income and any chosen level of income. This may be written in equation form as C = 20 + ¾Y. This theoretical consumption function may thus be thought of as the sum of two parts: an amount of consumption that is independent of the level of income, because it is the amount found even at zero income (20), and an amount of consumption that depends on the level of income, because it rises and falls by a constant fraction (3/4) of any rise or fall in income. The first part is commonly described as autonomous consumption, C_a, and the second part as induced consumption. The subscript is used here and elsewhere to designate a variable whose magnitude is autonomous or independent of the level of income.

This equation for the consumption function tells us everything that Figure 4-2 tells us. Just as we can find C for any level of Y by inspection in Figure 4-2, we can do the same by substituting any level of Y in the equation. Figure 4-2 shows that C is 80 when Y is 80, and the equation shows the same: C = 20 + ¾(80) = 80. Similarly, when Y is 160, the figure shows that C equals 140, and the equation shows the same: C = 20 + ¾(160) = 140. To find the APC or C/Y at any level of Y, we simply divide the original equation through by Y, or C/Y = 20/Y + ¾Y/Y, which is equal to 20/Y + 3/4. When Y equals 80, C/Y = 20/80 + 3/4 = 1. When Y equals 160, C/Y = 20/160 + 3/4 = 0.875.

---

[6] The standard linear equation is y = a + bx, where b is the slope of its graph and a is its y intercept (the value of y at the point where x = 0; that is, the point at which the graph cuts the y axis).

Because we will not restrict ourselves later to the consumption function with the intercept and slope of the function shown in Figure 4-2, a general equation for the linear consumption function may be given here:

$$C = C_a + cY$$

In this equation C_a is autonomous consumption or the amount of consumption when Y equals 0 and the constant c is the slope of the function or the MPC. If we divide this equation through by Y, we derive the general equation for the APC:

$$APC = \frac{C}{Y} = \frac{C_a}{Y} + c$$

The hypothesis as to the way people divide their income between consumption and saving was summarized above as a set of properties. To satisfy these properties, it is required that C_a be positive and that c be positive but less than 1. This may be verified by noting that if C_a is negative, the proportion of income consumed increases as income increases; if c is greater than 1, the increase in consumption accompanying an increase in income exceeds the increase in income; and if c is negative, there is a decrease in consumption with an increase in income. All these possibilities conflict with the hypothesis.

The Saving Function

Part B of Figure 4-2 shows the saving function, which is the counterpart of the consumption function shown in Part A. In Part A the amount of saving at any level of income is the difference between the consumption function and the guideline (the shaded area). The saving function shown in Part B can therefore be directly derived from Part A.

When income is 80, we see in Part A that consumption is 80 and saving is 0; this is depicted in Part B by the intersection of the saving function with the horizontal axis at income of 80. When income is 40, consumption is 50, and saving is − 10; the saving function lies 10 below the horizontal axis at income of 40. When income is 160, consumption is 140, and saving is 20; the saving function lies 20 above the horizontal axis at income of 160.

Average Propensity to Save The saving counterpart to the APC is the **average propensity to save,** or the APS. Whereas the APC is the ratio of C to Y, the APS is the ratio of S to Y. Because Y itself is devoted to either C or S, it follows that the two ratios, C/Y and S/Y, must add up to 1. Thus when Y is 40, $C/Y = 50/40$, or 1.25, and $S/Y = -10/40$, or -0.25. Similarly, when Y is 160, $C/Y = 140/160$, or 0.875, and $S/Y = 20/160$, or 0.125.

Marginal Propensity to Save There is also a saving counterpart to the MPC. If, instead of looking at the ratio of S to Y at any level of Y, we look at the ratio of the change in S to the change in Y for any change in Y, we have what is termed the **marginal propensity to save,** or the MPS. Given a change in Y, ΔY, then $\Delta S/\Delta Y$ is the ratio of the change in S to the change in Y, just as $\Delta C/\Delta Y$ is the ratio of the change in C to the change in Y. Because ΔY must be devoted to either ΔC or ΔS, the two ratios $\Delta C/\Delta Y$ and $\Delta S/\Delta Y$ must add up to 1.

If the MPC is positive but less than 1 and is the same for any change in income, then it follows by subtraction, because MPS $= 1 - $ MPC, that the MPS must also be positive but less than 1 and that it must also be the same for any change in income. Furthermore if the APC decreases steadily as income rises, then the APS must increase steadily as income rises, because these two ratios also add up to 1 at all levels of income. Finally, if the APC is always greater than the MPC, it follows that the APS is always less than the MPS.[7]

The Saving Function—Equations As is the case for a straight-line consumption function, a straight-line saving function can be described in terms of its vertical intercept and its slope with the aid of the equation of the straight line. The derivation of the equation for the saving function is analogous to that for the consumption function. When income is 0, saving is -20. For any level of income above 0, saving is -20 plus 1/4 of the difference between zero income and any chosen level of income. Therefore, $S = -20 + \frac{1}{4}Y$. To derive the equation for the APS, or S/Y, we simply divide through by Y, which gives us $S/Y = -20/Y + \frac{1}{4}Y/Y$, or $S/Y = -20/Y + 1/4$.

The general equation for the linear consumption function was given as $C = C_a + cY$; therefore, the general equation for the linear saving function may be given as

$$S = S_a + sY$$

S_a equals autonomous saving or the amount of saving at the theoretical zero level of income and s equals the marginal propensity to save.[8] If we divide this equation through by Y, we derive the general equation for the APS:

$$APS = \frac{S}{Y} = \frac{S_a}{Y} + s$$

The hypothesis about how people divide their incomes between consumption and saving was summarized previously with a set of properties. To satisfy these properties, the equation for the saving function, $S = S_a + sY$, requires that the value of S_a be negative and the value of s be positive but less than 1. This may be verified by noting that if S_a is positive, the proportion of income saved decreases as income increases; if s is greater than 1, the increase in saving

---

[7]Earlier, in describing the relationship between APC and MPC, we saw that for a consumption function of the type given in Figure 4-2, APC > MPC at all levels of income. Since APC + APS = 1 and MPC + MPS = 1, if APC > MPC at all levels of income, it follows that MPS > APS at all levels of income. For example, at $Y = 80$, APC = 1 and

MPC = 3/4, whereas APS = 0 and MPS = 1/4. At Y of 160, APC = 7/8 and MPC = 3/4, whereas APS = 1/8 and MPS = 1/4.

[8]S_a equals $-C_a$ and s equals $1 - c$. This can be shown as follows: Because $Y = C + S$, $S = Y - C$. Substituting $C_a + cY$ for C, we have $S = Y - (C_a + cY)$. From this, $S = Y - C_a - cY$, or $S = -C_a + Y - cY$, or $S = -C_a + (1 - c)Y$. Because we have written $S = S_a + sY$, it follows that $S_a = -C_a$, and $s = 1 - c$ as was to be demonstrated.

accompanying any increase in income exceeds the increase in income; and if s is negative, there is a decrease in saving with an increase in income. All these possibilities conflict with the hypothesis.

Determination of the Equilibrium Level of Income and Output

The GNP identity for a two-sector economy was given in Chapter 2 as $C + S \equiv GNP \equiv C + I$ in which S includes business saving in the form of capital consumption allowances and I includes business investment spending before deduction of capital consumption allowances. If both of these are measured net of capital consumption allowances, the final product so measured is net national product. Because there is no government in this economy, national income equals net national product.[9] If we further assume that all firms are noncorporate, there are no undistributed profits, and personal income equals national income.[10] Again, because there is no government, there can be no taxes, and all personal income becomes disposable personal income. In this economy, disposable personal income equals net national product; every dollar spent during the time period for either consumption or net investment produces a dollar of disposable personal income. Disposable personal income must be devoted either to personal consumption expenditures or to personal saving. Because disposable personal income equals net national product, personal saving (the amount of unconsumed disposable personal income) must then equal investment (the amount of unconsumed net national product).

If we measure the results for any time period in this economy, we have the following identities:

$$\text{Net National Product} \equiv C + I$$
$$\text{Disposable Personal Income} \equiv C + S$$

Here S and I are understood to be net amounts.

Because net national product and disposable personal income are identical in this economy in any time period, we may refer to them interchangeably, disposable personal income being identical with the value of output and the value of output being identical with disposable personal income. If we designate both by Y, we may write:

$$Y \equiv C + I$$
$$Y \equiv C + S$$

and

$$S \equiv I$$

These are the fundamental accounting identities with which we will work in the two-sector economy. Note that these are the same identities developed in Chapter 2 (except for the substitution of net investment for gross investment and correspondingly net national product for gross national product). As identities, they are composed of the *realized* values for the variables for any time period. Therefore, by our accounting definitions, realized saving is identical with realized investment. However, as we will see, realized investment may be greater or less than the amount of investment *planned* by business people, if the amount of investment planned by business people differs from the amount of saving planned by income recipients. In what follows, we will use the terms *realized* and *planned* to make this distinction. Later in the chapter, we will turn to a more detailed examination of realized and planned investment.

---

[9] Strictly, this also requires that business transfer payments be zero, an assumption we make here.

[10] In a two-sector economy in which all firms are noncorporate, personal income would exceed national income by the amount of interest paid by consumers. The easiest way to avoid the complications this factor would otherwise bring into the analysis is to assume that interest paid by consumers is zero.

Equilibrium Income and Output

What determines the economy's consumption and investment expenditures? According to the assumption we have worked with so far, disposable income is the sole determinant of consumption expenditures. What investment expenditures will be depends on factors yet to be considered. However, in order to get started, suppose that these factors are such that business people plan to spend a total of 20 (billion dollars) per time period for additions to plant and equipment and change in inventories. No matter how they may have arrived at these plans, we need only to assume for the time being that the plans are independent of the level of output. In other words, at all levels of output, planned investment expenditures are fixed at 20, or the investment function is simply $I = 20$.[11]

To derive a function or curve which will show aggregate expenditures or aggregate spending at each level of output, we must add together the consumption and investment functions. This is illustrated in Part A of Figure 4-3 by the curve labeled $C + I$. Here the consumption function is the same as that in Figure 4-2 which indicates the amount of planned consumption at each level of output. The investment function, which we have assumed is constant at 20 for all levels of output, is added to the consumption function. The resulting aggregate spending function is read as follows: If aggregate output and therefore aggregate real income were 120, aggregate spending would be 130 (110 + 20), or if aggregate output and therefore aggregate real income were 160, aggregate spending would be 160 (140 + 20).

Given this aggregate spending function, we can define the equilibrium level of income as that one particular level at which aggregate spending just equals aggregate output. In Figure 4-3, each dollar amount along the horizontal axis indicates a different possible level of aggregate output; the actual amount of goods and services for any given time period could be any of these amounts. However, only if the amount of output happens to be 160 will aggregate spending just equal aggregate output.

To see why this is the case, suppose that business people believe that during a given time period they can sell 160 in goods and that they produce this amount of goods during the period.[12] With output of 160, disposable income will be 160; and with disposable income of 160, the consumption function in Figure 4-3 indicates that consumers will spend 140. Adding to this the 20 that business people will spend, we have aggregate spending of 160 when output is 160. *Business people produced aggregate output of 160 in the expectation that sales of output would total 160, and sales turned out to be exactly 160, so the plans of both sellers and buyers were realized.* Consumers with income of 160 purchase the 140 of consumer goods they plan to buy when income is 160; business people purchase the 20 of investment goods they plan to buy. Both sectors purchase the amounts intended, and their purchases match exactly what business people intended to sell. In short, the amount of goods purchased equals the amount produced for sale—which is one way of stating the condition for equilibrium in the level of output.

In Part A of Figure 4-3, the aggregate spending function, $C + I$, intersects the guideline at the equilibrium level of output. Aggregate out-

---

[11] Although we are assuming for the time being that investment expenditures are not functionally related to any other variable, it is still convenient to use here the term "investment function" to parallel the term "consumption function." In Chapter 18, we will examine several theories of investment spending and will employ "investment functions" that express these specific theories.

[12] Not all goods, of course, are produced for sale to consumers and to other firms. Parts of some firms' production may be intended as additions to their own inventories. Such output may be viewed as if it were sales of goods by firms to themselves. Thus, some part of estimated sales of 160 is made up of planned "sales" by firms to themselves.

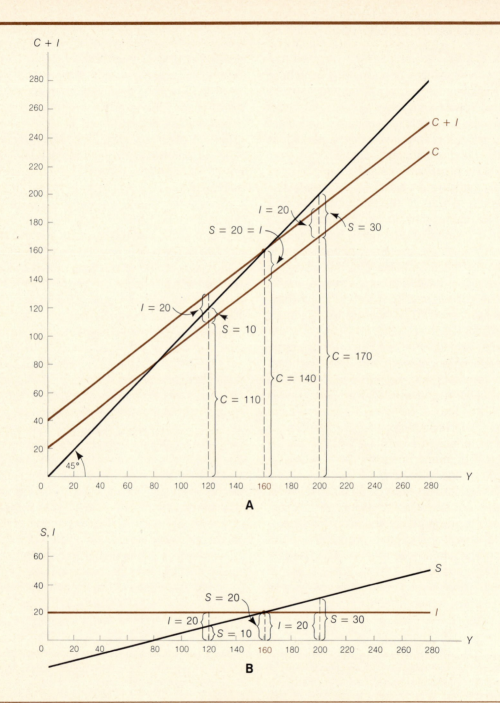

FIGURE 4-3
The Equilibrium Level of Income and Output: the $C + I$ Approach

put of 160, measured on the horizontal axis, is matched by an equal aggregate of spending, 160 (140 + 20), on the vertical axis. Because any point on the guideline is equidistant from both axes, and because the condition for equilibrium in the level of output is that $C + I$ be equal to Y, it follows that the equilibrium level of output must be that level of output at which the aggregate spending function intersects the guideline.

Equilibrium may also be defined as that level of output at which planned saving equals planned investment. In Part B of Figure 4-3, planned investment is shown by an investment curve horizontal to the output axis and 20 above that axis to conform with the assumption that investment is 20 at all levels of output. The construction of the saving curve was explained earlier. It will be seen that planned saving is 20 at the output and income level of 160. Because planned investment is also 20, the amount that business people choose to spend for investment goods exactly matches the amount of income of 160 that income receivers choose *not* to spend for consumer goods. In other words, given that the dollar amount of income generated during a time period is equal to the dollar amount of goods and services produced during that time period, it follows that aggregate spending will have to be equal to that aggregate output of goods and services for the period if each dollar of that period's income that is saved or not spent on consumption is matched by a dollar spent on investment. If planned saving and planned investment are equal, aggregate spending and aggregate output are also equal.

Equilibium Income and Output—Equations

Taking as our condition for equilibrium the equality between $C + I$ and Y, we may also determine this equilibrium income and output by solving the equation $Y = C + I$, in which C and I refer to *planned* consumption and *planned* investment. Solution of this equation identifies that level of output at which planned spending by people on

consumption out of the income earned in producing that output will, when added to the planned spending on investment, be just sufficient to purchase the total amount of output actually produced. The amount income receivers plan to spend on consumption at any possible level of income is given for our economy by the equation $C = 20 + \frac{3}{4}Y$. The amount business people plan to spend for investment is assumed to be fixed at 20 and is given by the equation $I = 20$. This gives us the following three equations:

$$Y = C + I \qquad [1]$$
$$C = 20 + \tfrac{3}{4}Y \qquad [2]$$
$$I = 20 \qquad [3]$$

Substituting [2] and [3] into [1] and solving for Y, we have

$$Y = 20 + \tfrac{3}{4}Y + 20$$

or

$$Y = 160$$

Alternatively, we find the equilibrium level of output to be that at which planned saving equals planned investment, or $S = I$. At this particular level of output, the amount of the income earned in producing that output *not* spent on *consumption* will be exactly offset by an amount spent by business people for *investment*. The amount income receivers plan to save at any possible level of income is given by the equation $S = -20 + \frac{1}{4}Y$. The amount business people plan to spend for investment is again assumed to be fixed at 20; that is, $I = 20$. This gives us the following three equations:

$$S = I \qquad [1]$$
$$S = -20 + \tfrac{1}{4}Y \qquad [2]$$
$$I = 20 \qquad [3]$$

Substituting [2] and [3] into [1] and solving for Y, we have

$$-20 + \tfrac{1}{4}Y = 20$$
$$Y = 160$$

This confirms that only when Y equals 160 will aggregate spending equal aggregate output and planned saving equal planned investment. With C, I, and S all referring to planned amounts, we may summarize as follows:

Output:

$$Y = C + I$$
$$160 = 20 + \tfrac{3}{4}(160) + 20$$

Income:

$$Y = C + S$$
$$160 = 20 + \tfrac{3}{4}(160) + [-20 + \tfrac{1}{4}(160)]$$
$$S = I$$
$$-20 + \tfrac{1}{4}(160) = 20$$

With the consumption function and investment function as given, we may further illustrate why 160 is the only equilibrium level of income and output by taking at random any other level of income and output and showing why it is necessarily a disequilibrium level.

Disequilibrium Income and Output

The actual level of output in any period is the result of the decisions of thousands of business people, and there is no reason to expect their collective decisions to result precisely in the equilibrium output. In our example, suppose these decisions result in output of 200. With an output of 200, disposable income will also be 200. The consumption function indicates that income receivers will now spend 170 on consumption. Adding planned investment of 20 to planned consumption of 170, we have aggregate spending of 190 when output and income are 200. Aggregate spending is clearly insufficient to buy the amount of goods business people expected to sell. What is required for equilibrium with output of 200 is aggregate spending of 200; what is found is aggregate spending of 190, or a deficiency of 10.

In Part A of Figure 4-3, this deficiency of aggregate spending is reflected in the difference in height between the aggregate spending function and the guideline. Instead of intersecting the guideline at 200, the aggregate spending function lines below the guideline at 200; the vertical distance between the two lines is the measure of the deficiency of aggregate spending. At this level of output, there is also necessarily disequilibrium between planned saving and planned investment; planned saving is 30 and planned investment is still the unvarying 20. Of the 200 of income earned in the course of producing 200 of output, the 30 that income receivers choose *not* to spend on consumer goods is greater than the 20 that business people choose to spend on investment goods. In Part B of Figure 4-3, the degree to which the saving function is positioned above the investment function at the income level of 200 is the measure of the deficiency of aggregate spending at this level of output.

The equations also indicate that income and output of 200 is a disequilibrium level. Here, rather than solving to find what level of Y is the equilibrium level, we assume a given level of Y and find whether it is the equilibrium level. In the following set of equations, we know that the equilibrium level of Y must satisfy Equation [2]. Equations [3] and [4] show that the equilibrium level could not be 200.

$$\begin{aligned} Y &= C + I & [1] \\ Y &= 20 + \tfrac{3}{4}Y + 20 & [2] \\ 200 &\neq 20 + \tfrac{3}{4}(200) + 20 & [3] \\ 200 &\neq 170 + 20 & [4] \end{aligned}$$

In terms of saving and investment, the equilibrium level of Y is that which satisfies Equation [2] in the following set of equations. Could the equilibrium level be 200? Equations [3] and [4] show that it could not.

$$\begin{aligned} S &= I & [1] \\ -20 + \tfrac{1}{4}Y &= 20 & [2] \\ -20 + \tfrac{1}{4}(200) &\neq 20 & [3] \\ 30 &\neq 20 & [4] \end{aligned}$$

The combination of an aggregate output of 200 and aggregate spending of 190 can mean only one thing: Business as a whole finds its inventories of goods 10 greater than it had planned.[13] If output is maintained at the 200 level period after period and the aggregate spending function remains as given ($20 + \frac{3}{4}Y + 20$), business people will experience an unplanned or involuntary addition of 10 to inventories in each period. Sooner or later, in order to get inventories down to a lower, desired level, business people will lay off workers and cut back output. This in turn will cause income to fall as fast as output. Once output and income are reduced to 160, equilibrium will be restored; aggregate spending will equal aggregate output, and planned saving will equal planned investment.

To consider another disequilibrium situation, suppose that business people err in the opposite direction and estimate that they can sell only 120 in output. If output is 120, income will be 120; if income is 120, planned consumption will be 110. Assuming an unvarying 20 of planned investment, aggregate spending will be 110 + 20, or 130, 10 in excess of aggregate output of 120. In Part A of Figure 4-2, with output at 120, the aggregate spending function at 130 is 10 above the guideline, and its vertical distance above the guideline is a measure of the excess in aggregate spending, just as its vertical distance below the guideline at output of 200 was a measure of the deficiency in aggregate spending. In Part B of Figure 4-3, with output at 200, planned saving is 10, and planned investment is 20. The 10 that income receivers choose *not* to spend for consumer goods is less than the 20 that business people choose to spend for investment goods.

The excess of planned investment over planned saving means that aggregate spending must be greater than aggregate output by the amount of this excess. The distance of the investment function above the saving function is the measure of the excess of aggregate spending at this level of output.

The equations also indicate that the income and output level of 120 is a disequilibrium level. The solution to Equation [2] would give us the equilibrium level, and Equations [3] and [4] show that this level could not be 120.

$$Y = C + I \qquad [1]$$
$$Y = 20 + \tfrac{3}{4}Y + 20 \qquad [2]$$
$$120 \neq 20 + \tfrac{3}{4}(120) + 20 \qquad [3]$$
$$120 \neq 110 + 20 \qquad [4]$$

Similarly, in terms of saving and investment, the solution to Equation [2] below would give us the equilibrium level. Again Equations [3] and [4] show that this equilibrium level could not be 120.

$$S = I \qquad [1]$$
$$-20 + \tfrac{1}{4}Y = 20 \qquad [2]$$
$$-20 + \tfrac{1}{4}(120) \neq 20 \qquad [3]$$
$$10 \neq 20 \qquad [4]$$

In each period during which output remains at 120 and spending at 130, there must be an unplanned decrease of 10 in inventories held by business people.[14] Sooner or later, in order to stop this unplanned drain of inventories, business people will hire more workers and expand output. If they raise output to the 160 level, equilibrium will be restored.

---

[13] Planned investment of 20 may include a planned increase in inventories. Perhaps plans call for 15 of net investment in plant and equipment and 5 in additional inventories. The result above would thus become an addition of 15 to plant and equipment and 15 to inventories, the planned addition of 5 plus the unplanned addition of 10.

[14] If plans had called for net investment of 10 in plant and equipment and 10 in inventories per time period, the addition to inventories would be 0. If plans had called for net investment of 20 in plant and equipment and no addition to inventories per time period, the results would be net investment of 20 in plant and equipment and −10 (a decrease) in inventories. In both cases, realized investment, or unconsumed output would be (120 − 110).

Investment—Planned Versus Realized

We have examined three levels of income and output for our simple economy, of which one (160) was the equilibrium level and the other two (120 and 200) were disequilibrium levels. Because income and output are flows, these three levels must all be amounts corresponding to specific time periods. The national income accountant who seeks to measure income and output for these three time periods (the order of which here has no relevance) would summarize the data for the periods as follows:

Period	Realized	Realized	Realized
	$C + S \equiv Y \equiv C + I$		$S \equiv I$
A	$140 + 20 = 160 = 140 + 20$		$20 = 20$
B	$170 + 30 = 200 = 170 + 30$		$30 = 30$
C	$110 + 10 = 120 = 110 + 10$		$10 = 10$

Notice that the figures in the accountant's identities reveal nothing about the *planned* investment of business people and nothing about the equilibrium or disequilibrium of the economy at each of these income and output levels. The accountant's identities show only what income and output actually were, how the actual income was divided into realized consumption and realized saving, how the actual output was divided into realized consumption and realized investment, and, from these, the identity between realized saving and realized investment. Whether or not realized investment is equal to, less than, or greater than planned investment cannot be determined from the accountant's identities.

Unlike the accountant, the economist seeks to determine the level of output at which the economy will be in equilibrium. We assume that the economist knows what planned consumption spending and planned investment spending will be at each level of income and output and that he or she therefore knows the aggregate spending function ($C + I$) for the economy. In contrast to the accountant's identities, our economist uses a set of equations that show planned consumption and planned investment for the actual income and output levels in each of these time periods. Realized saving and realized investment figures for each period are repeated in Table 4-1 for easy reference.

Comparing the economist's equations with the accountant's identities, we find, as before, that only when income and output are 160 does planned investment of 20 correspond with realized investment. When income and output are 200, business people discover that, contrary to their plans for investment of 20, realized investment is 30 (consumed output is 170, and the remainder of output or the unconsumed portion of output, 30, equals realized investment). Similarly, when income and output are 120, business people discover, again contrary to their plans for investment of 20, that realized investment is 10 (consumed output is 110, and unconsumed output of 10 equals realized investment). Because realized investment may be described as the sum of planned and unplanned investment, and because planned investment is the constant 20,

TABLE 4-1

Period	Planned Planned $C + S = Y = C + I$	Planned $S = I$	Realized $S \equiv I$
A	$140 + 20 = 160 = 140 + 20$	$20 = 20$	$20 = 20$
B	$170 + 30 = 200 > 170 + 20$	$30 > 20$	$30 = 30$
C	$110 + 10 = 120 < 110 + 20$	$10 < 20$	$10 = 10$

the economist may also express this in equation form as follows:

Period	Planned Invest-ment	+	Unplanned Investment	=	Realized Invest-ment	=	Realized Saving
A	20	+	0	=	20	=	20
B	20	+	10	=	30	=	30
C	20	+	−10	=	10	=	10

In Figure 4-3, the amounts of unplanned investment may be identified as the difference between realized investment and planned investment at each of the three levels of income and output.[15] When unplanned investment is 10, the excess of realized investment over planned investment amounts to an unplanned increase in inventories of 10; some of the goods produced simply are not sold and remain in inventory, even though the producers do not want them to. When unplanned investment is − 10, on the other hand, the excess of planned investment over realized investment amounts to an unplanned decrease in inventories of 10.

In short, if there is any unplanned investment, planned investment will not equal realized investment, and the economy will therefore be at a disequilibrium level of output. However, the identity between realized saving and realized investment is just as consistent with positive or negative unplanned investment as it is with zero unplanned investment.[16] The accounting identities, therefore, can tell us nothing about whether there is equilibrium or disequilibrium in a particular time period and therefore nothing about whether the level of income and output will rise or fall in succeeding time periods. To determine this we need equations that show the relation between planned saving and planned investment.

Therefore, we must work with definitions of saving and investment that at first appear to be contradictory. In the one definition, saving and investment (realized) are necessarily equal in any time period; in the other definition, saving and investment (planned) are not necessarily equal and in fact are typically unequal in any time period. In the introduction to national income accounting in Chapter 2, we used only the first definition of saving and investment and did not have to distinguish between planned and realized. From now on, however, they must be so distinguished. We must avoid saying that saving and investment can be both equal and unequal. We can, however, flatly and unambiguously say that realized saving and realized investment can only be equal, but that planned saving and planned investment can be unequal. *Throughout the remainder of this book, all references to consumption, saving, and investment not specifically designated as realized quantities should be understood to be planned quantities.*

---

[15] Realized investment at any level of output is the difference between the *C* curve and the guideline in Part A of Figure 4-3 and the difference between the horizontal axis and the *S* curve in Part B of Figure 4-3. Planned investment is the difference between the *C* curve and the *C + I* curve in Part A and the difference between the horizontal axis and the *I* curve in Part B.

[16] A discrepancy can appear only between planned investment and realized investment and not between planned saving and realized saving during a particular time period, because it has been implicitly assumed that income receivers succeed in saving the amount of income they plan to save at each level of income. One can drop this assumption and consider disequilibrium situations in which business people always succeed in investing the amount they plan to invest while income receivers fail to save the amount they plan to save at any given level of income. Disequilibrium will then appear as a result of planned saving being greater or less than realized saving.

5

Shifts in the Aggregate Spending Function and the Multiplier

OVERVIEW ——————————

Chapter 4 provided an explanation of the determination of the equilibrium level of output for a simple two-sector model. This chapter provides an explanation of *changes* in the equilibrium level of output in the same two-sector model.

Any such change is shown to be the result of a shift in the aggregate spending function—that is, an upward or downward shift in the $C + I$ curve—and the dollar amount of the change in the income and output level is ordinarily a multiple of the dollar amount of this shift. The ratio of the change in income and output to the change in the level of the spending function is called the *multiplier*. The primary purpose of this chapter is the development of the basic multiplier mechanism as it is found in the simple two-sector model.

The chapter discusses separately a *temporary* shift and a *permanent* shift in the aggregate spending function. Detailed numerical illustrations are provided to show that although in both cases the change in income and output is a multiple of the amount of the shift in the aggregate spending function, only in the latter case is there

a permanent change in the equilibrium level of income and output.

The multiplier is an important concept, and future chapters will expand it beyond the basic form in which it appears in this chapter. However, once the logic of the multiplier is understood in this basic form, students should encounter no great difficulty in following its elaboration in later chapters. To make its logic clear, the latter part of the chapter provides a discussion of the multiplier mechanism, in both verbal and equation form.

In Chapter 4, we saw that output may fluctuate above and below the equilibrium level as business people err in overproducing or underproducing. We also saw that they react to these errors in such a way as to make output move toward, if not actually to attain, that single equilibrium level of output which in the simple model is determined solely by the position of the aggregate spending function.

Shifts in the Aggregate Spending Function

From one time period to the next, it is not only possible but probable that the aggregate spending function in Part A of Figure 4-3 will shift upward or downward. In our two-sector economy, the aggregate spending function is the sum of the consumption function and the investment function. Although either or both of these functions can shift from one time period to the next, most observers agree that the consumption function is relatively stable and the investment function relatively unstable. The relative stability of the consumption function does not necessarily imply that the actual amount of consumption expenditures is relatively stable; this amount will change with every change in the level of income. It does mean, however, that the amount of consumption expenditures *at any given level of income* is relatively stable and that an initial change in the level of income itself is typically the result of a shift in the investment function.[1] In terms of Part A of Figure 4-3, this means simply

that the entire C curve does not bounce up and down over the short run, or, in terms of Part B, that the S curve does not bounce up and down over the short run. The C + I curve does fluctuate over the short run, but this is primarily due to instability in the investment component rather than in the consumption component. Consequently, the analysis in this chapter will concentrate on changes in the equilibrium level of income and output that result from shifts in the investment function. Note, however, that a parallel analysis applies to shifts in the consumption function.

To begin, assume that, due to an improvement in business expectations, investment expenditures rise permanently from 20 to 30 per time period, an amount that is, as before, the same at all levels of output. Part A of Figure 5-1 illustrates this shift in the investment function. The curves labeled C and C + I are the same as those found in Part A of Figure 4-3. To indicate the increase from 20 to 30 in investment expenditures, we simply vertically add the 10 of additional investment to the curve labeled C + I and label this new aggregate spending function C + I + ΔI. The curves labeled S and I in Part B of Figure 5-1 are the same as those found in Part B of Figure 4-3 (p. 76); we simply vertically add the 10 of additional investment to the curve labeled I and label this new investment function I + ΔI.

With the aggregate spending function, C + I, the equilibrium level of output was 160. With the new aggregate spending function 10 higher than the old, we might expect the new equilibrium level of output to be also 10 higher—an increase from 160 to 170. But 170 is not the new equilibrium level. At 170, aggregate spending exceeds aggregate output and investment exceeds saving. The equilibrium level, therefore, must be greater than 170. Part A of Figure 5-1 reveals that, with the higher aggregate spending function, aggregate spending and aggregate output are equal only at an output of 200. Part B reveals that, with the higher investment function, saving and investment are equal only at an output of 200. The fact that the increase of 10 in investment

---

[1] Given a stable consumption function of $C = 20 + \frac{3}{4}Y$, C can change only as a result of a change in Y. If Y were 100, C would be 95; if Y were 120, C would be 110. *Consumption expenditures* are not stable, because they change with the level of income; but, under these circumstances, the *consumption function* is perfectly stable. An unstable consumption function would show change in C with no change in Y, which could result only from a change in the value of the constant 20 or of the constant 3/4. Therefore, if Y is 120 and stays at 120, C can still change from one period to the next if the constant 20 rises to, say, 25.

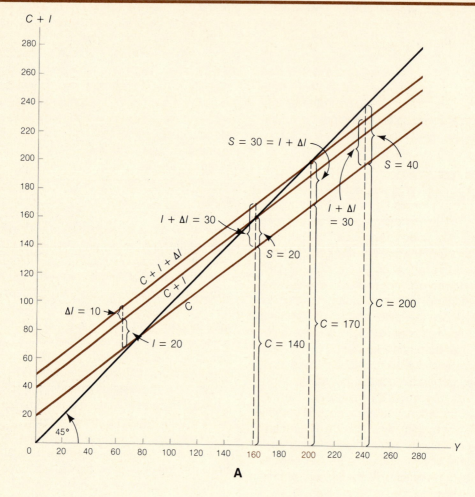

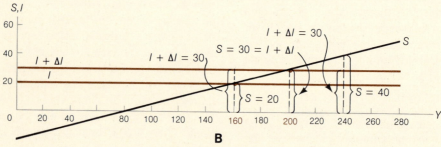

FIGURE 5-1
The Effect of a Change in Investment on the Equilibrium
Level of Income

has raised the equilibrium level of income and output not merely by 10 but by 40, perhaps surprising at first glance, will be explained in the following pages.

A Temporary Shift in the Aggregate Spending Function

The new equilibrium level in Figure 5-1 was established as the aggregate spending function shifted from $C + I$ to the higher level of $C + I + \Delta I$. We have assumed that this is a permanent shift. However, to understand better the implications of a *permanent* shift, let us first examine the implications of a *temporary* shift in the function. Unlike the results shown in Figure 5-1, if the rise in investment is a temporary one, the rise in income and output will also be temporary. When investment subsequently drops back to its original level, income and output will also eventually drop back to their original level.

Changes in the level of income and output take place over time. To trace the process set into motion by a temporary increase in investment spending, we may split up the time interval required for the system to reestablish equilibrium into a series of shorter, numbered time periods. Let us assume that in Period 1 we have the original equilibrium position described in the previous chapter and shown in Figure 5-1; aggregate output is 160 and aggregate spending, the sum of consumption spending of 140 and investment spending of 20, is also 160. In Period 2, we upset this equilibrium by introducing an increase in investment spending of 10, or a rise in investment spending from 20 to 30. We assume that business people do not attempt to anticipate changes in the demand for their output, but instead follow a simple rule of thumb of producing in each period an output equal to their sales in the preceding period. Given this behavior by business people, output in Period 2 will be equal to sales of Period 1; that is, output will be 160. Aggregate spending in Period 2, however, is found to be 170, because in this period we have

the increase of 10 in investment spending. Inventories serve as a buffer—the *excess* of aggregate spending of 10 is absorbed in Period 2 by an unplanned decrease of inventories.

In Period 3, business people expand aggregate output to 170, the figure for total sales in Period 2. Output of 170 in Period 3 generates disposable income of 170 during this period. Given the consumption function, $C = 20 + \frac{3}{4}Y$, consumption spending in Period 3 will be 147.5 (7.5 greater than in Period 2). If investment spending now drops back to its original level of 20 following its temporary rise to 30 in Period 2, we find in Period 3 consumption spending of 147.5 and investment spending of 20, or aggregate spending of 167.5. Because output in Period 3 is 170, there is now a *deficiency* of aggregate spending of 2.5, which is reflected in an unplanned increase in inventories. In Period 4, business people reduce aggregate output to 167.5, the total for sales in Period 3. This means a corresponding decline in income to 167.5, and the consumption function indicates that consumption in turn will be 145.6 in Period 4. Spending in Period 4 is accordingly 145.6 plus 20 for investment (an aggregate of 165.6). Because output in Period 4 is 167.5, there is again a deficiency of spending—now equal to 1.9—which again is reflected in an unplanned increase in inventories. In Period 5, there is a further reduction in output and again a deficiency of spending but one smaller than that of Period 4. In this way, the level of output declines period by period until Period n, assumed to be the last in what is actually an infinite number of periods. In Period n, output is 160, income is correspondingly 160, consumption spending is 140, and investment spending is 20—or aggregate spending of 160 is equal to aggregate output of 160. The system has returned to the same equilibrium position from which we started in Period 1.

Table 5-1 gives the period-by-period detail of the process just described. In this table, C and I indicate the values for consumption and investment spending in the original equilibrium of Period 1. The change in consumption spending

TABLE 5-1
A Temporary (One-Period) Increase in Investment Spending

Period	C	+	I	+	ΔC	+	ΔI	=	Aggregate Spending	$\overset{\geq}{\underset{<}{=}}$	Aggregate Output	=	Y	+	ΔY	Realized Investment	Planned Investment
1	140	+	20	+	0.0	+	0	=	160.0	=	160.0	=	160	+	0.0	20.0	20
2	140	+	20	+	0.0	+	10	=	170.0	>	160.0	=	160	+	0.0	20.0	30
3	140	+	20	+	7.5	+	0	=	167.5	<	170.0	=	160	+	10.0	22.5	20
4	140	+	20	+	5.6	+	0	=	165.6	<	167.5	=	160	+	7.5	21.9	20
5	140	+	20	+	4.2	+	0	=	164.2	<	165.6	=	160	+	5.6	21.4	20
6	140	+	20	+	3.2	+	0	=	163.2	<	164.2	=	160	+	4.2	21.0	20
7	140	+	20	+	2.4	+	0	=	162.4	<	163.2	=	160	+	3.2	20.8	20
8	140	+	20	+	1.8	+	0	=	161.8	<	162.4	=	160	+	2.4	20.6	20
9	140	+	20	+	1.3	+	0	=	161.3	<	161.8	=	160	+	1.8	20.5	20
.	.		.		.		.		.		.		.		.	.	.
.									.		.		.				.
.																	
n	140	+	20	+	0.0	+	0	=	160.0	=	160.0	=	160	+	0.0	20.0	20
n + 1	140	+	20	+	0.0	+	0	=	160.0	=	160.0	=	160	+	0.0	20.0	20
					30.0		10								40.0		

between Period 1 and any following period is shown by ΔC; and the change in investment spending between Period 1 and any following period is shown by ΔI. Total consumption spending in any period is then given by $C + \Delta C$, total investment spending by $I + \Delta I$, and aggregate spending by their sum. In the same way, Y indicates aggregate output in Period 1, ΔY the change in output between Period 1 and any other period, and $Y + \Delta Y$ the aggregate output for any period. The last two columns in the table show *realized* investment, which equals saving, and *planned* investment for each period. Planned investment for each period is the same as $I + \Delta I$. Realized investment or saving (or unconsumed output) in any period is the difference between that period's output and its consumption, or $(Y + \Delta Y) - (C + \Delta C)$.

In any time period, aggregate spending may be equal to, greater than, or less than aggregate output. Or what is the same thing, in any time period, planned investment may be equal to, greater than, or less than realized investment.

The level of output is an equilibrium level in Period 1, because aggregate spending of 160 is just equal to aggregate output of 160 and planned investment of 20 is just equal to realized investment of 20. The equilibrium of Period 1 is upset in Period 2 by the rise in planned investment, which is a rise in aggregate spending. Equilibrium is not restored until Period n, because in all intervening periods aggregate spending is either greater or less than aggregate output or—what is the same thing—planned investment is either greater or less than realized investment.

Disequilibrium occurs through all these periods, despite the fact that the cause of disequilibrium—the rise in investment spending—is limited to Period 2 alone. This one-period rise in investment spending, however, produces the changing level of output in all these later periods by initiating a series of changes in consumption spending starting in Period 3. Thus, ΔC of 7.5 in Period 3 results from ΔY of 10 in Period 3, which results from ΔI of 10 in Period 2. Similarly, ΔC of 5.6 in Period 4 results from ΔY of 7.5 in Period 4, which results from ΔC of 7.5 in Period 3, which results from ΔY of 10 in Period 3, which results from ΔI of 10 in Period 2. In other words, the ΔI of Period 2 initiates a process in which ΔC in each period is 3/4 (the MPC) of ΔY in that period. Furthermore, given that ΔC is equal to 3/4 of ΔY of that period and that ΔY of each period is equal to $\Delta C + \Delta I$ of the preceding period, the fact that the increase in investment (ΔI) is limited to Period 2 alone means that ΔY and ΔC become smaller each period until eventually, in Period n, ΔC becomes zero.[2] Because ΔI is also zero in Period n, ΔY becomes zero, and the level of income and output is back to the equilibrium found in Period 1, or 160.[3]

Although Table 5-1 shows that the equilibrium level of output established in Period n is the same as that of Period 1, it is important to note that the *cumulative* addition to income and output over the time interval in which the process works itself out is, in the present case, four times the size of the initiating increase in investment spending in Period 2. This cumulative addition to income and output is 40, as shown at the bottom of the column headed ΔY in Table 5-1. The 40 is composed of cumulative additions of 30 to consumption and 10 to investment, as shown at the bottom of the columns headed ΔC and ΔI in the table. There-

fore, although the one-period injection of extra investment spending does not lift income and output to a permanently higher level, the *cumulative* effect in the present case is a flow of extra income and output four times the amount of that one-period injection of investment spending.

A Permanent Shift in the Aggregate Spending Function

If the aggregate spending function shifts upward and remains at the new higher level period after period, the original equilibrium level of income and output will be replaced by a new, higher equilibrium level. This is the result shown in Figure 5-1.

To describe the process by which the system moves to a higher equilibrium level of output as a result of such a sustained increase in aggregate spending requires only that we extend the description of the process for a temporary increase in aggregate spending. In Table 5-1, ΔI of 10 in Period 2 called forth ΔY of 10 in Period 3. Because we then assumed that investment spending returned to its original level in Period 3, ΔY of Period 4 (equal only to ΔC of 7.5 of Period 3) dropped below ΔY of Period 3, which was equal to ΔI of 10 of Period 2. In the present case, however, with a permanent rise in investment spending of 10, we have ΔI of 10 as well as ΔC of 7.5 in Period 3, so that ΔY of Period 4 (now equal to ΔC of 7.5 plus ΔI of 10) is 17.5, greater than ΔY of 10 in Period 3. From ΔY of 17.5 in Period 4, we get ΔC of 13.1 in Period 4, so that ΔY in Period 5 is 23.1 (the sum of ΔC of 13.1 plus the constant ΔI of 10). With investment sustained at the new higher level, ΔY in each period continues to rise above ΔY of the preceding period until a new equilibrium is established with ΔY of 40.

Table 5-2 records the period-by-period detail of this process. The column headings are the same as those in Table 5-1. ΔI starts at zero in Period 1, becomes 10 in Period 2, and remains

[2] For a one-period increase in investment spending of \$1, the *differences* between each period's aggregate spending and spending in the original period are given by the series 1, c, c^2, c^3, c^4, . . . , c_n. Because c is less than 1, the differences become smaller and smaller. After the passage of an infinite number of time periods represented by n, c_n becomes infinitely small, so that income returns to its original equilibrium level.

[3] Actually, the cumulative addition to investment spending does not occur in Period 2 as is suggested by the column headed ΔI. An increase in investment of 10 was planned for Period 2, but the realized increase in investment was 0. As shown by the next to last column, realized investment in Period 2 is 20, the same as in Period 1. The *realized* increases in investment may be identified in this column as the differences between the indicated values and 20—that is, 2.5 in Period 3, 1.9 in Period 4, and so forth. The sum of these changes will total 10, equal to the increase in planned investment of 10 shown in Period 2.

TABLE 5-2
A Permanent Increase in Investment Spending

Period	C + I + ΔC + ΔI =	Aggregate Spending	$\gtrless$	Aggregate Output = Y + ΔY		Realized Investment	Planned Investment
1	140 + 20 + 0.0 + 0 =	160.0	=	160.0 = 160 + 0.0		20.0	20
2	140 + 20 + 0.0 + 10 =	170.0	>	160.0 = 160 + 0.0		20.0	30
3	140 + 20 + 7.5 + 10 =	177.5	>	170.0 = 160 + 10.0		22.5	30
4	140 + 20 + 13.1 + 10 =	183.1	>	177.5 = 160 + 17.5		24.4	30
5	140 + 20 + 17.3 + 10 =	187.3	>	183.1 = 160 + 23.1		25.8	30
6	140 + 20 + 20.5 + 10 =	190.5	>	187.3 = 160 + 27.3		26.8	30
7	140 + 20 + 22.9 + 10 =	192.9	>	190.5 = 160 + 30.5		27.6	30
8	140 + 20 + 24.7 + 10 =	194.7	>	192.9 = 160 + 32.9		28.2	30
9	140 + 20 + 26.0 + 10 =	196.0	>	194.7 = 160 + 34.7		28.7	30
.	. . . .	.		. . .		.	.
.							
.	. . . .	.		. . .		.	.
n	140 + 20 + 30.0 + 10 =	200.0	=	200.0 = 160 + 40.0		30.0	30
n + 1	140 + 20 + 30.0 + 10 =	200.0	=	200.0 = 160 + 40.0		30.0	30

10 in each succeeding period. As before, ΔY for any period is the sum of ΔI plus ΔC for the preceding period. In comparing the value of ΔY period by period, note that as ΔY becomes larger and larger, the change in ΔY becomes progressively smaller and in Period n becomes zero. In this period, ΔY stabilizes at 40, and the sum of $Y + \Delta Y$ stabilizes at 200. With aggregate output at 200, income is 200, and with income at 200, the consumption function ($C = 20 + \frac{3}{4}Y$) indicates consumption spending of 170. Investment spending is given at 30, so aggregate spending in Period n is 200 and equal to aggregate output. Similarly, as shown in the last two columns of Table 5-2, in Period n realized investment reaches 30 and is equal to planned investment of 30. Viewed in either way, in Period n a new equilibrium is established.

The same period-by-period detail recorded in Table 5-2 may be seen graphically in Figure 5-2. This graph shows only the change in Y and in C + I of 40 between the original equilibrium and the new equilibrium; it does not show the various possible absolute amounts of Y or C + I as is done in Figure 5-1. Specifically, in terms of that earlier figure, Figure 5-2 shows in greatly enlarged form only the small portion of the 45° line and the C + I + ΔI line running from 160 to 200—from the original equilibrium to the new equilibrium—on both axes.

Paralleling the description of Table 5-2, the initial equilibrium is upset by ΔI of 10 in Period 2 (line segment AB). Because output responds to increased spending with a one-period lag, Y rises by 10 in Period 3 (line segment BD). In Period 3, ΔY of 10 calls forth ΔC of 7.5 (line segment DE). This increase in spending leads to an increase in output of equal amount or ΔY of 7.5 (line segment EF). It is important to recognize here that ΔY is now 17.5 above the *original* equilibrium level because it first went up by 10 (B to D) and now by another 7.5 (E to F). That ΔY of 7.5 calls forth ΔC of 5.6 (line segment FG). Here ΔC is now 13.1 above the original amount because it first went up by 7.5 (D to E) and now by another 5.6 (F to G). The process moves ahead in this way period by period until the new equilibrium is established with ΔY of 40, as shown at the top of the diagram and with ΔI of 10 and ΔC of 30 as shown on the left side of the diagram.

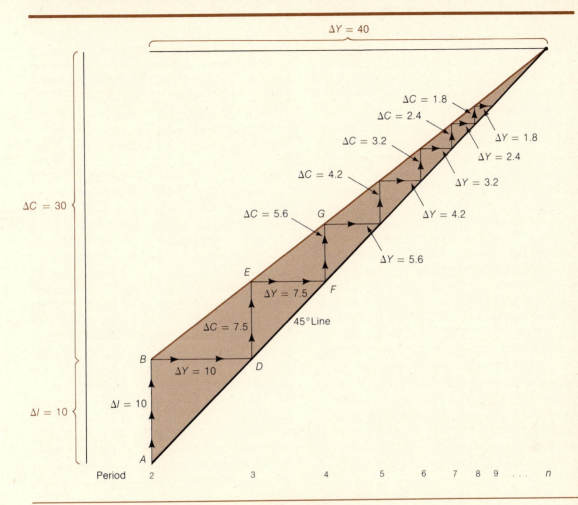

$\Delta Y = 40$

$\Delta C = 1.8$

$\Delta C = 2.4$

$\Delta C = 3.2$

$\Delta Y = 1.8$

$\Delta C = 4.2$

$\Delta Y = 2.4$

$\Delta C = 5.6$ G

$\Delta Y = 3.2$

$\Delta C = 30$

$\Delta Y = 4.2$

E

$\Delta Y = 7.5$ F

$\Delta Y = 5.6$

$\Delta C = 7.5$ 45°Line

B

$\Delta Y = 10$ D

$\Delta I = 10$ $\Delta I = 10$

A

$\Delta I = 10$

Period   2   3   4   5   6   7   8 9 ... n

FIGURE 5-2
The Period-by-Period Changes in Income
Resulting from a Change in Investment

The Multiplier—A Shift in the Aggregate Spending Function

In terms of Figure 5-1 and Table 5-2, a permanent upward shift in the aggregate spending function results in a movement of income and output to a new equilibrium level that is higher than the original equilibrium level by some multiple of the upward shift in the aggregate spending function. The value of this multiple is known as the *multiplier* and represents the number by which the shift in the aggregate spending function must be multiplied to determine the change in the level of income and output required to establish a new equilibrium.[4] Under present assumptions, this multiple is 4.

Why do Figure 5-1 and Table 5-2 show a multiplier of 4 and not some other? The reason is that income receivers choose to spend 3/4 of any change in income (MPC = 3/4) on consumption or that they choose to save, or not spend on consumption, 1/4 of any change in income (MPS = 1/4). With MPS = 1/4, only when income and output have risen by 40 will income receivers devote an additional 10 of their higher income to saving. Then $\Delta S = \Delta I$, 10 = 10, and a new equilibrium level of income and output is established.

For any given shift in the aggregate spending function, the change in income required to re-establish equilibrium is entirely dependent on the value of the MPC or the MPS. For example, still assuming that $\Delta I = 10$, we can simply determine the new equilibrium if MPC = 4/5 and MPS = 1/5. Instead of ΔY of 40 as before, we will now have ΔY of 50, because it is only when ΔY is 50 that ΔS will be 10 and therefore equal to ΔI of 10. Accordingly, until Y has risen by 50 (until ΔY equals 50), aggregate spending will exceed aggregate output and investment will exceed saving, forcing a further rise in income and output. By the same reasoning, if the MPC were 2/3 and the MPS 1/3, the rise in income would be 30.[5]

These and various other combinations of MPC and MPS are all possible and plausible. Although many combinations are not plausible,

a particular pair of these combinations can help clarify the multiplier mechanism. One of these is MPC = 0 and MPS = 1. The rise in Y necessary to reestablish equilibrium in this case will be exactly equal to the permanent rise in I. If ΔI in Period 2 and in each subsequent period is 10, ΔY in Period 3 and in each subsequent period will be 10 also, because, if MPS = 1, ΔS will be 10 as soon as ΔY is 10. Therefore, $\Delta S = \Delta I$ in Period 3, and the new equilibrium level is immediately established at a level of income and output exactly 10 above the original level. The increase in investment does not lead to an increase in income larger than itself, because with MPS = 1, the rise in income of 10 in Period 3 does not lead to a rise in consumption spending. Instead, the income receivers choose to devote all the increase in income of Period 3 to saving (MPS = 1). There being no induced rise in consumption spending in Period 3, ΔY of Period 4 and each subsequent period is simply equal to ΔI of 10 for each such period. Unlike the situation in Table 5-2, in which only a part of the enlarged income stream of Period 3 was diverted into saving, here all ΔY of Period 3 leaks out of the spending stream in Period 3, and the expansion process ends as quickly as it began. In a formal sense, the value of the multiplier is 1, but this is a far cry from the earlier results in which the multiplier was 4 (MPC = 3/4 and MPS = 1/4).

The other combination is MPC = 1 and MPS = 0. Starting off as before with ΔI of 10 in Period 2 (and in each subsequent period), none of the

[4] Although it was made famous by the role it plays in Keynes' *General Theory,* the term was coined by another British economist, R.F. Kahn. Kahn's multiplier was an *employment* multiplier, measuring the ratio of the increment of total employment associated with a given increment of employment in the capital goods industries. Keynes' multiplier is an *investment* multiplier, the ratio of the increment to total income associated with a given increment in investment. (See John Maynard Keynes, *The General Theory of Employment, Interest, and Money,* Harcourt Brace Jovanovich, 1936, pp. 113–15.)

[5] While we may ask such questions and give such answers to illustrate the principle, it should be noted that

if we were to assume some value other than 3/4 for the MPC (or 1/4 for the MPS) the original equilibrium would not have been 160. With an MPC of 4/5, the original equilibrium income and output would have been 200, equal to the aggregate spending function, $20 + \frac{4}{5}Y + I$, in which I equals 20. From this original equilibrium, ΔI of 10 would result in ΔY of 50 before equilibrium was restored with ΔS of 10 equal to ΔI of 10; ΔY would be 50 as described above, but the rise in Y would have been from an original equilibrium with $Y = 200$ to a new equilibrium with $Y + \Delta Y = 250$.

additional income of 10 flowing to income receivers in Period 3 is diverted from the spending stream. Therefore, the entire 10 of ΔY of Period 3 appears on the market as spending for consumption goods. In Period 3, $\Delta C = 10$, $\Delta I = 10$, and therefore in Period 4 $\Delta Y = 20$. In Period 4, all ΔY of that period appears as spending for consumption goods so that $\Delta C = 20$, $\Delta I = 10$, and therefore in Period 5, $\Delta Y = 30$. No new equilibrium would be possible in this case, and income would rise without limit. Equilibrium requires that $\Delta S = \Delta I$. But because all ΔY of any period is devoted to ΔC and none is diverted to ΔS, ΔS remains zero period after period and can never equal ΔI as required for equilibrium. Period after period, investment exceeds saving and aggregate spending exceeds aggregate output. In this special situation, we quickly have to drop our assumption that output expands proportionally with aggregate spending. This assumption is not too unreasonable for an economy with substantial unemployment of people and machines; but with spending growing without limit, unemployment would be quickly eliminated. As full employment approached, output would cease expanding proportionally with spending; once all available resources were fully utilized, output would not expand at all. Aggregate spending would continue to rise, but the rising expenditures would mean only continuously rising prices paid for an amount of output temporarily at its physical maximum. Such is the consequence of the assumption of an increase in I with MPC = 1 and MPS = 0.

In all the examples above, we have assumed that the aggregate spending function shifts upward. Shifts in the opposite direction are equally possible. In such cases, the multiplier works to produce a multiple contraction of income and output instead of a multiple expansion. With a downward shift in the aggregate spending function, our concern is not how much income will rise before equilibrium is restored but how much it will fall before equilibrium is restored. With MPC = 3/4 and MPS = 1/4, if investment spending falls from 20 to 10 ($\Delta I = -10$), the *drop*

in income and output necessary to restore equilibrium will be 40. The reasoning is the same as before. Income will drop until saving again equals investment. Because investment is reduced from 20 to 10 (by -10), saving must be reduced from 20 to 10 (by -10), to restore equilibrium. Given MPS = 1/4, only when income is reduced by 40 will saving be reduced by 10. As income receivers increase saving by 1/4 of any addition to income, they decrease saving by 1/4 of any reduction in income. From the original equilibrium of 160, the system reaches a new equilibrium level with income and output reduced by 40 to 120. Observe that the downward multiplier is 4 for the same reason that the upward multiplier is 4: because MPC = 3/4 and MPS = 1/4. If we assume different values for the MPC and the MPS, the results for a downward shift in the aggregate spending function parallel those just described, differing only in the size of the multiplier. With MPC = 2/3 and MPS = 1/3, a downward shift in the aggregate spending function of 10 ($\Delta I = -10$) will produce a decline in income and output of 30.

Because the MPC or the MPS determines the multiplier and because the multiplier determines the size of the increase or decrease in income and output that will follow any given upward or downward shift in the aggregate spending function, the practical importance of the MPC and the MPS is great. Given the variability of that portion of the aggregate spending function made up of investment spending, the degree of instability of the entire economic system depends to some extent on the values of the MPC and the MPS. As business spending for plant and equipment increases in one period and decreases in another, there is a direct impact on the level of income and output within each period. This in itself is a source of instability. Yet whatever the variability of investment spending, a relatively low MPC and a relatively high MPS will tend to produce less instability in the economy than will a relatively high MPC and a relatively low MPS.

Of the two extreme cases we discussed earlier, the one in which MPC = 1 and MPS = 0 will produce extreme instability in income and output, because any variability in investment spending from one period to the next will be greatly magnified by continuously rising induced consumption spending. At the other extreme, when MPC = 0 and MPS = 1, the instability in income and output will be far less, because the variability of investment spending from one period to the next will not be magnified at all by induced consumption spending. Any explanation of fluctuations in the level of income and output involves far more than just the variability of investment spending and the values of the MPC and the MPS. Nonetheless, these values play a vital role in explaining the amplitude of the upward and downward movements in income and output during business cycles.

The Multiplier— Equations_____

To determine the equilibrium level of income and output in the two-sector economy, we used the equation

$$Y = C + I \qquad [1]$$

Once given the consumption function and the investment function, the equation could be readily solved:

$$Y = 20 + \tfrac{3}{4}Y + 20$$
$$160 = 140 + 20$$

If we retain this same consumption function but assume an upward shift in the investment function, the equilibrium level of income and output will increase. Because any change in Y—that is ΔY—must be equal to $\Delta C + \Delta I$, we have the following equation, the solution to which gives us the new equilibrium level of income and output. (The column headings in Tables 5-1 and 5-2 were derived from this equation.)

$$Y + \Delta Y = C + I + \Delta C + \Delta I \qquad [2]$$
$$160 + \Delta Y = 140 + 20 + \Delta C + \Delta I$$

Subtracting Equation [1] from Equation [2], we have another equation, the solution to which indicates the *change* in the level of income necessary to produce the new equilibrium level of income.

$$\Delta Y = \Delta C + \Delta I \qquad [3]$$

The consumption function $(C = C_a + cY)$ indicates that consumption spending *(C)* rises or falls by an amount equal to the MPC or c (here $\tfrac{3}{4}$) times the change in income. That is, it says that $\Delta C = c\Delta Y$ or, in the present example, $\Delta C = \tfrac{3}{4}\Delta Y$. Substituting in Equation [3], we have the following:

$$\Delta Y = c\Delta Y + \Delta I$$
$$\Delta Y - c\Delta Y = \Delta I$$
$$\Delta Y(1 - c) = \Delta I$$
$$\Delta Y = \frac{1}{1 - c}\Delta I$$

and

$$\frac{\Delta Y}{\Delta I} = \frac{1}{1 - c}$$

or

$$\Delta Y = \tfrac{3}{4}\Delta Y + \Delta I$$
$$\Delta Y - \tfrac{3}{4}\Delta Y = \Delta I$$
$$\Delta Y(1 - 3/4) = \Delta I$$
$$\Delta Y = \frac{1}{1 - \tfrac{3}{4}}\Delta I$$

and

$$\frac{\Delta Y}{\Delta I} = \frac{1}{1 - \tfrac{3}{4}} = 4$$

If $\Delta I = 10$, $\Delta Y = 40$; the new equilibrium level of income and output will be 40 above the original level. Because $\Delta C = \tfrac{3}{4}\Delta Y$ and $\Delta Y = 40$, $\Delta C = 30$. The rise in income and output is divided between a rise in consumption of 30 and a rise in investment of 10.

Given any change in investment (ΔI), the change in income and output necessary to re-establish equilibrium is known as soon as the multiplier is known. The multiplier, in turn, is known as soon as the MPC is known. As we have just seen, the general expression for the multiplier is

$$\frac{\Delta Y}{\Delta I} = \frac{1}{1 - MPC}$$

In other words, the multiplier is the reciprocal of 1 minus the MPC; the larger the value of the MPC, the larger will be the value of the multiplier. This clearly agrees with our intuitive notion that the rise in income induced by a given rise in invest-ment will be larger if a larger fraction of additional income is spent on consumption and will be smaller if a smaller fraction of additional income is spent on consumption—that is, the rise in income will be larger or smaller for a larger or smaller MPC.

There is a second approach to the determi-nation of the multiplier. To determine the equilib-rium level of income and output, we earlier used $Y = C + I$ and

$$S = I \qquad [1]$$

Whereas $Y = C + I$ focuses on the equality between aggregate output and aggregate spending, $S = I$ focuses on the equality between saving and investment. Once given the saving function and the investment function, the equa-tion could be readily solved for the equilibrium level of income and output as follows:

$$S = I$$
$$-20 + \tfrac{1}{4}Y = 20$$
$$\tfrac{1}{4}Y = 40$$
$$Y = 160$$

The further development of the approach in terms of saving and investment is exactly parallel with the preceding development in terms of con-sumption and investment. Assuming an upward shift in the investment function, the new equilib-rium level of income and output is that at which

$$S + \Delta S = I + \Delta I \qquad [2]$$

Because $S = I$, we may subtract $S = I$ from Equation [2] which gives us

$$\Delta S = \Delta I \qquad [3]$$

The solution to this equation indicates the change in the level of income necessary to produce the new equilibrium level of income, given a speci-fied change in the investment function.

The saving function ($S = S_a + sY$) indicates that saving rises or falls by an amount equal to the MPS or s (here $\tfrac{1}{4}$) times the rise or fall in income. That is, $\Delta S = s\Delta Y$. Substituting in Equa-tion [3], we have:

$$s\Delta Y = \Delta I$$

$$\Delta Y = \frac{1}{s}\Delta I$$

$$\frac{\Delta Y}{\Delta I} = \frac{1}{s}$$

If, as before, $\Delta I = 10$, then $\Delta Y = 40$; the new equilibrium level of income and output will be 40 above the original level. Given any change in investment (ΔI), the change in income and output necessary to restore equilibrium is known as soon as the multiplier is known. The multiplier, in turn, is known as soon as the MPS is known. Therefore, we have as a second general expres-sion for the multiplier:

$$\frac{\Delta Y}{\Delta I} = \frac{1}{MPS}$$

Because $MPS = 1 - MPC$, $1/MPS$ as here derived is exactly equal to our earlier equation for the multiplier, $1/(1 - MPC)$. Thus, the multi-plier is the reciprocal of 1 minus the MPC or the reciprocal of the MPS.

Simple Income Determination— A Concluding Note

In this chapter we have examined the theory of income determination under some highly simplifying assumptions—hence the use of the adjective "simple." Some of these assumptions will be dropped in later chapters. Naturally, the more that are dropped, the more complicated the theory becomes and the closer it comes to describing the infinitely complex process by which income and output change in the real world.

There is no doubt, however, that the simple theory outlined in this chapter sheds considerable light on the aggregate economic process in the world about us; it explains things that are not immediately apparent. One may properly argue that it takes no high level of economic sophistication to recognize that output will be increased in an economy with idle workers and idle machines if either business people or consumers or both step up their spending for goods and services.

However, the completely unsophisticated will probably expect output to increase by the amount of this initial increase in spending. But merely by introducing the concepts of the consumption function, the marginal propensity to consume, and the multiplier, even the simple theory makes very clear the secondary consequences that produce an increase in income and output larger than the initial increase in investment or consumer spending.

Our simple theory not only shows the process by which an increase in autonomous spending will raise income and output by a multiple of that increase, but also indicates what determines the size of this multiple (admittedly under very restrictive assumptions). Although this simple theory cannot begin to explain the actual fluctuations in the level of income and output in the real world, it can explain an important truth, a truth necessary but not sufficient to an understanding of these fluctuations. To understand this is to understand the essence of what the simple theory has to tell us.

OVERVIEW

The analysis of the preceding two chapters has been limited to an economy that excludes government and the rest of the world. The major purpose of this chapter is to extend the theory of income determination that was developed in those chapters to include the effect of government spending and taxation on income.

The actions of government in varying its spending and taxes are called its fiscal policy. How do various fiscal policy actions affect the income level? This chapter views this question narrowly, emphasizing the mechanics of fiscal policy by working through the mechanics of three fiscal models of increasing complexity. The first model assumes that all government spending is for goods and services and that tax receipts are a fixed dollar amount, rather than an amount that varies with the level of income. Despite the unreality of its assumptions, this first model is valuable, not only as a point of departure but as the basis for the well-known balanced-budget theorem. The second model involves one basic change—it allows for government transfer payments as well as government purchases, and shows that changes in these two types of government expenditures have different effects on the income level. The third model makes one more basic change—it drops the assumption that tax receipts are a fixed dollar amount in favor of the assumption that they are a direct linear function of the income level.

Government Spending and Taxation

The three fiscal models outline how specific changes in government purchases, transfer payments, and tax receipts affect the level of income. The next part of the chapter examines the question of the particular fiscal changes required at any time to raise the level of income to its full employment value. Three routes to full employment through fiscal policy are described and illustrated. The concluding note sounds a necessary warning on the questionability of the conclusions indicated by simple fiscal models like those developed in this chapter.

When the model of income determination is expanded to include government, aggregate spending is composed of personal consumption, domestic investment, and government expenditures for final product; the aggregate flow of income is now allocated not only to consumption and private saving, but, in part, to taxes as well.

In general, government can expand aggregate spending in any time period by increasing the amount it adds to the stream of private spending through its purchases of goods and services or by decreasing the amount it diverts from the stream of private spending through its net tax collections. By the same token, it can contract aggregate spending by decreasing the amount it adds to private spending or by increasing the amount it diverts from private spending. The effect of government spending and taxation on aggregate spending depends, in the first instance, on how much government injects into the spending stream through its purchases and on how much it withdraws through net tax collections. Because the level of income and output depends on aggregate spending, government can clearly raise or lower that level through its policy with respect to spending and taxing.

This at least is a conclusion with which the vast majority of economists agree. A few extreme monetarists seem to say that government is powerless to affect aggregate spending via its spending and taxing except to the extent that these involve a deficit that is financed by an increase in the money supply or a surplus that is used to reduce the money supply. They believe that government spending and taxing can affect aggregate spending only through the money supply changes that may accompany that spending and taxing. Although everyone now grants that the way a government deficit is financed or a surplus is disposed of significantly affects aggregate spending, most economists still hold that deficits and surpluses have a considerable effect on aggregate spending in and of themselves and apart from any change in the money supply that accompanies them. In this

chapter, we study the way in which this takes place.

Fiscal Policy

Government policy with respect to spending and taxing is known as its fiscal policy. In the years since the Great Depression, it has become generally accepted that the fiscal policy of the federal government should contribute to the attainment of certain economic goals. If the economy is operating at a level of income and output below that at which there is reasonably full utilization of its resources, the appropriate fiscal policy is an expansionary one. If, on the other hand, the economy is at a level of income and output at which there is not only full utilization of resources but strong upward pressure on prices, the appropriate fiscal policy is a contractionary one. In other words, fiscal policy should operate in a countercyclical fashion, promoting the stabilization of economic activity at high levels of output and employment. Other goals of fiscal policy include rapid economic growth, greater equality in the distribution of income, and maximum economic "well-being." These goals overlap to a degree; some compete with each other and some complement each other. In order to avoid the complexities of dealing with a diversity of goals, we will assume that the goal of fiscal policy is simply the stabilization of economic activity at its full employment level. Taking full employment to mean full utilization of all of the economy's resources, we may refer to the corresponding output as the economy's full employment output.

Having accepted this as the goal of fiscal policy, we would next want to devise the set of fiscal policy actions that would best enable us to achieve this objective under the conditions with which the economy is confronted at a particular time. There are two sets of basic fiscal policy alternatives. If the need is for an expansion of income, the fiscal policy alternatives are to increase government spending, decrease taxes, or both. If, on the other hand, due to inflationary pressures, there is a need to contract income, the fiscal policy alternatives are to decrease government spending, increase taxes, or both.

How does the government select the most effective alternative in any given situation? If there is a need for an expansion of income, what is the difference between increasing government purchases by a given dollar amount and decreasing tax collections by an equal amount? Can government expand income by increasing its purchases if at the same time it increases its tax collections by an equal amount? Is there any difference between the expansionary effect of a given dollar increase in government purchases of goods and services and an equal increase in government transfer payments? Resolving questions of this sort requires some understanding of the essential mechanics of fiscal policy.

To explain the mechanics of fiscal policy, we will construct a series of three models, each of which is built on the models developed for the two-sector economy. In the first, only tax receipts (T) and government purchases (G) are added to the two-sector model; government transfer payments are in effect assumed to be zero. In the second model, government transfer payments are added. Both of these models assume that tax receipts are independent of the level of income— that they are "autonomous." In the third model, the breakdown of government expenditures into purchases of goods and services and transfer payments is retained, but tax receipts are recognized as being, in part, dependent on the level of income. Because increases and decreases in government expenditures have expansionary or contractionary effects on the level of income, this model reflects the fact that tax receipts depend in part on the level of government expenditures.[1]

---

[1]For a more detailed development of these same models, see N.F. Keiser, *Macroeconomics, Fiscal Policy, and Economic Growth,* Wiley, 1964, Ch. 8, especially pp. 135–47. A more advanced and theoretical treatment is found in B. Hansen, *The Economic Theory of Fiscal Policy,* Harvard Univ. Press, 1958, and in A. Peacock and G.K. Shaw, *The Economic Theory of Fiscal Policy,* 2nd ed., Allen and Unwin, 1976.

Although, as we mentioned earlier, one accepted goal of fiscal policy is to promote full employment of the economy's resources, we will not attempt to show specifically how the level of government spending and taxation might be varied to accomplish this particular objective. The models simply assume certain amounts of government spending and taxation and indicate the expansionary or contractionary effect of each. The emphasis in this chapter will be on the pure mechanics of the relationships between government spending, taxation, and the level of income. However, in a final section of the chapter we will note briefly, in terms of a fiscal model, how the level of government spending and taxation might be adjusted to raise the level of output to the full employment position. More will be said about full employment fiscal policy in Chapter 24, of the book, which is devoted in part to the question of economic stabilization.

First Fiscal Model— Including Net Taxes and Government Purchases

In working out accounting identities in Chapter 2, the GNP identity for a three-sector economy was given as $C + S + T \equiv GNP \equiv C + I + G$. For NNP, here also designated by Y, the only change is that I is net rather than gross private investment and S is net rather than gross private saving. On both sides, the net figure is obtained from the gross figure by subtracting an amount equal to capital consumption allowances. With I and S now understood to refer to net amounts, we may write

$$C + S + T \equiv C + I + G$$

From this net national product identity follows the identity for saving and investment:

$$S + (T - G) \equiv I$$

Here $(T - G)$ equals public saving.

In the two-sector economy in which we assumed there were no undistributed corporate profits, disposable personal income was found to be equal to net national product. In the three-sector economy, however, taxes absorb a portion of the income generated by expenditures on net national product. Therefore, disposable personal income is less than net national product by the amount of taxes. Letting Y represent net national product and Y_d disposable personal income, we now have

$$Y_d \equiv Y - T$$

or

$$Y \equiv Y_d + T$$

The consumption function for the two-sector economy, in which Y_d equaled Y, was $C = C_a + cY$. Now, with Y_d less than Y, the consumption function becomes $C = C_a + c(Y - T)$, or $C = C_a + cY_d$. With this consumption function, with investment assumed to be entirely autonomous ($I = I_a$) and with fixed amounts of government purchases and tax receipts assumed per time period, the equilibrium level of income is given by

$$Y = C_a + c(Y - T) + I + G$$

Expressed in terms of saving and investment, equilibrium will be found at that level of income and output at which planned saving plus taxes equals planned investment plus government purchases:

$$S + T = I + G$$

For example, assume that $c = 3/4$, $C_a = 20$, and $I = 20$ and, for the moment, that T and G are both 0 (which amounts to a two-sector economy). These are precisely the values assumed in the very first model of simple income determination in a two-sector economy, as illustrated in Figure 4-3. There we saw that the equilibrium level of income for the values given was 160. Now let us superimpose (1) a given level of government purchases and (2) a given level of taxes. Then we

can trace the effects of each on the equilibrium level of income and output.

In Figure 6-1, the C and $C + I$ curves in Part A and the S and I curves in Part B correspond exactly to their counterparts in Figure 4-3. The equation for C is $C = C_a + c(Y - T)$, in which $C_a = 20$, $c = 3/4$, and, for the moment, $T = 0$. The equation for I is simply $I = I_a$, in which $I_a = 20$. Investment is completely autonomous— that is, it is the same at all levels of income. The equation for the saving function in Part B follows from the consumption function: $S = S_a + s(Y - T)$, in which $S_a = -C_a = -20$, and $s = 1 - c = 1/4$. The equilibrium level of income for these assumed values is, of course, 160 in Figure 6-1 as it was in Figure 4-3. Now we insert G of 25 and assume that this amount is entirely deficit financed so that taxes remain at 0. This is shown in Part A of Figure 6-1; the "autonomous" public spending (G of 25) is added to private spending ($C + I$) to produce the aggregate spending function, ($C + I + G$). In Part B, G is simply added again to investment spending (I) to produce the function labeled $I + G$. The new equilibrium level of income is now 260, 100 above what it was before aggregate spending was increased by the 25 of public spending.

Why did the equilibrium level of income rise by 100 with the addition of government expenditures of only 25? With government now in the picture, the new equilibrium level of income must be that at which the amount of the income stream diverted from consumption into planned saving and tax payments equals the amount added to the income stream in the form of investment and government expenditures. Because taxes are assumed to be 0, to restore equilibrium following the injection of 25 in government spending, income must rise to the level at which planned saving alone is equal to the sum of planned investment and government expenditures. Given an MPC of 3/4 and an MPS of 1/4, only when income has risen by 100 will there be additional saving of 25 leaking out of the income stream to match the 25 injected into the income stream per period by government spending. Therefore, in

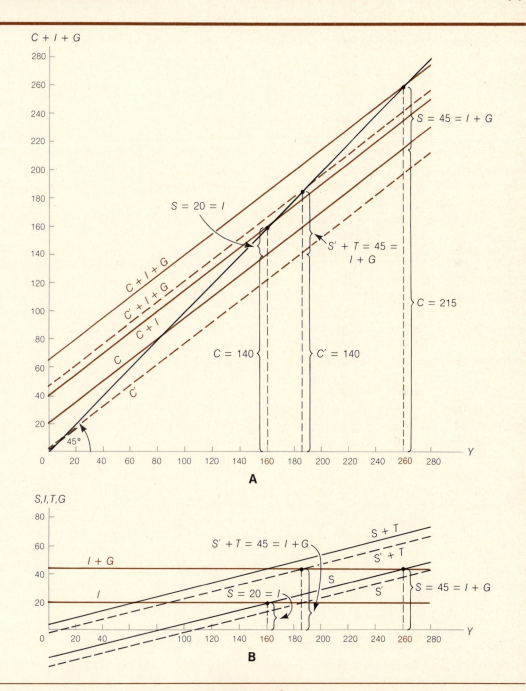

FIGURE 6-1
Equilibrium Level of Income, Including Government Expenditures and Taxation

Figure 6-1, we see that $S = 45 = I + G$ at Y of 260. Once income has risen by 100, a new equilibrium is established.

The effect of adding a given amount of government expenditures to the present model is essentially no different from the effect of an equal increase in C_a or I_a. Like C_a or I_a, G is here a part of autonomous spending. With $c = 3/4$, the ordinary multiplier is 4, and any increase in autonomous spending (G of 25) will, for example, other things being unchanged, raise income by four times the increase in autonomous spending to restore the system to equilibrium. The equation for the equilibrium level of income may be rewritten to show the multiplier explicitly. That is,

$$Y = C_a + c(Y - T) + I + G$$

may be rewritten as

$$Y = \frac{1}{1 - c}(C_a - cT + I + G)$$

Solving for the values we have assumed we have

$$260 = 4[20 - \tfrac{3}{4}(0) + 20 + 25]$$

Now let us suppose that government abandons its policy of deficit spending and that it collects 25 in taxes per time period to cover its expenditures of 25 per time period. With the imposition of this fixed amount of taxes, disposable income is 25 less than net national product at all levels of net national product. With an MPC of 3/4, it follows that taxes of 25 reduce consumption by 18.75 at each level of net national product. This is illustrated in Part A of Figure 6-1 by the new consumption function labeled C', which is positioned 18.75 below C. With an MPS of 1/4, taxes of 25 also reduce saving by 6.25 at each level of net national product. This is illustrated in Part B of Figure 6-1 by the new saving function labeled S', which lies 6.25 below S.

The new equilibrium level of income is now found in Part A by adding the 20 of I and 25 of G to C' to produce the new aggregate spending function, $C' + I + G$. This function intersects the guideline at Y of 185. The equilibrium level may also be found in Part B by adding the 25 of T to

S' to produce $S' + T$, which intersects $I + G$ at Y of 185. In Part A, equilibrium is indicated at the level of Y at which aggregate spending equals aggregate output ($Y = C' + I + G$). In Part B, equilibrium is indicated at the level of Y at which the aggregate diversions of income from consumption are offset by the aggregate of compensating expenditures ($S' + T = I + G$).

At first glance it is surprising to find that government injection of 25 into the income stream and the withdrawal in taxes of an exactly equal amount from the income stream still results in an expansion of the income stream from 160 to 185, an amount equal to the increase in the government budget. In the simplest terms, this result follows from the fact that the downward shift in the aggregate spending function due to T of 25 is less than the upward shift in that function due to G of 25. With the MPC of 3/4, T of 25 lowers the consumption function by 18.75 at each level of Y, or from C to C'. Because the upward shift of 25 is 6.25 greater than the downward shift of 18.75, the aggregate spending function with T and G both 25 is 6.25 above the aggregate spending function with T and G both 0. The net shift upward of 6.25 is subject to a multiplier of 4, which raises the equilibrium level of income by 25, from 160 to 185. As in previous models, this may also be explained in terms of saving and investment. Expressed in equation form, we have the following figures for the equilibrium positions, first with G and T both 0, and second with G and T both 25:

$$Y = C_a + c(Y - T) + I + G$$

$G = 0; T = 0:$
$$160 = 20 + \tfrac{3}{4}(160 - 0) + 20 + 0$$

$G = 25; T = 25:$
$$185 = 20 + \tfrac{3}{4}(185 - 25) + 20 + 25$$

$$S + T = I + G$$

$G = 0; T = 0:$
$$-20 + \tfrac{1}{4}(160 - 0) + 0 = 20 + 0$$

$G = 25; T = 25:$
$$-20 + \tfrac{1}{4}(185 - 25) + 25 = 20 + 25$$

Provided that G and T remain equal, substitutions of larger or smaller amounts of G and T in either equation will result in a rise or fall in the equilibrium level of income equal to the amount of the increase or decrease in the size of the government budget. This result is known as the **balanced budget theorem** or **unit-multiplier theorem.** We may see its meaning more clearly by again rewriting the aggregate spending equation to show the multiplier explicitly. That is,

$$Y = C_a + c(Y - T) + I + G$$

may be rewritten as

$$Y = \frac{1}{1 - c}(C_a - cT + I + G)$$

In this form, it may be seen that a change in any single value within the parentheses will produce a change in income equal to the change in that value times the ordinary multiplier, $1/(1 - c)$. Substituting the values from the previous example, we have

$$185 = \frac{1}{1 - 3/4}[20 - \frac{3}{4}(25) + 20 + 25]$$

If now, for example, we assume a change in I, the other values remaining unchanged, the new equilibrium level of Y is equal to the original level of Y plus the change in Y:

$$Y + \Delta Y = \frac{1}{1 - c}(C_a - cT + I + G)$$
$$+ \frac{1}{1 - c}\Delta I$$

Subtracting Y from both sides, there remains

$$\Delta Y = \frac{1}{1 - c}\Delta I = \frac{\Delta I}{1 - c}$$

In the same way, we will find that

$$\Delta Y = \frac{1}{1 - c}\Delta C_a = \frac{\Delta C_a}{1 - c}$$

and

$$\Delta Y = \frac{1}{1 - c}\Delta G = \frac{\Delta G}{1 - c}$$

Therefore, for equal sized changes in I, C_a, and G, we have

$$\Delta Y = \frac{\Delta I}{1 - c} = \frac{\Delta C_a}{1 - c} = \frac{\Delta G}{1 - c}$$

However, a change in T of the same size as the change in I, C_a, or G will produce a smaller change in Y and the change will be in the opposite direction, because

$$\Delta Y = \frac{-c\Delta T}{1 - c}$$

In the previous example, the equilibrium level of income with $G = 0$ and $T = 0$ was 160. Then, with $G = 25$ and $T = 0$, the equilibrium level rose from 160 to 260 or $\Delta Y = 100$. That is,

$$\Delta Y = \frac{\Delta G}{1 - c} = \frac{25}{1 - 3/4} = 100$$

However, with both $T = 25$ and $G = 25$ in the model, the new equilibrium level was 185. The addition of $T = 25$ to the model pulled income down, because

$$\Delta Y = \frac{-c\Delta T}{1 - c} = \frac{-\frac{3}{4}(25)}{1 - 3/4} = -75$$

Adding G of 25 raised the equilibrium level by 100, but adding T of 25 pulled the equilibrium level down by 75. Putting both together,

$$\Delta Y = \frac{\Delta G}{1 - c} + \frac{-c\Delta T}{1 - c} = 100 - 75 = 25$$

The change in Y is 25, as noted earlier.

The contractionary effect of an increase in taxes is therefore less than the expansionary effect of an equal increase in government spending for goods and services. A rise in G is, in its entirety, an addition to aggregate spending, but a rise in T is not, in its entirety, a decrease in aggregate spending. Some part of the rise in T is absorbed by a decrease in S, and only the remainder is absorbed by a decrease in C or in aggregate spending.

The different impacts of ΔG and ΔT on the level of Y may also be seen by comparing the multipliers that apply to each. The government purchases multiplier is the same as the multiplier applicable to a change in autonomous consumption or investment spending. For ΔG,

$$\Delta Y = \frac{\Delta G}{1 - c}$$

or

$$\frac{\Delta Y}{\Delta G} = \frac{1}{1 - c}$$

For ΔT, however, we derive the **tax multiplier**, which is smaller than the government purchases multiplier. Whereas a change in government purchases leads to a change in autonomous spending equal to the change in government purchases, a change in taxes leads to a change in autonomous spending that is only c times the change in taxes. For ΔT,

$$\Delta Y = \frac{-c\Delta T}{1 - c}$$

or

$$\frac{\Delta Y}{\Delta T} = \frac{-c}{1 - c}$$

If, as earlier, we assume c to be 3/4, a rise in government purchases is subject to a multiplier of 4, but a rise in taxes is subject to a multiplier of -3. In other words, an additional dollar of G will raise Y by \$4, an additional dollar of T will reduce Y by \$3, and the net effect of a rise of \$1 in both G and T is a \$1 rise in Y.

Regardless of the value of c, the government purchases multiplier ($\Delta Y/\Delta G$) will always be 1 greater than the tax multiplier ($\Delta Y/\Delta T$). This may be shown by combining the separate multiplier expressions for ΔG and ΔT:

$$\frac{\Delta Y}{\Delta G} + \frac{\Delta Y}{\Delta T} = \frac{1}{1 - c} + \frac{-c}{1 - c} = \frac{1 - c}{1 - c} = 1$$

Because $\Delta Y/\Delta G$ is always positive and $\Delta Y/\Delta T$ always negative, the sum of the two will always be unity, whatever the value of c.

A dramatic implication for fiscal policy seems to follow from the unit-multiplier theorem. If the level of the economy's output is below full employment, government should be able to raise the level to full employment by appropriately expanding its budget, covering every dollar of additional expenditures with a dollar of additional taxes. The desired rise in income and output could therefore be achieved through a fiscal policy that does not produce the real or alleged "evils" of deficit financing. However, as we have noted a number of times, in each case these crude mechanisms are subject to numerous qualifications that complicate the solution. The achievement of full employment is not as simple as the crude unit-multiplier theorem suggests. Although it is questionable that a rise in the size of the budget, with taxes and expenditures both up by \$5 billion, will raise the level of income by \$5 billion, it certainly will not be neutral in its effect on the level of income. Although proper analysis of the expansionary effects of a balanced budget involves more than the unit-multiplier theorem, the mechanical model of that theorem as developed here at least dispels the notion that a balanced budget is fiscally neutral, as was once thought to be the case.[2]

Second Fiscal Model— Including Gross Taxes, Government Purchases, and Transfer Payments

The first model emphasized the effects on income of changes in the net tax receipts of government and government purchases of goods and services. Now let us introduce a simple modification

[2] The literature on the unit-multiplier theorem is summarized in W.J. Baumol and M.H. Peston, "More on the Multiplier Effects of a Balanced Budget," in *American Economic Review*, March 1955, pp. 140–48. The more important studies in this extensive literature are also listed in R.A. Musgrave, *The Theory of Public Finance*, McGraw-Hill, 1959, p. 430.

that brings out the essential difference between the effects on income of changes in government purchases and transfer payments.

Net tax receipts *(T)* are equal to gross tax receipts minus government transfer payments or $T_g - R$.[3] Expressing this as $T = T_g - R$ underscores the fact that R is really negative taxes, in effect an amount of gross tax receipts that is returned to individuals through government transfer payments.[4] Substituting $T_g - R$ for *T*, the fundamental identity for net national product now becomes

$$C + S + T_g - R \equiv Y \equiv C + I + G$$

Disposable personal income, in turn, becomes

$$Y_d \equiv Y - T_g + R$$

The consumption function becomes

$$C = C_a + c(Y - T_g + R)$$

And the equilibrium level of income is given by

$$Y = C_a + c(Y - T_g + R) + I + G$$

which may be rewritten as

$$Y = \frac{1}{1 - c}(C_a - cT_g + cR + I + G)$$

This equation is identical to that for the first model, except that $T_g - R$ is now substituted for *T*. And the interpretation of this equation as rewritten is identical to that of its counterpart in the first model—any single change in the values within the parentheses will produce a change in income equal to the change in that value times the ordinary multiplier.

From the equation it is clear that the effect on *Y* of an increase in *R* will be less than the effect of an equal increase in *G*, as long as the MPC, or *c*, is less than 1. That is, where ΔG equals ΔR,

$$\frac{1}{1 - c} \Delta G > \frac{1}{1 - c} c\Delta R$$

The reason for this difference is that, in the first instance, all of any increase in *G* is an addition to aggregate spending, whereas only part of any increase in *R* becomes an addition to aggregate spending. ΔG affects aggregate spending directly, but ΔR affects aggregate spending only indirectly through its effect on disposable income. Assuming that there is no change in tax receipts, ΔR increases disposable income directly by the full amount of ΔR. The consumption function indicates, however, that not all of any increase in disposable income will be devoted to consumer spending; some portion will be devoted to personal saving. *In other words, at the first step, some portion of government transfer payments will fail to appear as spending for goods and services, but all government purchases will appear as spending for goods and services.* Therefore, in the case of *government purchases*, the full increase in government spending is subject to the ordinary multiplier; in the case of *government transfers*, only the part that is not diverted into saving is subject to the ordinary multiplier. These amounts may be designated ΔG and $c\Delta R$, respectively, as in the previous equation for the equilibrium level of income.

Instead of showing that all of ΔG and only part of ΔR are subject to the ordinary multiplier, we may express the same thing differently in terms of the government purchases multiplier and the government transfers multiplier. For government purchases, we developed the following multiplier:

$$\Delta Y = \frac{1}{1 - c} \Delta G$$

or

$$\frac{\Delta Y}{\Delta G} = \frac{1}{1 - c}$$

---

[3]More exactly, one must subtract the sum of transfer payments, government net interest payments, and subsidies less current surplus of government enterprises, as explained in Chapter 2, pp. 35–36. *R* will be referred to here simply as transfer payments; technically it includes the other transfer-type expenditures noted.

[4] With a balanced budget, $G = T$ and $G + R = T_g$. By showing *R* as a deduction from gross tax receipts, we have $G = T_g - R$. If there is a deficit or surplus, $G > T$ or $G < T$; the size of the deficit or surplus, of course, remains unchanged in the equation as restated.

For government transfers, we derive the multiplier to which the total of any change in transfers is subject as follows:

$$\Delta Y = \frac{1}{1-c}\, c\Delta R$$

or

$$\frac{\Delta Y}{\Delta R} = \frac{c}{1-c}$$

Regardless of the value of c, the government transfers multiplier is 1 less than the government purchases multiplier. Apart from the change in sign, it is the same as the tax multiplier. This equality between the tax multiplier and the government transfers multiplier has several important implications that will be noted below.

First, for a numerical example, let us compare the effects of ΔG of 5 with ΔR of 5, assuming that c equals 3/4:

$$\Delta Y = \frac{1}{1-c}\, \Delta G = 20$$

and

$$\Delta Y = \frac{1}{1-c}\, c\Delta R = 15$$

Expressed in terms of the government purchases multiplier and the government transfers multiplier, this means that ΔG is subject to a multiplier of 4 and ΔR to a multiplier of 3.

$$\frac{\Delta Y}{\Delta G} = \frac{1}{1-c} = 4$$

and

$$\frac{\Delta Y}{\Delta R} = \frac{c}{1-c} = 3$$

Because ΔG exerts a greater expansionary effect on Y than ΔR exerts when T_g remains constant, one would also expect the expansionary effect of ΔG on Y to exceed that of ΔR when ΔT_g matches the increase in government expenditures. The balanced budget theorem showed that an equal change in both G and T (for which we may now substitute T_g) would produce a change in Y equal to the change in the size of the budget.

For example, with ΔG and ΔT_g both 5 and with c of 3/4, we found the following:

$$\Delta Y = \frac{\Delta G}{1-c} + \frac{-c\Delta T_g}{1-c} = 20 - 15 = 5$$

Now, however, if the tax-financed increase in government expenditures is an increase in R rather than in G, we would have a different result:

$$\Delta Y = \frac{c\Delta R}{1-c} + \frac{-c\Delta T_g}{1-c} = 15 - 15 = 0$$

Unlike that of G, the expansionary effect of an increase in R is fully offset by the contractionary effect of an equal increase in T_g. In short, the expansionary effect suggested by the balanced budget theorem applies only to tax-financed changes in G, not to tax-financed changes in R.

In practice, the differences between the expansionary effects of an increase in purchases and those of an increase in transfer payments are not likely to be precisely those indicated by these crude models.[5] Despite the need for qualifications, the models still permit us to reach some tentative conclusions concerning the probable results of alternative fiscal policies: Assuming that, at its discretion, government may alter one or more of the variables according to plan, it may incur a deficit by (1) reducing tax receipts, (2) increasing purchases, (3) increasing transfer payments, or (4) any combination of these changes. In making a deficit of a given amount, an increase in purchases will have a greater expansionary effect than either a reduction in tax

---

[5] Crude models assume that the MPC is the same for all persons. However, the MPC of persons suffering a reduction in disposable income through additional tax payments may well be different from that of persons enjoying an increase in disposable income through receipt of transfer payments. The decrease in consumption of taxpayers will, therefore, not necessarily be the same as the increase in consumption of the beneficiaries of the transfer payments. The two sets of persons need not be the same. For example, unemployment compensation is financed through business taxes whose incidence may be on the owners or the customers of business or on both, but the beneficiaries of the compensation checks are the unemployed.

receipts or an increase in transfer payments. The expansionary effect of a deficit incurred by reducing tax receipts or raising transfer expenditures will be of the same order. Assuming that additional expenditures are to be covered by additional taxes, government can produce an expansionary effect only by increasing its purchases of goods and services. A reduction in its purchases accompanied by an equal reduction in tax receipts may be expected to be contractionary. In short, if government policy is to avoid a change in the size of the deficit or surplus, increasing or decreasing transfer payments and tax receipts in like amount will not directly affect the level of income.

Third Fiscal Model— Including Gross Tax Receipts as a Function of Income, Government Purchases, and Transfer Payments

In the second fiscal model, we developed the following equation for the equilibrium level of income, from which we may find, for any given value of c, the effect that a change in any one element within parentheses will have on Y if all the other elements remain constant:

$$Y = \frac{1}{1 - c}(C_a - cT_g + cR + I + G)$$

In reality, of course, a change in any one element is bound to affect the others through its effect on the level of income. A change in spending, whether directly through a change in autonomous consumption, investment, or government purchases, or indirectly through a change in government transfer payments or tax receipts will change the level of income; this change may call forth changes in other components of spending. The response of consumption spending to a

change in income is already built into the model because consumption is assumed to be equal to $C_a + cY_d$. The response of investment spending could also be built into the model by replacing the investment function in which investment is completely autonomous with one that makes investment depend in one way or another on the level of income or on changes in the level of income.[6] The response of government spending to changes in the level of income could also be built into the model, although there is no simple, meaningful relationship between government spending and the level of income (other than for transfer payments). To keep our discussion of this third model comparatively simple, we will continue to treat investment spending and government spending as completely autonomous.

One modification that may easily be made to bring our third model closer to reality is to allow for the fact that any change in income will typically affect tax receipts. In the previous model we assumed that tax receipts would remain constant in the face of a change in income. In practice, this would happen only if government took just the offsetting action necessary to prevent the change in tax receipts that otherwise would follow automatically from a change in income. In recent years, well over half the combined tax receipts of federal, state, and local governments have been from personal and corporate income taxes; the revenue produced by these taxes, far from being independent of income, varies more than proportionally with changes in income. Other mainstays in the tax structure, such as sales and excise tax receipts, are also related to income but less closely than income tax receipts. Given our present tax and rate structure, to prevent the changes in tax receipts that would automatically accompany a change in income would call for appropriate changes in the tax and/or rate structure. Now, assuming, as is found in practice, that tax receipts vary with changes in income, we

---

[6]Several functions of this kind are developed in Chapter 18.

may treat tax receipts roughly as a linear function of income. This gives us the following tax function:

$$T_g = T_a + tY$$

A tax function of this type is depicted by the T_g line in Figure 6-2. Notice that this function is of the same type as the consumption function, $C = C_a + cY$. Accordingly, it is interpreted in the same way. Just as c represents the MPC, so t stands for the MPT or the **marginal propensity to tax**. It indicates the marginal tax rate ($\Delta T_g/\Delta Y$)—that is, the fraction of any change in income that will be diverted from income receivers to government under a given tax structure and tax rates. It is comparable to the single rate in a proportional income tax. Graphically, the slope of the T_g function, drawn in Figure 6-2 as 1/5, tells us that for every change in Y of $5, there will be a change in T_g of $1. T_a, which is analogous to C_a, represents the amount of "autonomous" tax receipts—that is, the amount of tax receipts that is independent of the level of income. Although in practice income could not fall to zero, T_a indicates the amount of tax receipts at the theoretical zero level of income, which is depicted graphically by the intercept of the T_g function with the vertical axis.

The T_g function of Figure 6-2 shows T_a as a positive amount. Assuming that R remains the same at all levels of income and expressing the tax function in net terms, the net tax function,

labeled T in the figure, would lie below the gross tax function by the amount of R. As before, R appears as negative tax receipts or as a subtraction from gross tax receipts. The net tax function, $T = T_a + tY - R$, crosses the vertical axis below zero, indicating that at very low levels of income the amount of transfer payments would exceed the amount of gross tax receipts. Net tax receipts are shown to be negative at all income levels below $0b$. If we go a step further and recognize that transfer payments vary inversely with the level of income, the net tax function corresponding to the gross tax function given in Figure 6-2 would be one like the dashed line lying above T. This reflects the fact that as income rises, unemployment compensation and other expenditures under general relief programs decrease. This results in a narrowing of the spread between the gross tax function and the net tax function as income rises and a widening of the spread as income falls. For the sake of simplicity, however, we will assume that R is independent of Y, so that $T_g = T_a + tY$ and $T = T_a + tY - R$.

Substituting the tax function, $T_g = T_a + tY$, for T_g, we now have

$$C + S + T_a + tY - R = Y = C + I + G$$

Disposable personal income becomes

$$Y_d = Y - (T_a + tY) + R$$

or

$$Y_d = Y - T_a - tY + R$$

The consumption function becomes

$$C = C_a + c(Y - T_a - tY + R)$$

Retaining our assumption that investment and government expenditures are entirely autonomous, the equilibrium level of income is given by

$$Y = C_a + c(Y - T_a - tY + R) + I + G$$

or

$$Y = C_a + cY - cT_a - ctY + cR + I + G$$

which may be rewritten as

$$Y = \frac{1}{1 - c(1 - t)}(C_a - cT_a + cR + I + G)$$

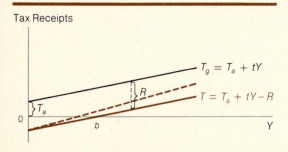

Tax Receipts

$T_g = T_a + tY$

R

$T = T_a + tY - R$

T_a

0

b

Y

FIGURE 6-2

Gross and Net Tax Functions

With tax receipts assumed to be independent of the level of income, the equation for the second model had a multiplier of $1/(1 - c)$. Recognizing that tax receipts are dependent on the level of income, the multiplier is reduced to $1/[1 - c(1 - t)]$. Assuming that $c = 3/4$ and that $t = 1/5$, we now have the smaller multiplier 2.5, instead of the previous multiplier 4. If the marginal propensity to tax (t) is greater than zero, the present model will always yield a smaller multiplier than the previous model.

Therefore, with $c = 3/4$ and $t = 1/5$, for a change in G of 10 we now have

$$\Delta Y = \frac{1}{1 - c(1 - t)} \Delta G$$

$$= \frac{1}{1 - (3/4)(1 - 1/5)}(10) = 25$$

instead of our earlier result,

$$Y = \frac{1}{1 - c} \Delta G = \frac{1}{1 - 3/4}(10) = 40$$

In the period in which G increases by 10, income increases by 10. If $t = 0$, disposable income also rises by 10, so that the full increase in income is available to consumers to spend or save. If we now assume that $t = 1/5$, disposable income does not rise by the amount of the increase in income. Instead, 1/5 of the income increase of 10 is diverted to the government in the form of tax payments, leaving only 8 as the increase in disposable income. With $c = 3/4$, instead of induced consumption of 7.5, or 3/4 of 10, as in the previous model, we now have induced consumption of 6, or $3/4 \times 4/5 \times 10$. Consequently, the marginal propensity to tax operates as a drag on consumption, reducing it to 6 from the 7.5 it would be if t equaled zero. In each of the subsequent periods required for the multiplier process to work itself out, 1/5 of the income generated in each period is also diverted to government in the form of tax payments. The final result is a new equilibrium level of income with ΔY of 25, made up of ΔG of 10 and ΔC of 15.

This process is described in detail in Table 6-1. Part A assumes $t = 1/5$ and traces the multiplier process given by the multiplier, $1/[1 - c(1 - t)]$. Part B assumes that tax receipts are independent of income, $t = 0$, and traces the familiar multiplier process given by the ordinary multiplier, $1/(1 - c)$. In both parts, an original equilibrium in Period t is upset in Period $t + 1$ by a permanent increase of 10 in government purchases. For use in this model, a lagged consumption function is assumed, so a change in disposable income in any one period does not lead to a change in consumption spending until the following period.

TABLE 6-1
Marginal Propensity to Tax and the Multiplier Process

A: $t = 1/5$, $c = 3/4$					
Period	ΔY	ΔG	ΔT_g	ΔY_d	ΔC
t	0	0	0	0	0
$t + 1$	10.0	10	2.0	8.0	0
$t + 2$	16.0	10	3.2	12.8	6.0
$t + 3$	19.6	10	3.9	15.7	9.6
$t + 4$	21.8	10	4.4	17.4	11.8
$t + 5$	23.0	10	4.6	18.4	13.0
....					
$t + n$	25.0	10	5.0	20.0	15.0

B: $t = 0$, $c = 3/4$					
Period	ΔY	ΔG	ΔT_g	ΔY_d	ΔC
t	0	0	0	0	0
$t + 1$	10.0	10	0	10.0	0
$t + 2$	17.5	10	0	17.5	7.5
$t + 3$	23.1	10	0	23.1	13.1
$t + 4$	27.3	10	0	27.3	17.3
$t + 5$	30.5	10	0	30.5	20.5
....					
$t + n$	40.0	10	0	40.0	30.0

NOTE: Figures are rounded to nearest tenth.

In Part A, ΔG of 10 in Period $t + 1$ generates ΔY of 10 but ΔY_d of only 8, because 1/5 of ΔY is diverted to government as ΔT_g. In Period $t + 2$, ΔY is 16, which consists of ΔG of 10 and ΔC of 6, the latter being 3/4 of ΔY_d of Period $t + 1$. Of ΔY of 16, 1/5 (or 3.2) is diverted to government, leaving ΔY_d of 12.8. In Period $t + 3$, ΔY is then the sum of ΔG of 10 and ΔC of 9.6. Income gradually rises by Period $t + n$ to a new equilibrium 25 above the original equilibrium. In Part B, the process is the same, except that no portion of ΔY is diverted into tax payments. Without additional taxes to be paid on the additional income, disposable income is greater, consumption spending is greater, and the level of income rises faster and farther than in Part A. In this situation, income rises to a new equilibrium level 40 above the old. Similarly, because consumption is not subject to the drag of additional taxes, induced consumption rises by 30 in Part B as compared with only 15 in Part A.

Although a positive marginal propensity to tax means that the expansion of income for any given increase in government spending will be smaller than it would be with a zero marginal propensity to tax, it also means that the deficit created by any increase in government spending will be less than the amount of the increase in government spending. For example, again in Part A of Table 6-1, the deficit created by ΔG of 10 is only 5 per time period, once the income equilibrium level has been reached—that is, $\Delta G - \Delta T_g = 5$ in Period $t + n$. In contrast, we see in Part B, with $t = 0$, that ΔG of 10 creates a deficit of 10 in each period. Part A is more relevant, because in the real world the MPT is positive. This suggests that an increase in government expenditures, with no change in tax rates or tax structure, normally will lead to a less than equal increase in the deficit.

This point is sometimes missed by persons who overlook the expansion of the income flow produced by the increase in government spending. With a positive MPT, some part of the expanded income flow automatically becomes additional tax receipts of government and as such becomes a check to what otherwise would be a change in the deficit equal to the increase in government spending. As we can see in the present model, the greater the MPC, the greater will be this check to the size of the deficit. If, for example, in Part A we substitute an MPC of 9/10 for the MPC of 3/4 and retain the same MPT of 1/5, the multiplier, $1/[1 - c(1 - t)]$ becomes 3.57. Then ΔG of 10 would produce a new equilibrium in Period $t + n$ with ΔY of 35.7. With ΔY of 35.7, ΔT_g would be 7.14 in Period $t + n$ and the deficit would be $10.00 - 7.14$ or only 2.86 in each period. Although an MPC of such size is unrealistic, in the present model an MPC that approaches 1 will produce a multiplier that approaches 5, given the same MPT of 1/5. In this case, ΔG of 10 would produce a new equilibrium in Period $t + n$ with ΔY of 50. The result would then be a "balanced budget" because ΔT_g would be 10 in Period $t + n$ or equal to ΔG. The increase in the equilibrium level of income induced by the increase in government spending would raise tax receipts by the same amount as the increase in government spending.

Fiscal Models and the Full Employment Level of Income

The several fiscal models developed to this point have shown how changes in G, R, and T_g, individually and in combination, affect the level of Y. We can summarize the implications of these simple fiscal models by demonstrating in terms of such a model how alternative fiscal policies may be used to lift an economy to its full employment level of income and output.

Let us begin with the most recently developed equation for the equilibrium level of income:

$$Y = C_a + c(Y - T_a - tY + R) + I + G$$

or

$$Y = \frac{1}{1 - c(1 - t)}(C_a - cT_a + cR + I + G)$$

We will assume that the following values apply:

$$C = 15 + \tfrac{3}{4}Y_d \quad R = 10.66 \quad T_g = 4 + \tfrac{1}{5}Y$$
$$I = 32 \qquad\qquad G = 50$$

Substituting in the equation for the equilibrium level of income, we have

$$Y = 15 + \tfrac{3}{4}(Y - 4 - \tfrac{1}{5}Y + 10.66) + 32 + 50$$
$$Y = 255$$

with $C = 173$, $I = 32$, and $G = 50$.

Let us further suppose that the full employment level of Y is 280 at the existing price level and that expansion of output from 255 to the full employment level will not raise the price level. The model suggests several possible routes by which this output level may be attained. An increase in government expenditures for goods and services is one route. To determine the needed increase in government expenditures, we insert Y of 280 into the equation and solve for the necessary G.

$$280 = 15 + \tfrac{3}{4}[280 - 4 - \tfrac{1}{5}(280) + 10.66]$$
$$+ 32 + G$$
$$G = 60$$

This could be found more simply and directly from the second equation given above, which shows the effective multiplier to be 2.5. To produce the required increase in Y of 25 would then call for an increase in G of 10 or from G of 50 to G of 60.

With Y at 255, T_g is 55 and $G + R$ is 60.66, indicating that there is a deficit of 5.66. If G rises by 10, resulting in a rise in Y of 25, T_g becomes 60, and the deficit increases to 10.66. Despite the increase in government expenditures of 10, the deficit increases by only 5; additional tax receipts of 5 are provided by the rise in income of 25.

A second route to full employment would be through tax reduction. Because tax receipts in the model depend on the level of income, tax reduction may take the form of a reduction in the marginal tax rate (t). To determine how far to reduce the tax rate, other things being equal, in

order to produce aggregate spending of 280 and so income and output of 280, we insert Y of 280 into the equation and solve for the necessary value of t:

$$280 = 15 + \tfrac{3}{4}(280 - 4 - 280t + 10.66)$$
$$+ 32 + 50$$
$$t = 0.15$$

A reduction in the marginal tax rate from 0.20 to 0.15 (or more precisely to 0.1523) will raise income by the required amount. Or, other things being equal, this tax rate will produce the level of disposable income at which, given the marginal propensity to consume, consumption spending will, when added to investment and government spending, yield the required level of aggregate spending of 280 and so the required income level of 280.

As before, the required tax rate may be found more simply and directly from the alternative equation that originally showed the effective multiplier to be 2.5:

$$\frac{255}{102} = \frac{1}{1 - \tfrac{3}{4}(1 - \tfrac{1}{5})} = 2.5$$

For Y of 280, the effective multiplier is therefore 280/102 or 2.75. To achieve this desired multiplier, t must be 0.15, as can be determined by solving the following for t:

$$\frac{280}{102} = \frac{1}{1 - \tfrac{3}{4}(1 - t)} = 2.75$$

As we mentioned earlier, the expansionary effect of a deficit incurred by way of tax reduction is less than that of an equal deficit incurred by way of increased government purchases. The same result is found here, except that the size of the deficit required to produce a specific expansion in income by way of increased government purchases must now be compared with that required to produce it by way of a decreased tax rate. Full employment was reached through increased purchases with an increase in the deficit from 5.66 to 10.66 per period. It is reached through a decreased tax rate with an increase in the deficit from 5.66 to 14.66 per period. In the present example, the deficit must increase (via tax reduction) by 9 per period to produce the expansion of income of 25 secured by an increase in the deficit (via increased government purchases) of 5 per period.

A third route to full employment would raise the income level by the required amount without any deficit financing. Because the expansionary effect of a dollar of government purchases is greater than the contractionary effect of a dollar of taxes, some amount of increase in government purchases and in taxes will raise income to the full employment level and produce a balanced budget at the same time. To determine this level of G and T (net taxes) at which $G = T$ with $Y = 280$, we start off with:

$$280 = 15 + \tfrac{3}{4}(280 - 4 - 280t + 10.66) + 32 + G$$

Given that T at Y of 280 equals $4 + 280t - 10.66$, we substitute G for this expression and solve the equation for G:

$$280 = 15 + \tfrac{3}{4}(280 - G) + 32 + G$$
$$280 = 257 + \tfrac{1}{4}G$$
$$G = 92$$

Therefore, we know that T must equal 92 to produce a balanced budget with Y of 280. Corresponding to net taxes of 92 are gross tax receipts (T_g) of 102.66. The required marginal tax rate is therefore derived from the tax function $102.66 = 4 + 280t$, or $t = 0.35$ (or more precisely 0.3523). The final solution is then

$$280 = 15 + 3/4[280 - 4 - 0.35(280) + 10.66] + 32 + 92$$
$$280 = 156 + 32 + 92$$

in which $C = 156$, $I = 32$, and $G = 92$.

In comparison with the first route, this one calls for a much greater expansion in government purchases. In comparison with the second route, it calls for an increase in the marginal tax rate. Although it manages to raise the income level without deficit financing, it does so only by enlarging both the share of the flow of goods and services and the share of the flow of income that are absorbed by government. A greater fraction of what is now a greater flow of final goods and services is made up of governmentally provided goods and services. A greater share of what is now a greater flow of income is diverted into taxes, and a smaller share is left for private consumption and saving.

The choice of which of these three fiscal policies to use in a given situation depends on what set of side effects is regarded as the least harmful. Government must evaluate the relative merits and demerits of spending, taxing, and changing the size of the public debt. In practice, the first and second routes or some combination of the two have received the most attention. Although both involve deficits and therefore some growth in the public debt, taxing does not enlarge the scope of government activities at all. Government spending produces the desired effect on the income level with a relatively much smaller enlargement of government activities than that necessitated by a fiscal policy with the budget-balancing restraint.

A Concluding Note

No matter how elaborate, Keynesian fiscal models are all essentially built along the lines of the simple Keynesian models discussed in this chapter. The chief purpose of devising such models is to shed light on the way in which government spending and taxing affect aggregate spending. Once this is explained, the effect on the equilibrium level of income and output is also explained, because in Keynesian models income and output depend on aggregate spending. However, even after accepting this basic premise, it should be emphasized that the conclusions suggested by the succession of models in this chapter are based on the assumption of "other things being equal." Of course, other things may change as a direct result of the government's taxing–borrowing–spending process. To the extent that they do change, the conclusions suggested by the models must be modified.

For one thing, while their effect on induced consumption is built into the models, changes in government spending and taxing may have other effects on consumption which are not built into the models. The fiscal process may alter the slope or level (the intercept with the vertical axis) of the consumption function. The expansionary effect of a tax-financed increase in government purchases will be greater than is shown in the models if it leads to a rise in the MPC or in the level of the consumption function. Conversely, it will be smaller than is shown in the models if it leads to a fall in the MPC or in the level of the consumption function. One way the government's fiscal actions might produce such results is through their effect on the distribution of income. For example, to the extent that the MPC of the "poor" is greater than that of the "rich," government expenditures financed through a progressive income tax will raise the aggregate MPC and have a greater expansionary effect on the income level than if the aggregate MPC remains unchanged. If the same government expenditures were financed instead by sales taxation, they might conceivably lower the aggregate MPC and thus have a smaller expansionary effect on the income level than if the aggregate MPC had remained unchanged.

Even more important are the possible effects of the government taxing–spending process on the investment function. A tax-financed increase in government expenditures covered by higher corporate or progressive personal income tax rates might have an adverse effect on the willingness of investors to spend on structures and durable equipment. The resultant downward shift in the investment function could offset the expansionary effect of the rise in government spending. Even the case in which the increased government expenditures are deficit financed is not without possible adverse effects on the investment function. With an increase in government borrowing added to the existing private demand for loanable funds, the interest rate may be expected to rise. The monetarists make much of this, arguing that the higher rate of interest will "crowd out" private investment spending of an amount equal to the debt-financed increase in government spending. In this event, the increase in government spending does not on balance have an expansionary effect on income. If the deficit is financed by an increase in the money supply, this offsetting may not occur. The central bank has the power to expand the money supply by the indicated amount; however, the central bank, rightly or wrongly fearful of inflation, often will not accommodate the increased demand for funds. In this event, the interest rate will tend to rise as it does with an increase in government borrowing from the public. Again, according to the "crowding out" argument, the resulting decrease in investment spending will offset the otherwise expansionary effect of the increase in government spending.

Another criticism of the basic Keynesian fiscal conclusions is much more severe. A group known as "supply side" economists has attacked the Keynesian single-minded attention to the demand-side effects of government spending and taxing and its almost complete neglect of the supply-side effects. From the viewpoint of supply-side economists, a tax cut will raise the equilibrium level of income and output, not by shifting the aggregate spending function upward, but through an effect which is outside the simple Keynesian model. They believe the expansionary effect of a tax cut results from raising labor productivity through more rapid capital formation, from encouraging greater work effort by allowing people to keep more of what they earn, and from stimulating saving (which in their world never goes to waste, but goes automatically into real capital formation). "Supply-siders" have attracted a good deal of attention over the past five years, but their views remain the views of a small minority of professional economists.

It is apparent from this glance at some of the criticisms of the conclusions drawn from the simple Keynesian fiscal models that these conclusions are by no means solidly established. The actual consequences of any change in the government's taxing–borrowing–spending program cannot be predicted with a high degree of accuracy. Yet, to the extent that a general statement is possible, most economists will agree that an increase in government spending or a reduction in taxes will encourage both consumption and investment and thereby produce a rise in income and output that is larger than the initial reduction in taxes or increase in government spending. The three models presented in this chapter are intended to suggest in very general terms how this expansionary process may work itself out in practice.

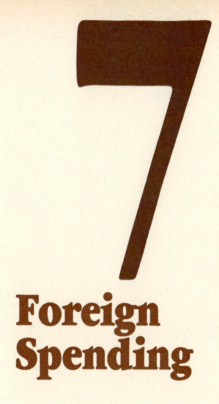

Foreign Spending

OVERVIEW

To this point, our analysis has assumed a "closed economy"—an economy considered in isolation from all others. In this chapter, we will relax that assumption and examine an "open economy"— a four-sector economy in which aggregate spending is measured by the spending of the three domestic sectors plus that of the foreign sector. Just as the income level is affected by spending originating with consumers, business, and government at home, so it is affected by spending originating with foreign consumers, foreign business, and foreign governments. This chapter introduces foreign spending into the system to build the full four-sector model.

Chapter 6 dealt only with the mechanics of government spending and taxes. The treatment here, too, is confined to the mechanics of the way in which imports, exports, and the net import or export balance affect the economy's income level. Just as a detailed analysis of the determinants of government spending and taxing was

omitted in Chapter 6, this chapter omits a detailed analysis of the determinants of an economy's imports and exports. In this chapter, we adopt a crude theory to explain the determination of the economy's aggregate imports and exports. We then turn to the major task of showing how imports and exports are worked into the simple Keynesian model of income determination that was built for two- and three-sector economies in the preceding chapters. Further attention will be given to the role of imports and exports in income determination in Chapter 14.

In Chapter 2 we saw that it is an economy's net rather than gross exports that measure the amount of its final product secured by the rest of the world and the amount of its GNP accounted for by the foreign sector. Gross imports must be subtracted from gross exports in measuring GNP, because gross imports are already included in the measurement of the amount of final product secured by the domestic sectors of the economy. Because both domestic and foreign goods and services are included in consumer, business, and government expenditures, $C + I + G$ no longer measures only the amount of domestically produced final goods and services secured by these three sectors. It measures this amount *plus* an amount equal to gross imports.[1] If we could separate C into the amounts spent for domestic and foreign output and do the same for I and G, then gross rather than net exports could be added to the resulting total for consumption, investment, and government spending on domestic output to yield aggregate expenditures by all four sectors of the economy for domestic output. Such a complete separation is, of course, impossible in practice. When a consumer purchases a ticket to see a foreign film or purchases a domestically produced automobile that consists in part of raw materials and parts that were produced abroad, he is purchasing simultaneously both domestic and foreign output combined in the same good or service. Similar cases also abound in domestic investment expenditures and in government purchases of goods and services.

In practice, therefore, we are forced to measure aggregate expenditures of the three domestic sectors by their expenditures on final product, regardless of whether it was produced domestically or abroad. For any time period, such expenditures will include gross imports of goods and services. Because this overstates the amount of domestically produced output secured by the domestic sectors, gross imports are subtracted in a lump sum to yield, in effect, the amount of domestically produced output secured by the domestic sectors. Expenditures by the rest of the world for the country's gross exports are then added to the figure obtained by subtracting the country's gross imports from the sum of expenditures by the domestic sectors. The resulting figure is a sum that accurately represents aggregate expenditures, domestic and foreign, for the economy's final output. If I is measured in net terms, we have the following identity for the net national product or Y on the expenditure's side:[2]

$$Y \equiv C + I + G + (X - M)$$

As always, corresponding to the flow of expenditures on the right is an equal flow of income on the left, which is split up as before into C, R_{pf}, S, and T. To show the breakdown on both the expenditures and income sides, we now have

$$C + R_{pf} + S + T \equiv Y \equiv C + I + G + (X - M)$$

Because R_{pf}, personal transfer payments to foreigners, is negligible in terms of net national product, we may simplify the identity by assuming such transfer payments to be zero. This gives

---

[1] As in the two- and three-sector economies, I is understood to be net private domestic investment. In the Department of Commerce accounting framework, net private investment is the sum of net private *domestic* investment and net *foreign* investment; the latter, in turn, is a part of the net export balance. For present purposes, it is not necessary to show net foreign investment explicitly, that is, to separate it from net exports. Therefore, we can manage without affixing a subscript to I as would be required if a second investment term, net foreign investment, were shown explicitly.

[2] If we could separate the amount made up of foreign *(f)* goods and services from each domestic sector's expenditures for final product, symbolically we would have in the four-sector economy

$$Y \equiv (C - C_f) + (I - I_f) + (G - G_f) + X$$

in which X equals gross exports and $C_f + I_f + G_f$ equals gross imports, or M. Because this separation cannot be made in practice, we subtract gross imports in a lump sum from $C + I + G$ and add gross exports:

$$Y \equiv C + I + G - M + X$$

This may then be rewritten in the standard form of the identity that follows in the text.

us a breakdown of the income flow into $C + S + T$, and the identity becomes

$$C + S + T \equiv Y \equiv C + I + G + (X - M)$$

Although in so doing we no longer have a net national product identity, we may rewrite the preceding identity as

$$C + S + T + M \equiv C + I + G + X$$

The sum of expenditures on the right exceeds net national product by the amount of gross imports or M, as does the sum of income on the left. The expression is still an identity, however, and if C is dropped from both sides, we have an identity that is useful in the explanation of the determination of the equilibrium level of income in a four-sector economy.

Equilibrium Level of Income and Output

All else being equal, the domestic economy's income and output will rise from one period to the next as its gross exports rise or as its gross imports fall, because both of these changes enlarge its net exports. Consequently, its income and output will fall from one period to the next as its gross exports fall or as its gross imports rise, because both of these changes decrease its net exports. Therefore, the effect of imports and exports on the equilibrium level of the domestic economy's income and output must be found in the factors that determine the economy's imports and exports.

In a very general way, the volume of any economy's gross exports depends on (1) the prices of goods in the domestic economy relative to the prices of the same or substitute goods in other economies, (2) tariff and trade policies existing between the domestic and other economies, (3) the level of income in other countries, (4) the level of the domestic economy's imports, and (5) various other less significant factors. Some of the more important factors influencing

an economy's exports are not directly related to conditions within that economy. Although this is a great simplification, we will assume that gross exports of the domestic economy are wholly determined by external factors. In other words, we may take gross exports as an autonomous variable, the value of which for any time period is wholly determined by forces outside the domestic economy.

The volume of imports is determined by a similar list of factors. However, many of these factors are much more closely related to conditions within the economy than are those that determine exports. If, in the case of imports, we assume an unchanging system of international price differences, unchanging tariff, trade, and exchange restrictions, and all other factors unchanging except the level of domestic income, we may concentrate on one of the most important factors affecting gross imports—namely, the level of income within the domestic economy.

The Import Function

All else being equal, as the level of income rises, we expect an induced rise in spending. We may also expect that some portion of the rise in spending will be for imported goods and services. As a rough approximation, we will assume that there is a linear relationship between income and imports, which gives us the import function:

$$M = M_a + mY$$

Here M_a represents autonomous expenditures for imports and m is the **marginal propensity to import,** abbreviated as MPM. As in the $C_a + cY$ function, M_a is the amount of expenditures for imports at a theoretical zero level of income, or the amount of import expenditures that are independent of the level of income; m is simply the fraction of any change in income that will be devoted to expenditures on imports, or $m = \Delta M / \Delta Y$.

The upward-sloping line shown in Figure 7-1 depicts the import–income relationship described by the import function given above. Because

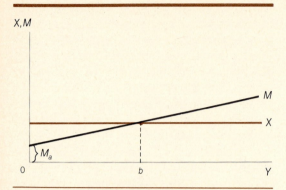

FIGURE 7-1
Import and Export Functions

exports are assumed to be externally determined, they are designated in the figure by a line parallel to the income axis. The level of the export line depends on the whole complex of external conditions. For the two functions as illustrated, at all income levels below $0b$ the economy has a net export balance, and at all income levels above $0b$ it has a net import (or negative net export) balance. Clearly, any change in the determinants of gross exports that shifts the export function upward will increase the net export balance or decrease the net import balance at each level of income. Similarly, any change that shifts the import function downward (decreases M_a) or reduces the slope of the import function (decreases m) will have the same effect.

The Equilibrium Level of Income—Equations

In the four-sector economy, the equilibrium level of income is that at which aggregate spending— the sum of consumption, investment, government, and net foreign expenditures—is equal to income. This gives us the following general equation for the equilibrium level of income:

$$Y = C + I + G + (X - M)$$

It can also be said that because $C + S + T = C + I + G + (X - M)$, the equilibrium level of income is that at which $S + T = I + G + (X - M)$, or, when it is rearranged,

$$S + T + M = I + G + X$$

In this formulation, $S + T + M$ represents the portion of the economy's gross income flow that is diverted from consumption expenditure on domestically produced output. If the amount of compensating expenditures on domestically produced output, $I + G + X$, just equals these diversions or "leakages" from the income stream, then aggregate spending must equal aggregate income. The particular level of income at which this equality occurs is the equilibrium level.

If we now recognize that the economy's gross imports depend to some extent on the level of its income and assume that its gross exports are externally determined, the equilibrium equation is modified as follows:

$$Y = C + I + G + X - (M_a + mY)$$

We could also say that the equilibrium level of income is that at which

$$S + T + (M_a + mY) = I + G + X$$

Finally, assuming that I, T, and G are all autonomous, and that $C = C_a + c(Y - T)$, the equation for the equilibrium level of income becomes[3]

$$Y = C_a + c(Y - T) + I + G + X - (M_a + mY)$$

---

[3]Apart from the addition of imports and exports, this equation is the same as that developed for the first fiscal model of Chapter 6. If the third fiscal model, which included government transfer payments and the tax function, were expanded to allow for exports and the import function, we would have

$$Y = C_a + c(Y - T_a - tY + R) + I + G + X \\ - (M_a + mY)$$

Alternatively, the equilibrium level of income would be that at which

$$S_a + s(Y - T_a - tY + R) + (T_a + tY - R) \\ + (M_a + mY) = I + G + X$$

The analysis in this text will be limited throughout to the simpler model in which G and T are both autonomous and R is assumed to be zero.

Because $S = -C_a + s(Y - T)$ and $-C_a = S_a$, we may also describe the equilibrium level of income as that level at which

$$S_a + s(Y - T) + T + (M_a + mY) = I + G + X$$

For a numerical example of the determination of the equilibrium level of income, assume the following values for the spending flows:

$G = 26$
$I = 20$
$X = 17$
$T = 25$
$M = M_a + mY = 2 + \frac{1}{10}Y$
$C = C_a + c(Y - T) = 25 + \frac{8}{10}(Y - 25)$

Substituting in the equation for the equilibrium level of income, we have

$Y = C_a + c(Y - T) + I + G + X - (M_a + mY)$
$Y = 25 + \frac{8}{10}(Y - 25) + 20 + 26 + 17$
$\qquad\qquad\qquad\qquad\qquad - (2 + \frac{1}{10}Y)$
$Y = 220$

or, in its alternative expression:

$S_a + s(Y - T) + T + (M_a + mY) = I + G + X$
$- 25 + \frac{2}{10}(Y - 25) + 25 + (2 + \frac{1}{10}Y) =$
$\qquad\qquad\qquad\qquad\qquad 20 + 26 + 17$
$\qquad \frac{3}{10}Y = 63 + 3$
$\qquad\quad Y = 220$

The Equilibrium Level of Income—Graphs

Figure 7-2 illustrates the determination of the equilibrium level of income. Apart from the addition of net exports, the figure is identical to Figure 6-1. The consumption function is plotted from the equation $C = 25 + \frac{8}{10}(Y - 25)$. (The vertical intercept is therefore 5.) Autonomous investment of 20 is then superimposed on C to produce the $C + I$ function, and autonomous government purchases of 26 are superimposed on $C + I$ to yield the $C + I + G$ function. Finally, superimposed on the $C + I + G$ function is the last component of aggregate spending, net exports or $X - M$. This gives the complete aggregate spending

function $C + I + G + (X - M)$. Because gross exports are assumed to be independent of the level of domestic income and because gross imports are partially dependent on the level of domestic income, the excess of exports over imports of 15 (that is, $17 - 2$) at the theoretical zero level of income gradually diminishes to zero at income of 150 [at which $X = 17$, and $M = 2 + \frac{1}{10}(150) = 17$]. Therefore, up to Y of 150, foreign trade results in a net addition to aggregate spending—that is, $C + I + G + (X - M) > C + I + G$. Above this level, however, imports exceed exports, and this excess grows larger at successively higher levels of income. Therefore, at income levels above 150, foreign trade results in a net reduction in aggregate spending—that is, $C + I + G > C + I + G + (X - M)$.

Because the net exports component of aggregate spending becomes negative at higher levels of income in our example, the aggregate spending function, including net foreign spending, lies below the spending function, which comprises only the spending of the three domestic sectors, at these higher levels of income.

The equilibrium income level is that level at which the aggregate spending function intersects the 45° guideline. In this case, when $Y = 220$, $C = 181$, $I = 20$, $G = 26$, and $X - M$

When $Y = 220$, the four components of aggregate spending add up to 220, an amount equal to the income flow; therefore, only 220 can be the equilibrium income level. Following the argument of previous analyses, Part A of Figure 7-2 shows that $C + I + G + (X - M) > Y$ at any level of Y below 220; this excess of spending over income leads to a rise in income and output. At any level of Y above 220, $C + I + G + (X - M) < Y$; this deficiency of spending leads to a fall in income and output.

Given the values we have assumed for the various expenditure flows, the inclusion of foreign trade means a lower equilibrium level than that which would be found in its absence. If $C + I + G$ were to remain the same in the absence of the availability of foreign-produced goods, the equilibrium level would occur at Y of 255, the

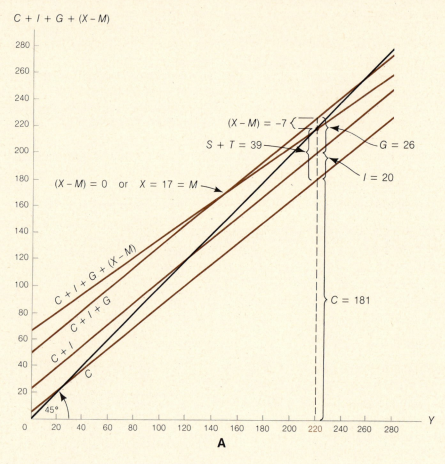

A

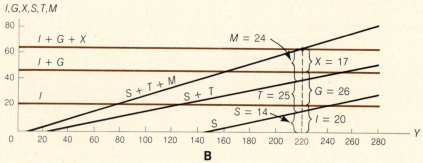

B

FIGURE 7-2
The Equilibrium Level of Income, Including Imports and Exports

income level at which the $C + I + G$ function cuts the 45° guideline.[4] The actual equilibrium in our example with foreign trade included is 220.

Part B of Figure 7-2 shows the alternative graphic approach to the determination of the equilibrium income level. Apart from the addition of gross imports and gross exports, the figure is identical to Part B of Figure 6-1. Imports now appear as a third diversion from the amount of consumer expenditure on domestically produced output; total diversions now equal $S + T + M$. Exports now appear as a third kind of expenditure compensating for the diversions of income into $S + T + M$; total compensating expenditures now equal $I + G + X$. With these modifications for foreign trade, the equilibrium level of income is accordingly that at which $S + T + M = I + G + X$. As shown in Part B, this is at $Y = 220$.

Part B of Figure 7-2 enables us to clearly identify each of these diversions from and the compensating injections into the spending stream. Putting them all together, at the income level of 220, we find that

$$S + T + M = I + G + X$$
$$14 + 25 + 24 = 20 + 26 + 17$$

It will be recalled from the analysis of the two-sector economy that if $I > S$, as here 20 > 14, there would be a disequilibrium and the level of income would rise. Similarly, in the three-sector economy, if $I + G > S + T$, as here 46 > 39, there would be a disequilibrium and the level of income would rise. However, in this four-sector economy, the income-expansionary effect of $I + G > S + T$ is offset by the income-contractionary effect of $M > X$, or 24 > 17. At the income level of 220, these forces offset each other precisely—total compensating injections match total income diversions—so income neither expands nor contracts.

---

[4] If foreign-produced goods were not available, C might be lower at each level of Y. Consumers with strong preferences for imported goods might transfer part of what was spent on such goods to saving rather than transferring it all to domestically produced goods.

The Foreign Trade Multiplier and Changes in the Level of Income____

In an open economy, where imports depend in part on the level of income, the overall expansionary effect of any increase in autonomous spending will be dampened by the "leakage" of some part of any expansion of income into the purchase of imports. Assume that as a result of a rise of incomes in other countries there is a rise in the exports of the domestic economy. This will cause an equal initial increase in domestic income as production is stepped up to meet increased foreign spending. The MPC indicates that this initial rise in income will induce an increase in consumption expenditures, but the MPM reveals that some of the additional consumption expenditures will be for imported goods. Therefore, at the second stage of the expansion process, domestic income rises by the amount of induced consumption expenditures less the rise in induced consumption expenditures for imported goods. The restricted increase in income at the second stage leads to a smaller third-stage increase in domestic income than would otherwise be the case, because, again, part of the increased expenditures at the third stage is for imported goods. Thus, for any given increase in autonomous spending, the size of the multiplier is reduced when there is a positive marginal propensity to import.

To trace the effect of the marginal propensity to import on the multiplier in terms of our earlier equations, we may begin with the equation developed in this chapter for the equilibrium level of income in the four-sector economy:

$$Y = C_a + c(Y - T) + I + G + X - (M_a + mY)$$

This may be rewritten as

$$Y = \frac{1}{1 - c + m}(C_a - cT + I + G + X - M_a)$$

Here $1/(1 - c + m)$ is the foreign trade multiplier for a system in which consumption expenditures and import expenditures are linear functions of the level of domestic income.[5] As in other equations of the same type, a change in any of the values within parentheses will result in a change in income equal to the change in that value times the multiplier. Let us suppose that there is a change in exports, ΔX:

$$Y + \Delta Y = \frac{1}{1 - c + m}(C_a - cT + I$$
$$+ G + X - M_a) + \frac{1}{1 - c + m}\Delta X$$

Subtracting Y from both sides, we have

$$\Delta Y = \frac{1}{1 - c + m}\Delta X$$

or

$$\frac{\Delta Y}{\Delta X} = \frac{1}{1 - c + m}$$

The same would be true for a change in C_a, I, or G and, with opposite sign, for a change in M_a.[6] Adopting the same values for the MPC and the

MPM used earlier and assuming ΔX of 18, we have

$$\Delta Y = \frac{1}{1 - \frac{8}{10} + \frac{1}{10}}(18) = 3.33(18) = 60$$

or

$$\frac{\Delta Y}{\Delta X} = \frac{60}{18} = \frac{1}{1 - \frac{8}{10} + \frac{1}{10}} = 3.33$$

If there were no marginal propensity to import or if this propensity were 0, the multiplier would be the ordinary one, $1/(1 - c)$, or, in this example, 5. The rise of 18 in exports would raise the level of income by 90 instead of by 60. Whatever its value, as long as the MPM is positive, it reduces the size of the effective multiplier. The MPM fits into the determination of the multiplier in the same way as the MPS.[7]

Another way of illustrating the effect of the MPM on the multiplier is to express the multiplier as $1/[1 - (c - m)]$. Here, as before, c is the marginal propensity to purchase both domestically produced goods and foreign-produced goods and m is the marginal propensity to purchase foreign-produced goods. The expression $c - m$ accordingly represents the marginal propensity to purchase domestically produced goods and is relevant to changes in the domestic level of income. If m were equal to c, the multiplier would be 1, because any rise in autonomous spending would raise income only by the amount of that rise in autonomous spending. The full

---

[5] A more complex foreign trade multiplier would emerge from the equation that recognized taxes as a function of the income level. Adding imports and exports to the equation developed for the third fiscal model in Chapter 6, we have the equation of footnote 3, p. 116:

$$Y = C_a + c(Y - T_a - tY + R) + I + G + X$$
$$- (M_a + mY)$$

This may be rewritten as

$$Y = \frac{1}{1 - c + ct + m}(C_a - cT_a + cR + I + G + X - M_a)$$

Here the multiplier $1/(1 - c + ct + m)$ is that for the model in which consumption, imports, and taxes are all linear functions of the level of domestic income.

[6] However, for a change in T in the present model, the multiplier becomes

$$\frac{\Delta Y}{\Delta T} = \frac{-c}{1 - c + m}$$

See p. 102.

[7] In these terms, $1 - c$ is the MPS, or s. The greater $1 - c$, the greater is s, the greater is the "leakage" into saving from any change in income, and therefore the smaller is the expansion in income for any increase in autonomous spending. In turn, $s + m$ is the sum of the MPS and the MPM. The greater this sum, the greater is the "leakage" into saving and imports from any change in income, and therefore the smaller is the expansion in income for any increase in autonomous spending. Finally, for the multiplier including the MPT, ct is added to $s + m$ to produce $s + ct + m$. This, then, is the sum of MPS, MPC $\times$ MPT, and MPM. The greater this sum, the greater is the "leakage" of any change in income into saving, imports, and taxes, and the smaller is the expansion in income for any increase in autonomous demand.

amount of the increase in income received at the first stage would be diverted to the purchase of foreign-produced goods; there would be no induced increase in the purchase of domestically produced goods. As long as m is less than c, which it usually is, the multiplier will exceed 1. Finally, if m were zero, c would become identical to the marginal propensity to purchase domestically produced goods—the multiplier $1/[1 - (c - m)]$ would in effect be the ordinary mutliplier $1/(1 - c)$.

Figure 7-3 depicts the method of determining the change in the equilibrium level of income that results from a change in autonomous spending.[8] In Part A, for the income range shown, the solid-line schedules are the same as those in Figure 7-2. The aggregate spending function, $C + I + G + (X - M)$, also intersects the 45° line at the income level of 220 as in Figure 7-2. Now, suppose that exports increase by 18.[9] The resultant aggregate spending function, now labeled $C + I + G + (X + \Delta X - M)$, lies 18 above its previous position at each level of income and intersects the 45° line at income of 280, the new equilibrium level. With a rise of 18 in autonomous spending and a consequent rise of 60 in income and output, the multiplier is $\Delta Y/\Delta X = 60/18 = 3.33$, as was determined earlier in terms of the equation for the equilibrium level of income.

Before exports rose by 18, foreign trade exerted a net contractionary effect on the income level (at the equilibrium level of 220, $X - M = 17 - 24 = -7$). The aggregate spending function lay below the spending function for the three domestic sectors alone. After the rise of 18 in exports and the establishment of the new equilibrium of 280, foreign trade exerts a net expansionary effect. At this new income level, $X + \Delta X - M = 17 + 18 - 30 = 5$. The new aggregate spending function now lies above the spending

function for the three domestic sectors. Notice, however, that the expansionary effect of the rise in exports is checked to some extent by the induced expenditures for foreign-produced output. The ordinary multiplier of 5, indicated by the MPC of 8/10, would produce a rise of 90 in income with ΔX of 18. But this greater rise in income is prevented by the MPM of 1/10, which reduces the effective multiplier to 3.33 and therefore holds to 60 the rise in income from ΔX of 18. This income-restraining effect of the MPM is depicted graphically as the narrowing of the spread at successively higher levels of income between the spending function of the three domestic sectors and the new aggregate spending function.

Part B of Figure 7-3 expresses these two equilibrium positions in terms of the equality between $S + T + M$ and $I + G + X$. Again, apart from the narrower income range shown here, the solid-line functions are the same as those shown in Part B of Figure 7-2. There the initial equilibrium, $S + T + M = I + G + X$, occurred at an income of 220. The increase of 18 in exports shifts the entire $I + G + X$ function, labeled $I + G + X + \Delta X$, upward by 18. The increase in exports (ΔX) sets the multiplier in operation and raises income to the new equilibrium level of 280. Because in the present model I, G, and T are assumed to remain unchanged despite changes in income, the new equilibrium must occur at that level of income where $\Delta X = \Delta S + \Delta M$. In other words, given the injection of ΔX, Y must rise to the level at which the diversions, $\Delta S + \Delta M$, from the income stream match the injection of ΔX into the income stream. Because the MPS $= 2/10$ and the MPM $= 1/10$, it is only when income rises by 60 that the sum of ΔS and ΔM will match ΔX $[^2/_{10}(60) + {}^1/_{10}(60) = 12 + 6 = 18]$. The rise in income must be 3.33 times the rise in exports, as we can see by expressing the multiplier in terms of the MPS, or s, and the MPM, or m: $\Delta Y/\Delta X = 1/(s + m)$. In the present example, $60/18 = 1/(2/10 + 1/10) = 3.33$.

If the rise in income generated by the rise in exports did not induce expenditures for foreign

---

[8] In order to show better detail over the relevant range of income, this figure shows each function only over this narrower range of income.

[9] This unrealistically large increase is chosen to avoid "congestion" in the figure.

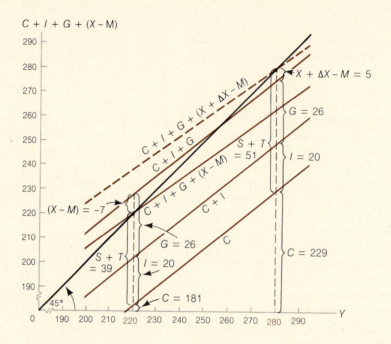

A

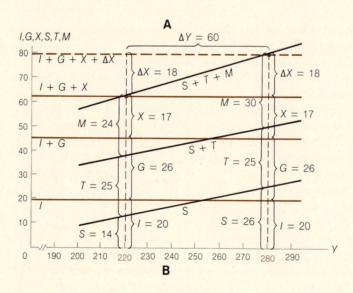

B

FIGURE 7-3
Effect of a Change in Exports on the Equilibrium Level of Income

goods as well as for domestic goods, the net effect on income and output would be an increase of 90, or the increase of 18 in exports times the ordinary multiplier of 5 indicated by the MPS of 2/10. The income-restraining effect of the MPM is indicated in Figure 7-3 as the widening spread at higher income levels between the schedule of "leakages" labeled $S + T$ and the schedule of "leakages" including imports labeled $S + T + M$.

All this suggests that the greater the MPM, the greater the reduction in the effective multiplier, and therefore the smaller the expansion of income that follows any specific increase in autonomous spending. In practice, the MPM varies considerably among countries. It tends to be higher in countries such as England, for which foreign trade is relatively more important than in countries such as the United States, for which foreign trade is relatively less important. This suggests further that, with allowance for any difference in the MPC, any increase in autonomous spending will have a smaller multiplier effect in a country such as England than in a country such as the United States. However, this conclusion is based on our assumption that a country's exports are entirely determined by external factors. If we drop this assumption and recognize that internal as well as external factors affect a country's exports, the probability that a country like England will have a smaller effective multiplier than a country like the United States does not necessarily follow. To see why this is so, we will next consider one of the ways in which a nation's exports are tied to domestic factors.

Exports as a Function of Imports

In any country, an increase in consumption, investment, or government spending will raise the level of income as long as there are no offsetting decreases in its net export balance or increases in its net import balance. With a positive marginal propensity to import, however, the rise in income leads to a rise in imports and, in the first instance, to a decrease in the net export balance or an increase in the net import balance. Such a rise in, say, U.S. gross imports is felt by all other countries combined as an equal increase in their gross exports. Because the rest of the world experiences an increase in gross exports with no simultaneous increase in gross imports (U.S. exports did not increase in the first instance), one or more countries in the rest of the world must show an increase in net exports or a decrease in net imports. This means that one or more countries will, all else being equal, show a rise in their domestic income levels. But these countries also have a positive marginal propensity to import, and some portion of the increase in their incomes will be diverted to the purchase of imported goods and services. The U.S. economy will probably secure some share of the increase in purchases made abroad by these foreign countries, and this will appear as a rise in U.S. gross exports. In this complicated fashion, changes in U.S. gross *exports* are indirectly influenced by changes in the income level in the United States.

If we recognize that changes in the U.S. income level are a factor determining changes in U.S. exports, the earlier assumption that exports are determined entirely by external factors appears to be invalid. This assumption is nonetheless a valid approximation for small economies, in which even a large percentage change in income will be relatively small in absolute terms. Even with a high marginal propensity to import, the effect of such an increase in income on the country's gross imports will not be large enough to affect significantly the aggregate exports and therefore the level of income in other countries. This being the case, the small country cannot expect an appreciable feedback in the form of increased exports to result from the increase in its imports. We must therefore distinguish between countries that are and those that are not large enough to influence perceptibly the income levels of other countries through changes in their imports. Size in this context is not measured merely by the real income level of the country; it is a compound of income level and marginal propensity to import. In terms of our earlier comparison, although the U.S. marginal propensity to import is smaller than England's, the relatively high income level of the U.S. economy means that a moderate percentage change in U.S. income may have a noticeable effect on the exports of the rest of the world. (Based on 1980 figures, a 5 percent increase in gross domestic product amounted to about $130 billion; an MPM of 1/20 would then mean an increase in imports of about $6.5 billion.) On the other hand, although the income level of England is far smaller than that of the United States, the higher marginal propensity to import of the English economy means that even a moderate percentage change in its income level can have a perceptible impact on exports of the rest of the world. (Based on 1980 figures—including an exchange rate of £1 = $2.33—a 5 percent increase in gross domestic product amounted to about $6.5 billion; an MPM of 1/5 would then mean an increase in imports of about $1.3 billion.)

When there is a vigorous business expansion in a large country like the United States, the rising level of income induces an increased flow of imports into the United States. The most recent illustration of this is what happened in the United States during the recovery that followed the severe recession of 1973–75. Imports increased from $127.6 billion in 1975 to $155.1 billion in 1976 or by 22 percent. The increased flow of imports is felt by some countries in the rest of the world as a rise in their incomes. This induces a rise in imports in these countries, and, to the extent that the United States shares in these expanding foreign markets, U.S. exports increase. This further raises the income level in the United States and further enlarges U.S. imports from the rest of the world. These repercussions continue to interact on the income levels of both the United States and countries in the rest of the world. However, because the marginal propensities to import both here and abroad are less than 1, the amount of spending at each succeeding stage of this expansion process will decrease until income in

the United States and in other countries tends to stabilize at new levels. In practice, of course, income changes of this sort occur continually as the result of changes in domestic spending in various countries. Therefore, before one series of repercussions can work itself out, a new series is initiated by further changes in domestic spending in one or more important countries.

This crude description suggests why the income levels of different countries are interdependent. A rising level of income in a large country like the United States tends to raise income levels of some other countries. By the same process, a falling level of income here is felt by other countries as shrinkage in their exports and declining levels of income. As nations become more and more closely linked through foreign trade, we encounter what economists have called the "international propagation of business cycles." Depression in one or more large countries tends to trigger depressions in other countries; prosperity in one or more large countries tends to promote prosperity in other countries.[10]

A Concluding Note

As we mentioned at the outset, the purpose of this chapter has been to describe the way in which an economy's net export or import balance enters into the determination of the equilibrium income level and the way in which changes in that balance can cause changes in the income level. The basic Keynesian model was developed on the assumption that exports are externally determined and imports internally determined; specific attention was paid to only one of the many internal factors that influence imports—the level of income. Although we did not develop a

---

[10] A formal algebraic statement of what has been loosely stated here will be found in books on international economics. See, for example, M.E. Kreinen, *International Economics: A Policy Approach,* Harcourt Brace Jovanovich, 3rd ed., 1979, Appendix III, pp. 404–407, and C.P. Kindleberger and P.H. Lindert, *International Economics,* 6th ed., 1978, Irwin, pp. 304–308.

formal model, we did note the way in which the exports of a large nation may depend indirectly on its level of income.

Many other factors also influence a nation's net export or import balance and thereby influence its income level. In a more thorough analysis, for example, we would recognize that differences in the relative prices of goods in different countries are the reason for international trade in such goods. If an economy finds its price level rising relative to the price levels of other economies, it may expect its imports to rise, even if its marginal propensity to import and its real income remain unchanged. (In terms of the import function, this would appear as an increase in M_a). At the same time that its imports rose, its exports would decline as foreign importers (like domestic buyers) shifted purchases to other countries that offered the desired products at lower prices. To show how this fits into a model clearly requires a model in which the price level is treated as a variable. Chapter 14 brings the foreign sector into an extended model with a variable price level.

A more thorough analysis would also have to consider variations in currency exchange rates, a factor that has become increasingly important in the years since 1973 when the foreign exchange values of many of the world's leading currencies were left to float more or less freely in response to short-run changes in their supply and demand. From the end of World War II until the turn to floating rates in the early seventies, the world economy had operated under a system usually referred to as the Bretton Woods system. (It came into being as a result of an international conference of the leading trading nations at Bretton Woods, New Hampshire in 1944.) That system was successful in providing short-run exchange rate stability through the post-World War II period until

1973. The following years of experience with the system of floating exchange rates, which includes a period of severe international recession, has led many observers to believe that such a system of floating rates will remain workable in the years ahead. Whatever the direction in which the international monetary system evolves during the eighties, it will continue to be one that provides much greater flexibility in exchange rates than was provided during the quarter of a century under the Bretton Woods system. What is relevant at this point is that an international monetary system in which exchange rates are adjusted more frequently would increase the influence of changes in exchange rates on net import and export balances. The fluctuation of exchange rates therefore becomes another important factor that must be taken into account in any thorough analysis. An introduction to the way that changes in the foreign exchange rates affect the economy's income and output levels is provided in the extended model in Chapter 14.

Some other factors at work are changes in tariffs, quotas, foreign-exchange controls, and other controls imposed by each economy. The effects on the net import or export balance that might otherwise follow from changes in price levels or in foreign-exchange rates could be offset, at least temporarily, by appropriate manipulation of these devices.

A thorough analysis of these and other such factors may be found in basic texts on international economics. We have mentioned such factors simply to emphasize the rigid assumptions on which the simple analysis in this chapter is based. Yet this analysis has provided some insight into the question we posed at the beginning of this chapter: How do an economy's foreign transactions affect the level of income and output within that economy?

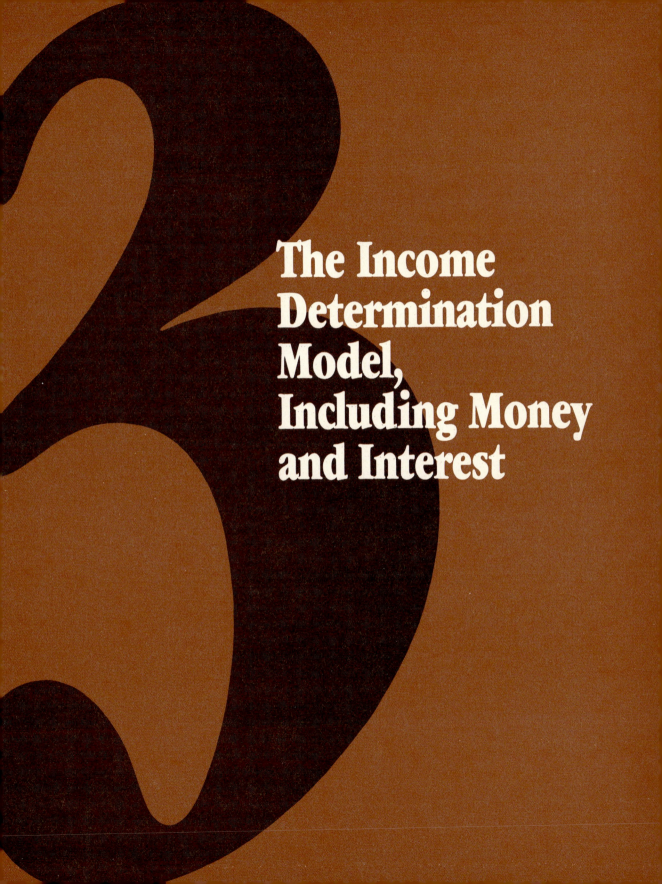

The Income Determination Model, Including Money and Interest

OVERVIEW

The primary purpose of this chapter is to explain the derivation of the aggregate supply function. This shows the varying amounts of aggregate output that business as a whole is ready to offer at each possible price level. Three different relationships between aggregate output and the price level result from three different combinations of assumptions. One combination of assumptions indicates an aggregate supply curve that is perfectly elastic up to the full employment level of output. In this case, shifts in the aggregate spending curve will have no effect on the price level in an economy operating below the full employment level of output. At the opposite extreme is the combination of assumptions that results in an aggregate supply curve that is perfectly inelastic at the full employment level of output—that is, the curve is simply a vertical line at the full employment level of output. Under the third combination of assumptions, the aggregate supply curve that is obtained begins to slope upward to the right below the full employment level of output. For both the second and third cases, shifts in the aggregate spending curve will affect the price level.

Because an aggregate supply curve is, in a sense, a summation of the supply curves of all the industries in the economy, we can better understand the nature of the aggregate supply curve if we look behind it at the industry's supply curve and behind this at the firm's supply curve. To this end, the first part of the chapter provides a sketch of the micro theory underlying the supply curves of the firm and the industry. The balance

The Aggregate Supply Function: Keynesian and Classical

of the chapter covers the derivation of the aggregate supply curve itself. This discussion is divided into three parts corresponding to the three basic types of aggregate supply curves: (1) the Upward-Sloping Aggregate Supply Curve, (2) the Perfectly Inelastic Aggregate Supply Curve, and (3) the Perfectly Elastic Aggregate Supply Curve.

We call the theory of income determination developed in Part 2 "simple" because it uses highly simplified assumptions to provide an answer to the core question of what determines the level of income and output. According to this simplified theory, aggregate spending is the sole determinant of whether or not the economy operates at the upper limit of output it is capable of producing with full employment of the labor force. Moreover, the theory assumes that changes in aggregate spending do not change the price level but lead to proportional changes in total output over the range of output up to the full employment level of output. As noted at the beginning of Chapter 4, this follows from the assumption that changes in aggregate spending produce a movement along an aggregate supply curve which is perfectly elastic over this range of output. In the simple theory, therefore, the aggregate supply curve merely sets the price level; the higher the position of the curve, the higher will be the price level, and vice versa. Furthermore, in earlier chapters, we were not concerned with factors that determine the position of the aggregate supply curve or that make it shift upward or downward. The curve was simply assumed to be given at some initial and unchanging position; this position determined the price level, which was also unchanging.

To assume the aggregate supply curve as a given presents no serious problem in the simple model where aggregate supply plays a purely passive role and aggregate spending is almost all that matters. However, as one moves ahead to less simple models, aggregate supply enters into the determination of both the price level and the output level. Consequently, the determinants of the position and shape of the aggregate supply curve take on major importance.

The curve takes three forms as illustrated in Figure 8-1. Starting at the bottom, the curve in Part C is perfectly elastic up to the full employment level of output. This is the form of the curve on which the simple Keynesian model is based. We will see in this chapter that this curve, in turn,

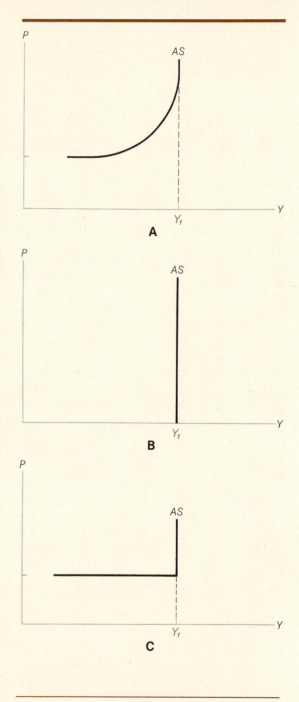

FIGURE 8-1
Aggregate Supply Functions

is based on the assumption that the money wage rate is fixed and the further assumption that the marginal product of labor is constant up to the full employment level of output. At the opposite extreme to the aggregate supply curve in Part C of Figure 8-1 is that in Part B—perfectly inelastic throughout and positioned at the full employment level of output. We will see in this chapter that such an aggregate supply curve follows from the assumption that the money wage rate is perfectly flexible downward, falling without limit in the event of an excess supply of labor. The model at the opposite extreme to the simple Keynesian model is the simple classical model. The form of the aggregate supply curve shown in Part B is based on the simple classical model. We will look at the simple classical model in some detail in Chapter 9. Lastly, Part A is the intermediate case in which the aggregate supply curve becomes less than perfectly elastic at some level of output below the full employment level. We will see in this chapter that this curve follows from the assumptions that the money wage rate is fixed and that the marginal product of labor begins to diminish before the full employment level of output is reached. The curve shown in Part A, like that in Part C, is also a form of the aggregate supply curve on which the Keynesian model is based, but the curve in Part A is the basis for a less simple Keynesian model than is the curve in Part C.

Whatever its form, an aggregate supply curve is, in a sense, the summation of the supply curves of all the industries in the economy. To understand the nature of the aggregate supply curve, an approach which looks first at the individual firm's supply curve and the individual industry's supply curve proves helpful. In looking at these curves, attention will be limited to the conditions that yield a supply curve with an upward-sloping segment for the firm and the industry and that for all industries combined yield a supply curve like that in Part A of Figure 8-1. However, as already noted, we will give attention to the conditions that result in each of the three kinds of aggregate supply curves when we turn

specifically to the derivation of the aggregate curve later in the chapter. We will discuss the cases shown in Parts A, B, and C of Figure 8-1 in that order.

The Supply Curve: Firm and Industry[1]

The supply curves we seek to derive are all short-run curves. Economists define the short-run period in the present context as a length of time too short to allow firms to vary the amount of plant and equipment with which they operate. If we assume that the technology, or the method of production, also remains constant over the short-run period, the only way a firm can change its output during this time is to change the amount of labor it employs. Therefore, in short-run analysis, the relationship between a firm's labor input and goods output is the first consideration.[2]

Production Function

This input–output relationship is described by the firm's production function, or total product curve, one possible form of which is shown in Part A of Figure 8-2. The linear portion may be said to indicate "proportional returns," because it indicates that output varies proportionally with labor input up to output of O_1 or up to labor input

---

[1] A minimal sketch of the relevant short-run micro theory is provided here. For a thorough treatment, see E. Mansfield, *Microeconomics: Theory and Application,* 3rd ed., Norton, 1979, Chs. 6–9, R.H. Leftwich, *The Price System and Resource Allocation,* 7th ed., Dryden Press, 1979, Chs. 8–13, or any other standard textbook on price theory.

[2] Except where we indicate otherwise, we will assume that all firms sell in purely competitive markets, that each firm attempts to maximize profits or minimize losses, that there is a constant money wage rate for each unit of labor provided by a perfectly homogeneous labor force whose services are sold in purely competitive markets, and that all firms are fully integrated. The last assumption means that, with the single exception of labor services, all variable inputs, including raw materials, necessary to the production of the firm's output are produced within the firm.

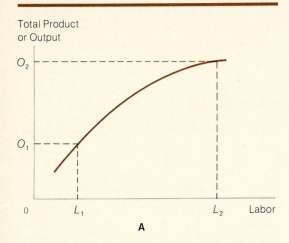

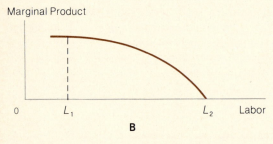

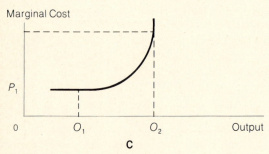

FIGURE 8-2
Derivation of the Firm's Supply
Curve

than proportional. Consequently, beyond labor input of L_1, total output increases less and less for each increment of labor input. The nonlinear portion of the total product curve, starting at L_1, illustrates this stage of diminishing returns. Finally, beyond labor input of L_2, further labor input will not increase total output at all; in fact, at some even higher level of labor input, output will begin to decrease as more workers are hired. In Figure 8-2 we see that diminishing returns that begin at L_1 have diminished all the way to zero at labor input of L_2. Given this production function, it should be clear that in the short run the firm would under no circumstances hire labor beyond the amount of L_2.[3]

The increment in total product that results from the addition of a unit of labor is termed the **marginal physical product** (MPP) of that unit of labor. Part B of Figure 8-2 shows the curve of the marginal physical product of labor derived from the total product curve of Part A.[4] Because the total product curve shows that the increment in output is the same for each increment of labor input over the linear portion of that curve (that is, up to labor input L_1), the MPP of labor is constant over this range of labor input. Between L_1 and L_2, however, the total product curve shows that the increments in total output become smaller and smaller and finally become zero. Therefore, the

---

[3]Readers familiar with the orthodox theory of the firm will recognize the modification of that theory in the present construction. Conventional theory shows the total product curve of Part A divided into three stages: more than proportional, proportional, and less than proportional (or diminishing) returns. Therefore, the marginal product curve of Part B has an initial stage in which marginal product is rising, and the marginal cost curve of Part C has an initial stage in which marginal cost is falling. This first stage, however, does not appear in Figure 8-2. For our purposes, we may simplify without serious error by suppressing this first stage and showing only the two stages, proportional and less than proportional. It may be added that the firm, if it produces at all, produces an output greater than that in the first stage so that this stage is, in any event, of no practical interest.

[4]The vertical scale of Part B is an expanded version of that scale in Part A.

of L_1. However, because more and more labor—the variable input—is being employed with a fixed amount of plant and equipment as we move along the labor axis, the proportional relationship between output of product and input of labor must eventually be succeeded by one that is less

MPP of labor diminishes as labor input increases from L_1 to L_2 and finally becomes zero when labor input reaches L_2.

Marginal Cost

Because output may be increased or decreased in the short run only by changing the amount of labor employed, the only cost that varies with changes in output is the amount the firm pays for labor. The costs associated with a fixed plant and equipment are constant in the short run because they will be incurred by the firm whether the plant and equipment are being used to capacity or are sitting idle. Because **marginal cost** (MC) is the cost of producing an additional unit of output, the marginal cost of a unit of output in our model is the additional labor cost incurred in its production. Part C of Figure 8-2 gives the firm's MC curve, showing the increase in total cost resulting from each additional unit of output. Because MC in this case is composed entirely of labor cost, it equals the money wage rate of labor *(W)* divided by labor's marginal physical product (MPP) at any level of output:

$$MC = \frac{W}{MPP}$$

Suppose, for example, that the total product curve shows that 10 worker-days of labor can turn out 100 units of total product and that 11 worker-days of labor can turn out 110 units. The MPP of the eleventh worker-day of labor would therefore be 10 units. If the increase in total cost resulting from the labor cost of a single worker-day of labor is $20, the marginal cost of a unit of output over the range from 100 to 110 is accordingly $2; that is, from the equation MC = W/MPP, $2 = $20/10. If the total product curve shows that 12 worker-days of labor can produce 120 units of output, the MPP of the twelfth worker-day of labor would also be 10, and the marginal cost of a unit of output over the range of output from 110 to 120 is again $2 per unit. In terms of Figure 8-2, this indicates that labor input of 11 or 12 days must be below L_1, because only below L_1

does output vary proportionally with labor input. Because output varies proportionally with labor input up to L_1, the marginal cost of output must remain constant over the range of output that can be produced with labor input up to L_1. This range of output is zero to O_1, and the MC curve in Part C accordingly shows the same marginal cost for all levels of output up to O_1.

If the firm were to expand output beyond O_1, the MPP of labor would start to decline, and the MC of output would start to rise. Suppose, for example, that when labor input is increased from 15 to 16 worker-days, total product rises from 145 to 150 units. The MPP of the sixteenth worker-day of labor is only 5 units, but the cost of the sixteenth worker-day of labor is, like all others, $20. This means that the marginal cost of a unit of output over this range of 145 to 150 is $20/5, or $4. In terms of Figure 8-2, the sixteenth worker-day of labor must lie between L_1 and L_2, and the output from 145 to 150 must lie between O_1 and O_2. For this output, as is evident in Part C, marginal cost rises.

If, in its attempt to expand output, the firm should employ worker-days of labor of L_2 or more, the MPP of labor would be zero. Marginal cost would accordingly become undefined at output O_2. With the given MPP curve, labor clearly would not be employed beyond L_2 in the short run, no matter how low the wage rate of labor and no matter how high the market price of output, as long as profit remained the guide to the firm's employment decision.

Profit-Maximizing Output

In a purely competitive market, the individual firm is only one of so large a number of producers of a homogeneous product that no one firm has any control over the price at which this product can be sold. This market price is determined by industry supply and demand. The individual firm simply adjusts its output to the market-determined price in order to maximize profits. The firm's short-run profit-maximizing level of output is the point at which the marginal cost of output

(MC) just equals the market price of output *(P)*.[5] Because of this and because at each possible level of output MC = *W*/MPP, the profit-maximizing output can also be expressed as that output at which

$$P = \frac{W}{MPP}$$

or that output at which

$$W = P \times MPP$$

This identifies the output at which the additional receipts from the sale of the additional output produced by an additional unit of labor (that is, *P* × MPP) just equals the wage rate of labor.

For example, if the market price were $2 per unit, output would be expanded to that level at which marginal cost was $2. If the fixed wage rate were $20 per worker-day, this would occur at that level of output at which the MPP of labor was 10. At this output, the MPP of labor at 10 multiplied by the price per unit of output at $2 equals the wage rate of labor of $20. If the market price of output were $4, output would be carried to the higher level at which MC was $4. With the same fixed wage rate of $20 per worker-day, this higher level of output would be that at which the MPP of labor had fallen to 5. (At this output the MPP of labor of 5 times the price per unit of output of $4 equals the wage rate.) Any level of output below that at which MC equals *P*—that is, at which receipts from the sale of the output produced by an additional unit of labor exceed the wage rate per unit of labor—would be a level of output whose expansion would increase profits. An expansion of output would add less to costs

than to sales receipts. On the other hand, any level above the one at which MC equals *P*—that is, at which the receipts from the sale of the output produced by the last unit of labor are less than the wage rate per unit of labor—would be a level of output whose contraction would increase profits. A reduction in output would subtract more from costs than from sales receipts.

The marginal cost curve of Part C of Figure 8-2, which is derived entirely from the MPP of labor and the wage rate of labor, is also the firm's supply curve. It shows the various quantities of output (measured along the horizontal axis) that the firm will supply to the market at each price (measured along the vertical axis) in order to maximize its profits.[6]

Once the profit-maximizing level of output has been determined, the amount of labor that should be hired by the firm in order to achieve this level may be found directly from the total product curve given in Part A of Figure 8-2. Given our assumptions that the money wage rate, the curve of the marginal product of labor, and the market price of output remain unchanged, the short-run equilibrium level of output and the amount of labor employed by the individual firm will remain unchanged. However, anything that reduces the money wage rate, alters the total product curve to raise the marginal product of labor, or raises the market price will increase the level of output at which the firm maximizes profits. The amount of labor to be hired at this new level of output may, as before, be determined graphically from the appropriate point on the firm's total product curve.

The relationships we have just described for the individual firm apply to all firms in a purely

---

[5]Instead of MC = *P*, the more general expression is MC = MR, in which MR is *marginal revenue*, the additional revenue from the sale of one more unit of output. Under our assumption of purely competitive markets, each individual firm in the industry can sell the amount of output it wishes to at the going market price, so that MR for it always equals *P*. Under imperfect competition the firm can sell more only by cutting *P*, so that MR is always less than *P*. For simplicity only, our analysis is limited to purely competitive markets, in which the individual firm finds MR always equal to *P*.

[6]Because MC is constant up to O_1, the firm's average variable cost is constant over this same range of output. If price is above P_1, the firm maximizing profits (or minimizing losses) will produce and sell something more than O_1. However, if price is below P_1, the firm will produce and sell no output, because this price does not even cover its variable cost (here, labor cost) per unit of output. If price were exactly P_1, the firm would incur a loss equal to its fixed costs, whether it produced no output or output O_1.

competitive industry. The industry's supply curve is then simply the horizontal summation of the marginal cost curves of all firms in the industry. As shown in Figure 8-3, it looks much like the firm's supply curve.[7] The vertical axis is now labeled "Price" to make clear that a supply curve shows the amount of the commodity supplied at each possible price for the commodity.

Because each firm in the industry operates in the short run with a fixed stock of plant and equipment and a fixed technology, the industry also operates with these fixed factors. For the same reason that the firm's supply curve eventually slopes upward to the right, the industry's supply curve must eventually slope upward to the right. Given these assumptions, beyond some point the industry can produce more output only at higher marginal cost; therefore, that output will be supplied only at higher prices.

The Supply Curve: Aggregate

To proceed from the derivation of the supply curve for a single firm and single industry to that for industry as a whole is essentially a matter of extending and, in some cases, modifying the theory sketched for the firm and the industry. The following pages will present the derivation of the three forms of the aggregate supply curve shown in Figure 8-1. The first section explains the derivation of the curve in Part A. This curve, which slopes upward to the right, is based on the assumptions of a fixed money wage rate and diminishing marginal productivity of labor. Because these are the same standard assumptions that underlie the short-run supply curve for the firm and industry, the relationship between output as a whole and the general price level

---

[7]Although this curve is similar in shape to that of the individual firm in Part C of Figure 8-2, it must be recognized that the scale of the two figures differs on the horizontal but not on the vertical axis. A given interval along the horizontal axis of the industry graph represents a much larger number of units of output than the same interval along the axis of the individual firm's graph.

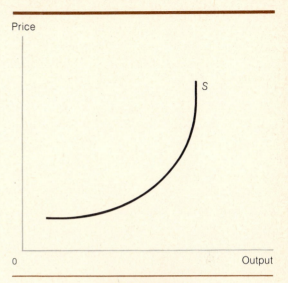

FIGURE 8-3
Industry Supply Curve

---

shown in Part A of Figure 8-1 is expectedly similar to that shown in Figure 8-3 for the single industry. The second section explains the derivation of the perfectly inelastic aggregate supply curve (that in Part B of Figure 8-1). This curve is based on the assumptions of a perfectly flexible money wage rate and, like that in Part A, a diminishing marginal productivity of labor. Finally, the third section explains the derivation of the aggregate supply curve, which is perfectly elastic up to the full employment level of output (that in Part C of Figure 8-1). This curve is based on the assumption of a fixed money wage rate, as is the curve in Part A, but, unlike the curve in Part A, allows for the assumption of constant marginal productivity of labor.

In each of the three cases, the derivation will be presented graphically through a four-part diagram adjusted as required to fit different cases.

The Upward-Sloping Aggregate Supply Curve

Production Function Part A of Figure 8-4 is the aggregate production function, or total product curve, for the economy as a whole. Apart from

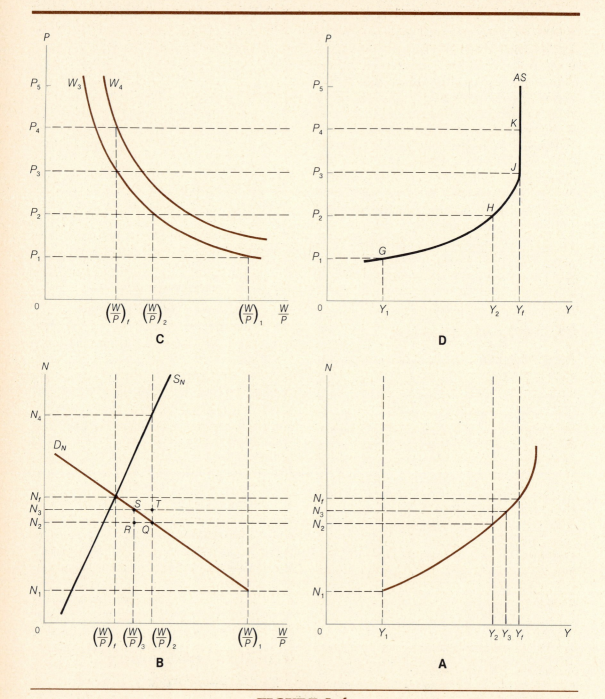

FIGURE 8-4
Derivation of the Aggregate Supply Curve: Fixed Money Wage Rate

the fact that the axes have been reversed for convenience, the curve has the same appearance and the same properties as the individual firm's production function given in Part A of Figure 8-2. If the composition of aggregate output is fairly stable, the aggregate production function will show a range of proportional returns followed by a range of diminishing returns essentially as shown for the individual firm. When a single firm or industry attempts to expand its output further and further, it runs into the short-run barrier of fixed plant and equipment; the same thing happens in an attempt to expand aggregate output.

Demand for Labor   Part B shows the curve of the marginal physical product of labor, which is now labeled D_N for reasons that will be noted. As in Part B of Figure 8-2, this curve is derived directly from the production function in Part A. For the uses to be made of Figure 8-4, the axes of Part B have also been reversed from those in Figure 8-2, but the meaning of Part B is the same in both figures. The MPP schedule for the individual firm indicates the additional output that results from the addition of each unit of labor input. Similarly, the MPP schedule for industry as a whole indicates the addition to the economy's aggregate output that results from the addition of each unit of labor input.[8]

Due to diminishing returns, the MPP of labor decreases as we move up the vertical axis of Part B to larger amounts of labor. Because employers maximize profits by hiring labor up to the point at which $W = P \times$ MPP, for any given W more labor will be hired beyond an initial equilibrium only at a higher P; conversely, for any given P more labor will be hired only at a lower W. Now divide both sides of the preceding equation by P to obtain $W/P =$ MPP. This says that the level of employment consistent with profit maximiza- tion may alternatively be described as the level at which W/P (the real wage) is equal to MPP (the marginal physical product of labor). $W = P \times$ MPP expresses *in dollar terms* both the cost of labor and what labor provides to the firm; in contrast, $W/P =$ MPP expresses *in real terms* both the cost of labor and what labor provides to the firm.

For example, suppose initially that the amount of labor employers hire is N_1. This means that W and P are such that W/P equals the MPP of labor at that level of employment. With the values of both W and P assumed given, to hire more or less than this number of workers would sacrifice maximum profits, and employers would not do so. Under what conditions would they be willing to expand the number of workers employed to, say, N_2? To do this is to encounter the lower MPP of labor at N_2, so employers will only expand to N_2 if W/P declines by the required degree. Consequently, the number of workers hired is an inverse function of the real wage. The lower the real wage, the larger will be the number of workers employed. Viewed in this way, the MPP curve becomes a demand curve for labor and for this reason is labeled D_N in Part B.

Allowing time for adjustment, changes in the real wage rate will lead to changes in the number of workers employed, as shown by movements along the D_N curve. However, firms (singly or in the aggregate) may be off the D_N curve. Increasing output in the short run requires the input of more labor, but this can be achieved only by employing a larger number of workers or by working the same number of workers for longer hours. In Figure 8-4 and the following figures, N is a measure of the number of workers—not a measure of the number of work hours—unless we assume an unvarying workweek for all workers. To the degree that firms vary the length of the workweek rather than the number of workers in order to turn out different levels of aggregate output, the result will be a temporary movement off the D_N curve.

For example, assume (as a result of an increase in aggregate demand, which is not shown

---

[8]In practice, of course, we would be dealing in units of thousands of workers when estimating actual changes in the labor input for the economy as a whole, but the same principle applies in both cases.

here) that there is a relatively small increase in aggregate output from Y_2 to Y_3 in Part A of Figure 8-4. It will only be profitable for firms to obtain the additional labor needed to produce this extra output if the real wage rate falls from $(W/P)_2$ to $(W/P)_3$ in Part B. If firms believe that this increase in output is transitory, they may find it cheaper to produce it with overtime work for the existing work force than to produce it by hiring more workers. Although the former method incurs higher hourly wage costs, it avoids the cost of screening applicants, training those hired, and dismissing them later. Therefore, in Figure 8-4, given the increase from Y_2 to Y_3, N may remain at N_2. However, because the real wage must decline to $(W/P)_3$ to make it profitable for firms to raise output to Y_3, the result must be a movement off the D_N curve from point Q to point R. If the increase in output is indeed transitory, this will be followed by a return to point Q as output falls from Y_3 to Y_2. On the other hand, if it becomes a lasting increase in output, firms will eventually increase employment from N_2 to N_3 and there will be a movement from point R to point S or again back on to the D_N curve.

The same thing may occur in the opposite direction. Assume initially the Y_3 level of output followed by a decline to Y_2, which firms regard as transitory. Rather than lay off unneeded workers and face the costs of rehiring workers later, firms may choose to incur the extra labor costs of "stockpiling" these workers over the temporary period of slack. In this case, there is a movement off the D_N curve from the initial point S to point T. If Y returns to Y_3 as firms expect, the movement is back to point S; if the decrease turns out to be persistent, layoffs will occur and the movement will be to point Q.

Because employers will act to minimize costs for any level of output over time, movements off the D_N curve are to be expected and evidence shows that they occur. However, although we have noted this characteristic of the demand for labor, in what follows we will simplify by assuming that the adjustments all occur by varying the number of workers employed or simply by movements along the D_N curve.

Supply of Labor   The other curve in Part B, which is labeled S_N, is the supply curve of labor. The model shows that the supply of labor, like the demand for labor, is a function of the real wage (W/P) with the supply of labor a direct function. This expresses the contention that a higher money wage rate will not call forth more labor if the price level rises proportionally, because in this event the real wage remains unchanged. For the same reason, a lower money wage rate matched by a proportional fall in the price level will not lead to a reduction in the quantity of labor supplied. The basis for this postulate of classical theory is the unpleasantness of more work; a larger *real* reward is necessary to induce labor to provide an ever larger supply of labor services.

Workers, as well as the firms that employ them, are maximizing units in this system—workers seek to maximize utility just as firms seek to maximize profits. Firms will not hire more labor at a lower money wage rate if the prices at which they can sell their output fall proportionally with the money wage rate. The cost of a unit of labor relative to the price at which the firm's output sells—the real wage—is what counts to the firm. By the same token, workers will not supply more labor at a higher money wage rate if the prices of the goods purchased with their wages rise proportionally with the money wage rate. The money wage received per unit of labor supplied relative to the prices of the goods that can be purchased with that money wage—the real wage—is what counts to the worker. This maximizing behavior on either side of the labor market gives us the demand curve for labor as an inverse function of the real wage and the supply curve as a direct function of the real wage.

Money Wage Rate   Part C does nothing more than graphically depict a relationship covered in earlier discussions of the theory of the firm and industry. In its attempt to maximize profits, the single firm will in the short run expand output to the level at which MC = P. Because MC = W/MMP, the profit-maximizing output is also that at which P = W/MMP. Therefore, for a fixed money wage rate (W) the firm will hire labor up to the amount at which labor's MPP multiplied by P equals the given W. For the single firm and, by the same argument, for the single industry, once the profit-maximizing output has been determined for the fixed wage rate, more labor will be hired and more output produced only if forces within the market produce a rise in P. The amount of labor employed by the firm can then expand until the MPP of labor (which will decrease as the amount of labor employed increases) multiplied by the new, higher P is equal to the unchanged W.

The same follows for industry as a whole. Curve W_3 in Part C of Figure 8-4 gives us nothing more than the various combinations of P and labor's MPP whose products equal the W that was assumed in drawing the fixed W_3 curve. For example, if the level of employment (N) were such that the MPP of labor was 8, P would have to be 3 before producers would provide this level of employment with W fixed at 24. If N were greater, so that MPP was smaller—for example, 6—P would have to be 4 in order to ensure that the employment of labor up to the amount at which its MPP fell to 6 would be consistent with the profit-maximization objective of producers.[9]

Derivation of the Aggregate Supply Curve

Part D rounds out the apparatus by showing how the aggregate supply function is derived from the other parts of the figure. Thus, for any level of N,

Part A gives the aggregate output (Y) corresponding to that labor input, but, as we will see, only the levels of N up to N_f are relevant. The D_N curve in Part B indicates the real wage (W/P) equal to the MPP of labor, for each possible level of N. And the W_3 curve of Part C identifies the price level (P) which is required to yield the indicated W/P on the basis of the money wage rate of W_3. The P indicated in Part C and the Y indicated in Part A then combine to determine a specific point in Part D that is one point on the aggregate supply function being derived. Such a specific point may also be determined by starting in Part C. Assuming W is given at W_3, for a selected level of P, the W_3 curve identifies a resultant W/P on the horizontal axis. The D_N curve in Part B then shows the amount of labor that will be employed at that W/P. And the production function in Part A shows the amount of output (Y) produced by that amount of labor. The P assumed in Part C and the Y found in Part A then combine to identify a specific point in Part D.

For example, start in Part A with N of N_1, an amount of labor that produces output of Y_1. The D_N curve in Part B shows the MPP of labor and therefore the W/P at which that quantity of labor will be demanded, $(W/P)_1$. Assuming a fixed money wage rate, specifically W_3 in Part C, producers must get a price level of P_1 for their output of Y_1 to yield $(W/P)_1$, the W/P at which they will hire N_1 and produce Y_1. Therefore, producers will supply the indicated amount of output—Y_1, at the price level of P_1. The P_1 in Part C and the Y_1 in Part A combine to identify the specific point G in Part D which is one point on the aggregate supply curve.

In the same way, other values of N up to N_f—for example, N_2 and N_f—will identify other points—H and J, respectively—in Part D which will be other points on the aggregate supply curve. Connecting such points as G, H, and J yields an aggregate supply curve that slopes upward to the right. Up to the limit of N_f, the greater N, the greater will be the Y and P indicated in Part D. A greater N will mean a greater Y as more labor

---

[9] The W_3 curve is one of a family of such curves that will be employed in Part C of a series of figures like Figure 8-4. Technically, each of the curves in question is a rectangular or equilateral hyperbola which is a curve such that all rectangles established by running perpendiculars from any point on the graph of the function to the axes will be equal in area. The general equation for this function is $xy = a$ in which $a > 0$. For the variables here, the specific equation becomes $(W/P)P = W$, and in the two illustrations given, $8 \times 3 = 24$ and $6 \times 4 = 24$.

produces more output up to the N at which the MPP of labor falls to zero. But a greater N must also be accompanied by a higher P. Given the assumption that W is fixed, a higher P is the only way to obtain a lower W/P, and, because the higher N means a lower MPP, employers will not find it profitable to hire the additional labor except at the correspondingly lower W/P.

What must next be seen is that once output reaches the level Y_f, which is the level produced with employment at N_f, the aggregate supply curve no longer slopes upward to the right but becomes vertical. Output has reached the maximum set by full employment of the labor force, the level of employment identified by the intersection of the S_N and D_N curves in Part B.[10] At the market-determined real wage established by this intersection, every worker who wishes to work at that real wage is able to find employment; the level of employment at this real wage is, therefore, full employment. However, examine any level of employment below this, such as N_2 in the preceding illustration. As shown by the D_N curve, N_2 will be employed at a real wage of $(W/P)_2$, but the S_N curve shows that N_4 will be available at that real wage rate. There is an excess supply of labor in the amount $N_4 - N_2$. Similarly, there is an excess supply at each lower real wage rate down to $(W/P)_f$, at which rate the supply of labor equals the demand for labor. Because the money wage rate is assumed to be fixed in the present case, the only way to move from a higher real wage rate to the lower rate

which will raise employment to N_f and output to Y_f is through a rise in the price level to P_3. As P rises toward P_3 with W stable at W_3, W/P falls and employment rises toward N_f.[11]

Rises in P beyond P_3 with a fixed W will mean declines in W/P below $(W/P)_f$. It might at first appear that the amount of labor employed will then fall below N_f because the S_N curve shows that less than N_f will be provided at a real wage below $(W/P)_f$. This would be true if the money wage rate were absolutely fixed. However, the notion of a fixed money wage rate precludes only downward adjustments, not upward adjustments. Or it is inflexible downward, but not inflexible upward. The idea of a fixed money wage rate reflects labor's opposition to a cut in that rate, but labor obviously has no opposition to a rise in its money wage rate.

What then happens if P rises above P_3 is that W rises proportionally with P. Such a rise in P with no rise in W would create an excess demand for labor as the real wage rate fell below $(W/P)_f$. The quantity of labor that employers sought to hire would exceed the amount provided and competition would bid up W to match each rise in P. For example, a rise from P_3 to P_4 would raise W proportionally as shown by the shift from W_3 to W_4 in Part C. P_4 and W_4 would keep W/P at $(W/P)_f$, N at N_f, and Y at Y_f. Consequently, in Part D of Figure 8-4, for any value of P above P_3, Y remains at Y_f. The points J and K show the same Y, that is, Y_f. In other words, the aggregate supply curve becomes perfectly inelastic upward starting at J.

[10] Note that this is not the maximum output the economy is capable of producing. Part A shows that output would continue to expand beyond Y_f with labor input greater than N_f. The existing stock of capital and state of technology are such that labor input greater than N_f still has a positive marginal physical productivity. Therefore, the aggregate supply curve in Part C becomes vertical before the production function in Part A does.

[11] No force automatically raises P toward P_3, and therefore N toward N_f. What P will be cannot be determined until we combine an aggregate demand curve with the aggregate supply curve in Part D. As will be covered in

detail in Chapter 12, there can be an equilibrium in the present model, for example, with P of P_2, output of Y_2, employment of N_2, and unemployment of $N_4 - N_2$, if the aggregate demand curve happens to intersect the aggregate supply curve at the point H. The economy would be in equilibrium with less than full employment. The aggregate supply curve identifies the P needed to provide the Y consistent with full employment as well as the P consistent with other levels of Y in the present case, but it cannot by itself determine what the actual level of P, Y, or N will be.

The Perfectly Inelastic Aggregate Supply Curve

In a world with no labor unions or other labor market imperfections, the money wage rate would be flexible downward. Any time that the supply of labor exceeded the demand for labor, competition for jobs among workers would eventually result in a decline in the money wage rate. In this case, the aggregate supply curve would turn out to be perfectly inelastic at the full employment level of output like the curve shown in Part B of Figure 8-1.

Derivation of the Aggregate Supply Curve

This is traced for the case of a flexible money wage rate in Figure 8-5. With the exceptions of the two additional curves in Part C to designate two more possible money wage rates of W_1 and W_2, Parts A, B, and C of Figure 8-5 are identical with those parts of Figure 8-4. The substantive difference is in Part D—the aggregate supply curve is perfectly inelastic throughout. To see the basis for this difference, assume that the money wage rate is W_3 in Part C. Now, to obtain the W/P consistent with full employment (N_f) calls for P of P_3 as P_3 and W_3 give $(W/P)_f$. Y_f in Part A and P_3 in Part C combine to identify point J in Part D. This is no different from the derivation of point J in the preceding part of this chapter.

Assume next that P falls to P_2. On the assumption of a fixed money wage rate, we found in Figure 8-4 that N would fall to N_2. The decline in employment would mean a decline in output, or at P of P_2 firms would produce output of Y_2 as shown in Figure 8-4 by point H. On the assumption of a flexible money wage rate, the result is quite different. W will not remain at W_3 as P falls to P_2, because this will create an excess supply of labor; a flexible money wage rate is one that falls in the face of an excess supply of labor as workers compete for the available jobs. Therefore, the money wage rate will decline from W_3 to W_2 in Part C of Figure 8-5. Because this decline in W is proportional to the decline in P, the preex-

isting real wage of $(W/P)_f$ is maintained. At that real wage, N is N_f and Y is Y_f. Combining Y_f in Part A with P_2 in Part C yields point Q in Part D. The only change is that P and W have fallen proportionally. In the same way, a further decline in P to P_1 would cause a decline in W to W_1. Therefore, W/P remains at $(W/P)_f$, N at N_f, Y at Y_f, and the combination of Y_f and P_1 yields point R in Part D. Again, the only change is that W and P have fallen proportionally. With a downwardly flexible money wage rate, the aggregate supply curve turns out to be perfectly inelastic at the full employment level of output. Whatever the level of P, W adjusts to it to maintain W/P at $(W/P)_f$, thereby maintaining employment at N_f, and output, in turn, at Y_f. The assumption of a flexible wage rate fixes the level of total production at Y_f because it makes the level of total production independent of the price level.

The Lag in Adjustment of a Flexible Money Wage Rate

The assumption of a flexible money wage rate is perfectly reasonable in a world with no labor unions or other labor market imperfections. However, the results shown in the present model go beyond this to the assumption of a completely frictionless system: Not only does the money wage rate fall freely in the face of unemployment, it falls *instantly* by whatever amount is needed to maintain uninterruptedly the full employment position. Even in the absence of labor market imperfections, the money wage rate would not fall in this way. Given that employers will lay off workers in the face of a rise in the real wage rate (an action which also may not occur immediately), the unemployed workers will not immediately offer their services in the market at whatever wage rate is offered by employers. Although workers may eventually learn that it is necessary for them to accept the lower money wage rate being offered if they are to secure employment, they do not know this at the time they become unemployed. For example, workers may attribute their dismissals to special problems of their particular employers, and believe

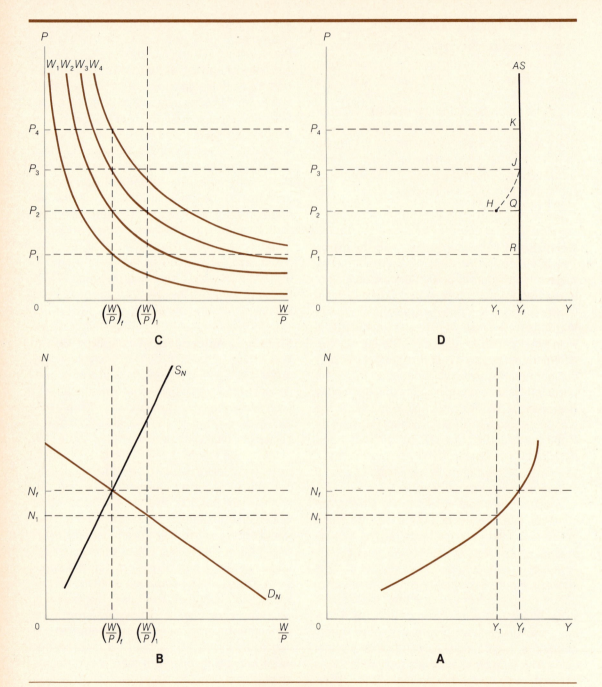

FIGURE 8-5
Derivation of the Aggregate Supply Curve: Flexible Money Wage Rate

that work is available elsewhere at an unreduced or even higher money wage rate. Information concerning opportunities in the labor market is not available without cost; discovering what offers are available requires search by workers.[12]

Expressed in terms of Figure 8-5, this kind of reaction by labor means that a rise in the real wage rate from $(W/P)_f$ to $(W/P)_1$, given the existing money wage rate of W_3, is not immediately followed by a drop in the money wage rate to W_2 as previously assumed. Workers initially react by choosing some unemployment rather than a lower money wage rate. For the time being, W remains at W_3 in Part C of Figure 8-5. W_3 combined with P_2 indicates a real wage of $(W/P)_1$. Employment at $(W/P)_1$ is seen to be N_1 in Part B, and the number of workers previously employed who are without jobs is measured by the distance between N_f and N_1. The production function in Part A shows $Y = Y_1$ with $N = N_1$. From Y_1 and P_2 in Part D, point H is identified.

Point H in Figure 8-5 corresponds to point H in Figure 8-4 where we assumed a fixed money wage rate. However, in the present case, the decrease in the amount of employment and the amount of output supplied will be temporary. When they search the job market, the unemployed will learn that the best they can do is the lower money wage rate of W_2 and they will accept that lower money return. Given P_2, this returns W/P to $(W/P)_f$ in Part C, increases employment to N_f in Part B, and output to Y_f in Part A. The system

is back to the full employment level of output. From Y_f and P_2 in Part D, point Q is identified.

This refinement of the flexible wage rate model merely shows that some temporary departure from the full employment of the labor force and the full employment level of output is to be expected as unemployed workers take time to search for acceptable wage offers. Given the decline in the price level, they can only return to employment by accepting a lower money wage rate; they learn this, accept it, and the full employment equilibrium is reestablished. For these reasons, in Part D of Figure 8-5, following the fall from P_3 to P_2, the system does not move directly from point J to point Q as earlier described, but goes first to point H, then to point Q. However, given that the money wage rate is flexible, the important point is that the system does, after some period of adjustment, return to the full employment equilibrium at point Q. Apart from a temporary sideways movement for such adjustments, the final movement is, as seen earlier, along a perfectly inelastic aggregate supply curve at the full employment level of output under a flexible money wage rate.

The Perfectly Elastic Aggregate Supply Curve

The perfectly elastic aggregate supply curve in Part C of Figure 8-1, like the curve in Part A which slopes upward to the right, assumes a fixed money wage rate. However, what makes it perfectly elastic instead of merely elastic like the curve in A is the additional assumption of a constant marginal productivity of labor. Part A of Figure 8-6 shows a production function that gives this result. Over a range of output up to and beyond that which can be produced with full employment of the labor force, the production function is perfectly linear. Each increment of labor employed produces the same increment to output so that the curve of the marginal product of labor in Part B is at the same height above the employment axis over the relevant range of

---

[12] In the present case, unemployment results from a rise in the real wage rate, which is produced by a fall in the price level. Even though a percentage cut in the money wage rate equal to the percentage decline in the price level would leave the real wage rate unchanged and would leave labor as well off as before, ordinarily labor will not fully recognize a fall in the price level, but it will fully recognize a lower money wage rate offered by employers. Labor has a money illusion (as described on pp. 354–55). Consequently, it may be expected that workers will search for work at the old money wage rate, even though such a wage rate, which cannot be obtained, would now be a higher real wage rate than was obtained earlier.

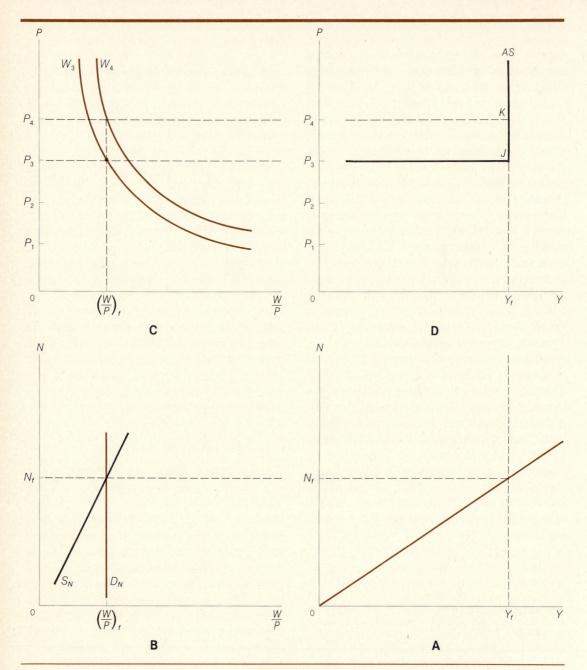

FIGURE 8-6
Derivation of the Aggregate Supply Curve: Fixed Money Wage Rate and Constant Marginal Productivity of Labor

employment. For previously explained reasons, the marginal product curve of labor is the demand curve for labor (D_N) and this D_N curve intersects the S_N curve to identify the full employment position (N_f). The S_N curve here is the same as in the preceding cases.

Assume an initial full employment equilibrium which occurs with W/P of $(W/P)_f$. N is N_f and Y in Part A is then Y_f. Assuming the fixed money wage rate given by W_3 in Part C, to secure W/P of $(W/P)_f$ requires P of P_3 in Part C. The combination of P_3 and Y_f identifies point J in Part D. Because this initial equilibrium is at full employment, a rise from P_3 to P_4 will yield the same results as those found in the preceding cases. As has been noted, the notion of a fixed money wage rate rules out decreases but not increases, and the effect of a rise in P is a proportional rise in W. W shifts to W_4; W/P, N, and Y all remain unchanged. P_4 and Y_f indicate point K on the aggregate supply curve. As before, the aggregate supply curve becomes perfectly inelastic at the full employment level of output.

Again, starting at the full employment equilibrium, assume now a decline from P_3 to P_2. Because the D_N curve is perfectly elastic at $(W/P)_f$, the slightest decrease in P with W fixed makes the total amount of labor supplied at the resultant higher W/P entirely an excess supply. Employers will hire any amount of labor over the range shown in Part B at the real wage rate of $(W/P)_f$, but they will hire none at all at any real wage above this. Consequently, with W perfectly rigid in the downward direction, the slightest decline in P below P_3 will reduce N to zero and therefore reduce Y to zero. Graphically, this is shown by a perfectly elastic aggregate supply curve positioned at the P_3 level.

An aggregate supply curve like this seems to be a limiting case. In practice, the aggregate production function may be approximately linear, and therefore the marginal product of labor may be approximately constant at relatively low levels of employment and output. As additional workers are hired over this limited range, the existing stock of capital is so large relative to the still low level of employment that each additional worker can be supplied with as much capital as he can effectively work with, and therefore his marginal product will not fall below that of workers hired earlier. In this event, the aggregate supply curve may be expected to have a perfectly elastic segment at low levels of output. However, as the economy moves toward full employment, the amount of capital available per worker is no longer the amount that enables each additional worker to produce the same additional output as was the case with fewer workers employed. The marginal product of labor will begin to decline—diminishing returns will set in. This will produce a segment of the aggregate supply curve that slopes upward to the right. This segment was derived as the first of the three cases considered here.

On the basis of this observation, the simple Keynesian theory of income determination developed in Part 2 best fits an economy producing output far below the full employment level. It has long been argued that the simple Keynesian model developed in Part 2 applies strictly during times of depression, one characteristic of which is a level of output far below the full employment level. At its far left, the aggregate supply curve does have a range over which it is perfectly elastic or very nearly so. If we happen to be operating within that range, the simple Keynesian model is not as much of an oversimplification as is otherwise the case. However, Keynes adopted an aggregate supply curve of this kind only as a first approximation. He also recognized that the marginal productivity of labor would decline short of full employment as firms sought to expand output by employing more labor with an unchanged amount of equipment, the result of which would be an upward-sloping segment of the aggregate supply curve.[13] In Chapter 12, as we develop the Keynesian model

---

[13]See the *General Theory*, pp. 299–300.

further, we will use the simpler or perfectly elastic curve; thereafter our work with the Keynesian model will use only the upward-sloping curve.[14]

A Concluding Note

The derivation of the aggregate supply curve in this chapter has shown how the aggregate amount of output supplied by industry as a whole varies with the price level in each of the three cases examined. The amount supplied at each price level, of course, will remain as shown by any given aggregate supply curve as long as the determinants of the curve remain unchanged. However, as the determinants change over time, the aggregate supply curve will shift accordingly. A rightward or outward shift in the production

---

[14]As the above analysis has shown for the case of a rigid money wage rate, whether the aggregate supply curve begins to slope upward at levels of output far below full employment or remains flat up to a level of output corresponding to full employment depends on the shape of the aggregate production function—that is, whether it is linear, as in Part A of Figure 8-6, or nonlinear, as in Part A of Figure 8-4. In other words, it depends on whether the marginal productivity of labor remains constant as aggregate employment varies or whether it decreases or increases as aggregate employment increases or decreases. Although diminishing marginal productivity of labor seems well established in microeconomics, it is less so in macroeconomics. Economists who have tried to measure the short-run relationship between aggregate output and aggregate labor input have seldom found diminishing marginal productivity of labor. More usually they have found that the marginal productivity of labor is constant or even that it increases with increases in employment. However, anyone who works through all the complications of what is actually being measured in the empirical work finds that the empirical findings are consistent with the theoretical aggregate production function that exhibits diminishing returns to labor. This form of the aggregate production function is found in most macroeconomic models. For further discussion of this question, see G. Ackley, *Macroeconomics: Theory and Policy*, Macmillan, 1978, pp. 69–74.

function in Part A of Figures 8-4 to 8-6—something that does occur in the long run—will produce an outward shift or an increase in aggregate supply in Part D of those figures. A leftward shift or increase in the labor supply in Part B will have the same effect on the vertical portion of the aggregate supply curve. Also, in Figures 8-4 and 8-6, which are based on the assumption of a fixed money wage rate, there will be an upward shift or an increase in the nonvertical part of the aggregate supply curve due to an autonomous increase in the money wage rate that fixes it at a new higher level. A shift cannot occur for this reason in Figure 8-5, because that is based on the assumption of a perfectly flexible money wage rate.

The mechanics of the process by which a shift of the curves in Parts A, B, and C brings about shifts in the aggregate supply curve could have been traced as a final part of this chapter. However, it is not very revealing to trace the process by which such shifts occur in isolation from aggregate demand. If one traces this process in a framework that contains an aggregate demand curve, one can see how the forces in question exert their influence not only on aggregate supply but on the output level and the price level. The following chapter examines the simple classical theory of income determination. In it, we will see how shifts in the production function and the supply of labor displace the perfectly inelastic aggregate supply curve that is a part of that theory. We will also see how, in combination with an aggregate demand curve based on classical theory, such displacement of the aggregate supply curve changes the output level and the price level. In later chapters, we will extend the Keynesian theory of aggregate demand developed in simple form in Part 2 and see how shifts in the aggregate supply curve in combination with an aggregate demand curve based on Keynesian theory cause changes in the output level and the price level.

The Simple Classical Model

OVERVIEW

The essential difference between the classical and Keynesian theories of income determination was noted in a general way in the introductory chapter. However, with respect to the details of the theory of income determination, attention to this point has been limited to the development of the Keynesian theory. The chapters of Part 2 covered the simple Keynesian model in some detail. The purpose of this chapter is to do the same, but in less detail, for the simple classical model of income determination. The essential difference between the classical and Keynesian theories, as noted in Chapter 1, is that the classical theory denies the possibility of a deficiency of aggregate demand and of equilibrium below full employment. The discussion of the classical theory in this chapter explains how these conclusions were reached.

In the simple Keynesian model, the aggregate supply curve is perfectly elastic up to the full employment level of output so that aggregate spending determines the actual level of output. In the classical model, the structure is reversed: The aggregate supply curve is perfectly inelastic at that level of output that can be produced with a fully employed labor force. This means that the actual level of output is at the full employment level, whatever the level of aggregate spending may be. In line with this approach, this chapter starts off with the perfectly inelastic aggregate supply curve derived in the preceding chapter. The aggregate demand curve implicit in classical theory is derived and combined with the supply curve.

In classical theory, aggregate demand is determined by both the supply and velocity of money; with the velocity of money held to be a constant, changes in aggregate demand are determined by changes in the supply of money. The aggregate demand curve corresponding to any supply of money slopes downward to the right, specifically in the form of a rectangular hyperbola. Combining this aggregate demand curve with the perfectly inelastic aggregate supply curve determines the price level at which the full employment level of output sells. Within this model, changes in the supply of money produce shifts in the aggregate demand curve that cause changes in the price level that are proportional to the changes in the supply of money.

After tracing how changes in the supply of money affect the equilibrium position, the chapter examines the effects of changes in the supply of labor and in the demand for labor on the equilibrium position. One foundation of the classical model is the assumption of a perfectly flexible money wage rate that yields the perfectly inelastic aggregate supply curve. The chapter next looks into what happens to the classical equilibrium if a rigid money wage rate replaces the flexible money wage rate.

The last part of the chapter introduces saving and investment as they appear in the basic classical model. As we saw in Part 2, shifts in saving and investment curves in the Keynesian model affect the position of the aggregate spending curve and thereby the equilibrium level of output. We find here that the level of output is independent of shifts in saving and investment curves; in the basic classical model, such shifts affect only the division of the existing full employment level of output between consumer goods and capital goods.

In the simple Keynesian theory of income determination covered in Part 2, we saw that the level of output is determined solely by aggregate spending. The perfectly elastic aggregate supply curve, which is part of that theory, does not influence the level of output; it determines only the price level. In Chapter 8, we introduced the concepts of the production function, the demand for and supply of labor, and wage flexibility. We now have the basis on which to develop the simple classical theory of income determination. This theory is at the opposite extreme to the simple Keynesian theory. In the classical theory, the level of output is determined solely by aggregate supply and aggregate demand determines only the price level, just the reverse of the result found in the simple Keynesian theory.

The classical model to be developed in this chapter is highly simplified. The form in which it is presented will not be found in the writings of Ricardo, Mill, Marshall, or any of the other nineteenth and early twentieth century economists who created and refined the classical theory. Not until after the appearance of Keynes' *General Theory*[1] did economists turn to the writings of the classical theorists to construct complete models that might be placed side by side with the Keynesian model for comparison. Because, for simplicity, we will limit ourselves to the broad outlines of

that classical model, we must note that our inattention to specific details amounts to inattention to the many qualifications that must be made to the conclusions we will draw. Nonetheless, the conclusions reached on this basis will at least suggest the directions in which the classical theory led.

The classical theory, the broad outlines of which are described in this chapter, is specifically classical theory as it was before Keynes' *General Theory*. As we will see, the quantity theory of money is an essential part of classical theory, but the "modern" version of the quantity theory differs markedly from the old version. We will touch on the modern version in a later chapter; here our purpose is to cover the essentials of classical theory before Keynes. Consequently, it is the "old" quantity theory that we examine.

The classical theory presented in this chapter is also different from the new classical or rational expectations theory. The new theory, like the old, assumes a vertical aggregate supply curve and downward wage and price flexibility. However, its emphasis on rational expectations leads it to other assumptions which differ from those of the old classical theory. Because these other assumptions are especially relevant to the issue of the effectiveness of fiscal and monetary policy, the rational expectations theory will be reviewed in a later chapter devoted specifically to policy.

Finally, the classical theory in this chapter is also limited to classical explanations of the determination of employment, output, and price levels,

---

[1] John Maynard Keynes, *The General Theory of Employment, Interest, and Money*. Harcourt Brace Jovanovich, 1936.

because these were the explanations attacked by Keynes and others. The other basic questions of what is to be produced, how it is to be produced, and for whom it is to be produced provoked no disagreement. In Keynes' words:

> If we suppose the volume of output to be given, i.e. to be determined by forces outside the classical scheme of thought, then there is no objection to be raised against the classical analysis of the manner in which private self-interest will determine what in particular is produced, in what proportions the factors of production will be combined to produce it, and how the value of the final product will be distributed between them.[2]

Output and Employment in Classical Theory

The equilibrium levels of output and employment are determined in the classical system as soon as we are given (1) the economy's production function from which is derived the demand curve for labor, and (2) the supply curve of labor. Apart from the inclusion in Part D of aggregate demand curves, AD_0 and AD_1, which will be explained below, all of the other curves in Figure 9-1 were explained in deriving Figure 8-5 in Chapter 8. The MPP of the labor curve given by D_N in Part B is, as before, derived from the production function in Part A, and Figure 9-1 shows the standard case of diminishing returns in which the MPP of labor decreases as the amount of labor employed increases. As previously explained, employers hire that amount of labor at which MPP = W/P. Therefore, the amount of labor hired is an inverse

function of the real wage. With a given production function and an initial equilibrium at which MPP = W/P, an increase in employment is not possible without a decrease in the real wage. As before, the curve labeled S_N in Part B is the supply curve of labor. This shows that the amount of labor supplied is a direct function of the real wage rate, the reasons for which were also considered earlier.

On the assumptions underlying the classical model, the intersection of the supply and demand curves for labor in Part B determines what the level of aggregate output will be. With a real wage of $(W/P)_0$ in Figure 9-1, there is equilibrium between the supply of and demand for labor. At this real wage, employers choose to hire N_0 of labor, and workers choose to provide N_0 of labor. With the aggregate production function of Part A, employment of N_0 indicates aggregate output of Y_0.[3]

In the classical scheme of things, any real wage other than $(W/P)_0$ will generate forces causing the real wage to rise or fall by the amount necessary to establish equilibrium in the labor market. To review the analysis of the preceding chapter, at a real wage rate greater than $(W/P)_0$, there is an excess supply of labor. To achieve equilibrium, the real wage must fall and, given a flexible money wage rate, this would be accomplished by the appropriate decline in the money wage rate. Once W has fallen by the amount required to reduce W/P to $(W/P)_0$, equilibrium is reached. If we had assumed instead an initial real wage below $(W/P)_0$, the adjustment process would be similar. However, in this case there would be an excess demand for labor, and competition among employers would bid up the

---

[2] Keynes, *General Theory*, pp. 378–79. This is not to say, however, that the theory of distribution that was developed by classical economists is the last word. Although Keynes accepted this part of classical theory for his purposes, the very ground broken by Keynes in the theory of aggregate output and employment gave rise to a new interest in the macroeconomic aspects of income distribution. See, for example, S. Weintraub, *A General Theory of the Price Level, Output, Income, Distribution, and Economic Growth*, Chilton, 1959, and N. Kaldor, "Alternative Theories of Distribution," in *Review of Economic Studies*, Vol. 23, 1955–56.

[3] Although N_0 and Y_0 are full employment values, they have not been labeled N_f and Y_f as in the preceding chapter. Shifts in the production function and in the supply of labor are introduced in the following text, and there is a different full employment value for N and Y for each position of these curves. For this reason, each value for N and Y, whether a full employment value or not, has been simply identified by a numerical subscript. The original set of equilibrium values is identified by the subscript 0.

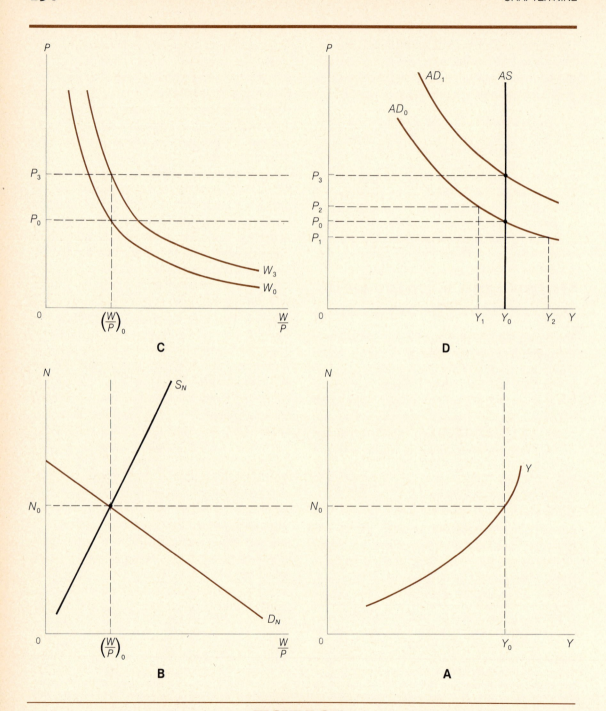

FIGURE 9-1
The Classical Model Without Saving and Investment

money wage rate by the amount necessary to raise the real wage to its equilibrium level.

Given such flexibility of the money wage rate, a displacement of the real wage from the equilibrium wage of $(W/P)_0$ that results from a change in P will be followed by a return to that real wage, because W will change as needed to offset that change in P. And as long as W/P is at $(W/P)_0$ for any value of P, Y also is at Y_0 for any value of P. This is the basis on which the perfectly inelastic aggregate supply curve in Part D of the diagram was derived for the classical case in Chapter 8.

Remember that the equilibrium level of employment found at $(W/P)_0$ is the full employment level; that is, at this level all those who are able, willing, and seeking to work at prevailing wage rates are able to find employment. This does not mean that there is no unemployment or unfilled vacancies. There will always be some workers who are between jobs for various reasons, but unemployment of this kind is consistent with a condition of full employment as long as persons so unemployed are able to find positions within a reasonable period of time. During the 1960s, there was considerable agreement among economists that the various sources of friction in the labor market accounted for unemployment equal to about 4 percent of the labor force. However, changes that have occurred since then have raised this percentage to between 5 and 6. As economists disagree as to whether the figure is closer to 5 or 6 percent, one may loosely say that under present conditions unemployment within the range of 5 to 6 percent may be described as full employment.

Because any level of employment other than the full employment level is a disequilibrium level, a familiar proposition of classical theory is that the equilibrium position in the labor market is necessarily one of full employment. Apart from frictional unemployment, whatever unemployment persists in the face of this equilibrium must be voluntary unemployment. For example, with the equilibrium real wage established at $(W/P)_0$, any persons who are unemployed are considered to be voluntarily unemployed if they are

seeking work but will accept work only at a money wage that, at the existing price level, means a real wage greater than $(W/P)_0$. They are seeking a real wage that is inconsistent with the marginal productivity of their labor, and in effect they are "pricing" themselves out of the market. Given the assumptions of the classical system, there is no barrier to full employment or to the elimination of involuntary unemployment in that system as long as labor is willing to reduce its money wage as required to produce that real wage at which all who wish to work will be hired.

The Quantity Theory of Money and the Price Level

As shown in Part D of Figure 9-1, the classical model yields a perfectly inelastic aggregate supply curve at the output level that is consistent with full employment. Although this curve specifies what the output level must be in this model, it does not specify which of the various price levels along this supply curve will be the prevailing price level. To do this, classical theory relied on the quantity theory of money. This theory of money holds that the quantity of money in the hands of the public determines how high or low the price level will be.

In dealing with money, we will accept the ordinary definition which states that money is anything that is generally accepted by the public in payment for goods, services, and other valuable assets and in the discharge of debts. The supply of money that exists on any date is, therefore, the sum total of those things that meet the condition stated in the definition. The following chapter is devoted to the question of the supply of money—including the full list of things that currently serve as means of payment. Of these things, currency, coin, and demand deposits made up about 90 percent of the total dollar amount early in 1981. For present purposes, we may simply think of the supply of money as the sum of currency (which is understood to include coin) and demand deposits.[4] Furthermore, we need not concern ourselves with the question of how changes in the supply of money come about. (This is the major topic of Chapter 10.) Here we simply accept such changes as given.

The Quantity Theory as a Theory of the Price Level

Although the public may choose to use currency and demand deposits as a store of value—that is, as a form in which wealth can be held—the classical view was that the public uses other assets like interest-bearing savings deposits and securities as a store of value. It was maintained that the assets that make up money (as narrowly defined) were used almost exclusively as a medium of exchange. In their role as a medium of exchange, the function of these assets is simply to overcome the difficulties unavoidable in barter exchange. But even with money's role thus limited, a question remains: Does a bushel of wheat exchange for $2 and a ton of coal for $20, or does a bushel of wheat exchange for $5 and a ton of coal for $50? The answer given by classical theory is that the absolute level of prices, $2 or $5 for wheat and $20 or $50 for coal, depends on the quantity of money in the economy. This relationship—in which the price level is made a function of the money supply—is known as the quantity theory of money. Furthermore, the relationship between changes in the money supply and changes in the price level was held to be strictly proportional. This conclusion depended on several assumptions that may most simply be revealed by examining the identity $MV \equiv PY$, in which M is the supply of money, V is its velocity or the number of times it turns

over per period in the purchase of final output Y, and P is the price level of this output.[5]

It should be emphasized that $MV \equiv PY$ is an identity. As such, it stands completely apart from the quantity theory or any other theory. $MV \equiv PY$ says simply that the quantity of money multiplied by the number of times each unit of money on the average is spent for final output in any time period equals the quantity of final goods and services sold during that period multiplied by the price level of those goods and services. If Y is the physical volume of goods and services represented by any period's GNP, P is the price level of these goods, and V is the number of times the money supply is used to purchase goods whose value is PY, the familiar GNP identity (neglecting net exports) $GNP \equiv C + I + G$ may be expanded to read $MV \equiv GNP \equiv C + I + G \equiv PY$. Each part of this expression set off by an identity sign is identical in value to every other part; each part is merely a different way of describing the same dollar amount.

The $MV \equiv PY$ identity is converted into the quantity theory of money under the assumptions that Y and V are constant or stable in the short run and that P is passive. The assumption that P is passive means that P depends on changes in M rather than that changes in M depend on changes in P. Given these assumptions, any short-run increase (or decrease) in M must lead to a proportional rise (or fall) in P.[6] Without these assumptions, however, it is equally inevi-

---

[4]It is convenient to use the letter M for the money stock, as is done in this and following chapters, as well as for imports, as done in Chapters 2 and 7 and in following chapters. In almost all cases it will be clear from the context which of the variables M refers to; where there may be any doubt, a specific statement will be made.

[5]M is a stock variable and Y a flow variable. If Y is defined for one quarter, M is the average stock of money in the economy during that quarter, V is the number of times that average stock of money is used to purchase final output during that quarter, and P is the average price level of output for that quarter.

[6]For example, begin with $100 \times 4 = 2 \times 200$. Increase M by 10 percent to 110. Assuming the constancy of V and Y, we have $110 \times 4 = 2.2 \times 200$, or a 10-percent increase in P, a rise proportional with the increase in M. Or, alternatively, rewrite the identity as $M(V/Y) \equiv P$, in which the assumed constancy of V and Y makes V/Y a positive proportionality constant, here equal to $4/200$, or 0.02. Then, whatever the value for M, P is always 0.02 times that value.

table that any increase (or decrease) in M will *not* lead to a proportional rise (or fall) in P (barring the unlikely case in which changes in V and Y are exactly offsetting).

The classical view that the level of output is stable in the short run simply reflects the fact that the fully employed labor force works with a fixed stock of capital and given production techniques in the short run. In terms of Figure 9-1, the production function in Part A can shift outward or to the right with growth in the capital stock and technological advances, resulting in a rise in the level of output consistent with full employment that appears in Part D as a rightward shift in the perfectly inelastic aggregate supply curve. However, these changes occur only gradually over the long run. The labor supply curve in Part B can shift to the left with the same result, but this change also occurs gradually with the growth in population over the long run. We will trace changes of these kinds through figures like Figure 9-1 later in this chapter. Finally, short-run variations in output could appear as a result of departures from the normal position of a fully employed labor force, but such departures were regarded as infrequent and subject to prompt correction in a system of competitive markets. Given the assumption that full employment of the labor force is normal, the assumption of a stable level of output for any short-run period follows logically.

The classical view that the velocity of money is constant is based on the argument that the institutional, structural, and customary conditions that determine velocity usually change very gradually. Among these conditions are the frequency with which economic units receive and make payments, the regularity of these receipts and payments, and the portion of such receipts and payments that is made on a money or barter basis.[7] Although these and all other conditions

affecting the size of V are subject to change, the quantity theory asserts the gradualness of such change in support of its conclusion that V is constant in the short run.[8]

The Quantity Theory as a Theory of Aggregate Demand

Whereas the simple Keynesian model is unable to say anything about the level of output without a theory of aggregate demand, the simple classical model is able to establish the level of output and apparently also the price level of output without such a theory. The output level is determined to be that output which is produced by a fully employed labor force and the price level at which that output sells is determined by the quantity of money. Although the classical theorists seemed to make do without explicitly bringing in aggregate demand, a theory of aggregate demand is

day, he does not typically spend the whole $200 on payday (and end up "broke" for the next thirteen days). If he spends the $200 evenly over the two-week period, his average cash balance will turn out to be $100. Because his biweekly spending is $200, this $100 average balance has a V of 2 biweekly; because his annual spending is $5,200, this $100 average balance has a V of 52 annually. If he were instead paid $100 every Friday, by the same line of argument his average cash balance would be $50. This $50 average balance has a V of 4 biweekly and a V of 104 annually. Generalizing for the economy as a whole, with a given supply of money, a change in which everyone were paid half as much twice as often would mean the existing supply of money could handle a much greater volume of final purchases. This rise in V with constant M would mean a rise in PY proportional with the rise in V.

This illustration covers frequency of receipts—only one of the many conditions that were believed to change very slowly and thus to make for stability in V. For a discussion of the determinants of V, see J.M. Culbertson, *Money and Banking*, 2nd ed., McGraw-Hill, 1977, pp. 125–32, and G. Garvy and M.R. Blyn, *The Velocity of Money*, Federal Reserve Bank of New York, 1969, Ch. 6.

[8]Even in its crude form, the quantity theory did not argue that short-run V and Y were as stable or P as passive as is here assumed. We will retain these assumptions in the extreme form in which they have been given so that we may proceed with the construction of the simplified classical model.

---

[7]Even though no one may choose to hold idle money, everyone holds some currency or demand deposits to even out the difference between receipts and payments. For example, if an employee is paid $200 every other Fri-

implicit in their quantity theory of money. This theory of aggregate demand may be described with an appropriate aggregate demand curve. Then the combination of that aggregate demand curve and the aggregate supply curve gives us a simple aggregate demand–aggregate supply classical model that can be compared with the simple Keynesian model developed in Part 2. The theory of aggregate demand in this classical model is crude, and the aggregate demand curve that describes it is easily derived.

To begin with, classical theory held that, whatever the size of the money supply, the full amount was in active circulation as a medium of exchange. This is the assertion that the public does not hold money as a store of value. The absence of idle money balances is a critical element in the rigid quantity theory; in the view of the classical theorists, the absence of such holdings was to be expected on the basis of rational human behavior. They could see no reason why people should choose to hold any portion of their money receipts in idle money form. As people acquired money, there was only one disposition for it: spending. Spending was either for consumption or for capital goods. As we will see, the act of saving, or not spending for consumption goods, was automatically transformed into an act of spending for capital goods. Money that was held back from consumption spending would be loaned to firms that would, in turn, spend all the money for capital goods. Therefore, although persons do save, classical theory held that they would not hold any amounts saved in the form of money and that consequently all money would remain in active circulation.

As long as money was used exclusively as a medium of exchange and thereby remained completely in active circulation, the velocity of money would remain stable. With V known and stable, MV or total spending on goods and services is known as soon as M is known. This brings us to the concept of aggregate demand as it appears in the simple classical model of Figure 9-1. It is portrayed graphically by a curve like AD_0 in Part D. That curve shows the various quantities

of output that can be purchased at various price levels with a certain fixed amount of total spending. As V is stable in the simple classical model, what that amount of spending will be in any time period depends entirely on M, the average stock of money held by the public during that time period. For each stock of M, there is a different aggregate demand curve: The greater the stock of money, the farther from the origin is the corresponding aggregate demand curve.

For any given AD curve, every combination of P and Y along that curve will be a combination whose product equals the same total spending, a property which reveals that the AD curve in question is of unitary elasticity throughout.[9] However, we have seen that the classical theory makes Y independent of total spending: Y is whatever a fully employed labor force is able to produce. It is shown in Part D by the position of the perfectly inelastic AS curve. Accordingly, the intersection of the AD curve with the AS curve does no more than determine the price level. Therefore, for AD_0, the equilibrium price level must be P_0. Any departure from this price level sets into motion forces that return P to P_0.

If, for example, P were P_2 instead of P_0, the level of total spending indicated by AD_0 would be able to purchase output of only Y_1, while the amount of output supplied would be unchanged at Y_0. This is a case in which $AS > AD$. Does this mean that producers will adjust by cutting back from the Y_0 to the Y_1 level of output and by laying off workers? Not at all. Production will remain at Y_0. Given the money wage rate of W_0, producers find it consistent with the requirement for profit maximization—$W = P \times \text{MPP}$—to supply Y_0 of output at a price level of P_0. At the higher price

---

[9]Like the W curves in Part C, the AD curves in Part D are rectangular hyperbolas. Each AD curve corresponds to a particular value of MV, and MV is by definition equal to PY. Given the identity between MV and PY, every rectangle found by running perpendiculars from any point on a given AD curve to the axes must be equal in area. Because the AD curve is such that PY is equal for every pair of P and Y values along it, price elasticity of demand is unity at every level of P.

level of P_2, they cannot sell all they can produce at full employment, but the result is not a reduction in production. It is the price level that adjusts downward as producers compete for customers, and once the price level has fallen to P_0, buyers can with the same total spending again purchase the full employment output that producers are prepared to supply at this price.

If we choose a disequilibrium level for P below rather than above P_0, an upward adjustment occurs. At the lower price level of P_1, the total spending represented by AD_0 calls for output of Y_2, which exceeds the output produced at full employment. The result in this case must be a rise in P. Competition among buyers who, per time period, spend the unchanged sum represented by AD_0 will force P up until equilibrium is restored at P_0.

To sum up, assuming competitive conditions in the markets for both output and labor, the classical model ensures that the equilibrium level of output will be the full employment level or Y_0, as shown in the illustration by the intersection of the AS and AD_0 curves. A deficiency of aggregate demand that would appear if P were above the level given by the intersection or an excess of aggregate demand that would appear if P were below the level given by the intersection is promptly removed as competitive forces drive P to the level at which $AS = AD$.

Classical Model Without Saving and Investment

The interconnected parts of Figure 9-1 enable us to identify the full set of equilibrium values for this simple classical system. These values are N_0, $(W/P)_0$, Y_0, W_0, and P_0. Barring any shift in the production function or the supply curve of labor or any change in the money supply or its velocity, the indicated set of equilibrium values will remain unchanged period after period. In practice, of course, these elements will change over time, but under classical assumptions, for each change new equilibrium values will be established for the variables of the system. Tracing through several such changes will illustrate the mechanics of the system.

Effects of a Change in the Supply of Money

Consider first the case of an increase in the money supply from M_0 to M_1, which produces the shift of the AD curve from AD_0 to AD_1 in Part D of Figure 9-1. The increase in M (with constant V) means an increase in total spending per time period of $V(M_1 - M_0)$ and a rise in the price level from P_0 to P_3. If the money wage does not rise proportionally with this rise in the price level, the real wage will fall. This will cause employers to try to expand output by hiring more workers, because a higher price for output without a higher money wage rate means greater profits with greater output. But a real wage below $(W/P)_0$ means that the quantity of labor available is too small to produce output Y_0, let alone to expand output beyond this. Competition among employers for workers will then force the money wage level up to W_3, or proportionally with the price level, leaving the equilibrium real wage unchanged at $(W/P)_0$ and output unchanged at Y_0. The net result of the expansion of the money supply is a proportional rise in the price level and in the money wage but no change in employment or output; the equilibrium values are N_0, $(W/P)_0$, Y_0, P_3, and W_3.

This, of course, is just what we should expect according to the quantity theory. The level of output is determined by the aggregate supply curve; the money supply only sets the price level for this output. Increasing or decreasing the money supply will cause the price level of output to rise or fall proportionally, but the level of output itself will remain unchanged at the full employment level. Any change in the money supply that is accompanied by a change in the velocity of money will break the proportional relationship between M and P but will still leave the level of output and employment unaffected by changes in either M or V.

Effects of a Change in the Supply of Labor

Now let us imagine an increase in the labor supply, as shown by the shift from S_{N_0} to S_{N_1} in Part B of Figure 9-2. With no shift in the production function and so no shift in the curve of the MPP of labor, any increase in employment will lower the MPP of labor. The full employment equilibrium was previously at N_0 with the real wage of $(W/P)_0$. The new full employment equilibrium is at N_1. To achieve this equilibrium, the real wage must decline from $(W/P)_0$ to $(W/P)_1$. At this real wage and level of employment, output is seen to be Y_1 in Part A and the AS curve in Part D is AS_1, a shift to the right from its original position at AS_0.

What is required to adjust to the new full employment equilibrium following the increase in the supply of labor? With MV unchanged, AD in Part D remains at its original position of AD_0. Therefore, the sale of the larger output produced by the larger number of workers employed at the new full employment position can only occur at the lower price level of P_1. One thing then required is the indicated decline in P. Producers will find it advantageous to produce this larger output and sell it at the lower price level if the money wage rate declines enough. Specifically, W must fall in Part C from W_0 to W_1 because it is only with W of W_1 that P of P_1 will yield $(W/P)_1$, the real wage consistent with full employment after the increase in the labor supply.

This decline in W must clearly be greater than the decline in P in order to cause the required decline in W/P. To see this graphically, suppose for the moment that W declines only by the amount indicated by the broken line between the W_0 and W_1 curves. This decline would be proportional with the decline in P as a horizontal line from P_1 intersects the broken W curve at the same W/P at which a horizontal line from P_0 intersects the W_0 curve. But if W fell only that far, there would be no decline in the real wage and therefore no incentive for employers to hire more labor and expand output in the first place. Furthermore, if W fell proportionally with P, maintaining Y at its original level of Y_0, there could be no basis

for P to fall in the first place. A decline in P below P_0 with AS remaining at AS_0 and Y therefore remaining at Y_0 would create excess demand, AD > AS, the result of which would be a return of the price level to P_0. However, given the classical theory's assumption of downward wage flexibility, W will fall any time there is less than full employment; given the increase in the supply of labor and the other assumptions, W will fall to W_1 to restore the system to full employment. At that point, a new full employment equilibrium with the following values is established: N_1, $(W/P)_1$, Y_1, W_1, and P_1.

A numerical "before" and "after" example may clarify the adjustments involved. The first row of the following table gives the equilibrium values for N, Y, W, P, and W/P when labor demand is D_N, labor supply is S_{N_0} (Figure 9-2), the money stock is $75, and velocity is 4. The second row gives the new equilibrium values after the shift from S_{N_0} to S_{N_1}. Full employment now calls for N of 150, at which the MPP of labor and therefore W/P is 1.66. With N of 150, the full employment Y is 400. If Y is 400, P must be 0.75. With MV and AD unchanged at 300, 400 of output can be sold only at P of 0.75. Finally, with P of 0.75, W must adjust downward to the degree required to achieve the new real wage of 1.66, if there is to be full employment.[10]

---

[10] On the assumption of profit maximization, employers will not expand employment unless greater profits are expected from the sale of the higher level of output. In this case, there will be greater profits, as may be seen from the figures. At the original equilibrium, labor's share of the real output of 300 is N × MPP, or 100 × 2, or 200. The remainder, Y − (N × MPP), or 100, may be called the "profit share." At the new equilibrium, labor's share of the real output of 400 is 150 × 1.66, or 250, leaving 150 as the "profit share," an increase in profits of 50. In dollar terms, the flow of income at the original equilibrium is $300, or 300 × 1, divided into $200 for labor and $100 for profits. At the new equilibrium, it is the same $300, or 400 × 0.75, now divided into $187.50, or 150 × $1.25 for labor and $112.50 for profits. Although labor's share is decreased in money terms from $200 to $187.50, the $187.50 adjusted for the fall in P from 1 to 0.75 is equal to $250 in "base period" prices. Similarly, the profits of $112.50 are equal to $150 in "base period" prices.

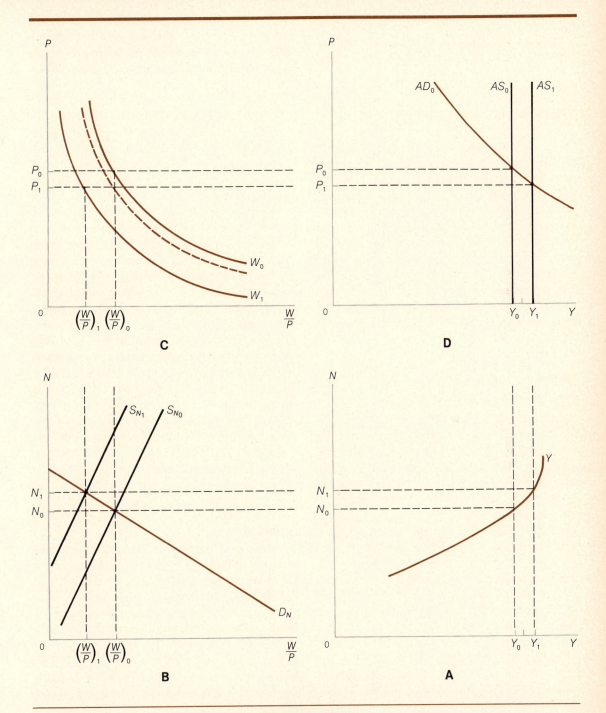

FIGURE 9-2
The Classical Model: Effects of a Change in the Supply of Labor

	N	Y	W	P	MPP = (W/P)	M	V
Original equilibrium (subscripts 0)	100	300	$2.00	1.00	2.00	$75	4
New equilibrium (subscripts 1)	150	400	$1.25	0.75	1.66	$75	4

Given an increase in the labor supply, the crucial element of the process by which the system moves to its new equilibrium position is the adjustments that occur in the money wage and the price level. Whether unemployment results from an increase in the labor supply or for other reasons, flexibility of the money wage and price level is indispensable to the correction of unemployment. As long as the money wage responds to unemployment and as long as the price level responds to changes in output, full employment can always be regained according to this simple classical model.

Effects of a Change in the Demand for Labor

Growth in the capital stock or technological advances will cause the production function to shift outward over time, as shown by the movement from Y to Y' in Part A of Figure 9-3. At each possible level of employment, the MPP of labor is now greater than it was, because at each level of N the slope of Y' exceeds the slope of Y. This is reflected in Part B of Figure 9-3 as an upward or rightward shift in the demand curve for labor, indicating that it is now profitable for employers to hire more labor at each possible real wage. The equilibrium real wage rises from $(W/P)_0$ to $(W/P)_1$, employment rises from N_0 to N_1; output rises from Y_0 to Y_1 and AS shifts from AS_0 to AS_1. With no change in the money supply, the greater output requires a fall in the price level from P_0 to P_1. At the new equilibrium real wage of $(W/P)_1$, price level P_1 calls for money wage W_1. In the present case, the rise in the real wage necessary to reestablish equilibrium is produced by a fall in P and a rise in W.

The first row of the following table repeats the set of figures previously used to describe the original equilibrium values; the second row gives a set of figures that describes the new equilibrium.

	N	Y	W	P	MPP = (W/P)	M	V
Original equilibrium (subscripts 0)	100	300	$2.00	1.00	2.00	$75	4
New equilibrium (subscripts 1)	105	333	$2.25	0.90	2.50	$75	4

In passing, we may note several basic propositions of economics that are clearly revealed by the present analysis. For one, the gradual rise in the real wage, or "standard of living," is primarily the result of the gradual outward shift in the production function, which is largely attributable to technological progress and a growing stock of capital. If, over the same period in which these developments raised the schedule of marginal productivity of labor from D_{N_0} to D_{N_1}, the supply curve of labor had also moved from S_{N_0} to S_{N_1}, the number of workers employed would have risen, but the real wage would have remained the same. The actual gradual rise in the real wage experienced over the long run in Western economies has occurred primarily because the growth in capital and the rate of technological advance have exceeded the rate of growth in the labor force.

A second proposition brought out by this analysis is that the long-run growth of output (whether produced as here by an outward shift in the production function, or as in the previous case by a shift to the left in the labor supply curve, or as in practice by both) leads to a falling price level unless accompanied by an expansion in the money supply. Although an expansion of output with no rise in the money supply will in practice cause V to rise, V cannot rise without limit. Therefore, as output expands in the long run, M must expand to avoid what otherwise must be a gradually falling P. Although these propositions have

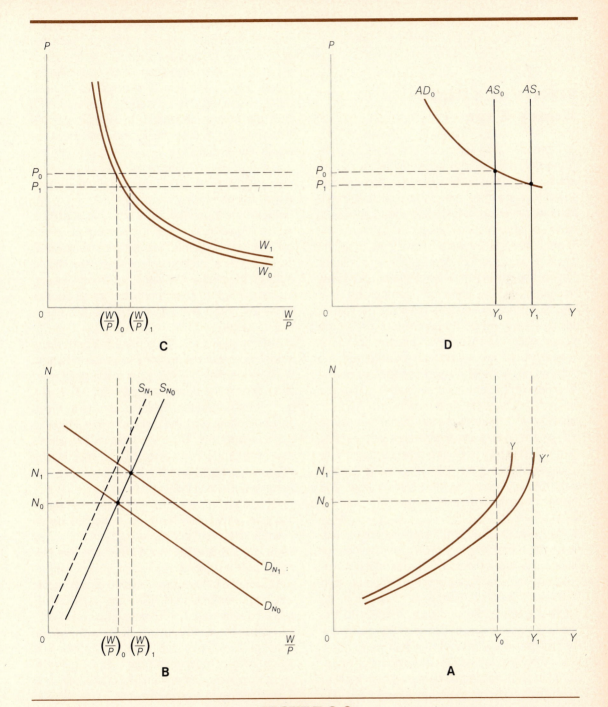

FIGURE 9-3
The Classical Model: Effects of a Change in the Demand for Labor

been brought out by the classical model, they are accepted in principle by most economists today.

Effects of a Rigid Money Wage

From an initial equilibrium with a given AD curve, an increase in the supply of labor calls for a fall in the price level and a larger fall in the money wage rate to establish a new full employment equilibrium at a lower real wage. Classical theory assumes perfectly competitive markets; an excess supply of labor in such markets will automatically depress the money wage. If we now drop the assumption of perfect competition in the labor market, the results may be different. Consider, for example, the imperfect competition that results when workers are organized into labor unions. There will be no barrier to a rise in the money wage when excess demand for labor appears, but there will now be a barrier to a fall in the money wage when excess supply appears. In other words, the money wage is flexible upward but may be rigid downward. Furthermore, in an imperfect market the money wage may be forced up even though there is no excess demand for labor. To illustrate, let us begin with a full employment equilibrium position for the economy and observe what follows when the money wage is arbitrarily pushed up, say by union pressure.

In Figure 9-4 there is full employment equilibrium with a real wage of $(W/P)_0$ and values for other variables indicated by subscript 0. Suppose now that the money wage is forced up from W_0 to W_1. If the price level were to remain at P_0, the real wage would rise proportionally to the rise in the money wage. But, with the given AD, P must rise. If it does not, the real wage rises, which means a decrease in the amount of Y supplied, and with aggregate demand given by AD_0, a smaller Y is accompanied by a higher P. However, P cannot rise as far as W, because if it did there would be no change in the real wage and consequently no change in output. The original

output cannot all be sold with unchanged aggregate demand at a higher P; therefore, P must rise in proportion to the fall in output.

In the process by which a new equilibrium is reached, P, Y, and N must all adjust to the fixed money wage, W_1. The new equilibrium values for P, Y, and N are designated by the subscript 1. As compared to the initial equilibrium, there are now a higher real wage, a lower output level, and a higher price level. The higher real wage, which was artificially caused by forcing up the money wage, forces employment down from N_0 to N_1. Because the amount of labor supplied is greater with a higher real wage, the amount of unemployment is not merely the difference between N_1 and N_0, but the larger difference between N_1 and N_2. With the higher real wage, those workers fortunate enough to keep their jobs are, of course, better off than they were before the rise in the money wage.

Although we will not go into this part of the model, note that the arbitrary increase in W from W_0 to W_1 makes the AS curve slope downward as shown by the dashed segment of AS. An AS curve that is perfectly inelastic throughout can only be obtained on the assumption of a flexible money wage rate. Drop that assumption as we have temporarily done here, and the effect on the AS curve is as shown, the basis for which was examined in detail in Chapter 8.

The table on page 162 provides a numerical example, similar to those given earlier, which illustrates the results of introducing a rigid money wage into the present model. Because the new equilibrium is not one of full employment, the last three columns have been added to show the resulting unemployment. (S is labor supplied; D is labor demanded; U is labor unemployed.) With full employment equilibrium defined by a real wage of 2, we can see from the figures that unemployment must result from the arbitrary raising of the money wage from $2.00 to $2.40.

As long as the money wage is arbitrarily held above the level consistent with full employment, we have an *equilibrium situation with unemployment*. Although we have noted several times

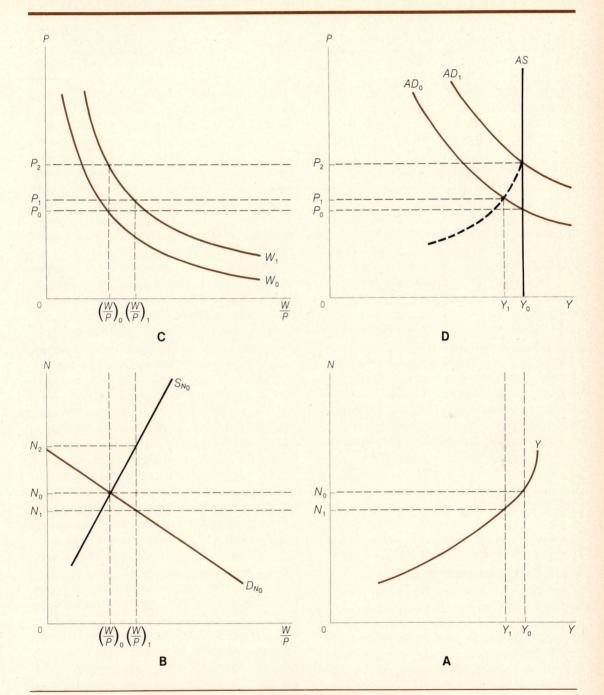

FIGURE 9-4
The Classical Model: Effects of a Rigid Money Wage

| | N | Y | W | P | MPP = W/P | M | V | Labor | | |
								S	D	U
Original equilibrium (subscripts 0)	100	300	$2.00	1.00	2.00	$75	4	100	100	0
New equilibrium (subscripts 1)	90	273	$2.40	1.10	2.18	$75	4	102	90	12

before that classical theory denied this possibility of equilibrium with unemployment, the denial was made only on the assumption that we were dealing with an economy in which the money wage was flexible. An equilibrium with less than full employment is therefore entirely consistent with classical theory when that theory is stripped of the assumption of flexible wage rates, an assumption indispensable to its full employment conclusion.

In the *General Theory*, Keynes replaced the classical assumption of a flexible money wage with that of a rigid money wage, an assumption certainly more closely in agreement with the facts of observation. In so doing, Keynes could easily enough show that equilibrium with unemployment is possible. Although a great deal more is involved, it should be clear from analysis of the present case that the corresponding change in assumption in the classical theory leads to the same possibility of equilibrium with unemployment reached by Keynes in the *General Theory*.

Monetary Policy and Full Employment

In the classical scheme, if the money wage is held artificially above the level necessary for full employment, an appropriate expansion of the money supply may be an antidote. According to the quantity theory, an increase in M, with V and Y stable, will raise P proportionally. With a rigid money wage, the rise in P reduces the real wage and provides the profit incentive for employers to expand employment and output toward the full

employment level. Therefore, some appropriate expansion in the money supply is sufficient both to raise P to the level that reduces W/P to the full employment equilibrium level and to provide the increase in AD needed to purchase the full employment output at that price level.

In terms of Part C of Figure 9-4, to achieve the full employment real wage of $(W/P)_0$ with the money wage inflexible at W_1 requires a price level of P_2, because at that level W_1/P_2 equals W_0/P_0, or $(W/P)_0$. With real wage of $(W/P)_0$, output is Y_0. Therefore, in Part D, MV must be increased to equal $P_2 Y_0$ in order to generate AD adequate to purchase full employment output Y_0 at price level P_2.[11] The AD curve must shift to AD_1.

The previous numerical example may be modified to show how an appropriately expansionary monetary policy may offset the effect of a rigid money wage. The first two rows of the table on page 163 are the same as before: The first describes the initial full employment equilibrium, the second the less-than-full employment equilibrium that results from an artificially raised money wage. The third row shows the return to a full employment equilibrium that results from the appropriate expansion of M.

Note that the strict quantity theory does not hold in this situation, because part of the increase in AD created by the expansion of M is absorbed by the expansion of Y that is called forth by the fall in the real wage. M rises from $75 to $90 (20 percent), so that the strict quantity theory would indicate a 20 percent rise in P or from 1.10 to

---

[11]With V constant, $\Delta M = M_1 V - M_0 V = P_2 Y_0 - P_1 Y_1$.

									Labor	
	N	Y	W	P	MPP = W/P	M	V	S	D	U
Original equilibrium (subscripts 0)	100	300	$2.00	1.00	2.00	$75	4	100	100	0
Second equilibrium (subscripts 1)	90	273	$2.40	1.10	2.18	$75	4	102	90	12
Third equilibrium (N_0, Y_0, W_1, P_2)	100	300	$2.40	1.20	2.00	$90	4	100	100	0

1.32. P actually rises from 1.10 to 1.20 (less than 10 percent) as Y rises from 273 to 300.

Apparently, monetary policy provides the solution to unemployment created by a rigid money wage. However, as we can see from the crude model before us, this method of securing full employment in the face of an artificially high wage rate works only as long as the increase in M is not offset by a decrease in V. Aggregate demand must increase with the increase in M. Classical theory saw no "leakage" between an increase in M and an increase in aggregate demand. We can begin to see why monetary policy was *the* policy weapon of classical economists. When we return to Keynesian theory in the next chapter, we will see that this simple tie between changes in the money supply and changes in aggregate demand disappears. In Keynesian theory, aggregate demand cannot be so simply increased or decreased by expansion or contraction of the money supply.

Classical Model with Saving and Investment

Although formally correct, the classical model we have been discussing is greatly oversimplified. It fails to break down aggregate demand into demand for consumption goods and demand for capital goods. This means that it does not recognize the processes of saving and investment.

Saving and Investment

Not every dollar of income earned in the course of production is spent for consumption goods; some part of this income is withheld from consumption, that is, a portion of income is saved. Clearly, unless there is a dollar of planned investment spending for every dollar of income saved, there is a deficiency of aggregate spending. Another part of classical theory provides the mechanism that presumably ensures that planned saving will not exceed planned investment. This mechanism is the interest rate.

Classical theory treated investment as an inverse function of the interest rate, as illustrated by the curve labeled I in Figure 9-5. The derivation of this important curve is explained in considerable detail in Chapter 17; for present purposes, merely note that, other things being equal, the lower the rate of interest, the greater will be the amount of investment spending. For every prospective investment project, management estimates the expected net rate of return before allowance for the interest cost on the funds tied up in that project. With a relatively high rate of interest, relatively few of the available projects promise a rate of return equal to or greater than the interest rate. Consequently, relatively few projects are undertaken and there is relatively little investment. With a relatively low rate of interest, the opposite result is found. For example, at the interest rate of 9 percent, investment is $50 billion per time period, but at the interest

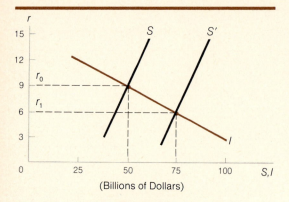

FIGURE 9-5
Classical Equilibria Between
Saving and Investment

rate of 6 percent, investment is $75 billion per time period. In other words, there is an additional $25 billion of investment on which the expected rate of return is between 9 and 6 percent.

If one drops the assumption of other things being equal, of course, shifts to the right or left in the investment curve will occur, for example, in response to those changes in technology, the adoption of which requires new capital equipment and therefore investment. Chapter 18 provides an examination of some factors that cause shifts in the investment curve. But again, for present purposes, it is sufficient merely to note that the investment curve of Figure 9-5 will shift to the right or left in response to changes in all factors affecting investment other than the rate of interest.

Keynes accepted the "investment as a function of the interest rate" part of classical theory; we will see how it fits into the extended Keynesian model in Chapter 12. However, another part of the classical theory shown in Figure 9-5 was rejected by Keynes—saving as a direct function of the interest rate. In Keynesian theory, saving is a direct function of the level of income. In that scheme, the interest rate may influence saving, but it is of minor importance. In classical theory, the interest rate is all-important, and the level of

income is of minor importance. Because the classical model argues that full employment is the normal state of the economy, the level of income is in effect ruled out as a variable in the short run. Consequently, it cannot influence the amount of saving. The problem in classical economics is to explain how saving will vary at the full employment level of income. The solution is provided by the interest rate. The higher the interest rate, the greater will be the amount of full employment income that is devoted to saving.

Given saving and investment curves such as S and I of Figure 9-5, competition between savers and investors would move the interest rate to the level that equated saving and investment. If the rate were above r_0, more funds would be supplied by savers than were demanded by investors, and the competition among savers to find investors would force the rate down. If the rate were below r_0, competition would force the rate up. When the rate is at r_0, equilibrium is established, with every dollar saved matched by a dollar devoted to investment spending.

It is important to see that this transfer of money from savers to investors also involves a transfer of resources. When income recipients decide to save part of current income, they are deciding not to exercise their claims to the full amount of output that results from their productive services. This releases resources from the production of consumption goods and makes them available for the production of capital goods. These resources will be fully absorbed in the production of capital goods only if investors choose to purchase the exact amount of capital goods that can thereby be produced. This means that if the rate of interest were above r_0 and somehow stayed there, unemployed resources would appear: The excess of S over I at an interest rate above r_0 reflects, in real terms, an excess of resources released from the production of consumption goods over the amount absorbed in the production of capital goods. One of these resources is, of course, labor; the excess of S over I also means that there is an excess of labor available over labor employed. In a word, there is unemployment. As we have seen, in the classical system, if the interest rate fails to equate saving and investment, it also fails in its assigned task of promptly reallocating the resources released from production of consumption goods to the production of capital goods; unemployed resources are the result.

Changes in Saving and Investment

As long as the interest rate adjusts upward and downward to correct any disequilibrium, shifts in the saving and investment functions will lead to the establishment of new equilibrium positions. Suppose that income recipients become more thrifty; at each interest rate they choose to save a larger part of their current income. This appears in Figure 9-5 as a shift to the right from S to S' in the saving curve and a decrease in the interest rate from r_0 to the new equilibrium level r_1. A numerical example such as those presented earlier reveals the effects of an increase in thrift in the classical system. The first row of the table below indicates the values of the variables at the original full employment equilibrium. Full employment of the labor force is N of 100; full employment output is Y of 300. With the interest rate at r_0, say 9 percent, the real income of 300 is divided into 250 of consumption and 50 of saving; r of 9 percent also produces equilibrium with saving of 50 and investment of 50. If the saving curve now shifts to the right and the interest rate drops to r_1, say 6 percent, a new equilibrium is established at which saving of 75 (in real terms, Y of 300 minus C of 225) equals investment of 75. With no shift in the production function or the supply of labor, full employment output remains at 300. The only change is in the distribution of out-

put between consumption goods and capital goods. The increased thrift of the public has produced a reallocation of resources—away from the production of consumption goods and to the production of capital goods—but with the total production of goods unchanged.

If the saving function shifted in the opposite direction so that there were less saving at each interest rate, we would have a higher interest rate at which a smaller flow of saving would be equated with a smaller flow of investment, but the flow of aggregate output would still be unchanged from the original full employment level. The effects of shifts in the investment curve may be traced in the same way. Whatever the shifts in the saving and investment curves, however, the possibility of "oversaving" or "underconsumption" could not arise so long as the interest rate succeeded in balancing saving and investment.

Does the interest rate always adjust promptly as required to maintain equality between saving and investment? The Swedish economist Knut Wicksell (1851–1926) was one of the first to point out that there are conditions under which it would not. However, even if the interest rate did not adjust promptly, the full employment level of output would be maintained if prices and wages were sufficiently flexible. If the interest rate did not adjust promptly, there would be an excess either of planned saving over planned investment or planned investment over planned saving. According to Keynesian theory, a fall or rise in income (output and employment) would be required at this point to bring saving and investment back into balance. This was not the case in classical theory, however. An excess of saving over investment would mean a deficiency of aggregate demand at the existing price level. This would lead to a deflation of prices and

	N	Y	C	I	W	P	MPP = W/P	M	V
Original equilibrium (r = 9 percent)	100	300	250	50	$2.00	1.00	2.00	$75	4
New equilibrium (r = 6 percent)	100	300	225	75	$2.00	1.00	2.00	$75	4

wages, but would not interfere with the maintenance of the real wage consistent with full employment. An unchanged aggregate demand that had become deficient at the original price level would now be adequate to purchase the full employment level of output at a lower price level. Conversely, an excess of planned investment over planned saving would mean an excess of aggregate demand at the existing price level. This would lead to an inflation of prices and wages, but again would not interfere with the maintenance of the real wage consistent with full employment.

Summary Statement

The purpose of this chapter has been to show, in terms of a simple model, how classical theory answered the fundamental questions of macroeconomics: What determines the levels of employment, output, consumption, saving, investment, prices, and wages? Our discussion may now be summarized in a list of the basic propositions of classical theory. Each of these propositions will be related to the graphic apparatus of Figure 9-6, which adds nothing new but brings together the saving–investment branch of the classical system with its other branches, presented in two steps in the preceding pages.

1. As shown in Part B, the supply, S_N, and demand, D_N, for labor are both functions of the real wage, W/P. Because of diminishing returns, the demand curve slopes downward to the right (that is, more labor is hired only at a lower real wage). Because of the essential disagreeableness of work, the supply curve slopes upward to the right (that is, more labor is offered only at a higher real wage). Therefore, the intersection of the supply and demand curves determines both the real wage $(W/P)_0$ and the level of employment N_0, which is the full employment level.

2. With fixed techniques of production and fixed capital stock, output in the short run becomes a function of employment, as shown by the production function in Part A. With employment determined in Part B as N_0, output is determined in Part A as Y_0.

3. On the assumption of a flexible money wage, the aggregate supply curve, AS, in Part D is perfectly inelastic at Y_0, the full employment level of Y. The aggregate demand curve, AD, is determined by the stock of money, M, given the assumption that the velocity of money, V, is stable. The price level, P_0, is then determined by the intersection of the AS and AD curves in Part D. Because AS is perfectly inelastic and because the position of AD depends on the size of the money stock, the size of the money stock determines the price level.

4. The money wage, W, adjusts to the equilibrium price level to produce the real wage required for full employment equilibrium. With the equilibrium real wage determined in Part B as $(W/P)_0$ and the equilibrium price level determined in Part D as P_0, the required money wage is determined in Part C as W_0.

5. As shown in Part E, saving, S, is a direct function of the interest rate; investment, I, is an inverse function of the interest rate. With the interest rate as a measure of the reward for saving, the higher it is, the greater will be the volume of saving. With the interest rate as the "price" of capital goods, the lower the interest rate, the greater will be the volume of investment. The interest rate is determined by the intersection of the saving and investment functions. It determines how real income is allocated between saving and consumption as well as how production (equal to real income) is allocated between consumption goods and capital goods.

These propositions are the basis for answers to the questions originally posed. They not only specify the levels of employment, output, consumption, saving, interest rate, price level, and money wage rate, but something much more: They show that the employment level is uniquely established at the full employment position. If both wages and prices are flexible, the money

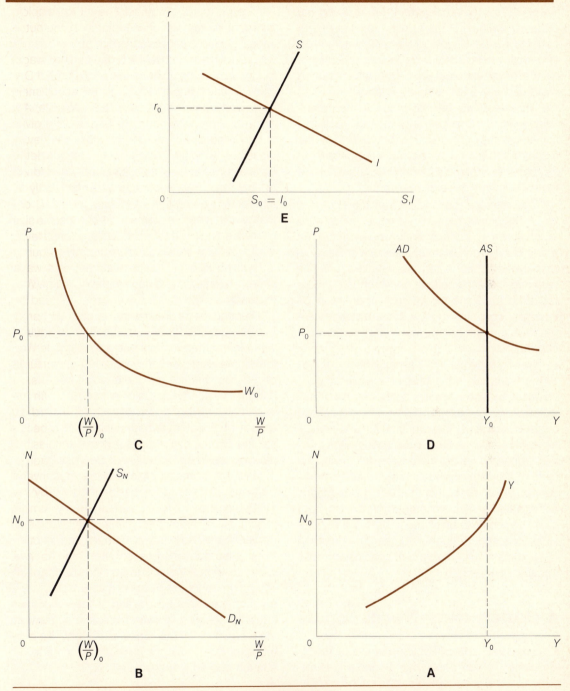

FIGURE 9-6
The Classical Model: Including Saving and Investment

wage will fall if unemployment appears and the price level will fall if the existing level of output cannot be sold at going prices. The automatic full employment conclusion follows logically. It also follows that output will be that which can be produced with a fully employed labor force, that the price level will be that at which the money supply with its given velocity will purchase this full employment level of output, and that the money wage will be so related to the price level as to make it profitable for employers to produce the full employment level of output.

The classical conclusion that the economy has an automatic tendency to move toward a full employment equilibrium is not widely accepted today. But this and other conclusions of classical employment theory can be rejected only by rejecting the assumptions on which that theory rests, because the theory itself appears to be internally consistent. Once its assumptions are granted, the theory inevitably leads to the indicated conclusions.

We will not enter into Keynes' specific attack on the assumptions that underlie classical theory. However, most economists agree that his attack was successful. Not only did he offer persuasive arguments against these critical assumptions—he replaced the rejected assumptions with others that appeared much more consistent with the facts of ordinary observation and statistical evidence. To the extent that the basic assumptions of the classical theory of employment and output could be shown to be unacceptable, the conclusions reached through that theory—including the automatic full employment conclusion—also became unacceptable.

A Concluding Note

If the classical analysis of the process by which the levels of employment, output, and prices are determined is unacceptable, at least in its application to the modern economy, it may appear that this chapter is basically unnecessary. To this there are a number of replies.

First, it is not altogether correct to label the classical theory as unacceptable or in some sense "wrong." Because the aim of this chapter was merely to introduce the broad outlines of that theory, it could do no more than draw broad conclusions and compare them with the conclusions so far derived from our study of Keynesian theory. The omission of refinements that would give us a more accurate picture of classical theory leaves us with little choice but to categorize the basic propositions of classical theory as correct or incorrect, but such categorization is itself inherently incorrect. Alfred Marshall once said that every *short* statement about economics is misleading (with the possible exception of this one). Our statement here, relative to what is involved in a complete treatment, is such a short statement and unavoidably somewhat misleading.

Second, one's understanding of a new theory is surely enriched when that theory is contrasted with the old theory that it seeks to displace. The classical system was the accepted explanation of macroeconomic phenomena for well over a hundred years. A discussion of this theory, which is partially correct and a product of the not so distant past, helps us understand and appreciate the changes in macroeconomic theory that have occurred since the Great Depression.

Finally, it is important to note that, despite the dramatic success of Keynesian theory from the 1940s to the 1970s, classical theory is still believed in by many people in positions of great responsibility, both in government and in business. It is not even necessary for them to have received formal training in economics; the stuff of which economics is made has a way of permeating people's minds and influencing their outlooks without any awareness on their part. At the very end of the *General Theory,* Keynes expressed this thought in what has come to be a much-quoted statement:

. . . the ideas of economists and political philosophers, both when they are right and when they are wrong, are more powerful than is commonly understood. Indeed the world is ruled by little else. Practical men, who believe themselves to be quite exempt from any intellectual influences, are usually the slaves of some defunct economist. Madmen in authority, who hear voices in the air, are distilling their frenzy from some academic scribbler of a few years back.[12]

The defunct economists who continue to influence many of these people today are the economists who constructed the classical theory.

In a similar vein, we find the very last sentence in Alexander Gray's classic little handbook on economic thought:

> No point of view, once expressed, ever seems wholly to die; and in periods of transition like the present, our ears are full of the whisperings of dead men.[13]

For more than one reason, the teachings of the classical economists are of something more than historical interest almost fifty years after the publication of the *General Theory*. The few reasons here given should be sufficient to make this point. The "Keynesian Revolution" did not so completely wipe out the "old order" that no sign of it remains. Today's monetarism evolved from that "old order." Although it has been influenced by and incorporates some of the insights of Keynesian economics, in general outline it bears a close resemblance to that "old order." For both academic and practical reasons, a proper introduction to macroeconomic theory must still include the fundamentals of the theory that held sway for more than a century before Keynes.

---

[12] Keynes, *General Theory,* p. 383.
[13] A. Gray, *The Development of Economic Doctrine,* Longmans, Green, 1931, p. 370.

10

The Money Supply Process

OVERVIEW

The most widely adopted definition of money counts as money anything that is generally acceptable in payment for goods, services, and other valuable assets and for the discharge of debts. The money supply on any day is therefore the total dollar amount of those things existing on that day which meet this requirement. This chapter begins by identifying a number of money supply measures for which the Federal Reserve publishes figures, including the measure known as M-1B (the one that includes all the items that fit the definition of money just given). There are also a still narrower measure, M-1A, and the broader measures, M-2, M-3 and L.

The chapter next turns to the question of what determines the supply of money at any given time. For simplicity, here we use the M-1A measure of money—that is, the sum of demand deposits at the commercial banks and the currency and coin in the hands of the public. To explain what determines the money supply we need only to explain what determines the amounts of these two components. Given certain simplifying assumptions, the amount of demand deposits held by the public depends on the amount of reserves held by the banks and the percentage reserve requirement against demand deposits. If the banks must hold 20¢ in reserves for each dollar of demand deposits and if they have a total of $25 billion in reserves, the maximum amount of demand deposits they may have on their books is $125 billion. When we add to this the amount of currency and coin held by the public at the time, we have the money supply known as M-1A.

The third part of the chapter describes the tools or instruments that the Federal Reserve uses in its efforts to control the money supply. The two principal tools used to effect changes in the dollar amount of reserves are open market operations and changes in the discount rate. The means by which it varies the amount of demand deposits that each dollar of reserves can back up are changes in the percentage reserve requirements.

The fourth part of the chapter describes the basic process by which the amount of demand deposits expands and contracts in response to a change in the amount of reserves held by the commercial banks. It is easy to see that $25 billion of reserves will support $125 billion of demand deposits, given a 20 percent reserve requirement, that $26 billion of reserves will support $130 billion of demand deposits, or that $24 billion of reserves will support $120 billion of demand deposits, given the same 20 percent reserve requirement. However, this in itself sheds no light on the process by which an increase in reserves from $25 billion to $26 billion or a decrease from $25 billion to $24 billion brings about a $5 billion increase or decrease in the total of demand deposits. That process is examined in this part of the chapter.

The fifth part of the chapter takes up three complications to the simplified money supply process described in the preceding parts of the chapter. There it was assumed that the public's holdings of currency do not change as the banks expand or contract demand deposits on the basis of an increase or decrease in their total reserves. It was also assumed that commercial banks have only demand deposits, no savings or time deposits, and that the deposits of the commercial banks equal the maximum amount consistent with the amount of their reserves and the existing percentage reserve requirement (in other words, that the banks hold no excess reserves). None of these assumptions is found in the real world. In practice, we find that the effect of dropping each assumption is that the increase or decrease in the amount of demand deposits and in the money supply that results from an increase or decrease in the total reserves of the commercial banks is smaller than would otherwise be the case.

The sixth part of the chapter examines the way that the three complications examined in the fifth part affect the ability of the Federal Reserve to control the money supply. The Federal Reserve's degree of control is appreciably diminished by its need to adjust to these complications.

The chapter next turns to the way in which financing the federal government's expenditures affects the money supply. First, the effect of a balanced budget is distinctly different from the effect of an unbalanced budget. Second, the effect of an unbalanced budget depends on whether the Treasury borrows the amount by which its budget is unbalanced from the public, the commercial banks, or the Federal Reserve Banks.

The concluding note to this chapter points out that for the Federal Reserve to control the money supply as closely as it can, it must sacrifice the degree of control it can otherwise exercise over interest rates. At times it chooses a closer degree of control over interest rates at the cost of a smaller degree of control over the money supply.

O n those occasions in the preceding chapters when the supply of money entered into the analysis, we simply accepted that supply as given and offered no explanation of what determined it. The present chapter will examine the question of the way in which changes in the supply of money come about. Note that, strictly speaking, there is a distinction between explaining what determines the money supply and what determines changes in the money supply. To explain why the money supply, according to the measure known as M-1B, was the absolute amount of $411.9 billion at the end of 1980 is a far more difficult task than to explain why it grew to this level from $386.9 billion one year earlier. Any explanation of why the absolute total is what it is at any date would call for a detailed historical study of the country's economic development with emphasis on the nature of its financial institutions and legislation. Our concern is with the much simpler question of what brings about changes in the total from one date to another.

Money Supply Measures

What is meant by *the supply of money?* For our purposes, the supply of money is the total dollar amount of all those things that are generally acceptable by the public in payment for goods, services, and other valuable assets and for the discharge of debts. The things that are most obviously money in this sense are currency (including coin) and demand deposits. Because checks are closely related to demand deposits, they are sometimes mistakenly identified as money. However, although demand deposits are definitely money, checks are just as definitely not money. A moment's thought shows that they are merely the device by which a transfer of a specific amount of money is made from the demand deposit of one party (person, firm, or governmental unit) to another party. It is the amount in the demand deposits of the nonbank public on any date that is to be counted as part of the money supply on that date.

For many years, currency and commercial bank demand deposits held by the public were the only assets that qualified as money according to the narrow definition of money just given. However, changes that occurred during the 1970s added some other assets to the list. These include NOW (negotiable order of withdrawal) accounts at savings and loan associations and commercial banks, ATS (automatic transfer service from savings to demand deposits) accounts, credit union share draft accounts, and demand deposit accounts at mutual savings banks. With the exception of the last mentioned, these are all technically kinds of savings deposits against which checks may be drawn either directly or indirectly. As such, because the amounts in such accounts may be used to make payment without any specific preliminary action by the depositor to convert such amounts into currency or demand deposits, balances in these accounts serve as, and must be counted as, means of payment.

Because of the appearance of these new kinds of accounts and other developments, the Federal Reserve in 1980 redefined the so-called monetary aggregates.[1] The aggregate that is equal to the sum of currency and demand deposits held by the nonbank public, previously known as M-1, is now called M-1A. This aggregate and the other items listed above (NOW and ATS accounts, share draft accounts, and demand

deposits at mutual savings banks) yield a new aggregate known as M-1B. The amounts for these two money stock measures as well as others at the end of selected years from 1960 to 1980 are shown in Table 10-1. The average annual rate of growth for each of the aggregates between the indicated years is also shown. Note that the difference between M-1A and M-1B becomes appreciable only in the 1970s.[2] Furthermore, because the assets that are added to M-1A to obtain M-1B have made up an increasing share of M-1B since 1970, the growth rate of M-1B has been above that of M-1A since then.

Because economists have a special interest in the measure that includes the total amount of deposits held by the public in a form directly usable in making payments, when one refers to the money supply without qualification, the M-1B total is now usually understood. However, to avoid certain complications one faces at various points in dealing with so heterogeneous a collection of means of payment as M-1B, we will find it convenient at such points to work with M-1A. In any event, wherever it makes a difference whether the aggregate is M-1A, M-1B, or any other, the particular one being used will be specified.

By adding to those items that are already means of payment other items that can be quickly converted into means of payment, we obtain a broader money stock measure than

---

[1]See T.D. Simpson, "The Redefined Monetary Aggregates," *Federal Reserve Bulletin,* February 1980, pp. 97–114.

---

[2]Until December 31, 1980, only depository institutions in the New England states, New York, and New Jersey were authorized to offer NOW accounts. Effective on that date, Congress extended that authority to depository institutions nationwide. Although M-1B was 5 percent greater than M-1A at the end of 1980, the difference has become substantially greater since most institutions in the other forty-two states offered and promoted NOW accounts beginning in 1981. As of April 1981, M-1B had become 17 percent greater than M-1A. For a review of the provisions of the landmark banking legislation, of which the extension of NOW accounts is only one part, see "The Depository Institutions Deregulation and Monetary Control Act of 1980," *Federal Reserve Bulletin,* June 1980, pp. 444–53 or *Economic Perspectives,* Federal Reserve Bank of Chicago, September–October 1980, an issue devoted entirely to this legislation. See also Chapters 22–24 of E.V. Bowden, *Revolution in Banking,* R.F. Dame, 1980.

TABLE 10-1
Money Stock Measures and Their Rates of Growth,
Selected Years, 1960—80
(billions of dollars)

December	M-1A Amount	M-1A Percent Rate of Growth	M-1B Amount	M-1B Percent Rate of Growth	M-2 Amount	M-2 Percent Rate of Growth	M-3 Amount	M-3 Percent Rate of Growth	L Amount	L Percent Rate of Growth
1960	$141.6		$141.6		$ 311.2		$ 313.3		$ 402.5	
1965	168.7	3.5	168.8	3.5	457.2	7.9	478.5	8.8	582.3	7.6
1970	215.3	4.9	215.4	4.9	625.2	6.4	671.7	7.0	812.5	6.8
1975	287.9	5.9	289.0	6.0	1022.4	10.3	1161.0	13.2	1369.6	11.0
1976	305.0	5.9	307.7	6.5	1166.7	14.1	1299.7	11.9	1523.5	11.2
1977	328.4	7.7	332.5	8.1	1294.1	10.9	1460.3	12.4	1720.2	12.9
1978	351.6	7.1	359.9	8.2	1401.5	8.3	1623.6	11.2	1934.9	12.5
1979	369.8	5.2	386.9	7.5	1526.0	8.9	1775.5	9.4	2151.8	11.2
1980	384.8	4.1	411.9	6.5	1673.4	9.7	1957.9	10.3	2373.5	10.3

Note: Dollar amounts are averages of daily figures, not seasonally adjusted.

SOURCE: Dollar amounts from Board of Governors of the Federal Reserve System; growth rates computed by author.

M-1B. The Federal Reserve defines M-2 as the sum of M-1B plus regular savings deposits and small denomination (less than $100,000) time deposits at all depository institutions. Such deposits can be immediately converted into currency or demand deposits (or another component of M-1B), although in the case of time deposits only by suffering a substantial interest penalty. M-2 also includes several other things, the most important being money market mutual fund shares. The volume of these shares grew very rapidly during the high interest rate period from 1979 to mid-1980 and again during the early months of 1981. On as little as $500, people could earn much higher interest rates by buying shares in these funds than were obtainable at depository institutions. The funds in turn purchased large-denomination certificates of deposit issued by commercial banks, commercial paper, Treasury bills, and other short-term obligations with high interest yields.

Yet another money stock measure, M-3, is obtained by adding to M-2 several other items, the most important being large-denomination ($100,000 or more) deposits at all depository institutions. A final measure, designated L, is obtained by adding to M-3 other liquid assets such as bankers acceptances, commercial paper, Treasury bills and other liquid Treasury securities, and U.S. savings bonds held by the public.

As noted above, we will generally work with the narrowest money supply measure, M-1A. Although the reason for focusing on M-1A is to avoid certain complications from working with a broader measure, it is still essential to pay attention to what is happening to the other measures of the money supply. Aggregate spending depends not only on the public's holdings of M-1A and M-1B, but on the amount held in the form of other assets added to M-1B to obtain M-2 (assets only one step removed from M-1B). For this reason, anyone who tries to make predictions about aggregate spending by looking at what is happening to the "money supply" finds it necessary to look not only at changes in M-1B, but at changes in M-2—and for that matter, M-3 and L as well. Although difficult questions arise when we attempt to evaluate the influence on spending of changes in the amounts shown by the different money stock measures, we will get a better view by doing this as thoroughly as possible than we would if we looked no further than M-1A and M-1B.

Although this last statement is clearly true, the question of what determines the money supply is ordinarily posed in terms of M-1B or, again to avoid unnecessary complications, in terms of M-1A. In other words, the usual point of departure is to explain what determines the amount of currency and commercial bank demand deposits held by the public. As we will see, this amount depends on actions taken by the Federal Reserve, the commercial banks, and the public. For an obvious example, M-1A will be smaller, other things being equal, to the degree that the public chooses to hold more of its assets in time deposits and less in demand deposits. For a less obvious example, M-1A will be smaller, other things being equal, to the degree that the commercial banks choose to hold excess reserves. As will be covered in the following pages, the decisions of commercial banks, the public, and—most importantly—the Federal Reserve, determine how M-1A changes from time to time.

The Federal Reserve, Bank Reserves, and Demand Deposits

With the narrowly defined money supply, here simply designated as M, equal to the sum of currency, C, and demand deposits, DD, held by the public,

it is apparent that we cannot explain what determines the amount of M on any date without first explaining what determines the amounts of C and DD.[3] The amount of C on any date is the amount the public chooses to hold: The public can, without restriction and without delay, switch out of DD into C or out of C into DD. However, the public does not control what the *total* of C plus DD—that is, M—will be, and therefore it does not have control over what DD will be (except to the minor degree that results from deposits to and withdrawals from its demand deposits). Therefore, the first step in explaining what determines M is to explain what determines DD.

We begin by assuming that the public is holding the amount of currency it wishes to hold and that this amount temporarily remains fixed. For simplicity, we also initially assume that the only deposits the public holds are demand deposits. Given these assumptions, what then determines the amount of DD on the books of the commercial banking system as of any date? The actual amount may at any time be less than the maximum amount, but we first identify what the maximum amount will be. That amount depends on two things—the dollar amount of reserves held by the banks and the size of the percentage reserve requirement imposed on the banks' demand deposits by the Federal Reserve.

Table 10-2 is an abbreviated balance sheet for a hypothetical commercial banking system which has the maximum amount of demand deposits consistent with its dollar amount of reserves and with an assumed percentage reserve requirement of 20. Actual reserves of $25 billion

---

[3]There is more than one possible approach to explaining the determination of the money supply, and there is almost no limit to the number of complications that can be taken into account in whatever approach is taken. The number of complications in the approach taken here is held to a minimum consistent with a meaningful explanation. For more complete explanations, see J.T. Boorman and T.M. Havrilesky, *Money Supply, Money Demand, and Macroeconomic Models,* Allyn and Bacon, 1972, Ch. 1, and A.E. Burger, *The Money Supply Process,* Wadsworth, 1971. See also L.C. Andersen, "Three Approaches to Money Stock Determination," *Review,* Federal Reserve Bank of St. Louis, October 1967, pp. 6–13.

TABLE 10-2
Balance Sheet: All Commercial Banks
(hypothetical figures in billions)

Assets		Liabilities and Capital Accounts	
Reserves	$ 25	Demand Deposits	$125
Loans and Securities	105	Non-deposit Liabilities	15
Other Assets	20	Capital Accounts	10
Total Assets	$150	Total Liabilities and Capital Accounts	$150

are just equal to the required reserves of $25 billion or to 20 percent of demand deposits of $125 billion. Under these conditions, the commercial banks as a group are said to be "loaned up" or that they can support no more than the existing $125 billion amount of demand deposits now on the books. In other words, given the dollar amount of reserves and the percentage reserve requirement, the upper limit to the demand deposit component of the money supply is $125 billion.

Only two assets held by commercial banks qualify as reserves—the currency in their vaults and their deposits with the Federal Reserve Banks.[4] As we will see, the Federal Reserve can

[4]Prior to the implementation of the Depository Institutions Deregulation and Monetary Control Act of 1980, banks that were not member banks of the Federal Reserve System were subject to reserve requirements set by the various state governments. Under this act, the system of reserve requirements is now in a transition that will not end until 1988. So-called transaction accounts (in brief, accounts in which amounts are subject to transfer by "check" or its equivalent) in *all* commercial banks and other financial institutions (including savings and loan associations and credit unions) have become subject to uniform reserve requirements set by the Federal Reserve under which required reserves must be held in the form of vault cash or deposits with Federal Reserve Banks. However, these requirements—which are significantly lower than those previously applied to member banks alone—are being phased in gradually over a four-year period for member banks and an eight-year period for others. In this chapter, our attention is limited to transaction accounts of commercial banks or to their demand deposits; for simplicity we assume that all commercial banks are currently subject to the same percentage reserve requirements.

control the total dollar amount of these two assets held by the commercial banks. With this power over the amount of these assets plus the power to set the minimum percentage of the demand deposit liabilities that the banks must hold in the form of these two assets, the Federal Reserve determines the maximum amount of demand deposits that can be outstanding for any time period.

If the outstanding amount of demand deposits is at its maximum, the following equation will be satisfied:

$$R = r_D DD$$

Here R is the dollar amount of reserves and r_D is the percentage reserve requirement against demand deposits. In the previous illustration we found

$$\$25 \text{ billion} = 0.20 \cdot \$125 \text{ billion}$$

All of the reserves are absorbed in meeting the requirement for the existing amount of demand deposits. We may rewrite this equation to show that DD depends on R and r_D by dividing both sides by r_D:

$$DD = \frac{R}{r_D}$$

In this form, the maximum amount of DD is immediately identified for any combination of values for R and r_D. For the same r_D of 0.20 but a different R of $24 billion, DD will be $120 billion; or for R of $25 billion but r_D of 0.25, DD will be $100 billion; or for R of $24 billion and r_D of 0.25, DD will be $96 billion.

The preceding equation may also be written as follows:

$$DD = (1/r_D)R$$

Here $(1/r_D)$—the reciprocal of the percentage reserve requirement—is called the *deposit expansion multiplier*. We determine the deposit expansion mutliplier from the value of r_D, and we determine the maximum amount of DD the banking system can support with any given amount of R by applying that multiplier to R.

Because $R = r_D DD$, it follows for any given value of r_D that

$$\Delta R = r_D \Delta DD$$

Dividing through by r_D and rearranging gives us

$$\Delta DD = (1/r_D)\Delta R$$

This is the maximum change in DD that will result from any change in R, assuming no change in r_D. The maximum change in DD that will result from any change in r_D, assuming no change in R, is calculated as follows:

$$\Delta DD = R\Delta(1/r_D)$$

To understand the full meaning of these equations, suppose now that the Federal Reserve takes actions to increase R by $100 million, but leaves the percentage reserve requirement unchanged. If that requirement happened to be 20 percent and if the banks as a group already had on their books the maximum amount of DD consistent with the preexisting amount of R, the maximum increase in DD is found by substitution:

$$\Delta DD = (1/r_D)\Delta R$$
$$\Delta DD = (1/0.20)\$100 \text{ million}$$
$$\Delta DD = \$500 \text{ million}$$

Given the same assumptions, if the Federal Reserve were to take actions to reduce R by $100 million, the result would be $\Delta DD = -\$500$ million.

To look at the case in which the Federal Reserve changes r_D but leaves R unchanged, assume r_D is cut from 0.20 to 0.19 at a time when

$R = \$25$ billion. A change in $1/r_D$ from $1/0.20$ to $1/0.19$ or from 5.0 to 5.263 means that $\Delta(1/r_D) = 0.263$. Again, the increase in DD is found by substitution:

$$\Delta DD = R \cdot \Delta(1/r_D)$$
$$\Delta DD = \$25 \text{ billion} \cdot 0.263$$
$$\Delta DD = \$6.575 \text{ billion}$$

Given the same assumptions, if the Federal Reserve were to raise the percentage reserve requirement from 20 to 21, $1/r_D$ would decline from 5.0 to 4.762 and Δr_D would be -0.238. With R of $25 billion, the result would be $\Delta DD = \$25$ billion $(-0.238) = -\$5.95$ billion.

The Instruments of Monetary Control

The changes in DD shown by the equations for changes in R and r_D are the end product of a process that works itself out as the commercial banks adjust to changes in the dollar amount of their reserves or to changes in their percentage reserve requirements. Before examining that adjustment process, we will look briefly at the instruments the Federal Reserve employs to produce changes in the reserve positions of the commercial banks. In its attempt to stabilize the economy by increasing or decreasing the money supply (via deposits), the Federal Reserve relies primarily on instruments that produce changes in R. We first will look at these instruments and then at the less frequently used instrument that produces changes in DD by varying r_D and therefore the deposit expansion multiplier.

Open-Market Operations

By far the most important instrument in the hands of the Federal Reserve is the *open-market operation*—the purchase and sale by the Federal Reserve Banks (all transactions are actually carried out by the Federal Reserve Bank of New York) of U.S. government securities in the so-called open market. These transactions are carried out between the Federal Reserve and sev-

TABLE 10-3
Balance Sheet Changes for Federal Reserve Open-Market Operations
(millions of dollars)

A: The Federal Reserve purchases securities:

Federal Reserve Banks

Assets		Liabilities and Capital Accounts	
U.S. Government Securities	+$100	Deposits of Commercial Banks	+$100

Commercial Banks

Assets		Liabilities and Capital Accounts	
Deposits at Federal Reserve Banks	+$100	Demand Deposits	+$100

B: The Federal Reserve sells securities:

Federal Reserve Banks

Assets		Liabilities and Capital Accounts	
U.S. Government Securities	−$100	Deposits of Commercial Banks	−$100

Commercial Banks

Assets		Liabilities and Capital Accounts	
Deposits at Federal Reserve Banks	−$100	Demand Deposits	−$100

eral dozen dealers in U.S. government securities. These dealers, in turn, sell to and buy from thousands of other members of the public who are active in the government securities market.

Part A of Table 10-3 shows the results of a purchase by the Federal Reserve of $100 million worth of U.S. government securities from dealers. The dealers receive checks in the amount of $100 million drawn against the buying Federal Reserve Bank and deposit them in their demand deposit accounts at commercial banks. The commercial banks send the checks to the Federal Reserve Banks for payment, which is made in the form of a $100 million addition to their deposit balances at the Federal Reserve Banks. The immediate results are a $100 million increase in M—the +$100 million of demand deposits is an increase in total DD of that amount—and a $100 million increase in the reserves of the com-

mercial banks. The public, which includes the securities dealers, shows a change in the composition of its assets: $100 million less of securities and $100 million more of demand deposits. Note that the Federal Reserve will always find dealers ready to sell, because it will bid up the price it is willing to pay by whatever amount is required to induce sales.

As a result of this $100 million open-market operation, the Federal Reserve has directly increased demand deposits, the money supply, and bank reserves by $100 million. Later in the chapter, we will look at the way in which an increase in reserves will lead to a further increase in the amount of DD and therefore an increase in M beyond the increase initially produced.

The Federal Reserve may use open-market purchases to supply the commercial banks with additional reserves when it deems such action to be appropriate, but it may use open-market sales to deprive the commercial banks of some of their reserves when it deems that to be appropriate. As shown in Part B of Table 10-3, an open market sale of $100 million worth of U.S. government securities by the Federal Reserve will have exactly the opposite effects of a $100 million purchase. The entries in the second half of the table are identical with those in Part A except that the signs accompanying each dollar amount are now reversed. The selling Federal Reserve Bank now receives checks drawn by the buying dealers against their accounts in the commercial banks. The $100 million will be deducted from the commercial bank deposits at the Federal Reserve Banks, and the commercial banks will deduct the $100 million from the demand deposits of those who wrote the checks. The public—which includes the dealers who bought the securities—will show a change in the composition of its assets: $100 million more of securities and $100 million less of demand deposits. Note that the Federal Reserve will always find dealers ready to buy, because it will cut its selling price by whatever amount is needed to attract buyers.

As a result of this operation, the Federal Reserve has directly decreased demand deposits, the money supply, and bank reserves by $100 million. Later in the chapter, we will look at the way in which a decrease in reserves will lead to a further decrease in the amount of *DD* and therefore a decrease in *M* beyond the decrease initially produced.

Changes in the Discount Rate

The Federal Reserve may also increase or decrease the amount of reserves held by the commercial banks by increasing or decreasing the dollar amount of loans provided to the commercial banks. Assume, for example, a $10 million increase in the amount of such loans that the borrowing banks take in the form of $10 million added to their deposit balances at the Federal

Reserve Banks. The statements of the Federal Reserve Banks and commercial banks will be changed as shown in Part A of Table 10-4. The Federal Reserve Banks have acquired an additional $10 million of promissory notes from the borrowing banks and have paid for these assets by creating $10 million more of deposit liabilities. The commercial banks have enlarged their total reserves by $10 million, but they have also incurred additional indebtedness of $10 million. Note that this transaction is between the Federal Reserve Banks and the commercial banks only; it does not in itself affect the balance sheet of the public. There is a $10 million increase in commercial bank reserves, but at this point the demand deposits held by the public have not changed. Later in this chapter, we will look at other changes that may follow from the change in total reserves.

Part B of Table 10-4 shows the repayment to the Federal Reserve Banks by the commercial banks of $10 million of loans. It is the same as the top half of the table except that all of the signs are now negative instead of positive. In repaying $10 million of loans, the commercial banks suffer a $10 million reduction in their deposit balances at the Federal Reserve Banks, but this is matched by a $10 million reduction in the amount owed to the Federal Reserve Banks. As we will see later, this reduction in reserves may in turn lead to other changes.

Unlike open-market operations for which the initiative rests entirely with the Federal Reserve, the initiative to borrow from the Federal Reserve Banks rests with the commercial banks. Because every dollar borrowed is a dollar of additional reserves, the Federal Reserve must obviously ensure that the amount of borrowing is kept within control. The principal control device is the interest rate the Federal Reserve Banks charge on loans, popularly known as the discount rate. If a large spread exists between the discount rate and other interest rates—for example, the yield on U.S. Treasury bills—the commercial banks have a strong profit incentive to borrow from the Federal Reserve Banks in order to put the funds

TABLE 10-4
Balance Sheet Changes for Federal Reserve Lending to Commercial Banks
(millions of dollars)

A: Commercial banks obtain loans:

Federal Reserve Banks

Assets		Liabilities and Capital Accounts	
Loans	+$10	Deposits of commercial banks	+$10

Commercial Banks

Assets		Liabilities and Capital Accounts	
Deposits at Federal Reserve Banks	+$10	Loans payable	+$10

B: Commercial banks repay loans:

Federal Reserve Banks

Assets		Liabilities and Capital Accounts	
Loans	−$10	Deposits of commercial banks	−$10

Commercial Banks

Assets		Liabilities and Capital Accounts	
Deposits at Federal Reserve Banks	−$10	Loans payable	−$10

out at the higher rate. The Federal Reserve discourages borrowing for this purpose; it is not deemed an appropriate use of the "discount window." In an effort to control the problem that would otherwise develop, the Federal Reserve raises the discount rate as necessary to prevent the development of too high a spread between the discount rate and other interest rates at times when other interest rates are rising.

However, given the way the Federal Reserve operates, the level of the discount rate, even when it rises as high as the 13 percent figure reached in 1980 and the 14 percent peak in 1981, is typically below the interest rates commercial banks can earn on various uses of funds. Therefore, if the Federal Reserve is to maintain control over bank reserves, it cannot stand ready to lend any amount commercial banks may want to bor-

row at the existing discount rate. The Federal Reserve lays down certain "nonprice" conditions that borrowing banks must meet. In general, the discount window is open to banks that must meet unforeseen problems such as a sudden withdrawal of currency or seasonal demands for loans beyond those that can reasonably be met with the banks' own resources. Because it is not always easy to determine whether or not a loan request arises for appropriate reasons, Federal Reserve Bank loan officers maintain surveillance over borrowing banks in an effort to restrict borrowing for inappropriate purposes. By varying the discount rate so that it closely parallels short-term market interest rates, the problem of surveillance is reduced, because the incentive for commercial banks to borrow in order to profit by relending is not as strong as it otherwise would be.

Changes in Percentage Reserve Requirements

Unlike open-market operations and changes in the discount rate, changes in percentage reserve requirements do not affect the amount of reserves, but alter the amount of demand deposits that each dollar of reserves can support. In other words, its use changes the deposit expansion multiplier. A dollar of R will support $5 of DD if r_D = 0.20, because r_D of 0.20 yields a multiplier of 5 or 1/0.20 = 5. A dollar of R will support a larger or smaller number of dollars of DD at a lower or higher value for r_D, respectively. As we saw in the earlier illustration, if total reserves are $25 billion, a cut in r_D from 20 to 19 percent will raise the previous maximum for DD by $6.575 billion; a hike in r_D from 20 to 21 percent will reduce the previous maximum for DD by $5.9 billion.

The Federal Reserve has seldom used changes in percentage reserve requirements in recent years. The last change was made at the end of 1976. There are various reasons for the minor role played by this instrument, one of which is suggested by our last illustration. Changes of even 0.25 percentage points—the authorities prefer not to make changes smaller than this—can change the money supply by several billion dollars. Declining membership in the Federal Reserve System had also been an important problem until 1980, when Congress empowered the Federal Reserve to take corrective action. From mid-1955 to mid-1978, member banks as a percentage of all commercial banks declined from 48 to 38; member bank deposits as a percentage of all commercial bank deposits declined from 85 to 72. The major reason for this exodus from membership was that member banks were subject to relatively higher percentage reserve requirements. Commercial banks, like other businesses, seek profits. Reserves of member banks are entirely nonearning assets. A higher percentage reserve requirement means that a larger fraction of these banks' total assets must be held in nonearning form. By relinquishing their membership, the banks could maintain a larger fraction of their total assets in earning form. Since the fifties, an increasing number of banks had believed that this gain was greater than the loss of the Federal Reserve services available to members.

Under the Depository Institutions Deregulation and Monetary Control Act passed by Congress in 1980, the Federal Reserve has taken action that will result in uniform percentage reserve requirements for all commercial banks at the end of a transition period. The same requirements also apply to nonbank financial institutions having nondemand deposit accounts such as NOW accounts that are transferable by the equivalent of checks. The 1980 act also gave the Federal Reserve substantial new powers. For example, now it may set reserve requirements at any level it considers necessary for up to 180 days under what it regards as extraordinary circumstances. Previously the Federal Reserve was limited to percentage reserve requirement changes within a specified range.

Although the Federal Reserve need no longer fear the loss of memberships from a rise in percentage reserve requirements, it is hard to say what use it will make of this instrument. Most economists working in this area agree that under practically all circumstances the Federal Reserve can effectively control the money supply without relying on changes in percentage reserve requirements. Its other tools are adequate for the job. In fact, according to some economists, open-market operations alone are sufficient. Whether the fact that it can now adopt higher percentage reserve requirements without losing members will lead it to make greater use of this instrument is something only time will tell.

Deposit Expansion and Contraction: The Basic Process

By the use of its instruments of control, primarily open-market operations, the Federal Reserve can increase or decrease the amount of reserves to the degree required to expand or contract the money supply by whatever amount it deems appropriate at the time. Given a 20 percent reserve requirement, $100 million added to reserves permits a $500 million expansion of demand deposits, whereas $100 million taken away from reserves forces a $500 million contraction of demand deposits, other things being equal. We will now examine the essentials of the process by which such expansion and contraction occurs. The assumptions made earlier remain in effect: The amount of currency held by the public does not change; the banks have only demand deposits; and the indicated change in demand deposits is not necessarily the actual change, but the maximum change possible for any given change in reserves. The expansion process will be explained first in some detail; the contraction process, which is almost exactly the reverse of the expansion process, will then be described in brief form.

Deposit Expansion

An open-market purchase of securities by the Federal Reserve will result in an increase in reserves that is gradually spread out among the thousands of banks in our system. As this occurs, the banks take actions that result in an increase in demand deposits equal to a multiple of the increase in reserves. To see how this process takes place, assume that before the process begins all banks have reserves exactly equal to the amount needed to meet the percentage reserve requirement against their demand deposits—that is, total reserves and required reserves are equal. Before going further, it is necessary to introduce another very important reserve concept: excess reserves. For an individual commercial bank as well as for all commercial banks combined, excess reserves are simply the amount derived by subtracting required reserves from actual reserves. The hypothetical balance sheet for all commercial banks in Table 10-2 shows actual reserves of $25 billion and demand deposits

of $125 billion. Assuming a 20 percent reserve requirement, required reserves are $25 billion; therefore, actual reserves of $25 billion minus required reserves of $25 billion equal excess reserves of zero. Required reserves can be less than or greater than actual reserves—that is, there may be (positive) excess reserves or (negative) deficient reserves.

A hypothetical balance sheet for one of the many banks in the system, Bank A, is shown in Table 10-5. For the convenience of working with small numbers, assume that the Federal Reserve Bank of New York purchases $1,000 worth of U.S. government securities in the open market from a securities dealer. The dealer, whose checking account is at Bank A, will deposit the $1,000 check received from the Federal Reserve Bank and Bank A will send the check to its Federal Reserve Bank for payment in the form of a credit to its account. As a result of this transaction, Bank A's balance sheet will be changed as shown by the entries marked (a) under Bank A's T-account in Table 10-6. We will refer to statements like those in Table 10-6 that show *changes* in the balance sheet as T-accounts.

Both the bank's demand deposit liabilities and its assets in the form of reserves have increased by $1,000. These increases may be broken down into an increase in required reserves of $200 (20 percent of the $1,000 increase in demand deposits) and an increase in excess reserves of $800 (or a rise from zero to $800). Note that at this point the money supply increases by $1,000 because the new $1,000 in demand deposits is offset neither by a decrease in demand deposits in any other bank nor by a decrease in the public's holdings of currency. The open-market purchase by the Federal Reserve of $1,000 worth of U.S. government securities from the public in and of itself is initially matched by a $1,000 increase in demand deposits and therefore a $1,000 increase in the money supply.

In the normal course of events, this initial increase of $1,000 in the money supply will be followed by a further increase as Bank A expands credit on the basis of its excess reserves. *An*

TABLE 10-5
Balance Sheet
Bank A
Dec. 31, 1981

Assets		Liabilities and Capital Accounts	
Reserves	$ 2,000,000	Demand Deposits	$10,000,000
Loans	5,000,000	Other Liabilities	1,500,000
Securities	3,000,000	Capital Accounts	500,000
Other Assets	2,000,000	Liabilities plus	
Total Assets	$12,000,000	Capital Accounts	$12,000,000

TABLE 10-6
Multiple Expansion of Demand Deposits: First Three Banks

Bank A

Assets			Liabilities and Capital Accounts		
Reserves	+$1,000	(a)	Demand Deposits	+$1,000	(a)
	− 800	(c)		+ 800	(b)
Loans	+ 800	(b)		− 800	(c)
net changes			net changes		
Reserves	+$ 200		Demand Deposits	+$1,000	
Loans	+ 800				

Bank B

Assets			Liabilities and Capital Accounts		
Reserves	+$ 800	(c)	Demand Deposits	+$ 800	(c)
	− 640	(e)		+ 640	(d)
Loans	+ 640	(d)		− 640	(e)
net changes			net changes		
Reserves	+$ 160		Demand Deposits	+$ 800	
Loans	+ 640				

Bank C

Assets			Liabilities and Capital Accounts		
Reserves	+ $ 640	(e)	Demand Deposits	+ $ 640	(e)
	− 512	(g)		+ 512	(f)
Loans	+ 512	(f)		− 512	(g)
net changes			net changes		
Reserves	+ $ 128		Demand Deposits	+ $ 640	
Loans	+ 512				

individual commercial bank may add to its holdings of loans and securities an amount no greater than the amount of its excess reserves. Assume that Bank A makes a loan for $800 to a customer who, as is customary, takes the $800 by having the bank credit that amount to her checking account at Bank A. As shown by the (b) entries in Bank A's T-account in Table 10-6, both loans and demand deposits have increased by $800. Note that at this point the money supply has been increased further, this time by $800, as a result of this loan transaction. The $800 added to Bank A's demand deposits is offset neither by a decrease in demand deposits in other banks nor by a decrease in the public's currency holdings.

Because interest must be paid on loans, no one borrows merely to let the loan proceeds remain idle in a checking account. The borrower will probably quite promptly write a check for $800 in payment of a bill, for the purchase of goods, or for some other purpose. That check will be received by a firm or person who probably has a checking account in a different bank, given the very large number of banks in the U.S. system. Assume that the recipient of this check deals with Bank B and accordingly deposits the check there. Assume also that Bank B collects from Bank A through the check clearing facilities of the Federal Reserve Banks with the result that Bank B has $800 added to its balance at a Federal Reserve Bank and Bank A has $800 deducted from its balance at a Federal Reserve Bank. The Federal Reserve Bank returns the check to Bank A, which deducts $800 from the balance of the borrower. Consequently, the (c) entries of Bank A's statement show decreases in both reserves and demand deposits of $800.

The net changes in Bank A's balance sheet as a result of the full series of transactions shown in its T-account are indicated at the bottom of that T-account. Bank A has additional liabilities in the form of an increase in demand deposits of $1,000 and additional assets in the form of an increase in reserves of $200 and an increase in loans of $800. Remember that Bank A had exactly the amount of reserves needed to meet its reserve

requirements before it obtained the $1,000 of additional deposits and the $1,000 of additional reserves through the Federal Reserve Bank's open-market operation. After the series of transactions shown, this is again true. If we updated Table 10-5, now its total deposits would be $10,001,000 and its total reserves would be $2,000,200—the minimum needed to meet its 20 percent reserve requirement. Bank A is "loaned up," as it was before the process began.

The basis for the rule that an individual commercial bank can add to its holdings of loans and securities an amount no greater than the amount of its excess reserves may be seen by noting the predicament Bank A would find itself in if it had violated this rule. Suppose it had made a loan of $900, thereby adding $900 to its demand deposits, and shortly thereafter had lost $900 of reserves to Bank B when that bank collected the check received from one of its customers who, in turn, had received it from the borrower at Bank A. The net changes in Bank A's balance sheet would then have been +$100 in reserves and +$900 in loans on the assets side and +$1,000 in demand deposits on the liabilities side. Before these changes, Bank A had zero excess reserves; after these changes, it would have negative excess reserves or a reserve deficiency of $100. (Total demand deposits would be $10,001,000 and total reserves would be $2,000,100; but required reserves would be $2,000,200, $100 more than actual reserves.) Clearly, the rule holds: Bank A could increase its loans at the maximum by $800.[5]

Returning now to the case in which Bank A does limit itself to the maximum of an $800 increase in loans, the $800 in demand deposits

---

[5] An individual bank could violate the rule without running into a reserve deficiency only if some portion of the dollar amount of checks written against the deposits created by its additional loans is received by firms and persons who have their accounts with that bank. That bank will not lose reserves equal to the amount of the newly created deposits, and therefore may increase loans and create deposits in an amount somewhat larger than its excess reserves.

that Bank A thereby creates is lost by Bank A, but not by the banking system; the $800 now appears as an addition to the deposits of Bank B. Bank B in gaining $800 of deposits previously in Bank A also gains $800 of reserves. These changes are shown by the (c) entries in Bank B's T-account in Table 10-6. Accompanying the $800 increase in its demand deposits is a $160 increase in its required reserves. Its excess reserves, which had been zero, are now $800 − $160, or $640. Bank B may now make loans in the amount of $640, thereby creating new demand deposits in that amount as shown by the (d) entries in Bank B's T-account. At this point, another $640 has been added to the money supply, because this is a net addition to the public's holdings of demand deposits and there has been no change in its holdings of currency.

We next assume that the borrower of the $640 writes a check against his account and that this check is received by a firm or person who deals with a different bank, Bank C. When that check is collected by Bank C, Bank B's reserves and its demand deposits both decrease by $640, as shown by the (e) entries in Bank B's T-account. The $640 of new demand deposits created through Bank B's loan of that amount is lost by Bank B, but appears as an addition to Bank C's demand deposits. The net changes in Bank B's balance sheet are shown at the bottom of that bank's T-account.

As shown by the (e) entries in Bank C's T-account, that bank now has gained $640 of additional demand deposits and $640 of additional reserves, of which $512 are excess reserves. Repeating the process already traced for Banks A and B yields the net changes in Bank C's balance sheet shown at the bottom of that bank's T-account in Table 10-6.

The first few lines of Table 10-7 bring together the net changes in the balance sheets of Banks A, B, and C. On the liabilities side, these three banks show a combined increase in demand deposits of $2,440, which is also that much of an increase in the money supply; on the assets side, they show an increase in reserves of $488 (equal to 20 percent of the increase in demand deposits of $2,440) and an increase in loans of $1,952. Of the $2,440 increase in demand deposits, the $1,000 at Bank A came into being as the direct result of the Federal Reserve Bank's purchase of $1,000 of securities in the open market, the $800 at Bank B as a result of Bank A's increase in loans of $800 (which was at first matched by an $800 increase in demand deposits at Bank A, followed by a loss of that amount in demand deposits to Bank B), and the $640 at Bank C as a result of Bank B's increase in loans of $640 (which was at first matched by a $640 increase in demand deposits at Bank B, followed by a loss of that amount to Bank C). As we have seen, each bank's ability to expand its loans depends on its

TABLE 10-7
Multiple Expansion of Demand Deposits: All Banks

	Assets		Liabilities and Capital Accounts
	Reserves	Loans	Demand Deposits
Bank A	+$ 200	+$ 800	+$1,000
Bank B	+ 160	+ 640	+ 800
Bank C	+ 128	+ 512	+ 640
Total—Banks A–C	+$ 488	+$1,952	+$2,440
Total—All Other Banks	+$ 512	+$2,048	+$2,560
Grand Total—All Banks	+$1,000	+$4,000	+$5,000

having acquired excess reserves; the initial provision of excess reserves of $800 to Bank A follows from the Federal Reserve Bank's purchase of $1,000 of securities from a securities dealer.

The transactions shown for Banks A, B, and C in Table 10-7 are repeated by Banks D, E, F, and so on. Consequently, loans and demand deposits expand even further. In Table 10-7, the totals for all banks beyond Banks A, B, and C are shown in the row labeled "Total—All Other Banks." The grand totals for all banks when the expansion process is fully worked out are shown on the last line. In this line we have the results which we can obtain quite easily from the equation: $\Delta DD = (1/r_D)\Delta R$. With $r_D = 0.20$, the deposit multiplier is 5; and with $\Delta R = \$1,000$, ΔDD is $5,000. The equation yields the value for ΔDD in one step; the preceding pages have shown through a series of steps how this total is generated by the lending actions of the many banks in the system.

Before leaving this part of the analysis, note that the change in both demand deposits and the money supply would have been the same if the banks had elected to expand credit by purchasing securities instead of by making loans. Bank A could have increased its security holdings by the amount of its excess reserves ($800) and in so doing would have lost that amount of reserves to another bank, which in turn could have increased its security holdings by the amount of its excess reserves ($640) and in so doing would have lost that amount of reserves to another bank—and so forth through the system. When the process was fully worked out, the final numbers would have been the same as those in the last line of Table 10-7 except that the $4,000 figure would refer to a change in security holdings instead of a change in loans. Finally, although the credit expansion could be made through loans or purchases of securities, it could also be made through a combination of each.

Deposit Contraction

Whereas an initial increase in reserves in a commercial banking system with no excess reserves sets into motion a process that culminates in an increase in demand deposits equal to a multiple of that increase in reserves, a decrease in reserves will set into motion a process that culminates in a decrease in demand deposits equal to a multiple of that decrease in reserves. Because the contraction process is almost exactly the reverse of the expansion process just explained, we need not describe it in detail.

To see the essentials, we start off with an open-market *sale* of $1,000 of U.S. government securities by a Federal Reserve Bank to a dealer. The dealer will pay the Federal Reserve Bank with a $1,000 check drawn against a demand deposit at Bank A; that check will be collected by deducting $1,000 from the deposit balance of Bank A at its Federal Reserve Bank. Bank A shows a decrease in reserves of $1,000, a decrease in demand deposits of $1,000, and therefore a reserve deficiency of $800 (all commercial banks are assumed to have zero excess reserves at the outset).

There are various ways in which Bank A could remove the deficiency, including the possibility of an $800 loan from its Federal Reserve Bank. However, that will meet the problem only temporarily. Barring an inflow of deposits, Bank A will have to reduce its earning assets. Suppose it sells $800 of securities to a buyer who happens to have a demand deposit at Bank B. Then Bank A will take away $800 of reserves from Bank B, and Bank A's reserve deficiency is no more. But now Bank B will have a reserve deficiency of $640, because its deposits and reserves will both have decreased by $800. Bank B may meet its deficiency by selling $640 of securities to a buyer who happens to have a demand deposit at Bank C.

The story is familiar by now. As this process is worked out to its end, the demand deposits for all commercial banks combined will decrease by $5,000. The commercial banks as a group have adjusted to the $1,000 decrease in their total reserves through a $5,000 decrease in demand deposits which reduces required reserves by

$1,000—an amount equal to the decrease in total reserves effected by the Federal Reserve's open-market sale. Both actual and required reserves are reduced by $1,000, so they are once again equal. In adjusting to the decrease in reserves, the commercial banks have reduced their holdings of securities by $4,000 (starting with Bank A's reduction of $800). The net changes for all commercial banks combined will be, on the assets side, a decrease in reserves of $1,000 and a decrease in securities of $4,000, and, on the liabilities side, a decrease in demand deposits of $5,000.

As previously noted, the expansion process in which a $1,000 increase in reserves is the basis for a $5,000 increase in demand deposits cannot occur in only one bank in a multi-bank system. However, the corresponding contraction process could occur in only one bank. In the previous illustration, Bank A initially lost $1,000 of reserves and $1,000 of demand deposits due to the Federal Reserve Bank's open-market sale, and it therefore had an $800 reserve deficiency. If Bank A were to try to remove that deficiency by reducing loans, it would probably have to reduce its loans by $4,000. Because most of Bank A's loans will be to borrowers who have their demand deposits at Bank A, these borrowers will probably draw down their deposits in repaying loans. In this special case, the full brunt of the contraction is borne by the single bank. The changes will be, on the assets side, a decrease in reserves of $1,000 and a decrease in loans of $4,000, and, on the liabilities side, a decrease of demand deposits of $5,000.

As we saw before, these results for the contraction case are obtained quite easily from the following equation:

$$\Delta DD = (1/r_D)\Delta R$$

With $r_D = 0.20$, the deposit multiplier is 5; and with $\Delta R = -\$1,000$, ΔDD is $-\$5,000$. What the equation shows in one step has been briefly described as a series of steps.

Deposit Expansion and Contraction: Three Complications

In the simplest possible case of deposit expansion and contraction to which our attention has so far been limited, the change in the money supply that results from a change in reserves (or from a change in the percentage reserve requirement) is equal to ΔDD—the assumption being that the public's holdings of currency do not change. However, in practice, these holdings do change; the public varies its holdings of currency as its holdings or demand deposits vary. This means the change in the money supply that results from a given change in reserves cannot be determined until we allow for the way in which changes in currency holdings vary with changes in demand deposits. This is the first complication that we will consider.

The assumption in the simplest case is that commercial banks have only demand deposits, no savings or time deposits (which will here be combined and referred to as time deposits). However, a second complication arises from the fact that they actually do have time deposits and that they are subject to percentage reserve requirements against some time deposits. Under the Monetary Control Act of 1980, the Federal Reserve has the power to abolish reserve requirements against all time deposits, but at present it does impose a requirement against time deposits other than those of individuals. To the degree that a portion of any increase in reserves is absorbed in backing up an increase in nonpersonal time deposits, that portion is not available to back up an increase in demand deposits. With the money supply defined as the sum of currency and demand deposits, the increase in the money supply that results from a given increase in reserves will be smaller to the degree that a portion of that increase in reserves is absorbed in supporting an increase in time deposits. Similarly, the decrease in the money supply that results from a decrease in reserves will be smaller to the degree that a decrease in time deposits releases reserves previously absorbed in meeting the requirement against those time deposits. To trace the effect of a given change in reserves on the money supply requires that the existence of time deposits be taken into account.

In the simplest case, it is assumed that the commercial banks expand demand deposits to the maximum amount consistent with any increase in reserves. A third complication arises because some banks do not do this; some choose not to be fully loaned up, but to hold some excess reserves. This means that the actual expansion of demand deposits will be less than the maximum possible with any given increase in reserves. Moreover, the actual contraction of demand deposits will be less than the maximum otherwise required in the case of a decrease in reserves. Before drawing any final conclusion on the change in the money supply that will follow from any given change in reserves, we must, therefore, consider the banks' propensity to hold excess reserves.

We will now examine the way each of these three complications modifies the simple equation so far derived to determine the change in the money supply generated by a change in reserves.

The Public Varies Its Currency Holdings

As the public's holdings of demand deposits increase year by year, its holdings of currency also increase.[6] The amount of each year's increase in the money supply that is held in currency or demand deposits is determined by the public, but the combined growth of currency and demand deposits is primarily determined by the Federal Reserve in line with what it believes to be an

appropriate growth of the money supply. Because a dollar of currency and a dollar of demand deposits are equal means of payment, the Federal Reserve's concern is with the total of the two, not with the particular division of the total from year to year.

However, the way in which the public chooses to divide its money holdings between currency and demand deposits greatly affects the amount of reserves the Federal Reserve must supply in order to hit any selected target money supply. Suppose that the actual money supply of $400 billion—the sum of $300 billion in demand deposits and $100 billion in currency—happens to be the target money supply. Assume that the reserve requirement against demand deposits is 20 percent and the banks have just the $60 billion in reserves needed to meet the minimum requirement. (As before, we assume no time deposits.)

If people and firms now want more currency, they draw checks against their demand deposits, and currency is drained from the banks. Suppose $100 million of demand deposits are exchanged for currency. The money supply is unchanged at $400 billion ($100.1 billion of currency and $299.9 billion of demand deposits) and is still on target. However, if the Federal Reserve fails to act, the money supply will not remain on target. For every dollar of currency withdrawn from the commercial banking system, a dollar of reserves is lost. In the illustration, both demand deposits and reserves will be down $100 million, required reserves will be down $20 million, and a reserve deficiency of $80 million will be created. Unless the Federal Reserve steps in to provide the additional $80 million of reserves needed, this will lead to a contraction of bank loans and securities and thereby contractions of both demand deposits and the money supply. Just as a drain of currency from the commercial banks requires that the Federal Reserve pump reserves into the banks to avoid a reduction in the money supply, an opposite movement—that is, a flow of currency into the banks from the public—requires that the Federal Reserve withdraw

---

[6]An exception to this rule occurred from 1956 to 1957 when currency holdings increased slightly while demand deposits decreased slightly.

reserves from the commercial banks to avoid an expansion of the money supply.

Over time, the Federal Reserve makes possible an expansion of the money supply to meet a growing economy's need. From the illustration presented here, we can see that the amount of additional reserves the Federal Reserve must supply to bring about a specific increase in the money supply depends on how much of the money supply the public chooses to hold in currency and how much in demand deposits. For example, if the public chooses to hold $1 of currency for every $3 of demand deposits, the increase in reserves needed to achieve any given increase in the money supply will be greater than if the public chooses to hold $1 of currency for every $4 of demand deposits. In recent years the ratio of currency to demand deposits has risen strikingly. In the early 1960s the ratio was around 0.25, by the mid-1970s it was around 0.30, and by 1980 it had risen to 0.40.[7] In the following analysis, we will work with a ratio of 0.40.

Given the assumptions that the banks have no time deposits and that they hold no excess

---

[7]An interesting explanation for the much greater use of currency in recent years is based on the rapid growth of the underground or subterranean economy in which transactions are settled in currency so as to leave no written record. For example, people like self-employed repairmen may be willing to accept lower payment from homeowners for their services if payment is made in cash. The recipients of such income may omit it from their tax returns with little danger of detection by the Internal Revenue Service. The greater the amount of such unreported activities relative to the total of all commercial activities, the greater will be the amount of currency needed relative to the amount of demand deposits. See N.N. Bowsher, "The Demand For Currency: Is the Underground Economy Undermining Monetary Policy?" *Review,* Federal Reserve Bank of St. Louis, January 1980, pp. 11–17; R.D. Laurent, "Currency and the Subterranean Economy," *Economic Perspectives,* Federal Reserve Bank of Chicago, March–April 1979, pp. 3–6; E.L. Feige, "How Big Is the Irregular Economy?" *Challenge,* November–December 1979, pp. 5–13; and P.M. Gutmann, "The Subterranean Economy," *Financial Analysts Journal,* November–December 1977, pp. 26, 27, 34.

reserves, part of any increase in total reserves will be absorbed in meeting the increased reserve requirements caused by the increase in demand deposits resulting from the banks' expansion of loans and securities on the basis of the increase in reserves; and part will be absorbed in meeting the public's demand as it converts into currency that portion of the increase in demand deposits needed to satisfy the public's desired ratio of currency to demand deposits. For any given increase in reserves, the increase in currency holdings and demand deposits that will result is determined from the expansion of an earlier equation. On p. 176 we had the following:

$$\Delta R = R_D \Delta DD$$

Given an increase in reserves, banks will expand demand deposits until all reserves are absorbed in meeting the requirement against demand deposits. Leaving that simplest case, we now consider the fact that the banks will not be able to retain all of the increase in reserves as they expand demand deposits; some of the reserves will be lost through withdrawals of currency. Because the increase in reserves will either be absorbed as an increase in required reserves or as an increase in currency in the hands of the public, we have

$$\Delta R = r_D \Delta DD + \Delta C$$

Here C refers to currency held by the public. The ratio, C/DD, will be designated by c, the value of which is assumed to be 0.40. Because $\Delta C = c\Delta DD$, by substitution in the preceding equation we have

$$\Delta R = r_D \Delta DD + c\Delta DD$$

Factoring out the ΔDD's yields

$$\Delta R = (r_D + c)\Delta DD$$

To show the change in demand deposits that will follow from a change in reserves, we earlier rewrote the equation $\Delta R = r_D(\Delta DD)$ to read ΔDD

$= (1/r_D)\Delta R$. For the same purpose, we now rewrite $\Delta R = (r_D + c)\Delta DD$ to read:

$$\Delta DD = \left(\frac{1}{r_D + c}\right)\Delta R$$

Allowing for the fact that the public chooses to hold an amount of currency equal to a fraction of its demand deposits, the deposit expansion multiplier is $1/(r_D + c)$ in contrast to $1/r_D$ before allowance for this fact. Because c is a positive figure, the deposit expansion multiplier has been reduced. Assuming as before that r_D is 0.20, the deposit expansion multiplier was 5 with c of zero. If c is 0.40, the multiplier drops from 5 to 1.666.

Using these assumptions, suppose that the Federal Reserve increases R by $100 million through open-market operations. By substituting this in the last equation, we have

$$\Delta DD = \frac{1}{.20 + .40} \times \$100 \text{ million}$$
$$\Delta DD = 1.6667 \times \$100 \text{ million} = \$166.67 \text{ million}$$

The $100 million of additional reserves are absorbed in part by the 20 percent reserve requirement against the additional demand deposits of $166.67 million and in part by the increase in the public's holdings of currency. The former takes $33.33 million (0.20 × $166.67 million), and the latter takes $66.67 million (0.40 × $166.67 million). After the expansion process is completed, the banking system's T-account indicates additional reserves of $33.33 million, which is just equal to 20 percent of the additional demand deposits of $166.67 million. It also indicates that the banks will have added $133.33 million to their loans and security holdings during the expansion process:

Before allowing for the fact that the public's cash holdings change with its demand deposit holdings, we were able to determine the change in the money supply that results from any change in reserves as soon as we knew the change in demand deposits. In other words, because ΔC was assumed to be zero, ΔM was equal to ΔDD. However, now ΔC is no longer zero. Therefore, given $\Delta M = \Delta DD + \Delta C$, to find ΔM that results from any ΔR, we must add ΔC to both sides of the equation for ΔDD. For ΔDD we have

$$\Delta DD = \frac{1}{r_D + c} \cdot \Delta R$$

For ΔM, we have

$$\Delta M = \Delta DD + \Delta C = \frac{1}{r_D + c} \cdot \Delta R + \Delta C$$

Because $\Delta C = c\Delta DD$ and ΔDD is as previously given, we have for ΔC,

$$\Delta C = \frac{c}{r_D + c} \cdot \Delta R$$

Therefore,

$$\Delta M = \left(\frac{1}{r_D + c} \cdot \Delta R\right) + \left(\frac{c}{r_D + c} \cdot \Delta R\right)$$

$$\Delta M = \frac{1 + c}{r_D + c} \cdot \Delta R$$

We saw earlier that the demand deposit multiplier is $1/(r_D + c)$. We see here that the *money supply multiplier* is $(1 + c)/(r_D + c)$; in other words, the money supply multiplier is equal to 1 + c times the demand deposit multiplier. Sub-

All Banks

Assets		Liabilities and Capital Accounts	
Reserves	+$ 33.33	Demand Deposits	+$166.67
Loans and Securities	+ 133.33		
Total Change	+$166.66	Total Change	+$166.67

stituting the values assumed earlier, the money supply multiplier is

$$\frac{1 + 0.40}{0.20 + 0.40} = 2.333$$

Contrast this with the demand deposit multiplier, which was

$$\frac{1}{0.20 + 0.40} = 1.666$$

A lower or higher value for c will mean a larger or smaller money supply multiplier, respectively. For example, for $c = 0.30$ and $c = 0.50$, the money supply multiplier will be 2.6 and 2.1, respectively. Each dollar of any addition to reserves that is retained by the banks will support a multiple of that amount in demand deposits, but each of these dollars lost by the banks through cash withdrawals adds only one dollar to the money supply. The higher the ratio of currency to demand deposits, the smaller will be the increment to the money supply that results from any increment to bank reserves.

Commercial Banks Have Time Deposits as well as Demand Deposits

Not only do the commercial banks have time deposits as well as demand deposits, but the amount of time deposits greatly exceeds the amount of demand deposits. At the end of 1980, time deposits were 75 percent greater than demand deposits. Although the percentage reserve requirement for time deposits is much lower than that for demand deposits, the fact that this percentage is greater than zero means that a portion of the banking system's total reserves is absorbed in meeting the reserve requirement against time deposits and is therefore not available to support what otherwise might be a larger volume of demand deposits and a larger money supply.

With a change in total reserves, how much of a change both in demand deposits and in the money supply will result after allowance for the complication introduced by the existence of time deposits? With two complications now being considered, an increase in reserves will be absorbed in meeting the reserve requirement against an increase in demand deposits, in meeting a cash drain, and in meeting the reserve requirement against an increase in time deposits. That is,

$$\Delta R = r_D \Delta DD + \Delta C + r_T \Delta TD$$

Here TD is time deposits and r_T is the percentage reserve requirement against time deposits.

Earlier we expressed ΔC as a ratio to ΔDD—$\Delta C = c\Delta DD$, in which $c = C/DD$. Here we do the same for ΔTD—$\Delta TD = a\Delta DD$, in which $a = TD/DD$. Many factors affect the size of this ratio—for example, the rate of return the public can earn on TD in contrast to the rate of return on DD, and the rate of return it can earn on TD in contrast to the rate of return on similar deposits in nonbank thrift institutions. Changes in these and other factors cause variations in the ratio over time; for the sake of illustration, here we assume the ratio to be 2.

Substituting $c\Delta DD$ and $a\Delta DD$ for ΔC and ΔTD in the preceding equation gives us

$$\Delta R = r_D \Delta DD + c\Delta DD + ar_T\Delta DD$$
$$\Delta R = (r_D + c + ar_T)\Delta DD$$

As before, the last equation is rewritten to show that ΔDD is equal to the demand deposit multiplier times ΔR:

$$\Delta DD = \frac{1}{r_D + c + ar_T} \cdot \Delta R$$

Assuming as before that $r = 0.20$, $c = 0.40$, and now that $r = 0.05$, the demand deposit multiplier is

$$\frac{1}{0.20 + 0.40 + 2(0.05)} = 1.43$$

The demand deposit multiplier has declined from 1.67 to 1.43 after taking into account the public's holdings of time deposits (specifically on the assumption that the public holds time deposits equal to twice its demand deposits and that the reserve requirement imposed on time deposits is 5 percent). A change in reserves of $100 million will lead to a change in demand deposits of $143 million.

To find the change in the money supply, $\Delta M = \Delta DD + \Delta C$, for any ΔR, we must add ΔC to both sides of the preceding equation. By the same procedure used earlier, we obtain

$$\Delta M = \left(\frac{1}{r_D + c + ar_T} \cdot \Delta R\right) + \left(\frac{c}{r_D + c + ar_T} \cdot \Delta R\right)$$

$$\Delta M = \frac{1 + c}{r_D + c + ar_T} \cdot \Delta R$$

For the given values of r_D, c, a, and r_T, the money supply multiplier is

$$\frac{1 + 0.40}{0.20 + 0.40 + 2(0.05)} = 2$$

A change in reserves of $100 million will lead to a change in the money supply of $200 million.

The change in reserves is absorbed as follows: Required reserves against ΔDD is $28.6 million (0.20 × $143 million). Given $\Delta DD = \$143$ million, there is a loss of reserves through a cash drain of $57.2 million (0.40 × $143 million). And given $\Delta TD = \$286$ million (2 × $143 million), required reserves against ΔTD is $14.3 million (0.05 × $286 million). After the expansion process is complete, the T-account for the banking system shows that of the additional $100 million of reserves, the banks retain just the $42.9 million needed to meet the increased reserve requirement caused by the increase in their deposit liabilities. The banks also will have added $386.1 million to their loans and securities during the process:

The Banks Choose to Hold Excess Reserves

Someone once said that banks abhor nonearning assets as much as nature abhors a vacuum. If that is correct, we might expect that banks would hold only the minimum amount of reserves (nonearning assets) needed to meet the percentage reserve requirements against their deposits—in other words, that banks would ordinarily be in a fully "loaned-up" position. However, in practice, the banks do hold excess reserves, although the amount is relatively small. Over the past ten years, excess reserves have averaged less than 1 percent of total reserves.

Why should banks hold any excess reserves at all? One reason individual banks do so is for protection in the event of unusually large withdrawals of currency or unusually large losses of reserves to other banks through adverse clearing balances. In an uncertain world where this may happen at any time, every bank must weigh the cost of holding excess reserves against the cost of avoiding the reserve deficiency that will follow a large loss of reserves. The cost of holding excess reserves is the amount of interest that could have been earned if the excess reserves had been used to make loans or buy securities. The cost of avoiding a reserve deficiency is the cost of borrowing that amount of reserves from the Federal Reserve or from other banks with excess reserves, that is, borrowing in the Federal funds market. Given the rate of interest earned on bank assets and the rate paid for borrowed reserves, some banks will decide that the policy of holding some excess reserves—and thereby holding less than the maximum amount of earning assets—generally implies lesser costs and

All Banks

Assets		Liabilities and Capital Accounts	
Reserves	+$ 42.9	Demand Deposits	+$143
Loans and Securities	+ 386.1	Time Deposits	+ 286
Total Change	+$429.0	Total Change	+$429

therefore greater earnings. The more variable a bank's inflow and outflow of currency and deposits, the more likely it is to decide that this is the appropriate course of action.

However, because the interest rates that are central to a bank's decision do change, today's decision to hold some amount of excess reserves may be followed by tomorrow's decision to hold more, less, or none at all. What counts here is not so much the absolute level of interest rates as the magnitude of the spread between the rate earned on bank assets and the rate paid to the Federal Reserve for borrowed reserves. Almost without exception, the former rate is greater than the latter. For example, with no change in the discount rate, a rise in the rate earned on bank assets increases the spread, increases the cost per dollar of holding excess reserves, and tends to reduce holdings of excess reserves.[8] With no change in the discount rate, a fall in the rate earned on bank assets will have the opposite effect. Although both rates do change over time, it is still the extent of the spread between the two rates that is primarily relevant to the decision in question.

Changes in the discount rate tend to lag behind changes in the Federal funds rate, Treasury bill rate, and other interest rates. This was especially true before the 1970s when the Federal Reserve changed the discount rate infrequently but by relatively large amounts. Since then, discount rates have been changed more frequently and in smaller amounts as the Federal Reserve adopted a policy of keeping the dis-

count rate more closely in line with other interest rates. However, because there is still a lag, the spread between other interest rates and the discount rate tends to widen when interest rates rise and to narrow when they fall.

Because of the way in which holdings of excess reserves respond to changes in the size of this spread, this relationship could in turn cause the money supply to vary directly with interest rates. Assuming no change in total reserves, a rise in interest rates that widens the spread and thereby makes excess reserves more costly will lead banks to expand loans and security holdings. Due to this expansion, deposits will increase and some of the reserves that were previously excess reserves will be converted into required reserves against the newly created deposits (and some of the reserves that were previously excess reserves may be lost by the banks through currency withdrawals). If the spread grows larger with each successive rise of interest rates, excess reserves may drop to zero as they all become required reserves. A fall in interest rates with the discount rate again lagging tends to produce the opposite result: The spread narrows and some of the total reserves become excess reserves as banks tend to contract loans and security holdings, reduce deposits, and cut down required reserves.

Although we recognize that holdings of excess reserves may be related to interest rates in the way described, we do not incorporate this refinement into the money supply equations of this chapter.[9] Instead, we assume that, whatever the level of interest rates on bank assets and the discount rate prevailing at any particular time, the banks will choose to hold excess reserves in amounts that will vary in direct proportion to the volume of their demand deposits.

---

[8]At the same time that excess reserves will tend to decrease in response to a widening of the spread, the amount of borrowing from the Federal Reserve Banks will tend to increase. As noted in the discussion of the discount rate as an instrument of monetary control, the inducement to borrow from the Federal Reserve Banks becomes stronger as the spread widens. Although borrowing solely for the purpose of relending at higher interest rates is an unacceptable use of the discount window, Federal Reserve surveillance of borrowers does not eliminate all such borrowing, especially during times when the profit incentive for such borrowing becomes unusually great.

---

[9]To do so would greatly complicate what are now quite simple but nevertheless very informative equations. Chapter 11 considers the interest elasticity of the demand for money in detail, and the question raised here concerning the interest elasticity of the supply of money will receive further attention there.

The rationale for this assumption is that the risk of a bank's losing reserves through cash withdrawals or adverse clearing balances will be greater, the greater the amount of that bank's demand deposits. (The bank's savings deposits—which in practice are convertible into cash without notice—also expose it to some risk of this kind, but this risk is minor in comparison to the other and will be omitted here.) Therefore, for the banking system as a whole, we may write

$$ER = eDD$$

Here ER is the desired amount of excess reserves and e is the desired ratio of excess reserves to demand deposits, or ER/DD. For a change in demand deposits, we have

$$\Delta ER = e\Delta DD$$

The now familiar questions may once again be posed: Given a change in reserves, what will be the change both in demand deposits and in the money supply? The answer may also be approached in the now familiar manner. Any change in reserves—for example, an increase—will now be absorbed in four ways: required reserves against demand deposits, cash withdrawals, required reserves against time deposits, and desired excess reserves. That is,

$$\Delta R = r_D\,\Delta DD + \Delta C + r_T\Delta TD + e\Delta DD$$

After substituting $c\Delta DD$ for ΔC and $a\Delta DD$ for ΔTD, then factoring out ΔDD, we obtain

$$\Delta R = (r_D + c + ar_T + e)\Delta DD$$
$$\Delta DD = \frac{1}{r_D + c + ar_T + e} \cdot \Delta R$$

The demand deposit multiplier which was simply $1/r_D$ before any complications were introduced is now the more complex expression derived here. Assuming the values chosen earlier for r_D, c, a, and r_T, and assuming now the value of 0.01 for e, the size of the demand deposit multiplier is

$$\frac{1}{0.20 + 0.40 + 2(0.05) + 0.01} = 1.41$$

A change in reserves of $100 million will lead to a change in demand deposits of $141 million.

As before, to find the change in the money supply, $\Delta M = \Delta DD + \Delta C$, for any ΔR, we must add ΔC to both sides of the preceding equation. By the same procedure used earlier, we obtain

$$\Delta M = \left(\frac{1}{r_D + c + ar_T + e} \cdot \Delta R\right)$$
$$+ \left(\frac{c}{r_D + c + ar_T + e} \cdot \Delta R\right)$$
$$\Delta M = \frac{1 + c}{r_D + c + ar_T + e} \cdot \Delta R$$

For the assumed values of r_D, c, a, r_T and e, the money supply multiplier is

$$\frac{1 + 0.40}{0.20 + 0.40 + 2(0.05) + 0.01} = 1.97$$

A change in reserves of $100 million will lead to a change in the money supply of $197 million.

With allowance now made for the desire of banks to hold excess reserves, the assumed $100 million change in total reserves is absorbed as follows: $28.2 million to meet the 20 percent reserve requirement against ΔDD of $141 million, $56.4 million (0.40 × $141 million) to cover the drain of currency, $14.1 million to meet the 5 percent reserve requirement against ΔTD of $282 million, and $1.4 million (0.01 × $141 million) to provide the desired excess reserves. The following T-account identifies the changes in the balance sheet for the banking system after the adjustments to the $100 million increase in reserves have all occurred. The banks retain $43.7 million of those reserves—$1.4 million more than enough to meet the requirements against the increase in deposits. Of course, the decision to hold excess reserves is also a decision to make less loans and buy fewer securities than would otherwise be the case. In the T-account on p. 191, which differs from this one only because this one allows for the banks' holdings of excess reserves, the change in loans and

All Banks

Assets			Liabilities and Capital Accounts	
Reserves		+$ 43.7	Demand Deposits	+$141
Required	+$42.3		Time Deposits	+ 282
against *DD*	+$28.2			
against *TD*	+ 14.1			
Excess	+ 1.4			
Loans and Securities		+ 379.3		
Total Change		+$423.0	Total Change	+$423

securities was $386.1 million. Here the change is $379.3 million. The decision to hold $1.4 million of excess reserves has reduced possible earning assets by $6.8 million.

Federal Reserve Control over the Money Supply

In the absence of the complications examined in the preceding section, the Federal Reserve's control over the money supply could be, at least potentially, as precise as its control over total reserves. However, once these three complications are taken into account, the Federal Reserve's power to effect any desired change in the money supply from one month to the next is significantly diminished.

Our last money supply equation provides a helpful framework through which to show how these complications restrict the Federal Reserve's ability to control the money supply:

$$\Delta M = \left(\frac{1 + c}{r_D + c + ar_T + e}\right) \cdot \Delta R$$

From a purely mechanical point of view, ΔM is rigidly linked to ΔR as long as the value of the multiplier remains fixed. If such were actually the case, the Federal Reserve's control over ΔM would be as precise as its control over ΔR, and its control over ΔR is in fact fairly precise. However, fairly precise control over ΔR will be accompanied by a control over ΔM, which is less precise to the degree that the values of the terms in the multiplier show frequent, sizable, erratic, and therefore unpredictable changes.

Of these terms, the Federal Reserve has complete control over r_D and r_T in the sense that these percentages may be set wherever the Federal Reserve thinks appropriate within the limits established by Congress. Neither the public nor the commercial banks have any power to change them. However, prior to the simplification of the reserve requirement structure under the Depository Institutions Deregulation and Monetary Control Act of 1980, R_D was a percentage that varied substantially between banks of different size. The requirement varied from a low of 7 percent on the first $2 million of a bank's demand deposits through five brackets to a high of 16.25 percent on a bank's demand deposits in excess of $400 million. Therefore, how much demand deposits any given amount of reserves could support depended significantly on how those deposits were distributed among banks of different size. Percentage reserve requirements against time deposits varied according to the maturity of deposits and, to a small extent, according to the size of the bank's time deposits. The requirement was 3 percent on the first $5 million and 6 percent on the amount over $5 million on maturities of 30 to 179 days, 2.5 percent on maturities of 180 days to 4 years, and 1 percent on maturities of 4 years or more. Therefore, how much time deposits any given amount of reserves could support somewhat depended on how these deposits were distributed by size of bank and by maturity.

Under the 1980 legislation, all transaction accounts (demand deposits as well as other accounts transferable by check or its equivalent held in commercial banks and other depository institutions) became subject to reserve requirements set by the Federal Reserve. The initial reserve requirements, which are to be phased in over a period of years, are 3 percent on a depository institution's first $25 million of transaction accounts and 12 percent on amounts over $25 million. There is no reserve requirement on personal time deposits; on other time deposits, the requirement is 3 percent for maturities less than 4 years and zero for maturities of 4 years or more.[10] Although more than half of the nation's commercial banks have deposits of less than $25 million, these banks hold no more than 10 percent of the total deposits of all commercial banks. Therefore, as the new requirements are phased in over time the great bulk of demand deposits will be subject to the same 12 percent requirement. From the point of view of the Federal Reserve's control over the money supply, how much in demand deposits any given amount of reserves can support will be little affected by the distribution of these deposits among banks of different size. Now that the Federal Reserve need not be concerned with member banks giving up membership in the system because of its higher reserve requirements, it can move toward setting uniform reserve requirements for all banks. (The earlier system relied on lower requirements for small and middle-sized banks, which were the ones most likely to give up membership in the system.) The limitation on the Federal Reserve's control over the money supply that existed under the previous reserve requirement structure will have been removed.

Unlike the limitation that resulted from the reserve requirement structure, a more serious limitation (which cannot be removed by legislation) results from the fact that the Federal Reserve has no direct control at all over the other terms in the money supply multiplier: c, a, and e. For any time period, the public decides the ratio it will maintain between its currency holdings and its demand deposits (the value of c); the public decides the ratio it will maintain between its time deposits and its demand deposits (the value of a); finally, the commercial banks decide the ratio they will maintain between their desired holdings of excess reserves and their demand deposit liabilities (the value of e). Actions taken by the Federal Reserve can indirectly affect the values of c, a, and e, but the public and the commercial banks still have the power to maintain larger or smaller values for c, a, and e from one time period to the next quite independently of actions taken by the Federal Reserve.

Consequently, despite a high degree of control over r_D and r_T, the Federal Reserve will be unable to ensure that ΔM will be the amount desired in any particular month if the public and the commercial banks cause frequent, large, and erratic variations in the values of c, a, and e. Suppose the Federal Reserve authorities want to increase the money supply by $500 million over the next month.[11] Given unchanged percentage reserve requirements, the amount of increase in R needed depends on the values of c, a, and e. However, if these vary significantly and unpredictably from month to month, the increase in legal reserves provided by the Federal Reserve may produce an increase in the money supply possibly twice as large or half as large as the one

---

[10] For percentage reserve requirements both before and after the implementation of the 1980 legislation, see Table 1-15, "Depository Institutions Reserve Requirements," in the Financial and Business Statistics section of the *Federal Reserve Bulletin*.

[11] Since 1975, the Federal Reserve has set targets for M-1A, M-1B and M-2 (and for the predecessors of these aggregates before the redefinitions of 1980) expressed as a range of growth rates, for example, 4–6.5 percent for M-1A. Therefore, reference here and elsewhere in this chapter to a target as a specific dollar amount does not describe actual procedure. However, for the introductory purposes of this chapter, that simplification conveys the idea in question. Target growth rates are discussed further in Chapter 26.

aimed for during that month. As the data on the change in the money supply become available, the error, if there is indeed one, will be revealed. If the Federal Reserve still has an unchanged money supply goal, say an increase of $500 million, it then takes the necessary corrective action— by providing still more reserves if the money supply did not increase sufficiently, or by taking away some reserves if the money supply increased too much. It is, of course, possible that this action, intended to be corrective, will turn out to be perverse if changes in a, c, and e now occur in the opposite direction from the earlier changes. This in turn calls for corrective action in the opposite direction by the Federal Reserve. Even under these most adverse hypothetical circumstances, however, control by the Federal Reserve does not become completely impossible. Through what in effect may be a continuing process of adjustment, over a long period of time, the Federal Reserve can still make ΔM come out close to the magnitude intended for that longer period of time.

The time period is critical here: The longer the time period under consideration, the closer the Federal Reserve can come to its objective as the short-term errors in one direction or the other are averaged out. If we take the very short-term period of a week, the Federal Reserve might take actions with the expectation that the actions will result in some particular increase in the money supply during the next week, but it would not be surprised to find that there is an actual decrease in the money supply in that next week (here ignoring the additional complication introduced by the unreliability of weekly money supply figures). Once we stretch the time period under consideration out to a month, errors in direction of change become less likely. On a quarterly basis, the magnitude of the change in the money supply may still be off target, but the direction of change would probably not be. Over a still longer period of time, the magnitude of the change in the money supply can probably be brought to within a fraction of 1 percent of the intended figure.

Treasury Financing and the Money Supply

The last money supply equation we developed shows how the change in the money supply that results from any change in bank reserves depends on the values of c, a, and e. These ratios may change from time to time and their values at any time are determined by decisions of the public and the commercial banks. Through changes in these ratios, the public and the commercial banks cause changes in the money supply, at least until such changes are offset by the Federal Reserve through changes in reserves.

In addition to the public (which includes state and local governments) and the commercial banks, the federal government also makes decisions that may affect the money supply. Thus, changes in the money supply depend on whether an unbalanced federal budget (deficit) is financed by borrowing from either the public, or the commercial banks or the Federal Reserve Banks. Contrary to popular opinion, the balance or imbalance in the federal government's budget is not the critical factor in determining whether or not federal government finance changes the money supply. However, we will approach the question of the effect of financing federal government expenditures on the money supply through this familiar classification, looking first at the effects of a balanced budget and then at the effects of an unbalanced budget (surplus as well as deficit). In the following discussion, all references to government are to the federal government alone.

Balanced Budget

Assume initially that the budget is in balance— that is, gross tax receipts equal government purchases of goods and services plus transfer payments—and that the government then simultaneously increases its spending and tax receipts by $1 billion to maintain a balanced budget. What is the effect of this tax-financed increase in government spending on the money supply? The answer is seen most clearly through sets of T-accounts. The first set shows the effects of the Treasury's collecting $1 billion of additional tax receipts. (Although the Treasury does not have capital accounts in the sense that the banks and other groups do, the same heading is used on the right side of each T-account.)

U.S. Treasury

Assets		Liabilities and Capital Accounts
Deposits at Federal Reserve Banks	+$1	
Taxes Receivable	−$1	

Federal Reserve Banks

Assets	Liabilities and Capital Accounts	
	Deposits:	
	Commercial Banks	−$1
	U.S. Treasury	+$1

Commercial Banks

Assets		Liabilities and Capital Accounts	
Deposits at Federal Reserve Banks	−$1	Demand Deposits of the Public	−$1

Public

Assets		Liabilities and Capital Accounts	
Demand Deposits	−$1	Taxes Payable	−$1

As the Treasury receives the taxpayers' checks for $1 billion, it deposits them in its accounts at the Federal Reserve Banks; the Federal Reserve Banks charge the $1 billion to the accounts of the commercial banks against which the checks were drawn.[12] The effects at this point are a $1 billion decrease in the money supply (the public

has $1 billion less in demand deposits and no change in its currency holdings) and a $1 billion decrease in commercial bank reserves.[13] The Treasury disburses the $1 billion, the effects of which are shown in the following set of T-accounts.

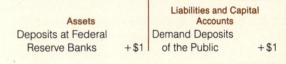

U.S. Treasury

Assets		Liabilities and Capital Accounts
Deposits at Federal Reserve Banks	−$1	
Goods and Services	+$1	

Federal Reserve Banks

Assets	Liabilities and Capital Accounts	
	Deposits:	
	Commercial Banks	+$1
	U.S. Treasury	−$1

Commercial Banks

Assets		Liabilities and Capital Accounts	
Deposits at Federal Reserve Banks	+$1	Demand Deposits of the Public	+$1

Public

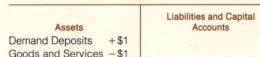

Assets		Liabilities and Capital Accounts
Demand Deposits	+$1	
Goods and Services	−$1	

The public receives checks from the Treasury for $1 billion in exchange for $1 billion worth of

---

[12]The Treasury will typically first deposit the checks in so-called Tax and Loan Accounts it maintains with commercial banks, each check deposited in the bank against which it is drawn (with the exception of those banks with which the Treasury does not carry Tax and Loan Accounts). However, the Treasury does not write checks against these accounts. When the time comes to disburse the funds, they are transferred to the Treasury's deposits at the Federal Reserve Banks; it is against these deposits that the Treasury writes all of its checks. The displayed T-accounts omit the intermediate step.

[13]If the commercial banks held no excess reserves to start with, this would result in a reserve deficiency. However, given our assumption that the disbursing and collecting of the $1 billion occur simultaneously, the creation of a reserve deficiency in this way is prevented because the Treasury is adding $1 billion to bank reserves at the same time that it is deducting $1 billion from bank reserves.

goods and services provided to the government.[14] These checks are deposited in the commercial banks, which send them to the Federal Reserve Banks where the amount in question is added to the commercial banks' deposits and subtracted from the Treasury's deposits. The effects at this point are a $1 billion increase in the money supply (the public has $1 billion more in its demand deposits and no change in its currency holdings) and a $1 billion increase in commercial bank reserves.

When the transactions in the two sets of T-accounts are combined to show the net effects of both the Treasury collection of an additional $1 billion of tax receipts and the Treasury disbursement of an additional $1 billion in payment for goods and services, we see that there is no change, on balance, in commercial bank reserves or in the money supply. The decreases in bank reserves and money supply that result from the additional tax collections equal the increases in bank reserves and money supply that result from the additional Treasury disbursements. All that occurs is a real transfer of goods and services from the public to the government in exchange for which the public obtains "tax receipts."

If we again start with a balanced budget and trace through the effects of a $1 billion *decrease* in tax receipts and a $1 billion *decrease* in government spending, there will again be no change in bank reserves or the money supply. The public will have provided $1 billion less in goods and services to the government than otherwise and the public will have received $1 billion less in "tax receipts" from government than otherwise.

Unbalanced Budget

An unbalanced budget, of course, may show a deficit or a surplus. Our recent history gives us repeated instances of deficits and rare instances of surpluses. Over the last twenty-five years, a surplus occurred only in 1969; even then it was a minor $3.2 billion. We will now examine the effects of the more relevant case of a deficit. The effects of a surplus are essentially the opposite.

A deficit has no single set of effects on bank reserves and the money supply—the effects vary with the way in which the deficit is financed. The three practical possibilities are (1) borrowing from the public, (2) borrowing from the commercial banks, and (3) borrowing from the Federal Reserve Banks.

Borrowing from the Public To the extent that they affect bank reserves and the money supply, the steps previously outlined for an increase in government tax receipts and an equal increase in government spending are duplicated in the case of an increase in borrowing from the public and an equal increase in government spending. Whatever the deficit in the preceding period, assume that the deficit for the current period is larger by $1 billion. Then specifically as a result of this $1 billion increase in the amount of borrowing, bank reserves and the money supply decrease by $1 billion as the Treasury deposits in the Federal Reserve Banks the checks received in payment for the $1 billion of securities sold to the public. This is then matched by a $1 billion increase in bank reserves and the money supply as the Treasury disburses these funds from its accounts at the Federal Reserve Banks. The net effect on bank reserves and the money supply is accordingly zero. The only difference between borrowing from the public and taxing the public is that at the end of the process the public holds interest-bearing government securities instead of tax receipts in exchange for the goods and services provided to the government. Or, from the viewpoint of the Treasury, instead of paying for an increase in goods and services with a decrease in taxes receivable, the Treasury pays with an increase in the amount of U.S. government securities outstanding. Although this is the only difference, it is an important difference with various implications. For example, to the degree that the public finances government

---

[14] The $1 billion could be received by the public as transfer payments, in which event the Treasury T-account would show on the liability side − $1 billion under "Transfers Payable" and the public's T-account would show on the asset side − $1 billion under "Transfers Receivable." Everything else would be the same.

spending by acquiring government securities rather than tax receipts, the public realizes an increase in its financial wealth. This in turn, as is examined in Chapter 16, can be expected to affect the position of the consumption function which has further implications. However, with respect to the narrow issue of bank reserves and the money supply, there is no difference between financing a deficit by taxing or borrowing from the public.

In actual experience, the question is not whether there will be a deficit or surplus, but whether the deficit will be larger or smaller from one year to the next. However, consider what happens in a year when there actually is a surplus. This excess of tax receipts over spending, say $1 billion, will result in a $1 billion decrease in bank reserves and the money supply, assuming as before that the Treasury deposits taxpayers' checks directly into its accounts at the Federal Reserve Banks. However, in the reverse of a deficit financed by selling securities to or borrowing from the public, the Treasury uses its $1 billion surplus to buy back that amount of securities held by the public. This adds $1 billion to bank reserves and to the money supply as the bond sellers deposit these checks in their demand deposits and the commercial banks add $1 billion to their balances at the Federal Reserve Banks. Generating a surplus and using that surplus to retire U.S. government securities held by the public will have, on balance, no effect on bank reserves and the money supply. However, it will affect the public's and the Treasury's T-accounts. The public's T-account will show a $1 billion decrease in the liability item, Taxes Payable, and a $1 billion decrease in the asset item, U.S. Government Securities Owned. The Treasury's T-account will show a $1 billion decrease in the asset item, Taxes Receivable, and a $1 billion decrease in the liability item, U.S. Government Securities Outstanding.[15]

Borrowing from the Commercial Banks   If the Treasury finances a deficit by selling securities to the commercial banks, the net effect will be no change in bank reserves but an increase in the money supply. However, before the Treasury can borrow from the commercial banking system, the system must have excess reserves that some banks will choose to use in this way. Assuming, as before, the financing of $1 billion, the following set of T-accounts shows the effect of the commercial banks' purchase of that $1 billion of securities from the Treasury.

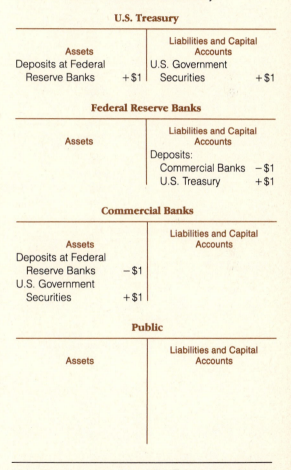

U.S. Treasury

Assets	Liabilities and Capital Accounts
Deposits at Federal Reserve Banks + $1	U.S. Government Securities + $1

Federal Reserve Banks

Assets	Liabilities and Capital Accounts
	Deposits:
	Commercial Banks − $1
	U.S. Treasury + $1

Commercial Banks

Assets	Liabilities and Capital Accounts
Deposits at Federal Reserve Banks − $1	
U.S. Government Securities + $1	

Public

Assets	Liabilities and Capital Accounts

of goods and services, the public's T-account would show a $1 billion increase in the asset item, Goods and Services, and a $1 billion decrease in the asset item, U.S. Government Securities Owned. The Treasury's T-account would show a $1 billion decrease in the asset item, Goods and Services, and a $1 billion decrease in the liability item, U.S. Government Securities Outstanding.

---

[15]This assumes that the $1 billion surplus results from a $1 billion increase in tax receipts with no change in expenditures. If it were the other way around, with no change in taxes and a $1 billion decrease in purchases

The commercial banks lose $1 billion of reserves as the Treasury's deposits at the Federal Reserve Banks rise by that amount and the commercial banks' deposits at the Federal Reserve Banks fall by that amount. The public is not party to this transaction, and there is no effect on the money supply.

Disbursement of the $1 billion by the Treasury in payment for goods and services produces the following entries in the T-accounts:

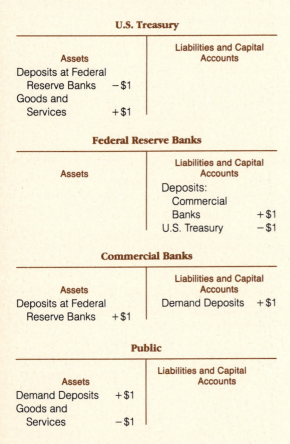

U.S. Treasury

Assets		Liabilities and Capital Accounts
Deposits at Federal Reserve Banks	− $1	
Goods and Services	+ $1	

Federal Reserve Banks

Assets	Liabilities and Capital Accounts	
	Deposits:	
	Commercial Banks	+ $1
	U.S. Treasury	− $1

Commercial Banks

Assets		Liabilities and Capital Accounts	
Deposits at Federal Reserve Banks	+ $1	Demand Deposits	+ $1

Public

Assets		Liabilities and Capital Accounts
Demand Deposits	+ $1	
Goods and Services	− $1	

With the disbursement, the total of bank reserves increases by $1 billion and thereby returns to its original level, while the total of demand deposits increases to $1 billion above its original level. Unlike the case of Treasury financing of a deficit by selling securities to the public, financing a deficit by selling securities to the commercial banks increases the money supply.

In the opposite case—a budget surplus of $1 billion the Treasury uses to buy back securities held by the commercial banks—the results will be no change in bank reserves, but a $1 billion decrease in the money supply. With a $1 billion surplus, the public will have drawn down its demand deposit balances by $1 billion more in payment of federal taxes than it will have built up through deposit of checks generated by federal government disbursements. In our first case, the Treasury used that $1 billion surplus to buy back U.S. government securities held by the public and thereby to return that extra $1 billion to the demand deposits of the public. However, in this case, the $1 billion decrease in demand deposits is not offset. In buying back securities held by the commercial banks, the effect on the commercial banks' T-account is a $1 billion decrease in security holdings and a $1 billion decrease in demand deposits. With no change in the public's currency holdings, this is a $1 billion decrease in the money supply.

Although this Treasury debt retirement transaction in itself has the indicated effects, these are not necessarily the final effects. Note that the commercial banks are in a position to replace the U.S. government securities bought back by the Treasury with loans or other securities. Because there has been no change in total bank reserves, there need not be a change in total deposits. If carried through this last step, the final effects will be no change in the money supply as well as no change in bank reserves. The Treasury, however, will have retired $1 billion of the national debt as a result of the budget surplus.

Borrowing from the Federal Reserve Banks Finally, the Treasury may finance a deficit by borrowing from the Federal Reserve Banks. Assume that it sells $1 billion of securities to the Federal Reserve Banks, for which it receives payment in the form of a $1 billion increase in its deposits at these banks, as shown by the following set of T-accounts:

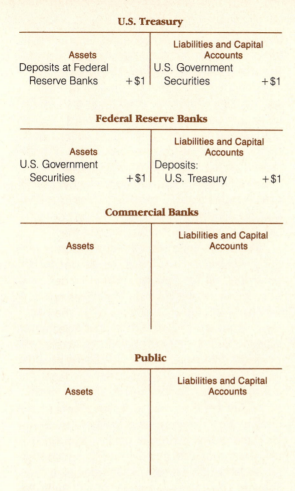

U.S. Treasury

Assets	Liabilities and Capital Accounts
Deposits at Federal Reserve Banks +$1	U.S. Government Securities +$1

Federal Reserve Banks

Assets	Liabilities and Capital Accounts
U.S. Government Securities +$1	Deposits: U.S. Treasury +$1

Commercial Banks

Assets	Liabilities and Capital Accounts

Public

Assets	Liabilities and Capital Accounts

When the Treasury disburses this $1 billion in payment for goods and services, the T-account entries will be the same as shown earlier for the disbursement of $1 billion borrowed from the commercial banks. The Treasury's deposits at the Federal Reserve Banks will decrease by $1 billion, and reserves of banks will increase by $1 billion. However, in this case the $1 billion added to bank reserves is a net increase, not an offset to a previous decrease. We previously noted that, on balance, Treasury borrowing from the commercial banks left bank reserves unchanged, because it first decreased reserves and then increased them by an offsetting amount. Treasury borrowing from the Federal Reserve

Banks increases reserves by an amount equal to the amount borrowed.

Therefore, as compared to financing a deficit by borrowing from the commercial banks, financing by borrowing from the Federal Reserve Banks not only increases the money supply by the amount of the deficit, but provides the potential for an increase equal to a multiple of the deficit. If the commercial banks had no excess reserves at the time of the $1 billion of deficit financing, they will now have excess reserves as their total reserves increase by $1 billion and their required reserves increase by some fraction of this $1 billion. In terms of its potential effect on the money supply, this method of financing a Treasury deficit is clearly the most expansionary.

The effects of this method are essentially the same as those of financing a deficit by having the Treasury print up an equal amount of paper money (although this old-fashioned way of covering a Treasury deficit is no longer used). The Treasury, of course, pays its bills not by issuing paper money but by writing checks against its deposits at the Federal Reserve Banks. However, it can acquire additional deposits at the Federal Reserve Banks by selling those banks newly-printed Treasury currency instead of selling them newly-printed securities. If it were to sell Treasury currency, the only differences in the preceding set of T-accounts would be the replacement of a noninterest-bearing Treasury liability (Treasury Currency) for an interest-bearing liability (U.S. Government Securities) on the liability side of the Treasury's T-account and on the asset side of the Federal Reserve Banks' T-account.[16]

In the opposite case—a budget surplus of $1 billion, which the Treasury uses to buy back securities of that amount held by the Federal Reserve Banks—the immediate results will be a $1 billion decrease in bank reserves and in the

---

[16] Although Treasury currency appears as a liability of the Treasury for bookkeeping purposes, realistically it is not a liability at all. As it is already the final form of money itself, it is not something the Treasury is obligated to exchange for money at some specified date.

money supply. However, if the commercial banks had no excess reserves at the time, they will now suffer a reserve deficiency as their total reserves decrease by $1 billion and their required reserves decrease by a fraction of that amount. Further decrease in the money supply will follow and the total decrease in the money supply will be equal to a multiple of the Treasury surplus.

This completes our review of the way in which alternative methods of financing a Treasury deficit (or of disposing of a Treasury surplus) will affect bank reserves and the money supply. In the case of a deficit, financing by selling securities to the public leaves both bank reserves and the money supply unchanged; financing by selling securities to the commercial banks leaves reserves unchanged, but increases the money supply by the amount of the deficit; and financing by selling securities to the Federal Reserve Banks increases reserves by the amount of the deficit and, at least potentially, increases the money supply by a multiple of the increase in reserves.

A Concluding Note

Any treatment of the money supply process naturally begins with a consideration of the meaning of the term *money supply* and then proceeds to the process through which changes in the money supply are effected. The explanation of that process involves what is often called "money mechanics," to which the major part of this chapter has been devoted. We have traced such particulars as how open-market operations and borrowing at the Federal Reserve Banks affect bank reserves, how the change in the money supply is determined by the change in bank reserves times the money supply multiplier, and how the money supply multiplier is altered by changes in the public's currency/demand deposit and time deposit/demand deposit ratios and by the commercial banks' desired excess reserves/demand deposit ratio. All of these and some other relationships not listed here are basically mechanical in nature.

We have also noted matters of a less mechanical nature, including the important matter of the degree of control that the Federal Reserve maintains over the money supply. Over any period of time, like a month, the money supply may differ from the amount targeted by the Federal Reserve, because the Federal Reserve in so short a time span is unable to offset actions by the public, the commercial banks, and the federal government—all of which influence the supply of money. However, over a longer period of time, the Federal Reserve can compensate for such influences and probably bring the money supply very close to the targeted figure.

Most economists would probably agree with this conclusion, if one adds the very important condition that the Federal Reserve is willing to sacrifice other objectives to that of exercising a very close degree of control over the money supply. At times, the growth of the money supply over a period of months or even years follows a path markedly different from that the Federal Reserve might have preferred. Some observers conclude from this that the Federal Reserve was powerless to prevent this unwanted outcome. However, the Federal Reserve may have deliberately sacrificed the closer degree of control it could have achieved over the money supply in order to realize what at the time was regarded as a more important outcome—the prevention of an undesirably large change in interest rates.

Consider a couple of illustrations, one from forty years ago and one from a few years ago. When the United States entered World War II at the end of 1941, the Treasury and the Federal Reserve recognized that the financing of the anticipated huge increase in government expenditures would be accomplished, in large part, through borrowing. All of that borrowing could have been from the public; the result then would have been no increase in the money supply from this source. The Federal Reserve could have kept close control over the growth of the money supply. But such a large increase in borrowing from the public would have drastically forced up interest rates over time and greatly complicated the

Treasury's problem of finding buyers among the public for successive new issues of its securities when the market values of its outstanding securities were being forced down by rising interest rates.[17] The Federal Reserve, therefore, sacrificed control over the money supply for the sake of holding interest rates down. Through purchases of securities in the open market, the Federal Reserve pumped additional reserves into the commercial banks, enabling them to buy a significant part of the newly issued Treasury securities. This made it possible for the Treasury to finance its borrowing without running into higher interest rates, but it meant that the Federal Reserve had sacrificed its control over the money supply.

More recently, in the months preceding October 1979, there was unusually rapid growth of the money supply because the Federal Reserve had been following a policy of keeping the Federal funds rate from moving above the upper limit of the range it had set, despite market pressures working to push it higher. To restrain the rise in the Federal funds rate—and through this the rise in other short-term interest rates—the Federal Reserve found itself expanding reserves to a degree that resulted in an unacceptably rapid rate of growth of the money supply. In a dramatic change of approach, on October 6, the Federal Reserve announced that it would begin to pay

---

[17] The basis for the inverse relationship between interest rates and the market prices of outstanding securities is explained on pp. 213–16.

much more attention to bank reserves and much less attention to interest rates. In the following months, it failed to provide additional reserves at the rate needed to meet the growing demand for money; consequently, by the spring of 1980, interest rates had soared to the highest levels in a hundred years. The Federal Reserve had reasserted its control over the money supply, but under the conditions then existing was only able to do this at the price of temporarily extraordinarily high interest rates.

Why interest rates will rise in response to an increase in the demand for money under conditions of an unchanged supply of money will be discussed in detail in the following chapter. There the demand for money is examined, and the supply of and demand for money are brought together in a model of interest rate determination. Our concern here is merely to point out that the closeness of the degree with which the Federal Reserve can control the supply of money, to a large degree, depends on its willingness to forgo control over interest rates. Although some structural changes would make its instruments of control more effective than they are, the Federal Reserve already has the tools needed to control the money supply over a period of months. What occasionally appears to be a *failure* to do so should not automatically be interpreted as an *inability* to do so. At the time, the Federal Reserve may have acted as it did because it regarded control over interest rates as more important to the stability of the economy than control over the money supply.

11

The Supply of and Demand for Money and the Rate of Interest

OVERVIEW

As developed in Part 2, the Keynesian model did not explicitly include the supply of and the demand for money in its discussion of what determines the income, output, and price levels. In contrast to classical theory, which could not even tentatively deal with these matters without introducing money into the system, the incomplete Keynesian theory could at least provide provisional answers without including money. In the complete Keynesian model, however, the supply of and demand for money together determine the rate of interest. This chapter, accordingly, discusses the Keynesian theory of money and interest. The following chapters will complete the Keynesian model, building on the earlier presentation of Keynesian theory to show how it incorporates money and interest in the determination of the economy's income, output, employment, and price levels.

As we saw in Chapter 10, there are a number of measures of the money supply. The measure adopted for use here, M-1A, is the narrowest. The chapter briefly discusses the obvious but important fact that money is one among many assets that people may move into or out of by moving out of or into other assets. The chapter then turns

to its first major topic—the demand for money. Our approach follows Keynes in identifying three types of demand—transactions, precautionary, and speculative. Because of their importance here, the transactions and speculative demands are examined in some detail. Classical theory denied the existence of what Keynes called the speculative demand, and it is here that we find the basis for the most radical departure of Keynesian theory from classical theory.

From the analysis of the demand for money is derived a demand function for money. In the next section of the chapter, we explain how the supply of and demand for money determine the equilibrium rate of interest. Then we review how such factors as changes in the supply of money, the level of income, and the speculative demand for money cause changes in the equilibrium rate of interest.

The final section of the chapter provides a sketch of the theory of the demand for money from simple classical theory through Keynesian theory to the modern quantity theory. The major part of this section is devoted to a nontechnical explanation of Milton Friedman's modern quantity theory of money, which is contrasted with both simple classical quantity theory and Keynesian theory.

In Keynesian theory, the rate of interest depends on the supply of and demand for money. As this theory is developed in this chapter, we will see that it differs sharply from the classical theory of interest rate determination discussed in Chapter 9. There the interest rate was seen to depend on the "real" factors of the supply of saving ("thrift") and the demand for investment ("productivity of capital"). Although these real factors indirectly enter into the determination of the interest rate in Keynesian theory, the monetary factors of the supply of and demand for money are at the forefront of the theory.

With regard to the supply of money, any number of measures are possible. The Federal Reserve measures of the supply of money vary from the narrowest (M-1A, which limits money to currency and demand deposits held by the public) to succcessively broader measures (M-1B, M-2, and M-3).[1] M-1B includes M-1A plus amounts in NOW, ATS, and similar accounts. Unlike M-1A assets, the amounts held in NOW, ATS, and similar accounts are means of payment on which holders receive an interest return. Ordinarily the rate of return on these accounts is lower than that on the deposits that are added to M-1B to get to M-2 and added to M-2 to get to M-3. However, unlike the amounts held in M-1B assets, the additional amounts included in M-2 and M-3 assets are not part of the economy's means of payment.

To understand what follows, we must be completely clear as to the measure of the money supply with which we will be working. Some statements that are incorrect on the basis of a narrow measure are correct on the basis of a broad measure. In developing the theory of the demand for money, we will use the very narrow measure of M-1A. This limits money to the public's holdings of currency and demand deposits at commercial banks; it also limits money to noninterest-bearing assets.[2] It therefore distinguishes money from other financial assets on which interest is earned. Moreover, because this measure includes no assets that do not serve as means of payment, it is made up of what may be described as *noninterest-bearing means of payment.*

Each person on any date has some amount of wealth, and each person may hold wealth in a number of forms, including money as here defined, regular savings and time deposits, interest-bearing securities such as bonds, equity securities or stock shares, real estate, and physical assets of other kinds. He or she may distribute total wealth in various ways among these assets, and each will seek his or her optimal portfolio. The amount of any one asset in the portfolio may be expected to vary directly with the rate of return on that asset and inversely with the rates of return on substitute assets. Money as here defined has no explicit rate of return (so many cents of interest per dollar per year), but it has an implicit rate of return in the form of the convenience, security, and maneuverability that goes

---

[1] See pp. 171–73.

[2] There are deposits at commercial banks which are the equivalent of interest-bearing demand deposits, but these are NOW and ATS accounts, which are part of M-1B but not of M-1A.

with having immediately available purchasing power. Whatever the implicit rate of return on money may be at any time, if that rate remains constant while the rates on one or more alternative assets rise, portfolio balance suggests that a smaller proportion of total assets should be held in the form of money and a correspondingly larger proportion should be held in one or more other assets. Furthermore, given the large number of different kinds of assets available, a change in the yield on any one of these will often involve more than an offsetting switch between this particular asset and another. Assembling the portfolio that maximizes the wealth-holder's utility may involve numerous changes.[3]

An approach to money and interest that considers all of the assets a person may choose to hold as alternatives to holding money is consistent with what people do in practice. However, this approach is complex, because it involves such complications as the rates of return on many different kinds of assets and on different maturities of the same kind of asset. The simpler approach, which we will be working through in this chapter, involves only one of the alternative assets—long-term bonds. In other words, we will focus on two assets—money and long-term bonds. At any time, a wealth-holder may either supply bonds to the market and demand money or supply money and demand bonds. This way of looking at the demand for money as the opposite side of the supply of bonds is critical to the theory of interest. Once we understand the reasons why people demand the amount of money they do at any one time, given the money supply that exists at that time, we can explain why the rate of interest is what it is.

The Demand for Money

One reason people demand money is that it is needed in any economy in which almost every

person and firm sells goods and services (including factor services) for money and in turn uses money to buy the goods and services offered by others. Functionally, this amounts to the use of money as a medium of exchange. Classical theory explained the demand for money as essentially a demand resulting from this need for money as a medium of exchange.

In Keynesian theory, money becomes much more than a medium of exchange, much more than a device for mediating transactions in the marketplace. People also demand money for speculative purposes and as security against unforeseen needs for cash reserves. The breakdown of the demand for money into transactions and precautionary and speculative demands plays a vital part in the theory Keynes advanced to explain the interest rate.

Transactions Demand

Everyone needs to hold some amount of money to carry out ordinary day-to-day transactions. However, the closer the synchronization between the timing of one's receipts and the timing of payments, the smaller will be the average money balance one must hold for this purpose. If the amount that a person received at each point in time equaled the amount that he or she paid out at each point in time, no money balance at all would be required for transactions. In practice, of course, no person or firm even approaches this limiting case, despite the ability of each to exercise some control over the timing of receipts and payments. Everyone must, therefore, hold some amount of money to cover the unevenness between the timing of what comes in and what goes out.

No two persons have identical time patterns of payments, and few find their total payments for any month evenly distributed over the month. Particular days include above-average payments: The day the mortgage payment or the rent is due, the day the car payment must be made, the day for payment of all or part of the balance on department store charge accounts, MasterCard, Visa, and so forth. However, as a

---

[3]An introduction to the process of portfolio balance is provided in Chapter 26 as part of the analysis of how monetary policy works. See pp. 509–92.

first approximation, let us assume that there is an even distribution of payments over the month. What we want to see is that, with this pattern of payments, a person whose receipts for the month all come in on the first day of the month will require a larger average money balance over the month than would be the case if these same total receipts came in at intervals during the month. As a general rule, the average money balance a person or firm must hold over time for transactions declines as the frequency of receipts rises.

For example, assume an individual has receipts of $1,400 per month and that he makes payments of an equal amount each month. For convenience, assume that each month has exactly four weeks. Monthly receipts of $1,400 may arrive in a number of different time patterns, such as $1,400 on the first day of the month, $700 on the first and fifteenth days of the month, or $350 on the first day of each week. (An amount of $2,800 bimonthly would also technically qualify.) If this individual actually receives the $1,400 on the first day of the month and disburses the full amount evenly over the month, he will have a money balance of $1,400 at the beginning of the first week, $1,050 at the beginning of the second week, $700 at the beginning of the third week, and $350 at the beginning of the fourth week. His balance shrinks to zero at the end of the fourth week, but then jumps back again to $1,400 the next day. His *average* money balance for the month in this case is $700—an amount equal to half of his *monthly* receipts. His actual money balance at each point during the month is shown by the curve in Part A of Figure 11-1.

Suppose now that this individual receives the same monthly receipts at a rate of $350 per week paid to him on the first day of each week. Assuming as before that his payments equal his total receipts, his money balance at the beginning of the first day of the week will be $350, at the beginning of the second day $300, and so forth with an *average* money balance of $175 for the week—an amount equal to one-half of his *weekly* receipts. In this case, his actual money balance at each point during each week is shown in Part B

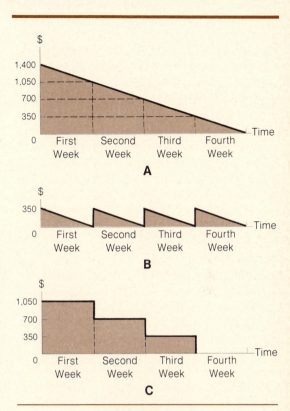

FIGURE 11-1
Hypothetical Allocation of an Individual's Transactions Balance Between Money and Earning Assets

of Figure 11-1. The switch from an arrangement in which all of the month's income is received at the beginning of the month to that in which one-fourth of the same income is received at the beginning of each of the month's four weeks (4 × $350 instead of 1 × $1,400) means a fourfold rise in the frequency of receipts and a reduction in this person's average money balance to one-fourth ($175 instead of $700) of what it would be in the monthly case. If we extend the illustration to the case in which the monthly receipts of $1,400 arrive at $50 per day, we would find that this sevenfold increase in the frequency of receipts (7 × $50 instead of 1 × $350) would be accompanied by a reduction in this person's average money balance to one-seventh ($25 instead of $175) of what it would be in the weekly case. In pushing this illustration all the way to the daily case, we reach a point of synchronization between each day's receipts of $50 and each day's payments of $50. The person holds an average balance of $25 during each day, but does not carry over any balance from one day to the next as is required in the weekly case and a fortiori in the monthly case. The general rule noted ealier should now be clear: *The average money balance a person or firm must hold in order to mediate transactions decreases as the frequency of receipts increases.*[4]

This general rule holds true with the usual assumption that other things remain equal. In our illustration, a person's balance drops from $700 to $175 as he switches from monthly receipts to weekly receipts on the assumption that his total receipts and payments remain at $1,400 for the period of a month. If these should somehow jump fivefold at the same time that there is a switch from monthly to weekly receipts, this person's average money balance would rise from $700 to $875. In this case, the effect that the rise in the dollar amount of receipts and payments has in

increasing his average money balance more than offsets the effect that the switch from monthly to weekly receipts has in decreasing it. If this fivefold increase in receipts and payments had occurred with no change in the frequency of receipts and no change from the same even distribution of payments, the average money balance needed to handle the larger volume of transactions would be five times what it was before. This leads us to another general rule: *The average money balance a person or firm must hold in order to mediate transactions increases proportionally with the dollar volume of transactions.* Here again we hold other things equal, in this case including the frequency of receipts of each person and firm.

In summary, over time the amount of money needed to handle transactions will tend to shrink to the extent that some persons and firms achieve a closer degree of synchronization between receipts and payments; over time the amount of money needed will tend to increase to the extent that the dollar volume of transactions to be mediated increases. The dollar volume of transactions has, of course, doubled and redoubled over the long run. Whatever the strength of the forces working in the other direction may have been, the rising volume of transactions has many times outweighed it to give us an almost uninterrupted increase year after year in the amount of money balances that all persons and firms combined find it necessary to hold in order to mediate the total volume of transactions.

Transactions Demand as a Function of Income   The actual growth in the total volume of transactions has been accompanied by a growth in the size of the gross national income or gross national product. Because the dollar volume of transactions for each time period includes all kinds of transactions in intermediate product and in securities and existing real property, it far exceeds each period's gross national income or product. However, in the belief that the ratio of GNP to the dollar volume of all transactions is reasonably stable, we may say as a first approx-

---

[4] It must be emphasized that this general rule applies on the assumption that the pattern of a person's *payments* over time is even or at least approximately so. A person's *purchases* may be spaced out evenly over time, but *payment* may occur at discrete points in time. Suppose a person's purchases of $50 per day are all on credit, with the settlement date of all accounts falling on a particular day each month. If his receipts of $1,400 per month all come in on the same day that payment of the $1,400 falls due, his average money balance for the month will be close to zero. He may hold money for only a matter of hours or minutes on that one day. On the other hand, if this person's receipts came in evenly at $50 per day, it will be seen that his average money balance for the month would be $700. His balance would rise by $50 per day to $1,400 at the end of 28 days, at which time he would pay the $1,400 which then falls due. In this case, the more frequent his receipts, the larger his average money balance would be. Although this is plainly an extreme illustration, it does indicate that there can be special conditions under which the general rule as stated does not hold.

imation that the amount of money balances that the public as a whole wishes to hold for transactions purposes depends directly on the level of income. We can thereby relate money balances to the variable with which we have been working throughout the preceding chapters.

In this relationship, the actual dollar amount the public seeks to hold to carry out the transactions associated with any given level of output, Y, will vary proportionally with the price level, P, at which that output sells. Obviously twice as much money is needed to buy a commodity when the price is \$100 as it takes to buy the same commodity when the price is \$50. The same is true for the grand total of purchases designated by PY. Any change in PY will require the same change in transactions balances, whether that change is entirely in P, entirely in Y, or in any combination of the two. For example, if the public needs \$1 to handle the transactions represented by \$4 of income, required transactions balances will be \$100 billion when income is at the \$400 billion level, whether that level of PY is \$4 × 100 billion units, \$2 × 200 billion units, or any other combination equal to \$400 billion.

This relationship may be expressed in equation form as $M_t = k(PY)$. Here M_t is the amount of money demanded for transactions and, assuming M_t and (PY) are linearly related, k is the fraction of money income over which the public wishes to hold command in the form of transactions balances. Following the illustration above in which k is assumed to be 1/4, M_t will be \$100 billion when PY is \$400 billion. In the same way, M_t would be \$125 billion if PY were \$500 billion.

The amount of money demanded for transactions may be expressed either in *nominal* or in *real* terms. The equation above, $M_t = k(PY)$, which is in nominal terms, may also be written as $M_t = P \cdot k(Y)$ on the customary assumption that a change in P will cause a proportional change in the dollar amount of transactions balances demanded. Then, to convert from a demand for nominal balances to a demand for real balances, one merely divides $M_t = P \cdot k(Y)$ through by P to get $M_t/P = k(Y)$. Here M_t/P is the amount of real

balances demanded for transactions. This amount will also be designated by m_t.

The way in which the amount of these real money balances demanded varies with the level of Y and the size of k is illustrated in Figure 11-2. The line labeled $k(Y)$ indicates the amount of m_t for various levels of Y with k assumed to be 1/4. If Y were \$400 billion, m_t would be \$100 billion; if Y were \$500 billion, m_t would be \$125 billion. If k were 1/5, we would have the line $k'(Y)$ in this figure. For real incomes of \$400 and \$500 billion, real transaction balances demanded would then be only \$80 and \$100 billion, respectively.

The size of k depends on institutional and structural conditions within the economy. These conditions include the previously emphasized degree of synchronization between receipts and payments for each person and firm; the time required for payments originating in one location to become receipts in other locations, or the speed of movement of money; the degree of integration of industry, integration converting what were money payments between firms into mere intrafirm bookkeeping entries; and other such factors. Some of these factors do not change significantly even over a decade, but it appears that the speed of money's movement does. The 1960s and 1970s have witnessed revolutionary changes in the technology of moving money. Developments like the checkless transfer

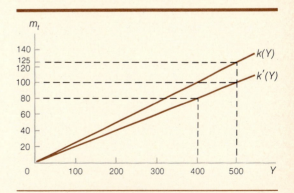

FIGURE 11-2
Transactions Demand for Money

of wages and salaries by computer, the lock-box system of mail delivery of checks, and the use by the Federal Reserve of a fleet of jets to transport checks between Federal Reserve Banks have resulted in the fact that each dollar of demand deposits at the start of the 1980s mediated about three times the dollar amount of transactions that it did at the beginning of the 1960s. In terms of Figure 11-2, this suggests that the slope of the straight line may show more than a negligible decrease over a few years. However, in order to simplify the present analysis, we will assume that k is stable in the short run. In other words, we will assume that the chief determinant of changes in the amount of real balances held for transactions is changes in the level of real income. Graphically, changes in m_t are then primarily the result of movements along a line like $k(Y)$ rather than changes in k, that is, changes in the slope of the line.

Transactions Demand as a Function of the Rate of Interest   The amount of real balances demanded for transactions purposes will vary directly with the level of real income. It may also vary inversely with the rate of interest. Consider again the case of a person who receives $1,400 on the first of each month and spends his total receipts evenly over the 28 days of the month. As previously noted, at any point during the month, this person's holdings of money for transactions would be as shown in Part A of Figure 11-1. It may be seen that this person holds $1,050 of completely idle money for transactions during the first week, $700 during the second, and $350 during the third. Could he not convert this temporarily idle money into an interest-bearing asset? Parts B and C of the figure illustrate what he might do. On the first day of the first week (payday), he retains $350 to cover the first week's payments (see Part B), and uses $1,050 to acquire earning assets (see Part C). On the first day of the second week, he cashes in $350 of his earning assets to obtain money to cover payments of the second week, and so forth for the third and fourth weeks, after which the cycle

repeats itself. In this fashion, the individual reduces his average transactions balances to $175 for the month (Part B) and makes his average earning-asset balance $525 for the month (Part C). These, of course, add up to the same $700 average balance shown in Part A.

Do people do this? Yes. In practice, people—at least some people, under some conditions—have more alternatives than the simple choice between holding money and holding long-term bonds. For example, the person in the previous illustration could put his $1,400 into an ATS account on the first day of each month and the bank would transfer funds (usually in $50 minimum amounts) into his checking account as needed to cover the checks presented for payment. This person would earn interest on the balance in his ATS account at the current rate paid on savings accounts. However, the bank imposes a charge for the services provided in connection with an ATS account. If the interest earned on the balance in the account is less than the service charge, this person would have been better off in money terms by keeping the full amount in a checking account. Alternatively, he could earn interest and avoid any service charge by keeping the balance in a regular savings account, but now he would have to visit the bank periodically to transfer funds from the savings account to the checking account to cover the $350 in checks written each week. The cost is no longer in the form of a service charge, but in the form of time and inconvenience. There are differences of detail among different assets of this kind, but a cost of one kind or another typically must be paid in order to earn interest on transactions balances placed in such accounts. Whether or not anyone will find it advantageous to follow the course noted in the illustration depends on how these costs compare with the benefits.

This comparison has been analyzed in detail in economics literature. It involves the choice between holding idle transactions balances in interest-bearing securities (like U.S. Treasury bills, commercial paper, or other short-term money market instruments) and holding such balances in money. Among other things, the cost per purchase and sale of such instruments, the rate of interest earned on them, and the frequency of purchases and sales determines the profitability of placing idle transactions balances in Treasury bills and similar assets.[5] Nonetheless, with the cost per purchase and sale given, there is clearly some rate of interest at which it becomes profitable to switch transactions balances into interest-bearing securities, even if these funds may be spared from transactions needs for only weeks or even days. The higher the interest rate, the larger will be the fraction of any given amount of transactions balances that can profitably be diverted into securities.

During the 1979–80 period of record high short-term interest rates, the number of "money market" or "liquid asset" mutual funds multiplied.

Through these funds, individuals who are usually unable to make direct purchase of money market instruments because of the large minimum purchase can participate indirectly in the market for these instruments with as little as $1,000. However, prospective purchasers face financial costs because the operators of such funds pass on their costs and add a charge for their services in the form of a "management fee." But the higher the interest rate being paid on such instruments—and therefore the higher the rate being paid by this kind of mutual fund—the more profitable it is for people to divert transactions balances into this kind of fund. With the return on such funds as high as 20 percent in the spring and fall of 1980, it is safe to say that the amount of transactions balances being held in money form had been reduced close to the absolute minimum.

The relationship between the level of income, the rate of interest, and the transactions demand for money for the economy as a whole is depicted in Figure 11-3. If $Y = \$400$ billion and $k = 1/4$, m_t is $100 billion as shown by the curve Y_1. This

---

[5] See J. Tobin, "The Interest-Elasticity of the Transactions Demand for Cash," in *Review of Economics and Statistics,* August 1956, pp. 241–47, and W.J. Baumol, "The Transactions Demand for Cash: An Inventory Theoretic Approach," in *Quarterly Journal of Economics,* Nov. 1952, pp. 545–56. The following simple illustration will bring out the basic point. Assume an individual is holding $1,000 for the purpose of paying a bill that falls due one month later. Even if he were able to buy so small an amount, would it pay for him to put this $1,000 into a security for the one month? If the dealer imposes a flat charge of $1 per purchase and sale plus an additional charge of 10¢ per $100, it will cost our individual $2, or $1 + (10 × 10¢), to buy a $1,000 security at the beginning of the month and an equal amount to sell at the end of the month. Total cost is $4. If the interest rate that he can earn is 6 percent per annum, for one month he will receive 1/12 × 0.06 × $1,000, or $5, to leave him with a gain of $1 over costs. At a 4 percent interest rate, he will earn $3.33, or an amount less than his costs. A 4.8 percent rate is that at which the interest earned will just cover costs. It does not, however, follow that the individual will buy at any rate above 4.8 percent. With only $1,000 involved, the $1 to be earned at a 6 percent rate or even the $2 to be earned at a 7 percent rate may not be worth the trouble of the record-keeping and paper work required. At the same time, if the amount involved is relatively large, a 6 percent rate will be quite attractive. On $1 million for the month, there will be a gain of $3,998. Even for the wealthy individual, this amount will offset the minor problem involved in arranging the purchase and sale of securities.

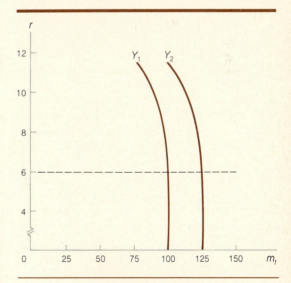

FIGURE 11-3
Interest-Elastic Transactions
Demand for Money

figure of $100 billion, however, is valid only as long as the interest rate is not above 6 percent, for example. As the rate rises above 6 percent, the transactions demand for money becomes interest elastic, indicating that given the costs of switching into and out of securities, an interest rate above 6 percent is sufficiently high to attract some amount of transactions balances into securities. For still higher rates, the amount so diverted becomes larger, as indicated by the backward slope of the Y_1 curve. For a level of income of $500 billion, the transactions demand curve shifts to Y_2 but again slopes backward at an interest rate above 6 percent. The curves Y_1 and Y_2 correspond to incomes of $400 and $500 billion on the $k(Y)$ curve of Figure 11-2.

It is difficult to generalize concerning the interest elasticity of the transactions demand for money for the economy as a whole. A giant corporation that this week holds millions of dollars not needed for transactions until next week will not forgo the oppportunity to put these funds into earning assets for a week or even less if the interest rate is high enough to yield a profit. An individual whose average transactions balance is moderate is less likely to be so interest rate conscious. His transactions demand will probably be almost completely interest inelastic at other than irresistibly high interest rates like those experienced in 1974, 1980, and 1981.

Most economists agree that in practice there is some interest rate at which the transactions demand curve for money for the economy as a whole begins to slope backward (as in Figure 11-3). This means that our equation for transactions demand should become $m_t = f(Y, r)$ and that there is no longer a simple linear relationship between m_t and Y. To simplify our analysis, however, we will assume that this demand is perfectly inelastic with respect to the interest rate and retain our simple equation for this demand: $m_t = k(Y)$. In terms of Figure 11-3, the transactions demand for money becomes a function of the level of income alone. Changes in the level of income shift the demand curve, as from Y_1 to Y_2, but the curve is perfectly inelastic with respect to the interest rate at high as well as low rates.

Precautionary Demand

Transactions demand for money stems largely from a lack of synchronization between receipts and expenditures; similarly, precautionary demand arises primarily because of the uncertainty of future receipts and expenditures. Precautionary balances enable persons to meet unanticipated increases in expenditures or unanticipated delays in receipts.

This type of demand for money varies to some extent with one's income. Individuals need more money and are better able to set aside more money for this purpose at higher income levels. The precautionary demand also varies inversely with the interest rate. Unlike a transactions balance (something definitely scheduled for use in the near future), a precautionary balance secures one against a "rainy day" that may never come. At a high enough interest rate, one may be tempted to assume the greater risk of a smaller precautionary balance in exchange for the high interest rate that can be earned by converting part of this balance into interest-bearing assets.[6]

---

[6]Although precautionary demand may vary with the income level and the interest rate as transactions demand does, the individual's need that precautionary balances satisfy may nowadays be met quite well at little or no cost in ways other than by holding money balances. For many individuals, the recent development of credit cards has reduced the amount of money they would ordinarily hold for both precautionary and transactions purposes. Many emergency expenses can be met with a credit card—it can even be used to get cash immediately, and cash can, of course, be used to meet any kind of expenditure. For larger amounts, individuals can now do what business firms have long done: establish "lines of credit" with banks. Because a $1,000 line of credit means that this amount is immediately available at the individual's request, it is as if he had this amount sitting in his checking account as a precautionary balance. Although banks may charge a fee for setting up a line of credit whether the person draws on the line or not, some charge a fee only if one draws on the line. These banks, of course, limit this "free" service to those who maintain a deposit account with the bank; it is a device to attract new depositors to these banks. To the individual, however, it is a way of maintaining what amounts to a precautionary money balance at little or no extra cost to himself.

Although precautionary demand may be formally distinguished from transactions demand, the total amount of money held to meet both demands is viewed primarily as a function of the level of income and, to some extent, of the interest rate. As in the case of the transactions demand, we will assume, for the sake of simplicity, that precautionary demand is interest inelastic and that it too depends solely on the level of income. If both transactions demand and precautionary demand are functions of income, the two may be combined so that our earlier equation, $m_t = k(Y)$, may now be understood to include in m_t both transactions and precautionary balances.

Speculative Demand

The proposition that money is held for transactions and precautionary purposes does not conflict with the classical view. A transactions balance is nothing more than money in its function as a medium of exchange. A precautionary balance can be added to the classical system without materially affecting its conclusions. But this is as far as the classical theory went. The speculative demand for money, a systematic part of the demand for money in Keynesian theory, represents a distinct break with classical theory.

Classical theory assumed that a person would hold no money in excess of the amount needed to meet his transactions (including precautionary) requirements. To do otherwise would be to forgo the interest that could be earned by putting that money into a bond. Classical theorists reasoned that, even if the interest rate were very low, it would be better to get some return than none at all. Keynes, however, pointed out that one who buys a bond is "speculating" that the interest rate will not rise appreciably during the period in which he intends to hold the bond. If he believes that it will rise, he would be wise to hold noninterest-bearing money. This uncertainty as to the future interest rate causes people to hold money for speculative purposes. If the future interest rate were known with certainty, there would be no speculative demand for money, and there could be no objection to the classical concept of the demand for money.

Security Prices and the Interest Rate   To understand speculative demand, we must examine the relationship between the interest rate and the market price of a debt security. Take, for example, a marketable U.S. government bond on which a purchaser faces no "credit risk"—that is, no risk of default. There is no credit risk because the federal government can, if it so chooses, meet its obligations by merely creating the money needed for this purpose. Also for a U.S. government bond—and for most other direct Treasury obligations—there is negligible "marketability risk" or "liquidity risk." An organized nationwide market exists for such securities; a holder may at any time sell at a price close to the last quoted price. Unlike the markets for some other securities, the price variations on successive transactions are ordinarily minor. However, although a U.S. government bond is practically free of credit and marketability risks, like other securities, it is subject to "market risk"—the risk that the market interest rate may change.

These U.S. government bonds, like any other bonds freely traded in the market, have a dollar amount and an interest rate, commonly referred to as the coupon rate, printed on the face of the obligation. This coupon rate times the face amount is the yearly amount the issuer will pay the holder. For example, assume a 25-year, $1,000 bond with a 5 percent coupon issued in 1965. The U.S. Treasury promises to pay $50 interest each year from 1966 through 1990 and the face amount of $1,000 at maturity in 1990. Assuming it is now the year 1985, how much would that bond sell for in the market? In other words, what would be the present market value of the stream of interest income of $50 per year to be received from 1986 through 1990 and the $1,000 of principal to be received in 1990? To answer the question, we insert the interest rate the U.S. Treasury has to pay in 1985 to borrow money for a five-year maturity and the other figures into the general equation for the present value of a future income stream.

To develop this equation, we start with the ordinary compound interest equation. Suppose that the market rate of interest is 5 percent. If one lends $95.24 at 5 percent for one year, he will receive $100 at the end of the year.

$$\$95.24 + (0.05 \times \$95.24) = \$95.24(1 + 0.05)$$
$$= \$100$$

In general, at the end of one year, a lender will get back

$$P_1 = P_0(1 + r)$$

Here r is the rate of interest and P_0 is the amount lent. If he lends the P_1 amount for the second year, at the end of that year, he will get back

$$P_2 = P_0(1 + r)(1 + r) = P_0(1 + r)^2$$

The rule is that a sum of P_0 loaned at interest rate r for n years will grow to

$$P_n = P_0(1 + r)^n$$

The process of finding the present value of a future sum is the reverse of the process of accumulation. For example, what is the present value of $100 receivable one year from today when the market rate of interest is 5 percent? We are given P_1 of $100 and r of 0.05 and wish to find P_0. Because $P_1 = P_0(1 + r)$, it follows that

$$P_0 = \frac{P_1}{(1 + r)} = \frac{\$100}{(1 + 0.05)} = \$95.24$$

What is the present value of $100 receivable two years from today? Because $P_2 = P_0(1 + r)^2$, we have

$$P_0 = \frac{P_2}{(1 + r)^2} = \frac{\$100}{(1 + 0.05)^2} = \$90.70$$

In general, we can find the present value of the series of future sums generated by any bond by discounting each portion of that series back to the present by the appropriate rate of interest. Using V for present value, $R_1, R_2, \ldots R_n$ for each part of the stream of interest income, and A for

the face or principal amount to be paid in Year n, we have

$$V = \frac{R_1}{(1 + r)} + \frac{R_2}{(1 + r)^2} + \cdots + \frac{R_n}{(1 + r)^n} + \frac{A}{(1 + r)^n}$$

Let's return to the illustration of the U.S. Treasury bond issued in 1965 and maturing in 1990. Assuming today is 1985, what is the present value of that bond? Remember that, as of 1985, the Treasury promises future sums of $50 each year from 1986 through 1990, and $1,000 at maturity in 1990. Suppose that for this five-year maturity the rate of interest the Treasury must pay in 1985 is 8 percent. We find the present (1985) value of that outstanding bond by inserting the 8 percent interest rate and the other figures into the previous present value equation.[7]

$$V = \frac{\$50}{(1 + 0.08)} + \frac{\$50}{(1 + 0.08)^2} + \frac{\$50}{(1 + 0.08)^3}$$
$$+ \frac{\$50}{(1 + 0.08)^4} + \frac{\$50}{(1 + 0.08)^5} + \frac{\$1,000}{(1 + 0.08)^5}$$
$$= \$46.29 + \$42.87 + \$39.69 + \$36.75$$
$$+ \$34.03 + \$680.58$$
$$= \$880.21$$

The bond sells at approximately a 12 percent discount from its face value of $1,000. If the interest rate had been higher than 8 percent, the present value would have been smaller or the discount would have been larger. On the other hand, if the rate had been below 5 percent, the present value of the bond would have been greater than $1,000 (it would have sold at a pre-

---

[7] One need not make any calculations like these. The present value of a dollar discounted at various rates and for various time periods may be found from tables provided in financial handbooks and finance textbooks. See, for example, *Comprehensive Bond Values Table,* Financial Publishing Co., 1958, and H. Bierman, Jr., and S. Smidt, *The Capital Budgeting Decision,* 5th ed., Macmillan, 1980.

mium).[8] Given the stream of interest income and the principal amount to be paid at maturity, the present value of this U.S. Treasury bond can change for essentially only one reason—a change in the interest rate. In contrast, corporate, state, and local bonds—which carry some credit risk—can fluctuate in price as the market evaluation of credit risk varies. In other words, on such securities there is some risk that the interest (R) and principal (A) may not be paid as promised. For many such securities, there is also a substantial marketability risk. The thinness of the market sometimes results in an inability to sell at a price very close to that of the last transaction in the same security. However, if we limit ourselves to federal government bonds, changes in the interest rate are virtually the only cause of price fluctuations.

The arithmetic relationship between the price of a bond and the interest rate is most clearly brought out by the consol, a type of security issued by the British government. This security promises only to pay a specified number of dollars in interest per year. It has no redemption value or maturity date; an investor can convert it into money only by selling it to another investor. If at a particular time market conditions are such that 5 percent is the rate being earned on securities of this type, a consol will sell for $1,000 if it pays $50 in interest each year. A buyer who pays $1,000 will get a 5 percent return on his funds. For consols, the present value equation reduces to:

$$V = \frac{R}{r}$$

or

$$\$1,000 = \frac{\$50}{0.05}$$

---

[8] Finding the present value of the stream of income generated by a bond is similar to finding the present value of the stream of income generated by a capital good. For a discussion of the latter, including illustrations of the way in which present values vary with different interest rates, see pp. 368–71.

Nonetheless, no matter how attractive the 5 percent yield may appear at the time, if a prospective purchaser believes that the interest rate will rise, he may be better off to hold his $1,000 completely idle, as a speculative balance, rather than buy this security. Suppose, for example, that he believes the interest rate one year from now will be 5.26 percent. The security must then sell at the lower price that yields 5.26 percent to its purchaser, or $V = \$50/0.0526 = \$950$. To buy the security today and hold it for one year promises interest income of $50 and capital loss of $50 or (apart from tax considerations) neither a net gain nor a net loss. In other words, a prospective purchaser who holds his $1,000 as idle cash for a full year and then buys the security will be as well off as one who buys it today, if the rate does in fact rise to 5.26 percent. If a prospective purchaser anticipated that the rate a year hence would be anything above 5.26 percent, it would clearly be to his advantage to hold cash rather than buy the security. If the expected rate were anything less than 5.26 percent, there would clearly be a gain in buying the security rather than in holding the cash.[9] For example, if the expected rate were 6 percent, the price of the bond would fall to $833.33, with a net loss to the purchaser of $116.66 for the year. On the other hand, if the expected rate were 4 percent, the price of the bond would rise to $1,250, with a net gain of $300 for the year. Including interest and capital gain or loss, a 1 percent rise in the rate results in a negative yield of 11.66 percent; a 1 percent fall results in a positive yield of 30 percent for the year.

The same inverse relationship between the interest rate and price applies to conventional debt securities with specified maturity dates. However, in contrast to the case for a consol, the closer a conventional security is to its specified maturity date, the less sensitive its price will be to changes in the interest rate. A rise in the rate from 5 to 6 percent reduced the market value of the consol, which pays $50 interest per year, from

---

[9] See *General Theory*, p. 202.

$1,000 to $833.33. For a $1,000 bond paying $50 interest per year and maturing in ten years, the same rise in the interest rate would reduce market value to $926.39. If it were five years from maturity, the value would fall to $957.88, and if it were only one year from maturity it would fall to $990.57.[10]

In summary, combining interest rate, maturity, and market value, the market value of a debt security is inversely related to the interest rate, and any given change in the interest rate will exert a greater effect on that market value the more distant the security is from maturity.

Expectations and the Interest Rate   Anyone who buys a long-term bond is unavoidably speculating to some extent on future changes in the interest rate and must face the possibility of a financial gain or loss that comes with such changes. Although other considerations affect their decisions, persons who switch at any time from money to such bonds expect the interest rate to fall and bond prices to rise; they regard the present interest rate as "high" and present bond prices as "low." Those who switch from bonds to money hold opposite expectations; they regard the present interest rate as low and bond prices as high. Clearly, anyone who views the current interest rate as high or low must have some "normal" rate in mind against which the current rate is being compared. The normal rate itself is constantly changing. Nothing has done more to cause such changes than the inflation experience of the past fifteen years. The normal

rate in the early 1980s is several times that of the early 1960s. And if somehow the inflation rate later in the 1980s were to fall to the very low inflation rate of the early 1960s, the interest rate that would then be viewed as normal would be at a level not much different from the rate that was considered normal in the early 1960s. Although changes in the rate of inflation and other factors cause wealth-holders to revise their view of what is a normal rate of interest, at any time these people may decide that the actual interest rate is higher than, lower than, or equal to that normal rate.

Given the notion of a normal rate, if wealth-holders view the current rate as high, they then expect the rate to drop as it returns to normal. At this high rate, wealth-holders will accordingly hold bonds rather than money. Thereby they not only currently enjoy the high rate of return provided by bonds, but can expect capital gains as bond prices rise and the interest rate falls to normal.[11] If, on the other hand, wealth-holders view the current rate as low, they anticipate a rise in the rate as it returns to normal. They accordingly hold money rather than bonds. The penalty paid in interest forgone is relatively small when the interest rate is low; the prospective capital loss

---

[10] This assumes that 5 percent was the original yield on the consol and on the three securities with varying maturities. Because yields customarily vary directly with maturity, a yield of 5 percent on the consol might be accompanied by yields of, say, 4, 3, and 2 percent, respectively, on the 10, 5, and 1 year maturities. If the consol sold for $1,000 to provide a yield of 5 percent, the other three securities would probably have sold at successively greater premiums over $1,000. But it still follows that the fall in value that would result from an equal rise in the interest rate on each maturity will be less for the shorter maturity than for the longer.

[11] Although wealth-holders could possibly view the current rate as "high" in the sense that it is somewhere above "normal," they might still expect it to go higher. Therefore, before they will spurn cash and hold bonds, they must not only view rates as above normal but also expect that the next movement will be downward toward the normal level. Although wealth-holders may under certain circumstances expect one rise in rates to be followed by another, they will sooner or later expect this movement to reverse itself. The historical record does not show interest rates moving uninterruptedly to ever higher levels. Note, however, that if they did indeed expect interest rate movements to be cumulative instead of self-reversing, each rise in the rate would cause a further shift out of bonds into money. This would give us a direct relationship between the amount of speculative balances held and the interest rate—the reverse of the relationship, which will be found in the demand curve for speculative balances shown in Figure 11-4. Although expectations of a cumulative movement in interest rates may be held for a short period of time, at some point the expectations of a reversal will prevail.

is relatively large if the rate should rise as expected from its low to its normal level. Holding idle money becomes the financially prudent policy.

Clearly, the amount of speculative balances that people will want to hold varies inversely with the interest rate. To accompany our equation $m_t = k(Y)$ for the transactions and precautionary demand for money, we must now write an equation for the speculative demand for money. If the amount of nominal balances held for speculative purposes is designated by M_{sp}, we have $M_{sp} = P \cdot h(r)$ for this equation. Unlike the relationship in the transactions demand equation in which M_t varies directly with Y, the relationship between M_{sp} and r is inverse. As with the equation for transactions demand, the amount of speculative balances demanded may be expressed in real terms by dividing $M_{sp} = P \cdot h(r)$ by P. This yields $M_{sp}/P = h(r)$. In other words, the amount of real speculative balances demanded is a function of the interest rate. For a shorter form, M_{sp}/P will be designated by m_{sp}.

In the case of the transactions demand for money, the nominal amount of such balances demanded will probably vary proportionally with the price level as shown in the equation $M_t = P \cdot k(Y)$. Other things being equal, the public simply needs proportionally larger (or smaller) nominal transactions balances to handle the transactions associated with a given level of output when the price level of that output is higher (or lower). However, should we expect the nominal amount of speculative balances demanded to vary with the price level as suggested by $M_{sp} = P \cdot h(r)$? The answer here is less clear-cut. To see what is involved, consider the case of a one-time, overnight doubling of the price level. If a wealth-holder's income and wealth also double in money terms, nothing has changed in real terms. The wealth-holder would now want to hold twice the number of dollars in his speculative balance that he previously held at any given interest rate or he would adjust the nominal amount of that balance in line with the change in the price level so as to leave the real balance unchanged.

Although this seems reasonable enough, not all wealth-holders will find that their income and wealth increase in nominal terms proportionally with the general price level. At the extreme, suppose that an individual's wealth is held entirely in currency and consols and his only income is the interest earned on holdings of consols. An overnight doubling of the price level would leave his nominal income unchanged but would cut real income in half. It would leave the nominal value of his wealth unchanged, but would reduce it in real terms by approximately the same degree that it reduced income. Whatever the speculative demand for money by the wealth-holder in these circumstances, it is not reasonable to expect him to adjust the size of his speculative balance proportionally with the change in the price level.

There are, of course, few wealth-holders who fit this extreme. The answer to the question seems to be that the amount of speculative balances that wealth-holders as a group will want to hold at any particular interest rate will depend to a degree on the price level, but that the amount may not vary proportionally with the price level. However, the usual treatment today is to show speculative balances varying in the way indicated by the equation $M_{sp} = P \cdot h(r)$.

Working with this equation in the form that shows the amount of real speculative balances demanded, $M_{sp}/P = m_{sp} = h(r)$, we may show the relationship graphically by the curve in Figure 11-4. The higher the market interest rate, the smaller will be the amount of real balances that wealth-holders choose to maintain for speculative purposes. At some high interest rate, the curve indicates that they will hold no money in speculative balances. As drawn here, at a rate of 14 percent or higher, the speculative demand curve in effect coincides with the vertical axis—m_{sp} is zero. This amounts to saying that all wealth-holders believe that the rate is so high that it can only fall or that even if it should creep still higher, the current high interest rate will more than offset any capital loss that may result. At this rate, no one prefers money to bonds; bonds become perfectly "safe." At the other end of the

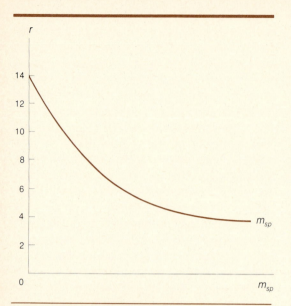

FIGURE 11-4
Speculative Demand for Money

curve, speculative demand becomes perfectly elastic. In the present figure, this occurs at a rate of 4 percent. Although under different conditions 4 percent would not be regarded as a "low" rate, conditions at the time are assumed to be such that wealth-holders believe the rate can go no lower. To hold bonds at this interest rate instead of money is to face almost certain capital loss as interest rates rise. The interest income that is provided when the interest rate is that low would only partially offset this loss. This section of the curve, known as the "liquidity trap," will be discussed later in the chapter.[12]

_____

[12] Although we have here limited ourselves to Keynes' approach which stresses the concept of a normal rate of interest in explaining a downward-sloping speculative demand curve, later writing has shown that the demand for money as an asset will be interest elastic without resorting to the concept of a normal interest rate. (See J. Tobin, "Liquidity Preference as Behavior Towards Risk," in _Review of Economic Studies,_ Feb. 1958, pp. 65–86, reprinted in M.G. Mueller, ed., _Readings in Macroeconomics,_ 2nd ed., Holt, Rinehart & Winston, 1971, pp. 173–91.)

The focus here has been on Keynes' theory of the speculative demand for money. This theory has an important shortcoming. Keynes gives the wealth-holder a choice between holding risky bonds and riskless money. However, in practice, the wealth-holder could also hold other debt forms that do not require that he incur risk in order to avoid the zero return on money holdings. He may, for example, hold wealth in savings deposits, savings and loan shares, commercial paper, Treasury bills, and similar forms. All of these alternative debt forms provide a rate of return, are immediately convertible into money, and are either absolutely fixed in dollar value regardless of changes in the market interest rate, or, in the case of a debt form like Treasury bills, are of such short term as to be virtually unaffected by changes in the market interest rate.

This brings us to a point emphasized at the beginning of this chapter: Some statements that are incorrect on the basis of a narrow definition of money are correct on the basis of a broad definition of money. On the one hand, when working with the M-1A measure of money as we have been doing, it is correct to say that wealth-holders have a speculative demand for money balances as long as the only alternative to holding money is holding long-term bonds. Then the alternative carries a risk of loss in the event of a rise in market interest rates. However, if we recognize that in practice other interest-bearing assets without this risk are available to wealth-holders, the speculative demand for M-1A disappears. On the other hand, if we work with the M-2 measure of money, the existence of a speculative demand for M-2 is apparent. The M-2 measure includes interest-bearing assets such as savings deposits and money market mutual fund shares which are completely or largely free of risk of loss in the event of a change in market interest rates. Wealth-holders will hold speculative balances in such components of M-2 and this amount will vary inversely with the market interest rate on long-term bonds. They will choose relatively large amounts of the interest-bearing assets found in M-2 when the interest rate on long-term bonds is believed to be below normal, but will choose relatively smaller amounts when the interest rate is believed to be above normal. Now we have wealth-holders switching between very short-term and long-term interest-bearing assets. In this way speculative demand for money becomes part of the explanation of the term or maturity structure of interest rates.

Specifically, when the interest rate on long-term bonds declines to a level that wealth-holders regard as below normal, they shift into certain interest-bearing assets included in M-2 and other short-term money market instruments included in broader measures of the money stock. They don't shift into the assets included in M-1A. The rise they expect in the long-term interest rate will mean a capital loss on holdings of long-term bonds, but they can avoid this danger and still earn a return by holding interest-bearing assets included in M-2 and broader measures of the money stock. As wealth-holders shift into short-term debt for this reason, the prices of short-term obligations, like Treasury bills and commercial paper, are bid up and the yields on such obligations are forced down. In terms of the maturity structure of interest rates, this means that short-term yields will tend to fall relative to long-term yields.

Consider the opposite situation, in which the interest rate on long-term debt rises to a level that wealth-holders regard as above normal. They then anticipate a fall in the long-term interest rate, which will give them a capital gain on any holdings of long-term debt—something they will not get on holdings of short-term debt. Consequently, they tend to switch out of holdings of short-term debt into long-term debt. This raises the price of long-term debt and reduces its yield. Therefore, in this case, short-term yields tend to rise relative to long-term yields.[13]

Given the actual availability of interest-bearing assets that do not confront wealth-holders with the risk of long-term bonds, we concluded that in practice there is no speculative demand for money, if we hold to the M-1A definition of money. However, even though there would be no speculative demand in the sense of idle M-1A balances being held in expectation of changes in the long-term interest rate, the amount of M-1A balances held would still vary inversely with the interest rate. Practically all persons and firms do, of course, hold currency and demand deposits (M-1A) for transactions purposes. As we noted earlier, the amount of such balances held at any level of income will become interest elastic at some level of the interest rate, because individuals and firms will find ways of economizing on transactions balances in order to gain the rate of return available on riskless short-term debt when that rate becomes high enough to make such effort worthwhile. With respect to demand for transactions balances, a recognition of this behavior is all we need to produce a demand curve for real money balances that slopes downward to the right. In what follows, we could, therefore, completely discard the Keynesian speculative demand for money and work only with an interest-elastic transactions demand for money. We would still reach results similar to those reached with a speculative demand for money included. However, we will follow the conventional procedure, which treats the transactions demand as interest inelastic and which allows the wealth-holder to choose only between riskless money and risky long-term bonds, and

---

[13]The maturity structure with the short-term rate below the long-term rate—the first case described above—is commonly found in recession periods, because in such periods the overall structure of interest rates, both short- and long-term, declines below what it was during the

boom, and the long-term rate comes to be viewed by wealth-holders as below normal. The opposite situation, by the same argument, is found during boom periods. For an introduction to this subject, see W.L. Smith, "The Maturity Structure of Interest Rates," in W.L. Smith and R.L. Teigen, eds., *Readings in Money, National Income, and Stabilization Policy*, 3rd ed., Irwin, 1974, pp. 432–37, and B.G. Malkiel, *The Term Structure of Interest Rates: Theory, Empirical Evidence, and Applications*, McCaleb-Seiler, 1970, reprinted in T. M. Havrilesky and J. T. Boorman, *Current Issues in Monetary Theory and Policy*, 2nd ed., AHM Publishing, 1980, pp. 395–418.

therefore does create a speculative demand for narrowly defined (M-1A) money. The transactions demand is thus $m_t = k(Y)$, and the speculative demand is $m_{sp} = h(r)$.

Total Demand for Money

The total demand for money expressed in real terms may be designated by m_d, where $m_d = m_t + m_{sp}$. Therefore, combining the equation $m_t = k(Y)$, which we understand to include precautionary demand, and the equation $m_{sp} = h(r)$ we now have an equation for the total demand for money:

$$m_d = k(Y) + h(r)$$

For any given price level, we know from k what m_t will be for each level of Y. Similarly, for any given price level, we know from h what m_{sp} will be for each level of r. We therefore know from k and h what the total demand for money will be for every possible combination of Y and r. This may be shown as in Figure 11-5.

Part A of the figure shows the transactions demand for money as $100 billion when the level of income is $400 billion, assuming that k is 1/4. Part B shows the speculative demand for money as an inverse function of the interest rate. Part C shows the total demand curve for money, the sum of the separate demands of Parts A and B, or the sum of m_t and m_{sp}. For example, at an income level of $400 billion and an interest rate of 8 percent, total money demanded is $110 billion; at the same income level, but with an interest rate of 10 percent, total money demanded is $105 billion.

The Supply of and the Demand for Money

Regardless of the demand for money, the nominal amount of money that people and firms hold at any time clearly cannot exceed the stock of money in the system at that time. Furthermore, it cannot be less. Whatever the stock of money may be at any time, someone must hold that amount.

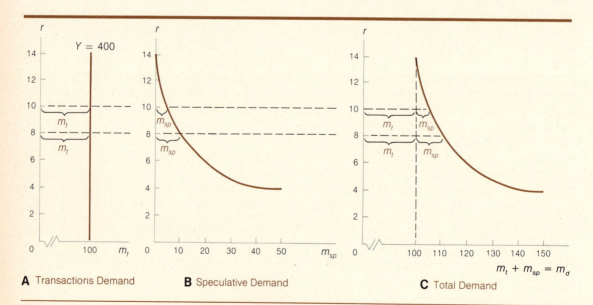

A Transactions Demand   **B** Speculative Demand   **C** Total Demand

FIGURE 11-5
Total Demand for Money

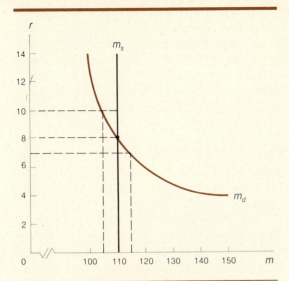

FIGURE 11-6
Equilibrium Between Supply of and Demand for Money

Equilibrium in the market for money requires that the supply of money equal the demand for money. If M_s represents the nominal amount of existent money, equilibrium requires that $M_s = M_d$ and that, in real terms, $m_s = m_d$.

The nominal money stock, of course, changes over time as the result of actions taken by the Federal Reserve. The real money stock corresponding to any nominal money stock changes with the level of prices. For the moment, assume that the real stock of money is some given amount. This appears in Figure 11-6 as the perfectly inelastic supply curve, m_s. The demand curve, $m_d = (m_t + m_{sp})$, is carried over, with the scale expanded but otherwise unchanged, from Part C of Figure 11-5.

The Equilibrium Interest Rate

Given the money supply and the income level, at some particular interest rate the sum of the trans-

actions and speculative demands for money will just equal the supply of money. The interest rate that equates the supply of and demand for money is the **equilibrium interest rate.** When the supply of money is $110 billion, as in Figure 11-6, only at an interest rate of 8 percent is the amount of money demanded equal to the amount supplied. At a higher rate, say 10 percent, disequilibrium occurs, because money demanded is $105 billion and money supplied is still $110 billion. Because someone must hold the total money supply, in such a situation the public finds that its actual holdings of money exceed the desired amount. After allowing for $100 billion required for transactions, the $10 billion remaining is more than people choose to hold in the form of idle money balances at so high an interest rate.

People will therefore enter the market to buy bonds with the excess cash. The increased demand for bonds will drive up the prices of bonds and reduce their yield. This will continue until bond prices have been pushed up by the amount necessary to reduce their yield to 8 percent, at which point people will be content to hold the $10 billion of speculative balances. Conversely, at any rate below the equilibrium rate, say at 7 percent, there is also a disequilibrium. However, in this case, money demanded is $115 billion and money supplied is only $110 billion. At this low interest rate, people would rather hold less in bonds and more in money. Therefore, they try to sell bonds and get into money. The increase in the supply of bonds drives down their prices and raises their yield. This continues until bond prices have fallen by the amount necessary to raise their yield to 8 percent, at which point people will be content to hold the $10 billion of speculative balances.

Like other prices, the interest rate—which is the price of money—will rise or fall in response to changes in supply and demand. Assuming no off-setting change in the price level, the real supply of money changes as the Federal Reserve increases or decreases the nominal stock of money. On the same assumption, total demand changes as the level of income or the speculative demand for money changes. As a first step, we may therefore trace changes in the interest rate to changes in the money supply, the level of income, and the speculative demand for money. Changes in one of these variables may influence the value of another. For example, an increase in the money supply will reduce the interest rate, stimulate investment spending, and raise the level of income, thereby increasing the transactions demand for money and raising the interest rate above the level to which it fell as a result of the increase in the money supply. How all these interdependent variables fit together in a general model will be explained in Chapter 12. At this point, we will consider one change at a time, assuming that other things remain equal.

Changes in the Money Supply

The process by which changes in the money supply occur was covered in some detail in Chapter 10. Here we merely assume that the Federal Reserve seeks to bring about particular changes in the money supply and increases or decreases the amount of reserves by the amount needed for that purpose. Remember that the commercial banks may support a larger or smaller amount of demand deposits with a given amount of reserves, depending on whether they choose to expand to the limit or to hold some excess reserves. To the degree that they choose to hold some excess reserves, that amount tends to vary inversely with the interest rate. This is similar to the behavior of individual wealth-holders with respect to the amount of speculative balances they choose to hold at different interest rates. Consequently, with no change in the total amount of reserves held by the banks, the amount of their deposit liabilities outstanding will vary directly with the interest rate. Graphically, instead of a supply curve perfectly inelastic throughout as in Figure 11-6, the supply curve slopes upward to the right. If we allow for this

aspect of bank behavior, the supply of money as well as the demand for money depends on the interest rate. However, because the supply elasticity is not crucial in what follows and in any event appears to be quite low, for simplicity we will assume as before that the supply of money consistent with any given amount of bank reserves is interest inelastic.[14]

Monetary Expansion and the Interest Rate The m_s and m_d curves of Figure 11-7 are the same as those of Figure 11-6. As we saw there, with demand as given, the money supply of \$110 billion produces an equilibrium interest rate of 8 percent. The m_{s_1} curve shows the supply of money after a \$10 billion increase. This forces the interest rate down to 6 percent. As long as there is no shift in the total demand curve for money, further increases in the supply of money will continue to lower the interest rate; decreases will raise it. Although our model is highly simplified, it shows in general how the Federal Reserve can raise and lower the interest rate by producing changes in the money supply. These changes are usually brought about by means of open-market operations as described in Chapter 10.

This ability rests in turn on the ability of the Federal Reserve to find sellers when it seeks to buy securities and to find buyers when it seeks to sell securities. As long as the Federal Reserve does not try to buy low and sell high in order to show a profit or avoid a loss in open-market transactions, there will be no shortage of buyers or sellers, whatever the scope of Federal Reserve operations in the open market.

For example, suppose the Federal Reserve purchases \$2 billion of securities from the public. Security prices may have to rise to induce secu-

---

[14]For an introduction to the relationship between the interest rate and the supply of money, see W.R. Hosek and F. Zahn, *Monetary Theory, Policy, and Financial Markets*, McGraw-Hill, 1977, pp. 90–103, and R.L. Teigen, "The Demand for and Supply of Money," in W.L. Smith and R.L. Teigen, eds., *Money, National Income and Stabilization Policy*, 4th ed., Irwin, 1978, pp. 54–81.

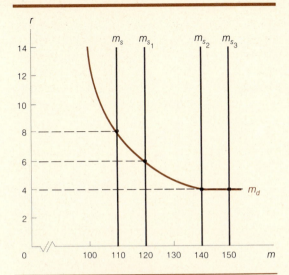

FIGURE 11-7
Changes in the Supply of Money and the Rate of Interest

rity holders to exchange interest-bearing securities for noninterest-bearing money. The Federal Reserve is prepared to pay the higher price to carry out its policy. This purchase by the Federal Reserve adds $2 billion to demand deposits and $2 billion to bank reserves, and, assuming a 20 percent reserve requirement, provides the banks with $1.6 billion of excess reserves. On certain assumptions, these excess reserves in turn provide the basis on which the banks may purchase $8 billion of securities and add $8 billion more to demand deposits. As this occurs, some further rise in security prices may be necessary to induce the exchange of this amount of interest-bearing assets for money. In terms of Figure 11-7, for the complete sequence that involved an increase in the money supply of $10 billion, security prices had to rise enough to force the interest rate down from 8 to 6 percent. Only at this lower interest rate were people content to hold the additional $10 billion of money in place of an equal amount of securities.

The "Liquidity Trap" How much change in the interest rate may be expected from any specific increase in the money supply depends, other things being equal, on the elasticity of the speculative demand curve. If it is more elastic over the range from 8 to 6 percent than the m_d curve of Figure 11-7, the decrease in the interest rate effected by the $10 billion increase in the money supply would be less. If less elastic, it would be more.

There may be some relatively low rate at which the curve in Figure 11-7 becomes perfectly elastic, indicating that virtually all wealth-holders believe that the interest rate is so low that it can go no lower and that security prices are so high that they can go no higher. The absolute level of the interest rate at which this occurs, if it occurs at all, may vary substantially over long periods of time, depending in large part on the absolute interest rate viewed as normal at any time. In Figure 11-7, it is assumed that the demand curve for money becomes perfectly elastic at 4 percent.

Although the Reserve authorities could, through open-market operations, expand the money supply from m_{s_2} to m_{s_3}, in so doing they could not succeed in reducing the interest rate below that set by the "liquidity trap." At this rate, the demand of wealth-holders for money is perfectly elastic, or the wealth-holders' supply of securities is perfectly elastic. The Reserve Banks could continue to buy more securities in the open market, but the prices paid for them would stay the same. Monetary expansion is completely incapable of reducing the interest rate below the rate set by the liquidity trap.

Although it is an interesting and presumably possible phenomenon, the actual appearance of a liquidity trap is obviously a rarity. It was something much discussed during the 1940s and 1950s, but it is doubtful that the U.S. economy was ever actually in a liquidity trap. Interest rates seldom reach the low level at which wealth-holders hold the expectations necessary to produce a liquidity trap. The closest approximation to a liquidity trap in U.S. experience occurred during the years immediately following the Great Depression.[15] In recent years, interest rates have been far above whatever rate would at the time be identified with a liquidity trap. Although it is now viewed as an extreme case, the liquidity trap plays an important part in Keynes' *General Theory,* interestingly enough written at a time when the existence of a liquidity trap seemed more than a mere possibility. We will discuss the liquidity trap further when we develop an extended model of income determination in Chapter 12.

Changes in the Level of Income

If we accept the money supply and speculative demand for money as given, the interest rate will vary directly with the level of income. Handling the larger dollar volume of transactions associated with a higher level of income calls for larger transactions balances. Let us retain the assumption that $k = 1/4$; with income at \$400 billion, the m_d curve of Figure 11-8 is the same as that in preceding figures. A rise in income from \$400 to \$420 billion raises transactions demand from \$100 to \$105 billion. As long as speculative demand does not change, the total demand curve shifts \$5 billion to the right at each interest rate to produce the new total demand curve m_{d_1}. With an increase in the demand for money and no change in supply, the interest rate rises to a new equilibrium level of 10 percent.

[15]The existence or nonexistence of the Keynesian liquidity trap has been investigated by J. Tobin in his study, "Liquidity Preference and Monetary Policy," in *Review of Economics and Statistics,* May 1947, pp. 124–31, and in a more sophisticated form by M. Bronfenbrenner and T. Mayer, "Liquidity Functions in the American Economy," in *Econometrica,* Oct. 1960, pp. 810–34. See also D. Laidler, "The Rate of Interest and the Demand for Money—Some Empirical Evidence," in *Journal of Political Economy,* Dec. 1966, pp. 543–55, and K. Brunner and A. Meltzer, "Liquidity Traps for Money, Bank Credit, and Interest Rates," *Journal of Political Economy,* Jan.–Feb. 1968, pp. 1–35. For a more recent study, see J.L. Scadding, "An Annual Money Demand and Supply Model for the U.S.: 1924–1940/1949–1966," *Journal of Monetary Economics,* Jan. 1977, pp. 41–58.

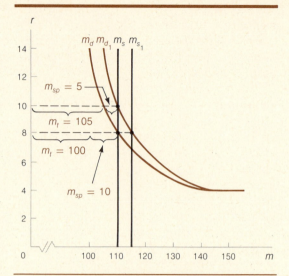

FIGURE 11-8
Changes in the Income Level and the Rate of Interest

The underlying process by which this rise in the interest rate takes place is not revealed by Figure 11-8. Basically, the process involves the diversion of money from speculative to transactions balances. As people and firms find that more money is needed to handle the greater volume of transactions accompanying a rise in income, they sell some of their security holdings in the market in order to secure the additional transactions balances needed. Because we are assuming that there is no change in the total supply of money, the additional transactions balances can come only from speculative balances. This transfer will occur as the prices of securities fall and their yields rise, the result of the increase in the supply of securities offered on the market. With the fall in prices and rise in yields, holders of speculative balances who were fearful of bonds at higher prices and lower yields will be tempted to switch to bonds at the more attractive price-yield combination now available. In our illustration, bond prices must fall enough to raise the interest rate from 8 to 10 percent in order to draw the required $5 billion out of speculative balances into transactions balances.

By the same reasoning, with the money supply given, a fall in the income level means a decline in the interest rate. When the income level falls, the public discovers that it is holding more in transactions balances than it needs. This excess money will seek a return in securities, thus pushing up the prices of securities and reducing their yields to the point at which the public willingly holds the larger, idle money balances. The results of a decline in income from $420 to $400 billion are indicated in Figure 11-8 by a shift in the total demand curve from m_{d_1} to m_d. The equilibrium interest rate falls from 10 to 8 percent.

We are now in a position to tie together changes in the money supply and changes in the income level. As a rise in real income and the accompanying rise in employment are desirable, public policy in this situation will oppose a rise in the interest rate because of its adverse effect on investment spending and on the further expansion of real income. Given a $20 billion rise in income, open-market purchases of $1 billion of securities by the Reserve Banks would (on certain assumptions) provide the additional commercial bank reserves necessary for an overall increase of $5 billion in the money supply. This increase would provide the additional transactions balances called for by the $20 billion rise in income. There would be no rise in the interest rate and no danger of restraining the expansion of income through a restrictive monetary policy. This increase in the money supply is depicted in Figure 11-8 by the shift in the supply curve from m_s to m_{s_1}. As a result, the interest rate is held constant at 8 percent.

In the opposite situation—a decline in income—public policy will favor a fall in the interest rate as a means of stimulating investment and arresting and possibly reversing the decline in output and the decline in employment that accompanies it. The model shows that some "easing" of the interest rate occurs even without action by the Reserve authorities. The decline in

income will of itself automatically bring some reduction in the interest rate, but this will only prevent the decline in income from being greater than it otherwise would have been. For the typical downturn, the Reserve authorities will go beyond a passive role and pursue an active, expansionary policy: More money will be pumped into the system in an effort to bring about an upturn.

Changes in the Speculative Demand for Money

In our earlier discussion of Keynes' speculative demand, we noted that wealth-holders develop a concept of what are "normal," "low," and "high" interest rates. This does not mean that all wealth-holders make the same evaluation. There will be and must be diversity of judgment if the concept of a speculative demand function is to have any meaning.[16] Despite this diversity of judgment, there will also be a consensus among wealth-holders as a group. References to high, low, and normal rates are to what average opinion holds these rates to be at any given time.

If the consensus is that the normal rate will rise from near 8 percent to 9 percent, there will be a movement out of securities into money, which will raise the interest rate to 9 percent. If

---

[16] If all wealth-holders held identical views as to the normal interest rate at any particular time, and if each went "whole hog" into bonds at any rate above this rate and "whole hog" into cash at any rate below it, the speculative demand curve would be a perfectly elastic function at the level of this normal rate. Regardless of the size of the money supply, as long as it was greater than that needed for transactions purposes, the interest rate would remain unchanged. With the actual rate equal to what wealth-holders regard as the normal rate, there would be no reason for this perfectly elastic function to shift upward or downward and therefore no way for the interest rate to change in response to any change in the money supply. Since the interest rate does actually change, it follows that the speculative demand curve must be less than perfectly elastic if it is to have any meaning. This does not conflict with the possibility that a portion of the curve may be perfectly elastic. A liquidity trap may exist, but the whole curve cannot amount to a continuous liquidity trap.

there is no decrease in the money supply and no rise in the level of income, the interest rate will in fact rise if wealth-holders expect it to and act on their expectations. The same is true in the other direction. If there is no increase in the money supply and no fall in the level of income, the interest rate will fall from near 8 percent to 7 percent, if wealth-holders expect it to fall and act on their expectations.

In Figure 11-8, with money supply given by m_s and demand for money given by m_d, the actual rate is 8 percent. We may assume that wealth-holders regard this as near the normal rate. If now general opinion should come to hold that rates near 10 percent will be normal, rates above 10 percent will be viewed as high and rates below 10 percent will be viewed as low. This amounts to an upward shift in the whole demand curve from m_d to m_{d_1}. With no change in the money supply or in the level of income, a new equilibrium interest rate is established at 10 percent.

It is easy enough to trace the simple mechanics of the process by which a change in the equilibrium interest rate will follow from a change in wealth-holders' opinions as to what the normal interest rate will be. It is not so easy to explain specifically what causes wealth-holders' opinions to change. To begin with, the particular opinions concerning normal interest rates at any time cannot be separated from the actual rates observed over the near and more distant past. In an economy that has never experienced a rate above 8 percent on high-grade long-term bonds, for example, wealth-holders are not likely to believe such a rate can be a normal rate. But the economy with that experience could not have been one that experienced years of "double-digit" inflation. After experiencing more than fifteen years of high inflation rates, including some years of "double-digit" inflation, wealth-holders in the United States have adjusted their view of the normal rate to include a substantial inflation premium. If wealth-holders believed that the future inflation rate would be a steady 10 percent per year, their idea of a normal long-term interest

rate would be around 13 percent. In contrast, if wealth-holders believed the economy would return to the kind of price stability of the early 1960s in which the inflation rate was 1 to 2 percent per year, they would adjust their idea of a normal rate downward over time to the 4 to 6 percent range it was under those relatively stable price conditions. (The liquidity trap interest rate, if one exists, might then be around 2 percent.)

The normal rate is also affected by wealth-holders' views concerning future Federal Reserve policy, partly because some view that policy as an important factor in determining the inflation rate, and partly because the Federal Reserve can, at least for a period of time, act to prevent interest rate changes. If there were no offsetting Federal Reserve action, the interest rate would usually begin to rise during a period of vigorous business expansion following a recessionary low. Unless met by an expansion in the money supply, the increased transactions requirements would tend to force the interest rate up, as it did before World War II. But compare this, for example, with the experience during the first four years of the economic expansion that began early in 1961. GNP at annual rates in current dollars rose by almost $160 billion from the first quarter of 1961 to the first quarter of 1965. However, the interest rate on long-term U.S. bonds fluctuated over a range of less than 0.5 percentage point during this period because the Federal Reserve acted to prevent the long-term rate from rising sharply. The rate averaged 3.8 percent during the first quarter of 1961, but averaged no higher than 4.1 percent during the first quarter of 1965, despite four continuous years of business expansion.

How does such experience affect wealth-holders' views of the normal interest rate? Changes in such views now become dependent on (1) the expected changes in all domestic and international factors that affect the business forecast and (2) the expected response of the Reserve authorities to such changes, if they actually occur. Expected changes that would otherwise lead wealth-holders to anticipate a higher normal rate will not cause an upward shift in the speculative demand function if wealth-holders also expect Federal Reserve policy to offset the rise in the rate.

An interesting result of this is the way the Reserve authorities may exploit wealth-holders' recognition of their power to maintain, raise, or lower the interest rate over limited periods of time. If, for example, a rise in the rate is deemed necessary by the Reserve authorities, instead of actually selling securities in the open market, they may achieve the desired rise through public statements by the Chairman of the Board of Governors and other high officials of the Federal Reserve, warning that inflation represents a dangerous threat to the stability of the economy. Wealth-holders will interpret this as an announcement of a pending "tight money" policy. The higher rate that the Reserve authorities seek may then be produced simply as a result of the upward shift in the speculative demand for money that will occur as wealth-holders respond to the statements made by the Reserve authorities. In this way, the Reserve authorities may accomplish, with nothing more than a few words, what could otherwise be accomplished only by positive open-market action.

To illustrate in terms of Figure 11-8, assume that the Reserve authorities have planned to induce a desired tightening with the money supply unchanged at m_s. With the equilibrium rate at 8 percent, wealth-holders need only believe that the Reserve authorities will raise the rate to 10 percent. This expectation can in itself shift the demand function from m_d to m_{d_1}. This will yield the desired rise in the rate, enabling the Federal Reserve to achieve its goal without actually intervening in the market.

The Demand for Money— from Simple to Modern Quantity Theory

The simple quantity theory of money described in Chapter 9 includes a simple theory of the demand for money. People supply goods and services and demand money rather than other goods in exchange, because only money is generally acceptable in exchange for other goods and services. As money is received, it is spent. The number of times per time period that the existing money supply appears in the market as demand for goods and services is its velocity. The simple quantity theory regarded velocity as stable in the short run. For a system whose output was at the full employment level, output too was stable in the short run. This meant that the price level varied proportionally with the money supply. Any additional money flowing into the hands of the public through a money-creating expansion of bank credit would flow into the market and raise the price level of goods proportionally. Therefore, it could be said that the price level equates the supply of and demand for money. Any rise in the supply of money will raise the price level sufficiently to create an increase in the demand for money equal to the increase in supply. The higher P is, the greater is PY; the greater PY is, the greater is the amount of M required to purchase PY with a stable V.

However, the concept of the demand for money does not emerge very clearly when the quantity theory is approached, as it was here, in terms of the $MV = PY$ equation. An equilibrium between M_d and M_s is only implicit in the equation. The concept of the demand for money is hidden from view. If we rewrite this equation to read $M = 1/V(PY)$ and then substitute k for $1/V$, we have $M = k(PY)$. $MV = PY$ is known as the velocity formulation and $M = k(PY)$ as the cash-balance formulation.[17] Because $V = 1/k$ and $k = 1/V$, the two formulations are algebraically equal. But there is a fundamental difference

---

[17] The $MV = PY$ formulation is also known as the Fisher equation, after Irving Fisher. More correctly, it is an adaptation of the original Fisher equation, $MV = PT$, in which T included all monetary transactions, not only final product, Y. The $M = k(PY)$ formulation is known as the Marshallian equation, after Alfred Marshall. It is also popularly known as the Cambridge equation, after the university at which Marshall, A.C. Pigou, D.H. Robertson, and Keynes (before the *General Theory*) developed this approach.

between the analyses that underlie the two: "The central question in . . . velocity analysis was *how rapidly money is spent*. The central question in cash-balances analysis is why holders of cash *haven't spent it yet*."[18] D.H. Robertson expressed this distinction colorfully as money "on the wing" and money "sitting."[19] Money sitting leads one to ask why it is sitting and, more specifically, why people demand money.

If $V = 4$, then $k = 1/4$. The former expression means that each dollar in the money supply is on the average used four times during the period to purchase final product. The latter means that people want to "keep by them" money equal in value to a certain stock of real goods and services, in this case an amount equal to one-fourth of the economy's output for the period.[20] The concept of the demand for money here appears explicitly. For example, given an initial equilibrium situation in which people's actual money holdings are equal to desired money holdings, assume an increase in the money supply. As a result of the increase, the public holds more money than it wants to hold at the existing price level, and attempts to rid itself of this excess money by spending. Assuming a full employment level of output, the additional spending forces up the price level until the actual, larger money holdings become desired money holdings. To hold enough money to command one-fourth of the period's output requires more money at a higher price level for output; therefore the rise in P with given Y equates the demand for M with the enlarged supply of M. A decrease in the money supply causes a similar adjustment through a fall in the price level.

The basic assumption here is the same as in the velocity formulation of the simple quantity theory covered in Chapter 9—people hold money for transactions purposes. Earlier in this chapter, the transactions demand for money in nominal terms was designated as M_t. Therefore, we had

$$M_t = k(PY)$$

Assuming here that k is a constant, we may also write

$$M_t = P \cdot k(Y)$$

If nominal balances are demanded only for transactions purposes—that is, $M_d = M_t$—then the total money supply, M_s, is absorbed in M_t and equilibrium between the supply of and demand for money is given by

$$M_s = P \cdot k(Y)$$

Simple Quantity Theory and Keynesian Theory

Like the quantity theorists, Keynes believed that the transactions demand for money depended on the level of income and not in any specific way on the interest rate. Keynes has $M_t = P \cdot k(Y)$. However, by adding the speculative demand for money, $M_{sp} = P \cdot h(r)$, Keynes denied that $M_d = M_t$. Therefore, he rejected the proposition that equilibrium between M_s and M_d can be stated as $M_s = P \cdot k(Y)$. As a result, Keynes' theory becomes far different from the quantity theory in the conclusions to which it leads.[21] Equilibrium between the supply of and demand for money now occurs when

$$M_s = P \cdot k(Y) + P \cdot h(r)$$

Therefore, a rise in M_s may be absorbed in part by speculative demand. To show how an increase in M_s will be divided between the two demands

[18]A.G. Hart, P.B. Kenen, and A.D. Entine, *Money, Debt and Economic Activity*, 4th ed., Prentice-Hall, 1969, p. 216.
[19]D.H. Robertson, *Money*, Univ. of Chicago Press, 1959, Ch. 2.
[20]See A. Marshall, *Money, Credit, and Commerce*, Macmillan, 1923, pp. 44–45.

[21]In the *General Theory*, Keynes implied that the demand for nominal transactions (and precautionary) balances varies with the price level, but that the demand for nominal speculative balances does not. (See the *General Theory*, p. 199.) As noted earlier, post-Keynesian writers generally maintain that the speculative demand also varies with the price level. That is the treatment followed here.

requires the apparatus that will be developed in the following chapter. However, we can see here that a rise in M_s will no longer mean a rise in PY equal to 4 times the rise in M_s, assuming that k is a constant of one-fourth so that the public wants to hold transactions balances equal to $(1/4)(PY)$. In Keynesian theory, an increase in M_s will affect PY only to the extent that it reduces r and to the extent that the reduction in r raises investment spending (and possibly consumption spending). Given a less than perfectly elastic speculative demand function, the increase in M_s will lead to some fall in r; given a less than perfectly inelastic investment curve, the fall in r will lead to some rise in investment spending and therefore some rise in PY. But the ratio of the rise in PY to the rise in M_s may be any figure less than 4.[22] In short, changes in PY are no longer determinable from changes in M_s alone, as is true when transactions demand is the only demand for money.

The importance of this conclusion cannot be overemphasized. Because the addition of the speculative demand for money to the quantity theory's demand for money equation rules out what otherwise is proportionality between changes in M_s and changes in PY, one can no longer satisfactorily explain changes in aggregate demand, and therefore in PY, through changes in M_s. This calls for an alternative theory of aggregate demand and income determination—one that Keynes supplied. When we look at it in this way, we see the great importance of Keynes' addition of a speculative demand for money to the transactions demand (which had been the only demand recognized by the simple quantity theory).

Although Keynes treated the transactions (and precautionary) demand as interest inelastic, we saw that it actually becomes interest elastic at sufficiently high interest rates. Keynes made the speculative demand for money a function of the interest rate only, but under certain conditions it may also become a function of the level of income. If the transactions, precautionary, and speculative demands all depend to some extent on both the level of income and the interest rate, the separate demand functions for M_t and M_{sp} may be combined and written as

$$M_d = P \cdot f(Y,r)$$

This consolidated demand function avoids the artificiality of separating the demand for money into the three parts set forth by Keynes. People obviously do not divide their money holdings into three or more neat compartments to satisfy each of the three or more motives for holding cash. Statistically, for the economy as a whole, there is no way of separating the total money supply into active and idle balances without relying on very arbitrary assumptions. The consolidated equation, although general, has the advantage of showing that the demand for money for all purposes is a function of income level and interest rate.

Modern Quantity Theory

Expressed in its most basic form, the simple quantity theory of money makes the demand for nominal money balances depend only on the nominal income level: $M_d = P \cdot f(Y)$. The Keynesian theory adds the interest rate as a determinant to give us a different function: $M_d = P \cdot f(Y,r)$. During the post-Keynesian period, another theory was developed. It is now known as the new or modern quantity theory. Its creator, Milton Friedman, holds that its closest links are with the old-fashioned quantity theory, although it clearly involves notable differences. Other economists,

---

[22] For a crude numerical illustration, assume an initial equilibrium between the supply of and demand for money and that k is equal to 1/4. A \$10 rise in M_s could then lead to a rise in PY of various possible amounts. If the speculative demand for money is very inelastic and the investment curve is very elastic, a possible outcome could be $\Delta(PY)$ equal to \$38 with $k[\Delta(PY)]$ equal to \$9.50 and $h(\Delta r)$ equal to \$0.50. The ratio of the rise in PY to the rise in M is then 3.8. On the other hand, with the opposite combination of elasticities, a possible outcome could be $\Delta(PY)$ equal to \$4 with $k[\Delta(PY)]$ equal to \$1 and $h(\Delta r)$ equal to \$9. The ratio of the rise in PY to the rise in M in this case is 0.4.

however, find Professor Friedman's quantity theory in many ways closer to the Keynesian theory than to the old quantity theory that Keynes sought to displace.[23]

Although it is possible to distinguish clearly between the simple quantity theory and the Keynesian theory without great difficulty, the same is not true of the modern quantity theory vis-à-vis these other theories. The fact that Friedman sees the modern quantity theory as a restatement of the old one, whereas others see it as an elaborate statement of Keynesian theory attests to the complexities present in it. We will not go into these complexities here, but will note only some of the essentials needed to provide a perspective on how the modern quantity theory is related to the simple quantity theory and the Keynesian theory that we have already examined.[24]

As we have seen, one way of expressing the demand for money in the simple quantity theory is $M_d = k(PY)$, where k is a constant. This equation may now be used as the point of departure for a sketch of some elements in Friedman's restatement of the quantity theory. This is not to imply that this equation correctly expresses Friedman's theory of the demand for money. He insists that the demand for money be treated as a demand for real balances, just as a consumer's demand is a demand for real consumer goods; he makes use of permanent rather than current income; he does not hold that k is a constant; and he introduces other differences. Several of these differences will be considered in our discussion, but the demand for money equation of the simple quantity theory is not so different from Friedman's to preclude its use for the limited purposes of this sketch.[25]

The simple quantity theory held k to be stable so that exact proportionality existed between M_s and PY. Furthermore, the simple quantity theory was a part of classical theory, which argued that full employment was the normal position of the economy. Therefore, in the short run, Y was fixed at whatever output a fully employed economy could produce. This meant that the rigid link between M_s and PY became a rigid link between M_s and P: the quantity theory was a theory of the price level. Like Keynesian theory, the new or modern quantity theory recognizes that output may be below its full employment level other than temporarily so that Y is a variable in the short run. It also recognizes that k in the simple quantity theory is a variable so that changes in M_s do not necessarily lead to proportional changes in PY. With k a variable, the value of PY will vary not only due to changes in M_s but also due to changes in k. However, although the modern quantity theory recognizes that k is not stable in the sense of being an unvarying numerical value, like 1/3 or

[23]This is the convincing contention made by Don Patinkin in "The Chicago Tradition, the Quantity Theory, and Friedman," in *Journal of Money, Credit and Banking,* Feb. 1969, pp. 46–70. In Patinkin's words, "Milton Friedman provided us in 1956 with a most elegant and sophisticated statement of modern Keynesian theory—misleadingly entitled 'The Quantity Theory of Money—A Restatement.'" In a 1964 article, Friedman had practically said as much in the following words: "A more fundamental and more basic development in monetary theory has been the reformulation of the quantity theory of money in a way much influenced by the Keynesian liquidity preference analysis." "Postwar Trends in Monetary Theory and Policy," in *National Banking Review,* Sept. 1964, p. 4.

[24]Professor Friedman's own formulation is found in his short (but difficult) essay, "The Quantity Theory of Money—A Restatement," in M. Friedman, ed., *Studies in the Quantity Theory of Money,* Univ. of Chicago Press, 1956, pp. 3–21, reprinted in M. Friedman, *The Optimum Quantity of Money and Other Essays,* Aldine, 1969. For a longer and more readable presentation that also goes into the complexities, see S. Rousseas, *Monetary Theory,* Knopf, 1972, Chs. 9 and 10.

[25]We here refer to the equation that Friedman maintains gives a satisfactory explanation of the demand for money when applied to the aggregate time series data. This equation, used in his empirical work, is very different from the far more complex equation used to express his theoretical formulation of the demand for money. However, the latter equation involves variables like wealth and the ratio of nonhuman to human wealth on which there are either inadequate data or no data at all and is therefore not directly testable. It is approximated by one that resembles $M_d = k(PY)$, which can be tested.

1/4, it argues that k is a stable *function* of a limited number of other variables that determine it. This means that although k will vary from time to time, its variations are not arbitrary but are explainable in terms of these other variables. In other words, it is the function determining k that is stable, not the value of k itself. Unlike the old-fashioned quantity theory, the modern quantity theory does not hold that PY may be predicted from M_s alone, but that PY may be predicted from M_s and the several variables that determine k.

However, in order to predict PY in this way, not only must k be a stable function of a limited number of variables, but, under ordinary conditions, the elasticity of the demand for money with respect to these variables must not be great. If it does exist, such a stable function implies only that k will not fluctuate unpredictably over time— that is, k will change by some specific amount in response to a change of some specific amount in any of the variables determining it.

In the simplified version of Friedman's theory, the two major variables determining k are the interest rate and the rate of change in the price level. In the simple quantity theory, M_d/P is equal to M_t/P because the only demand for money is the transactions demand. In that case, the equation is simply $M_d/P = k(Y)$, in which k is a constant determined by certain institutional and structural characteristics of the economy that ordinarily do not change significantly in the short run. The demand for money equation in the version of Friedman's theory being presented here is

$$M_d/P = k(r, \dot{P}) \cdot Y$$

Here $\dot{P}$ is the rate of change of the price level. Therefore, the quantity of real balances the public wants to hold is no longer a fixed amount at any level of real income, but an amount that varies with the interest rate and the rate of change of the price level.

In this equation, Friedman says the function $k = k(r, \dot{P})$ is stable. Even if we accept that this function is indeed stable, the closeness of the tie between the demand for real balances and real

income will still be less, the greater the elasticity of demand for real balances with respect to r and $\dot{P}$. If the demand for money is highly elastic with respect to r, relatively small changes in r will produce relatively larger changes in M_d/P. Given the fact that the interest rate does change frequently and sometimes appreciably and that M_d/P may therefore change likewise, it may well be that *there is no longer a stable relationship between M_d/P and Y in the equation $M_d/P = k(r, \dot{P}) \cdot Y$, although k may be a perfectly stable function of r and $\dot{P}$ which determine it.* In order to satisfy the modern quantity theory contention that real balances are a stable function of real income, not only must the k function be stable, but the relevant elasticities must also be sufficiently small. There are conditions under which the modern quantity theory predictions will hold even with high elasticities, but these conditions are not generally prevalent.

However, as Friedman reads the empirical record, the problem does not arise in practice because the relevant elasticities are too small to significantly influence M_d/P. In the case of the elasticity with respect to the rate of interest (or, in Friedman's complete formulation, several rates of return—those on money, bonds, and equities), Friedman grants that economic theory would lead one to expect that interest rates are one of the variables influencing the public's desired money balances and therefore affecting k. In this regard, his theoretical formulation of the quantity theory closely resembles Keynesian theory with its inclusion of the interest rate in the demand for money equation. But what one would expect from theory is not, according to Friedman, what one actually finds in the empirical record. As he interprets that record, the influence of the interest rate on the demand for money, though present, is quite minor.[26] In other words, he holds that the

---

[26] See his "The Demand for Money: Some Theoretical and Empirical Results," in *Journal of Political Economy*, Aug. 1959, pp. 327–51, reprinted in R.A. Gordon and L.R. Klein, eds., *Readings in Business Cycles*, Irwin, 1965, pp. 427–55.

interest rate need not be included in a demand for money equation in order for it to provide a satisfactory explanation of the demand for money. In contrast, all other empirical investigations find that the interest rate has more than a minor influence on the demand for money.[27] These studies uniformly find interest elasticities significantly different from zero and of a magnitude capable of producing instability in the size of k. To the degree that the results of these studies are the more correct—and the degree of uniformity in their results suggests that they are—they represent a damaging blow to Friedman's quantity theory.

The second major variable affecting k is the percentage change in the price level. This variable and the interest rate together determine the cost of holding money. The interest rate reflects the rate of return one forgoes by holding money; the rate of change in the price level reflects the rate of change in the real value of the money one holds. The rate of change in the price level must be carefully distinguished from alternative absolute price levels. Because the demand for money is expressed here as a demand for real balances, the influence of the absolute price level is already reflected in M_d/P. Other things being equal, a higher P will mean a correspondingly higher M_d or no change in the demand for real balances. The absolute level of P does not affect k. However, while prices rise, the rate at which they rise—that is, the size of $\dot{P}$—does alter the amount of real balances demanded. The greater $\dot{P}$ is, the greater is the rate at which the real value of each

dollar held shrinks or the more rapid is the rise in the cost of holding money. Accordingly, the greater $\dot{P}$ is, the greater is the decline in k.

In his empirical work, Friedman was unable to establish that the percentage rate of change of prices had any influence on k (and, through k, on the demand for money), although a historical analysis persuades him that such an effect is present. When he combines this empirical finding with his empirical finding that the interest rate does not appreciably affect the demand for money, he concludes that changes in the cost of holding money do not significantly affect the amount of money held. Because the two variables that measure the cost of holding money are the principal variables that determine the size of k, Friedman contends that there is no significant elasticity in the demand for money with respect to these variables. This brings him to the modern quantity theory conclusion that k, although not stable in itself, does not vary sufficiently to cause an unstable relationship between the demand for real money balances and the level of real income.

As previously noted, the empirical record as read by other investigators reveals a sufficiently high interest elasticity of demand to make Friedman's position unacceptable. Because the rate of interest plays a significant role in the demand for money, they maintain that it is not permissible to simplify Friedman's equation, $M_d/P = k(r, \dot{P})\, Y$, to obtain $M_d/P = k(Y)$. They insist on a demand for money equation that assigns a role to the rate of interest. One such equation is the Keynesian $M_d/P = k(Y) + h(r)$.

The particular aspect of the modern quantity theory that we have reviewed in the preceding paragraphs is the most widely known and probably the most important from a practical viewpoint. If the Friedman demand for money equation does in practice reduce to essentially $M_d/P = k(Y)$—or in nominal terms, to $M_d = k(PY)$—we are led to the monetarist conclusion that the supply of money is overwhelmingly important in determining the level of income. From an initial equilibrium in which $M_s = M_d$, the disequilibrium caused by any change in M_s will be corrected by

---

[27] For further discussion of this question and a review of the empirical evidence, see J.T. Boorman, "The Evidence on the Demand for Money: Theoretical Formulations and Empirical Results," in J.T. Boorman and T.M. Havrilesky, *Money Supply, Money Demand, and Macroeconomic Models*, Allyn and Bacon, 1972, pp. 248–86. As shown by the table on p. 266, single equation studies employing a long-term rate of interest find elasticities in the range from −0.4 to −0.9 and those employing a short-term rate of interest find elasticities in the range from −0.1 to −0.5. These studies unanimously conclude that rate of interest is an important factor in explaining variations in the demand for money.

an equal change in M_d. Therefore, we may substitute M_s for M_d in the preceding equation and write $M_s = k(PY)$. Last, divide through by k and rearrange to obtain

$$PY = (1/k)M_s$$

This is equal to $PY = VM_s$ (or $MV = PY$ in the more familiar arrangement). Given that k or its reciprocal, V, is relatively stable and that causation runs from M_s to PY, we have the conclusion that the supply of money is the supremely important determinant of the level of money income.

This conclusion, which follows from the quantity theory view of the demand for money, is quite different from the conclusion that follows from the Keynesian view of the demand for money. As previously noted, the demand for money in the Keynesian theory is significantly influenced by the rate of interest; this breaks the very close link between the money supply and changes in the income level postulated by the quantity theory. For purposes of our work in the chapters ahead,

we must have a theory of the demand for money. We accept the Keynesian theory that was developed in the first part of this chapter and that is described by the general equation $m_d = M_d/P = f(Y, r)$. However, we will find it convenient to identify a transactions demand that depends only on Y and a speculative demand that depends only on r. This returns us to the equation in which we dichotomize the total demand:

$$m_d = \frac{M_d}{P} = k(Y) + h(r)$$

With this as our theory of the demand for money and with the liquidity preference theory of the interest rate that is derived from it, we can now proceed to combine the theory of money and interest developed earlier in this chapter with the theory of income determination developed in earlier chapters. This will provide us with a model that simultaneously determines the equilibrium level of income and the equilibrium interest rate.

12

The Extended Model: Fixed Price Level

OVERVIEW

This chapter combines the theory of income and output and the theory of money and interest in a two-market equilibrium model that shows how the goods and money markets interact to determine the level of output and the rate of interest. The price level is not a variable in this model because the model retains the assumptions of Part 2: The aggregate supply curve is perfectly elastic up to the full employment level of output and does not shift; and the economy's level of output varies along the range below the full employment level. Therefore, changes in aggregate spending can affect only the output level; the price level is fixed.

The first part of the chapter explains the derivation of the *IS* and *LM* functions on which the model is built. At the particular combination of income level and interest rate at which *IS* equals *LM*, there is equilibrium in both the goods and the money markets. The *IS* and *LM* functions have long been the most basic tools of macroeconomics. The balance of the chapter uses them to examine questions that could not be handled adequately with the tools at hand in earlier chapters. Following the derivation of the *IS* and *LM* functions is the derivation of the aggregate demand function or curve. This is found from the intersection formed by the *IS* and *LM* functions. To simplify in this chapter, the assumptions are such as to produce a perfectly inelastic aggregate demand curve.

The next part of the chapter analyzes the separate and combined effects of increases in investment and the money supply on the income level and the interest rate. The conclusions reached through the use of the *IS–LM* tool differ from those reached when the goods and monetary aspects of the analysis were considered separately. For example, the simple Keynesian multipliers developed for the two-sector economy in Chapter 5 are now seen to apply only when events in the monetary sector are such that the interest rate remains constant as aggregate spending for goods and services changes.

The same sort of general analysis is carried out in the next part of the chapter for changes in government spending and taxation. Here again the simple government spending and tax multipliers presented in Chapter 6 are found to apply only when the monetary authority acts to maintain a constant interest rate.

The last part of the chapter turns to the question of the elasticities of the *IS* and *LM* functions, and to the closely related question of the effectiveness of monetary and fiscal policies. The elasticities of the two functions are analyzed to clarify the difference between the extreme version of the classical theory—which argues that only monetary policy can be effective in raising the income level—and the extreme version of the Keynesian theory—which argues that only fiscal policy can be effective. On the basis of this analysis, the *LM* function, if it is assumed to vary from perfect inelasticity at one extreme to perfect elasticity at the other, can be divided into a segment consistent with classical theory, a segment consistent with Keynesian theory, and an intermediate segment lying between the extreme versions of the two theories.

In previous chapters, we developed separately the theories of income determination and money and interest. Although this procedure provided an orderly introduction to the relevant theory, it must now be recognized as highly simplistic. The two parts are actually so related that what happens in one depends on what happens in the other. In developing the simple Keynesian theory of income determination in Chapters 4–7, we found that a rise in investment spending would raise the equilibrium level of income by an amount equal to the multiplier times the rise in investment spending. However, we implicitly assumed that the interest rate was given. If we now admit the interest rate as a variable in the system, the rise in investment spending will, by raising the level of income, also force up the interest rate. This in turn will discourage investment, and the actual rise in the equilibrium level of income will be less than it would otherwise be. Similarly, in developing the theory of money and interest in Chapter 11, we saw that an increase in the money supply would reduce the interest rate, as shown by the movement down the given demand curve for money. However, this curve assumed a given level of income. If we now admit the income level as a variable in the system, the increase in the money supply will, by lowering the interest rate, stimulate investment spending and raise the level of income. This will increase the transactions demand for money, and the actual fall in the interest rate will be less than it would otherwise be. Therefore, it appears that the interest rate and the level of income are linked in a complicated manner. In this and the following two chapters, we will construct and employ an extended model that can accommodate this and other complications.[1]

The Goods Market and the Money Market

Our model consists of two parts: The first draws together the determinants of equilibrium in the market for goods, and the second draws together the determinants of equilibrium in the market for money. For a two-sector economy, we found in Chapter 4 that goods market equilibrium is found at that level of *Y* at which the sum of *C* + *I* is just equal to that level of *Y*. Goods market equilibrium is also defined by an equality between saving

---

[1] The construction here will be almost entirely graphic. For an algebraic formulation of the same elementary model covered in this chapter, see the Appendix to Chapter 12 of E. Shapiro, *Macroeconomic Analysis—A Student Workbook,* 5th ed., Harcourt Brace Jovanovich, 1982. A concise algebraic treatment of a less elementary *IS–LM* model is provided in W.L. Smith and R.L. Teigen, *Readings in Money, National Income, and Stabilization Policy,* 4th ed., Irwin, 1978, pp. 1–22. The model, including a variable price level, is developed in R.S. Holbrook, "The Interest Rate, Price Level, and Aggregate Output," in the same volume, pp. 38–54.

and investment. At the level of Y at which $S = I$, the leakage from the income stream into S is exactly offset by I. Money market equilibrium is defined by an equality between the supply of and the demand for money—$m_s = m_d$—the condition that gave us the equilibrium interest rate. In other words, at the interest rate at which $m_s = m_d$, there is money market equilibrium.[2]

The particular level of income at which there is goods market equilibrium depends in part on conditions in the money market. The particular interest rate at which there is money market equilibrium depends in part on conditions in the goods market. For a preliminary look at what is involved, let us briefly review the simplest possible Keynesian model as shown in Figure 12-1. Given the $C + I_1$ curve in Part A and the S and I_1 curves in Part B, the equilibrium level of Y is Y_1. If investment depends at all on the interest rate, the $C + I_1$ curve in Part A and the I_1 curve in Part B must have been drawn on the assumption of some particular interest rate. Other things being equal, a lower interest rate would indicate a different position for the $C + I$ curve—say $C + I_2$ instead of $C + I_1$—and a different position for the I curve—say I_2 instead of I_1. This, in turn, would indicate a different equilibrium income level, Y_2 instead of Y_1. Figure 12-1, however, does not reveal what the interest rate may be—it assumes some rate and proceeds from there.

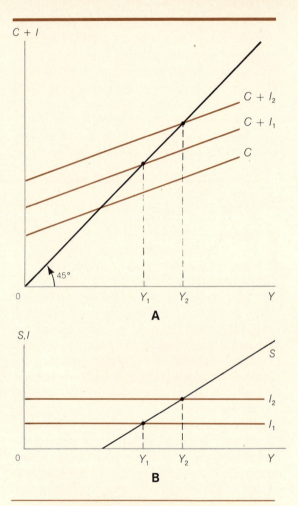

FIGURE 12-1
Equilibrium Levels of Income

[2]A more complete general equilibrium model will also include the market for factors of production, which, because of the short-run assumption of a fixed capital stock, becomes the market for labor. Equilibrium in this market requires equality between the supply of and the demand for labor. From a Keynesian viewpoint, disequilibrium in this market in the form of an excess supply of labor—that is, unemployment—can be corrected by policies designed to raise the level of output—that is, to shift the equilibrium in the goods market to a higher level of goods output whose production in turn calls for employment of more labor. From a classical viewpoint, the same disequilibrium would be removed automatically by falling wages and prices in a system characterized by such flexibility. Following the development of the basic model, which is limited to the goods and money markets, attention will be given to these other questions in Chapter 13.

Figure 12-2 shows the determination of the equilibrium interest rate. Given the m_s and m_{d_1} curves, the equilibrium rate is r_1, at which the demand for and the supply of money are equal, or $m_{t_1} + m_{sp_1} = m_{d_1} = m_s$. However, the demand for money is composed in part of the transactions demand which depends on the level of income. Therefore, the m_{d_1} curve must have been drawn on the basis of some assumed income level that defined m_{t_1}. Other things being equal, a higher income level would indicate a different position

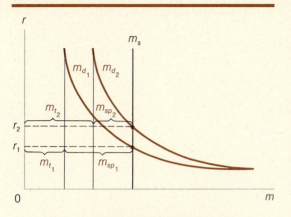

FIGURE 12-2
Equilibrium Levels of the
Interest Rate

for the curve—say m_{d_2} instead of m_{d_1}. This would indicate a different equilibrium rate of interest, r_2, at which $m_{t_2} + m_{sp_2} = m_{d_2} = m_2$. Figure 12-2, however, does not reveal what the level of income may be—it assumes some income level and proceeds from there.

It appears that we cannot determine the equilibrium income level without first knowing the interest rate and that we cannot determine the equilibrium interest rate without first knowing the income level. Somehow Y and r must be determined simultaneously. Although this cannot be done through Figures 12-1 and 12-2, there are nonetheless a particular income level and interest rate that simultaneously provide equilibrium in the goods market behind Figure 12-1 and in the money market behind Figure 12-2. The model to be developed in this chapter provides this simultaneous solution of the two equilibrium values and clarifies some other important problems and policy questions.[3]

---

[3]This model was originally developed by J.R. Hicks in his article "Mr. Keynes and the 'Classics': A Suggested Interpretation," in *Econometrica*, April 1937, pp. 147–59, reprinted in W. Fellner and B.F. Haley, eds., *Readings in the Theory of Income Distribution*, Irwin, 1946, pp. 461–76.

Equilibrium in the Goods Market

Because equilibrium in the goods market requires that $Y = C + I$ and $S = I$, all the factors that cause the consumption function and therefore the saving function to shift and all the factors that cause the investment function to shift influence the determination of this equilibrium. Although other factors may be introduced once the basic model is developed, we assume here that investment is a function of the interest rate alone and that consumption and therefore saving is a function of income alone. From the $C + I$ approach, we then have, in general terms, the following three equations to cover the goods market:

$$\text{Consumption function: } C = C(Y)$$
$$\text{Investment function: } I = I(r)$$
$$\text{Equilibrium condition: } Y = C(Y) + I(r)$$

From the S, I approach, we have, in general terms, the following three equations to cover the goods market:

$$\text{Saving function: } S = S(Y)$$
$$\text{Investment function: } I = I(r)$$
$$\text{Equilibrium condition: } S(Y) = I(r)$$

One may develop the diagrammatic analysis that follows on the basis of either or both of the approaches, but attention here will be limited to that based on the S, I approach.

The set of equations for that approach may be shown graphically as in Figure 12-3. Part A gives the investment spending schedule, showing that investment spending varies inversely with the interest rate. The straight line in Part B is drawn at a 45° angle from the origin. Whatever the amount of planned investment measured

---

See also F. Modigliani, "Liquidity Preference and the Theory of Interest and Money," in F.A. Lutz and L.W. Mints, eds., *Readings in Monetary Theory*, Irwin, 1951, particularly pp. 190–206.

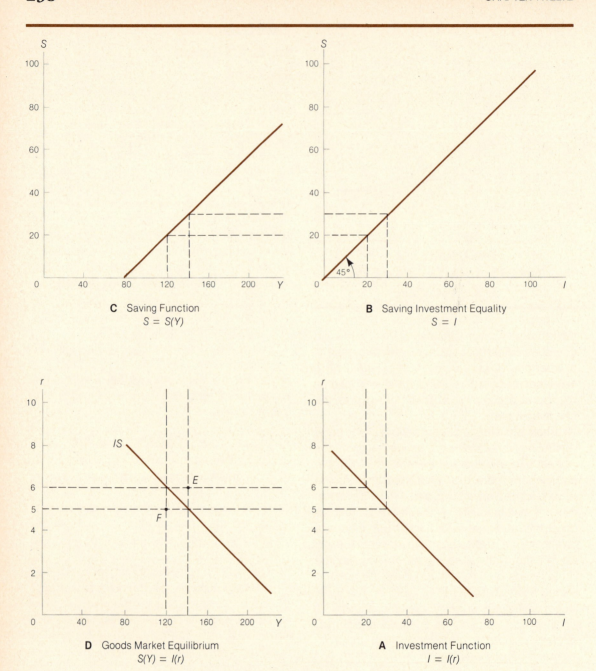

C Saving Function
$S = S(Y)$

B Saving Investment Equality
$S = I$

D Goods Market Equilibrium
$S(Y) = I(r)$

A Investment Function
$I = I(r)$

FIGURE 12-3
Goods Market Equilibrium

along the horizontal axis of Part B, equilibrium requires that planned saving measured along the vertical axis of Part B be the same. Therefore, all points along the 45° line in Part B indicate equality of saving and investment. Part C brings in the saving function, showing that saving varies directly with income.

The *IS* curve in Part D is derived from the other parts of the figure. For example, assume an interest rate of 6 percent in Part A, indicating that investment is $20 per time period.[4] In Part B, to satisfy the equality between *S* and *I*, saving must also be $20, as shown on the vertical axis. In Part C, saving will be $20 only at an income level of $120.[5] Finally, bringing together *Y* of $120 from Part C and *r* of 6 percent from Part A yields one combination of *Y* and *r* at which *S* = *I* (and *Y* = *C* + *I*). If we assume the lower interest rate of 5 percent, Part A indicates that investment will be $30, which yields an income level of $140 in Part C. Therefore, *Y* of $140 and *r* of 5 percent is another combination of *Y* and *r* at which *S* = *I*. Other combinations could be found in the same way. Connecting these combinations gives us the *IS* curve in Part D.[6]

There is no longer a single level of income at which *S* = *I*, but a different level for each different interest rate. The higher the interest rate, the lower will be the level of income at which *S* = *I*. Viewed in one way, this follows from the fact that a high *r* means a low *I*. A low *I*, through the multiplier, means a low *Y*. Viewed in another way, it follows from the fact that a low *Y* means a low *S*. Because equilibrium requires that *S* = *I*, a low *S*

means a low *I*. A low *I* is the result of a high *r*. Although the *IS* function indicates that equilibrium in the goods market will be found at a lower level of income for a higher interest rate, it alone does not reveal what particular combination of *Y* and *r* will be found in any specific time period. All combinations on the *IS* function are equally possible equilibrium combinations of *Y* and *r* in the goods market.

Identifying all equilibrium combinations does not, however, mean that the actual combination in each time period will be one of them. There may be disequilibrium in the goods market. Suppose that the actual combination is the disequilibrium combination of *Y* = $140 and *r* = 6 percent indicated as point *E* in Part D of Figure 12-3. At the income level of $140, *S* will equal *I* only if the interest rate is 5 percent. Therefore, given this $140 income level and an interest rate of 6 percent, *S* must exceed *I* because *I* will be smaller at a rate higher than 5 percent, but *S* will be unchanged. *S* depends only on the level of income, which is here unchanged at $140. The combination of *Y* = $140 and *r* = 6 percent is also a disequilibrium from a second point of view. At the interest rate of 6 percent, *S* will equal *I* only if the income level is $120. Therefore, given the combination of this 6 percent interest rate and an income level of $140 as at point *E*, *S* must exceed *I* because *S* will be larger at an income level above $120, but *I* will be unchanged. *I* depends only on the interest rate, which is here unchanged at 6 percent. It follows that for any combination of *Y* and *r* located anywhere in the space to the *right* of the *IS* curve, the same conclusion may be drawn that was drawn for point *E:* There is a disequilibrium in which *S* exceeds *I* and *Y* exceeds (*C* + *I*).

By the same line of reasoning, the combination of *Y* = $120 and *r* = 5 percent indicated as point *F* is a disequilibrium of the opposite kind: Here *I* must exceed *S*. Generalizing as before, for any combination of *Y* and *r* anywhere in the space to the *left* of the *IS* curve, there is a disequilibrium in which *I* exceeds *S* and (*C* + *I*)

---

[4]All dollar amounts are in billions.

[5]The saving function $S = S_a + sY$ is here $S = -\$40 + \frac{1}{2}Y$.

[6]Alternatively, the combinations of *Y* and *r* at which *S* = *I* could just as well be determined graphically by starting with assumed levels of *Y*. Assuming *Y* of $120, Part C shows that *S* will be $20. Moving from Part C through Part B to Part A, *I* of $20 is consistent with *r* of 6 percent. Therefore, in Part D, *Y* of $120 and *r* of 6 percent identify one combination at which *S* = *I*.

exceeds Y. In other words, the aggregate spending on goods exceeds the aggregate output of goods.

Equilibrium in the Money Market

Equilibrium in the money market requires an equality between the supply of and the demand for money. The Keynesian theory of the demand for money makes the transactions demand (here combined with the precautionary demand) a direct function of the income level alone, or $m_t = k(Y)$. It makes the speculative demand an inverse function of the interest rate alone, or $m_{sp} = h(r)$. Total demand for money is $m_d = m_t + m_{sp} = k(Y) + h(r)$. The supply of money m_s is determined outside the model—it is exogenous. This may be written $m_s = m_a$, in which m_a is simply the amount of money that exists, an amount determined by the monetary authorities. (The monetary authorities determine only the nominal stock of money, M_s, but with P assumed to be stable, determination of M_s also determines m_s.) This gives us three equations to cover the money market:

$$\text{Demand for money: } m_d = k(Y) + h(r)$$
$$\text{Supply of money: } m_s = m_a$$
$$\text{Equilibrium condition: } m_d = m_s$$

This set of equations is shown graphically in Figure 12-4. Part A shows the speculative demand for money as a function of r. Part B is drawn to show a total money supply of $100, all of which must be held in either transactions or speculative balances. The points along the line indicate all the possible ways in which the given money supply may be divided between m_t and m_{sp}. Part C shows the amount of money required for transactions purposes at each level of income on the assumption that $k = 1/2$. The LM curve of Part D is derived from the other parts as follows.

Assume in Part A an interest rate of 6 percent, at which the public will want to hold $40 in speculative balances. In Part B, subtracting the $40 of speculative balances from a total money supply of $100 leaves $60 of transactions balances, an amount consistent with an income level of $120 as shown in Part C. Finally, in Part D, bringing together Y of $120 from Part C and r of 6 percent from Part A yields one combination of Y and r at which $m_d = m_s$ or at which there is equilibrium in the money market. If we assume the lower interest rate of 5 percent, Part A indicates that speculative balances will be $50, Part B indicates that transactions balances will be $50, and Part C indicates the income level of $100 as that consistent with transactions balances of $50. This yields another combination of Y and r—$100 and 5 percent—at which $m_d = m_s$. Other such combinations can be determined in the same way. In Part D, the function labeled LM results when these combinations are connected.[7]

Although particular characteristics of the LM function will call for attention later, in general the function slopes upward to the right. With a given stock of money, money market equilibrium is found at combinations of high interest rates and high income levels or low interest rates and low income levels. Viewed in one way, this follows from the fact that a high level of income calls for relatively large transactions balances, which, with a given money supply, can be drawn out of speculative balances only by pushing up the interest rate. Viewed in another way, it follows from the fact that at a high interest rate speculative balances will be low; this releases more of

---

[7] As with the IS curve, the combinations of Y and r at which $m_d = m_s$ could just as well be determined graphically by starting with assumed levels of Y. Therefore, assuming Y of $120, Part C shows that m_t will be $60. Subtracting $60 from the total money supply of $100 leaves $40. As Part A shows, this is an amount the public will be willing to hold in speculative balances, m_{sp}, at r of 6 percent. In Part D, Y of $120 and r of 6 percent therefore identify one combination of Y and r at which $m_d = m_s$.

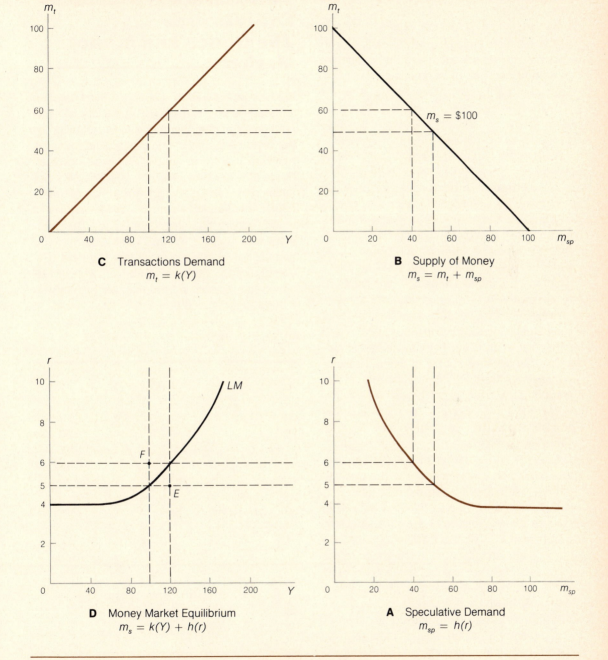

C   Transactions Demand
$m_t = k(Y)$

B   Supply of Money
$m_s = m_t + m_{sp}$

D   Money Market Equilibrium
$m_s = k(Y) + h(r)$

A   Speculative Demand
$m_{sp} = h(r)$

FIGURE 12-4
Money Market Equilibrium

the money supply for transactions balances. This money will be held in such balances only at a correspondingly high level of income. Although the *LM* function indicates why equilibrium in the money market will occur at a higher interest rate for a higher level of income, it alone cannot reveal what particular combination of *Y* and *r* will be found in any given time period. All combinations on the *LM* function are equally possible equilibrium combinations in the money market.

As with the *IS* curve, identifying all combinations at which $m_d = m_s$ does not mean that the actual combination in each time period will be one of them. The actual combination may involve a disequilibrium in the money market. For example, consider the disequilibrium combination indicated by point *E* in Part D of Figure 12-4. At the income level of $120, m_d will equal m_s only if *r* is 6 percent. Therefore, if we combine this $120 income level with an interest rate of 5 percent, m_d must exceed m_s because m_d will be larger at $r = 5$ percent. The quantity of money demanded for speculative purposes rises with a lower interest rate, but the total supply of money is fixed. Alternatively, if we start with the interest rate of 5 percent, m_d will equal m_s only if the income level is $100. Therefore, if we combine this 5 percent interest rate with an income level of $120 shown as point *E*, m_d must exceed m_s because m_d will be larger at an income level above $100 than it will be at $100. The quantity of money demanded for transactions rises with a higher income, but the total money supply is, as before, fixed. What has been concluded for the combination indicated by point *E* holds true for any combination located in the space to the right of the *LM* curve; any combination of *Y* and *r* in this space is necessarily a disequilibrium combination in which m_d exceeds m_s.

By the same reasoning, the combination of $Y = \$100$ and $r = 6$ percent indicated as point *F* is a disequilibrium of the opposite kind: m_s must here exceed m_d. Generalizing as before, there is a disequilibrium in which m_s exceeds m_d for any combination of *Y* and *r* located in the space to the left of the *LM* curve.

Two-Market Equilibrium— The Goods and Money Markets

Equilibrium between the supply of and demand for goods is possible at all combinations of *Y* and *r* indicated by the *IS* curve; similarly, equilibrium between the supply of and demand for money is possible at all combinations of *Y* and *r* indicated by the *LM* curve. However, there is only one combination of *Y* and *r* at which the supply of goods equals the demand for goods *and* the supply of money equals the demand for money. This combination is defined by the intersection of the *IS* and *LM* curves derived in Figures 12-3 and 12-4 and brought together in Figure 12-5. In this illustration, equilibrium in both markets occurs with $Y = \$120$ and $r = 6$ percent.

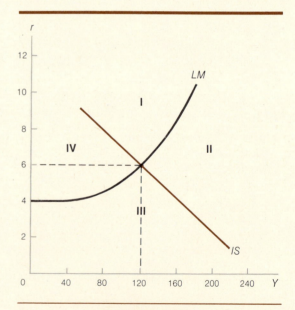

FIGURE 12-5
Equilibrium in the Goods and Money Markets

From Disequilibrium to Equilibrium

Every possible combination of Y and r in Figure 12-5 other than that given by the intersection of the IS and LM curves is one at which there is disequilibrium in the goods market, the money market, or both. All those combinations that do not lie on either the IS or the LM curve fall into this last category. Because all such combinations do not lie on a line, they necessarily lie in one of the four areas identified by the Roman numerals I through IV. As we saw earlier, any combination of Y and r that lies anywhere to the right of the IS curve is a combination at which $S > I$ and $Y > (C + I)$. The opposite is true for any combination of Y and r anywhere to the left of the IS curve. Similarly, any combination of Y and r anywhere to the right of the LM curve is a combination at which $m_d > m_s$. The opposite is true for any combination to the left of the LM curve. Accordingly, each of the four spaces may be distinguished from the other three in terms of the relationships between the supply of and demand for goods and between the supply of and demand for money for any combination of Y and r that falls within that space:

	Goods Market	Money Market
In Space I:	$I < S, (C + I) < Y$	$m_d < m_s$
In Space II:	$I < S, (C + I) < Y$	$m_d > m_s$
In Space III:	$I > S, (C + I) > Y$	$m_d > m_s$
In Space IV:	$I > S, (C + I) > Y$	$m_d < m_s$

From the analysis of the goods market considered in isolation, we know that a situation in which $I > S$ or $(C + I) > Y$ will lead to a rise in income and vice versa. From the analysis of the money market considered in isolation, we know that a situation in which $m_d > m_s$ will lead to a rise in the interest rate and vice versa. What we now have in the four spaces laid out in Figure 12-5 are various combinations of IS and LM disequilibrium situations. Because we know the direction in which the income level tends to move in response to an excess supply or excess demand

for goods and the direction in which the interest rate tends to move in response to an excess supply or excess demand for money, we can trace out in a nonrigorous fashion a possible path that the income level and the interest rate may follow in response to any given disequilibrium situation.

In Figure 12-6 we assume the economy is located at the disequilibrium combination of Y and r indicated by A, which is in Space III. Here there is an excess demand for goods and an excess demand for money. The excess demand for goods tends to raise the income level, as indicated by the horizontal arrow originating at A. The excess demand for money tends to push up the interest rate, as indicated by the vertical arrow originating at A. With these forces at work, it is not unreasonable to expect the economy to move along the path designated by the arrow from A to B. Next, with the economy at B, the supply of and demand for goods are equal,

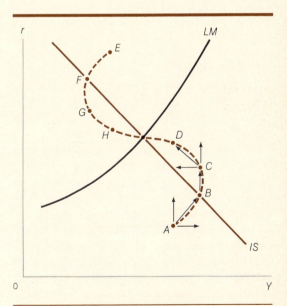

FIGURE 12-6
Possible Paths of Movement to Equilibrium in the Goods and Money Markets

because we are on the *IS* curve. But we are still at a point to the right of the *LM* curve, so the demand for money exceeds the supply of money. Therefore, a force is at work to push up the interest rate and the next movement may be along the arrow from *B* to *C*. At *C* there is still an excess demand for money, which again tends to push up the interest rate as indicated by the vertical arrow originating at *C*. However, at *C* there is an excess supply of goods, which tends to reduce the income level as shown by the horizontal arrow originating at *C*. These forces may on balance cause the economy to move along the path described by the arrow running from *C* to *D*. At *D*, the forces are the same as at *C*; the result is a movement of the same kind. The combination of income level and interest rate may change in this way over time until finally the system reaches that one combination of *Y* and *r* at which both markets clear. Although the several discrete steps traced out here help reveal the underlying process at work, the actual process would be a continuous one in which *Y* and *r* might move along a path like that indicated by the dashed line running from *A* to *D* and then to the intersection of the two curves.

Instead of starting at *A*, we could start at any other disequilibrium point in Figure 12-6 and trace the movement of *Y* and *r* toward the single pair of equilibrium values in the same way. No matter what disequilibrium point one starts with, all one need do is (1) identify whether $I > S$, $I < S$, or $I = S$, or in terms of aggregate spending whether $(C + I) > Y$, $(C + I) < Y$, or $(C + I) = Y$, which tells whether *Y* will tend to rise, fall, or remain unchanged; (2) identify whether $m_d > m_s$, $m_d < m_s$, or $m_d = m_s$, which tells whether *r* will tend to rise, fall, or remain unchanged; and (3) establish the direction of movement of the *Y*, *r* combination indicated by the forces found to be at work in (1) and (2). For example, starting with any point in Space I such as *E*, forces tend to reduce both the income level and the interest rate. The reader may trace the discrete steps from *E* through *H*, which are different in direction but exactly symmetrical with those from *A* through

D. As was shown for the movement from *A* to the intersection, the continuous path that the economy might follow from *E* to *H* and then to the intersection is indicated by a dashed line. Once at the intersection, the combination of *Y* and *r* provides equilibrium in both markets; the income level and the interest rate will remain unchanged until the existing equilibrium is upset by a shift in the *IS* or *LM* curve, or in both.[8]

IS–LM Equilibrium and the Aggregate Demand Curve

In the simple classical theory of Chapter 9, the aggregate demand curve was derived from the quantity of money and appeared graphically as a downward sloping curve (rectangular hyperbola). Given the classical theory's conclusion that the aggregate supply curve is a perfectly inelastic line situated at the full employment level of output, the intersection of the *AD* curve with the *AS* curve did no more than determine the price level of the full employment output.

The model being constructed in this chapter includes the opposite extreme for the *AS* curve—that is, one that is perfectly elastic up to the full employment level of output but perfectly inelastic at that level. This kind of *AS* curve is shown in Part B of Figure 12-7. The present model also assumes that the economy operates below the full employment level of output—that is, along the perfectly elastic portion of the *AS* curve. Some

---

[8]Although it is quite illuminating to trace the path followed by *Y* and *r* as we have done here, the *IS–LM* model now before us does not in itself reveal that *Y* and *r* will follow the path here described or any other particular path from an initial disequilibrium position like *A* or *E*. As briefly explained in Chapter 3, to trace the process of change in the values of a model's variables from one period to another can be done only with a dynamic model. The *IS–LM* model is not dynamic, but completely static. It identifies the values the variables must exhibit in order that there be equilibrium, but it does not show the sequence of changes by which these values will be reached if we start off with any values other than these equilibrium values.

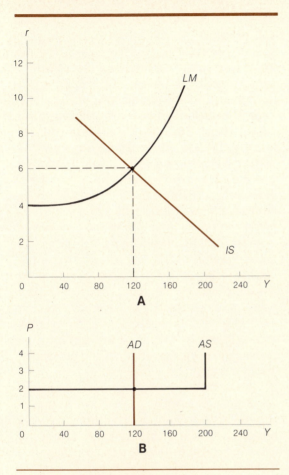

FIGURE 12-7
The *IS–LM* Curves and the
Aggregate Demand Curve

ular *IS* and *LM* curves, and it is from the intersection of this pair of curves that the *AD* curve is derived in the present model. To derive the *AD* curve, we make one final assumption—that neither the *IS* nor the *LM* curve shifts with changes in the price level. This assumption enables us to postpone dealing with some major complications until Chapter 13.

With this assumption, whatever the price level might be—1, 2, 3, 4, or any other level in Part B of Figure 12-7—the *IS* and *LM* curves remain in the position shown in Part A. Therefore, corresponding to each possible price level on the vertical axis of Part B, we have the same pair of *IS* and *LM* curves and the same equilibrium figure of 120 for the output level found in Part A. The *AD* curve shows the total amount of goods demanded at various price levels, but on the present assumption that amount is a constant 120. Therefore, the aggregate *AD* curve is perfectly inelastic at the output level of 120, as shown in Part B. Throughout the balance of this chapter we will assume that the *IS* and *LM* curves do not shift with the price level; therefore all of the *AD* curves will be perfectly inelastic. However, these *AD* curves can shift to the right or the left, and we next look at some of the factors that will produce such shifts.

Changes in Aggregate Demand

other assumptions finally yield the conclusion that the level of output is determined entirely by aggregate demand. In this case, aggregate supply only determines the price level at which that output will sell.

In this model, the derivation of the *AD* curve is more complicated than in the simple classical model in which it only depends on the supply of money. Here it depends on all the factors that determine the positions of the *IS* and *LM* curves. The supply of money is only one of these factors. At any time, these factors will determine partic-

The equilibrium combination of *Y* and *r* identified by the intersection of the *IS* and *LM* functions will, of course, change in response to any shift in those functions, and the *AD* curve will shift to the level of *Y* identified by the new intersection. Shifts in the *IS* function are caused by shifts in the investment or the saving function (Parts A and C of Figure 12-3); shifts in the *LM* function are caused by shifts in the money supply, transactions demand, or speculative demand functions (Parts B, C, and A, respectively, of Figure 12-4). Finally, a shift in any of the functions on which the

IS and LM curves are based may result from a change in the factors that determine the positions of these functions. This gives us a method of analyzing the effects of a change in any of these underlying factors. We can trace a change in any factor through the system to its final effect on the income level and interest rate—assuming, of course, that all other factors remain unchanged. Given the assumed shape of the aggregate supply curve, none of these changes will affect the price level.

A Change in Investment

Among the various possibilities, a shift in the investment curve is one of the most important. Suppose a change in an underlying factor—for example, an improvement in business expectations—causes this curve to shift $20 to the right *at each rate of interest.* In Part A of Figure 12-8, the original curve is labeled I_1 and the new one I_2. In Figure 12-3, an IS curve was derived graphically from the investment and saving curves given there. Similarly, in Figure 12-8, a separate IS curve may be derived from each of the investment curves in combination with the given saving curve. In Part D, the IS_1 and IS_2 curves are based on the I_1 and I_2 curves, respectively. *At each interest rate, IS_2 lies $40 to the right of IS_1.* In other words, at each interest rate the level of income at which $S = I$ is now $40 greater than it was before the shift in the investment schedule. This follows from the fact that, with an increase of $20 in investment, income must rise by $40 to induce an increase of $20 in saving, given that the MPS is 1/2. This is nothing more than the simple multiplier in action, $\Delta Y(1/MPS\Delta I$, which gives us $40 = 2 \cdot $20.

The original equilibrium was earlier found at Y of $120 and r of 6 percent. Here it is shown again by the intersection of IS_1 and LM in Part D of Figure 12-8. As before, this gives us the AD_1 curve positioned at Y of $120 in Part E. The LM curve here is the same as the one derived in Figure 12-4. The new equilibrium that results from the shift in the investment curve is at Y of $140 and r of 7 percent (an increase of one percent-

age point) as shown by the intersection of IS_2 and LM in Part D. As the increase in investment spending starts an upward movement in income, the rising income level increases the money balances needed for transactions purposes. This leads to a rising interest rate, which in turn feeds back to make the increase in investment spending less than the $20 and the increase in income less than the $40 they would have been with no rise in the interest rate. In the present illustration, with the LM curve as given, the shift in the IS curve caused by a rightward shift of $20 in the investment curve raises Y by $20 and r by one percentage point. The $20 rise in Y means an increase of $10 in required transactions balances, given $k = 0.5$. The rise in r of one percentage point is just sufficient to reduce the amount of money the public wishes to hold in speculative balances by $10, thereby supplying the additional $10 needed for transactions balances. Therefore, with $\Delta Y = $20 and Δr of one percentage point, the supply of and demand for money will again be in balance.

The same one percentage point rise in r will decrease investment from $20 to $10. As may be seen in Part A of Figure 12-8, investment—which would have risen from its original $20 at r of 6 percent (point E) to $40 with no change in r (Point F)—only rises from $20 to $30 (point G) because one half of what would have been the larger increase is choked off by the rise in r from 6 to 7 percent. The final increase in investment of $10 turns out to be the same amount as the increase in saving that occurs with a rise in income of $20. From $\Delta S = s(\Delta Y)$, we here have $10 = 0.5($20)$. With $\Delta Y = $20 and Δr of one percentage point, S will again equal I and Y will again equal $C + I$. No other combination of changes in Y and r will be consistent with equilibrium in both the goods and money markets, assuming the indicated rightward shift in the investment schedule with all else as given.

For a leftward shift in the investment schedule, the results will be the opposite. If the investment schedule of Part A were to shift to the left by $20 or from I_1 to I_3, the new equilibrium in Part D would show Y of $100 and r of 5 percent.

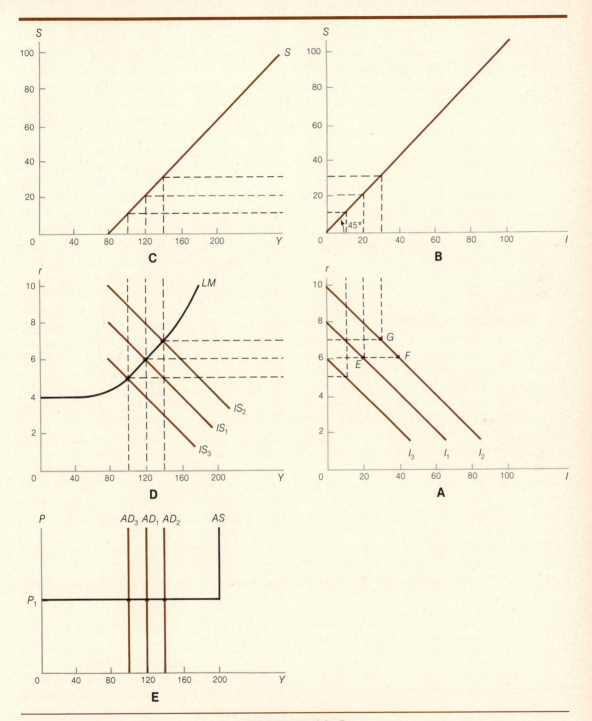

FIGURE 12-8
A Change in Investment and the Change in Aggregate Demand

Relative to the original equilibrium, this would be a decrease in Y of $20 and in r of one percentage point.[9] No other combination of changes in Y or r would be consistent with equilibrium in both the goods and money markets, assuming the indicated shift in the investment schedule with all else as given.

Just as the intersection of IS_1 and LM in Part D established the AD_1 curve in Part E, the intersections of the IS_2 and LM curves and of the IS_3 and LM curves establish the AD_2 and AD_3 curves, respectively, in Part E. Given the LM curve in Part D, the shifts in the I curve of Part A which cause the indicated shifts in the IS curve in Part D also produce the shifts here noted in the AD curve in Part E.

A Change in the Money Supply

As a second illustration of a shift in the AD curve, assume a $20 increase in the money supply. This shifts the m_s curve in Part B of Figure 12-9 from its original position of m_{s_1} to the new position m_{s_2}. With no change in the speculative demand function or the transactions demand function, the $20 increase in m_s shifts the LM function rightward by $40 *at each rate of interest,* or from LM_1 to LM_2. What lies behind this may be seen as follows. Equilibrium between m_d and m_s requires a rise in Y sufficient to absorb the m_s increase of $20 in transactions balances, m_t, if the interest rate is assumed to be given. Because $m_t = k(Y)$, we have $Y = m_t/k$ and $\Delta Y = \Delta m_t/k$. Accordingly, with k given as 0.5, ΔY must be $40 to produce a new equilibrium between m_d and m_s at each interest rate.

---

[9]For simplicity, here we assume that the LM curve is linear over the range of interest rates (5 to 7 percent) relevant to our illustrations. (This requires that we also assume that the underlying speculative demand curve is linear over this same range.) Specifically, the slope of LM is taken to be 0.05 (r changes by 0.05 percentage point for each $1 billion change in Y or by 1.00 percentage point for a $20 billion change in Y). Any departure from linearity would give actual numerical results different from the symmetrical ones found in the illustrations.

The original equilibrium at Y of $120 and r of 6 percent is shown here again by the intersection of IS and LM_1 in Part D of Figure 12-9. The IS curve here is the same as the one originally derived in Figure 12-3. The new equilibrium that results from the increase in the money supply is at Y of $140 and r of 5 percent. Although the $20 increase in m_s will shift the LM curve $40 to the right at each interest rate, it will not raise the equilibrium level of Y by $40, because, with no shift in the IS curve, a rise in the equilibrium level of income cannot occur unless r falls. However, a fall in r will increase the amount of money people choose to hold in speculative balances. In the present illustration, $10 of the $20 increase in M will be absorbed in speculative balances as r falls from 6 to 5 percent (as may be seen from Part A of Figure 12-9). This same fall in r is also just sufficient to raise I by $10 (as may be seen from Part A of Figure 12-8) and, through the multiplier, raise Y by $20. A rise in Y of $20 increases required transactions balances by $10, which accounts for the balance of the $20 increase in m_s. No other possible combination of changes in Y and r but this $20 increase and one percentage point decrease will be consistent with equilibrium, assuming the indicated increase in the money supply with all else as given.

If the change were in the opposite direction— a $20 decrease in the money supply that shifts the curve from m_{s_1} to m_{s_3}—the new equilibrium combination of Y and r would be at $100 and 7 percent, or a decrease in Y of $20 and a rise in r of one percentage point. By the reasoning of the preceding paragraph, no other combination of changes in Y and r will provide a new equilibrium within the assumptions of the present illustration.

Because the LM_1 and IS curves in Figure 12-9 are identical with the LM and IS_1 curves in Figure 12-8, they intersect at $Y = $120 and $r = $ 6 percent. With the equilibrium interest rate set at 6 percent, $S = I$ and $Y = C + I$ at Y of $120. As in Figure 12-8, this establishes the AD_1 curve in Part E at $Y = $120. An increase from m_{s_1} to m_{s_2} shifts the LM curve from LM_1 to LM_2, lowers the equilibrium interest rate, and makes $S = I$

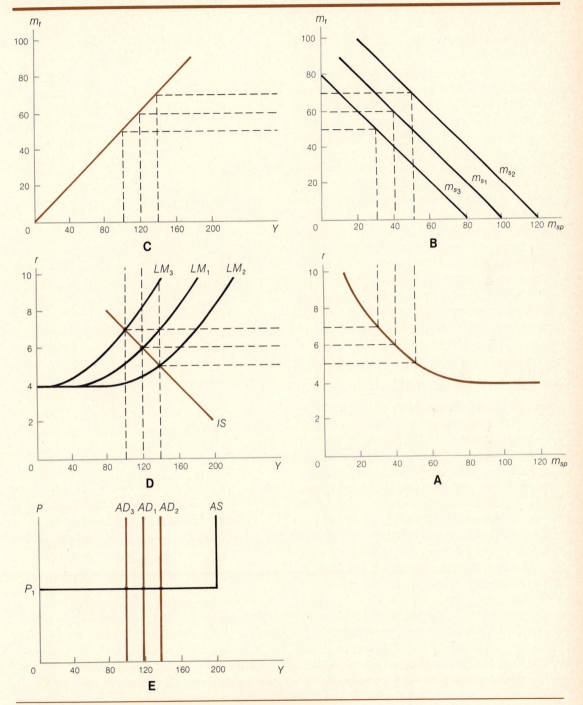

FIGURE 12-9
A Change in the Money Supply and the Change in Aggregate Demand

and $Y = C + I$ at Y of $140. This establishes the AD_2 curve at Y of $140 in Part E. In the same way, the LM_3 curve based on m_{s_3} yields the AD_3 curve at Y of $100 in Part E.

Although the present illustration involves nothing more than a purely *monetary* change, one result is still a change in the level of *real* income. In short, given the *IS* and *LM* curves as in Figure 12-9, monetary policy can influence the economy's level of output. As will be explained later, the effect on the income level of an increase in the money supply depends on (1) how great the fall in the interest rate is, which in turn depends on the elasticity of the speculative demand function, and (2) how much investment spending rises as a result of any given drop in the interest rate, which in turn depends on the interest elasticity of the investment function. If the interest rate falls with a rise in the money supply and if investment spending rises with a fall in the interest rate, the income level will rise.

A Simultaneous Increase in Investment and the Money Supply

Now suppose that the two increases we have discussed separately occur simultaneously. The rise in the investment function moves the *IS* curve from IS_1 to IS_2, and the rise in the money supply moves the *LM* curve from LM_1 to LM_2, as shown in Part A of Figure 12-10. The result is a shift in the equilibrium position from Y of $120 and r of 6 percent to Y of $160 and r of 6 percent. The *AD* curve of Part B correspondingly shifts from its position at Y of $120 to a position at Y of $160. A rise in investment spending, with no change in the money supply, produces a rise in income that is dampened by a rise in the interest rate resulting from it. If the money supply increases by just the amount necessary to prevent this rise in the interest rate, the full income-expansionary effect of the rise in investment will be realized. The increase in Y from $120 to $160, with an increase in investment of $20 and an MPC of 1/2, is just the result we found in the simple Keynesian

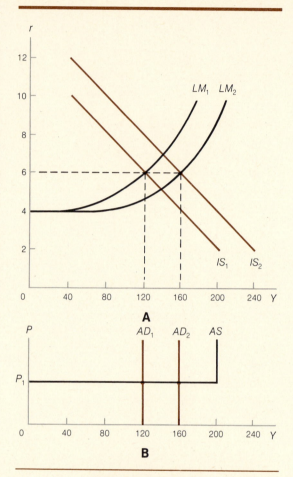

A

B

FIGURE 12-10
Effect on Aggregate Demand of a Simultaneous Increase in Investment and the Money Supply

model in Chapter 5. Now we see that this result will be realized only if an appropriately expansionary monetary policy—here an increase in m_s of $20—is pursued to prevent what otherwise would be a rise in the interest rate and consequently a smaller rise in the income level.

The effects of shifts in other functions may be traced in the same way. For example, an increase in "thrift," which appears as an upward shift in the saving function (Part C of Figure 12-3), will shift the *IS* curve to the left and lower *r* and *Y*. An increase in the demand for money to be held in idle balances, which appears as a shift to the right in the speculative demand function (Part A of Figure 12-4), will shift the *LM* curve to the left, raise *r*, and lower *Y*. A change in payments practices that makes it possible for each dollar of money to handle a larger volume of transactions per time period reduces *k* and appears as a less steeply inclined transactions demand function (Part C of Figure 12-4). This will shift the *LM* curve to the right, lower *r*, and raise *Y*.

Government Spending, Taxation, and Aggregate Demand

Once government spending and taxation have been added to the model, the equilibrium condition *S* = *I* in the goods market for a two-sector economy becomes *S* + *T* = *I* + *G* for a three-sector economy. This simply means that the aggregate spending for goods and aggregate output of goods will be equal when the sum of the diversions, *S* + *T*, from the real income stream is just matched by the sum of compensating injections, *I* + *G*, into the real income stream. Alternatively, the equilibrium condition in the goods market may be expressed as *Y* = *C* + *I* + *G*. The equilibrium condition in the money market is $m_d = m_s$, as before.

As in the first fiscal model of Chapter 6, both government purchases of goods and services and net tax receipts are assumed to be independent of the level of income. Part A of Figure 12-11 shows $20 of government purchases added to the investment schedule of Figure 12-3. Because these purchases are also regarded as independent of the interest rate, the *I* + *G* curve lies $20 to the right of the *I* curve at all interest rates. Whatever the interest rate, the sum of *I* + *G* will be $20 greater than *I* alone. In terms of its effect on *Y*, a dollar of *G* is no different from a dollar of *I*. Adding $20 of *G* therefore shifts the

IS curve $40 to the right, from IS_1 to IS_2, for the same reason that the increase in investment of $20 shifted the *IS* curve to the right by $40 in Figure 12-8.[10] Part D of Figure 12-11 includes the same *LM* function derived in Figure 12-4.

Other things being equal, the introduction of deficit-financed government purchases of $20 moves the *Y, r* equilibrium in Part D from $120 and 6 percent to $140 and 7 percent and shifts the *AD* curve in Part E from AD_1 to AD_2. Again the result shown is the same as that in Figure 12-8 for a $20 shift in the investment demand schedule. What otherwise would be an expansion in *Y* of $40, as indicated by the simple multiplier of 2, becomes the lesser expansion of $20 due to the effect of the rise in *r* that accompanies the rise in *Y*. However, there is a difference: *G* of $20 is unaffected by the rise in *r* it causes, but the rise in *r* reduces *I* by $10, which makes the net change in *I* + *G* only $10 and the rise in income only $20. The full income-expansionary effect of *G* is not realized, because the resulting rise in *r* crowds out $10 of private investment spending. Therefore, a fiscal policy designed to raise the income level through a deficit-financed expansion of government spending may not produce the maximum possible rise of income unless it is accompanied by an appropriately expansionary monetary policy.[11]

Let us now suppose that there is a balanced budget and that the government collects taxes of $20 to match its spending of $20, thereby

---

[10] It would be more correct to designate the curve as *IG–ST* instead of *IS*, but the simpler notation will be retained. Note, however, that in Parts A–C the axes previously labeled *I* are now *I* + *G*, and the axes previously labeled *S* are now *S* + *T*.

[11] Because government spending in this example is entirely deficit financed, we are concerned with the method of deficit financing employed. If entirely financed by the sale of government securities to the public, there will be no increase in the money supply; the results are as described above. If financed by the appropriate "mix" of sales to the public and the banking system, there will be an increase in the money supply that permits the full $40 potential expansion in *Y*.

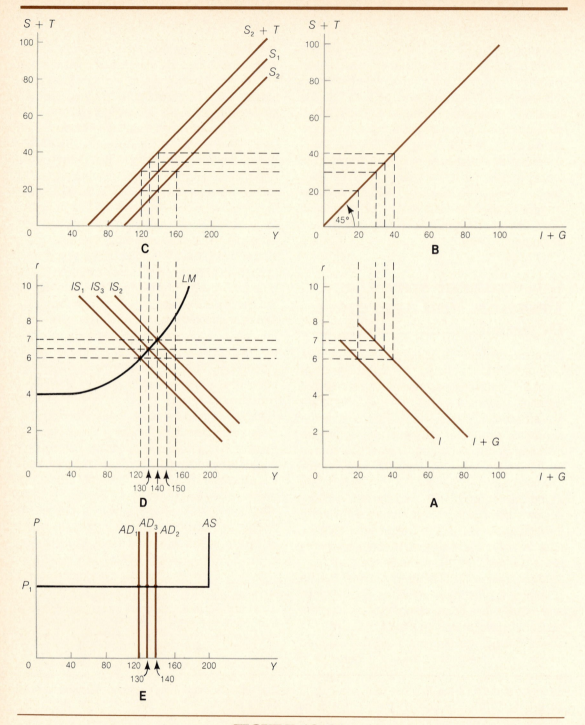

FIGURE 12-11
**Effect on Aggregate Demand of Changes in Government Spending
and Taxation**

avoiding deficit spending. In the present model, taxes of $20 reduce disposable income by $20. With the MPS of 1/2, the reduction in saving is one-half of this amount. Consequently, at each level of Y, T of $20 reduces S by $10 and C by $10, which appears in Part C of Figure 12-11 as a downward shift of $10 from S_1 to S_2 in the saving function. To the leakage from income made up of saving must now be added the leakage of $20 for taxes. This gives us the curve $S_2 + T$, the sum of saving and taxes, or that portion of the income flow that does not appear as consumption spending at each level of income.[12]

I of Part A and S_1 of Part C gave us IS_1 of Part D; $I + G$ of Part A with T of zero gave us IS_2 of Part D; finally, $I + G$ of Part A with $S_2 + T$ of Part C gives us IS_3 of Part D. The new equilibrium position indicated by the intersection of IS_3 and LM in Part D is found at Y of $130 and r of 6.5 percent. Corresponding to this is AD_3 positioned at Y of $130 in Part E. In our illustration, adding G of $20 and an equal amount of T raises the equilibrium level of Y by one-half the increase in the size of the budget.[13]

With G and T both independent of the level of Y, we have a model similar to the one that gave us the unit multiplier in Chapter 6. In that model, the rise in Y was equal to the increase in the size of the budget. However, because the interest rate is now part of the model, we find that the actual multiplier is less than the balanced-budget multiplier of 1 that appears in the simpler model. An expansion in the size of the budget, with the budget balanced, will raise the income level, but the rise in income—which would otherwise be equal to the expansion in the size of the budget—will be dampened by the tendency for the interest rate to rise with the rise in income. In other words, **a fiscal policy designed to produce a rise in income while maintaining a balanced budget will produce the maximum possible income increase only if it is accompanied by an expansionary monetary policy that prevents what otherwise might be a rise in the interest rate and a consequent reduction in private investment spending.**

We have seen that a rise in the income level may be expected from an expansion in G with no change in T and even from an expansion in G that is matched by T. The third possibility, of course, is a reduction in T with no reduction in G, a commonly cited example of which was the tax cut of 1964. This major reduction cut federal tax receipts about 10 percent below what they otherwise would have been; in contrast, the more recent anti-recessionary Tax Reduction Act of 1975 reduced receipts about 5 percent below what they otherwise would have been. Figure 12-11 may be used to illustrate an aspect of the 1964 tax cut much discussed at the time. Suppose the original equilibrium is defined by the intersection of IS_3 and LM at Y of $130 and r of 6.5 percent; this is the equilibrium consistent with $I + G$ of Part A and $S_2 + T$ of Part C of Figure 12-11. With no change in G but a tax cut of $20, the $I + G$ curve remains as is, and the $S_2 + T$ curve shifts downward to S_1. This in turn causes the IS curve to shift from IS_3 to IS_2. But the full expansionary effect of the tax cut—a rise in Y from $130 to $150—is not realized because the interest rate rises. Therefore, in judging the prospective effectiveness of the 1964 tax cut, one consideration was whether or not the expected increase in aggregate spending would be smaller than otherwise obtainable due to adverse monetary effects. In President Johnson's words, "It would be self-defeating to cancel the stimulus of tax reduction by tightening money. Monetary and debt policy should be directed toward maintaining interest rates and credit conditions that encourage private investment."[14] The model in

---

[12]For example, with Y of $140 and T of zero, Y_d, or $Y - T$, would be $140; C would be $110, or $40 + ½($140 − 0); and S would be $30, or −$40 + ½($140 − 0), the last figure as shown on the S_1 curve of Part C of Figure 12-11 at Y of $140. The imposition of T of $20 reduces Y_d to $120 when Y is $140. This reduces C to $100, or $40 + ½($140 − $20), and S to $20, or −$40 + ½($140 − $20), the latter figure as shown on the S_2 curve at Y of $140. Finally, adding T of $20 makes total diversions from income $40 at Y of $140, as shown on the $S_2 + T$ curve.

[13]The original budget was one in which both G and T were zero.

[14]*Economic Report of the President*, Jan. 1964, p. 11.

Figure 12-11 is far too simple to come to grips with the questions involved, but it suggests, in very general terms, that what is called for is an increase in the money supply. This increase should be sufficient to shift the *LM* curve to the right by the amount necessary to secure the greater rise in income—from $130 to $150—that will follow from the increase in aggregate spending to be expected at a stable interest rate.

Although we will not go beyond the simple model in which both *G* and *T* are assumed to be independent of *Y*, the *IS–LM* analysis of Figure 12-11 may be elaborated by introducing more realistic fiscal assumptions. In Part C, for example, *T* may be treated as a function of *Y*, and the effects of this more realistic fiscal assumption on the *Y, r* equilibrium combination may readily be traced. This model will show how the potential income-expansionary effect of, say, a rise in investment spending may be restrained by both a rise in the interest rate and a rise in tax receipts as income expands. Although it adds something to the simpler model of this section, like any other model of this kind it will again bring out our principal conclusion: An increase in aggregate spending—whether it is the result of a shift in the investment function, consumption function, or a change in government spending or taxation—will not produce the effect on income suggested by the crude multipliers in earlier chapters. When we recognize the role played by money and interest, we see how an otherwise greater expansion of income suggested by crude multipliers may be prevented by the rise in the interest rate that may accompany a rise in income.

The *IS* and *LM* Elasticities and Monetary-Fiscal Policies

So far, we have intentionally avoided specific reference to the elasticities of the *IS* and *LM* functions so that we might concentrate on the general

characteristics of the present stable-price model and the general conclusions it suggests. As we allow for the elasticities of these functions, we will find that some of these conclusions must be qualified and that some must even be abandoned in the extreme cases of perfectly elastic or inelastic functions. For example, an expansionary fiscal policy may raise only the interest rate and leave the income level unchanged; conversely, it may raise only the income level and leave the interest rate unchanged. An expansionary monetary policy may lower only the interest rate and leave the income level unchanged; or it may change neither the interest rate nor the level of income. The reverse is possible for contractionary policies.

Elasticity of the *IS* and *LM* Functions

With a fixed money supply, the *LM* function as derived in Figure 12-4 slopes upward to the right. However, at one extreme the function may become perfectly elastic, and at the other extreme it may become perfectly inelastic, with a range of varying elasticities in between. In general, the higher the interest rate, the less elastic the corresponding point on the *LM* function will be. These three ranges are delineated in Part A of Figure 12-12, in which the perfectly elastic section is the "Keynesian range," the perfectly inelastic section is the "classical range," and the section between is the "intermediate range."

Why this particular shape with perfect elasticity at one extreme and perfect inelasticity at the other? Remember that at some very low interest rate the speculative demand for money may become perfectly elastic due to a consensus by wealth-holders that the interest rate will fall no lower and that security prices will rise no higher. Wealth-holders accordingly stand ready to exchange securities for cash at existing security prices, which produces the liquidity trap on the speculative demand function. Here, on the *LM* function, it produces what is known as the Keynesian range. At the other extreme, at some very high interest rate, the speculative demand for

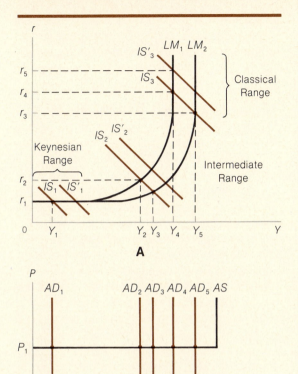

A

B

FIGURE 12-12
Effects of Shifts in the *IS* and
***LM* Functions with Various**
Elasticities of the *LM* Function

money may become zero and perfectly inelastic at interest rates above this if wealth-holders believe the interest rate will rise no higher and that security prices will fall no lower. At this or any higher rate, wealth-holders accordingly prefer to hold only securities and no idle cash. This perfectly inelastic section of the speculative demand function is known as the classical range on the *LM* function.

Why are the three sections into which the *LM* function has been divided labeled in this fash-

ion? In our simplified version of the classical theory, money is demanded only for transactions purposes. Therefore, in Figure 12-4, classical theory assumes that the speculative demand for money is zero at each interest rate. In effect, Part A of that figure vanishes. If the total money supply given in Part B is $100, that $100 will be held in transactions balances or $m_{sp} = 0$ and $m_s = m_t$. With k of 1/2 in Part C, the *LM* curve of Part D becomes a perfectly vertical line at the income level of $200. If the public holds money only for transactions purposes and if it holds money balances equal to one-half of a period's income, money market equilibrium is found at an income level of $200 at all interest rates.[15]

With the exception of the perfectly inelastic section—the so-called classical range—it would not be altogether incorrect to include the remainder of the *LM* function in the Keynesian range. However, because of Keynes' emphasis on the ineffectiveness of monetary policy, the liquidity-trap section alone has been identified as the Keynesian range. Within this range, monetary policy is completely ineffective; therefore, this range most closely fits Keynes' emphasis.

The *IS* function as derived in Figure 12-3 slopes downward to the right. Its elasticity depends on the responsiveness of investment spending to changes in the interest rate and on the magnitude of the multiplier. If the investment spending schedule is perfectly inelastic (indicating that investment spending is completely insensitive to the interest rate), the *IS* curve derived in Part D will be perfectly inelastic, regardless of the magnitude of the multiplier. If, on the other hand, the investment demand schedule shows some elasticity, as seems to be the case, the *IS* curve will be more elastic, the lower the MPS. The lower the MPS, the higher will be the mutliplier and the greater will be the change in income for any increase in investment resulting from a fall in the interest rate. Part A of Figure 12-13 shows three pairs of *IS* curves, each

---

[15]The graphic derivation of a perfectly inelastic *LM* curve is shown in Chapter 13 on p. 268.

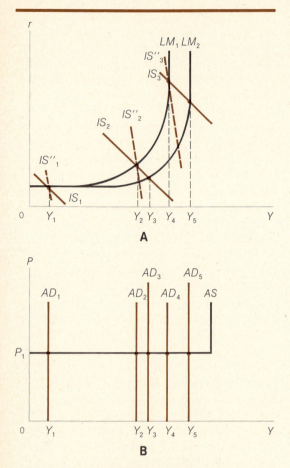

FIGURE 12-13
Effects of Elastic and Inelastic *IS*
Functions in Different Ranges of
the *LM* Function

made up of one highly inelastic and one elastic *IS* curve.

Parts B of both Figures 12-12 and 12-13 show *AD* curves corresponding to the various levels of *Y* set off on the *Y* axis in Part A of each of those figures. As in previous figures of this chapter, the *AS* curve is assumed to be perfectly elastic up to the full employment level of output. Also as before, the full employment level is assumed to be greater than the highest level of

output attained, Y_5 in Part A. Consequently, all of the changes in *AD* shown in each figure from Y_1 to Y_5 are accompanied by proportional changes in Y.[16]

Monetary and Fiscal Policy

Monetary policy is the exercise of the central bank's control over the money supply as an instrument for achieving the objectives of general economic policy. Fiscal policy is the exercise of the government's control over public spending and tax collections for the same purpose. We will confine ourselves here to the single policy objective of raising the level of real income. The *IS–LM* framework then provides a basis for comparing the effect of the two types of policy on the income level and the interest rate and for comparing conditions under which each type of policy will be effective or ineffective in producing the desired change in income. For this purpose, the discussion is conveniently divided into three parts, each corresponding to a range of the *LM* function in Part A of Figure 12-12.

The Keynesian Range   Consider first the Y_1, r_1 equilibrium in the Keynesian range. An increase in the money supply shifts the *LM* curve to the right, from LM_1 to LM_2. This means that *for each possible level of income* $m_d = m_s$ only at a lower interest rate; the rate must fall by the amount necessary to make the public willing to hold larger idle cash balances. But this is not true in the

---

[16]Although the present model contains a classical element in the form of the perfectly inelastic range of the *LM* curve, the model is essentially Keynesian because it shows that the equilibrium level of output may be below the level consistent with full employment. Remember from Chapter 9 that the simple classical model with its assumption of perfect wage and price flexibility yields a perfectly inelastic *AS* curve, which is located at the full employment level of output. This makes the full employment level of output the only equilibrium level, a result altogether different from that found in Figures 12-12 and 12-13. Further comparisons between the classical and Keynesian models in terms of the *IS—LM* framework will be presented in the following chapter.

"liquidity trap." Here the interest rate is already at an irreducible minimum for the time being. As the monetary authority purchases securities, security-holders are willing to exchange them for cash at the existing prices. Therefore, expansion of the money supply cannot cause the interest rate to fall below the rate given by the trap. All that happens is that the public holds more in speculative balances and less in securities. Further increases in the money supply would shift the LM curve still farther to the right, but the lower end of the curve would remain anchored in the same liquidity trap. If the economy is already in the trap, monetary policy is powerless to raise the income level. It cannot reduce the interest rate any further to produce a movement down the IS_1 curve to a higher equilibrium income level. The belief that the economy was in the trap during the early thirties led Keynes to his then unorthodox fiscal policy prescriptions. Because government cannot raise the income level through monetary policy, it can only try to do so through fiscal policy. If a rise in income cannot be achieved by producing a movement down the IS_1 curve through monetary expansion, it can be achieved by producing a shift in the IS_1 curve itself, say from IS_1 to IS'_1. Fiscal measures such as increased government spending or reduced taxes that could shift the IS curve become the order of the day.

To the extent that monetary policy operates by raising investment spending through a reduction in the cost of money, the impasse of monetary policy for an economy caught in the trap means that the elasticity or inelasticity of the IS function is no longer relevant. In Part A of Figure 12-13, for example, it does not matter whether the IS function is the elastic IS_1 or the inelastic IS''_1.[17]

The liquidity trap is an extreme case that could occur only during a deep depression, if even then. A prosperous economy and a liquidity trap do not go hand in hand. Because the pure Keynesian range is the range of the liquidity trap, one can now appreciate what Professor Hicks meant by his observation, made shortly after the appearance of Keynes' book, that "the General Theory of Employment is the Economics of Depression."[18]

The Classical Range   Next let us examine the Y_4, r_4 equilibrium defined by the intersection of IS_3 and LM_1 in Part A of Figure 12-12. Some increase in the money supply will shift the LM_1 curve to LM_2. In contrast to the result in the Keynesian range, the result is now an increase in the income level from Y_4 to Y_5 and a fall in the interest rate from r_4 to r_3. In the classical range, the interest rate is so high that speculative balances are zero; money is held for transactions purposes only. Under these circumstances, if the monetary authority enters the market to purchase securities, security-holders can be induced to exchange securities for cash only at higher prices. As security prices are bid up and the interest rate is pushed down, investment is stimulated (and, in classical theory, saving is discouraged). Because nobody chooses to hold idle cash, expansion of the money supply will produce a new equilibrium only by reducing the interest rate by whatever amount is necessary to increase the income level sufficiently to absorb the full increase in the money supply in transactions balances. If in the present case we assume that $\Delta m_s = \$20$ and $k = 1/2$, equilibrium will be restored only when Y has risen by $\$40$, or, in general, when $\Delta Y = \Delta m_s/k$. In the classical range, the result follows the simple classical quantity theory of money as a theory of aggregate demand. Y rises proportionally with the increase in m_s. If $V = 2$ or $k = 1/2$, the rise in Y must be twice the rise in m_s in order to satisfy the equilibrium condition: $m_s V = Y$ and $m_s = k(Y)$.

---

[17]As we will see, the elasticity of the IS function does become relevant elsewhere, but not in the Keynesian range.

[18]J.R. Hicks, "Mr. Keynes and the 'Classics': A Suggested Interpretation," reprinted in W. Fellner and B.F. Haley, eds., *Readings in the Theory of Income Distribution*, Irwin, 1946, p. 472.

In contrast to the Keynesian range, in which monetary policy is completely ineffective, in the classical range it appears to be completely effective. No part of any increase in the money supply disappears into idle cash balances. The increase in the money supply leads to increased spending that raises the income level to the point at which the total increase in the money supply is absorbed into transactions balances. Because all income changes are real changes in the present model, the increase in the money supply that shifts LM_1 to LM_2 causes an increase from Y_4 to Y_5 in output as well as in income.

Again in contrast to the Keynesian range, in which fiscal policy alone can be effective, fiscal policy in the classical range is completely ineffective. An upward shift in the IS function from IS_3 to IS'_3 in Part A of Figure 12-12 can raise only the interest rate, from r_4 to r_5; the income level stays unchanged at Y_4. Given the increase in spending that lies behind the upward shift in the IS function, the interest rate will rise sufficiently to crowd out enough spending to leave aggregate spending unchanged. Therefore, if the rise in spending resulted from increased government spending, the rise in the interest rate would crowd out an amount of private spending equal to the rise in government spending. The level of income is as high as the given money supply can support. In the classical range, an increase in income is therefore impossible without an increase in the money supply, and monetary policy becomes an all-powerful method of controlling the income level.

How does the elasticity of the IS function affect the equilibrium positions in the classical range? Let us compare the elastic IS_3 function and the inelastic IS''_3 function shown in Part A of Figure 12-13. Given the IS''_3 function, no increase in the money supply and no reduction in the interest rate is capable of raising the income level from Y_4 to Y_5. Monetary policy will raise Y, but not by the multiple of m_s given by $1/k$. Although this seems to upset the result suggested by classical theory, classical theorists would deny that the IS curve could be so inelastic. Remember that in

both classical and Keynesian theory investment is a function of the interest rate, but that in classical theory saving also is a function of the interest rate. Consequently, only if both saving and investment are quite insensitive to the interest rate could there be an inelastic curve of the sort described by IS''_3 in Part A of Figure 12-13.[19] As long as one or the other is elastic, the resulting IS function will also be elastic; with an elastic IS function, the result of a change in the money supply in the present model is $\Delta Y = \Delta m_s/k$.

The Intermediate Range   Finally, let us examine the equilibrium of Y_2, r_2, as defined by the intersection of IS_2 and LM_1 in Part A of Figure 12-12. Here again we see that some increase in the money supply will shift the LM_1 function to LM_2. In the Keynesian range, this increase in the money supply left both Y and r unchanged because that total increase was absorbed in speculative balances at the existing interest rate. In the classical range, this increase in the money supply raised Y by the amount necessary to absorb the full increase in transactions balances. This worked itself out through the interest rate reduction that raised spending by the amount needed to produce the required rise in income. In the intermediate range, however, the increase in the money supply is partially absorbed in both speculative and transactions balances. The level of income rises, but by an amount less than that which would require the full increase in the money supply for transactions purposes.

For example, suppose that the increase in the money supply is $20 and k is 1/2. Although the resultant shift in the LM function is $40, here the rise in income ($Y_3 - Y_2$) is only half that amount.

---

[19] In terms of Part C of Figure 12-3, we may show saving as a function of both Y and r by drawing in a similar fashion successively higher saving functions to correspond with successively higher interest rates. An inelastic investment function in Part A combined with this income-elastic and interest-elastic saving function in Part C will still produce an elastic IS function in Part D.

In reducing the interest rate by the amount that produces the increase in spending needed to raise the income level by $20, $10 (one-half of the increase in the money supply) is absorbed in speculative balances. The remaining $10 is exactly the additional amount of money needed for transactions purposes with the income level up by $20.

In the intermediate range, monetary policy has some degree of effectiveness but not the complete effectiveness it has in the classical range. In general, the closer the equilibrium intersection is to the classical range, the more effective monetary policy becomes; the closer the intersection is to the Keynesian range, the less effective it becomes.

Within this range, fiscal policy is also effective to some extent. Fiscal measures that shift the IS function from IS_2 to IS'_2, for example, will raise the level of income and the interest rate to the new equilibrium defined by the intersection of IS'_2 and LM_1. If the shift in the IS function stems from a deficit-financed increase in government spending, the interest rate must rise. We are assuming a fixed money supply described by LM_1, so the increased government spending is being financed by borrowing from the public. The sale of additional securities by the government depresses security prices, raises the interest rate, and chokes off some amount of private spending. The rise in the interest rate following any given increase in government spending will be greater or smaller depending on how high in the intermediate range the equilibrium happens to be. Although fiscal policy is somewhat effective anywhere in the intermediate range, in general it will be more effective the closer equilibrium is to the Keynesian range and less effective the closer equilibrium is to the classical range.

Although both monetary and fiscal policies have varying degrees of effectiveness in the intermediate range, the relative effectiveness of each depends in large part on the elasticity of the IS function. If the IS function is the inelastic IS''_2 in Part A of Figure 12-13, monetary policy can do very little to raise the level of income, even in the intermediate range; fiscal policy alone is effective in such a situation. Furthermore, an expansionary fiscal policy need not be concerned with adverse monetary effects in this case. A shift in an inelastic IS function will raise the interest rate, but this higher rate will have little feedback on spending. Keynes maintained that the investment schedule (as well as the saving schedule) was interest inelastic. If this is the case, the IS schedule must also be inelastic, and fiscal policy, which is completely effective in the Keynesian range, must be almost as effective in the intermediate range. If the IS schedule is indeed interest inelastic, then the Keynesian range becomes, in effect, the complete LM curve, more applicable at the lower end than at the upper end, but with some applicability throughout.

13

The Extended Model: Variable Price Level

OVERVIEW

This chapter builds on the analysis of Chapter 12 by relaxing some major assumptions made there. First, we assumed that the aggregate supply curve is perfectly elastic up to the full employment level of output and that the economy operates below the full employment level. Those assumptions result in a stable price level. Relaxing them yields a model in which the price level is a variable. We also assumed that the aggregate demand curve was perfectly inelastic—that is, the amount of goods and services demanded in the aggregate was the same at each price level. This assumption was necessary in that chapter's simplified analysis. The results that follow from relaxing it and recognizing that the aggregate demand curve slopes downward to the right are examined in the present chapter.

The first part of this chapter traces the derivation of the downward-sloping aggregate demand curve. The intersection between this downward-sloping aggregate demand curve and an upward-sloping aggregate supply curve (the derivation of which was explained in Chapter 8) determines the equilibrium level of output and the equilibrium price level. Unlike the model of Chapter 12 in which the price level was stable, the present model does not permit us to identify the equilibrium level of output from only the *IS–LM* portion of the system. Now equilibrium is found at the

intersection of an upward-sloping aggregate supply curve and a downward-sloping aggregate demand curve in another portion of the system.

Keynes assumed a downwardly inflexible money wage rate. As explained in Chapter 8, given diminishing returns to labor, such a wage rate leads to an aggregate supply curve that slopes upward to the right. If the aggregate demand curve intersects the aggregate supply curve along this upward-sloping portion, there is an equilibrium with less than full employment. This result is consistent with classical theory, but classical theory maintained that such a conclusion could not follow if the money wage rate were perfectly flexible downward. The foundation for this classical conclusion was explained as part of the development of the basic classical model in Chapter 9. The second part of the present chapter begins by showing that the same classical conclusion emerges when the same classical assumptions are inserted into the *IS–LM* framework. However, Keynes contended that the less-than-full employment equilibrium could occur even if the money wage rate were perfectly flexible downward. The *IS–LM* framework is therefore employed to show how the Keynesian conclusion will follow in his special cases—that is, in the event of an inconsistency between saving and investment or in the event of a liquidity trap. Finally, the second part of the chapter concludes with a presentation of the classical reply to the Keynesian argument—that even in the event of a liquidity trap, wage flexibility would move the economy to full employment through the influence of the real balance effect.

The last part of the chapter returns to the question of employing expansionary monetary and fiscal policies to raise the level of output. Given the Keynesian case of a downwardly inflexible money wage rate and therefore an upward-sloping aggregate supply curve, such policies can move the economy from a less-than-full employment to the full employment position. However, unlike the effects of expansionary monetary and fiscal policies as discussed in the preceding chapter, the effects here are not only a higher level of output but a higher price level. This clearly is a much closer approximation to the real world.

At the end of Chapter 12 we saw that either fiscal or monetary policy may be employed in varying circumstances to shift the *IS* and *LM* functions to the right. The result is a rightward shift of the *AD* curve, which raises the equilibrium level of *Y*. Because our model assumed that the *AS* curve is perfectly elastic up to the full employment level of income, each of the illustrated policy-generated shifts in the *AD* curve along that *AS* curve identified a new equilibrium level of *Y* at an unchanged *P*.

The assumption of this kind of *AS* function must be recognized as no more than a convenient simplification, although in the early days of Keynesian economics it was accepted as much more than that. Economists then believed that changes in *AD* would not affect *P* over a range of *Y* from a depression level to a level practically up to the full employment level. However, there is little doubt today that an increase in *AD* will have some upward effect on *P,* even though that increase still leaves the level of output somewhat below the full employment level. The difficulty lies in distinguishing the point at which the curve begins to slope upward and how fast it does so.

For example, in mid-1980 with the unemployment rate near 8 percent and the rate of capacity utilization about 85 percent, some economists asserted that fiscal and monetary actions to shift the *AD* curve rightward would result almost entirely in lower unemployment and greater output and in only negligible pressure on prices. Other economists, emphasizing considerations other than the spread between actual and potential aggregate output, predicted a sharp rise in prices as a result of the same actions.

For present purposes, we need only recognize that the *AS* curve does display an upward-sloping range between a perfectly elastic range at depression levels of output and a perfectly inelastic range at the full employment level of output. As noted in the derivation of various *AS* curves in Chapter 8, the upward slope must be a part of the curve, if one assumes a fixed money wage and a diminishing marginal product of labor. Firms will then offer a larger amount of output only at a price level sufficiently higher to offset the diminishing marginal product of the additional labor that must be employed to produce it. Because the marginal product of labor becomes increasingly smaller before it reaches zero, the assumption of a fixed money wage rate means that the AS curve becomes increasingly steeper before it reaches the vertical.[1]

Assuming a fixed money wage rate, the AS curve with an upward-sloping range is closer to reality than one without such a range. We will employ this form hereafter. (Conversely, assuming a perfectly flexible money wage rate—and we will be returning to the classical theory in which this is a basic assumption—the AS curve is perfectly inelastic throughout at the full employment level of output.)

On the other side of the analysis, the aggregate demand curve may take two forms: perfectly inelastic or less than perfectly inelastic (that is, downward sloping to the right). In all of our work with the Keynesian model, we have so far assumed that the AD curve is perfectly inelastic. Formally, such a curve results if neither the IS nor the LM curve shifts with changes in the price level.

Like the perfectly elastic AS curve, the perfectly inelastic AD curve is a simplification. If total nominal spending increases or decreases proportionally with any rise or fall in the price level, total real spending is unchanged. The same amount of goods is demanded whether the price level is higher or lower. There is some reason to expect this to occur if the real income received by resource suppliers as a group does not change with a change in the price level. For example, a doubling of prices makes goods twice as costly in nominal terms, but if income recipients as a group receive twice as much income in nominal terms as before, they may be expected to maintain real spending at the same level as before. This kind of conclusion is reasonable as far as it goes, but it omits various other ways in which a change in the price level may influence total real spending. We will see that there are ways in which changes in the price level cause shifts in both the IS and LM curves. In such cases, the AD curve derived from the intersections of IS and LM curves will show more goods demanded at a lower price level—that is, it will slope downward to the right.

It was a simplification of the Keynesian model to assume in the preceding chapter that the AD curve was perfectly inelastic. In the classical model presented in Chapter 9, another simplification gave us an AD curve that did slope downward to the right without limit, specifically in the form of a rectangular hyperbola—that is, with unitary elasticity throughout. That AD curve was

---

[1] In terms of the present construction, despite the diminishing marginal product of labor, P could remain stable all the way up to the full employment level of Y, if the money wage rate were to decrease by just the amount needed to offset the decrease in the marginal product of labor. Any one AS curve is drawn on the assumption of a given money wage rate. As shown in the following figure, successive reductions in the money wage rate could shift the AS curve downward from AS_1 to AS_2 and so forth as needed to permit expansion of Y along a path with a stable price level of P_1.

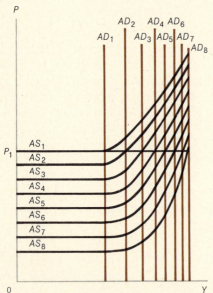

Of course, there is no tendency for money wage rates to behave in any such fashion. On the contrary, the closer the economy gets to the full employment level of output, the tighter labor markets become and the greater becomes the upward pressure on the money wage rate. Wage rates tend to increase and thereby shift the AS curve upward and make the price level at which a given level of output is supplied higher than it otherwise would be.

based on the simple quantity theory of money in which nominal spending is determined by the stock of money, given the theory's asumption of a stable velocity of money. As long as the stock of money remains unchanged, nominal spending remains unchanged. If M were $100 and V a stable 5, nominal spending per time period would be established at $500. A few points along the resulting unitary elasticity AD curve would be Y of 200 and P of 2.5, Y of 250 and P of 2, and Y of 300 and P of 1.67. In the simple quantity theory, this downward-sloping AD curve is fully specified by nothing more than the supply of money, given a stable V. Now we will turn to the way in which a downward-sloping AD curve is derived from the IS and LM curves. With the LM curve based on the demand for money that underlies the quantity theory of money, the AD curve will show unitary elasticity only over a limited range of output. With the LM curve based on the demand for money of the Keynesian theory, the elasticity of a downward-sloping AD curve will ordinarily vary at each price level.

Derivation of the Aggregate Demand Curve and Determination of the Equilibrium Price and Output Levels

In the IS–LM framework, the LM curve shows the various combinations of Y and r at which the real supply of money, m_s, and the real demand for money, m_d, are equal. As $m_s = M_s/P$, an increase in M_s is accompanied by a proportional increase in m_s as long as P is unchanged. Therefore, assuming an unchanged P, changes in M_s cause shifts to the right in the LM curve in the way explained on pages 248–50 and illustrated in Figure 12-9.

Unlike the case in those pages, here P is a variable. Now m_s can change because of a change in M_s, or in P, or in both. For a numerical illustration, suppose that initially $M_s = 100$ and

$P = 2$ so that $m_s = 50$. There will be a 20 percent increase in m_s, if there is a 20 percent increase in M_s with no change in P. We will have $m_s = 120/2 = 60$, a 20 percent increase over the initial m_s of 50. The same increase in m_s results with M_s unchanged at 100 but P reduced to 1.67 (or by 16.7 percent). That is, $m_s = 100/1.67 = 60$, a 20 percent increase over the initial m_s of 50. In terms of the LM curve, the same shift to the right will occur in both of these cases because there is the same increase in the real money supply. The IS and LM curves in Part A of Figure 13-1 are like

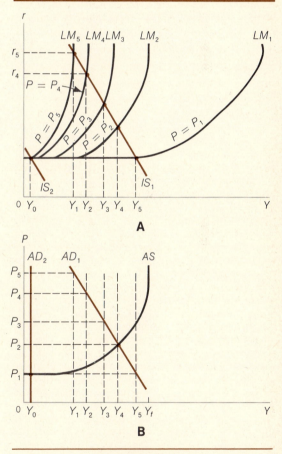

FIGURE 13-1
Equilibrium in the Keynesian Model

those derived in the preceding chapter. In what follows, the nominal money supply, M_s, remains unchanged and the initial price level of P_5 combined with this nominal money supply establishes the LM curve at LM_5. Successively lower price levels from P_4 through P_1 establish LM_4 through LM_1, respectively.[2] Here we assume that the IS curve is unaffected by the price level; its position is the same for all values of P shown. Suppose that the IS curve is that labeled IS_1 and that P is P_5. The equilibrium level of Y in Part A is at Y_1, given by the intersection of IS_1 and LM_5. Output of Y_1 will be demanded at P_5 because that is the price level underlying the LM curve which in combination with the IS curve identifies output of Y_1. Therefore, one point on the aggregate demand curve that is being derived in Part B must be at P_5 and Y_1. A decline in P to P_4 shifts

the LM curve from LM_5 to LM_4 and in Part A establishes a new equilibrium level at Y_2. Because an output of Y_2 will be demanded at P_4, a second point on the aggregate demand curve must be at P_4 and Y_2. Further reductions to P_3, P_2, and P_1 shift the LM curve to LM_3, LM_2, and LM_1, respectively, and as before identify equilibrium levels at Y_3, Y_4, and Y_5. These three levels of output will be demanded at P_3, P_2, and P_1, respectively, and thereby establish three more points on the aggregate demand curve. Connecting all the points now established yields the downward-sloping aggregate demand curve labeled AD_1 in Part B.

By what process does a decrease in the price level result in an increase in the aggregate quantity of goods demanded? Consider an initial equilibrium in Part A at Y_1, r_5 given by LM_5 and IS_1. Assume then the decrease from P_5 to P_4 that shifts the LM curve from LM_5 to LM_4. The adjustment of Y and r in Part A to this change is not instantaneous; at the existing combination of Y_1, r_5, the public is holding larger real money balances than it wishes to hold. (Equilibrium between m_s and m_d is now given by the combinations of Y and r along the LM_4 curve, but the existing combination of Y_1, r_5 is to the left of the LM_4 curve.) The excess real balances spill over into the purchase of bonds, bid up bond prices, and lower the interest rate. As the interest rate falls, investment increases, and, other things being equal, the total amount of goods demanded increases. Once the adjustment is completed, the increase in the real money supply that results from the decline in P ceases to be an excess supply. The demand for money is $m_d = k(Y) + h(r)$. A fall in r to r_4 and a rise in Y to Y_2 increase m_d by just the amount of the increase in m_s, and there is again an equilibrium in the money market. Any number of other combinations of Y and r along LM_4 would also provide equilibrium in the money market, but all of these would be off IS_1. At any point off the IS curve, the amount of goods demanded is different from the amount of goods corresponding to that level of Y. To have simultaneous equilibrium in the money and goods markets, the new

---

[2] It is assumed that $P_5 - P_4 = P_4 - P_3 = P_3 - P_2 = P_2 - P_1$. This will be seen on the P axis in Part B of Figure 13-1. On this assumption, measuring on an arithmetic scale, the horizontal distance between LM_4 and LM_3 must exceed that between LM_5 and LM_4, that between LM_3 and LM_2 must exceed that between LM_4 and LM_3, and so forth. For example, suppose that M_s is given as 100. With $P = P_5$, $m_s = 100/5 = 20$. LM_5 indicates all combinations of r and y at which $m_s = 20 = m_d$. A decline in P to P_4 increases m_s to 25 and LM_4 indicates all combinations of r and y at which $m_s = 25 = m_d$. Apart from the liquidity trap range, at each rate of interest the Y value indicated by LM_4 is 25 percent greater than that indicated by LM_5. With a further decline in P to P_3, $m_s = 33.33$ and LM_3 indicates all combinations of Y and r at which $m_s = 33.33 = m_d$. In this case, the Y value indicated by LM_3 at each interest rate above the liquidity trap is 33.33 percent greater ($33.33/25 = 1.33$) than that indicated by LM_4. In the same way, with a P of P_2, the Y value indicated by LM_2 at each interest rate is 50 percent greater than that indicated by LM_3. Finally, with a P of P_1, the Y value indicated by LM_1 at each interest rate is 100 percent greater than that indicated by LM_2. If the LM curves in Part A were drawn equidistant horizontally, the values of P would be such that $P_5 - P_4 > P_4 - P_3 > P_3 - P_2 > P_2 - P_1$. We will later have occasion to work with LM curves that are equidistant horizontally, but for our present purposes we want to work with equal absolute changes in P, and these give us the unequal spreads between the LM curves in Part A.

combination of Y and r must be Y_2, r_4. Therefore, although the aggregate amount of goods demanded was Y_1 with a P of P_5, a decline to P_4 sets into motion a process that increases the aggregate amount of goods demanded from Y_1 to Y_2.

Specifically how much of an increase in the amount of goods demanded will occur with the rightward shift in the LM curve produced by any particular decrease in the price level? The less elastic the IS curve, the smaller the increase in the amount of goods demanded that would result from any given decrease in P. If the IS curve were perfectly inelastic, the AD curve would also be perfectly inelastic. In this case, the decline in r resulting from the fall in P would call forth no increase in investment and therefore no increase in the total amount of goods demanded.

There is a special case in which the AD curve is perfectly inelastic, no matter how elastic the IS curve may be. The IS curve labeled IS_2 intersects the LM curves in the Keynesian range of the LM curve. Although declines in P shift the LM curve downward or rightward in the intermediate and classical ranges, they cannot do this in the Keynesian range. Therefore, such declines in P cannot reduce the interest rate below the rate in the liquidity trap. This means that there can be no increase in investment via a lower interest rate and therefore no movement down an elastic IS curve. Consequently, in Part B, an aggregate demand curve based on an IS curve that intersects the LM curves in the Keynesian range will be perfectly inelastic, regardless of the elasticity of that IS curve. Thus, the perfectly inelastic AD_2 curve in Part B of Figure 13-1 is derived from the IS_2 curve and the LM curves in Part A.

Once an aggregate demand curve has been derived in Part B, whatever its position and elasticity, its intersection with the aggregate supply curve, assuming there is an intersection, determines the equilibrium levels of output and price. In the present illustration, these are Y_4 and P_2 with IS_1 but Y_0 and P_1 with IS_2. In all of our previous work with the Keynesian model, the AS curve we

employed was perfectly elastic up to the full employment level of output. As noted earlier, hereafter in working with the Keynesian model, we will employ an AS curve with an upward-sloping range.[3] The particular AS curve shown in Part B of Figure 13-1 assumes that the fixed money wage rate is such that only at a price level of P_4 or higher will firms supply the amount of output, Y_f, that is produced with full employment of the labor force.

For the two illustrative AD curves derived in Part B of Figure 13-1, the equilibrium level of output is below the full employment level. This follows our earlier work with the Keynesian model, which also showed that equilibrium could be below full employment. However, now there is a range over which rightward shifts in the AD curve affect not only the output level as in the earlier Keynesian models but also the price level. A shift in the IS curve, for example, from IS_2 to IS_1 increases the equilibrium level of output, but also raises the equilibrium price level.

Although the Keynesian model shows that equilibrium below full employment is a real possibility, it does not at all rule out equilibrium at full employment. In Part A of Figure 13-1, a sufficiently large rightward shift of the IS curve from the position at IS_1 will give rise to an AD curve in Part B that intersects the given AS curve at the full employment level of Y. However, although full employment may occur in the Keynesian model, it need not necessarily occur in that model. The classical economists also granted that it need not occur if the money wage rate was inflexible downward, but they insisted that it must occur if the rate was perfectly flexible downward. As long as the money wage rate falls freely in the face of unemployment, it was their view that unemployment would be eliminated. Although Keynes assumed a downwardly inflexible money wage

---

[3]The derivation of this aggregate supply curve was described on pp. 135–40 of Chapter 8. A review of these pages will be very helpful to an understanding of what follows.

rate in his model—an assumption that all agree is consistent with unemployment—he also asserted that the classical conclusion of automatic full employment does not necessarily follow even in a system in which the money wage rate is perfectly flexible downward. In the following section, we will examine how Keynes and the classical economists arrived at these different answers to a central question in macroeconomic theory: Does an economy characterized by downwardly flexible money wage rates and prices automatically achieve equilibrium at the full employment level of output?

Wage–Price Flexibility and Full Employment Equilibrium

The basis on which classical economics concluded that the equilibrium level of output would be only at the full employment level was examined in Chapter 9 in some detail, but in terms of a simple classical model. In that model, the aggregate demand curve is of unitary elasticity throughout as shown in Figure 13-2. This follows from the quantity theory of money assumption that the velocity of money is stable. Given V, MV or total spending is known as soon as M ($= M_s$) is known. Because $MV = PY$ and $AD = MV$, any indicated MV or AD will buy various quantities of Y depending on P. The various possible combinations of Y and P consistent with a given AD are identified in the classical model by a curve with unitary elasticity that graphically appears as a rectangular hyperbola.

The classical theory, of course, assumes a flexible money wage rate. However, as a first step, let us here note briefly the result that follows from combining the aggregate demand curve of the basic classical model with the Keynesian assumption of a downwardly inflexible money wage rate.[4] In Figure 13-2, suppose that the rigid

---

[4]Fuller development of this brief statement is provided in Chapter 9, pp. 160–62.

W is such that P_4 gives the W/P at which S_N, the supply of labor, equals D_N, the demand for labor; in other words, there is full employment. Therefore, at P_4 or above, the AS curve is perfectly inelastic. However, with the downwardly inflexible W, at any P below P_4, W/P exceeds that consistent with full employment; therefore, firms provide a lower level of employment and supply a smaller aggregate quantity of goods. In brief, the AS curve slopes downward to the left below P_4 as shown by the broken-line AS curve in Figure 13-2. With the nominal money supply being such as to yield the AD curve shown in this figure, the result is an intersection between the AD curve and the broken-line AS curve below Y_f. In the illustration, full employment requires a Y of 200; actual Y is 160. Consequently, with a rigid money wage rate, equilibrium can occur in the classical model at an output level below the full employment level.

However, once we return to the classical assumption that the money wage rate falls freely whenever there is unemployment, the AS curve that emerges is a perfectly inelastic curve at the full employment level of output, as shown by the

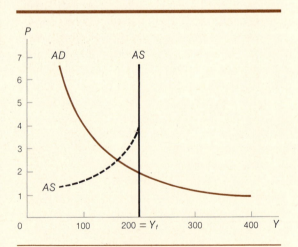

FIGURE 13-2
Full Employment Equilibrium in the Basic Classical Model

solid-line *AS* curve in Figure 13-2.[5] With an *AD* curve of the kind given by the simple quantity theory of money, there must necessarily be an intersection between that curve and the perfectly inelastic *AS* curve. Moreover, the level of output at which this intersection occurs is necessarily the full employment level. In the illustration, Y_f is 200 and *P* is 2. Of course, if the price level were above 2, say at 4, and if for some reason the price level were inflexible downward, the existing total spending would be unable to purchase the full employment output of 200. The amount purchased would be 100; reduced production and unemployment would follow. However, in a system of competitive markets for labor and goods, the money wage rate will fall freely in the face of unemployment and the pursuit of profits by competitive sellers can be depended on to lead to a falling price level also. Given the assumptions of the classical model, the system will move to the full employment equilibrium indicated by the intersection between the *AD* curve and solid-line *AS* curve.

Combining the simple quantity theory of money with a downwardly flexible money wage rate and price level makes the full employment equilibrium shown in Figure 13-2 inevitable. Keynes could not accept a downwardly flexible money wage rate and still reject the classical conclusion unless he rejected the simple quantity theory of money in which total real spending is directly and proportionally related to the real money supply. Reject this he did. But how does the rejection of the quantity theory of money lead to Keynes' conclusion that output may be below the full employment level even with a downwardly flexible money wage rate? The key here is that the shape of the *LM* curves that are derived from the quantity theory of money are distinctly differ-

ent from the shape of those earlier derived from Keynesian theory.

Keynes made the demand for money a function of both the income level and the interest rate or $M_d/P = m_d = k(Y) + h(r)$. The derivation of the *LM* curve for this money–demand function was shown in Figure 12-4 on p. 241. If the demand for money is interest-elastic as in the Keynesian function, there is a range of the *LM* curve over which it slopes upward to the right. In the simple quantity theory, the demand for money is not interest-elastic. The quantity theory suppresses the speculative demand function for money, $M_{sp}/P = h(r)$, or makes the demand for money equation $M_d/P = m_d = k(Y)$. For a given price level, the *LM* curve based on $m_d = k(Y)$ is a vertical or perfectly inelastic line with respect to the interest rate, as shown in Part D of Figure 13-3. Unlike Figure 12-4, m_{sp} in Part A of Figure 13-3 is zero at all interest rates and the m_{sp} curve disappears. In Part B, whatever m_s happens to be, it is all necessarily held in transactions balances, m_t. Running a horizontal line from the point on the m_t axis at which $m_t = m_s$ across to the $m_t = k(Y)$ function in Part C identifies the level of *Y* at which $m_s = k(Y)$. It is the level of *Y* so identified at which $m_s = m_d$, whatever the interest rate, as $m_d = m_t$ and $m_t = m_s$. The *LM* curve becomes a perfectly inelastic line at that level of *Y* at which $m_t = k(Y)$.[6] Its position will change with a change in m_s or a change in *k*, but the curve itself will remain perfectly inelastic. Its position along the *Y* axis is simply equal to m_s/k.

Assume now that M_s/P and *k* are such as to locate the *LM* curve at LM_5 in Part A of Figure 13-4. With no change in M_s or in *k*, decreases in *P* will increase the real money supply and shift the *LM* curve to the right. This is the same relationship noted in connection with Part A of Figure 13-1. As in that figure, the present figure shows

---

[5]The derivation of this aggregate supply curve was described on pp. 141–43 of Chapter 8. As with the derivation of the upward-sloping supply curve in Figure 13-1, a review of the pages on the derivation of the perfectly inelastic supply curve will be very helpful to an understanding of what follows.

[6]The real money supply, M_s/P, is also assumed to be interest-inelastic in this model or it would provide a slope to the *LM* curve despite the interest inelasticity on the demand side.

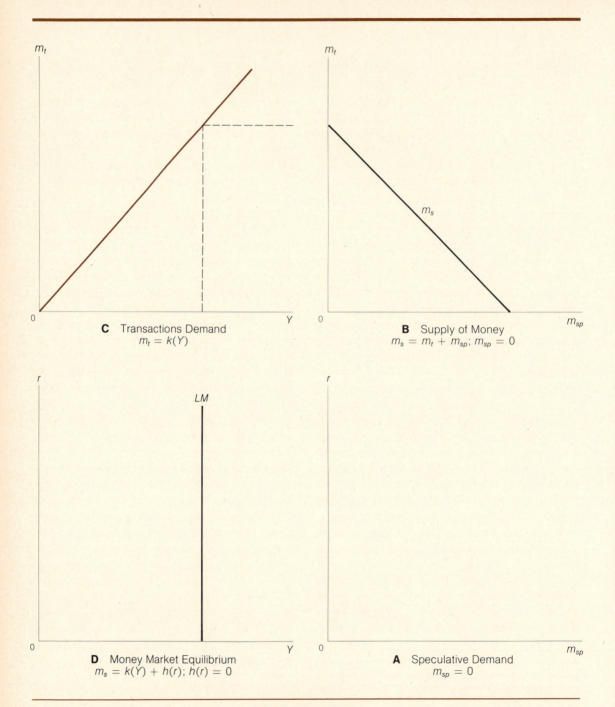

C   Transactions Demand
$m_t = k(Y)$

B   Supply of Money
$m_s = m_t + m_{sp}; m_{sp} = 0$

D   Money Market Equilibrium
$m_s = k(Y) + h(r); h(r) = 0$

A   Speculative Demand
$m_{sp} = 0$

FIGURE 13-3
Money Market Equilibrium with Speculative Demand Equal to Zero

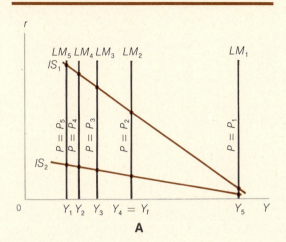

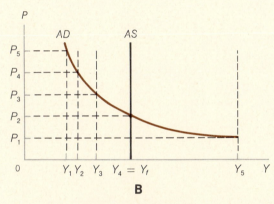

FIGURE 13-4
Full Employment Equilibrium in the Classical Model Within the *IS–LM* Framework

five *LM* curves corresponding to five levels of *P*. Also as before, the intersections with an *IS* curve identify five points in Part B which are connected to form the *AD* curve. Two *IS* curves, IS_1 and IS_2, are shown in Part A, but both yield the same *AD* curve in Part B because both intersect each of the series of *LM* curves at the same level of *Y*. The *AD* curve derived in Part B is of unitary elasticity *over the range shown* in the figure. As with the *AD* curve in Figure 13-2 derived directly from

the simple quantity theory of money, the *AD* curve in Figure 13-4 shows that output may be raised from a less-than-full employment level such as Y_3 to the full employment level of Y_4 by a decline in the price level from P_3 to P_2. With the *AD* and *AS* curves as shown in Part B, unemployment will necessarily be eliminated by an appropriate decline in the price level.

Wage–Price Flexibility and the Interest Rate Effect

In the simple quantity theory on which Figure 13-2 is based, an increase in the real money supply that results from a reduction in the price level leads *directly* to an increase in the quantity of goods demanded. Successive increases in the real money supply lead directly to successive increases in the quantity of goods demanded. The relationship is different in Figure 13-4. There the increase in the real money supply leads to an increase in the quantity of goods demanded, but not directly. It achieves this by first causing a decline in the interest rate. In Part B of Figure 13-4, the increase in the quantity of goods demanded that occurs with a decline in *P* from P_3 to P_2 is explained in Part A through the shift in the *LM* curve from LM_3 to LM_2—the result of the simple quantity theory—*and* through the fact that this reduces the interest rate and thereby raises the quantity of capital goods demanded. This rise in the quantity of capital goods demanded is the source of the increase in the total quantity of goods demanded from Y_3 to Y_4.

The simple quantity theory of money on which the *AD* curve of Figure 13-2 is based does not require a reduction in the interest rate as a part of the process by which an increase in the real money supply causes an increase in the quantity of goods demanded. However, such a reduction is required in the Keynesian theory on which Figure 13-4 is based. This difference in turn brings us to one of the bases for the Keynesian conclusion that full employment may be unattainable even with wages and prices perfectly flexible downward.[7]

Inconsistency Between Saving and Investment

In Figure 13-4, assuming initially that output is below the full employment level, that level may be attained via a decline in the price level to P_2. However, this requires that the IS curve be positioned far enough to the right—for example, like the IS_1 curve—or that the IS curve be sufficiently interest-elastic—for example, like the IS_2 curve. Instead of the IS curves in Part A of Figure 13-4, suppose that the IS curve is that shown in Figure 13-5. In Figure 12-8 on p. 247, the position of the IS curve depends on the position of the investment curve in Part A and the position of the saving curve in Part C. A leftward shift of the investment curve or the saving curve will cause a leftward shift of the IS curve. If the position of the investment and saving curves are such as to yield an IS curve in the relatively low position of that in Part A of Figure 13-5, declines in the price level cannot restore to full employment a system suffering from unemployment.

To see this, in Part A, start with P_5. Given the nominal money supply and the value of k, P_5 establishes the LM curve at LM_5. As in Figure 13-4, in Part B with a P of P_5, the quantity of goods demanded is found to be Y_1, a quantity well below Y_4, the full employment level of output. There is unemployment. On the assumption of flexible wages and prices, the money wage rate falls and the price level falls in turn. As P falls step by step from P_5 to P_3, the quantity of goods demanded increases, as shown by the portion of the AD curve in Part B derived from that range of price levels in Part A. Over this particular range, the AD curve is of unitary elasticity as in the preceding figure. However, once P falls below P_3, the AD curve in the present figure becomes perfectly inelastic. Such decreases cause no further

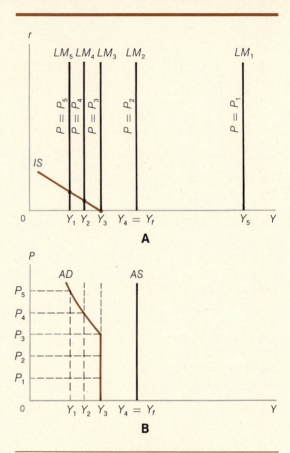

A

B

FIGURE 13-5
Unemployment Due to Inconsistency Between Saving and Investment

increases in the quantity of goods demanded. The quantity demanded reaches a maximum of Y_3, short of the Y_4 produced at full employment. Therefore, full employment is not attainable through a falling price level.

If the increase in the real money supply effected by a decrease in the price level always led to an increase in real demand proportional to the increase in the real money supply, a result like this could not occur. However, in Part A of Figure 13-5 an increase in the real money supply

---

[7]These different views of the process by which a change in the real money supply is transmitted through the system to affect the real income level are considered further in Chapter 26, pp. 590–92.

affects real demand only by first reducing the interest rate and boosting investment. In the simple case of a two-sector economy, even if the interest rate could be reduced to zero, the amount of investment called forth would be equal to the amount of saving at Y_3, because this is the level of Y at which the IS curve in Part B hits the Y axis. To achieve a Y of Y_4 would require that an interest rate of zero call forth an amount of investment equal to what saving would be at Y_4. Then the IS curve would hit the Y axis at Y_4. However, the underlying saving and investment curves give us the IS curve as shown; the maximum attainable output level is the less-than-full employment level of Y_3.[8]

It is an open question whether the relationship between the investment schedule and the saving schedule could be such that the amount of saving generated at full employment output would exceed the amount of investment generated by a zero interest rate. But it must be recognized as a possibility which would preclude the attainment of the full employment output through a deflation of wages and prices.

Liquidity Trap   There is a second basis for the Keynesian conclusion that downward flexibility of wages and prices may fail to correct unemployment. On this basis, one need not deny that a sufficiently low positive interest rate can call forth investment equal to what saving will be at full employment. What one does deny on this basis is that the interest rate can fall to the level at which this occurs. The concept of the liquidity trap, which sets a lower limit to the decline in the interest rate, is now brought into the picture. The perfectly inelastic LM curves of Part A of Figure 13-5 follow from the demand for money of the simple quantity theory in which $M_d/P = k(Y)$. In their place now are the LM curves of Part A of Figure

[8]It appears from the diagram that a negative interest rate could get the output level to Y_4, but a negative rate cannot be secured. While the interest rate might approach zero, it surely could not become negative (in which event lenders would be required to pay interest to borrowers to use the lenders' funds).

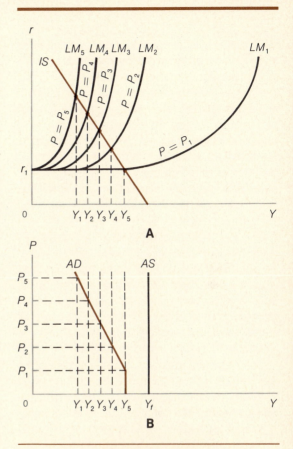

**FIGURE 13-6
Unemployment Due to a
Liquidity Trap**

13-6, which follow from the demand for money of Keynes' theory in which $M_d/P = k(Y) + h(r)$ and in which at a sufficiently low rate of r the speculative component of the demand for money becomes perfectly elastic.

As before, assume that P is initially P_5, which places the LM curve at LM_5. The LM_5 curve intersects the IS curve at Y_1 and gives us a point on the AD curve in Part B at P_5 and Y_1. For P_4, P_3, P_2, and P_1, other points on the AD curve are identified as before. With each decline from P_5 to P_1, there is an increase in the quantity of goods demanded. However, at P_1, the quantity demanded, Y_5, is still below Y_f. Apparently still more deflation is needed to increase the quantity of goods demanded. However, the deflation-generated increase in the real money stock has already pushed the interest rate down to r_1, which in the present illustration is the minimum rate set by the liquidity trap. To increase the quantity of goods demanded beyond Y_5 requires an increase in investment, which in turn requires a decline in the interest rate. However, further declines in P below P_1 and the resulting further rightward shifts in the LM curve beyond LM_1 cannot reduce the interest rate below r_1. Because they call forth no increase in investment, declines in P below P_1 leave the total quantity of goods demanded at Y_5; in other words, the AD curve becomes perfectly inelastic below P_1. In this illustration, the quantity of goods demanded reaches a maximum of Y_5, short of the quantity produced at full employment, Y_f. Therefore, full employment is not attainable through a falling price level.

Keynes' conclusion that a deflation of wages and prices could fail to produce the result asserted by the classical economists rests on his view of the way that deflation affects the quantity of goods demanded. As he saw it, any increase in the quantity of goods demanded at a lower price level was essentially the result of the lower interest rate that results from a lower price level. Although there are other ways in which a decline in the price level may affect the quantity of goods demanded, this interest rate effect has come to be associated with Keynes' name and is sometimes referred to as the Keynes effect.

A Policy Question: Price Deflation Versus Nominal Money Supply Expansion

have now reviewed the bases on which Keynes argued that deflation may be unable to bring the system to full employment: The IS curve may lie so far to the right that not even a zero interest rate will be sufficient; the liquidity trap may prevent the needed decline in the interest rate which otherwise would be sufficient. However, Keynes and his followers also argued that, as a policy

matter, there is in any event little to be said for trying to achieve full employment in this way. If one accepts Keynes' position that whatever favorable effect on output follows from wage and price cuts comes through their effect on the interest rate, then to achieve a reduction in the interest rate through the painful process of deflation is "patently absurd," as the late Professor Hansen, Keynes' foremost American disciple, once put it. As we have seen, the shift in the LM function necessary to reduce the interest rate may be caused by an increase in the nominal money stock or by a decreae in the price level. The objective of reducing the interest rate can be achieved much more simply through an increase in the nominal money supply. The central bank can do this with no direct interference with the wage and price structure. Working toward the same objective through wage and price cuts is doing it the "hard way." It was for this reason that Keynes identified wage cuts as "monetary management by the Trade Unions, aimed at full employment."[9]

Leaving monetary management to the banking system also avoids many difficult problems that arise in achieving the goal of a lower interest rate through wage and price reductions. In the first place, one must consider all the institutional barriers that stand in the way of a fall in wages and prices. One must also consider all the economic inequities and distress that inevitably result from wage and price cuts: All wages and prices do not fall at the same rate; some groups benefit and others suffer as income and wealth are redistributed in the course of a deflation. Businesses that are saddled with heavy fixed debt may be unable to weather the storm; bankruptcies are bound to result. Most important of all, because in practice a decline in wages and prices does not occur in one quick step, one wage cut and one price cut often give rise to expectations of further cuts, and such "bearish"

---

[9] John Maynard Keynes, *The General Theory of Employment, Interest, and Money,* Harcourt Brace Jovanovich, 1936, p. 267.

expectations will lead to a postponement of some investment spending (and probably also some consumption spending on durable goods). In this fashion, the favorable effect on the quantity of goods demanded, which otherwise occurs in response to the lower interest rate that results from the reduction in the price level, could easily be swamped by the unfavorable effect on the quantity of goods demanded of the decline in spending that results from expectations of further declines in wages and prices. For these and other reasons, most economists agree that if a falling price level affects the quantity of goods demanded through its effect on the interest rate, the goal of a lower interest rate and higher output and employment levels is assuredly better achieved by expansionary monetary policy than by a falling price level.

Wage—Price Flexibility and the Pigou Effect

As we have seen, if the limit to the reduction in the interest rate set by the liquidity trap is reached before the quantity of goods demanded can be raised to the full employment level or if even a reduction in the interest rate to zero is unable to raise the quantity of goods demanded to the full employment level, wage and price flexibility working through the Keynes effect is repudiated as a means of achieving the full employment level of output. However, this conclusion is based on the argument that a decline in wages and prices exerts its influence only through the interest rate. An attempt to counter the Keynesian argument and rehabilitate the classical theory's conclusion of automatic full employment through wage—price flexibility is found in the Pigou effect or the real balance effect, first advanced by Professor A.C. Pigou in the early 1940s and later the subject of a sizable literature.[10]

How does the Pigou effect work? Suppose that investment falls off so that output and employment drop as in the ordinary Keynesian model. Unemployment causes money wages to fall, which means lower costs and lower prices. The prices of assets such as goods, buildings, land, and common-stock shares may be expected to fall with other prices so that there will be no change in their real value. However, the fall in the price level means a rise in the real value of assets that are fixed in dollar terms, such as money, savings deposits, and bonds. This increase in the real value of fixed-dollar assets makes the holders less anxious to continue to build up their asset holdings. They devote a smaller fraction of their current income to saving and a larger fraction to consumption, which amounts to a downward shift in the saving function or an upward shift in the consumption function. In terms of Figure 13-7, this appears as a rightward shift in the IS function. With each successive drop from P_5 to P_4 and so forth, the IS curve shifts from IS_5 to IS_4 and so forth. The LM curves and the IS_5 curve in Figure 13-7 are the same as the LM curves and the IS curve in Figure 13-6; the AD_1 curve derived from them shows that the liquidity trap sets an upper limit of Y_5 to the quantity of goods demanded. However, allowing for the Pigou effect, both the IS and LM curves now shift to the right with each decline in P, and the AD curve in Figure 13-7 shifts from AD_1 to AD_2. The AD_2 curve is derived from the intersections of IS_5 and LM_5, IS_4 and LM_4, and so forth. Because of the Pigou effect, the quantity of goods demanded is now

---

[10]A.C. Pigou, "The Classical Stationary State," *Economic Journal,* Dec. 1943, pp. 345–51, and "Economic Progress in a Stable Environment," *Economica,* Aug. 1947, pp. 180–88, reprinted in *Readings in Monetary Theory,* pp. 241–51; and D. Patinkin, "Price Flexibility and Full Employment," *American Economic Review,* Sept. 1948, pp. 543–64, also reprinted in *Readings in Monetary Theory,* pp. 252–83. See also D. Patinkin, *Money, Interest, and Prices,* 2nd ed., Harper & Row, 1965, and B.P. Pesek and T.R. Saving, *Money, Wealth and Economic Theory,* Macmillan, 1967. As is commonly done, the terms, Pigou effect and re-balance effect, are here used as synonyms, although this is not altogether proper. For an explanation of the difference between them, see G.E. Makinen, *Money, The Price Level, and Interest Rates,* Prentice-Hall, 1977, pp. 160–62.

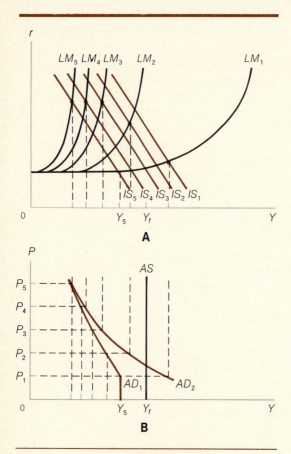

FIGURE 13-7
Full Employment
via the Pigou Effect

higher than before at each price level below P_5. The AD_2 curve intersects the AS curve and therefore yields equilibrium at the full employment level of output. According to this argument, a large enough decline in the price level will raise the real value of a given stock of fixed-dollar assets sufficiently to shift the saving function downward by the amount necessary to shift the IS curve so as to produce an AD curve consistent with the full employment level of output.

To the extent that the Pigou effect achieves this result, it may be said that Keynes was met on his own ground and there, at least in terms of

pure theory, Pigou won a "triumph" for classical theory by showing that, if flexible wages and prices are incorporated, even the Keynesian model gives us the automatic full employment conclusion of classical theory. This seems to invalidate the Keynesian position that such flexibility cannot yield the classical conclusion. But economists in general concede no such victory to Pigou and the classical theory. They raise a number of criticisms of the Pigou effect and of the attempt to rehabilitate classical theory through its use.

A first criticism is that the Pigovian argument cannot apply, in the simple form given here, to all fixed-dollar assets. Although the real value of all such assets held by a creditor increases as the price level falls, the real value of the corresponding debtor's obligations also increases. Conceivably the rise in the creditor's average propensity to consume could be just offset by the fall in the debtor's, leaving the APC of the system as a whole unchanged. The Pigovian reply to this attack is to limit the argument to fixed-dollar obligations issued by the government, on the reasonable assumption that this debtor's expenditures will not be affected by changes in the real burden of its debt resulting from changes in the price level. In other words, deflation increases the real value of government debt holdings, the sum of currency and interest-bearing government securities, and therefore stimulates consumption spending by those who hold these assets, without being offset by any decrease in government spending. The net effect, as argued by Pigou, is an increase in aggregate spending.

However, even if it is granted that a deflation-created rise in the real value of consumer holdings of currency and government securities will increase consumption spending at any given level of real income, the crucial issue then becomes how great the rise in consumer spending will be for any given decrease in the price level. In the face of a certain amount of unemployment, it is one thing if a 10 percent decline in the price level and the accompanying increase in the real value of the stock of currency and government securities is sufficient to raise consumption spending by the amount needed to restore full employment; it is quite another if the Pigou effect is so weak that the same result can be achieved only with an 80 percent decline in the price level. If a major deflation is required, this in itself effectively rules out reliance on the Pigou effect as a practical means of restoring an economy to full employment.[11] A hyperdeflation may satisfy the purely theoretical requirements of the Pigou effect, but in practice it might also produce economic distress leading to riots and even revolution.

If anything more than a minor deflation is required for the Pigou effect to do its work—and this seems to be the case—we have the final and decisive objection to the Pigovian theory: It neglects the role played by expectations. We noted the same objection earlier in discussing deflation as a means of reducing the interest rate. An instantaneous once-and-for-all deflation needed to give credibility to the Pigou effect simply cannot be obtained in practice. Wages and prices cannot be substantially deflated without creating expectations of further deflation. An initial fall in wages and prices will often generate pessimistic forecasts and cause business people and consumers to reduce their expenditures.

It may even be argued that a once-and-for-all deflation would not work, assuming that such a thing could be engineered. The public might well view the lower price level as a temporary situation. A return to the earlier higher price level may be expected as unemployment declines and the economy moves into a recovery. This means that the public will also view the increase in the real value of their fixed-dollar assets as a temporary increase. Although a permanent increase in the value of these assets is another matter, it is doubtful that such a temporary increase will raise expenditures above the level they would otherwise attain.

A final issue is whether or not it is realistic to believe that the effects of a lower price level on private creditors and private debtors cancel out as suggested earlier. Is it likely that the increase in spending that we may expect from creditors in response to a rise in the real value of their fixed-dollar assets will be as large as the decrease in spending that we may expect from business and personal debtors in response to the rise in the real burden of their fixed-dollar debts? Short of resorting to bankruptcy, there is no escape from the increase in this real burden; other things being equal, the real income of the debtors remaining after paying interest is reduced and their real spending is fairly likely to change in line. It is doubtful that creditors whose real income has been increased, at least temporarily, will increase their real spending in an offsetting manner. Therefore, there is real pressure on debtors to cut back, but no corresponding pressure on creditors to do the opposite. The net effect may well be a reduction in private spending.

All things considered, the Pigovian argument appears impractical as an approach to the solution of the unemployment problem. In fact, Professor Pigou himself did not really see it being used for this purpose. He described certain aspects of his argument as "academic exercises, of some slight use for clarifying thought, but with very little chance of ever being posed on the chequer board of actual life."[12]

---

[11] Empirical testing has given mixed results. That the Pigou effect is too weak to have any practical significance is suggested by T. Mayer's study, "The Empirical Significance of the Real Balance Effect," in *Quarterly Journal of Economics,* May 1959, pp. 275–91. A study that indicates a Pigou effect of considerable strength is Ta-Chung Liu, "An Exploratory Quarterly Econometric Model of Effective Demand in the Postwar U.S. Economy," in *Econometrica,* July 1963, pp. 310–48, and especially pp. 331–32. See also D. Patinkin's discussion of some other investigations in *Money, Interest, and Prices,* pp. 651–64. Patinkin estimated the elasticity of consumption with respect to the price level at -0.2—that is, for every 1 percent change in the price level, consumption expenditures change by 0.2 percent in the opposite direction.

---

[12] A.C. Pigou, "Economic Progress in a Stable Environment," *Economica,* Aug. 1947, reprinted in F.A. Lutz and L.W. Mints, eds., *Readings in Monetary Theory,* p. 251.

Wage–Price Flexibility and Other Effects

The Keynes (interest-rate) effect and the Pigou (real-balance) effect have received the most attention in discussions of wage–price flexibility as a cure for unemployment, but several other effects deserve mention.

Income-Redistribution Effects Wage and price deflation involves some redistribution of real income in favor of fixed-income groups. For any level of real income, the share of the total that goes to wage and profit recipients will decrease, and the share going to recipients of interest, rents, and pensions will increase. Some fixed-income flows, such as interest payments, may go predominantly to upper-income groups; others, such as pensions, may go predominantly to lower-income groups. However, knowledge of the income distribution of these total flows is limited. To the extent that redistribution favors lower-income groups, some rise in the consumption function is to be expected, and therefore some shift to the right in the *IS* and *AD* functions. But the extent of this effect in turn depends on whether or not there is a sizable difference between the marginal propensities to consume of upper- and lower-income groups, and there appears to be no such difference.[13] Because we cannot be sure whether redistribution favors lower- or upper-income groups, and because the difference in the MPCs is not appreciable in the first place, we can do no more than note the existence of fixed incomes as a factor to be considered in appraising the effects of wage–price declines on consumption spending. However, this factor, in any event, is probably of no great importance except during a drastic deflation.

Tax and Transfer-Payment Effects Through their tax effects, wage–price declines may be expected to favorably affect consumption. With the progressive income tax as the mainstay of the federal revenue system, deflation automatically shifts taxpayers into lower brackets and reduces the fraction of their real income that is paid in income taxes. Then both real disposable income and consumption increase. To some extent, this favorable effect is offset by the existence of specific taxes (such as 10¢ per pack of cigarettes), the burden of which increases with deflation. The net effect is favorable, however, in a system whose overall tax structure is progressive. In those government programs that call for purchase of a fixed quantity of goods and services, expenditures on goods and services will tend to decline in line with the fall in price level. However, because some transfer payments are at any time fixed in dollar terms, a fall in the price level means a rise in the real income represented by a given dollar flow of these transfer payments. Therefore, we may expect an increase in real consumption by the beneficiaries of such payments.

Notice that government could provide the same stimulus to consumption spending, with an unchanged price level, by reducing taxes and raising transfer payments. The situation is comparable to that discussed earlier in connection with the Keynes effect. Just as an expansionary monetary policy is an alternative to deflation as a means of reducing the interest rate, so an expansionary fiscal policy of cutting taxes and raising transfer payments is an alternative to deflation as a means of increasing after-tax incomes and thereby raising consumption expenditures. But, specifically in reference to the wage–price flexibility argument, if there is deflation, tax and transfer-payment effects must be recognized as another stimulus to aggregate spending.

Foreign Trade Effects The final effect to consider is that on a nation's imports and exports. A decline in a nation's prices relative to the level of prices in other nations encourages exports and discourages imports, increasing the net export (or decreasing the net import) component of

[13]Redistribution of income as a means of altering consumption spending is discussed in Chapter 16. See pp. 356–59.

aggregate spending. In an open economy, aggregate spending is the sum of $C + I + G + (X - M)$. A rise in $(X - M)$ will shift the IS function to the right, just as a rise in C, I, or G would. Because imports and exports play a relatively much more important role in countries like England than in a country like the United States, the foreign trade effect is more important there than here. But in any open economy some shift in the IS function and stimulus to demand may be expected from a decline in its price level relative to the price level in other countries.

In summary, classical theory argued that an economy with flexible wages and prices would be self-equilibrating at the full employment income level. We have examined this argument in terms of the various effects of wage–price flexibility: the Keynes effect (or interest-rate effect), the Pigou effect (or real-balance effect), and the effects of income redistribution, tax and transfer payments, and foreign trade. Keynes' position that deflation affects the output level through a shift in the LM function and a reduction in the interest rate amounts to a repudiation of deflation as a sure road to the full employment level of output. All the other effects operate not through shifts in the LM function, but through shifts in the IS function. Output-expanding shifts in the IS function as a result of deflation are not limited by a barrier such as the liquidity trap. A sufficient decline of wages and prices could—as classical theory said it would—restore the economy to full employment, but not in the manner indicated by the crude quantity-theory reasoning examined in Chapter 9. Furthermore, the whole wage–price flexibility argument holds up only if the required deflation occurs without creating widespread expectations of further deflation.

Although there is some theoretical basis for the conclusion that an economy suffering general unemployment may be cured through flexible wages and prices, it does not necessarily follow that this should be the medicine prescribed. Deflation may possibly bring the patient around, but so may other measures. Fiscal policy has been the most popular of these since the appear-

ance of the *General Theory*. Beyond fiscal policy and, of course, monetary policy, lie other measures that reach an extreme with the outright socialization of investment. Whatever the appropriate policy for any set of circumstances, the classical policy of wage–price flexibility is unlikely ever again to receive serious practical consideration, certainly not after the revolution in economic theory of the past four decades. It is almost inconceivable that government would stand by passively in the face of deflation

> to test the proposition that if a deflating economy is left alone long enough, it will eventually, via a deflationary wage and price spiral, dig itself deeply enough into the mire to extricate itself. It is a political axiom of the mid-twentieth century that a government that conscientiously pursued this policy would not be around to observe the outcome.[14]

Beyond this, the prospect that any deflation at all will occur has grown extremely remote. Our world has known little else but inflation since World War II; our acquaintance with it has been especially severe during the past decade. When recessions occur, as in 1973–75, 1980, and looking ahead, 1981–82, we do not expect deflation but at best some deceleration in the rate of inflation.

Although deflation as a solution to unemployment is no longer a conversational topic for policy makers, the *theoretical* support for reliance on the classical solution of wage and price deflation has not been so completely swept away as Keynes and his disciples believed it was in the early days following the appearance of the *General Theory*. This question is still disputed by Keynesian and anti-Keynesian theorists, but it has now become a question of pure theory removed from the province of applied economics. Few economists today, however anti-Keynesian, would prescribe the classical theory's medicine as a cure for general unemployment—not because it will necessarily fail to effect a cure,

---

[14] J.P. Lewis and R.C. Turner, *Business Conditions Analysis*, 2nd ed., McGraw-Hill, 1967, p. 288.

but because it is less palatable than the medicines of expansionary monetary and fiscal policies.

Monetary–Fiscal Policies and the Full Employment Equilibrium

At the end of Chapter 12, we looked briefly at the way monetary and fiscal policies shift the LM and IS curves to affect the output level in a model with a stable price level. There we assumed that the aggregate supply curve was perfectly elastic up to the full employment level and that the economy was operating below the full employment level so that shifts in the aggregate demand curve could affect the output level but not the price level. Here we replace the perfectly elastic aggregate supply curve with one that slopes upward to the right. Consequently, shifts in the aggregate demand curve produced by shifts in LM and IS curves affect not only the output level, but the price level. Because the positions of the IS and LM curves are in turn affected by changes in the price level, to trace the process by which monetary and fiscal policies raise the level of output, allowance must be made for the changes in the price level that may occur as a result of those policies. This is something that can be done here but was ruled out in the preceding chapter by the assumption that the economy was operating along the perfectly elastic portion of the aggregate supply curve.

In Part A of Figure 13-8, the three solid-line LM curves are those for a given nominal money supply, M_s, and three different price levels, P_3, P_2, and P_1.[15] A decrease in P is an increase in the real money supply. Other things being equal,

an increase in the real money supply shifts the LM curve to the right. The LM curve will also shift to the right with an increase in M_s and an unchanged P. Therefore, with P at P_3, there is some increase in M_s, which will shift the LM curve from LM_3 to the broken-line LM_3'. Similarly, this same increase in M_s accompanied by a price level below P_3 will shift the LM curve rightward from its previous position. With P of P_2, the position will be LM_2' instead of LM_2; and with P of P_1, the position will be LM_1' instead of LM_1. In other words, for each M_s there is a different LM curve for each P. In Part A, there are two amounts of M_s and three levels of P—two sets of three curves each. To work, for example, with three different amounts of M_s and five levels of P would require three sets of five curves each (some of which might coincide).

Part A of the figure also includes a set of IS curves similar to the set of LM curves. The three solid-line IS curves are the original curves corresponding to the three different price levels, P_3, P_2, and P_1. A decline in P shifts the IS curve to the right via the Pigou effect, the income redistribution effect, and the other effects discussed in the preceding section. The IS curve also shifts to the right at an unchanged price level as a result of an increase in the investment function— business people invest more at each interest rate—or a decrease in the saving function— income recipients save less at each level of income. Lastly, the IS curve shifts to the right as a result of expansionary fiscal actions such as a decrease in tax receipts or an increase in government spending. Some specific fiscal action will shift the IS_3 curve to the broken-line IS_3' curve and will similarly shift the IS_2 curve to IS_2' and the IS_1 curve to IS_1'. As with the LM curves, there are two sets of three IS curves in the illustration.

Suppose now that M_s happens to be the amount that gives us the solid-line set of LM

---

[15]Unlike the assumption made in the preceding section, here it is *not* assumed that $P_3 - P_2 = P_2 - P_1$, a condition which, as we saw there, requires that the spread between the LM curves increase with each decrease in P. Here the spread between the LM curves is the same, but $P_3 - P_2$

$> P_2 - P_1$. Also, here the LM curves are not drawn to show a Keynesian and a classical range. The inclusion of these properties is not needed for present purposes and would needlessly complicate the diagram.

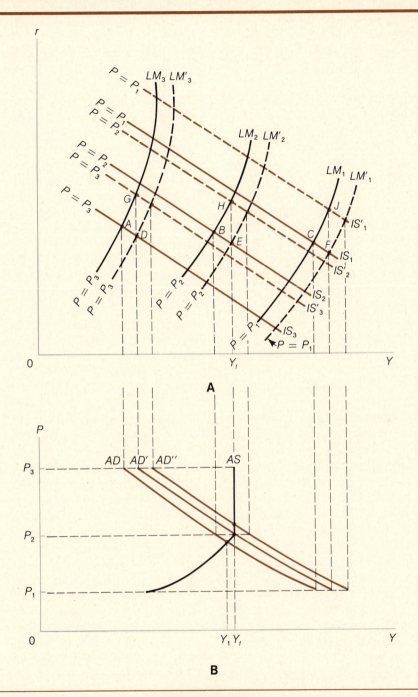

FIGURE 13-8
Monetary–Fiscal Policies and the Full Employment Equilibrium

curves. Combining this set with the solid-line set of IS curves produces the intersections A, B, and C that yield the curve labeled AD in Part B. The equilibrium levels of P and Y are given by the intersection of this curve with the AS curve. This intersection shows a Keynesian less-than-full employment equilibrium with actual output of Y_1 being less than Y_f. If instead of the rigid money wage rate which gives us the AS curve as shown, the money wage rate were perfectly flexible downward, the AS curve would be perfectly inelastic at Y_f, and Y_1 would not be an equilibrium position. According to the self-correcting mechanism of classical theory, a decline in P would occur to produce an intersection of AD with the perfectly inelastic AS at Y_f; equilibrium at full employment would be automatically achieved via deflation. However, it is this classical mechanism that was questioned by Keynes and others and has led us here to examine the result that follows with a rigid money wage rate and therefore with an AS curve like that in Part B of Figure 13-8.

With the AS curve as there given, less-than-full employment equilibrium occurs at Y_1, as already noted. In Keynesian theory, the solution to unemployment is an appropriate rightward shift in the AD curve. But there is nothing in the Keynesian system to automatically cause the increase in investment spending, the increase in consumption spending, or the combination of the two that will produce the required rightward shift. To accomplish this calls for an expansionary policy by government. Assuming the economy is not in a liquidity trap, one such policy is monetary—an increase in M_s, which results in the broken-line or LM' set of curves in Part A. With no simultaneous governmental action taken to shift the IS curve, the intersections between the set of LM' curves and the set of IS curves at D, E, and F yield the AD' curve in Part B. The increase in M_s has raised the AD curve by just the amount that provides an intersection between that curve and the AS curve at Y_f. There is now an equilibrium with full employment and a higher price level. To

reach the full employment position, note that the price level must rise under present assumptions. The increase in employment that raises Y from Y_1 to Y_f will only occur with a decline in the real wage rate. As long as the money wage rate is inflexible downward as is assumed, such a decline can only occur with a rise in the price level.

Return now to the original less-than-full employment equilibrium given by the intersection of the AD and AS curves. A second policy to lift output to the full employment level is fiscal—an increase in government spending, a reduction in tax receipts, or a combination of both which results in the broken-line or IS' set of curves in Part A. Assuming a balanced budget before these fiscal actions are taken, a deficit results. Assuming also that the deficit so created is not financed by an increase in the nominal money supply, there is no shift in the LM curves; the relevant set is the original solid-line set. The intersections between these sets of IS' and LM curves occur at G, H, and J; the AD curve derived from these intersections is AD' in Part B of Figure 13-8. This curve intersects AS at Y_f. As before, there is equilibrium with full employment.

It is apparent that Part A of the figure has been drawn so that the shift from the IS set to the IS' set of curves and the shift from the LM to the LM' set produces the same rightward shift in the AD curve. Of course, the figure reveals nothing about the relative magnitudes of the money supply increase or the government expenditures increase or tax decrease that is required for this purpose. However, some amount of monetary expansion and some amount of fiscal expansion by themselves will produce the indicated shift in the AD curve. An appropriate mixture of the two composed of less monetary expansion and less fiscal expansion will also produce the same result. Less monetary stimulus would reduce the extent of the rightward shift of the LM' curves, and less fiscal stimulus would reduce the extent of the rightward shift of the IS' curves. If the shifts are such that the LM_2' curve and the IS_2' curve intersect at Y_f, the AD' curve that is derived will intersect the given AS curve at Y_f and P_2 as now shown. They will therefore yield a full employment equilibrium with the minimum necessary increase in the price level. As a final word, note that a mixture of monetary and fiscal policies which shifts the LM curves rightward to the positions shown by the LM' curves and *also* shifts the IS curves rightward to the positions shown by the IS' curves will produce a shift in the AD curve to AD''. This expansion would clearly be more than is needed to achieve full employment; the excess would be entirely absorbed in pulling the price level above the level needed to reach the full employment output level.

Just as Keynes and others criticized the classical argument that a system of flexible wages and prices would automatically correct lapses from full employment, some economists have criticized the argument that monetary and fiscal policies can be used to restore to full employment an economy suffering unemployment. Some of the questions raised concerning the appropriateness and efficacy of monetary and fiscal policies will be examined in later chapters. This brief section has merely traced the bare mechanics of the process by which monetary and fiscal policies can shift the IS, LM, and AD curves in a model in which the position of the IS and LM curves depends on the price level.

14

The Extended Model: Foreign Sector Included

OVERVIEW

Chapters 12 and 13 developed the extended model for a closed economy; this chapter does the same for an open economy. In so doing, it builds on the simple model of an open economy presented in Chapter 7. That earlier chapter took into account only the economy's imports and exports of goods and services and traced the way that its net export or import balance affected aggregate spending and the equilibrium level of income and output. There is, however, much more to economic relationships between economies than imports and exports of goods and services. There are transfer payments between governments and individuals in different countries and, more important, there are capital flows in which persons and firms in one country acquire financial assets issued by and purchase real assets located in other countries. The statement summarizing these international transactions in combination with the imports and exports of goods and services is the nation's balance of payments.

Chapter 14 starts by limiting attention to imports and exports as does Chapter 7, but it here fits these flows into the *IS–LM* apparatus developed in the preceding chapters. In so doing, it shows how changes in the net export balance affect not only the output level but also the interest rate.

Once imports and exports have been fitted into the *IS–LM* apparatus, that apparatus is expanded by adding to its *IS* and *LM* functions a third function for the balance of payments—the *BP* function. This is a curve like the *IS* and *LM* curves in the sense that each combination of output and interest rate along it indicates an equilibrium combination. In this case, the combination provides equilibrium in the balance of payments. To obtain this equilibrium requires certain relationships among an economy's net export balance, net foreign transfers, and net capital flows. Each point along the *BP* function is a combination of *Y* and *r* at which such an equilibrium relationship is found.

Just as certain factors cause shifts in the *IS* and *LM* functions, certain factors do the same to the *BP* function. After tracing the derivation of the *BP* function in some detail, the chapter examines the way that shifts in this function result from changes in the economy's price level and the foreign exchange value of its currency.

With the inclusion of the *BP* function in the model comes the distinction between internal and external equilibrium. The combination of *Y* and *r* at which the *IS* and *LM* curves intersect provides domestic or internal equilibrium; but if this combination is not on the *BP* curve, there is an external disequilibrium—that is, there is either a surplus or deficit in the balance of payments. Given such a surplus or deficit, an adjustment process takes place. Because the adjustment process works differently under a system of flexible exchange rates and fixed exchange rates, the process is examined for both systems.

The next section of the chapter brings in the issue of full employment. The concept of internal equilibrium refers to an equality between aggregate demand and aggregate supply. In the classical model, these can only be equal at full employment. However, in such a model, if the wage–price structure is too high, there will be less-than-full employment; to reach the equilibrium at full employment requires wage–price deflation. Assuming initially a disequilibrium situation, the process by which both external and internal equilibrium are simultaneously achieved is first examined for the classical model in which flexible wages and prices play the key role. In the Keynesian model, with its inflexible money wage rate and resultant upward-sloping aggregate supply curve, equilibrium between aggregate demand and aggregate supply can occur at any level of output. If that equilibrium is below full employment, to achieve external and internal equilibrium simultaneously and also to achieve that internal equilibrium specifically at the full employment level of output requires an increase in aggregate demand. The process by which the two objectives may be simultaneously achieved is next explained for this model in which monetary and fiscal policies play the key role.

The concluding note to this chapter is devoted to it and the preceding two chapters. It presents two summary formulations of the many elements that make up the extended model of income determination. The first is a flow-type formulation. On one side is aggregate demand behind which are the *IS* and *LM* functions and in turn the large number of factors that lie behind these functions. On the other side, of course, is the aggregate supply function and the factors behind that function. By assuming a change in any of the many factors on the two sides, it is possible to trace the effect of such a change on the primary variables of aggregate output and the price level, although this formulation does not show the extent of the effect on each.

The second summary formulation brings together in one fourteen-part figure different parts of the diagrammatic apparatus found in these last few chapters. This figure adds nothing new, but shows how the many parts of the extended model fit together. As with the other summary formulation, but in a more formal way, we can see how individual changes work through the system of diagrams to affect the primary variables of aggregate output and the price level. In both of these formulations, we can trace the changes only by assuming that other things remain equal. Despite this restraint, tracing the changes is still helpful in that it allows us to bring together in one place the major elements that comprise the extended income determination model.

As we turn from the explanation of what determines aggregate income and output in a closed economy to the same in an open economy, we are likely to think first of the domestic economy's exports of goods and services to the other economies of the world and its imports from them. However, in an open economy, other international transactions also affect income and output—for example, transfer payments and capital flows between persons, firms, and governments in different countries. These transactions combined with import and export transactions may be brought together to produce a summary statement known as a nation's balance of payments. Through an elaboration of the preceding chapters' *IS–LM* apparatus that adds a *BP* (balance of payments) function, we may trace the effect of various transactions that enter into the *BP* function on a nation's income and output level as well as other variables.

The *IS–LM* Model Including Imports and Exports

The first step in elaborating the earlier *IS–LM* apparatus to include foreign transactions is to show the way that imports and exports fit into that apparatus. Just as the *IS* curve for the two-sector economy and the three-sector economy, respectively, show all combinations of r and Y at which $S = I$ and $S + T = I + G$, the *IS* curve for the four-sector economy shows the combinations of r and Y at which $S + T + M = I + G + X$. If $S + T + M = I + G + X$, the leakages from the income stream are equal to the injections into it; the quantity of goods demanded remains unchanged. However, as for the two- and three-sector economies, the *IS* curve for the four-sector economy will show a different level of Y at which $S + T + M = I + G + X$ for each different interest rate, assuming, of course, that no part of the *IS* curve is perfectly inelastic. For a given *IS* curve, the level of Y identified by a particular

interest rate is the specific amount of goods that will be demanded by the four sectors combined at that rate. If the economy is operating at that level of Y, the amount of goods demanded is equal to the amount supplied, and the goods market clears. At a lower (higher) interest rate, the quantity of goods demanded is larger (smaller) and the goods market will correspondingly clear at a higher (lower) level of Y.

Derivation of the *IS* Function

Figure 14-1 shows the derivation of the *IS* curve for both a three- and a four-sector economy in order to demonstrate the change that occurs with the introduction of the fourth sector. The derivation for the three-sector case was illustrated in Figure 12-11 and discussed on pages 251–54. In Figure 14-1, the IS_c curve for the three-sector or closed (c) economy is derived from the $I + G$ curve in Part A and the $S + T$ curve in Part C in the way earlier explained. To introduce exports, the amount of X is added horizontally to the $I + G$ curve in Part A to produce the $I + G + X$ curve. Because the amount of X is assumed to be determined entirely by factors outside the domestic economy, the interest rate in the domestic economy does not affect exports. The $I + G + X$ curve is accordingly equidistant from the $I + G$ curve at each interest rate. To introduce imports, M is added vertically to the $S + T$ curve in Part C. In the model of Chapter 7 carried over here, $M = M_a + mY$, so that the spread between $S + T$ and $S + T + M$ varies directly with the level of Y. The difference between the slope of $S + T$ and the slope of $S + T + M$ is equal to m or the marginal propensity to import. The various combinations of r and Y at which the sum of the leakages, $S + T + M$, equals the sum of the injections, $I + G + X$, are identified in the usual way. The points in the Y, r space corresponding to these combinations are connected with a line that is the IS_o curve for the open (o) economy.

The IS_o curve slopes downward to the right as does the IS_c curve, but the slope of the IS_o

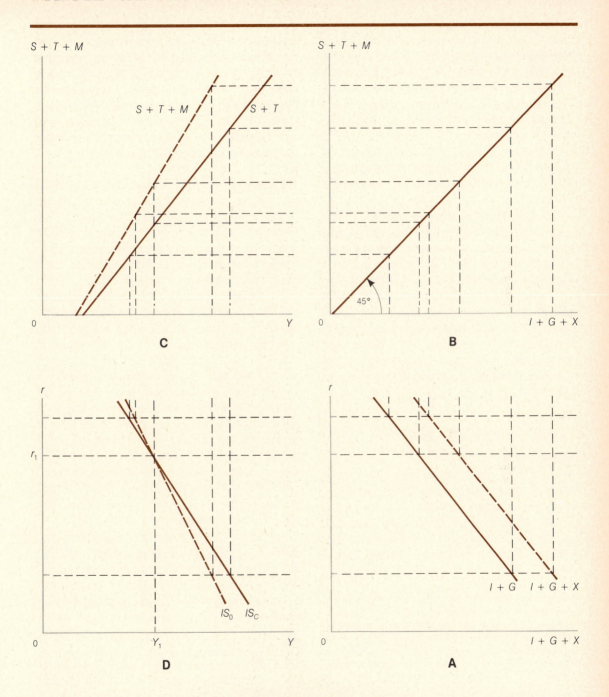

FIGURE 14-1
Derivation of the *IS* Function

curve is seen to be greater than that of the IS_c curve. A decline in the interest rate raises investment spending. The resulting increase in income will be that at which the sum of leakages from the income stream grows by an amount equal to the increase in injections—that is, to the increase in investment spending. With the leakage into imports now added to the leakage into saving, the indicated increase in the sum of leakages will occur with a smaller increase in income than would be the case if there were only the leakage into saving.[1]

The relationship between the curves in Parts A and C of Figure 14-1 is such that the IS_o and IS_c curves intersect. If the fixed spread between the $I + G$ and the $I + G + X$ curves in Part A were greater than the maximum spread between $S + T$ and $S + T + M$ in Part C, the IS_o curve would lie to the right of the IS_c curve throughout. In the opposite case, the IS_o curve would lie to the left of the IS_c curve throughout. However, over a sufficient range of income, it is most likely that the curves intersect at some point as shown in Figure 14.1.[2]

Shifts in the *IS–LM* Functions

The IS curve for the open economy will shift as a result of any change in autonomous spending, whether that change originates with any of the domestic sectors or with the foreign sector. To focus on the foreign sector, assume that the $I + G$ and $S + T$ curves remain constant. Then a rightward shift in the IS curve will result from

either an increase in X or a decrease in M_a in the equation $M = M_a + mY$; a leftward shift in the IS curve will result from either of the opposite changes. Because X is simply equal to X_a or is completely autonomous, the subscript a has not been attached to it. The amount by which the IS curve will shift in the present model is equal to the change in X or in M_a times $1/(1 - c + m)$, the foreign trade multiplier developed in Chapter 7.

Because our present extended model does not assume the stable price level of the earlier model, it allows us to examine the effect on the IS curve of a change in the domestic price level relative to foreign price levels. Assuming no offsetting change in the foreign exchange rates between currencies, a relative decline in the domestic price level makes domestic goods relatively less expensive to foreign buyers, thereby stimulating exports; and it makes foreign goods relatively more expensive to domestic buyers, thereby discouraging imports. Consequently, a relative decline in the domestic price level usually will increase sales of domestic goods abroad (increase X) and decrease the amount of goods purchased abroad (decrease M at each level of income by decreasing M_a). A relatively lower domestic price level will shift the IS curve rightward by shifting the $I + G + X$ curve rightward and the $S + T + M$ curve downward. A relative increase in the domestic price level will naturally have the opposite effects.

Figure 14-2 shows some of the effects of a shift in the IS curve caused by foreign trade. IS_1 and LM_1 are the original positions of the curves. The intersection identifies Y_1 and r_1. Assume now a rightward shift of the IS curve resulting from an increase in X, the cause of which might be an

---

[1] Following the model presented in Figure 12-11, p. 252, the amount of leakage into T is assumed to be a fixed dollar amount. It therefore does not influence the increase in income required to raise the sum of $S + T + M$ by the increase in the sum of $I + G + X$ that results from the increase in I.

[2] The combination at which Y_1 and r_1 intersect is a combination at which both $S + T = I + G$ and $S + T + M = I + G + X$ and therefore $X = M$. At any lower level of Y, $X > M$. Because a net export balance has an expansionary effect on the income level, other things being

equal, foreign trade makes the income level higher than it otherwise would be; the IS_o curve must lie to the right of the IS_c curve at each relevant interest rate. At any level of Y above Y_1, $X < M$. Because a net import balance has a contractionary effect on the income level, other things being equal, foreign trade makes the income level lower than it otherwise would be; the IS_o curve must lie to the left of the IS_c curve at each relevant interest rate.

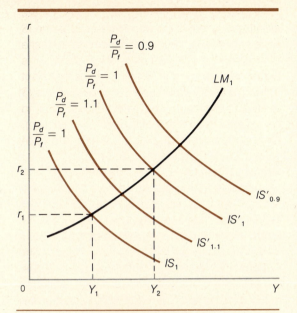

FIGURE 14-2
Shifts in the *IS* Function

price level, P_d, to foreign price levels, P_f. Assume that P_d/P_f is initially 1 and that this ratio is one of the factors that initially establishes the position of the *IS* curve at IS_1. At the same time that the shift from IS_1 to IS_1' occurs, assume that the relative price ratio changes from 1 to 1.1—in other words, that domestic goods become relatively more expensive, or foreign goods become relatively less expensive. Taken by itself, this change in P_d/P_f will ordinarily increase real imports and reduce real exports and thereby shift the *IS* curve leftward from IS_1.[3] However, combining this change with the change that shifts *IS* from IS_1 to IS_1' and assuming that the strength of the change in the price level ratio is less than the strength of the other change, the *IS* curve on balance will shift rightward to a position between the original position and IS_1', say to the position shown by $IS_{1.1}'$. In the same way, if the change in the relative price ratio were from 1 to 0.9, domestic goods would become relatively less expensive and foreign goods relative more expensive. This change, taken by itself, would shift the *IS* curve rightward

---

increase in incomes in other countries, a decrease in import duties in other countries, or a change in the tastes of people in other countries in favor of foreign goods and travel. The shift in the *IS* curve could also result from a decrease in M_a, the cause of which might be an increase in import duties in the domestic economy or a change in tastes by people in the domestic economy away from foreign goods and travel. Suppose one or more such changes shifts the IS_1 curve to IS_1'. Assuming no change in relative price levels or other things, the new equilibrium is given by the intersection of IS_1' and LM_1, at which $Y = Y_2$ and $r = r_2$. This merely introduces another variation of the basic analysis of Chapter 12. There we traced the same kind of change in the *Y, r* equilibrium as a result of a shift in the investment curve, an increase in government purchases, or a decrease in tax receipts, each of which shifts the *IS* curve to the right.

We may now examine the effects of a change in relative price levels or the ratio of the domestic

[3]Empirical studies suggest that this is the usual result. Although it is the result we will accept here, it is theoretically possible that the relative rise in the price level of domestic goods could lead to an increase in net exports or a decrease in net imports and thereby cause a rightward shift in the *IS* curve. The relatively higher cost of domestic goods will reduce the *quantity* of goods exported, but the amount of the reduction depends on the elasticity of demand for exports. At the same time, the relatively lower cost of foreign goods will increase the *quantity* of goods imported, but the amount of the increase again depends on the elasticity of the demand for imports. If the demand for exports were sufficiently inelastic and the demand for imports sufficiently elastic, the money value of imports could decline more than that of exports, resulting in a larger net export balance or a smaller net import balance than existed before the relative rise in the domestic price level. However, the empirical evidence does not indicate this kind of result. One study estimated the elasticity of demand for U.S. imports at 0.9 and that for U.S. exports at 1.5, a combination of elasticities that will clearly result in a decrease in the value of U.S. net exports with a relative rise in the U.S. price level. See H.S. Houthakker and S.P. Magee, "Income and Price Elasticities in World Trade," *Review of Economics and Statistics*, May 1969, pp. 111–25.

from IS_1. In combination with the shift in the curve to IS_1' due to the other change, the total shift will be to a position to the right of IS_1', say to the position shown by $IS_{0.9}'$.

In order to identify the equilibrium Y and r resulting from changes in relative price levels, we must also observe what happens to the absolute price level at the same time. Changes in the absolute price level, assuming an unchanged nominal money supply, also cause shifts in the IS and LM curves. The IS curve will shift due to a change in relative price levels as previously described, but it will also shift due to a change in the absolute price level for reasons described in Chapter 13. Relative price levels are what matters for imports and exports or foreign trade effects, but the absolute domestic price level is what matters for the Pigou, income-redistribution, and tax and transfer-payment effects. However, although the IS curve will shift in response to both a relative and an absolute price level change, the LM curve will shift only in response to an absolute price level change, again assuming a given nominal money supply.

Because a change in relative price levels is consistent with an increase, decrease, or no change in the domestic price level, various effects on the Y, r combination may follow. For example, a decrease in the P_d/P_f ratio from 1.0 to 0.9 will in itself tend to shift the IS curve rightward. If the decrease occurs in part or in whole via a decline in the domestic price level, there is an increase in the real money supply on the assumption of an unchanged nominal money supply. Therefore, the rightward shift in the IS curve due to foreign trade effects will be reinforced by a shift due to the Pigou and other effects that depend on the absolute price level. Moreover, in this case, the LM curve will shift rightward and the IS–LM intersection must occur at a higher Y than otherwise. On the other hand, if the decline in the ratio from 1.0 to 0.9 is entirely the result of a smaller absolute increase in the domestic price level than in foreign price levels, there is a decrease in the real money supply, assuming an unchanged nominal money supply.

The rightward shift in the IS curve due to the foreign trade effect will be accompanied by a leftward shift due to the Pigou and other effects that depend on the absolute price level, which is now higher than before. Whether the IS curve shifts rightward or leftward depends, of course, on the relative strengths of these effects. The LM curve in this case will clearly shift leftward. The new Y and r may be higher or lower than the original values, depending on the particular shifts in the IS and LM curves.

Just as we have so far used the IS–LM apparatus to trace the effects on Y and r of changes in variables like autonomous exports, autonomous imports, and relative and absolute price levels, we can use it to trace the effects on Y and r of changes in yet other international variables, for example, foreign exchange rates. Although much can be seen with the IS–LM apparatus alone, much more can be seen by supplementing its IS and LM functions with a third function, a balance of payments or BP function. The IS–LM–BP apparatus is much more illuminating, and it is to the development and application of this broader apparatus that we turn next.

The Balance of Payments Function

The only international transactions considered so far have been the purchases and sales of goods and services between firms and people in different countries—in other words, imports and exports. These included goods such as wheat and computers and services such as tourism and transportation. In addition to these commercial transactions are private and public transfers. These include remittances by people in one country to relatives and friends in other countries, government transfers to foreign governments of both military goods and money, and government transfers of money in payments of pensions to persons abroad. Like goods and services, transfers flow in both directions. A net figure for transfers is reached in the same way that a net figure for exports and imports is reached. The sum of the figures for net exports of goods and services *and* net transfer payments to foreigners is, in balance of payments terminology, called the **balance on current account.**[4]

Beyond the transactions in goods and services and the private and government transfers which are combined to arrive at the balance on current account is a second major set of transactions. People and firms in one country spend abroad not only to import goods and services provided by foreign firms, but to acquire such things as land, dwellings, plant and equipment in foreign countries, and stocks and bonds issued by foreign corporations and governments. The purchases of real assets physically located abroad or financial assets issued by foreign governments and firms (including bank accounts issued by foreign firms in the banking business) are described as capital transactions. The balance for any time period—the difference between such purchases by persons and firms of one country in all other countries and the purchases by persons and firms of all other countries in the first country—is called the **balance on capital account.**[5]

The Balance of Payments Deficit or Surplus

During any year, each country will have a deficit or a surplus in its current account and a deficit or a surplus in its capital account. (A balance in either or both of these accounts for a year is, of course, possible, but not common.) The sum of these two figures is called the **deficit or surplus in the balance of payments** for that period. If there is a surplus in one account and a deficit in the other and if they are of the same absolute size, the sum of the two is, of course, zero. Such a zero sum is required for **equilibrium in the balance of payments,** although economists differ as to the number of years within which that zero sum should be achieved in order to conclude that there is equilibrium in the country's balance of payments. If we simplify by omitting transfers, the surplus on current account is $X - M$. If we designate the deficit on capital account or the net capital outflow by H, we have the following equation for B, the balance of payments surplus: $B = (X - M) - H$. If $X - M$ equals H, B is zero and the balance of payments is in equilibrium.

If during a year the U.S. were to show exports of goods and services of $305 billion and imports of $300 billion, the surplus on current account would equal $305 - $300 or + $5 billion. If during the year U.S. holdings of assets in foreign countries were to increase by $30 billion and foreign holdings of assets in the U.S. were to increase by $25 billion, there would be a net capital outflow of $5 billion; the deficit on capital account would be $5 billion. This set of figures would indicate equilibrium in the balance of payments or $B = 0$, as ($305 - $300) - ($30 - $25) = 0.

Assuming in this illustration that all transactions are settled in foreign currencies, the U.S. would have received $5 billion more in foreign currencies through its exports than it would have paid in foreign currencies for its imports. Consequently, it would show a gain in holdings of foreign currencies of $5 billion for the period as a result of its transactions on current account.

---

[4]In the GNP identity of Chapter 2, $C + S + T + R_{pf} \equiv$ GNP $\equiv C + I + G + (X - M)$, where $X - M$ is the balance on goods and services and R_{pf} is net transfer payments made abroad by private parties. The remaining items in the balance on current account, government transfer payments abroad, do not appear explicitly in the basic GNP identity.

[5]A nation's GNP is a measure of currently produced goods and services, not of assets or changes in ownership of assets. The international transactions that directly enter the GNP are found in the current account; the international transactions covered in the capital account entail purchases and sales of assets and as such do not direclty affect the GNP total or its separate components.

However, its purchases of foreign assets call for the payment to foreigners of $5 billion more in foreign currencies than the amount of foreign currencies received from foreign purchases of assets in the U.S. Consequently, it would show a decline in holdings of foreign currencies of $5 billion as a result of its transactions on capital account. In sum, the balances in the current and capital accounts offset each other; U.S. holdings of foreign currencies are unchanged. Viewed from one perspective, a nation's balance of payments is in equilibrium if there is neither an accumulation nor a decumulation of that nation's holdings of foreign currencies during the time period. In a brief but rough way, this conveys the meaning of the concept of balance of payments equilibrium.

This illustration has shown an equilibrium in which a current account surplus is matched by a capital account deficit. An equilibrium may also result with the opposite pairing. Reversing the same set of numbers, we have $X - M = \$300 - \$305 = -\$5$ billion balance on current account and $H = \$25 - \$30$ (capital outflow minus capital inflow) or a balance on capital account of $-\$5$ billion. With $X - M = -\$5$ billion and $H = -\$5$ billion, the sum of $(X - M) - H$ is zero, and there is again a balance of payments equilibrium.

Of course, various changes in the illustrative numbers will convert the equilibrium into a deficit or a surplus. In general, starting from a balance of payments equilibrium, any reduction in the net export balance or increase in the net import balance will result in a balance of payments deficit, assuming no change in the balance on capital account. And any increase in the net export balance or decrease in the net import balance will result in a balance of payments surplus on the same assumption. Starting again from a balance of payments equilibrium, any increase in the net capital outflow or decrease in the net capital inflow will result in a balance of payments deficit, assuming no change in the balance on current account. And any decrease in the net capital out-

flow or increase in the net capital inflow will result in a balance of payments surplus on the same assumption.

Derivation of the Balance of Payments Function

Given the simplification that the balance on current account is equal to the net import or net export balance, the determination of the balance on current account may be explained with the model of Chapter 7. That simple model makes exports entirely a function of factors outside the domestic economy and makes imports a function of the income level within the domestic economy. In line with this model, Part C of Figure 14-3 shows that the $X - M$ balance varies inversely with the domestic income level. The higher Y is, the smaller will be $X - M$ or the smaller the net export balance or the larger the net import balance.

What determines the balance on capital account? People and firms purchase those assets that provide the highest yield, given the risk involved, and they will switch from domestic assets to foreign assets if the difference in yield, adjusted for differences in risk, makes such a switch advantageous. Therefore, the net capital outflow, H, may be written as an inverse function of the rate of interest, r, in the domestic economy. With interest rates assumed given in other countries, the lower the rate in the domestic economy, the larger is the net capital outflow or the smaller is the net capital inflow. The curve in Part A of Figure 14-3 shows this relationship between H and r.

Part B of the figure provides a 45° line needed to link H in Part A and $X - M$ in Part C. Each point along the 45° line shows an equality between the value of $X - M$ on the vertical axis and H on the horizontal axis and therefore a zero value for B.

In the same way that the IS function was derived in Part D of Figure 12-3 (page 238), the BP function in Part D of Figure 14-3 is derived

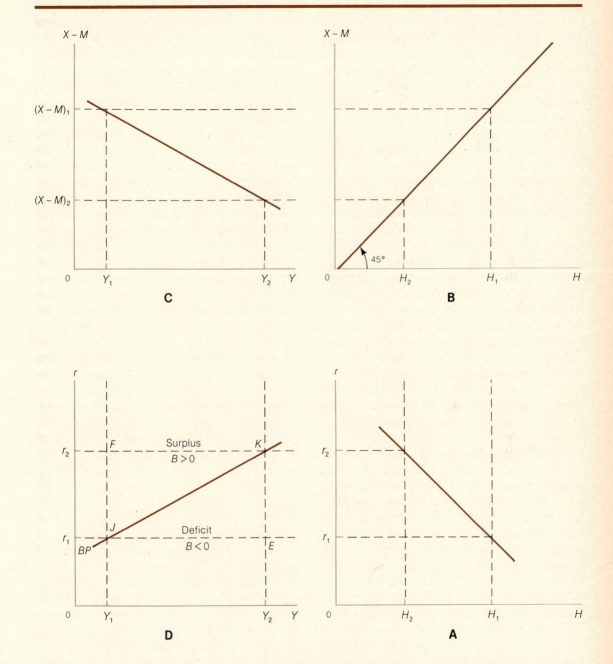

FIGURE 14-3
Derivation of the *BP* Function

from the other parts of this figure. Suppose that the interest rate in Part A is r_1. This indicates a capital outflow of H_1. To secure B of zero needed for equilibrium in the balance of payments, $X - M$ must equal H. Tracing from Part A through Part B to Part C indicates that $X - M$ will be equal to H_1 if Y is equal to Y_1. Bringing together in Part D the values of r_1 from Part A and Y_1 from Part C yields one combination of r and Y at which $B = 0$. To vary the approach, start this time in Part C to derive a second combination. Suppose the income level is Y_2, which indicates $(X - M)_2$. Balance of payments equilibrium requires that H equal $(X - M)_2$. Tracing from Part C through Part B to Part A indicates that H will equal $(X - M)_2$ if r is r_2. Bringing together in Part D the values of r_2 and Y_2 yields a second combination of r and Y at which $B = 0$. Connecting the points identified by these and other such combinations yields the BP function.

The BP function will always slope upward to the right—that is, balance of payments equilibrium will be found at combinations of relatively high interest rates and relatively high income levels or relatively low interest rates and relatively low income levels. This follows from our assumptions that a relatively high income level will mean a relatively low net export surplus; equilibrium in the balance of payments then requires a relatively low net capital outflow, which will be secured with a relatively high domestic interest rate. Or starting with a relatively low domestic interest rate, there will be a relatively large net capital outflow; equilibrium in the balance of payments then requires a relatively large net export balance, which will occur with a relatively low level of income.

Every point along the BP curve identifies a combination of r and Y at which $X - M = H$ or $B = 0$. Every combination not on the curve is one at which $X - M \gtreqless H$ or $B \gtreqless 0$. Specifically, all combinations above the BP line are combinations at which $X - M > H$, indicating a balance of payments surplus; all combinations below the BP line are combinations at which $X - M < H$, indicating a balance of payments deficit.

This may be seen as follows. The combination of Y_2, r_2 represented in Part D of Figure14-3 by K, for example, indicates an equilibrium. Because the combination of Y_1, r_2 shown as F includes the same interest rate as at K but a lower income level than at K, H will be the same as at K, but $X - M$ will be larger than at K. Therefore, because $X - M = H$ at K, $X - M$ must exceed H at F. There must be a balance of payments surplus at F. The same may be seen by comparing the combination at point F with that at J. The combination of Y_1, r_1 shown as J indicates an equilibrium. Because the combination of Y_1, r_2 shown as F includes the same income level as at J but a higher interest rate than at J, $X - M$ at F will be the same as at J, but H will be smaller at F than at J. Because $X - M = H$ at J, $X - M$ must exceed H at F. There must be a balance of payments surplus at F. The same conclusion—a balance of payments surplus—will be found for any other combination of Y and r that lies above the BP curve.

By the same reasoning, a comparison of the Y, r combination shown as E, for example, with the equilibrium combinations shown as J and K will reveal that there must be a balance of payments deficit for the Y, r combination given by E. The same will be found for any other combination of Y and r that lies below the BP curve.

Shifts in the Balance of Payments Function

If the actual interest rate and income level are at a point like E or F or at any other point not on the BP function, the deficit or surplus in the balance of payments automatically tends to cause an equilibrating shift in the BP function. Therefore, in the case of a surplus, the BP function in Part D of Figure 14-3 will shift upward or leftward; in the case of a deficit, it will shift downward or rightward. We conclude this section by examining the way changes in the price level and the foreign exchange rate will shift the BP function. Here we will merely see why such changes shift the BP

function. Later we will look at the automatic forces in the system that tend to cause changes in the price level and the foreign exchange rate.

A Change in the Price Level   Part C of Figure 14-4 shows an initial net export curve labeled $(X - M)_1$ in which the subscript 1 identifies P of P_1. What is the effect of an absolute change in the domestic price level on the BP function, all else being equal? We have seen that an absolute rise in the domestic price level decreases the net export balance and shifts the IS curve leftward and also decreases the real money supply and shifts the LM curve leftward. Figure 14-4 shows that an absolute rise in the domestic price level from P_1 to P_2 shifts the $(X - M)$ curve leftward from $(X - M)_1$ to $(X - M)_2$; this, in turn, shifts the BP curve in Part D leftward from BP_1 to BP_2. Consequently equilibrium in the balance of payments at any level of Y now requires a higher r; alternatively, equilibrium at any r now requires a lower Y. Because the rise from P_1 to P_2 reduces the level of X and increases the level of M at each level of Y, equilibrium in the balance of payments requires that Y fall enough to restore $X - M$ to what it was before the rise in P (a decrease of FJ in Part D), that r rise enough to reduce H by an equal amount (an increase of FK in Part D), or any combination of the two. A decline in the domestic price level from P_1 to P_0 will naturally have the opposite effect, as shown by the rightward shift from $(X - M)_1$ to $(X - M)_0$ in Part C and the resulting rightward shift from BP_1 to BP_0 in Part D.

A Change in the Foreign Exchange Rate   A foreign exchange rate is simply the price of one currency in terms of another. For example, in the years 1977–80, the price of the West German currency unit, the Deutsche mark (DM), averaged approximately $0.50 in terms of the U.S. currency unit, the dollar. Expressed the other way, the price of the U.S. dollar has been approximately 2 DM. For this pair of currencies, an appreciation or rise in the dollar means that the buyer of dollars

pays more than 2 DM per dollar. From the other side, an appreciation or rise in the dollar—which is a depreciation or fall in the DM—means that the buyer of Deutsche marks pays less than $0.50 per DM. To prospective West German buyers, the attractiveness of U.S. goods and services depends, among other things, on their prices in terms of dollars and on the price of the dollar in terms of the DM. Basically, a 10 percent rise in dollar prices of U.S. goods with no change in the price of the U.S. dollar in terms of the DM is the same to the prospective German buyer as a 10 percent rise in the price of the U.S. dollar in terms of the DM and no change in the prices of U.S. goods in terms of dollars. For example, if a U.S.-manufactured computer is priced at $100,000 and the U.S. dollar is priced at 2 DM, the computer will cost a German importer 200,000 DM. To that importer, a 10 percent rise in the price of the computer to $110,000 with no change in the price of the dollar ($1 = 2 DM) will raise the cost to 220,000 DM and a 10 percent rise in the price of the dollar ($1 = 2.20 DM) with no change in the price of the computer will also raise the cost to 220,000 DM.

Let us now assume a rise in the foreign exchange rate of the dollar against other currencies in general—in other words, that it takes more Deutsche marks, pesos, francs, lira, yen, and so forth than before to buy a U.S. dollar in the foreign exchange markets. This will cause the BP curve to shift leftward, just as a rise in the U.S. price level will cause the BP curve to shift leftward. With no change in the price levels of the other countries, U.S. exports will decline, because it now takes more of each foreign currency unit to purchase the U.S. currency unit. U.S. imports will grow, because the U.S. currency unit will purchase more of each foreign currency unit. In Part C of Figure 14-4, a rise of the dollar in terms of other currencies will shift the $X - M$ curve from $(X - M)_1$ to $(X - M)_2$—the same kind of movement that occurs with a rise in the price level. This leftward shift in the $X - M$ function, in turn, shifts the BP function leftward from BP_1 to BP_2. Consequently balance of payments equilibrium

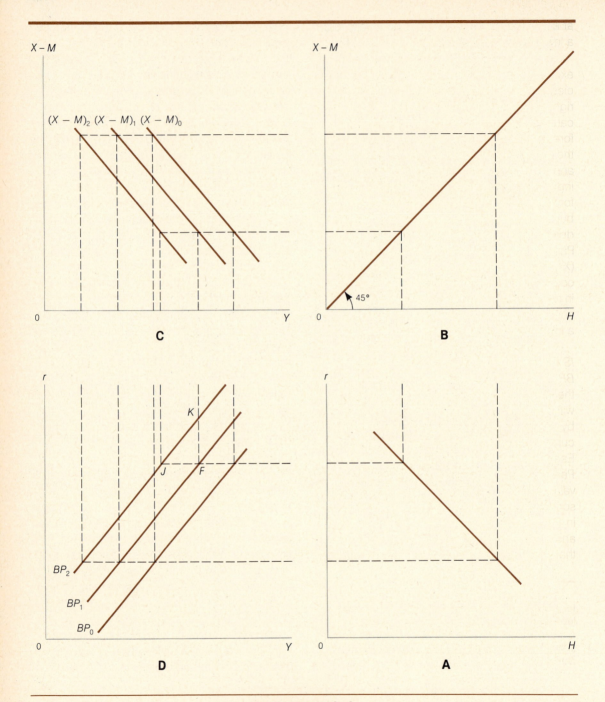

FIGURE 14-4
Shifts in the *BP* Function

at any Y requires a higher r, or at any r requires a lower Y.[6]

By the same argument, a fall in the foreign exchange rate of the dollar against other currencies in general will cause the BP curve to shift rightward, just as a fall in the U.S. price level will cause the BP curve to shift rightward. Because foreigners can now purchase dollars with less of their own currency, they will buy more U.S. goods and U.S. exports will increase. Because U.S. individuals and firms can now purchase fewer foreign currency units with each dollar, they will buy less foreign goods and U.S. imports will decrease. For this case, the $X - M$ curve in Part C of Figure 14-4 will shift rightward from $(X - M)_1$ to $(X - M)_0$—the same kind of shift that occurs with a lower price level. The BP function, in turn, shifts from BP_1 to BP_0. Consequently, balance of payments equilibrium at any Y requires a lower r or at any r requires a higher Y.

Changes in foreign exchange rates affect the IS function in the same way that they affect the BP function. In terms of Figure 14-1, a decline in the foreign exchange value of a nation's currency will shift the $I + G + X$ curve rightward in Part A by increasing X and will shift the $S + T + M$ curve in Part C downward by decreasing M_a. Each of these shifts tends to shift the IS_0 curve in Part D rightward. A rise in the foreign exchange value of a nation's currency will by the same reasoning bring about a leftward shift in the IS_0 curve in Part D. Later, when we combine the IS, LM, and BP functions in one diagram, we will note that changes in the foreign exchange value of a nation's currency, like changes in its price level relative to foreign price levels, affect the position of both the BP and IS functions.

Balance of Payments Disequilibrium and the Money Supply

If the balance of payments is in equilibrium, the total payments to foreigners for goods and services imported and for real and financial assets acquired abroad are exactly equal to the total receipts from foreigners for their imports of goods and services from the domestic economy and for their real and financial assets acquired in the domestic economy. However, a surplus means that receipts from abroad exceed payments made abroad, and a deficit means that payments made abroad exceed receipts from abroad. Such an imbalance between outpayments and inpayments may cause changes in the economy's money supply, and changes in the money supply play a role in the process by which a nation achieves external and internal equilibrium. We will examine this process in the next section; here we will look at the way that payments imbalances may cause changes in a country's money supply.

Exporters and others who receive foreign currencies (generally in the form of bank drafts or claims to foreign currency rather than actual money) sell these currencies to commercial banks in exchange for their own currency. Importers and others who make payment in foreign currencies buy the needed foreign currencies from the banks with their own currency. If a country has a balance of payments surplus for any given time period, the commercial banks as a group will experience an increase in their overall holdings of foreign currencies over that period. The amount of foreign currencies purchased each day is added to the banks' assets; the payments for these currencies (typically in the form of credits to the demand deposit balances of the sellers)

---

[6]As explained in footnote 3, it is theoretically possible for a rise in a country's price level relative to foreign price levels to result in an increase in the money value of its net exports or a decrease in the money value of its net imports, if that country's demand for imports is sufficiently elastic and other countries' demand for its exports is sufficiently inelastic. The same is true for foreign exchange rates. It is theoretically possible for a rise in a country's foreign exchange rate to result in an increase in the money value of its net exports or a decrease in the money value of its net imports, if the price elasticities of demand are as described.

are added to the banks' demand deposit liabilities. Similarly, the amount of foreign currencies sold each day is deducted from the banks' assets; the payments for these currencies (typically in the form of reductions in the demand deposits of the currency buyers) is subtracted from the banks' demand deposit liabilities. With a balance of payments surplus, there is a net increase in the amount of foreign currencies held by the country's banks. All else being equal, there is then a net increase in the banks' assets and an equal net increase in their demand deposit liabilities to the public. Thus, with a net increase in the public's holding of demand deposits and no change in its holdings of currency, the country's money supply increases due to the surplus in its balance of payments.

One may object that this conclusion is valid only if the commercial banks are willing and able to hold larger amounts of foreign currencies among their assets. What if these banks choose not to or cannot do so? For example, assume that all countries show an increase in holdings of French francs—in other words, that France has a deficit in its balance of payments for the period. If U.S. commercial banks choose not to hold the additional francs they have purchased but not sold, how may they dispose of them? Under the Bretton Woods international payments system which prevailed from the end of World War II until 1973, unwilling holders of francs could in effect sell them to the French central bank, the Bank of France. In practice, the U.S. commercial banks would sell the francs to the Federal Reserve Banks at a fixed price of so many francs per dollar in exchange for additional reserve balances. The Federal Reserve Banks would in effect present the francs to the Bank of France in exchange for dollars at the same fixed price. If the Bank of France did not have dollars or other acceptable currencies, it would have to make payment in gold, again at a fixed price of so many francs per ounce of gold. The international monetary system maintained fixed foreign exchange rates. Under this system the Bank of France would exchange its holdings of U.S. dollars or gold for francs presented to it by foreign central banks in order to prevent a decline in the value of the franc in terms of the U.S. dollar or gold.

Carrying the story through this second step actually reinforces our conclusion that a country with a surplus in its balance of payments will show an increase in its money supply, all else being equal. This second step involves not only the original increase in the money supply, but now the potential for a further increase. The U.S. commercial banks have converted foreign currency holdings into additional reserves at the Federal Reserve Banks. These additional reserves increase the banks' ability to extend credit to their regular customers and thereby further increase demand deposits and the money supply. Because each dollar of reserves can support a multiple of that amount in demand deposits, the amount of credit extended and the new money created is also a multiple of the increase in commercial bank reserves.

Consider now a deficit in a country's balance of payments. This should have the opposite effect of a surplus—a reduction in the country's money supply, assuming, of course, that all else remains equal. During a period of deficit, the amount of foreign currencies the nation's banks sell to importers and others who make payments abroad will exceed the amount they buy from exporters and others who receive payments from abroad. Consequently, with a net decrease in the public's holdings of demand deposits and no change in its holdings of domestic paper money and coin, the country's money supply decreases as a result of the deficit in its balance of payments.

Things may work out this way, but only if commercial banks can keep enough foreign currency "in stock" to compensate for the difference between the purchase demands of importers and the selling needs of exporters. If they do not have this stock, the deficit may be financed out of the foreign currency holdings that the central bank maintains to meet such needs. The central bank could sell the needed foreign currencies to importers and others whose requirements could not be met by the commercial banks. The central bank would receive payment in the form of checks drawn against the demand deposits of the buyers in the commercial banks. The central bank will deduct the amount of these checks from the reserve balances of the commercial banks at the central bank. We are now at the step that parallels the other case. In the process as described, the commercial banks lose reserves equal in amount to the foreign currencies sold to importers and others in the domestic economy by the central bank. All else remaining equal, the loss of reserves may force the commercial banks to contract credit by a multiple of this loss. This results in a corresponding decrease in demand deposits and the money supply.

Under the Bretton Woods international payments system, those who sought to purchase foreign currencies with their own currency could do so at a fixed rate. Each country was obligated to maintain a fixed value for its currency in terms of other currencies. For a deficit country to prevent a decline in the external value of its currency, its central bank had to use its reserves of foreign currencies or gold to meet the demands of those who wished to convert the domestic currency into foreign currencies. As long as the central bank had the reserves to meet such demands and was willing to use them, the external value of the nation's currency could be maintained.[7]

Although it bypasses many complications, our review is sufficient to show the way in which a balance of payments deficit or surplus tends to decrease a deficit country's money supply and increase a surplus country's money supply under an international monetary system of fixed

exchange rates. However, in 1973, the Bretton Woods system was abandoned in favor of a system of flexible exchange rates. Under the new system, central banks do not stand ready to use their holdings of foreign currencies to stabilize the value of their currency at a fixed level in terms of other currencies. Instead, a deficit country lets the external value of its currency depreciate and a surplus country lets the external value of its currency appreciate. If this process is permitted to run its course freely, any balance of payments deficit or surplus that appears will be a short-lived phenomenon. In a free market, the foreign exchange rate established by the forces of supply and demand will move to the level that eliminates a deficit or a surplus. To the degree that deficits and surpluses are corrected in fairly short order under a system of flexible exchange rates, there is no automatic tendency for a deficit or a surplus to cause a decrease or increase in the money supply as it did under the old system of fixed exchange rates.

Balance of Payments Disequilibrium and the Adjustment Process

Using the groundwork laid in the preceding pages, we will now examine the processes by which a surplus or deficit in the balance of payments may be eliminated. In Part A of Figure 14-5, internal equilibrium is defined by the Y_1, r_1 combination at which the IS and LM curves intersect. However, because the Y_1, r_1 intersection lies

---

[7]Suppose the deficit country is France. The Bank of France will be faced with demands from French importers for foreign currencies, say U.S. dollars, to settle transactions in which payment must be made in dollars. The central bank accordingly sells dollars to its own nationals in exchange for francs, as in the present illustration. In the earlier illustration in which commercial banks in the U.S. and other countries found themselves with enlarged holdings of francs due to the French deficit, U.S. and other exporters had accepted payment for goods sold to France

in francs and had sold those francs to their commercial banks for domestic currency. The U.S. commercial banks exchanged these francs for dollars at the Federal Reserve Banks, which in turn presented the francs to the Bank of France for payment in dollars. The only difference in the two illustrations of the French deficit is that the demand for dollars from the Bank of France originates in the first illustration with U.S. exporters who accepted francs in payment and in the other illustration with French importers who have agreed to make payment in dollars.

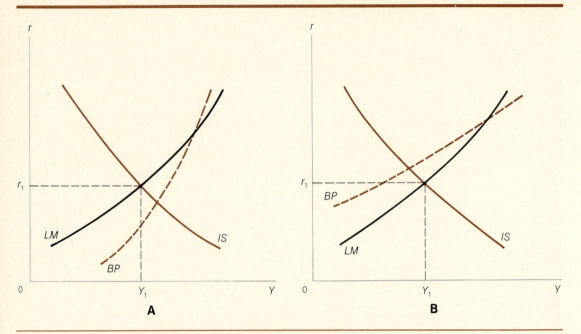

FIGURE 14-5
Balance of Payments Disequilibria

above or to the left of the *BP* function, there is external disequilibrium, specifically a surplus in the balance of payments. In Part B of Figure 14-5, because the Y_1, r_1 intersection that provides internal equilibrium lies below or to the right of the *BP* function, there is the opposite kind of external disequilibrium, a deficit.

In terms of Figure 14-5, to eliminate a balance of payments deficit or surplus, the *IS–LM* intersection must lie neither above nor below the *BP* function—inversely stated, the *BP* function must lie neither below nor above the *IS–LM* intersection. To achieve this result requires that shifts in one or more of the three functions produce an intersection of all three functions at one *Y, r* combination. The adjustment process that causes shifts in one or more functions varies according to whether the international monetary system is one of flexible or fixed exchange rates. From the end of World War II to 1973, the international

economy operated under the fixed exchange rate system established by the major powers at Bretton Woods, New Hampshire in 1944. However, the Bretton Woods system weakened during the 1960s and collapsed in 1973. Since then, the world has lived with a flexible (floating) exchange rate system, but a return to a form of a fixed exchange rate system is possible in the 1980s. The process of adjustment to a balance of payments disequilibrium differs under the two systems, or, in terms of Figure 14-5, the shifts in the functions differ under the two systems. We will trace the basic mechanics of the adjustment process under each of the two systems.

The Flexible Exchange Rate System

The *LM*, IS_1, and BP_1 set of curves in Part A of Figure 14-6 indicate a surplus. The quantity of foreign currencies received from foreign purchasers of goods, services, and real and financial assets exceeds the amount of foreign currencies needed to make payment for goods, services, and assets purchased from foreign countries during the period. Under the flexible exchange rate system, the foreign exchange value of the economy's currency is not stabilized within a narrow band by the central bank, but is essentially allowed to find its own level in response to the forces of supply and demand in the free market. In the case of a surplus, the excess supply of foreign currencies means that it will take more units of such currencies than before to exchange for a unit of the domestic economy's currency. The foreign exchange value of the domestic economy's currency will rise. This discourages exports and encourages imports. Consequently, both the *BP* and *IS* functions shift to the left, say, from IS_1 and BP_1 to IS_2 and BP_2 in

Part A of Figure 14-6. With these two shifts, the *IS, LM,* and *BP* functions all intersect at Y_2, r_2. At this income level and interest rate there is both internal and external equilibrium.

Part B of Figure 14-6 shows the adjustment in the case of a deficit. In this case, the amount of foreign currencies needed to make payments abroad exceeds the amount received from abroad; in terms of the domestic currency, the prices of foreign currencies are bid up. The foreign exchange value of the domestic currency falls. Accordingly, exports are encouraged and imports are discouraged. The *BP* and *IS* functions both shift rightward from IS_1 and BP_1 to IS_2 and BP_2 in Part B of Figure 14-6. After this, the *IS, LM,* and *BP* functions all intersect at Y_2, r_2. At this income level and interest rate there is both internal and external equilibrium.

Under the flexible exchange rate system, the economy's money supply does not automatically

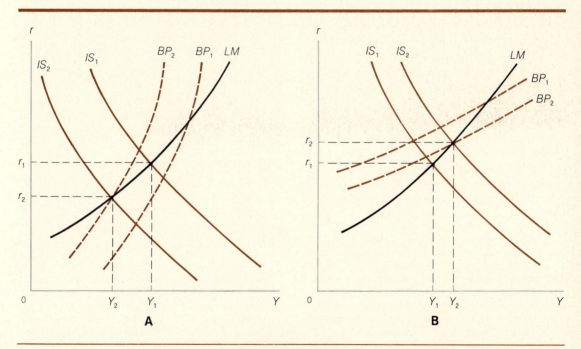

FIGURE 14-6
Balance of Payments Equilibrium under Flexible Exchange Rates

tend to increase if there is a surplus or to decrease if there is a deficit. However, suppose the central bank sought to maintain a fixed exchange rate in the face of a surplus. The central bank would have to put more of its currency into the economy as it bought foreign currencies to prevent the excess of foreign currencies from raising the value of its currency. If it sought to maintain a fixed exchange rate in the face of a deficit, it would have to take the opposite action, which would reduce the amount of its own currency in its economy. Because the central bank does not add to or subtract from its own money supply under the flexible exchange rate system, the LM curve does not automatically tend to shift as a part of the balance of payments adjustment process. The adjustment occurs through shifts in the BP and IS functions.[8]

The Fixed Exchange Rate System

Given the initial set of curves labeled IS_1, LM_1, and BP_1 in Part A of Figure 14-7, there is a balance of payments surplus. The initial Y, r equilibrium is at Y_1, r_1. To prevent a rise in the foreign exchange value of its currency that otherwise will result with a surplus, the central bank must absorb the excess foreign currencies; in the process, it increases the amount of its currency and the nominal money supply held by the public. This shifts the LM curve to the right. If the price level remained stable in the face of the expanding money supply, it would be possible to

eliminate the surplus and achieve equilibrium solely through a shift from LM_1 to LM_3. The LM_3, IS_1, and BP_1 curves all intersect at the Y_3, r_3 combination. However, a significant increase in the price level may result from the increase in demand generated by what can be a sizable expansion of the money supply. The resulting decrease in exports and increase in imports will cause the IS and BP curves to shift leftward from their original positions. With a rise in the price level as a result of a rightward shift in LM, the shift in LM needed to achieve equilibrium is less than the shift from LM_1 to LM_3. In Part A of Figure 14-7, equilibrium is achieved with whatever expansion of the money supply is required to shift from LM_1 to LM_2. This results in that rise in the price level that shifts IS_1 and BP_1 leftward to IS_2 and BP_2.[9] IS_2, LM_2, and BP_2 intersect at Y_2, r_2 and equilibrium is established.

The initial set of curves, IS_1, LM_1, and BP_1, in Part B of Figure 14-7 indicates a deficit. The initial Y, r equilibrium is at Y_1, r_1. With a deficit, the foreign exchange value of the currency will tend to fall. However, to maintain a stable exchange value, the central bank must dip into its holdings of foreign currencies to buy up the excess supply of its own currency being offered in the market. This support policy reduces the amount of its currency or the nominal money supply held by the public. The balance of the argument then parallels that traced for the surplus case. If there were no decrease in the price level in response to the decrease in the money supply, equilibrium could be achieved at Y_3, r_3 by a leftward shift in the LM curve from LM_1 to LM_3. However, with a decline in the price level, there is a smaller leftward shift

---

[8]Under a fully flexible exchange rate system, deficits or surpluses tend to be corrected relatively quickly. Although the adjustment process calls for some shift in the IS curve and therefore some shift in the AD curve, the effects on the domestic price level of the shift in the AD curve will not be so large as to make the price level change play a major part in the adjustment process. Consequently, the LM curve may be assumed to remain in its initial position—an assumption that would not be permissible with a significant change in the price level, because that would change the real money supply and the position of the LM curve.

[9]The greater the effect on the price level of any increase in the nominal money supply, the greater will be the increase in the nominal money supply needed to produce a given rightward shift in the LM curve. The LM curve shifts rightward only if there is an increase in the real money supply. A nominal increase in the money supply will shift the curve in this direction only if it more than offsets the tendency of the rise in the price level it generates to shift the LM curve in the opposite direction.

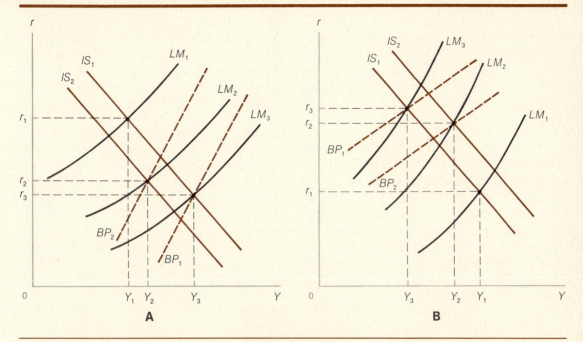

FIGURE 14-7
Balance of Payments Equilibrium under Fixed Exchange Rates

in the *LM* curve and a rightward shift in both the *IS* and *BP* curves. Equilibrium occurs at Y_2, r_2 where IS_2, LM_2, and BP_2 intersect.

Balance of Payments Equilibrium and Full Employment Equilibrium

The combination of Y and r at which the *IS* and *LM* curves intersect has been described as consistent with internal equilibrium, but the level of Y so identified may be at or below full employment. If it is below, there is an equilibrium in the sense that an upward-sloping *AS* curve is intersected by the *AD* curve to the left of the output level at which the *AS* curve becomes perfectly inelastic. That is, the *AS–AD* intersection is below

the full employment level and there is a Keynesian less-than-full employment equilibrium. However, on the classical assumption of downwardly flexible wages and prices, the *AS* curve is a vertical line at the full employment level of output and a level of output below this is not an equilibrium level. In Chapter 13, we examined the process by which a deflation of wages and prices, according to the classical argument, would move the actual output level to the full employment level as the deflation caused rightward shifts in the *IS* and *LM* functions. Here we want to do the same thing for the model that includes a *BP* as well as *IS* and *LM* functions, thereby showing how both full employment equilibrium and balance of payments equilibrium may be achieved. We also saw in Chapter 13 that with the downwardly rigid wages and prices assumed in the Keynesian model, expansionary monetary and fiscal policies are needed to shift the *IS* and *LM* functions rightward to get to the full employment equilibrium. As a second step, here we will explain how monetary and fiscal policies may be used to achieve both full employment equilibrium and balance of payments equilibrium in the model that contains a *BP* as well as *IS* and *LM* functions.

Wage–Price Flexibility and Full Employment

The IS_2, LM_2 and BP_2 curves in Part A of Figure 14-8 all intersect at Y_1, r_2. Therefore, we find both internal and external equilibrium at this income level and interest rate. The initial positions of the curves at IS_2, LM_2, and BP_2 are based on an initial price level of P_2. Because the IS_2 and LM_2 curves in Part A intersect at Y_1, Part B of the figure shows that at the P_2 price level the amount of goods demanded is Y_1—an amount below the full employment output of Y_f. On classical assumptions, the unemployment that exists with actual output at Y_1 leads to falling money wage rates followed by falling prices. In Chapter 13, we found that the fall in the price level would shift the *LM* curve rightward via the real-balance effect and would shift the *IS* curve rightward via the real-balance, foreign trade, and other effects. The foreign trade effect—an increase in exports relative to imports—will also shift the *BP* curve rightward. There is some decrease in the price level, specifically from P_2 to P_1 in the illustration, which shifts each of the three curves to produce a new intersection of the three curves at the Y_f level of output. With a P of P_1, the IS_1 and LM_1 curves show that the amount of output demanded will be Y_f. In other words, there is equilibrium at the full employment level of output.

The decline in the price level stimulates exports and reduces imports, thereby increasing net exports and the level of domestic output and income. However, the rise in income in turn enlarges the amount of imports, which has the opposite effect on domestic output and income. The domestic economy must be importing a

greater real amount of goods at Y_f than at Y_1, given a positive marginal propensity to import; but the illustration indicates that the increase in its exports created by the decline in the price level exceeds the increase in its imports created by the rise in income. This follows from the fact that the new balance of payments equilibrium is at a lower interest rate and therefore has a larger net capital outflow. Given the equation for balance of payments equilibrium, $B = (X - M) - H$, because H has risen with a lower r, $X - M$ has risen by an equal amount. In absolute terms, both X and M have risen with the rise in X exceeding the rise in M by the amount of the rise in H.[10]

The rise from Y_1 to Y_f is due only in part to the rise in $X - M$. In a closed economy, the same decline in the price level would shift the *IS* and *LM* curves rightward and raise the level of output above Y_1. To separate out the amount of the expansion in output due to changes in real domestic and real foreign spending requires that one examine the curves from which the *IS* and *LM* curves are derived.

Monetary–Fiscal Policies and Full Employment

Some of the problems confronted in relying on wage–price deflation as the solution to unemployment were noted in Chapter 13. To Keynes, the problems ruled out deflation as a realistic

---

[10] In one aspect, the adjustment process would be different if we had started with an initial set of curves which, like Parts A and B of Figure 14-5, showed a balance of payments surplus or deficit, instead of the balance of payments equilibrium shown by IS_2, LM_2, and BP_2 in Figure 14-8. However, assuming that the *IS* and *LM* curves were initially as in Figure 14-5, a decrease from P_2 to P_1 would shift the *IS* and *LM* curves to IS_1 and LM_1, as in Figure 14-8. The *AD* curve is determined by the *IS* and *LM* curves, not by the *BP* curve. If there were an initial surplus, a larger decrease in the interest rate than that from r_2 to r_1 in Figure 14-8 would then be required to achieve the full employment equilibrium and balance of payments equilibrium. On the other hand, if there were an initial deficit, a smaller decrease, no change or possibly an increase in the interest rate would be required to achieve the two objectives.

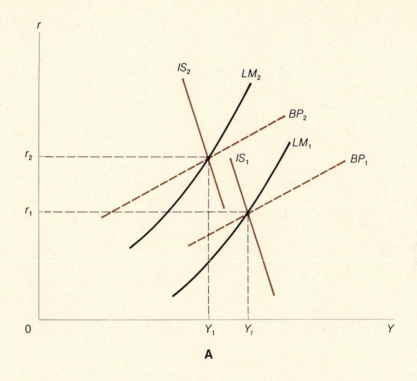

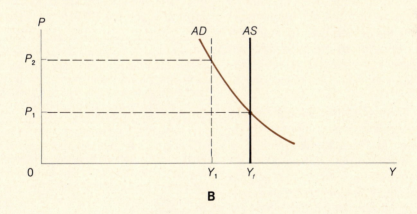

FIGURE 14-8
Balance of Payments and Full Employment Equilibria Through
Wage–Price Flexibility

course of action, even if the wage and price cuts that it calls for could be secured in practice. Consequently, Keynes looked at the economy as it would operate with downwardly rigid wages and prices. In place of the perfectly inelastic AS curve at Y_f in the classical model of Part B of Figure 14-8, there is the upward-sloping AS curve in the Keynesian model of Part B of Figure 14-9.

Part A of Figure 14-9 shows an initial set of curves, IS_1^a, LM_1^a, and BP_1, all of which are consistent with a price level of P_1 in Part B. This set yields neither a full employment equilibrium nor a balance of payments equilibrium. The intersection of the IS_1^a and LM_1^a curves at J indicates that Y_1 of goods are demanded at P_1. This identifies the P_1, Y_1 point on the AD_1 curve in Part B. The AS curve shows that Y_1 of goods are supplied at P_1; therefore, $AD = AS$ at Y_1. There is an internal equilibrium, albeit a less-than-full employment equilibrium. On the external side, there is a disequilibrium, a deficit, because the intersection of IS_1^a and LM_1^a at J occurs below the initial BP function, BP_1.

The full employment level of output identified in Part B is carried up as the Y_f vertical line running through Part A. Now we see that to meet *only* the objective of full employment equilibrium requires that the IS and LM curves intersect anywhere along the Y_f line, but to meet the objective of balance of payments equilibrium requires in addition that the IS, LM, and BP functions all intersect at the same point along the Y_f line.

We saw in Chapter 13 that through expansionary monetary policy (barring either an inconsistency between saving and investment or a liquidity trap) government could presumably shift the LM curve rightward as needed to reach the full employment output, or that through fiscal policy it could presumably shift the IS curve rightward to achieve the same objective. The same may be seen here. Through an appropriate expansion of the nominal money supply, the LM curve may be shifted from LM_1^a to LM_1^b to intersect IS_1^a on the Y_f line at G, thereby achieving full employment output through monetary policy

alone.[11] Similarly, through an appropriate expansion of government expenditures, a cut in tax receipts, or some combination of these measures, the IS curve may be shifted from IS_1^a to IS_1^b to intersect LM_1^a on the Y_f line at F, thereby achieving full employment equilibrium through fiscal policy alone.

Monetary policy may also be used alone to achieve balance of payments equilibrium. A sufficiently restrictive monetary policy will shift the LM curve leftward from LM_1^a to LM_1^c so that LM_1^c and IS_1^a intersect on the BP_1 curve at E.[12] The deficit in the balance of payments that occurs at the original point J has been removed. However, this has only been done by reducing output below the Y_1 level, which was already below the full employment level; consequently, this is not a policy that would likely be adopted. The restrictive monetary policy raises r enough to establish balance of payments equilibrium, but the same rise in r reduces interest-sensitive spending enough to cause the indicated reduction in the output level.[13]

One way to achieve both objectives—full employment equilibrium and balance of payments equilibrium—is through coordinated use of both monetary and fiscal policies. Given the point at which the BP function cuts the Y_f line,

---

[11] Not shown in the figures is the feedback on the IS and BP functions that will result from the higher price level caused by the expansionary monetary policy. In shifting the LM curve to the right, that policy also shifts the AD curve in Part B to the right or up the AS curve to a higher price level. A higher price level will produce leftward shifts in both the IS and BP functions.

[12] Here, too, the figure does not show the feedback on the IS and BP functions. In shifting the LM curve to the left, monetary policy also shifts the AD curve in Part B to the left or down the AS curve to a price level below P_1. A lower price level will produce a rightward shift of both the IS and BP functions.

[13] As Figure 14-9 is drawn, fiscal policy—no matter how restrictive—could not by itself bring about equilibrium in the balance of payments. It would not be so used in any event, but it will be seen that fiscal policy alone could achieve balance of payments equilibrium only if the LM curve were to cut the BP curve from below, somewhere to the left of the IS curve.

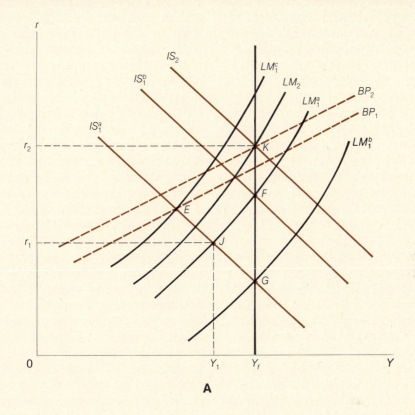

A

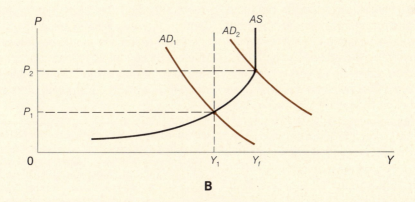

B

FIGURE 14-9
Balance of Payments and Full Employment Equilibria Through
Monetary–Fiscal Policies

the dual objective calls for both a higher interest rate and level of income. Expansionary fiscal policy may be relied on to raise the income level, but the higher income level it produces will reduce the net export balance and enlarge the existing deficit in the balance of payments. This larger deficit will be offset somewhat as the expansionary fiscal policy also forces up the interest rate and reduces the net capital outflow. However, a deficit will remain. Elimination of the deficit requires a monetary policy sufficiently restrictive to raise the interest rate to the level at which the net capital outflow and the net export balance that occur at the full employment income level are equal.

In Figure 14-9, fiscal policy must be sufficiently expansionary to shift IS from IS_1^a to IS_2 and monetary policy must be sufficiently contractionary to shift LM from LM_1^a to LM_2. These shifts cause a shift from AD_1 to AD_2 in Part B and a rise in the price level from P_1 to P_2.[14] The IS_2 and LM_2 curves are understood to be those consistent with the new equilibrium price level of P_2. The BP_2 curve is consistent with the new equilibrium price level. The higher price level produces a leftward or upward shift of the BP function by reducing exports and increasing imports and tends to increase the size of the deficit. To achieve the dual objectives, fiscal policy must be more expansionary and monetary policy must be more contractionary than would be required in the absence of a rise in the price level. The end product is the balance of payments equilibrium and the full employment equilibrium given by the intersection of IS_2, LM_2, and BP_2 on the Y_f line at K. Output has risen from Y_1 to Y_f, the interest rate from r_1 to r_2, and the price level from P_1 to P_2.[15]

Figure 14-9 merely traces the mechanics of the process by which an appropriate mix of monetary and fiscal policies may achieve the dual objectives of a full employment internal equilibrium and an external equilibrium. In practice, the process is anything but mechanical. There are limitations on the efficacy of monetary and fiscal policies as instruments for achieving full employment in a closed economy. Moreover, there are further limitations on the efficacy of monetary and fiscal policies in an open economy as instruments to achieve the dual objectives of full employment and external equilibrium.

Basically, the policy approach in a balance of payments deficit situation relies on a rise in the interest rate obtained by restrictive monetary policy to meet the external objective. It relies on an expansion of aggregate demand by fiscal policy to meet the internal objective. Although both objectives may be attained, the fact that a rise in the interest rate is required to do so introduces other problems. For example, in the judgment of many economists, the mix of output will be altered in an unfavorable direction. A problem encountered repeatedly during the post–World War II period has been the severely depressing effect of a rise in interest rates on construction, especially residential construction. Other investment spending has also been curtailed. Fiscal policy may succeed in expanding output, but because of the rise in interest rates, too little of the additional output may be in capital goods or the kind of goods that increase the economy's long-run capacity to produce. Too much of the

---

[14] Remember that there must be a rise in the price level to reach full employment in this model. With a fixed money wage rate, the only way to get the reduction in the real wage rate at which firms will hire the unemployed labor is through a higher price level.

[15] Although this topic is not covered in this book, the present analysis offers a clear-cut application of an impor-

tant principle in the theory of economic policy: The number of policy instruments must be equal to the number of policy goals or objectives. Here the two objectives of full employment output and balance of payments equilibrium could not be achieved with the fiscal policy instrument alone or with the monetary policy instrument alone, but they could be achieved with the two instruments together. The seminal work in the theory of economic policy was done by J. Tinbergen. See his *On the Theory of Economic Policy*, North-Holland, 1952, and *Economic Policy: Principles and Design*, North-Holland, 1956. See also L. Johansen, *Public Economics*, Rand-McNally, 1965.

additional output may be in public projects with little value beyond the fact that they provide jobs—however important that may be. If they are to devise monetary and fiscal policies that will achieve the most desirable results, economists must continue to seek ways to offset consequences such as the one here noted that follows from these policies. For example, one technique tried back in 1961–62 came to be called "operation twist." The Federal Reserve sought to twist the interest rate structure to secure higher short-term interest rates that would induce an inflow of short-term capital from abroad and reduce an existing balance of payments deficit. At the same time, it sought to secure lower long-term interest rates that would induce construction and other investment spending to alleviate the recessionary or near-recessionary conditions at home.

Beyond a specific problem like this is a whole range of more general problems faced in the use of monetary–fiscal policies: for example, the difference in the time lags between the date at which monetary and fiscal actions are taken and their impact is felt and variations in the length of these lags from one case to another; the lack of knowledge of what is the proper degree of monetary or fiscal stimulus or restraint in any situation, with the danger of overshooting on the expansion side to bring on inflation or overshooting on the contraction side to bring on recession; the delays faced in getting Congress to act on whatever fiscal actions economists think best under the circumstances; and so forth. Some problems of this kind are covered briefly in the last two chapters of the book.

As long as we recognize that the application of monetary–fiscal policies faces many difficult problems to which there are anything but perfect solutions, we are not likely to be misled by the simple mechanics of this section and to read into the analysis of the kind presented here more than is in it. However, the analysis here presented is surely informative and in general indicative of certain basic relationships, the understanding of which enables us to take our first steps in the macroeconomics of the international economy.

The Extended Income Determination Model: A Concluding Note

This chapter concludes the analysis we began in Chapter 4. Although any number of related questions have been introduced along the way—for example, in this chapter the question of simultaneous equilibrium in the balance of payments and the level of output—our basic question has been what determines the economy's real income or output of goods and services and what determines the price level of that output. As we have seen, the question of what determines the economy's output is closely related to the question of what determines the level of employment. The further question of what explains the long-run rate of output growth will be discussed in Part 5.

Clearly, the answer to the basic question of short-run output and price level determination is not so simple that we can now pack it into a summary formulation that is at once neat, brief, and comprehensive. Because our detailed analysis has repeatedly relied on simplifying assumptions, any summary formulation necessarily compounds the simplifications. Recognizing this limitation, Figure 14-10 offers one summary formulation of the theory developed over the preceding chapters. This figure provides an informal flow-type presentation of the basic structure of the theory and resorts to neither equations nor curves. Figure 14-11 offers a more formal approach that condenses in one integrated fourteen-part figure the complete diagrammatic apparatus constructed in the course of developing the theory. We will look at these two figures in turn.

A Flow-Type Summary Formulation

Our major objective is to explain the output level and the price level; therefore, Figure 14-10 focuses on these two variables: Y and P. As

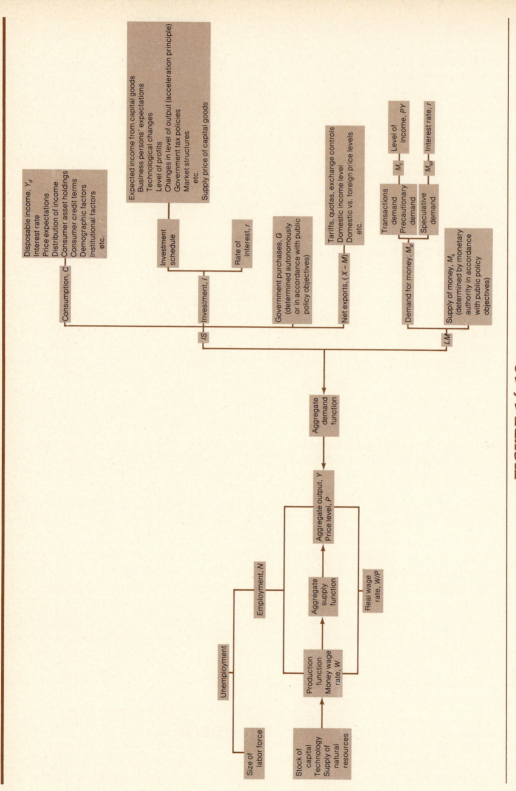

FIGURE 14-10

A Flow-Type Summary Formulation

indicated by arrows, all of the flows point to these two variables. The immediate determinants of the output level and the price level are the aggregate supply and aggregate demand functions. In the basic classical theory, the level of output is determined entirely on the supply (left) side of Figure 14-10. That level of output is the level which can be produced by a fully employed labor force. The amount of output that can be produced by this number of workers, given their education, training, and skills, depends on the economy's capital stock, technology, and supply of natural resources—all of which are fixed in the short run. In the classical case, aggregate demand merely determines the price level at which the full employment level of output will sell in the market. In Keynesian theory, beyond its simplest version, aggregate demand affects the price level as well as the output level; if aggregate demand is not adequate, the amount of output produced will be below the amount that provides full employment for the labor force. It is in the Keynesian case that the portion of Figure 14-10 showing unemployment, a difference between the size of the labor force and the number employed, becomes relevant.

In this and other ways, Figure 14-10 has been constructed to fit the Keynesian theory. It shows the following:

$$\left.\begin{matrix} \text{Aggregate} \\ \text{supply} \\ \text{function} \end{matrix}\right\} \begin{matrix} \text{Aggregate output, } Y \\ \text{Price level, } P \end{matrix} \left\{\begin{matrix} \text{Aggregate} \\ \text{demand} \\ \text{function} \end{matrix}\right.$$

Here Y and P are simultaneously determined by the aggregate supply and demand functions. To correspond with the simple classical theory, it would be more accurate to present this part as follows:

$$\left.\begin{matrix} \text{Aggregate} \\ \text{supply} \\ \text{function} \end{matrix}\right\} \begin{matrix} \text{Aggregate output, } Y \\ \text{Price level, } P \end{matrix} \left\{\begin{matrix} \text{Aggregate} \\ \text{demand} \\ \text{function} \end{matrix}\right.$$

In classical theory, Y, the output produced at full employment, is determined on the supply side,

and P, the price level at which the full employment output sells, is determined on the demand side.

In terms of Figure 14-10, the difference between the two theories becomes more striking when we consider the determinants of aggregate demand. In the simple classical theory, almost everything that now lies to the right of the Aggregate demand function disappears; all that remains is the part which shows

Demand for money, M_d
Supply of money, M_s

and some of the items under these headings. Beyond this, in the classical theory, changes in aggregate demand result from changes in the supply of money rather than the demand for money. Accepting the demand for money of the classical theory, we have $M_{sp} = 0$ or $M_d = M_t$ and therefore $M_d = k \cdot PY$. To accept that theory is also to accept k as a constant. In equilibrium, $M_s = M_d$ or $M_s = k \cdot PY$. With k constant, PY varies proportionally with M_s. The aggregate demand side reduces to the one variable, the supply of money, which in conjunction with the constant k establishes the aggregate demand function.

In contrast, for the extended Keynesian model developed in the last few chapters, everything to the right of the Aggregate demand function is needed to explain aggregate demand. We have seen in these chapters that shifts in the aggregate demand function occur with shifts in either the IS function, LM function, or both. We have explained the changes in aggregate demand through the various factors that cause shifts in these two functions. Although it could not there be expressed in these terms, the shifts in aggregate demand that were considered in the simple Keynesian model of Part 2 were shifts explained solely in terms of the factors that lie behind the IS function. The supply of and demand for money that lie behind the LM function were no part of the simple Keynesian model.

Although the interest rate affects I and perhaps also C (as shown by the inclusion of the

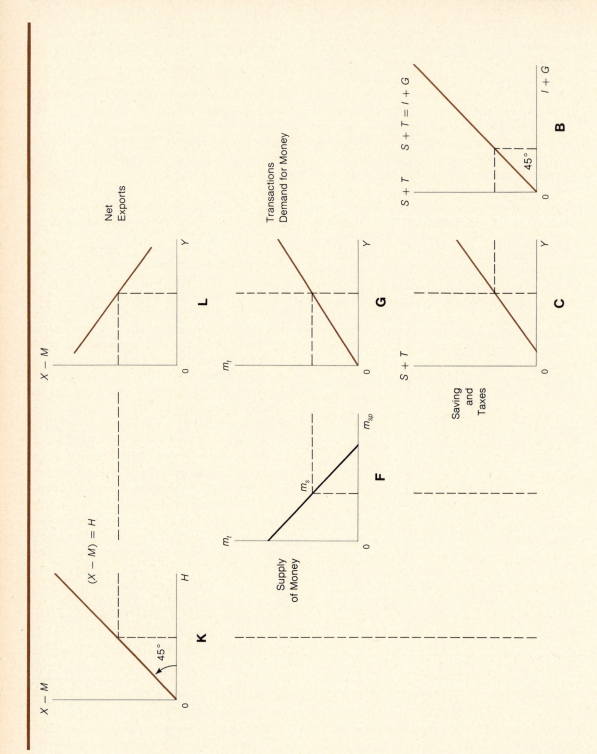

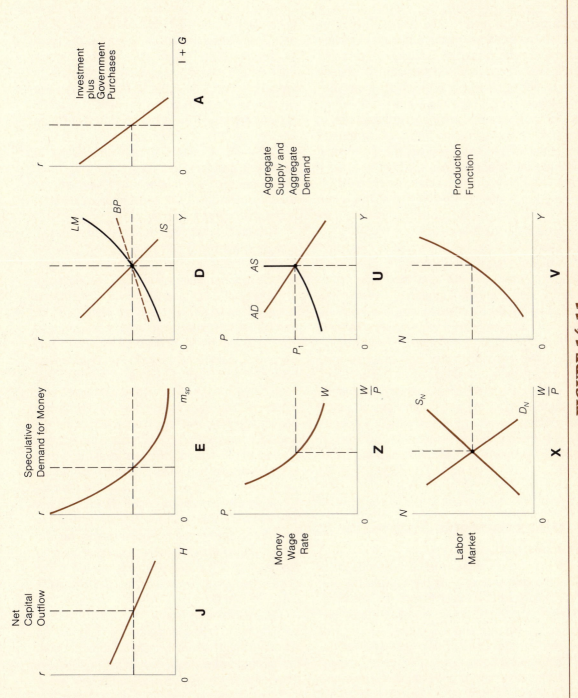

FIGURE 14-11

The Complete Extended Model—A Graphic Formulation

interest rate among the determinants of both of these spending streams), the interest rate was assumed to be given in the simple Keynesian model. The extended model summarized in Figure 14-10 incorporates the supply of and demand for money. These in turn determine the interest rate, which is no longer a given but a variable that affects I and C. The interest rate itself in turn is affected by other determinants of these spending streams and also of the G and $X - M$ spending streams, because changes in any of these determinants affect total spending, which affects the level of income, which affects the demand for money, which affects the interest rate. This is the kind of interaction noted repeatedly in the $IS–LM$ analysis of the last few chapters.

Even though we limit ourselves to the determinants specifically listed under the IS and LM headings, our list is still fairly long. The "etc." inserted here and there suggest that it is anything but complete. A rise or fall in the price levels of other countries, technological advances, changes in the distribution of income, money supply, speculative demand for money or consumer asset holdings, expectations of a rising or falling price level, and many other such developments produce shifts in the aggregate demand function. With a given aggregate supply function, shifts in the aggregate demand function cause changes in output, employment, and the price level.

A Diagrammatic Summary Formulation

As in the version above, the centerpieces here are the output level and the price level—the primary variables that we seek to explain. These are determined in Part U of Figure 14-11 by the intersection of the AD and AS curves, which are derived from the curves in the other thirteen parts of the complete figure.

A first step toward understanding what initially looks like a formidable diagram is to break it down into its component parts, which are individually familiar from earlier work. The IS curve in Part D of Figure 14-11 is built from Parts A, B, and C (as it was in Parts A, B, and C of Figure 12-11, page 252). The LM curve in Part D is built from Parts E, F, and G (which correspond to Parts A, B, and C of Figure 12-4, page 241). The BP curve in Part D is built from Parts J, K, and L (which correspond to Parts A, B, and C of Figure 14-3, page 291). The AS curve in Part U is built from Parts V, X, and Z (which correspond to Parts A, B, and C of Figure 8-4, page 136). Thus, twelve parts of the fourteen-part diagram are used to obtain the IS, LM, and BP curves in Part D and the AS curve in Part U.

Remember that there are sets of the IS, LM, and BP curves in which each curve in any set identifies the position of that curve which corresponds to a particular price level. The positions of the single IS, LM, and BP curves in Part D are assumed to result from a price level of P_1 in Part U. For any other price level, each of these curves would be in a different position. Also remember that the AD curve in Part U is derived from intersections of IS and LM curves and that each curve in each set of IS and LM curves corresponds to a different price level. Finally, having derived the AD curve, the intersection of the AD and AS curves in Part U establishes the equilibrium output level and the price level—and provides the answer to the basic question with which we started. It need not be this way, but the particular equilibrium level of output shown in Figure 14-11 is consistent with full employment of the labor force. It also need not be this way, but the curves are so drawn that there is equilibrium in the balance of payments—that is, the BP curve passes through the intersection of the IS and LM curves in Part D.

As was done in Figure 14-10, this figure is constructed to fit Keynesian theory. Instead of an AS curve that is perfectly inelastic throughout at the full employment level of output as in classical theory, the AS curve here has a range over which it slopes upward to the right. Consequently, any leftward shift of the *AD* curve from this position would not only reduce the price level (as in classical theory), but would reduce the output level and, with it, the employment level.

Now that we understand how the complete model is derived and recognize the fact that it incorporates Keynesian rather than classical assumptions (and therefore yields Keynesian rather than classical conclusions), we can introduce various changes into the model and trace their effects on the output level and the price level in Part U. A few of the changes that will shift the *AD* curve to the left and thereby lower the output and price levels are a decrease in the money supply (inward shift of the curve in Part F), a decrease in investment demand (inward shift of the *I* plus *G* curve in Part A), and an increase in the demand for idle money balances (outward shift of the curve in Part E). A few of the changes that will shift the *AS* curve to the right and thereby both raise the output level and lower the price level are technological advances (outward shift of the curve in Part V), increase in the supply of labor (upward or leftward shift of the S_N curve in Part X), and, however unlikely this may be, a decrease in the money wage rate (downward shift of the *W* curve in Part Z). As suggested by standard supply and demand analysis, a combination of changes that produce such shifts in the *AD* and *AS* curves leads to a lower price level but a higher, lower, or unchanged output level depending on the relative strength of the changes on the two sides.[16] Various other changes may

be inserted into the diagram and the effect of each may be traced on the *AS* or *AD* curves and thereby on the equilibrium output level and price level.

Although Figures 14-10 and 14-11 (and other possible presentations of this kind) are highly valuable in tracing changes in particular variables through to their effects on the output and price variables, these figures serve only as points of departure; they do not begin to suggest the complex interrelationships among all the variables identified in Figure 14-10 or the smaller number of variables incorporated in the diagrams of Figure 14-11. The inclusion of these interrelationships in Figure 14-10 would result in a bewildering maze of arrows crisscrossing in all directions. Their inclusion in Figure 14-11 would rule out the kind of integrated system of diagrams that is possible only because it simplifies to the degree needed for this purpose. Furthermore, the relationships among variables are dynamic; to understand the way successive changes occur, the time sequence in which they occur must be considered. The present figures stop short of this. Nonetheless, they are most helpful in tying together the broad dimensions of the theoretical structure developed in the preceding few chapters.

---

[16] Any changes that cause shifts in the curves in Parts A, C, E, F, or G—some examples of which were here noted—directly affect the position of the *IS* and *LM* curves in Part D and thereby affect the position of the *AD* curve in Part U. However, any changes that cause shifts in the curves in Parts J and L directly affect the position of the *BP* curve in Part D and only indirectly affect the position of the *IS*

and *LM* curves and thereby affect the position of the *AD* curve that is determined by them. As discussed earlier in this chapter, depending on whether there is a deficit or surplus in the balance of payments and whether there is a system of fixed or flexible exchange rates, the adjustment to a disequilibrium in the balance of payments includes a shift not only in the *BP* curve but also in the *IS* or *LM* curves. Therefore, shifts of the curves in Parts J and L indirectly lead to shifts in the *AD* curve. In the simpler model that limits the foreign sector to only imports and exports, there is a direct effect on the *IS* curve, as shown in Figure 14-1. This simpler model is part of Figure 14-10, in which net exports are one of the determinants of the *IS* curve.

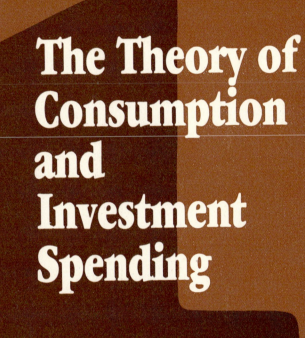

The Theory of Consumption and Investment Spending

The Income Level and Consumption Spending: Four Hypotheses

OVERVIEW

The relationship between income and consumption was introduced in Chapter 4, but developed no further than was necessary to present the simple Keynesian theory of income determination. This chapter will examine this very important relationship much more closely, including the body of theory that it has called forth and some of the empirical data bearing on it.

There are four major hypotheses concerning the ways income influences consumer spending: the *absolute income, relative income, permanent income,* and the *life-cycle* hypotheses. The first half of the chapter approaches these four hypotheses in terms of the theory of individual consumer or micro behavior that underlies each. For testing purposes, the data relevant to this approach are cross-sectional; they show how spending varies at different levels of family income in any one time period. The second half of the chapter approaches the same four hypotheses in their generalized, aggregative, or macro form; this form attempts to explain how aggregate consumption varies with the aggregate income of all consumers. The data relevant here are time series data; they show the magnitude of these two aggregates for the economy as a whole on a period-to-period basis. In line with this separation, the first part of the chapter is labeled Consumer Behavior: Microanalysis and the second part Consumer Behavior: Macroanalysis.

Throughout the chapter, a basic question unifies the overall analysis: Does aggregate consumption vary proportionally or less than proportionally with changes in consumer income? All the rival hypotheses do not give the same answer to this question. Students may find it helpful to use this particular question as a reference point as they work through the analysis of the hypotheses. As emphasized in the concluding note to the chapter, the answer to this question of proportionality or nonproportionality has substantial bearing on the question of the long-run health of the economy. Clearly, the question is of more than academic interest.

In developing the simple Keynesian model of income determination in Part 2, we worked with a consumption function in which the MPC was constant, positive, and less than 1—and in which the APC exceeded the MPC at all levels of income. Although we suggested that such a relationship between consumption and income seemed plausible, no real evidence was submitted in its support; the relationship was simply derived from a particular theory of consumer behavior (described briefly in Chapter 4). The major tenets of this theory are that consumers devote a fraction of any increase in income to saving and that they save a larger fraction of a higher income than of a lower income. This specific theory of consumer spending, apart from some simplifications of a noncritical nature, is essentially that advanced by Keynes in his *General Theory*.

As elaborated by others, Keynes' theory has become known as the *absolute income hypothesis*. Rival hypotheses have also been developed—the *relative income, permanent income,* and *life-cycle* hypotheses. Each of these four hypotheses involves a quite specific but different view of consumer behavior—that is, each assigns a different role to income as an influence on consumer spending.

The economists who have constructed these hypotheses have all begun with individual consumer behavior and then generalized to cover aggregate behavior. Here we discuss the four hypotheses in turn, first from the perspective of individual consumer behavior or microanalysis, and then from the perspective of aggregate consumer behavior or macroanalysis.

Consumer Behavior: Microanalysis

At the micro level, the relevant data are those that show how much of the individual family's income is devoted to consumption and saving for samples of families at various income levels. Table 15-1 shows such data from a survey of family expenditures by income class for 1972–73. Column 1 gives the average disposable income for samples of families in various income classes; column 2 gives the average consumption expenditures of those families. Individual families in any income class, of course, will have disposable income and consumption expenditures above and below the averages shown for that class. But it is the average and not the individual variations to which we must look to discern whatever pattern exists.

Column 3 was derived by dividing the dollar amounts in column 2 by the dollar amounts in column 1. The values in column 3 may be related to our earlier concept of the average propensity to consume, if we recognize, however, that these values relate to different levels of family income rather than different levels of aggregate income. The values in column 3 show that as we move from lower to higher family incomes, the percentage of income devoted to consumption expenditures, the *apc*, decreases. (To differentiate the family from the aggregate average propensity to consume, *apc* is used for the family and, as before, APC for the aggregate.) Column 4 was also derived from the dollar amounts in columns 1 and 2. Here the change in consumption between each pair of disposable income figures is divided by the change in income between that pair of disposable income figures. Again, recognizing that the values relate to different levels of family rather than aggregate income, we may relate the values in column 4 to our earlier concept of the marginal propensity to consume. These values show that as we move from lower to higher income classes, consumption expenditures increase—but by less than the increase in income. With minor variations, other family budget studies made at different times reflect the same properties: The *apc* decreases with higher levels of family income, and the *mpc* (here using *mpc* for the family marginal propensity to consume) is positive, but less than 1.

The data in columns 1 and 2 of Table 15-1 have been plotted in Figure 15-1. The dots for these data have been connected by a smooth

TABLE 15-1
Family Consumption Expenditures by Size of Family Income, 1972–73

(1) Average Disposable Income	(2) Average Consumption Expenditures	(3) *apc*	(4) *mpc*
$ 1,636	$ 3,039	1.86	—
3,347	4,000	1.20	0.56
4,252	4,531	1.07	0.59
5,084	5,100	1.00	0.68
5,928	5,725	0.97	0.74
6,715	6,148	0.92	0.54
7,911	6,921	0.87	0.65
9,491	7,889	0.83	0.61
11,485	8,890	0.77	0.50
14,541	10,639	0.73	0.57
18,370	12,591	0.69	0.51
30,461	16,738	0.55	0.34

Note: The figures for disposable income and consumption expenditures are averages for all families and single consumers in before-tax income classes. The figures are also annual averages for two years, 1972 and 1973. Consumption expenditures do not include expenditures for personal insurance, gifts, and contributions.

SOURCE: Consumer Expenditure Survey Series: *Interview Survey, 1972–73, Report 455–4*, pp. 4–7, U.S. Department of Labor, Bureau of Labor Statistics, 1977.

line that may be called a *family consumption function.* The familiar 45° line has been inserted as a guide.

Because the family consumption function crosses the 45° line at a family income level in the neighborhood of $5,000, we may deduce that in 1972–73 a family income level of about this amount represented the break-even income—the income level at which consumption equaled income, so that there was neither family saving nor family dissaving. At successively lower family income levels, the average family had increasing dissaving. Conversely, at successively higher family income levels, the average family had increasing saving. Apart from some curvature of the family consumption function of Figure 15-1—which indicates that the *mpc* was not constant—there is a general similarity between the position

and shape of this function and of those in Part 2. They reflect the same properties: decreasing dissaving as we move from very low income to the break-even income, then increasing saving as we move up to higher income.

Having demonstrated that, apart from some curvature, the properties of the empirically derived family consumption function are the same as those of the aggregate consumption function earlier assumed, we might be tempted to conclude that the earlier aggregate consumption function is a reasonably accurate description of how expenditures actually do vary as the level of aggregate income varies. This simple conclusion is ruled out, however, when we remember that we are talking about two completely different types of consumption function. One shows how families at different income levels divide their respective

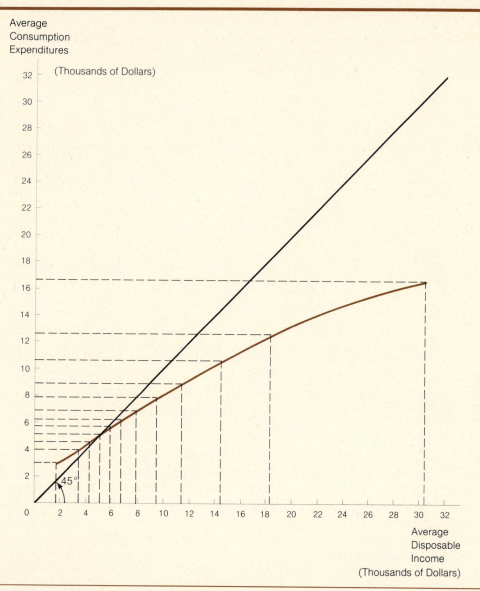

Average
Consumption
Expenditures

(Thousands of Dollars)

Average
Disposable
Income
(Thousands of Dollars)

FIGURE 15-1
Family Consumption Function, 1972–73

incomes between consumption and saving. The other shows how all families combined would divide different *alternative* levels of aggregate income between consumption and saving. Whether or not conclusions drawn from cross-sectional studies of *family* income differences apply to *aggregate* income differences can only be decided after examining individual consumer behavior and the various hypotheses of consumer spending.

The Absolute Income Hypothesis

The basic tenet of the absolute income hypothesis is that the individual consumer determines the fraction of current income he will devote to consumption on the basis of the *absolute* level of that income. All else being equal, a rise in absolute income will lead to a decrease in the fraction of that income devoted to consumption. As we have noted, the first statement of this hypothesis is probably that made by Keynes in the *General Theory*. Its subsequent development is primarily associated with James Tobin and Arthur Smithies.[1]

For a simple illustration, assume that we were able to ascertain the average consumption expenditures of all families at three different income levels, specifically $4,000, $8,000, and $12,000, for a given year. We would expect these average consumption figures when plotted to show up as points like D, E, and F on curve C in Figure 15-2. (Disregard the curve labeled C'.) Such a pattern for the three points is clearly what cross-sectional data from actual budget studies typically show. Suppose next that all families at these income levels—as well as all families at all other income levels—somehow double their income between this initial year and a subsequent year. Assuming no other changes, how do families at each income level, on the average, divide their doubled incomes between consumption and saving? The behavioral hypothesis that underlies the absolute income hypothesis suggests that families would, on the average, divide their now doubled incomes in the same way as did the average family that previously occupied that income position. This would mean that the three families would move along the family consumption function in Figure 15-2 from D to E, from E to G, and from F to H, respectively. Families at

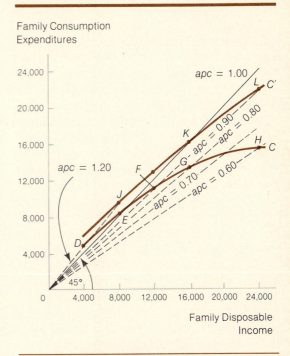

Family Consumption Expenditures

FIGURE 15-2
Family Consumption Function: Absolute and Relative Income

other income levels would move along the function in a similar manner. Because the absolute level of the family's income is held to control the division of income between consumption and saving, this hypothesis predicts a decline in the average propensity to consume of the average family when families move up to a higher income level.[2]

---

[1]See J. Tobin, "Relative Income, Absolute Income, and Saving," in *Money, Trade, and Economic Growth,* Macmillan, 1951, pp. 135–56, and A. Smithies, "Forecasting Postwar Demand: I," in *Econometrica,* Jan. 1945, pp. 1–14.

[2]Therefore, the $4,000 family whose *apc* was 1.2 (or $4,800/$4,000) now becomes an $8,000 family whose *apc* is 1.0 (or $8,000/$8,000). The $8,000 family whose *apc* was 1.0 ($8,000/$8,000) now becomes a $16,000 family whose *apc* is 0.8 (or $12,800/$16,000). And the $12,000 family whose *apc* was 0.9 (or $10,800/$12,000) now becomes a $24,000 family whose *apc* is 0.6 (or $14,400/$24,000).

If consumers do, in fact, respond this way to changes in income, it follows that, of the aggregate income received by all consumers, the fraction spent decreases as the aggregate income increases. This relationship between aggregate income and aggregate consumption is one of the properties of the aggregate consumption function we employed in Chapter 4. Because that function was drawn to correspond with Keynes' hypothesis of consumer behavior, that hypothesis was essentially what later came to be called the absolute income hypothesis.

The absolute income hypothesis of individual consumer behavior seems plausible. A noneconomist would probably accept it without hesitation. Presented with the question before us, he would probably say that high-income families save a larger fraction of their incomes than low-income families because they obviously have a relatively large fraction of their incomes left after meeting consumption needs, whereas low-income families find that consumption needs absorb or even exceed their total incomes. It would be equally obvious to the noneconomist that as families move up the income scale, they can save a larger fraction of their income at each higher income level. In the first years following the appearance of the *General Theory,* economists also generally accepted the absolute income hypothesis. But this widespread acceptance was short-lived. Practically all economists today lean toward one of the other hypotheses. Some reasons for this will become apparent as we continue.

The Relative Income Hypothesis

The relative income hypothesis argues that the fraction of a family's income devoted to consumption depends on the level of its income *relative* to the income of other families with which it identifies rather than on the *absolute* level of its income.[3] If a family's income rises but its *relative*

position on the income scale remains unchanged because the incomes of other families with whom it identifies have risen at the same rate, its division of income between consumption and saving will remain unchanged. The family's absolute income has risen, so its absolute consumption and saving will also rise, but the *fraction* of income devoted to consumption will be the same as it was at the lower level. On the other hand, if a family's income remains unchanged but the incomes of these other families rise, its income position relative to that of the other families has then changed. According to the relative income hypothesis, the deterioration in the relative position of this family would lead to a rise in the fraction of its income devoted to consumption, despite the fact that there has been no change in its absolute income.

In its focus on relative income, this hypothesis emphasizes the imitative or emulative nature of consumption. A family with any given level of income will typically spend more on consumption if it lives in a community in which that income is relatively low than if it lives in a community in which that income is relatively high. This tendency arises in part from the pressures on the family to "keep up with the Joneses" and in part from the fact that as the family observes what seem to be the superior goods of other families it will be tempted to spend as a result of what James S. Duesenberry calls the "demonstration" effect. Studies have shown that black families with an income of, say, $15,000 will, on the average, spend less than white families with an equal income, because the black family will probably live in a neighborhood in which $15,000 is a relatively high income, whereas the white family will probably live in a neighborhood in which this income is farther down the scale of incomes.

[3] See J.S. Duesenberry, *Income, Saving, and the Theory of Consumer Behavior,* Harvard Univ. Press, 1949. See also D.S. Brady and R. Friedman, "Savings and the Income Distribution," in *Studies in Income and Wealth,* Vol. 10, National Bureau of Economic Research, Princeton Univ. Press, 1947, pp. 247–65, and F. Modigliani, "Fluctuations in the Saving-Income Ratio: A Problem in Economic Forecasting," in the same series, Vol. 11, 1949, pp. 371–443.

If families behave as suggested by the relative income hypothesis, the division of their income between spending and saving will clearly be different from the division suggested by the absolute income hypothesis. This basic difference may be seen by turning back to Figure 15-2. Assume as before that the absolute income of all families doubles between an initial year and a subsequent year. There is then no change in the distribution of income. The top 1 percent of all families gets the same percentage of the aggregate income in both years, the bottom 1 percent gets the same percentage in both years, and similarly for every other percentile. Therefore, despite the doubling of each family's income, its relative position on the income scale is the same as it was before. The relative income hypothesis then argues that there would be no reason, on the basis of the income change alone, to expect a change in the fraction of income consumed by the average family.

Accordingly, each family would not move upward along the function labeled C, as suggested by the absolute income theory, because such a movement indicates a decrease in the ratio of income spent by each family. The relative income hypothesis argues instead that each family moves in such a way as to create the new consumption function labeled C'. That is, the $4,000 family would move from D to J; the $8,000 family would move from E to K; and the $12,000 family would move from F to L. If the average family at each income level responded to this doubling of income as indicated by the relative income hypothesis, its apc would be the same before and after the doubling of its income. Each family is on the same apc curve (depicted in Figure 15-2 by broken straight lines drawn from the origin) that it was on before the rise in its income.[4]

According to the relative income hypothesis, each family, in deciding on the fraction of its income to be spent, is uninfluenced by the fact that it is twice as well off in *absolute* terms and is influenced only by the fact that it is no better off in *relative* terms. Being no better off in this sense, its decision is to "live" as it did previously, devoting the same fraction of its income to consumption as before.

Like the absolute income hypothesis above and the other hypotheses to be discussed later, the relative income hypothesis relates consumer spending to income on the assumption that no change occurs in any of the other factors influencing consumption. Under this assumption, the relative income hypothesis shows that the family consumption function shifts upward in proportion with changes in aggregate income received by all families. This result, therefore, turns out to be inconsistent with the result indicated by the absolute income theory. If relative income controls the fraction of income spent by the family, an equal percentage change in the incomes of all families will produce no change in the fraction of that enlarged aggregate income that is devoted to consumption. On the other hand, if absolute income controls it, the fraction of aggregate income consumed declines as aggregate income increases. The results reached by the absolute and relative income theories will be compared further in the time series analysis later in this chapter.

The Permanent Income Hypothesis

Both the absolute and relative income hypotheses focus on the individual family's "current" income as the income concept relevant to its spending. What is the meaning of current income in this context? Is the family's current income its measured income for a week, a month, a year, two years? Does the family adjust its consumption upward or downward from one week or month to the next in the face of a rise or fall in its measured income? A family's weekly spending is not closely

---

[4]The $4,000 family whose apc was 1.2 (or $4,800/$4,000) is now an $8,000 family whose apc is still 1.2 (or $9,600/$8,000). The $8,000 family whose apc was 1.0 (or $8,000/$8,000) is now a $16,000 family whose apc is still 1.0 (or $16,000/$16,000). And the $12,000 family whose apc was 0.9 (or $10,800/$12,000) is now a $24,000 family whose apc is still 0.9 (or $21,600/$24,000).

related to its measured income during that specific week; its consumption would not be drastically affected in any one week, even if its measured income for that week should be zero. The same is true to a lesser degree for a time span of one month. Where is the line to be drawn? Most studies that take current income as the appropriate income concept use the current year, or sometimes the current and the preceding year, as the relevant time span.

A quite different approach to the role of income in the theory of consumer spending has been developed by others, including Milton Friedman. Friedman's point of departure is the rejection of the usual concept of "current" income and its replacement with "permanent" income.[5] A family's permanent income in any one year is in no sense indicated by its current income for that year, but is determined by the expected or anticipated income to be received over a long period of time, stretching out over a number of future years. In Friedman's words, permanent income "is to be interpreted as the mean income regarded as permanent by the consumer unit in question, which in turn depends on its horizon and farsightedness."[6]

More technically, each consumer arrives at an approximation of his or her permanent income on the basis of his or her total wealth, human and nonhuman. Each person makes a smaller or larger investment in human wealth by acquiring training or skills of various kinds. Such investments vary from the relatively small investment by the person who trains to be a waiter to the relatively large investment by the person who trains to be a surgeon. From this point of view, the wealth embodied in a waiter is a small fraction of that embodied in a surgeon. Correspondingly, the permanent income that the waiter can expect to derive from his human wealth is a small fraction of that which the surgeon can expect. For some people, the wages and salaries from human cap-

ital make up almost all of their income; for some others there is rental, interest, and dividend income derived from nonhuman wealth in the form of real property and financial assets. Each person looks ahead as best he or she can and derives estimates of the streams of income to be received from human and nonhuman capital. The sum of the present discounted values of these two streams of income constitutes the person's current wealth.[7] Finally, the figure for his or her permanent income for the current year is equal to that wealth figure multiplied by a rate of interest. From one year to the next, a person's permanent income will change in response to changes in his "horizon and farsightedness" and his evaluation of the future flows from human and nonhuman capital.

Given this meaning of permanent income, a family's measured or observed income in any particular year may be larger or smaller than its permanent income. Friedman divides the family's measured yearly income into permanent and transitory components, so that its measured income is larger or smaller than its permanent income, depending on the sum of positive and negative transitory income components. For example, if a family wage earner receives an unexpected special bonus at work in one year and has no reason to expect the same bonus in following years, this income element is regarded as positive transitory income; it raises measured income above permanent income. On the other hand, if this person suffers an unexpected loss of income—due, say, to a plant shutdown as a result of fire—this income element is regarded as negative transitory income; it reduces measured income below permanent income. These unforeseen additions to and subtractions from a family's income usually cancel out over the longer period, but they are present in any shorter period.

In the same way, Friedman divides measured consumption into permanent and transitory com-

[5]See M. Friedman, *A Theory of the Consumption Function,* Princeton Univ. Press, 1957.

[6]*Ibid.*, p. 93.

[7]The concept of the present value of an income stream is explained on p. 241. See also pp. 368–70.

ponents.[8] A good purchased because of an attractive sale price or a normal purchase deferred due to unavailability of the good are examples of positive and negative transitory consumption. As with measured income, a family's measured consumption in any particular period may be larger or smaller than its permanent consumption.

With these definitions at hand, we may turn to Friedman's basic argument that permanent consumption depends on permanent income. Specifically, the relationship he proposes is that permanent consumption is a constant proportion of permanent income which depends only on the interest rate, the ratio of "nonhuman" wealth to total (human plus nonhuman) wealth, and tastes. Tastes are affected by factors such as age and family composition. The permanent consumption of different families with the same permanent income will therefore vary according to their specific characteristics. However, if there is no reason to expect these characteristics to vary with the level of income, it may be assumed that the average ratio of consumption to permanent income for groups of families at different levels of permanent income will be the same. In its extreme form, the hypothesis states that the average fraction of permanent income devoted to consumption will be the same for groups of families with permanent income near the bottom or the top of the income scale. In other words, the *apc* of families at all levels of family income is held to be the same when the *apc* is expressed as a ratio of permanent consumption to permanent income. This, of course, also means that the average propensity to save of families at all levels of family income is the same. The "rich" and the "poor" devote the same fraction of their incomes to saving!

This conclusion, which appears to conflict with what ordinary observation shows, follows from the argument that saving is primarily for the

purpose of providing future consumption for the family. The family's intent is to even out consumption over a time period that is substantially longer than the single year but not necessarily as long as its remaining life span. Although this behavior is necessary if families at all income levels are to smooth out consumption, most economists question whether this is a correct description of actual behavior. It may be granted that most families make some attempt to even out consumption in this way, but it is questionable whether the preference for present over future goods is not greater for low-income families than it is for high-income families. However strong the desire of low-income families to avoid a level of consumption that is even lower in later years than the low level of the current year, it is difficult to believe that such families feel able to save the same fraction of their meager incomes that high-income families save of theirs. The pressures toward present consumption at the low-income levels are such that the preference for present goods over future goods seems substantially stronger here than at the high-income levels. These pressures would probably keep consumption by low-income families high and saving by high-income families high, relative to their respective incomes.

Another basic argument of Friedman's permanent income hypothesis is that the transitory component of consumption is not correlated with the transitory component of income. This amounts to saying that in a period in which a family's measured income contains a negative transitory component, it does not reduce its consumption in response, nor, under the opposite circumstance, does it raise its consumption. Unexpected increases or decreases in income therefore result in equivalent increases or decreases in saving; consumption is unaffected by "windfall" gains or losses. In other words, the marginal propensity to consume out of transitory, or "windfall," income is held to be zero. As they have questioned the argument that the fraction of family income saved is the same at all levels of family income, most economists have questioned

---

[8]Friedman also defines consumption as spending on services and nondurable goods plus the depreciation and interest cost on consumer durable goods. A net addition to the family's stock of durable goods is treated as saving.

whether this too is a correct description of actual consumer behavior.[9] In the words of one critic, the hypothesis says, "The man who has a lucky day at the races does not buy his friends a drink, and the poor fellow whose wallet is stolen does not postpone the purchase of a new overcoat."[10] This critic argues, and submits some evidence to suggest, that "the lucky winner does not run to the savings bank but to the tavern, and the victim of theft does cut his coat according to his cloth."[11]

However, to the degree that the marginal propensity to consume out of transitory income is indeed zero or at least very small, the permanent income theory carries a far-reaching implication—the marginal propensity to consume out of measured income may be quite unstable. In any time period, millions of individuals realize changes in their measured incomes. How they view the nature of that income change becomes a major determinant of the marginal propensity to consume out of measured income for all people combined. The larger the portion of the income change perceived by its recipients to be transitory, the smaller the marginal propensity to consume, and vice versa. Because the perception of those particular individuals whose incomes change will not be the same from one period to

the next, the marginal propensity to consume will not be stable from one period to the next. The existence of a relatively stable marginal propensity to consume was a major building block of Keynesian theory. The absolute income hypothesis yielded a stable marginal propensity to consume. But because the permanent income hypothesis denies any such stability, it has dealt a damaging blow to the Keynesian model. Still, the conclusion of an unstable marginal propensity to consume depends on the argument that the marginal propensity to consume out of transitory income is zero or at least very small. As noted, that argument is not without its critics.

The various basic arguments of the permanent income hypothesis have raised considerable controversy.[12] Our purpose here is not to pursue this debate, but merely to set forth some essentials of the permanent income hypothesis and to relate these to the simple cross-sectional evidence provided by empirical family consumption functions.

Cross-sectional data such as those plotted in Figure 15-1 clearly do not form a pattern that would be expected on the basis of the permanent income hypothesis. The data given in the 1972–73 study, as well as data from similar studies made

---

[9]However, Friedman's contention turns out to be more reasonable than it may at first appear, once one takes into account his definition of consumption. Consumption is not the same as expenditures by consumers. As indicated in footnote 8, consumption excludes spending that adds to a family's stock of durable goods. Therefore, a family that uses a "windfall" gain to purchase a new automobile has devoted this transitory income to consumer expenditure, but not to consumption (apart from an amount equal to the value of the services rendered by the car during the time period—an amount approximated by the depreciation and interest cost of the car). The exclusion of expenditures on durable goods (adjusted for depreciation and interest cost) from consumption makes the argument that transitory income is not devoted to consumption more reasonable, especially because consumers tend to devote sizable "windfalls" to the purchase of durable goods they otherwise would not acquire.

[10]H.S. Houthakker, "The Permanent Income Hypothesis," in *American Economic Review*, June 1958, p. 398.

[11]*Ibid.*, p. 404.

[12]See, for example, I. Friend and I.B. Kravis, "Consumption Patterns and Permanent Income," in *American Economic Review*, May 1957, pp. 536–55; H.W. Watts, "Long-Run Income Expectations and Consumer Saving," in T.F. Dernburg, R.N. Rosett, and H.W. Watts, *Studies in Household Economic Behavior*, Yale Univ. Press, 1958, pp. 103–44; H.W. Watts, *An Analysis of the Effects of Transitory Income on Expenditure of Norwegian Households*, Cowles Foundation Discussion Paper 149, 1962; R.C. Bird and R.G. Bodkin, "The National Service Life Insurance Dividend of 1950 and Consumption: A Further Test of the 'Strict' Permanent Income Hypothesis," in *Journal of Political Economy*, Oct. 1965, pp. 499–515; R. Bodkin, "Windfall Income and Consumption," in *American Economic Review*, Sept. 1959, pp. 602–14; and M.E. Kreinen, "Windfall Income and Consumption," in *American Economic Review*, June 1961, pp. 388–90. See also T. Mayer, *Permanent Income, Wealth, and Consumption*, University of California Press, 1972, a book devoted to a synthesis of previous tests of the permanent income theory and the presentation of some new tests.

in other years, uniformly show the *apc* declining as we move from lower to higher levels of family income. However, this relationship emerges from data on the "current" income and the "current" consumption of families at different levels of income. The permanent income hypothesis does not deny the relationship shown by such studies; but it does deny the appropriateness of this relationship as a description of the way that family consumption varies with family income. According to this hypothesis, the use of current or measured income improperly mixes permanent and transitory income. The fact that the *apc* is relatively high at relatively low levels of measured income and relatively low at relatively high levels of measured income is held to be attributable to the influence of the transitory component of income that varies from a relatively large negative amount at a relatively low level of measured income to a relatively large positive amount at a relatively high level of measured income.

Figure 15-3 shows both permanent and measured values. The consumption axis is marked C for measured and C_p for permanent family consumption. The income axis is marked Y for measured and Y_p for permanent family income. The curve labeled C, like that in Figure 15-1, shows how C varies with the level of Y. (Because it simplifies the diagram without affecting the conclusions drawn from it, the C curve here appears as a straight line rather than what is actually a curved line as in Figure 15-1.) The C_p curve shows how C_p varies with the level of Y_p. Given the assumptions of the permanent income hypothesis that yield the conclusion that the *apc* out of permanent income is the same at all levels of permanent income, the C_p curve appears as a straight line from the origin. Only a straight line through the origin displays the property of a constant *apc*. The C curve that intercepts the vertical axis above the origin displays an *apc* that decreases at successively higher levels of family income.

The C curve in Figure 15-3 shows how measured consumption will vary with measured income for a sample of families drawn from a

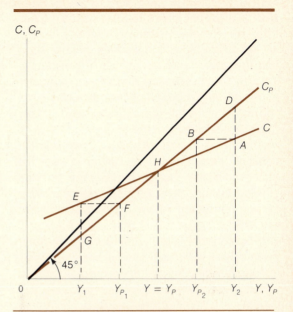

FIGURE 15-3
The Relationships Between Measured Consumption and Measured Income and Between Permanent Consumption and Permanent Income

roughly normal income distribution. Given the measured incomes of families in each income class, we may say that families in the upper income classes will tend to have positive transitory income, whereas those in the lower income classes will tend to have negative transitory income. Families at the average income level will tend to have zero transitory income—that is, for such families measured income equals permanent income, or $Y = Y_p$. This is to be expected because for any above average income class in a normal distribution, there are more families with permanent incomes *below* that income class who can move up into that income class because their transitory income is positive than there are families with permanent incomes *above* that income class who can drop down into that income class because their transitory income is negative. Therefore, positive transitory income will be more common in such an income class than negative transitory income. Again on the assumption of a roughly normal income distribution, a parallel argument indicates why families with incomes below average will tend to have negative transitory income. Some families with income equal to the average will have positive transitory income and some will have negative transitory income, but, on the average, families at this particular level will have zero transitory income (measured income equal to permanent income).

The consumption of some families in each income class will have a positive transitory component; that of some others will have a negative transitory component. However, because the hypothesis assumes that transitory consumption is not correlated with transitory income, there is no reason to expect the positive transitory component of consumption for the families in any income class to be greater or less than the negative transitory component of consumption of families in that income class. In other words, the average transitory component of consumption for all families within an income class is zero. Therefore, the measured consumption for each income class equals its permanent consumption.

With this background, let us examine any level of measured income in Figure 15-3 other than the average level—for example, Y_2. Because transitory income is correlated with measured income, families at this measured income level will generally have permanent income below measured income (positive transitory income). From the basic argument that permanent consumption is proportional to permanent income, illustrated in Figure 15-3 by the C_p curve, it would follow that consumption at measured income of Y_2 would have been that shown by D on the C_p curve if Y_2 had included no transitory income—that is, if it had been permanent income. However, because there is a positive transitory component in Y_2, consumption is indicated by A rather than D. The fact that consumption is the

amount shown by A establishes that the average permanent income of families with measured income of Y_2 is Y_{P_2}. This follows because at this level of permanent income, consumption will be the amount indicated by point B on the C_p curve, which is an amount equal to A on the C curve.

If we examine a level of measured income below the average—for example, Y_1—the relationships parallel those noted for the Y_2 income level. However, families at the Y_1 income level, on the average, will have permanent income above measured income (negative transitory income). Families with income of Y_1 have measured consumption shown by point E. As before, permanent consumption equals measured consumption, or equals E. If Y_1 had included no transitory income—that is, if it had been permanent income—consumption at Y_1 would have been that shown by point G on the C_p curve. However, because there is a negative component of transitory income in Y_1, consumption is the larger amount shown by E. As in the preceding paragraph, the fact that consumption is the amount shown by E indicates that the average permanent income of families with measured income of Y_1 is Y_{P_1}. At this level of permanent income, consumption will be the amount indicated by point F on the C_p curve, which is an amount equal to E on the C curve.

Having looked at measured income levels with negative and positive components of transitory income, we may return to the average income level, at which the average transitory income is zero or $Y = Y_P$. It should now be clear why the C and the C_p curves in Figure 15-3 intersect at this level. Of the various income levels along the axis, only at this income level is there no difference between the level of measured income and the corresponding level of permanent income. For the measured income level of Y_2, the corresponding permanent income level was Y_{P_2}; for the measured income level of Y_1, the corresponding permanent income level was Y_{P_1}. But for the families at the average income level, measured income indicates permanent income and the amount of consumption shown at H is consistent with both that level of measured income and that level of permanent income.

We have emphasized that **the basic argument of the permanent income hypothesis is that consumption depends on permanent income and that the average propensity to consume out of permanent income is the same, on the average, for families at different income levels.** By reversing this argument, we may note an important implication of the hypothesis. On the average, the consumption of families with a permanent income of Y_{P_2} will be indicated by point B in Figure 15-3. Assume that their incomes jump from Y_{P_2} to Y_2, but that the increased income is entirely transitory. This results in no change in consumption, because consumption at Y_2 is indicated by point A, which is the same level indicated by point B. In terms of the permanent income theory, there is no change in consumption because consumption depends on permanent income; there was no change in permanent income in this instance. Similarly, we may start off with families whose permanent income is Y_{P_1}. Assume their incomes drop from Y_{P_1} to Y_1, but that the decreased income is entirely transitory. This results in no change in consumption, because consumption at Y_1 is indicated by point E, which is the same level indicated by point F. To the extent that the marginal propensity to consume out of transitory income is zero (or close to zero) as held by the permanent income hypothesis, the changes in consumption as families move to different income levels is critically dependent on whether the change in income is permanent or transitory. Although the permanent income hypothesis has been subjected to criticisms, it correctly reveals that the simple relationship between measured consumption and measured income is inadequate to explain how consumption will change as the measured incomes of families change.

The C curve in Figure 15-3 shows how measured consumption varies with measured income for families at different income levels during a specific time period. Because aggregate measured income will usually increase faster than the number of families, average family income will rise above the initial level shown as $Y = Y_P$. Because the consumption of families with *average* income increases proportionally with their measured income—average transitory income being zero for families at the average income level—the income level at which $Y = Y_P$ will shift along the axis with the rise in average family income. The C curve may in turn shift upward and intersect the unshifting C_P curve at correspondingly higher points. In each time period, there is a curve that intersects the C_P curve as does the C curve in Figure 15-3. What the permanent income hypothesis says about the relationship between the C curve for each time period and the C_P curve is the same as what was outlined in connection with the C curve and C_P curves of Figure 15-3.

The Life-Cycle Hypothesis

This hypothesis—developed by Franco Modigliani, Richard E. Brumberg, and Albert Ando[13]— is like Friedman's permanent income hypothesis in that the individual's consumption in any given time period does not depend to a significant degree on his income during that period but depends on the present value of his expected income or his wealth. As suggested by the name given to it, the life-cycle hypothesis is based on the argument that "the rate of consumption in any given period is a facet of a plan which extends over the balance of the individual's life, while the income accruing within the same period is but one element which contributes to the shaping of such a plan."[14] Furthermore, it is argued that this plan finds the typical individual maintaining a roughly constant or perhaps slightly increasing

---

[13]See F. Modigliani and R.E. Brumberg, "Utility Analysis and the Consumption Function: An Interpretation of Cross-section Data," in K. Kurihara, ed., *Post-Keynesian Economics*, Rutgers University Press, 1954, and A. Ando and F. Modigliani, "The Life-Cycle Hypothesis of Saving: Aggregate Implications and Tests," in *American Economic Review*, March 1963, pp. 55–84.

[14]Modigliani and Brumberg, pp. 391–92.

level of consumption over his life cycle, although his income displays a quite different pattern over the same years. In other words, from the perspective of the individual's life cycle, there is little connection between income and consumption in any one year.

In Figure 15-4, the *Y* curve is a profile of the life-time income stream of a typical person. Measuring time from the year in which he begins full-time employment, his income in each following year rises until it reaches a peak in his middle or late working years; thereafter it declines. The *C* curve shows his life-time consumption stream, here drawn to show a gradually increasing level of consumption from year to year. Assuming that he plans zero bequests, he will seek to make the present value of his consumption over the life cycle equal to the present value of his income. The shaded area at the left of the figure shows that the individual's consumption exceeds his income in the early years of his working life—he is a dissaver, or net borrower. In the middle years, his income exceeds his consumption—he is a

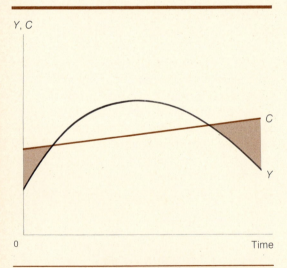

FIGURE 15-4
The Life-Cycle Hypothesis of
Consumption

saver. He not only repays the debt earlier incurred, but acquires assets on which he earns interest. Finally, in the late years indicated by the shaded area at the right, his consumption again exceeds his income—he is again a dissaver. However, here the dissaving is financed not by borrowing but out of the savings accumulated during the middle years.

If the profile of the life-cycle income stream and consumption stream of the average consumer is, in general, like that in Figure 15-4, the life-cycle hypothesis concludes that the *apc* will decrease with higher levels of family income. In any budget study in which we draw a random sample of families and classify them by income, it follows from the life-cycle hypothesis that the family consumption function will look like that in Figure 15-1: The *apc* will be lower at the higher income levels and vice versa. This is because the higher income families in the sample will contain a relatively large proportion of families who are there only because the family income earner is in his or her middle or late working years. As shown by Figure 15-4, those in this range of the life cycle exhibit a relatively low *apc*. Correspondingly, the lower income families in the sample will contain a relatively large proportion of families who are there only because of their positions in the early and late stages of the life cycle. As shown by Figure 15-4, the *apc* is at its highest at the ends of the range. The life-cycle hypothesis thereby explains the empirical finding that the *apc* falls as disposable family income rises. This has been demonstrated repeatedly by cross-sectional studies made in various countries at various times.

According to the life-cycle hypothesis, how will consumption be affected when individual families enjoy an increase or suffer a decrease in income? In brief, for most such changes, there will be little effect on consumption. Changes in income like those increases from year to year up to the late working years and decreases thereafter are expected as part of the life-cycle income stream; the change in consumption that occurs from any one year to the next is not significantly determined by these changes in income. The life-cycle stream of consumption has already allowed for such expected changes in income. Naturally, few families can predict their stream of income over the life cycle with any certainty; many families will realize unexpected changes in income in some years. However, such unexpected changes will have only minor impact on consumption in the year they occur, if they are viewed as temporary deviations from the life cycle of expected income. At the same time, an unexpected change in current income (for example, due to a promotion at work years before it was expected) that has a major effect on the level of income expected over the future working years will have more than a minor effect on current consumption. The parallel here with the conclusions reached by the permanent income hypothesis is apparent.

The preceding pages have been concerned with this micro-level question: What is the effect on an individual family's consumption as it moves along the family income scale? We now turn to the following macro-level question: What is the effect on the aggregate consumption of all families as their aggregate income changes? Our further examination of the life-cycle and other hypotheses will be from the macroeconomic perspective.

Consumer Behavior: Macroanalysis

Prior to World War II, empirical evidence on the consumption–income relationship at the macro level was limited to such evidence as could be drawn from family budget-study data. During World War II, however, estimates of national totals for personal consumption expenditures and disposable personal income became available for the first time on a comprehensive basis. Unlike cross-sectional data, these data show specifically how aggregate consumption expenditures have varied with aggregate disposable personal income.

Data for the years 1929–80, in constant (1972) dollars, are listed in columns 2 and 3 of Table 15-2. Column 4 shows the average propensity to consume, obtained by dividing the figures in column 2 by the figures in column 3. Column 5 shows the marginal propensity to consume, obtained by dividing the change in consumption from one year to the next by the change in disposable income for the same two years. In one simple table we have data which show how aggregate consumption has varied with aggregate income over the past fifty years.

In Chapter 4, we assumed that the consumption–income relationship has the following properties: (1) the MPC is positive but less than 1, (2) the MPC is the same for all changes in income, and (3) the APC decreases as income increases. How do these properties check out against the actual data? For the first, column 5 shows that in 16 of 51 cases the MPC is either negative, equal to, or greater than 1; these are shown in color in the table. For the second, there is considerable variability in the magnitude of the MPC; far from being the same for all annual changes in income, it seems to be different for every annual change in income. The third property is far from fully satisfied. In 15 of 52 cases, the APC rises with a rise in income, although in many cases the rise is such a small fraction of one percentage point, that it hardly qualifies as a rise. It could easily be accounted for by statistical error. These are shown in color. In no case does the APC fall with a decline in income. Seven of the 15 exceptions are found in the ten-year period 1954–63. The evidence here set forth appears to be inconsistent with the consumption–income relationship we earlier assumed. Does not this contrary evidence force us to reject that relationship?

Properly interpreted, these apparently pronounced differences do not necessarily lead to this conclusion. It was almost inevitable that there would be differences, even pronounced differences for some years, between the consumption–income relationship we adopted in developing the simple theory of income determination and the relationship revealed by the aggregate

TABLE 15-2
Disposable Personal Income and Personal Consumption Expenditures, 1929–80
(billions of 1972 dollars)

(1) Year	(2) Personal Consumption Expenditures	(3) Disposable Personal Income	(4) APC	(5) MPC	(1) Year	(2) Personal Consumption Expenditures	(3) Disposable Personal Income	(4) APC	(5) MPC
1929	215.1	229.5	0.937	—	1955	394.1	426.9	0.923	1.021
1930	199.5	210.6	0.947	0.825	1956	405.4	446.3	0.908	0.582
1931	191.8	201.9	0.950	0.885	1957	413.8	455.6	0.909	0.903
1932	173.9	174.4	0.997	0.651	1958	418.0	460.7	0.907	0.824
1933	170.5	169.6	1.005	0.708	1959	440.4	479.7	0.918	1.179
1934	176.9	179.8	0.984	0.627	1960	452.0	489.7	0.923	1.160
1935	187.7	196.8	0.954	0.635	1961	461.4	503.8	0.916	0.667
1936	206.2	220.5	0.935	0.781	1962	482.0	524.9	0.918	0.976
1937	213.8	227.7	0.939	1.056	1963	500.5	542.3	0.923	1.063
1938	208.8	212.6	0.982	0.331	1964	528.0	580.8	0.909	0.714
1939	219.8	229.8	0.956	0.640	1965	557.5	616.3	0.905	0.831
1940	229.9	244.0	0.942	0.711	1966	585.7	646.8	0.905	0.925
1941	243.6	277.9	0.876	0.404	1967	602.7	673.5	0.895	0.637
1942	241.1	317.5	0.760	−0.063	1968	634.4	701.3	0.905	1.140
1943	248.2	332.1	0.747	0.486	1969	657.9	722.5	0.911	1.108
1944	255.2	343.6	0.743	0.609	1970	672.1	751.6	0.894	0.488
1945	270.9	338.1	0.801	−2.855	1971	696.8	779.2	0.894	0.895
1946	301.0	332.7	0.905	−5.907	1972	737.1	810.3	0.910	1.296
1947	305.8	319.0	0.959	−0.350	1973	768.5	865.3	0.888	0.571
1948	312.2	336.0	0.930	0.376	1974	763.6	858.4	0.890	0.710
1949	319.3	336.9	0.948	7.890	1975	780.2	875.8	0.891	0.954
1950	337.3	362.9	0.929	0.692	1976	823.7	907.4	0.908	1.377
1951	341.6	372.7	0.916	0.438	1977	863.9	939.8	0.919	1.241
1952	350.1	383.2	0.913	0.810	1978	904.8	981.5	0.922	0.981
1953	363.4	399.1	0.911	0.836	1979	930.9	1,011.5	0.920	0.870
1954	370.0	403.3	0.917	1.571	1980	934.2	1,018.0	0.917	0.465

SOURCE: *Economic Report of the President*, January 1981, and *Survey of Current Business*, U.S. Department of Commerce, February 1981.

data. In the simple theory of income determination, the relationship between income and consumption is drawn on the assumption that all the factors that influence consumption, other than the level of income, remain unchanged. The income–consumption relationship indicated by the aggregate data, on the other hand, is based on the measured year-to-year values for consumption, which result from all the factors that influence consumption. In other words, the changes in actual consumption are certainly influenced by the changes in income, but other factors are at work such as the price level, interest rates, income distribution, consumer asset holdings, and consumer credit terms. These factors themselves also change; in so doing, they influence the level of consumption spending from year to year.

Ideally, we need a way of isolating the portion of the actual changes in consumption that were due to changes in income from the portion that were due to the changes in all the other factors. Although advanced statistical techniques enable us to derive quantitative approximations of this kind, for present purposes a simpler approach will suffice.

The data from columns 2 and 3 of Table 15-2 are plotted in Figure 15-5. Each dot on the chart indicates the combination of personal consumption expenditures and disposable personal income for a given year between 1929 and 1980. A glance at the scatter reveals that consumption does not vary with income exactly as suggested in Chapter 4. To do so, a straight line with an intercept above zero on the vertical axis and a positive slope of less than 1 would have to pass through every dot in the figure. Although no straight line will do this, one will come close if we ignore the six dots for the years 1941–46. Omitting these six years, the straight line drawn is fitted to the data for 1929–40 and 1947–80 by the method of least squares.[15] The equation for this empirical consumption function is $C = 12.4 + 0.89Y$. This equation is the one used in Chapter 4 ($C = C_a + cY$). Now, however, instead of hypothetical figures for C_a and c, actual values yield the empirical consumption function. C_a, which is here \$12.4 billion, indicates the point at which the consumption function intercepts the

vertical axis. As earlier described, it is the amount of consumption spending at the zero level of income, recognizing that in reality the level of income could not fall to zero; c, which is here 0.89, is the MPC (or $\Delta C / \Delta Y$ with Y being disposable personal income), or the slope of the consumption function. If consumption were to change with every change in income as given by the equation, then for every change of \$100 million in income, consumption would change by \$89 million.[16]

The vertical differences between the dots and this straight line are quite apparent. However, in view of the number of other factors that influence consumption spending, what is surprising is not that such differences exist but how small these differences actually are. The relationship between disposable income and consumption expenditures is remarkably close and seems to suggest that consumption is very largely explained by income. Because consumption so closely follows income, the combination of other factors that influence consumption spending seems to influence consumption spending much less than the single factor of the level of disposable income.[17]

A glaring exception to this conclusion is the period 1941–45 and perhaps also 1946, when the otherwise close relationship between consumption and disposable income seems to have broken down completely. The unusual distance

---

[15]This is the straight line of "best fit" in the sense that the sum of the squares of the deviations between actual consumption and consumption indicated by the line—known as a *regression line* or simply as a *regression*—will be less than for any other line that could be fitted to the data.

[16]Actual empirical work on the consumption function involves much more complex functions than the simple equation in one variable used here. For an introduction to empirical estimates of the consumption function, see M.K. Evans, *Macroeconomic Activity*, Harper & Row, 1969, Ch. 3, and the references given there.

[17]Conclusions such as these, suggested by the single-equation, least-squares method used here, must be interpreted with great caution. This statistical method is acceptable for dealing with independent variables, but the consumption and income variables are interdependent. Consumption depends on income, and income also depends on consumption. Therefore, we cannot conclude that the changes in income are the causes of changes in consumption from the fact that a line of regression indicates a close relationship between consumption and

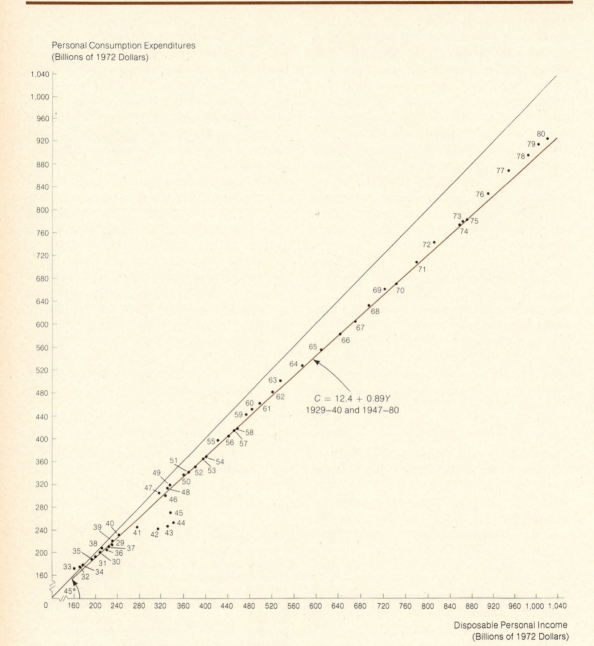

FIGURE 15-5
Relationship Between Personal Consumption Expenditures and Disposable Personal Income, 1929–40 and 1947–80

from the regression line of the dots for these years is readily explained by the extraordinary impact of certain nonincome factors in operation during World War II.[18] It is statistically proper to disregard these years in determining the "normal" consumption–income line. The remaining years may be somewhat arbitrarily divided into four periods of approximately equal length: 1929–40, 1947–57, 1958–69, and 1970–1980. A separate regression line fitted to the data for each of these periods will allow us to see how the fit of the line for each of these shorter periods compares with that for the overall period and how

the shorter periods compare with one another.[19] The lines for the four shorter periods are shown in Figure 15-6, where the equation for the 1929–40 line is $C = 33.8 + 0.80Y$; for the 1947–57 line, $C = 41.6 + 0.81Y$; for the 1958–69 line, $C = 20.4 + 0.88Y$; and for the 1970–80 line, $C = -90.2 + 1.01Y$. The striking difference between the equation for the 1970–80 period and those for the three earlier periods will be considered later.

In comparing each of these regression lines with that for the overall period in Figure 15-5, it is apparent that the regression lines for the shorter periods provide a better fit to the years on which each is based. Of course, factors other than income still influence consumption during each of these four periods. In no year, however, did these factors produce a level of consumption spending that was widely different from that which would be expected on the basis of the regression line.

It is also apparent in Figure 15-6 that the regression line for the 1947–57 period has shifted noticeably upward relative to that for the

---

income. The line of causation could run in the other direction—changes in income caused by changes in consumption. What we have is a relationship of mutual interaction in which higher income means higher consumption and higher consumption means higher income. Furthermore, when we note that consumption expenditures typically constitute about 90 percent of income, it is apparent that we would find a close relationship between income and consumption, even if consumption were completely unrelated to income. D.B. Suits has indicated that the correlation between consumption and income in these circumstances may be expected to be about 0.9, even if income changes do not cause consumption changes. See D.B. Suits, "The Determinants of Consumer Expenditure: A Review of Present Knowledge," *Impacts of Monetary Policy,* Commission on Money and Credit, Prentice-Hall, 1963.

Where interdependence exists between variables, the customary terminology of independent variable (income) and dependent variable (consumption) and the single-equation, least-squares method of deriving the relationship between the two are inappropriate. Each variable should have an equation of its own to explain the way it varies in a system of equations that are solved simultaneously. This is the method most frequently used today by econometricians in consumption-function estimation. For the introductory purpose of this chapter, we will limit ourselves to the simple one-equation, least-squares method, but this method is inherently defective in handling interdependent variables; conclusions reached by means of it cannot be taken at face value. For a discussion of this problem, see Evans, pp. 48–55.

[18]Consumers spent much less than would have been expected solely on the basis of their incomes during 1941–45 because of the complete unavailability of certain durable goods like automobiles and the limited availability of other goods. To a lesser degree, consumers also spent less than would have been expected because of government pleas to save and purchase U.S. Savings Bonds.

Less pronounced but still sizable departures from the regression line are found in the early postwar years. Although disposable income dropped to successively lower levels in 1945, 1946, and 1947, consumption expenditures rose sharply in 1945 and 1946 and moderately in 1947. As goods that had been unobtainable or obtainable only in limited quantities during the war years began to reappear on the market, the public went on a spending spree to meet long-unfilled needs. Although real disposable income showed a small net decline from 1944 to 1949—decreasing from 1944 to 1947 and increasing from 1947 to 1949—consumption expenditures rose in each of these years. The vast accumulation of wartime savings made the financing of these expenditures no problem. During the war years, and to a lesser extent during the early postwar years, consumption spending temporarily lost its close tie with income, as first it dropped far below (1941–45) and then rose above (1946–47) the amount that might have been expected solely on the basis of the level of disposable income.

[19]The comparison would be more illuminating if each of the three periods began with the economy at the upper or lower turning point in the business cycle and ended similarly. However, the distortion introduced by our choice of periods does not appear to be serious for the present purpose.

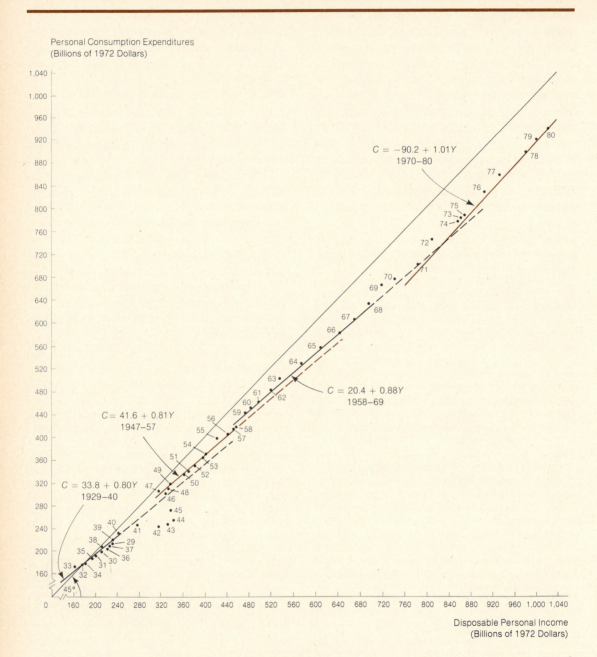

FIGURE 15-6
Relationship Between Personal Consumption Expenditures and Disposable Personal Income, 1929–40, 1947–57, 1958–69, and 1970–80

prewar period. To show this more clearly, the line for the prewar period has been extended by a broken line to levels of income reached in the 1947–57 period. If consumers had chosen to allocate their income between consumption and saving in the same way after the war as they did before the war, the dots for 1947–57 would have been scattered just above, just below, or right along this extended broken line. Instead, the dots all lie above the extended line. Apparently, in the early postwar period, consumers did not choose to maintain the same relationship between income and consumption found in the prewar period. The same is true between the 1947–57 and 1958–69 periods; the regression line for 1958–69 has shifted noticeably upward relative to that for the 1947–57 period. (Although C_a, the intercept, is smaller for 1958–69 than for 1947–57, the slope for 1958–69 is greater than that for 1947–57; on balance, this results in a 1958–69 regression line positioned above the extension of the 1947–57 line.)

In general, the regression line calculated for any random 10 consecutive years of the postwar period will lie above the regression line for the preceding 10 years (excluding World War II years). In other words, the regression line based on data for successive periods about 10 years in length clearly drifts upward. However, this is not clearly the case for the most recent period of this length for which data were available at the time of writing. The equation for the 1970–80 period was $C = -90.2 + 1.01Y$. An extrapolation of the 1959–69 line, $C = 20.4 + 0.88Y$, will cut the 1970–80 line from above. Therefore, only part of the 1970–80 line lies above the extension of the 1959–69 line. The well-defined upward shift of the regression line from one period to the next does not hold here.

The line for 1970–80 differs from those for the earlier periods here considered as well as others in its negative value for C_a and its slope greater than one. (Lines calculated for 1967–77, 1968–78, and 1969–79 also have relatively large negative values for C_a, but they have slopes less than 1.) These properties do not conform with the properties of the income–consumption relationship

assumed in Chapter 4 in developing the simple Keynesian theory of income determination. The assumption in that model was an MPC less than 1 and an APC that decreases as income increases. For 1970–80 the MPC is slightly greater than 1. Because C_a is negative, the APC here increases as income increases. This may turn out to be a temporary phenomenon due to the income–consumption relationship of the late 1970s. However, a continuation of this unusual result in the years ahead will require qualification of certain well-established relationships between cyclical and secular consumption functions that are considered in the next section.

Cyclical and Secular Consumption—Income Relationships

The regression lines, or empirical consumption functions, derived from the time series data for 1929–40, 1947–57, 1958–69, and 1970–80 may be described as cyclical consumption functions. Although each period covers more than a single business cycle, we may designate them as cyclical to distinguish between a period of limited duration in which the changes in consumption spending may be related to the cyclical ups and downs in disposable income and a much longer period, running over many decades, in which the changes in consumption spending may be related to the secular growth in disposable income. In such a long period, we may abstract from the cyclical fluctuations and derive what may be described as the secular consumption function. We may also describe the cyclical consumption function as the short-run consumption function and the secular as the long-run.

In the previous section, we saw that the theoretical consumption function adopted in Chapter 4 received support from the aggregate time series data, at least through the mid-1970s. It may be asked why this does not end the matter. Why now cyclical and secular consumption functions? In a formal sense, the empirical consumption function revealed by the data for a long-run period is different from that revealed by the data for a short-run period. What is the basic relationship between disposable income and consumption if all factors that influence consumption—other than income—are absent? If the time series data suggest a different relationship according to the time interval examined, our question remains unanswered until we explain this difference.

Figure 15-6 has already shown the nature of the problem. The regression line for 1929–40 gives a good fit to the data for that short-run period, and the regression lines for 1947–57, 1958–69, and 1970–80 give good fits to the data for those periods. However, the line for each later period lies above the line we get by simply projecting the line for the preceding period (with some qualification for the 1970–80 period). This suggests that the 1929–40 line may have shifted upward from a regression line for a preceding short-run period, say 1919–28, and that a regression line to be computed for 1981–91 will also have shifted upward from the 1970–80 line. If this indeed is what takes place over the long run, the argument that the APC decreases with a rise in income is supported by the data *only* if we limit the application of that argument to a description of the typical short-run relationship between disposable income and consumption. Only then does the APC plainly decrease with increases in income. On the other hand, if from one short-run period to the next the entire function shifts upward, it does not necessarily follow that the APC will decrease with long-run increases in income. *The upward shift in the function could be such as to produce an APC that remains roughly unchanged in the long run.*

In fact, the data suggest that this is what actually does happen over the long run. To demonstrate this empirical long-run relationship, we will look at two sets of data. The first is an alternative presentation of the data in Table 15-2 for the fifty years from 1929 to 1978; the second is data from a 1946 study by Simon Kuznets for the seventy-year period from 1869 to 1938. What is now needed is a presentation of data that shows changes between successive short-run periods, say of decade length, rather than changes between individual years as in Table 15-2. Based on the data in Table 15-2, Table 15-3 gives the average annual disposable income, average annual personal consumption expenditures, and the average APC for overlapping decades from 1929 to 1978. The dollar figures have been obtained by simply adding total yearly disposable personal income and consumption expenditures for the decade and dividing each total by ten. The APC is the ratio of the ten-year total for consumption expenditures to the ten-year total for disposable personal income.

A comparison of the average APCs for the successive decades in Table 15-3 does not seem to support the proposition that the APC remains roughly unchanged in the long run. There is a very sharp drop from an average APC of 0.96 in the 1929–38 decade to an average APC of 0.86

TABLE 15-3
Average Disposable Personal Income and Personal Consumption Expenditures by Decade, 1929–78
(billions of 1972 dollars)

Decade	Disposable Personal Income	Personal Consumption Expenditures	APC
1929–38	202.4	194.8	0.96
1934–43	243.5	218.1	0.89
1939–48	307.1	263.3	0.86
1944–53	351.8	316.3	0.90
1949–58	403.8	372.1	0.92
1954–63	471.2	434.7	0.92
1959–68	572.4	525.1	0.92
1964–73	707.7	642.6	0.91
1969–78	837.4	763.5	0.91

SOURCE: *Economic Report of the President,* Jan. 1981, and *Survey of Current Business,* U.S. Department of Commerce, Feb. 1981.

in the 1939–48 decade. Of course, these are two of the most exceptional decades in the country's history—the first dominated by the Great Depression, which forced the consumption ratio sharply upward, and the second dominated by World War II, which forced the consumption ratio sharply downward. If we omit the rows in the table that include all or part of the periods covered by these two events, we drop down to the row for 1949–58. For the periods starting with 1949–58, the average APC shows very little variation. While disposable personal income more than doubled from the 1949–58 period to the 1969–78 period, the APC remained virtually unchanged. Although three decades do not make up a very long-run period in the present sense of that term, the figures tend to support the argument that the APC remains roughly unchanged in the long run. More support is provided by the data in Table 15-4 for the much longer period from 1869 to 1938, again after omitting the last two periods of this table that include the years of the Great Depression. While national income increased more than sevenfold from the 1869–78 period to the 1919–28 period, the APC varied only over the narrow range of 0.84 to 0.89.[20]

Therefore, in the long run, as the level of income rises, the APC remains quite stable. This is in sharp contrast to the result for the short run in which the APC typically tends to decline as the level of income rises. In other words, instead of an ever smaller fraction of income being devoted to consumption as the level of income doubled and redoubled over the decades, an approximately stable proportion of income was devoted to consumption.[21]

---

[20]Note that Table 15-4 shows national income rather than disposable personal income. For these early years, no satisfactory estimates of disposable personal income are available. Also, for the decades 1869–78 through 1914–23, estimates are for decades; and for the decades 1919–28, 1924–33, and 1929–38, estimates are averages of annual estimates.

[21]The findings of another study agree with those summarized in Table 15-4. See R. Goldsmith, *A Study of Saving in the United States,* Vol. 1, Princeton Univ. Press, 1955, pp. 393, 400.

TABLE 15-4
Average National Income and Personal Consumption Expenditures by Decade, 1869–1938
(billions of 1929 dollars)

Decade	National Income	Personal Consumption Expenditures	APC
1869–78	9.3	8.1	0.86
1874–83	13.6	11.6	0.86
1879–88	17.9	15.3	0.85
1884–93	21.0	17.7	0.84
1889–98	24.2	20.2	0.84
1894–1903	29.8	25.4	0.85
1899–1908	37.3	32.3	0.86
1904–13	45.0	39.1	0.87
1909–18	50.6	44.0	0.87
1914–23	57.3	50.7	0.89
1919–28	69.0	62.0	0.89
1924–33	73.3	68.9	0.94
1929–38	72.0	71.0	0.99

SOURCE: Simon Kuznets, *National Product Since 1869,* National Bureau of Economic Research, Princeton Univ. Press, 1946, p. 119, and Simon Kuznets, *National Income: A Summary of Findings,* National Bureau of Economic Research, Princeton Univ. Press, 1946, p. 53.

The differences between the cyclical and secular relationships become more apparent when the dollar amounts in Table 15-4 are plotted, as in Figure 15-7. Apart from the dots for the 1924–33 and 1929–38 periods, a visually fitted straight-line consumption function drawn *from the origin* comes very close to passing through all the other dots in the figure. Unlike the general equation ($C = C_a + cY$) for the *cyclical* straight-line consumption function, the general equation for the *secular* straight-line consumption function is simply $C = bY$, in which the long-run MPC is designated by b to distinguish it from the short-run MPC, which is designated by c. The C_a constant becomes zero in the long-run function; the straight line intercepts the vertical axis at the

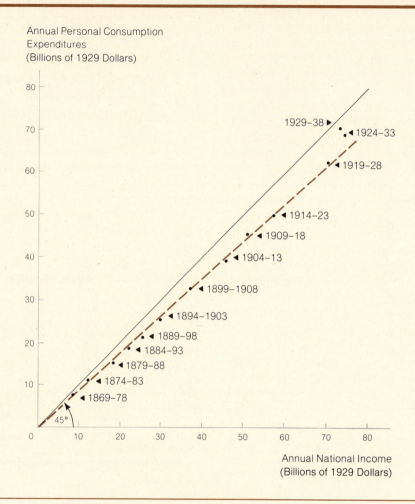

Annual Personal Consumption
Expenditures
(Billions of 1929 Dollars)

1929–38 ▶
◀ 1924–33
◀ 1919–28
◀ 1914–23
◀ 1909–18
◀ 1904–13
◀ 1899–1908
◀ 1894–1903
◀ 1889–98
◀ 1884–93
◀ 1879–88
◀ 1874–83
◀ 1869–78

45°

Annual National Income
(Billions of 1929 Dollars)

FIGURE 15-7
Secular Consumption Function

origin. As in any straight-line consumption function that intersects the vertical axis at the origin, in this long-run consumption function APC = MPC at all levels of income, in contrast to the typical short-run function in which APC > MPC at all levels of income. Another way of distinguishing the two functions is to describe the short-run straight-line function as *nonproportional* and the long-run straight-line function as *proportional*. This simply refers to the fact that, in the short run, consumption does not change proportionally with income; this proportion instead typically rises with falling income and falls with rising income. In the long run, consumption changes proportionally with income; it remains roughly the same proportion of income as the level of income doubles and redoubles over the decades of the long run.

On the basis of the empirical consumption functions in Figures 15-6 and 15-7 (disregarding the 1970–80 function in the belief that it is a temporary departure from the typical function), we may now construct Figure 15-8 to illustrate in general the nature of the short-run and long-run functions suggested by the time series data. Below the 45° line lies line *LR;* it depicts the proportional relationship between disposable income and consumption suggested by the data for the long-run period. Each of the family of lines labeled *SR* represents the nonproportional relationship between disposable income and consumption suggested by the data for a short-run period. Figure 15-6 showed that the short-run consumption function very clearly shifted upward from the 1929–40 period to the 1947–57 period and from the 1947–57 period to the 1958–69 period. Each successively higher *SR* line in Figure 15-8 represents such a shift in the function from one short-run period to the next.

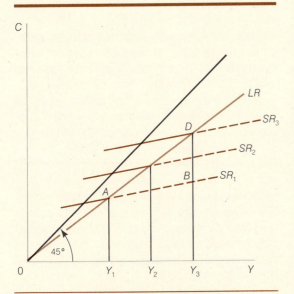

**FIGURE 15-8
Secular and Cyclical
Consumption Functions**

Reconciling the Cyclical and Secular Relationships

The statistical record shows that the consumption function is nonproportional in the short run and proportional in the long run. Therefore, the various hypotheses that attempt to explain the relationship between aggregate income and aggregate consumption must reconcile this difference, if they are to win any acceptance. The balance of this chapter reviews the way each of the four hypotheses explains the relationship between aggregate income and aggregate consumption shown by the data and describes how each of these hypotheses reconciles the difference between the short-run and long-run relationships.

The Absolute Income Hypothesis

The basic tenet of the absolute income hypothesis is that the individual consumer's spending depends on the absolute level of his income. When this theory is extended to aggregate behavior, it indicates that increases in the aggregate income of all consumers should result in a decline in the APC, or the fraction of this aggregate income devoted to consumption. Because the actual level of aggregate income grows larger and larger in the long run, the APC should become smaller and smaller.[22] In terms of Figure 15-8, as income increases in the long run, the theory would lead us to expect consumption to

[22]When the period under consideration stretches out over decades as it does here, it is essential to express the consumption and income variables in per capita form. If aggregate real income grows no faster than total population, real income *per capita* remains unchanged, and there is no reason to expect a change in the APC on the basis of income alone. The situation that is relevant here is that in which real income per capita grows larger and larger; in this situation, the absolute income theory holds that the ratio of real consumption per capita to real income per capita will become smaller and smaller.

follow the path of an *SR* curve projected out to the right. However, the long-run data show clearly that this is not what happens. One way of reconciling the position that the basic relationship is nonproportional with the data that show the long-run relationship to be proportional is through an upward shift in the basic, nonproportional consumption function as a result of changes in factors other than income. A number of factors work in this direction: (1) With the increase in the accumulated wealth of households that has accompanied the long-run growth of income, households have tended to spend a larger fraction of any given level of income, thereby contributing to an upward shift in the consumption function. (2) Over the present long-run period, there has been a continuing movement of population from the farms to the cities. Because urban wage earners have a substantially higher propensity to consume than farm proprietors, this shift in population has contributed to an upward shift in the consumption function. (3) The percentage of older people in the population has increased over the long-run period. Because per capita consumption in this age group does not drop off as rapidly as does per capita income, the consumption function tends to shift upward. (4) New consumer goods have been introduced at a rapid rate over this long-run period. As more and more of these goods become regarded as "essentials" by the typical household, the consumption function tends to shift upward.

According to the absolute income hypothesis, factors like these have caused the consumption function to shift upward by roughly the amount necessary to produce a proportional relationship between consumption and income over the long run and thereby to prevent the nonproportional relationship that would be expected on the basis of the income factor alone.

The Relative Income Hypothesis

When this hypothesis is extended from individual consumer behavior, to aggregate behavior, the ratio of consumption to income becomes dependent on the ratio of the *current income level* to the *peak income level* previously attained. In developing the peak income argument of the relative income hypothesis, Duesenberry takes as his point of departure the known fact that income does not grow at an even pace over the long run but instead displays cyclical ups and downs. These short-run income fluctuations push the economy off the *LR* curve and onto the successive *SR* curves in an unbroken series over time.

To illustrate Duesenberry's hypothesis in terms of Figure 15-8, suppose that a recession strikes when the economy is at income Y_1, which we will assume represents the highest level of income yet reached by the economy. As income falls over the course of the recession, consumers as a group will attempt to maintain the consumption level they enjoyed when income was at its peak but will gradually cut back their expenditures as their aggregate income falls. Consequently, consumption falls, but not proportionally, with the fall in income. As the economy moves down the SR_1 curve, the APC rises and the APS falls. This reflects the fact that in an attempt to maintain the previously established higher standard of living, consumers will cut down their saving more than proportionally and consumption less than proportionally. Then, as recovery succeeds recession and the income level begins its move back toward its previous peak, consumption rises but less than proportionally with the rise in income. Consequently, the APC falls and the APS rises. The movement of consumption upward along the SR_1 curve is just the reverse of the earlier downward movement. Just as consumers cut down saving more than proportionally to defend the level of consumption on the downswing, so they increase saving more than proportionally on the upswing in order to restore saving to its previous level.

As the level of income rises to its previous peak and pushes on to higher ground, consumption does not follow the SR_1 line to the right past the peak income but instead shifts over to follow the *LR* line. Because income is now rising to levels not previously attained, consumers no longer feel the increased urge to save that they felt during the period of recovery. They feel free to consume a larger fraction of this income than they consumed of the below-peak income of the preceding recession. As income grows to ever higher peaks, consumption increases proportionally; the APC and APS remain unchanged. However, since it is the nature of the economy that a business downturn will succeed an upturn (and vice versa), instead of an uninterrupted movement along LR, the economy will slide into another recession after having established a new peak income of Y_2. The sequence now repeats itself along the SR_2 curve as the recession causes consumption to move down that curve; recovery then causes it to move back up that curve to the previous peak at Y_2. At this point, consumption again will shift over to the LR curve, and the economy will move ahead to a new peak at Y_3.[23]

---

[23]Although we earlier described 1929–40, 1947–57, 1958–69, and 1970–79 as cyclical periods, we noted that each such period is actually made up of more than one complete business cycle. For example, over the years 1948–80, GNP in constant dollars moved from peak, P, to trough, T, to peak as follows (Roman numerals indicate quarters): P–1948 IV, T–1949 IV, P–1953 II, T–1954 II, P–1957 III, T–1958 I, P–1960 I, T–1960 IV, P–1969 III, T–1970 IV, P–1973 IV, T–1975 I, P–1980 I and T–1980 II. Whether we measure from peak to peak or from trough to trough, each such period is a full business cycle, if we simply date the turning points of the cycle by the peaks and troughs in real GNP. It is to such cycles that the SR curves of Figure 15-8 most meaningfully apply. If we examine the consumption and disposable income data quarter by quarter for each of the full cycles during 1948–80, we find a marked tendency for the APC to rise and the APS to fall quarter by quarter during business cycle contractions and vice versa during expansions, which is consistent with the nonproportional SR curves of Figure 15-8. However, this is a tendency and not a rule. An exception is found in the recession from 1969 III to 1970 IV during which the APS rose from 0.086 to 0.104 as the recession continued. During the expansion from 1970 IV to 1973 IV, the APS fell from 0.104 to 0.082 in 1972 III but then rose to 0.112 by the last quarter of that expansion. For the contraction, 1973 IV to 1975 I, the APS changed in line with the tendency noted; it fell from 0.112 in 1973 IV to 0.089 in 1975 I.

The aggregate behavior suggested by the relative income theory may be expressed in a single consumption function that combines the properties of the long-run function ($C = bY$) and the short-run function ($C = C_a + cY$) as follows:

$$C = \overline{Y}(b - c) + cY$$

The peak level of income is indicated by $\overline{Y}$ and the current level of income by Y. Accordingly, for any time period Y must be equal to or less than $\overline{Y}$. As long as income is steadily attaining new peaks during prosperity, peak income will be equal to current income, and the combined function will reduce to the long-run consumption function ($C = bY$).[24] The consumption–income relationship described by this function is the same as that described graphically by a movement along the LR line of Figure 15-8.

If a recession strikes and the current level of income drops below the peak attained earlier, $\overline{Y}$ is constant and greater than Y. With $\overline{Y}$ constant, $\overline{Y}(b - c)$ is also constant; therefore the constant C_a may be substituted for it. With current income below peak income, the combined function reduces to the short-run consumption function ($C = C_a + cY$). As long as current income is below peak income, the consumption–income relationship described by this function is the same as that described graphically by a movement along an SR line of Figure 15-8.

With recovery and the expansion of income beyond the previous peak, the combined function again reduces to the long-run function and consumption again increases proportionally with income along the LR line.

The Permanent Income Hypothesis

The permanent income hypothesis holds that the basic relationship between aggregate consumption and aggregate income is proportional, but

---

[24]$C = b\overline{Y} - c\overline{Y} + cY$. As long as $\overline{Y} = Y$, $-c\overline{Y} + cY = 0$, and $C = b\overline{Y}$ or bY.

the relationship here is expressed in terms of permanent income and consumption. The figures given in Table 15-3 show long-run proportionality between consumption and measured income. To discover what the empirical relationship between the corresponding permanent quantities may be, we must first obtain figures for these permanent quantities.

The concept of permanent income inherently involves expected or anticipated income, which cannot be estimated in any direct manner. In his time series analysis, Milton Friedman's procedure is to define the permanent income of any one year as a weighted average of actual or measured income over a 17-year period. Measured income of the current year is weighted at 33 percent, that of the preceding year at 22 percent, and so forth for the remaining fifteen years, with the weights rapidly declining. On the basis of such estimates of permanent income for each year back to the early part of the century, Friedman found that the ratio of consumption to permanent income was approximately constant year after year. Excluding the war years, the relationship for 1905–51 is $C = 0.88\,Y_P$ (in which Y_P refers to permanent income). The average propensity to consume equals the marginal propensity to consume and the function corresponds to a line like LR in Figure 15-8, which has a specific slope of 0.88. Accordingly, we find a long-run relationship of proportionality whether the relationship is derived as earlier described from figures of the decennial measured kind given in Tables 15-3 and 15-4 or from estimates produced by Friedman's method.

How does the permanent income hypothesis reconcile its assertion that over a long period of years there is a proportional relationship between permanent income and consumption with the data on measured income and consumption that show a nonproportional relationship over any short period of years? In Figure 15-9, the long-run relationship is indicated by the curve labeled $C = 0.88\,Y_P$ (the relationship found by Friedman). The permanent income hypothesis argues that the economy departs from this long-run

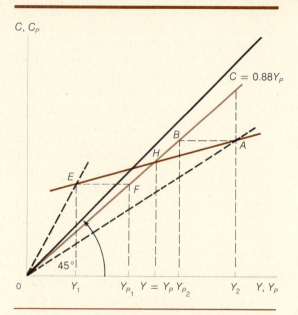

FIGURE 15-9
Relationship Between Aggregate Consumption and Aggregate Income According to the Permanent Income Hypothesis

growth path in the short run as it is buffeted by business cycles. Suppose that in an initial year the income level is indicated by $Y = Y_P$—that is, aggregate measured income and aggregate permanent income are equal. This average year is followed, say, by an above average year during which measured income rises to Y_2. For all families combined, part of this surge in measured income will be positive transitory income. With consumption out of transitory income equal to zero, the result will be consumption, say, at point A and a drop in the economy's APC below what it is at point H along the long-run consumption function.

If we apply Friedman's assumptions here, we may say that 33 percent of the increase in measured income for the year in question is an increase in permanent income; the balance is transitory income. For example, assume that the increase in measured income was $10 billion ($Y_2$ exceeds $Y = Y_P$ by $10 billion). The change in consumption will then be $0.88 \times 0.33 \times \$10$ billion—approximately $2.9 billion. With an increase in measured income of $10 billion and an increase in consumption of $2.9 billion—that is, a "one year" marginal propensity to consume of 29 percent—the APC at Y_2 will be smaller than the 0.88 value of the APC at the original income level of $Y = Y_P$. (This is shown by the slope of the dashed line from the origin to point A in comparison with the 0.88 slope of the solid line consumption function from the origin.) Because the marginal propensity to consume out of permanent income is 0.88 and the increase in permanent income is $3.3 billion (33 percent of the increase in measured income), the increase in consumption is also $0.88 \times \$3.3$—that is, $2.9 billion. This is shown by point B, which lies above the new level of income, Y_{P_2}. Relative to consumption indicated by point H, this is the same increase in consumption shown by point A, which lies above the new level of measured income, Y_2.

A related result follows from a cyclical decline in income during a year that carries income to Y_1 from the initial level at $Y = Y_P$. In this case, part of the decline in income will be negative transitory income. With consumption out of transitory income equal to zero, the result will be consumption, say, at point E and a rise in the APC relative to what it is at point H. If we assume that the decrease in income was $10 billion ($Y_1$ is $10 billion less than $Y = Y_P$), the change in consumption will be $0.88 \times 0.33 \times (-\$10 \text{ billion})$—approximately $2.9 billion. As before, the "one year" marginal propensity to consume is 29 percent. The APC at point E will be greater than the 0.88 value of the APC at the original level of income. The decline in permanent income is that from $Y = Y_P$ to Y_{P_1}, which will here be $3.3 billion. Because $\Delta C = 0.88(\Delta Y_P)$, we have $\$2.9 = 0.88$ ($3.3 billion). The decrease in consumption corresponding to this decrease in permanent income takes us from point H to point F (the same decrease as that from H to E).

As shown by these two illustrative cases of cyclical departures from the long-run growth path of income, according to the permanent income hypothesis, the nonproportional relationship between consumption and measured income found in the short run is based on the positive and negative transitory income components that appear respectively in the aggregate measured income of above- and below-average years.[25] If income were to grow at a steady trend rate or without cyclical variations, permanent income would equal measured income. Consumption would be a stable fraction of measured income—that is, the APC would be stable rather than rising during the below-average years and falling during the above-average years of the business cycle. This stable fraction, it is argued, is the result that we do get in the long run or over the course of successive business cycles as the short-run cyclical function shifts upward along the long-run proportional function. The long-run relationship averages out positive and negative transitory income components; in the long run, consumption is a stable fraction of income.

Note that the permanent income hypothesis effects a reconciliation of the aggregate consumption functions somewhat as does the relative income hypothesis. In the relative income hypothesis, the behavior of consumption over the business cycle is also central to the reconciliation, but the key was the effect on consumption as income recedes from the previous *peak*

---

[25]This, it may be noted, parallels the microanalysis of the permanent income hypothesis presented in connection with Figure 15-3. There we saw that changes in the level of permanent family income result in changes in consumption shown along the C_P curve, which intersects the origin, indicating a proportional relationship between different levels of family income and consumption. In contrast, changes in the level of measured family income that include positive and negative transitory components result in changes in consumption shown along the C curve of Figure 15-3. This function intersects the consumption axis above the origin, indicating a nonproportional relationship between different levels of family income and consumption.

income level. In the permanent income hypothesis, the key is the effect on consumption of the positive and negative transitory income components that appear as income departs from the long-run growth path during business cycles.

The Life-Cycle Hypothesis

The life-cycle hypothesis holds that the individual family seeks to maintain a stable or gradually increasing level of consumption over its life cycle and that its income displays a distinctly different pattern over the same period of years. Consequently, the *apc* varies significantly from a maximum at the early and late years to a minimum at the peak earning years of the life cycle. When we ask what happens to the aggregate consumption of all families as their aggregate income varies over time, the answer depends, among other things, on what happens to the distribution of families by age and by income over time. If there is an increase in the proportion of all families who are at the early and late stages of the life cycle (and thus a decrease in the proportion between those stages), the result would appear to be a rise in the fraction of the larger total income that is consumed, assuming no change in the distribution of income by income class. The opposite shift in the age distribution would appear to have the opposite effect, all else being equal. However, the actual record for the United States shows that the age and income distributions have changed quite gradually; therefore, the life-cycle hypothesis introduces no large error by assuming that these distributions are stable.

As this hypothesis holds that the family's consumption depends on the present value of the family's expected income over its life cycle, the hypothesis also holds that aggregate consumption depends on the present value of the expected income of all families. Because the number of families changes over time, aggregate consumption will not be stable, but will grow proportionally with aggregate expected income. The aggregate consumption function may therefore be expressed as

$$C_t = cV_t$$

Here V_t is the value in year t of aggregate current plus expected income of future years. V_t may be written as

$$V_t = A_t + Y_{L_t} + Y_{L_t}^e$$

$A_t =$ the value of all property assets as of that year

$Y_{L_t} =$ labor or nonproperty income for that year

$Y_{L_t}^e =$ the present or year t value of expected labor or nonproperty income of future years

Therefore,

$$C_t = c(A_t + Y_{L_t} + Y_{L_t}^e)$$

A_t and Y_{L_t} can be measured directly, but $Y_{L_t}^e$ cannot. To obtain estimates of actual consumption from this function, values for Y_L^e must be found for each year. Ando and Modigliani tested various possible assumptions as to how expected labor income varies with different measurable values and adopted the assumption that average expected labor income is equal to current labor income multiplied by a scale factor, or

$$Y_{L_t}^e = \beta Y_{L_t}$$

in which β is some positive fraction. If there is an increase in current labor income from one period to the next, the recipients raise their estimate of average expected labor income by an amount equal to the change in current labor income multiplied by β. Total expected labor income, of course, varies directly with the remaining years of employment. On the assumption of an average worker age of 35 and an average retirement age of 65, the remaining years would be 30. Designating the remaining years by T, the total of expected labor income for the current period is then equal to $(T - 1) \beta Y_{L_t}$.

With expected labor income expressed in terms of current labor income, the consumption function may then be written as

$$C_t = c[A_t + Y_{L_t} + (T-1)\beta Y_{L_t}]$$

or

$$C_t = cA_t + c[1 + \beta(T-1)]Y_{L_t}$$

In this form, the coefficients of A_t and Y_{L_t} can be estimated. On the basis of annual U.S. data, Ando and Modigliani found

$$C_t = 0.06A_t + 0.7Y_{L_t}$$

This formula reveals that an increase of $1 billion in property assets would raise consumption by $60 million and that an increase of $1 billion in current labor income would raise consumption by $700 million.

Now we may see the way in which the life-cycle hypothesis reconciles the data that show a nonproportional short-run consumption function with the data that show a proportional long-run consumption function. In the short run, property assets remain approximately unchanged and the $0.06A_t$ term in the function may be taken as a constant. However, in the short run, labor income will vary. Figure 15-10 shows *labor* income along the income axis and, as usual, consumption along the vertical axis. The intercept of the short-run function labeled SR is given by $0.6A_t$, a constant in the short run; the slope of that function is 0.7, the marginal propensity to consume out of labor income. The relationship indicated is nonproportional—that is, the average propensity to consume out of labor income varies inversely with changes in labor income.

Over the long run, the growth in property assets will shift the SR function upward and raise its intercept as shown by the dashed lines in Figure 15-10. Although this is not inherent in the life-cycle hypothesis, the statistical record indicates that the short-run function has shifted upward over time to produce a series of points along a

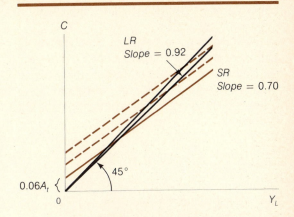

FIGURE 15-10
Short-Run and Long-Run Aggregate Consumption Functions of the Life-Cycle Hypothesis

curve like that labeled LR in Figure 15-10. The LR function shows a constant ratio of consumption to labor income as labor income reaches successively higher levels in the long run. To see this numerically, divide the preceding equation by Y_{L_t}. This yields

$$\frac{C_t}{Y_{L_t}} = 0.06\frac{A_t}{Y_{L_t}} + 0.7 = 0.06\left(\frac{A_t}{Y_t}\cdot\frac{Y_t}{Y_{L_t}}\right) + 0.7$$

If the A_t/Y_t and Y_t/Y_{L_t} ratios are constant, the C_t/Y_{L_t} ratio will also be constant—the LR function will intersect the origin in Figure 15-10. The record shows that the two ratios have indeed been fairly stable. The ratio of property assets to total income has been about 2.8 and the ratio of labor income to total income (the reciprocal of Y_t/Y_{L_t}) has been about 0.76. If we now substitute these values for the ratios in the preceding equation, we have

$$\frac{C_t}{Y_{L_t}} = 0.06\left(2.8\cdot\frac{1}{0.76}\right) = 0.92$$

The slope of the *LR* line in Figure 15-10 is therefore about 0.92.

This indicates the ratio of consumption to total labor income in the long run. As a final step, we may derive the ratio of consumption to total income. Given the earlier equation, $C_t = 0.06A_t + 0.7Y_{L_t}$, divide through by total income (Y_t) to obtain

$$\frac{C_t}{Y_t} = 0.06\frac{A_t}{Y_t} + 0.7\frac{Y_{L_t}}{Y_t}$$

Now we substitute the values for A_t/Y_t (2.8) and Y_{L_t}/Y_t (0.76).

$$\frac{C_t}{Y_t} = 0.06(2.8) + 0.7(0.76) = 0.70$$

The APC is about 0.70. If this were plotted, the function would be a straight line from the origin with a slope of 0.70. For C_t/Y_{L_t}, the slope was found to be about 0.92, but this function relates consumption to labor income alone instead of to labor plus property income.

The conclusions that follow from this analysis may be stated as follows: Because the ratio of property assets to total income and the ratio of labor income to total income have been reasonably stable in the long run, the life-cycle hypothesis does explain the long-run proportionality found between consumption and income. The fact that the amount of property assets is roughly stable in the short run, while labor income varies over that same time interval, explains the short-run nonproportional relationship indicated by the actual data. Lastly, as we saw in the microanalysis part of this chapter, the hypothesis also explains the observed relationship between consumption and income at different family income levels—the *apc* declines with the level of family income.

Although the life-cycle hypothesis scores well in explaining the various relationships revealed by the cross-sectional and time series data, the importance it assigns to current labor income as a determinant of expected labor income is regarded by some critics as a major weakness. Although this hypothesis indicates that a change in current labor income will in itself lead to a relatively small change in consumption, it makes the change in current labor income the cause of a relatively large change in consumption by so closely linking changes in the much larger figure for expected labor income to changes in current income. In so doing, it treats what may be temporary changes in current labor income as if they were permanent changes. The marginal propensity to consume out of labor income of 0.7 applies to all changes in labor income, but the actual propensity may be much smaller for some changes. The best illustration of this is the 10 percent income tax surcharge of 1968, which Congress passed as a strictly temporary tax. When changes in labor income, like those that resulted from this tax, appear to be temporary, the changes in consumption indicated by the coefficient of the labor income component of the estimating equation may substantially overstate the changes that will actually occur.

Income and Consumption: A Concluding Note

Empirical data covering a century reveal that the long-run relationship between consumption and income is approximately proportional. The data also show that the short-run or cyclical relationship is typically nonproportional. Before the long-run data became available, many economists concluded on the basis of the Keynesian absolute income hypothesis that the nonproportional relationship applied not only in the short run but also in the long run. If that were the case, an ever larger fraction of income would be saved as income grew over the long run.

The implications of such a relationship in terms of the simple Keynesian model of income determination are apparent. If the consumption function is nonproportional in the long run, then the higher the level of income grows over the years, the greater will be the percentage of that income devoted to saving. Assuming a simple two-sector economy, to maintain any given level of income, planned investment must equal planned saving. Therefore, to provide an ever-growing level of income, an ever-growing percentage of the economy's production would have to be channeled into investment in order to absorb the ever-growing percentage of the economy's income that goes into saving. Whether or not business people will find it profitable to carry planned investment to the required level will, in the absence of government intervention, decide the crucial issue of whether or not the economy can continue to grow and generate ever higher levels of income and output.

If, on the other hand, the long-run consumption function is proportional, this problem does not appear. Growth in income alone will not affect the fraction of income that is saved. Therefore, the fraction of production that must be devoted to investment remains the same. Assuming that government's relative role remains unchanged, the economy faces the much less serious problem of expanding investment *proportionally* with the growth of income and output. Whereas the whole complex of conditions that determine the amount of investment expenditures planned by business might be sufficiently favorable to produce a growth of investment spending proportional with the growth of income, it is less likely that these conditions will be sufficiently favorable to produce a growth of investment spending that is more than proportional with the growth of income. The inability of the economy to absorb such saving would stop the growth of income and output dead in its tracks.

Not only does this problem not carry the forbidding implications it did thirty or forty years ago, but to many economists the very reverse has become the problem in the United States over recent years. The problem they see is not whether investment will grow fast enough to absorb saving, but whether saving will grow fast enough to make possible the amount of investment needed to provide a satisfactory rate of growth of output. In the last few years, an often-expressed fear has been that the economic future is bleak unless we find ways to reverse the recent tendency of saving to grow more slowly than income. This is the opposite of the fear expressed by Keynes almost fifty years ago. Then he could see only more stagnation unless massive government deficits offset the volume of saving that was expected to grow more rapidly than income. Of the several villains in the dismal picture he painted, the belief in a nonproportional consumption function was one of no small importance.

Although saving has grown less than proportionally with income in recent years, the record still suggests that there is a proportional relationship between saving and income or between consumption and income over the long run. This amounts to a rejection of the major tenet of the absolute income hypothesis. If this indeed is the "true" nature of the long-run consumption function, we may expect consumption to absorb a relatively constant proportion of an ever-growing national output of goods and services over the decades ahead. Assuming that the government's relative role remains unchanged, we may also expect saving to result in investment equal to a relatively constant proportion of output, as long as there is no Keynesian problem of getting that much saving into investment.

Although consumption shows a proportional relationship to income over the long run, there is more to the explanation of consumption spending than the level of income. In Chapter 16 we will examine some other factors that influence consumption.

16

Other Factors Influencing Consumption Spending

OVERVIEW

Any attempt to explain consumption spending understandably begins with income, the most important factor. However, many other factors influence consumption. This chapter will examine a few of these in some detail.

The first factor is the rate of interest. Although at first glance it seems reasonable that a higher rate of interest earned on savings would result in the saving of a larger fraction of income, this result does not necessarily follow. There are forces working in both directions, and the net result is not clear.

The second factor considered is the price level and expectations of changes in it. All else being equal, a higher or lower price level should not affect aggregate real consumption if aggregate disposable income increases or decreases proportionately. However, if there is "money illusion"—a failure on the part of consumers to see that their real income is unchanged—a change in real consumption will occur with no change in real income. Moreover, a change in real consumption may also occur as a result of a change in price expectations. If consumers expect the rate of inflation to accelerate, they will tend to increase the amount of an unchanged real income they currently consume.

The next factor looked into is the distribution of income. The fraction of disposable income that goes into consumption will vary according to the distribution of that income by income class. The effect of a redistribution of income on consumption will differ according to whether we follow one or another of the various income hypotheses examined in Chapter 15.

The last factor considered is the volume of financial assets held by consumers. To what degree do changes in these holdings cause consumers to change the fraction of their income that is consumed? Some aspects of this large question are considered here. The chapter concludes with a brief look at a few other nonincome factors that influence consumption.

350

The empirical evidence on the consumption–income relationship examined in Chapter 15 suggests that disposable income is by far the most important factor influencing consumption spending. More specifically, it suggests that disposable income is of far greater importance in explaining consumption on a decade-to-decade basis than it is on a year-to-year basis, and of far greater importance on a year-to-year basis than on a quarter-to-quarter basis. In other words, the shorter the time period under consideration, the more clearly do factors other than the level of income influence the level of consumption spending.

We cannot expect with any certainty that a change in income from one quarter to the next will be accompanied by a change in consumption in the same direction; the MPC is frequently negative. On the other hand, a change in income from one year to the next, if it is at all sizable, will almost certainly be accompanied by a change in consumption in the same direction. Even on a yearly basis, however, the change in consumption may be anywhere from a small to a large fraction of the change in income; the MPC is positive, but highly variable.[1] In short, for annual and quarterly changes, income alone is not the complete explanation of the changes in consumption we observe in the real world. Other factors are clearly at work.

Rate of Interest

Although it is reasonably certain that the rate of interest influences the way in which any given level of aggregate disposable income is allocated between consumption and saving, it is not equally certain that a higher interest rate means that less disposable income will be allocated to consumption and more to saving, or vice versa.

---

[1]As was shown in column 5 of Table 15-2, the MPC for year-to-year changes (omitting 1942–47) varied from a low of 0.331 in 1938 to a high of 7.890 in 1949. Large changes are found in adjoining years: from 0.376 in 1948 to 7.890 in 1949 and from 1.108 in 1969 to 0.488 in 1970.

A change in the interest rate may cause an increase *or* a decrease in the total amount saved.

By first examining the saving behavior of the individual, we may see why the response, in the aggregate, may go in either direction. Apart from saving prompted by a desire to leave an estate, the individual's current saving may be viewed as deferred consumption. Because the typical individual prefers a dollar of present consumption to a dollar of future consumption (a positive time preference), he is willing to abstain from a dollar of current consumption only in exchange for something more than a dollar of future consumption. Assuming a stable price level, the rate of interest a person can receive on saving indicates the amount of future consumption he can secure in exchange. For example, at a rate of 5 percent, he can exchange one dollar of current consumption for approximately one and a half dollars of consumption eight years later. The individual who aims at maximizing total utility over time will substitute future consumption for present consumption up to the point at which the marginal utility derived from the expenditure of the interest-augmented future dollar is just equal to or just greater than that derived from the expenditure of the current dollar.

Given the typical individual's schedule of preferences, it appears that the amount of saving is directly dependent on the rate of interest. However, while a higher interest rate tends to produce a substitution toward more future and less present consumption, it also increases the individual's future income beyond what it would have been otherwise. Therefore, a higher interest rate raises his future income relative to his current income, which in turn may lead him to take part of this larger future income in the form of present consumption. Whether an individual with a given current income will save more on balance at a higher interest rate then depends on the relative strength of the *substitution effect,* which works toward more saving at higher interest rates, and the *income effect,* which works toward less saving at higher interest rates. For those lower-income individuals who will save only a relatively small part of their incomes even at high interest rates, the substitution effect will outweigh the income effect; their saving will vary directly with the rate of interest. For individuals with large incomes who tend to save relatively large parts of these incomes, the income effect may outweigh the substitution effect; higher interest rates may decrease the amount of current saving. For low-income savers, a supply curve relating the amount of saving to the rate of interest will slope upward to the right over any realistic range of interest rates. For high-income savers, this supply curve may at some rate of interest bend backward, indicating that saving decreases for all rates above that at which this backward bend appears.[2]

A special case in which an individual's supply curve will be backward sloping at *all* rates of interest occurs when the individual saves whatever amount is needed to realize the goal of accumulating a fixed dollar sum by a particular future date. The higher the interest rate, the smaller then is the amount that he must save per time period in order to realize his goal.

The argument that a higher interest rate may cause some individuals to save more and others to save less receives its strongest support when limited to individuals who actually save some positive amount (as opposed to dissavers who "save" a negative amount). The interest rate, however, may also affect dissavers. For these individuals, a higher interest rate will in practically all cases discourage dissaving and encourage saving. Dissavers finance current consumption in excess of current income either by drawing down past savings or by borrowing. Because, all else being equal, no one wants to borrow at a higher rather than a lower interest rate, higher interest rates—which mean higher rates on installment credit purchases of cars and the like and on personal loans—will, if anything, discourage borrowing.[3] To the extent that higher

rates make dissaving smaller than it otherwise would be, the amount of saving to this extent varies directly with the interest rate.

Although the supply curves of dissavers will therefore probably vary directly with the interest rate, the supply curves of savers may vary directly or inversely with the interest rate for reasons noted earlier. Consequently, the general shape of the aggregate supply curve, which is a summation of all these individual supply curves, can hardly be specified *a priori*. No simple, systematic relationship can be established between aggregate personal saving and the rate of interest on theoretical grounds. Few empirical studies of the relationship have been made; most of these show that the interest rate has a negligible effect on saving.[4] In view of the available evidence, many economists have taken an essentially agnostic position. They recognize that a change in the interest rate may change the amount of aggregate saving out of any given level of disposable income. But they also insist that although the change in saving is most likely to be in the same direction as the change in the interest rate, it may possibly change in the opposite direction.[5] This amounts to saying that inter-

---

[2]For a detailed analysis in terms of indifference curves, see R.L. Crouch, *Macroeconomics*, Harcourt Brace Jovanovich, 1972, pp. 49–60, esp. 57–60.

[3]For the influence of interest rates on consumer demand, see M.J. Hamburger, "Interest Rates and the Demand for Consumer Durable Goods," in *American Economic Review*, Dec. 1967, pp. 1131–53, and W. Weber, "The Effect of Interest Rates on Aggregate Consumption," in *American Economic Review*, Sept. 1970, pp. 591–600.

[4]An exception is that by M.J. Boskin, "Taxation, Saving, and the Rate of Interest," in *Journal of Political Economy*, April 1978, pp. S3–S27. He concludes that a good deal of evidence suggests a positive relationship between saving and the rate of interest.

[5]This contention should not be confused with the contention that saving will tend to be placed in those institutions or in those forms that pay the highest rate of interest consistent with savers' other objectives. This says that individuals, *once having saved,* will tend to seek the highest rate of interest for their savings; it does not say that a higher rate of interest will necessarily induce more saving at any given level of disposable income. The intense competition, including "price (interest-rate) competition," among savings institutions does not necessarily influence the amount of income saved, but may affect only its allocation among the competing institutions.

est rate changes of the size found in actual experience do not, on balance, greatly influence the amount of personal saving at any level of disposable income. Forces working in both directions are partially offsetting and produce a net effect that is believed to be small.

Price Level and Price Expectations

Another factor that influences aggregate consumption expenditures is the price level of consumer goods and services. As it changes, will aggregate consumption expenditures change in the same direction, the opposite direction, or not at all?

To answer this question, several distinctions must initially be made. First, we are concerned with aggregate consumption expenditures and not expenditures on any particular good or service or group of goods and services. A rise in the price of any single good or service for which there are close substitutes will lead to a transfer of expenditure to substitutes and a decrease in expenditures on the good that has risen in price. A decline in the price of such a good would, by the same reasoning, lead to a transfer of expenditures away from substitutes and increased expenditures on the good whose price has declined. However, for a rise or fall in the *price level* of consumer goods and services, there are no substitutes to which expenditures may be diverted.[6] It is possible now only to substitute

personal saving for consumption expenditures or consumption expenditures for personal saving. In other words, consumers may react to any rise or fall in the price level by spending either more or less of their incomes for goods and services.

How consumers as a group may react basically depends on a second distinction—that between a price level change accompanied by a proportional change in aggregate current-dollar disposable income as distinguished from a change accompanied by a nonproportional change in aggregate current-dollar disposable income.[7] If current-dollar disposable income rises or falls proportionally with the consumer price level, constant-dollar (real disposable) income remains unchanged. If it rises more or less than proportionally, real disposable income, of course, increases or decreases, respectively.

Given a rise in the price level of consumer goods and services, will aggregate consumption expenditures rise or fall? If a change in the consumer price level is offset by a proportional change in aggregate current-dollar disposable income, in terms of real income, consumers as a group are no better or worse off than before. All else being equal, they presumably will hold real consumption expenditures and saving unchanged.[8] This conclusion is based on the

---

[6]Because a rise in the consumer price level does not involve proportional changes in the prices of all goods and services, there may be some degree of substitution of goods that have risen relatively little or possibly even fallen in price for goods that have risen relatively sharply in price. However, the cost to the average consumer of any likely assortment of goods and services, even after substitutions have been made, will be higher after the rise in the price level than it was before. The greater the rise in the price level, the more certain this is to be true. This is all that is needed to qualify here as a rise in the price level as seen by the average consumer.

[7]There is no simple or unvarying relationship between a change in the consumer price level and a change in the level of current-dollar disposable income. The two may change in opposite directions, although quarter-to-quarter data for recent years show, with few exceptions, changes in the same direction. Periods in which prices, not only of consumer goods and services but of the other goods and services included in GNP, are rising are typically periods during which GNP in current dollars will be rising. Disposable income will rise along with GNP, but whether it rises more or less rapidly than GNP depends especially on how much of the enlarged gross income flow is diverted into tax receipts and retained corporate profits and how much the remaining gross income flow is supplemented by government transfer payments.

[8]Among other things that may not remain equal is the distribution of income. If current-dollar income is redistributed between the fixed income group and other income groups as a result of a changing price level, incomes of some groups may rise or fall faster than prices,

Keynesian argument that real consumption is a function of real income.[9]

"Money Illusion"

Although there is no change in real income, a change may nonetheless occur in real consumption if consumers are subject to what economists call "money illusion."[10] Suppose, for example, that during a given time period the consumer price level rises 10 percent and the current-dollar disposable income of each family rises 10 percent. Those families that recognize that their money income is unchanged in real terms suffer no money illusion, and, all else being equal, will probably maintain their consumption and saving unchanged in real terms, that is, they will increase both spending and saving in current dollars by 10 percent. Other families may be subject to a money illusion in either of two ways. Some may see only that the price level has risen and somehow overlook the fact that their current-dollar disposable income has risen proportionally. They are actually no worse off, but they believe that they are and act accordingly. To the extent that families reduce the fraction of income saved in

response to a decrease in real income, the families whose money illusion leads them to believe they have suffered a decrease in real income will reduce the fraction of income saved or increase the fraction consumed. This, of course, involves an increase in real consumption, because their real income was actually unchanged. Other families may see only the rise in their current-dollar disposable income and overlook the proportional rise in the price level. These families will feel better off and, accordingly, may increase the fraction of income saved or reduce the fraction consumed. This involves a decrease in real consumption, because their real income was actually unchanged.

If we assume that no widespread money illusion exists among consumers, we may expect no appreciable change in the fraction of aggregate current-dollar disposable income devoted to consumption expenditures as a result of a change in the consumer price level accompanied by a proportional change in current-dollar disposable income. In terms of the aggregate consumption function diagram, if we measure real income and real consumption on the two axes, the economy remains at the same points on the income and consumption axes.

What about changes in the consumer price level that are not matched by compensating changes in current-dollar disposable income? Such changes mean changes in real disposable income, and a change in real disposable income should directly affect real consumption expenditures. A rise in prices that leads to a fall in real disposable income should move consumers as a group back down the aggregate short-run consumption function. At this new point on the function, there will be an absolute decrease in real consumption expenditures and an increase in the fraction of real disposable income devoted to consumption expenditures. Conversely, a fall in prices that leads to a rise in real disposable income moves consumers as a group up along the function. There will be an absolute increase in real consumption expenditures and a decrease in the fraction of real disposable income devoted to consumption expenditures.

---

of others slower than prices, and of still others not at all. To the extent that the marginal propensity to consume of these groups differs, an impact on real consumption expenditures would be expected. Income redistribution as a specific factor influencing real consumption expenditures will be considered in a later section of this chapter.

There is also the real balance or Pigou effect discussed in Chapter 13. A rise in the price level reduces the value of money balances and other fixed-dollar assets and thereby reduces consumer wealth. This will tend to reduce the amount of real consumption at any level of real disposable income. We will return to this later in this chapter.

[9]Although our attention is limited here to the effect of price level changes, aggregate consumer spending as well as spending on individual goods and services may be affected by *relative* price changes quite apart from changes in the price level. (See G. Ackley and D.B. Suits, "Relative Price Changes and Aggregate Consumer Demand," in *American Economic Review,* Dec. 1950, pp. 785–804.)

[10]This term was coined by Irving Fisher, who used it to describe "a failure to perceive that the dollar or any other unit of money expands and shrinks in value." (See *The Money Illusion,* Adelphi, 1928, p. 4.)

Although these are valid conclusions, the changes in real consumption expenditures that occur under these circumstances are not caused directly by the changes in the consumer price level. They are caused by the changes in real disposable income that accompany changes in the consumer price level. We already know from the empirical short-run consumption function that real consumption expenditures fluctuate with real income in this fashion. In short, a changing price level may affect real consumption expenditures to the extent that the changing price level is not offset by changes in current-dollar disposable income, provided that consumers are not subject to money illusion.

Price Expectations

In the preceding discussion, we were concerned with the relationship between *realized* changes in the consumer price level and *realized* changes in aggregate disposable income. We assumed that consumer spending behavior was determined *only* by the realized changes experienced by consumers in any time period. There are periods, however, in which the consumer price level is rising, current-dollar disposable income is rising to match prices, and real consumption expenditures are increasing. Note that we are now suggesting an increase in real consumption expenditures with no change in real disposable income. This frequently occurs when the consumer price level has been rising sharply for some time. It reflects the fact that consumers are devoting a larger fraction of real income to consumption expenditures "today" in *expectation* of still higher prices "tomorrow." Conversely, expectations of a lower price level in the future can lead to a postponement of real consumption expenditures, even though real disposable income has not fallen in the current period.

For example, during the last quarter of 1979 and the first quarter of 1980, the percentage of disposable personal income devoted to consumption rose to 92.5 from less than 92.0 during the first three quarters of 1979. (A one percentage point change was then equal to about $17–$18 billion dollars at an annual rate.) This spurt in consumer spending appears to have been driven by the acceleration of the inflation rate, which to the average consumer is the best guide to what the inflation rate will be later. The month-by-month changes in the 1979 Consumer Price Index had jumped to a double-digit annual rate, the first time that had happened since 1974. In the first quarter of 1980, the rate had soared to 18 percent. Until President Carter's consumer credit restraint program was introduced in the spring of 1980, credit was readily available, and the "buy now" mentality took hold with a vengeance. This surge in consumer spending may have delayed the beginning of a recent recession from 1979 to 1980. The consensus among economists in early 1979 was that a recession would start later that year, but this view failed to allow for the increased fraction of income devoted to consumption.

Price level expectations are only one of a number of types of expectations that may influence real consumption expenditures. For many families, an important factor may be expectations as to the future level of their income. Consumption expenditures are also influenced to some extent by general expectations concerning the short-run outlook for expansion or contraction in business activity. Finally, any developments that lead to expectations of large-scale war will produce expectations of shortages and higher prices. These expectations in turn will increase real consumption expenditures in the current period.

Consumer expectations with respect to economic, social, or political changes can all affect real consumption expenditures in any period. Although noted here in connection with the price level, expectations in this more general sense may properly be considered as a separate and at times very important factor influencing consumption.[11]

---

[11]See G.E. Angevine, "Forecasting Consumption with a Canadian Consumer Sentiment Measure," in *Canadian Journal of Economics,* May 1974, pp. 273–89, G. Briscoe, "The Significance of Financial Expectations in Predicting Consumer Expenditures: A Quarterly Analysis," in *Applied*

Distribution of Income[12]

The level of aggregate disposable income is the most important factor that influences the level of aggregate consumption expenditures. However, with any given *level* of disposable income, the resulting level of consumption expenditures also depends on the *distribution* of that income by income class. In general, the more equal that distribution, the larger the fraction devoted to consumption tends to be. For example, an economy in which the 25 percent of the families with the highest income receive 30 percent of total income and the 25 percent of the families with the lowest incomes receive 20 percent of total income is more likely to show a larger fraction of total income devoted to consumption than if the top 25 percent of the families received 45 percent of the total income and the bottom 25 percent of the families received only 5 percent. This is suggested by the fact that the fraction of disposable income allocated to consumption is higher at low levels of family income and lower at higher levels of family income. The family budget data of Table 15-1 gave us in Figure 15-1 an empirical family consumption function that showed this relationship.

Although we may say that the more equal the distribution of income, the higher the fraction of income devoted to consumption tends to be, it does not necessarily follow that any change in the distribution of a given level of income against higher-income families and in favor of lower-income families will increase the fraction of that income that is allocated to consumption.[13] Although at first glance a redistribution would seem to work this way, several qualifications limit the quantitative importance of such changes and even question their direction.

1. Changes in the distribution of income in any short period, even a period as long as a decade, are moderate.[14] There is little yearly change in the existing occupational wage differences, distribution of property ownership, differences in productive ability, and the whole complex of institutional factors that determine the distribution of income. Therefore, changes in the distribution of income from year to year are correspondingly small and can have only a small effect on the fraction of aggregate disposable income devoted to consumption. Apparently the effect becomes significant only over a decade or several decades. Of course, a deliberate public

---

Economics, June 1976, pp. 99–119, A.A. Tait, "Savings, Real Balances, Inflation and Expectations—Further Empirical Evidence," *Manchester School of Economics and Social Studies,* Dec. 1978, pp. 311–21, and R.J. Cooper and K. McLaren, "Inflationary Expectations in Intertemporal Consumer Demand Systems," *Australian Economic Papers,* June 1980, pp. 193–202.

[12]Discussion here is limited to personal distribution or distribution by income group. For distribution by occupational group and functional share, see I.B. Kravis, "Relative Income Shares in Fact and Theory," in *American Economic Review,* Dec. 1959, pp. 917–49, and I. Friend and I.B. Kravis, "Entrepreneurial Income, Saving, and Investment," in *American Economic Review,* June 1957, pp. 269–301. At the same income levels, the marginal propensity of business owners and farmers to save is found to be greater than that of others. This suggests that shifts in the functional distribution of income over the business cycle may explain part of the short-run changes observed in consumption spending.

[13]Because the long-run trend in the distribution of income in the U.S. and other free economies has been toward less inequality, unless otherwise indicated all references to changes in distribution will be to changes toward less inequality.

[14]The share of aggregate income received by the 20 percent of families with the lowest incomes changed from 4.9 percent in 1960 to 5.5 in 1970 and 5.3 in 1979. For the next higher quintile, the percentage was 12.0, 12.0, and 11.6, respectively for these three years. For the middle quintile, it was 17.6, 17.4, and 17.5 percent, respectively; for the next, 23.6, 23.5, and 24.1 percent, respectively; and for the top quintile, 42.0, 41.6, and 41.6 percent, respectively. (SOURCE: U.S. Department of Commerce, Bureau of the Census, *Current Population Reports,* Series P-60, No. 80, "Income in 1970 of Families and Persons in the United States," p. 28, and Series P-60, No. 125, *Money Income and Poverty Status of Families and Persons in the United States: 1979,* p. 15.)

policy designed to reduce income inequality rapidly, regardless of its consequences, could alter this conclusion. Past experience, however, indicates that even with a progressive tax structure and other governmental measures that have contributed noticeably to less inequality, even decade-to-decade changes in income distribution have not greatly influenced the amount of consumption expenditures at any given level of income.

2. Given any change in income distribution, a second qualification arises from the fact that the increase in the fraction of income devoted to consumption may be much less than is suggested by a comparison of how families at different income levels divide their total incomes between consumption and saving. Redistribution of a *given* aggregate income involves additions to the incomes of some families and reductions in the incomes of others. Families do not ordinarily allocate an addition to or a reduction in their incomes between consumption and saving in the same way as they allocate their total incomes between consumption and saving. The *mpc* describes the allocation of additions to or reductions in the family's disposable income; the *apc* describes the allocation of the family's total disposable income. This distinction is important, because the differences in the *mpc* at various family income levels are much smaller than the differences in the *apc*.[15] If the immediate effect of any redistribution of income on aggregate consumption expenditures depends on the *mpc* rather than the *apc* at various family income lev-

els, it follows that the prospective expansionary effect on consumption may be overestimated if this effect is gauged from differences in the *apc* rather than from differences in the *mpc*.

In fact, the *mpc* may be virtually the same at each level of family income. In such a case, even though the *apc* at higher incomes may be much below what it is at lower incomes, a change in distribution would have virtually no effect on consumption expenditures. According to some findings, something approaching this result may be found in actual U.S. experience.[16] Without pushing the argument to this extreme, however, the absence of pronounced differences in the *mpc* at different levels of family income has been used to support the argument that income redistribution, at least of the order realized in recent years, does not significantly increase the fraction of disposable income allocated to consumption expenditures.

3. The effect on consumption to be expected from a given redistribution of income differs according to which income hypothesis we follow. As we will see, the relative income hypothesis suggests that a decrease rather than an increase in consumption expenditures may result from redistribution. The absolute income hypothesis suggests just the opposite result. The permanent income hypothesis suggests that the amount of permanent consumption out of any given level of

[15]Evidence supplied by budget studies relate measured consumption to measured income as in Figure 15-1. There the moderate curvature of the empirical family consumption function indicates moderate differences in the *mpc* at different family income levels. If the function were a straight line, the *mpc* would be the same at all levels. The *apc* at different levels of family income could be shown in Figure 15-1 by the slopes of a set of straight lines from the origin to various points on the consumption function. (Such a set of *apc* lines is given in Figure 15-2.) A comparison of the difference between the slopes of the two lines from the origin with the difference in the slope of

the consumption function itself at any two income levels will show that the difference in the *apc* is greater than the difference in the *mpc*.

[16]See H. Lubell, "Effects of Redistribution of Income on Consumers' Expenditures," in *American Economic Review,* March 1947, pp. 157–70, and "Correction," in *American Economic Review,* Dec. 1947, p. 930. See also M. Bronfenbrenner, T. Yamane, and C.H. Lee, "A Study in Redistribution and Consumption," in *Review of Economics and Statistics,* May 1955, pp. 149–59; M. Bronfenbrenner, *Income Distribution Theory,* Aldine, 1971, pp. 107–109; A.S. Blinder, "Distribution Effects and the Aggregate Consumption Function," in *Journal of Political Economy,* June 1975, pp. 447–75; and J. van Doorn, "Aggregate Consumption and the Distribution of Incomes," in *European Economic Review,* October 1975, pp. 417–23.

permanent income will be unaffected by redistribution. Finally, the life-cycle hypothesis suggests a relatively small effect on consumption as a result of redistribution.

Consider first the case in which spending and saving depend exclusively on absolute income. If a redistribution takes place with no change in the level of income, higher-income families will move down and lower-income families will move up the family consumption function in Figure 15-1. If each family regards its new position as permanent and immediately adjusts its spending to the amount that families at this income level customarily spend, we may expect an increase in the *apc* of the higher-income families after they move down and a decrease in the *apc* of the lower-income families after they move up. Because the *apc* of the lower-income families is still above the *apc* of the higher-income families, the net effect will be an increase in aggregate consumption expenditures.[17]

Consider next the case in which relative income completely controls consumption. With no change in aggregate disposable income, redistribution by definition means a change in relative incomes. All along the income scale, each family adjusts its spending to its new income level, not in accordance with the new absolute level of that income, but in relation to the spending patterns of the families whose consumption standards it emulates. As the income

of the higher-income families is reduced through redistribution, the pressure on families just below to "keep up with the Joneses" is reduced downward in accordance with their reduced incomes. This process will continue all the way down the income scale. The lowest-income families may still have no choice but to spend all their higher incomes, because these incomes are just sufficient to cover basic necessities. Other families, however, may now be able to save a part of their income that was previously used to purchase goods and services that were largely emulative purchases. A redistribution, instead of leading to increased consumption, may actually decrease consumption, because the lessening of inequality wipes out some of society's emulative spending.

The case in which permanent consumption is related to permanent income as indicated by the permanent income hypothesis gives yet a different result. Remember that this theory holds that the ratio of permanent consumption to permanent income is the same at all levels of family income and that there is zero correlation between transitory consumption and transitory income. A redistribution toward greater equality will provide increments of income to lower-income families and the opposite for higher-income families. These additions to and subtractions from income may at first be regarded by these families as positive and negative transitory-income components. In this case, the permanent income hypothesis holds that neither the lower-income families nor the higher-income families will change the amount of their consumption, so that the redistribution has no effect on consumption. A program of redistribution that is maintained year after year will eventually cause the families gaining or losing income to regard these as permanent changes in income, thereby raising the permanent incomes of lower-income families above what they otherwise would have been. However, the aggregate of permanent consumption is unaffected to the extent that the ratio of permanent consumption to permanent income is, as the hypothesis holds, the same for all otherwise sim-

---

[17]For example, as a result of redistribution a $21,000 family that had saved $6,300 (*aps* = 0.30) and spent $14,700 (*apc* = 0.70) becomes a $20,000 family that now saves $5,600 (*aps* = 0.28) and spends $14,400 (*apc* = 0.72). A $4,000 family that had saved nothing (*aps* = 0) and spent $4,000 (*apc* = 1) now becomes a $5,000 family that saves $200 (*aps* = 0.04) and spends $4,800 (*apc* = 0.96). The increase in saving of the low-income family will not be as great as the decrease for the high-income family; the decrease in consumption of the high-income family will not be as great as the increase for low-income family. The two families that showed total consumption of $18,700 and total saving of $6,300 before the redistribution show total consumption of $19,200 and total saving of $5,800 after the redistribution, although the combined income of the two families is $25,000 in both cases.

ilar families, regardless of the level of their permanent income. The result therefore appears to be the same in the short period, when the redistribution may be viewed by those who gain or lose from it as transitory changes in income, and in the longer period, when the redistribution is viewed by those who gain or lose from it as permanent changes in income.

Last is the life-cycle hypothesis. Because this hypothesis makes current consumption depend not on current income but on the expected flow of income over the balance of a person's life, barring a massive redistribution, the person who gains income and the person who loses income as a result of redistribution will not see this change in income as a relatively large amount in terms of their life-cycle incomes. Consequently, the effect on aggregate current consumption will not be large. This at least is the result that follows for a redistribution that was expected and therefore an income change that people had taken into account in their life-cycle consumption plan. If a redistribution came unexpectedly, the effect on aggregate consumption would be larger. Overall, however, the conclusion here is close to that noted for the permanent income hypothesis. Both make current consumption depend on income extending years into the future—in the case of the life-cycle hypothesis extending for the balance of peoples' lives. Therefore, the life-cycle hypothesis suggests that redistribution will have no sizable effect on current consumption.

Because several of the hypotheses suggest quite different results, one cannot choose one result over another without first choosing one hypothesis over another. The relative merits of the competing hypotheses are still debated. So far, few economists have accepted the permanent income theory in its extreme form; therefore few economists would deny that redistribution has some effect on consumption. However, there is little disagreement as to the importance of this effect. Although in the early years following the appearance of Keynes' *General Theory*, economists generally believed that raising the level of aggregate consumption spending by redistri-

bution was a simple matter, it has been many years since anyone took that position.

Financial Assets

Some economists have attached considerable importance to the volume of financial assets accumulated by consumers as a factor influencing consumption expenditures. It seems reasonable to expect that, on the average, the family with a larger accumulation of cash, demand deposits, savings deposits, stocks, bonds, and other kinds of financial assets will spend more than the family with a smaller accumulation of financial assets, other things (including the disposable income of each family) being equal.[18] The rationale here is that a family's urge to add still more to its financial assets diminishes as its holdings of these assets increase. If most families reacted this way, as the total holdings of financial assets of all families increased over the years, a larger fraction of aggregate disposable income would be devoted to consumption and smaller fraction to saving or to the accumulation of still more financial assets. In terms of the aggregate consumption function, the entire curve would shift upward with the growth in the volume of financial assets, thereby producing a higher

---

[18]As a factor influencing consumption expenditures, economists usually count only "liquid assets," which exclude any financial assets, such as conventional mortgages, that cannot be quickly converted into cash at fixed prices. Liquid assets supposedly influence consumption more than illiquid assets because the possession of the former allows a consumer to dissave very readily. Some economists, however, include all financial assets and also make allowance for financial liabilities of consumers, the major part of which is debt outstanding as the result of purchases of houses and durable consumer goods. Beyond this, one need not limit attention to financial assets but may include real assets like housing and personal property and may allow for all liabilities to derive a *net worth* figure as in a consumer's balance sheet. However, the brief discussion here will consider financial assets alone.

APC at each possible level of aggregate disposable income.

As a case in point, the upward shift in the aggregate consumption function in the first of the postwar periods shown in Figure 15-6 (page 336) may be attributed to the huge amount of savings bonds, bank deposits, and other liquid assets accumulated by consumers during World War II. The upward shift in consumption was not limited to the first few postwar years when it could be readily attributed to spending to satisfy deferred demand. This shift characterizes later years as well. It may be argued that during the war years families built up a volume of liquid assets that they regarded as adequate or more than adequate to meet any future emergencies. With this accumulation of cash equivalents to rely on, families felt free in the postwar period to devote a larger fraction of their current disposable income to consumption. In contrast, a smaller fraction of disposable income had been devoted to consumption in the prewar period, because then only a small minority of the nation's families had an appreciable amount of such assets.

At first glance, this explanation suggests a clear-cut connection between the volume of financial assets held by consumers and the fraction of their disposable income devoted to consumption. As before, however, qualifications are necessary as soon as we examine this theory a little more closely.

For one thing, the size of the consumption-inducing effect depends on the ownership distribution of these financial assets by income class. An increase in the volume of these assets, if concentrated in the hands of upper-income families, may give little or no stimulus to consumption. Upper-income families save a large fraction of their incomes in any event; it is doubtful that further growth in their holdings of financial assets would cause them to decrease the fraction of their income that is saved.

A related qualification, which applies regardless of ownership distribution, is the possibility that for many families a taste of financial assets

simply whets the appetite for more. Even families of moderate income may react this way. Their original preference for consumption over saving may, after the first taste of financial assets, change to a preference toward saving as the means of accelerating the accumulation of financial assets.[19] Although this may be far from common, particularly for low-income families, it is still sufficient to raise some doubt as to the direct connection posited between the volume of financial assets held by consumers and the level of consumer expenditures at any given level of income.

Finally, the mere dollar volume of financial assets may suggest incorrect relationships; only the real value of the dollar volume held at any time is pertinent. A changing price level will raise or lower the real value of a given volume of financial assets. Except for holdings of stocks, shares in mutual funds, or other such assets whose current-dollar valuation tends to rise and fall with the price level, all financial assets are fixed-dollar assets. Barring money illusion, a family with $10,000 in fixed-dollar assets will recognize a rise in the price level as a decrease in the real value of its fixed-dollar assets and a fall in the price level as an increase in the real value of these assets. For example, a doubling in the price level will be seen to cut in half the purchasing power of the $10,000. If a rise in the price level is matched by a proportional rise in the family's current-dollar disposable income so that its real income remains unchanged, it may nevertheless reduce its real consumption expenditures due to the depressing effect of the price level change on the real value of its fixed-dollar assets. Conversely, if a fall in the price level is matched by a proportional fall in the family's cur-

___

[19] A revision of preferences toward saving and away from consumption is also toward income and away from consumption. Less consumption and more saving, with the saving devoted to the acquisition of income-producing financial assets, is a means of raising the level of family income and making possible still more saving.

rent-dollar disposable income, it may still increase its real consumption expenditures due to the expansionary effect exerted by the rise in the real value of its holdings of fixed-dollar assets. This, it may be recalled, describes the Pigou effect.

Of a related nature but still distinct from the Pigou effect is the consumption-stimulating effect of an increase in the real value of financial assets brought about by a fall in interest rates. As explained in Chapter 11, outstanding debt obligations that promise to pay a fixed number of dollars of interest each year and the principal amount at maturity will vary inversely in value with market interest rates. For example, a family that today holds a high-grade, 10 percent corporate bond with a $10,000 face value and maturity in the year 2005 would receive $1,000 interest each year and the $10,000 principal in 2005. If market interest rates on bonds of this kind were to rise substantially between now and, say, 1990, there would be a sizable decrease in the real value of that bond as of that date. In the opposite case of a substantial decline in market interest rates as of 1990, there would be a sizable increase in the real value of that bond as of that date.[20] In the first case, the decrease in the real value of its financial assets could cause the family to reduce the amount of consumption out of an unchanged real income; in the other case the opposite, of course, would be true. This interest-induced effect on consumption is seen to parallel the price-induced (Pigou) effect just described.

Depending on the quantity of financial assets held and the magnitude of changes in interest rates, the real value of these assets may change considerably over time. Therefore, potentially at least, changes in interest rates could significantly affect consumption spending. This is an interesting possibility, because it means that the interest rate is at least potentially important as an indirect influence on consumption spending through its effect on the value of assets, whereas it does not appear to be at all important as a direct influence. In other words, although people may not be directly induced to save a larger portion of their income because a higher interest rate yields a greater return on their saving, they may be indirectly induced to do so because a higher interest rate decreases the value of some of the assets they already hold.

Although we are primarily concerned with the influence of the amount of financial assets held by consumers on the level of their spending, as we have seen, any consideration of this factor is closely related to the price level and the rate of interest. The real value of the financial assets held by consumers changes not only because consumers devote part of their saving to the acquisition of more such assets but also as a result of revaluations due to changes in the price level and the interest rate. Whatever the cause of any particular change in the real value of these assets, the relevant issue is whether or not such a change produces a change in consumption spending. There is little doubt that there is a direct relationship here, but the quantitative strength of the relationship is another matter.[21]

---

[20] Although we are concerned with financial assets, the relationship in question applies in general to all assets that produce fixed income streams. A rise or fall in market interest rates means a rise or fall in the rate at which the income stream from any such asset will be capitalized. For example, the owners of an office building that produces a given income flow per time period (under long-term leases) would see the price at which they could sell this building decline in the face of rising interest rates, other things being equal.

[21] For a quantitative estimate of the influence that consumers' liquid asset holdings have on consumption expenditures, see A. Zellner, "The Short-Run Consumption Function," in *Econometrica,* Oct. 1957, pp. 552–67, and "Further Analysis of the Short-Run Consumption Function with Emphasis on Liquid Assets," in *Econometrica,* July 1965, pp. 571–81. See also K. Marwah, "Measuring the Role of Liquid Assets in Consumption: A Cross Country View of the World Economic Periphery," in *Journal of Development Studies,* April–July 1974, pp. 332–46. A list of consumption functions with liquid asset terms included is provided in D. Patinkin, *Money, Interest and Prices,* 2nd ed., Harper & Row, 1965, Appendix M.

The evidence is not clear, but it would appear that these assets are not ordinarily a major influence on consumption spending.[22] The holding of such assets is, nonetheless, one of the major *nonincome* factors that influence consumption spending.

Other Factors, in Brief

In any time period, relatively easy consumer credit terms can stimulate consumer expenditures for durable goods, and relatively tight terms can do the opposite.[23] The explosion in consumer purchases of automobiles far back in 1955 is credited in large part to the unusually easy credit terms offered in that year. When we recall that an increase in expenditures for durables tends to be largely at the expense of a decrease in saving, we can understand how easy credit, which stimulates purchases of durables, can increase the fraction of aggregate disposable income that is spent in any time period.[24]

---

[22]For an introductory statement on the general concept of the price-induced and interest-induced wealth effects and an argument supporting the importance of assets or wealth on consumption spending, see B.P. Pesek and T.R. Saving, *Money, Wealth, and Economic Theory,* Macmillan, 1967, pp. 11–21. See also M.J. Bailey, *National Income and the Price Level,* McGraw-Hill, 2nd ed., 1971, Ch. 6.

[23]Easier consumer credit is not the same as a lower rate of interest, although the latter may be one characteristic of easier consumer credit. Consumer installment credit may be said to be "easier," with no reduction in rates charged, if there is a lengthening of the repayment period on installment purchase contracts or if there is a relaxation of credit standards that makes credit available to applicants previously rejected.

[24]See P.W. McCracken, J.C.T. Mao, and C. Fricke, *Consumer Instalment Credit and Public Policy,* Bureau of Business Research, Univ. of Michigan, 1965. An appendix provides a case study of the role of installment credit in the 1955 auto sales year. See also D.B. Eastwood and R.C. Anderson, "Consumer Credit and Consumer Demand for Automobiles," in *Journal of Finance,* March 1976, pp. 113–23.

The difference between the growth rates of aggregate disposable income and population over a period of years also influences the fraction of aggregate disposable income devoted to consumption. If the nation's population is growing faster than aggregate disposable income, disposable income per capita is decreasing; this in turn tends to raise the fraction of aggregate disposable income that is consumed. Changes in certain characteristics of the population, such as its age distribution, will also affect the fraction of aggregate income spent. For example, an increase in the percentage of persons past or under working age will tend to increase the percentage of disposable income spent, because the average propensity to consume in these age groups is higher than the average for all age groups combined.

Deferred demand, especially on the scale displayed in the years immediately following World War II, tends to push consumption expenditures above the level that would be expected on the basis of disposable income alone. However, this factor has little application in normal peacetime periods.

Over recent decades, institutional changes have occurred that also affect the spending–saving patterns of consumers. For many families, saving has become largely automatic with the popularization of long-term saving commitments through life insurance, private pension funds, and mortgage loans on homes, the repayment of which is amortized over many years. Once families are committed, the amount of such quasi-compulsory saving is largely immune to changes in income. Because income does change, the stability of this portion of personal saving also influences the fraction of income that is devoted to consumption. For the portion of saving that remains a matter of current decision by the family each week or month, the diversity of forms in which personal saving may be placed is now so great that savers may find outlets for their savings that are virtually tailor-made to their requirements. To some degree, this also affects the spending–saving patterns of consumers.

Consumption Demand— A Concluding Note_____

In attempting to explain what determines the level of consumption spending, one is tempted, as were many economists in the early years following the appearance of Keynes' *General Theory,* to begin and end the explanation with the level of disposable income as *the* determinant. The time-series data that first became available during World War II gave empirical support to disposable income as the major factor in any explanation, but at the same time these data showed disposable income to be less than a total explanation. Many other factors were found to influence consumption spending, particularly in the short run; these dispelled any notion of a stable relationship between changes in consumption and changes in disposable income on a quarter-to-quarter or even a year-to-year basis.

However, despite the influence of these other factors, the data still clearly suggested that the level of disposable income dwarfs any nonincome factors and, except for short-term changes in income and consumption, is more important than all these nonincome factors combined.

One purpose of this chapter has been to provide some understanding of what the nonincome factors are, what their importance is, and how each one may influence consumption spending. Such an understanding puts into perspective the simplified relationship in which consumption is assumed to be a function solely of the income variable. In an introductory treatment of macroeconomic theory, one focuses on the income variable through an equation like $C = C_a + cY$ to simplify what would otherwise be a complex relationship. This was the focus of all the models in the earlier chapters. This review has revealed that consumption depends on many other variables in addition to current income.

17

Capital and Investment

OVERVIEW

Chapters 17–19 are concerned with the broad question of what determines the level of aggregate investment expenditures in any time period. Investment expenditures were brought into the simple model of income determination in Part 2 and into the extended model in Part 3. In the simple model, investment was merely assumed to be some fixed-dollar amount in a given period or was assumed to change by some fixed-dollar amount from one period to the next without benefit of any explanation. In the extended model, investment was shown to be a function of the interest rate, but the question of how responsive investment is to the interest rate was not considered. Nor was consideration given to the factors that cause the investment curve to shift and thereby increase or decrease the amount of investment at any particular interest rate. The following two chapters turn to such considerations. But before undertaking this task, we must have a framework within which investment theory may be formulated. The present chapter provides this framework.

Following a brief discussion of the meaning of investment and capital, this chapter takes up the major topic of the *decision to invest.* The business person's decision as to whether or not to undertake a given investment project depends on the relationships among the expected income flow from the project, the cost of the project, and the market interest rate. The chapter works through the mechanics of these relationships and shows how they lead to the very important concept of the *marginal efficiency of capital.*

The final section of the chapter is an analysis of the process of capital accumulation, a description of how a discrepancy between the desired and the actual capital stock is corrected over time through net investment expenditures.

Investment, a word with many meanings in popular usage, has only one meaning in national income analysis—the value of that part of the economy's output for any time period that takes the form of new structures, new producers' durable equipment, and change in inventories. In practice, apart from the change in inventories, the value of this output is measured by the amount of expenditure on these items. Investment can be viewed in either gross or net terms. If we deduct from gross investment expenditures an allowance for the amount of the existing total of structures and producers' durable equipment used up in producing the period's output, we have net investment.

The amount of gross investment that is made up of new structures and new producers' durable equipment is called gross fixed investment. This may be divided into nonresidential investment, which is essentially business fixed investment, and residential investment, the largest component of which is single-unit houses. The balance of gross investment—the nonfixed component—is the change in business inventories. Figure 17-1 shows this breakdown of gross investment with each component expressed as a percentage of GNP for each of the years since World War II.

Gross investment itself has, with a few exceptions, fluctuated between 14 and 18 percent of GNP. The highest percentage figure, 18.8, came in 1950, the year in which the share of GNP accounted for by residential investment also peaked. The lowest percentage figure, 13.3, came in 1975, the last year of the severe 1973–75 recession and also the year in which the share of GNP accounted for by residential investment hit its post-World War II low.

Of the three components, nonresidential is the largest and the most stable. Inventory investment is the least stable; for example, it fell from 1.4 percent of GNP in 1973 to − 0.5 percent in 1975. In 1975, as during earlier recessions, inventory investment became negative as businesses not only stopped adding to inventories but reduced the amount already on hand. Fixed investment, it will be seen, remains positive in all of the years shown.

In any attempt to explain aggregate investment expenditures for any time period, one difficulty is the fact that different factors determine the different types of investment expenditure. No single investment theory can reasonably apply to all forms of investment expenditure. The amount of expenditures people make for single-unit housing is not dominated by profit considerations as is the amount of expenditures made by businesses for commercial and industrial structures and for durable equipment. Similarly, the amount of expenditures made by businesses for new plant and equipment is affected by factors different from those that determine the amount they spend for additions to inventories, even though the expectation of profit dominates in both cases. Although some attention will be paid to other types of investment in Chapter 19, in this chapter investment will refer specifically to nonresidential investment or business expenditures for plant and equipment. In recent years this component has made up roughly two-thirds of gross investment.

Investment is a flow variable; its counterpart stock variable is capital. Capital, another word with many meanings, should here be understood to mean only the accumulated stock of plant and equipment held by business. If, for the economy as a whole, gross investment in any period equals the amount of capital used up during that period, there is neither net investment nor disinvestment—and consequently no change in the stock of capital. If gross investment exceeds replacement requirements, the difference equals positive net investment, which represents an increase in the stock of capital. If gross investment is less than replacement requirements, the difference is negative net investment, or disinvestment, which represents a decrease in the stock of capital.

Therefore, by definition, net investment is an addition to the stock of capital. All else being equal, an addition to the stock of capital increases

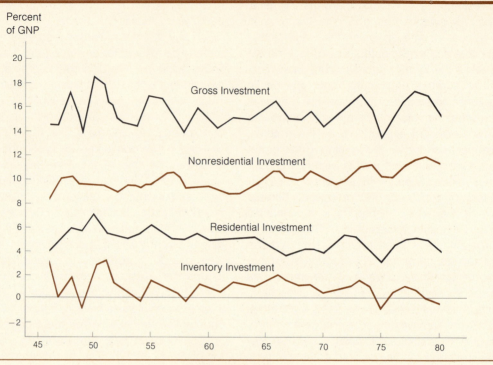

FIGURE 17-1
Gross Investment and Its Components as a Percentage of GNP, 1946—80

SOURCE: *Economic Report of the President,* Jan. 1981, pp. 233 and 249

the productive capacity of the economy. This must be the result when a larger physical stock of capital is available for use with an existing labor force, natural resources, and technology. In the same way, an increase in productive capacity must result when the labor force increases with no change in the stock of capital, natural resources, or technology or when there is an improvement in technology with no change in the stock of capital, labor force, or natural resources. As suggested by the "law of diminishing returns," the only plausible exception to this rule is the case in which the variable factor is so plentiful relative to the fixed factors that its marginal productivity falls to zero. This situation is very unusual.

The stock of capital for the economy as a whole tends to grow; the labor force, at least so far, also has tended to grow and technology to improve. In practice, other things do not remain equal as the capital stock grows. However, for analytical purposes, the growth in the capital stock must be isolated from the growth in other factors in order to specify the increase in potential output associated with the growth in the capital stock. To assume an unchanged technology or a given "state of the arts" presents no serious conceptual difficulty; we must simply understand that the same methods of production are employed. Net investment and the resultant growth in the stock of capital then means that more of the existing kinds of capital goods are employed in the same way as existing capital goods. To assume an unchanged labor force, however, presents some conceptual difficulty. Although the stock of capital might conceivably grow virtually without limit even in the absence of technological change, it is more difficult to imagine unlimited growth in the stock of capital of this kind without a growth in the labor force. More workers would be needed to utilize an enlarged stock of capital that involves no labor-saving changes in technology.

If the stock of capital, the state of technology, and the labor force are all treated as variables, this conceptual difficulty disappears and others appear. With all treated as variables, technological improvements may lead to a growth in the stock of capital without any corresponding increase in the amount of labor required for the efficient use of the now larger stock of capital. With the state of technology as a variable, there may also be a growth in the stock of capital that is intended not as a means of increasing capacity but as a means of reducing the cost of producing the level of output attained with existing capacity. "Modernization" of a firm's plant and equipment through net investment expenditures may amount to the adoption of technologically superior and therefore lower cost-per-unit methods of producing an unchanged level of output. Such cost-cutting net investment may be distinguished conceptually from net investment that is designed simply to expand the productive capacity of the firm's plant and equipment. However, for the economy as a whole, whether net investment is undertaken for "modernization" or for capacity expansion, all net investment increases the productive capacity of the economy as a whole. If a plant is "modernized" to produce a given level of output with less labor, the labor so released is available to enlarge production elsewhere in the economy and thereby enlarges the economy's productive capacity.

To avoid the complications inherent in simultaneously treating all these factors as variables, we will assume for the present that the state of technology, the size of the labor force, and the

amount of the economy's natural resources are all constant. As we develop the theory of net investment spending for the economy as a whole, we may simply identify the resultant expansion in the capital stock as an expansion in the productive capacity of the economy.

The Decision to Invest

Because most capital goods remain useful for many years, one can learn only after several years whether the investment in these long-lived goods will turn out to be profitable or unprofitable. However, if a particular investment expenditure is made, for replacement as well as for expansion, it generally means that the business person who invests has estimated that the investment will be profitable.[1]

Three Elements Involved
The business person's estimate of the profit or loss that will accrue from any particular investment is based on the relationships among three elements: the expected income flow from the capital good in question, the purchase price of that good, and the market rate of interest. Because a forecast of what lies in the future is unavoidable, the crucial factor in the business person's evaluation of the prospective profitability of any investment expenditure is his estimate of the income flow the capital good will yield over

---

[1] We make the standard assumption that the firm's objective is "profit maximization." Although it is well known that firms are influenced by other objectives, for simplicity "profit maximization" will be assumed here to be the exclusive objective. For an introduction to the question of the validity of this assumption, see R.M. Scherer, *Industrial Market Structure and Economic Performance*, Rand McNally, 2nd ed., 1980, pp. 29–41. The leading contributions to the literature in this area are identified in the footnotes on these pages. See especially F. Machlup, "Theories of the Firm: Marginalist, Behavioral, Managerial," in *American Economic Review*, March 1966, pp. 1–33.

its life. This uncertainty arises not only from uncertainty as to the amount of income the good will generate each year of its life but also from the number of years in that life. The good may turn out to be less durable than was originally anticipated, or it may become obsolete due to technological changes well before it is physically worn out. Beyond this, in some cases even the purchase price is uncertain. If instead of a single capital good like a piece of machinery, we think of the construction and equipping of a complete new plant, its full cost to the firm at the time of its completion several years later may well turn out to be substantially different from what was anticipated at the time the decision was made to go ahead with the project.

To trace through the basic relationships among the three elements involved in the investment decision, let us for the moment ignore the matter of uncertainty. Suppose that in considering the purchase of a particular machine management estimates that it can remain in use for a five-year period, at which time it will have only a negligible scrap value. Management will estimate its physical productivity—the increase in the number of units of final output made possible in each of the five years because of the addition of this machine to its stock of capital. Then to obtain the figure for the gross income flow expected from the machine each year, the estimated marginal physical productivity for each year is multiplied by the estimated price per unit (net of indirect taxes) at which each year's additional output can be sold or, more exactly, is multiplied by the marginal revenue per unit. However, in producing and selling this additional output, extra raw materials, power, advertising, and labor will probably be required.[2] When the total cost of these extra inputs for each year is subtracted from the estimated gross income flow for each year, the remainder is the estimated net income produced by the machine in each year. In computing this figure, all costs that will be incurred in using the machine and in producing and selling its output are deducted, with two notable exceptions: (1) the annual depreciation expense, which on a straight-line basis equals one-fifth of the purchase price of the machine; and (2) the annual interest cost on the amount of funds tied up in the machine, a cost equal to the undepreciated portion of the purchase price times the market rate of interest. Accordingly, if in the first year one-fifth of the original outlay is covered by setting aside in a depreciation reserve one-fifth of the purchase price of the capital good, the interest cost in the second year will equal the market rate of interest times four-fifths of the purchase price. The estimated net income figures for the five years make up a series of figures that may be designated as R_1, R_2, R_3, R_4, and R_5.[3]

Suppose that the sum of R_1, R_2, R_3, R_4, and R_5 exceeds the purchase price of the capital good. Can this excess over the amount required to replace the machine be taken as the dollar amount of estimated profit from the machine over its five-year life? Can we divide this figure by 5 and call this amount the average profit per year? Can we divide this average amount by the purchase price of the machine and call this the rate of return on the investment? The answer to all these questions is no. Not all the excess of the income flow over the purchase price is profit. We made no allowance for the fact that the income flow from the capital good will trickle in over the next five years, whereas the outlay for the capital

---

[2]Although we have assumed that the labor force, natural resources, and technology are all unchanged, the individual firm can always get more labor and raw materials by bidding them away from other firms. This is patently impossible for all firms together, but all firms may still redeploy the available labor force and the supply of raw materials so as to make optimum use of them in combination with a growing stock of capital. Of course, as all firms taken together increase the stock of capital, the additional output per additional unit of capital must eventually decrease, if the quantity of labor and other factors remains unchanged. Diminishing returns enter the picture.

[3]Of course, if we choose to express net income after income taxes, a deduction for this would have to be made in computing the R values.

good is made in one lump sum at the time of purchase. To disregard the time difference between income and outlay would be to equate today's dollar with tomorrow's; as long as a positive rate of interest can be earned by any lender, a dollar to be received tomorrow will necessarily be worth less than one received today. To compare properly the number of dollars paid out today in purchasing the capital good with the number of dollars of income that the good will earn over its life, we must compute the *present value* of those future dollars. This requires that we *discount* each of those future dollars for the number of years it is removed from the present; the present value depends on the rate at which the future dollars are to be discounted. Discounted at 4 percent, the sum of $100 to be received five years from today has a present value of $82.19; at 5 percent, the present value is $78.35; and at 6 percent, the present value is $74.73. Part A of Figure 17-2 shows this graphically. The higher the rate that is used, the lower

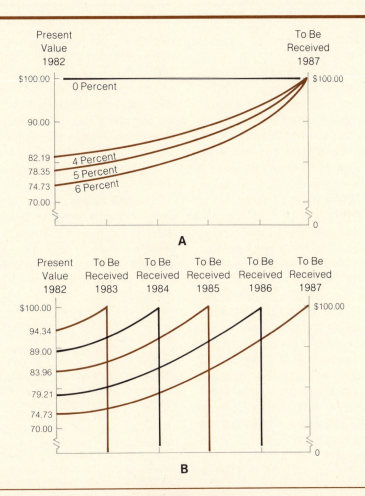

FIGURE 17-2
Present Value of $100 for Selected Discount Rates and Time Periods

TABLE 17-1
Present Value of an Income Stream at Various Discount Rates

Estimated Income	Discounted at		
	4%	5%	6%
R_1 $100 at end of 1st year	$ 96.15	$ 95.24	$ 94.34
R_2 $100 at end of 2nd year	92.46	90.70	89.00
R_3 $100 at end of 3rd year	88.90	86.38	83.96
R_4 $100 at end of 4th year	85.48	82.27	79.21
R_5 $100 at end of 5th year	82.19	78.35	74.73
Total of Present Values	$445.18	$432.94	$421.24

is the present value. In the interesting but non-existent case of a zero rate, the present value is identical with the future value.

The present value of any future dollar also varies inversely with the time period involved. Assuming a 6 percent rate, the present value of $100 to be received five years from today is $74.73, but the present value of the same number of dollars to be received one year from today is $94.34. Part B of Figure 17-2 shows the present value of $100 to be received 1, 2, 3, 4, and 5 years in the future, in each case discounting at 6 percent.

As explained in Chapter 11, this discounting process—the process by which a future sum shrinks as it is translated into present value—is simply the reverse of the more familiar process by which a sum grows as it is carried into the future. If the present value of $100 to be received five years from today is $82.19 when it is discounted at 4 percent, $82.19 put out today at 4 percent interest will grow to $100 at the end of five years. This is shown by the uppermost curve of Part A, in which we visualize the growth over time of $82.19 today to $100 five years from today. Similarly, if the present value of $100 to be received four years from today is $79.21 when discounted at 6 percent, then $79.21 put out today at 6 percent interest will grow to $100 at the end of four years. This is shown by the curve for the four-year period in Part B.

Let us assign specific dollar values to R_1, R_2, R_3, R_4, and R_5 and determine the present values

of these amounts at 4, 5, and 6 percent discount rates. Suppose that for each of the five years the estimated income from the capital good is $100 after deduction of all expenses other than interest and depreciation. (To simplify, assume also that each year's income appears in one lump sum at the end of that year.) The results for each of the three discount rates are given in Table 17-1. Note that the series of five figures in the final column corresponds with the five figures at the left side of Part B of Figure 17-2.

The total for the present values at the bottom of each column is the amount which, if put out today at the rate at the head of each column, would generate $100 at the end of each of the next five years and then nothing.[4] That is, this income stream provides a yield of 4 percent if

---

[4] If one invests $445.18 at 4 percent for one year, he earns $17.81 in interest for that year, making his investment at the end of the first year $462.99. Withdrawing $100 from investment at the end of the first year, he invests $362.99 for the second year, on which he receives $14.52 of interest, making his investment at the end of the second year $377.51. Withdrawing another $100 from investment, he invests $277.51 for the third year, on which he receives $11.10 in interest, making his investment at the end of the third year $288.61. Withdrawing another $100 from investment, he invests $188.61 for the fourth year, on which he receives $7.54 in interest, making his investment at the end of the fourth year $196.15. Withdrawing another $100 from investment, he invests $96.15 for the fifth year, on which he receives $3.85 in interest, making his investment at the end of the fifth year $100, which amount he withdraws to close out the investment.

the machine can be purchased for $445.18, a yield of 5 percent if it can be purchased for $432.94, and a yield of 6 percent if it can be purchased for $421.24.

Suppose that the machine that promises this income stream can actually be purchased for $432.94. Will it be a profitable investment? All we know so far is that if we buy the machine for $432.94 and if it produces net income of $100 per year for five years, we will have a 5 percent rate of return on the funds invested. Is a prospective rate of return of 5 percent high enough to induce the business person to make the investment expenditure? Here the market rate of interest enters the picture. If the firm must borrow the funds to purchase the machine and the rate it must pay for such funds exceeds 5 percent, the interest rate then exceeds the expected rate of return, and the investment would be unprofitable. If, on the other hand, the market rate of interest is below 5 percent, the investment would be profitable. If the firm need not borrow but has on hand its own funds, the comparison is between the rate of interest it could earn by simply lending these funds in the market at interest and the rate of return it expects from an investment of these funds in the machine. If the rate of interest it can secure by lending these funds exceeds 5 percent, the firm will be wiser to lend than to invest in the machine. If the rate at which it can lend funds in the market is less than 5 percent, it will be wiser to invest in the machine than to lend the funds. As a general rule, it pays to invest in a capital good if the rate of return expected from that capital good over its life exceeds the current market rate of interest. This "rule," however, is subject to a number of qualifications, some of which we will consider later.

All this may also be expressed in terms of the general equation for the present value of a future income stream. This is the equation used earlier to find the present value of a bond.[5] A bond returns a yearly amount of income until maturity and the principal amount at maturity. A capital good returns a yearly amount of income (which, unlike that from a bond, is necessarily an estimated amount) over its life and an amount (also necessarily estimated) equal to its scrap value, if any, at the end of its life. Assuming no scrap value for the capital good, the present value equation is

$$V = \frac{R_1}{(1+r)} + \frac{R_2}{(1+r)^2} + \ldots + \frac{R_n}{(1+r)^n}$$

Here $R_1, R_2, \ldots R_n$ are the estimated amounts of net income that will be generated by the capital good during each year of its life. For a capital good that is expected to generate $100 per year for five years and to have no scrap value, Table 17-1 shows the values discounted at 4, 5, and 6 percent. For example, if the market interest rate were 6 percent, the present value of the income stream would be $421.24.

The Marginal Efficiency of Capital

To find the present value figure, we started out with a given income stream and an interest rate that was assumed to be the actual market rate at the time. Given $R_1, R_2, \ldots, R_n$, and r, we could find V. Suppose now that we are given the purchase price or cost of a capital good, designated as C, and the income stream to be produced by that good, designated as before. In this case, we want to find the interest rate that will make the present value of the income stream produced by the capital good just equal to the cost of the capital good. In terms of the following equation, we want to find the value of i for given values of C and $R_1, R_2, \ldots, R_n$.

$$C = \frac{R_1}{(1+i)} + \frac{R_2}{(1+i)^2} + \ldots + \frac{R_n}{(1+i)^n}$$

Note that the rate we find in this way is designated i to distinguish it from the market rate of interest, r. The relationship between i and r will be examined later.

For a numerical illustration, assume a capital good that cost $427.02 is expected to produce

---

[5]For the derivation of this equation, see pp. 213–14.

an income stream of $100 at the end of each year for five years. Substituting these figures in the equation just above gives us

$$\$427.02 = \frac{\$100}{(1+i)} + \frac{\$100}{(1+i)^2} + \frac{\$100}{(1+i)^3}$$
$$+ \frac{\$100}{(1+i)^4} + \frac{\$100}{(1+i)^5}$$

Solving will give us 5.5 percent as the value for i.

We could substitute any other possible price for the capital good and solve for i on the basis of that price. For a given income stream, the higher the price of the good, the lower will be the value of i; the lower the price of the good, the higher will be the value of i. For example, if the good cost $485.35, i would be a mere 1 percent, but if it were "bargain priced" at $299.00, i would be 20 percent.

In solving for the rate that will make the present value of the returns from a capital asset just equal to its cost, we have found the rate that Keynes called the **marginal efficiency of capital**. This term has become part of the language of the theory of capital and investment; we will use it hereafter to indicate the rate of return expected from a capital asset.

We may compute the marginal efficiency of capital (MEC or i) for any capital good once we are given its cost and the stream of income expected from it. By comparing the MEC with the current market rate of interest, r, we can tell at once whether the contemplated investment promises to be profitable or unprofitable. In the previous illustration, given that the capital good in question costs $427.02, we found its MEC to be 5.5 percent. If the interest rate were 6 percent, the investment would be unprofitable; but if the interest rate were 5 percent, it would be considered profitable. Furthermore, the difference between the MEC and r is the net rate of return expected after allowance for all costs, including the interest cost on the funds tied up in the capital good over its life and the depreciation cost of the asset itself. With the MEC at 5.5 percent and r at 5 percent, purchase of the capital good promises a net return of 0.5 percent over and above all costs; with r at 6 percent, a net return of -0.5 percent.

Because the MEC and r are both percentages, they are sometimes confused or identified as the same thing. The two percentages are distinctly different. The business person's estimate of the MEC for any capital good in no way depends on r. Once the MEC has been estimated, the profitability of the capital good in question can be gauged only by comparing its MEC with r, but this step is altogether distinct from that of estimating the MEC itself. The level of r determines whether or not the good will be purchased, once its MEC is given, but r does not determine the MEC of that good.

We may now note how all three elements—the income flow expected from a capital good, the supply price of that good, and the market rate of interest—fit together. An improvement in the business outlook that causes the business person to revise upward his estimate of the expected income flow from a capital good will, given an unchanged price for the good, raise the MEC of that good. Alternatively, if there is no change in the income flow expected from the good, a drop in its price will raise its MEC. A fall in r will not affect the MEC of that good, but if $r >$ MEC before the fall and if MEC $> r$ after the fall, the purchase of the capital good, which previously appeared unprofitable, will now appear profitable. A downward revision in the expected income flow from the good, a rise in its price, or a rise in the market rate of interest will all work in the opposite direction—decreasing the expected profitability of the good or even turning it into expected loss.

Stock of Capital and the Rate of Investment

At any point in time, a firm is confronted with a long list of possible investment projects. Apart from projects that arise as a result of changing technology, there are projects such as expansion of its existing factory building, construction of a new and larger building, purchase of more of the same equipment to expand production of existing lines, purchase of different equipment to produce a new line of goods, and purchase of trucks to handle its own deliveries. If the firm already has or can borrow the necessary funds, the investment expenditures for each possible project will or will not be made depending upon the MEC of each and the current level of r. After estimating the MEC of each of the diverse investment projects it might undertake, the firm could prepare a schedule like Figure 17-3 to show the possibilities.

Figure 17-3 assumes that at a selected point in time the firm's stock of capital net of depreciation is valued at $500,000. If the market rate of interest is 13 percent, only the first project in the schedule promises to be profitable. This project requires net investment expenditures of $50,000 and will increase the firm's capital stock to $550,000. If the market interest rate is 7 percent, the next three projects shown would also be profitable. Net investment expenditures of another $150,000 would raise the firm's stock of capital

to $700,000. Once the stock of capital has been expanded to the level at which the MEC of the last project has dropped to the level of r, the firm has its profit-maximizing or desired stock of capital.[6] No further change is to be expected, barring the appearance of new projects with MEC above r or barring a fall in r itself. The firm's net investment in each succeeding period will be zero; its gross investment will be whatever is required for replacement purposes only.

What is true of one firm is true of others—management of every profit-conscious firm continuously seeks investment opportunities that will improve the profit and loss statement. If each firm were to prepare a schedule of the kind shown in Figure 17-3 and if all these schedules were added together, we would have an aggregate schedule of the MEC such as that shown in Part A of Figure 17-4.[7] The "lumpiness" of the investment projects available to the individual firm that

---

[6]It is not true in all cases that the firm will maximize profits by always selecting a project with a higher MEC rather than an alternative with a lower MEC. There is a weakness in the approach that compares the MEC and r such that, under certain circumstances, this approach will fail to rank projects consistently. An alternative approach, free of this deficiency, will not be developed here. For analysis of this particular problem, see A.A. Alchian, "The Rate of Interest, Fisher's Rate of Return Over Cost, and Keynes' Internal Rate of Return," in *American Economic Review,* Dec. 1955, pp. 938–43, and J. Hirschliefer, "On the Theory of the Optimal Investment Decision," in *Journal of Political Economy,* August 1958, pp. 329–52. For a textbook presentation, see W.H. Branson, *Macroeconomic Theory and Policy,* 2nd. ed., Harper & Row, 1979, pp. 219–22.

[7]In a strict sense, the aggregate schedule cannot be derived in so simple a manner. A drop in the rate of interest from 10 to 8.5 percent in Figure 17-3 may call forth more than $25,000 of net investment by the firm in question. Because the same drop in the interest rate will trigger investment by other firms, the resultant increase in aggregate spending may improve the outlook of this firm sufficiently to increase the MEC of its other prospective projects. In general, when we allow for this interdependence, the effect is to make the individual firm's schedule more elastic than otherwise. The determination of the aggregate schedule, however, becomes a problem in general equilibrium analysis, which allows for the interdependence between each firm's schedule and those of all other firms.

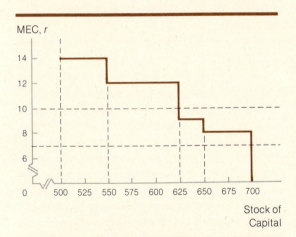

**FIGURE 17-3
Schedule of the Marginal
Efficiency of Capital for a Firm**

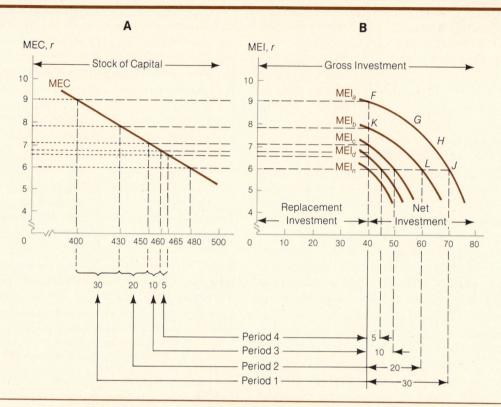

FIGURE 17-4
**The Process of Capital Accumulation in Response to a Fall
in the Interest Rate**

produces the stair-like curve of Figure 17-3 evens out in aggregation to produce the smooth curve of Part A of Figure 17-4.

At any point in time, all firms combined have some existing aggregate stock of capital, say $400 billion. At the same point in time, there is some particular market rate of interest, say 9 percent (here assuming that a single rate prevails for all borrowers and for loans of all maturities and for all purposes). With the aggregate MEC schedule as given in Part A of Figure 17-4 and with r at 9 percent, any expansion in the aggregate stock of capital beyond the existing $400 billion level promises a net return of less than

9 percent—that is, below the market rate of interest. Under these conditions, business as a whole has that stock of capital that maximizes profits; there is no reason to expand or contract the capital stock, and so there is no net investment or disinvestment. Some individual firms may have net investment, but others will have an equal amount of disinvestment, making net investment zero for all firms combined. Under these conditions, there can be no net investment for all firms combined until there is either a drop in the interest rate that produces a movement down the MEC schedule to a higher stock of capital, or a shift to the right of the MEC schedule that will,

with an unchanged rate of interest, make the stock of capital consistent with profit maximization larger than it was.

A Fall in the Rate of Interest

In our example, we have assumed that with a capital stock of $400 billion, MEC is 9 percent. If r is also 9 percent, this would be the profit-maximizing stock of capital, and net investment spending would be zero. Assume now a drop in r from 9 to 6 percent.[8] At this lower rate, the profit-maximizing stock of capital as given by the MEC schedule of Figure 17-4 is $480 billion. This means that $80 billion of net investment expenditures is needed to raise the capital stock to the higher, desired level. How much will all firms combined actually invest per time period? And how long will it take these firms to build up the capital stock from the $400 billion to the $480 billion level?

In considering the individual firm, we were able to bypass this kind of question. When a firm decides to increase its stock of capital, it can conceivably accomplish this virtually overnight. If the capital goods required are held in inventory by firms in the capital goods industries, the firm can move up to the higher capital stock desired as quickly as these goods can be delivered. If new construction is required, the firm can move up to the higher capital stock as quickly as this construction can be completed. Furthermore, it is unlikely that its investment expenditures would exert more than a negligible upward pressure on the supply prices of the capital goods in question.

For firms as a group, we cannot, however, bypass this kind of question. To expand the aggregate stock of capital from $400 to $480 billion must take time. Although some firms may

increase their stock of capital immediately by simply buying capital goods from other firms, there will be no increase in the stock of capital goods held by all firms combined unless more capital goods are produced. Naturally, the rate at which these goods can be produced is limited by the existing productive capacity of the capital goods industries.[9] Furthermore, as all firms combined step up their investment expenditures, the capital goods industries, in expanding output to meet this higher demand, will eventually experience rising marginal costs that may lead to higher prices for capital goods. These rising prices will in turn slow the rate of investment spending and thereby lengthen the time required to effect any given increase in the aggregate stock of capital.

Assume that the capacity output of the capital goods industries is $80 billion per time period, valuing capital goods at the prices in effect when their output equals the amount needed for replacement requirements.[10] With an existing capital stock of $400 billion, replacement requirements are $40 billion per time period, assuming that 10 percent of these goods wear out in each time period. Therefore, the capital goods industries, operating at capacity output, can supply a net addition to the capital stock of $40 billion per time period. In other words, it will take two time periods *at capacity output* to raise the capital stock from $400 to $480 billion. Will the rate of net investment spending be sufficient to push the capital goods industries to

---

[8]This large change is chosen because it will show clearly in chart form the results that follow a fall in the interest rate.

[9]The productive capacity of the capital goods industries may grow over time as these industries expand through net investment, but, for simplicity, we assume no such change, or constant productive capacity in the capital goods industries.

[10]Because the MEC schedule will shift with every change in the supply price of capital goods, to produce the stable MEC schedule necessary to the following analysis requires that we assume that the MEC schedule is based on the fixed supply price for capital goods that is in effect when output of capital goods is, say, the amount necessary for replacement purposes only. This amount can reasonably be assumed to be stable in the short run.

capacity output? To find out what net investment expenditures will be per time period for all firms combined, turn to Figure 17-4.[11]

Part B of Figure 17-4 introduces the schedule of the marginal efficiency of investment, or MEI schedule. This schedule indicates the rate of investment spending per time period at each possible market rate of interest. It is therefore the same schedule that appeared in earlier chapters where it was referred to simply as the investment schedule or investment curve. However, nothing was said earlier about its derivation. We will explain its derivation here.

Separate MEI schedules are shown for a number of different levels of the stock of capital. With the MEC schedule as given in Part A, with r at 9 percent, and with the capital stock at $400 billion, the actual capital stock is profit maximizing and net investment is zero. Therefore, a schedule relating investment expenditures to the rate of interest must show zero net investment at an interest rate of 9 percent, which the MEI schedule labeled MEI_a shows (at point F). If r falls to 6 percent, net investment expenditures will appear. In the first time period after the drop in r, curve MEI_a reveals that net investment will be $30 billion (or gross investment will be $70 billion), even though the capacity of the capital goods industries permits $40 billion of net investment (or $80 billion of gross investment) per time period. Investment spending is checked at a rate short of the capacity output of the capital goods industries by the rise in prices of these goods, which occurs as their rate of output is expanded in response to investment demand. It is specifi-

cally the upward-sloping supply curve of capital goods that produces the downward-sloping MEI curve. Furthermore, the more sharply the supply curve of capital goods slopes upward, the more sharply the MEI curve slopes downward.[12]

We can see more clearly why net investment in the first period following the fall in r will be exactly $30 billion by following the MEI_a schedule from point F down to point G. At G the MEI is 8 percent because the rise in net investment spending from a rate of zero to a rate of about $15 billion has so raised the prices of capital goods as to reduce to 8 percent the rate of return on investment in these goods. This, however, is still an MEI above r, which is 6 percent, so a higher rate of net investment spending is warranted. At point H the MEI has fallen to 7 percent because the still higher rate of net investment spending, now about $25 billion, has pushed the prices of capital goods to the still higher level at which the rate of return on investment is reduced to 7 percent. The MEI is still above r, so a still higher rate of net investment spending is warranted. At point J, the MEI is 6 percent, again because the still higher rate of net investment spending, now $30 billion, has pushed the prices of capital goods to the still higher level at which the rate of return on investment is reduced to 6 percent. To push the rate of net investment spending beyond $30 billion would reduce the MEI still further, or below 6 percent and so below r. Accordingly, net investment will be at the $30 billion rate, no higher and no lower, in the first time period following the drop in r.

From the beginning to the end of this first time period, with net investment of $30 billion during

[11]This figure is adapted from G. Ackley, *Macroeconomic Theory*, Macmillan, 1961, pp. 481–85. See also his *Macroeconomics: Theory and Policy*, Macmillan, 1978, pp. 628–31. For alternative treatments, see A.P. Lerner, "On Some Recent Developments in Capital Theory," in *American Economic Review, Proceedings*, May 1965, pp. 284–95, *The Economics of Control*, Macmillan, 1944, pp. 330–38, and R.L. Crouch, *Macroeconomics*, Harcourt Brace Jovanovich, 1972, pp. 66–86.

[12]Suppose the supply curve were perfectly elastic up to the capacity output. Then the MEI_a curve, instead of sloping downward, would be perfectly horizontal (perfectly elastic) up to gross investment of $80 billion. The same would be true for the other MEI curves that are explained below. An MEI curve that is perfectly elastic over an unlimited range will be encountered in the following chapter's discussion of the simple acceleration principle.

the period, the capital stock will have risen to $430 billion from its beginning level of $400 billion. As shown in Part A, this increase of $30 billion reduces the MEC to about 8 percent (actually 7.87) from its previous level of 9. Because r is still 6 percent, further growth in the capital stock is called for. The amount by which it grows in the second period, or the rate of net investment spending in the second period, depends on the MEI schedule. With MEC now at 8 percent, the new MEI schedule, relating investment expenditures to the interest rate, must show zero net investment at an interest rate of 8 percent (point K). Therefore, MEI_b, the new schedule, lies below MEI_a because of the increase in the stock of capital in the first time period; the whole MEI schedule must fall to a lower level with each movement to a lower point on the given MEC schedule. MEI_b slopes downward for the same reason that MEI_a sloped downward—the rising supply price of capital goods as the rate of output of these goods is expanded in response to investment spending.

The rate of net investment spending in the second period is determined in the same way as the rate in the first period was. It will be the rate that reduces the MEI to equality with r. Schedule MEI_b shows that net investment for the second period will be $20 billion (point L). Note that this is below the $30 billion of the first time period. Given that the prices of capital goods rise with their rate of output, as soon as net investment reaches the rate of $20 billion per time period, the rise in prices of capital goods reduces the MEI from 8 to 6 percent, or to equality with r. In the first period, only when net investment reached the $30 billion rate was the rise in prices of capital goods sufficient to produce the greater drop in MEI from 9 to 6 percent, or to equality with r. In other words, the greater spread between MEI and r at the beginning of the first period permitted the higher rate of investment spending in that period.

Net investment spending of $20 billion during the second period raises the stock of capital to $450 billion from its level of $430 at the beginning

of the second period. The increase in the stock of capital reduces the MEC further to about 7 percent (actually 7.12), which produces the new, lower MEI schedule, MEI_c. The rate of net investment spending in the third period as given by this schedule is $10 billion. This again raises the stock of capital, now from $450 to $460 billion. This in turn reduces the MEC and creates the new, still lower MEI schedule, MEI_d. The rate of net investment spending in the fourth period is then $5 billion. With no shift in the MEC schedule and with no further fall in r, net investment spending, lower in each succeeding period, eventually raises the stock of capital to $480 billion, at which level the MEC equals r. The actual stock of capital is now the profit-maximizing stock for the interest rate of 6 percent. With the capital stock at $480 billion, the relevant MEI schedule is MEI_n, which shows net investment to be zero and gross investment equal to replacement investment per time period. We have reached a new equilibrium, which will be upset only by a shift in the MEC schedule or by a change in the market rate of interest.

In summary, given an unshifting MEC schedule, the appearance of a positive rate of net investment depends in the first instance on the size of the stock of capital and the interest rate. Given the stock of capital, we know MEC; given r we know whether MEC $> r$, MEC $< r$, or MEC $= r$. A prerequisite to net investment is that MEC $> r$. In this situation, an increase in capital stock is called for. This increase can occur only through net investment spending. The rate of net investment spending per time period depends on how steep the downward slope of the MEI schedule is (or more correctly its elasticity); this in turn depends on how steep the upward slope (or the elasticity) of the supply curve of capital goods is. If the supply curve slopes sharply upward, the rate of investment spending will fall sharply downward with respect to the interest rate. In any event, the capital stock will grow to the new profit-maximizing level, but its growth rate will be slower the steeper the MEI schedule is.

A Shift in the MEC Schedule[13]

A lowered interest rate with no shift in the MEC schedule will raise the profit-maximizing stock of capital from its previous level. An upward shift in the MEC schedule with no change in the interest rate will have the same result. Schedule MEC_a of Figure 17-5 is identical with the MEC schedule shown in Figure 17-4. In both cases, assuming that r is 9 percent and the actual capital stock is $400 billion, the actual stock is profit maximizing and net investment spending is zero. If the MEC schedule now shifts upward to MEC_b, the profit-maximizing stock of capital becomes $480 billion. Net investment now appears, because, with the capital stock at $400 billion, the MEC has risen from 9 to 12 percent. In other words, due to a rise in the expected income flow from capital goods, which is assumed here to be the cause of the upward shift in the MEC schedule, the rate of return expected from the first increment to the stock of capital is 12 percent. Because r is still 9 percent, the MEC now exceeds r by 3 percent. Note that this is the same relationship between MEC and r as was given in Figure 17-4, except that here the 3 percent spread between MEC and r is caused by a rise in MEC from 9 to 12 percent instead of by a drop in r from 9 to 6 percent.

As in the previous illustration, net investment expenditures of $80 billion are required to raise the capital stock to its new profit-maximizing level. The rate of net investment in each time period is the same in both illustrations, as is the number of time periods required to increase the capital stock by $80 billion. Part B of Figure

17-5 differs from Part B of Figure 17-4 only in being higher above the horizontal axis. In Figure 17-4, the investment rate in the first period after the fall in r reduced the MEI from 9 to 6 percent; in Figure 17-5, the investment rate in the first period after the shift upward in the MEC schedule reduces the MEI from 12 to 9 percent. The significant factor is the spread between MEI and r rather than the absolute level of either. Because this spread is the same in both of our illustrations, the rate of net investment in each period will be the same.

Of course, shifts in the MEC schedule could occur at the same time as changes in the market interest rate. For example, the upward shift in the MEC schedule of Figure 17-5 could be accompanied by a fall in the interest rate like that shown in Figure 17-4. If this happened, the new profit-maximizing capital stock would be greater than $480 billion. A rise in the interest rate might be sufficient to offset the rise in the profit-maximizing capital stock that otherwise would result from an upward shift in the MEC schedule. Conversely, a fall in the interest rate could offset the decrease in the profit-maximizing capital stock that otherwise would result from a downward shift in the MEC schedule.

Unless these combinations of changes are exactly offsetting, however, they will change the profit-maximizing capital stock. Given such a change, the net investment process is that by which the economy moves to the higher profit-maximizing capital stock, whatever it may be and whatever may have caused it to change.[14]

---

[13]Although the intent here is simply to distinguish between a change in the interest rate and a shift in the MEC schedule, note that these two changes are not independent of each other. An increase in investment spending resulting from a fall in the interest rate raises the income level, which in turn (via the acceleration principle to be examined in Chapter 18) tends to cause a shift to the right in the MEC schedule. A movement along the schedule may, in other words, set into motion forces that cause a shift in the schedule.

[14]Apart from several years during the Great Depression, the profit-maximizing capital stock has grown uninterruptedly. Therefore, we have not here specifically entered into the process by which the capital stock would be reduced over time below the actual capital stock at any point in time. In brief, if the movement were, say, from an actual capital stock of $480 billion to a desired capital stock of $400 billion, gross investment would drop to zero and net investment would accordingly become negative. The maximum possible rate of negative net investment (disinvestment) is set by the rate at which the capital stock is used

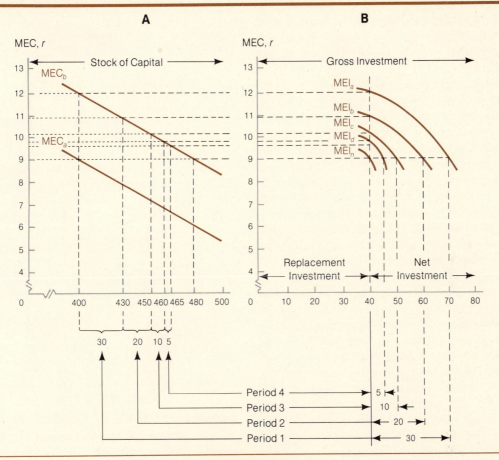

FIGURE 17-5
The Process of Capital Accumulation in Response to a Shift in the Schedule of the Marginal Efficiency of Capital

A Summary Formulation

The portion of aggregate spending that is accounted for by the business sector of the economy is measured by the investment expenditures of business for newly produced capital goods. To explain aggregate spending for any time period, we must concentrate on business investment expenditures for that time period rather than on the actual stock of capital held by business at any point within that time period. Net investment expenditures are the means by which a change in the capital stock is effected. In other words, net investment, which is zero when the actual capital stock equals the profit-maximizing

up. If, as earlier assumed, this were simply 10 percent per time period, it would then take a little less than two time periods to reduce the actual stock from $480 billion to the desired stock of $400 billion. Because no capital goods are being purchased, the shapes of the supply curve of capital goods and the MEI schedule have nothing to do with the maximum disinvestment rate.

capital stock, becomes positive when the profit-maximizing stock exceeds the actual stock. A prerequisite to the appearance of net investment expenditures is a rise in the profit-maximizing capital stock.

What produces such a change in the profit-maximizing capital stock? Once such a change occurs, the rate of net investment expenditures determines the time necessary to raise the capital stock to its profit-maximizing level. What determines this rate? In the preceding pages we have attempted to lay the conceptual groundwork for answering these two questions. Figure 17-6 presents in schematic form the various factors we have introduced so far. If the difference between the actual and profit-maximizing capital stock is zero, the rate of net investment expenditures will be zero. In this case, the portion of the chart below the vertical arrow is not really relevant; it becomes relevant only when a change somewhere above the arrow produces a difference between the actual and the profit-maximizing capital stock. Whether such a difference will appear depends on the relationship between the MEC schedule and the market rate of interest. The MEC schedule in turn depends on the supply price of capital goods and the expected income flow from such goods.[15] If there is a change in any of these factors that is sufficient to produce a difference between the actual and the profit-maximizing capital stock, then the lower portion of the chart gives us the factors that determine the rate of net investment and therefore the time required to raise the actual capital stock to the profit-maximizing level. Remember that the rate of net investment expenditures depends on the

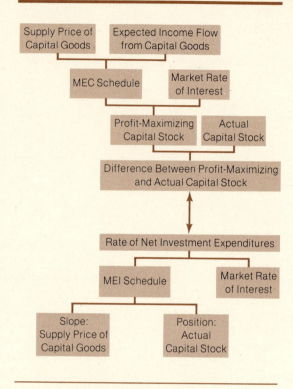

FIGURE 17-6
From the Stock of Capital to the Rate of Investment

---

[15]As noted earlier, in order to derive an MEC schedule, a particular price level of capital goods must be assumed. This means assuming the price level to be given at some point along the supply–price schedule. For each different price level selected, there will be a different MEC schedule; but for any one price level, there will be a unique MEC schedule. To derive the MEI schedule, on the other hand, the complete supply–price schedule is employed; it determines the overall slope of the MEI schedule.

relationship between the interest rate and the MEI schedule, that the overall slope of the MEI schedule depends in turn on the supply price of capital goods, and that its position vis-à-vis the axes depends on the actual stock of capital.

The MEI Schedule: Long Run and Short Run

So far we have discussed one factor that influences the rate of net investment spending—the growth in the stock of capital, represented graphically by a movement down the MEC schedule. This factor becomes important only in the long run; then the growth in the stock of capital is large enough, relative to the preexisting stock of capital, to cause an appreciable movement down the MEC schedule. For this reason, it is necessary that we now distinguish between the MEI schedule in the long run and in the short run.

The process illustrated by Figures 17-4 and 17-5 takes place over the long run. Given a one-time drop in r and no shift in the MEC schedule, Figure 17-4 showed how, over the course of the first few of an endless series of time periods, the stock of capital would grow toward the new profit-maximizing stock as a result of each period's net investment expenditures. Figure 17-5 showed the same process for a one-time shift in the MEC schedule with no change in r.

In both cases, we deliberately exaggerated the changes involved to clarify the process. The net investment expenditures of each period were sizable relative to the capital stock at the beginning of each period; this in turn meant that the resulting change in the stock of capital in each period would push down the MEI schedule perceptibly in the next period until that schedule eventually reached the level at which net investment expenditures became zero. This explanation must now be qualified to describe the MEI schedule in the short run. In the short run, the addition to the stock of capital resulting from net investment expenditures will be insignificant relative to the large existing capital stock. Therefore, the downward shift in the MEI schedule shown in Parts B of Figures 17-4 and 17-5 will be correspondingly insignificant. As a matter of fact, a short-run period in the present context is usually defined as a time interval of such length that the changes in capital stock, relative to the size of the capital stock before the changes, are too small to influence the level of net investment expenditures.

For short-run analysis we can, without appreciable error, abstract from the effect of changes in the capital stock on the position of the MEI schedule. In terms of Figure 17-4, when r falls from 9 to 6 percent, net investment is $30 billion in the first period following the fall in r. However, instead of the long-run results described by Figure 17-4, we may assume that the preexisting stock of capital is so large that the addition of $30 billion does not cause a perceptible movement down the MEC schedule. Consequently, the MEI schedule in the second period is virtually in the same position. Therefore, the rate of investment expenditures in the second and subsequent periods that make up the short run may remain virtually the same as that of the first period. This, it may be noted, is precisely what Keynes assumed in his *General Theory*.

In Chapter 20 we will be concerned with long-run analysis; we will have to look both ways in the manner originally described in connection with Figures 17-4 and 17-5. In the long run, net investment expenditures do move the economy along the MEC schedule. With the MEC schedule sloping downward, the result must be a downward shift of the MEI schedule and, assuming an unchanging supply curve for capital goods, a decrease in the rate of net investment expenditures. However, in this part of the book, we need look only one way—a difference between the actual and the profit-maximizing capital stock affects net investment expenditures, but these expenditures *in the short run* do not appreciably affect the economy's position along the MEC schedule.

A Concluding Note

Our concern in this chapter essentially has been the meaning of capital and investment and the mechanics of the relationships between the stock of capital and the rate of investment. If at any point in time the actual stock equals the profit-maximizing stock, an excess of the latter over the former will appear subsequently only if the market rate of interest falls or if the MEC schedule shifts upward. Either change will produce a positive rate of net investment spending. For short-run analysis, the indicated rate of net investment spending may continue unchanged. However, in the long run, the rise in the stock of capital resulting from net investment spending will depress the MEI schedule and with it the rate of net investment spending. This long-run result assumes that the growth in the stock of capital produces a movement along an unshifting MEC schedule that necessarily slopes downward. In reality, however, long before net investment spending raises the actual stock of capital to the profit-maximizing level indicated by a given market rate of interest and a given MEC schedule, this schedule may have shifted. From such a shift would follow a shift in the MEI schedule and from it a change in the rate of net investment spending.

Now that we understand the mechanics by which changes in the profit-maximizing capital stock are translated into changes in the rate of investment, we are free to concentrate on the factors that produce shifts in or movements along the MEC schedule and thereby produce changes in the profit-maximizing capital stock.

OVERVIEW _____

Investment Spending: The Profits and Accelerator Theories

Of the various theories that have been advanced to explain investment demand, the profits theory and the accelerator theory have received the most attention from economists.

As explained in Chapter 17, a prerequisite to net investment is a desired capital stock that exceeds the actual capital stock. The profits theory argues that the desired capital stock is a function of the level of profits—that is, an increase in the level of profits increases the desired capital stock. Graphically, a rise in the level of profits gives this result by causing a rightward shift in the MEC schedule, which causes a shift in the MEI schedule from which one can read the higher rate of investment spending that is then in effect at the existing interest rate.

Because the level of profits is closely related to the level of income, the profits theory of investment makes investmant a function of the level of income. Through an expansion of the graphic apparatus developed in Chapter 17, a simple model of the profits theory is constructed that enables us to go from the level of income to the level of profits, from the level of profits to the desired capital stock, from the desired capital stock to the rate of investment, and thus back to the rate of investment consistent with any given income level. This yields an investment function, $I = I_a + eY$, which parallels the standard consumption function, $C = C_a + cY$, in that investment, like consumption, is made a function of the income level.

In the *IS–LM* models of Part 3, investment was made a function of the interest rate only. Here we see that investment is also a function of the level of income. The earlier graphic *IS–LM* model may be extended to show investment as a function of both variables, or $I = I(r, Y)$. With this investment function, the *IS* curve does not nec-

essarily slope downward as before; it may exhibit this slope, no slope, or an upward slope. An upward-sloping *IS* curve leads to conclusions quite different from those reached on the basis of the familiar downward-sloping curve. These conclusions are identified and explained. To keep all of this in the perspective of this chapter, remember that this extension of the earlier *IS–LM* model follows from the fact that the profits theory of investment is here the basis for the upward-sloping *IS* curve.

The accelerator theory, the other theory of investment examined in this chapter, argues that the desired capital stock is a function of the economy's output level. Like the profits theory, the accelerator theory explains changes in investment through shifts in the MEC schedule. But its explanation of the causes of shifts in the schedule is altogether different from that submitted by the profits theory. In very general terms, the accelerator theory holds that the incentive for business people to acquire more capital goods is found in the pressures that increasing output at times exerts on the existing capital stock. The fact that profits are higher or lower is not regarded as crucial.

The chapter's analysis of the accelerator theory begins with the development of a basic accelerator-type investment function, which is then expanded to take into account the distinction between gross and net investment and the influence of excess capacity. To show the way that investment will behave in response to various assumed changes in output, a numerical illustration is examined in detail. Although subject to considerable qualification, some important and striking conclusions are brought out by this examination. The last part of the analysis offers a graphic apparatus that enables us to see certain relationships between the accelerator theory and the MEC and MEI schedules.

W hat was said in the mid-1960s by two prominent students of investment spending is probably equally true today: "The theory and measurement of investment behavior is one of the most controversial areas of professional economic study. . . . the subject is inherently difficult and complex."[1] In view of these characteristics, it is not surprising that a plethora of theories to explain investment demand still exists. We will not attempt to present here all the major theories, but will limit our attention to the profits theory and the accelerator theory.[2]

In the simplified version that we will develop, it may even be incorrect to classify the profits

theory as one of the major theories. However, because most laymen think of a simple profits theory first (it is often the only one they think of), it is worth consideration as long as appropriate criticism is included. Practically all economists assign a place of major importance to the accelerator theory, at least in one of its more refined versions, although many disagree with those economists who hold that this theory by itself provides an adequate explanation of investment demand.

In terms of the apparatus developed in Chapter 17, we can classify all theories of investment or all of the individual factors influencing investment into those that exert their influence by producing a movement along an existing MEC

[1] J.R. Meyer and R.R. Glauber, *Investment Decisions, Economic Forecasting, and Public Policy,* Harvard Business School, 1964, p.1.

[2] The number of theories obviously goes up from here. A five-way classification of theories has been employed in one empirical study: (1) neoclassical I, (2) neoclassical II (the difference being in the treatment of capital gains and losses on capital goods), (3) accelerator, (4) expected profits, and (5) liquidity. See D.W. Jorgenson and C.D. Siebert, "A Comparison of Alternative Theories of Corporate Investment Behavior," *American Economic Review,* September 1968, pp. 681–712. For a detailed examination of how alternative theories of investment have performed

in the explanation of business investment spending, see P.K. Clark, "Investment in the 1970s: Theory, Performance and Prediction," *Brookings Papers on Economic Activity,* 1979, No. 1, pp. 73–114, and R. Eisner, *Factors in Business Investment,* (National Bureau of Economic Research), Ballinger, 1978. See also R.W. Kopcke, "The Behavior of Investment Spending during the Recession and Recovery, 1973–76," *New England Economic Review,* November–December 1977, for an evaluation of the performance of different theories of investment during the severe contraction of 1973–75 and early part of the recovery.

schedule and those that exert their influence by producing a shift in the schedule itself. The profits theory and the accelerator theory are both of the latter type. In the profits theory, the desired capital stock is a function of profits. Accordingly, a rise in profits causes a rightward shift in the MEC schedule, indicating a larger desired capital stock at each rate of interest. In the accelerator theory, the desired capital stock is a function of the economy's output. Accordingly, a rise in output causes a rightward shift in the MEC schedule, indicating a larger desired capital stock at each rate of interest. According to these two theories, a decrease in profits or in the level of output will, of course, produce leftward shifts in the MEC curve.

As we saw in the preceding chapter, a rise in the desired capital stock and thereby a rise in investment expenditures may also occur without a shift in the MEC curve. If there is a reduction in the market rate of interest, there is then a movement down along the existing MEC curve to a larger desired capital stock. All the factors that affect the market interest rate thereby become factors affecting the desired capital stock and through it investment expenditures. How important these may be depends in large part on the elasticity of the MEC schedule. The more elastic it is, the more important are changes in the interest rate as an influence on the rate of investment expenditures. Although there is some difference of opinion among economists as to the elasticity of the schedule, there is virtual unanimity of opinion that shifts in the schedule are much more important in explaining the observed changes in investment expenditures than the movements along a given schedule that result from changes in the interest rate.

The Profits Theory[3]

At first glance, it may seem that the profits theory is the only possible theory of investment because,

in an economy in which profit maximization is the primary goal of business, firms will rarely spend money for capital assets that are not expected to add to their profits (or reduce their losses). In terms of the framework of the preceding chapter, this will be the case as long as the MEC exceeds the rate of interest.

This basically incontrovertible proposition is not, however, what is meant by the profits theory of investment. The profits theory holds that the amount of investment spending depends on the amount of profits that firms are making. We may all agree that investment spending will be undertaken only in the expectation that it will be profitable, but we cannot find in this any explanation of the actual volume of investment spending that will take place in any time period. We are not likely to agree so unanimously that a higher dollar amount of profits will give rise to a higher dollar amount of investment, but we will unanimously agree that this hypothesis deserves investigation as a possible explanation of what determines investment spending.

There are various measures of profits and investment, one pair of which is corporate profits (with inventory valuation and capital consumption adjustments) and gross fixed nonresidential investment (a measure that approximates the concept of investment in "plant and equipment"). The relationship between these measures for 1961–80 is shown in Figure 18-1. The diagram shows, in general, a direct association between the level of profits and the level of investment, although investment and profits do change in

---

[3]Among the major studies that deal with the effect of profits on investment are the following: J. Tinbergen, *A Method and Its Application to Investment Activity,* League of Nations, 1939; C.F. Roos, "The Demand for Investment Goods," in *American Economic Review, Papers and Proceedings,* May 1948, pp. 311–20; L.R. Klein, "Studies in Investment Behavior," in *Conference on Business Cycles,* Universities–National Bureau Committee for Economic Research, 1951; J.R. Meyer and E. Kuh, *The Investment Decision,* Harvard Univ. Press, 1957; and Yehuda Grunfeld, "The Determinants of Corporate Investment," in A.C. Harberger, ed., *The Demand for Durable Goods,* Univ. of Chicago Press, 1960.

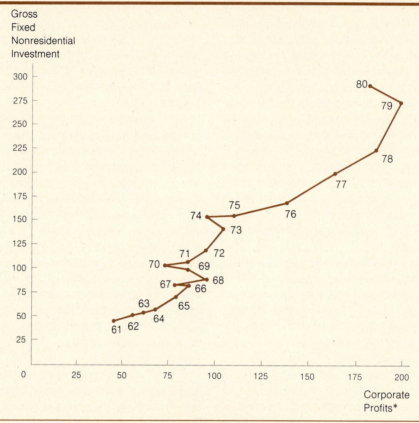

FIGURE 18-1
Relationship Between Corporate Profits and Fixed Nonresidential Investment, 1961—80
(billions of dollars)

*Corporate profits include inventory and capital consumption adjustments. Values for 1980 are preliminary.
SOURCE: *Economic Report of the President,* Jan. 1981, pp. 249 and 253.

opposite directions in some years. Data for other periods, as well as for other definitions of profits and investment, show relationships similar to that in Figure 18-1. However, the existence of this kind of direct relationship does not automatically validate the profits theory position that the level of investment depends on the level of profits. The opposite is possible. One may argue that profits depend on investment because investment determines income and profits depend on income.

What then is the basis for the position of the profits theory that investment expenditure depends on the level of realized profits? A key element in the answer lies in the fact that one of each firm's guides to the probable future level of its profits is simply the level of profits of the current period and of the recent past. An increase in the level of profits actually experienced over a period of time may well lead to the expectation of continued increases in the future. In estimating the stream of net income $(R_1 + R_2 + R_3 + \ldots + R_n)$ of any prospective investment, business people are likely to come up with higher dollar figures if these estimates are being made at a time when the absolute levels of their company profits and economy-wide profits are rising than they would under the opposite set of conditions. A high level of profits thereby leads to higher estimates of the MEC of various investment projects than would otherwise be the case. In terms of the graphic apparatus of Chapter 17, this means an upward or rightward shift in the MEC schedule, which amounts to an increase in the profit-maximizing capital stock. This in turn translates into a rise in the level of investment spending.

This, at least, is what lies at the heart of the profits theory. Plausible as it sounds, it is still not difficult to find fault with it. For one thing, it is not obvious that the firm's realized profits of this year or of the last few years can provide a measure of the profits of next year or of the next few years. A rise in currently realized profits may be the result of unexpected changes of a transitory nature. If there is no reason to expect this situation to continue, the mere appearance of such profits does not provide an incentive to invest. Or suppose that a rise in profits is not the result of an unexpected change, but is the normal payoff on past investment spending. Although this does say that the past investment spending turned out satisfactorily, it does not necessarily give the firm an incentive to invest further.

From this point of view, the profits theory is as good an explanation of investment spending as realized profits are an indicator of all those future conditions that determine the profitability of an investment. The firm's current profits reflect the current conditions of demand for its products and the current conditions of supply for the various inputs it uses. However, they do not adequately reflect the many changes that may occur in supply and demand conditions in the future. Conditions will, of course, vary drastically from industry to industry and from firm to firm, but even firms operating in near-monopolistic markets may not be able to expect that the demand that

made possible the realized profits of the present and near past will do the same in the future. A satisfactory level of profits today reflects satisfactory demand conditions today, but management can hardly conclude from this that the increase in demand will be there tomorrow to provide the increase in profits necessary to justify investment by the firm today. The same is true for supply conditions. For example, future technological developments may substantially affect methods of production and business profits, but these changes are not reflected in today's profit figures.

These considerations are sufficient to convince us that firms must assuredly look beyond their realized profits before deciding on changes in their capital stock. On the other hand, another consideration leads us to continue to assign considerable importance to current profits. Higher current profits make possible the internal financing of a larger volume of investment, and the total amount of investment actually undertaken may depend in part on how much can be internally financed. Without the internal funds generated by profits, certain investment projects that are otherwise attractive will not be undertaken; business may not invest if it can do so only by raising funds externally.[4] Furthermore, business may even go ahead with investment projects that are distinctly marginal as long as internal funds are available for their financing. The alternative is the commitment of all such funds to extra dividends or additions to cash, bank account, or short-term security holdings—none of which may appear as attractive to management as the available investment projects.

To the extent that some investment projects that would not otherwise be undertaken are undertaken because current profits provide the means of their financing, we have another reason why the level of profits, or more exactly the level of profits remaining after taxes and dividends,

---

[4]The broader question of the cost and supply of investment funds in general will be touched on in Chapter 19.

may be important in determining the level of investment spending.

Insofar as the level of investment spending responds to the level of profits, it also responds to the level of income because the aggregate profits earned by business vary directly with the level of the economy's income. For a simple illustration, suppose that the change in profits was always equal to one-fifth of each change in income and that the change in investment was always equal to three-fourths of each change in profits. There would then be a rigid link between a change in income and a change in investment. A $10 billion rise in income would mean a $1.5 billion rise in investment [$1.5 billion = (1/5) × (3/4) × $10 billion].

No such rigid link, of course, exists. The profits theory is based on a link between investment and profits, but it does not require a rigid link in order to be a worthwhile theory. As Figure 18-1 suggests, increases in investment are associated with increases in profits, but the relationship is not proportional. The historical record also shows no rigid relationship between aggregate

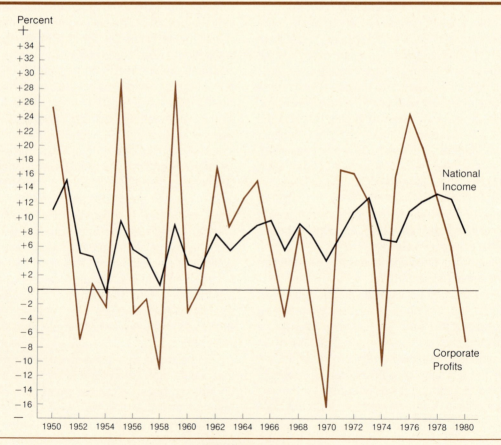

FIGURE 18-2
Percent Change in Corporate Profits and Percent Change in National Income, 1950–80

SOURCE: *Economic Report of the President,* January 1981, Table B-18, p. 253 and Table B-80, p. 280.

profits and the level of income. The two vary in the same direction, but not proportionately. The total amount of profits is much lower when the economy is operating at the relatively low income level of a recession than it is when the economy is enjoying the relatively high income level of prosperous periods. However, as the income level rises and falls over the course of business fluctuations, profits typically vary more than proportionally with the change in income. This relationship is quite apparent in Figure 18-2, which shows the year-to-year percentage change in corporate profits and national income from 1950 to 1980. Consider, for example, the period of 1973 to 1977, which covers the severe recession from late 1973 to early 1975 and the first years of recovery from that recession. Profits decreased by 12.4 percent from 1973 to 1974 while the growth of national income slowed from 12.7 percent in the preceding year to 6.9 percent in 1974. From 1974 to 1977, corporate profits shot up 73.6 percent while the national income increased only 33.2 percent.

What we then have here are relationships in which the level of aggregate profits varies with the level of the economy's income and, according to the profits theory of investment, the desired capital stock varies with the level of aggregate profits. If the level of profits indicates a desired capital stock that exceeds the actual capital stock, net investment occurs to correct the shortage of capital, a process examined in detail in the preceding chapter.

The Level of Profits, the Desired Capital Stock, and the Investment Function

We can tie together the analysis from the preceding chapter and the profits theory of investment introduced here with the help of Figure 18-3. The curve in Part A shows that total profits, designated by Z, vary directly with the income level, Y. In accordance with the profits theory, for each level of profits shown in Part A there is a particular capital stock desired by business. However, we cannot identify that particular capital stock in Part B without also knowing the market rate of interest, because this model includes the rate of interest as well as the level of profits as a determinant of the desired capital stock. We meet this problem in Part B by constructing a family of curves, each corresponding to a different interest rate. The upward slope of each of these curves shows that the desired capital stock measured on the horizontal axis varies directly with the level of profits measured on the vertical axis. However, for any particular level of profits, the desired capital stock will be smaller the higher the rate of interest; therefore, the higher the rate of interest, the further to the left lies the curve relating desired K to realized Z. Curves for 8, 6, and 4 percent interest rates are shown in Part B.

In Part C, we can derive an MEC curve for each possible level of profits in Part A. If the existing profit level is $15, we see in Part B that the desired capital stock will be $340 if $r = 8$ percent, $400 if $r = 6$ percent, and $460 if $r = 4$ percent. Plotting these pairs of values in Part C gives us the MEC curve labeled $Z = \$15$. The MEC curve for $Z = \$40$ is derived in the same way. This could be repeated for any other level of profits in Part A.

Now suppose that profits are actually $15, the market rate of interest is 6 percent, and the actual capital stock is $400. We see in Part C that the desired capital stock is $400, so the actual is equal to the desired.[5] Net investment will be

---

[5]It may be objected that this is a highly implausible supposition because profits of $15 on a capital stock of $400 provide a return to stockholders of less than 4 percent, or less than the market interest rate of 6 percent. The answer is that we cannot say anything here about the return to stockholders on the basis of the information given. A major consideration is the amount of capital stock that is debt-financed. For example, if it is $300 of the $400, the profits figure of $15 (which is arrived at after deducting interest paid on debt as well as all other expenses) turns out to provide a 15 percent return on the capital stock that is equity-financed.

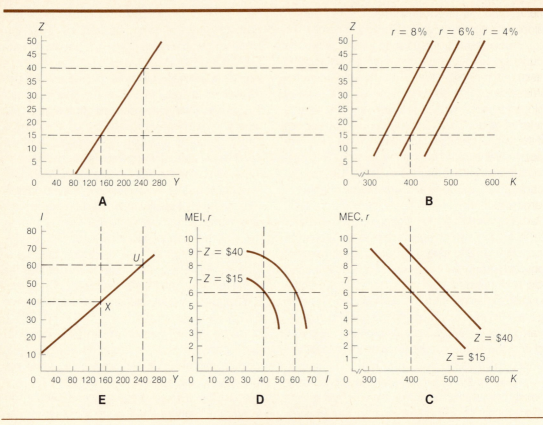

FIGURE 18-3
The Level of Profits, the Desired Capital Stock,
and the Investment Function

zero. As was explained in Chapter 17, in this case the MEI curve in Part D will be positioned like the curve labeled $Z = \$15$. That curve shows, at the existing interest rate of 6 percent, net investment of zero and replacement investment of $40, assuming that one-tenth of the existing capital stock of $400 requires replacement during the period. Finally, noting in Part A that Z of $15 is found with the economy operating at the $150 level of Y, it follows that the I of $40 in Part D is also found with Y of $150. This combination of $I = \$40$ and $Y = \$150$ identifies the point marked X in Part E and establishes one point on the investment function toward which we are working.

By finding other such combinations of I and Y, we can fully specify the investment function in Part E. If we start with the profit level of $40 in Part A, we will find in Part C that at a 6 percent interest rate the desired capital stock is $480. With the existing capital stock again assumed to be $400, the desired exceeds the actual and the MEC exceeds the market rate of interest. The MEI curve in Part D shifts upward to the position shown by the curve labeled $Z = \$40$; this indicates net investment of $20 and gross investment of $60. Because Z of $40 is found in Part A with the economy operating at Y of $250, it follows that I of $60 in Part D is also found with Y of $250. This identifies the point marked U in Part E. Connecting points like X and U yields the upward-sloping investment curve.

The position and slope of the investment curve shown in Part E follow from the specific assumptions made in other parts of the model. With different assumptions, the position and/or slope will be different. For example, if Z made up a larger fraction of Y at each level of Y—that is, if the curve in Part A were located above the one now shown—the I curve in Part E would then be located above its present position. If the desired capital stock for any given level of profits were larger than now shown—that is, if the curve in Part B for any given rate of interest were located to the right of its present position—again the I curve in Part E would be located above its present position. If all functions were as shown but the market rate of interest were lower than the assumed 6 percent, the I curve again would be located above its present position. If the curve in Part A were steeper, indicating that the fraction of any change in income that goes into profits is larger than that shown by the present curve, the I curve in Part E would be steeper than the one now shown. If the MEI curve in Part D were flatter (the supply curve of capital goods more elastic), indicating a greater rise in I for any given shift in an MEC curve, again the I curve in Part E would be steeper than the one now shown. However, for present purposes, it is sufficient to see that the profits theory produces an investment curve of the general type shown in Part E.

One property of this type of curve is an intercept with the vertical axis above zero, but it may appear that the investment curve should have a negative intercept with the vertical axis just as the profits curve does. The profits curve is drawn this way to reflect the fact that at a sufficiently low level of income, aggregate profits will become negative (a rare situation but one that did occur during the Great Depression). A depression so severe that aggregate profits become negative will probably cause negative net investment, but gross fixed investment will be a positive amount. Some firms will still find it necessary to undertake at least some replacement investment merely to maintain minimal operations. Because the verti-

cal axis of Part E shows gross and not net investment, an investment curve with a positive intercept like the one shown seems appropriate.

The amount of investment indicated by the vertical intercept, $10 in Part E, is ordinarily described as **autonomous**, meaning independent of the level of income. Although in practice income could not fall to zero, the intercept shows what investment would be in this hypothetical case. Then starting at zero and moving to successively higher levels of income, total investment becomes successively greater. The difference between autonomous investment and total investment is ordinarily called **induced** investment, meaning investment that is called forth by or dependent on the level of income. Accordingly, in Part E, at Y of $150, total investment of $40 is composed of induced investment of $30 and autonomous investment of $10, and at Y of $250, total investment of $60 is composed of $50 of induced investment and the unchanged $10 of autonomous investment. According to this terminology, a shift in the investment curve with no change in its slope involves a change in autonomous investment only; a change in the slope of the curve with no change in its intercept involves a change in induced investment only.

The investment curve in Part E has the same properties as the short-run linear consumption function developed in Chapter 4 as part of the simple Keynesian model. The general equation for that consumption function was $C = C_a + cY$, in which C_a represented autonomous consumption and cY represented induced consumption. In a parallel fashion, the general equation for the investment function in Part E of Figure 18-3 is $I = I_a + eY$, in which I_a represents autonomous investment and eY represents induced investment. Paralleling c is e, the marginal propensity to invest, which is equal to $\Delta I/\Delta Y$.[6] Note that the investment curve in Part E has an MPI of 0.20. With income of $150, I is $40, and with income of

---

[6]Because c has been used for the MPC and s for the MPS, this mnemonic approach suggests i for the MPI. Because this letter has already been used with another meaning in Chapter 17, e will be used instead.

$250, I is $60. Or $\Delta I/\Delta Y = 20/100 = 0.20$. Although both c and e refer to kinds of induced spending, in what follows we will want to compare induced investment with induced saving. As induced consumption is cY, induced saving is $(1-c)Y$ or sY—from the saving function $S = -C_a + (1-c)Y$. For any change in Y, the change in induced S (which is also the change in total S) equals $(1-c)\Delta Y$ or $s(\Delta Y)$ and the change in induced I (which is also the change in total I) equals $e(\Delta Y)$. Therefore, if $e > s$, $\Delta I > \Delta S$ for any ΔY, and vice versa. In what follows the relative sizes of e and s are critical.

The Profits Theory of Investment and the Equilibrium Income Level and Equilibrium Interest Rate

In the *IS–LM* models of Part 3, the only determinant of investment taken into account was the interest rate. We there had the investment equation $I = I(r)$. The profits theory of investment here developed makes investment depend on the level of income. By now introducing this investment theory into the *IS–LM* model so that investment depends on both the rate of interest and the level of income or $I = I(r,Y)$, we arrive at some results that are surprisingly and interestingly different from those earlier reached.

Derivation of the *IS* Curve with Induced Investment

To obtain these results, the first step is to fit the induced investment curve derived in Part E of Figure 18-3 into the graphic framework for the derivation of the *IS* curve. For this purpose, the four-part diagram originally used in Figure 12-3 (p. 238) is extended as in Figure 18-4. Parts A through D of this figure correspond with Parts A

through D of Figure 12-3; Parts E and F have been added. Part E duplicates Part E of Figure 18-3. As there, the investment function is $I = 10 + 0.20 Y$. The investment function in Part E shows how I will vary with Y, *assuming a given interest rate* (for this function, 6 percent). For example, if Y were 150, I would be 40, and if Y were 250, I would be 60. Part F has no economic content; its 45° line serves only as a means of transferring amounts of I identified on the vertical axis of Part E to the horizontal axis of Part A. For example, if Y is 150 in Part E, I is 40, remembering that the values for I in Part E are based on the assumption that r is 6 percent. The I of 40 from Part E corresponds with point H in Part A, which is one point on an MEI curve labeled MEI_a.[7] In the same way, at Y of 250 in Part E, I is 60, and this corresponds with point J in Part A, which is one point on another MEI curve labeled MEI_b. A number of other MEI curves could be inserted for other values of Y, but two are sufficient.

Look next at the solid line saving function in Part C, which shows S for each possible income level. This saving function is $S = -4 + 0.10Y$. To illustrate with the two income levels earlier noted, when $Y = 150$, $S = 11$; when $Y = 250$, $S = 21$. In this model, S depends only on Y, but I now depends on both Y and r. Therefore, *if income is 150, S will be 11; to obtain equilibrium between S and I at the income level of 150 requires that the interest rate be whatever higher rate is needed to reduce I from 40 to 11*. Given the slope of the MEI_a curve, that interest rate is 9 percent. Therefore, $S = 11 = I$ at Y of 150 and r of 9 percent—a combination which yields point K on the *IS* curve, which is being derived in Part D of Figure 18-4. Similarly, if we started with the income level of 250, I would be 60, but S would be 21. Again, there is some higher interest rate that will reduce I from 60 to 21 at the income level

---

[7]Unlike the MEI curves in Part D of Figure 18-3, the MEI curves are here made linear in order to simplify. To simplify further, the distinction between replacement investment and net investment made in Figure 18-3 is dropped here because it is not essential to the model.

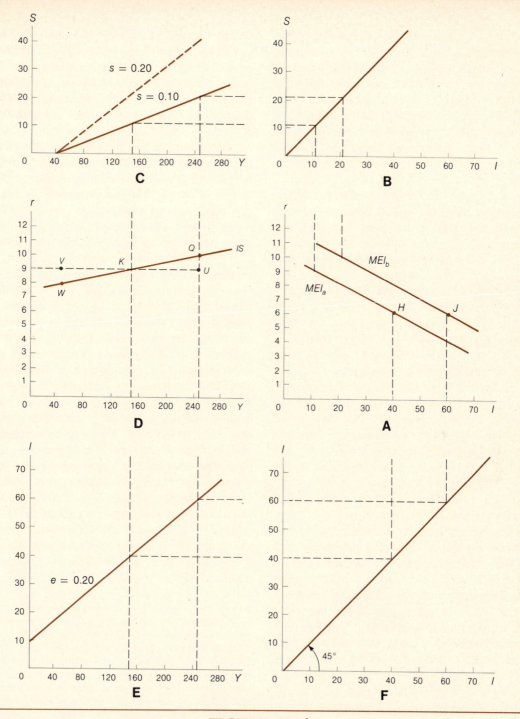

FIGURE 18-4
Derivation of *IS* Curve with Induced Investment

of 250. As shown by the MEI_b curve, this occurs at the interest rate of 10 percent. The combination of $S = 21 = I$ at Y of 250 and r of 10 percent yields point Q on the IS curve being derived in Part D of Figure 18-4. With all functions linear, connecting points K and Q with a straight line gives us the IS curve as shown. This IS curve is different from all those we have seen in earlier chapters: *This IS curve slopes upward to the right.*

In Chapter 12, for the model in which I depended only on r, the IS curve necessarily sloped downward to the right. A higher Y is accompanied by a higher S, but to call forth the higher I to match the higher S required a lower r. The combinations of Y and r at which $S = I$ formed an IS curve in which higher levels of Y were accompanied by lower levels of r. In the present model, I varies directly with Y and, as before, also inversely with r. Again a higher Y will be accompanied by a higher S, but it will now also be accompanied by a higher I.

To see the implications of this, suppose that the system is initially at Y of 150 and r of 9 percent (point K on the IS curve in Part D). Here $S = I$ and there is goods market equilibrium. For comparison, take point U, which is at the same r of 9 percent but the higher Y of 250. In this figure, $e = 0.20$ and $s = 0.10$; therefore, a change in Y from 150 to 250 raises S by 10 and I by 20. The excess of I over S will tend to raise Y still higher, thereby producing even greater excess of I over S. It appears that goods market equilibrium cannot be reattained. However, equilibrium can be achieved through the interest rate. In the present illustration, goods market equilibrium will occur at Y of 250 if r rises from 9 to 10 percent (the Y and r combination labelled Q). That rise in r chokes off 10 of I—exactly the amount of difference between I and S that results from the rise in Y from 150 to 250 with $e = 0.20$ and $s = 0.10$.

For the opposite case, compare the disequilibrium combination of Y and r indicated by V with the equilibrium combination indicated by K. A movement of Y from 150 to 50 reduces S by 10 and I by 20. Consequently, S exceeds I by 10 at point V. This will tend to lead to a further reduction in Y at which S will exceed I by an even greater amount. However, as before, equilibrium may be reattained at the 50 level of Y by an appropriate change in the interest rate. In this illustration, a decrease in r from 9 to 8 percent will raise I by 10 to bring S and I into equality at point W.[8]

This illustrates the general conclusion that goods market equilibrium requires that the interest rate must rise or fall as the income level rises or falls when the marginal propensity to invest exceeds the marginal propensity to save. In other words, under these conditions, the IS curve must slope upward to the right. On the other hand, suppose the marginal propensity to invest is smaller than the marginal propensity to save. Then any increase in income will be accompanied by a larger increase in saving than in investment, thereby necessitating a lower interest rate to reattain equilibrium between saving and investment. (Any decrease in income will be accompanied by a greater decrease in saving than in investment, thereby necessitating a higher interest rate to reattain equilibrium.) This will produce the earlier result of an IS curve that slopes downward to the right. Finally, for the special case in which the two marginal propensities are equal, the result will be a horizontal IS curve. For example, the dashed line in Part C indicates a marginal propensity to save of 0.20, which is equal to the marginal propensity to invest of 0.20 in Part E. The slopes and the positions of these saving and investment functions will yield a horizontal IS curve that lies just below the 8 percent interest rate.

---

[8]In originally deriving the IS curve in Chapter 12, we made the rule that any point to the right of the IS curve identified an income level at which $S > I$ and any point to the left of it identified an income level at which $I > S$. The forces were such as to reattain equilibrium by pushing the income level toward the IS curve. That rule holds as long as I does not depend on Y; it also holds even if I does depend on Y, provided that e is smaller than s. However, where e exceeds s, the saving and investment forces push the income level away from rather than toward the IS curve. That is the case we have considered here.

The *IS–LM* Model with Induced Investment

Although the introduction of the investment function in which *I* depends on *Y* as well as *r* is consistent with an *IS* curve with upward, downward, or no slope, the most interesting case is that of an upward slope resulting from a marginal propensity to invest that exceeds the marginal propensity to save. Combining an *IS* curve of this kind with an *LM* curve (the *LM* curve always slopes upward) raises some new problems in tracing the process by which the economy returns to equilibrium following a shift in the *LM* or *IS* curve that upsets an existing equilibrium.

To make graphical analysis of this process readily manageable, we simplify by assuming that adjustment to any disequilibrium in the money market is so rapid that the supply of and demand for money are always equal. This amounts to saying the interest rate adjusts instantaneously or that the economy is always on the *LM* curve. On the other hand, adjustment to a disequilibrium in the goods market takes place gradually.[9] Although no adjustment is instantaneous in practice, the typical adjustment in the money market occurs far more rapidly than the typical adjustment in the goods market. The money market is financial and requires only those changes in the prices of financial claims needed to raise or lower the interest rate to its equilibrium level. The goods market is, of course, real and requires the expansion or contraction of production in order to raise or lower output to the equilibrium level.

In practice, changes in output are typically accompanied by changes in the price level.

---

[9]In the description of the adjustment process in Chapter 12 (pp. 243–44), we considered the case of a disequilibrium in both the goods and money markets—a position off both curves—and traced a possible series of steps by which the system would move to the *Y* and *r* equilibrium indicated by the intersection of the two curves. Now the only disequilibrium positions we consider are positions off the *IS* curve. Because disequilibrium positions in the money market are instantaneously removed, in effect there are no such positions.

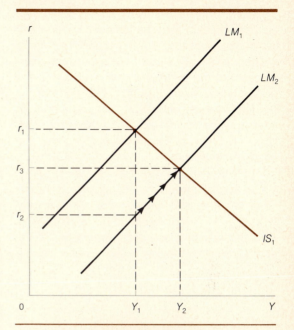

**FIGURE 18-5
The Adjustment Process:
Downward-Sloping *IS* Curve**

Again, to keep the graphical analysis easily manageable, we bypass this aspect by assuming the stable price level case of Chapter 12 in which the aggregate supply curve has a perfectly elastic range within which the economy is assumed to be operating. Therefore, in what follows, aggregate supply and demand curves are not required.

To clarify the adjustment process, first consider an adjustment for the familiar case of earlier chapters in which the *IS* curve slopes downward to the right as in Figure 18-5. From an initial equilibrium at Y_1 and r_1 given by the intersection of IS_1 and LM_1, assume an increase in the money supply that shifts the *LM* curve to LM_2. Because we have assumed that the interest rate adjusts instantaneously whereas the level of output adjusts gradually, the interest rate drops immediately from r_1 to r_2. At Y_1 and r_2, the economy is to the left of the downward-sloping *IS* curve;

therefore, investment exceeds saving. As income starts to rise, so does the transactions demand for money. Consequently, the interest rate starts to rise above r_2. Both the income level and interest rate rise along the LM curve as shown by the arrows until a new equilibrium is attained at the IS_1–LM_2 intersection with Y of Y_2 and r of r_3. In relation to the original equilibrium, the new equilibrium is one with a higher level of income and a lower interest rate.

Turn next to the new case in which the IS curve slopes upward to the right as in Figure 18-6. As before, an increase in the money supply shifts the LM curve from LM_1 to LM_2 and the interest rate instantaneously drops from r_1 to r_2. At Y_1 and r_2 investment exceeds saving, and income

starts to rise. Furthermore, unlike the case in Figure 18-5, now each rise in income produces a further rise in investment (because investment depends on the level of income). Because the marginal propensity to invest exceeds the marginal propensity to save, the induced rise in investment exceeds the induced rise in saving. To attain equilibrium in the goods market, saving and investment are brought into equality by a rise in the interest rate which chokes off more investment than the rise in income calls forth. In Figure 18-6, given the underlying response of investment to income and the interest rate, the rise from r_2 to r_3 will squeeze out an amount of investment equal to the amount by which the increase in investment exceeds the increase in saving. Saving will again equal investment with r of r_3 and Y of Y_2.

In relation to the initial equilibrium, the new equilibrium has both a higher level of income and a higher interest rate. This is an interesting result because the disequilibrium occurred as a result of an expansionary monetary policy, which ordinarily would produce a new equilibrium with a lower interest rate. However, here expansionary policy leads to a higher rather than a lower interest rate. The possibility of this outcome has been noted by monetarists for some time, but they attribute it to the effect that expansionary monetary policy has in raising inflationary expectations and the effect that heightened inflationary expectations have in raising the interest rate. The present model indicates the possibility of a rise in the interest rate without relying on any change in inflationary expectations, although it does rely on a marginal propensity to invest that is greater than the marginal propensity to save. That is, if the rise in income that results from the initial decline in the rate of interest leads to a greater increase in induced investment than in induced saving—if $e > s$—the new equilibrium r will be higher than the original equilibrium r.

One other case must be noted: In Figure 18-7, the IS curve slopes upward to the right as in Figure 18-6, but its slope is now greater than that of the LM curve. As before, the existing equi-

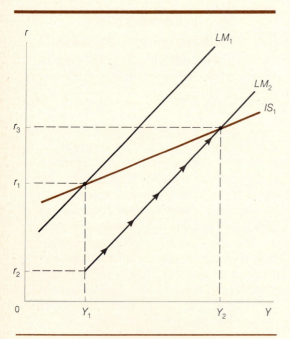

FIGURE 18-6
The Adjustment Process:
Upward-Sloping *IS* Curve with
Stable Equilibrium

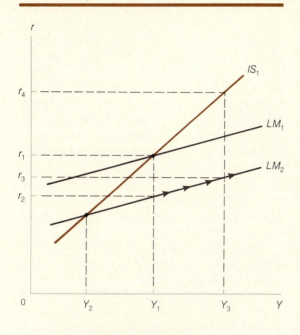

FIGURE 18-7
The Adjustment Process: Upward-Sloping *IS* Curve with Unstable Equilibrium

librium at r_1 and Y_1 is upset by an increase in the money supply that shifts the *LM* curve from LM_1 to LM_2. As before, this produces an immediate drop in the interest rate from r_1 to r_2. The comparative statics of the diagram may tempt us to conclude that the system will move to a new equilibrium given by the intersection of the IS_1 and LM_2 curves. However, this would imply a decline in the income level, whereas we know that disequilibrium is such as to lead to a rise in the income level. With the immediate effect of the shift of the *LM* curve being a decrease in r from r_1 to r_2 and no change in Y, investment exceeds saving and this raises the income level. (Because $S = I$ on the *IS* curve at r_1 and Y_1, I must exceed S at r_2 and Y_1, given that I varies inversely with r.)

As before, the excess of investment over saving drives the system upward along the *LM* curve. The resulting increase in income increases the transactions demand for money and raises the interest rate. However, unlike the case in Figure 18-6, the rise in the interest rate is not now great enough to bring investment into equality with saving. For example, there could be equality between saving and investment (goods market equilibrium) at Y_3 with r of r_4, but there is money market equilibrium at Y_3 with the lower interest rate of r_3. As the income level rises, the gap between the higher interest rate needed for goods market equilibrium and the lower interest rate needed for money market equilibrium grows ever larger. Under this condition, equilibrium cannot be reestablished. The initial equilibrium at Y_1 and r_1 is unstable in the sense that any departure from it is not followed by the establishment of a new equilibrium. Although this unstable case is interesting, note that it is only possible with an upward sloping *IS* curve—and only then if the *LM* curve has a lesser upward slope than the *IS* curve. In the earlier case of the downward sloping *IS* curve, there will always be a stable equilibrium, no matter how slight the upward slope of the *LM* curve.

This completes our consideration of the profits theory of investment and how its incorporation affects the results of our extended model of income determination. To sum up, the profits theory of investment is the basis for an investment function that relates investment directly to the level of aggregate income. Inserting this function into the income model produced a model the results of which differ in important ways from those of the earlier analysis where attention was limited to investment as a function of the interest rate only. The specific results that follow for the interest rate and the income level when an existing equilibrium is upset by an increase in the money supply depend in part on the strength of induced investment (as measured by the marginal propensity to invest) relative to the strength of induced saving (as measured by the marginal propensity to save).

The Accelerator Theory[10]

The rationale of the profits theory is that the behavior of realized profits guides business people in judging what future profits will be. In the absence of clear-cut evidence to the contrary, higher current profits promise higher future profits; they therefore provide business people with the incentive (and also all or some of the funds needed) to acquire the additional capital goods that will provide the greater output, the sale of which will generate those greater future profits. The accelerator theory denies that the level of profits plays this strategic role. Its rationale is that the incentive to acquire more capital goods arises not because the current profit record is favorable but because increases in output are putting pressure on firms' existing productive capacity. An increase in productive capacity requires an expansion of the capital stock, which in turn calls for a higher rate of investment spending than would otherwise be needed. Accordingly, the rate of investment spending is made to depend on *changes* in the level of output.

Industry and company statistics reveal that profits and investment spending are directly correlated. Industries and firms with greater profits spend more on investment than those with smaller profits. Some people might therefore conclude that the greater investment spending is *due to* the greater profits. The supporters of the accelerator theory see it quite differently. Those industries and companies with relatively high current profits are also those in which sales and output have been expanding relatively rapidly. They then acquire additional plant and equipment not because the level of profits is high but because the growth in sales and output is rapid.

From this point of view, investment is explained largely on a physical or input–output basis; increases in the desired capital stock occur because a growing demand for output necessitates a growing supply of the services of capital goods. If the existing capital goods are already utilized, a growing supply of the services provided by such goods can be secured only through an expansion in their stock. This brings us back to the accelerator theory argument that the rate of investment spending is tied to changes in the level of output.

The dispute between those who find profits to be the explanation and those who find the changes in output and degrees of capacity utilization to be the explanation, as well as between these and others who offer still different explanations, can only begin to be resolved through econometric study. For example, the particular dispute here noted is illuminated through the following fairly crude approach. Given the available data on profits, sales, output, and plant and equipment expenditures of thousands of firms, we may compare firms that have quite similar changes in sales and output but quite different profit records. To the extent that the investment behavior of these firms is similar, there is some indication that changes in output are more important than the level of profits as a determinant of investment. On the other hand, if we were to compare a group of firms with similar profits but dis-

---

[10]There is a large body of literature on the accelerator theory or the acceleration principle, some of which goes back to the early years of this century. The best known of the early studies is J.M. Clark, "Business Acceleration and the Law of Demand," in *Journal of Political Economy,* March 1917, pp. 217–35. Among the more recent studies are R. Eisner, "Capital Expenditures, Profits and the Acceleration Principle," in *Models of Income Determination, Studies in Income and Wealth,* Vol. 28, Princeton University Press, 1964; E. Kuh, *Capital Stock Growth: A Microeconomic Approach,* North Holland, 1963; and B. Hickman, *Investment Demand and U.S. Economic Growth,* Brookings Institution, 1965. For coverage of the pre-1952 literature as well as an examination of the principle itself, see A.D. Knox, "The Acceleration Principle and the Theory of Investment: A Survey," in *Economica,* Aug. 1952, pp. 269–97. Considerable econometric work has been done on the accelerator theory in more recent years; references to this work will be found in D.W. Jorgenson, "Econometric Studies of Investment Behavior: A Survey," in *Journal of Economic Literature,* Dec. 1971, pp. 1111–47.

similar sales and output, a finding of similar investment behavior would suggest that profits are more important than changes in output.

Although this approach would help separate the effect of the two factors, it does not consider other factors that may be correlated with one or the other of these two and that may actually be the major factors in any explanation. For this purpose, sophisticated statistical techniques are required. In recent years, with the aid of modern computers, these techniques have been applied to masses of time series and cross-sectional data on firms and industries. Even so, the complications and difficulties are so great that findings are still not beyond dispute.[11] However, the findings are clear enough to lead to the conclusion that in refined form the accelerator theory is one of the most worthwhile theories of investment spending. Because of the difficulties involved, in what follows we will not get into the econometric testing of the theory or discuss the theory itself beyond its basic form. Even in this form, the fairly straightforward statement that investment spending depends on changes in the level of output is not without its share of complications.

The Capital–Output Ratio

According to the accelerator theory, investment occurs to enlarge the stock of capital because more capital is needed to produce more output. Within limits, firms may be able to produce more output with existing capital through more intensive use of that capital, but there is a particular ratio of capital to output that firms consider optimum. This ratio will vary considerably from industry to industry—much more capital is used per

dollar of output in the automobile industry than in the barbering industry—but at any time we will find a particular ratio that is the desired ratio for the economy as a whole. This ratio will change as the mix of output changes—more cars and fewer haircuts or vice versa—and as technological changes and changes in relative factor costs alter the least-cost combination of labor and capital used in the production of different kinds of goods and services. But to reduce the complications, we will assume that this ratio remains unchanged over time.

With K representing the capital stock, Y the level of output, and w the capital–output ratio (the desired number of dollars of capital per dollar of output per time period), we have

$$K = wY$$

If the capital–output ratio is 2, then K of \$400 is desired for Y of \$200, and K of \$450 for Y of \$225.[12] Because we are assuming an unchanging capital–output ratio, the desired stock of capital will change over successive time periods *only* with changes in output. Designating some particular time period as t, preceding time periods as $t - 1$ and $t - 2$, and subsequent time periods as $t + 1$ and $t + 2$, let us suppose that in Period $t - 1$ precisely the desired capital stock was on hand to produce the level of output of Period $t - 1$. That is,

$$K_{t-1} = wY_{t-1}$$

If output then rises from Period $t - 1$ to Period t, the desired capital stock will also rise or

$$K_t = wY_t$$

---

[11]For an impression of what is being done in this area, see D. W. Jorgenson, "Econometric Studies of Investment Behavior: A Survey," in *Journal of Economic Literature*, Dec. 1971, pp. 1111–47. For an essay on the extraordinary difficulties faced by those working in this area, see R. Eisner, "Investment and the Frustration of Econometricians," in *American Economic Review*, May, 1969, pp. 50–64.

[12]Note that K is a stock and Y is a flow. Because flows can be expressed in terms of different time periods, the capital–output ratio will vary with the time period employed. If it takes \$400 of K to produce \$200 of Y over the course of a year, it will also take \$400 of K to produce \$50 of Y over the course of a quarter of a year (assuming production is at a constant rate). The former indicates a capital–output ratio of 2 and the latter a ratio of 8, but these amount to the same thing when allowance is made for the difference in the time periods over which output is being measured.

The increase in the desired stock is $K_t - K_{t-1}$. To increase the capital stock, net investment expenditures are needed. To increase the capital stock from K_{t-1} to K_t, the net investment expenditures required equal the change in capital stock, or

$$I_t = K_t - K_{t-1} \qquad [1]$$

Here I_t is *net* investment for period t. By substituting wY_t for K_t and wY_{t-1} for K_{t-1}, we may also describe net investment expenditures required in Period t as

$$I_t = wY_t - wY_{t-1} = w(Y_t - Y_{t-1}) \qquad [2]$$

This equation simply indicates that net investment during t depends on the change in output from $t - 1$ to t multiplied by the capital–output ratio, w.[13] If $Y_t > Y_{t-1}$, the equation indicates that there is positive net investment during Period t; If $Y_t < Y_{t-1}$, there is negative net investment, (disinvestment) during Period t. In short, for any assigned value of w and for any change in Y from $t - 1$ to t, the equation indicates the amount of net investment, positive or negative, for Period t that is attributable to the change in the level of output.[14]

If we wish to show gross rather than net investment, we merely add replacement invest-

ment to both sides of the equation. Assuming replacement investment to be equal to depreciation and letting D_t represent depreciation in Period t, we have

$$I_t + D_t = w(Y_t - Y_{t-1}) + D_t$$

Because negative net investment in plant and equipment is limited to the amount of depreciation of the capital stock, the sum of I_t and D_t cannot be less than zero. If I_{g_t} represents gross investment in Period t, we may also write

$$I_{g_t} = w(Y_t - Y_{t-1}) + D_t \qquad [3]$$

Investment will respond to changes in the level of output as indicated by the equation only if certain assumptions are satisfied. Others will be noted later, but one of the crucial assumptions is best introduced here. This is the absence of excess capacity. We may allow for this factor by letting X_t stand for excess capacity at the beginning of Period t and rewriting Equation [3] to read

$$I_{g_t} = w(Y_t - Y_{t-1}) + D_t - X_t$$

Whatever the level of gross investment might otherwise be in Period t, it will be reduced by the amount of X_t. If the value of $w(Y_t - Y_{t-1}) + D_t$ happened to be equal to or less than X_t, I_{g_t} would

---

[13]It may be noted that Equations [1] and [2] represent our first encounter with so-called difference equations. By assuming that our variables have only a discrete set of possible values and that these values are available at certain uniformly spaced time intervals, we may date all the variables in our equations. Equations with variables dated in this fashion are one type of difference equations. A set of such difference equations makes up a dynamic model— "dynamic" in that the value of a variable, say, for the Period t, is made dependent on the values of one or more other variables for Periods $t - 1$, $t - 2$, and so forth. For a discussion of the use of difference equations in economics, see W.J. Baumol, *Economic Dynamics*, 3rd ed., Macmillan, 1970, Part 4.

[14]This formulation may be criticized because it requires that the change in the stock of capital goods occur instantly, whereas in practice this is a production process that requires time. The problem is this. From Equation [2], we do not know what I_t will be until we know what the change from Y_{t-1} to Y_t is, and we cannot know this before

the end of Period t when we have the figure for Y_t. This hardly leaves time during Period t to carry out the investment, I_t, that is indicated for that time period, and thus constitutes a valid objection to Equation [2]. The problem may be met by making the desired capital stock in any period depend on the output of the preceding period, or $K_t = w(Y_{t-1})$ and $K_{t-1} = w(Y_{t-2})$, from which we derive the investment equation, $I_t = w(Y_{t-1} - Y_{t-2})$, which is not subject to the objection noted. However, this lag system introduces other problems that are better avoided here. Another way of meeting the problem is to make the output of any period depend on the *sales* of the preceding period. In simplest form, business in each time period chooses to produce output equal to sales of the preceding period, or $Y_t = Sales_{t-1}$. (This also introduces problems of its own, but these will not bother us here.) Therefore, at the beginning of Period t, business knows how much it wants to produce during that period (it knows what Y_t will be). It therefore also knows how much net investment is needed to make the actual capital stock equal the desired stock—$I_t = w(Y_t - Y_{t-1})$—so that Equation [2] as given above is now acceptable.

be zero, the minimum possible figure for gross investment in plant and equipment.

These relationships, which we have here little more than listed in terms of equations, will be discussed more fully and traced through with the help of numerical examples in the following sections.

The Acceleration Principle

The basic relationship between the change in the level of output and the volume of investment spending is known as the **acceleration principle.** The capital–output ratio, w, is known as the **accelerator.** The theory of investment based on this relationship is known as the **accelerator theory.**

The acceleration principle as expressed in equation form in the preceding section is straightforward. If the economy is already producing the most that can be produced with the existing capital stock (that is, there is no excess capacity or $X_t = 0$), and if there is a fixed ratio between output and capital (that is, w is a constant), any expansion of output requires an expansion of the capital stock. Furthermore, if the accelerator has a value greater than 1, the needed increase in capital stock must exceed the increase in output, so that the increase in investment spending will be greater than the increase in output that causes it. Otherwise expressed, to the extent that the demand for additional plant and equipment is derived from the demand for output, a change in the demand for output, given an accelerator greater than 1, leads to a magnification of the derived demand for the plant and equipment necessary to the production of additional output.

To observe the acceleration principle in operation, let us now trace changes in output and gross investment over a number of time periods. In Table 18-1, column 1 simply indicates a series of time periods; column 2 gives the assumed level of income and output in each period. The specific period-to-period values in this column have been deliberately selected to bring out certain relationships indicated by the acceleration

principle; the table does not at all explain why these values are what they are, but merely takes them as given.[15] We assume a constant capital–output ratio, w, of 2 so the desired stock of capital given in column 3 is double the output given in column 2. The table includes conditions under which the actual capital stock will exceed the desired capital stock, so column 4 has been inserted to show the actual stock. The average durability of capital goods is here assumed to be 20 time periods instead of 10 as before, so that in each time period there is replacement investment equal to 5 percent of the capital stock in existence in Period 1. This gives us in column 5 an unvarying replacement investment of 20 per time period.[16] Net investment in any period, as shown in column 6, equals w times the change in output between that period and the preceding period. Gross investment of column 7 is the sum of replacement and net investment of columns 5 and 6.

With the demand for output unchanged from Period 1 to Period 2, firms need simply maintain the existing capital stock of 400. This is done by replacing the 20 that wears out during the period. However, when demand for output increases by 10 in Period 3, new capital facilities of 20 are wanted. In terms of the equation in which I measures *net* investment only, we have $I_t = w(Y_t - Y_{t-1})$ or $20 = 2(210 - 200)$. Total expenditures for capital goods—made up of 20 of replacement and 20 of net investment—accordingly rise from

---

[15]According to footnote 14, the output figure for any period is equal to the sales figure for the preceding period; however, these sales figures are not explained here either, but are taken as given.

[16]Replacement investment remains at 20 per time period despite the rise in capital stock in Period 3 and subsequent periods. The 20 added to the capital stock in Period 3 does not need replacement until Period 23, the 20 added in Period 4 does not need replacement until Period 24, and so forth. These are all time periods beyond those given in the table. Note also that the capital stock of 400 on hand in Period 1 must have been built up through net investment of 20 during each of the 20 periods preceding Period 1 in order to produce the constant 20 of replacement.

TABLE 18-1
The Working of the Acceleration Principle, $w = 2$

(1) Period	(2) Output	(3) Desired Capital	(4) Actual Capital	(5) Replacement Investment	(6) Net Investment	(7) Gross Investment
1	200	400	400	20	0	20
2	200	400	400	20	0	20
3	210	420	420	20	20	40
4	220	440	440	20	20	40
5	250	500	500	20	60	80
6	270	540	540	20	40	60
7	260	520	520	20	−20	0
8	256	512	512	20	− 8	12
9	250	500	500	20	−12	8
10	230	460	480	—	—	0
11	200	400	460	—	—	0
12	190	380	440	—	—	0
13	210	420	420	—	—	0
14	220	440	440	20	20	40

20 in Period 2 to 40 in Period 3. With an accelerator of 2, the increase of 10 in expenditures for final output produces an increase of 20 in expenditures for capital goods. In percentage terms, a 5 percent increase in expenditures for final product calls for a 100 percent increase in expenditures for capital goods. It is this relationship that gives the acceleration principle its name.

From Period 3 to Period 4, output rises by 10, as it did from Period 2 to Period 3. This indicates net investment of 20 in Period 4 to effect the increase of 20 in desired capital. Net investment in Period 4 is therefore the same as in Period 3, and gross investment in Period 4 is 40, as it was in Period 3. This brings out one of a number of relationships between changes in output and the level of investment suggested by the acceleration principle. In order for gross investment merely to be maintained at the same higher level after it has been increased (to remain at 40 in Period 4 after increasing from 20 in Period 2 to 40 in Period 3), output must continue to rise.

Gross investment can stand still period after period only if output rises period after period. To be more precise, gross investment will remain unchanged from one period to the next if the absolute increase in output remains unchanged from one period to the next.[17]

Under what conditions will gross investment increase from one period to the next? Expenditures for output must increase by ever larger absolute amounts from one period to the next. Gross investment in Period 5 rises above that in

[17]This requires qualification, because it is true for only a limited number of periods. In the present illustration, in order for gross investment to remain at 40 from Period 3 through, say, Period 22, output must rise by 10 in each succeeding period. However, in Period 23, gross investment will remain at 40 even though output does not rise above its level (400) reached in Period 22. In Period 23, the 20 of net investment of Period 3 comes up for replacement, and replacement investment jumps abruptly from 20 to 40. Similarly, the 20 of net investment of Period 4 comes up for replacement in Period 24, to make replacement investment 40 in Period 24. And so forth.

Period 4 because the absolute increase in output from Period 4 to Period 5 exceeds that from Period 3 to Period 4. However, note next that despite the further increase in output from Period 5 to Period 6, gross investment actually declines. The absolute increase in output from Period 4 to Period 5 was 30, but the absolute increase from Period 5 to Period 6 was only 20. This illustrates another relationship that follows from the acceleration principle. A mere decrease in the absolute amount of increase in the level of output will lead to an absolute decrease in the level of gross investment. For gross investment to show any absolute increase period after period, the economy's output must show successively larger absolute increases period after period. Roughly speaking, the economy must run faster and faster in order for gross investment spending to move ahead at all.

As a next step, the economy's output is assumed to begin a decline in Period 7. Output in that period drops 10 below the output of Period 6, which means that desired capital in Period 7 is 20 less than in Period 6. *Net* investment is therefore -20 in Period 7. Because 20 of the capital carried over from Period 6 will wear out during Period 7, business is able to work down the capital stock to the desired lower level simply by not replacing the 20 that wears out during Period 7. Gross investment is zero for the period.

Output continues to decline in Period 8, but gross investment actually increases. This is the result of the fact that there is a smaller absolute decrease in output in Period 8 than there is in Period 7. This is just the reverse of the relationship in Periods 5 and 6, where gross investment decreased because, although output was increasing in both periods, the absolute increase was less in Period 6 than in Period 5. Viewed on the downside, this relationship suggests that an upturn in gross investment need not necessarily await an upturn in output—it may occur even in the face of a decline in output once that decline begins to proceed more slowly. This helps to explain a phenomenon observed in some business cycles: The peaks and troughs in real

expenditures for capital goods will occur earlier than the peaks and troughs in real expenditures for final output as a whole.

To bring out another important feature of the acceleration principle, it is next assumed that the slowing of the decline in output is followed by a speedup in the decline. Starting in Period 8, the absolute decrease in output in the next three periods is 6, 20, and 30. A decrease in output greater than 10 in any period presents a situation not confronted earlier. For example, the decrease in output from 250 in Period 9 to 230 in Period 10 reduces desired capital from 500 to 460. However, for the economy as a whole, the maximum amount by which the capital stock can be reduced in any period is the amount of the goods that wear out. Individual firms may be able to cut back more rapidly by selling unwanted capital goods to other firms, but this is plainly not possible for all firms combined. In our illustration, the amount that wears out in each period is 20, so 20 becomes the maximum possible net disinvestment per period. Therefore, in Period 10 a discrepancy appears between desired capital and actual capital, the former having declined by 40 from Period 9 but the latter by only the maximum possible 20. Another decline in output greater than 10 occurs in Period 11; this further enlarges the discrepancy between required and actual capital stock. Finally, the figures assumed in the subsequent periods are such that the discrepancy is fully removed in Period 13.

The discrepancy over Periods 10 through 12 means that firms are operating with excess capacity during these periods (that X_t exceeds $w(Y_t - Y_{t-1}) + D_t$ in each period). Therefore, the slowing in the absolute amount of decline in output in Period 12 is not sufficient to raise gross investment to a positive figure as it did in Period 8 when there was no excess capacity present. Not even an absolute increase in the level of output as in Period 13 is sufficient to lift gross investment above the zero level. It is not until the excess capacity is eliminated that the acceleration principle becomes operative once again; this occurs in Period 14.

Although the acceleration principle becomes temporarily inoperative during periods of excess capacity, the simple mechanics traced for the other periods of Table 18-1 still show that the principle can explain the relatively wider fluctuations that occur in the expenditures for capital goods than in the expenditures for final goods in general (a real-world phenomenon that economists have long recognized). However, even in those periods during which the economy is operating with no excess capacity, the results shown by the table can be produced only by making certain other assumptions, some of which may be unrealistic. It is clearly necessary to look at these assumptions in order to evaluate the practical significance of the principle.

Closely related to the assumption that firms are operating without excess capacity is the assumption that firms will increase capacity to meet every increase in real spending. In effect, this means that business people act as automatons, responding to an increase in the quantity of goods sold by increasing investment spending and to a decrease in the quantity of goods sold by decreasing investment spending. In practice, however, even if their capital facilities are operating at capacity, business people will try to squeeze additional output from existing plant and equipment unless and until they are convinced that the observed increase in the quantity of goods sold is likely to be permanent.

Similarly, if and when an expansion of capital facilities appears warranted, the expansion may not be exactly that needed to meet the *current* increase in sales; it will probably be sufficient to meet the increase in sales anticipated over a number of years. Piecemeal expansion of facilities in response to short-run increases in quantity of goods sold may be uneconomical or even, depending on the industry, technologically impossible. (One cannot add one-half of a blast furnace.)

The assumption of a constant capital–output ratio or accelerator, *w,* is necessary to our simple mechanical model, but it also is rather unrealistic. Even if firms could automatically adjust their capital stock to each change in current sales, the capital–output ratio would not be constant. An increase in sales might be concentrated at one time on the output of industries whose technology calls for high capital–output ratios and at another time on the output of industries with low ratios. Consequently, even in the absence of technological changes, the degree to which investment spending responds to any increase in quantity of output sold depends on the distribution of that increase among the goods of different industries in which output is subject to different capital–output ratios.

This point suggests another qualification. Investment for the economy as a whole may increase even without an increase in the quantity of output sold. Through the acceleration principle, a redistribution of a given total of expenditures among available goods may lead to more net investment in industries enjoying the increased spending than disinvestment in those suffering the decreased spending—because, at the limit, disinvestment in any industry cannot exceed the rate at which capital facilities are used up.

Another assumption of the simple acceleration principle is that any gap between the amount of capital desired by business people and the amount they actually have is closed within a single time period. This may be physically impossible. As we saw earlier, if the desired capital stock falls below the actual by an amount greater than the amount of depreciation for the period, it will require more than the current period to reduce the actual capital stock to the desired level. During that interval, the acceleration principle becomes inoperative. Note now that a related situation may be confronted in the other direction. If the capacity output of the capital goods industries for one time period is less than the sum of that period's replacement investment and the excess of the desired over the actual capital stock, the gap cannot be closed in one time period. For example, if the capacity of these industries is $50 billion per year with replacement investment currently absorbing $20 billion per year, a gap greater than $30 billion between desired and actual capital cannot be filled within one single year. However, the simple acceleration principle will show net investment of $40 billion for a gap of $40 billion, despite the fact that this rate of net investment may be impossible.

Moreover, even if the production capacity of the capital goods industries were always physically sufficient to close any gap in one time period, it does not follow that this would happen. As we saw in Chapter 17, the amount of net investment spending in one time period may fall below the amount needed to close an existing gap during that time period, not because the capital goods industries do not have the physical capacity to produce the amount of capital goods needed but because net investment spending itself is restrained below that amount by the effect on the MEI of the rising cost of capital goods as these industries expand output closer to their capacity levels. We may illustrate the simple acceleration principle and this particular qualification of it by building on the graphic apparatus developed in Chapter 17.

The Acceleration Principle and the MEC and MEI Schedules

The accelerator theory of investment and the acceleration principle on which it rests make the desired capital stock proportional to the level of output. If the accelerator is 2, as in Part A of Figure 18-8, the desired capital stock is equal to twice the level of output. The curve in Part A also shows that for any change in the output level—for example, a rise from $200 to $220—there is a rise in the desired capital stock equal to twice the output change—a rise from $400 to $440. Because the acceleration principle in its rigid form assumes that any gap between the desired and actual capital stock is filled within a single time period, it follows that net investment in that single time period will equal the accelerator

times the change in the level of output. In terms of the equation derived earlier,

$$I_t = K_t - K_{t-1} = w(Y_t - Y_{t-1})$$

In terms of the numerical illustration just given,

$$\$40 = \$440 - \$400 = 2(\$220 - \$200)$$

This result, in which the actual capital stock grows to the desired capital stock within the same period that a gap between the two appears, can occur only if the conditions noted earlier are satisfied. Parts B and C of Figure 18-8 show graphically what is involved.

These two parts bring in the familiar MEC and MEI curves. In Part B, two MEC curves are plotted, one corresponding to Y of $200 and one to Y of $220. The acceleration principle alone indicates that the desired capital stock will be $400 with Y of $200 and an accelerator of 2. However, the desired capital stock will also vary with the rate of interest. With Y of $200, the curve so labeled shows that desired capital will be $400 when r is 6 percent, $420 when r is 5 percent, and $380 when r is 7 percent. With Y of $220, desired capital will vary with the rate of interest as shown by the MEC curve labeled $Y = \$220$.

Suppose now that the actual level of Y is $200, the market rate of interest is 6 percent, and the actual capital stock is $400. Because the actual and the desired capital stocks are equal, net investment is zero and gross investment is equal to replacement investment. Assuming, as in Table 18-1, that the average life of capital goods is 20 years, replacement investment is $20. The MEI curve in Part C labeled $Y = \$200$ therefore shows gross investment of $20 and net investment of zero at the market interest rate of 6 percent.

Suppose, next, that the output level rises from $200 to $220 so that we move from the lower to the upper MEC curve in Part B. With the interest rate at 6 percent and the actual or existing capital stock still at $400, desired capital exceeds actual capital by $40. The MEI curve in Part C labeled $Y = \$220$ shows that in the first time period gross

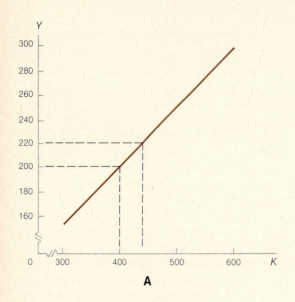

A

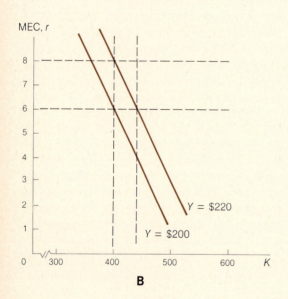

B

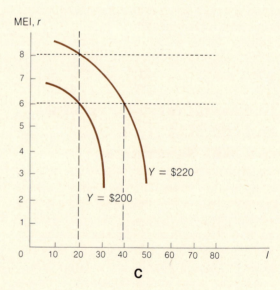

C

FIGURE 18-8
The Level of Output, the Desired Capital Stock,
and the MEC and MEI Schedules

investment will be $40 and, accordingly, *net* investment will be $20 (less than the full amount of the desired increase in the capital stock). It will therefore actually take a series of time periods to adjust the capital stock to the desired level.

Because the simple acceleration principle assumes that net investment sufficient to close the gap between actual and desired capital stock will occur in a single time period, no matter how large the amount involved ($40 in the present illustration), it must also assume, quite unrealistically, that the short-run supply curves of the capital goods industries are perfectly elastic over an unlimited range. In other words, it must assume not only that these firms do not run into short-run rising costs as they expand output but also that their capacity to expand output is unlimited in the short run. This would be described graphically in Part C by the dotted-line MEI curves, which remain perfectly flat over an unlimited range. The assumed rise in output in Part A would then lead to a shift in the MEI curve in Part C from the lower to the upper dotted line. Gross investment, which had been equal to $20 for the time period in which output was $200, would now jump to $60 in the next time period in response to the increase in output to $220 in that time period. If the MEI curve were actually perfectly elastic, there would be no barrier to achieving the amount of net investment needed to close the gap between actual and desired capital stock in one time period.

Although the MEI curve may not turn down as soon or as sharply as the solid-line MEI curves illustrated, it must turn down at some level of investment. Expansion of output by the capital goods industries must sooner or later run into rising marginal costs, given the fact that the productive capacity of these industries is limited in the short run. The assumption of the simple acceleration principle that any increase in the desired capital stock will be met in a single time period, therefore, cannot always be satisfied. The answer to this and other problems that arise from the simple version of the acceleration principle is to resort to a more flexible and refined version that can handle them.[18]

Both the simple version of the accelerator theory of investment and the profits theory of investment considered earlier operate on investment spending by first causing a shift in the MEC curve, as has been seen in Figures 18-3 and 18-8. In Chapter 19, we turn to the rate of interest and the role of finance—forces that operate on investment spending by first causing a movement along an *existing* MEC curve.

---

[18]This more advanced version of the acceleration principle is not developed in this book. For an introduction to this version, see M.C. Lovell, *Macroeconomics: Measurement, Theory, and Policy,* Wiley, 1975, pp. 193–98, and R. Dornbusch and S. Fischer, *Macroeconomics,* 2nd ed., McGraw-Hill, 1981, pp. 192–96.

19

Investment Spending: The Rate of Interest and the Role of Finance

OVERVIEW

The rate of investment spending will be affected by a shift in the MEC schedule or by a movement along an existing MEC schedule. In Chapter 18, we looked at two theories of investment, both of which seek to explain changes in investment by explaining what causes shifts in the MEC schedule. In this chapter, we will look at changes in investment that result from a movement along an existing MEC schedule.

How large a movement along the MEC schedule—and therefore how large a change in the desired capital stock—occurs as a result of any given change in the interest rate depends on the elasticity of the MEC schedule. For any given movement along the MEC schedule, in order to find how much of a change in investment occurs we must look at the MEI schedule. The first part of this chapter brings together again the MEC and MEI schedules and examines how the elasticity of the MEC schedule affects the rate of investment spending.

Because the elasticity of the MEC schedule is of some importance as an influence on investment spending, we look into the determinants of this elasticity in the second part of the chapter. In the third part, we briefly examine the elasticity of the MEC schedule when that schedule is conceptually disaggregated into separate schedules for structures, producers' durable equipment, and business inventories. To what extent are the desired stock of structures, producers' durable equipment, and inventories affected by changes in interest rates and therefore to what extent is investment in these three kinds of goods affected by interest rates?

Although a focus on the interest rate is a helpful and informative first step, the influence of finance on investment goes far beyond the interest rate. In the last part of the chapter, we look at the role of finance in a larger perspective. In so doing, we recognize, for example, that borrowing in the market at the market rate of interest is not the only means by which firms may secure funds to finance investment spending, although this is what is implied as long as one does not look beyond the rate of interest. Internal funds and equity funds are also available. The total amount of funds available is the sum of funds available from these three sources, and this total and its composition may be shown through a curve called the marginal cost of funds or MCF curve. The construction of the MCF curve is explained in some detail, and this curve and the familiar MEI curve are then brought together. This gives us a framework through which we can learn far more about the role of finance as an influence on investment than is possible from looking only at the rate of interest. Several illustrations of the way this framework can be used conclude the chapter.

The extent to which a change in the rate of interest causes a change in the rate of investment spending depends on the elasticity of the MEC schedule. The more elastic the schedule, the greater the increase or decrease in the profit-maximizing capital stock that follows from any decrease or increase in the rate of interest. In order to specify the relationship between a change in the rate of interest and a change in the rate of investment spending, we must proceed from a change in the rate of interest through the resultant change in the profit-maximizing capital stock to the resultant change in the rate of investment.

The Rate of Interest and the Rate of Investment

As a first step, it will be helpful to review the relationships found in Chapter 17 between the rate of interest, the MEC schedule, and the MEI schedule. Figure 19-1 parallels Figure 17-3 except for changes in the numerical values and the omission of replacement investment. As in Figure 17-3, with the MEC schedule given in Part A, the actual capital stock given as $400 billion, and the interest rate given as 9 percent, the actual capital stock is also the profit-maximizing capital stock. The rate of net investment as shown in Part B is accordingly zero. Now, if we assume

a drop in the rate of interest from 9 to 8 percent, the profit-maximizing capital stock in Part A of Figure 19-1 becomes $600 billion, and net investment in Part B becomes $5 billion for the first time period following the drop in the rate of interest. The addition of $5 billion to the stock of capital during the first period does not move the economy perceptibly down the MEC schedule. Therefore, the MEI schedule does not shift downward appreciably, and the rate of investment remains virtually the same in the second and third periods and in as many periods as may properly be included in the short run.[1]

Figure 19-2 differs from Figure 19-1 only in the elasticity of its MEC schedule. In Figure 19-2 the MEC declines relatively more rapidly with increases in the stock of capital than in Figure 19-1. Assuming for Figure 19-2 the same initial equilibrium given in Figure 19-1, a drop in the interest rate from 9 to 8 percent will increase the profit-maximizing capital stock from $400 billion to only $420 billion. Note, however, that, despite the inelasticity of the MEC schedule of Figure 19-2, the rate of investment in the first time period following the drop in the interest rate is $5 billion in Figure 19-2, just as it is in Figure 19-1. Starting from a position in which the profit-maximizing

---

[1] The short run, as defined in Chapter 17, is a time interval in which the growth in the stock of capital is not great enough to depress the MEI schedule appreciably.

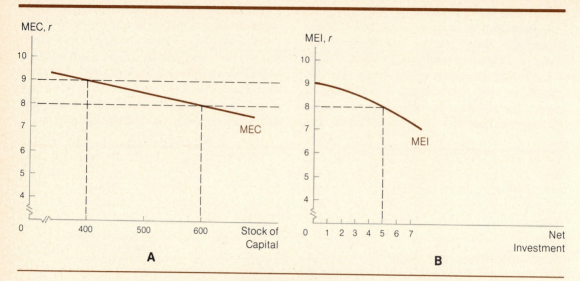

FIGURE 19-1
**Net Investment with an Elastic Marginal Efficiency
of Capital Schedule**

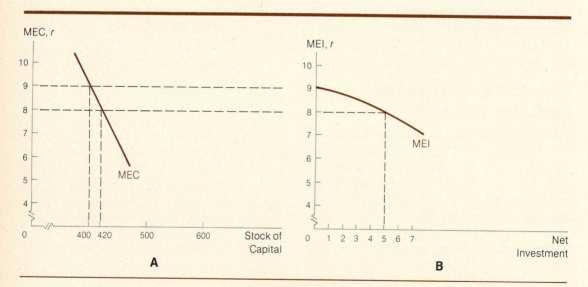

FIGURE 19-2
**Net Investment with an Inelastic Marginal Efficiency
of Capital Schedule**

capital stock equals the actual stock, the *initial* impact of a drop in the rate of interest on the rate of investment spending is independent of the elasticity of the MEC schedule. The initial impact of such a drop depends only on the elasticity of the MEI schedule, which is independent of the elasticity of the MEC schedule.[2]

Nonetheless, the elasticity of the MEC schedule must eventually influence the rate of investment spending. If the MEC schedule is relatively inelastic, additions to the stock of capital that result from each period's net investment will move the economy quickly down such a schedule. This will push down the MEI schedule and with it the rate of investment at the given market rate of interest. In short, all else being equal, the more inelastic the MEC schedule is, the sooner appreciable downward pressure on the MEI schedule will appear as a "feedback" from the growth in the stock of capital.

Although this analysis shows that the effect of a change in the interest rate on the rate of investment spending in any time period depends on the elasticity of the MEC schedule, it does not reveal anything about what determines that elasticity. We cannot appraise the significance of changes in the interest rate as one of the factors influencing the rate of investment unless we know something about what determines the elasticity of the MEC schedule.

Determinants of the Elasticity of the MEC Schedule

Assuming again that a firm buys capital goods only in the expectation that each purchase will add to its profits, the elasticity of the MEC schedule for the economy as a whole may be said to depend on the significance of any given change

in the interest rate as a factor altering the profit-maximizing or desired capital stock for all firms combined. A fall in the interest rate may lead some firms to expand their stock of capital goods substantially, whereas other firms may not expand at all. The elasticity of the aggregate MEC schedule depends on the combined responses of all firms to any change in the interest rate.

What determines whether any given change in the interest rate will lead to a larger or smaller change in the profit-maximizing capital stock? Although it is immediately apparent that a lower interest rate, all else being equal, is also a reduction in one cost of doing business, different businesses respond differently to such a drop. In seeking an explanation for this disparate reaction, we will get at the factors that determine the elasticity of the MEC schedule.

All else being equal—especially the existing state of technology—one factor that determines the extent of an increase in the profit-maximizing capital stock resulting from any given reduction in the interest rate is the extent to which firms find it technologically possible to substitute the now relatively cheaper capital input for the now relatively more expensive labor input. In terms of the cost of factor units, the comparison is between the rate of interest as the cost of capital and the wage rate as the cost of labor. Because we express the rate of return from an addition to the stock of capital as a percentage—the MEC—we must for comparability express the cost of capital as another percentage—the market rate of interest. A fall in the interest rate is then a decrease in the cost of capital. In contrast, because we express the return from an addition of a unit of a given type of labor as the dollar value of the output that will be produced because of that unit, the cost of labor is also expressed as a dollar value—the dollar cost of the services of a unit of the given type of labor. A fall in the wage rate paid labor is then a decrease in the cost of labor.[3]

---

[2]Remember that the elasticity of the MEI schedule depends on the elasticity of the supply schedule of capital goods. The latter may be assumed to be the same in both cases, so the elasticity of the MEI schedule is the same in both figures. See pp. 375–77.

---

[3]If we express the productivity of a capital good by its MEC, which is a percentage, we must measure the "price" of that capital good not by the number of dollars paid for

With a fall in the interest rate and no change in the wage rate, there will be a tendency throughout the economy to substitute the cheaper input (capital) for the more expensive input (labor) in the production of any constant level of output. Although such a tendency will be present throughout the economy, the extent to which substitution of this sort actually takes place will vary widely from industry to industry and, to a lesser extent, from firm to firm within a particular industry.

For some firms, the state of technology may be such that, regardless of the fall in the cost of capital, substitution is severely limited or even impossible. At the extreme, for firms whose technology is such that production requires a rigidly fixed combination of workers and machines, a fall in the rate of interest will lead to no substitution of capital for labor.[4] For such firms, the amount of capital employed in the production of a given level of output is virtually independent of the interest rate. In this case, as far as substitution goes, a fall in the interest rate will have no effect on the size of the profit-maximizing capital stock consistent with a constant level of output.

the good but by the rate of interest, explicit or implicit, paid for the funds used to purchase that good. The cost element represented by its supply price has already been allowed for in the computation of its MEC. The MEC is the percentage rate of return expected on the capital good after allowance for all costs other than interest cost. Once given the MEC, the decision to buy or not to buy the capital good requires a comparison of its price, which is the rate of interest, with its return, which is its MEC.

This is not the only approach to this question. In contrast to this widely used Keynesian formulation is the neoclassical formulation in which the price of capital is expressed as the price of a unit of capital services; that in turn is the cost to the firm of using that unit of capital for a period of time. From this approach, the cost of a unit of capital services is expressed as a dollar value, as is the cost of hiring a unit of labor services. See D.W. Jorgenson, "The Theory of Investment Behavior," in R. Ferber, ed., *Determinants of Investment Behavior*, National Bureau of Economic Research, 1967, pp. 129–55.

[4]Even here, however, there is some opportunity for substitution. For example, if a firm has 100 machines and must have 100 workers to operate the machines and if the machines are subject to intermittent breakdown, the fall in

This also means that the rate of investment spending will be unaffected by a drop in the interest rate.

For other firms, the amount of capital employed may be more or less sensitive to changes in the interest rate. Their technology may be such that, within limits, each drop in the interest rate can make further substitution of capital for labor profitable. For a crude example, suppose that the existing technology permits the firm a choice between a one person–one machine, one person–two machine, or one person–three machine combination. However, to switch to the one person–two machine combination requires purchase of an "Adapter A," which links two of the original machines so that one worker may operate both. To switch to a one person–three machine combination requires a second "Adapter A" plus one "Adapter B" to link three of the original machines so that one worker may operate all three simultaneously. After the linkage, each of the original machines will turn out the same number of units of output as before. Before the fall in the interest rate, the then current costs of capital and labor made the one person–one machine combination the least-cost combination. But with an initial fall in the interest rate, capital becomes relatively cheaper, so one "Adapter A" may be purchased for every two machines; one-half of the labor force employed in operating the machines may be replaced by capital. With some further fall in the interest rate, the least-cost combination may call for the purchase of another "Adapter A" and one "Adapter B" for every three original machines; one-third of the remaining labor force employed in operating the machines

the price of capital may lead to the purchase of one or more additional machines to be pressed into use when any of the 100 in use at any time breaks down. With the fall in the price of capital, this increase in the capital stock may be cost saving, for the relatively more expensive input, labor, will not remain idle while the relatively less expensive input, capital, is being repaired. It is true that one or more machines will always be idle or in repair, but this "idleness" may, with the lower interest rate, be less costly than the otherwise idle labor.

may be replaced by capital. The firm's output remains the same in all cases.

Our first factor is essentially technological in nature. With a given state of technology but with some opportunity for firms to vary factor combinations within this given state of technology, one way in which a drop in the interest rate is translated into an increase in the profit-maximizing capital stock is through a substitution of capital for labor. The greater the possibilities available within the existing state of technology, the more elastic the MEC schedule will be.

Closely related to this factor is the cost saving represented by a switch toward greater use of capital as a result of a drop in the interest rate. Even though the existing technology may permit

variation in the capital–labor combination, the extent to which such variation will occur depends on the cost advantage offered by such variation. Two illustrations may be traced through to outline the operation of this factor. In the first, presented in Table 19-1, a fall in the interest rate leads to a cost advantage through the substitution of capital for labor in the production of a given level of output; in the second, presented in Table 19-2, a fall in the interest rate leads not to reduction in the quantity of labor employed but to the use of more durable capital goods in combination with an unchanged quantity of labor.

In the first illustration, suppose that there are two firms, with outputs of identical value and with identical costs of $1,000 per year. As shown in

TABLE 19-1
The Substitution of Capital for Labor as a Result of a Fall in the Interest Rate

		Capital Stock	Annual Depreciation	Annual Interest Cost	Annual Labor and Other Costs	Total Costs
Market Interest Rate 6 Percent	Firm A	$ 500	$ 50	$ 30	$920	$1,000
	Firm B	4,000	400	240	360	1,000
Market Interest Rate 4 Percent	Firm A	$ 500	$ 50	$ 20	$920	$ 990
	Firm B	4,000	400	160	360	920

TABLE 19-2
The Use of More Durable Capital as a Result of a Fall in the Interest Rate

		Capital Stock	Annual Depreciation	Annual Interest Cost	Annual Labor and Other Costs	Total Costs
Market Interest Rate 6 Percent	Firm Y	$1,000	$500	$ 60	$440	$1,000
	Firm Z	3,500	350	210	440	1,000
Market Interest Rate 4 Percent	Firm Y	$1,000	$500	$ 40	$440	$ 980
	Firm Z	3,500	350	140	440	930

Table 19-1, Firm A's method of production emphasizes labor and Firm B's method emphasizes capital. Firm A's method may be described as more labor intensive and less capital intensive than Firm B's, and vice versa. The first part of the illustration assumes a market interest rate of 6 percent, the second part, one of 4 percent. In both parts, straight-line depreciation with a ten-year life for capital goods is assumed, making annual depreciation cost 10 percent of the value of the capital stock. Annual interest cost is simply the market rate times the capital stock. A drop in the interest rate from 6 to 4 percent reduces Firm A's total costs for the given output from $1,000 to $990, a reduction of 1 percent, and reduces Firm B's total costs for output of the same value from $1,000 to $920, a reduction of 8 percent. Because both firms are assumed to have output per period of equal value, the drop in the interest rate produces a 1 percent reduction in cost per unit of Firm A's output and an 8 percent reduction in cost per unit of Firm B's output.

With the interest rate at 6 percent, Firm A's method of production, on a strict cost basis, is as good as Firm B's.[5] But with a drop in the interest rate, Firm B's more capital-intensive method of production has a significant cost advantage over Firm A's more labor-intensive method. Insofar as we can generalize from this illustration for the economy as a whole, the fall in the interest rate will produce some tendency toward greater use of capital and less use of labor in the production of any given level of aggregate output.

In this first illustration, the two firms' methods of production are essentially different: Firm A uses up $50 of capital goods and $920 of labor services in producing its output per year; Firm B uses up $400 of capital goods and $360 of labor services in producing output of the same value in the same time period. In our second illustration, let us assume two firms whose methods of production are identical in that each uses up the same amount of labor services in the production of output of the same value, but whose methods of production differ in terms of the *durability* of the capital goods they employ in combination with the same quantity of labor services.

In Table 19-2, Firm Y has capital stock of $1,000 made up of capital goods with an average life of two years; Firm Z has capital stock of $3,500 with an average life of ten years. Because both firms produce output of the same value and incur labor costs of the same amount, the capital stocks of the two firms make an equal contribution to output. At first glance, one may object that it is then better to invest $1,000 than $3,500 in capital, if both investments provide capital goods with equal capacity to produce. Is not interest cost at 6 percent on $1,000 only $60, whereas on $3,500 it is $210? This, however, overlooks the fact that the more expensive capital goods, though no more productive per year than the less expensive, are more expensive only because they are more durable and will make the same contribution to production over a greater number of years. Our figures are deliberately selected to show that they are not proportionally more expensive. The purchase price of the more durable capital goods is only 3.5 times that of the less durable, but their life is 5 times that of the less durable. This in turn means that the cost of the more durable capital goods, as measured by annual depreciation, $350, is less than the depreciation cost of the less durable goods, $500—the output from both collections of capital goods being the same for each year.

As in the previous illustration, on a strict cost basis, Firm Y's method of production is as good as Firm Z's when the interest rate is 6 percent.[6]

---

[5]Considerations other than total cost per unit would, of course, be relevant in choosing the "better" method. For example, the percentage of costs that are fixed is much lower for Firm A than for Firm B. This puts Firm A in a much better position to meet a decrease in demand, because it can reduce total costs almost proportionally with a reduction in output. On the other hand, if wage rates are subject to constant upward pressure, Firm B may be in a better position, because Firm A's costs for any level of output will rise much more sharply.

[6]This is subject to other considerations of a type noted in footnote 5. Especially relevant would be Firm Z's greater exposure to the dangers of obsolescence.

Each has output of the same value produced at the same total cost. However, with a drop in the interest rate from 6 to 4 percent, the second part of the illustration in Table 19-2 shows a decrease in total cost from $1,000 to $980, or 2 percent, for Firm Y and from $1,000 to $930, or 7 percent, for Firm Z. Because the value of output is the same for both firms, Firm Y has a 2 percent and Firm Z a 7 percent reduction in cost per unit of output. With a drop in the interest rate, there is clearly a cost advantage in Firm Z's method, which employs more durable capital goods. Insofar as we can generalize from this illustration for the economy as a whole, the fall in the interest rate will produce some tendency toward production of any given level of aggregate output with more durable capital goods. In other words, there will be a tendency to produce any given level of output with a larger stock of capital goods.

In both illustrations, a fall in the interest rate results in a tendency toward more capital-intensive production. In the first illustration, this was due to a substitution of capital for labor; in the second, it was due to the use of more durable capital goods with no reduction in the quantity of labor used. A fall in the interest rate would, of course, tend to encourage substitution of capital for labor *and* the use of more durable capital goods simultaneously. Both tend to increase the profit-maximizing capital stock consistent with any given level of output. Therefore, both work toward a higher rate of investment spending.

These, then, are the factors through which a change in the interest rate will affect the profit-maximizing capital stock. Whether the change in the profit-maximizing capital stock will be large enough to produce an MEC schedule that is elastic with respect to any given interest rate change depends on the combined responses of all firms to that change. It is one thing to indicate the factors that determine the responses of firms and quite another to conclude that the combined responses of all firms for any time period and for any change in the interest rate will produce an aggregate MEC schedule that is elastic or inelastic.

Elasticity of the MEC Schedule—Structures, Producers' Durable Equipment, and Business Inventories

Since the 1930s, most economists have argued that the rate of investment spending for an industrially advanced economy such as that of the United States is interest-inelastic. Although this appears to be the consensus, this general conclusion is not equally applicable to all forms of investment spending.

To the extent that investment does respond to changes in the interest rate, the most pronounced response seems to occur in the field of investment spending for residential and business structures. The reasons for this are implicit in the previous illustrations. For example, an additional one million square feet of living space or factory space per year can be provided only by the construction of the required quantity of houses, apartments, or factories.[7] Because the product yielded by construction as such is measured in square feet of floor space available per year, production of this product is technologically very capital intensive.[8] The sum of depreciation cost and interest cost per unit of output is a large fraction of total cost per unit of output of this kind. Furthermore, production is not only very capital intensive, but it is carried out with capital goods that are durable. To provide another one million square feet of floor space this year requires the construction of buildings that will provide this same output for many years. Because the interest

---

[7]An existing amount of floor space cannot be substantially "enlarged" by altering factor proportions. More labor applied to an unchanged quantity of floor space can facilitate more rapid repairs and redecoration and therefore higher utilization of the existing quantity, but possibilities in this direction are very limited.

[8]This is not to be confused with the capital intensity in the production of the buildings that in turn produce the output in the form of a number of square feet of floor space per year. The production method employed in constructing the buildings is an altogether different question.

cost on durable capital goods goes on for many years, even small changes in the interest rate can mean a substantial difference in the cost per unit of output (square foot of floor space per year). In other words, where the technology makes for capital-intensive production and where the nature of the capital employed is very durable, a change in the interest rate can make a great difference in cost per unit of output. This will markedly affect the rate of investment expenditures for this type of capital goods.

The responsiveness of inventory investment to changes in the interest rate is of a different nature. Just as there is a profit-maximizing stock of plant and equipment, there is also a profit-maximizing stock of inventories. However, unlike the case of structures, the profit-maximizing stock of inventories is not likely to be very responsive to typical interest-rate changes. A lower interest rate reduces the carrying cost of any given amount of inventories, of course, and therefore may be expected to increase the profit-maximizing stock of inventories, all else being equal. However, a fall in the interest rate primarily affects the profit-maximizing capital stock consistent with any level of output by inducing substitutions of capital for labor or by inducing the use of more durable capital equipment. Neither of these factors has any real applicability to the determination of the profit-maximizing stock of inventories, which is determined primarily by the firm's sales, interest cost, and other carrying costs, rather than by its method of production.[9] However, the interest rate will play some role in the determination of the firm's profit-maximizing inventory. All

else being equal, when interest rates rise, firms will attempt to maintain their rate of production and sales with a smaller ratio of inventories to sales and therefore a necessarily higher rate of inventory turnover, particularly if interest rates rise sharply or to unusually high levels. For example, in 1979 the cost to business of funds to carry inventories was over 10 percent and the average book value of inventories held by all businesses was over $400 billion. This meant that the interest cost of carrying inventories during 1979 was over $40 billion. Although $40 billion was only a bit over 1 percent of total sales for the year, it was approximately 13 percent of the before-tax profits of corporate and noncorporate business. A rise in interest rates can therefore cut sharply into profits and it is to be expected that businesses will react as noted. The response will clearly vary with different firms, depending in part on how large the interest cost of carrying inventories is as a percentage of the firm's total costs for any level of output.

Consequently, the response to changes in the interest rate for the economy as a whole will probably have the greatest impact on the stock of structures, less on the stock of producers' durable equipment, and least on the stock of business inventories. Because different types of investment spending show different responses to changes in interest rates, it is obviously difficult to generalize with respect to the elasticity of investment spending in the aggregate. This is further complicated by other considerations. Among these is the likelihood of less inelasticity at high levels of the interest rate than at low levels, so that a change in the interest rate from 10 to 9 percent will probably lead to a greater increase in the profit-maximizing capital stock than will an interest rate change from 5 to 4.5 percent. In other words, whatever the elasticity of the overall schedule, it will be more inelastic at low interest rates than at high.[10] Its actual elasticity, however, remains an unsettled question.

[9]For a simple model of the determination of the firm's optimal inventory, see W.J. Baumol, *Economic Theory and Operations Analysis,* 4th ed., Prentice-Hall, 1977, Ch. 1. On the question of the responsiveness of inventory investment to interest rates, see, for example, M. Feldstein and A. Auerbach, "Inventory Behavior in Durable-Goods Manufacturing: The Target-Adjustment Model," in *Brookings Papers on Economic Activity,* 2, 1976, pp. 351–96, and L. Rubin, "Aggregate Inventory Behavior: Response to Uncertainty and Interest Rates," in *Journal of Post-Keynesian Economics,* Winter 1979–80, pp. 201–11.

[10]See A.H. Hansen, *Business Cycles and National Income,* Norton, 1964, pp. 113–38.

In summary, we may note what was then the generally accepted conclusion reached two decades ago by Meyer and Kuh:

It is difficult to say how sensitive the investment–interest rate relationship is likely to be in the short run, other than presuming it is something greater than zero. Available evidence, none of which is terribly satisfactory, suggests that the interest elasticity of demand is not large, at least in the historically relevant range of roughly 3 to 10 percent *per annum* charged for long-term capital.[11]

This conclusion is probably as generally accepted today as it was then, although the historically relevant range of interest rates charged for long-term capital should be adjusted upward on the basis of the experience of the past two decades.

The Role of Finance—Beyond the Interest Rate

So far in this chapter, the role of finance in the investment decision has been drastically simplified by assuming that it involves only one element, the market rate of interest. Investment spending in any time period has been determined from the MEI schedule by drawing a hor-

---

[11]E. Kuh and J.R. Meyer, "Investment, Liquidity and Monetary Policy," in *Impacts of Monetary Policy,* Commission on Money and Credit, Prentice-Hall, 1963, pp. 340–41. See also L. Tarshis, "The Elasticity of the Marginal Efficiency Function," in *American Economic Review,* Dec. 1961, pp. 958–85, and R. Hall, "Investment, Interest Rates, and the Effects of Stabilization Policy," *Brookings Papers on Economic Activity,* 1977, No. 1, pp. 66–103. For a survey of the econometric literature on the investment–interest rate relationship and a bibliography thereon, see M.J. Hamburger, "The Impact of Monetary Variables: A Survey of Recent Econometric Literature," in *Essays in Domestic and International Finance,* Federal Reserve Bank of New York, 1969, pp. 37–49, reprinted in W.L. Smith and R.L. Teigen, *Readings in Money, National Income, and Stabilization Policy,* 3rd ed., Irwin, 1974, pp. 376–90.

izontal line at the prevailing market rate of interest to an intersection with the MEI schedule. With a given MEI schedule, only a change in the interest rate would produce a change in investment demand.

Without denying the underlying correctness of this basic relationship, we must recognize the oversimplification that it involves. By showing that aggregate investment spending is determined by the intersection of the MEI curve with a horizontal line drawn at the prevailing interest rate, we are assuming for one thing that funds are available in unlimited amounts to borrowers of every description at the market rate of interest. A first objection to this is the fact that, in reality, there is no such thing as *the* market rate of interest. There is a whole complex of rates. The rate paid by any particular borrower depends on such variables as the term and size of the loan, the collateral offered, and especially the credit worthiness of the borrower. Moreover, there is not an unlimited supply of funds available to any single borrower in any time period at this rate; there is some tendency for the rate he pays to rise with each addition to his indebtedness per time period, all else being equal.

A more fundamental objection to this formulation is its implication that the only way in which firms may secure funds to finance investment spending is by borrowing in the market and paying whatever interest rate they must pay. Actually there are three sources of funds for investment, only one of which involves borrowing in the usual sense of that word. These are (1) undistributed profits and depreciation allowances or so-called internal funds; (2) borrowing from banks or in the bond market, the source usually thought of in connection with the market rate of interest; and (3) equity financing or the sale of new stock issues.

Figure 19-3 shows total sources of corporate funds and the amount of funds derived from each of the three sources for each year from 1972 to 1980. Over this period, internal funds have clearly predominated, accounting for more than the sum of borrowed and equity funds in each

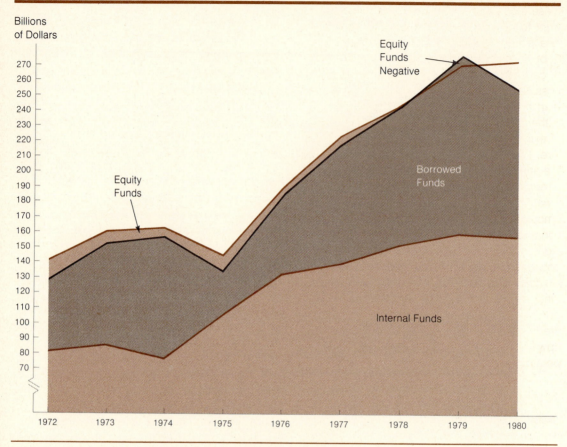

Billions
of Dollars

FIGURE 19-3
Sources of Corporate Funds, 1972—80

SOURCE: *Prospects for Financial Markets, 1981* and *Prospects for the Credit Market 1978*, Salomon Brothers, Inc., New York.

year, except 1974. In turn, of the external funds raised, borrowed funds have far exceeded equity funds. In 1979, corporations on balance retired about $5 billion more of stock than was issued (equity financing was − $5 billion). Of the $1,793 billion total for sources of funds for these years, $1,090 billion or 61 percent was internal, $656 billion or 37 percent was borrowed, and only about 2 percent came from equity. Equity funds have not always been so relatively small, but that was the way it was in the 1970s.

How do the three sources of funds compare in terms of their cost to the firm?[12] The funds that are lowest in cost to the firm are internal funds. The cost of using these funds for investment purposes is the opportunity cost measured by the rate that the firm could otherwise earn by putting

[12]The approach to be sketched in the following paragraphs is that developed by J.S. Duesenberry in his *Business Cycles and Economic Growth*, McGraw-Hill, 1958, Ch. 5. It has since become widely used.

these funds into securities. If the firm does not want to risk purchasing stock, the appropriate rate is the rate it would earn on the purchase of debt issues of other firms or of the government. Because firms that are not in the lending business usually must pay a higher rate as borrowers than they can receive as lenders, the implicit cost to them of internal funds will be less than the cost of external funds secured by borrowing. Therefore, if we set out to build a supply curve showing the amount of funds available to the firm at different costs, we will show that the funds with the lowest cost are those internally generated. This amount, equal to retained profits and depreciation allowances for the time period, is shown in Figure 19-4 by segment A of the firm's marginal cost of funds schedule or MCF curve.

To secure a quantity of funds greater than that generated internally, the firm must resort to borrowing or to equity issues. Borrowed funds are shown in the figure by segment B. The upward slope of this segment indicates that the percentage rate paid for borrowed funds rises with the amount of borrowing. This is in part a reflection of the need to pay a higher rate the more heavily in debt the firm becomes within any time period, but more importantly it is the reflection of an imputed risk factor that rises with increased debt servicing.[13]

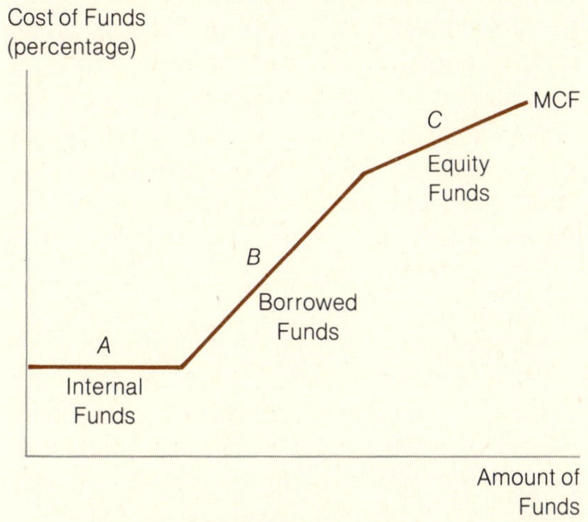

Because the cost of borrowing increases with the amount of borrowing, a point is reached at which it pays the firm to resort to equity financing rather than to more debt financing. This is shown by the C segment, which lies above the B segment of the curve. The cost of equity funds is greater than the cost of borrowed funds for a number of reasons, one of the most important being the differential tax treatment of interest and dividends. The firm's interest payments are deductible in arriving at taxable income; its dividend payments are not. Because the federal corporate income tax rate is close to 50 percent (46 percent at time of this writing), this in itself may make a dollar of equity funds almost twice as expensive as a dollar of borrowed funds. For example, suppose a firm can sell additional bonds at a 10 percent rate. If it can sell additional stock only at a price that provides the purchaser with earnings per share equal to 10 percent of the price paid (a 10 price–earnings ratio), it will have to earn about 20 percent on

Cost of Funds
(percentage)

C — MCF

Equity
Funds

B

Borrowed
Funds

A

Internal
Funds

Amount of
Funds

FIGURE 19-4
A Firm's Marginal Cost of Funds Curve

[13]The firm incurs debt to finance the acquisition of capital, which is expected to add to its profits after meeting all expenses, including the interest on the debt incurred. However, the risk faced by the firm is that profits may not rise or may even decline, whereas interest costs will rise as debt rises. If profits do not rise, the firm can then meet the higher fixed cost of debt service in each time period only by cutting dividends, reducing the amount added to surplus, or incurring more debt to pay interest on the existing debt. All of these will adversely affect the cost of raising funds in the future through both debt and equity, and therefore involve risks that firms will take into account.

Applying this same argument, the A segment of the supply curve might also be drawn with an upward slope for firms with outstanding debt. Because debt is assumed to involve risk, the use of internal funds to finance investment entails rising costs inasmuch as these funds could alternatively be used to reduce the firm's outstanding debt.

the capital goods financed by the stock issue to meet this 10 percent return. This is double the rate of earnings needed to meet the same 10 percent return on debt financing. A factor of a quite different nature that helps to explain the higher position of the equity-financing portion of the supply curve is an imputed cost in the form of the dilution of an existing group's control that results from an increase in the number of shares outstanding. Bond financing avoids this kind of cost. Apart from its higher average position, note also that the C segment of the curve slopes upward as does the B portion. However, the upward slope of the C segment does not reflect imputed risk as in the case of borrowing, because the firm does not have to pay dividends but it does have to pay interest. It reflects a rising yield on the firm's stock (a declining price–earnings ratio), which will result from the fall in the market price of its stock as the firm issues more and more of it.

Various other considerations that underlie the shape of this curve could be noted, but it is sufficient for present purposes to note that a three-segment curve with the general shape of that in Figure 19-4 provides a reasonable description of how the cost of funds varies for the individual firm. The curve will differ considerably in shape and position from one firm to another, but in general will resemble that in the figure. When the separate curves for individual firms are aggregated, a smooth S-shaped curve like MCF_1 of Figure 19-5 will result.

Instead of the unrealistic assumption of a perfectly elastic or unlimited supply of funds at an ill-defined "the" interest rate, we now have an aggregate schedule that shows that an ever-larger total amount of funds is available only at successively higher cost. The concept of the interest rate still plays a major role here, because a rise or fall in the prevailing interest rate will shift the curve bodily upward or downward. A lower interest rate decreases the cost of both internal funds and equity funds, not merely the cost of borrowed funds. The cost of internal funds is clearly affected because this cost is measured

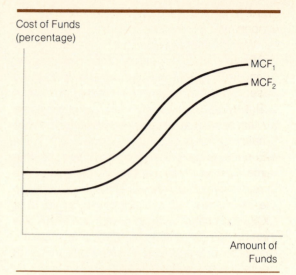

Cost of Funds (percentage)

MCF_1
MCF_2

Amount of Funds

FIGURE 19-5
Aggregate Marginal Cost of Funds Curves

by and varies directly with the market rate of interest. The cost of equity funds is affected because lower interest rates lead to a rise in the price of equities to restore the normal relationship between the interest rate on bonds and the price–earnings ratio on stock. A lower interest rate therefore shifts the MCF curve as a whole downward—for example, from MCF_1 to MCF_2 in Figure 19-5.

The position of the MCF curve may also be altered with no change in the interest rate. An increase in corporate profits that results in an increase in retained earnings or a change in the method of charging depreciation that increases depreciation allowances would shift the supply curve to the right by elongating the elastic segment of the curve that measures internal funds. The MCF curve would therefore move from MCF_1 to MCF_2 in Figure 19-6. The leftward portion of the MCF curve remains unaffected—the new and old curves coincide over the elastic range of the old curve—but the rest of the curve shifts downward much as the curve shifts downward in response to a lower interest rate.

We can now see how shifts in the MEI or the MCF curve or both affect the level of investment spending. Figure 19-6 illustrates one possible case. Suppose that the MEI curve shifts from MEI_1 to MEI_2—a movement that may be explained by the profits theory or the accelerator theory. Whatever the cause of the righward shift in the MEI curve, there is likely to be at the same time some increase in corporate profits, some increase in retained earnings, and therefore some shift in the MCF curve—for example, from MCF_1 to MCF_2. Assuming a greater shift in the MEI curve than in the MCF curve, which is more likely, the marginal cost of funds is driven up from 6 to 8 percent. This rise in the cost of funds chokes off

some investment spending that otherwise would have occurred. If the cost of funds had remained at 6 percent instead of rising to 8 percent, investment would have risen to $70 instead of being held to $60.

The rise in investment spending would be even smaller if the interest rate increased at the same time. This would not be unreasonable in the present illustration; the expansion of economic activity that underlies the shift in the MEI curve would also work toward a higher interest rate. A rise in the interest rate will shift the whole MCF schedule upward, as from MCF_2 to MCF_1 in Figure 19-5. A shift of this kind in Figure 19-6 would move the MCF_2 curve upward to produce an intersection with MEI_2 at a cost of funds higher than 8 percent and a level of investment spending lower than $60.

The results suggested by this illustration are plausible, but are not the only ones possible. As we have seen, the same economic forces that affect the position of the aggregate MEI curve also affect the position of the aggregate MCF curve, although the relative impacts may differ from time to time and give quite different results. During severe recession, the MEI curve may shift far to the left to a position like MEI_1 in Part A of Figure 19-7. At the same time, the elastic portion of the MCF curve will become shorter as retained profits shrink or possibly disappear. However, depreciation allowances will still provide an elastic range to this curve. Under these conditions, a shift in the MEI curve in the other direction that occurs as recovery gets under way need not run into an increase in the cost of funds. For example, the shift from MEI_1 to MEI_2 results in an increase in investment spending that is financed entirely out of internal funds. Therefore, to the degree that this is the typical result during recession, it may be argued that the interest rate is not an important financial determinant of investment during recession; retained earnings and depreciation allowances or internal funds constitute the important financial determinant. On the other hand, as the economy moves toward a boom level, the MEI curve may intersect the MCF curve as shown by

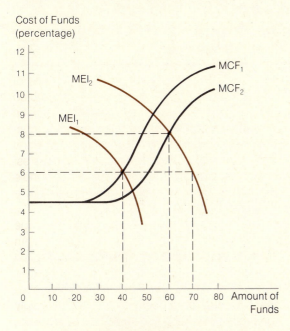

FIGURE 19-6
Shifts in the MEI and MCF Schedules and the Rate of Investment

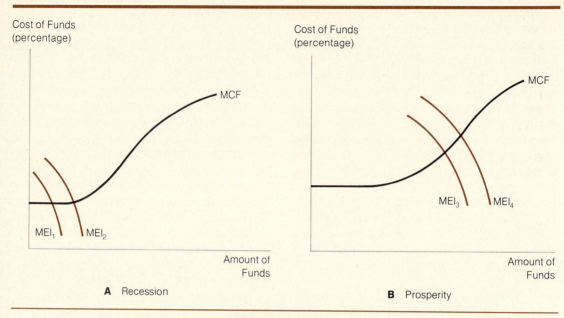

FIGURE 19-7
**Comparison of Possible Effect of Shift in the MEI Schedule
During Recession and Prosperity**

MEI_3 in Part B. Investment is now greater than can be financed out of internal funds; borrowing is taking place. At this stage, the interest rate becomes the important financial determinant of investment spending. The size of the particular increase in investment spending that results from the shift from MEI_3 to MEI_4 depends on the elasticity of the MCF curve in this range that covers borrowed funds. The interest rate is the price of borrowed funds and here becomes the important financial influence on investment.

Consequently, we cannot evaluate the influence of finance on investment demand from information on the level of market interest rates alone. As we have just seen, changes in interest rates may be of little influence at some times and of considerable influence at other times. It would, therefore, have been clearly more accurate in the earlier chapters to have taken into account

refinements on the side of finance such as the one here noted. However, in the interest of working with readily manageable models, that was not done. Accordingly, the conclusions suggested by such models are subject to additional qualifications.

A Concluding Note

In Chapter 17, we worked through the pure mechanics of the process by which changes in the profit-maximizing or desired capital stock are translated into changes in the rate of investment spending. In Chapter 18, we saw how the profits and accelerator theories explain changes in the desired capital stock. In the first part of this chapter, we looked at the way a change in the interest rate does the same thing.

Whatever may have brought it about, a divergence in which the desired capital stock exceeds the actual capital stock will cause a rightward shift in the MEI curve. The greater the shift, the greater will be the rate of net investment spending. Once we have explained the shift in the MEI curve, we need look no further if we assume that the supply of funds available to finance investment is perfectly elastic at the prevailing market interest rate. However, as we saw in the last part of this chapter, the supply of funds is actually described by an upward-sloping MCF curve. It follows that any given shift in the MEI curve will have a larger or smaller effect on investment spending depending on the elasticity of the MCF curve in the relevant range. Although we simplify everywhere else in this book by assuming that the role of finance is adequately indicated by a cost of funds curve that is perfectly elastic at the market interest rate, we see from the foregoing pages that the role of finance involves more than this.

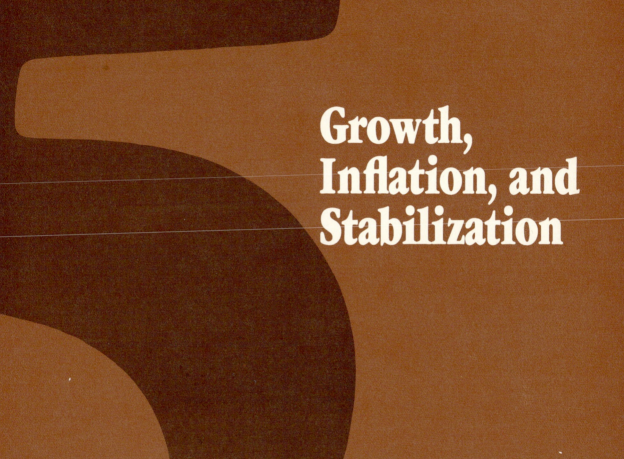

5

Growth, Inflation, and Stabilization

20
Economic Growth

OVERVIEW

In this chapter, we will discuss several theories of economic growth that have been developed since the 1930s. However, before turning to growth theory, some background material is provided in the first part of this chapter.

Like so many other familiar terms in economics, economic growth has been defined in a number of ways. The first part of the chapter begins with the matter of definition. Compared to definition, the form in which growth is measured is more uniform in practice: It is measured as an average annual rate between a beginning and a terminal period. The concept of an average annual rate and the importance of the choice of beginning and terminal years are explained. Following this, we briefly examine the actual growth record of the U.S. economy, including the growth rate for each full business cycle over the period from 1910 to 1979.

The second part of this chapter presents the Harrod–Domar theory of economic growth. A distinguishing feature of this theory is the assumption that labor and capital are combined in fixed proportions. Because capital is the only factor of production explicitly considered, the production function is a simple one in which output is related explicitly to this one input. If the average productivity of capital is assumed to remain constant, the rate of increase in the economy's capacity to produce output therefore depends on the rate of growth of the capital stock. If the average propensity to consume is constant, the rate of increase in the demand for output depends on the rate of growth of investment. The basic theory then works through the determination of the equilibrium rate of growth, the rate at which demand for output and capacity to produce output remain in balance period after period. If investment grows at just this rate, investment will increase the capital stock and will also increase capacity output per time period, via the average productivity of capital, by the same amount that it increases the aggregate demand for output per time period via the multiplier. This equilibrium growth process is

427

presented first in terms of the basic Domar equations and then illustrated with tables and graphs.

The work of Harrod and Domar on growth is similar enough so that economists combine the two and speak of Harrod–Domar growth theory. However, there are differences—the most basic one being that Harrod includes a theory of investment in his approach and Domar does not. The first part of the discussion on the Harrod–Domar theory basically follows Domar; it shows the rate at which investment must grow if there is to be equilibrium, but it does not say anything about the rate at which investment will actually grow. The last part of the discussion brings in the Harrod investment equation and examines the significance of this addition to the model.

In the third part of the chapter, we present the neoclassical theory of growth. This theory is readily distinguishable from the Harrod–Domar theory by its assumption that labor and capital can be combined in any proportion. This difference alone means that capacity output can no longer be related to the single factor of the capital stock, but must bring the labor supply explicitly into the model. Accordingly, the first section of the discussion of the neoclassical theory is devoted to the issue of how capacity output grows in response to varying rates of growth in both the capital stock and the labor force. In this first section, the analysis is simplified by assuming that no technological progress takes place. The next section of the analysis brings in the very important factor of the rate of technological progress, initially on the simplifying assumption that all such progress is "disembodied." The final section of the analysis drops the assumption that all technological progress is "disembodied" and works through the changes in the conclusions that follow when technological progress is recognized to be at least in part embodied in plant and equipment.

The fourth part of the chapter considers not another formal growth theory but the views of "supply-side" economics on the question of growth. As in formal growth theory, the labor supply and the capital stock are recognized as basic, but to "supply siders" the critical factor in how much work is done and how much saving and capital formation occur is how heavily people and businesses are taxed. The more extreme among them argue that economic behavior is almost completely determined by tax rates. A simple graphic model is constructed to set out the way in which labor input and investment respond to tax cuts and to show through these responses how the growth rate of income varies inversely with the tax rate. This part of the chapter concludes with a questioning look at the preconditions that must be met to get the kind of responses to tax cuts that the supply-side economists are so sure will follow.

The chapter concludes with two brief parts, the first of which presents estimates of the sources of economic growth. To obtain such numbers requires that the estimator dissect the growth rate for various time periods into the percentage points attributable to growth in the size of the labor force, in education, in advance of knowledge, and other such factors. The most ambitious work along this line has been that by Edward F. Denison, whose estimates for the United States are examined.

The last part of the chapter provides a short introduction to the exceedingly important issue of the growth rate and environmental quality. Since the late 1960s, many people have questioned the desirability of such a high rate of growth as that which we worked toward and achieved during the 1960s. The question that is asked more and more is whether or not there is a "trade-off" between the rate at which the economy expands the output of goods and services and the rate at which the quality of the environment deteriorates. Some of the many factors that enter into the answer to this question are considered.

What is economic growth? What has been the growth record of the U.S. economy? What theories have been advanced to explain why an economy grows at one rate rather than another? What has been the relative importance of the growth in the labor force, the growth in the capital stock, and advances in knowledge in explaining the growth record of the U.S. economy? Is deterioration in the quality of the environment an unavoidable consequence of economic growth? These are some of the many questions found under the general heading of economic growth.

Introduction

Definition of Economic Growth

Economic growth can be most simply defined as the increase in the economy's output over time. Our best measure of the economy's output is real GNP or GNP in constant dollars. The reason for specifying constant dollars is, of course, that changes over the years in GNP in current dollars are the result of a mixture of price changes and output changes. Therefore, if growth is defined as the expansion of the economy's output and if we are to use GNP as a measure of growth, then price changes must be removed from GNP as in the constant-dollar series. Furthermore, if we are interested not merely in how much the economy's aggregate output expands over time but in how much the amount of output produced per person expands over time, real GNP must also be corrected for population increases. These two adjustments will give us what is for some purposes the most useful concept of economic growth—expansion in real GNP per capita.

From the basic concept of real GNP per capita, various related concepts of economic growth have been derived, each of which emphasizes a different facet of growth. One is "real consumption per capita," a concept that indicates the growth in consumer economic welfare. Such figures are derived initially from the deflated data for the personal consumption expenditures component of GNP converted to a per capita basis and sometimes adjusted for the changes in leisure that may be regarded as a part of real consumption. A further adjustment could be made by adding to personal consumption expenditures that portion of deflated government purchases of goods and services that is "clearly" in the nature of public consumption, such as public parks and recreation. However, a large part of government purchases cannot be classified as "clearly" of a consumption or of an investment nature. A second and somewhat different growth concept is "real GNP per unit of labor input" or per combined unit of labor and capital input, a concept that stresses the changes in the economy's efficiency or productivity over time. These are but two of a number of growth concepts, each of which emphasizes a particular feature of the economy over time.

Each of these growth concepts is based on the actual real GNP of the economy. An altogether different concept of economic growth is based not on the actual but on the potential real GNP. It considers not what the economy did produce, but what the economy could have produced if it had fully utilized its labor force and capital stock. This distinction was noted in Chapter 1 in terms of Figure 1-1, which showed potential and actual output over the years from 1952 to 1980. We will turn to this distinction shortly as we consider growth theory. It will then be seen that actual output may depart from potential output in Harrod–Domar theory, whereas they are assumed to be always equal in neoclassical theory, which therefore concentrates on explaining the growth path that will be followed by an economy that fully utilizes its resources as their quantity grows over time.

The U.S. Growth Record

Whatever concept of economic growth one works with, growth is usually expressed as an average annual rate between the initial and terminal years of each period rather than in terms of the absolute dollar change over the period. For example, consider the actual real GNP figures (in 1972 dollars) of $315.7 billion for 1929 and $1,483.0 billion for 1979. These figures indicate an increase of 370.0 percent for the fifty-year period. Expressed as an average annual rate of growth, real GNP increased at a 3.1 percent rate over this period. In terms of per capita real GNP, the increase was from $2,593 in 1929 to $6,723 in 1979—159.3 percent over the fifty year period, an average annual growth rate of 1.9 percent.[1] Over a much longer period, the hundred years from 1870 to 1970, the average annual rate of growth for real GNP has been estimated at 3.7 percent and for per capita real GNP at 2.0 percent.[2]

For growth rates over shorter periods of time, Table 20-1 shows the average annual growth rate of real GNP and also the implicit price deflator

---

[1]Data are from the *Economic Report of the President, January 1981,* Table B-2, p. 234, and Table B-26, p. 263. Each average annual growth rate may be determined from a compound interest table by finding the interest rate required to produce the percentage change in the indicated time period. For the above example, in terms of aggregate real GNP, the rate required for $1 to grow to $4.70 in fifty years will be a rate between two of the rates given in the headings of such a table. In the ordinary compound interest table, interpolation is then required to find the growth rate to the nearest tenth of a percent. This need for interpolation may be avoided by using a specially prepared growth-rate conversion table from which the growth rate to the nearest tenth of a percent may be read off directly. (See *Long Term Economic Growth, 1860–1970,* Bureau of Economic Analysis, U.S. Dept. of Commerce, 1973, pp. 114–43.)

Alternatively, one can directly compute the growth rate by using the compound interest formula:

$$GNP_t = GNP_b(1 + r)^n$$

where t designates the terminal year, b the beginning year of the period, n the number of years in the period, and r the average annual rate to be determined. Solve by converting the equation to logarithms:

$$\log(1 + r) = \frac{(\log GNP_t - \log GNP_b)}{n}$$

[2]*Long Term Economic Growth, 1860–1970,* Bureau of Economic Analysis, U.S. Dept. of Commerce, 1973, p. 99.

TABLE 20-1
Growth Rates and Price Changes During U.S. Business Cycles, 1910–1979

Business Cycle (Peak to Peak)	Average Annual Growth Rate of Real GNP	Average Annual Change in GNP Implicit Deflator
1910–13	4.4%	1.4%
1913–18	2.5	11.7
1918–20	1.8	6.8
1920–23	5.4	− 6.4
1923–26	3.9	0.2
1926–29	2.8	− 0.5
1929–37	−0.2	− 1.1
1937–44	9.0	3.3
1944–48	−3.3	9.3
1948–53	4.9	2.1
1953–57	2.3	2.5
1957–60	2.5	1.9
1960–69	4.4	2.6
1969–73	3.6	5.0
1973–79	2.8	7.5

SOURCE: 1910–29 from J.W. Kendrick, "Concepts and Measures of Economic Growth," Table IV-1, pp. 268–69, in *Inflation, Growth, and Employment,* in the Commission on Money and Credit series, Prentice-Hall, 1964; 1929–79 computed by author from data in Table 7, p. 17, *Survey of Current Business,* Dec. 1980.

over each business cycle from 1910 to 1979, measuring the rate in each case from peak to peak of the cycles.[3] Over the fifteen business cycles of this seventy-year period, the highest growth rate, 9.0 percent, occurs during the cycle that includes the years of World War II; the highest peace-time growth rate, 5.4 percent, occurs during the cycle of the early 1920s. The slowest growth rate, actually a negative rate of − 3.3 per-

---

[3]To obtain the fairest representation of the actual growth rate, the beginning and terminal years of the period should be similar in terms of the business cycle phase. For example, if in the 1929–79 illustration above we had measured from 1933, a business cycle trough year when real GNP

cent, occurs during the adjustment from the extraordinary war-time output level of 1944, a year in which the unemployment rate reached an all-time low of 1.2 percent, to the more normal peace-time output of 1948. The relatively high rate of 4.9 percent during the 1948–53 cycle reflects the impact of the Korean War and some still unsatisfied demand pent-up from World War II. Following the relatively low rates of 2.3 and 2.5 during the two cycles from 1953 to 1960, the rate during the long cycle from 1960 to 1969 rose to 4.4 percent, then fell off to 3.6 percent in the cycle from 1969 to 1973 and still lower to 2.8 percent in the most recent cycle from 1973 to 1979. (Measurement here is from peak to peak; from trough to trough, the most recent cycle is 1975–80 from March to July.)

The experience of the 1960s and 1970s well illustrates the huge difference in real output that results from a growth rate like 2.8 percent and a more rapid rate like 4.4 percent. If the 4.4 percent growth rate of the 1960–69 cycle had continued over the following two cycles, the cumulative gain in output (valued in 1972 dollars) over the decade from 1969 to 1979 would have been *over one trillion dollars*. The gain in 1979 alone would have been almost $200 billion; instead of the actual GNP of $1,483.0 billion (in 1972 dol-

---

was $222.1 billion, to 1979, a business cycle peak year, the growth rate for real GNP would have been 3.8 percent, a far larger figure than the 3.1 percent found when 1929, a business cycle peak year, was used as the initial year. The higher figure overstates the growth rate because it reflects not only the long-run growth of output but the cyclical recovery of output from the deepest business cycle trough in our history. Measuring from peak to peak or from trough to trough avoids what can be a serious distortion. In contrast to Table 20-1, which limits rates to those between peaks of business cycles, detailed tables called growth-rate triangles, each including about 3,000 entries, are available. These show the growth rate of aggregate real GNP for every possible combination of initial and terminal years for the years from 1890 to 1969. Those rates for periods in which the initial and terminal years are similar in terms of business cycle phase differ from the rates for periods in which the initial and terminal years are different in terms of business cycle phase. (See *Long Term Economic Growth, 1860–1970*, pp. 105–10.)

lars) recorded for that year, the figure would have been $1,673.6 billion. This amounts to almost $1,000 per capita for that one year alone.

The difference between 2.8 and 4.4 percent is obviously quite large; 2.8 percent is a 36 percent decrease from 4.4 percent. However, the results that follow from smaller differences are still dramatic. If the growth rate during 1973–79 had merely been maintained at the more normal 3.6 percent rate of the preceding cycle, it would have meant approximately an extra $464 billion (in 1972 prices) of goods and services for the six year period of the last business cycle. Figures like these make clear why persons who favor rapid rates of growth may become concerned about changes as small as 1/10 of a percentage point in growth rates.

The Background of Growth Theory

Growth theory went through a period of unusually rapid development from the 1940s to the 1960s, but economists' concern with the question of economic growth goes back at least as far as 1776, to Adam Smith's *An Inquiry into the Nature and Causes of the Wealth of Nations*. The very title of this classic suggests the author's interest in the long-run question of the accumulation of wealth, one aspect of any study of economic growth. In Smith's view of the process by which the economy's wealth expands, an important role is assigned to the "division of labor," or specialization. The idea of diminishing returns had not yet been "discovered," and Smith saw no obstacle to the increase of returns to labor through increased specialization. Increased specialization would lead to a rising standard of living for a growing population. This optimistic conclusion was replaced a few decades later by a pessimistic one as a result of the work of Thomas Malthus and David Ricardo: The Malthusian population principle and the Ricardian diminishing returns and rent theory combine to force the great majority of the economy's population down to a subsistence standard of living. Between the writings of classical economists such as these and the writings of the economists of the past forty years are such major contributions as the growth systems of Karl Marx and Joseph Schumpeter, both of whom saw the capitalistic process as one in which business people are engaged in an unrelenting drive toward accumulation that would one day end with the destruction of the system.[4]

The phrase "modern growth theory" is usually applied to the large body of theory which began to appear a few years after the publication of Keynes' *General Theory* in 1936. In view of the impact made by the *General Theory,* it was only to be expected that economists would proceed to construct theories that would secularize and make dynamic the short-run static theory presented by Keynes. Some of this growth theory evolved directly from Keynes' work; some evolved in an altogether different direction.

Three major branches of modern growth theory have been identified. One relates the growth rate of the economy's aggregate output to that of its capital stock. In this approach, capital is the only factor of production explicitly considered, and it is assumed that labor is combined with capital in fixed proportions. With regard to the rate at which capital accumulates, this theory is Keynesian in nature and appeared a few years after the *General Theory.* It holds that under laissez faire conditions there is no effective adjustment mechanism to equate investment with full employment saving. If it is true that changes in thriftiness do not automatically lead to equal changes in investment, the rate of growth will not be that which would occur with capital accumulation determined by full employment saving. This fixed-proportion, Keynesian-based growth theory to be examined in the next part, is most commonly known as the **Harrod–Domar theory**.

So rapid and so varied has been the development of modern growth theory that the Harrod–Domar theory may now be described as a relatively early and relatively simple approach to the growth question. Most of the growth theory that followed and the theory that then dominated the area is known as **neoclassical growth theory**. In this theory, which we will study in a later part of this chapter, a production function is employed in which capital and labor may be combined in varying proportions. Unlike the Harrod–Domar model, substitutability among factors is allowed for in the production process. Also unlike the other theory, the neoclassical theory assumes that capital will accumulate at a rate set by the thriftiness of the economy operating at full employment. The issue of whether or not the amount of saving forthcoming at full employment will be matched by an equal amount of planned investment, a prerequisite to the continued full utilization of the factors of production, is therefore answered in terms of classical rather than Keynesian theory.

A third branch of recent growth theory is commonly described as the **modern Cambridge theory** because of its close association with the names of Joan Robinson and Nicholas Kaldor of Cambridge University. This theory is highly critical of the neoclassical theory in many ways. For example, it rejects that theory's classical approach to saving and investment and returns to the Keynesian approach in which investment is determined not by saving propensities but by business persons' decisions, which are held to depend on such things as their experiences in the recent past, governmental policies, and sociocultural influences on the willingness to bear risk. It also rejects the neoclassical production function and with it the entire marginal productivity theory of income distribution, offering alternative macroeconomic theories as substitutes. The theory of the Cambridge school is therefore both a theory of income distribution and a theory of growth in which one of the unique features of the growth theory is its incorporation of a "Keynesian" theory of income distribution. Although the attack of Robinson and Kaldor and

---

[4]For an analysis of classical growth theory and the growth theory of Marx and Schumpeter, see, for example, B. Higgins, *Economic Development,* rev. ed., Norton, 1968, Chs. 3–5; W.J. Baumol, *Economic Dynamics,* 3rd ed., Macmillan, 1970, Chs. 2–3; and D. Hamberg, *Economic Growth and Instability,* Norton, 1956, Ch. 1.

others on the neoclassical growth theory and the defense thereof by its supporters have filled the journals with dozens of articles since 1960, space does not permit us a more detailed examination of the modern Cambridge theory.[5]

Harrod–Domar Growth Theory[6]

A basic principle emphasized by Harrod and Domar and incorporated in all modern growth theory is the dual effect of net investment: Net investment constitutes a demand for output, and it also increases the capacity of the economy to produce output. For example, constructing and equipping a new factory generates a demand for steel, brick, and machinery; the factory once constructed and equipped increases the economy's productive capacity. The economy's net investment in any period thus has a *demand* and a *capacity* effect. If the amount of net investment in any period equals that period's net saving, it has the demand effect of removing from the market that portion of output not purchased by consumers, thereby making aggregate demand equal to aggregate output for the period and making that period's actual level of income and output the equilibrium level. This is nothing more than the familiar Keynesian principle that planned saving and planned investment must be equal if there is to be equilibrium in the level of income and output. What is not familiar from the Keynesian model is the fact that this period's net investment also has a capacity effect: It increases the economy's productive capacity in this period and thereby increases the next period's potential output. If this expanded capacity is to be fully utilized, aggregate demand in the next period must exceed that of this period. In general, as long as there is net investment in one period after another, aggregate demand must rise period after period if the expanding productive capacity resulting from net investment is to be fully utilized.

Increase in Capacity Output

The basic theory involves a simple production function that relates the generation of total output to the stock of capital via the capital–output ratio. Taking the techniques of production as given, some specified amount of capital goods is necessary to produce a given amount of output. If we let K represent the capital stock and Y the level of output, we may define the average capital–output ratio as K/Y. Therefore, if it takes $3 worth of capital goods to produce $1 worth of final output, a capital stock of $300 billion is required to produce aggregate final output of $100 billion, and the capital–output ratio is 3 to 1.[7] In contrast, the marginal capital–output ratio

[5]For an analysis of the modern Cambridge models, see D. Hamberg, *Models of Economic Growth,* Harper & Row, 1971, Ch. 3, and H.Y. Wan, Jr., *Economic Growth,* Harcourt Brace Jovanovich, 1971, Ch. 3. Further references will be found in these chapters.

[6]The basic elements of the Domar model are found in Evsey Domar, "Expansion and Employment," in *American Economic Review,* March 1947, pp. 34–55. See also his "Capital Expansion, Rate of Growth, and Employment," in *Econometrica,* April 1946, pp. 137–47, and "The Problem of Capital Accumulation," in *American Economic Review,* Dec. 1948, pp. 777–94. These and related essays by Domar are reprinted in his *Essays in the Theory of Economic Growth,* Oxford Univ. Press, 1957. For the Harrod model, see Roy F. Harrod, "An Essay in Dynamic Theory," in *Economic Journal,* March 1939, pp. 14–33, reprinted in A.H. Hansen and R.V. Clemence, eds., *Readings in Business Cycles and National Income,* Norton, 1953, pp. 200–19, and revised and expanded in Harrod's *Towards a Dynamic Economics,* St. Martin's, 1948 (see particularly pp. 63–100). The 1939 essay is refined but unchanged in essentials in Harrod's "Second Essay in Dynamic Theory," in *Economic Journal,* June 1960, pp. 277–93. On both models, see also D. Hamberg, *Models of Economic Growth,* Ch. 1, and H.Y. Wan, Jr., *Economic Growth,* Ch. 1.

[7]Note that the ratio depends on the time period chosen for the measurement of output. Capital stock of $300 billion will produce, say, $100 billion of output *per year*—that is, the 3 to 1 ratio. The same capital stock will produce $25 billion of output *per quarter,* a 12 to 1 ratio, and $8.3 billion *per month,* a 36 to 1 ratio. One year is the time period usually selected for measurement of flows. Note also that our analysis makes use of the average capital–output ratio for the economy as a whole; the capital–output ratio will, of course, vary among the different goods into which aggregate output may be broken down.

$\Delta K/\Delta Y$ reveals how much additional capital is necessary to produce a specified addition to that flow of output. The marginal ratio need not be equal to the average ratio as long as technology changes over time. It would rise with capital-using technological changes and fall with capital-saving technological changes. In the model, however, we assume a constant technology, so that $\Delta K/\Delta Y$ remains constant. To simplify the analysis still further, we assume that the constant $\Delta K/\Delta Y$ equals K/Y, so that K/Y is also constant.

The reciprocal of the average capital–output ratio, Y/K, represents the average productivity of capital. If $3 of capital goods are required to produce $1 of final output—that is, if $K/Y = 3$—the average productivity of capital, Y/K, will be 1/3, or 0.33. Given an increase in the capital stock, ΔK, $\Delta Y/\Delta K$ indicates the ratio of the increase in capacity output to the increase in capital stock. Just as $\Delta K/\Delta Y$ need not be the same as K/Y, so $\Delta Y/\Delta K$ need not be the same as Y/K. The pace of technological advance will affect these ratios, but the simple model does not treat them as variables, so that $Y/K = \Delta Y/\Delta K$. This ratio of output to capital stock is designated by σ (sigma), which Domar calls the "potential social average productivity of capital."

Because ΔK in any period equals that period's net investment, I, $\Delta Y/\Delta K = \sigma$ may also be expressed as $\Delta Y/I = \sigma$ or $\Delta Y = \sigma I$. Therefore, if $\sigma = 1/3$, $1 of net investment will increase capacity output by 33.3¢. Consequently, the cumulative net investment of any period increases capacity output by σI. This is the most important relationship in the model. By defining capacity output in terms of the capital stock, we find that the increase in capacity output for any period equals σI, or the average productivity of capital multiplied by that period's cumulative net investment. Note that ΔY is not necessarily the *actual*, or *realized*, increase in output, but the *potential* increase with full utilization of the expanded productive capacity. Because the actual increase need not necessarily equal the potential, let us now distinguish the actual, or realized, increase from the potential by appending subscripts: ΔY_r and ΔY_p.

Increase in Aggregate Spending

In a two-sector economy, aggregate spending equals the sum of consumption and investment expenditures. With a stable consumption function, consumption expenditures will rise only as a result of a rise in income. Therefore, a rise in investment expenditures is necessary to initiate a rise in income. Consequently, we may determine the total rise in income that will result from any given rise in investment by using the simple multiplier expression

$$\Delta Y = \frac{1}{s}\Delta I$$

in which s is the MPS.[8] This rise in income is matched by an equal rise in actual output, because, with a stable price level, output responds in proportion to the rise in spending. With subscript r designating realized, or actual, we have

$$\Delta Y_r = \frac{\Delta I}{s}$$

This brings us to a crucial asymmetry of the demand and capacity effects of investment. On the demand side, an increase in actual output, ΔY_r, is a function not of investment but of the *increment* to investment. (Remember from the basic Keynesian model that if net investment remains unchanged period after period, aggregate spending will remain unchanged and so will aggregate output.) But, on the supply side of the system, each period's net investment represents an addition to the capital stock and therefore an addition to the economy's productive capacity. If we assume constant net investment, potential

---

[8]In the long run, which we must use for growth analysis, it is reasonable to treat the marginal propensity to consume as equal to the average propensity to consume and, therefore, the marginal propensity to save as equal to the average propensity to save. As we saw in Chapter 15, the long-run empirical consumption function based on Kuznets' data showed this relationship between "average" and "marginal." In what follows, we may therefore refer only to the propensity to save, without distinguishing between marginal and average.

output expands period by period, but actual output remains unchanged; therefore, unused productive capacity must result. The assumed constant net investment will not be maintained by business period after period in the face of such excess capacity. This underscores the essential paradox of investment: To justify today's net investment, tomorrow's must exceed today's in order to provide the additional aggregate spending needed to purchase that part of the enlarged potential output that is not purchased by consumers. In other words, as long as net investment is positive, it must increase in order not to decrease. The economy cannot stand still period after period with a constant net investment; either it will move ahead (for example, if autonomous consumption or government spending increases), or it will fall back. Only a stationary economy neither moves ahead nor falls back, but by definition there is zero net investment in a stationary economy. Zero net investment is not characteristic of any developed real-world economy. If, then, a real-world economy must be growing, what is the rate at which it must move ahead to avoid falling back? In other words, what is its equilibrium rate of growth?

The Equilibrium Rate of Growth

There is some rate of growth at which the increase in actual output in each period, ΔY_r, will just equal that period's increase in capacity output, ΔY_p. This rate is called the **equilibrium rate of growth**. Of course, ΔY_r and ΔY_p are not rates as such but absolute amounts of change measured from one period to the next. However, by relating each such absolute amount of change to the absolute actual amount of output and to the absolute capacity output of the preceding period, each may be expressed as a rate. Accordingly, from an original period in which there is equilibrium as given by $Y_r = Y_p$, it follows that if the rate $\Delta Y_r/Y_r$ remains equal to the rate $\Delta Y_p/Y_p$ period after period, Y_r will remain equal to Y_p. In such a situation, aggregate realized output grows as fast as aggregate potential output,

thereby producing a path of equilibrium growth over time.

Because $\Delta Y_r = \Delta I/s$ and $\Delta Y_p = \sigma I$, the equilibrium rate is also that at which $\Delta I/s = \sigma I$. The left side shows the increment to aggregate realized output for the period; because this is equal to the increment of aggregate spending, it may be called the demand side. The right side shows the increment to productive capacity for the period and as such may be called the supply side. Note that investment appears on both sides of the equation, although not in the same form. On the left side we have the increment to net investment, or the difference between the net investment of any one period and that of the preceding. This absolute change of net investment times the multiplier determines the change in aggregate output. On the right side of the equation, however, we find not the *change* in net investment for the period but the *total* net investment for the period. This happens, of course, because total net investment for the period times the average productivity of capital determines the change in productive capacity.

We may solve this equation by multiplying both sides by s and then dividing both sides by I. Given that

$$\frac{\Delta I}{s} = \sigma I$$

multiplying by s yields

$$\Delta I = s\sigma I$$

Then, dividing by I,

$$\frac{\Delta I}{I} = s\sigma$$

In this form, the left side of the equation now gives the required rate of growth of net investment. If actual output is to rise as fast as potential output, the growth rate of net investment must be $s\sigma$, or the propensity to save multiplied by the productivity of capital.

Although ΔI is subject to a multiplier that makes ΔY greater than ΔI, the growth rate of actual output, $\Delta Y_r/Y_r$, must be the same as the growth rate of investment, $\Delta I/I$. Because in equilibrium $\Delta Y_r = \Delta Y_p$ and because $\Delta Y_p = \sigma I$, it follows that $\Delta Y_r = \sigma I$. Furthermore, because $I = sY$ in equilibrium, then by substitution $\Delta Y = \sigma s Y$ and $\Delta Y/Y = s\sigma$. Therefore,

$$\frac{\Delta I}{I} = \frac{\Delta Y}{Y} = s\sigma$$

The rate at which actual output and investment must grow in order that actual output remain equal to potential output is determined by the propensity to save and the productivity of capital. The higher the propensity to save, the greater is the required growth rate, and vise versa. The higher the productivity of capital, the greater is the required growth rate, and vise versa. The meaning of these relationships will be revealed most clearly through the series of numerical illustrations that follow.

Numerical Illustrations of the Growth Process

Assume an economy in which for a given year aggregate spending equals the aggregate potential output that economy can produce with the capital stock existing at the beginning of the year. This defines an equilibrium for the year (say Year 1) in which $Y_r = Y_p$ and provides a take-off point from which we can trace the growth process over the next few years. Remembering that the equilibrium growth rate is given by $s\sigma$, we find in Table 20-2 the growth process for three different

TABLE 20-2
Illustrations of the Growth Process: Equilibrium Situations

(1)	(2)	(3)	(4)	(5)	(6)	(7)	(8)
		Potential Output	Realized Output		Change in Consumption	Investment (Autonomous)	Change in Investment (Autonomous)
Year	Capital Stock			Consumption			
	K	$Y_p = \sigma K$	$Y_r = C + I$	$C = (1-s)Y_r$	$\Delta C = (1-s)\dfrac{\Delta I}{s}$	I	ΔI
		Model 1: $s = 0.20$, $\sigma = 0.25$, and $\Delta I/I = \Delta Y/Y = 0.05$					
1	400.00	100.00	100.00	80.00	—	20.00	—
2	420.00	105.00	105.00	84.00	4.00	21.00	1.00
3	441.00	110.25	110.25	88.20	4.20	22.05	1.05
4	463.05	115.76	115.76	92.61	4.41	23.14	1.09
		Model 2: $s = 0.10$, $\sigma = 0.25$, and $\Delta I/I = \Delta Y/Y = 0.025$					
1	400.00	100.00	100.00	90.00	—	10.00	—
2	410.00	102.50	102.50	92.25	2.25	10.25	0.250
3	420.25	105.06	105.60	94.56	2.31	10.51	.256
4	430.76	107.69	107.69	96.62	2.36	10.77	.263
		Model 3: $s = 0.20$, $\sigma = 0.50$, and $\Delta I/I = \Delta Y/Y = 0.10$					
1	200.0	100.0	100.0	80.0	—	20.0	—
2	220.0	110.0	110.0	88.0	8.0	22.0	2.0
3	242.0	121.0	121.0	96.8	8.8	24.2	2.2
4	266.2	133.1	133.1	106.5	9.7	26.6	2.4

combinations of s and σ that yield growth rates of 5, 2.5, and 10 percent per year.

In Model 1 the productivity of capital is taken to be 0.25 and the propensity to save to be 0.20. The capital stock in place (column 2) at the beginning of Year 1 is 400, the stock necessary with σ of 0.25 for production of potential output, Y_p, of 100 (column 3). Let us also assume that in Year 1 actual, or realized, output, Y_r (column 4), was 100. Consumption (column 5), equal to $(1 - s)Y_r$, was 80, so saving, equal to sY_r, was 20. Investment (column 7) was also 20, yielding aggregate spending of 100, the amount necessary to make realized output equal to potential output. This much is the ordinary, short-run Keynesian model. Now allow for the fact that I of 20 in Year 1 increases by 20 the capital stock in existence at the beginning of Year 2. This increases capacity output of Year 2 by σI (or $\sigma \Delta K$)—that is, by 5. Consequently, aggregate spending in Year 2 must also increase by σI to make use of the increase in capacity. But aggregate spending will increase only if investment increases. To secure the required increase in aggregate spending of 5 in Year 2, investment must rise from 20 to 21. Given the multiplier of 5 ($s = 1/5$), we then find an increase in spending of 5 composed of $\Delta C = 4$ (column 6)[9] and $\Delta I = 1$. If investment in Year 2 does in fact rise at the required rate of 5 percent, or from 20 to 21, Y_r in Year 2 will equal Y_p in Year 2. Or, given that $\Delta I / I = s\sigma$, numerically for Year 2 we have $1/20 = 0.20 \times 0.25$. The growth rate of output, $\Delta Y / Y = s\sigma$, is then $(4 + 1)/100 = 0.20 \times 0.25$, where 4 represents the increase in consumption and 1 represents the increase in investment. With s and σ as given in Model 1 and as long as investment rises 5 percent per year, aggregate spending will rise as fast as potential output, and actual output will grow accordingly at the capacity rate of 5 percent. At this constant rate of growth, investment and consumption represent the same proportions of the expanding output, but the abso-

lute increase in the amount of investment and of consumption grows larger each year. This means that the amount of investment in any given year must always exceed the saving of the preceding year if aggregate spending is to rise as fast as potential output.

Models 2 and 3 show how different values of σ and s affect the equilibrium growth rate.[10] The choice of the particular values of σ and s in these three models brings out the following points. First, the growth rate in Model 1 is twice that in Model 2 because the propensity to save is twice as large (0.20 instead of 0.10) with the same productivity of capital in both cases. An economy that can double the fraction of its resources diverted from the production of consumer goods can double the fraction of its resources devoted to capital accumulation. Therefore, if the productivity of capital remains unchanged, the economy can grow *potentially* at twice its previous rate with what amounts to a doubling of its propensity to save. Next, the growth rate in Model 3 is twice that in Model 1 because the productivity of capital is twice as great (0.50 instead of 0.25) with the same propensity to save in both cases. This suggests that if the amount of output obtainable per unit of capital can somehow be doubled, an economy can double its *potential* rate of growth with the unchanged rate of capital accumulation set by its propensity to save. Finally, the growth rate in Model 3 is four times the growth rate in Model 2 because both the productivity of capital and the propensity to save are twice what they are in Model 2.

Each of the models of Table 20-2 traces an equilibrium growth path, the sole difference between them being in the values of σ and s, which determine the rate of equilibrium growth. In each model, the economy follows an equilibrium growth path as a result of growth in aggregate spending equal to the growth in capacity output, a result that in turn depends on growth of

---

[9]In column 6, $\Delta C = (1 - s)\Delta I/s$. In equilibrium, this equals $\sigma I/(1 - s)$.

[10]Because output in Year 1 is set at 100 in all three models, the original capital stock in Model 3 is only 200 with productivity of capital assumed to be 0.50.

the required rate.

investment at the required rate. Model 1-A of Table 20-3 repeats Model 1 of Table 20-2, in which investment grows at the required rate of 5 percent. Models 1-B and 1-C, however, show what happens to growth if investment fails to grow at the rate required to make full use of the growing capacity. In Model 1-B, net investment remains constant, and in Model 1-C, net investment grows but at less than the required rate.

The last two models describe disequilibrium situations. In Model 1-B, there is a constant net investment of 20 per year and a constant addition to capacity of 5 each year. Because changes in aggregate spending depend on changes in net investment and not on the level of net investment, aggregate spending remains constant as long as net investment is constant. Because with each passing year 5 more is being added to excess capacity under these circumstances, it is unlikely that net investment will be maintained even at 20 year after year. A decrease in net investment will follow, which will cause aggregate spending to fall; depression and stagnation may ensue. In Model 1-C, investment does grow but at a rate too slow to absorb that part of growing capacity output that is not absorbed by consumption. This will also cause excess capacity to pile up year by year, which means that even the indicated lower-than-required growth rate probably cannot be maintained.

TABLE 20-3
Illustrations of the Growth Process: Disequilibrium Situations

(1) Year	(2) Capital Stock K	(3) Potential Output $Y_p = \sigma K$	(4) Realized Output $Y_r = C + I$	(5) Consumption $C = (1-s)Y_r$	(6) Change in Consumption $\Delta C = (1-s)\frac{\Delta I}{s}$	(7) Investment (Autonomous) I	(8) Change in Investment (Autonomous) ΔI
\multicolumn{8}{c}{Model 1-A: Investment grows at the required rate of 5 percent.}
1	400.00	100.00	100.00	80.00	—	20.00	—
2	420.00	105.00	105.00	84.00	4.00	21.00	1.00
3	441.00	110.25	110.25	88.20	4.20	22.05	1.05
4	463.05	115.76	115.76	92.61	4.41	23.14	1.09
\multicolumn{8}{c}{Model 1-B: Investment is constant.}
1	400.00	100	100	80	—	20	—
2	420.00	105	100	80	—	20	—
3	440.00	110	100	80	—	20	—
4	460.00	115	100	80	—	20	—
\multicolumn{8}{c}{Model 1-C: Investment grows at the too slow rate of 3 percent.}
1	400.00	100.00	100.00	80.00	—	20.00	—
2	420.00	105.00	103.00	82.40	2.40	20.60	0.60
3	440.60	110.15	106.09	84.87	2.47	21.22	.62
4	461.82	115.45	109.28	87.42	2.55	21.86	.64

A Graphic Representation of the Growth Process[11]

With a few modifications, the familiar Keynesian short-run saving-investment figure for the determination of the equilibrium level of output can be adjusted to illustrate the growth process described in Table 20-2. In Figure 20-1, the intersection of S and I_1 defines an original equilibrium level of output at Y_1.[12] The short-run analysis suggested that the equilibrium level of output would remain at Y_1 as long as neither the saving nor the investment function shifted. With no such shift, investment would be just equal to the leakage into saving at the given level of income and output; whatever part of income was not spent for consumption would be offset by an equal (planned) amount spent for investment. With no change in total spending, there would be no change in the equilibrium level of income and output. As we now know, this is an unrealistic conclusion except for very short-run situations, because it neglects the capacity effect of that part of spending composed of net investment. If we can incorporate this capacity effect into the figure, it can be used to illustrate the growth process in which capacity output rises and full use of capacity is possible only if the amount of investment rises as required per time period.

Let us assume, as in Table 20-2, that $Y_r = Y_p$ at the output level Y_1 in Year 1. Net investment for the year is I_1, which raises the capital stock at the beginning of Year 2 by the same amount, so Y_p of Year 2 exceeds Y_p of Year 1. How large this increase in capacity output will be depends on I_1 and σ. The year's net investment is, of course, represented by the height of the I_1 function above

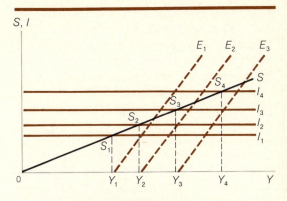

[11]The figures in this section follow those developed by H. Pilvin in "A Geometric Analysis of Recent Growth Models," in *American Economic Review*, Sept. 1952, pp. 594–99.

[12]This portion of the figure differs from the familiar Keynesian figure only in that the short-run nonproportional saving function has been replaced by a long-run proportional function. As drawn, MPS = APS, in contrast to the short-run nonproportional function, in which MPS > APS.

FIGURE 20-1
The Equilibrium Growth Process

the horizontal axis. The value of σ is represented by the reciprocal of the slope of the E_1 function. The higher the value of σ, the less will be the slope of the function. If $\sigma = 3/4$, the slope will be $4/3$; if $\sigma = 1/4$, the slope will be 4; and in the special case in which $\sigma = 1$, the slope will be 1 (a 45° line), with the increase in capacity output just equal to net investment. With the slope of E_1 in Figure 20-1, I_1 raises productive capacity by Y_1Y_2. This is determined graphically by moving along the I_1 curve from S_1 to the intersection with the E_1 curve and dropping a vertical line to locate Y_2 on the output axis.

For Year 1 we assumed that $Y_r = Y_p$, but now Y_p of Year 2 exceeds Y_p of Year 1. If there is to be full utilization of the increased productive capacity in Year 2, Y_r must rise by an amount equal to the rise in Y_p. This in turn requires that aggregate spending rise by the same amount. With a stable saving function, the required rise in aggregate spending can occur only if investment rises in Year 2 by the amount necessary to offset the rise in saving at the higher level of output. In other words, if Y_r is to rise from Y_1 to Y_2, net investment must rise from I_1 to I_2 to offset the rise in saving from S_1 to S_2 that will accompany a rise in output to Y_2. If such a rise in investment occurs, the economy will then operate at full capacity in Year 2; $Y_r = Y_p$ at the output level Y_2. The process then repeats itself. Investment of I_2 during Year 2 raises the capital stock at the beginning of Year 3 by the amount I_2. With an unchanged value for σ, this increase in capital stock raises the productive capacity of the economy in Year 3 from Y_2 to Y_3, as indicated by the E_2 line. Again, to make full use of the expanded productive capacity, investment will have to rise from I_2 to I_3 in Year 3.

As revealed by Table 20-2, equilibrium growth requires that the absolute increase in investment in each period exceed the absolute increase in investment of the preceding period. In terms of Figure 20-1, $I_3I_2 > I_2I_1$ and $I_4I_3 > I_3I_2$. With a constant value for σ, the increase in capacity output in each period also exceeds that of the preceding period, or $Y_3Y_2 > Y_2Y_1$ and $Y_4Y_3 > Y_3Y_2$. If numerical values were inserted on the axes of Figure 20-1, the percentage changes from Y_1 to Y_2 and Y_2 to Y_3 and from I_1 to I_2 and I_2 to I_3 would prove to be equal to $s\sigma$, the slope of the S function multiplied by the reciprocal of the slope of the E function.

The Addition of a Theory of Investment

The model, as developed so far, shows the rate at which investment *must* grow if aggregate spending is to grow at the rate needed to provide full utilization of a growing capital stock. Accordingly, column 7 of Table 20-2 showed the dollar amounts of investment, and Figure 20-1 showed the successive positions of the autonomous investment curve that must be attained if productive capacity is to be fully utilized period after period. However, indicating what *must* happen in order to meet this objective tells us nothing about what *will* happen. There is nothing within the model itself to indicate what the actual value of investment will be period after period. It is specifically a model of this kind that Domar developed. He chose an approach that did not enter into the question of what determines the rate of

investment but limited itself to identifying what the rate of investment would have to be period after period in order to provide an equilibrium rate of growth.

We may now expand the Domar-type model by adding a theory of investment such as the accelerator theory so that the model will then contain a theory of what investment will be in each period. In combination with the theory of consumption already in the model, this addition will give us a model that contains a theory to cover both components of aggregate spending. It is specifically the inclusion of an accelerator theory of investment that, in a formal sense, is the major difference between the approach taken by Harrod and that taken by Domar. Because these two approaches are essentially the same apart from this, they are commonly lumped together under the heading of the Harrod–Domar model. Still, the difference is important; its full implications can be seen only by developing Harrod's approach in detail. We will not do that here, but we can gain some understanding of the effect of the addition of the accelerator investment equation to the model developed so far merely by comparing Figure 20-1, which showed what investment must be if the system is to follow an equilibrium growth path, with Figure 20-2, which includes a theory of what investment will be.

One form of the accelerator theory of investment makes investment of any period equal to the accelerator times the change in the level of output between the current and the preceding period, or, as an equation, $I_t = w(Y_t - Y_{t-1})$.[13] This is the version presented in Chapter 18, the one used by Harrod, and the one on which Figure

---

[13]Algebraically the accelerator w, or K/Y, is the reciprocal of σ, or Y/K, the output–capital ratio or average productivity of capital, which appears above in the analysis that follows Domar's approach. If we rewrite $I_t = w(Y_t - Y_{t-1})$ in the simpler form, $I = w(\Delta Y)$, Domar's $\Delta Y = \sigma I$ may in turn be rewritten as $I = (1/\sigma)\Delta Y$—that is, in a form algebraically equal to Harrod's acceleration investment equation. However, although w and $1/\sigma$ are equal algebraically, their economic meanings are quite different. The rewritten Domar equation cannot be interpreted like the Harrod

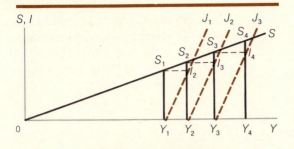

FIGURE 20-2
The Growth Process with an
Accelerator Theory of
Investment

20-2 is based. In this figure, the change in output from Period 1 to Period 2 is given by the distance between Y_1 and Y_2 on the income or output axis. How much investment this induces in Period 2 depends on the size of the accelerator, which is shown diagrammatically by the slope of the line labeled J_1. This and the other J lines are all drawn with a slope of 2 to conform with the assumption that the accelerator is 2. Given a rise in output from Y_1 to Y_2, induced investment in Period 2 is equal to the vertical distance I_2Y_2 or twice the change in output, Y_1Y_2. The figure is so drawn that the rise in output, Y_1Y_2, is just sufficient to induce investment of I_2Y_2, which is just equal to the saving made available in Period 2. A lagged saving function is assumed in which each period's saving equals the propensity to save times the preceding period's income. Accordingly, saving made available in Period 2 is equal to S_1Y_1, which is matched in Period 2 by investment of I_2Y_2.

equation, in which I is made a function of ΔY and w refers to the ratio that business people *desire* to establish between I and ΔY. No such intended or desired relationship between I and ΔY is present in the Domar approach. The equation from that model as originally given, $\Delta Y = \sigma I$, expresses the relationship that Domar employs—a simple production function in which the change in the period's capacity output is technologically equal to some fraction of the period's net investment.

The rate of growth of income and output from Period 1 to Period 2 is equal to $(Y_2 - Y_1)/Y_1$. In Figure 20-2 the same rate of growth of income is maintained in succeeding periods, so that $(Y_2 - Y_1)/Y_1 = (Y_3 - Y_2)/Y_2$ and so forth. If income grows from period to period as described by the figure, the economy may be said to be moving along an equilibrium path. The only growth rate that will carry the system along such a path is the particular rate that is consistent with the values of the accelerator and propensity to save adopted in drawing the figure. Harrod calls this particular growth rate the *warranted* rate of growth, which suggests that the given combination of accelerator and propensity to save "warrant" the rate of growth indicated. If the propensity to save were higher (a greater slope to the S curve), it could be seen that a higher rate of output growth would be required to keep the economy moving along an equilibrium growth path. A smaller accelerator (a lesser slope to the J curve) would have a similar effect. In the same way, a smaller propensity to save or a larger accelerator would each mean that a lower rate of output growth would be required to keep the economy moving along an equilibrium growth path.

This equilibrium growth path has been commonly described as a "razor's edge"—the slightest departure of the actual growth rate from the equilibrium (warranted) rate throws the economy off the equilibrium growth path into either "stagnation" or "exhilaration." For example, assume that income has risen by less than Y_1Y_2 from Period 1 to Period 2. Induced investment in Period 2 would then be less than I_2Y_2 and therefore less than the amount of saving forthcoming in Period 2. This means a deficiency of spending, which means excess capacity—a situation in which the existing capital stock is greater than that desired by business at the then current level of output. Paradoxically, this excess capacity results from the fact that business did not invest enough or acquire enough additional capacity. An appropriately higher level of investment would have prevented the deficiency of demand and the appearance of excess capacity. However, the fact is that excess capacity has appeared, which causes a contraction of income and output, which in turn, via the accelerator, causes a further reduction in investment. But then saving again exceeds investment, and there is a still greater deficiency of aggregate spending. Once given an initial divergence in which the actual growth rate falls below the equilibrium (warranted) growth rate, forces push the system, not back toward the equilibrium growth rate, but farther and farther away from it. In the event of such a divergence, the result is deep, prolonged depression or stagnation.

In the case of the opposite divergence, suppose that output has risen by more than Y_1Y_2 from Period 1 to Period 2. Induced investment in Period 2 would then be greater than I_2Y_2 and therefore more than the amount of saving made available in Period 2. This means an excess of spending, which in the present context means a capital shortage—a situation in which the existing capital stock is less than that desired by business at the then current level of output. As before, there is a paradox here: The capital shortage results from the fact that business invested too much. An appropriately lower level of investment would have prevented the excess spending that resulted in the capital shortage. However, once a capital shortage appears, investment rises as business tries to make up for the shortage. Investment again exceeds saving, and there is a still greater excess of spending. Once the actual rate exceeds the equilibrium (warranted) growth rate, forces push the system farther and farther away from the equilibrium growth rate. Where the divergence is an actual rate above the equilibrium rate, the result is secular exhilaration.

Because the actual growth rate is subject to all sorts of influences, it can be expected that it will depart from the equilibrium rate of growth dictated by the values of the propensity to save and the accelerator. Harrod's formulation therefore suggests an economy with an inherently unstable pattern of growth, marked by a tendency toward long periods of boom or stagnation. As we have seen, once the economy

departs from the equilibrium growth path, it moves farther and farther away from it over time. It is a focus on this alleged tendency toward secular instability that is the most striking feature of Harrod's formulation of the basic capital-accumulation theory known as the Harrod–Domar theory.

The Employment of Labor

In the basic Harrod–Domar theory the equilibrium (warranted) growth rate is that which provides full utilization of a growing capital stock or results in neither shortage nor excess of capital. Although capital is the only factor of production that is explicitly considered, the model of course recognizes that labor too is needed in order to produce. Labor as a factor of production is, however, brought in through the assumption of fixed factor proportions, so it may be said that the amount of labor employed is indicated by the amount of capital in use. In other words, labor and capital are assumed to be perfectly *complementary* in the production process, but the focus of the model is on the stock of capital. The model also assumes constant returns to scale, so that, for example, a 1 percent increase in the amount of labor and capital will result in a 1 percent increase in the economy's capacity output.

If the economy grows at the equilibrium (warranted) rate, the amount of labor employed will grow at the same rate, assuming perfect complementarity. This suggests that there will be full employment of labor only if the warranted growth rate is equal to the growth rate of the labor force and only if the actual growth rate corresponds with the warranted growth rate. In the previous section we noted that the actual and warranted rates may be expected to diverge; here the warranted growth rate and the labor force growth rate may also be expected to diverge, given the essentially demographic factors that determine the long-run growth of the labor force.

If the actual growth rate equals the warranted growth rate but the warranted growth rate exceeds the labor force growth rate, the result is accumulation of idle plant and equipment; there would be more new capital added than new workers to operate it. Because business people quite plainly will not long continue to produce new plant and equipment that cannot be utilized for want of workers, the ceiling to the actual rate of growth in this case would appear to be a rate set by the growth of the labor force. The warranted rate might be 4 percent when the labor force growth rate is only 1 percent. Given the model's assumption of fixed proportions between labor and capital, the ceiling to the actual rate of growth of output would then be 1 percent.

The actual growth rate would not be limited to this 1 percent ceiling if we added to our illustration an allowance for the influence of technological advance. Technological advance of a labor-saving nature enables a smaller amount of labor and an unchanged amount of capital to produce an unchanged amount of output. In a growth context, this means that capital may now grow at a faster rate than the labor force because technological advance is continuously releasing some labor from the existing capital stock, which *in effect* is equivalent to a rise in the growth rate of the labor force. The process may be viewed as one in which the labor so released becomes available for employment with new capital goods that would not have been produced if this labor had not been made available by labor-saving technological advance. If this rate of technological advance is, say, 2 percent and the growth rate of the labor force is 1 percent, the ceiling growth rate becomes 3 percent instead of the 1 percent set by the actual growth of the labor force alone. However, because this ceiling is still below the 4 percent rate assumed as the warranted rate, the actual rate must still fall below the warranted rate, resulting in economic stagnation as noted earlier.

In the opposite case, the labor force growth rate may be greater than the warranted growth rate. For example, if the propensity to save were relatively low and the investment of the amount of income saved permitted only a 2 percent growth rate for the capital stock, a labor force growth rate of more than 2 percent would mean insufficient plant and equipment to employ the full labor force. The ceiling to the actual rate of growth would then be imposed by the warranted rate. With the labor force growth rate greater than this rate, the rate of growth of the capital stock would not be sufficient to provide full employment for the growing labor force. The dual objective of full utilization of both labor and capital cannot be satisfied under the conditions described, because labor and capital are employed in fixed proportions—and the labor force in this situation is simply growing faster than the capital stock. In short, full employment of labor becomes impossible.

These and other conclusions reached in the preceding discussion of the Harrod–Domar theory follow at least partially from the fact that the theory assumes fixed factor proportions. If we were to drop the assumption that labor and capital are combined only in this way, it would no longer necessarily follow that full employment of the labor force would become impossible. If the labor force growth rate exceeds the warranted growth rate, the ratio of labor to capital in the production process might increase to permit full employment of the labor force. From a much broader point of view, if we drop the assumption of fixed factor proportions, it is no longer meaningful to say that we can explain the economy's growth rate in terms of the propensity to save and the productivity of capital. With the possibility of variable proportions, the approach to an explanation of the growth rate must bring the labor force explicitly into the analysis.

Once we introduce this possibility of variable factor proportions into the picture, we leave the world of Harrod–Domar. As noted in the introduction to this chapter, it is the adoption of the assumption of variable factor proportions that characterizes a body of more recent growth theory. The economists who returned to this neoclassical assumption of substitutability between factors built a new type of growth theory that differs basically from the Harrod–Domar type; it is generally known as neoclassical growth theory.

Neoclassical Growth Theory[14]

In one sense, neoclassical growth theory stands at an opposite extreme from Harrod–Domar. In place of the Harrod–Domar assumption of a single production process that imposes a fixed ratio between capital and labor is the assumption of an indefinitely large number of production processes, one shading off from another in a way that permits any combination of labor and capital to be employed. Capital is regarded as a unique, abstract agent of production that can be adjusted at any time to absorb into employment a labor force of any size. With the combination of labor and capital capable of varying in this way, it follows that, instead of the fixed ratio between output and capital employed by Harrod and Domar, the output–capital ratio can vary continuously. Therefore, the larger the labor force absorbed into employment with a given stock of capital, the greater will be the output–capital ratio, or the productivity of capital, and the smaller will be the output–labor ratio, or the productivity of labor. Similarly, the smaller the labor force absorbed into employment with a given stock of capital, the lower the productivity of capital and the higher the productivity of labor. These results follow simply as a matter of diminishing returns.

---

[14]A sizable literature has developed since the mid-1950s. Among the major contributions are R.M. Solow, "A Contribution to the Theory of Economic Growth," in *Quarterly Journal of Economics*, Feb. 1956, pp. 65–94; "Technical Change and the Aggregate Production Function," in *Review of Economics and Statistics*, Aug. 1957, pp. 312–20; T.W. Swan, "Economic Growth and Capital Accumulation," in *Economic Record*, Nov. 1956, pp. 334–61, and E.S. Phelps, "The New View of Investment: A Neoclassical Analysis," in *Quarterly Journal of Economics*, Nov. 1962, pp. 548–67. For less technical and nonmathematical expositions of neoclassical growth theory, see H.G. Johnson, "The Neo-Classical One-Sector Growth Model: A Geometrical Exposition and Extension to a Monetary Economy," in *Economica*, Aug. 1966, pp. 265–87, and J.E. Meade, *A Neo-Classical Theory of Economic Growth*, Oxford Univ. Press, 1961. See also D. Hamberg, *Models of Economic Growth*, Ch. 2, and H.Y. Wan, Jr., *Economic Growth*, Ch. 2.

The neoclassical theory also differs from Harrod–Domar in its assumption of automatic full utilization of capital and labor. The issue of whether or not the amount of saving generated by an economy with factors fully utilized will be matched by an equal amount of planned investment, a requisite to continued full utilization of factors, is answered in terms of classical theory: All economic activity is carried out in conditions of perfect competition, with flexible prices of inputs and outputs serving to balance supply and demand in all markets along the lines discussed in Chapter 9. Output then depends simply on the supply of inputs, because all inputs available will find employment. With the question of full utilization of inputs thereby resolved, the neoclassical theory focuses on the growth path that will be followed by a system in which labor and capital resources remain fully utilized as the quantity of these resources grows over time. Consequently, there is no need to distinguish in this discussion between the growth rate of the economy's potential output and the growth rate of its actual output because the latter becomes the same as the former.

The Rate of Output Growth Without Technological Progress

The rate at which the output of the economy grows basically depends on the rate at which its capital stock, labor force, and technological know-how grow over time. The relationship for any particular period of time may be simply expressed in the form of the following production function:

$$Y = f(K, L, A)$$

Here K is the capital stock, L the labor force, and A an index of technological know-how whose magnitude will grow at some rate over time. As a first step, however, we will temporarily simplify the relationship by assuming that no technological progress takes place. The production function is then

$$Y = f(K, L)$$

In this simplest case, how does Y vary as K and L vary, all else being equal? In the Harrod–Domar theory, if both K and L increased by 1 percent, Y would increase by 1 percent. The neoclassical theory indicates the same result, because both theories assume a production function with constant returns to scale. However, in Harrod–Domar, a 1 percent increase in L with no increase in K (and with all the existing K already in full use) would mean no increase in Y because of the fixed proportion between L and K. However, in neoclassical growth theory, the same set of conditions would lead to some increase in Y because the enlarged L could be absorbed into employment with an unchanged K.

If the increase in L is not very great, the increase in Y will be approximately equal to the increase in L times the marginal physical product of L, or $\Delta Y = MPP_L \cdot \Delta L$ in which MPP_L is the marginal physical product of labor, or the increase in Y that accompanies a unit increase in L with K held constant. If we had assumed an increase in K with no change in L, under the same assumptions we would have had $\Delta Y = MPP_K \cdot \Delta K$ in which MPP_K is the marginal physical product of capital, or the increase in Y that accompanies a unit increase in K with L held constant. Finally, for changes in both K and L in a given time period, we may write

$$\Delta Y = MPP_K \cdot \Delta K + MPP_L \cdot \Delta L$$

Dividing both sides by Y, we have

$$\frac{\Delta Y}{Y} = \left(\frac{MPP_K}{Y}\right)\Delta K + \left(\frac{MPP_L}{Y}\right)\Delta L$$

which may also be written as

$$\frac{\Delta Y}{Y} = \left(\frac{MPP_K \cdot K}{Y}\right)\frac{\Delta K}{K} + \left(\frac{MPP_L \cdot L}{Y}\right)\frac{\Delta L}{L} \qquad [1]$$

If we recall our earlier assumption of perfect competition in all markets and now adopt the marginal productivity theory of factor pricing, each unit of a factor will be paid its marginal product, and the total earnings of capital and labor will equal $MPP_K \cdot K$ and $MPP_L \cdot L$, respec-

tively. Given that factors are paid their marginal products, the total earnings of capital and labor will exactly absorb the total output in the case of the present production function with constant returns to scale. That is,

$$MPP_K \cdot K + MPP_L \cdot L = Y$$

Because

$$\frac{MPP_K \cdot K}{Y} + \frac{MPP_L \cdot L}{Y} = \frac{Y}{Y} = 1$$

we may substitute b for the first term on the left and $(1 - b)$ for the second term and rewrite Equation 1 as

$$\frac{\Delta Y}{Y} = b\left(\frac{\Delta K}{K}\right) + (1 - b)\frac{\Delta L}{L} \qquad [2]$$

The magnitude of b indicates the proportion of the total product or of total income that would be received as a return on capital if capital were paid its marginal product. This is the same as saying that b measures the elasticity of output with respect to changes in the amount of capital used.[15] If $b = 0.25$, either the owners of capital would receive 25 percent of the economy's income if capital earned a return equal to its marginal product or a 1.0 percent increase in the amount of capital in use would produce a 0.25 percent increase in output. These amount to two ways of saying the same thing. The same kind of statement may, of course, be made for labor by making the appropriate substitution.[16]

Assuming a value for b, say 0.25, we may read from Equation [2] the percentage change

---

[15] The general concept of elasticity refers to a percentage change in one variable divided by the percentage change in another. If L is not changing, $b = \Delta Y/Y \div \Delta K/K$, or the percentage change in Y over the percentage change in K, or b is an elasticity.

[16] That $(1 - b)$, or $(MMP_L \cdot L)/Y$, is equal to labor's share of total output follows the analysis of Chapter 13. We saw there that under competitive conditions, employers will hire labor up to the point at which $MPP_L \cdot P = W$, or $MPP_L = W/P$. Substituting W/P for MPP_L in $MPP_L \cdot L/Y$ gives us WL/PY, or the total money wage income of labor as a fraction of the total money income for the economy.

in output that will follow from a given percentage change in capital, labor, or both. If both K and L rise by 3 percent, output also rises by 3 percent, because the underlying production function has constant returns to scale. In this case, we have $\Delta Y/Y = 0.25 \times 3 + 0.75 \times 3 = 3$. However, note that capital and labor do not contribute equally to the growth in output, even though each factor grows at the same rate. In the illustration, 2.25 percentage points of the 3 percent growth rate are due to labor; the remaining 0.75 percentage point is due to capital. Labor is given three times the weight of capital, because the weights correspond with their output elasticities; these show that a 1 percent increase in labor will produce a percentage increase in output three times as large as a 1 percent increase in capital. Therefore, a 3 percent increase in K and a 1 percent increase in L would indicate a 1.5 percent increase in output, but a 1 percent increase in K and a 3 percent increase in L would indicate a 2.5 percent increase in output.

These results are very different from those indicated by the Harrod–Domar theory. In terms of our numerical example, if we started from a position of full utilization of labor and capital, a 3 percent growth rate for K and a 1 percent growth rate for L—or vice versa—would in both cases mean a ceiling growth rate for Y of 1 percent. This again is the necessary result if we rule out the substitutability between factors that is not ruled out in neoclassical growth theory. In a more general way, we may bring out the basic difference between the Harrod–Domar and neoclassical theories by rewriting Equation [2] to incorporate the Harrod–Domar theory. Because $\Delta K = I = sY$ and because $Y/K = \sigma$ in which σ is the symbol used earlier for the output–capital ratio, we may rewrite Equation [2] to read

$$\frac{\Delta Y}{Y} = b(s\sigma) + (1 - b)\frac{\Delta L}{L}$$

In the Harrod–Domar theory, $s\sigma$ defined the equilibrium rate of growth; that is, the growth equation was simply $\Delta Y/Y = s\sigma$. In the neoclassical theory, with its allowance for substitutability between factors, the growth rate of labor has its own influence on the rate of growth of output. The propensity to save, s, and the productivity of capital, σ, the product of which equals the growth rate of capital, are in themselves no longer sufficient to explain the rate of growth of output. Actually, the growth rate of capital is not only insufficient to explain the growth rate of output, but may be far less important than the labor force in this regard. This follows from the fact that the influence of capital accumulation on the growth rate depends heavily on the size of b, and b may be relatively small. To trace through a numerical illustration, suppose that the economy's output is growing at 3 percent over a period when s is 0.10 and σ is 0.30, so that $s\sigma$ equals 0.03, or 3 percent. If the economy became twice as thrifty and raised s to 0.20, would the growth rate of output also double to 6 percent? According to the Harrod–Domar theory, a doubling would result, but here we find that it results only if b equals 1.[17] But b is actually in the neighborhood of 0.25 to 0.33, the range of the share of capital in total income. If b were 0.25, the doubling of the saving ratio would raise the growth rate of output only from 3.0 to 3.75 percent; if b were 0.33, such a doubling would raise the growth rate of output only from 3.0 to 4.0 percent. The fixed link between the growth rate of capital and the growth rate of output given by Harrod and Domar is replaced here by a link in which the growth rate of output depends on the rates of growth of both capital and the labor force and, further, on the output elasticities of capital and labor.

The Rate of Output Growth per Capita

Although there is obvious interest in how the growth rate of aggregate output (or $\Delta Y/Y$) will vary

---

[17]If b were to equal 1, the neoclassical equation would reduce to $\Delta Y/Y = s\sigma$—the Harrod–Domar equation. However, for b to equal 1 requires a surplus of labor that is not at all substitutable for capital in production, so output can grow only at the rate of growth of capital, or $\Delta Y/Y = \Delta K/K = s\sigma$.

with different growth rates of labor and capital, of much greater interest is how the growth rate of output per worker will vary under the same circumstances. If we subtract $\Delta L/L$ from $\Delta Y/Y$, we have the difference between the growth rate of aggregate output and the growth rate of the labor force, a difference that is approximately equal to the growth rate of output per worker. Therefore, we can convert Equation [2] to show the growth rate of output per worker by subtracting $\Delta L/L$ from both sides. The same subtraction will show the growth rate of output *per capita,* if the growth rate of the population is the same as the growth rate of the labor force. Making the indicated subtraction gives us

$$\frac{\Delta Y}{Y} - \frac{\Delta L}{L} = b\left(\frac{\Delta K}{K} - \frac{\Delta L}{L}\right) \qquad [3]$$

The growth rate of output per worker ($\Delta Y/Y - \Delta L/L$) is equal to the growth rate of capital per worker ($\Delta K/K - \Delta L/L$) weighted by the elasticity of output with respect to capital. In order for the growth rate of output per worker to be above zero, the equation shows that there must be an increase in the stock of capital per worker—that is, a growth rate of capital greater than the growth rate of the labor force. For example, suppose that $\Delta Y/Y$ equals 2 percent and $\Delta L/L$ equals 1 percent, a combination that indicates a 1 percent rise in output per worker per period. The right-hand side of Equation [3] shows that, to secure this 1 percent rise in output per worker per period, the growth rate of capital must be 5 percent if we assume a value for b of 0.25, or 4 percent if we assume a value of 0.33. Given a value of b in this range, a growth rate of capital four to five times the growth rate of the labor force is required to produce a 1 percent rate of growth in output per worker per period.[18]

---

[18] If we had assumed $\Delta Y/Y$ of 4 percent and $\Delta L/L$ of 3 percent, the growth rate of output would again be approximately 1 percent, but this would demand an even higher growth rate of capital: 7 percent for b of 0.25 and 6 percent for b of 0.33.

Is it possible for the capital stock to grow at a higher rate than the growth rate of the labor force period after period, which, according to Equation [3], is a prerequisite to a rising output per worker period after period? Due to diminishing returns, a growth rate of the capital stock greater than the growth rate of the labor force must result in a decline in the average productivity of capital, or in the output–capital ratio. Correspondingly, a rise in the average productivity of labor, or in the output–labor ratio, must result. The decline in the average productivity of capital amounts to a fall in the rate of return on capital. This may be seen through a variation of Equation [3]. The growth rate of output per worker was expressed there as $\Delta Y/Y - \Delta L/L$. In a similar way, we may express the growth rate of output per unit of capital as $\Delta Y/Y - \Delta K/K$. If we subtract $\Delta K/K$ from both sides of Equation [2], as we earlier subtracted $\Delta L/L$ from the same equation, we find

$$\frac{\Delta Y}{Y} - \frac{\Delta K}{K} = (1 - b)\left(\frac{\Delta L}{L} - \frac{\Delta K}{K}\right) \qquad [4]$$

If b is 0.25, growth rates of 5 percent for capital and 1 percent for labor produce a 3 percent *decline* in the productivity of capital per time period. Whatever the level from which the decline starts, if our periods are years, this means that in less than fifteen years the return on capital will have fallen to less than two-thirds of its previous level. As a matter of fact, Equation [4] indicates that for any value of b less than 1 and for any values of $\Delta K/K$ and $\Delta L/L$ in which $\Delta K/K > \Delta L/L$, the growth rate of productivity of capital will be negative and the rate of return on capital will be a declining figure. Under these conditions, capital will not grow more rapidly than labor. In the very long-run adjustment in the present case, both capital and labor ultimately will grow at the same rate.

However, we saw that growth in output per worker cannot be achieved unless there is growth in capital per worker. Here we see that the very long-run tendency is for capital to grow at the same rate as labor. Because we know from the historical record both that capital has grown faster than labor and that there has been growth in output per worker, there appears to be something wrong with our formulation. It is actually correct, given its assumptions, but one of the critical assumptions it makes is that no technological progress occurs. If this were indeed the case, the neoclassical model would lead to a so-called steady-state growth in which capital, labor, and output all grow at the same rate. It is only when allowance is made for technological progress that we find the real-world result of a rising output per worker, or a rising "standard of living."

Technological Progress and Output Growth

There is no question that technological progress contributes significantly to the growth rate of output, but there are difficult questions in establishing precisely how it works out its effect on the output growth rate. We will touch on this issue later in this section. As a first step, however, it is helpful to simplify things by viewing technological progress as a force that merely raises the growth rate of output above what it otherwise would be. It is therefore viewed as a factor that is independent of the labor and capital factors with which it actually collaborates to some degree in production. With this simplification, we may refer to the rate of technological progress as a 2 percent rate if, during the time period, such progress makes possible the production of an aggregate output 2 percent greater than would otherwise have been possible with an unchanged amount of labor and capital. Designating the rate of technological progress by $\Delta A/A$, we have in place of Equation [2] the following:

$$\frac{\Delta Y}{Y} = \frac{\Delta A}{A} + b\left(\frac{\Delta K}{K}\right) + (1-b)\frac{\Delta L}{L} \qquad [5]$$

and in place of Equation [3] the following:

$$\frac{\Delta Y}{Y} - \frac{\Delta L}{L} = \frac{\Delta A}{A} + b\left(\frac{\Delta K}{K} - \frac{\Delta L}{L}\right) \qquad [6]$$

It is no longer true that growth of output per worker can occur only if there is growth in capital per worker. We now find that even if $\Delta K/K = \Delta L/L$, $\Delta Y/Y - \Delta L/L$ will be greater than zero by an amount equal to $\Delta A/A$. Indeed, the growth rate of output per worker will be still higher if $\Delta K/K > \Delta L/L$, but this is not a prerequisite to a positive growth rate in output per worker as it was before technological advance was brought into the equation.[19]

The growth rate of output per worker therefore depends on the capital stock per worker and the rate of technological advance. These two sources are all-inclusive if we view technological advance as a residual catchall that includes all sources of growth other than the rise in capital per worker. Because the growth rate of output per worker is $\Delta Y/Y - \Delta L/L$ and because we know from Equation [3] that the growth rate of output per worker due to the growth in capital per worker is $b(\Delta K/K - \Delta L/L)$, the ratio of the latter to the former gives the proportion of the total growth rate of output per worker that is due to the growth in capital per worker. The proportion of the total growth rate of output per worker that is due to technological advance is then obtained as a residual, or the difference between this proportion and 1. The proportion due to growth in capital per worker, here designated by e, may be expressed as follows:

$$e = \frac{b\left(\dfrac{\Delta K}{K} - \dfrac{\Delta L}{L}\right)}{\dfrac{\Delta Y}{Y} - \dfrac{\Delta L}{L}}$$

---

[19] In the same way that Equation [6] replaces Equation [3], we may replace Equation [4] with the following:

$$\frac{\Delta Y}{Y} - \frac{\Delta K}{K} = \frac{\Delta A}{A} + (1-b)\left(\frac{\Delta L}{L} - \frac{\Delta K}{K}\right)$$

which indicates that the productivity of capital need not necessarily fall in the event the capital stock grows at a faster rate than the labor force. The innovations and technical changes that give $\Delta A/A$ its value may be sufficient to raise the productivity, or real return on new capital, more rapidly than it is reduced by a growing ratio of capital to labor—that is, by diminishing returns.

If $\Delta K/K = \Delta Y/Y$, then $e = b$. We have seen that a realistic value for b is in the range from 0.25 to 0.33, so in this case e would be 0.25 to 0.33. To the extent that $\Delta K/K$ is smaller than $\Delta Y/Y$—and this appears to have been the case for the last sixty years—e declines to less than 0.25 for b of 0.25 and to less than 0.33 for b of 0.33. Figures such as these have led economists to conclude that less than one-third of the growth rate of output per worker over the years from the turn of the century can be attributed to the rise in capital per worker. Over two-thirds of the growth rate of output per worker therefore *must* be attributed to all the other factors covered by the catchall called technological advance. This same conclusion may be expressed alternatively by stating that less than one-third of the growth rate of total output can be attributed to the growth rate of the labor and capital inputs, so over two-thirds of the growth rate of total output must be attributed to increased output per unit of labor and capital inputs, or again to all the factors included under the catchall heading of technological advance.

The Embodiment of Technological Progress

Technological progress was introduced into the preceding analysis in the simplest possible way —as a factor completely independent of the capital stock growth rate and the labor force growth rate. This amounts to viewing technological progress as know-how which falls like manna from heaven and applies equally and impartially to all units of the economy's labor force and capital stock. Such technological progress— for example, organizational improvements—is formally described as **disembodied**, because it yields its benefits without the necessity of embodiment in newly produced capital goods or newly trained workers. As long as technological progress is disembodied, we may assume in theory that the labor force is homogeneous, because the productivity of all workers, regardless of age,

training, or education, will benefit proportionally from technological progress. Similarly, we may assume that all units of capital are homogeneous because all units of capital, regardless of age and design, will benefit proportionally from technological progress.

By contrast, **embodied** technological progress must be physically incorporated in newly produced capital goods or newly trained workers before it can contribute to the rate of growth of the economy's output. (For example, jet engines required embodiment in newly produced capital goods, namely, jet airplanes.) Capital can then no longer be assumed to be homogeneous. The capital stock becomes a mixed stock of different "vintages." Because they embody more technological progress, newer machines are more productive than older ones. Similarly, the labor force can no longer be assumed to be homogeneous. Like units of the capital stock, different individuals in the labor force are distinguished by age and training or education. Individuals of the current vintage are then more productive than individuals of earlier vintages.

Although embodied technological advances refer to those that are embodied in either the capital stock or the labor force—that is, in "physical capital" or "human capital"—in what follows we will limit attention to technological advance of a kind that either is or is not embodied in physical capital. Advances of this kind have been described as "design" or "organizational," the former requiring new capital goods and the latter requiring only new procedures or methods.

Economists working in this area disagree as to what part of actual technological advance is design and what part is organizational. If it is true, as some argue, that the larger part is of a design nature that must be embodied in new capital goods if its benefits are to be gained, then it also appears true that the real importance of the capital stock cannot be indicated merely by the fraction of the growth rate of output that is directly explained by the growth rate of the physical stock of capital. Its real importance is much greater, because the capital stock is the vehicle through which technological progress is worked into the production process and without which the growth rate of output would be only a fraction of what it actually is. From this point of view, the capital stock, which otherwise could be downgraded to a minor role, reassumes the position of primacy that most people always thought it occupied.

A numerical illustration will clarify the difference between the earlier approach, in which technological advance was assumed to be completely disembodied, and the present approach, in which it is in part embodied. We assume an economy in which the capital stock is equally divided into one-year through twenty-year vintages. All capital goods last exactly twenty years, so at the end of each year the capital goods then of twenty-year vintage come up for replacement. This will be 5 percent of the capital stock. We also assume that gross investment is equal to replacement investment—that is, net investment is zero. This means that each year's gross investment is equal to 5 percent of the capital stock, which in turn is a physical stock that does not change in amount from year to year.

Some part of the economy's technological advance is embodied in newly produced capital goods. Assume that technological advance is such that the capital goods produced each year show a 3.5 percent quality improvement, or productivity increase, over the capital goods produced during the preceding year. Any variable that grows at a 3.5 percent compound rate per annum will double in size in twenty years. Therefore, a capital good newly produced in Year t and embodying the improvements of Year t and all preceding years will have twice the productivity of the capital good of Year $t - 20$ that it replaces. The comparison is, of course, between capital goods of equal real cost; the physical makeup of the old and the new may be completely different.

Because gross investment is by assumption equal to replacement investment and because replacement is understood to be the amount of capital goods that must be produced during the period in order to maintain the total capital stock, we appear to have a case of zero growth rate in the capital stock. However, even though each unit of capital is replaced at the end of twenty years by another unit of equal real cost, the replacement unit is twice as productive as the replaced unit and therefore in effect is equivalent in real terms to two of the replaced units. For example, if the total capital stock is thought of as 100 units, this year's gross investment of 5 units for replacement equals the 5 units that wear out during this year and keeps the total capital stock unchanged at 100 units; but, because the 5 replacement units are equivalent in productivity to 10 of the replaced units, in effect the capital stock has been enlarged from 100 to 105 units. In our simple case, this increase would not be revealed to the statistician who measured merely the number of units or the physical quantity of capital. An increase in the capital stock is nonetheless there but not in explicit form. In the present example, this implicit, or effective, increase of 5 in the capital stock indicates a 5 percent growth rate ($\Delta K/K = 5/100 = 5$ percent). Otherwise viewed, gross investment that is equal to replacement—that is, to 5 percent of the capital stock—is effectively gross investment equal to 10 percent of the capital stock, one half of which is 5 percent for replacement and the other half of which is, in effect, 5 percent for net investment.

On the basis of all the preceding assumptions and if we now add the final assumption that b equals 0.25, we find that the part of technological advance that is embodied in the capital stock accounts for 0.25(5/100), or about 1.2 percentage points of the rate of output growth. This figure of 1.2 is derived from a whole series of assumptions, some quite arbitrary, and is likely to be far wide of the true figure that is unknown. Nonetheless, even if the actual figure is well above or below 1.2, we still reach conclusions quite different from those reached in the earlier discussion in which technological advance was completely disembodied. Without knowing what the correct figure really is, many economists still feel, on the basis of available evidence, that the contribution of the capital stock to the rate of output growth comes in large part, if not primarily, from the role of capital as a vehicle for the embodiment of technological advance. There is, in sum, much more to the role of the capital stock in the growth process than the mere growth in the quantity of capital goods.

Although we chose to limit attention in this section to the question of the embodiment of technological advance in physical capital, the embodiment of technological advance in "human capital" involves a parallel analysis. Just as the mere growth in the quantity of physical capital accounts for part of the growth of output, so the mere growth in the quantity of human capital does the same. But, as in the case of the capital stock, over and above the mere growth in the amount of labor input is the question of the improvement in its quality as the result of the embodiment of education and training in people. It may well be that this is a more important factor in explaining the growth rate of output than is the embodiment of technological advance in the capital stock.

Economic Growth: The View of "Supply-Side" Economics

We did not include the role of taxation in our review of Harrod–Domar and neoclassical growth theories, because that role is not critical to those theories. In recent years, however, a group of economists, journalists, and politicians have advanced the proposition that taxes are indeed the critical factor in economic growth. The more extreme among them argue that economic behavior is almost completely determined by tax rates.[20]

Members of this group are popularly known as "supply-side" economists. Their major tenet

[20]A detailed statement of this is found in J. Wanniski, *The Way the World Works,* Simon and Schuster, 1978. See also B. Bartlett, *Reaganomics,* Arlington House, 1981.

is that tax reduction is an effective means of raising the growth rate, because it both enhances the incentive of people to work and calls forth increased saving that is matched by increased investment and thereby an enlargement of the economy's capital stock. With greater labor input and greater capital stock, more output will surely be produced. This simple but basic tenet of supply-side economics is contrary to the equally simple Keynesian tenet—which has thoroughly dominated the view of economists for decades—that a tax cut is effective because it stimulates aggregate spending. According to the Keynesian view, income and output increase in response to the tax-induced increase in aggregate demand. Proponents of this view are naturally described as "demand-side" economists.

In relation to the formal growth theory presented earlier, supply-side economics is, therefore, not related to Harrod–Domar, but it is related to neoclassical theory. It assumes automatic full utilization of labor and capital—that is, it rules out any Keynesian problem of deficient aggregate demand. As in neoclassical theory, whatever amount of saving is generated by an economy operating with full utilization of its resources will be matched by an equal amount of planned investment. Growth becomes essentially a matter of greater work effort and increased saving and capital formation; the way to achieve these objectives is through appropriate tax cuts.

Will tax reductions result in a higher growth rate, as supply-side economists assert? The effects of tax reductions on labor supply, saving, and investment were, of course, studied by economists long before any of today's "supply-siders" were born. However, the supply-side people have made the issue of tax cuts not just *a* factor affecting work, saving, and investment, but *the* factor, almost the *sine qua non*. This, of course, does not necessarily mean that they are correct. Their policy prescriptions may indeed raise the growth rate as they say, but these prescriptions *may* also reduce it.

This issue is the crux of supply-side economics. Here we examine it through a graphic model designed to show how a tax cut may change the rate of growth both by influencing labor input and by affecting saving, investment, and thereby the capital stock.[21] These are the two primary avenues through which supply-side economists see a tax cut affecting the growth rate. We will trace through an illustration that assumes a set of responses to a tax reduction that, on balance, produces a rise in the growth rate as asserted by the supply-side economists. This is not to imply that these are necessarily the responses to be expected in practice, only that these are the responses needed to obtain the effect on income growth claimed by the supply-side economists. Following this, we will briefly examine the prerequisite conditions for obtaining those responses and we will indicate in terms of the graphic model how the failure to meet some of these conditions rules out those responses.

Increasing the Growth Rate: The Supply-Side Prescription

In Figure 20-3, the effect of a tax-induced change in labor input on income growth, or what will be called the work effect, is traced through Parts A, B, and C; the effect of a tax-induced change in saving, investment, and the capital stock on income growth, or what will be called the capital formation effect, is traced through Parts A, D, E, and F. These two effects are then combined in Part G and are carried down to Part H, which shows the net supply-side effect on the income growth rate that results from any particular tax cut assumed in Part A at the outset. The derivation of the work effect is traced first, the capital formation effect second, and then the two effects are combined.

The Work Effect of a Tax Cut   In Part A, Y_{at}/Y is the ratio of after-tax income to pre-tax income

or, with T standing for net tax receipts, $Y_{at}/Y = 1 - T/Y$.[22] Assume that an initial T/Y of oa is cut to ob. This raises Y_{at}/Y from oc to od.

Part B of Figure 20-3 shows how $\Delta L/L$ varies with Y_{at}/Y. Because supply-side economics adopts the neoclassical growth theory assumption that there is full utilization of the labor force, $\Delta L/L$ is both the growth rate of labor supply and the growth rate of labor input. As here used, the concept of labor input is broader than "hours of work," because a change in the tax rate will affect labor input not only through hours of work but in other ways. For example, it will affect the time of retirement—and there is some evidence that higher personal income tax rates raise the probability of retirement before 65. It will also affect the intensity of work by altering the fraction of on-the-job time devoted to socializing and other unscheduled work breaks. It will also affect the quality of work by affecting human capital investment, the return on a person's expenditures for education and other means of expanding his or her human capital depending in part on personal income tax rates.[23] Because the term "work effort" may better describe what is here involved, that term is frequently used by supply-side economists, but labor input will serve as well with the understanding that it refers not only to quantity but also quality and intensity of work.

In Part B, the relationship between a change in the tax rate and the growth rate of labor input

---

[21]The presentation follows that in E. Shapiro, "'Supply-Side' Economics: A Diagrammatic Exposition," *Nebraska Journal of Economics and Business,* Spring 1981, pp. 37–46.

[22]Y_{at} is quite different from the familiar Y_d, disposable personal income. In terms of the national income accounting of Chapter 2 with GNP here represented by Y, we have $Y_{at} = Y - T$, and $Y_d = Y_{at} -$ (undistributed corporate profits + capital consumption allowances + statistical discrepancy) + interest paid by consumers. Y_{at} is clearly more relevant than Y_d to the question of the effect of taxation on saving and investment because Y_{at} includes the personal saving component of Y_d as well as the business saving components of capital consumption allowances and undistributed corporate profits.

[23]See H.S. Rosen, "What is Labor Supply and Do Taxes Affect It?" *American Economic Review,* May 1980, pp. 171–76, for a statement of the problem noted here and a summary of the relevant empirical literature.

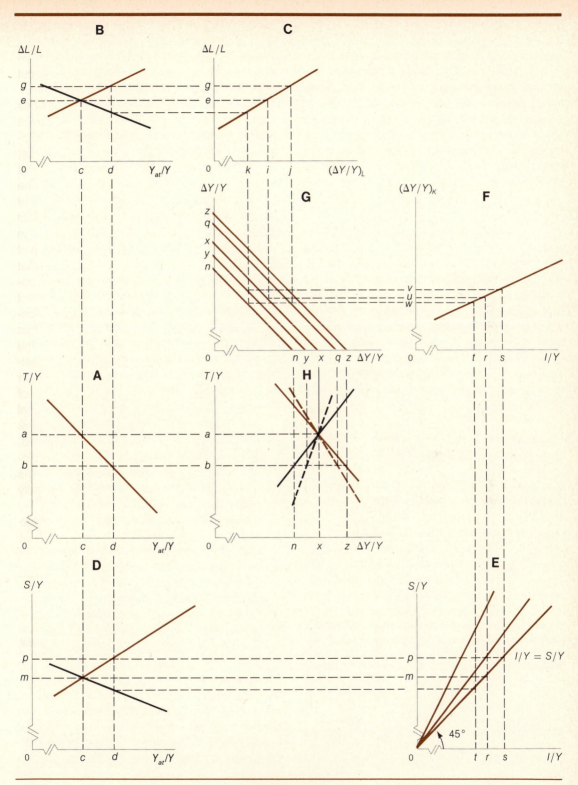

FIGURE 20-3
Tax Cuts and the Growth Rate of Income

is assumed to be that given by the colored line (one of many possible positively sloped lines consistent with supply-side economics). At any time, there is some growth rate in the labor supply and in labor input. If people are permitted to retain a larger share of their income, supply-side economics argues, there will be an increase in the rate at which labor input grows in the economy as a whole. In the present illustration, the rise in Y_{at}/Y from oc to od raises $\Delta L/L$ from oe to og in Part B.

Part C indicates a relationship between $\Delta L/L$ and $(\Delta Y/Y)_L$—that is, between the growth rate of labor input and the growth rate of total income attributable to the growth rate of labor input. At the initial $\Delta L/L$ of oe, $(\Delta Y/Y)_L = oi$; at the higher $\Delta L/L$ of og, $(\Delta Y/Y)_L = oj$. As shown in the previous development of the neoclassical growth theory, what the increase in $\Delta Y/Y$, here designated as $(\Delta Y/Y)_L$, will be for an increase in $\Delta L/L$ (from oe to og in the illustration) depends on (MPP_L/Y).[24] Part C shows one possible relationship that is consistent with supply-side economics.

The Capital Formation Effect of a Tax Cut
Assuming as before in Part A a cut in T/Y

---

[24] See p. 445 where it is shown that on neoclassical assumptions

$$\frac{\Delta Y}{Y} = \left(\frac{MPP_K \cdot K}{Y}\right)\frac{\Delta K}{K} + \left(\frac{MPP_L \cdot L}{Y}\right)\frac{\Delta L}{L}$$

If $\Delta K/K$ is zero, then

$$\frac{\Delta Y}{Y} = \left(\frac{MPP_L \cdot L}{Y}\right)\frac{\Delta L}{L}$$

However, this is true only for small changes in $\Delta L/L$. With no increase in $\Delta K/K$, a large increase in $\Delta L/L$ will significantly raise the ratio of L to K, reduce MPP_L, and thereby reduce the $\Delta Y/Y$ attributable to $\Delta L/L$. However, the supply-side economists envision large changes in both $\Delta L/L$ and $\Delta K/K$ as a result of the tax revisions they propose. To the extent that these results follow and to the extent that $\Delta K/K$ and $\Delta L/L$ increase at approximately similar rates, the MPP_L will not fall as it otherwise would with an increase in $\Delta L/L$. That increase will, therefore, produce an increase in $(\Delta Y/Y)_L$.

from oa to ob and the resultant rise in Y_{at}/Y from oc to od and assuming now the relationship between S/Y and Y_{at}/Y indicated by the colored line in Part D, S/Y rises from om to op. Although a change in Y_{at}/Y will probably result in a change in S/Y in the same direction as shown, that result is not certain. The tax cut will tend to raise the saving ratio by raising the Y_{at}/Y ratio, but the tax cut may work in the other direction through its effect on variables other than Y_{at}/Y. We will touch on this later; here, accepting the supply-side position, we take the final effect of the tax cut on S/Y to be one like that shown by the colored line in Part D.

Presumably the same lower tax rates that result in a higher saving ratio in Part D, when combined with lower interest rates caused by the higher saving ratio, will generate an expansion of planned investment to absorb the expansion of saving. Assuming, as in neoclassical growth theory, that there is no Keynesian problem of investment demand deficiency, I/Y will match S/Y. Therefore, the appropriate line in Part E is the 45° line; at every point along this line, $I/Y = S/Y$. Accordingly, the rise in S/Y from om to op in Part D will result in an equal rise in I/Y from or to os in Part E. (We may insert demand-side problems into the system here by representing the relationship in Part E with a line of slope greater than 45°. For example, the center line in Part E shows $I/Y = 0.75 (S/Y)$ and the steepest line shows $I/Y = 0.50 (S/Y)$. However, we here take the assumption of the supply-side economists: A higher saving ratio, whatever its magnitude, is matched by a correspondingly higher investment ratio.)

As long as income is growing at all, a higher I/Y ratio means a larger increment than before to the capital stock per time period. Because the productivity of labor varies directly with the capital stock per worker, the larger the increment to the capital stock per time period, *ceteris paribus*, the greater the productivity of labor and the greater the growth of income per time period that is attributable to the growth of the capital stock. (This naturally assumes that the fraction of each period's increment to the capital stock that takes the form of antipollution, safety, and similar equipment does not grow larger.) The line in Part F shows one possible way that $(\Delta Y/Y)_K$ or the growth rate of income attributable to the capital stock may respond to a change in I/Y—a rise in $(\Delta Y/Y)_K$ from ou to ov is caused by a rise in I/Y from or to os.

The Work Effect and the Capital Formation Effect Combined

The effect of a tax cut on $\Delta Y/Y$ has now been traced through the work effect of the tax cut, shown in Part C, and through the capital formation effect of the tax cut, shown in Part F.[25] Part G is next introduced as a device to identify $\Delta Y/Y$. Each line in Part G indicates a particular value for $\Delta Y/Y$. Only a few of these lines are shown, but Part G is dense with such lines. Because $\Delta Y/Y = (\Delta Y/Y)_K + (\Delta Y/Y)_L$ on neoclassical assumptions,[26] the $\Delta Y/Y$ in Part G corresponding to any combination of $(\Delta Y/Y)_L$ in Part C and $(\Delta Y/Y)_K$ in Part F may be identified graphically as follows. Before the tax cut, $(\Delta Y/Y)_L$ was found to be oi in Part C and $(\Delta Y/Y)_K$ was found to be ou in Part F. A line drawn downward from oi and a line drawn leftward from ou intersect in Part

G on line ox and thereby identify $\Delta Y/Y$ as ox. After the tax cut, $(\Delta Y/Y)_L$ was found to be oj and $(\Delta Y/Y)_K$ to be ov; carried into Part G, this combination forms an intersection on line oz. Therefore, $\Delta Y/Y$ rises from ox before the tax cut to oz after the tax cut.

The final part of the system is Part H, in which the relationship between T/Y and $\Delta Y/Y$ is identified. It has been seen through Parts B, C, D, E, F and G that T/Y of oa and ob in Part A result in $\Delta Y/Y$ of ox and oz respectively in Part G. Because all relationships have been taken to be linear, carried over to Part H these two combinations identify two points from which the colored line in that part is obtained. With that line in place, $\Delta Y/Y$ may be identified for values of T/Y other than oa and ob.

If the final relationship is one like that shown by the solid colored line in Part H, then one conclusion of the supply-side economics is correct: A cut in tax rates will raise the growth rate of income through its effects on the supply-side of the economy. Although the present illustration has limited attention to the tax cut case only, the solid colored line in Part H also indicates that a rise in tax rates will lower the growth rate of income through its effects on the supply-side of the economy.

The specific relationship shown by the solid colored line in Part H is, of course, the product of the particular relationships portrayed in the other parts of the system. The critical issue is whether or not the actual relationships in these parts are such that in combination they will yield a curve in Part H that does in fact slope downward to the right. Supply-side economists apparently have no doubt that this will be the result; but critics contend that we have little or no theoretical or empirical basis for drawing any such conclusion. The curve may slope downward to the right, but it may also slope downward to the left. We turn next to the preconditions that must be met if the variables are to behave in a way that supports the particular conclusion of the supply-side economists considered here.

---

[25]Attention is here limited to these two effects of a tax cut. Omitted is the influence on the growth rate that will follow from the effect of a tax cut on the rate of technological advance. However, this omission does not appear to be a serious problem in the present context because it is in line with the emphasis of supply-side economists. In their view, labor input and capital formation are the principal avenues through which tax cuts will effect more rapid income growth.

[26]As shown in footnote 24,

$$\frac{\Delta Y}{Y} = \left(\frac{MPP_K}{Y}\right)\frac{\Delta K}{K} + \left(\frac{MPP_L}{Y}\right)\frac{\Delta L}{L}$$

Substituting $(\Delta Y/Y)_K$ for the first term on the right and $(\Delta Y/Y)_L$ for the second term on the right yields the expression used here:

$$\frac{\Delta Y}{Y} = \left(\frac{\Delta Y}{Y}\right)_K + \left(\frac{\Delta Y}{Y}\right)_L$$

Preconditions to the Conclusion of the Supply-Side Economics

Supply-side economists maintain that a cut in T/Y, by raising Y_{at}/Y, will increase labor supply and labor input as indicated by a movement upward along the colored line in Part B of Figure 20-3, and vice versa. In the case of a tax cut, they believe that the substitution effect of more labor and less leisure will more than offset the income effect of less labor and more leisure. However, theory does not predict the relative strengths of these two effects and therefore does not predict whether a tax cut or a tax increase will lead to more labor and less leisure or vice versa.[27] Supply-side economists are naturally well aware that the conventional theory does not provide an answer here, but they have restated the basic theory in a way that they believe supports their case.[28] However, most economists so far seem to hold to the traditional agnostic view on this question.

There appears to be much less uncertainty that a tax cut will increase the saving ratio for most people, but there are exceptions. The most familiar of these is that of people whose goal is the accumulation of a fixed savings total as of a certain future date. Because they will be able to achieve this goal by reducing the fraction of their after-tax income saved when that income is enlarged by a lower tax rate, inducing such people to raise their saving ratio requires an increase in tax rates.[29] People with such savings programs are almost surely a minority, but there are people who react to a tax cut by reducing their saving ratio.

As in the case of the uncertain effects of taxes on labor input, supply-side economists are well aware of the uncertain effects of taxes on the saving ratio. However, the likelihood of raising the saving ratio may be greatly improved by reliance on tax rates designed to achieve this specific goal.[30] A tax cut in the form of a tax exemption on the first \$1,000 of interest and dividends (in place of the 1981 exemption of \$200) will, according to some, raise the saving ratio. In the case of corporate saving, more rapid depreciation provisions will probably do the same. Although it may mean a tax structure that does not meet the "good" tax structure's requirement of an equitable distribution of the tax burden, the existing tax structure can be altered to raise the ratio of income devoted to private saving by individuals and businesses.

However, even with such changes, there is still no assurance that the saving ratio will rise. The immediate effect of the tax cuts will be a rise in the deficit (government dissaving), unless the revenue loss is offset by a reduction in government spending. Even if everything works out the way the supply-side economists envision, the rise in tax revenue generated by the growth of income that follows the tax cuts will only appear some time after the tax cuts. When we combine the negative change in government saving and

[27] For a review of the literature, theoretical and empirical, on the effect of taxation on the work–leisure choice, see G.F. Break, "The Incidence and Economic Effects of Taxation," in A. Blinder et al., *The Economics of Public Finance,* The Brookings Institution, 1974, pp. 181–91.

[28] See J. Wanniski, *The Way the World Works,* Simon and Shuster, 1978, for a short, clear statement. It is granted that a tax increase tends to make the *typical laborer* work harder (the income effect tends to outweigh the substitution effect), but the tax increase will cause certain *entrepreneurs* to work less hard. The tax increase will tip those firms that were on the margin of profitability below that margin, and the affected entrepreneurs will choose to close down their firms and shift into leisure. Therefore, despite the willingness of the many laborers employed by such firms to work harder to increase production, all of the production of such firms will be lost by the decision of the few entrepreneurs whose decisions are critical.

[29] This parallels the argument in Chapter 16 that a higher interest rate will result in a higher saving ratio. Because people with a fixed savings goal can reach that goal with a lower saving ratio at a higher rate of interest, inducing such people to raise their saving ratio requires a lower interest rate.

[30] For an analysis of the effects of various tax changes on total saving, see G.F. Break, "The Incidence and Economic Effects of Taxation," in A. Blinder, et al, *The Economics of Public Finance,* Brookings, 1974, pp. 191–203.

the positive change in private saving, the outcome is not so clearly a rise in the fraction of national income that goes into total saving (private plus public saving), which is what S/Y measures in Part D. Some part of the additional income left in people's pockets by a tax cut will unavoidably go into consumption spending; but every dollar of tax cut will, in the short run, add a dollar to the deficit as long as government spending is not reduced. It is, therefore, quite possible for the overall saving ratio to decline as a result of a tax cut. If that occurs, we find a relationship like that shown by the black line in Part D.

If there is a reduction in the tax ratio from oa to ob in Part A and if the work effort response in Part B and the saving ratio response in Part D are given by the black lines, $\Delta Y/Y$ in Part G will equal on and the relationship in Part H will be given by the solid black line. *What is then found in Part H is contrary to what is indicated by supply-side economics.*

Finally, the work effort response and the saving ratio response need not be in the same direction. If the work effort response were the positive one shown in Part B and the saving ratio response were the negative one shown in Part D, $\Delta Y/Y$ in Part G would be oq; for the opposite combination, $\Delta Y/Y$ in Part G would be oy. From these values and the reduction in the tax ratio in Part A are derived the two dashed lines in Part H, one consistent with the supply-side conclusion and the other not. Obviously, any number of other slopes for the relationship between a change in the tax ratio and the income growth rate may be derived in Part H by introducing different slopes for each of the relationships in the other parts of Figure 20-3.

The considerable uncertainty as to the slopes of the underlying relationships contributes to the wide disagreement and continuing debate on the issue of whether a tax cut will raise or lower the growth rate of real income through its effects *on the supply side.* At the one extreme are supply-side supporters like economist Arthur Laffer, Congressman Jack Kemp, and Jude Wanniski,

who foresee an explosion of work, saving, and investment as an almost certain response to the kind of tax cuts (thirty percent in three years) proposed in the Kemp–Roth Bill. At the other extreme are liberal economists like Walter Heller, whose perspective is demand-side or Keynesian. To him, tax cuts of the Kemp–Roth Bill magnitude would produce a tidal wave of increased demand that would overwhelm existing productive capacity and sweep away all hopes of containing inflation. Even some conservative economists like Herbert Stein lean in this direction.[31]

The answer to the question posed depends on a multitude of factors and their complex interrelationships. Figure 20-3 presents in a purely static framework the relationships among several of the major factors that must be considered. To the degree that we can draw meaningful conclusions on the basis of these few relationships, the figure provides a graphic exhibition of what the relationships must be to obtain the conclusion that a tax cut like that proposed by the Kemp–Roth Bill will raise the growth rate of real income through its effects on the supply side in the way argued by its supporters.

Estimates of the Sources of Economic Growth

So far in our discussion of the growth rate, only a few very general quantitative statements have been offered concerning the relative importance of the various factors that together determine the growth rate. On p. 449 we noted that, based on what seem to be reasonable assumptions, less than one-third of the growth rate of total output can be attributed to the growth rate of the labor and capital inputs, and that consequently over two-thirds of that growth rate must be attributed

---

[31]For a sampling of views on the Kemp–Roth Bill of the above individuals and others, see A.B. Laffer and J.P. Seymour, editors, *The Economics of the Tax Revolt,* Harcourt Brace Jovanovich, 1979, pp. 45–68.

to increased output per unit of labor and capital inputs, or to all the factors included under the catchall heading of technological advance. Although such a statement is informative as far as it goes, it obviously says nothing about the separate contributions of the labor and the capital inputs nor about whether the labor contribution was due merely to a larger number of people working, to better educated people working, or to still other characteristics of the labor force. It also puts the contribution of everything but the labor and capital inputs under the catchall heading of technological advance; it says nothing about the contributions of the individual factors that may be identified under this catchall heading.

We here look at some specific detailed estimates (prepared by Edward F. Denison) of the contributions of various sources to the economic growth rate.[32] Formidable conceptual and statis-

tical problems have been faced by those economists who have undertaken the preparation of estimates of this kind, but from these attempts to dissect the growth record of the past, come clues to what the growth record of the future may be. If we accept, for example, Denison's finding that for the four decades from 1929 to 1969 the expanded amount of labor accounted for more than one-third of the growth of output, the enlarged stock of capital for more than one-eighth, and increased output per unit of input or increased productivity for the remainder, estimates of the changes expected in these sources in the future will give us at least some idea of what to expect.

Denison's dissection of the growth rate for the U.S. economy has been the most ambitious of these various studies. Table 20-4 provides some summary data for the 1929–69 period and for the 1929–48 and 1948–69 periods into which the overall period has been divided. In the first set of three columns, we see that the growth rate of national income is 3.41 percent for the overall period, 2.75 percent for 1929–48, and 4.02 percent for 1948–69.[33] The column of figures for each of these three growth rates shows the estimated portion of each accounted for by each of a number of sources to which that growth rate can be attributed. In broad terms, of the 3.41 percent growth rate for 1929–69, 1.82 percentage points are accounted for by total factor input

[32]E.F. Denison, *Accounting for United States Economic Growth, 1929–1969,* Brookings Institution, 1974. In an earlier study, *The Sources of Economic Growth in the United States,* Supplementary Paper No. 13, Committee for Economic Development, 1962, Denison published a similar set of estimates for the United States for 1909–57. He also applied the viewpoint and methodology developed in the original study to the 1950–62 experience of the United States and eight western European countries in *Why Growth Rates Differ,* Brookings Institution, 1967. In both of the studies for the United States, he identifies a large number of sources of growth (nineteen in Table 20-4) and estimates the portion of the growth rate attributable to each. In earlier studies, other economists worked with only three or four, their major objective commonly being to identify the portion of growth due to changes in output per unit of input and the portion due to changes in the total amount of input. Among these studies are M. Abramovitz, *Resources and Output Trends in the United States since 1870,* National Bureau of Economic Research, 1959; F.C. Mills, *Productivity and Economic Progress,* Occasional Paper 38, National Bureau of Economic Research, 1952; J. Schmookler, "The Changing Efficiency of the American Economy, 1869–1938," in *Review of Economics and Statistics,* Aug. 1952, pp. 214–31; J.W. Kendrick, *Productivity Trends in the United States,* National Bureau of Economic Research, 1961; and R.M. Solow, "Technical Progress, Capital Formation, and Economic Growth," in *American Economic Review,* May 1962, pp. 76–86.

[33]The output measure here is national income rather than the more familiar GNP. Note also that national income is potential rather than actual. Based on actual national income, the growth rates for the indicated periods are 3.33, 2.75, and 3.85 percent respectively. A difference between the growth rate for actual national income and potential national income in any period reflects the fact that the first and last years of that period are not comparable in terms of business cycle phase or of short-term demand pressures. Although 1929, 1948, and 1969 are all peak years of business cycle expansions, demand pressure was nonetheless less strong in 1969 than in the other two years. Therefore, increases in actual output from 1929 to 1969 and from 1948 to 1969 were less than increases in potential output. To secure growth estimates unaffected by the short-term status of demand in the

and 1.59 percentage points by output per unit of input (or productivity). Of the 1.82 percentage points, 1.32 are accounted for by labor and 0.50 by capital. Further breakdowns are given for each of these input headings as well as for output per unit of input.

The breakdowns for the 1929–48 and 1948–69 periods reveal that capital and advances in knowledge are primarily responsible for the marked rise of 1.27 percentage points in the growth rate from 2.75 percent in 1929–48 to 4.02 percent in 1948–69. From the earlier to the later period, capital increased its contribution by 0.67 percentage points and advanced knowledge increased its contribution by 0.57 percentage points. Denison observes that the latter change is probably due largely to a faster rate of advances in knowledge relevant to production in the later period but that an end to the depression-induced restrictions against efficient practices also contributed to it. According to the figures, the 0.14 percentage point increase from 0.29 in 1929–48 to 0.43 in 1948–69 in the growth rate attributed to economies of scale makes this source next in importance in accounting for the rise in the growth rate between the two periods. The increase assigned to economies of scale was the consequence of the faster expansion of markets, but in turn the changes in the contribution of capital and advances in knowledge made the faster expansion possible.

The second set of three columns converts the first set into percentages of the growth rate (3.41 = 100) accounted for by each of the sources. This permits a direct comparison of the relative

importance of each of the sources in accounting for the growth rate in any period and of the relative importance of each of the sources in different periods. Accordingly, the first of these columns shows that for the 1929–69 period total factor input—increasing the quantity of labor and capital—was responsible for 53.4 percent of total growth and that productivity—getting more output per unit of input—was responsible for 46.6 percent. Of the inputs, labor was responsible for 38.7 percent of total growth and capital for only 14.7 percent. The 1929–48 and 1948–69 columns reveal major changes in the percentages. The percentage for capital was atypically small in 1929–48, a period during which it accounted for only 4.7 percent of total growth in comparison with 19.9 for 1948–69. The percentages accounted for by total factor input in 1929–48 and 1948–69 are similar, 54.5 and 52.5 percent respectively; but the unusually low percentage contribution for capital in the 1929–48 period gives an unusually high percentage contribution for labor in the same period.

The figures for the subheadings reveal that advances in knowledge—technological, managerial, and organizational—contributed a little more to the growth rate than the increase in the amount of work done by the labor force for the 1929–69 period and contributed substantially more for the 1948–69 period. A major part of the contribution made by labor is not measured by the amount of work done but by the education of the labor force. Using the sum of the percentages for employment and hours as the percentage for work done, for 1929–69 the percentage for work done is 25.5 or somewhat less than the percentage of 27.0 for advances in knowledge. If the same is done for the 1948–69 period alone, the 29.6 percentage attributed to advances in knowledge exceeds by far the 23.9 percent for employment and hours or work done. When Denison's estimates are classified in this way, advances in knowledge emerge as the most important source of growth.

However, if we view the contribution of labor not just in terms of the amount of work done by

beginning and terminal years of the periods chosen, Denison estimated potential national income for the years bounding the periods and calculated growth rates on the basis of these figures. It was pointed out in footnote 3 on p. 430 that growth rates of actual output for periods that start or end at different phases of the business cycle are not strictly comparable. We see here that one approach to this problem is to replace the figures for actual output with figures for potential output as Denison has done. See *Accounting for United States Economic Growth, 1929–1969*, pp. 9, 127–28.

TABLE 20-4
Allocation of Growth Rate of National Income among the Sources of Growth

	Percentage Points in Growth Rate			Percent of Growth Rate		
	1929–69	1929–48	1948–69	1929–69	1929–48	1948–69
National income	**3.41**	**2.75**	**4.02**	**100.0**	**100.0**	**100.0**
Total factor input	**1.82**	**1.50**	**2.11**	**53.4**	**54.5**	**52.5**
Labor	1.32	1.37	1.31	38.7	49.8	32.6
Employment	1.09	1.05	1.15	32.0	38.2	28.6
Hours	−0.22	−0.23	−0.19	− 6.5	− 8.4	4.7
Average hours	−0.49	−0.64	−0.34	−14.4	−23.3	− 8.5
Efficiency offset	0.19	0.33	0.06	5.6	12.0	1.5
Intergroup shift offset	0.08	0.08	0.09	2.3	2.9	2.2
Age-sex composition	−0.05	0.00	−0.10	− 1.5	0.0	− 2.5
Education	0.41	0.39	0.42	12.0	14.2	10.4
Unallocated	0.09	0.16	0.03	2.6	5.8	0.7
Capital	0.50	0.13	0.80	14.7	4.7	19.9
Inventories	0.09	0.05	0.12	2.6	1.8	3.0
Nonresidential structures and equipment	0.20	0.03	0.36	5.9	1.1	9.0
Dwellings	0.19	0.06	0.29	5.6	2.2	7.2
International assets	0.02	−0.01	0.03	0.6	− 0.4	0.7
Land	0.00	0.00	0.00	0.0	0.0	0.0
Output per unit of input	**1.59**	**1.25**	**1.91**	**46.6**	**45.5**	**47.5**
Advances in knowledge and n.e.c.[a]	0.92	0.62	1.19	27.0	22.5	29.6
Improved resource allocation	0.30	0.31	0.31	8.8	11.3	7.7
Farm	0.26	0.28	0.24	7.6	10.2	6.0
Nonfarm self-employment	0.04	0.03	0.07	1.2	1.1	1.7
Dwellings occupancy ratio	0.01	0.02	−0.01	0.3	0.7	− 0.2
Economies of scale	0.36	0.29	0.43	10.6	10.5	10.7
Irregular factors	0.00	0.01	−0.01	0.0	0.4	− 0.2
Weather in farming	0.00	0.01	−0.01	0.0	0.4	− 0.2
Labor disputes	0.00	0.00	0.00	0.0	0.0	0.0

[a] n.e.c. Not elsewhere classified.

SOURCE: E.F. Denison, *Accounting for United States Economic Growth, 1929–1969*, Brookings Institution, 1974, pp. 127–28.

employed people but also allow for education of employed people, the contribution of labor becomes that shown in the table under the heading "labor." It emerges as the most important source of growth in all three periods, especially in the 1929–48 period, during which it accounts for almost one-half of the growth rate. From this view, advances in knowledge then take second place. Third in importance for the 1929–69 and the 1948–69 periods is the growth in the country's capital stock. Fourth comes economies of scale, which largely reflect the expansion of markets. Next is improved resource allocation, which for the most part is the correction of the misallocation of labor to farming and to small and inefficient family enterprises in the nonfarm sector. Because the other sources are of negligible importance, we may conclude that the five sources listed account for practically all of the growth of the U.S. economy over the forty-year period, according to the estimates made by Denison.

Although Denison has provided the most detailed allocation of the growth rate of the U.S. economy among its various subsources, his basic conclusion on the initial allocation between total factor input and output per unit of input is in line with that reached in other, earlier studies. However output per unit of input may be allocated into the parts attributable to advance of knowledge, economies of scale, and other subsources, the output per unit of input in itself accounts for nearly half of the growth rate. Although different studies assign a somewhat different importance to increases in productivity, they all conclude that, in the words of Moses Abramovitz, "to explain a very large part of the growth of total output and the great bulk of output *per capita,* we must explain the increase in output per unit of conventionally measured inputs. . . ."[34]

The Growth Rate and Environmental Quality

From the late 1950s through the mid-1960s, no economic issue received more attention than the country's growth rate. The relatively slow rate during the Eisenhower years was not infrequently described as a national disaster. A major goal of the Kennedy administration was to "get the country moving again." As shown by the annual growth rate of 4.3 percent for the 1960–69 period in Table 20-1, there was success in this direction. But at the same time that this success was achieved, doubt began to arise as to whether this was indeed a success in a more complete sense of that word. By the late 1960s there was serious questioning of a proposition that had long been practically taken for granted—that the national well-being is enhanced by an increase in the rate of output of the goods and services designed to satisfy the needs of ultimate consumers currently and in the future. By then economists were asking whether or not there is a "tradeoff" between the rate at which we expand the output of goods and services and the rate at which the quality of the environment deteriorates. A more rapid rate of growth means more goods and services, but it also means more air, water, land, and noise pollution and environmental damage. With the awakening to the seriousness of the pollution problem in the late 1960s, economic growth, which had long been generally viewed as an unmixed blessing, came to be viewed by the more extreme environmentalists as an unmixed evil.[35]

---

[34]M. Abramovitz, "Economic Growth in the United States," *American Economic Review,* Sept. 1962, p. 776.

[35]In order to evaluate the cost of economic growth in terms of environmental damage, it is necessary to some-
how define each of the concepts in quantitative dimensions that permit an analysis of their relationship. Defining economic growth is relatively easy compared with defining environmental deterioration. First, the latter concept is in itself much more elusive than that of economic growth, and, second, the problem of evaluating those changes in the ecosystem that involve environmental deterioration in a way that can be related, quantitatively if possible, to the process of economic growth is extremely difficult.

Of course, pollution did not suddenly appear in the late 1960s. Pollution problems were reported in London as early as 1285 as a result of the burning of soft coal. What did appear for the first time in the late 1960s was the widespread awareness of the fact that pollution had reached such proportions that, if allowed to grow completely unchecked, it could destroy civilization within only a few more generations. Accompanying real GNP (valued in 1972 dollars) of $534.8 billion in 1950 was a level of pollution that was apparently close to the assimilative capacity of the natural environment and therefore caused no great concern. However, eighteen years later, in 1968, real GNP had doubled to $1,058.1 billion and with it probably came a more than proportional increase in the amount of lead, mercury and other poisons deposited annually in the air and water. A growth rate of 3 percent will produce another doubling of real GNP by 1992. Because we have already passed the tolerable levels for certain kinds of pollution, the prospect of a doubling of 1968 levels understandably strikes fear into almost everyone. It is easy to understand the opposition to growth voiced by those who believe there is inevitably a close relation between the rate of growth of GNP and the rate of decay of the environment.[36]

---

[36]That there is such a close relation was the belief of the membership of the Club of Rome which sponsored the research set forth in the widely publicized bombshell of a book, *The Limits to Growth*, Universe Books, 1972, by D.H. Meadows, D.L. Meadows, et al. The authors constructed an elaborate computer model of the world that involves five basic quantities: capital stock, population, food production, nonrenewable resources, and pollution. Among the relationships in the model are complex "feedback loops" that register the effects of changes in one variable such as food production on another such as birth rates. Into the model went past data on such things as rates of growth of population, industrial output, and agricultural yields, and estimates of rates of technological advance that would allow the use of new resources, raise agricultural productivity, and control pollution. The primary conclusion that the authors reach is that unchecked growth can have only one outcome: a rather sudden and uncontrollable collapse in both population and industrial

Whether or not growth is indeed at the heart of the problem is an issue we will turn to in a moment. However, even if it is, it should be seen that a cessation of growth will not provide a solution to the problem. To drop all the way down to a zero rate of economic growth would not stop the deterioration of the environment; it would only slow the rate at which it deteriorates. A zero rate of growth means an unchanged total of goods and services produced each year. To the degree that the amount of pollution depends on the amount of output, the amount of pollutants

---

capacity some time before the year 2100. No matter which way one turns, the conclusion is always the same: collapse from shortage of food, from exhaustion of resources, or from pollution. The only possible escape is to stop the rate of growth of output and of population within the next fifteen years and achieve what is called a "global equilibrium" with zero growth. But with the likelihood that this will happen not being very great, what seems to await mankind in the next century is doomsday. The basis on which this apocalyptic vision was reached was subjected to a well-deserved barrage of criticism from prominent economists and ecologists. None of the critics denies the seriousness of the problem, but they disagree with the forecast of almost inevitable disaster. Whatever the scientific shortcomings of *The Limits to Growth,* the study had a great impact when it appeared and provided a scientific basis of sorts for an increase in the antigrowth sentiment that had already been rapidly developing over the preceding several years. However, this antigrowth sentiment has probably weakened over the years since the appearance of *The Limits to Growth.*

The Second Report to the Club of Rome, a volume by M. Mesarovic and E. Pestel entitled *Mankind at the Turning Point,* E.P. Dutton, 1974, did not conclude, as did the first report, that collapse was inevitable unless growth was stopped. With the second report, the Club of Rome modified its view and declared that it could find some hope in the future and spoke optimistically of an organic growth that takes prudent account of environmental and other dangers.

The Global 2000 Report to the President by the U.S. Council on Environmental Quality and other government agencies published in the summer of 1980 was pessimistic, but not to the extent of the First Report of the Club of Rome. This report resulted from a three-year study requested by President Carter in 1977, and was the first attempt by any government to make long-term projections on population, food production, energy, endangered species, forests, farmlands, water supply, and the like.

dumped into the system will be no larger next year than this year. However, preventing an ever larger amount of damage from being inflicted on the environment year after year is obviously not the same as protecting the environment from all damage. The problem remains: If a positive rate will lead to doom, a zero rate will do the same but on a slower timetable.

Moreover, even if a cessation of economic growth would mean a cessation of environmental deterioration, it is unlikely that the problem could be solved in this way. Because it is a world problem, it would do little good to stop growth in the United States and other affluent countries if it continued unrestrained in the less affluent countries. Because the people of some poor countries see in economic growth the only possibility of rising out of poverty, it is fanciful to believe that their governments would voluntarily adopt a no-growth policy. The very suggestion of such a policy would be interpreted by them as a conspiracy by the affluent countries to lock them into perpetual poverty. To try to meet this problem through a redistribution of wealth is another unworkable solution. Redistribution on the scale required both within and between countries could not occur without force, which would mean revolutions and wars.

If the preceding is essentially correct—that a zero-growth policy in itself will not stop the deterioration of the environment but only put it on a slower timetable and that, in any event, a zero-growth, world-wide policy could not be implemented in a world of nations that differ so widely in wealth—the answer to the problem of the deterioration of the environment is not to be found in stopping economic growth. However, if continuing growth means continuing environmental decay, there would seem to be no escape from eventual disaster. This, at least, would be the inevitable result if economic growth over the years ahead were of the same kind as that over the years since World War II. On the other hand, if it is possible to change the composition of the growing output and the technology employed to produce that output, growth in the future may do

more to slow the deterioration in the environment than a situation of no growth could, assuming that the latter could be realized in practice. It may even be possible that, within limits, the more rapid the rate of growth, the better the job that can be done to slow the deterioration of the environment. If pushed to this extreme, this argument stands the argument of the zero-growth proponents on its head.

It is generally conceded that the know-how exists to provide procedures and produce systems capable of greatly reducing most kinds of pollution.[37] The particular way or ways in which the reallocation of resources needed to provide the required pollution-control facilities may be brought about is another of the many difficult questions faced in this area. Perhaps even more basic is the question of whether or not it can be brought about in a capitalistic system in which the profit incentive is so important in deciding what shall and what shall not be produced. However, assuming for the moment that society can

[37] In the case of pollutants emitted into the air, the ones of central concern are carbon monoxide, hydrocarbons, sulfur dioxide, oxides of nitrogen, and particulates. In the United States, the greatest tonnage of these pollutants comes from the transportation sector, and almost all of this from the internal combustion engine. Some of these may be reduced by engine changes to achieve more complete combustion of fuel; others, like oxides of nitrogen, that are not a result of incomplete combustion, may be controlled by the installation of catalytic afterburners, which add substantially to the complexity and cost of engines. Another possibility is a changeover to the Wankel engine. Beyond this is the complete abandonment of the internal combustion engine in favor of steam or electric engines if and when either of the latter is made practical. Still another alternative is greater reliance on mass transit. Control of airborne residuals from stationary sources (utility power, industry, and households) involves approaches such as (a) fuel preparation, for example, removal of sulfur-bearing pyrites from coal before burning; (b) redesign of burners to reduce oxides of nitrogen; and (c) treatment of stack gases, for example, scrubbing with water, to remove sulfur and particulates. See A.V. Kneese, "Background for the Economic Analysis of Environmental Pollution," in *Swedish Journal of Economics,* March 1971, pp. 1–24, reprinted in P. Bohm and A.V. Kneese, eds., *The Economics of Environment,* Macmillan, 1971.

effect a shift in the composition of output such that a substantially larger portion of total output is made up of investment in antipollution devices and facilities of various kinds, a large step would have been taken in the right direction. Systems would be acquired for recycling, which reduces pollution by channeling wastes of the production and consumption processes back into these processes. Also, systems would be acquired to augment the natural environment's assimilative capacity through such means as stream aeration and chemical waste treatment.[38]

An idea of the magnitude of the required investment in facilities and the costs of operating them is provided by the following estimates of the Council on Environmental Quality. To meet the standards established by federal environmental legislation, the estimated amounts (in billions of 1978 dollars) for both operation and maintenance costs and capital costs for the decade 1978–87 are as follows: air pollution, $305.7; water pollution, $281.7; solid waste, $93.3; drinking water, $12.5; noise, $6.6; and other, $10.7; for a total of $710.7 for the decade.[39]

Devotion of more of the nation's resources to producing output whose sole purpose is to control the amount of pollution generated by the production and use of other output can be effected more easily under conditions of a positive growth rate. Although there will be virtually universal agreement that there must be greater investment in output devoted to the control of pollution, there will be far less agreement on how the real cost of this control shall be apportioned among various sectors of society. This is why some economists argue that a growth rate well above zero is, at least in this regard, preferable to one closer to zero. With a higher growth rate, the amount of other goods that must be given up is less, and therefore it will be easier to smoothly effect the necessary shift in the composition of output.

Although a sizable shift of this kind in the composition of output is essential to meet the problem of environmental deterioration, it is not the only shift required. The composition of output should also be altered to move us back toward the way things were in the pre-World War II economy. A major factor in explaining the environmental damage over the years since World War II has been the change in the composition of output from natural to synthetic products (soaps to detergents, paper to plastic), of power-conservative products to relatively power-consumptive products (railroads to automobiles), and of reusable to "disposable" containers. These and other changes of this kind have been part of the postwar technological transformation of the economy. According to the prominent ecologist, Barry Commoner, in most of these changes that have been part of our economic growth since 1946, the new technology has an appreciably greater damaging impact on the environment than the technology it displaced.[40] On the basis of his studies, he concludes that the postwar technological transformation of productive activities is the chief reason for the present environmental crisis.[41]

---

[38]Of course, the production of the aluminum, copper, steel, asbestos, and beryllium components for things like air pollution control systems and sewage plants contributes to the problem it seeks to solve. The pollution contributed by the production and operation of huge amounts of pollution control systems may thus be substantial, but still it will be only a fraction of the amount of the present pollution that it eliminates.

[39]Figures are from Table 12-5, p. 667 of *Environmental Quality—The Tenth Annual Report of the Council on Environmental Quality,* 1980.

[40]See B. Commoner, "The Environmental Costs of Economic Growth," in R. Dorfman and N.S. Dorfman, eds., *Economics of the Environment,* 2nd ed., Norton, 1977, pp. 331–53. The discussion here closely follows this article.

[41]Although the change in the product is plainly seen in a case like the change in the automobile, the technological change does not in all cases involve an appreciable change in the product itself. This is especially true in agriculture. For example, the beef from a range-fed steer is not readily distinguishable from beef from a feedlot steer. However, range-fed cattle are integrated into the soil ecosystem and produce almost zero environmental damage, whereas cattle maintained in feedlots have a considerable damaging effect.

The argument that productive activities with a large damaging effect on the environment have displaced those with much less serious damaging effect does not imply that technology is by its very nature detrimental to the environment. It does not mean that the advantages that accompany technology must be sacrificed. What must be done is to develop new technologies that incorporate ecological wisdom as well as scientific prowess. This calls for restructuring many of the technological transformations that have occurred since 1946 in order to bring the nation's technology into balance with the undeniable demands of the ecosystem. In Professor Commoner's words:

> This will require the development of massive new technologies, including systems to return sewage and garbage directly to the soil; the replacement of synthetic materials by natural ones; the reversal of the present trend to retire soil from agriculture and to elevate the yield per acre; the development of land transport that operates with maximal fuel efficiency at low combustion temperatures; the sharp curtailment of the use of biologically active synthetic organic agents. In effect, what is required is a new period of technological transformations of the economy which will reverse the counter-ecological trends developed since 1946.[42]

The cost of this new technological transformation will run into hundreds of billions of dollars. If this transformation is undertaken, as it must be if the environment is to be saved, it will obviously have far-reaching effects on the economy. Unlike the technological transformation that occurred during the quarter century following World War II, this new one will not be undertaken in response to the profit motive. Large parts of it will occur only because it is forced through governmental regulations. It will unquestionably increase the cost of many goods and probably price some completely out of the market. Although it will

---

[42]B. Commoner, "The Environmental Costs of Economic Growth," in R. Dorfman and N.S. Dorfman, eds., *Economics of the Environment,* 2nd ed., Norton, 1977, p. 353.

bring handsome profits to those firms that win out in the competition to produce the most effective antipollution systems, it may result in shrinking profit margins in much of the rest of the business sector. This in turn could lead to a slowing of the traditional kinds of investment spending and introduce an era in which the growth rate is much slower than it was during the quarter century following World War II. It is possible that in this way a movement toward the objective of the no-growth proponents will occur automatically. Still, for reasons discussed earlier, it is to be hoped that such a movement, if it does occur, does not carry the growth rate close to zero. There is a much better chance of solving the many problems involved in carrying out a very costly full-scale technological transformation under conditions of economic growth than without growth. It appears that economic growth, which has long been recognized as a major objective of every economy, does not cease to be such an objective because of the pollution problem. Economic growth and improvement in environmental quality are not only not necessarily inconsistent but may be mutually reinforcing.

A Concluding Note

Among the various subject areas of macroeconomics, economic growth is probably beset with more unanswered questions than any other. The primary purpose of this chapter has been the presentation of two formal theories of economic growth, but neither of these theories (nor any other) is universally accepted. Furthermore, beyond the theories, our empirical knowledge of the sources of growth remains painfully inadequate, despite the impressive work of Denison and others who, it may be noted, reach conclusions somewhat different from Denison's. Even with regard to so basic a question as whether or not growth is desirable, there is no clearcut answer. A number of highly respected economists conclude that a positive rate of growth necessitates a sacrifice of well-being for a nation's people. At the same time, many others, equally respected, devote their energies to devising ways to achieve a more rapid rate of growth.

Beyond the differing views of the antigrowth and progrowth camps, yet another view is that we are perhaps getting to the point where we do not actually have a choice between those two points of view. It is argued that other forces have come into play that have taken the decision out of our hands and resolved it in favor of the antigrowth side. The soaring price of energy since the early 1970s, which is not exclusively OPEC's doing, has reminded us of the fact that supplies of oil and other natural resources are limited in quantity. Unless technological breakthroughs not now visualized can be made, growth rates of the future may simply not be able to match those of the past.

It is interesting to note that neoclassical growth theory makes growth a function of technological advance, the supply of capital, and the supply of labor—but not of the supply of natural resources, which are treated like a free good or something available to society in unlimited quantity. In a similar way, in Denison's allocation of the growth rate among factor inputs, part of the total rate is credited to labor, part is credited to capital, but none is credited to land. This procedure may be appropriate so far, but the constraint of natural resources may have to be taken into account before long. In growth theory, an equal percentage increase in the labor and capital inputs may no longer be expected to result in a proportional increase in output, unless technological advances are of a kind and occur at a rate to offset the influence of the limited supplies of natural resources. If technological progress does not provide the offset, the unpleasant prospect is that output per capita may decline over time. But technological progress may be such as to enable us not only to prevent this outcome but to make possible the continuation of a rising output per capita. This is surely one of the biggest questions in the area of economic growth; we can know the answer only with the passage of time.

Inflation: Definition, Measures, and Effects

OVERVIEW

Of the many questions that may be asked on the subject of inflation, perhaps of first importance to economists is that of causation. For to understand the cause of something is ordinarily a prerequisite to taking appropriate action to control it, and inflation is assuredly something that we want to control. The following two chapters are devoted in large part to this question of causation. In this chapter, we introduce the topic with discussions of the definition of inflation, measures of inflation, and the effects of inflation.

The first part of this chapter examines some of the problems economists face in defining inflation. Because of these problems, we almost unavoidably end up with a somewhat vague definition: Inflation is a persistent and appreciable rise in the general level of prices. This is the definition with which we will work.

The second part of the chapter takes up measures of inflation: the Consumer Price Index (CPI), the Producer Price Index (PPI) (formerly called the Wholesale Price Index), and the GNP Implicit Price Deflator. Recently, a fourth measure—the Personal Consumption Expenditures Implicit Price Deflator or the PCE Deflator—has gained popularity as an alternative to the CPI. The nature of each of these indexes is noted and the record of price increase that each shows for the period from 1950 to 1980 is presented. The man on the street is obviously interested primarily in what is happening to the prices of the goods and services he buys or to his "cost of living." The last pages of this second part of the chapter consider the question of whether the CPI or the PCE Deflator is a better measure of this.

The final part of the chapter deals with the economic effects of inflation. In any list of the evils of inflation, the arbitrary way in which inflation redistributes income and wealth among different income classes comes first. If inflation had no such effect, there would be much less reason to be as concerned with it. To study this effect, two definitions of income are first introduced—a narrow definition that limits income to the sum of wages and salaries, interest, dividends, transfer payments, and other such flows; and a broader definition that includes the sum of these flows as well as changes in wealth or net worth. To clarify the meaning of redistribution, illustrations are provided of the way in which inflation causes a redistribution of income. With the mechanics of the process in place, we then turn to some empirical evidence of the impact of inflation on households at different income levels. Do high income households gain and low income households lose as a result of inflation or vice versa? According to a study reviewed here, the redistribution with income

narrowly defined is quite different from the redistribution with income broadly defined.

The effects of inflation are not limited to the income redistribution it causes. The chapter concludes with a look at inflation's impact on output, employment, and the growth rate. We discuss here whether, in an economy operating below potential, inflation will raise next year's output closer to potential than this year's. We also consider the long-run effect of inflation on the accumulation of wealth and the potential growth rate of output.

If we were to discuss subjects in order of their importance, inflation would deserve a position in the first rather than the last part of a book on macroeconomics written during the 1980s. However, a prerequisite to any study of the process and causes of inflation is an analytical framework within which such a study may be undertaken. It was not until the development of the extended model in Part 3 of this book that such a framework became available to us.

Although the term "inflation" appeared a few times in earlier chapters, we basically ignored it as a phenomenon in itself. In this and the following two chapters, we turn specifically to the phenomenon of inflation.

Definition of Inflation

The obvious definition of inflation is that inflation is a rising price level, the price level being a figure that changes as the outlay needed to purchase an assortment of specific quantities of different goods changes. However, this familiar definition of inflation is far from unambiguous. For one thing, there is the question of how rapid the rise in the price level must be to qualify as infla-

tion. If we measure the rate of inflation by the GNP implicit price deflator, the third index in Table 21-1, does the approximately 1.5 percent average annual rate of price increase over the years from 1958 to 1964 qualify as inflation? (The year-to-year rate varied from 0.9 to 2.2 over this period.) Or must the rate be something greater than this to qualify as inflation? Some people who regard inflation as an economic evil believe that a price level rising at a rate of around 1.5 percent is so gradual that it assists in achieving and maintaining full employment and a satisfactory rate of economic growth. Such people would apply the term "inflation" only to what they regard as an "unhealthy" or "excessive" rise in the price level. Other people agree that inflation is an economic evil, but they go further and label any rise in the price level as inflation, even the rise during the 1958–64 period, slow as it was.

Unless we adopt this latter viewpoint and describe any rise in the price level as inflation, we are forced to admit the possibility of a noninflationary rise in the price level. If we accept this, it then appears that there is some rise in the price level per period at which a price movement becomes inflationary. The problem is to determine how rapid the rise must be. Many writers tend to fall back on words such as "appreciable,"

TABLE 21-1
Consumer Price Index, Producer Price Index, GNP Implicit Price Deflator, and Personal Consumption Expenditures Implicit Price Deflator, and Percent Change in Each for Selected Years, 1929–80

Year	Consumer Price Index 1967 = 100	Percent Change	Producer Price Index 1967 = 100	Percent Change	GNP Implicit Price Deflator 1972 = 100	Percent Change	Personal Consumption Expenditures Implicit Price Deflator 1972 = 100	Percent Change
1929	51.3		49.1		32.8		35.9	
1933	38.8	−5.6	34.0	−6.9	25.1	−5.4	26.9	−5.7
1940	42.0	1.1	40.5	2.5	29.1	2.1	30.9	2.0
1945	53.9	5.1	54.6	6.1	37.9	5.4	44.1	7.3
1948	72.1	10.2	82.8	14.9	53.0	11.8	56.0	8.2
1950	72.1	0.0	81.8	−0.5	53.6	0.6	56.9	0.8
1951	77.8	7.9	91.1	11.4	57.1	6.5	60.6	6.5
1952	79.5	2.2	88.6	−2.7	57.9	1.4	62.0	2.3
1953	80.1	0.8	87.4	−1.4	58.8	1.6	63.2	1.9
1954	80.5	0.5	87.6	0.2	59.6	1.4	63.7	0.8
1955	80.2	−0.4	87.8	0.2	60.9	2.2	64.4	1.1
1956	81.4	1.5	90.7	3.3	62.8	3.1	65.6	1.9
1957	84.3	3.6	93.3	2.9	64.9	3.3	67.8	3.3
1958	86.6	2.7	94.6	1.4	66.0	1.7	69.2	2.1
1959	87.3	0.8	94.8	0.2	67.6	2.4	70.6	2.0
1960	88.7	1.6	94.9	0.1	68.7	1.6	71.9	1.8
1961	89.6	1.0	94.5	−0.4	69.3	0.8	72.6	1.0
1962	90.6	1.1	94.8	0.3	70.6	1.9	73.7	1.5
1963	91.7	1.2	94.5	−0.3	71.7	1.6	74.8	1.5
1964	92.9	1.3	94.7	0.2	72.8	1.5	75.9	1.5
1965	94.5	1.7	96.6	2.0	74.4	2.2	77.2	1.7
1966	97.2	2.6	99.8	3.3	76.8	3.2	79.4	2.8
1967	100.0	2.9	100.0	0.2	79.1	3.0	81.4	2.5
1968	104.2	4.2	102.5	2.5	82.5	4.3	84.6	3.9
1969	109.8	5.4	106.5	3.9	86.8	5.2	88.4	4.5
1970	116.3	5.9	110.4	3.7	91.4	5.3	92.5	4.6
1971	121.3	4.3	113.9	3.2	96.0	5.0	96.5	4.3
1972	125.3	3.3	119.1	4.6	100.0	4.2	100.0	3.6
1973	133.1	6.2	134.7	13.1	105.7	5.7	105.7	5.7
1974	147.7	11.0	160.1	18.9	114.9	8.7	116.3	10.0
1975	161.2	9.1	174.1	9.2	125.6	9.3	125.2	7.7
1976	170.5	5.8	182.9	5.1	132.1	5.2	131.6	5.1
1977	181.5	6.5	194.2	6.2	139.8	5.8	139.5	6.0
1978	195.4	7.7	209.3	7.8	150.0	7.3	149.1	6.9
1979	217.4	11.3	235.6	12.6	162.8	8.5	162.3	8.9
1980	246.8	13.5	268.6	14.0	177.4	9.0	178.9	10.2

Note: Percent change is the average annual rate of change from the previous year. Consumer price index data for 1978–80 are for all urban consumers; earlier data are for urban wage earners and clerical workers.

SOURCE: *Economic Report of the President*, Jan. 1981, *Survey of Current Business*, U.S. Department of Commerce, and *Monthly Labor Review*, U.S. Department of Labor.

"considerable," or "sizable," and some such question-begging is unavoidable. The only alternative is to resort to some fixed percentage rate, but the arbitrariness of any such figure would be worse than the ambiguous adjectives.

Still, unless we resort to some fixed percentage rate, the matter is complicated further by the fact that the rate we view as the minimum needed to qualify as inflation has a tendency to rise over the years. We resist this tendency, but after suffering through so many years with prices rising at near or actual "double digit" rates, we tend to say that a return to a 3 or 4 percent price advance would be a return to a practically inflation-free period. It would surely be a great improvement, but it just as surely would not be inflation-free. To accept such a notion is to equate a sufficient slowdown in the rate of price advance with a cessation of inflation, and thereby possibly in the future to not even count a "double digit" rate of price advance as deserving of the title of inflation.

We encounter another definitional problem when we consider the time dimension. A 2 percent rise in the GNP deflator over any one quarter would, if sustained, amount to more than an 8 percent rise over a full year. An 8 percent rise in a year would be regarded by almost everyone as an appreciable and therefore inflationary rise in the price level. But suppose the 2 percent rise in one quarter were to reverse itself in the following quarter. Shall we describe the first quarter as a period of inflation? Or must an upward price movement be not only appreciable but prolonged in order to qualify as an inflationary price movement? If so, we must again fall back on question-begging qualifications such as "continuing," "persistent," or "sustained" rises in the price level. The only alternative is to resort to some fixed calendar period, but the arbitrariness of the selection of any such period would be worse than the adjectives.

In short, as long as we define inflation in terms of price level changes, no fully satisfactory definition is available. However, this problem is not too serious. What matters is not how fast and how long the price level must rise before the rise is called inflationary, but what causes the price level to rise in the first place and what are the consequences of different rates of price level change for the distribution of income, the level of output and employment, the growth rate, and other critical variables used to measure the economy's performance. Recognizing the ambiguities of our terminology, we will define inflation simply as a persistent and appreciable rise in the general level of prices.[1]

Measures of Inflation

Even if we agree on the minimum rate at which the price level must rise and the minimum period over which that rise must continue in order for that rise to be called inflation, what is inflation according to one measure may not be inflation according to another measure for some periods of time. A month is far too short a period on which to base any conclusion, but the month of July 1980 is interesting as an extreme example of the differences that can appear in different measures of price change. Due to a special development, the consumer price index (CPI) showed a zero percent change for that one month, whereas the producer price index (PPI) soared at an annual rate of over 17 percent. Relatively large month-to-month differences among measures are not unusual, but appreciable differences also appear among different measures

---

[1]At least one of a number of other developments may be called inflation but are not covered by our definition. If an almost surely otherwise persistent and appreciable rise in the general price level is prevented during wartime by price controls and rationing, the underlying inflation is described as "suppressed" or "repressed." Although all may agree that there is some amount of suppressed or repressed inflation in such a period, the extent of such inflation is no more measurable than anything else that is not observable. The conventional definition adopted here is limited to observable and so to measurable changes in prices.

over a period of years (the kind of time period more relevant to the present question). For example, as shown in Table 21-1, there was no inflation at all over the 1958–64 period according to the PPI, but there was what some would call a very mild or "creeping" inflation according to the CPI.

Once we get beyond 1964, there is no longer any ambiguity among the measures as to whether or not there is inflation. All four measures shown in Table 21-1 agree on this. This is more easily seen in Figure 21-1, which shows the average annual rate of price change for each of the four

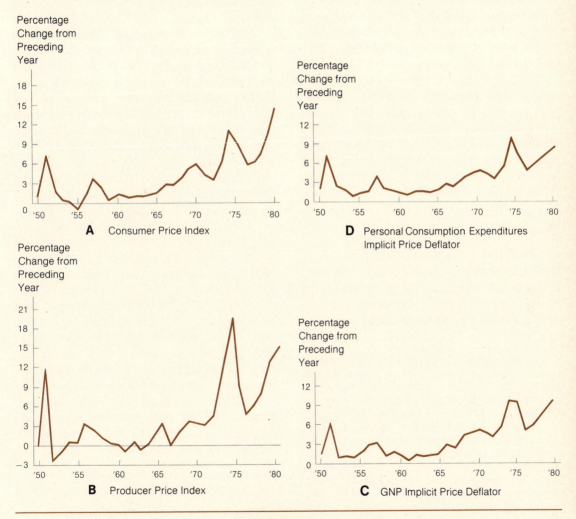

FIGURE 21-1
Annual Rate of Change of Consumer Price Index, Producer Price Index, GNP Implicit Price Deflator, and Personal Consumption Expenditures Implicit Price Deflator, 1950–1980

measures in Table 21-1 for the thirty years from 1950 to 1980. The measures not only unambiguously agree that we have been faced with inflation since the mid-1960s, but they also agree that the rate has clearly accelerated since that time. As compared with the fifteen year period from 1950 to 1965, which shows the rate of price change fluctuating for the most part between 0 and 3 percent (the 1951 Korean war experience is the notable exception), the fifteen years since 1965 show a definite uptrend in the inflation rate, no matter which of the four parts of Figure 21-1 we examine.

Because discussions of inflation run in terms of the different measures in Table 21-1 and Figure 21-1, we note the basic features of these four measures and then turn to the question of how rapidly consumer prices in particular have risen.[2] Two of the four measures shown are indexes of consumer prices, but in recent years they have shown markedly different rates of price increase.

Four Measures of Inflation

The Consumer Price Index (CPI)   This index is designed to reflect changes in the prices of a "market basket" of about 400 goods and services purchased by all urban consumers.[3] The

---

[2]Detailed descriptions of the different price indexes are provided in the *Handbook of Methods,* Bureau of Labor Statistics, U.S. Department of Labor, and in the biennial edition of *Business Statistics,* U.S. Department of Commerce. See also *The Consumer Price Index: Concepts and Content Over the Years,* Report 517, revised ed., Bureau of Labor Statistics, U.S. Department of Labor, 1978; *The Revision of the Consumer Price Index* by W.J. Layng, reprinted from the *Statistical Reporter,* Feb. 1978, No. 78-5, U.S. Department of Commerce; J.F. Early, "Improving the Measure of Producer Price Change," *Monthly Labor Review,* April 1978, pp. 7–15; and J.F. Early, "The PPI Revision: Overview and Pilot Survey Results," *Monthly Labor Review,* Dec. 1979, pp. 11–19.

[3]The consumer price index with this broad coverage was first published in 1978. Before 1978, the coverage of the index was limited to urban wage earners and clerical

basic data are collected from over 50,000 stores and other reporters located in 85 cities in all parts of the United States. A single index is calculated for all the goods and services in the basket as well as separate indexes for groups of items like food, housing, apparel and upkeep, and transportation. In addition to an index for the country as a whole, the data for different cities permits the preparation of price indexes for certain large cities.

Each of the goods and services in the basket is weighted according to its importance in consumers' budgets in 1972–73. Because some new items enter and old items leave consumers' budgets and because other items become more or less important over time, it is necessary to periodically update the market basket. To obtain the data for this purpose, a Consumer Expenditures Survey is carried out about every ten years by the Bureau of Labor Statistics. At present, the items included and the weights assigned to each item reflect consumers' spending patterns during 1972–73 when the last survey was conducted. Accordingly, the index number for 1980 which averaged 246.8 reveals that the cost in 1980 of purchasing the fixed collection of goods and services in the 1972–73 market basket was 246.8 percent of the cost of purchasing that same collection of goods and services in 1967, currently the base year for the index (1967 = 100). Otherwise expressed, this index number indicates that the cost of this collection of goods and services increased 146.8 percent from 1967 to 1980. The index number for 1972 was 125.3; therefore, the cost of purchasing this same collection increased by 97.0 percent or almost doubled from 1972 to 1980.

The Producer Price Index—PPI   The second price index in Table 21-1, the producer price

---

workers. The new index extends coverage to about 80 percent of the total noninstitutional population from the approximately 45 percent of the total covered by the other index. The Bureau of Labor Statistics, which prepares this index, continues to publish both versions.

index, formerly called the wholesale price index, is similar to the CPI in construction. It, however, measures the prices of some 2,200 commodities (no services are included) at the level of their first commercial transaction. The old name of wholesale price index was, therefore, a misnomer because the index does not attempt to measure prices received by wholesale sellers or jobbers. Like the CPI, this index has fixed weights that, in this case, are derived from the 1963 censuses of manufactures and mineral industries as well as other sources. The weights are expenditures for items measured by net value of shipments of producers in particular industries. The interpretation of this index is similar to that of the CPI. The index number for 1980, which averaged 268.6, indicates that the cost in 1979 of purchasing the specific amounts of the 2,200 commodities in the 1963 collection was 268.6 percent of the cost of purchasing the same amounts of those commodities in 1967, which, as with the CPI, is the base year for this index number (1967 = 100).

The GNP Implicit Price Deflator

In Chapter 2, we described how current dollar GNP is deflated to derive constant dollar GNP. A byproduct of the deflation procedure is a price index officially known as the GNP implicit price deflator, the third index shown in Table 21-1. It is called *implicit* because it is not obtained directly as are the CPI and PPI; instead, it is calculated by dividing current dollar GNP by constant dollar GNP.

The total for constant dollar GNP is obtained by separately deflating each of the many components of current dollar GNP by a price index appropriate for each and then totalling all of the deflated component values. At present, the constant dollar GNP for all years is expressed in terms of prices in effect in 1972 (1972 = 100). For any year—1980, for example—the constant dollar GNP therefore represents the amount that it would cost to purchase the actual amounts of goods and services found in the 1980 GNP, *if* the prices of all those goods and services were those that prevailed in 1972. Because the current dollar

GNP reflects 1980 prices, we obtain the price index number for 1980 by dividing the 1980 current dollar GNP by the 1980 constant dollar GNP and multiplying by 100—that is, \$2,628.8 billion/\$1,481.8 billion = 1.774 × 100 = 177.4 in which 177.4 is the implicit price deflator for 1980. The deflator is found in the same way for any other year.

Unlike the CPI or the PPI, the GNP implicit price deflator is not based on a fixed "market basket" or collection of commodities. For example, if the personal consumption expenditures component of GNP rises relative to the investment expenditures component, greater weight is automatically given to the price changes of consumer goods and less weight is automatically given to the price changes of investment goods. In other words, the weights assigned to different items change continuously as buyers vary their spending among different items. For the CPI and the PPI, the weights remain unchanged over whatever number of years pass between revisions. Therefore, even though expenditures for the items covered by these indexes shift away from some and toward others, in the case of the CPI each of the 400 items continues to carry a weight that is based on how much was spent for it relative to other items in the 1972–73 survey period.

The PCE Implicit Price Deflator

The PCE deflator, the last index shown in Table 21-1, is an alternative to the CPI as a measure of the change in consumer prices. It is an index of price change for all of the goods and services included in the personal consumption expenditures (PCE) component of the GNP, and is derived as is the implicit price deflator for GNP as a whole. Although our interest here is in the index for this particular component of GNP, which incidentally makes up almost two-thirds of the total, implicit price deflators are also computed for other components (and subcomponents) of GNP such as gross private domestic investment (and the subcomponents of producers' durable equipment and structures). For an example of the PCE deflator, we obtain the value for 1980 by dividing the 1980 current dollar figure for PCE by the 1980 constant dollar figure for PCE and multiplying by 100—that is, $1,671.1 billion/$934.2 billion = 1.789 × 100 = 178.9. With constant dollar figures for every year expressed in 1972 dollars (1972 = 100), this deflator reveals that the prices of the goods and services included in the PCE component of GNP rose by 78.9 percent from 1972 to 1980.

Like the GNP deflator, the deflator for each of the components of GNP is not a fixed-weight price index. Accordingly, in the PCE deflator, as consumer expenditures for gasoline declined relative to consumer expenditures for clothing, the price changes for gasoline automatically received less weight and the price changes for clothing automatically received more weight.

Of these four indexes, the GNP deflator has the broadest coverage and therefore most closely approximates the concept of the general price level of all final goods and services. Consequently, economists regard it as the best single indicator of the rate of inflation in the United States. However, the average consumer who is concerned with what is happening to the purchasing power of the dollar ordinarily looks to the CPI for an answer. Beyond this, to tens of millions of consumers, changes in this index number are directly translated into changes in their income, because their wage rates and pensions are automatically adjusted in response to such changes. Approximately 9 million workers are covered by collective bargaining agreements with escalator clauses that provide for automatic wage increases as the CPI goes up. For a far larger number of persons who receive civilian and military pensions as former federal employees, social security benefits, or food stamps (and some receive more than one of these), the amounts received are periodically adjusted upward or *indexed* to cover in full the rise in prices shown by the CPI. If the average consumer follows any price index at all, it is understandable that it will be the CPI.

How Fast Have Consumer Prices Risen?

In recent years, the answer to this question would depend on whether we looked at the rate of change of the CPI or the PCE deflator. For example, as shown in Table 21-1, from 1979 to 1980 the CPI increased by 13.5 percent and the PCE deflator by 10.2 percent. Some of this difference arises from the differences in items covered and in definitions of items covered by the two indexes. But much of the higher rate of inflation shown by the CPI was the result of several other characteristics of the CPI that critics maintain resulted in sizable overstatement of the true increase in consumer prices in the year noted as well as in other recent years.[4]

Before examining these characteristics, note that, from one point of view, what a consumer price index should measure is the rate at which consumers must increase their spending in order to maintain a given level of utility or standard of living. This increase is usually described as the increase in the "cost of living." However, despite its designation by the press and the general public as a cost of living index, the CPI is no such thing; it is officially known as the Consumer Price Index. (Years ago the National Industrial Conference Board did publish an index called a Cost of Living Index.) The CPI measures the change in the cost of purchasing an unchanged collection of goods and services, specifically the collection in the 1972–73 market basket. But to maintain the same standard of living in 1980 that one had in 1972 obviously does not require that

---

[4]A detailed reconciliation of the factors accounting for the difference between the changes in the two indexes is presented in the *Survey of Current Business,* U.S. Department of Commerce, each quarter. The preliminary reconciliation for the second quarter of 1980 and the revised reconciliation for the first quarter of 1980 are given in the August 1980 issue, p. 3. Corresponding reconciliations appear every three months. The explanation of the reconciliation is provided in "Reconciliation of Quarterly Changes in Measures of Prices Paid by Consumers," *Survey of Current Business,* March 1978.

one consume the same amounts of the same collection of goods and services that were consumed in 1972. Numerous changes in both the collection of goods and services and amounts of each consumed are consistent with an unchanged standard of living. Such changes continuously occur in response to changes in individual tastes and the availability of different goods and services.

Therefore, although the cost of purchasing the 1972–73 market basket rose by 97.0 percent from 1972 to 1980, the cost of living increased by less than that percentage. This follows from the way that consumers make substitutions in response to relative price changes. They tend to buy less of the items whose prices have risen in relation to other prices and more of the items whose prices have fallen in relation to other prices. For example, changes in relative food prices since 1972 have caused people to substitute poultry and eggs for beef. The quadrupling of the price of gasoline since 1972 has led people to substitute public for private transport, small cars for large cars, vacations at nearby locations for cross-country auto trips, and the like. In the other direction, because the relative prices of shoes and clothing have fallen, consumers have tended to substitute more of such goods for other goods whose relative prices have risen. Through such substitutions, the average consumer did not have to increase spending by 97 percent from 1972 to 1980 to maintain the 1972 standard of living. This indicates that the CPI has an upward bias—that it overstates the actual increase in the cost of living, however accurately it may measure the increase in the cost of purchasing the 1972–73 market basket.[5]

A second way in which the CPI will at times overstate the rise in consumer prices is in its measurement of the cost of housing services.[6] The cost of rental housing is based on a sampling of rentals actually paid; the cost of owner-occupied housing is based on a combination of the prices of houses and mortgage interest rates. With housing services given a weight of almost 30 percent in the CPI, the rapid rise in the prices of houses and the even more rapid rise in mortgage interest rates in 1979 and early 1980 contributed significantly to the rise in the CPI over this period. For example, the Bureau of Labor Statistics in its October 1979 CPI release stated, "The housing component, primarily reflecting higher mortgage interest rates and house prices, continued to advance sharply and accounted for about two-thirds of the increase in the October CPI." The CPI rose in that month at a 12.5 percent annual rate; without the housing component included, the rate of increase would have been only between 4 and 5 percent.

Nobody would argue that housing costs did not rise substantially during this period, but there is considerable agreement that the BLS procedure for measuring the cost of owner-occupied housing seriously distorts the true increase in

---

sis Using Estimated Cost-of-Living Indexes," *American Economic Review,* March 1980, pp. 64–77. Brathwait found for the period 1958–73 that the substitution bias for all categories of consumption goods combined was 1.5 percentage points. Instead of a 47.5 percent increase, he estimates a 46.0 percent increase. In the case of the food category, he found a 55.4 percent increase instead of a 56.1 percent increase (a relatively small bias of only 0.7 percentage points). In contrast, in the case of the recreation and entertainment category, he found a 39.9 percent increase instead of a 46.9 percent increase (a relatively large bias of 7.0 percentage points).

[6]See T.K. Rymes, "The Treatment of 'Home Ownership' in the CPI," *Review of Income and Wealth,* Dec. 1979, pp. 393–412. Note that the cost of housing services refers to the cost of obtaining living space, whether rental or owner-occupied. It does not include any of the costs of household operation such as electricity, gas, telephone, cleaning supplies, furniture, appliances, and the like.

---

[5]On this bias, see P.J. Lloyd, "Substitution Effects and Biases in Nontrue Price Indices," *American Economic Review,* June 1975, pp. 301–13; N.N. Noe and G. Von Furstenberg, "The Upward Bias in the Consumer Price Index Due to Substitution," *Journal of Political Economy,* Nov.–Dec. 1972, pp. 1280–94; and S.D. Brathwait, "The Substitution Bias of the Laspeyres Price Index: An Analy-

these costs. The rub arises from the fact that the reported increases in the cost of housing for any time period substantially exaggerate the actual increase for all those households who do not purchase a new or existing home during that time period. Because the vast majority of today's home owners purchased their houses in the past and obtained their fixed interest rate mortgages in the past, the rise in the price of houses and in mortgage interest rates at later dates do not directly increase their housing costs. Under conditions like those of 1979–80, the increases in housing costs reported in the CPI are reasonably accurate only for the small minority who did buy a house at the time. But the reported increases should apply to more than this small group.

No price index is without its defects, but to many economists the defects of the CPI as a measure of the change in consumer prices are more serious than those of the PCE deflator. In recent years, this deflator has been accepted by many as an alternative to the CPI, especially since this deflator became available on a monthly basis starting in late 1979.[7] For one thing, as we have seen, the weights assigned to the various items in the PCE deflator are automatically adjusted as consumer spending patterns change in response to changes in relative prices, tastes, and other factors. For example, because of the sharp rises in the price of gasoline since 1973, consumers have reduced their use of this item. Instead of the 4.2 percent weight assigned to gasoline in the CPI, a figure appropriate in 1972–73 when gasoline was relatively cheap, the implicit weight assigned by the deflator in 1979 was only 2.9 percent. In contrast, clothing, which is assigned a 4.8 percent weight in the CPI, had an implicit weight of 8.2 percent in the deflator in 1979, a reflection of the smaller rise in the price of clothing relative to other items. With the CPI market basket now ten years old and with substantial differences in the rate at which the prices

of some consumer goods and services have risen over the last ten years of inflation, consumers have made some major substitutions in their spending patterns. The PCE deflator takes them into account and avoids the exaggerated measure of price increases that result in the CPI. Of course, at the time of the next Consumer Expenditures Survey, this problem will be corrected, at least temporarily.

The other shortcoming of the CPI—its overstatement of the increase in the cost of housing services—is also avoided by the PCE deflator. The cost of rental housing is there measured by the actual rentals paid (as is done in the CPI), but the cost of owner-occupied housing is measured by an imputed value for rentals, not by the price of houses and mortgage interest rates. The nature of this imputation was briefly described in Chapter 2; it is an estimate of the rental that would have been paid if the owner-occupied house had been rented rather than purchased. If rent rates rose at the same rate as housing prices, the increase in the cost of housing services would be the same, whether measured by rentals or by housing prices. But in recent years of rapidly rising property values, rents have gone up less rapidly than property values. Renters have been getting a bargain because owners of rental properties have expected to receive part of the return on their investment from the rise in the value of the property. Partially for this reason, in recent years the PCE deflator, which determines the increase in the cost of housing entirely on the basis of rentals, has shown a significantly smaller rate of increase for the cost of housing services than has the CPI. For reasons noted above, this rate of increase is closer to the actual rate. Of course, this particular shortcoming of the CPI could be corrected by estimating the cost of housing services in the CPI as this is done in the PCE deflator.[8]

---

[7]See J.C. Byrnes et al., "Monthly Estimates of Personal Income, Taxes, and Outlays," *Survey of Current Business*, Nov. 1979, pp. 18–38.

[8]For a detailed analysis of how the differences in weighting and treatment of homeownership contribute to the differences in the two indexes, see A.S. Blinder, "The Consumer Price Index and the Measurement of Recent

The arguments here considered lead many economists to conclude that, on balance, in recent years the PCE deflator has been a more accurate measure of consumer prices than the CPI as now constructed. Because the PCE deflator has risen less rapidly than the CPI over this time span, the widespread acceptance of the CPI as *the* measure of inflation in consumer prices has led the American people to believe that the rate of increase in these prices has been greater than it actually was. The federal government has also paid out billions of dollars more in social security benefits and federal employee pensions than it would have paid out if the CPI had more accurately measured the rise in consumer prices. As one step toward controlling federal expenditures, President Carter in his final budget message submitted in January 1981 proposed that the cost of living adjustment for social security beneficiaries and others be based on something other than the CPI.

If the PCE deflator has indeed been the more accurate measure in recent years, how much has the CPI overstated the rise in consumer prices? The gap between the average annual rate of change in these two index numbers can be seen in Table 21-1. A general impression of the record from 1965 through 1980 is provided by Figure 21-2, which shows the absolute difference between the two rates (percentage change in CPI minus percentage change in PCE deflator). Over this time span, the difference was positive or zero in all years except 1968 and 1972, but it did not exceed 1.4 percentage points through 1978. In 1979 and 1980 the difference became much larger: 2.4 and 3.3 percentage points respectively. It is understandable that the issue of CPI overstatement of the rise in consumer prices received a great deal of attention in recent years.

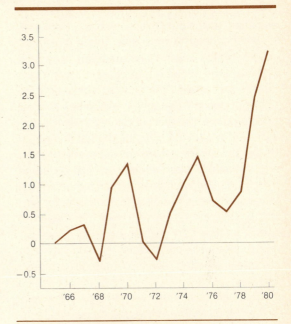

FIGURE 21-2
Percentage Change in the CPI minus the Percentage Change in the PCE Deflator, 1965–80

SOURCE: Based on figures from Table 21-1.

Economic Effects of Inflation

Although some members of society gain from inflation, others get hurt; the major measure of how badly they get hurt is the amount of their income and wealth that inflation takes away from them. In an economy in which the prices of everything, including the prices of assets and debt instruments, changed proportionally with the price level, nobody would be hurt by or benefit from changes in the price level, unless those changes affected the economy's output and the rate at which that output grew. However, in the real economy, all prices do not change at the same rate. Consequently, inflation does provide

Inflation," *Brookings Papers on Economic Activity*, No. 2, 1980, pp. 539–65. On this and related questions, see also the nontechnical paper by R.J. Gordon, "The Consumer Price Index: Measuring Inflation and Causing It," *The Public Interest*, Spring 1981, pp. 112–134.

gains to some and losses to others, apart from any effect on the output level and its growth rate.

The popular view is that the middle and especially the lower income groups lose and that the upper income groups gain. Even more loosely expressed, "the rich get richer and the poor get poorer." Because the incomes of most people do not qualify as upper incomes (by definition), it is perhaps only natural that this would be the popular view. In recent years, inflation has unquestionably been especially hard on some people with lower incomes because much of the advance in prices has been for food, energy, and shelter on which people with lower incomes must spend a large part of their incomes. However, due to less well-known facts, inflation has also adversely affected some people with higher incomes.

Surprising as it may seem to those who hold to the popular view, allowance for all the facts suggests that some people high on the income scale were big losers, at least in the earlier years of the present inflation that began in the mid-1960s. These people did not reach this unhappy state so much because their incomes (in the ordinary sense of wages and salaries, self-employment earnings, royalties, interest, and the like) failed to grow roughly in line with inflation, but because such incomes *adjusted for inflation-induced changes in their net worth* fell far behind inflation. As will be covered in detail below, the biggest factor here is the decline in the market value of their holdings of fixed-dollar, long-term, interest-bearing securities. As inflation drives up yields on such securities, the market value of these securities declines (as described on pp. 213–15), and the owners suffer corresponding losses in wealth.

Person by person, from poor to rich, who gains and who loses from inflation depends in part on who anticipates inflation and who does not. In any income group, those who correctly anticipate inflation and find ways to protect themselves against the loss of income and wealth that would otherwise occur obviously do not get hurt in the process. However, few people from the lower or upper income groups are able to do this. Actually, before the 1970s, few people thought about taking any specific steps to protect themselves against inflation. In the years preceding the prolonged inflation that began in 1965, the general public usually anticipated price stability. There was a series of inflationary experiences during the first twenty or so years following World War II, 1946–48, 1950–51, and 1956–58, but none was so prolonged as to replace in the public's mind the existing belief that relative price stability was the norm and inflation was the exception. However, by 1970, there had been five years of uninterrupted inflation, each year worse than the last. By then, most respondents of consumer surveys, such as the Survey of Consumer Finances conducted by the University of Michigan, expected that inflation for the coming year would equal or exceed the existing rate. This widespread expectation of inflation has now persisted for more than a decade. The actual record of inflation over these years has given the public little basis to expect anything but more of the same.

As measured by the impact of inflation on one's income and wealth, anyone who is able to increase his money income and the market value of his wealth as fast as prices rise is, from this point of view, not hurt by inflation. However, in order to say that such a person does not suffer a loss, his income and wealth increases must result automatically from inflation—for example, a money wage rate increase that results from a cost of living adjustment, and not for any other reason. If the decrease in a person's real income and real wealth that otherwise would result from inflation is not offset automatically but rather by his working the extra number of hours per week needed to achieve that result, then this person's real income and real wealth are unchanged. However, he has clearly suffered a loss from inflation in the form of the sacrifice of leisure or in the form of extra real income he would have had from this same sacrifice of leisure under a stable price level. As we examine the effects of inflation on different groups, the answer to the question of whether a group is worse off or better off as a result of inflation must be viewed in this sense. One obviously cannot conclude that all those families that were better off in absolute terms in 1980 than in 1970 were for this reason not hurt by the decade of inflation. One also cannot deny that some of those families that were worse off in 1980 than in 1970 were, despite this fact, still helped by the same decade of inflation.

To investigate this question of who gains and who loses from inflation, we will first examine the way that inflation results in a redistribution of income and wealth among different income classes.[9] We will then briefly look at the way that inflation may benefit some people and hurt others through its effects on the level of output, employment, and the growth rate.

The Effects of Inflation on the Distribution of Income and Wealth

It is necessary at the outset to introduce several definitions of income that will be used here. One definition counts as a household's income its receipts of wages and salaries, self-employment earnings, interest, dividends, rents and royalties, government transfer payments, unemployment compensation, private and government pensions, and the like for a specified time period. This definition of income is used by the U.S. Census Bureau in its income distribution data. A broader definition of income counts not only flows like those noted, but the change during the time period in a household's net worth.[10] The change in a household's net worth from one date to another is the difference between the changes in the dollar amounts of its assets and liabilities. Although this is conceptually a broader definition, it may yield a smaller income figure than the other because the change in net worth may be negative. For convenience in what follows, we will refer to these definitions of income simply as the narrow and broad definitions respectively.

In terms of the narrow definition, inflation affects the distribution of income only to the degree that it alters the way that the flow of total income is distributed by income class. If this

[9]The literature on this question includes the following: G.L. Bach and A. Ando, "The Redistributional Effects of Inflation," in *Review of Economics and Statistics,* Feb. 1957, pp. 1–13; A. Brimmer, "Inflation and Income Distribution in the United States," in *Review of Economics and Statistics,* Feb. 1971, pp. 37–48; J. Foster, "The Redistributive Effects of Inflation—Questions and Answers," in *Scottish Journal of Political Economy,* Feb. 1976, pp. 73–98; A.M. Maslove and J.L. Rowley, "Inflation and Redistribution," in *Canadian Journal of Economics,* Aug. 1975, pp. 399–409, G.L. Bach and J.B. Stephenson, "Inflation and the Redistribution of Wealth," in *Review of Economics and Statistics,* Feb. 1974, pp. 1–13; E.C. Budd and D.F. Seiders, "The Impact of Inflation on the Distribution of Income and Wealth," in *American Economic Review,* May 1971, pp. 128–38; and S.E. Harris, *The Incidence of Inflation: Or Who Gets Hurt?* Study Paper No. 7, Study of Employment, Growth, and Price Levels, Joint Economic Committee, U.S. Congress, 1959; H. Niida, "The Redistributive Effects of the Inflationary Process in Japan, 1955–75," *Review of Income and Wealth,* June 1978, pp. 195–219; J.J. Minarik, "The Size Distribution of Income During Inflation," *Review of Income and Wealth,* Dec. 1979, pp. 377–92; W.D. Nordhaus, "The Effects of Inflation on the Distribution of Economic Welfare," *Journal of Money, Credit and Banking,* Feb. 1973, Part 2, pp. 465–96.

[10]This definition follows the Haig–Simons definition of income as consumption plus the change in net worth. (R.M. Haig, "The Concept of Income—Economic and Legal Aspects," in R.M. Haig, ed., *The Federal Income Tax,* Columbia University Press, 1921, and H.C. Simons, *Personal Income Taxation: The Definition of Income as a Problem of Fiscal Policy,* University of Chicago Press, 1938.) For example, if a man receives a salary of $20,000 for a year (but receives no interest, dividends, transfer payments, and the like) and spends $19,000, his income will be $20,000—the sum of consumption of $19,000 plus an increase in net worth of $1,000. Again, if a man receives a salary of $20,000 (but no other flows) and spends $19,000 for consumption but now also suffers a decrease in net worth of $10,000—for example, due to a stock market decline—his income will be $10,000—consumption of $19,000 minus a decrease in net worth of $9,000. (His net worth is down $10,000 due to a decrease in the market value of his assets and is up $1,000 due to the addition of $1,000 to his assets through saving.)

remains unchanged despite inflation, then by definition inflation does not affect the distribution of income. However, by the broad definition, inflation may leave the flow covered by the narrow definition unchanged, but still significantly alter the distribution of income by causing changes in the distribution of the net worth of households by income class. Of course, in practice inflation is likely to simultaneously change the distribution of income by changing the distribution of both income flows and net worth. Later we will look at some estimates of the way in which the distribution of income narrowly defined and broadly defined is affected by inflation. First, however, to be sure that the bare mechanics of the processes are understood, we will work through an illustration of each.

Income Redistribution Through Inflation: Income Narrowly Defined

Assume the simple case of a community in which the number of households is the same at each income level and all households are at the three income levels of $20,000, $30,000, and $50,000. Assume also that the community's total real income is the same after inflation as before inflation; whatever real changes are indicated in the incomes of households at different income levels are assumed to be entirely due to inflation. If the prices of all goods and services double and the nominal incomes of all households double over the same

time interval, inflation causes no change in the distribution of income as here defined. Every household has twice the nominal income as before, but each faces prices twice as high as before. Both nominal income and prices have increased by 100 percent, as shown in columns 2 and 3 of Table 21-2 for households at each of the three income levels.

For a quite different case, suppose now that when prices double, the incomes of each of the $20,000, $30,000, and $50,000 households go to $36,000, $57,000, and $107,000 respectively, as shown in column 4. The increases are 80, 90, and 114 percent respectively, as shown in column 5. Now there is a redistribution of income. Households at these income levels needed $40,000, $60,000, and $100,000 respectively in nominal income to stay even. Measured in the cheaper dollars of column 4, each $36,000 household is $4,000 worse off than before the inflation, each $57,000 household is $3,000 worse off than before the inflation, and each $107,000 household is $7,000 better off than before the inflation. (Measured in pre-inflation dollars, these gains and losses would be one-half of those given here.) Redistribution has been in favor of the $107,000 households, each of which gained $7,000 by in effect obtaining $4,000 from a $36,000 household and $3,000 from a $57,000 household. In percentage terms, the changes in real income are a decrease of 10

TABLE 21-2
Hypothetical Incomes Before and After Inflation

Incomes Before Inflation (1)	Without Redistribution		With Redistribution	
	Incomes After Inflation (2)	Percentage Change in Incomes (3)	Incomes After Inflation (4)	Percentage Change in Incomes (5)
$20,000	$ 40,000	100	$ 36,000	80
30,000	60,000	100	57,000	90
50,000	100,000	100	107,000	114

percent for each $36,000 household ($-$4,000/$40,000), a decrease of 5 percent for each $57,000 household ($-$3,000/$60,000), and an increase of 7 percent for each $107,000 household ($7,000/$100,000).

If we simplify here by assuming that households at each income level spend their incomes on the same things, this illustration implies that households at the $50,000 level of initial income derive their income from sources that increase the amount paid to income recipients by 114 percent while the price level rises by 100 percent. Correspondingly, households with initial incomes of $30,000 and $20,000 derive their incomes from sources that increase the amount paid to income recipients by 90 and 80 percent respectively while the price level rises by 100 percent. The winners are those who are fortunate enough to derive their incomes from sources that more than match the inflation rate; the losers are those in the opposite circumstances. In the present illustration, the numbers chosen are such that the top income receivers are the winners. Obviously, another set of numbers might result in the bottom income receivers being the winners. Later we will take up the issue of who actually wins and loses and the extent of their winnings and losses; our purpose here is merely to illustrate the simple mechanics of the redistribution process for the case of narrowly defined income.

Income Redistribution Through Inflation: Income Broadly Defined

To see how changes in net worth by themselves affect the distribution of broadly defined income, assume that the narrowly defined incomes of all households double as the price level doubles. There is then no redistribution of narrowly defined income. Now the redistribution that results from changes in net worth can be distinguished conceptually from the redistribution that results from other changes.

How the net worth or wealth positions of households are affected by inflation depends on how inflation affects the money value of the particular assets owned by each household and the money value of the debts owed by each household. The debts found on any household's balance sheet are, with negligible exceptions, fixed in dollar terms. The balances it owes on the house mortgage, the car, bank loans and the like do not become larger or smaller in money terms as prices rise or fall. They are fixed-claim debts. Among its assets, however, some are fixed claims it holds against others and some are variable-price assets, the latter including all kinds of physical assets like houses, land, automobiles, and other personal property, and financial assets like shares of stock. Among holdings of fixed-claim assets are savings and demand deposits in banks, share accounts in savings and loan associations, and bonds issued by governmental units and private corporations. Although not a claim like the others, currency is also a fixed-claim asset because it is fixed in dollar terms like the other items.

Because a household's net worth is the difference between the value of its assets and debts, its net worth will be adversely or favorably affected by inflation depending primarily on how its assets are divided between variable-price assets and fixed-claim assets and on how large its fixed-claim assets are relative to its debts, which are all fixed-claim debts. Some households will be adversely affected and others favorably affected; in other words, inflation will result in some transfer of net worth.

Part A of Table 21-3 shows hypothetical balance sheets for a negative, a moderate, and a high net worth household before inflation. Starting with these balance sheets, what will be the effect on the relative position of each of these households if the price level doubles? A major difficulty in arriving at an answer is that different variable-price assets rise at different rates as prices in general rise. For example, over recent years the value of residential property has risen much more rapidly than the general price level, but the value of stock shares has not. However, we must here simplify by assuming that all variable price assets rise at the same rate and that that rate is equal to the rate of increase in the

TABLE 21-3
Hypothetical Balance Sheets of Negative Net-Worth, Moderate Net-Worth and High Net-Worth Households

A. Before Inflation

Negative Net-Worth Household

Fixed claim assets	$ 100	Debts	$ 3,500
Variable price assets	2,900	Net worth	− 500
Total assets	$ 3,000	Debts plus net worth	$ 3,000

Moderate Net-Worth Household

Fixed claim assets	$ 1,000	Debts	$ 10,000
Variable price assets	14,000	Net worth	+ 5,000
Total assets	$ 15,000	Debts plus net worth	$ 15,000

High Net-Worth Household

Fixed claim assets	$ 30,000	Debts	$ 15,000
Variable price assets	70,000	Net worth	+ 85,000
Total assets	$100,000	Debts plus net worth	$100,000

B. After Inflation

Negative Net-Worth Household

Fixed claim assets	$ 50	Debts	$ 1,750
Variable price assets	2,900	Net worth	+ 1,200
Total assets	$ 2,950	Debts plus net worth	$ 2,950

Moderate Net-Worth Household

Fixed claim assets	$ 500	Debts	$ 5,000
Variable price assets	14,000	Net worth	+ 9,500
Total assets	$ 14,500	Debts plus net worth	$ 14,500

High Net-Worth Household

Fixed claim assets	$ 15,000	Debts	$ 7,500
Variable price assets	70,000	Net worth	+ 77,500
Total assets	$ 85,000	Debts plus net worth	$ 85,000

general price level. This means that the *real* value of each household's original holdings of variable-price assets remains unchanged. On the other hand, given a doubling of the price level, the *real* value of each household's fixed-claim assets and debts is cut in half.

Part B of Table 21-3 shows the balance sheets of Part A adjusted for the real changes in the assets and debts of each that occur due to the inflation. The negative net-worth household shows a rise in real net worth from − $500 to + $1,200. Inflation has wiped out its insolvency! The real net worth of the moderate net-worth household has risen from $5,000 to $9,500 and that of the high net-worth household has fallen from $85,000 to $77,500.

Later, we will look at actual estimates, but note here that the negative net-worth households, which are in general the households that are also poor in terms of narrowly defined income, are among the major beneficiaries of inflation. On the average, they do not show large amounts of debt—they are poor credit risks and find it difficult to borrow—but they also show even less of fixed-claim assets. What little assets they have are primarily in their household possessions and an automobile. This composition of assets and the low ratio of fixed-claim assets to debt bring them out ahead in a period of inflation. From this it is easy to appreciate why, on the average, they show no concern about inflation so far as its effect on their net worth is concerned.

The net worth of the moderate net-worth household shows a gain of $4,500 in real terms. The major factor here is that households at this net worth level typically show large amounts of debt relative to fixed-claim assets. Many will own their own homes and a major part of their debt will be a mortgage balance owed on it. They will have some fixed-claim assets in the form of bank accounts and the like but will hold by far the major part of their assets in the variable-price form. In most cases, their single largest asset will be their home.

The high net-worth household shows a decline of $7,500 in its real net worth. It is a loser. Relative to its net worth, the amount of its debt typically will be small. It ordinarily does not find it necessary to borrow to cover purchases that lower net-worth families can only cover by borrowing. On the asset side, it will tend to hold a sizable part of its total assets in fixed-claim form like bonds. For one thing, if a very high net-worth household is also a very high income household by the nar-row definition of income, there is a great advantage in holding state and local government securities because the interest on these is not subject to federal income tax.

Given the assumptions made, the changes in the real net worth of the three illustrative households will be as shown. However, an important qualification is not covered by the illustration: The indicated gains and losses are based on the assumption that the inflation was unanticipated. If at any time inflation is generally anticipated, households and others will make longer-term loans and buy bonds and other fixed-claim instruments only if they are able to secure an interest rate high enough to compensate, at least in part, for the fact that the dollars they will get back when the loans come due and the bonds mature will be of smaller real value. Households that seek to obtain loans and others that seek to issue bonds and other fixed-claim instruments will be willing to pay higher interest rates because they expect to repay the amounts borrowed in dollars of smaller real value. However, as noted earlier, although practically everyone had come to anticipate more inflation by the beginning of the 1970s, not everyone anticipated the same rate. For any time period, that rate can only be known after the fact. Therefore, unless a lender arranges with a borrower that the principal amount to be repaid shall be adjusted to reflect purchasing power equal to that supplied at the beginning of the contract, wealth will be redistributed between debtors and creditors to the degree that the actual rate of inflation differs from the anticipated rate. However unlikely this may be, there is even the following possibility under certain conditions: The consensus view of the anticipated rate of inflation turns out to be so much higher than the actual rate of inflation that the redistribution of wealth between creditors and debtors turns out to be larger than it would have been if inflation had not been anticipated.

A final note on our illustration in Table 21-3. The figures there have been chosen to be consistent with the fact that all households combined occupy a net creditor position in the economy.

The sum of fixed-claim assets of the three households in Part A of Table 21-3 is $31,100; the sum of debts is $28,500 for a net-creditor position of $2,600. Part B shows that the net-creditor position in real terms is cut in half (to $1,300) after prices double. Although we found a decrease in real net worth for the high net-worth household and an increase for the other two as a result of the inflation, for all three combined we find a decrease in real net worth, as would be true for all households in the actual economy. In the redistribution of wealth effected by inflation, households as a group at this stage appear to lose to business firms and to government units, which as a group are in a net-debtor position.

Income Redistribution Through Inflation: Some Empirical Evidence The empirical studies of this question are fewer than one would expect for so important a question, at least partially because of the limitations imposed on researchers by the available data. One recent study that makes use of a large set of microdata available for 1970 is that by J.J. Minarik.[11] He ran simulations to trace the effects of different increases in the inflation rate and for different lengths of time. We will show the results here for the base case of a 2 percentage point increase in the inflation rate (for example, 6 to 8 percent) over a one-year time span. (Hereafter this will simply be referred to as a 2 percent increase instead of a 2 percentage point increase.) Given this rise in the inflation rate, some households will experience no change in real income; with the 2 percent increase in inflation, their nominal incomes will be 2 percent greater than without it. Therefore, for these households the ratio of real income with inflation to real income without inflation is 1.0. Other households will win or lose respectively through inflation to the extent that their ratio is above or below one.

The results of this simulation are shown in Figure 21-3. The relatively flat curve indicates the ratio at each level of narrowly defined income. This curve lends some support to the proposition that "the rich get richer and the poor get poorer" as a result of inflation. At low income levels (below $10,000), there is a slight decrease in real income—the ratio is less than 1.0. At middle income levels ($10,000 to $20,000), there is almost no effect—the ratio is very close to 1.0. However, at higher income levels, there is a rise in real income with inflation. The ratio reaches its peak at income levels close to $1 million.

This suggests that the average household at low income levels receives a large part of its income from sources that do not increase the amount paid as rapidly as the price level rises. Minarik notes that this happens because some transfer income (a kind of income highly concentrated at the low income levels) lags behind prices. Households in the middle-income range had a ratio very close to 1.0, because the primary source of their income is labor—a source of income that tended to increase closely in line with prices. Finally, the ratio above 1.0 for incomes from $25,000 to $1 million is accounted for by a high concentration of interest income in this range—a source of income that tended to grow faster than the inflation rate. The dip in the ratio above the $1 million level is due to increased relative amounts of dividend income—a source that did not grow as fast as inflation.

The other curve reveals the effects of a 2 percent increase in the inflation rate on the distribution of broadly defined income. Although there was some redistribution shown for narrowly defined income, it is minor in relation to that revealed for the broad definition of income. At low income levels, instead of the loss shown under the narrow definition of income, there is a sizable gain. The ratio reaches almost 1.02 (an increase of about 2 percent in real income) with the 2 percent increase in the inflation rate. This follows from the increase in net worth realized through appreciation in the value of homes. (Just over half of all households with incomes below

---

[11]See footnote 7 for this reference as well as other references to the empirical and theoretical literature.

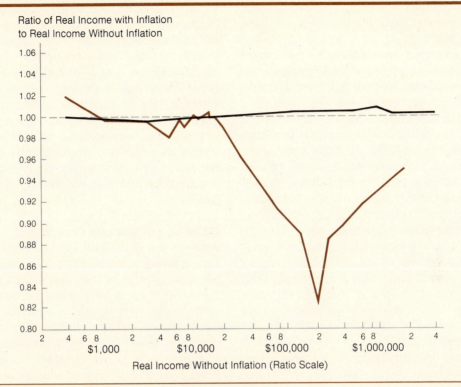

Ratio of Real Income with Inflation
to Real Income Without Inflation

Real Income Without Inflation (Ratio Scale)

FIGURE 21-3
Ratio of Real Income with Inflation to Real Income without Inflation by Income Class for Two Definitions of Income

SOURCE: J.J. Minarik, "The Size Distribution of Income During Inflation," *Review of Income and Wealth* Series 25, No. 4, Dec. 1979.

$10,000 owned their own homes in 1975.) The gain here swamps the loss previously noted under narrowly defined income.

For middle income households—the range from $10,000 to $20,000—there is little effect under either definition of income. For example, they gained in their balance sheets through appreciation in the value of their homes, but lost in their ordinary incomes through the rise in the burden of income taxes. High income households reflect a dramatic difference between the effects under the two income definitions. Although other factors are involved, the large depreciation

in the value of assets in fixed-claim form, like holdings of government and corporate bonds, primarily produced the large negative changes in the net worth that occur in the high income households. Holdings of fixed-claim securities are heavily concentrated among the high income households. Losses in the values of securities that are picked up in the broad definition of income far outweighed the gains shown by the high income families under the narrow definition of income. Minarik's simulation shows that over the income range from $50,000 to $1 million, the ratio was 0.94 or lower; consequently, the decrease in real income for households within this range was 6 percent or more for a 2 percent rise in the inflation rate.

The findings differ somewhat for the different simulations carried out by Minarik. To note merely one of the others, consider how the distribution of 1970 incomes before and after inflation is affected by a simulated 2 percent increase in the inflation rate over the actual inflation rate each year from 1965 to 1970. As in the case of the simulation for a 2 percent increase in the inflation rate for just one year, the high income households again suffer substantial income losses when changes in net worth are taken into account. Furthermore, in this five-year simulation, the very high income households ($200,000 and over) lose under both definitions of income.

The general conclusion that emerges from the various simulations is that inflation hurts mostly those with high incomes when incomes are measured to include the changes in net worth caused by inflation. This is not to deny that some low income households, especially those of the elderly, are clearly hurt by inflation, but many of these are somewhat protected by indexed social security benefits and other programs. Although Minarik's results are far from the final word on this question, they do suggest that the problems faced by the poor have not been created to any significant extent by inflation. On the contrary, the findings indicate that the problems created by inflation are primarily problems of the rich.

The Effects of Inflation on Output, Employment, and the Growth Rate

In an economy operating below full employment, will a spurt of inflation get some of the unemployed back to work? Will it mean that next year's output will be closer to the economy's potential than was this year's? For some people, the issue of whether they personally gain or lose from inflation is resolved right here. If they would not have a job but for inflation, they clearly gain from inflation, regardless of whether they gain or lose in

terms of the inflation-caused redistribution of income and wealth. Another issue is how inflation affects the economy's real wealth. Does it speed or slow the rate at which the economy builds up its stock of real assets? If it speeds it, wealth grows faster than it otherwise would and the potential rate of growth of output becomes greater than it otherwise would be. The first part of this section examines the issue of inflation's impact on output and employment in the short run; the second part examines its impact on the accumulation of capital and the rate of long-run growth.

Inflation's Impact on Output and Employment in the Short Run   For an economy producing below potential, many economists maintain that inflation of the creeping or crawling variety will have a tonic effect on output and employment. Here again it is essential to draw the distinction between anticipated and unanticipated inflation. The alleged beneficial effects in large part disappear if inflation is anticipated. In the event of unanticipated inflation, prices rise faster than money wage rates, and the resulting reduction in the real wage rate gives business the profit incentive to hire more workers and expand output. Consequently, a rise in the inflation rate, if unanticipated, may lead to a reduction in the unemployment rate. This line of argument will be developed in detail in Chapter 23. It is sufficient to note here that, in general, an expansionary effect on employment and therefore on output, at least of a temporary nature, is to be expected from unanticipated inflation.

An increase in output results not only from getting the unemployed back to work, but from reallocating labor and other resources to achieve the maximum output these resources can produce. Although inflation may lead to an increase in output by reducing unemployment, some economists would argue that inflation also tends to prevent the optimum allocation of resources and thereby tends to hold down output. The industries that have the strongest incentive to expand during a period of inflation will be those whose prices rise most rapidly relative to costs, but there will be some whose prices are restrained from rising, despite the inflation, and in which little expansion or possibly even contraction may result.

A couple of examples will make the point. Although electric utilities in some states now get automatic rate adjustments to cover changes in their fuel costs, they can only get rate increases to cover inflation of other costs after a delay the length of which varies with the time taken by state regulatory commissions to act. Because prices charged by some industries—for example, coal company sales to large industrial buyers—are on a contract basis, the inability of firms in such industries to adjust prices may mean losses instead of larger profits and contraction rather than expansion of output. Distortions like these in the price system result in resource misallocation. However, the resource allocation effect on output is not necessarily negative; there is a counterargument that inflation works in another way to effect a better allocation of resources than would occur with stable prices. As the price system functions, most prices are flexible upward but inflexible downward. Therefore, the only way in practice to get the relative price changes needed to achieve a better allocation of resources is by having some prices rise. This amounts to saying that the only way that the price system can achieve a better allocation of resources is through inflation.

If the net effect of these forces on resource allocation is a better allocation, the resources employed will turn out a greater total output than otherwise. Therefore, whatever increase in output results from the fuller utilization of resources, some additional amount will result from the better allocation of the resources used. In the opposite case in which the forces, on balance, result in a worsening of the allocation of resources, some decrease in output must be subtracted from the increased output gained through a fuller utilization of resources.

What then is the answer to the question? If the economy is suffering from unemployment,

will a moderate inflation cut unemployment below and raise output above what they otherwise would be? All things considered, most economists would probably answer yes, but many would quickly add important qualifications. Perhaps the most important is that, according to some, the reduction in unemployment achieved through the rise in the rate of inflation will only be temporary. The lag of the money wage rate behind prices, which brings about the reduction in unemployment, will be short-lived. Labor eventually anticipates inflation and acts to prevent the reduction of the real wage rate that can result from unanticipated inflation. Again, we will deal with this question more thoroughly in Chapter 23.

Another important qualification is that at the same time that inflation may reduce unemployment and raise output, it creates distortions of various kinds that will culminate in a downturn. A key role in the process is played by changes in inventories. If the consensus opinion is that there will be a continuation or even acceleration of an already high rate of inflation, business people may seek to build up inventories far in excess of what they need to meet any expected near-term increase in sales. The purpose, naturally, is to secure that large additional profit some time later by selling the goods at the much higher prices expected. Beyond building inventories, some businesses may also be encouraged by such expectations to expand expenditures for new plant and equipment. In all likelihood, the cost of borrowing and the purchase price of capital goods will be higher next year and the year after. Consumers also participate in the surge of overbuying. They don't maintain stocks of goods for resale as do businesses, but expectations of continuing inflation will lead some to accumulate durables and nonperishable goods.

Depending on the extent of the excesses, the eventual adjustment will produce anything from a minor slowdown to a serious recession. Some adjustment is inevitable in a process for which the foundation is predominantly speculation. If the major reason that buyers as a group expand their buying at today's prices is that they expect to be able to sell tomorrow at substantially higher prices, an unsustainable process has been set into motion. Its end may come because of the inability of business people to finance the amount of inventories they seek to accumulate. The monetary authorities may in due time refuse to permit credit expansion to continue at the rate needed to accommodate business demands. Bank loans become increasingly hard to get and interest rates soar. The profit possibilities in building inventories still higher begin to look less promising and firms under pressure begin to reduce instead of build inventories. If this occurs on any scale, prices may not only stop rising, contrary to what was generally expected, but there may even be some scattered decreases in prices. As the signs of a reverse like this become clear, many businesses become as anxious to reduce inventories as they were a short time earlier to enlarge them. The inventory adjustment that follows may be orderly and cause no more than a slowdown in the economy—or it may turn into something more serious.

We have noted that most economists would probably answer yes to the question of whether inflation will raise employment and output. Then we inserted some qualifications they would add to this answer. With the qualifications taken into account, what we are left with is anything but a conclusive answer to the initial question. Only in the case of an extremely rapid inflation can the answer be fairly conclusive. Although such an inflation may at first stimulate production and reduce unemployment, it will probably lead eventually to a more or less violent adjustment with production lower and unemployment higher than before. On the other hand, a short spurt of moderate inflation will stimulate production and raise employment without generating massive overbuying, excessive inventory accumulation, and the wild speculative activity that come with a prolonged, sharp rise in prices. The economy may adjust to such a moderate inflation with only a ripple instead of a wave; the gain in production and employment, even though only temporary,

need not be offset by a later loss. Believing this to be the case, some economists maintain that intermittent spurts of moderate inflation should be deliberately engineered for an economy that has continuing difficulty in maintaining full employment. To others, this sounds like playing with fire. A little inflation at times has a way of growing into a lot.

Inflation's Impact on the Rate of Long-Run Economic Growth When one observes the rate at which an economy's output grows over the long run, is the rate of growth higher during those extended periods that are marked by moderate inflation or during those marked by price stability? Looking back to the record of the eighteenth and nineteenth centuries, some economists find a positive relationship between inflation and economic growth in various countries. The driving force in rapid progress has been identified as large and long-lasting profit margins. As we have seen, such margins can be maintained only as long as wages lag substantially behind prices. In today's world, it will not take years for labor to remove such a lag, but some argue that in the past such lags at times prevailed over stretches of many years. To the extent that such lags did occur, they made possible massive shifts of resources away from the production of consumer goods for wage earners to the production of that much more of capital goods. This rapid accumulation in turn provided the increase in productive capacity and labor productivity that made possible extended periods of rapid economic growth.[12]

According to this argument, this shift in resources comes about through the effect of inflation on saving. Given an inflation in which wages lag behind prices, the wage share of total income shrinks and the fraction of total income

[12]On the question of the wage lag, see A.A. Alchian and R.A. Kessel, "The Meaning and Validity of the Inflation-Induced Lag of Wages behind Prices," in *American Economic Review,* March 1960, pp. 43–66, and T.F. Cargill, "An Empirical Investigation of the Wage-Lag Hypothesis,"

saved expands. This follows from the fact that a larger portion of the total income goes to profits and other nonwage income, the recipients of which are typically upper income groups with a relatively high propensity to save. That a greater saving will occur under the conditions here specified is well established. On the classical assumption that investment expands to absorb whatever volume of saving is forthcoming, the portion of output that takes the form of capital goods then grows in line with the portion of income that goes into saving.

However, as is the case with so many arguments, a counterargument maintains that inflation may discourage saving and thereby slow the accumulation of capital. Although some people see their incomes rise rapidly because they share in the rapid growth of the profits share, they will also see their real net worth shrink to the extent that they are net creditors. In the face of this, there is some doubt as to whether inflation is likely to increase the fraction of their income devoted to saving. The more rapid the inflation, the less likely it is to increase the saving fraction. There is no doubt but that inflation at the breakneck speed called hyperinflation discourages saving. However, as long as wages continue to lag behind prices, it is likely that moderate or even somewhat more than moderate inflations will still raise saving relative to consumption spending. For one thing, an inflation premium tends to be built into interest rates to give new purchasers of fixed-claim assets some protection against loss. Apart from this, protection is provided by avoiding ordinary fixed-claim assets. Savers may purchase an assortment of variable-price assets that provide varying degrees of protection against loss due to inflation.

Barring the special case of hyperinflation, on balance, the crucial factor in whether or not saving is encouraged by inflation is the existence or nonexistence of a wage lag. Although there is considerable evidence of such a lag for the earlier part of this century and for centuries preceding, there is little evidence of this in the United States for the period since World War II. The corporate profits and noncorporate business shares of national income declined substantially while the employees' compensation share increased substantially over these years of almost uninterrupted inflation. To the extent that the rate of long-run economic growth depends on the rate of capital accumulation, a major basis for the conclusion that inflation promotes rapid economic growth is undermined, given that wages no longer lag during inflation as they apparently did in times past.

There are, of course, many factors other than the rate of capital accumulation that influence an economy's long-run growth rate. As we saw in Chapter 20, advances in knowledge, for example, are judged to have been more important than the growth in the stock of capital over the 1929–69 period. However, whatever the importance of capital accumulation may be, with substantial wage lags a thing of the past in industrialized countries, inflation no longer appears to contribute to growth as it apparently once did. When one compares the rate of inflation and the rate of growth of real gross national product in major industrialized countries over the period since World War II, one finds no clear pattern. For example, West Germany (with the lowest rate of inflation) has shown one of the highest rates of growth and Japan (with a high rate of inflation) has shown by far the highest rate of growth. The United Kingdom (with the lowest rate of growth) is among the highest in terms of the rate of inflation. There are problems of interpretation here due to the impact of World War II on different countries, but in general the evidence hardly enables one to say that inflation has either speeded or slowed the rate of economic growth

in *American Economic Review,* Dec. 1969, pp. 806–16; and on the question of the wage lag as a factor in the rate of economic growth, see D. Felix, "Profit Inflation and Industrial Growth," *Quarterly Journal of Economics,* Aug. 1956, pp. 441–63, and E.J. Hamilton, "Prices as a Factor in Business Growth," *Journal of Economic History,* Dec. 1952, pp. 325–49.

in the major industrialized countries during the long period of inflation since World War II.[13]

The Effects of Inflation: A Concluding Note

In looking at the broad question of the effects of inflation, we have gone far enough to see that inflation is a pervasive economic process. Its effects are felt to some degree by every citizen and in every corner of the economy. Some of the effects are quite certain, at least when stated as broad generalizations; others are just as much uncertain. We know that inflation causes a redistribution of income and wealth.

The one study reviewed in these pages suggests, as a generalization, that it imposes losses on the high-income households and provides gains to the low-income households, but this evidence is by no means conclusive. It would perhaps be incorrect to say that we know that inflation causes short-run changes in the economy's output and employment levels and long-run changes in its growth rate, but it would be hard to believe that inflation leaves these unaffected. But whether inflation raises output and employment in the short run without being followed by declines equal to or greater than the increases is an issue on which economists disagree. Similarly, in connection with inflation's impact on the long-run growth rate, it is not clear for today's advanced economies whether inflation makes for a faster or a slower growth rate than would occur with stable prices.

Taking into account all the effects considered, the question of whether inflation is beneficial or harmful has a ready answer only when inflation proceeds at a rapid rate. A rapid rate that is unanticipated and to which there is therefore no chance to adjust is undoubtedly damaging. When inflation proceeds at a mild rate of not more than a few percentage points per year, there is no ready answer to the question posed. In view of this uncertainty, the best policy to many economists appears to be one aimed at achieving and maintaining a stable price level or a zero rate of inflation. Considering the record since the mid-1960s, such an achievement looks like a remote possibility, but it does not mean that it is not the best ultimate goal toward which policy should aim.

---

[13]For several empirical studies of this question, see M. Paldam, "An Empirical Analysis of the Relationship between Inflation and Economic Growth in 12 Countries, 1950 to 1969," in *Swedish Journal of Economics* (retitled *Scandinavian Journal of Economics* in 1976), Dec. 1973; G.S. Dorrance, "Inflation and Growth: The Statistical Evidence," *IMF Staff Papers,* March 1966, pp. 82–102; and A.P. Thirwall and C.A. Barton, "Inflation and Growth: The International Evidence," *Banca Nazionale del Lavoro-Quarterly Review,* Sept. 1971, pp. 263–75.

Demand-Side and Supply-Side Inflation

OVERVIEW

This is the first of two chapters devoted to the causes of inflation. The traditional approach to this issue has run in terms of a dichotomy: demand or demand–pull theory and supply or cost–push theory. Although the approach in recent years has emphasized the Phillips curve or the inflation–unemployment relationship, the traditional approach still illuminates some basic features of the inflation process. This approach provides the framework of this chapter; the Phillips curve approach provides the framework of Chapter 23.

As there is a dichotomy between demand-side and supply-side inflation theory, demand-side theory in turn presents another dichotomy—that between theories that explain demand–pull inflation as a phenomenon originating with real factors and theories that explain such inflation as a phenomenon originating with monetary factors. The analysis here is conducted with the tools developed in Part 3. Demand–pull inflation occurs as the aggregate demand curve shifts upward along an upward-sloping or vertical aggregate supply curve. To the degree that such shifts in aggregate demand originate with real factors, they emerge from the *IS–LM* framework as a result of rightward shifts in the *IS* curve. To the degree that such shifts originate with monetary factors, they emerge from the *IS–LM* framework as a result of rightward shifts in the *LM* curve.

The discussion of supply-side inflation theory begins with analysis of the three principal causes of upward shifts in the aggregate supply curve and therefore of causes of inflation on the supply side: wage–push inflation caused by increases in money–wage rates in excess of labor productivity made possible by the exercise of market power held by labor unions; profit–push inflation caused by the exercise of market power held by monop-

olistic and oligopolistic firms; and supply-shock inflation caused by such events as crop failures or OPEC price increases.

Following the analysis of the three principal causes of cost–push, we turn to the problem of controlling this kind of inflation. The problem here is quite different from that faced in controlling demand–pull inflation. Conventional monetary and fiscal policies operate on the demand side and therefore are most effective in controlling demand–pull inflation. However, they have been used at times in the attempt to conquer cost–push inflation. One experience of this sort occurred during 1969–71. In recent years, economists have been exploring the possibilities of using fiscal policy in an unconventional way to combat cost–push inflation. This is called supply management and works through variations in a tax rate such as the social security contribution rate, the direct effect of which is a shift in the aggregate supply curve. Conventional fiscal policy works through changes in income tax rates that cause shifts in the aggregate demand curve and therefore is known as demand management.

The chapter concludes with an examination of how supply-side inflation is related to demand-side inflation. Here included is a discussion of the generally accepted proposition that an inflationary process may begin on the supply side through a wage push, for example, but that it cannot be long sustained on the supply side unless there is a "validation" of wage push by expansionary monetary and fiscal policies that increase aggregate demand.

Like any other phenomenon, inflation has causes and effects. In the preceding chapter, we examined its effects; in this and the following chapter, we will examine its causes.[1] Of these two chapters, the first seeks to explain causation by use of the aggregate supply –aggregate demand model developed in Part 3. As we will see in Chapter 23, the aggregate supply–aggregate demand model, however useful in handling other questions, is not ideally suited to handling the question of inflation. Nonetheless, certain basic characteristics of the inflation process are clearly demonstrated by this model; it is an essential first step in any approach to explaining the causes of inflation.

In this model, the price level varies in response to shifts in the aggregate supply or aggregate demand curves. Therefore the model naturally lends itself to discussion under two headings: changes in the price level that originate on the demand side and changes in the price level that originate on the supply side. Although interdependence between aggregate demand and aggregate supply argues against treating them separately, such a separate treatment provides a reasonably clear first view of the inflationary process. Accordingly, apart from a brief discussion at the end of this chapter on the relation of supply inflation to demand inflation, the chapter is divided into two major parts—"Inflation: The Demand Side" and "Inflation: The Supply Side." Inflation originating on the demand side is commonly referred to as demand–pull inflation; whereas that originating on the supply side is cost–push inflation. These alternative terms will be used frequently in the following pages.

Inflation: The Demand Side

One main branch of inflation theory runs in terms of generalized excess demand, sometimes loosely

---

[1] Our examination will be limited to what can be seen by means of the two basic models presented in these two chapters. Through these models we will deal with a few very fundamental ideas in the theory of inflation. These ideas, however fundamental, are still only a few of the many in this complex area. The presentation of these many ideas has generated a vast literature that persistently grows more vast. Extensive bibliographies will be found at the end of the article by M. Bronfenbrenner and F.D. Holzman, "Survey of Inflation Theory," in *American Economic Review*, Sept. 1963; at the end of the article by D.E.W. Laidler and J.M. Parkin, "Inflation—A Survey," in *The Economic Journal*, Dec. 1975; and at the end of the book by E.J. Bomhoff, *Inflation, the Quantity Theory, and Rational Expectations*, North–Holland, 1980. A detailed bibliography of the Phillips curve literature will be found at the end of the article by A.M. Santomero and J.J. Seater, "The Inflation-Unemployment Trade-off: A Critique of the Literature," in *Journal of Economic Literature*, June 1978.

and not very accurately described as "too much money chasing too few goods." According to this theory, the general price level rises because the demand for goods and services exceeds the supply available at existing prices. In terms of the *IS–LM* framework, the excess demand that pulls up the price level may originate with any one or a combination of a number of changes that can shift the *IS* or the *LM* curve to the right. Real factors shift the *IS* curve; monetary factors shift the *LM* curve. Among the real factors are fiscal actions like changes in government spending and taxes; among the monetary factors are changes in the money supply. In the last section of Chapter 13, we saw how expansionary government actions could be used to shift the *IS* and *LM* curves to the right, thereby shifting the aggregate demand curve to the right, and, in an economy operating below full employment, raising the level of output and employment.

In Figure 13-8, page 279, we worked with an aggregate supply curve that slopes upward to the right before becoming perfectly inelastic at the full employment output level. Therefore, starting below full employment, rightward shifts in the aggregate demand curve raised the price level as well as the output level. But the question on which we focused was how full employment might be attained. The rise in the price level was mentioned only in passing. In here focusing specifically on inflation, we will employ the same graphic apparatus presented in Figure 13-8. Unlike in Figure 13-8, we will here assume that the economy is already operating at full employment. Consequently, rightward shifts in the aggregate demand curve affect only the price level; their effect is exclusively inflationary. Keynes described rises in the price level that occur under this condition as pure inflation.

We noted in a preceding paragraph that real and monetary factors shift the *IS* and *LM* curves, respectively. Because demand–pull inflation may originate with either, it is convenient to divide the discussion of demand–pull inflation into two parts according to whether the inflation originates with real or monetary factors.

Demand–Pull Inflation Originating with Real Factors

Among the various factors that may produce a rightward shift in the *IS* curve are an increase in government spending with no change in tax receipts, a decrease in tax receipts with no change in government spending, a downward shift in the saving function, an upward shift in the export function, a downward shift in the import function, and an upward or rightward shift in the MEI or investment function. The essence of the process by which demand–pull inflation may result from any of these factors is revealed in Figure 22-1.

Assuming that the other determinants of the positions of the *IS* and *LM* curves in Part A of Figure 22-1 are given, there will be a set of *IS* and *LM* curves with each curve in the set corresponding to a different price level. As covered in detail in Chapter 13, all else being equal, a decrease in the price level will shift the *LM* curve to the right because the decrease in the price level is an increase in the real money supply. By reducing the money supply, an increase in the price level will have the opposite effect of shifting the *LM* curve to the left. Figure 22-1 shows three positions for the *LM* curve corresponding to a given nominal money supply, but for three different price levels. As the price level rises from P_1 to P_2 to P_3, the corresponding position of the *LM* curve becomes LM_1, LM_2, and LM_3. In the same way, we saw in Chapter 13 that a decrease in the price level will shift the *IS* curve to the right via the Pigou effect, tax and transfer payments effects, and foreign trade effects. An income redistribution effect may also work in this direction, but that is uncertain; it may work in either direction. An increase in the price level will have the opposite effect, shifting the *IS* curve to the left. Accordingly, IS_1, IS_2, and IS_3 in Figure 22-1 make up an initial set of *IS* curves corresponding to three different price levels, P_1, P_2, and P_3, the position of the set reflecting the combined influence of the various effects listed.

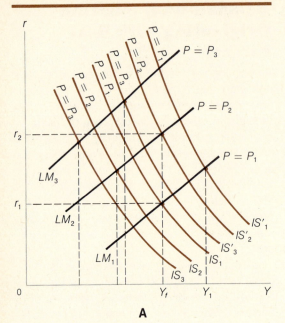

A

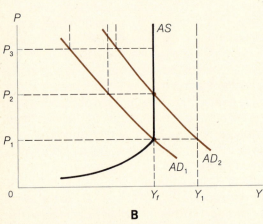

B

FIGURE 22-1
Demand–Pull Inflation
Originating with Real Factors

The intersections of IS_1 and LM_1, IS_2 and LM_2, and IS_3 and LM_3 indicate the amount of goods demanded at price levels of P_1, P_2, and P_3, respectively, and thereby provide the information

needed to draw the aggregate demand curve labeled AD_1 in Part B. This AD curve intersects the AS curve at P_1 and Y_f. Initially there is a full employment equilibrium at the price level P_1.

One of the real factors that can cause a demand–pull rise in the price level is an increase in investment demand—that is, an upward or rightward shift in the MEI or investment function. Suppose such a shift in the investment function in turn shifts the IS_1 curve to IS'_1 and the IS_2 and IS_3 curves to IS'_2 and IS'_3, respectively. The set of LM curves remains as given because there has been no change in the determinants of this set. We now find that at each price level saving plus taxes plus imports will equal investment plus government purchases plus exports at a higher Y for any r or at a higher r for any Y than before the shift in the investment function.

Following the shift in the set of IS curves, the AD curve derived from the intersections of the IS'_1 and LM_1, IS'_2 and LM_2 and IS'_3 and LM_3 is AD_2. The AD_2 curve intersects the AS curve at P_2, which is the new equilibrium price level. The rise from P_1 to P_2 is that required to eliminate the excess demand that exists at P_1 after the IS curves shift in response to the greater investment spending. At P_1 there is excess demand of $Y_1 - Y_f$. As this excess demand pulls up P, there is a decrease in the quantity of goods demanded. At P_2, the quantity of goods demanded is identified by the intersection of the IS'_2 and LM_2 curves in Part A. This is the full employment quantity. Excess demand has been eliminated and there is full employment equilibrium at P_2. Note also that the process of restoring equilibrium requires not only a rise in the price level but also a rise in the interest rate. As shown in Part A, before the shift in the IS curves, equilibrium was found at r_1; after the shift, equilibrium is found at r_2.

The same sequence would follow from any other change that produces a one-time rightward shift in the set of IS curves. For any such one-time shift, there will be a one-time rightward shift in the aggregate demand curve. Given an original position at the full employment level of output, that increase in aggregate demand must create an excess demand at the existing price level, which in turn must raise the price level. However, each rise in the price level identifies an *IS* and *LM* curve to the left of those with a lower price level and therefore a reduction in the quantity of goods demanded. Equilibrium will be restored automatically by that rise in the price level that reduces the quantity of goods demanded to the amount supplied at full employment.

Although this analysis reveals how the price level will be pulled up from one particular equilibrium level to another by a specific increase in aggregate demand, it does not deal with the disequilibrium process of inflation, which is a persistent rather than a one-time rise in the price level. However, if we return to Figure 22-1, it would appear that such a persistent rise in the price level comes out of this model by merely extending the argument already presented. If there is another and then another rightward shift in the set of *IS* curves, there will be another and then another increase in aggregate demand and in the price level.[2] Such a process may indeed continue up to a point, but the successive increases in the price level must eventually stop if the nominal money supply is fixed, an assumption that has been made in connection with Figure 22-1. With Y at Y_f, each rise in P raises the transactions demand for money proportionally with the rise in P. Additional transactions balances can be secured only by drawing them from speculative balances, given that the total nominal money supply is fixed. Once the interest rate has risen to the level at which idle cash balances have been reduced to zero, no additional money is available to generate still higher price levels for the full employment level of output. Unless the velocity of money were to increase without limit, the price level must stop rising due to the sheer inability of the existing stock of money to support a higher level of spending and money income.

Demand–Pull Inflation Originating with Monetary Factors

On the monetary side, demand–pull inflation may originate either through a decrease in the demand for money or an increase in the supply of money, but the supply of money is of overwhelming importance in this connection.[3] The essence of demand–pull inflation originating through increases in the money supply may be revealed through Figure 22-2.

This figure is similar to Figure 22-1. Assuming that the other determinants of the *IS* and *LM* curves are given, there is an initial set of *IS* and *LM* curves with each curve in a set corresponding to a different price level. The intersections between the curves in the sets, IS_1 and LM_1, IS_2 and LM_2, and IS_3 and LM_3, yield AD_1, and given the *AS* curve, indicate a full employment equilibrium with the price level at P_1. There is some increase in the money supply that shifts the LM_1 curve rightward to LM'_1 and the LM_2 and LM_3 curves to LM'_2 and LM'_3, respectively. The set of *IS* curves in this case will remain as given because there has been no change in the determinants of this set. With the shift in the set of *LM* curves, *at each price level* the supply of money will equal the demand for money at a higher Y for any r and at a lower r for any Y than before the increase in the supply of money.

---

[2]Starting from the new equilibrium established at P_2, we would want to identify the positions of a new set of initial curves, IS_2, IS_3, and IS_4, and then, following a change in some real factor, the shift of this set of curves to IS'_2, IS'_3, and IS'_4, a process paralleling that shown in Figure 22-1 for the shift from IS_1, IS_2, and IS_3 to IS'_1, IS'_2, and IS'_3. If the changes in real factors persist, the next set of curves would become IS_3, IS_4, and IS_5, and so forth.

[3]A decrease in the demand for money is not likely to originate an inflation, but it is almost certain to intensify an ongoing inflation that has reached a rapid rate. The greater the rate of inflation, the more costly it becomes to hold money, and the smaller the amount of real balances the public will want to hold at any level of real income and any interest rate. The velocity of money increases, which acts on the price level like an increase in the supply of money.

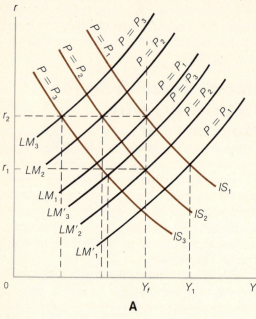

A

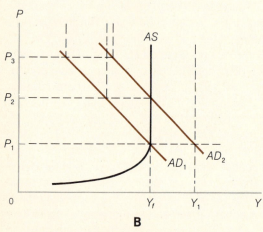

B

FIGURE 22-2
Demand–Pull Inflation
Originating with Monetary
Factors

With the new set of LM curves, there is a shift in the AD curve from AD_1 to AD_2. At the existing

price level of P_1, excess demand equal to $Y_1 - Y_f$ appears. The changes that follow from excess demand are the same for the present case in which the excess demand originates on the monetary side as they were for the previous case in which the excess demand originated on the real side. The excess demand will force a rise in the price level of a magnitude needed to eliminate the excess demand. The AD_2 curve intersects AS at P_2 and a rise from P_1 to P_2 is accordingly the rise needed to restore the system to equilibrium. In this case, because the excess demand originates with an increase in the money supply, the interest rate of r_1 at the new equilibrium is lower than the original interest rate of r_2.[4]

Following the analysis of a one-time shift in the set of IS curves due to a change in some real factor, we asked whether another and yet another such shift in the IS curves could lead to another and yet another rise in the price level. The answer was that rises in the price level would at some point be limited by the fixity of the money supply, although a sizable rise in the price level might be possible before this limiting point was reached. Now we ask whether another and yet another rightward shift in the LM curves caused by another and yet another increase in the money supply can lead to another and yet another rise in the price level. The answer is yes. Unlimited expansion of the money supply will mean an unlimited rise in the price level.

There is no disagreement among economists regarding this last statement: Persistent expansion of the money supply is a sufficient condition for a persistent rise in the price level. Disagreement arises over the importance of real factors in originating and supporting a persistent rise in the price level. Some will agree with Milton Friedman's position: "Inflation is always and every-

---

[4]This is the way the interest rate is expected to respond in the short run to an increase in the supply of money. However, we will see that the kind of monetary expansion that leads to a persistent rather than a one-time rise in the price level will be followed by a rise rather than a decline in the interest rate.

where a monetary phenomenon . . . and can be produced only by a more rapid increase in the quantity of money than in output."[5] This seems to leave little room for inflation to originate with or to be driven by real factors. Others will agree with J.R. Hicks, who assigns to money at best a supportive role. After noting that "it was true in the old days that inflation was a monetary matter; prices rose because the supply of money was greater than the demand for it," he then adds that "money is now a mere counter, which is supplied by the banking system (or by the government through the banking system) just as it is required."[6] Here the view is that in recent experience real factors have played the crucial role and that government has been merely permissive or accommodative in not restraining the growth of the money supply as required to prevent the inflation that originates with or is caused by changes in real factors.

The relative role of real and monetary factors in modern demand–pull inflation is therefore a matter on which some of the world's leading economists take opposite positions. However, whatever the origin of excess demand, the underlying mechanism by which that excess demand pulls up the price level is illustrated by Figures 22-1 and 22-2. Our purpose here has been limited to outlining that mechanism. In these two figures, we assumed that the aggregate supply function was given and thereby ruled out any changes on the supply side of the economy. Inflation resulted from excess demand as the aggregate demand curve shifted upward along the fixed aggregate supply curve. As a next step, we turn to the inflation that may result from upward shifts in the aggregate supply function. This branch of inflation theory is called supply, or cost–push, inflation.

Inflation: The Supply Side

For many years before the 1950s, inflation theory ran predominantly in terms of generalized excess demand. The origin of the excess demand was explained either in terms of changes in real or monetary factors. During the 1950s there occurred a revival of supply or cost theories of inflation. Although then commonly referred to as the "New Inflation," the general notion that price inflation can arise on the supply side is far from new. In their survey of inflation theory, M. Bronfenbrenner and F.D. Holzman note that

> Cost inflation has been the layman's instinctive explanation of general price increases since the dawn of the monetary system. We know of no inflationary movement that has not been blamed by some people on "profiteers," "speculators," "hoarders," or workers and peasants "living beyond their station."[7]

Of course, we now know much that is "new" about the nature of cost–push inflation as a result of the research of the last several decades that recognizes the structural and institutional changes during this period, but the general notion that inflation can be caused by supply or cost is an old one.

Until the 1970s, explanations of the causes of supply-side inflation ran almost entirely in terms of the exercise of market power by specific groups within the economy. There are two such groups: Labor unions maintain power over wage rates, and firms in monopolistic and oligopolistic industries maintain power over prices. Inflation originating through the exercise of the power of these two groups is commonly referred to as wage–push and profit–push inflation. As a result of the developments of the 1970s, attention has

[5]M. Friedman, *The Counter-Revolution in Monetary Theory,* Occasional Paper No. 33, Institute of Economic Affairs, London, 1970, p. 24.

[6]J.R. Hicks, "The Permissive Economy," in *Crisis '75. . . ?,* Occasional Paper Special, No. 43, Institute of Economic Affairs, London, 1975, p. 17.

[7]M. Bronfenbrenner and F.D. Holzman, "Survey of Inflation Theory," in *American Economic Review,* Sept. 1963, p. 613.

also been given to another source of supply-side inflation; this source is usually referred to as **supply shocks**. In 1973–74, such a shock resulted from crop failures and the surging foreign demand for U.S. agricultural commodities. Also in 1973–74 and to a lesser degree in 1979, we felt the shock of the drastically higher oil prices imposed by the OPEC cartel. Developments like these have the same impact on the price level as wage-push and profit-push. We will now examine each of these three sources of supply-side inflation: wage-push, profit-push, and supply shocks.

Wage—Push
Inflation

A sizable segment of the general public, excluding, of course, the segment made up of labor union members, believes that rising prices are the result of **wage-push**: labor unions' extracting money-wage rate increases greater than the increase in the productivity of labor. The idea has a simple plausibility: If firms find the labor cost per unit of output rising, they in turn raise their prices to cover the higher cost. A series of increases in wage rates leads to a series of increases in prices—inflation. The wage—push explanation of inflation also appeals to many because it appears to provide an easy solution to a perplexity of recent years. Some of our recent recessions have exhibited the phenomenon of a rising rate of increase in the price level in the face of a rising rate of unemployment, a combination of changes variously described as stagflation and inflationary recession. Although this phenomenon cannot be explained by simple wage-push alone, as we will see here, that theory of inflation is at least consistent with this phenomenon. In the following chapter we will examine specifically how inflationary recession occurs.

Wage-push can only occur in imperfectly competitive labor markets, and the foremost imperfection is the existence of labor unions. A usual characteristic of such markets is that the money-wage rate is inflexible downward, the result of which is an aggregate supply curve of

the kind shown by AS_1 in Part D of Figure 22-3. To clarify how a change in the money-wage rate causes a shift in the aggregate supply curve, the complete four-part diagram used in Chapter 8 for the derivation of the AS curve is repeated here. To start with, we assume that the existing money-wage rate is indicated by W_1 in Part C. On the assumption that the money-wage rate does not fall below W_1, the AS_1 curve is derived from this money-wage rate in Part C and from the other parts of the diagram as explained in Chapter 8 (see pp. 135–40). The equilibrium price level and output levels are determined in Part D by the intersection of the AD curve and the AS_1 curve. Suppose the IS and LM curves are positioned so as to produce the AD_1 curve in Part D. The result is $P = P_1$, $Y = Y_f$, and $N = N_f$; the equilibrium level of output is one of full employment of the labor force. (An AD curve to the left of AD_1 would produce an intersection with AS_1 below Y_f and would result in an equilibrium with less than full employment.)

With the initial AS_1 and AD_1 curves in place, we can turn to the process by which increases in the money-wage rate push up the price level. Assume that an increase in the money-wage rate results entirely from the exploitation of the market strength of labor unions and in no part from increased productivity of labor or increased demand for labor. This change appears in part C as a shift in the W curve from, say, W_1 to W_2. With the curves in Parts A and B as given, the AS curve derived in Part D is now AS_2. The increase from W_1 to W_2 has pushed AS upward from AS_1 to AS_2. The price level at which each possible level of output will be supplied increases proportionally with the increase in the money-wage rate.[8] With aggregate demand of AD_1, the result

---

[8]To maximize profits, firms selling in competitive markets hire labor up to the point at which the real wage rate is equal to the marginal physical product of labor or W/P = MPP. Or given W, they hire labor up to the point at which $W = P \cdot$MPP. Pick a level of output and suppose that the MPP at that level happens to be 10. If W is $20, that level of output will be supplied at a P of $2, because only then

of the higher money-wage rate and the resultant upward shift from AS_1 to AS_2 is a rise in the price level from P_1 to P_2 and a fall in the output level from Y_f to Y_1 as shown in Part D. In place of full employment of the labor force, N_f, in Part B, there is no employment of N_2 and unemployment equal to $N_4 - N_2$. The rise in the price level has been accompanied by the appearance of unemployment.

Although not shown in Figure 22-3, further increases in the money wage will shift the W curve upward in Part C and, all else being equal, will cause further upward shifts in the AS curve in Part D. With the AD curve given, once the adjustments have been worked out, each increase in the money-wage rate leads to a higher price level, lower output, and higher unemployment. If left to itself, such increases in the money-wage rate cannot continue indefinitely; the worsening unemployment that follows each such increase may restrain the unions' demands for ever higher money-wage rates. We will comment further on this later, but it will be seen here that, at least over some range, a rising price level may result from rising money-wage rates.

Cost–push inflation is classified as wage-push if a rising price level is caused by rising money-wage rates. However, although a rising money-wage rate may cause a rising price level, not all increases in money-wage rates are inflationary. Bypassing the complications that lie behind it, the basic relationship is that percentage increases in the money-wage rate that do not exceed those in the marginal productivity of labor are not inflationary. Given the rule for firms' profit maximization under competitive conditions ($W = P \cdot MPP$), if W rises by 5 percent in any time period and MPP rises by 5 percent,

W/MPP (marginal cost) remains unchanged. Firms will offer any particular quantity of output at the same price level as before, or an unchanged P is consistent with profit maximization at any given level of output.

Without tracing the relationships in detail, what basically occurs in terms of Figure 22-3 is a rightward shift in the production function of Part A, the result of technological advance or an increase in the capital stock. This raises the MPP at each level of N and shifts the D_N curve in Part B to the right. With a given money-wage rate in Part C, the result will be a downward or rightward shift in the AS curve of Part D.[9] If an increase in W which *in itself* causes the AS curve to shift upward is just matched in percentage terms by an increase in the MPP which *in itself* causes the AS curve to shift downward, the two are offsetting and the price levels at which the various output levels are supplied by industry as a whole remain unchanged. Of course, to the extent that the percentage changes differ, the AS curve, on balance, will shift upward or downward, although recent experience has shown no cases in which W did not rise at least as fast as MPP and therefore no cases in which the AS curve, on balance, shifted downward.

That increases in money-wage rates matched by increases in labor productivity are not inflationary is perhaps a familiar fact, but is it also a fact that increases in money-wage rates unmatched by increases in labor productivity are necessarily inflationary? This clearly looks like all one needs to identify a wage-push, but that is not necessarily the case. The rise in the money-wage rate may not be the result of the exploitation of the power held by labor unions but the result of an excess demand for labor. In this event, the money-wage rate would rise whether or not there were labor unions and the rise cannot meaningfully be described as inflationary.

---

will $W = P \cdot MPP$ ($\$20 = \$2 \cdot 10$). Assuming now that labor unions push W up to $\$30$ in the absence of any other change, the same level of output will be supplied at P of $\$3$, because only then will $W = P \cdot MPP$ ($\$30 = \$3 \cdot 10$). The price level will rise proportionally with the rise in the money-wage rate. The same will hold true if one starts with any higher or lower level of output and the lower or higher MPP that exists at that level of output.

---

[9]The process is illustrated by Figure 9-3, p. 159, although the model there assumes a perfectly inelastic AS curve instead of the one here that is less than perfectly inelastic over a range.

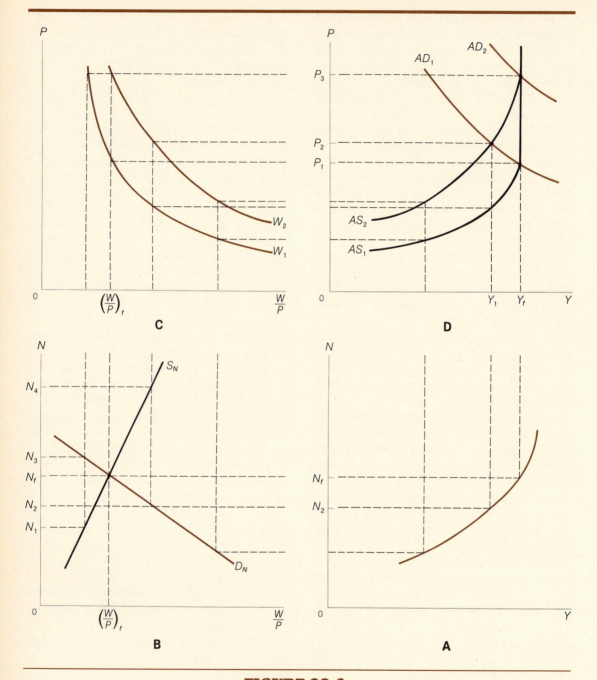

FIGURE 22-3
**Cost—Push Inflation Originating with Autonomous
Money Wage Rate Increase**

To see this, start in Part D of Figure 22-3 with an original equilibrium of Y_f and P_1 established by the intersection of AS_1 and AD_1. Assume then a shift to AD_2, which is purely inflationary and pulls P up to P_3. This, of course, is a standard case of demand–pull inflation. However, note the developments that follow from this. The higher P clearly means a larger profit per unit of output and a larger total profit for firms because the total receipts from the sale of an unchanged amount of output have risen proportionally with P. The greater profits spur firms to expand output, and they seek more labor for this purpose. With P at P_3 and W for the moment at W_1, W/P has declined to the extent that the amount of labor demanded increases from N_f to N_3 and the amount supplied decreases from N_f to N_1 in Part B. There is an excess demand for labor of $N_3 - N_1$. This excess demand forces W from W_1 to W_2 in Part C. With P at P_3, the increase from W_1 to W_2 raises W/P to its original level, $(W/P)_f$, and eliminates the excess demand for labor. At the same time, the increase in W shifts the AS curve upward from AS_1 to AS_2. At the new equilibrium, the supply of goods equals the demand for goods, and the supply of labor equals the demand for labor.

In this sequence, there has been a rise in the money-wage rate with no rise in the productivity of labor. Consequently, there has been a rise in the labor cost per unit of output. However, the rise in labor cost per unit of output is not the *cause* of the rise in the price level but the *result*. The money-wage rate rose as a result of an excess demand for labor derived from the upward shift in the aggregate demand function for goods; the rise in the money-wage rate would have occurred whether or not labor was organized. Although this conclusion may be obvious, recognition of it is necessary if we are to see the fallacy in the argument of those who contend that any rise in wage rates in excess of the rise in labor productivity causes a rise in the price level.

The concept of wage–push inflation must then be limited to increases in labor costs that are the cause and not the result of higher prices. Wage–push inflation can follow only from "spon-

taneous" or "autonomous" upward shifts in the supply function, as opposed to those that are "induced" by excess demand for labor. Induced shifts may occur with or without a strong labor movement, but spontaneous shifts require organized labor with sufficient strength to push up wage rates in the absence of any excess demand for labor. Where unions have this strength, a rise in wage rates may produce a spontaneous shift in the supply function from AS_1 to AS_2 even though there is no shift in AD. As a first approximation, therefore, we can say that a rise in prices is the result of wage-push if the existing AD function cannot support the rise in wage rates without a reduction in output and employment. This is illustrated by the reduction in output from Y_f to Y_1 that results from the shift from AS_1 to AS_2. On the other hand, a shift from AS_1 to AS_2 will not reduce output if that shift is induced by excess demand for labor that follows from a shift from AD_1 to AD_2.

Wage–push inflation is impossible in an economy in which wage rates are determined by purely competitive market forces. In such a situation, wage rates will rise or fall only in response to variations in labor supply and demand, the latter in turn depending on variations in aggregate demand for final output. However, the labor force need not be completely unionized to obtain the conditions needed for wage-push. It is sufficient that a substantial portion of the labor force be organized and that these organizations be strong enough to force increases in money wages that exceed productivity increases. With a partially organized labor force, as is the case in the U.S. and most other free economies—and to the extent that nonunion wages are closely tied (with established differentials) to union wages— wage-push may originate in unionized industries and the higher wages gained there may spread to other industries.

There are a number of reasons to expect this spread of higher wages to nonunion workers. Employers of nonunion labor may raise the wages of their employees in order to discourage unionization, prevent employee discontent, and avoid loss of valued employees. However, to the extent that nonunion wages are *not* adjusted to union wages, a wage–push process in unionized industries leads to an ever greater gap between union and nonunion wages. This gap will mean relatively higher prices on the goods produced by unionized industries, which may induce a shift of demand away from these goods in favor of the relatively lower-priced goods produced by non-unionized industries. This gap also increases the possibility that new firms will enter the unionized industries and operate with nonunion labor. Developments such as these represent threats to the jobs and the higher wage rates of union employees. As such they must act as a restraint on the push for higher wages in the unionized industries. Therefore, a wage–push inflationary process that creates a constantly widening gap between union and nonunion wage rates probably cannot be sustained. In sum, the initiation of an economy-wide wage–push inflation requires at least a partially organized labor force. The rate at which such an inflation will proceed and whether it can be sustained depends on, among other factors, the extent of unionization and the degree to which union-won gains spread to the balance of the labor force.

These results are based on the assumption that employers post higher prices for their products as rapidly as the forced increases in wage rates raise the cost of those products. Although the presence of labor unions on the supply side of the labor market is a prerequisite to wage–push inflation, the success of a union drive to increase wages depends in part on the demand conditions faced by the firms subjected to these wage demands. The individual firm, operating under monopolistically competitive conditions, cannot raise prices to offset higher wage rates without losing much of its sales, because under monopolistically competitive conditions the demand curve for its output is quite elastic. Whether they are organized or not, workers cannot force such an individual firm to grant higher wages without eventually driving it out of business (unless the particular firm enjoys some special advantage that provides extraordinary profits). If, on the other hand, the same increase in wage rates is secured from all firms in a monopolistically competitive industry, wage-push is at least possible. Despite the elasticity of the demand curve facing each firm, no one firm need fear loss of sales to competitors by raising prices to cover higher wages, because all other firms in the industry may be expected to follow a similar policy. The industry as a whole still faces a less than perfectly inelastic demand curve. Therefore, if wage rates do not show similar rises in other industries, the industry in question may lose sales to others. Nonetheless, labor may still be able to force through a wage-push, albeit at the cost of some decrease in the output of this industry and in the employment it provides. Because the demand curves facing oligopolists are less elastic than those in monopolistically competitive markets, such firms present unions with the best opportunities for securing wage increases in excess of productivity increases with a minimum loss of jobs. Largely for this reason, wage-push, if it occurs, tends to be most pronounced in unionized oligopolistic industries. Although initiated in and offset by higher prices for the output of these industries, higher wages usually spread to other unionized industries as unions there seek to follow the "pattern" and to match the gains that have been won by other unions. The same increases may in turn spill over in large degree into non-unionized industries, as we mentioned earlier.

Given strong aggressive unions in the major oligopolistic industries, one can see how wage pressures originating there and wage gains won there can possibly spread through the system as a whole to produce some degree of wage–push inflation in the absence of any increase in current demand for output of the economy as a whole.

Profit–Push Inflation

Profit-push is another variant of supply inflation. Just as labor unions may exercise their market power by forcing wage increases, so oligopolists and monopolists may, in their drive toward greater profits, raise prices more than enough to offset any cost increases. Again, just as labor unions are a prerequisite to a generalized wage–push inflation, so the existence of imperfectly competitive markets in the sale of goods and services is a prerequisite to profit–push inflation. Where prices of goods are set by the competition of buyers and sellers, as in agricultural commodities and raw materials, the seller cannot do very much about the price at which he sells. But many goods do not move through such markets, and the sellers of these goods "administer" prices. In an economy in which so-called administered prices abound, there is at least the possibility that these prices may be administered upward faster than costs in an attempt to earn greater profits. Graphically, the process may be represented by an upward shift in the AS curve like that described for wage-push in Part D of Figure 22-3. To the extent that the process of administering prices upward more rapidly than costs move upward is widespread, profit–push inflation will result.

Although there is this similarity between the administered prices at which labor unions supply labor to firms and the administered prices at which firms supply goods and services to their customers, the responsibility for supply inflation has still generally been placed with labor unions. One reason for this lies in the differences between the wage-setting process followed by unions and the price-setting process followed by business. It is argued that unions commonly press for higher wages with an objective that is little more specific than Samuel Gompers' classic goal of "more." This is either because unions regard the demand curve for labor as highly inelastic or because they are more concerned with higher wage rates than with the amount of unemployment that higher wage rates will produce with given aggregate demand. In contrast to the officers of labor unions, those who administer prices of goods have a more or less definite objective in the form of profit maximization. Profits of a firm depend not only on prices but on sales and unit costs as well, and the latter depend in part on prices charged. Therefore, although there is always the possibility of raising prices where

prices are administered, the argument is that market realities enter more systematically into the setting of prices than into the setting of wage rates by labor unions. Firms with administered prices may generally respond promptly to wage increases by raising prices, but they are unlikely, when faced with unchanged demand and stable costs, to raise prices above those that are already "equilibrium" prices according to the profit maximization or other objectives of the firm.

Critics of business who assert that "giant corporations" price their output to squeeze out the last dollar of profit sometimes also accuse the same companies of pricing their output in a way that produces profit–push inflation. From the preceding, it should be clear that one cannot have it both ways. If the companies have already fully exploited whatever market power they have, they cannot also price their output to produce a profit–push inflation without some sacrifice in those profits. On the other hand, if they have a reserve of unexploited market power, they can then price to produce a profit–push inflation. But in this case, the charge that they regularly squeeze out the last dollar of profit cannot also be supported.

A qualification to this line of argument appears if the degree of market power held by business increases continuously or over certain intervals of time. There is no completely satisfactory measure of monopoly or oligopoly power, but the one most commonly used is the concentration ratio, the share of an industry's total output accounted for by its 4 largest firms. A study of 209 manufacturing industries shows that from 1947 (or 1954) to 1963 the concentration ratios in 85 increased, in 81 decreased, and in 43 remained relatively stable. Based on later data, from 1947 (or 1954) to 1967, for the same 209 industries, the ratios increased in 95, decreased in 75, and remained relatively stable in 39.[10] Another study of 213 manufacturing industries

---

[10] See *Concentration Ratios in Manufacturing, 1967, Special Reports*, 1970, Part 1, Table 5, Bureau of the Census, Department of Commerce.

shows that the average concentration ratio increased from 41.2 percent in 1947 to 41.9 percent in 1966, an increase of 0.7 percentage point. The 132 of these industries classified as capital goods industries showed a decline in the average ratio over these years from 45.1 to 43.4, or by 1.7 percentage points; the 81 classified as consumer goods industries showed a rise from 34.8 to 39.6 percent or of 4.8 percentage points.[11] Such evidence suggests some overall increase in concentration in manufacturing for this particular period of time, but not an increase of major magnitude. Some of the U.S. economy's bouts with inflation over this period have been attributed to cost–push forces, but evidence like this does not lend much support to the argument that the cost-push was of the profit–push variety.

Supply-Shock Inflation

A third source of supply-side inflation is supply shock. The mechanics of the process by which supply-shocks push up the price level are the same as those for wage-push or profit-push. The AS curve in Part D of Figure 22-3 is pushed upward as described in our discussion of wage-push. What is different is the nature of the driving force. Although the action of OPEC that raised the price level in the United States was an exercise of market power—a power far greater than that exercised by any American firm—this kind of market power is different from that held by either labor or domestic firms. It is wielded by a foreign organization over which the U.S. government can exert only very limited influence. In contrast, U.S. labor unions and firms must always be concerned with the possibility that their selfish actions can result in punitive labor legislation and stricter enforcement of existing antitrust legislation or even new antitrust legislation. Shocks in the form of crop shortages stemming from developments such as bad weather are clearly altogether beyond the control of the U.S. government.

---

[11]See *Studies by the Staff of the Cabinet Committee on Price Stability,* Washington, D.C., Jan. 1969, p. 58.

To a much greater degree than the other sources of supply-side inflation, supply shocks are unforeseen. We can anticipate wage-push to occur whenever the conditions for it are appropriate, but something like the OPEC action of 1973–74 came as a total surprise. Similarly, the shutdown of oil production in Iran at the end of 1978 and the subsequent fall of the Shah were not widely anticipated, but these events triggered further sharp increases in oil prices in early 1979. This qualified as a supply shock, though a smaller one than that of 1973–74.

Although there is little that government can do to prevent the inflationary impact of the unforeseen disturbances called supply shocks, the government may be able to neutralize the impact of such disturbances through the use of fiscal policy as a tool of "supply management." This and other aspects of controlling supply-side inflation are considered in the following section.

Supply-Side Inflation: The Problem of Control

Restrictive monetary and fiscal policies are the standard weapons used to curb demand–pull inflation. If a burst of investment spending, foreign purchases, or other such forces shifts the AD curve in Figure 22-1 upward from AD_1 to AD_2, the resulting rise in the price level may be countered by restrictive monetary and fiscal policies that shift the AD curve back down to AD_1. In carrying out such policies, there are difficult questions of timing and degree, but there is little question that such policies are appropriate to combat demand–pull inflation. In a supply inflation, however, restrictive monetary and fiscal policies of the conventional kind are not so clearly appropriate. Such measures have their immediate impact on aggregate demand, but supply inflation is not the result of aggregate demand pressing against the economy's full employment output. As a matter of fact, in attempting to distinguish between demand and supply inflation, the most telling evidence of a supply inflation is a rising price level with output appreciably below the level indicated by full employment.

In Figure 22-4, starting at the full employment equilibrium given by the intersection of AS_1 and AD_2, if the aggregate supply curve is pushed upward to AS_2 as a result of, say, an autonomous rise in wage rates, the price level will rise from P_1 to P_2 and output will fall from Y_f to Y_1. The diagram suggests that we can prevent this rise in the price level by adopting monetary and fiscal policies restrictive enough to force the AD curve leftward from AD_2 to AD_1. However, it is also apparent that maintaining the price level unchanged at P_1 in this way is achieved only at the cost of further reduction in output from Y_1 to Y_2. In practice, the problem is that neutralizing the rise in the price level that comes with cost-push may require a reduction in output and a rise in unemployment so large as to be economically and socially unacceptable. In other words, we might be purchasing price stability only at the cost of considerable social distress and a slowed rate of economic growth. If sustained periods of 7 or 8 percent unemployment are necessary to achieve price stability, it would seem to many people the lesser of two evils to accept the higher price level that accompanies the lower unemployment, assuming that such lower unemployment can be obtained without setting into motion a continuing series of price increases.

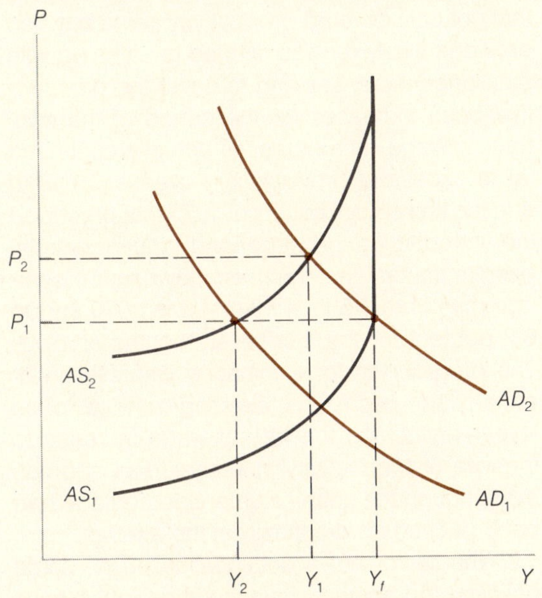

Supply-Side Inflation and U.S. Policy Since the Mid-1960s

U.S. experience over the period since the mid-1960s provides several illustrations of the problem of adjusting stabilization policies to conform with different types of inflation. The inflation during 1965–68 could be explained largely by the excessively rapid growth of aggregate demand. Of course, this growth was, in turn, initiated by the rapid expansion of military expenditures at the beginning of the Vietnam buildup in 1965. Prices rose considerably over these years, but output also rose quite sharply; the rise in output was sufficient to push unemployment below 4 percent in 1966, the first year a rate below 4 percent had been achieved since the Korean War. However, with further reductions to a 3.6 unemployment rate by 1968, most of the slack in the economy had been absorbed and further increases in aggregate demand could be expected to exert their impact predominantly on prices with little gain in output. If the existing inflation was not to go from bad to worse, it became imperative that demand be brought under control. Although the policy pursued by the government may surely be criticized for coming too late and perhaps also for being too little—

FIGURE 22-4
Combating Cost–Push Inflation with Restrictive Monetary and Fiscal Policies

action had been recommended by many economists as early as 1965—the increase in corporate and personal income tax rates through the 10 percent surtax imposed by the Congress in 1968 was a step in the right direction. There could be little doubt that demand–pull forces were at work in the ongoing inflationary process. The 1968 action was therefore an appropriate move.

In January 1969, the incoming Republican administration inherited the ongoing inflation, but it also inherited an economy with no serious unemployment problem. The January 1969 unemployment figure was 3.3 percent. The policy of the new administration, which was steadfastly adhered to for over two years, was to limit its attack on the inflation problem to what could be done with monetary and fiscal policies alone. Wage and price controls or guideposts or any other version of an incomes policy, even something as moderate as "jawboning," were rejected out of hand. The Nixon administration's opposition to such measures was almost theological in its fervor. Although the administration never spelled out exactly how this was to be accomplished, it held that through monetary and fiscal policies the rate of inflation would be reduced to an acceptable level without at the same time producing any appreciable rise in the unemployment rate. What actually happened is, of course, now in the record books: The economy went through its first recession since 1960–61 and suffered a rise in the unemployment percentage from an average of 3.5 in 1969 to 4.9 in 1970 and 5.9 in 1971. In exchange for this sacrifice, the economy received no substantial slowing in the rate of inflation. The restrictive monetary and fiscal policies had their effect predominantly on output and employment and only moderately on prices, just the opposite of what was to have been expected according to the administration's so-called "game plan."

The difficulty arose from the fact that what by 1969 had come to be an inflation driven in large part by wage–push forces was being attacked by the administration with weapons that are not well-suited to combat this kind of inflation. As we have seen, the wage–push element in an inflationary process can only be checked by restrictive monetary and fiscal policies through the capacity of those policies to restrain output and raise unemployment enough to prevent wage increases in excess of productivity increases. This fact gave rise to the widespread skepticism among economists that the administration could, by resort to any conceivable combination or variety of restrictive monetary and fiscal policies, check the existing strong inflationary movement without producing severe unemployment. Moreover, there was considerable doubt whether even a pronounced increase in unemployment would be adequate. The inflation had become progressively worse since 1965 and the public quite generally expected more of the same. Therefore, labor unions were understandably determined to settle for nothing less than wage rate increases that not only covered productivity gains but also provided whatever was needed to catch up with past price increases and to cover the prospective price increases for the period of the contract.[12] Wage rate increases actually continued far in excess of productivity increases in 1970 and the first seven months of 1971 that preceded the introduction of wage and price controls, despite the fact that the unemployment percentage rose from 3.5 in 1969 to 4.9 in 1970 and to 6.2 percent for the first seven months of 1971. The prerequisite for eliminating whatever influence wage-push was exerting on the price level—restraining the rate of wage increase to the rate of productivity increase—was not met, even though the unemployment percentage had been pushed up drastically in the attempt.

Whether or not a continuation of the same policies for another few months would have begun to produce the intended results will never

---

[12]The role of expectations and their effect on wage rates and the rate of inflation will be examined more fully in Chapter 23.

be known, although many within the administration believed it would have. In any event, in August 1971, the administration adopted an incomes policy or a policy of direct intervention in wage and price setting. This amounted to an admission that the monetary and fiscal policies that had been relied on over the preceding two and a half years had not worked as expected. Without entering into the question of the degree to which the wage and price controls, maintained in various forms until April 1974, were in their turn successful, what is relevant here is that a policy of controls at least offered some hope of slowing down a wage price spiral without putting the economy "through the wringer," something that restrictive monetary and fiscal policies are unable to do where strong cost–push forces are at work.

From August 1971, the month in which controls were introduced, to December 1972, the Consumer Price Index rose at an annual rate of only 3.3 percent; but from December 1972 to December 1973 the rate jumped to 8.8 percent and from December 1973 to December 1974 it reached the "double digit" rate of 12.2 percent. For the following year, the rate declined to 7.0 percent and for the year ending December 1976 it declined to 4.8 percent. Like the sharp rise in prices in 1969–70, the later surge of prices, especially the "double digit" experience of 1974, is another episode of cost–push inflation. However, although wage-push was to some degree exerting its influence during these years, the cost–push forces at work during 1973–74 were in large part of a special, nonrecurrent nature. 1974 was a year of worldwide economic recession, but 1973 was a year of worldwide economic boom. At the same time that they enjoyed high prosperity at home, most industrialized countries suffered poor agricultural crops during 1973, which led to a great surge in demand for U.S. farm output. The farm products component of the U.S. wholesale price index shot up 36 percent during 1973! The resulting rise in the overall U.S. price level was only one part of the inflation of

that year accounted for by international transactions. Another part resulted from the two devaluations of the U.S. dollar in December 1971 and February 1973. Import prices, which had risen at a 7 percent rate from 1971 to 1972, more than doubled to about 17 percent from 1972 to 1973. Although the devaluations had the intended effect of stimulating U.S. exports, they were responsible for a large part of the increase in import prices and through this contributed significantly to the inflation during 1973.

Then there was the supply shock without parallel: the quadrupling of oil prices by the OPEC cartel following the lifting of the embargo on oil shipments to the U.S. by Arab oil-producing nations imposed in October 1973. The 44 percent rise in U.S. import prices in 1974 made what had been a very sharp rise of 17 percent in the preceding year look small in comparison. As the huge increase in the price of imported oil worked its way through the economy—not merely in the form of higher gasoline and home heating fuel prices but in higher prices of the hundreds of other products for which oil is a basic raw material—its impact on the general price level in 1974 was of major importance. Estimates of the impact differ, but it is safe to say that the "double digit" inflation rate of 1974 would not have occurred in the absence of this explosive increase in costs imposed by OPEC. Although this is another matter, there are those who maintain that it was the sudden severe jolt of the huge increase in payments made for oil that was primarily responsible for the worst recession that the U.S., western Europe, and Japan suffered since the 1930s.

Throughout the Nixon administration and through the Ford administration from its beginning in August 1974 into the fall of that year, priority was given to combatting inflation. This was replaced by the priority of reducing unemployment and expanding output as the severity of the decline in economic activity came to be recognized by late 1974. The inflation problem itself, at least temporarily, became much less important. From the 12.2 percent rate in 1974, the CPI fell to 7.0 percent in 1975 and to a reasonable 4.8 percent in 1976 (annual rates from December to December).

In early 1975, fiscal policy clearly became expansionary with an income tax rebate for individuals, a rise in the investment tax credit for business, and new employment programs. Monetary policy, which had brought a continual slowing of the rate of growth of the money supply from 1973 through the first quarter of 1975, turned sharply in the other direction in the spring of 1975. Partially because of the surge in the growth of total spending from an 8.0 percent rate in 1975 up to a 12.4 percent rate by 1978, the deceleration of inflation from 1974 to 1976 ended. The CPI jumped from the 4.8 percent rate in 1976 to 6.8, 9.0, and 13.3 percent rates over the next three years. In 1979 the economy suffered a higher rate of inflation than that of 1974, which at the time had been viewed as an anomaly unlikely to recur. Although not quite as bad as 1979, 1980 was also a year with worse inflation than 1974.

As was the case in 1974, the acceleration of inflation in 1979 and early 1980 was dominated by a major supply shock: the huge increase in oil prices that followed from political developments in Iran. However, the spurt of the inflation rate during 1977 and 1978 cannot be attributed to this factor. The two devaluations of the dollar in 1971 and 1973 boosted import prices early in the decade; the substantial depreciation of the dollar from mid-1977 to 1979 did the same late in the decade. The rise in import prices in short order appeared as a rise in the inflation rate.

Another part of the acceleration of inflation in these years is explained by what happened to wage rates and labor productivity. Hourly compensation of labor increased 7.7, 8.4, and 9.9 percent respectively for the years 1977–79. Over the same period, the rate of growth of labor productivity fell from 3.3 percent in 1976 to 2.1, −0.2, and −0.4. Apart from 1974, 1979 and 1980 are the only years in the post-World War II period during which the rate of growth of labor productivity turned negative. One might expect that the poor productivity record of these years

would have slowed wage rate increases, but inflationary expectations led labor to seek and obtain large increases in wage rates at the same time that labor's productivity was diminishing. The resultant rise in the rate of growth of labor cost per unit of output forced up the aggregate supply curve and made a rise in the inflation rate practically inevitable.

From this brief look at some of the major developments in the story of inflation since the mid-1960s, we find that a good part of the inflation over these years has been the result of supply-side developments. The most spectacular spurts in the inflation rate, those of 1974 and 1979–80, were closely associated with supply shocks originating outside the country. Such occurrences present special obstacles to a policy of trying to hold down price advances. Although a policy of wage and price controls may be able to restrain, at least for some time, cost-push of the wage–push or profit–push varieties, it is unable to do much at all when confronted with cost-push due to supply shocks like those considered. The U.S. government obviously can not impose price controls on the goods supplied by foreign producers. It can do something to control increases in prices due to sudden, large increases in foreign demand—for example, grain prices in 1973—by imposing an embargo or setting limits on quantities that may be exported. However, in the case of agricultural products, this runs into the political problem of enraging the nation's farmers. The next section looks at a possible way of meeting inflation that occurs as a result of supply shocks.

Supply-Side Inflation and Supply Management Through Fiscal Policy

We began the discussion of the problem of controlling supply-side or cost–push inflation with the observation that restrictive monetary and fiscal policies of the conventional kind are not appropriate to combat supply-side inflation, but are well-suited to combat demand-side inflation. This, of course, follows from the fact that conventional monetary and fiscal policies work on aggregate demand, but not on aggregate supply. However, fiscal policy may also be employed in an unconventional way to work on aggregate supply. Economists in the 1970s began to explore the possibilities of using fiscal policy in this way. The use of fiscal policy to produce changes in aggregate supply is often referred to as "supply management" to parallel the term "demand management" commonly used to describe the use of monetary and fiscal policies to produce changes in aggregate demand.

Although government may not be able to prevent the upward shift in the supply curve that results from a supply shock—again the best example is the upward shift that resulted from the quadrupling of OPEC oil prices in 1974—it may be able to offset such supply disturbances by fiscal policy actions that operate on the supply side. It is generally accepted that increases in sales taxes, excise taxes, and payroll taxes on employers appear directly in price levels with little delay. It is also believed that reductions in such taxes will appear in price levels without great delay.[13] Therefore, increases in sales, excise, and employer payroll taxes will shift the aggregate supply curve upward and decreases will do the opposite.

However, the federal government's ability to effect such deliberate shifts as an anti-inflationary tool is quite limited under present arrangements. The only sizable excise taxes it has, other than those earmarked for particular purposes such as the highway and airport trust funds, are those on alcohol and tobacco. Neither of these

is well-suited to the purpose at hand, because the initial impact of changes in tax rates on these items would be very unevenly distributed through the population. Because the federal government has no sales tax, this tax is not directly available for this purpose. However, here an arrangement might be made through which the state governments would reduce sales tax rates when asked to do so by the federal government and the federal government would provide them with grants to offset the lost revenue. Although not impossible, this approach runs into serious administrative and equity problems arising from the fact that five states do not have sales taxes and those which do have widely different tax bases (for example, some include food, but others do not). Under present arrangements, what the federal government can do directly through fiscal policy on the side of supply is largely limited to what it can do through changes in the employer payroll tax.

The specific way in which supply management may be used to offset the effect of a supply shock is probably apparent. In the face of a disturbance that pushes the aggregate supply curve upward, an appropriate fiscal policy response would be a reduction in employer payroll taxes. An exactly offsetting response would shift the aggregate supply curve downward by precisely the distance that the supply shock would have shifted it upward and there would then be no rise in the price level and no fall in the level of output. In terms of Figure 22-4, the upward shift in the aggregate supply curve from AS_1 to AS_2 that would have resulted from a supply shock could be offset by a reduction in employer payroll taxes of an amount that would shift the curve downward from AS_2 to AS_1. To the extent that this is achieved, it appears at first glance that the level of output and the price level would remain unchanged at Y_f and P_1 respectively.

However, this conclusion does not take into account a second effect of the reduction of employer payroll taxes—the effect on the aggregate demand curve. With the price level and the output level unchanged but with lower employer

---

[13]The same statement cannot be made for payroll taxes on employees. Unlike the tax on employers, the nominal incidence—that is, the impact on the price level—of payroll taxes on employees is very uncertain. Although these taxes have no direct impact on the price level, they may indirectly affect the price level to the degree that they are offset by changes in wages. However, the degree to which this occurs is uncertain.

payroll taxes, the government's total tax receipts will be smaller and the public's disposable income will be larger. With larger disposable income, there will be some upward shift in the aggregate demand curve at each possible level of output. In Figure 22-4, such a shift will be purely inflationary as the AD curve moves up along the vertical portion of the AS_1 curve. One way to prevent such a shift in the AD curve and thereby maintain the equilibrium at Y_f and P_1 is through an increase in income taxes sufficient to exert downward pressure on the AD curve equal to the upward pressure exerted on it by the effect on disposable income of the decrease in employer payroll taxes. Another way would be through a decrease in government purchases of goods and services or in transfer payments, again of an amount sufficient to exert an offsetting effect on the AD curve. In practice, of course, it is not very likely that policy makers could determine the exact set of changes that would be offsetting in the sense described.

Although the *modus operandi* of supply management as an anti-inflationary tool is clear enough in principle, it is beset with a number of difficulties, several of which have already been mentioned. The first is that the scope of operations is severely limited by the fact that the employer payroll tax is practically the only tax the federal government can use in this way under present arrangements. A second is the difficulty of determining the income tax increase or expenditure decrease that would just offset the effect of the payroll tax decrease on disposable income and through this on the aggregate demand curve. Another difficulty is the detrimental effects on the allocation of resources that may result from the kinds of changes in the tax structure that are required. The loss in terms of distortions of resource allocation must be weighed against whatever gain may be achieved in terms of a more stable economy. Still, despite all the difficulties that it presents, the use of supply management offers the possibility of a benefit that may more than compensate for its costs—holding down inflation without suffering the decrease

in output and rise in unemployment that must accompany the attempt to hold down inflation through demand management. This outstanding advantage of supply management goes far to explain the growing attention it has received during the 1970s.

Supply-Side Inflation: Its Relation to Demand-Side Inflation

Up to this point, we have examined separately the two parts of a well-established dichotomy in inflation theory: demand-side or demand-pull and supply-side or cost-push. Although this dichotomy is now a part of the language of economics, some economists object to its implication that an inflation is *either* demand-pull *or* cost-push. They argue that any actual inflationary process contains some elements of both. Expressed in this fashion, their argument can hardly be denied. However, if the dichotomy is accepted as nothing more than a convenient twofold classification of types of causation, their objections do not apply: It is at least helpful in separating two distinct sets of forces that are usually simultaneously and interdependently at work in any actual inflationary process.

In terms of this dichotomy, there is a lack of symmetry between the demand–pull and cost–push theories. An inflationary process may begin with generalized excess demand and may persist as long as excess demand is present, even though no cost–push forces whatsoever are at work. Excess demand will raise prices, which in turn will raise wage rates, but the rise in wage rates in this case is not the result of cost-push. However, this does not rule out the possibility that cost–push forces may also be at work to produce an even greater rise in wage rates. On the other hand, an inflationary process may begin on the supply side, but it will not long persist unless there is an increase in demand. For example, an autonomous rise in wage rates will raise prices in the absence of any increase in demand. For a cost–push inflation so initiated to be sustained, however, one wage increase must be piled on top of another; but, in the absence of an increase in demand, this would mean ever smaller production and ever greater unemployment. Sooner or later this must limit any inflationary process that solely depends on changes on the supply side.

This asymmetry can be illustrated by Figure 22-5. With output at Y_f, shifts in the aggregate demand function from AD_1 to AD_2 to AD_3 and beyond can carry the price level ever higher, from A to E to G, and so forth, in a sustained

inflationary process. With full employment, wage rates will rise along with prices as producers, encouraged to expand output by the enlarged profits that result from the rising aggregate demand, increase their demand for labor. As long as the forces feeding the demand for final output continue to shift the AD function ever higher, inflation will continue unchecked. In the extreme case, a runaway price level known as "hyperinflation" may result. However, starting again from Y_f, a cost-push that shifts the aggregate supply function from AS_1 to AS_2 will, with the AD function still at AD_1, produce an intersection at B and reduce output below the full employment level. A further upward push on the supply side to AS_3, unless accompanied by a shift in AD above AD_1, will move the intersection to C and further reduce output and employment. The successive reductions in output and the growing unemployment that result under these conditions will stop the inflation. Unlike demand-pull, inflation may originate on the supply side, but it cannot be sustained unless there is an appropriate increase on the demand side.

The crucial point, of course, is the shift, if any, that occurs in the aggregate demand function as the aggregate supply function shifts in the way described. At one extreme, the AD function may shift upward proportionally with the upward shift in the AS function. If we assume rising money wages are the cause of the upward shift on the supply side, as firms raise prices in response to higher wage rates, aggregate spending rises proportionally to maintain output and employment unchanged at the higher price level. This is equivalent to no decrease in real demand, a result that can follow only if there is, for example, a sufficient expansion of the money supply and therefore no rise in interest rates that would reduce real investment spending. Or, combining the interest-rate effect and other effects such as the Pigou effect, this result can follow only if these effects do not produce a decrease in real demand—that is, if they do not prevent a rise in aggregate spending proportional with the rise in the price and wage structure. But, because of

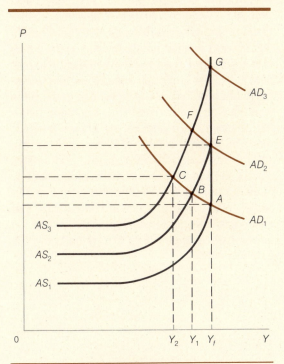

FIGURE 22-5
Shifts in the Aggregate Supply Function and Cost–Push Inflation

these effects and for other reasons, it seems most likely that aggregate spending will *not* rise in line with the rise in wages and that as a result there will be some decline in output and employment and a lesser rise in prices than would be the case under the assumptions stated. To the extent that this is the economy's characteristic response to the cost-push, successive cost-pushes can indeed force up wages and prices, but only at the cost of reduced employment and output. Consequently, we conclude that pure cost-push cannot in itself produce a sustained inflationary process.

If this conclusion is correct, the prospects of an inflationary process being fed in a sustained way from the supply side alone seem quite limited. But this overlooks one crucial consideration: Although a cost-push will probably not lead to a spontaneous increase in aggregate demand of the extent needed to prevent a reduction in output and employment, the required rise in aggregate demand may follow as the result of expansionary monetary and fiscal policies. Because cost-push left to itself can produce a reduction in output and aggravate any existing unemployment, this very fact may lead the monetary and fiscal authorities to react. They may choose policies designed to support output and employment, even though the result of such policies is an inflationary process that cost–push forces alone could not cause. This brings us face to face with a well-known dilemma: the apparent impossibility of simultaneously achieving full employment and avoiding some amount of infla-

tion in an economy in which strong cost–push forces are at work.

Viewed from this perspective, cost-push can mean a sustained inflationary process to the extent that "full employment at all costs" becomes the overriding economic objective of public policy. Such a policy requires the "validation" of an upward push of wages in order to prevent what otherwise would be an unacceptably high level of unemployment; but the validation of one wage-push is an open invitation to labor unions to bring off another wage-push. In terms of Figure 22-5, a "ratchet" is traced out by the movements from A to B to E to F to G as the price level moves up in a persistent inflationary process. This same process can also begin and proceed in an economy below full employment. Starting at B, a wage-push might shift us to C. An upward shift from AD_1 to AD_2 moves us to F, at which another wage-push (not shown) could shift the AS function upward another notch. As long as the policy is to validate each wage-push in the effort to prevent the worsening of an already existing unemployment problem, a sustained rise in the price level may occur in an economy operating below full employment. Because the choice typically made by government is to validate the cost-push, labor unions, oligopolistic business and foreign cartels such as OPEC with the market power to force up the price level and the willingness to exploit that power produce a combination that can sustain an inflationary process at the full employment position or at a position below full employment.

OVERVIEW

The two variables that receive the most attention in contemporary macroeconomics are inflation and unemployment. Probably no question in macroeconomics has received more attention in the last twenty years than the relationship between these two variables. Suppose the rate of unemployment is above the rate that at the time is judged to be the full employment rate. To what extent will government measures that raise the growth rate of aggregate spending spill over into a higher rate of inflation? To what extent will such measures result in a higher rate of growth of output and a lower rate of unemployment? There is no simple answer. Among other things, the answer depends heavily on the state of inflationary expectations at the time that the growth rate of aggregate spending rises.

This chapter constructs a model to help answer this question. Because we are interested in showing how the inflation rate and the unemployment rate change in relation to each other, the basic diagram that we will derive in a series of steps is the following:

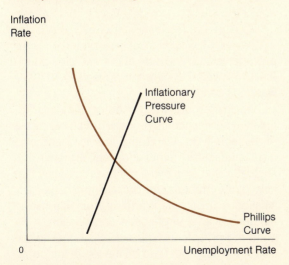

The diagram shows two curves: The Phillips curve, in this case the version of that curve which slopes downward to the right, and the inflationary pressure curve, which always slopes upward to the right. The intersection of these two curves indicates the inflation and unemployment rates at a point in time when forces are such as to put the two curves in the positions indicated. Changes in these forces will, of course, cause shifts in these curves and changes in the inflation rate and the unemployment rate.

In the first part of this chapter, we derive those two curves that are the elements of our model. We discuss why the Phillips curve, in one version, slopes downward to the right and why the inflationary pressure curve slopes upward to the right. With this understood, one can also understand

23
Inflation and Unemployment

why the intersection between the two curves identifies the inflation rate and the unemployment rate.

In the second part of the chapter, we take up the argument that the Phillips curve will slope downward to the right only in the short run and will become vertical in the long run. A downward-sloping curve indicates a tradeoff in the sense that a lower unemployment rate may be achieved at the cost of a higher inflation rate or a lower inflation rate may be achieved at the cost of a higher unemployment rate. However, a vertical Phillips curve permits no tradeoff: Every point along that curve is at the same unemployment rate. If the curve is indeed vertical in the long run, attempts to reduce the unemployment rate by raising the rate at which spending grows—an action which shifts the inflationary pressure curve upward—can only cause a higher inflation rate in the long run with no decrease in the unemployment rate.

In the final part of the chapter, we use the chapter's model to examine some developments of recent years. First, we note the existence of a cyclical pattern of inflation and unemployment from 1963 to 1980. Next, we focus on a special phase in this cyclical pattern—stagflation (infla-

tionary recession) or the phenomenon of a rising unemployment rate accompanied by a rising inflation rate. Historically, as unemployment increased during recessions, there was also deflation, or at least a deceleration of inflation; but we have run into exceptions to this in recent experience. An explanation for the existence of an acceleration of inflation in the face of a rising unemployment rate is offered here. Third, we examine the upward drift in the inflation rate over time. During or following recent recessions, the inflation rate has declined—but it has not dropped back to the rate prevailing before its rise during the preceding business expansion. This means that over time each episode of inflation starts from a higher base rate of inflation and there is therefore an upward drift in that rate. Last, we discuss the upward drift in the natural rate of unemployment, a concept close in meaning to the concept of the full employment rate of unemployment. The natural rate of unemployment has drifted upward because of such changes as the larger percentage of the labor force made up of women and teenagers and the provision of more generous unemployment compensation. Why such developments raise the natural rate of unemployment is explained.

The analysis of the inflationary process in Chapter 22 is acceptable as far as it goes, but it fails to focus specifically on the foremost macroeconomic concern of the past decade or more—the relationship between the inflation rate and the unemployment rate. So important are these two rates as a measure of our economic well-being that the late Arthur Okun of the Brookings Institution once suggested that the total of these two rates could be used as an index of discomfort. If this measure has any accuracy at all, our discomfort during the 1970s greatly exceeded our discomfort during the 1960s. The

average value of the sum of the two rates during the 1960s was 7.3 percent; during the 1970s, it was 13.3 percent.

We saw through the preceding chapter's Figure 22-5 an inflationary process traced out by the movements from A to B to E to F to G and also the fluctuations in output and, implicit therein, the fluctuations in employment that accompany that inflationary process. As defined in Chapter 21, inflation is a persistent and appreciable rise in the general level of prices. A continuation of the price movements in Figure 22-5 from G to the end of the alphabet (and off the top of the page) would surely meet the requirements of this definition. However, because discussions of inflation almost invariably proceed not in terms of absolute changes in the price level but in terms of the rate of change of the price level, it is desirable to work with diagrams that plot the rate of change of the price level—that is, the rate of inflation—on the vertical axis in contrast to all of the preceding chapter's diagrams, which plot the absolute price level on that axis.

In a similar way, discussions of the economy's record with respect to output and employment do not typically run in terms of absolute levels of output or employment but in terms of the growth rate of output and the rate of unemployment. In place of the preceding chapter's diagrams that plot the level of output and therefore implicitly the level of employment, it is desirable to work with diagrams that plot the unemployment rate. Then every point on a diagram that plots the inflation rate on the vertical axis and the unemployment rate on the horizontal axis identifies a combination of an inflation rate and an unemployment rate. What determines the particular combination that is found in the economy at any time? What causes changes in that combination from one time to the next? Included here is that perplexing change in which the new combination has both a higher inflation rate and a higher unemployment rate than existed before; this condition is popularly described as stagflation. This chapter constructs a model to deal with questions like these.

The Elements of the Model

The model contains two basic elements—a Phillips curve and an inflationary pressure curve. With the rate of inflation measured along the vertical axis and the unemployment rate measured along the horizontal axis, the Phillips curve in the short run slopes downward to the right, indicating a relationship in which a lower rate of inflation

is accompanied by a higher rate of unemployment. The inflationary pressure curve slopes upward to the right, indicating a relationship in which a higher rate of inflation is accompanied by a higher rate of unemployment. The intersection of the two curves identifies the inflation rate and the unemployment rate for that point in time. Shifts in either or both of these curves may result in changes in the inflation rate, the unemployment rate, or both. Accordingly, we have a model into which we can insert various factors that produce shifts in either of these two curves and trace their effect on the inflation rate and the unemployment rate.[1]

The Phillips Curve

As we saw in Chapter 22, one approach to an explanation of inflation runs in terms of wage-push—that is, wage increases not matched by increases in labor productivity are converted into increases in the price level. Expressed in terms of rates, an increase in the growth rate of wage rates not matched by an equal increase in the growth rate of labor productivity is converted into an increase in the inflation rate. For example, all else being equal, if initially money-wage rates are increasing by 7 percent per year and labor productivity is increasing by 3 percent per year, a 4 percent rate of increase in the price level, that is, a 4 percent inflation rate, will tend to result. A rise in the rate at which money-wage rates are increasing from 7 to 9 percent per year with no change in the 3 percent growth rate of labor productivity will tend to raise the inflation rate from 4 to 6 percent per year.

This relationship between the rate of increase of wage rates and the inflation rate leads us to examine another relationship—that between the rate of increase of wage rates and the rate of unemployment of the labor force. If in addition to the direct relationship between the rate of price

---

[1] The model is here presented in a simplified form with a number of complications omitted. For an examination of a similar model in full detail, see R.J. Gordon, *Macroeconomics*, 2nd ed., Little Brown, 1981, Chs. 7 and 8.

increase and the rate of wage increase, there is also an inverse relationship between the rate of wage increase and the rate of unemployment, it follows that there is an inverse relationship between the inflation rate and the unemployment rate. Because the data for various countries and various time periods do show this inverse relationship between the rate of wage increase and the unemployment rate, in this indirect way the unemployment rate becomes a factor of major interest in the study of inflation. The analysis of the particular relationship between the rate of wage increase and the unemployment rate proceeds in terms of the Phillips curve, named after A.W. Phillips, the British economist who pioneered in the investigation of this relationship for the United Kingdom.[2]

In its simplest form, a Phillips curve may be derived from an economy's data for a period of years by plotting for each year the percentage of money-wage rate increase, $\Delta W/W$ (vertical axis), against the percentage of the labor force that is unemployed, U (horizontal axis). A curve fitted to the points so plotted for certain periods of years will slope downward to the right like the curve in Figure 23-1. Any curve of this general shape suggests that the rate of wage rate increase is inversely related to the unemployment rate—that relatively high unemployment rates are accompanied by lower rates of wage rate increase than are relatively low unemployment rates. The hypothetical curve in Figure 23-1 reveals that $\Delta W/W$ will be 3 percent at the high U of 9 percent, but that $\Delta W/W$ will be 9 percent at the lower U of 6

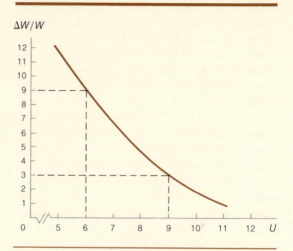

FIGURE 23-1
Phillips Curve

percent. There is, in other words, a tradeoff between the rate at which wage rates increase and the rate of unemployment. We will discuss the implications of this relationship later, but it is first necessary to examine how a relationship of this kind may be explained.

Explanations of the Phillips Curve Relationship   There are two principal explanations for the Phillips curve relationship. One relates to the behavior of organized labor. The argument here takes off from the one presented in the preceding chapter under the heading of wage–push inflation. Organized labor can cause autonomous increases in wage rates in excess of increases in productivity. This leads to rising prices of goods in a process that is accordingly called wage–push inflation. To the argument that organized labor can push through autonomous increases in wage rates greater than productivity increases, we now add the following: The degree to which labor can do this will vary inversely with the unemployment percentage and the ease of labor markets. With lower unemployment and

[2]See "The Relation between Unemployment and the Rate of Change in Money Wage Rates in the United Kingdom, 1862–1957," in *Economica*, Nov. 1958, pp. 283–99, reprinted in M.G. Mueller, ed., *Readings in Macroeconomics*, 2nd ed., Holt, Rinehart and Winston, 1971, pp. 245–56. Although Phillips' name has been attached to the relationship, an article by the American economist, Irving Fisher, anticipated Phillips by decades. See "A Statistical Relation Between Unemployment and Price Changes," in *International Labour Review*, June 1926, pp. 785–92, reprinted in *Journal of Political Economy*, March/April 1973, pp. 496–502.

tighter labor markets, organized labor will become more aggressive and press for larger wage increases; under the opposite conditions, organized labor will be less demanding. Furthermore, because times of low unemployment and tight labor markets are ordinarily times of buoyant demand for goods and abundant profits, business will usually grant the "excessive" wage increase demands rather than face the possibility of a strike and a shutdown of such profitable production. Under the opposite set of conditions—high unemployment and low profits—business would have much less to lose and would show considerable resistance to even moderate wage increase demands. With the relative bargaining strength of labor unions and employers varying in this way, we can expect an inverse relationship between the percentage wage increase and the unemployment percentage of the kind shown by the Phillips curve.

A second explanation, which is general and not dependent on the relative bargaining powers of organized labor and business, relates to excess demand for labor.[3] The explanation is somewhat involved and we will sketch only the bare essentials here. For this purpose, an abbreviated two-part graphic system is used instead of the four-part system needed to show the complete analysis graphically.

The explanation begins with supply and demand curves for labor, as shown in Part A of Figure 23-2. For the curves as given, the wage rate W_3 equates the supply of and demand for labor. Although this wage rate indicates an equilibrium in the labor market, it does not indicate an absence of unemployment. It is an equilibrium in the sense that the number of unemployed workers is just equal to the number of vacancies

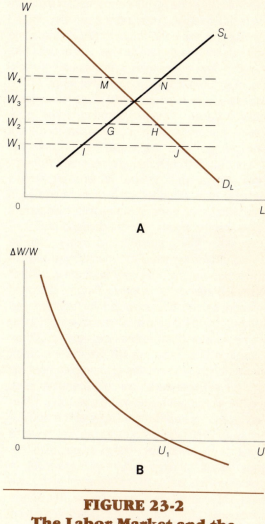

FIGURE 23-2
The Labor Market and the Phillips Curve

[3]This explanation is advanced by R.G. Lipsey in "The Relation between Unemployment and the Rate of Change of Money Wage Rates: A Further Analysis," in *Economica*, Feb. 1960, pp. 1–31, reprinted in R.A. Gordon and L.R. Klein, eds., *Readings in Business Cycles*, Irwin, 1965, pp. 456–87.

that employers seek to fill. It would be an equilibrium with zero unemployment only if frictional unemployment were always zero. This would require, for example, that no workers ever changed jobs or, if they did, that not a day's work was lost in the process—a situation obviously not realized in practice.

At any wage rate below this equilibrium—for example, W_2—the number of vacancies exceeds the number seeking jobs; there is excess demand for labor, in this case equal to GH. In the same way, at any wage rate above the equilibrium, there are fewer vacancies than the number seeking jobs; there is excess supply of labor. At W_4, excess supply is equal to MN. If we look specifically at cases of excess demand, a key argument in the present explanation is that the rate at which wage rates rise varies directly with the extent of the excess demand for labor. Accordingly, with a wage rate of W_1 and an excess demand of IJ, there will be a more rapid rise in wage rates than there would be with a wage rate of W_2 and the smaller excess demand of GH.

Another key argument is that the average period of time required for unemployed people to find jobs varies inversely with the extent of excess demand for labor. In Figure 23-2, the average search time involved for unemployed workers to find the kind of job they are looking for will be shorter when excess demand is IJ than when it is GH. From this follows the important conclusion that the amount of unemployment will vary inversely with the amount of excess demand. In other words, with a given labor supply, whatever rate of unemployment exists at the equilibrium wage rate will be smaller as we move to successively lower wage rates or successively larger levels of excess demand. However, a greater excess demand for labor will also raise the rate at which wage rates increase. This brings in the earlier argument that the speed with which wage rates rise in the face of excess demand depends on the magnitude of that excess demand. When we put together this relationship in which the rate of increase in the wage rate depends directly on the amount of excess demand and the rate of unemployment depends inversely on the amount of excess demand, we have the Phillips curve relationship, in which the rate of wage increase and the unemployment rate are inversely related.

For example, suppose that when there is neither excess supply nor excess demand—that is,

a wage rate of W_3 in Part A of Figure 23-2—there is an amount of unemployment that yields the unemployment rate U_1 in Part B of that figure. This unemployment rate is accompanied by a zero percentage rate of wage increase, because there is neither an excess supply of nor an excess demand for labor at that wage rate. At any wage rate below W_3, we have excess demand. This means a lower unemployment rate or a leftward movement in terms of the horizontal axis in Part B, and also a higher percentage rate of wage increase or an upward movement in terms of the vertical axis in Part B. We therefore find a movement to a point back up the Phillips curve. The greater the excess demand, the further from the originally selected point at U_1 will we be. The same reasoning may be applied to a wage rate above W_3. In this case, there is excess supply, which means a higher unemployment rate than U_1 and a rate of wage increase lower than zero, or a movement to a point down the Phillips curve from the originally selected point at U_1.[4]

The two explanations of the Phillips curve relationship noted here are not alternatives. The factors involved in the union power explanation and those in the excess demand explanation may be operating at the same time. The tendency of the rate of increase in money-wage rates to rise with a falling unemployment percentage may therefore be explained in terms of both these causes (as well as some lesser causes we have not examined here).

Our concern here has been limited to an explanation of the inverse relationship between

---

[4]The unemployment rate at which the curve in Part B of Figure 23-2 cuts the axis will be much lower than the rate at which the curve in Figure 23-1 cuts the axis. The curve in Figure 23-1 has been positioned to make rough allowance for the rate of price inflation of recent years, but that in Figure 23-2 does not take price inflation into account. The fact that the curve in Figure 23-1, if extended, would cross the U axis at an extremely high rate does not mean that at that rate there is equilibrium in the labor market. If the rate of inflation were zero, the curve in Figure 23-1 would be positioned far below that shown and would cut the U axis much farther to the left.

the rate of increase of the money-wage rate and the unemployment rate—that is, with the fact that the Phillips curve slopes downward to the right.[5] Another matter is the position of the curve: Does this curve shift upward or downward from one time period to another? Apart from the fact that a lower unemployment rate will be accompanied by a higher rate of wage increase, will the rate of wage increase corresponding to any particular unemployment rate be higher or lower from one time period to the next? This question of the stability of the Phillips curve is of the greatest importance. During most of the 1960s, it was widely believed that the curve was quite stable; but in the 1970s, the statistical and theoretical evidence supported the opposite belief. In a later part of the chapter, shifts in the Phillips curve become critical to our discussion.

A Modified Phillips Curve Relationship
Phillips' work focussed on the relationship between wage rates and unemployment rates, but the link between the rates at which wage rates and prices rise is so close that the Phillips curve may also be presented in a modified form as a relationship between the inflation rate and the unemployment rate. The link between the rates at which prices and wages rise is the rate at which output per manhour of labor or labor productivity rises.[6] If labor productivity grows at about 3 percent per year, then a 3 percent rate of increase of wage rates corresponds with a zero rate of price increase. Although the rate of productivity growth declined sharply to between 1 and 2 percent per year in recent years, the average for most of the period since World War II has been approxi-

mately 3 percent. For illustration, we have adopted the 3 percent figure.

In Figure 23-3, both the rate of change of wage rates, $\Delta W/W$, and the rate of inflation, $\Delta P/P$, are measured along the vertical axis. The upper curve, which relates $\Delta W/W$ to U, is identical with the curve in Figure 23-1. The lower curve, which relates $\Delta P/P$ to U, is the modified Phillips curve based on the assumption of a 3 percent increase in labor productivity per year. The relationship between the wage rate and the unemployment rate assumes that $\Delta W/W$ will be 3 percent per year if U is 9 percent. Accordingly, the modified Phillips curve reveals that $\Delta P/P$ will be zero or the price level will be stable if U is 9 percent. For another example, because $\Delta W/W$ is 9 percent with U of 6 percent, $\Delta P/P$ is 6 percent with U of 6 percent. Given our assumptions, the Phillips curve relating $\Delta P/P$ to U lies 3 percentage points below the Phillips curve relating $\Delta W/W$ to U for each value of U. Because in most of what follows our interest is with the curve relating $\Delta P/P$ and U, our diagrams will show only $\Delta P/P$ on the vertical axis. As is customary, the Phillips curve in such diagrams will be referred to simply as a

---

[5]We might also ask whether the slope is linear or nonlinear, as shown in Figure 23-2. This technical question is beyond the scope of our introduction to the subject, but explanations have been offered for a nonlinear relationship. See A.M. Santomero and J.J. Seater, "The Inflation-Unemployment Trade-Off: A Critique of the Literature," *Journal of Economic Literature*, June 1978, p. 503 and the references there cited.

[6]For more on this, see pp. 550–52.

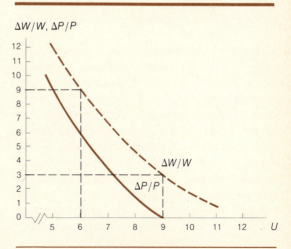

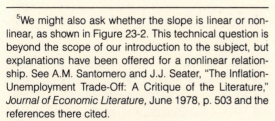

FIGURE 23-3
Modified Phillips Curve

Phillips curve without regard for the fact that it is a modification of the original Phillips curve.

Like the original Phillips curve, the modified Phillips curve may also shift over time. If over time there is an increase in the rate of money wage rate increase corresponding to any unemployment rate, we have seen that the original Phillips curve shifts upward. Assuming no change in labor productivity, we may expect an equal upward shift in the modified Phillips curve. Therefore, at any unemployment rate, the inflation rate will rise by the same amount as the rise in the rate of money wage rate increase. If the curve relating the rate of wage rate increase to the unemployment rate is unstable, the curve relating the rate of inflation to the unemployment rate will also be unstable. Furthermore, because there are forces other than changes in the rate of increase of wage rates that enter in here—for example, the quadrupling of the price of OPEC oil in 1974—the curve relating the inflation rate to the unemployment rate may shift independently of the curve relating the rate of wage rate increase to the unemployment rate. As previously noted, the stability of the Phillips curve is of utmost importance; we will discuss it in a later part of this chapter. For the time being, however, we assume that there is a stable relationship between $\Delta P/P$ and U of the form shown by the curve in Figure 23-3.

Given this assumption, society may exchange a higher unemployment rate for a lower inflation rate or a lower employment rate for a higher inflation rate on reasonably well defined terms. Each point along the curve identifies a combination of unemployment and inflation; a comparison of such combinations identifies the terms of the tradeoff between unemployment and inflation. For the time being, we will accept the existence of a tradeoff like that shown by the curve. The curve, however, does not reveal anything about which of the various possible combinations will actually occur in any time period. To determine this we must work the inflationary pressure curve into the diagram. This curve slopes upward to the right to intersect the downward-sloping Phillips curve, thereby specifying the actual $\Delta P/P$ and U.

The Inflationary Pressure Curve

To explain how the inflationary pressure curve fits into the model, we must start with a definitional relationship among three variables: the growth rate of nominal income, real income, and inflation. It can be shown mathematically that, in general, if $y = x/z$, (in which each refers to an absolute amount), the growth rate of y is equal to the growth rate of x minus the growth rate of z, or $\Delta y/y = \Delta x/x - \Delta z/z$. The economy's real income in any time period may be defined as the ratio of nominal income to the price level. The growth rate of real income or output is then equal to the growth rate of nominal income minus the growth rate of the price level. For example, assume that nominal income is $100 billion and an index of prices is 2.00; therefore, real income is $50 billion. If nominal income grows at a rate of 10 percent per time period (from $100 billion in the first period to $110 in the second period), output will also grow by 10 percent (from $50 billion to $55 billion), assuming that the price level grows at a zero rate. On the other hand, the same growth in nominal income will be accompanied by a zero growth rate of output, if the price level grows at a 10 percent rate—that is, the price index rises from 2.00 to 2.20. In other words, any growth rate of nominal income is absorbed by an equal growth rate of output, an equal growth rate of the price level, or some combination of the two rates. In every case, the rates of growth for the price level and output add up to the rate of growth of nominal income. Note that the rates of growth of output and the price level may be other than zero even if the growth rate of nominal income is zero. For example, if the price level grows at a 5 percent rate, output must grow at a -5 percent rate to satisfy the relationship.

The Slope of the Inflationary Pressure Curve: Okun's Law One would expect that a decrease in the unemployment rate will, in general, be accompanied by an increase in the growth rate of total output and vice versa. Over the years, such a relationship has been found to be so close that it has been termed **Okun's Law** (after the economist who brought it to the attention in 1962).[7] The basic relationship in the Okun analysis can be stated in several ways. For our purposes, we can say that a one percentage point increase (or decrease) in the unemployment rate will in the short run be accompanied by approximately a 2.5 percent decrease (or increase) in actual total output relative to the economy's potential output for that year.

For example, the sharp business downturn in the second quarter of 1980 raised the unemployment rate to 7.3 percent, an increase of 1.5 percentage points from the third quarter of 1979. The official estimates put potential and actual GNP (in 1972 dollars) for the second quarter of 1980 at $1,493.0 billion and $1,408.6 billion respectively (at annual rates); actual output was then 94.3 percent of potential output. The corresponding numbers for the third quarter of 1980 were $1,465.6 and $1,433.0 billion; actual was 97.8 percent of potential.[8] The decrease in the ratio of actual to potential from 97.8 to 94.3 is a 3.6 percent decline. Applied to the figures for this case, Okun's Law indicates that the decline in the ratio of actual to potential output should be 2.5 times the 1.5 percentage point change in the unemployment rate, or 3.75. The figure of 3.6 found here is quite close to that indicated by Okun's Law.

If we make calculations like these based on the year-to-year values for potential GNP, actual GNP, and the unemployment rate since the early 1960s, in some cases the percentage change in the ratio of actual to potential GNP will be very close to 2.5 times the change in the unemployment rate and in some cases not very close. However, the overall results are sufficiently close to those indicated by Okun's Law to warrant the conclusion that this law has been quite sturdy for recent U.S. experience. Even so, the relationship does not have the precision that one usually associates even with laws in economics and might better be described as a rule of thumb or a tendency.[9]

Having made this qualification, we will proceed here on the basis that there is a fixed relationship in which a 2.5 percent change in the growth rate of actual output relative to potential output and a 1 percentage point change in the

---

[9]From his 1962 study, Okun derived the following equation:

$$Y_p = Y_r [1 + 0.032 (U - 4)]$$

in which Y_p equals potential output or output produced under conditions of full employment, defined in the 1960s as 4 percent unemployment, Y_r equals realized or actual output, and U is the unemployment rate. Due to various changes that have occurred since the 1960s, the 0.032 coefficient is now about 0.025 and the unemployment rate now consistent with full employment is about 5.5 percent. Current application of the equation substitutes these figures for those shown in the equation above. By definition, when actual U is equal to the U consistent with full employment, $Y_p = Y_r$; a discrepancy between actual U and full employment U results in a difference between Y_p and Y_r. In the equation above, if we substitute 5.5 for 4 and 0.025 for 0.032, then divide each side of the equation into Y_r, we have the following:

$$\frac{Y_r}{Y_p} = \frac{Y_r}{Y_r[1 + 0.025(U - 5.5)]} = \frac{1}{1 + 0.025(U - 5.5)}$$

If the economy is operating at full employment or $U = 5.5$, then $Y_r/Y_p = 1$ or $Y_r = Y_p$. However, a decrease in U from 5.5 to 4.5 gives us

$$\frac{Y_r}{Y_p} = \frac{1}{1 + 0.025(4.5 - 5.5)} = \frac{1}{0.975} = 1.025$$

Y_r equals 1.025 percent of Y_p or a one percentage point decline in the unemployment rate increases real output relative to potential by 2.5 percent. On the other hand, a rise in U from 5.5 to 6.5 results in a value for Y_r/Y_p of 0.975 or a 2.5 percent decrease in real output relative to potential.

---

[7]See A.M. Okun, "Potential GNP: Its Measurement and Significance," in *1962 Proceedings of the Business and Economic Statistics Section of the American Statistical Association*, reprinted in W.L. Smith and R.L. Teigen, eds., *Readings in Money, National Income, and Stabilization Policy*, 3rd ed., Richard D. Irwin, 1974, pp. 285–92. A more recent study of the relationship is found in G.L. Perry, "Potential Output and Productivity," in *Brookings Papers on Economic Activity*, No. 1, 1977, pp. 11–47.

[8]Data for GNP are from the *Survey of Current Business*, Nov. 1980, p. 17, and data for the unemployment rate are from the *Economic Report of the President*, Jan. 1981, p. 269.

unemployment rate go together. From this we may derive the second curve in this chapter's model—the inflationary pressure curve. The curve labeled I_1 in Figure 23-4 is such an inflationary pressure curve. Underlying this particular curve are the following assumptions: an initial unemployment rate of 6 percent and an initial nominal income growth rate of 8 percent. This nominal income growth rate comprises a 2 percent growth rate of output and a 6 percent growth rate of prices. The U of 6 percent and the $\Delta P/P$ of 6 percent identify point B in Figure 23-4, which is one point on the inflationary pressure curve that is being derived. With no change in the growth rate of nominal income, a change in the unemployment rate would cause a change in the inflation rate.

For example, a reduction in the unemployment rate from 6 to 5 percent would lower the inflation rate from 6 to 3.5 percent, identified by point C. According to Okun's Law, the 1 percentage point change in U will raise the growth rate of output by approximately 2.5 percent—

from 2 to 4.5 percent. Now because 4.5 percent of the 8 percent growth rate of nominal income is absorbed by the growth of output, only 3.5 percent is absorbed by the growth of prices. Therefore, the inflation rate declines from 6 to 3.5 percent. By the same argument, starting again at point B, an increase in the unemployment rate from the initial rate of 6 percent to 7 percent would raise the inflation rate from 6 to 8.5 percent, identified by point A. Finally, a 2 percentage point decrease in the unemployment rate from the initial rate of 6 percent would cause the inflation rate to decline from the initial level of 6 percent to 1. This combination of U and $\Delta P/P$ is identified as point D. The inflationary pressure curve labeled I_1 is obtained by connecting points like A, B, C, and D. It shows all the combinations of U and $\Delta P/P$ that are consistent with the assumed 8 percent growth rate of nominal income and the assumed initial unemployment rate of 6 percent. The inflationary pressure curve has a slope of $+2.5$—that is, a 1 percentage point change of the unemployment rate is accompanied by a 2.5 percentage point change of the inflation rate in the same direction. This, of course, is the graphic representation of what was stated above.

The Position of the Inflationary Pressure Curve   The slope of the inflationary pressure curve remains unchanged at 2.5, but the position of the curve is subject to frequent change. As we will explain later, changes in the actual rate of inflation depend in part on shifts in the inflationary pressure curve. Consequently, it is essential to understand what causes shifts in that curve. One cause is a change in the growth rate of nominal income; an increase shifts the line to the left, and a decrease shifts it to the right. For example, suppose that as a result of expansionary monetary and fiscal policies the growth rate of nominal income rises from 8 to 10.5 percent and that when this occurs the unemployment rate is initially at 6 percent. In Figure 23-4 the curve labeled I_2 corresponds to these new values. The 2.5 percentage point rise in the growth rate of nominal income shifts the I curve upward by 2.5

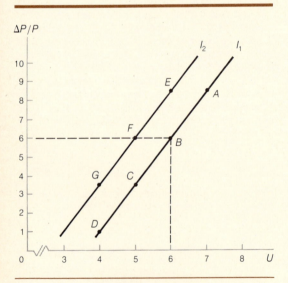

FIGURE 23-4
Inflationary Pressure Curves

percentage points along the $\Delta P/P$ axis or leftward by 1 percentage point along the U axis. This reveals that a rise in the growth rate of nominal income with no change in the unemployment rate will be matched by an equal rise in the inflation rate. Because the original position on the I_1 curve indicated a 6 percent inflation rate, or point B, the position on the I_2 curve indicates an 8.5 percent inflation rate, or point E. The 2.5 percentage point rise in the growth rate of nominal income is entirely absorbed by a higher inflation rate and not at all by a higher output growth rate. On the other hand, 1 percentage point decline in the unemployment percentage would mean a 2.5 percent rise in the output growth rate; the 2.5 percentage point rise in the growth rate of nominal income would be entirely absorbed by a higher output growth rate and the inflation rate would remain unchanged. The change is from the original position at point B on the I_1 curve to the position at point F on the I_2 curve. Points E and F are, of course, only two possible combinations of inflation rate and unemployment rate; every other point along the I_2 curve is another possibility, given the 10.5 percent growth rate of nominal income and an initial unemployment rate of 6 percent.

A change in the initial unemployment rate is a second and less apparent cause for a shift in the inflationary pressure curve. In Figure 23-4, the I_1 curve is based on the assumption of an initial unemployment rate of 6 percent and a nominal income growth rate of 8 percent. Suppose now that the unemployment rate we start with is 5 percent, but as before the growth rate of nominal income is 8 percent and that this 8 percent rate is divided as before into a 6 percent inflation rate and a 2 percent output growth rate. With these assumptions, the I curve will now be that labeled I_2 in Figure 23-4. There will be a 6 percent inflation rate at the initial 5 percent unemployment rate now assumed, just as there was a 6 percent inflation rate at the initial 6 percent unemployment rate earlier assumed. To reduce the inflation rate from, say, 6 to 3.5 percent now requires a reduction in the unemploy-

ment rate from 5 to 4 percent, as will be seen by comparing points F and G. This incidentally reveals that a reduction in the inflation rate from, say, 6 to 3.5 percent via a reduction in the unemployment percentage is more difficult at a lower initial unemployment rate than at a higher initial unemployment rate. It is much easier to reduce unemployment from 6 to 5 percent than it is to reduce it from 5 to 4 percent.

Phillips Curve, Inflationary Pressure Curve, and the Rate of Inflation

Now that we understand the derivation of the Phillips curve and the inflationary pressure curve, we may proceed to consider the question of what causes changes in the rate of inflation. Figure 23-5 reproduces the Phillips curve from Figure 23-3 and the inflationary pressure curve labeled I_1 from Figure 23-4. The inflationary pressure curve

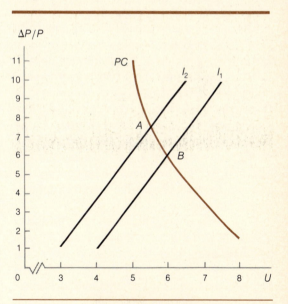

FIGURE 23-5
Phillips Curve and Inflationary Pressure Curves

is drawn on the assumptions of a given growth rate of nominal income and a given initial unemployment rate. If we assume that this initial unemployment rate is 6 percent, we have all that we need to find from the Phillips curve what the inflation rate must be. Running a line up to the Phillips curve at the 6 percent unemployment rate gives us an inflation rate of 6 percent. We do not need the inflationary pressure curve as such to establish just this. However, the inflationary pressure curve comes into play when we ask: What will be the effect of actions such as expansionary monetary and fiscal policies that raise the rate of growth of nominal income? The intersection of the inflationary pressure curve, which will shift from its initial position as a result of such actions, and the given Phillips curve identifies the changes in the inflation and unemployment rates. The initial rate of unemployment that was the basis for the initial inflationary pressure curve will have changed.

Figure 23-5 provides an illustration of the specific effects of this kind of action. At first, I_1 intersects PC at the 6 percent unemployment rate because the inflationary pressure curve was drawn assuming the 6 percent unemployment rate in effect at the time. Now introduce government actions that raise the growth rate of nominal income from 8, the rate assumed in drawing I_1, to 11 percent. I_1 shifts to I_2. From its original intersection with the Phillips curve at point B, the inflationary pressure curve now intersects the Phillips curve at point A. The inflation rate has risen from 6 to approximately 7.5 percent and the unemployment rate has fallen from 6 to approximately 5.5 percent.

This is the only combination of $\Delta P/P$ and U consistent with the given Phillips curve and the new inflationary pressure curve. To verify this, assume, for example, that the inflation rate rises from 6 to 9 percent instead of from 6 to 7.5 percent. The Phillips curve shows that at the inflation rate of 9 percent the unemployment rate will be approximately 5.25 percent—a drop of 0.75 percentage points. Such a decrease in the unemployment rate implies approximately a 1.9 per-

cent increase in the growth rate of total output (2.5×0.75) over and above the 2 percent growth rate we initially assumed. The rate of growth of output will now be near 4 percent. However, because the growth rate of nominal income is 11 percent and because that rate is definitionally equal to the sum of the growth rate of output and the rate of inflation, the indicated growth rate of output of almost 4 percent is only consistent with an inflation rate of just over 7 percent. This in turn is plainly inconsistent with the inflation rate of 9 percent assumed in the first place. The assumption of a rise in the inflation rate from 6 to 9 percent is therefore inconsistent with the change in the unemployment rate that the Phillips curve shows will result from that increase in the inflation rate.

The same kind of inconsistency will appear if we assume, for example, that the decline in the unemployment rate was 1 percentage point instead of 0.5 percentage point. This would indicate a 2.5 percent increase in the growth rate of output per time period over and above the initial growth rate of 2 percent. The rate of growth of output will now equal 4.5 percent. However, because the growth rate of nominal income is 11 percent and because that rate is definitionally equal to the sum of the growth rate of output and the rate of inflation, the indicated 4.5 percent rate of growth of output is only consistent with a 6.5 percent rate of inflation. This in turn is inconsistent with the increase of approximately 5 percentage points in the inflation rate that the Phillips curve shows will result from that decrease in the unemployment rate. The assumption of a 1 percentage point decrease in the unemployment rate is therefore inconsistent with the change in the inflation rate that the Phillips curve shows will result from that decrease in the unemployment rate.

These illustrations should clarify the basic conclusion to which we are led when we bring together the Phillips curve and the inflationary pressure curve: The actual inflation rate and unemployment rate will be that particular combination of these two rates identified by the intersection of the two curves. This conclusion may be contrasted with the conclusion reached in Chapter 22's model. There the intersection of the aggregate supply and aggregate demand curves identified what the particular combination of price level and output level would be. In that model, an increase in aggregate demand with no change in aggregate supply typically results in a rise in the price level and a rise in the output level.

As we have seen, this chapter's model does not work with aggregate demand but with the percentage growth rate of nominal income. However, shifts in the inflationary pressure curve result from changes in the growth rate of nominal income, and such shifts are a demand-side phenomenon just as shifts in Chapter 22's aggregate demand curve obviously are. The inflationary pressure curve may therefore be viewed as a more complicated kind of aggregate demand curve. Similarly, this chapter's model does not work with aggregate supply but with the Phillips curve, which shows how the rate of inflation varies with the unemployment rate. However, here too there is a relationship between the Phillips curve and Chapter 22's aggregate supply curve. The aggregate supply curve shows that a higher level of output will be offered only at a higher price level because cost per unit of output begins to rise with falling productivity of labor. The Phillips curve relating the inflation rate to the unemployment rate implies a related result, although it reaches it in a different way. The lower the unemployment rate, the higher the per unit cost of output becomes, because the rate of increase of money wage rates varies inversely with the unemployment rate. At the same time, the lower the rate of unemployment, the higher will be the actual growth rate of output in relation to the potential growth rate of output (Okun's Law). In this way, the Phillips curve is related to Chapter 22's aggregate supply curve, although the Phillips curve runs in terms of the rate of change of the price level instead of the absolute change in the price level and runs in terms of the unemployment rate, which may also be expressed as

a rate of growth of output, instead of the absolute change in output.

The model in this chapter may therefore be viewed as a kind of aggregate demand-aggregate supply model, although that is obscured by the fact that the unemployment rate is used instead of its counterpart output measure. This has been done in order to permit a direct focus on the relationship between the unemployment rate and the inflation rate—the relationship on which so much public attention has been focused in recent years.

It is apparent in this model that any change in the inflation rate or the unemployment rate or both will be the result of shifts in either the inflationary pressure curve or the Phillips curve or both. We have examined shifts in the inflationary pressure curve. A major matter that we have not yet considered is that of shifts in the Phillips curve or the stability of that curve. Whether or not the economy can trade off on a continuing basis more inflation for a lower unemployment rate or vice versa depends on the stability of the Phillips curve.

The Phillips Curve: Tradeoff and Non-Tradeoff

Introduced at the end of the 1950s, the Phillips curve became almost a household term by the end of the 1960s; its disappearance from popular discussion over the following decade was as dramatic as its appearance had been. However, the Phillips curve continues to be an essential device used by economists to organize their thinking on inflation and unemployment. A 1976 article by one of this country's foremost economists starts off with the words: "Any time seems to be the right time for reflections on the Phillips curve."[10]

---

[10]R.M. Solow, "Down the Phillips Curve with Gun and Camera," in D.A. Belsley, E.J. Kane, P.A. Samuelson, and R.M. Solow, eds., *Inflation, Trade, and Taxes*, Ohio State University Press, 1976, p. 3.

What is, in a sense, the "rise and fall" of the Phillips curve corresponds to what was a widely-held belief in the 1960s that the downward-sloping Phillips curve was a stable relationship—that is, that over the years a particular rate of unemployment would be accompanied by a particular rate of inflation. The widely held belief in the 1970s was that such a downward-sloping curve described only a short-run relationship or that the curve was subject to shifts over the long run—that is, that a particular rate of unemployment would be accompanied by a higher or lower rate of inflation over the years as the Phillips curve shifted upward or downward.

If there is a stable relationship, there is a tradeoff in the sense that the economy can, on fairly well defined terms, achieve a lower rate of unemployment by accepting a higher rate of inflation or it can achieve a lower rate of inflation by accepting a higher rate of unemployment. However, if the relationship is unstable, this does not follow. We may only temporarily at best gain a reduction in the unemployment rate by accepting a higher inflation rate. The unstable Phillips curve may shift upward and over time the economy may return to the unemployment rate from which it started or, even worse, it may back up to an unemployment rate even higher than the one from which it started.

As we have seen, the Phillips curve and the inflationary pressure curve introduced in the previous section identify by their intersection the inflation rate and the unemployment rate. That intersection will obviously change with any shift in either or both curves. In the following pages, we employ the model built out of the Phillips curve and the inflationary pressure curve. The analysis is divided into two parts: First, the assumption of a stable Phillips curve gives us the tradeoff results that economists believed were available to us in the 1960s. Second, the unstable Phillips curve, which denies that there can be more than a temporary tradeoff, gives the results that most economists came to accept in the seventies and accept today.

The Tradeoff Curve

In his 1958 study based on data for England for the long period from 1861 to 1957, Phillips had found a long-run stable relationship between the rate of unemployment and the rate at which wage rates increase. As we saw earlier, apart from special shocks to the system such as the OPEC quadrupling of oil prices in 1974, a stable relationship between the unemployment rate and the rate of increase of wage rates implies a stable relationship between the rate of unemployment and the rate of increase of prices. The spread between the rate of price increase and rate of wage rate increase is approximately equal to the rate of growth of labor productivity. There was widespread belief in the existence of such a stable relationship in the early 1960s. Furthermore, as the 1960s unfolded, the data for the U.S. economy very solidly supported this belief. The dots in Figure 23-6 show the combination of the inflation and unemployment rates for the years 1963–69. Straight lines have been drawn to connect the dots for consecutive years. The overall line from 1963 to 1969 shows that a decline in the unemployment rate was accompanied by a rise in the inflation rate each year without exception.

How does the previous section's model explain what we see in this figure? At first glance, the results appear to be the product of an inflationary pressure curve shifting persistently leftward over the years to intersect the Phillips curve at successively lower unemployment rates but successively higher inflation rates. During the first few years of the period, the decrease in the unemployment rate was pronounced and the rise in the inflation rate was moderate. In the last several years, there was little additional decline in the unemployment rate, and the shift of the line was matched almost entirely by a rise in the inflation rate.

It is understandable that a diagram like this would have led economists of the 1960s to the belief that the economy had a "menu of choices" between inflation and unemployment. Econo-

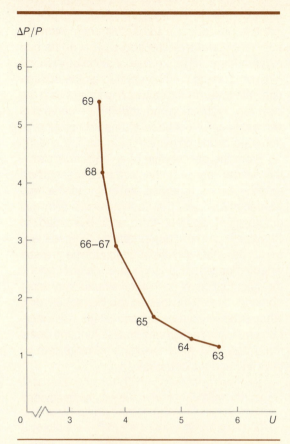

$\Delta P/P$

69

68

66–67

65

64

63

FIGURE 23-6
Phillips Curve for 1963–69

the difficulties of measuring the costs and benefits of specific changes in the inflation rate and the unemployment rate, there was also the problem of pinning down the terms on which any tradeoff could be obtained.

One study at the beginning of the 1960s suggested that to reduce the unemployment rate to 3 percent—a commonly accepted definition of "full employment" at the time—would require an inflation rate of 4 to 5 percent, a rate that looked like "galloping" inflation when the current rate was about 1.5 percent.[11] Readings of the terms of the tradeoff at the end of the 1960s were still more pessimistic. They suggested a 5 percent inflation rate could be expected to accompany a 4 percent unemployment rate, rather than the 3 percent unemployment rate that had earlier been matched with this inflation rate. These readings also suggested that to hold the rate of inflation down to a low 2 percent—it was running 5 to 6 percent at the end of the 1960s—would require an unemployment rate of 5.5 percent—it was less than 4 percent at the end of the 1960s.[12] However, despite the marked differences in estimates of the terms of the tradeoff, there was a widespread belief through the 1960s that the choice was there to be made.

The Non-Tradeoff Curve

Although the record for the 1960s suggests a systematic tradeoff between the inflation rate and the unemployment rate, at the time some economists disputed the conclusion drawn from this

mists generally agreed that monetary and fiscal policies could be employed to increase or decrease the growth rate of nominal income and thereby move the economy leftward or rightward along the Phillips curve to whatever choice had been made. A major disagreement at the time was what the choice should be; this was essentially a disagreement over costs and benefits. Does the benefit of a lower unemployment rate exceed the cost of a higher inflation rate or does the benefit of a lower inflation rate exceed the cost of a higher unemployment rate? Apart from

---

[11] See P.A. Samuelson and R.M. Solow, "Analytical Aspects of Anti-Inflation Policy," in *American Economic Review*, May 1960, p. 192. Another study of this sort drew more pessimistic conclusions for the U.S. economy: See R.J. Bhatia, "Unemployment and the Rate of Change in Money Earnings in the United States, 1900–1958," in *Economica*, Aug. 1961, pp. 285–96.

[12] G.L. Perry, "Changing Labor Markets and Inflation," in *Brookings Papers on Economic Activity*, 3, 1970, pp. 411–41 and R.J. Gordon, "Inflation in Recession and Recovery," *Brookings Papers on Economic Activity*, 1, 1971, pp. 105–58.

record and from other evidence, namely, that policy makers could choose among various combinations of inflation rate and unemployment rate.[13] These critics maintained that the alleged "menu of choices" did not exist. Society could at best only temporarily trade off more inflation for less unemployment by pursuing policies to change the economy's position along a downward-sloping Phillips curve. To them, this downward-sloping curve itself is a short-run or transitory phenomenon that is valid only as long as a discrepancy between the expected inflation rate and the actual inflation rate prevails. According to these economists, once such a discrepancy has been removed, the downward-sloping Phillips curve ceases to exist. In the long run, the Phillips curve becomes a vertical line—that is, in the long run, the rate of unemployment is independent of the rate of inflation.

The Natural Rate of Unemployment   How is this conclusion of a vertical Phillips curve reached? A first step toward an explanation is the introduction of the concept of the natural rate of unemployment, which, defined in one way, is that unemployment rate below which the inflation rate tends to increase and above which the inflation rate tends to decrease. At this rate there is neither a tendency for inflation to accelerate or decelerate. As we will see, this is equal to saying that the natural rate is the unemployment rate that exists when the actual rate of inflation is equal to the expected rate of inflation. A discrepancy between the actual and expected rates of inflation and the consequence of such a discrepancy,

an acceleration or deceleration of the rate of inflation, will occur if the actual unemployment rate is either below or above what is at that moment its equilibrium rate. The natural unemployment rate is thereby defined as the equilibrium rate toward which the economy moves in the long run. In the long run, the Phillips curve is a vertical line positioned at the natural or equilibrium rate of unemployment.

From the perspective of an equilibrium rate, the natural rate of unemployment, in simplified terms, can be regarded as equal to the rate of unemployment that corresponds with full employment as that term was described in Chapter 9 on the classical theory. It essentially would be whatever rate of unemployment exists when employment is at the level determined by the intersection of the labor supply and labor demand curves in that chapter's model, with labor supply a direct function of the real wage rate and labor demand an inverse function of the real wage rate. More exactly and more technically, in Friedman's words,

> At any moment of time, there is some level of unemployment which has the property that it is consistent with equilibrium in the structure of *real* wage rates. . . . The "natural rate of unemployment," in other words, is the level that would be ground out by the Walrasian system of general equilibrium equations, provided there is imbedded in them the actual structural characteristics of the labor and commodity markets, including market imperfections, stochastic variability in demands and supplies, the cost of gathering information about job vacancies and labor availabilities, the costs of mobility and so on.[14]

Because the characteristics of the economy are continuously changing, the natural rate of unemployment, contrary to the connotation of the word "natural," is not a God-given, immutable rate or a rate beyond the influence of public policy. A

---

[13]Foremost among these are Phelps and Friedman. See E.S. Phelps, "Money-Wage Dynamics and Labor-Market Equilibrium" in *Journal of Political Economy,* July–Aug. 1968, Part II, pp. 678–711 and *Inflation Policy and Unemployment Theory,* W.W. Norton, 1972, Ch. 2; M. Friedman, "The Role of Monetary Policy," in *American Economic Review,* March 1968, pp. 1–17. For a relatively nontechnical comparison of the view of these economists with the tradeoff view, see R.W. Spencer, "The Relation Between Prices and Employment; Two Views," in *Review,* Federal Reserve Bank of St. Louis, March 1969, pp. 15–21.

[14]M. Friedman, "The Role of Monetary Policy," *American Economic Review,* March 1968, p. 8.

change such as the computerization of job vacancies in state employment offices makes possible a more efficient matching of job openings and job seekers, thereby reducing the natural rate of unemployment. A change like that in the composition of the labor force over the past decade toward a larger share made up of women and teenagers (who have relatively high unemployment rates) raises the natural rate of unemployment. The combined effect of the changes in the many forces at work has been to raise the natural rate of unemployment over the years.[15]

The Process of Adjustment to a Shift in the Inflationary Pressure Curve

For the analysis that follows, the natural rate of unemployment is assumed to be U_n in Figure 23-7. We assume initially that the Phillips curve and the inflationary pressure curve are PC_1 and I_1, respectively. These indicate an inflation rate of 6 percent and an actual unemployment rate equal to the natural rate or an initial equilibrium at point E_1. By the definition of the natural rate of unemployment, the actual rate of inflation that exists with the economy operating at this rate of unemployment is equal to the expected rate of inflation. In this case, the two rates are equal at 6 percent. Starting from this position, will an increase in the growth rate of nominal income, say, of 3 percentage points, reduce the unemployment rate? We know that this increase in the income growth rate will shift the inflationary pressure curve leftward. As long as the downward-sloping Phillips curve remains stable, there will be some reduction in the unemployment rate as the inflationary pressure curve moves leftward along that stable Phillips curve. Will the increase in the income growth rate raise the inflation rate? Again, given that the leftward-shifting inflationary pressure curve moves upward along a stable, downward-

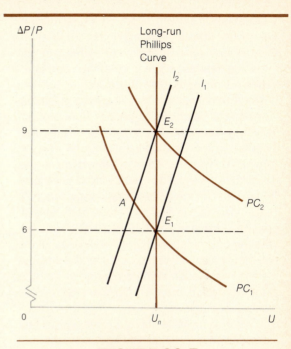

FIGURE 23-7
Long-Run Phillips Curve

sloping Phillips curve, there will be some increase in the inflation rate. If the 3 percent increase in the growth rate of nominal income in the first time period shifts the I curve from I_1 to I_2, the unemployment rate and inflation rate in that period will be those indicated by point A.

What is the process by which these results occur? We started with the inflation rate at 6 percent and the economy at the natural rate of unemployment. However high or low that inflation rate may have been at the time, it was equal to the expected inflation rate. This expected rate had entered into the determination of the money-wage rates negotiated by labor unions and employers. With the money-wage rates negotiated on the basis of this expected inflation rate and other factors, the real wage rate was such that the actual unemployment rate was the natural unemployment rate, or U_n. The reduction in

---

[15]Robert J. Gordon's estimates of this rate are 3.4 percent in the first few years of this century, 4.0 percent just after World War II, and 5.6 percent as of 1980. See his *Macroeconomics*, 2nd ed., Little, Brown, 1981, Appendix B.

the unemployment rate below the natural rate that now results from the leftward shift of the inflationary pressure curve is explained by the fact that the actual real wage rate is lower than had been expected or lower than is consistent with an unemployment rate of U_n. An increase in the real wage rate to match the increase in labor productivity may have been expected; the unexpected increase in the inflation rate reduces or even eliminates this. In its effect on employment, this is similar to the situation of a rise in the price level (P) with no change in the money wage rate (W). Here, however, we are concerned with rates of change rather than absolute amounts of change. With the cost of labor now relatively lower, firms find that profit maximization calls for the employment of more labor. With no change in the size of the labor force, the unemployment rate falls as the level of employment rises.

Critics of the tradeoff Phillips curve grant that this may occur. They quickly add, however, that the fall in the unemployment rate will only be temporary. Labor will recognize before long that the earlier negotiated increase in its money wage rate is not sufficient to provide the increase in the real wage rate that was expected. To get that expected increase in the real wage rate required that the inflation rate not exceed the expected 6 percent; but the actual inflation rate has turned out to be greater than the expected 6 percent. Once labor realizes what has happened, it will demand and will secure the higher rate of increase in the money-wage rate needed to offset the unexpected rise in the inflation rate. A higher rate of increase in the money-wage rate at each rate of unemployment results in an approximately equal increase in the inflation rate at each rate of unemployment. There is an adjustment process in which the Phillips curve in Figure 23-7 shifts upward from PC_1 to PC_2 through a series of steps. In the short run, the leftward-shifting inflationary pressure curve moves along a downward-sloping Phillips curve, but in the long run the downward-sloping Phillips curve shifts rightward or upward offsetting the effect on the unemploy-

ment rate of the leftward shift of the inflationary pressure curve. The end product is a return to the natural rate of unemployment with the inflation rate higher by the same number of percentage points that the growth rate of nominal income is higher. As that rate increases by 3 percentage points, the rate of inflation also increases by 3 percentage points—from 6 to 9 percent, as shown in Figure 23-7. The new equilibrium is shown by point E_2. **In the long run, there is no tradeoff of a lower unemployment rate for a higher inflation rate; the effect of an increase in the growth rate of nominal income is only a higher inflation rate.** In the long run, the Phillips curve is a vertical line with E_1 and E_2 indicating only two of any number of possible inflation rates consistent with the natural rate of unemployment at which the vertical Phillips curve is positioned.

Figure 23-7 is limited to simple comparative statics or to the identification of an original equilibrium, E_1, and a new equilibrium, E_2. An interesting but more difficult matter is one of dynamics—the path followed by the economy in moving from one equilibrium position to another. If an initial equilibrium like that at E_1 in Figure 23-7 is upset by a rise in the growth rate of nominal income, the particular path followed by the economy in adjusting to this change depends on the speed with which people revise whatever inflation rate they were expecting at the time. Do they respond quickly or slowly to a change that makes the actual rate different from the rate they expected? The sooner they revise the expected rate upward in response to an unexpected rise in the actual inflation rate, the sooner the Phillips curve will shift upward.

How expectations are formed is a controversial matter, but everyone will agree that people are not likely to expect a permanently higher rate of inflation if a moderate rise in the inflation rate occurs after a period of years during which the inflation rate was stable. For example, from 1958 to 1963, the average annual rate of growth of prices shown by the Consumer Price Index was 1.2 percent. In 1963, most people probably expected that rate to continue. It did so in 1964, but then jumped to 1.7 percent in 1965.[16] However, it is not likely that the jump in 1965 caused many people to revise upward the rate of inflation they expected; the one year spurt could have been a fluke. But the additional rises in the next two years probably did substantially increase the number of people who revised the expected rate upward. By 1968, with the rate up to 4.2 percent and with the experience of four continuous years of an accelerating rate behind them, few, if any, people expected that the rate ahead would be anything like the steady 1.2 percent annual rate of the 1958–64 period.

An Illustration of the Adjustment Process: 1963–70

The inflation record for the years covered in Figure 23-6 can now be explained to some degree by the public's changed expectations of inflation, assuming our description is approximately correct. Figure 23-8 roughly depicts the nature of the shifts in the inflationary pressure curve and the Phillips curve that produced the particular combinations of inflation rate and unemployment rate for this period and for the year 1970 not included in Figure 23-6. The subscripts identify the year or years during which the curve to which they refer was approximately in the position shown.

From 1963 to 1965 the inflationary pressure curves labeled I_{63}, I_{64}, and I_{65} shifted leftward along a stable (or nearly stable) downward-sloping Phillips curve labeled PC_{63-65}. The result of the shifting inflationary pressure curve over these years was primarily a sizable reduction in the unemployment rate and only a slight increase in the inflation rate. During these years, the economy was moving from an actual rate of unemployment above the natural rate down to an actual rate equal to the natural rate (at the time, about 4.5 percent). In 1965, the economy was

operating at or near its natural rate of unemployment. The intersection of I_{65} and PC_{63-65} at point E_1 identifies this equilibrium unemployment rate. From this equilibrium position, an increase in the growth rate of nominal income shifted the inflationary pressure curve to I_{66-67}. (There was a "mini-recession" in early 1967 and for the 1967 year as a whole the curve shifted little from its 1966 position.) Over these years, the leftward shifts in this curve had more impact on the inflation rate and less on the unemployment rate than in the preceding years. In 1966–67 the economy was operating below its natural rate of unemployment, whereas before 1965 it was operating above its natural rate. Statistical estimates of the short-run Phillips curve show that it becomes steeper at lower rates of unemployment; consequently, this combination of a relatively larger increase in the inflation rate and a relatively smaller decrease in the unemployment rate would be expected even if the Phillips curve remained stable. However, during 1966–67, people had revised upward their expected rate of inflation in view of what had been an appreciable increase in the inflation rate in 1965. The upward pressure on money-wage rates that followed from these revised inflationary expectations shifted the Phillips curve up to PC_{66-67} from PC_{63-65}. If the Phillips curve had remained stable, the new intersection would have been at point F with little increase in the inflation rate; because it did shift, the new intersection was actually at point G with a sizable increase in the inflation rate. Even so, there was a significant decrease in the unemployment rate from 1965 to 1967. However, the shifts in the inflationary pressure curve to I_{68} and I_{69} produced little further reduction in the unemployment rate, mostly a sharp rise in the inflation rate.

Over 1967–69, it appears that the Phillips curve shifted rightward or upward almost as fast as the inflationary pressure curve shifted leftward or upward. Expectations of inflation were being revised upward more sharply during these years; from such revisions followed the actions that

---

[16]See Table 21-1, p. 469, for the changes in the inflation rate for selected years.

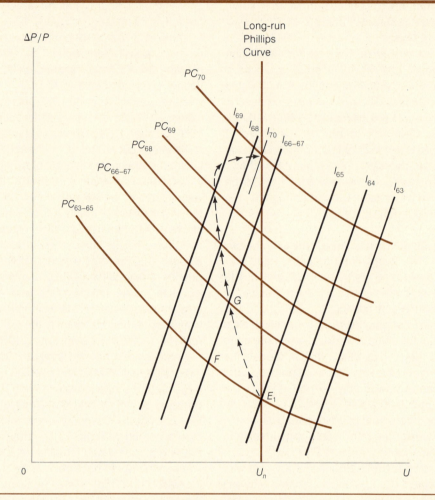

FIGURE 23-8
Phillips Curve and Inflationary Pressure Curve, 1963–70

again shifted the Phillips curve upward. As indicated by Figure 23-7, upward shifts in the Phillips curve, if large enough, will return the unemployment rate to its natural rate. That this did not occur from 1967 to 1969 has been explained by leftward shifts in the inflationary pressure curve sufficiently large to keep the rate at which inflation was rising one jump ahead, so to speak, of the rate of inflation expected by the public.

Although the public expected higher inflation rates, it was fooled because the inflationary pressure curve shifted upward so rapidly as to raise the actual rate of inflation above that which was expected. While this occurred—and it cannot occur indefinitely because the public cannot be fooled indefinitely—the unemployment rate was held at a level well below the natural rate to which it tends to return. The real wage rate was kept below the rate it would otherwise have reached and the lower real wage rate meant a lower unemployment rate.

All of this ended in 1970. The Phillips curve shifted upward again in that year in response to the further upward revision by the public of the expected rate of inflation. At the same time, there was a slowing in the rate of growth of nominal income, which before 1970 had been growing fast enough to keep the actual rate of inflation ahead of the expected rate. In terms of Figure 23-8, these changes may be roughly portrayed by the upward shift in the Phillips curve from PC_{69} to PC_{70} and the *downward* shift in the inflationary pressure curve from I_{69} to I_{70}. The magnitudes of these two shifts were such as to raise the 1970 unemployment rate roughly to the natural rate and also to raise the inflation rate above its 1969 level. The long-run result that the critics of the tradeoff view assert must occur seems to have occurred: The decline in the unemployment rate below the natural rate following 1965 was a temporary decline.[17] The critics would add that the unemployment rate was held below the natural rate as long as it was only at the expense of a rapidly accelerating rate of inflation. Furthermore, even this was only able to work because the public, having come through a long period of fairly stable prices in the late 1950s and early 1960s, was relatively slow in appreciating what was taking place and in adjusting its expected rate of inflation upward.

To try to reduce the unemployment rate during the 1980s by such a device would probably not be very successful, given the public's experience with inflation in the 1970s. Any actual change in the inflation rate will be promptly and fully reflected in money-wage settlements. The basic mechanism by which a higher inflation rate reduces the unemployment rate will cease to work. Apart from the possibility of some temporary reduction in the unemployment rate, the final result of a public policy of speeding up the growth rate of nominal income will be to raise the rate of inflation correspondingly. Again, the conclusion is that the rate of unemployment in the long run is independent of the rate of inflation. In the long run, the Phillips curve is not only steeper than in the short run, but is very close to vertical or vertical.

Reducing Unemployment by Reducing the Natural Rate of Unemployment This nontradeoff argument has been increasingly accepted in recent years. The pendulum has swung a long way from the opposite view so popular in the 1960s. With this swing has come more questioning of the government's ability to reduce the rate of unemployment below the natural rate through monetary and fiscal policies. But if such policies cannot succeed, the conclusion seems to be that the economy must live with a 5.5 to 6.0 percent unemployment rate, the range within which the estimates of most economists put the natural rate under present conditions. However, this conclusion does not necessarily follow. To argue that we cannot reduce the unemployment rate by forcing it below the natural rate is not to argue that we cannot reduce it by reducing the natural rate itself. As noted in a different context in Chapter 22, some reduction in unemployment can be achieved by policies that make labor markets more efficient in bringing together those seeking employment and those offering employment. These include retraining programs, improved dissemination of information concerning job vacancies, and relocation grants to the unemployed. In a quite different way, the natural rate of unemployment can be reduced by eliminating minimum wage laws, which are quite generally recognized as a cause of unemployment, especially among teenagers. In their place could be other types of income assistance programs, if they are found to be needed. Also along this line would be changes in unemployment compensation laws to provide benefits for a shorter

---

[17]From the early 1960s to 1970, the natural rate may have risen by about 0.5 percentage point, but no attempt has been made to incorporate this in the diagram. The assumption, in other words, is an unchanged natural rate over the full period of years shown.

period of time and in tax laws to make unemployment compensation fully subject to the personal income tax—two of a number of changes in unemployment compensation which would increase the incentive of some people to accept employment.[18]

Some such steps to reduce the unemployment rate were being recommended on their own merits well before the belief in a durable tradeoff between the inflation rate and the unemployment rate had been replaced with the belief that no such durable tradeoff existed. However, with this change in belief, such steps taken to reduce the natural rate of unemployment assume much greater importance than otherwise. They become not merely one way of achieving a sustainable reduction in the unemployment rate, but the only way. To realize a permanent reduction in the unemployment rate requires a reduction in the natural rate itself. At best, only a temporary reduction in the unemployment rate below the existing natural rate can be achieved by expansionary monetary and fiscal policies. Such policies will succeed in shifting the inflationary pressure curve leftward along a downward-sloping Phillips curve with some reduction in the unemployment rate and some rise in the inflation rate. When this occurs, expectations adjust more or less promptly, the Phillips curve shifts upward or rightward, and the unemployment rate tends to return to the natural rate.

The Relationship Between Inflation and Unemployment, 1963–80

The period from 1963 to 1980 exhibits a cyclical pattern of inflation and unemployment, one phase of each cycle being stagflation or inflationary recession. The period also shows that each time the economy goes through a new acceleration of the inflation rate, it starts that acceleration from a higher rate than it did the preceding time. And each time the economy gets into another period of a rising unemployment rate, it starts from a higher unemployment rate than it did the preceding time.

The Cyclical Pattern of Inflation and Unemployment

According to those who maintain that in the long run the Phillips curve is vertical at the natural rate of unemployment, any drop below this unemployment rate caused by leftward shifts in the inflationary pressure curve will only be temporary. The review of the record of the 1960s showed that in each year from 1965 to 1969, the unemployment rate fell farther below the natural rate and then from 1969 to 1970 returned to the natural rate. That review also showed that during these years the inflation rate increased year after year. The path traced by inflation and unemployment over that period is described in a general way by an arc like that from A to B in Figure 23-9.[19] The economy did not move along a stable downward-sloping curve like PC_1. The Phillips curve gradually shifted upward to PC_2, and the path followed by the economy was like the one from point A to point B. The same line of reasoning that gives us the movement along the arc from point A to point B (upward-sloping arrows) should theoretically yield a movement along the

---

[18]See M.S. Feldstein, "The Economics of the New Unemployment," *Public Interest,* Fall 1973, pp. 3–42, and R.E. Hall, "Prospects for Shifting the Phillips Curve through Manpower Policy," *Brookings Papers on Economic Activity,* 3, 1971, pp. 659–701, and E. Shapiro, "Wage Inflation, Manpower Training, and the Phillips Curve: A Graphic Integration," *The American Economist,* Spring 1981, pp. 17–21.

[19]The only differences are that the rise in the inflation rate from 1965 to 1970 started from a rate somewhat above zero, whereas Figure 23-9 starts from zero and that the path followed from 1965 to 1970 did not trace out a perfectly even arc like that from point A to point B in Figure 23-9.

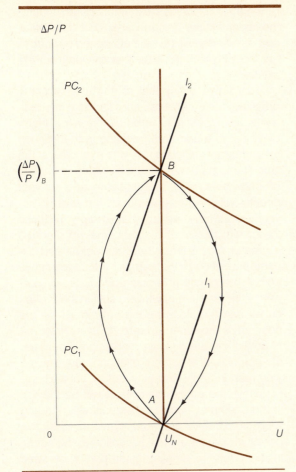

**FIGURE 23-9
A Cyclical Movement of the
Unemployment Rate and
Inflation Rate**

rate for a limited period of time at the cost of a higher inflation rate (as occurs along the path from point *A* to point *B*), so it may be possible to achieve a lower inflation rate at the cost of a higher unemployment rate for a limited period of time. Start with the economy in equilibrium at point *B* given by the intersection of PC_2 and I_2. Reversing the analysis of the preceding section, assume now restrictive policy actions to reduce the rate of growth of nominal income which will produce a rightward shift in the inflationary pressure curve from its position at I_2. If the Phillips curve were to remain stable at PC_2, the unemployment rate would rise and the inflation rate would fall by amounts identified by successive shifts of the inflationary pressure curve along such a stable downward-sloping Phillips curve.[20]

However, the economy will only temporarily move down that Phillips curve, because downward movement produces results that cause the curve itself to shift. The decline in the actual inflation rate that occurs as the economy starts to move from point *B* down the PC_2 curve opens a gap between the actual and expected inflation rates. People therefore revise their expected rate of inflation downward; this change in expectations in turn causes the Phillips curve to shift downward. A continuation of restrictive policy will cause a continuing downward shift in the Phillips curve. The economy will move along a path like that from point *B* to point *A* (downward-sloping arrows) until it reaches point *A*, at which point

[20]The process described on pages 529–30 explains the change in the unemployment rate, in the present case a rise in that rate. With the economy in equilibrium at point *B*, the expected rate of inflation is equal to the actual rate of inflation, $(\Delta P/P)_B$. The money wage rates arrived at in negotiating labor contracts are based on that inflation rate. As the actual inflation rate falls in response to rightward shifts in the inflationary pressure curve, the rates of increase of money-wage rates and prices are such that the rate of increase of real wages becomes greater than was expected in setting the terms of money-wage settlements. With the cost of labor now relatively higher, firms find that profit maximization calls for the employment of less labor. With no change in the labor force, the unemployment rate rises as the level of employment falls.

arc from point *B* to point *A* (downward-sloping arrows), although we will see that this is not the kind of movement we have actually experienced.

At point *B*, the economy is at its natural rate of unemployment and in this sense is in equilibrium. The inflation rate is the positive rate $(\Delta P/P)_B$, shown along the vertical axis. Just as it may be possible to achieve a lower unemployment

there is again equilibrium. At the end of the process, the inflation rate is lower than it was at the start and the unemployment rate is once again equal to the natural rate as it was at the start. However, during the process, the unemployment rate is temporarily above the natural rate.

Combining the movement from point A to point B, earlier described, with the movement from point B to point A, here described, produces a complete cycle of unemployment and inflation. In the unemployment cycle, the actual unemployment rate at first drops below, then rises above the natural rate; in the inflation cycle, the inflation rate rises while the unemployment rate is below the natural rate, then falls to its original level while the unemployment rate is above the natural rate.

A major objective of public policy in recent years has been that of wringing some of the inflation out of the economy. Just as the supporters of the non-tradeoff argument assert that policy actions to reduce the unemployment rate below the natural rate will lead only to a higher inflation rate in the long run, they also assert that policy actions that raise the unemployment rate above the natural rate will lead only to a lower inflation rate in the long run. The latter case we have just seen in the movement along the downward-sloping arrows from point B to point A in Figure 23-9. In both cases, there is a short-run but no long-run effect on the unemployment rate, but there is a long-run effect on the inflation rate. Therefore, it appears that restrictive monetary and fiscal policies may be employed to shift the inflationary pressure curve to the right and thereby wring inflation out of the economy at the cost of a temporary increase in the unemployment rate.

If the inflation rate can be reduced in this way, how much must the unemployment rate increase and for how long? As we saw in the preceding section, the particular path followed by the economy in adjusting to shifts in the inflationary pressure curve depends on the speed with which people revise their inflationary expectations upward. In the present case, the faster people

revise their inflationary expectations downward, the faster will the Phillips curve shift downward, and the shorter will be the time period needed to get from point B to point A or to wring out the inflation.

Restrictive policy that shifts the inflationary pressure curve rightward from its initial intersection at point B will result in some rise in the unemployment rate and some decline in the inflation rate. Whatever inflation rate was expected at the time of this shift, the amount by which the actual rate now falls below the expected rate will vary directly with the magnitude of that shift. A severely restrictive policy that sharply reduces the growth rate of nominal income will produce a greater discrepancy between actual and expected inflation rates than will a less restrictive policy. The greater this discrepancy, the greater will be the resulting downward shift in the Phillips curve, and therefore the more rapid will be the economy's movement toward point A. However, to obtain a relatively large discrepancy between the actual and expected inflation rates requires a correspondingly restrictive policy, but the more restrictive the policy, the greater will be the rise in the unemployment rate. Alternatively, starting again from point B and applying a less restrictive policy will cause a smaller decline in the actual inflation rate, a smaller discrepancy between actual and expected rates, and a smaller downward shift in the Phillips curve. But the less restrictive policy will impose a smaller increase in the unemployment rate than does the more restrictive policy.

This suggests that there are alternative routes from B to A that differ as to duration and degree of unemployment. A less restrictive policy will produce a route with a relatively small rise in the unemployment rate for a relatively long period of time; a more restrictive policy will produce a route with a relatively large increase in the unemployment rate for a relatively short period of time. In Figure 23-9, if we assume that the arc from point B to point A describes the path followed under the less restrictive policy, then the path followed with a more restrictive policy will be described by an arc bowed out farther to the right from the vertical line erected at the natural rate of unemployment.[21]

If we accept the argument that the inflation rate can be wound down by the application of restrictive policy and if we believe that it is worth paying the price of temporarily higher unemployment to achieve that goal, we are left with the problem of alternative routes to that goal. Which is preferable—a short but severe recession in which the unemployment rate rises substantially above the natural rate, or a long but mild recession in which the unemployment rate rises little above the natural rate? As a practical matter, this question is largely academic; it is not posed in real life. Apart from the question of whether or not they will succeed in wringing out inflation, monetary and fiscal policies sufficiently restrictive to produce a sharp recession are ruled out on political grounds. Congressmen, at least members of the House who are almost continuously running for reelection, will see such policies as political suicide. Less restrictive policies that would produce only a moderate recession may not be rejected out of hand, but such policies take a long time to work. Such policies may not only fail to bring a prompt decline in the inflation rate; in practice, they may at first be accompanied by a rise in the inflation rate. If the inflation rate fails to decline in short order—or, even worse, if it continues to rise for a while—the restrictive policies will be widely condemned as a failure in winding down inflation. At the same time, the price paid in the form of a higher unemployment rate and a slowdown in the growth rate

of output will be all too apparent—and the cry will go up to "get the economy moving" again.

In part because of the monetary and fiscal policies followed and in part for other reasons, the actual cyclical pattern of inflation and unemployment over the last two decades does not conform with the symmetrical cyclical pattern described by Figure 23-9. The record has not indicated that a rise in the inflation rate that accompanies a temporary decline in unemployment below the natural rate—that is, the path from A to B in Figure 23-9—has been followed by an offsetting decrease in the rate of inflation achieved through a temporary rise in the unemployment rate above the natural rate—that is, the path from B to A in Figure 23-9. Instead, the actual record indicates an upward drift in the inflation rate in which the rate takes two steps up and then only one step down and a rightward drift in the actual unemployment rate in which that rate fluctuates around successively higher natural unemployment rates. Of course, in the real world, we do not expect a perfectly symmetrical pattern like that in Figure 23-9, although this is roughly the kind that would exist, according to the non-tradeoff argument, in the absence of certain public policies and institutional changes. We will conclude this chapter with a look at the actual pattern of inflation and unemployment over the past two decades, including a review of several features of that pattern and an explanation of why it diverged so markedly from Figure 23-9.

Figure 23-10 adds to the 1963–69 record shown in Figure 23-6 the record for 1970–80. The tradeoff that appeared so clearly in the 1960s vanished in the following years. If we looked only at the dots for the individual years without the connecting lines, we would get the impression that no systematic relationship existed at all between the inflation rate and the unemployment rate from 1969 to 1980. However, there is a clear pattern traced out by the lines connecting the dots from 1963 to 1980. Two full cycles and part of a third appear. The first is from 1963 to 1972, the next from 1972 to 1976, and 1976 to 1980

---

[21] If one looks at these arcs alone, the one closer to the vertical line appears to be preferable, but this does not allow for the fact that it takes more time to get from point B to point A by traveling along that arc than it would take to reach the same point by traveling along an arc farther bowed out. A diagram showing arcs like these reveals nothing in itself about the time periods required to move from point B to point A; it shows only the unemployment rate and the inflation rate experienced each step along the way.

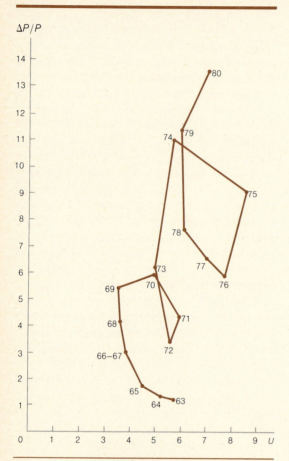

$\Delta P/P$

**FIGURE 23-10
Inflation Rate and
Unemployment Rate,
1963–1980**

ployment decreases (71–72, 75–76) and phases during which the rate of inflation increases as the unemployment rate increases (69–70, 73–74, 79–80). This last phenomenon, known as stagflation or inflationary recession, has probably been the most discussed and was for a long time the most perplexing feature of the cyclical pattern of inflation and unemployment.

Stagflation

Historically, a rising unemployment rate has usually been accompanied by a fall in the price level or at least by a decline in the rate at which the price level was rising.[23] The 1969–70 and 1973–74 experiences of a rising inflation rate in an economy suffering a rising unemployment rate were understandably the source of great consterna-

---

[22]We will not pursue this aspect, but we must note that the cycles would have been, to some degree, different from what they were in the absence of the wage–price controls program that ran from August 1971 to April 1974. Accordingly, the decline in the inflation rate from 1970 to 1971 may have been due in part to the 90-day freeze on prices from August to November 1971. As we will see, there was apparently a downward shift in the Phillips curve from 1971 to 1972; this may have been due in part to the relatively effective Phase II of the controls program that ran from November 1971 to February 1973. The effectiveness of the program declined greatly in Phases III and IV that ran from February 1973 to the end of the program in April 1974. To some degree, this accounts for the sharp rise in the inflation rate over this period, but there were also other very strong forces at work to push up prices (for example, crop shortages and OPEC oil pricing) that the actual controls program was powerless to do anything about.

[23]The sharp increases in the unemployment rate during the two business cycle contractions of 1957–58 and 1960–61 were accompanied by a rise in the price level, but not by a rise in the rate of inflation. The rate of increase of the price level declined. During the business cycle contractions before 1957–58, even the absolute price level declined. But with the rise in the unemployment rate during the contraction of 1969–70, the first year of the 1973–75 contraction and the contraction of 1980, not only did the price level continue to rise, but it rose at an accelerated rate. This distinguishes recent experiences from earlier experience.

may turn out to be the first part of a third full cycle.[22] In each of the two full cycles, we find, as would ordinarily be expected, phases during which the inflation rate decreases as the unemployment rate increases (70–71, 74–75) and phases during which the inflation rate increases as the unemployment rate decreases (63–69, 72–73). However, we also find, as would not ordinarily be expected, phases during which the rate of inflation decreases as the rate of unem-

tion at the time. Economists were hard put to explain the phenomenon in the early 1970s. A recently developed explanation has become the most generally accepted; it is based on the lag between a change in the actual inflation rate and the public's adjustment of its expected inflation rate and thereby the lag between a change in the actual inflation rate and the shift in the Phillips curve that occurs once the expected inflation rate adjusts to a change in the actual rate.

In Figure 23-11, assume the economy is initially at point A. Public policy is directed at reducing what is an unacceptably high inflation rate. Monetary and fiscal policies reduce the growth rate of nominal income and thereby cause a shift in the inflationary pressure curve from I_1 to I_2. If the Phillips curve were to remain at PC_1, the restrictive policies would reduce the inflation rate as the economy moved from point A to point B.

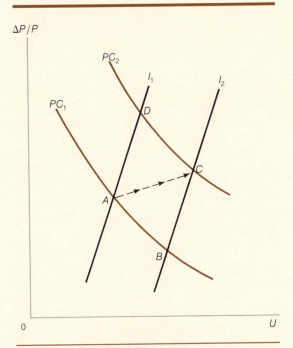

FIGURE 23-11
Stagflation

However, if the point A is the latest point in a series that trace out a sustained acceleration in the inflation rate, the PC_1 position of the Phillips curve would be the latest in a series of successively higher positions. Although the shift from I_1 to I_2 would in itself reduce the inflation rate, that potential reduction is more than offset by the upward shift in the Phillips curve from PC_1 to PC_2. Therefore, the movement is from point A to point C or to a higher rather than a lower rate of inflation.

According to this view, it is the lag in adjustment that results in a rising inflation rate accompanying a rising unemployment rate. At the time the restrictive policy was exerting its impact, expected inflation was still catching up with actual inflation; the upward pressure on the inflation rate exerted by the catching up exceeded the downward pressure exerted by the slower growth rate of nominal income.

It should be clear that a rising inflation rate and a rising unemployment rate would not occur if the unemployment rate corresponding to point A happened to be the natural rate. In that case, an equilibrium would have existed in which the expected inflation rate equaled the actual. There would be no catching up and therefore no upward shift in the Phillips curve. Point A in Figure 23-11 would then be like point B in Figure 23-9; the anti-inflationary effect of restrictive policies would not be offset as shown in Figure 23-11. The result would rather be that earlier discussed in explaining the movement from B toward A in Figure 23-9. It appears, however, that the episodes of 1969–70, 1973–74, and 1980 did not start from such an equilibrium position. Preceding both of these periods was an acceleration in the inflation rate. Therefore, the expected inflation rate during both of these periods was probably being adjusted upward or catching up was taking place. Hence, the upward shift in the Phillips curve.

Although these three periods are alike in that all were periods of worsening unemployment and worsening inflation, there was a striking difference between the rise in the inflation rate in the first and the other two cases. The much greater rise in the inflation rate in the 1973–74 and 1980 periods is explained largely by the extraordinary supply shocks that occurred at those times.

As from 1969 to 1970, some increase in both the unemployment rate and the inflation rate were to be expected from 1973 to 1974. Monetary and fiscal policies had turned contractionary to control the boom that had developed in 1973 in part as a result of the highly expansionary policies of 1972. However, we got a good deal more than the simple increase in the inflation rate that would result as the Phillips curve shifted upward in response to higher rates of increase in money wage rates induced by a sharp rise in the inflation rate from 1972 to 1973. Combined with the wage-induced upward shift in the Phillips curve was an upward shift that resulted from supply shocks. The elements in this have been mentioned before—bad weather caused poor harvests in 1972–73 resulting in a sharp rise in agricultural prices, and the quadrupling of crude oil prices by OPEC in early 1974 produced a sharp rise in the prices of gasoline, heating oil, plastics, chemicals, and many other things. A rise in the prices of farm products, oil, and other materials used in production enter into the cost structure in the same way as a rise in wage rates. In terms of the model of this chapter, they all push the Phillips curve upward.

As in 1974, the OPEC price increases of 1979 and early 1980 contributed significantly to the sharp increases in the inflation rate in 1979 and 1980. Although the percentage increase in OPEC prices in 1979–80 was nothing like the quadrupling of 1974, in relation to the size of the U.S. economy the later increase was larger than the earlier increase. The 1974 OPEC price increases had added about $18 billion to U.S. expenditures for imported oil, approximately 1.4 percent of GNP. The 1979–80 price shock added about $50 billion to the cost of U.S. imported oil, approximately 2 percent of GNP. Because an oil price shock that raises the cost of imported oil by an amount equal to 2 percent of GNP has much the same effect on prices as a 2 percent national sales tax, the 1979–80 OPEC action had a larger

impact on the inflation rate than the 1974 action with its 1.4 percent figure.

Episodes like those of 1969–70, 1973–74 and 1980 gave us the worst of both worlds—more unemployment and more inflation—but there have also been episodes like those of 1971–72 and 1975–76, that gave us the best of both worlds—less unemployment and less inflation. The latter experiences may be explained in the same way as the former by reversing the argument. With the decline in the inflation rate from 1970 to 1971 preceded by years of a rising inflation rate, the expected inflation rate in 1971 was greater than the actual rate. However, the actual decline led to some downward revision of the expected inflation rate and therefore to some downward shift of the Phillips curve from 1971 to 1972. The growth rate of nominal income increased from 1971 to 1972; as is so often the case, monetary and fiscal policies become expansionary in presidential election years. The inflationary pressure curve accordingly shifted leftward, but not up the Phillips curve that it intersected in 1971. As the Phillips curve shifted downward from 1971 to 1972, the leftward shifting inflationary pressure curve intersected that lower Phillips curve at a combination of a lower unemployment rate and a lower inflation rate. This explanation of the 1971–72 experience may also be applied to the 1975–76 experience.

What occurred in both cases may be seen graphically in Figure 23-11 by merely reversing the earlier argument. Starting from point C, the leftward shift from I_2 to I_1 did not move the economy upward along PC_2 to point D. PC_2 shifted downward to PC_1 as the public revised downward its expected inflation rate in a lagged response to the earlier decline in the actual rate. Accordingly, the movement was from point C to point A, as shown by the line between these two points but with the arrows now pointing in the opposite direction.

In the spring of 1981, it appeared that 1980–81 would resemble the episodes of 1970–71 and 1974–75. The long and severe recession from late 1973 to early 1975 exerted strong downward pressure on prices in 1975 and 1976. In contrast, the downturn of 1980 was one of the shortest on record, although real GNP did fall at a record-breaking annual rate of 9.9 percent during the second quarter of that year. The 1980 recession was not the kind to generate expectations that a significant slowing of the inflation rate would follow from it. However, whatever downward price pressures resulted from the 1980 recession were supplemented in early 1981 by other favorable developments.

In the spring of 1981, the OPEC decision to freeze the price of oil for the balance of the year was expected to result in the price of oil, both domestic and imported, remaining essentially flat for the rest of the year. Food price prospects also had improved as a result of expected abundant harvests. An easing in the upward trend of housing prices and mortgage interest rates had appeared; these had made a major contribution to the double-digit inflation rates of 1979 and 1980. Finally, the dramatic increase in the foreign exchange value of the U.S. dollar in early 1981 reduced the prices of imports and exerted downward pressure on the prices of domestic goods that compete with imports.

Barring a reversal in these developments, 1981 and 1982 could show a deceleration in the inflation rate like those in 1975 and 1976, but smaller in magnitude. However, it is less likely that either 1981 or 1982 will show the kind of decrease in the unemployment rate that followed the high 8.5 percent average rate for 1975. What appeared most likely in the spring of 1981 was that the dots for 1981 and probably for 1982 would not only lie below the dot for 1980 but to its right. With a slowdown in the second quarter of 1981 and signs that it would worsen, came the probability of another recession beginning in 1982.

The Upward Drift of the Inflation Rate

Another important, and one might say distressing, feature that appears in the pattern of Figure 23-10 is that each cycle begins with a higher inflation rate. There has been an upward drift in the price level since World War II, but only in the last half of this period has there clearly been an upward drift in the rate at which the price level is rising. Over the last half of this period, 1963, 1972, and 1976 are the years in which a movement to a lower unemployment rate and a higher inflation rate began. Each of these movements began from a higher inflation rate than the preceding—from 1.6 percent in 1963, from 3.4 percent in 1972, and from 4.8 percent in 1976. A continuation of this sort of pattern indicates that the next movement of this kind may start off from a 6–7 percent rate and rise from there.

What causes this upward drift in the inflation rate? The answer appears to be more political than economic. Unemployment has long been viewed as a greater evil than inflation by our elected representatives, especially Democratic representatives and administrations. A movement away from this one-sided view began in the late 1970s and may affect the pattern of the next inflation–unemployment cycle. However, the earlier cycles shown in Figure 23-10 were what they were in part because monetary and fiscal policies were designed in accordance with the prevailing view that the evil of a rising unemployment rate was to be avoided even at the cost of a sizable acceleration in the inflation rate.

With the decision as to whether monetary and fiscal policies at any time should be expansionary or contractionary based predominantly on what was happening to the unemployment rate, expansionary policies were introduced early in a recession to check rising unemployment, even though by so doing the decline in the inflation rate was also checked. For example, the decline in the inflation rate from 1970 to 1971 was most welcome, but it was accompanied by an increase in the unemployment rate that was added on to an even greater increase that occurred from 1969 to 1970. With attention riveted on the unemployment rate, the restrictive policies that had contributed to the recession and to the subsequent decline in the inflation rate were reversed. However, the decline in the inflation rate was also subsequently reversed. After declining from 1970 to 1972, it began to rise; in 1973, it exceeded the previous peak rate that had been reached in 1970.

According to those economists who maintain that public policy actions can produce only temporary departures of the actual from the natural unemployment rate, the upward drift in the inflation rate exhibited in Figure 23-10 is the cumulative result of not persisting in contractionary actions long enough to wring out the higher rate of inflation that resulted from earlier policy actions in the other direction. In other words, in each case we fail to get a complete movement like that from point B to point A in Figure 23-9 because the rise in the unemployment rate that is part of that movement generates political pressures that force a prompt reversal of the policies that cause that movement. According to the argument examined earlier in connection with Figure 23-9, a continuation of restrictive policies would not mean a continuation of the rise in the unemployment rate. The rise in the unemployment rate would be reversed for reasons earlier noted, but the decline in the inflation rate would continue. A continuation of such restrictive policies would therefore move the system toward point A. However, what actually occurs is that, with the economy perhaps halfway along the path from point B to point A, the restrictive policies are replaced with expansionary policies that swing the economy around to a northwesterly path and it is off on another cycle. In terms of the experience shown in Figure 23-10, a continuation of the restrictive policies that began in 1969 for a longer time period would have yielded a decline in the inflation rate to something like the 1963–64 rate with only a temporary increase in the unemployment rate above the rate reached in 1971 and with an eventual return to a lower unemployment rate that at the time was the natural rate. If then another cycle were to start in the mistaken attempt to get the actual unemployment rate below the natural rate to which it had returned, at least the inflation rate in that next cycle would

begin its rise from approximately the level it began at in the previous cycle and perhaps end up no higher than it had in the previous cycle.

If this correctly explains the upward drift in the inflation rate over the past two decades, we may expect a continuation of that upward drift if we get the same kind of policy reaction during the next recession. On the other hand, if we permit the recession with its accompanying rise in unemployment to run its course, there could be a pronounced effect on inflationary expectations, a sharp downward shift in the Phillips curve, and a marked reduction in the inflation rate. If the argument is correct, the economy may have to tolerate a somewhat higher unemployment rate for a somewhat longer period of time than would be the case if expansionary fiscal and monetary policies are implemented shortly after the recession begins. However, this would have the decided advantage of reducing and possibly stabilizing the inflation rate while the other policy simply puts the economy once again on the path of a rising inflation rate. On such a path, it is necessary sooner or later to reverse policy in order to combat what eventually becomes an unacceptably high rate of inflation and in the course of so doing to bring on yet another recession.

The Upward Drift of the Natural Unemployment Rate

Another feature that will be observed in Figure 23-10 is an upward drift in the unemployment rate. The low reached by the rate during each period of economic expansion, 1963–69, 1971–73, and 1975–79, is higher than the low during the preceding period of expansion. The low was 3.1 percent in 1969, 4.1 percent in 1973, and 5.8 percent in 1979. A major factor in the explanation of this phenomenon is the fact that the natural rate of unemployment has increased considerably since the 1960s. Some reasons for this were earlier discussed and need not be repeated here.

What is relevant here is that, for these reasons, the unemployment rate at which the inflation rate tends to accelerate has increased since the 1960s. Whereas it was earlier possible for an expansion to proceed until the unemployment rate was 4 percent or even less without triggering an acceleration of inflation, now the unemployment rate at which that occurs is about 5.5 percent or in the judgment of some even 6.0 percent. As was also noted earlier, the only answer to this is to pursue measures that will reduce the natural unemployment rate itself. However, if instead of reductions we experience increases, we may expect that the low for the rate of unemployment in future cycles of inflation and unemployment will be a successively higher rate.

A Concluding Note

The U.S. economy has experienced four *sharp* upward movements in prices since World War II: 1946–48, 1950–51, 1956–58, and the long period starting in 1965. With the last period now having run longer than a decade and a half, it might be more appropriate to pick out particular years within this span as years of *sharp* upward movement, but practically every one of them qualifies as a year of sharp increase in relation to the overall record of increase for the postwar period up to 1965. Naturally, if this period runs much longer, we will be compelled to include under the heading of years of sharp upward movement only those years in which the inflation rate exceeds, say, 8 or 9 percent, and adopt some other words to describe lower rates like 5 or 6 percent. Although in the past 6, 5, or even 4 percent rates were recognized as *sharp,* they will then have become rates recognized as *moderate* or even *low.*

People may disagree as to what word is appropriate in describing the movement of prices in a particular period, but they will not disagree that the past decade and a half as well as the earlier noted post-World War II periods were periods of inflation. To do something about inflation requires some understanding of the causes and the process of inflation; to gain such understanding we have developed and employed in this and the preceding chapter two models: the aggregate supply–aggregate demand model, and the Phillips curve–inflationary pressure curve model. The former is the simpler of the two models, but it can still shed a good deal of light, in general, on the causes of inflation and, in particular, on the way in which inflation may originate on the side of demand and on the side of supply. Accordingly, we saw how demand-side inflation may originate with either real or monetary factors and how supply-side inflation may originate with wage-push and possibly with profit-push and also with supply shocks.

The Phillips curve–inflationary pressure curve model enables us to see things that cannot be seen through the simple aggregate supply–aggregate demand model, especially the way in which the inflation rate and the unemployment rate change relative to each other under different conditions. At the same time, this model, like the aggregate supply–aggregate demand model, also permits us to deal with demand-side and supply-side inflation, although from a different perspective. Aggregate demand and aggregate supply do not appear explicitly in this model, but they lie behind the inflationary pressure curve and the Phillips curve respectively. On the demand side, inflation occurs as a result of leftward shifts of the inflationary pressure curve that may be caused by either real or monetary factors that produce a higher rate of growth of nominal income. On the supply side, inflation occurs as a result of upward shifts of the Phillips curve that occur for various reasons. Most important of these are those upward shifts that occur with the economy operating below the natural unemployment rate. In this kind of disequilibrium situation, an expected inflation rate above the actual inflation rate results in a wage-induced upward shift in the Phillips curve as labor obtains wage rate increases to catch up with the earlier rise in the actual inflation rate. There are also those shifts in the Phillips curve that occur even with the economy operating at the natural unemployment rate or in an equilibrium situation as a result of supply shocks such as the sharp increases in oil prices put through by the OPEC cartel.

Models like those developed in these two chapters provide an indispensable framework for systematic thinking about the process of inflation. In so doing, they yield some valuable insights on the causes and process of inflation. Still, however valuable, they cannot begin to take into account the multitude of political, social, and economic pressures that are part of what has become an exceedingly complex process. Inflation has always been a complex process, perhaps with the exception of hyperinflations in which we hardly need to look beyond the massive overissue of money for an explanation. But whatever the complexity before, over the period of the long inflation that began in 1965, that process has become even more complex as inflation has become deeply embedded in the political, social, and economic fabric of the country. Day-by-day decisions throughout the private sector, from those of the ordinary wage earner to those of the giant corporation, are influenced and in some cases determined by the current and expected inflation rate. Decisions in the government sector, from those of a small town council to those of the United States Congress, are what they are in part because of what begins to look like an endless inflation. After all these years, this inflation has taken on a life of its own; most members of society have long been busily engaged in finding ways to protect themselves as best they can from its consequences.

In this forbidding contest, the strong exploit the weak, the organized gain at the expense of the unorganized, debtors exploit creditors, and so forth. Planning by individuals and businesses becomes far more difficult. Savings set aside by people for their futures are rapidly reduced by

accelerating inflation. Investment lags as inflation inserts a large element of guesswork into the calculation of the risks inherent in long-term commitments. The list could go on, even to include the threat that accelerating inflation poses to our democratic form of government, free institutions, and personal freedoms.

Why not then bring this pernicious process to an end? One school of thought argues that we must simply learn to live permanently with what in relation to the past is a high rate of inflation, because there is no way of purging it from the system short of a catastrophic depression. Such a cure might be worse than the disease. Like an accelerating inflation, it too carries with it great danger to our democratic form of government. Other economists maintain that the repair job is manageable, but that it can only be done gradually over a period of five to ten years and only then if we are fortunate enough to avoid serious errors in policy and not suffer major supply shocks over which we have no control. As these people like to point out, it took us years to get into this fix and it will take years to get out of it. Still others believe that a turnabout can be achieved in relatively short order without suffering a disaster in the process, although this group appears to be in the minority.

The relatively short-lived spurts of sharp inflation we experienced in 1946–48, 1950–51, and 1956–58 left moderate damage in their wake in part because they were relatively short-lived. The inflation that began in 1965 and has continued at a faster, slower, but always substantial rate since then is, by virtue of its longevity, an inflation of a different kind. How do we cope with this kind of inflation? Its roots now spread into every nook and cranny of the economy. Can this now chronic disease be cured without causing the patient even more distress than that caused by the disease? Or, if we don't try a cure, will the disease get worse and so too the patient's distress? The total lack of any agreement on answers suggests that these are anything but easy questions.

OVERVIEW

In the area of macroeconomic policy, we hear the most about fiscal and monetary policy. However, this dominating duet may before long be expanded to a trio as more and more economists, some quite reluctantly, conclude that the deep-seated inflation problem now facing the economy cannot be solved solely by reliance on fiscal and monetary actions, however well these may have worked in the past. A more and more convincing case is being made for incomes policy, specifically for some variant of what is known as tax-based incomes policy. Our coverage of the three kinds of macroeconomic policy puts incomes policy in this chapter, fiscal policy in Chapter 25, and monetary policy in Chapter 26.

Before discussing the first of these three kinds of policy in this chapter, a few pages are devoted to some background on policy in general. Each kind of policy takes the form of some kind of intervention by government aimed at achieving full employment, stable prices, and satisfactory economic growth. Specific legislative sanction to intervene first came with the Employment Act of 1946 and this was reinforced in 1978 by the Humphrey–Hawkins Act. These acts and the circumstances that led Congress to put them on the books are reviewed.

We begin our examination of incomes policy by setting out its rationale. In brief, if money-wage rates rise no faster than the productivity of labor, unit labor costs will not rise and the prices of goods and services in turn will not rise. Central to incomes policy is control over the rate of increase in the money-wage rate. U.S. experience with incomes policy during the presidencies of Johnson, Nixon, and Carter are summarized.

Experience with incomes policy in this country has been entirely with what may be called conventional incomes policy. A major issue in incomes policy today is the possible adoption in this country of an unconventional or innovative form known as tax-based incomes policy or TIP. Two plans for such a policy are described: the Wallich–Weintraub (W–W) or penalty ("stick") plan and the Okun or reward ("carrot") plan. The two plans are compared, and the discussion of incomes policy concludes with a brief look into the question: Is there a TIP in our future?

24
Incomes Policy

Macroeconomic policy, depending on the forms it takes at any time, means that government does such things as slow down or speed up the growth rate of the money supply, raise or cut tax rates and/or the level of government spending, and impose or withdraw controls on prices and wages. The degree to which government has resorted to such actions in its effort to stabilize the economy grew tremendously in the years following World War II. By way of introduction to macroeconomic policy in general, in the first few pages of this chapter we consider some of the reasons for this. In the balance of the chapter, we go on to our main task of examining incomes policy—one set of actions that government at times takes for stabilization purposes.

The Background of Macroeconomic Policy in General

Since 1946 it has been the responsibility of the federal government to work toward the achievement and maintenance of maximum employment, price level stability, and a satisfactory rate of economic growth. The Employment Act of that year called on the government for the first time to

> use all practicable means consistent with its needs and obligations and other essential considerations of national policy . . . to coordinate and utilize all its plans, functions, and resources for the purpose of creating and maintaining, in a manner calculated to foster and promote free competitive enterprise and the general welfare, conditions under which there will be afforded useful employment opportunities, including self-employment, for those able, willing, and seeking to work, and to promote maximum employment, production, and purchasing power.

The wording of the act, it will be noted, explicitly covers only the single goal of maximum employment. However, as interpreted by numerous executive department statements and actions in which the Congress has concurred, the goals are generally understood to include price stability and satisfactory economic growth as well as the one directly stated.

Although the Employment Act is a landmark in economic legislation, its passage in 1946 does not mean that the federal government was not previously aware of a responsibility in the area to which the act refers. Still, there is a great difference between a mere awareness of a responsibility to work toward the goal of maximum employment and legislation that specifically directs that "all practicable means" be used to achieve this goal. The 1946 act does in this sense replace what at best was a vague and undefined sense of responsibility with an obligation that is somewhat more precisely defined. In this regard, it is interesting to speculate on what differences there would have been in the actions taken by the federal government during the years of the Great Depression if the Employment Act of 1946 had appeared instead in 1926. Perhaps the Great Depression would have been much less great!

It may well be argued, however, that an act of this kind could not have been passed in 1926 and that it was passed in 1946 only because, over the preceding decade, legislators had become convinced that the federal government not only had the responsibility to work toward the attainment of the specified goals but could make a truly significant contribution to their attainment. The power of the federal budget to eliminate unemployment had been revealed in dramatic fashion during World War II. By 1946 it was generally believed that the budget could and should be used as a means of helping to provide employment opportunities in peacetime. This conviction stands in sharp contrast to one held by many before World War II—a conviction that underlay what one writer has described as the *moralistic economics* of those earlier years.[1]

---

[1] See J.M. Culbertson, *Macroeconomic Theory and Stabilization Policy,* McGraw-Hill, 1968, pp. 371–73.

Those who accepted this moralistic economics adopted a "boom and bust" attitude toward business fluctuations. The causes of the bust were found in the excesses and maladjustments of the boom—speculation, unsound uses of credit, high living, and the like. The severity of the downturn also depended on the severity of the "economic sins" committed during the boom. Most importantly, because the moralistic economics did not recognize that with the necessary tools government could contribute substantially to the stabilization of the economy, it could offer little help toward eliminating "boom or bust" except to preach an economic piety that might somehow reduce that instability. This kind of thinking appeared to reach a high point in the late 1920s and early 1930s. To combat it was undoubtedly one of Keynes' purposes in writing the *General Theory*.

Keynes' book was a success with few equals in the history of economics. Without its impact on the world of practical affairs, we would probably not have had the Employment Act of 1946. Moreover, it is doubtful that we would have had many of the federal government actions taken to attain high employment and promote economic growth during the years since World War II. With the passage of the act came the establishment of the Council of Economic Advisers in the executive branch and the Joint Economic Committee in the legislative branch. Through them and their research studies, committee hearings, and the annual Economic Report of the President came a better understanding on the part of the Congress, business, and the general public as to what actions by the federal government might help in achieving these goals and what actions might work in the opposite direction.

Of course, throughout the almost forty years since the passage of the act there have been differences of opinion as to the degree of responsibility that government should assume in trying to achieve these goals. As might be expected, these differences even go back to the debate that preceded the passage of the act in 1946. The original bill, known as the Murray Bill, after

Senator Murray of Montana, was formally submitted in 1945 as the "Full Employment Bill." Most important among its various provisions, this bill declared in effect that the United States, as a nation and a government, had the responsibility to step in and provide jobs for all those who were willing and able to work, but who could not find work. In the debate on this bill, the position of those who favored provisions that imposed less responsibility on government as a guarantor of jobs was the one that prevailed. The final bill signed into law by President Truman nowhere contained the term "full employment," although the original Murray Bill had repeatedly used that term but oddly had in no place defined it. As noted in the previous excerpt from the bill as passed, the government's responsibility was limited to the less specific objective of promoting "maximum employment."

Those who maintained that the government's responsibility goes far beyond that imposed on it by the 1946 act continued to work for legislation that would impose that greater responsibility. Foremost among these was the late Senator Hubert H. Humphrey. Through his and others' efforts, Congress finally passed the Full Employment and Balanced Growth Act of 1978, popularly known as the Humphrey–Hawkins Act. As is apparent from its formal title, this new legislation explicitly uses the term "full employment" that was avoided in the earlier legislation.

The 1978 act strengthens the 1946 act by explicitly identifying national economic priorities and objectives, by directing the establishment of goals based on these priorities and objectives, and by creating new procedures through which the President, Congress, and the Federal Reserve may improve the coordination and development of policies. The setting of specific numerical goals, something not before done legislatively, has probably attracted the most attention. The goals for 1983 set in 1978 included the following: unemployment rate, 4.0 percent (with a supplemental goal of 3.0 percent for all those 20 years and older); inflation rate (CPI), 3.0 percent; and growth rate of real GNP, 4.2 percent.

The widely held view among economists at the time these initial goals were announced was that they were unrealistic, inconsistent, and unattainable. The inflation goal became even more unrealistic in 1979 as a result of the huge OPEC oil price increases of that year. In his Economic Report transmitted to Congress in January 1980, President Carter faced the facts and decided under the authority provided to him by the Humphrey–Hawkins Act to extend the target year for achieving the 4 percent unemployment rate to 1985 and the target year for achieving the 3 percent inflation rate to 1988. Further revisions were made a year later. In the 1981 Annual Report of the Council of Economic Advisers, the projections set forth are a decline in the unemployment rate from 7.7 percent in 1981 to 5.9 percent by 1986, still well over the 4.0 percent Humphrey–Hawkins goal. The projection for inflation (CPI) is a decrease from 12.6 percent for 1981 to 6.0 percent for 1986. Lastly, the growth rate of real GNP is projected to increase from 1.7 percent in 1981 to 3.7 percent in 1986. It may well be that even these less ambitious figures will also have to be scaled down when the Council of Economic Advisers makes its next projections.

Although the Humphrey–Hawkins Act went beyond the Employment Act of 1946 in one way by calling for the establishment of specific goals, it did not take the giant step of directing the government to do all it could in the effort to achieve the goals that were established, for example, to become the "employer of last resort" and hire all those seeking work who were unable to find satisfactory jobs in the private sector. The very ambitious goals established under the act were only goals. To have gone beyond this would have raised a great storm. The Humphrey–Hawkins Act was passed during the time that a growing number of people, economists and others, had begun to question the effectiveness of government actions aimed at stabilizing the economy. Franco Modigliani, one of the country's foremost economists and one who sees a clearcut need for government actions of this kind, devoted his presidential address before the American Economic Association in 1976 to an answer to the critics. Part of the title of his paper was "Should We Forsake Stabilization Policies?"[2] This is not a question he would have asked ten years earlier.

Under the moralistic economics of the 1920s, "boom and bust" instability was almost unavoidable, given the excesses of human behavior. It was believed that government could do little to control it. Modern critics of the government's efforts to provide stability through activist policies do not see "boom and bust" as the alternative. In their view, the economy is inherently stable; the Great Depression was a glaring exception that is now fifty years behind us. At the extreme, this view holds that much of the instability actually experienced in the post-World War II period has been the result of government's activist policies, which are repeatedly trying to undo the damage done by earlier activist policies, which in turn were trying to undo earlier damage caused in the same way. The argument is that the economy has self-correcting powers capable of handling, in a reasonably short time, the smaller disturbances that would arise if these disturbances were not aggravated by activist policies that seek to correct quickly each disturbance that occurs. In this view, there is little role for stabilization policies, barring the rare occurrence of major shocks to the system.

This issue of the role of stabilization policies in today's economy will be further considered in the following chapters. The point here is that, regardless of the fact that the passage of the Humphrey–Hawkins Act is an affirmation by the U.S. Congress of support for such policies by the U.S. government, the almost unquestioned and widespread acceptance during the 1950s, 1960s, and early 1970s of the proposition that activist policies contribute to greater stability had by the mid-1970s become much more questioned and

---

[2]See *American Economic Review*, March, 1977, pp. 1–19.

its acceptance much less widespread. That proposition so long challenged by only a few had by then become the subject of a debate in which a growing number of economists are found on the opposition side. However, the pro-activist view definitely remains the majority view so far. Activist macroeconomic policies are unlikely to disappear for some time, if ever. This and the following two chapters will examine some aspects of the three principal forms of macroeconomic policy.

As economists refer in the broadest of categories to the three basic macroeconomic goals of full employment, price stability, and satisfactory economic growth, they similarly refer in equally broad categories to monetary, fiscal, and incomes policy as the basic types of policy employed in working toward one or more of the specified goals. However, our macroeconomic goals, quite apart from the problem of what is really meant by such loose terms as "full employment," "price stability," and "satisfactory growth," cannot really be held within the confines of the three terms that comprise the standard list. At least two more major goals should be identified— the goal of economic justice, the principal characteristic of which is an "equitable" distribution of income, and the goal of economic freedom, characterized by the right of every person to change jobs, join a labor union, enter a business, own property, purchase desired goods, and do endless other things.

A discussion of a full list of macroeconomic goals would require an entire book or even several books. In our restricted coverage, we will bypass such goals as economic justice and economic freedom, not because they are unimportant but because we have limited space and because we have not developed in even the crudest form a theoretical framework needed for an analysis of policies appropriate to these goals. From earlier chapters we do have a theoretical framework adequate for an analysis of certain policies aimed at the specific goals of full employment, price stability, and economic growth.

We will limit our attention to these three goals. We will also limit our attention to the three principal forms of policy: incomes, fiscal, and monetary.

Monetary and fiscal policy have already been introduced in various contexts in earlier chapters. In developing the model of income determination in Parts 2 and 3, we considered specific monetary and fiscal policies designed to raise the levels of real income and employment. Similarly, in the preceding chapters of Part 5, we referred at several points to monetary and fiscal policies relevant to the problems of economic growth and inflation. However, all such references were incidental to the development of the basic theory of income and employment and of certain growth and inflation theories. Furthermore, what we covered earlier in no way got us into the practical problems of formulating policy in the real world.

It is necessary to explore some of these practical problems. For example, we saw earlier through the *IS–LM* framework that in a depression fiscal policy will be more effective than monetary policy in raising the income level. But to formulate specific fiscal policies to meet these conditions we need much more information than a theoretical framework like *IS–LM* can give us. Policies formulated for the actual economy must face many practical problems that arise out of complex political, social, and economic institutions, procedures, and practices. Although all these must be considered, the theoretical framework is still the foundation of rational policy making and is absolutely indispensable to it. Without an underlying theory, a policy-maker would have no notion of what consequences to expect from any proposed policy and therefore no way of knowing whether the policy in question would be a help or a hindrance in achieving the goal that is the very reason for adopting the policy. In other words, there can be no intelligent policy in the absence of a well-reasoned theoretical framework. As we proceed in these three chapters, it will become apparent both how the theoretical framework developed in earlier chapters lies at the bottom of policy formulation and why much more than just that theoretical framework is required for policy formulation.

Although no one who believes that there is a role for incomes, fiscal, and monetary policy in overall stabilization policy questions that the various policies must be coordinated to yield the best results, it is very convenient and also quite possible, up to a point, to discuss them separately. In the balance of this chapter, we will examine incomes policy; in the following two chapters, we will discuss fiscal and monetary policy.

The Rationale for Incomes Policy

If through an appropriate expansion of aggregate demand, an economy in recession could be restored to full employment without running into inflation, and if through an appropriate contraction of aggregate demand, an economy suffering inflation could have that inflation wrung out without suffering unemployment, monetary and fiscal policy would be all that is needed. These policies are alike in that they both operate by changing aggregate demand. Some combination of the two will produce an appropriate increase or decrease in aggregate demand in any set of circumstances. However, if a contraction of aggregate demand can only wring out inflation by putting the economy through several years of severe unemployment and zero or slow growth, fiscal and monetary policies are inappropriate because they work by altering aggregate demand.[3]

This brings us to incomes policy, which, according to its supporters, can control an inflation like the one that is now so deeply embedded in the economy, not without some pain but without putting the economy "through the wringer." Incomes policy advocates don't question the

need for proper fiscal and monetary policies, but they maintain that such policies alone are not enough. In addition, we need the incomes policy approach that gets right down to the microeconomics of what determines the prices of goods. The rationale of incomes policy is inherent in the argument that there is a stable relationship over time between the prices of particular goods and the unit labor cost of producing each of those goods. Consequently, if money-wage rates rise no faster than the productivity of labor, unit labor costs will not rise and therefore the prices of goods will not rise. To slow the inflation rate accordingly requires that increases in the growth rate of the money wage, in one way or another, be cut back until it is no greater than the growth rate of labor productivity. This is the essence of incomes policy.

In an economy in which the money-wage rate rises faster than the productivity of labor, why does the price level tend to adjust upward by the amount necessary to cover the difference? This follows from the basic profit maximization rule introduced earlier: $W = P \cdot \text{MPP}$. Given the money-wage rate, employers hire the amount of labor for which the price of output times the marginal physical product of labor is equal to the money-wage rate. For example, if W rises by 5 percent in any year but the MPP of labor also rises by 5 percent in that year, W/MPP (the marginal cost) remains unchanged. An unchanged P is still consistent with profit maximization. On the other hand, a percentage rise in W that exceeds the percentage rise in the MPP of labor indicates that a higher price level is necessary for profit maximization. In this case, W/MPP has increased, and, unless prices rise to allow for the rise in cost, the rise in the wage rate occurs at the expense of the profit margin. In practice, the price level tends to adjust by the amount necessary to cover any difference between the percentage changes in W and the MPP of labor.

The data for the years since World War II attest to this tendency. However, the data are not for W and MPP used in our general model but for labor compensation per hour and for average

---

[3]There is, however, a limited role for fiscal policy to alter aggregate supply as we saw in Chapter 22. See pp. 508–10.

output per hour. Given MC = W/MPP, MC increases if W rises relative to MPP; here unit labor cost increases if compensation per hour rises relative to average output per hour. Expressed in terms of rates, the percentage change in unit labor cost is approximately equal to the difference between the percentage change in compensation per hour and the percentage change in output per hour. For example, in 1978, compensation per hour rose at an 8.4 percent rate, output per hour or labor productivity rose at a −0.2 percent rate, and unit labor cost rose by the difference between these two rates, an 8.6 percent rate. Table 24-1 shows these percentage changes for 1948–79 as well as the percentage change in the GNP deflator for these years.

There is clearly more to the explanation of the percentage change in the GNP deflator in any year than the percentage change in the unit labor cost of producing goods and services during that year—for example, the percentage change in OPEC oil prices. However, the percentage change in the unit labor cost remains the most important factor; percentage changes in the GNP deflator will not differ too widely from the percentage change in unit labor cost over a period of years. The percentage changes in the deflator and unit labor cost were respectively 6.6 and 6.9 percent in 1951, 2.4 and 2.7 percent in 1959, 4.4 and 4.2 percent in 1968, and 5.2 and 5.1 percent in 1976. In some other years, the difference was larger, for example, 1.4 and 3.0 percent in 1952, 8.7 and 11.9 percent in 1974, and 8.5 and 10.4 percent in 1979.

Given the relatively close linkage between the rate of change in labor cost per unit of output and the rate of change of the price level, there is little doubt that the goal of reasonable stability in the price level cannot be attained in an economy in which the compensation of labor per manhour is pushed up at a rate well in excess of the rate of increase in productivity per manhour. This is why a money-wage rate that rises at the same rate as "labor productivity" is popularly described as "noninflationary," or consistent with price level stability. A money-wage rate that rises at a more

rapid rate is described as "inflationary," or inconsistent with price level stability.

Because this relationship is indicated by the theory and supported by the post–World War II data, the Council of Economic Advisers, in its January 1962 *Annual Report,* officially advanced for the first time the idea of general wage and price guideposts for price stability. In recent years, the word "standard" has been more commonly used than guidepost or guideline, but they all mean the same thing and will be used interchangeably here.[4] In its briefest form, the general wage guidepost for annual increases in total compensation per employee manhour is that such increases in percentage terms should not exceed the trend of labor productivity.[5] If so limited, increases in labor compensation will be consistent with stable prices and an unchanged distribution of income between labor and others.

An arithmetic example will show these results. Assume that a worker is paid $6.00 per hour, or $240.00 for a forty-hour week, and that output per worker per week is 200 units. Output per manhour is 200 divided by 40, or 5 units. Labor cost per unit of output is $240 divided by 200, or $1.20; or, what is the same thing on an hourly basis, $6.00 divided by 5 equals $1.20. If as a result of a technological advance, better capital equipment, or any other reason, output rises by 3 percent to 206 units per week for the same 40 hours of labor, output per manhour is also higher by 3 percent, or is now 5.15 units. If the worker

---

[4] *Annual Report of the Council of Economic Advisers,* Jan. 1962, pp. 185–90. The genesis and principles of the guideposts are reviewed in the *Annual Report,* Jan. 1967, pp. 120–34. For subsequent statements, see the *Annual Report,* Feb. 1968, pp. 120–28, and Jan. 1969, pp. 118–21. The development of the guideposts as seen in the *Annual Reports* from 1962 to 1967 is examined in R.E. Slesinger, *National Economic Policy—The Presidential Reports,* Van Nostrand, 1968, pp. 100–27.

[5] Because the productivity change in any one year can be influenced by short-run transitory factors, the Council used the trend productivity, which is the annual average percentage change in output per manhour during the latest five years.

TABLE 24-1
Changes in Output per Hour, Compensation per Hour, Unit Labor Cost, and GNP Implicit Price Deflator, 1948—79

Year	Output per Hour	Compensation per Hour	Unit Labor Cost	GNP Implicit Price Deflator
1948	5.3	8.5	3.0	6.9
1949	1.5	1.6	0.1	−0.9
1950	7.9	7.1	−0.8	2.1
1951	2.8	9.8	6.9	6.6
1952	3.2	6.4	3.0	1.4
1953	3.2	6.4	3.1	1.6
1954	1.6	3.2	1.6	1.2
1955	4.0	2.5	−1.4	2.2
1956	1.0	6.5	5.5	3.2
1957	2.5	6.5	3.9	3.4
1958	3.1	4.4	1.3	1.7
1959	1.6	4.3	2.7	2.4
1960	3.1	4.2	1.1	1.6
1961	3.3	3.8	0.5	0.9
1962	3.8	4.6	0.7	1.8
1963	3.7	3.7	0.0	1.5
1964	4.3	5.2	0.8	1.5
1965	3.5	3.9	0.3	2.2
1966	3.1	7.0	3.8	3.2
1967	2.2	5.5	3.2	3.0
1968	3.3	7.7	4.2	4.4
1969	0.2	7.0	6.7	5.1
1970	0.9	7.4	6.4	5.4
1971	3.6	6.6	2.9	5.0
1972	3.5	6.5	2.9	4.2
1973	2.7	8.0	5.2	5.7
1974	−2.3	9.4	11.9	8.7
1975	2.3	9.6	7.2	9.3
1976	3.3	8.6	5.1	5.2
1977	2.1	7.7	5.5	5.8
1978	−0.2	8.4	8.6	7.3
1979	−0.4	9.9	10.4	8.5

Note: Change is percent change from the preceding year. All figures are for private business sector.

SOURCE: *Economic Report of the President*, Jan. 1981, pp. 237 and 277.

receives an increase in compensation equal to the increase in productivity, he will get $6.18 per hour, or $247.20 for the forty-hour week. Labor cost per unit of output, however, remains unchanged at $1.20, or $6.18 divided by 5.15. If the price at which the product is sold remains unchanged, the difference between price per unit and labor cost per unit, which is the amount available for payment to others including stock-holders, will also remain unchanged. However, with a 3 percent increase in the number of units produced and sold, the total amount remaining after labor cost is also higher by 3 percent. The wage guidepost therefore indicates that a rise in the wage rate equal to the gain in productivity is consistent with a stable price for the product and a percentage increase in the earnings of the non-labor factors equal to that received by labor.

Because productivity gains vary widely by industry and firms, the guidepost approach requires a price as well as a wage guidepost. The general price guidepost, in its simplest form, is that those firms that grant wage increases equal to the national trend productivity but experience a rise in productivity greater than the national trend productivity should reduce prices by an amount to reflect this difference. Conversely, those firms that experience an increase in productivity smaller than the national trend productivity, but nonetheless grant wage increases equal to the national trend productivity, would appropriately raise prices to cover that portion of the compensation increase that is not matched by the productivity increase. Although some prices would accordingly fall and others rise, the overall result should be approximate price stability.

If an incomes policy of this kind is to have any chance of success in providing price stability, labor in general must settle each year for an increase in compensation no greater than the wage guidepost figure announced for that year, and firms in general must set prices that correspond to the price guidepost. The failure of firms to observe the price guidepost can lead to a rising price level in the same fashion as the failure of labor to limit its demands to the wage guidepost. The exercise of market power to raise prices to exploit what firms regard as favorable demand conditions for their output differs in kind but not in result from the exercise of market power by organized labor to raise wage rates to exploit favorable demand conditions in the market for labor.

U.S. Experience with Incomes Policy

The Johnson Years

The original official proposal for an incomes policy in the United States came in the January 1962 *Annual Report of the Council of Economic Advisers.* However, at that time, no specific trend productivity was set forth. Two recessions, 1957–58 and 1960–61, had occurred in the preceding five years, and it was difficult to identify the trend productivity for this period. Although no specific figure was stated in the next two *Reports,* in the 1964 *Report* the subsequently well-known figure of 3.2 percent appeared as the latest figure in a column labeled "trend productivity." In that year, the 3.2 percent figure became the recognized general guidepost for wages. In following *Reports,* the Council gave increasingly clear indications of what it regarded as the trend of productivity. In the January 1966 *Report,* the Council specifically recommended that the general wage guidepost be 3.2 percent for that year.

In the same year, there began a process that in effect temporarily marked the end of this incomes policy. Until mid-1966 the guideposts had been observed reasonably well by labor and business. On the part of labor, this to some degree may be attributed to a level of unemployment that averaged more than 5 percent during 1962–65. With increases in labor compensation in most cases limited to the guidepost figure and with business pricing decisions generally in line with the price guidepost, the consumer price index rose less than 2 percent per year during 1962–65. Then the rapid upward surge in the economy in 1966 reduced unemployment to 3.8 percent, and the resulting tightness in the labor market subjected the 3.2 percent wage guidepost to pressures unknown in the preceding years. More and more labor settlements were reached at figures in excess of the guidepost. Although it is more difficult to generalize on the side of prices, price decisions of firms with price discretion more frequently than in preceding years also appeared to be inconsistent with the decisions called for by the price guidepost. Consequently, consumer prices rose by 3.3 percent during 1966, which meant that in January 1967 the Council was effectively barred from announcing a wage guidepost for 1967 equal to the trend productivity. A figure in the neighborhood of 3.2 percent would, on the average, have provided the worker with an increase in compensation no more than sufficient to cover the rise in living costs and therefore would have permitted no increase to reflect the rise in worker productivity. This would be clearly unacceptable to the unions. For a case in point, a story in *Business Week* of November 26, 1966, was headlined "Unions Call Five Percent a Minimum for 1967." On the other hand, for the Council to have officially announced a guidepost figure that was adjusted upward by the amount needed to allow for all or part of the rise in living costs would have been inconsistent with the basic guidepost objective of preventing a rising price level. For example, a guidepost of 5.5 percent made up of 3 percent for productivity gain and 2.5 percent for the rise in the cost of living would have amounted to the adoption of a guidepost that officially accepted approximately a 2.5 percent rate of inflation. Because the guideposts had been popularized over the preceding years as a means of maintaining price stability, a wage guidepost that actually sanctioned inflation, however moderate, would not have been favorably received by the general public. Conditions being what they were, the Council reacted to the further 3 percent increase in consumer prices in 1967 as it had to the similar rise in the year before: As in its 1967 *Report*, no guidepost figure was announced in its 1968 *Report*. For the time being, the incomes policy was dead.[6]

---

[6]For more on the experience with incomes policy in the 1960s, see J. Sheahan, *The Wage-Price Guideposts*, Brookings Institution, 1968; the various papers in G.P. Schultz and R.Z. Aliber, eds., *Guidelines, Informal Controls and the Market Place,* University of Chicago Press, 1966; G.L. Perry, "Wages and the Guideposts," in *Ameri-*

The Nixon Years

There was little likelihood of a return to an incomes police under the new administration that took power in January 1969. President Nixon's Council of Economic Advisers and others in high positions wasted little time in making known their opposition to incomes policies. For more than two years, the new administration steadfastly limited its attack on inflation to what could be done through monetary and fiscal policies. Then with these policies apparently showing little success, in a sudden surprising about-face, on August 15, 1971, the President adopted the most extreme form of the kind of policy that had been denounced uninterruptedly for about two years. He imposed a 90-day freeze on practically all prices and wages, the ultimate form of intervention in the marketplace. This came to be known as Phase I. The 90-day freeze was followed by the establishment of a system of wage and price standards with mandatory rules and with compliance required by law. This system, in effect from November 13, 1971, to January 11, 1973 was Phase II. On the latter date, the system of standards was modified to a predominantly quasi-voluntary form under which the standards were to be self-administered and voluntary behavior consistent with these standards was to be expected. In the President's words, the system would be "as voluntary as possible . . . but as mandatory as necessary." This arrangement, Phase III, was in effect from January 11, 1973, to June 1973.

With the abrupt rise in the cost of living during the early months of 1973, primarily the result of the extreme increase in food prices, Phase III came under heavy attack by the public and Congress. The administration had originally turned to Phase III as a step toward a return to the pre-August 1971 system of no wage and price controls; but the sharp rise in prices that occurred in 1973 suggests, to say the least, that this transition had begun too soon. In response to price increases that grew greater month by month, the

---

can Economic Review, Sept. 1967, pp. 897–904, and M. Bronfenbrenner, "Guidepost-Mortem," in *Industrial and Labor Relations Review,* July 1967, pp. 637–49.

President again reversed direction. On June 13, 1973, he imposed the second price freeze in less than two years. This ran for two months, and was succeeded on August 12 by Phase IV, a system that was stricter in certain ways than Phase II for the industries it covered. However, this system at the same time incorporated a new strategy to achieve a return to free markets: decontrol of selected industries where that was deemed appropriate. Decontrol was authorized for some industries on reaching an agreement that the firms in those industries would expand output or capacity or limit exports and in this way ease price pressures in the domestic market by increasing supplies. Some other industries were decontrolled on the grounds that there had been no build-up of cost pressures in those industries. In such cases, decontrol would not lead to a spurt in prices and therefore no advantage would be gained by maintaining controls. Although there was a move toward a tightening of controls in some areas, there was also a move toward decontrol in others. In any event, the system known as Phase IV came to an end on April 30, 1974, the expiration date of the Economic Stabilization Act, the extension of which the administration did not request (except in the health and construction fields). Congress did not choose to provide an extension on its own. For all practical purposes, after April 30, 1974, prices and wages in the U.S. economy were again permitted to reach their free-market levels as had been the case before August 15, 1971, when the 32-month episode of controls began.

Looking back over the actual course of wages and prices during the almost three years of Phases I–IV, some economists maintain that the actual record of price and wage rate advance was little influenced by the fact that an incomes policy was in operation. They grant that there was an impressive slowing in the rate at which wage rates and prices rose during the first year under Phase II. However, they assert that this may simply have been the effect of the considerable slack in the economy that remained from the 1970 recession. Apart from this, it is usually the first year or so of a prolonged period of wage and

price standards that shows the best results. There will often be a degree of support and cooperation by labor and business at first, but as the distortive and discriminatory effects of the standards, some of which are unavoidable, begin to be felt, support is replaced by opposition. Also, as time passes, circumvention of the regulations increase as the public works out ways in which this can be accomplished. As the anti-incomes policy people see it, the inflation record over the full life of the program would have been little different if there had never been such a program at all. And there are, of course, defenders of the program who not only give major credit to the Phase II wage and price guideposts for favorable results in 1972, but also argue that the results in 1973 would have been much better if Phase II had not been replaced by the much weaker Phase III. In reply, the other side contends that no system of this kind could effectively cope with the shortage situation that had developed in 1973 with many industries operating at capacity. There were then very rapid increases in prices of raw commodities that were entirely outside the program from its inception. And then with 1974 came the staggering increase in the price of imported oil, something entirely beyond the reach of the program. It is obviously not an easy matter to decide which side has the better case.[7]

---

[7]For some analyses of the operation and effectiveness of parts or all of the 1971–74 incomes policy experience, see the following: *Annual Report of the Council of Economic Advisers,* Jan. 1974, Chapter 3, pp. 88–109; "Two Years of Wage-Price Controls," a series of papers in the *American Economic Review,* May 1974, pp. 82–104; B. Bosworth, "Phase II: The U.S. Experiment with an Incomes Policy," in *Brookings Papers on Economic Activity,* 2, 1972, pp. 343–83; R.J. Gordon, "The Response of Wages and Prices to the First Two Years of Controls," in *Brookings Papers on Economic Activity,* 3, 1973, pp. 765–78; D.J. Mitchell "Phase II Wage Controls," in *Industrial and Labor Relations Review,* April 1974, pp. 351–75; D.Q Mills, "Some Lessons of Price Controls in 1971–73," in *Bell Journal of Economics,* Spring 1975, pp. 3–49, and "Recent Experience with Wage and Price Controls," in *Sloan Management Review,* Fall 1974, pp. 48–57; R.E. Azevedo, "Phase III— A Stabilization Program That Could Not Work," in *Quarterly Review of Economics and Business,* Spring 1976, pp.

When Gerald Ford succeeded Richard Nixon as President in August 1974, to many observers inflation appeared to be the most serious problem facing the country. The new president immediately began a jawboning attack to Whip Inflation Now (WIN), complete with big red WIN buttons. A tax increase was also recommended as part of the attack on inflation. However, it shortly became clear to almost everyone but the administration that the economy was in a severe recession, the beginning of which was later dated back to November 1973. The rapid rise in the inflation rate that began in 1973 had slowed substantially by late 1974 under the pressure of recession. The 12.2 percent increase in the CPI from December 1973 to December 1974 dropped to 7.0 percent in the next twelve months and to 4.8 percent for the twelve months following that. At the same time, unemployment jumped from 4.9 percent in 1973 to a shocking 8.5 percent in 1975, then eased off to a still high 7.7 percent in 1976. Apart from the Ford administration's ideological opposition to incomes policy, these were not the kind of conditions to call forth any support for such a policy.

The Carter Years

During the first year of the Carter administration, the deceleration of the inflation rate from its 1974 peak was replaced by an acceleration. For the twelve months ending December 1977, the CPI increased by 6.8 percent in contrast to the 4.8 percent over the preceding twelve months. In his economic report of January 1978, President Carter called on the business community and the nation's workers to participate in a voluntary program to decelerate the rate of price and wage increases. This was a loosely-structured program, the objective of which was expressed no more specifically than a reduction in the rate of

7–21; D. Robinson, "Wage-Price Controls and Income Policies," in *Monthly Labor Review*, March, 1974, pp. 34–39; and A.R. Weber, "Making Wage Controls Work," in *The Public Interest*, Winter, 1973, pp. 28–40.

wage and price inflation in 1978 below the average rate of 1976–77. The administration did not establish a uniform set of numerical standards or guideposts against which each wage or price change was to be measured. By the fall of 1978, it was apparent that the deceleration program was not generally effective. Whatever its other weaknesses, a major one was the lack of a clear guide for wage and price decisions.

In October of 1978 the administration announced a new program that would include explicit numerical wage and price standards. In brief, the wage standard called on labor to hold the increases in wages and fringe benefits to 7 percent for the first year of the program; the price standard called on firms to hold their price increases over the first eighteen months of the program to a rate one-half of a percentage point below the average annual rate of increase of their prices during 1976–77. The program was voluntary, but the administration intended to improve compliance by relating the federal government's procurement of goods and services to the standards. Where the government had a choice of more than one supplier, the government would transfer orders from regular suppliers that were not in compliance with the price standard to other firms that were. This provision generated a great deal of resentment in parts of the business community because it appeared to be a back-door device to mandate a program that was supposed to be voluntary. In practice, actual procurement was not significantly changed by this provision.

The wage and price standards in the October 1978 program were similar to those used in earlier experience. However, something new was proposed for adoption this time—a so-called real wage insurance provision designed to encourage compliance by labor. Under this proposal, employee groups that met the 7 percent pay limitation would receive a federal tax credit, if the CPI increased by more than 7 percent over the year. The rate of the tax credit would be equal to the percentage point difference between the actual increase in the CPI and 7 percent up to a maximum of 3 percentage points (10 percent inflation rate) and would be applied to each employee's wages up to a maximum of $20,000 for the year. Accordingly, if the inflation rate turned out to be 10 percent or higher, an eligible employee with a $20,000 wage income for the year would receive a tax credit of $600, or 3% × $20,000.

Unlike the voluntary wage and price standards, implementation of the real wage insurance proposal required Congressional approval. Although its implementation would have helped to reduce inflation by inducing greater labor cooperation with the 7 percent pay standard, its cost to the Treasury was highly uncertain, and the proposal did not get very far in Congress. This proposal is one form of what is called tax-based incomes policy (TIP), and will be considered in some detail in the next part of this chapter.

Whatever contribution the October 1978 wage and price standards may have made to holding down inflation in 1979, the rate—13.3 percent from December 1978 to December 1979—was even higher than the 12.2 percent rate for 1974, which as of then had been the only other year since 1947 with a double-digit rate. Most of the 1979 price increase came in energy, especially OPEC oil, in other raw materials, and in food—all areas in which wage and price standards cannot effectively limit price increases. However, as labor suffered a decline in real wages in 1979, labor tended to blame the wage standard and to seek relaxation of that standard. In the attempt to win support from labor for the standards program, the administration worked out a national accord with leaders of American labor in September 1979, which in turn led to the creation of a tripartite Pay Advisory Committee on which labor would have a voice in setting the wage standard for the next year.

Although the standards program was continued in a half-hearted way through the remainder of the Carter administration, it was virtually a dead horse by late 1980. Both labor and business increasingly doubted that adherence to the standards would restrain inflation. Consequently they became increasingly unwilling to moderate wage and price increases. By then, even the economists in the Council on Wage and Price Stability, the agency in charge of administering the standards, agreed that the standards would not be effective if continued in their existing voluntary form. This question became academic with the election of Ronald Reagan; the end of this experiment with incomes policy was then assured. One of the new president's first actions after taking office on January 20, 1981, was to do away with the Council on Wage and Price Stability.[8]

From Conventional to Tax-Based Incomes Policy

Apart from the abortive attempt to introduce a system of real wage insurance in 1979, incomes policy in the United States has all been of the conventional kind. Direct controls have been the means of trying to hold price and wage increases to the explicit figure set as the standard for each. In the 1970s, several tax-based incomes policies, TIPS, were advanced: the Wallich–Weintraub (W–W) plan and the Okun plan. Both use taxes instead of direct controls to restrict the rate of wage rate increase. The W–W approach relies on a penalty or a "stick" in the form of a tax increase for noncompliance; the Okun approach relies on a reward or a "carrot" in the form of a tax credit for compliance. Our attention here will be limited to these two novel plans, although there are other related novel plans, perhaps the

---

[8]For description and analysis of the incomes policy of the Carter administration, see R. Higgs, "Carter's Wage-Price Guidelines: A Review of the First Year," *Policy Review,* Winter 1980, pp. 97–113; P. Bennett and E. Greene, "Effectiveness of the First-Year Pay and Price Standards," *Quarterly Review,* Federal Reserve Bank of New York, Winter, 1979–80, pp. 50–53; *Pay and Price Standards: A Compendium,* Council on Wage and Price Stability, June 1979. See also *Economic Report of the President,* Jan. 1981, pp. 14–15, 59, Jan. 1980, pp. 32–41 and 79–82, and Jan. 1979, pp. 80–85.

most "far out" being Abba Lerner's MAP or Market Anti-Inflation Plan. The W–W and Okun tax-based variants of incomes policy have been described as tax analogues to the equivalent market-based incomes policy proposed by Lerner.[9]

Economists who believe that the solution to the inflation problem is only to be found through appropriate monetary and fiscal policies list all kinds of objections to incomes policy, one of the strongest being that incomes policy seriously distorts the allocation of resources. As we saw in the review of U.S. experience with incomes policy, the regulations basically set a single national standard for wages and a single national standard for prices applicable to practically all employees and firms. For example, the October 1978 standards were a 7 percent pay increase limitation for the first year and a price limitation that over eighteen months would hold price increases one-half of a percentage point below the average rate for 1976–77. There are always some exceptions to these standards—for exam-

ple, a different approach is needed for firms not in business during the base period—but the general policy is a single national percentage standard.

Under these conditions, what happens to firms in a rapidly growing industry that seeks to attract more labor? The semiconductor industry may be unable to attract more technicians without offering more than the maximum allowed by the pay standard, but to offer more is not allowed. (The rules usually permit firms to exceed the standard for some employees, if that is offset in the other direction for other employees. This, however, provides very limited flexibility to most firms.) Consequently, the semiconductor industry is unable to hire the labor needed to meet the demand for its product, and the market's increased demand for the product goes unsatisfied. (The rules may allow exceptions in such cases, but each of these has to be handled on its own merits with the red tape that this generates.) By preventing the higher wages and prices needed to bring about shifts of labor and other resources into expanding industries, the standards prevent the reallocation of resources that otherwise automatically occurs in response to changes in demand. Because the relative prices of different commodities and kinds of labor are continuously changing in response to changing supply and demand conditions in free markets, a system of conventional wage and price standards maintained over any length of time must unavoidably impose a high cost on the economy through its distorting effect on resource allocation. Anyone who would propose anything more than a temporary use of incomes policy—and some argue for incomes policy on a permanent basis—cannot make a very convincing case unless the proposal is designed so as not to interfere with the essential resource allocation function performed by changes in relative wages and prices. As we will see as we now turn to the two major TIP proposals, the creators of those proposals argue that, among other advantages, the interference with the workings of the price mechanism is minimal in their systems.

<hr />

[9]Apparently the first proposal for a tax-based incomes policy was that in England by M.F.G. Scott, "A Tax on Price Increases," *Economic Journal,* June 1961, pp. 350–66. Since the first proposal for a tax-based incomes policy was published in the United States in 1971, a vast literature has been generated. On the W–W plan, see the original statement by its creators in H.C. Wallich and S. Weintraub, "A Tax-Based Incomes Policy," *Journal of Economic Issues,* June 1971, pp. 1–18. A book that gets into the details of the W–W plan, as well as into other matters, is Weintraub's *Capitalism's Inflation and Unemployment Crisis,* Addison-Wesley, 1978. On the Okun plan, see A.M. Okun, "A Reward Tip," *Statement before the Committee on Banking, Housing and Urban Affairs, U.S. Senate,* May 22, 1978 (reprinted in the Colander volume noted below), and A.M. Okun and G.L. Perry, "Innovative Policies to Slow Inflation," *Brookings Papers on Economic Activity,* 2, 1978. A series of articles on TIP is found in Part IV of D.C. Colander, ed., *Solutions to Inflation,* Harcourt Brace Jovanovich, 1980. An extensive bibliography on tax-based incomes policy is found at the end of A.P. Lerner and D.C. Colander, *MAP—A Market Anti-Inflation Plan,* Harcourt Brace Jovanovich, 1980. This volume provides a detailed statement of the MAP proposal. See also the *Economic Report of the President,* Jan. 1981, pp. 57–68.

The Wallich– Weintraub (W–W) Plan

The W–W proposal is based on the familiar proposition that an effective way of discouraging specific activities that impose costs on society is to tax those responsible. For example, firms that dump wastes into the air and water impose the costs of waste disposal on society in general in the form of polluted air and water. A widely recommended way of controlling pollution is to impose an effluent tax that makes firms pay for the use of a scarce resource—clean air and clean water. As firms must obviously pay a price for labor and other resources acquired in the marketplace, so they will pay a price for the use of air and water resources in the form of a tax, the amount of which will vary with the amount of waste put into the air and water. Firms, and individuals as well, do what is in their own self-interest. The tax gives firms an incentive or makes it in their self-interest to reduce the amount of effluents released into the air and water. The same objective of controlling pollution may be met by direct controls, but this approach is less efficient, less flexible, more complicated, and more costly to administer than the approach through tax incentives and the market mechanism.

This argument for taxing firms that impose a cost on society by polluting is the same argument on which the W–W plan rests. (All references to TIP in this section are to the W–W plan.) Firms that grant pay increases greater than the increase in labor productivity impose a cost on society in the form of inflation. To prevent or reduce this cost, impose a tax on the firms responsible for it. At present, it is in the self-interest of many corporations to grant large pay increases after only token resistance and then seek to pass the higher labor costs on through higher prices for their output. If the rate of a corporate profits tax varies with the rate of pay increase granted by a corporation, management will find it is in its self-interest to vigorously resist employees' demands for large pay increases, at times even to the point of taking a strike. So doing will hold down the unit labor cost of output. With firms typically setting prices for their output by taking a reasonably stable markup on unit labor cost, holding down the increase in unit labor cost will hold down the rate at which prices of goods and services are increased. Generalizing for the economy as a whole, holding down the increase in unit labor cost will hold down the rate of inflation.

How would the TIP tax be set up? Essentially, a surcharge will be levied on the income tax of corporations that grant pay increases in excess of the percentage established as the standard. If that rate were 7 percent and a firm granted a pay increase of 9 percent, the corporate profits tax for the firm would rise above the regular 48 percent rate by some multiple of the 2 percentage points excess. If the multiple were 4, the surcharge would be 8 percent and the tax rate would be 56 percent. If the standard were 6 percent, the excess would be 3 percentage points; if the multiple were 5, the surcharge would be 15 percent and the tax rate would be 63 percent. The surcharge can, within limits, be whatever rate is required to hold the actual percentage increase in the money-wage rate close to the rate established as the standard. Facing the threat of a sizable penalty, firms will resist excessive wage increases that otherwise would be granted. To the degree that this result is realized, price increases in turn will be lower than otherwise, and the inflation rate will be reduced.

Although this happy result is expected by its advocates, at first glance it seems unlikely that this program would ever be adopted. It appears well designed to elicit a hostile reaction from both labor and business. It seems to penalize labor by restricting the growth of labor's money income while not restricting the growth of profit income, and it appears to add a corporate income tax surcharge to what owners and managers of corporations already regard as an onerous tax load. Because a program to which both business and labor are opposed stands little chance of being tried, the supporters of the plan hasten to point out that these characteristics of the program are apparent but not real.

The program will indeed slow the growth of labor's money income, but this is not the same as saying that it will penalize labor. What matters to labor is its real income; over time real income must grow at the same rate as the productivity of labor. As we saw in Table 24-1, the inflation rate closely corresponds to the excess of the growth rate of labor compensation over the growth rate of labor productivity. Increases in money-wage rates unmatched by increases in labor productivity are offset by higher prices with no real gain to the wage earner. TIP supporters maintain that TIP will actually reward rather than penalize labor by achieving a full employment economy, raising the rate of growth of labor productivity, and thereby boosting labor's real income.

Furthermore, labor's fear that the profit share of income will increase at the expense of the wage share is not warranted, according to TIP supporters. Although TIP imposes a standard for wage rate increases but no standard for price increases, the growth rate of prices will, on the average, be roughly equal to the growth rate of unit labor cost. This has been true in the past and there is no reason to expect it to change in the future. As we saw on p. 151, as long as the increase in the growth rate of the money wage is equal to the gain in productivity, unit labor cost will remain stable and prices will then also remain stable. If the growth rate of the money wage exceeds the gain in productivity, unit labor cost will rise and the price level will rise at the same rate. However, whether the price level is stable or rising, the shares of total income going to labor and profit recipients are not affected. The profit share does not gain at the expense of the wage share.

What about the objection by business to another tax? The plan does not actually impose another tax on business. Unlike the corporate income tax, the surcharge is not intended to raise revenue for the government; by and large, business is expected to avoid paying this tax by holding the rate of wage increase to that set by the standard. Only those firms that grant excessive wage increases will find their taxes increased by TIP. When allowance is made for other details of the plan not here considered, the total tax burden on corporations and the share of national income made up of after-tax corporate profits are expected to be what they would be in the absence of TIP. However, if the share of income represented by after-tax corporate profits and the share represented by after-tax labor earnings are actually changing in an undesirable way, offsetting adjustments may be made by altering the rates of the personal, corporate, or payroll tax.

No matter how valid these and other responses to labor and business objections may be, they are not likely to convert labor and business into enthusiastic supporters of TIP. However, for the sake of argument, suppose the opposition from these groups was moderate enough and support by Congress and the President was strong enough to allow the program to be tried. Would it work? The likely answers of economists run the full spectrum from the enthusiastic yes to the emphatic no. These opposed answers to the broad question are naturally based on the opposed answers to the many narrower questions that must be faced. A few of these are noted here.

Will the Surcharge Be Shifted? Wouldn't firms grant increases in wage rates just as if there were no TIP and then simply pass on the surcharge this subjects them to by raising prices as required to maintain their after-tax profits? The surcharge amounts to an increase in the tax rate paid on corporate profits, and there is considerable disagreement among economists on the incidence of this tax. However, there is much less disagreement that this tax will be more fully shifted in the long run than in the short run. Because few firms will plan on paying a TIP tax continuously (most firms will meet the wage standard most of the time), supporters of TIP argue that it will be viewed by firms that do pay it as a short-run tax, and this reduces the likelihood of its being shifted. Furthermore, unlike the regular corporate income tax that treats all firms with equal profits the same, the surcharge will vary widely among firms with equal profits. Because competing firms in an industry will not incur the same surcharge, those with larger surcharges will find it more difficult to shift the charge than will the others. Overall, supporters of TIP believe that large-scale shifting is unlikely. However, to the extent that there is shifting, TIP will not work, because the surcharge then loses its restraining effect on wage increases. If firms can shift the tax, they will have little more reason to resist wage increases after TIP than before. The question of the shifting of the surcharge therefore becomes critical in any evaluation of whether or not the W–W TIP will work.

Is the Plan Administratively Feasible? The basic problem here is to establish the exact amount of a firm's increase in compensation per worker or per hour of labor employed. This obviously cannot be done accurately until the end of a firm's fiscal year; the surcharge, if any, cannot be computed until then. If a firm's increase turns out to be 9 percent for a year in which the standard is 7 percent, the 2 percent excess times the multiple is then the surcharge percentage. A multiple of 4 would make the surcharge 8 percent, and a firm with a $100 million corporate income tax obligation would add to this a surcharge of $8 million. Firms obviously have an incentive to arrive at a figure for the percent increase in labor compensation that is not greater than the standard. Suppose a simple way of measuring an increase in labor compensation was adopted. For example, total wages, salaries, bonuses, fringe benefits, and related payments divided by the number of employees on a particular date would give the average compensation per employee. Comparing this figure with that for the preceding year calculated in the same way gives the increase. This method is plainly unsatisfactory because the result it gives may be readily distorted by firms' increasing the number of employees on the date the calculation is made. That reduces the increase in compensation and thereby reduces or eliminates the surcharge.

To avoid some problems of this kind, Wallich and Weintraub have suggested the following as a fairly water-tight specification of the increase in labor compensation: total wages and related payments in each job classification and grade, divided by the number of manhours worked in the respective categories, and combined into a weighted index of increase in labor compensation. They grant that this kind of calculation would impose a considerable burden on a large firm with numerous plants as changes in the product mix and the geographical mix of the firm's output occur, given that there are different pay scales and different job classifications for the firm's plants in different localities. However, any simpler specification allows firms to engage in tax avoidance by manipulating the increase in labor compensation reported.

With the surcharge tied to the corporate income tax, the IRS would be the agency in charge of collection and enforcement of the surcharge. Just as some large firms would find it difficult to distill a single figure for the increase in compensation from the increases in many labor classifications in many different plants, the IRS would find it difficult to determine by audit if the final figure arrived at by any such firm was reasonably correct. There is room for honest differences of opinion between the firms and the IRS on some aspects. For example, it would be necessary to estimate the percentage gain in compensation that takes the form of an improvement in working conditions, one of the elements included in compensation by Wallich and Weintraub. Firms would seek to put as low a value on this as possible—perhaps a lower figure than the IRS would judge appropriate.

Some firms would resort to "sham" devices that the IRS would disallow, but the IRS would have to detect such ploys. For example, a firm might agree with its employees to reduce their regular work day to seven hours, then work one hour of overtime each day at double pay. In this way, larger increases in compensation could be given without exposing the firm to the surcharge.

Finally, consider a set of conditions that the IRS could not so readily classify as a "sham." A firm cuts back its employment of workers for whom demand is relatively strong and increases its employment of workers for whom demand is relatively weak. Because the former get higher rates of wage increase than the latter, the change in the composition of its labor force may enable the firm to end up with an overall increase in compensation below the standard. Given the way in which the firm happened to stay below the standard, should the firm, nonetheless, be subject to a surcharge?

Will the Plan Seriously Distort the Allocation of Resources? A major defect of wage and price standards of the kind so far employed is that they interfere with the right of firms to set their prices and the right of firms and employees to mutually agree on wage rates. Market forces may call for a large rise in some prices and some wage rates, but such adjustments are forbidden because they will violate the price and wage standards. If prices and wages are not permitted to respond to market forces, they cannot bring about the reallocation of resources that is called for by those forces. As noted earlier, this is what happens under conventional wage and price standards; but proponents of TIP argue that their plan is not subject to this defect.

If there is a large increase in the demand for a firm's product, that firm will offer higher wage rates to attract the additional labor needed to expand output. Unlike conventional incomes policy, the W–W plan will permit this to happen. The firm is completely free to exceed the wage standard as needed to attract the labor it needs. It is also subject to no price standard and the increase in demand for its product will result in a higher price for that product at the new profit-maximizing level of output. However, exceeding the wage standard does subject it to the surcharge and does raise its total corporate income tax over what it would otherwise be. The firm will not ignore this extra tax. Critics of the plan point out that this tax is likely to slow the rate at which labor is reallocated to the firm in question as well as to other firms faced with growing demand and away from firms faced with declining demand. Accordingly, the surcharge introduces another eco-

nomic inefficiency into the system. This inefficiency may be small in comparison with that under conventional incomes policy, but it still would not exist in the absence of any incomes policy.

The critics of the W–W plan have not conclusively proved that the plan will not work, but they have demonstrated that efficiency, administrative, and other costs could be substantial. The standard response of the plan's supporters is that all of these costs add up to a total much smaller than the cost of the alternative. Inflation cannot be controlled without incurring some cost. If it is to be controlled by restrictive monetary and fiscal policy, it will only be done at the cost of a great sacrifice of output and prolonged severe unemployment. On a cost basis, supporters of the Wallich–Weintraub program see it as a far preferable way of doing what has to be done.

The Okun Plan

In principle, the Okun plan is like the W–W plan except that it relies on a reward rather than a penalty to obtain compliance with the pay standard. In brief, a pay standard would be set—say, 6 percent—for the year ahead. All firms that choose to participate in the program would have to pledge to limit the average compensation increase of employees to 6 percent for that year. The pledge would not deny any firm the right to give individual workers increases in excess of 6 percent for merit or through promotion so long as its overall average pay increase did not exceed the standard. (The same problem of defining compensation and measuring the increase in compensation that is faced under the W–W plan is faced here.) Each participating firm would qualify all of its employees for a tax reduction for the coming year equal to, say, 1.5 percent of each employee's compensation up to some limit, say, $20,000. The $300 tax credit on $20,000 would more than equal a $400 pre-tax pay increase for the average worker at this level—that is, the 1.5 percent credit would be equal to a pay raise of a little over 2 percent. Therefore, the employee would be better off with the combination of the 6 percent pay increase and the 1.5 percent tax credit than with an 8 percent pay increase and no tax credit. For employees of participating firms, the amount of tax credit would be obtained in the form of a reduction in the employee's withholding tax.

Okun argued that all firms would want to participate because the tax credit to their workers—a cost to the Treasury and not to the firm—would help them to slow down the rate of increase in wages and salaries. But to make it even more attractive to firms, he proposed a tax credit to firms of, say, one-fourth of the total credits obtained by each firm's employees. This credit would be granted only to those firms that pledge in advance of the beginning of the program to meet the 6 percent pay standard. However, employees of firms that did not sign up in advance would also be eligible for the tax credit, if their employers reported after the year that they did not exceed the 6 percent standard. These employees would get the amount of the credit as a tax refund.

As with the W–W plan, under the Okun plan no employer is forced to limit the average compensation increase of its employees to the standard. Some firms faced with acute labor shortages may find it necessary to offer, say, a 12 percent annual raise to hold their workers and attract more workers; they are free to grant that large increase, but the workers in such firms are, of course, not then entitled to the anti-inflationary tax credit. With compensation rates thereby permitted to respond to market forces, this version (like the W–W version of TIP) greatly reduces the problem of distortion in the allocation of resources that occurs under an incomes policy which is not tax-based.

The Two Plans Compared

Although the penalty and reward plans both rest on the same principle, there are notable differences that affect their acceptability and workability.

Coverage   The W–W plan would apply to only the largest 2,000 firms in the country, but the Okun plan of necessity would apply to all firms from the largest corporation to the smallest neighborhood store. This is unavoidable if the tax credit is to be made available to all employees, wherever employed (including governmental units). All firms with employees who are to be covered would be required to keep the records and file the reports needed to qualify their employees for the tax credit. Critics say that the administrative and compliance problems faced under the W–W plan would be multplied a thousand times under the Okun plan with its universal coverage. The audit problems handed to the IRS would involve millions of reports. To reduce the reporting burden on very small firms and the audit load on the IRS, Okun suggested that firms with fewer than 20 employees might be given a special exemption. This would enable them to qualify their employees for the tax credit merely by signing a pledge to adhere to the anti-inflationary spirit of the program, the result of which should be some slowing of the rate of pay increase among employees of these very small firms. Of course, an exemption like this is bound to create suspicion and resentment among the owners and employees of somewhat larger firms, which might affect the credibility of the program itself.

Shifting of the W–W Surcharge   Because it imposes no tax, the Okun plan avoids a problem faced by the W–W plan. If the surcharge imposed under the W–W plan is shifted to customers through higher prices, it will fail to perform its function of restraining the rate of pay increase.

Cost to the Treasury   The W–W plan will increase the government's tax receipts; the Okun plan will increase the government's outlays. A major reason for the failure of Congress to consider President Carter's 1978 proposal for real wage insurance for 1979—a version of the Okun plan—was the great uncertainty of its cost to the Treasury. Under the insurance program, the tax credit to employees would have been the difference between the 1979 pay standard of 7 percent and the actual percentage increase in the CPI for that year, up to a limit of 3 percentage points (10 percent inflation rate). The credit would have been computed on a person's labor income only to a maximum of $20,000.

If the insurance program had been adopted for 1979 and a large fraction of all employees had complied with the 7 percent standard, that in itself would have gone far toward holding the rate of inflation well below what it would have been in the absence of the standard. However, even then the inflation rate would have surged due to sharply rising food and energy prices. As it turned out, the CPI rose by 13.3 percent from December 1978 to December 1979; it had risen only 9.0 percent over the preceding twelve months. If Congress had adopted the real wage insurance program and if there had been widespread participation in that program, the CPI might still have risen from the 9.0 percent rate to a 10.0 percent or higher rate for 1979. The Treasury would have faced the huge cost of an overall tax credit equal to 3 percent of the wage and salary income ($20,000 maximum per employee) of a large fraction of all employees in the country.

Equity for Employees   Neither the W–W plan nor the Okun plan has a price standard. In both, the rate of price level increase is decelerated through a deceleration of the rate of pay increase. Contrary to appearances, this does not make these approaches "anti-labor"; it merely recognizes that a wage standard is the more practical approach to the problem. There is considerable evidence that a slowdown in the rate of pay increase will be converted, with a fairly short lag, into a matching slowdown in the rate of price level increase; there is much less evidence for the opposite case. The slowdown in the rate of pay increase that follows from a slowdown in the rate of price level increase will probably be longer

delayed and less complete than the reverse case.

Because a successful attack on inflation through TIP must rely on a pay standard, the Okun plan has an advantage over the W–W plan in terms of fairness to employees. Workers will get a tax credit through reduced withholding immediately on the implementation of the program. Okun's view was that the take-home pay of workers would probably slightly increase initially. Under the W–W plan, workers would receive no benefit until their sacrifice in the form of a lower rate of pay increase was reflected in a lower rate of price increase. During the course of that lag, the burden of the program would fall on workers alone. The result could be a redistribution of income from wages to profits over that time period. This time period would not be longer than the first year of the program, and, as was noted in describing the W–W program, the problem created during that period could be met by an upward adjustment in the tax rate on profits to recover the income shifted from wages to profits. It could perhaps better be met by granting all low- and middle-income workers an income tax reduction for that year or by reducing the social security tax for that year. On this point, the Okun plan seems preferable to the W–W plan, because such a shift from wages to profits is not likely to appear at all under the former plan.

Is There a TIP in Our Future?

During the course of their election campaigns, recent Presidents, Democratic as well as Republican, made their opposition to incomes policy in any form emphatically clear. Nonetheless, as we saw earlier, Presidents Nixon and Carter both found it advisable to resort to wage and price guidelines, including Nixon's mandatory standards under Phase II of his program. At the time he took office in January of 1981, President Reagan faced a forbidding inflation problem. As outlined early in his term, the new administration's plan of attack on inflation differed from the conventional "demand-side" attack in which the weapons of restrictive fiscal and monetary policy are first brought into the battle. Instead, the emphasis was on the "supply side" with fiscal policy designed to stimulate work effort, saving, and capital formation and thereby a more rapid growth rate of output, as outlined in Chapter 20. However, this plan of attack had no place at all for incomes policy.

If the advocates of TIP are correct in their belief that price and wage setting procedures now in use make it impossible for almost any fiscal–monetary strategy to cure inflation without a disastrous depression, there is nothing else to turn to but incomes policy. Despite President Reagan's stated opposition to such policy, past experience suggests that it would not be at all surprising if his administration turned to it. Although it appeared unlikely in the spring of 1981 that 1981 would be the third consecutive year of double-digit inflation, if the inflation rate continued near the double-digit level over his first year or two in office, the public would probably judge his attack on the problem a failure. It is hard to believe that an incomes policy would not follow and that that incomes policy would not take advantage of the benefits that go with a tax-based version. At the time of writing, TIP appears to be more than a remote possibility.

25

Fiscal Policy

OVERVIEW

Fiscal policy has received attention at a number of points in earlier chapters; in this chapter, our attention is limited to a few selected aspects not earlier considered. Here we first introduce the concept of the high employment or full employment budget surplus (FEBS). Every quarter of every year, economists ask themselves whether the federal government's budget program has been stimulative or restrictive. A first approximation to an answer is provided by what happens to the FEBS from one quarter to the next and from one year to the next. We consider the meaning, shortcomings, and the 1956–80 figures for the FEBS in turn. The first part of this chapter ends with an examination of fiscal drag and fiscal dividend, which are related to the FEBS.

The next topic we consider is the flexibility of fiscal policy. Is it possible to adjust government spending and taxes with the degree of flexibility that may be needed, if those adjustments are to be useful in combatting cyclical fluctuations in the economy? We review this large question under the three headings of built-in flexibility, formula flexibility, and flexibility through discretionary actions.

Whether adjustments in any period are in the direction of stimulus or restraint, these adjustments necessarily take the form of changes in government purchases of goods and services, transfer payments, and taxes. To what extent can the federal government increase or decrease each of these as part of a counter-cyclical fiscal policy? In the final section of the chapter, we explore the limitations on the ability of the government to effect variations in each of these tools of fiscal policy.

The deliberate use of federal government spending and taxing as a possible means of attaining and maintaining full employment, a stable price level, and a satisfactory rate of growth now dates back fifty years. Activist fiscal policy began during the 1930s, largely as a result of three developments: the apparent ineffectiveness of monetary policy as a means of overcoming the severe unemployment of the Great Depression, the "new economics" advanced by Keynes with its emphasis on aggregate demand, and the growing importance of government spending and taxation in relation to the economy's total income and output. From its relatively modest beginnings, fiscal policy has become a major means by which the government attempts to achieve high employment and to prevent inflation. As noted, the Employment Act of 1946 directed legislatively that fiscal policy be used toward the achievement of these ends.

The success of the Keynesian economics was such that from the 1940s into the 1960s few people doubted that government could raise or lower aggregate demand through appropriate changes deliberately brought about in government purchases, transfers, and tax collections. Starting in the 1960s, monetarism—a doctrine that will be outlined in Chapter 26—achieved some success in its general attack on Keynesian economics. As part of the attack, the monetarists questioned the basic tenet of Keynesian economics which had long gone unquestioned. They revived an old classical notion that holds that, except under certain conditions, increases in government spending do not add to total spending but simply supplant or "crowd out" an equal amount of private spending. A parallel argument is made for decreases in tax rates. To the extent that such crowding-out occurs on anything like a dollar-for-dollar basis, fiscal policy becomes powerless to affect aggregate demand. All the other problems encountered in trying to use fiscal policy to deliberately influence aggregate demand then have no practical importance.

Most economists, however, do not accept the crowding-out argument as advanced by some

monetarists; in other words, most economists agree that fiscal policy can be used to vary aggregate demand in a way and to a degree that contributes to economic stabilization. If it can indeed be so used, it then becomes necessary to face the many real-world problems that complicate the planning and execution of actual fiscal policies. A few of these problems are discussed in this chapter.

In a sense, a problem that underlies all other such problems is that of evaluating the impact of any overall fiscal program on the level of economic activity. To measure in a meaningful way the stimulative or restrictive influence of any actual federal fiscal program or of the federal budget as a whole for any time period requires recourse to what is called the full employment budget surplus, also referred to as the high employment budget surplus.

The full employment budget surplus gives us a measure of the stimulus or restraint exerted by a particular fiscal program, but suppose that our objective is to provide more or less stimulus or more or less restraint than that indicated by a given fiscal program. The practical problem then faced is whether the program can be altered fairly promptly to yield the desired result. This is essentially the problem of flexibility in fiscal policy.

Any adjustment in the fiscal program to vary the restraint or stimulus exerted by that program calls for changes in the level and perhaps the composition of government purchases, transfer payments, or taxes or in various combinations. What are the practical difficulties involved in varying expenditures and taxes as may be required if fiscal policy is to contribute to the stabilization of the economy?

The Full Employment Budget Surplus

On the basis of the elementary fiscal models presented in Chapter 6, we reached the straightforward conclusion that fiscal changes that involve a deficit are expansionary and fiscal changes that involve a surplus are contractionary. If we work with this kind of model, it would seem that all we need do to determine whether the impact of the government budget is expansionary or contractionary in any period is to note whether it shows a deficit or a surplus for that period. If it shows a smaller deficit than in the preceding period, the rule suggests that the budget is still expansionary but less so than it was in the preceding period. The same logic holds for other period-to-period changes in the size of the surplus or for changes from surplus to deficit and deficit to surplus.

However, a major qualification to this rule shows that, under certain circumstances, a rise in the deficit from one period to the next is not indicative of a more expansionary budget, but of a contractionary budget.[1]

The federal government's budget program for each year fixes both planned expenditures and tax rates. This program cannot, however, fix in advance but can only estimate the size of the deficit or surplus, because the actual size will depend in part on the level of economic activity, which is not known in advance. Given the possibility that economic activity may vary over a sizable range, an unchanged program of planned government expenditures and tax rates is accordingly consistent with a whole range of possible surpluses or deficits. Although this is perhaps self-evident, we will take several steps beyond this that are not self-evident. It is therefore necessary to express the relationships in a formal manner.

The Absolute Budget Surplus and the Full Employment Budget Surplus

If we let ABS stand for the actual budget surplus of the federal government (and, if negative, for

---

[1] A review of the third fiscal model presented in Chapter 6 will contribute to an understanding of the material that follows.

the actual federal budget deficit), we have

$$ABS = T_g - G - R$$

in which T_g is gross federal tax receipts, G is federal purchases of goods and services, and R is federal transfer payments. T_g is a direct function of Y—that is, $T_g = tY$, in which it will be recalled that t is the marginal propensity to tax. (In Chapter 6, we wrote $T_g = T_a + tY$, but for simplicity here we drop the autonomous component.) Substituting tY for T_g in the preceding equation,

$$ABS = tY - G - R$$

Assuming given dollar amounts for G and R and a given rate for t, it follows that the ABS varies directly with the level of Y.

In Figure 25-1, the two upward-sloping lines shown are two of any number of possible lines of this kind, each of which is defined by a specific set of values for t, G, and R. As each such line identifies a different budget program, the line corresponding to each such program may be referred to as a budget program line or simply as a B line. (To avoid confusion with the BP or balance of payments line used earlier, the letters BP are avoided here.) For the set of values that give us the B_2 line, there is a deficit of C at the relatively low income level of Y_1 and a surplus of A at the relatively high income level of Y_2. If the economy were at the full employment level or potential output level of Y designated as Y_f, there would be a surplus of D.

It is assumed that the amounts of G and R remain the same at each possible level of Y. Therefore, with the budget program identified by any B line, the changes in the size of the deficit or surplus from one level of Y to another are due entirely to the changes in tax receipts that accompany changes in Y with an unchanged t. A shift in the B line is similarly assumed to be due to a change in t with unchanged G and R. In Figure 25-1, the two B lines differ in that B_2 is based on a higher t than is B_1. Consequently, for the B_1 line, there is a smaller surplus or larger

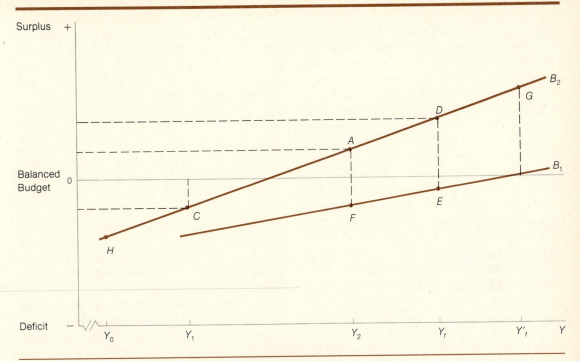

FIGURE 25-1
The Federal Surplus or Deficit and the Level of Income

deficit at any income level than the surplus or deficit indicated by the B_2 line.

We next define a new concept, the full employment budget surplus or FEBS:

$$FEBS = tY_f - G - R$$

The FEBS is the federal budget surplus that would be generated by a given budget program if the economy were operating at full employment throughout the year.[2] The actual level of Y in any year may be equal to, less than, or greater than

Y_f. Therefore, the actual budget surplus will differ from the full employment budget surplus in every year in which the economy is not operating at the full employment output level.

This is seen from the equations by subtracting the equation for the ABS from the equation for the FEBS to obtain

$$FEBS - ABS = tY_f - tY = t(Y_f - Y)$$

[2]The concept was first used by E.C. Brown, "Fiscal Policy in the Thirties: A Reappraisal," *American Economic Review,* Dec. 1956, pp. 857–79, but it received emphasis by the Council of Economic Advisers starting in 1962. (See the *Annual Report of the Council of Economic Advisers,* Jan. 1962, pp. 78–84.) A more thorough discussion is found in

M.E. Levy, *Fiscal Policy, Cycles and Growth,* National Industrial Conference Board, 1963, Ch. 6 and A.M. Okun and N.H. Teeters, "The Full Employment Surplus Revisited," in *Brookings Papers on Economic Activity,* 1, 1970, pp. 77–110. This article, on pp. 84–102, provides a good discussion of some of the major problems associated with the full employment surplus. See also A.S. Blinder, *Fiscal Policy in Theory and Practice,* General Learning Press, 1973, pp. 6–12.

The FEBS differs from the ABS only if Y_f differs from Y. For the case of the upper B line in Figure 25-1, the ABS of A is less than the FEBS of D because Y_2 is less than Y_f. Because the economy in practice so often operates below full employment—that is, because so often $Y_f > Y$—the FEBS commonly exceeds the ABS. The greater the amount by which Y falls below Y_f, the greater will be the amount by which the FEBS exceeds the ABS. For those less frequent years in which the economy operates at full employment, the FEBS and ABS are equal. In measuring the ABS from the recorded federal budget amounts in years of full employment, we also obtain in that same step the figure for the FEBS. However, for each year in which Y differs from Y_f (most years), the FEBS can only be obtained by estimating, among other things, what tax receipts would have been if the economy had been operating at full employment. Because estimates of this kind are unavoidably subject to sizable errors, estimates of the FEBS are less than highly accurate.

The actual estimating procedure takes into account refinements not covered by our simplified equation. For example, we assumed that G and R would be the same whether or not Y was equal to Y_f. This is not too unreasonable for G, but it is for R. Certain transfer payments—such as unemployment compensation and welfare benefits—vary inversely with Y. The closer Y is to Y_f, the smaller the amount of such payments. In the actual estimates of the FEBS made by the Council of Economic Advisers, allowance is made for this behavior of transfer payments.[3]

Is the Budget Program Stimulative or Restrictive?

With this understanding of the meaning of the ABS and FEBS, we may return to the basic question: Why do economists estimate the FEBS as well as measure the ABS? The short answer is

that the FEBS is a much more reliable indicator than the ABS of whether the federal budget in any time period is exerting stimulus or restraint on the economy and the extent of that stimulus or restraint. We noted earlier that it could be a serious mistake to measure the expansionary or contractionary impact of the federal budget by the actual deficit or surplus in that budget. We may see this by referring again to Figure 25-1.[4]

Suppose that the economy is operating at Y_2 in the current period and that it is expected to remain at this level in the following period (assuming the absence of monetary and fiscal policy actions taken to move it closer to Y_f). The budget program gives us the B_2 line and therefore a surplus of A exists. Suppose, however, that in the next period, due to a decline in private spending, the income level is only Y_1 rather than the Y_2 that was expected. With an unchanged budget program, the budget has shifted from the surplus of A to the deficit of C. In this case, what must be seen is that the deficit is solely the result of unplanned, nondiscretionary, or automatic changes in tax receipts. The deficit is passively induced by the slowdown in economic activity. Graphically, this is simply a movement down the B_2 line that designates the given unchanged budget program.

Consider next the opposite case of a discretionary change in the budget program—a change that involves a shift in the B line. Again, we begin with the economy operating at Y_2 and with the budget programs shown by the B_2 line in Figure

Department of Commerce, in late 1980. Current quarterly estimates are now published in the *Survey of Current Business*.

[4]Because the level of income which corresponds to full employment is continuously growing and because the significance of a surplus or deficit of any size varies with the level of income, the following analysis is often presented by measuring on the vertical axis the surplus or deficit as a percentage of the full employment level of income and by measuring on the horizontal axis the actual income level as a percentage of the full employment level of income. However, for ease of understanding, the simpler presentation that works with absolute amounts is employed here.

[3]Responsibility for the maintenance and improvement of current and historical full employment budget estimates was assumed by the Bureau of Economic Analysis, U.S.

25-1. As before, this results in the surplus of A. Now, however, we assume a discretionary change in the budget program, specifically, a change in the tax rate from t_2 to t_1, which shifts B_2 to B_1. If the income level were to remain at Y_2, this new budget program would result in the deficit of F instead of the surplus of A.

Note now that *the deficit of C is equal to the deficit of F, but they nonetheless differ completely in what they say about the impact of the budget program on the economy.* The movement from the surplus of A to the deficit of C is the result solely of the automatic decrease in tax receipts. A deficit that originates in this way does not indicate any change in the impact of the existing budget program on the economy. On the other hand, the movement from the surplus of A to the deficit of F is the result solely of discretionary changes in the budget program that make the impact of that program on the economy more expansionary or less contractionary than it was previously.

In practice, a given change in the actual deficit or surplus from period to period may result from changes in both the budget program and the level of output. Furthermore, a change in the level of output may itself result from a change in the budget program such as a change in the tax rate used for illustration in Figure 25-1. For example, begin with the economy operating at Y_2 with a budget program that gives us the B_1 line and a deficit of F. Then assume a change in the budget program that shifts B_1 to B_2. If there were no change in the level of output, there would be a movement from the deficit of F to the surplus of A, but the same increase in the tax rate that produces the shift in the B line is likely to cause a change in the level of output.

Suppose this change in the tax rate were sufficiently restrictive, all else being equal, to cause output to fall all the way to Y_0 at which we find the deficit of H. In this event, we have a movement from the initial deficit of F to the even larger deficit of H. If the impact of the budget program is judged solely in terms of the size of the actual deficit or surplus, we would conclude that the

budget program is more expansionary. However, at the same time that the actual budget *deficit* has increased from F to H, the full employment budget *surplus* has increased from E to D. If the impact of the budget is judged in terms of the full employment budget surplus, we would conclude that the budget program is more restrictive. Of the two conclusions, the more correct one is that given by the change in the FEBS: The budget program has become more restrictive, despite the fact that the ABS suggests the opposite.

This illustration resorts to an extreme case to emphasize the point, but the change in the size of the ABS is not a reliable guide to the change in the impact of the budget program in the general case as well. We have seen that one way to obtain a more reliable guide is to remove the influence of changes in the level of output on the deficit or surplus consistent with any given budget program. We did this to derive the FEBS, a measure that reflects only changes in the budget program and therefore indicates changes in the contractionary or expansionary impact of the budget program itself.

Shortcomings of the FEBS

Although the change in the FEBS from one period to the next is a more accurate indicator of the change in the stance of fiscal policy than is the change in the ABS, the change in the FEBS is not without its shortcomings as such a measure. One shortcoming is its failure to allow for the fact that a decrease in its size will have a larger or smaller expansionary effect on the level of income, depending on whether that decrease is, on the one hand, the result of a discretionary decrease in the tax rate or, on the other hand, the result of an increase in government purchases. This returns us to the concept of the balanced budget multiplier. As noted in Chapter 6, the multiplier for an increase in government purchases is one greater than that for a decrease in tax receipts.[5] Accordingly, a decrease in the FEBS of $5 billion

---

[5] See p. 102.

from one period to the next will raise the income level $5 billion more if that change is the result of a $5 billion increase in purchases than if that change is the result of a $5 billion decrease in tax receipts. Depending on how it is incurred, it is therefore possible for a smaller decrease in the FEBS to indicate a more expansionary change in fiscal policy than a larger decrease in the FEBS does. If we examine only the change in the FEBS, we fail to see that that change may be associated with a larger or smaller contractionary or expansionary change in income.

Another shortcoming of the change in the FEBS as an indicator of the change in the stance of fiscal policy arises from the fact that growth occurs in the economy. With unchanged tax rates, a growing economy will generate ever rising tax receipts at the full employment level of income (as well as at any other constant fraction of the full employment level of income). This will appear as an increase in the FEBS and therefore as evidence of a less stimulative or a more restrictive budget program. But such an interpretation would be incorrect. Although the FEBS meets the problem created by the fact that the economy does not continuously operate at the same percentage of its full employment output, it does not meet the problem created by the fact that, whatever the year by year variation in the percentage of full employment output at which it operates, the economy's total output tends to grow to ever larger absolute amounts over the years. To interpret an increase in the FEBS that tends to occur in this manner as something attributable to a contractionary budget program would be as incorrect as to interpret a decrease in the ABS that occurs due to a recession as something attributable to an expansionary budget program. The FEBS corrects for the variations in the economy's operating rate below full employment but not for the growth in the economy's output, whatever its operating rate may be.[6]

---

[6]Alternative measures of fiscal influence which are not subject to these and other shortcomings of the FEBS are developed by A.S. Blinder and R.M. Solow in "Analytical

The Absolute Budget Surplus and the Full Employment Budget Surplus: 1956—80

Whatever its shortcomings, the FEBS remains the figure that economists generally employ as the measure of the expansionary or contractionary impact of the federal budget on the economy. Consequently, it is interesting to see how the FEBS has varied over the years and how its variations compare with those of the ABS. However, to allow for the complication introduced by growth in the economy over the years, it is preferable to work not with the absolute amount of the FEBS but with the absolute amount expressed as a percentage of the full employment or potential output. By so doing, if the FEBS increases from $10 billion to $12 billion over a period of years during which the full employment GNP increases from $1,000 billion to $1,200 billion, the FEBS as a percentage of the full employment GNP will remain the same. The rise in the absolute amount of the FEBS can be misinterpreted as evidence of a less stimulative or more restrictive budget program; the constancy in the ratio suggests no change of this kind in the budget program. Figure 25-2 presents the record of the ABS and FEBS from 1955 to 1980 with the ABS shown for each quarter as a percentage of that quarter's actual GNP and the FEBS shown for each quarter as a percentage of that quarter's full employment GNP.

Note first in this figure that in most years the FEBS exceeds the ABS. This follows simply from the fact that in most years Y_f exceeds Y. As is to be expected, the spread between the lines for

---

Foundations of Fiscal Policy," in A.S. Blinder et al., *The Economics of Public Finance*, The Brookings Institution, 1974, pp. 3–115. The relevant portion of this study is reprinted in R.L. Teigen, ed., *Readings in Money, National Income, and Stabilization Policy*, 4th ed., Irwin, 1978, pp. 247–57. See also A.S. Blinder and S.M. Goldfeld, "New Measures of Fiscal and Monetary Policy, 1958–73," *American Economic Review*, Dec. 1976, pp. 780–96.

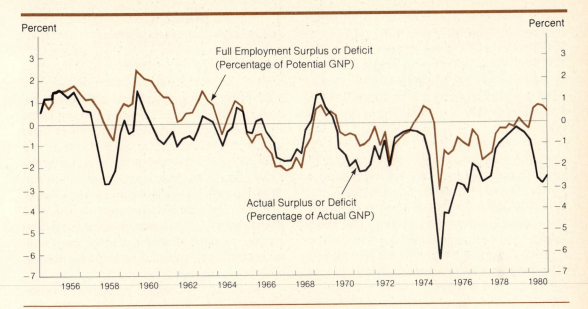

Percent   Percent

Full Employment Surplus or Deficit
(Percentage of Potential GNP)

Actual Surplus or Deficit
(Percentage of Actual GNP)

1956   1958   1960   1962   1964   1966   1968   1970   1972   1974   1976   1978   1980

FIGURE 25-2
Actual and Full Employment Surplus or Deficit

SOURCE: *Survey of Current Business*, Nov. 1980, p. 15, and *Survey of Current Business*, April 1981.

the ABS and FEBS is most pronounced in recession years, in which almost by definition Y falls most markedly below Y_f. Note next that the two lines practically coincide from 1964 to 1969, because in these years Y equaled Y_f. Actually, in the mid-1960s, the ABS > FEBS because $Y > Y_f$, the actual unemployment rate having fallen below the rate then used to define full employment. Note also that approximate equality between the ABS and FEBS may occur with the ABS in surplus, as in 1955–56, as well as with the ABS in deficit, as in 1965–68. All that is needed for this equality is that $Y = Y_f$; this may occur with either a surplus or a deficit in the actual budget.

A feature of Figure 25-2 that catches the eye is what happened during the 1973–75 recession. Better than any other episode, this most strikingly illustrates how seriously misleading it can be to measure the impact of the federal budget program on the economy by the ABS. The specific

dollar amounts underlying the chart are a 1974 ABS of −$10.7 billion and a 1974 FEBS of +$6.0 billion.[7] Therefore, despite an actual deficit, the effect of the budget program was still contractionary in that recession year. Furthermore, the ABS changed from −$6.7 billion in 1973 to −$10.7 billion in 1974, which would suggest that the budget program was changing in an expansionary direction. However, at the same time, the FEBS changed from −$9.0 billion to +$6.0 billion. In fact, the impact changed from one of expansion in 1973 to one of contraction in 1974. This change toward contraction—a one year swing in the FEBS of $15.0 billion—was the opposite of what the economy needed during

---

[7] These and the following dollar amounts are based on the federal government receipts, expenditures, and deficit in the national income and product accounts and differ from the dollar amounts in the unified budget.

recession. As a result of a tax rebate and other discretionary fiscal actions in 1975, the FEBS of + $6.0 billion for 1974 was replaced by a FEBS of − $25.2 billion in 1975, providing a $31.2 billion swing in the expansionary direction between those two years, a swing that contributed to the economic recovery that began in the spring of 1975.

Unlike the experience during the 1973–75 recession, that during the 1980 downturn suggests that the budget had an expansionary impact. Based on preliminary estimates, the 1980 FEBS was − $18.3 billion and the 1980 ABS was − $61.2 billion. Furthermore, the FEBS swung from − $2.2 billion in 1979 to − $18.3 billion in 1980 or by $16.1 billion in the direction of expansion. There was a much larger swing in the ABS from − $14.8 billion to − $61.2 billion or by − $46.4 billion. However, as is now familiar, that larger swing includes both the effect of the decrease in economic activity (a *movement down* a B line in Figure 25-1) and the effect of a change in the budget program (a *downward shift* of a B line in Figure 25-1). In rough terms, $30.3 billion of the $46.4 billion swing in the ABS was due to declining economic activity; the remainder, equal to the swing in the FEBS, was due to a change in the budget program toward expansion.

Fiscal Drag and the Fiscal Dividend

The level of output produced at full employment will naturally increase as the labor force and the productivity of labor increase. With an unchanged tax rate, federal tax receipts will increase, as will the FEBS so long as federal expenditures do not grow. If the economy is operating below full employment, the ABS will increase and become equal to the FEBS if and when the economy moves to the new full employment level of output. However the fact that the ABS increases in this way will itself restrain the growth of income and make it more difficult for the actual income level to reach the new full employment level.

This is roughly illustrated in Figure 25-1. Suppose that the economy is initially producing at Y_f. Therefore, the ABS and FEBS are equal and both are indicated by D. At a later date, Y_f has risen to Y_f' via an increase in the labor force and its productivity. But suppose that Y remains temporarily at the initial output level that is now below full employment. With an unchanged tax rate and government spending, the FEBS will have risen to G. This exerts restraint on the growth of actual Y, because more and more of income is drawn off by government in taxes as actual Y moves toward Y_f'. The difference between the surplus at D and that at G is a measure of the **fiscal drag** imposed on the economy in moving from the initial position to the new full employment position of Y_f'.

The concept of fiscal drag entered the language of fiscal policy in the early 1960s. The economy was then operating below full employment, but the federal tax structure and expenditures program were such that an expansion of output toward the full employment level would automatically increase the budget surplus, which in turn acted as a barrier to the attainment of full employment. If planned private investment had exceeded private saving at the time, this problem would not have appeared, because the rise in the government surplus (or in public saving) would then have been absorbed by the excess of private investment over private saving. However, this was not the situation at the time. To meet fiscal drag required an increase in the government spending program, a cut in taxes, or a combination of the two.

The argument advanced at the time by Walter W. Heller, Chairman of the Council of Economic Advisers, and supported by President Kennedy, was that a tax cut would reduce the ABS (that is, it would not increase the federal deficit, which had been $3.4 billion in 1961 and $7.1 billion in 1962), because the tax cut would overcome the fiscal drag, lift the economy toward full employment, and increase the tax base sufficiently to generate more revenue at the lower tax rate than was earlier generated at the higher tax rate. It took until 1964 to sell the tax cut to Congress, but once the cut was put through, its effects were much like those that had been predicted by Heller and others.[8]

The existence of a fiscal drag suggests the need to pay what is called a fiscal dividend. The dividend is paid either through a tax cut or an increase in government spending; in 1964 a tax cut was chosen. Things have changed substantially since then. Because of the pressure to increase spending for various federal programs over the years starting with President Johnson's Great Society and continuing through the Carter administration, fiscal drag has been avoided because the fiscal dividend has been paid as quickly as it appeared. Moreover, the country apparently obligated itself in the 1970s to pay fiscal dividends through various spending programs in advance of the appearance of those dividends. For example, commitments to more generous welfare programs were made with the expectations that the funds to cover them would come out of the fiscal dividends in the years ahead.

A growing real income is not the only source of a fiscal dividend. As we have learned over the years since the mid-1960s, inflation can also produce a substantial fiscal dividend. We have already recognized that real federal tax receipts will increase with the rise in real income, but now we note that with inflation real federal tax receipts can increase with no rise in real income. This occurs as nominal tax receipts increase faster than prices to provide an increase in real tax receipts. For example, if the price level rises by 10 percent, government will have to increase its spending by 10 percent to purchase an unchanged total of goods and services and maintain an unchanged total of real transfer payments. However, if there is a 10 percent increase in prices but no increase in real government spending, there will be a fiscal dividend because federal tax receipts will rise by more than 10 percent. Given the federal government's progressive tax structure, with no increase in their real income but a 10 percent increase in their nominal income, income recipients as a group will move into higher tax brackets and a larger fraction of their unchanged real income will be taken by taxes. It is through this "bracket creep" that inflation generates a fiscal dividend.

If the federal tax system were to be indexed, taxpayers would move into higher brackets only if they enjoyed an increase in real income; inflation would cease to be a source of a fiscal dividend. The dividend would appear only as a result of the growth over time in real income. So far, however, because Congress has chosen not to index the federal tax structure, we continue to have the two sources of a fiscal dividend described here. The reluctance of Congress to index is understandable: The present system allows it to pay fiscal dividends in the form of new and expanded old programs without seeking tax increases to finance them. Retention of the present system also permits Congress from time to time to pay a fiscal dividend in the form of a "tax cut," although the so-called tax cuts since the large one of 1964 have in fact been no more than partial offsets to the unlegislated tax increases that resulted from "bracket creep" caused by inflation.

President Reagan has recommended indexation of the federal income tax. Although this would

---

[8]The fact that the large tax cut of 1964 worked out as expected under the conditions prevailing in the early 1960s does not mean that a large tax cut would necessarily do the same under other conditions—for example, those prevailing in the early 1980s. The supporters of the Kemp–Roth proposal for the massive 30 percent across-the-board cut in federal income tax rates over three years with the first installment in 1981 defended that proposal by referring back to the success of the 1964 tax cut. Just one difference between then and 1981 should have been sufficient to give them pause. Inflationary expectations were nonexistent during the early 1960s; for 1961–64, the CPI rose at an average annual rate of about 1.2 percent. In 1981, it was quite different with the double digit inflation rates of 1979 and 1980 leading to expectations of more of the same. In this climate, a massive tax cut, even though accompanied by some cut in government spending, would probably aggravate inflationary expectations and thereby probably lead to even more rapid inflation.

make life more difficult for our congressmen, it would make taxpaying more equitable for the many millions penalized by the way the federal income tax now works. If the federal income tax were to be indexed, the only fiscal dividend would be the genuine one in which enlarged federal tax receipts arise from the greater real income of a growing economy.

Flexibility of Fiscal Policy

Economists generally rely on the FEBS to indicate whether the federal budget program is expansionary or contractionary from period to period. An increase in the FEBS from one quarter to the next suggests that the federal budget program is turning more contractionary or less expansionary; a decrease from one quarter to the next suggests that it is turning less contractionary or more expansionary. If at one time the intent of the policy-makers is to use fiscal policy to combat an ongoing recession, how much it is doing in this direction will be indicated by the extent to which the FEBS falls from one quarter to the next. Some measure like the FEBS is essential to give the policy-makers an indication of the expansionary or contractionary effect of the policy actions they have taken.

We here turn to another matter faced by policy-makers: Is it possible to secure the required degree of flexibility in government expenditures and/or tax rates to produce at one time the change in the FEBS in one direction and at another time the change in the opposite direction that may be required to meet the needs of the situation? This same question will arise in Chapter 26 in connection with monetary policy.

If we start off with a comparison of the relative flexibility of fiscal and monetary policy, it is generally conceded that monetary policy has the advantage. Although this is due in part to the inherent flexibility of the tools of monetary management discussed in Chapter 10, it is also due in part to the fact that the decision-making

authority lies in an essentially independent agency the political aims of which are limited to its own perpetuation and the preservation of its customary role and the power of which is concentrated in the hands of a few people. The seven-member Board of Governors of the Federal Reserve System or the twelve-member Federal Open Market Committee (which includes the same seven people plus the presidents of five of the Federal Reserve Banks) makes the monetary policy decisions in the United States. The presidents of the other Federal Reserve Banks, the Secretary of the Treasury, the Council of Economic Advisers, and others influence these decisions, but the power is nonetheless concentrated in these few hands. As we will see in Chapter 26, in a series of steps beginning in 1975, Congress has somewhat restricted the complete discretionary power previously possessed by these men, but they still have the power to alter policy promptly and over a wide range. Their performance record is, of course, another matter; here we simply note the flexibility with which discretionary changes can be made in the area of monetary policy.

In contrast, the decision-making process in the area of fiscal policy involves, in a sense, the whole of the executive and legislative branches of the federal government. The political motivation here is also obviously of an altogether different kind. Decisions in the fiscal policy area, especially decisions involving higher tax rates, are not made without allowance for their effect on the electorate in the next election. Apart from this political bias, which is perhaps unavoidable in a system like ours, a certain lack of maneuverability follows simply from the fact that the decision-making power in the fiscal area does not rest in the hands of a small group. The President has some limited power through his limited ability to control the timing of federal fiscal actions by speeding up or delaying expenditures and tax refunds. However, to get flexibility of a degree at all comparable with that found in the area of monetary policy would require that the President or some small group be given limited but discretionary power to vary certain tax rates and perhaps also some expenditure programs. Back in the 1960s, Presidents Kennedy and Johnson both made proposals along this line. In his final budget message in January 1969, President Johnson suggested that "consideration should be given to establishing as a permanent part of our tax system an element of flexibility under which the President . . . subject to congressional veto, would have discretion to raise or lower personal and corporate income tax rates within specified limits—such as 5 percent in either direction." [9]

Congress traditionally has closely guarded its power over the tax structure, tax rates, and expenditure programs. It did not act favorably on either the Johnson proposal or a very similar proposal made earlier by President Kennedy. As long as Congress retains almost complete power to make significant discretionary changes, it is clear that discretionary fiscal policy will remain less flexible than it might be. It will then continue to depend on legislative action, and legislative action, at least that which calls for the politically unpopular decision to raise tax rates or cut back on various spending programs, will probably continue to be preceded by time-consuming congressional hearings and debate.

Under these conditions, we will primarily depend on the built-in or automatic stabilizers for whatever real, short-run flexibility we have in fiscal policy. These, we will see, underlie the discussion earlier in this chapter of the way in which the ABS automatically increases or decreases with increases or decreases in the level of income, although there our attention was limited to only one of these stabilizers, the federal tax structure. Beyond automatic flexibility is formula flexibility, a type of flexibility that would not require Congress to give the President the amount of power he would acquire with even limited discretionary authority. In the following pages we will briefly examine how fiscal policy now

operates, with some flexibility provided by built-in stabilizers and the formula approach.

Built-in Flexibility

Built-in flexibility is achieved when changes in tax collections and government spending vary automatically, promptly, and in the right direction to produce a stabilizing effect on aggregate demand. Automatically means that no specific action need be taken; promptness means that changes in government spending and tax collections do not lag far behind changes in aggregate demand; right direction means that decreases in aggregate demand call forth additional government spending and reduced tax collections, whereas increases in aggregate demand call forth the opposite. In general, when aggregate demand and income are rising, automatic and prompt increases in tax receipts and decreases in transfer payments tend to dampen the expansion; when aggregate demand and income are falling, automatic and prompt decreases in tax receipts and increases in transfer payments tend to dampen the contraction.

These tendencies follow from the way in which total tax collections and government transfer payments automatically vary to prevent disposable personal income from rising or falling as much as GNP. In the case of a recession and falling GNP, for example, disposable personal income is protected somewhat because tax collections automatically fall and transfer payments automatically rise. Disposable personal income, therefore, falls less than it would if these stabilizers were not in operation. With disposable personal income so protected, personal consumption expenditures will fall less than they would if these stabilizers were not in operation. Finally, by avoiding what would otherwise be a sharper decline in consumption expenditures, the cumulative fall in GNP itself is less than it would be if these automatic stabilizers were not in operation. In simplest terms, this is the way built-in stabilizers produce a smaller fluctuation in GNP than would be the case in their absence.

[9]*The Budget of the United States Government,* Fiscal Year 1970, U.S. Government Printing Office, 1969, p. 12.

This dampening of income movements is the usual consequence of the operation of built-in stabilizers, but it is also possible for some to turn into built-in destabilizers and operate perversely or accentuate income movements. Such was the case in 1974, the year of an extraordinary combination of a sizable drop in real GNP and a "double-digit" rate of inflation. The dollar volume of transfer payments in the form of unemployment compensation benefits responded in a stabilizing manner, because this amount varies directly with the number of eligible unemployed workers, a number that increased with the real decrease in real GNP. However, income tax collections responded in a perverse or destabilizing manner. From 1973 to 1974, real GNP decreased 0.6 percent while nominal GNP increased 8.1 percent. Over the same period, personal income tax payments increased by 19.5 percent. Many taxpayers found that their nominal incomes increased substantially at the same time that their real incomes decreased, and it is nominal income on which their income taxes are based. Therefore, instead of the tax system taking a smaller fraction of such smaller real incomes— the result needed for the tax system to act in a stabilizing way—it took a larger share of such smaller real incomes, a result that shows the tax system acted in a destabilizing way.

The experience in 1980 provides an interesting contrast. Due largely to a collapse of residential construction and domestic automobile sales during the second quarter, real GNP fell during that quarter at an extraordinary 9.9 percent annual rate. However, real disposable personal income fell at a 5.0 percent rate or approximately half as fast as real GNP. The major difference between this result and that in 1973–74 was that, for this quarter at least, taxpayers were not forced into higher brackets. The rate of decline in real GNP more than offset the rate of increase in the GNP price deflator of 9.5 percent during the quarter. Nominal GNP remained practically unchanged, and federal personal income tax receipts increased at only a 1.8 percent annual rate. If the decrease in real GNP had not

been so severe and if the inflation rate had been the same 9.5 percent rate noted, federal personal income tax receipts would have soared and the rate of decline in real disposable personal income would have been closer to the rate of decline in real GNP. The result would then have been like that in 1973–74.

Even when the built-in stabilizers live up to their name, the dampening effect they can exert on income movements is not an unmixed blessing. Whereas the resistance the built-in stabilizers provide to a downward movement is desirable in an underemployed economy, the resistance they provide to an upward movement in the same economy is undesirable. This, as we saw earlier, is termed fiscal drag and calls for appropriate offsetting actions in the form of discretionary changes in government expenditures or tax rates. In an economy at full employment, the built-in stabilizers would tend to have a stabilizing effect in both directions. They would offer resistance to the worsening of any downturn brought on by a sharp decline in demand and to a worsening of any inflationary movement brought on by a sharp expansion in demand. In an economy operating at full employment, they provide a limited but helpful buffer against cumulative movements in either direction.

Economists quite generally favor the greatest possible use and strengthening of built-in stabilizers. If we could ignore other public policy objectives, any number of changes could be adopted that would strengthen existing stabilizers. In the case of the personal income tax, for example, a reduction in the size of the personal exemption and a tightening of deduction provisions would put a larger part of personal income into the base on which personal income taxes are computed, thereby increasing the cyclical variability of the revenue from this tax. A more progressive rate structure might contribute somewhat to the same end. In the case of indirect taxes, an *ad valorem* tax would increase the effectiveness of these stabilizers, because the revenue yield would vary more over the cycle under *ad valorem* than under *specific* taxes. In the case of government transfer payments, unemployment compensation payments could be made a more effective stabilizer by enlarging weekly benefits, lengthening the period over which these benefits may be received, and increasing the number of workers covered—actions that were taken during the especially severe recession that ended in 1975. Although each of these and a number of other changes can be made for the purpose of improving the effectiveness of an automatic program of stabilization, many such changes are ruled out because they conflict with and are judged subordinate to other aims of public policy.[10]

Partly because there are limits to how much automatic stabilization can be built into the system without causing conflict with other aims of public policy, most economists and many business people today are unwilling to limit the use of stabilizing fiscal policy to what can be accomplished through its passive role in an automatic program alone. Instead, some favor an active role in which taxes and government spending (purchases of goods and services as well as transfer payments) are made to vary according to formula or executive discretionary action.

---

[10]For an analysis of the quantitative impact of specific built-in stabilizers over a series of business cycles, see M.O. Clements, "The Quantitative Impact of Automatic Stabilizers," in *Review of Economics and Statistics,* Feb. 1960, pp. 56–61. An analysis of the actual behavior of each of the major built-in stabilizers will be found in the second chapter of W. Lewis, Jr., *Federal Fiscal Policy in the Postwar Recessions,* Brookings Institution, 1962. See also P. Eilbott, "The Effectiveness of Automatic Stabilizers," in *American Economic Review,* June 1966, pp. 450–65. For a study of the amount of built-in flexibility provided on the side of federal government spending, see N.H. Teeters, "Built-in Flexibility of Federal Expenditures," in *Brookings Papers on Economic Activity,* 3, 1971, pp. 615–48. For example, the Medicaid program with its close connection to the welfare rolls works as a built-in stabilizer. Another stabilizer results from the growth in the number of older people eligible for benefits under retirement programs. When jobs are lost during recession, for many older persons retirement is frequently more socially acceptable than unemployment.

The argument for a more active role for fiscal policy is substantially strengthened when we take into account a major limitation of the most complete system of built-in stabilizers: The stabilizers in themselves cannot prevent a downturn from occurring, because they do not come into effect until there already is some downturn in spending and income. True, they can help prevent a downturn from growing cumulatively worse, but they cannot *in themselves* reverse a downturn and initiate an expansion. On the other hand, although subject to other limitations, nonautomatic programs in which expansionary fiscal measures are initiated in the expectation of a downturn may in themselves (assuming correct forecasting) prevent downturns. Formula flexibility is like the built-in stabilizers in the sense that it is essentially automatic. However, it may be designed to allow a greater scope for stabilizing action than is provided by the built-in stabilizers, and, unlike the built-in stabilizers, may be able to reverse a downturn once begun.

Formula Flexibility

Formula flexibility relies on changes in selected indexes such as the unemployment rate or the consumer price level as indicators of a need for specific changes in income tax rates, transfer payments, or even public works expenditures. Formula flexibility is like built-in flexibility in that action takes place automatically in response to realized changes in the business situation. However, the two differ in that built-in flexibility is obtained within the existing tax and transfer payments structure, whereas formula flexibility, once activated, changes the structure itself. For example, in oversimplified form, the formula could require a specified reduction in personal income tax rates when the unemployment percentage equaled or exceeded 5 percent for two consecutive months; or it might call for an increase in those tax rates when the consumer price index rose 5 percent in a specified time interval. Similarly, a formula could call for liberalizing unemployment compensation and other kinds of government transfer payments in response to increases in the unemployment rate. A number of small-scale public works projects could also be kept "on the shelf" until there were specific changes in the unemployment rate or in other indexes of business conditions. Apart from public works with their focus on construction, emergency employment programs that hire extra people for things like park, recreation, fire protection, and security services may similarly be triggered in the same way. For example, an act was passed during the severe 1974 recession year that provided unemployment benefits during 1975 for some workers ineligible for the regular state or federal programs in the event that the local area unemployment rate averaged 6.5 percent or more for three consecutive months or the national unemployment rate averaged 6.0 percent or more for the same time period. By relying on a formula, changes in tax rates and expenditure programs would occur with minimum administrative delay and without forecasts of future business conditions—forecasts that, as is well known, are often wrong.

Yet, despite the automaticity of action associated with rigid adherence to a formula, the action so triggered may be wrong just as often as action that is based on forecasts. If an unemployment rate that is above some specified level for a period of a few months is the signal for action, for example, corrective action may come just at the time when the forces that caused the high unemployment are dying out. There is no way of knowing such things with certainty in advance, but detailed study of the situation may provide, at the minimum, some understanding of the cause or causes of the business downturn and the high unemployment and therefore some clue as to whether or not a turnabout may be imminent. For example, if study suggests that the downturn resulted primarily from an inventory liquidation, an end to the downturn may not be many months off. If, on the other hand, decreasing plant and equipment expenditures are the cause, the situation may be more serious—the action indicated by the formula or even more vig-

orous action may be in order. Without in any way detracting from the advantages of the formula device, action triggered by formula alone, without study of the total business situation, would receive the support of few economists. Actually, some economists support formula flexibility more for political than for economic reasons. They would favor granting the President limited authority to take discretionary action, but realize that Congress is not likely to delegate such authority.

Flexibility Through Discretionary Action

Although discretionary action is taken from time to time by Congress, such action has typically not been sufficiently flexible to be useful against short-run fluctuations in economic activity. Although this was not strictly an anti-cyclical action, a classic illustration of belated action is the 1964 tax cut. That cut requested by President Kennedy in 1962 to raise the economy's growth rate did not occur until after almost two years of deliberation by Congress. Another illustration is the experience of a few years later when the reverse kind of action was needed to meet the threat of inflation following the large rise in military expenditures for Vietnam. It again took about two years for action to take place.

However, a change may have occurred in the 1970s. Congress seemed able to take discretionary action much more quickly than theretofore, at least when the kind of action called for was a tax cut or an increase in spending. Once the seriousness of the 1974 downturn was finally recognized, Congress in fairly quick order passed the Tax Reduction Act of 1975 in March of that year. This act reduced that year's tax collections about 5 percent below what they otherwise would have been. However, it is interesting to note that the delay by Congress in enacting this tax cut placed the passage of the tax cut legislation in the same month that was later identified as the last month of the 1973–75 recession! The next tax cut came with the Revenue Act of 1978. The purpose of this cut in personal income tax rates was not to combat a recession but to offset the increase in the effective tax rates caused by "bracket creep." The earlier recession-induced tax cut of 1975 in effect was largely of this nature also, given the fact that the double-digit inflation rate of 1974 had pushed personal income tax payments up by 14.5 percent, despite the severity of the recession during that year.

To get more flexibility into fiscal policy than is now provided by the built-in stabilizers requires that Congress respond more promptly than in the past by changing tax rates and government spending or by giving the President some power to take such actions. At the time of this writing, Ronald Reagan was the new occupant of the White House. This combined with a Republican-controlled Senate and a conservatively-leaning House will obviously affect the flexibility of fiscal policy in the early 1980s. However, it seems certain that to the degree that fiscal policy is used to help stabilize the economy, stimulus will be provided predominantly by tax cuts rather than by increased spending. At the extreme in this direction is the Kemp–Roth proposal for a 30 percent across-the-board cut in income taxes. As was noted in the last part of Chapter 20, this tax action, according to the brand of "supply-side" economics preached by its proponents, will be a virtual cure-all for our economic ills. In their view, it will increase saving, investment, the will to work, and the productivity of the economy sufficiently to simultaneously bring inflation under control and provide the American people with a high level of prosperity. In the view of the critics, any such program is far more likely to produce an even more serious inflation than the one it is supposed to cure. Because of the great uncertainties as to what will work best, it is very unlikely that the complete Kemp–Roth proposal will be accepted by Congress. Still, whatever action is taken on the side of stimulus will be almost completely in the form of tax cuts. If and when a policy of restraint appears to be called for, the aim will be to effect that policy by reducing government spending. In this case, the only appreciable real increase in spending will be that for national defense—and that for reasons unrelated to stabilization.

To the degree that it can be carried out, an activist fiscal policy that attempts to limit its expansionary action to decreases in taxes and to limit its contractionary action to decreases in spending will achieve the goal of reducing the size of the government's role in the economy while contributing to the goal of stabilization. However, it may not be possible to achieve the stabilization objective if the government denies itself the use of higher tax rates for contractionary purposes and higher government spending for expansionary purposes. Because there are limitations on the use of all of the instruments of fiscal policy—taxes, government purchases, and transfer payments—those who seek the maximum contribution to economic stability that an activist fiscal policy may provide do not approve of an approach that makes the policy-makers tie one hand behind their backs. All tools should be available for use. The final section of this chapter explores some of the limitations on the use of each of these tools.

Variations in Government Purchases, Transfer Payments, and Taxes

We noted earlier that to a limited extent built-in flexibility provides appropriately timed, helpful responses to recessionary and inflationary developments. In order to secure greater fiscal response, discretionary action is required. Broadly classified, such action calls for variations in government purchases, transfer payments, and taxes; our discussion here will run essentially in terms of those broad classes. However, we will make some note of the fact that there are various possibilities under each of these headings. Government purchases may be for large- or small-scale public works, manpower training programs, or federal housing; transfers may be for unemployment compensation, various kinds of grants to state and local governments, or employment subsidies to private firms; and tax measures may include income tax rebates or surcharges, changes in such things as personal and/or corporate income tax rates, the size of personal exemptions and standard deductions under the personal income tax, social security contribution rates, the investment tax credit, accelerated depreciation provisions, maximum weekly unemployment compensation benefits, and so forth.

Given the available tools, can federal expenditures and taxes in practice be varied by the large amounts that may at times be necessary for successful stabilization policy? The answer to this question is certainly quite different today from what it would have been had it been asked before fiscal policy had become a generally accepted means of trying to achieve stabilization. For example, federal government purchases made up somewhat over 1 percent of GNP in 1929—$1.4 billion out of GNP of $102.4 billion. This percentage rose during the 1930s, reached almost 40 percent during the years of World War II, and for the decade of the 1970s averaged 7.9 percent. To the extent that purchases of the federal government can be promptly reduced by, say, 5 percent as an anti-inflationary measure or raised 5 percent as an antirecessionary measure, the impact on the economy will be far greater today than a similar percentage change would have been in the days of relatively smaller federal budgets. As federal purchases have grown in importance relative to GNP, so too have federal transfer payments. These rose from less than $1 billion in 1929 to $210 billion fifty years later, although GNP in the meantime had increased only 23 times. Roughly paralleling the growth of both types of federal spending has been, of course, the growth in federal tax receipts.

Although the monetarists and rationalists stand in opposition, most economists still appear to believe that variations in government purchases, transfer payments, and tax receipts can

be used in various combinations to produce desired expansionary or contractionary effects on aggregate demand and the level of income. In what follows we accept this view and go on to briefly examine some of the practical limitations on the use of variations in spending and taxing as tools of fiscal policy.

Purchases of Goods and Services

One way of reducing demand-side inflationary pressures is to reduce the level of government purchases, thereby releasing resources to meet private demands. Because it looms so large in the total, the most likely candidate for reduction would appear to be purchases for national defense. Although the fraction of total federal government purchases made up of purchases for national defense ran much higher during the peak years of the Vietnam war, for the years 1974–80 it has averaged two-thirds. With the Reagan administration's objective of reducing other spending and raising defense spending, that fraction is likely to run over the two-thirds average of the late 1970s.

Whatever the level at which the defense budget is set in any year, what is relevant here is that it is unlikely that it would be deliberately cut below this level for stabilization purposes. In other words, people will differ as to what level of purchases is required for adequate defense, but once that level is determined, few will argue that we should cut below it as a means of meeting inflationary pressures. Although almost all of the defense budget is subject to annual review through the normal appropriations process, the figure that emerges each year therefore reflects predominantly what those in power regard as the amount needed for national defense and only to a minor degree the figure that would contribute to the needs of economic stabilization. To the extent that this is true, it would appear that variations in federal government purchases deliberately engineered for stabilization purposes would have to be focussed on the one-third of purchases that are of a nondefense nature.

However, there are problems here also. For example, sharp slashes in these expenditures are plainly not administratively feasible in the short run. Moreover, placing the major burden of fiscal adjustment on the nonmilitary public sector is clearly unjust. Although it may be possible to reduce or stretch out some kinds of nondefense purchases of goods and services, those that are aimed at meeting such urgent problems as urban blight and pollution control should not be subject to cutting or stretching out. It also should be noted that because many of these expenditures are for services of government employees, adjusting spending of this kind to meet inflation means discharging workers who are performing worthwhile services. In times of inflationary pressures, it therefore does not seem that any major effect can be realized via cuts in nondefense purchases except at a high social cost. Inflation must be attacked primarily through increases in tax rates, which places the major burden of the stabilization policy on the almost 80 percent of GNP that represents private uses of output rather than on the 2.5 percent of GNP that has represented federal nondefense uses of output in the last few years.

One way of combating a recession is to increase the level of government purchases, thereby increasing government demand for goods and services and absorbing idle resources in their production. Unless more government purchases are to be made just for the sake of purchases (disregarding the usefulness of what is purchased), the major part of expanded purchases to meet the problem of recession will have to be for public works such as roads, dams, public buildings, and the like. This brings us to the problem of the limited flexibility of public works projects.[11] Even with preplanning, some

lag is unavoidable between the decision to undertake a project and the actual initiation of expenditures on it. Furthermore, few public works projects are of a type that can be completed in a matter of months or even a year. Consequently, it is possible that the economy will recover and even enter a vigorous expansion just when many antirecessionary public works projects are half completed. To abandon them at this point would be wasteful; to complete them would accelerate the expansionary movement at a time when this would be undesirable. This lack of flexibility is not a serious problem in the face of a prolonged depression such as the one during the 1930s, but it does mean that public works projects are of limited value in coping with short, cyclical downturns of the type the economy has suffered in the post-World War II period.

Transfer Payments

Transfer payments by the federal government would appear to allow greater maneuverability than purchases, because they can be more quickly expanded or contracted as conditions require. But we encounter problems here too. To achieve a substantial reduction in transfer payments as a part of an anti-inflationary program would mean cutting benefit provisions under old age, survivors, and disability insurance, food stamps, aid to families with dependent children, supplemental security income, unemployment insurance, and retirement programs (which account for almost all federal government transfer payments apart from Medicare and Medicaid). Some of these payments are contractual obligations of government and cannot be touched; others, such as old age benefits, although subject to change by congressional action, occupy

[11]See, for example, S. Maisel, "Varying Public Construction and Housing to Promote Economic Stability," in Joint Economic Committee, *Federal Expenditure Policy for Economic Growth and Stability,* Papers, 1957, pp. 382–97.

See also his "Timing and Flexibility of a Public Works Program," in *Review of Economics and Statistics,* May 1949, pp. 147–52; J. Margolis, "Public Works and Economic Stability," in *Journal of Political Economy,* Aug. 1949, pp. 293–303; and R.L. Teigen, "The Effectiveness of Public Works as a Stabilization Device," in W.L. Smith and R.L. Teigen, eds., *Readings in Money, National Income and Stabilization Policy,* 3rd ed., Irwin, 1974, pp. 305–10

a place in the social fabric of this country that effectively rules out reductions. Like certain kinds of federal government purchases, certain kinds of transfer payments are in practice relatively uncontrollable outlays. According to definitions used in President Carter's last budget submitted in January 1981, the "uncontrollable" portion of the budget grew from about 60 percent of outlays in fiscal year 1967 to more than 75 percent of outlays in fiscal year 1982. However, some of what is uncontrollable under earlier commitments or existing law can be made controllable if Congress is willing to change the laws affecting eligibility for certain benefits. For example, as discussed in Chapter 21, a case can be made for the use of the PCE price deflator instead of the CPI for indexing social security benefits. This would slow the growth of this transfer payment without truly denying the beneficiaries anything they were promised. As a result of their victories in the 1980 election, the Republicans were talking about changing the rules in this and other ways in 1981 and beyond.

If the need is to stimulate the economy, expansion of transfer payments would not appear to be subject to the limitations faced in contracting such payments. Not only can the amount be readily increased without any complaints from the recipients, but the major part of these amounts will flow to low-income recipients who will promptly use most of such funds to increase consumption spending. Although transfer payments have this significant advantage on the side of stimulation, any increase in transfer payments tends to be viewed by their recipients as permanent, which could present a problem if restrictive action is subsequently indicated. This problem, referred to in the preceding paragraph, limits the usefulness of transfer payments for short-run stabilization purposes that at times require expansionary action to be followed before long by action in the opposite direction.

Taxes

As variations in government purchases and transfer payments may be used to increase or

decrease aggregate demand, so too may variations in taxes. Furthermore, variations in taxes may also be used to effect changes in aggregate supply, a consequence of variations in taxes that has been emphasized in recent years by supply-side economics.[12] However, as discussed in Chapter 20, the degree to which lower taxes will raise people's incentive to work, encourage an increase in saving, and increase the investment rate are all uncertain, especially the first two. It is primarily through these effects of lower taxes that supply-side economics expects the increase in output to solve our long-lived inflation problem. But even if the cuts in taxes are successful in increasing saving, they will also produce an increase in consumption, which of course has inflationary consequences. Even if the cuts in taxes are successful in increasing the investment rate, the anti-inflationary effect of the increase in productivity that accompanies greater investment will not be felt for a year or two. In the meantime, the deficit will have grown larger—which has inflationary consequences.

In contrast, the effects of variations in tax rates on aggregate demand are more certain. Attacking inflation via cuts in tax rates—the supply-side prescription—stands an excellent chance of increasing aggregate demand much more than it increases aggregate supply and therefore of worsening the inflation. Attacking inflation via increases in tax rates—a conventional fiscal policy prescription—would probably decrease aggregate demand much more than it decreases aggregate supply and therefore ease the inflation, albeit at the price of some reduction in output and some increase in unemployment.

In the conventional case in which a rise in taxes is viewed as the prescription to meet the problem of an overheated economy, the only limitation to the use of tax rates for this purpose is

---

[12]Variations in transfer payments have also been used to affect the supply side for many years. Government subsidies, a kind of transfer payment, have long been employed to affect the supply of agricultural products and have been used in shipbuilding and elsewhere. However, as a practical matter, the use of transfers for this purpose is quite limited, which is not the case with taxes.

the willingness of Congress to impose higher rates, a willingness often absent except in cases of extreme emergency, such as wartime. But, even if this reluctance to raise taxes is overcome, there is the complex problem of deciding which rates are to be raised and the amount by which each is to be raised. An overly restrictive tax policy may not only bring an inflationary expansion to an end but precipitate a severe decline.

To the extent that the problem is excessive aggregate demand which can be attributed to developments in a particular sector of the economy, it may be possible to direct tax policy toward this sector without putting the brakes on the system as a whole. For example, if a boom in investment spending is under way, a rise in corporate income tax rates with unchanged personal income tax rates may be in order. In such a case, the dampening effect will fall, at least initially, on the sector that needs dampening.[13] If, on the other hand, the excess is primarily the result of a surge in consumption spending, the personal income tax would probably be a better vehicle through which to effect the required degree of restraint.

When the economy faces deficient aggregate demand and recession, appropriate fiscal policy may, of course, be to cut tax rates. Here again, how should any given cut be allocated over various types of taxes in order to get the maximum stimulative effect? In simplified form, the question is often approached as a choice between, or a combination of, tax cuts designed directly to stimulate consumption spending or investment spending. Because the cyclical fluctuations in investment spending are relatively greater than those in consumption spending, investment spending will usually be the more depressed of the two during recession. Consequently, some people argue that tax cuts should be aimed at encouraging investment, because the principal need is to raise the rate of investment spending in order to move the industries that are engaged in producing capital goods closer to their prosperity levels of output. Increased activity will mean rising income for consumers, from which, by way of the multiplier, will come the rise in consumption necessary to keep the upward movement rolling. Viewed from this perspective, tax cuts aimed directly at raising consumption spending will not, except after an unacceptably long lag, raise activity in the capital goods industries. Therefore, the immediate stimulus is not being applied where it is most needed.

Other people argue, however, that there is no better stimulus to investment spending than that provided by increased consumption spending. These economists claim that unless and until business people see an increase in the rate at which goods are moving into the hands of consumers, they will be little influenced in their investment decisions by tax inducements. Consequently, for these people, the maximum stimulative effect of a given amount of tax reduction will be secured through tax changes that leave more after-tax income in the hands of consumers than in the hands of corporations. The specific arguments on both sides could be examined in detail and in more precise form, but our purpose is simply to point out that this is one of the basic questions to be answered in selecting the most effective expansionary tax policy when policy is aimed at affecting aggregate demand. It should also be noted that the answer need not be the same in every situation; investment-stimulating tax changes may look more promising in one recession, consumption-stimulating tax changes in another.

---

[13]The decrease in after-tax profits of corporations may not, however, restrict the funds available to corporations to finance an expanding rate of investment spending. For example, if the outlook for growing corporate profits remains sufficiently favorable, corporations, despite the fact that government is now taking a larger share of this total, may offset the restraint of higher taxes by reducing the share of after-tax profits paid out in dividends. In addition, they may resort to borrowing as another source of additional investment funds. However, when the boom is being fed by investment spending, a restrictive monetary policy can play an important role by reducing the availability and raising the cost of funds borrowed to finance the splurge of investment spending. Some of these questions were discussed in Chapter 19 in connection with the role of finance as an influence on investment spending.

Whether an expansionary tax policy is to be aimed primarily at consumption or investment spending, a number of techniques may be employed for either purpose. To stimulate consumption spending, the principal reliance will be on cuts in the personal income tax, but cuts in excise tax rates may also help. To the extent that prices of taxed goods fall with lower excises, unchanged money expenditures will increase the total amount of goods that can be purchased, which will stimulate an increase in the production of goods and an expansion of employment. Within the personal income tax structure, a stimulative effect may be gained either through cuts in rates or through such changes as increases in the size of personal exemptions or larger standard deductions. Within the rate structure, the cut may be limited to the first bracket (the "basic rate"), it may be an across-the-board cut, or it may be still another variant. If the sole objective is to obtain the maximum stimulative effect on consumption for a given reduction in tax revenue, the most effective technique will probably be a reduction in the first-bracket rate of the personal income tax. This is the only rate paid by taxpayers with the smallest taxable incomes, and these taxpayers are those most likely to devote any increase in take-home pay to additional consumption spending. Investment spending may also be stimulated through a number of tax-related techniques. The most familiar are a reduction in corporate income tax rates, liberalization of depreciation allowances and an increase in the investment tax credit.

From the 1940s through the 1960s, most economists accepted the proposition that changes in income tax rates can and should be employed to increase or decrease aggregate demand in the interest of economic stabilization. Although this acceptance has by no means turned into a complete rejection, the confidence economists once had in the efficacy of demand management through fiscal policy has declined since the end of the 1960s. This decline has caused much more attention to be paid to supply management. The earlier confidence in demand

management perhaps reached a peak with the success achieved by the tax cut of 1964 in stimulating the economy. It began its decline with the apparent failure of the 10 percent surtax of 1968 to exert the contractionary effect on consumption spending that was expected from it.[14] It is interesting to note that this development understandably gave a great boost to the monetarists' stock. Although there are various other possible explanations, this development was widely accepted as a confirmation of the monetarist argument.

Another explanation advanced by some Keynesian economists is based on an application of the permanent income hypothesis. The unsuccessful 1968 tax increase was temporary and widely advertised as such, whereas the successful 1964 tax decrease was permanent. As we would expect from the permanent income hypothesis, a given reduction in after-tax income that results from an increase in tax rates as in 1968 but that the consumer believes will be in effect for only a year or two calls forth a very much smaller downward adjustment in his consumption over that year or two than would the same reduction in income if it were expected to be in effect indefinitely. What consumers actually did in 1968–69 was to absorb much of the increase in their tax bill by reducing saving, thereby robbing the personal income tax increase of most of its intended contractionary effect on spending.[15]

If the 1968 experience is correctly explained by the permanent income hypothesis, it raises the question of whether future temporary tax

---

[14]See A.M. Okun, "Measuring the Impact of the 1964 Tax Reduction," in W.W. Heller, ed., *Perspectives on Economic Growth*, Random House, 1968; A. Ando and E.C. Brown, "Personal Income Taxes and Consumption Following the 1964 Tax Reductions," in A. Ando et al., eds., *Studies in Economic Stabilization*, The Brookings Institution, 1968; A.M. Okun, "The Personal Tax Surcharge and Consumer Demand, 1968–70," in *Brookings Papers on Economic Activity*, 1, 1972, pp. 211–20; and W.L. Springer, "Did the 1968 Surcharge Really Work?" in *American Economic Review*, Sept. 1975, pp. 644–59.

[15]See R. Eisner, "Fiscal and Monetary Policy Reconsidered," in *American Economic Review*, Dec. 1969, pp. 897–905.

increases or decreases can be effective in changing aggregate demand. If the correct explanation lies elsewhere, the same question of effectiveness may not arise.

Although the experience with the 1968 tax increase came as a jolt to the many economists whose analysis suggests that it did not produce anything like the contractionary effect that they expected, this experience by no means warrants abandonment of tax changes as a device to alter aggregate demand. Further study may lead to the development of appropriate techniques to meet the problems encountered in such cases. If the workings of the permanent income hypothesis do indeed make temporary income tax changes ineffective, an alternative could be the use of a federal value-added tax the rates of which would be temporarily raised as an anti-inflationary measure. Although such a tax would not be subject to the permanent income problem noted for a temporary increase in income tax rates, it is regressive and raises the issue of equity. Consequently, an approach that may satisfy the objective of stabilization can be ruled out by the fact that it results in what most people feel is an unfair distribution of the tax burden.

If short-term variations in personal income tax rates are ineffective for stabilization purposes, and if a tax like the value-added tax is unacceptable on the grounds that it is inequitable, we must turn to other alternatives or to modifications that are acceptable. An approach can probably be devised that provides an acceptable compromise between economic stabilization and the other goals of public policy. Because of the limitations on the use of short-term variations in government spending for stabilization purposes, the ability to use short-term variations in taxes is especially important. However, as we have seen in our discussion of the variables through which fiscal policy as a device to control aggregate demand is carried out—government purchases, transfer payments, and taxes—there are difficult problems associated with the use of each. The better these and other problems are solved, the more effective fiscal policy will be and the more likely that it will be able to make a contribution to achieving a more stable economy.

26
Monetary Policy

Because monetary policy is concerned with government's attempts to provide a more stable economy by regulating the rate of growth of the money supply, a natural first question is: How does monetary policy work? In the first part of this chapter, we attempt to answer this question. Specifically, what is the transmission process by which a change in the money supply causes a change in the level of money income? Although there are more than two theories of the transmission process, we may still identify a basic two-way cleavage as Keynesianism versus monetarism. The Keynesian theory sees changes in the money supply working their way through the system in a way that does not result in a close and stable linkage between changes in the money supply and changes in the money income level. The monetarists do see such a close and stable linkage. To the extent that the monetarist view is correct, money is an extremely important influence on the level of money income; to the extent that the Keynesian view is correct, money is that much less important.

The difference between the two sides on the linkage between money and income was much less pronounced by the beginning of the 1980s than it had been in the 1960s. Although this difference had by no means disappeared, some observers of the continuing debate believe that the major difference in that debate had by then

become the question of whether or not there is a role for counter-cyclical monetary and fiscal policies. Some monetarists have long insisted that efforts by the Federal Reserve authorities to stabilize the economy, on balance, make for less stability than would occur if they did not make such efforts. Starting in the 1970s, an offshoot of monetarism known as rational expectations advanced a view that goes somewhat beyond that of the monetarists. To the "rational expectationists," counter-cyclical monetary and fiscal policies will not make the economy more or less stable than it would otherwise be; they believe that such policies simply have no systematic effect on the economy's real variables such as output and employment. In opposition to both the monetarists and the rational expectationists, the Keynesians hold to the view that has long been their gospel: Counter-cyclical policy can make a positive contribution to the stability of the system. In the second part of this chapter, we briefly discuss whether or not there is a role for counter-cyclical or stabilization policies.

Despite the arguments of the monetarists and rational expectationists, there is little likelihood that the day of activist monetary and fiscal policies will soon be over. The belief held by many in the 1960s that such policies could be used to "fine tune" the economy is assuredly over, but the belief that we can get better overall results by pursuing counter-cyclical policies in the face of major disturbances is still widely held. This raises another question: If the Federal Reserve is to pursue an activist monetary policy, how is it to determine when it is appropriate to adopt an easier policy—that is, to increase the rate at which it is expanding the money supply—and when it is appropriate to adopt the opposite policy? In the last part of this chapter, we explore four issues related to this question.

First of these is the issue of whether the money supply or interest rates should be the guide to Federal Reserve policy. Before 1970, the Federal Reserve authorities used the movement of interest rates or, more broadly, credit conditions, or the "tone and feel" of financial markets, as their almost exclusive guide to what appropriate policy should be. This approach, apart from other considerations, is consistent with the Keynesian view of the transmission process. The monetarist view, however, is that Federal Reserve policy guided by the movement of interest rates will contribute to instability of the economy. To the monetarists, the money supply or some similar monetary aggregate is the only proper kind of guide to monetary policy.

This brings us to the issue of regulating the money supply by rule. According to certain monetarists, the Federal Reserve should not only adopt the money supply as its guide to policy but should adopt a monetary rule of making the money supply grow at a predetermined rate and see to it that it does, regardless of what may happen to interest rates in the process. The case for a rule is the second issue considered in the last part of this chapter.

Although the Federal Reserve is unlikely to adopt anything as restrictive as a rule for some time, it was closer to doing so at the beginning of the 1980s than it had been at the beginning of the 1970s. It had then first publicly stated that the growth rate of the money supply would play a more important role in its policy making than it had theretofore. In 1975, Congress took the first of a series of actions that pushed the Federal Reserve farther and faster toward emphasis on the growth rate of the money supply than it apparently would otherwise have gone. In 1975, for the first time, during each quarter the Federal Reserve announced target growth ranges for a number of monetary aggregates. These target growth ranges are the third issue considered in the last part of this chapter.

With more emphasis on the money supply as a policy guide, another issue is the particular strategy that will most effectively enable the Federal Reserve to achieve its chosen growth rate of the money supply. This issue is usually described as operating procedures. From 1970 to 1979, the Federal Reserve's procedure was to target the federal funds rate; then, starting in October 1979, it switched to targeting reserves. Federal funds targeting and reserve targeting is the final issue examined in this chapter.

Monetary policy is the exercise of the central bank's control over the money supply as an instrument for achieving the objectives of general economic policy. Monetary policy primarily contributes to the achievement of such objectives as full employment, stable prices, and economic growth by influencing the level of aggregate demand and thereby the level of money income. Although the central bank's influence over the level of aggregate demand and money income stems from its ability to control the money supply, there are various measures of the money supply: M-1A, M-1B, M-2, and M-3. In carrying out monetary policy, the Federal Reserve seeks to keep the growth rate of each of these monetary aggregates within a range that it believes will contribute most to the achievement of the ultimate objectives. For certain purposes, it is necessary to refer to more than one of these aggregates, but more generally it is sufficient to refer merely to the money supply. When this is done, it is to be understood that reference is to M-1B, the most widely used measure of the money supply.

How Does Monetary Policy Work? Keynesianism Versus Monetarism[1]

We begin with a basic question: How does monetary policy affect the economy's income level? In other words, what is the transmission process by which a change in the money supply causes a change in the level of income? It is one thing to outline, as in the basic Keynesian model of earlier chapters, how an increase in the money supply will cause a decline in the interest rate and why, with a given MEC schedule, a lower interest rate will lead to a rise in investment spending and therefore to a rise in income. This is satisfactory as far as it goes, but it does not come to grips with the actual transmission process. A major development in monetary theory during the 1950s and early 1960s was the development of an explanation of that transmission process in terms of a systematic theory of portfolio adjustments. A change in the money supply produces a change in the income level

by setting off a complex sequence of substitutions among the financial and real assets that make up wealth-holders' portfolios.[2]

The Portfolio Adjustment Process[3]

In a broad sense, there is a rate of return on all assets in that all assets provide their owners with benefits. This is quite apparent in the case of plant and producers' durable equipment for which a specific rate of return may be readily computed and for interest-bearing financial assets like bonds for which yields are reported each day in the pages of financial newspapers. Although less apparent, it is also true for money and goods held by consumers. The family automobile and home appliances provide obvious flows of services to their owners. Less obvious but still present is the flow of services provided to its owners by money in the form of the convenience and security that immediately available purchasing power offers. Although the flows of services provided by such assets cannot be expressed as a rate of return as we express the income from a capital good or a bond, a rate of return nonetheless exists for these other assets.

Given then that all assets have rates of return or yields, suppose now that the Federal Reserve purchases Treasury bills in the open market. This purchase leads to a rise in the price of bills and a decline in their yield. With yields on other securities unchanged at the moment, a process of arbitrage begins in which wealth-owners execute portfolio adjustments that tend to push down yields on financial assets in general. Further-

---

[1]Our analysis focuses on the basic distinction between the transmission process as found in Keynesianism and monetarism. For a survey that makes more detailed distinctions, see R.W. Spencer, "Channels of Monetary Influence: A Survey," in *Review,* Federal Reserve Bank of St. Louis, Nov. 1974, pp. 8–26.

[2]The portfolio balance theory of monetary behavior is primarily associated with the name of James Tobin. For an outline of this approach, see his "Money, Capital, and Other Stores of Value," in *American Economic Review,* May 1961, pp. 26–37.

[3]We will here give only a minimum outline of the process. For a somewhat fuller statement, see M. Friedman and A.J. Schwartz, "Money and Business Cycles," in *Review of Economics and Statistics,* Supplement, Feb. 1963, pp. 59–63.

more, the Federal Reserve's initial purchase, all else being equal, has added to the reserves of the banks; they will now purchase more securities and make more loans. The banks' purchases of securities will add to the downward pressure on the yields provided by these assets, and their increased supply of loan funds will permit lower interest rates to borrowers.

As far as individual wealth-holders are concerned, the initial disequilibrium created by the increase in the amount of money in their portfolios is corrected as the process of trading money for other financial assets is carried to the point at which they find no advantage in further substitution of this kind. At the relative yields now in effect, their portfolios contain that amount of money and distribution of other financial assets that provide portfolio balance. This, however, is by no means a full equilibrium. It neglects the fact that the expected yields on various real assets are initially unchanged by the increase in the money supply and by the decline in yields on financial assets in general. Although wealth-holders may first tend to substitute other financial assets for what have become excess holdings of money, they will sooner or later also substitute real assets for financial assets. This constitutes an increase in the demand for real assets. Some may acquire existing assets directly by purchasing such things as apartment buildings and other commercial real estate; others will acquire ownership claims to various kinds of real assets, including plant and producers' durable equipment, by purchasing shares of stock. Increased demand for the existing stock of real assets will mean higher prices for them, and this will stimulate the production of more such goods. Increased demand for stock shares will mean higher prices, and this will encourage corporations to issue more stock to finance expansion of their productive facilities. This will lead to the production of more such goods. Similarly, corporations may choose to issue more bonds for this same purpose because the rate at which they can borrow in the bond market is now lower than it was.

Although this appears to be the more important component, the increased demand for real assets is not limited to the purchase of capital goods used in business operations or to ownership claims to such goods. The portfolio adjustment process will also lead wealth-holders to increase the demand for durable consumer goods. An increase in the supply of money will bring about a series of substitutions in portfolios which when completed will mean an increase in holdings of such assets as consumer durable goods as well as of other real assets and financial assets.

Subject to an important qualification for the wealth effect, which we will consider later, the step in these portfolio adjustments at which there is an increase in the demand for real assets or a substitution out of financial assets and into goods will take place *only* as a result of changes in relative yields on different assets. The substitution into real assets must be the result of the fact that the yields on financial assets have fallen relative to the expected yields on real assets. If wealth-holders are responsive to the changes in relative yields, they will, in the present example, adjust their balance sheets to include more real assets and less financial assets. This adjustment will stimulate production of more capital goods and raise the level of income.

This proposition is fundamental because, in the judgment of at least some economists, it leads to the heart of the difference between the Keynesians and the monetarists. Although Friedman and other monetarists trace the effect of changes in the money supply through a portfolio adjustment process much like that described, they do not hold that changes in interest rates are a prerequisite to changes in the demand for goods and services. Following an increase in the money supply, there can be a portfolio adjustment involving a movement out of money directly into goods. This is suggested by the following kind of statement: "The end result need not be a change in interest rates at all; it may be a change in the general price level or in output. An increased amount of water may flow through a lake without raising its level more than momentarily."[4] An increase in the money supply can, in other words, lead directly to spending for real assets. Consequently, the monetarists do not accept the Keynesian view that spending can be affected only indirectly as changed rates or yields on financial assets alter the prospective profitability of acquiring real assets and thereby affect the rate of spending for the various kinds of real assets.

It is one thing for monetarists to reject the Keynesian explanation; it is another to present an acceptable alternative explanation. Most economists who have followed the debate to the depths it reached do not believe that the monetarists have really provided a convincing alternative explanation to support the contention that a change in the money supply in and of itself can lead promptly and directly to a change in the demand for goods. In the absence of wealth effects, there appears to be no way to explain how a change in money can directly affect the income level.

Consider again the case in which the Federal Reserve purchases U.S. government securities in the open market. As it bids up the prices of government securities in order to persuade wealth-holders to exchange some of their holdings for new deposits, it effects a change in the composition of their assets but not at this point in their wealth or income. In bidding up prices, it also causes a fall in the yields on government securities. If the wealth-owners now choose to convert some of their deposits into goods, they must do so because the amount of goods they wish to hold, like the amount of money they wish to hold, is affected by the change in the yields on government securities and similar financial assets. Recall that the lower yield on government securities will, via a process of arbitrage, lead to lower yields on other securities. At the lower yield on

securities, portfolio equilibrium calls for substitution involving not only more money and less securities, but more goods and less securities. Without the change in yields, there seems to be no explanation of why the demand for goods increases, but with it we do have such an explanation. However, it is an explanation that shows that the connection between changes in the supply of money and the level of income is indirect. And if this is the only explanation, there is no direct connection as suggested by the monetarists.

Set forth in this manner, this conclusion seems to fly in the face of common sense. After all, to noneconomists the monetarist conclusion of a direct relation is one of the most self-evident propositions in all of economics. As they see it, because an increase in the amount of money means that the public as a whole now has more money than before, such an increase must mean the public will raise its total spending above what it was before. An increase in the money supply from one period to the next is, after all, that much additional "disposable income." There is an unquestioned direct relationship between a change in disposable income and the level of demand, so there must be a similar relationship between a change in the money supply and the level of demand.

Changes in Money and Changes in Wealth

Not even the staunchest antimonetarist denies that there may indeed be a relation of the kind just described. However, he will hold that this relation is not a unique result of the fact that there has been a change in the money supply but is rather a result of the fact that the change in the money supply involved a change in the public's total wealth. He will hold that, in the absence of a change in wealth, a change in the money supply has no direct effect on the demand for goods. Accordingly, whether or not a change in the money supply causes a change in wealth

[4]M. Friedman and D. Meiselman, "The Relative Stability of Monetary Velocity and the Investment Multiplier in the United States, 1897–1958," in *Stabilization Policies*, Commission on Money and Credit, Prentice-Hall, 1963, p. 221.

becomes a very important issue. The answer is that some changes in the money supply do and others do not.

The Interest-Induced Wealth Effect Because an increase in the money supply will tend to cause a decline in interest rates, it thereby tends to cause an increase in the discounted value of the streams of income yielded by assets. Assets for which values are determined by capitalizing the income streams they produce will rise in value when those streams are capitalized at a lower interest rate. Then, as the public sees the market value of its assets grow larger by way of these capital gains, it may be expected to increase its demand for goods and services. This interest-induced wealth effect was discussed in Chapter 16 in connection with consumption demand. It is one way in which a link may be established between changes in the stock of money and the level of demand that does not depend on *relative* interest rates.

Although this interest-induced wealth effect is clearly present, its strength—like that of the price-induced wealth effect or Pigou effect—does not appear to be large for the kinds of changes in interest rates ordinarily experienced. However, there are exceptional times during which changes in interest rates are so pronounced that the interest-induced wealth effect surely becomes significant. For example, in 1980, interest rates shot up to the highest levels in a hundred years. This was due to a more restrictive monetary policy adopted by the Federal Reserve authorities in October of 1979, to the sharp rise in the inflation rate in early 1980, and to other factors. In any event, the virtual collapse of long-term bond prices that accompanied the dramatic rise in interest rates, according to some estimates, amounted to a loss of $500 billion to holders of such securities over the period of a few months. An interest-induced wealth effect of this magnitude, even in a $2.7 trillion dollar economy, will probably have a significant effect on the aggregate demand for goods and services.

A Direct Wealth Effect A change in the money supply may not only produce a wealth effect by changing interest rates, but may *sometimes* produce such an effect directly. The general public believes that this effect *always* accompanies an increase in the money supply, because it believes that the creation of more money, in and of itself, adds that much to the public's wealth. Unlike other things, it is assumed that the public gets an increase in the total money supply without giving up anything in exchange. This is simply not true of most of the increases that occur in the money supply—they do not cause any such direct increase in the public's wealth.

Federal Reserve Open-Market Purchases Take first the case of an increase in the money supply that occurs as the Federal Reserve purchases securities in the open market. As we saw in Chapter 10, assuming that the sellers are not banks, the public now holds more money and less securities. There is a change in the composition of the public's assets, but no change in its total assets or total liabilities and therefore no change in its wealth. The wealth-holders in question shifted out of securities and into money because of the attractive price at which they could sell the securities, but the mere fact that they now hold more money is no reason to expect them to proceed to switch out of money into goods. However, as we have seen, such a switch may indeed follow not because of the increase in money holdings but because of the changes in relative yields the increase produces. The unchanged yields on real assets or goods will now be relatively attractive in comparison with the lower yields on financial assets.

Commercial Bank Lending Unlike the wealth-holders in the first case who secured additional money by giving up securities for it, consider now wealth-holders who secure additional money by borrowing at the commercial banks. All else being equal, Federal Reserve Bank or commercial bank purchases of securities in the open market and commercial bank purchases of customers' promissory notes result in an increase in the economy's total money supply. The cases differ, however, in this respect: Wealth-holders who were induced to switch out of securities into money are under no special pressure to use the money immediately. Individuals and firms who secure additional money by borrowing at the banks are, however, quite certain to make immediate use of that money. Why else would they go into debt to get it? The interest rate they must pay on the debt incurred is almost sure to be higher than the rate of return on holdings of demand deposits. Some borrowers may have incurred debt to pay off other debt, but many will do so to finance the purchase of goods. Accordingly, we presume that an increase in the supply of money resulting from an expansion of loans by the commercial banks will be used promptly and that it will lead quite directly to an increase in the demand for goods.[5]

Although money created by loans is therefore likely to have a greater effect on the demand for goods than money created by the monetization of existing financial assets such as U.S. government securities, the effect in both cases is achieved essentially via changes in relative interest rates. In neither case can we argue that a direct effect on the demand for goods arises from a wealth or income effect. In these cases,

increasing or decreasing the money supply does not mean adding to or subtracting from the public's wealth or income.

Treasury Deficit Financing   This brings us to the case in which an increase or decrease in the money supply may directly affect the demand for goods by adding that much to or subtracting that much from the wealth of the public. We will have such a case in the event that the public increases or decreases its money holdings without giving up or gaining an equal amount of other assets or without incurring an equal increase or decrease in its liabilities. This will happen only in the event that the U.S. Treasury finances a U.S. government deficit in a way that increases the money supply. As we saw in Chapter 10, there will be such an increase in the money supply if the Treasury meets the deficit by issuing newly printed currency or by obtaining newly created deposits at the Federal Reserve Banks or the commercial banks in exchange for Treasury interest-bearing obligations. As the Treasury pays out the currency to the public or transfers these deposits to the public, the public will find itself with an increase in its money holdings which, from its point of view, is a net increase in its financial assets. This in turn gives rise to a wealth-induced increase in the demand for goods.

Keynesians and monetarists agree that such a change in the money supply will directly affect spending on goods via a change in the public's wealth. However, apart from whatever interest-induced wealth effect may result, this is not true for all those changes in the money supply that occur as the banking system makes loans to or purchases securities from the public. Here the Keynesians insist that the effect is indirect and works through portfolio adjustments as previously described. They also grant that one effect of such an increase in the money supply will be an increase in the income level.[6]

---

[5]Although, quite apart from interest rates charged, increased availability of loans at banks will lead to loans that otherwise would not have been made, interest rates charged relative to other rates or yields still play the same kind of role here that was described earlier. Portfolio adjustments in response to changes in relative yields include more than substitutions among an existing total of assets; they also include varying the amount of liabilities and thereby the total amount of assets. In the present case, a decline in interest rates charged by banks on loans, with no decline in the prospective rates of return on the real assets to be acquired with the borrowed funds, explains why many loans are made. From an initial portfolio equilibrium, the public will be induced to enlarge its assets and liabilities by borrowing if the rates paid on borrowed funds relative to the rates expected on the goods purchased with these funds are such as to make these changes in portfolios advantageous.

---

[6]This was not always true. As late as the 1950s, ultra-Keynesians seemed to believe they were living in a liquidity trap world in which ordinary monetary policy was pow-

From this perspective, it almost seems that the Keynesians and monetarists differ not as to whether changes in the money supply affect the income level but as to how they affect it. There is some truth in this observation, but going one step further reveals that the way changes in the money supply affect the income level makes a critical difference in terms of how close and how stable the relationship is between changes in the money supply and the income level. The Keynesians find a loose relation, subject to considerable variation over time; the monetarists maintain that the relation is fairly close, subject to only moderate variation over time. What is the source of this difference?

Substitutability Among Assets

The Keynesians and the monetarists present very similar descriptions of the process of portfolio adjustment, but they disagree on a critical aspect of this process: the closeness of substitution between money and other financial assets and between money and real assets. As the Keynesians see it, money and other financial assets are close substitutes. Accordingly, because a rise in the price of any good will increase the demand for another good that is a close substitute, the rise in the prices of other financial assets—here caused by an increase in the money supply—will produce an increase in the amount of money wealth-owners wish to hold. But at the same time that higher prices and lower yields on other financial assets will induce the public to hold more money as a substitute for those assets, the public will also want to hold more real assets. As sketched earlier, the increase in the demand for real assets will lead to an increase in the production of goods and therefore to an increase in the income level. But what we have here is a loose connection between a change in the

money supply and the change in the level of income. Depending on the elasticities involved, a given increase in the money supply can give rise to a wide range of possible changes in the income level.

This is not so in the monetarist theory, at least not in Friedman's version of it. In his theory, real assets rather than financial assets are close substitutes for money. An increase in the money supply sets into motion a process of portfolio adjustment, but somehow through all the substituting that takes place in the process, there is no substitution of money for financial assets. That is, despite lower rates of return on other financial assets, the public does not choose to hold more money and fewer other financial assets. The demand for money is not interest elastic. Instead, the public chooses to hold more real assets and less money—that is, to substitute real assets for money. Again such an increased demand for real assets will lead to an increase in the production of these assets and therefore to an increase in the income level. In the Keynesian theory, the public seeks to substitute goods for only a part of any change in the money supply, and a part that can vary from time to time. In Friedmanian theory, substitution of goods for money will continue until the rate of production of goods or the income level is such that the amount of money actually held equals the constant proportion of income that the public wants its money holdings to equal. Otherwise expressed, at this point all of the money actually held by the public will be required to mediate the volume of transactions associated with that higher level of income.

Until the 1970s, the crux of the difference between Keynesian and Friedmanian theory seemed to be found in this difference on the matter of substitutability among assets. From this difference flow Friedman's quantity theory conclusions and the Keynesians' rejection of those conclusions. In terms of the elementary formulation employed in Chapter 11, if we deny that there is a substitution between money and other financial assets as their relative yields change, there will be equilibrium between the nominal

erless to affect interest rates and income levels. No one today denies that changes in the money supply will affect these variables.

supply of money, M_s, and the demand for money when $M_s = P \cdot k(Y)$. If we accept that there is substitution between money and other financial assets when their relative yields change, there will be equilibrium when $M_s = P \cdot k(Y) + P \cdot h(r)$. The first equation yields the quantity theory conclusion of a stable relationship between M_s and $P \cdot Y$; the latter yields no such relationship. Because such a relationship is the essence of monetarism, the issue of the closeness of the substitution between money and financial versus real assets is crucial. If real assets are closer substitutes for money than other financial assets, we are led toward the quantity theory; otherwise we are led toward the Keynesian theory and rejection of the quantity theory.

Until the 1970s, economists generally agreed that the essential difference between the sides was the one here described. Friedman had not provided a theoretical framework that would have clearly revealed the difference that existed between himself and the Keynesians, but his writings suggested that the difference over the interest elasticity of the demand for money was central. In answer to the critics who kept asking for a theoretical framework that would explain how money produced the effects on income that Friedman alleges the empirical record shows, Friedman published a major article in 1970.[7] Perhaps in the attempt to improve communication

with other economists who are accustomed to thinking in these terms, he made use of the IS–LM apparatus in this framework.

The early reaction to Friedman's framework was one of confusion and consternation on the monetarist side as well as the Keynesian side. For example, James Tobin stated:

> I have been very surprised to learn what Professor Friedman regards as his crucial theoretical differences from the neo-Kenyesians. . . . First, let me explain what I thought the main issue was. In terms of the Hicksian IS–LM language . . . I thought (and I still think) it was the shape of the LM locus.[8]

However, in the 1970 article, Friedman explicitly disavowed his earlier belief that the demand for money is interest inelastic and thereby accepted the Keynesian-shaped LM curve that slopes upward to the right. Apparently no less an economist than James Tobin had come to believe that the foundation for Friedman's monetarist propositions was a vertical or near vertical LM curve. Then to be told that these propositions do not

---

[7]For years, Friedman supported his monetarist propositions solely on the empirical regularities he detected in his extensive studies of the historical relation between changes in the money supply and changes in the income level. In connection with the assertion that monetary changes are the key to major movements in money income, he and Anna J. Schwartz wrote, "We have great confidence in this assertion. We have little confidence in our knowledge of the transmission mechanism, except in such broad and vague terms as to constitute little more than an impressionistic representation rather than an engineering blueprint." ("Money and Business Cycles," p. 54.) This great confidence that money is the key rested on evidence of various kinds: historical case studies—for example, the monumental *Monetary History of the United States, 1867–1960*, National Bureau of Economic Research, Princeton Univ. Press, 1963, by Friedman and Anna J.

Schwartz; summary regressions of time series in which changes in income are regressed against changes in money—for example, that by M. Friedman and D. Meiselman; and studies of the timing relationship between changes of the money supply (or changes in the rate of change in the money supply) and changes in the level of money income—for example, Friedman's "The Lag in the Effect of Monetary Policy," in *Journal of Political Economy*, Oct. 1961, pp. 447–66. This impressive body of empirical evidence has been subjected to much criticism. For example, on the matter of the crucial timing relationships, see J. Kareken and R. Solow, "Lags in Monetary Policy," in *Stabilization Policies*, Commission on Money and Credit, Prentice-Hall, 1963, pp. 14–25, and J. Tobin, "Money and Income: Post Hoc Ergo Propter Hoc?" in *Quarterly Journal of Economics*, May 1970, pp. 301–17. There was clearly a real need for Friedman to provide a theoretical framework to supplement his voluminous empirical work; this was done in "A Theoretical Framework for Monetary Analysis," in *Journal of Political Economy*, March–April 1970, pp. 193–238, and a follow-up article, "A Monetary Theory of Nominal Income," *Ibid.*, March–April 1971, pp. 323–37.

[8]J. Tobin, "Friedman's Theoretical Framework," in *Journal of Political Economy*, Sept.–Oct. 1972, p. 853.

rest at all on this ground gave many economists, including the leaders, great trouble trying to detect what ground, if any, they do rest on.

Two leading monetarists, K. Brunner and A.H. Meltzer, whose work is otherwise fairly close to Friedman's, found that Friedman's framework is in important ways neo-Keynesian. In their words, Friedman's "view of the transmission mechanism brings him into general agreement with the neo-Keynesians about the transmission of monetary policy. . . . We regard Friedman's discussion as either misleading or a complete reversal of his often stated position." [9]

Although Friedman's acceptance of an upward-sloping *LM* curve appeared to put him on the side of the Keynesians, Friedman contended that the major conclusions of monetarism did not depend on the slope of the *LM* curve.[10] The heart of the disagreement was elsewhere.[11] A leading critic of monetarism, Franco Modigliani, took this same point of view in stating, "There are in reality no serious analytical disagreements between leading monetarists and leading non-monetarists."[12] In accepting an upward sloping *LM* curve, monetarists had recognized that fiscal

variables can at least temporarily affect aggregate output; nonmonetarists had reciprocated in assigning a major role to the supply of money in determining aggregate output and the price level.

Is There a Role for Stabilization Policies? Keynesianism, Monetarism, and Rational Expectations——

If by the late 1970s Keynesians and monetarists believed that they were not seriously divided on analytical grounds, what did divide them? To some, the answer seems to be that the point had been reached at which they were divided not by monetarism itself, in the narrow meaning usually given to that term, but by the role that should be assigned to stabilization policies. As Modigliani has described the division, Keynesians accept

> the fundamental practical message of *The General Theory:* that a private enterprise economy using an intangible money *needs* to be stabilized, *can* be stabilized, and therefore *should* be stabilized by appropriate monetary and fiscal policies. Monetarists by contrast take the view that there is no serious need to stabilize the economy; that even if there were a need, it could not be done, for stabilization policies would be more likely to increase than to decrease instability. . . .[13]

---

[9]K. Brunner and A.H. Meltzer, "Friedman's Monetary Theory," in *Journal of Political Economy,* Sept.–Oct. 1972, p. 846.

[10]Thus, if certain conditions are met, one may retain the major monetarist conclusion that expansionary fiscal policy will not raise the level of income even with an upward sloping *LM* curve. Such policy will shift the *IS* curve upward or to the right and produce an intersection with an upward-sloping *LM* curve at a higher level of output. However, this higher level of output will not result, other than temporarily, if the expansionary fiscal policy produces a sufficiently large rise in the price level. Such a rise in the price level will produce that decrease in the real money supply and that leftward or upward shift in the *LM* curve that results in an intersection between this higher *LM* curve and the higher *IS* curve at the original level of output. *If this price increase occurs, the final result in terms of the level of output is the same as is obtained with a perfectly vertical LM curve.* From this point of view, the effect of the fiscal action on output is independent of the slope of the *LM* curve. Of course, what is needed to get this is the required rise in the price level. But according to the monetarist view this is just what will happen.

[11]Friedman had actually taken this position as early as 1966 when he wrote that ". . . no 'fundamental issues' in either monetary theory or monetary policy hinge on whether the estimated elasticity of demand for money with respect to the interest rate can for most purposes be approximated by zero or is better approximated by −0.1 or −0.5 or −2.0, provided it is seldom capable of being approximated by −∞." See his *The Optimum Quantity of Money and Other Essays,* Aldine, 1969, p. 155.

[12]F. Modigliani, "The Monetarist Controversy or, Should We Forsake Stabilization Policies?" *American Economic Review,* March 1977, p. 1.

[13]*Ibid.*

In the same vein, James Tobin wrote in 1980 that economists

> are deeply divided on essential points, on how to model the structures of our economies and on what government policies can improve their performance. Since the mid 1960s the degree of consensus once commanded by the post-Keynesian "neoclassical synthesis" has decayed, along with confidence in the stabilizing potential of active fiscal and monetary intervention.[14]

The view that the economy is inherently stable and that much of the instability actually experienced since World War II has been the result of active fiscal and monetary intervention has long been advanced by Friedman and other monetarists.[15] Keynesians, in general, reject this view.

The monetarist contention that the economy is inherently stable does not deny that the economy is subject to fluctuations, but these fluctuations are attributed primarily to destabilizing variations in the money supply caused by the monetary authorities. If that source of disturbance is removed, most of the instability will be removed, according to this point of view.[16] On the other side, the Keynesian rejection of the argument that the economy is inherently stable is not an acceptance of the opposite argument that the economy is explosively unstable. The argument is that it is subject to frequent, erratic shocks due primarily to the variability of investment spending and that these shocks are sufficiently strong to produce business cycles of significant amplitude. To reduce the damage that accompanies such fluctuations requires appropriate counter-cyclical monetary and fiscal policies, according to the Keynesian point of view.

From both points of view, counter-cyclical monetary and fiscal policies will affect output, employment, and prices. The critical difference is that monetarists believe that attempts to make things better through policy actions more often than not end up making them worse, whereas Keynesians believe just the opposite. Therefore, to monetarists there is no active role for stabilization policy, and to Keynesians there is. This two-way division has been given a third dimension in recent years by the rational expectationists who take issue with both the Keynesian and monetarist views. These economists reject the Keynesian position that monetary policy, if appropriate to the conditions, can have a beneficial effect on output and employment; they also reject the monetarist position that monetary policy, if inappropriate to the conditions, can have a detrimental effect on output and employment. Rational expectationists maintain that monetary policy has negligible systematic effects on output and employment—period. And this is not only true in the long run, as is generally accepted by all, but also in the quite short run. Varying the money supply affects prices of goods, not the total quantity of goods produced. This being the case, activist monetary policies designed to stimulate the economy are unlikely to do anything but raise the rate of inflation.[17]

---

[14]J. Tobin, *Asset Accumulation and Economic Activity: Reflections on Contemporary Macroeconomic Theory,* University of Chicago Press, 1980, p. 1.

[15]For Friedman's description of the way in which activist policy can turn out to be destabilizing rather than stabilizing, see "The Effects of a Full Employment Policy on Economic Stability: A Formal Analysis," in *Essays in Positive Economics,* University of Chicago Press, 1953, pp. 117–32.

[16]This leads to the argument long advanced by Friedman that the money supply should grow at a fixed rate. This argument for a so-called monetary rule will be discussed later in this chapter.

[17]A few of the major articles in the rational expectations literature are two articles by T.J. Sargent and N. Wallace, "Rational Expectations and the Theory of Economic Policy," in *Journal of Monetary Economics,* April 1976, pp. 169–83 and " 'Rational Expectations', the Optimal Monetary Instrument, and the Optimal Money Supply Rule," in *Journal of Political Economy,* April 1975, pp. 241–54; R.E. Lucas, Jr., "An Equilibrium Model of the Business Cycle," in *Journal of Political Economy,* Dec. 1975, pp. 1113–44; R.J. Barro, " 'Rational' Expectations and the Role of Monetary Policy," in *Journal of Monetary Economics,* Jan. 1976,

These economists are referred to as rational expectationists because their attack on the proposition that there is a role for stabilization policy is based on the application of the concept of *rational expectations* to the area of macroeconomic policy. The idea of rational expectations is, in short, that households and firms form their expectations of the future magnitudes of economic variables like the price level, GNP and disposable personal income by using all the information available to them. This includes whatever information they have on what government fiscal and monetary policies will be in the future, because a rational person recognizes that these policies will tend to affect the values of economic variables. In contrast, the conventional approach to the explanation of the way households and firms formulate their expectations, so-called *adaptive expectations,* makes the expected magnitude of these economic variables equal to a weighted average of their present and past values. Therefore, the expected values so determined do not allow for the influence of all the information that rational households and firms take into account in formulating their expectations.

Consequently, in broad terms, because the public's current spending, saving, investing, and other economic decisions are affected by their expectations of what is going to happen in the uncertain future and because their expectations of this depend in part on their expectations of what macroeconomic policy is going to be, the public's current decisions are what they are, in part, because of what it expects macroeconomic

policy will be. Accordingly, any widely expected policy action—for example, a slower rate of monetary growth—will have little effect on the public's behavior because it will already have been taken into account and acted on by the public. However, any unexpected policy action will for this reason cause the public to change its current behavior. Thus, the policy action will be effective in modifying the public's current behavior as the policy-makers intended only if it comes as a surprise to the public. An analogy is provided by the price of a share of stock. That price on any date already reflects all known information that investors regard to be relevant; the only thing that will change the price of the stock is the appearance of information that was not already taken into account or information that appears as a surprise.

Specifically in the area of monetary policy, the Federal Reserve authorities since 1975 have publicly announced monetary growth targets for the year ahead. Based on this and expected values of other variables like the federal government deficit, the public forms expectations of the inflation rate. The terms of wage agreements, the level of interest rates, and other variables are then adjusted to reflect the expected inflation rate. However, the argument of the rational expectationists is that, because of such adjustments, the policy actions when carried out will not be followed by changes in the level of employment and output, because the public responded to the indicated rate of monetary growth before the steps were taken to produce that rate. On the other hand, if the public expects a certain rate of monetary growth and the monetary authorities without warning boost that rate well above the expected rate, the policy will raise employment and output. Whatever the expected inflation rate had been before, there will be a higher rate as businesses react to the unexpected actions of the monetary authorities by raising the prices of their output. Because wage rates will lag under these conditions, the reduction in real wages and the rise in profits will mean

pp. 1–32; T.J. Sargent, "A Classical Econometric Model for the United States," in *Journal of Political Economy,* April 1976, pp. 207–37; and S. Fischer, *Rational Expectations and Economic Policy,* University of Chicago Press. A November 1980 supplement to the *Journal of Money, Credit and Banking* is devoted entirely to papers on rational expectations by nine economists. For a nontechnical introduction to the subject, see B. McCallum, "The Significance of Rational Expectations Theory," *Challenge,* Jan.–Feb. 1980, pp. 37–43.

some increase in employment and output. But the key to this result is the element of surprise. A counter-cyclical monetary policy the success of which rests on surprise, or some would say trickery, cannot be effective on a continuing basis.

According to rational expectations, a similar impediment to the effectiveness of counter-cyclical fiscal policy is faced. Because the public has learned from experience that there will be tax cuts and/or increases in government spending in the event of an economic downturn or slow-down, signs of such a development create expectations of such counter-cyclical action. As the public acts on these expectations, the timing of their actions need not provide the desired stabilizing effect. Although it may be an extreme illustration, the investment tax credit has been used to show that not only does business behavior guided by rational expectations rob this device of any counter-cyclical effect but actually turns it into one with a procyclical effect. The investment tax credit, which has been used off and on since 1962, permits firms to take as a credit against their income taxes a percentage of their outlays for new capital equipment. It appeared to have worked well when it was first used in 1962 because it came as a surprise. However, after a couple of rounds in which businesses found that it is taken off as the economy recovers and put back in when the economy slows, it ceases to work. Worse than this, this particular device becomes perverse. The current investment decisions of business people depend in part on their expectations of what macroeconomic policy will be. They come to expect that the investment credit will be reintroduced whenever the economy turns down. This leads to postponement of investment spending any time the economy shows signs of a downturn as people seek to take advantage of the expected tax credit. What may not actually have been the beginning of a downturn can be turned into one as the public acts on its expectations of what government policy will be. The downturn comes, Congress provides business with the expected

investment tax credit, and investment rises sharply. It looks as if the credit produces its intended counter-cyclical effect, but the opposite is actually the case. Its effect may be perverse: It starts or accelerates a downturn, then it does the same in the other direction. Instead of being counter-cyclical, this device turns out to be procyclical, a result that follows from the expectation that government will try to use it in a counter-cyclical way.

This may be sufficient to point out the basis for the major tenet of the rational expectations argument: Activist macroeconomic policy cannot systematically succeed in affecting the economy's employment and output levels. To affect these levels, the authorities must alter policy unexpectedly, but a continuing policy of this kind must lead to uncertainty by the public as to what policy will be. As the public's expectations of policy actions become more uncertain, the policy makers have no way of knowing whether any particular action they take will surprise the public and therefore be effective or whether that action has already been taken into account by the public and will therefore be ineffective. Without being able to know what public reaction will follow from any policy step it takes, the policy makers are bound to be in a quandary as to what the appropriate policy at any time should be. Policy making becomes dice-shooting. Therefore, according to the rational expectations argument, it is futile to try to affect output and employment through activist monetary and fiscal policies.

Although the rational expectationists have raised some new and interesting questions concerning the feasibility of counter-cyclical policy, the majority view among economists so far remains that activist policy is *not* powerless. The likelihood that counter-cyclical monetary and fiscal policies will be abandoned in the near future is slight, barring the development of a much stronger case than has so far been presented by the monetarists and the rational expectationists and barring the acceptance of this case by the fiscal and monetary authorities. As long as we continue to use counter-cyclical policies, all of the practical questions faced by policy makers will remain. The balance of this chapter considers a number of these questions.

Determining Monetary Policy

Monetary policy was defined at the beginning of this chapter as the exercise of the central bank's control over the money supply as an instrument for achieving the objectives of general economic policy. A change in policy accordingly calls for a change in the money supply—or more accurately for a change in the growth rate of the money supply—but this obviously reveals nothing about what monetary policy should specifically be at any time. What is needed is a guide or guides to direct those whose responsibility it is to answer this question.

We earlier noted the major goals of macroeconomic policy—full employment, price stability, and satisfactory growth—and one might argue that these should be the guides to follow in setting monetary policy. For example, as the economy suffers a downturn and the unemployment percentage rises, monetary policy should become expansionary; that is, the authorities should carry out those open-market purchases and/or take other steps that will increase the rate at which the economy's money supply is growing. Although at first glance this may seem to be obviously the appropriate policy, taking a so-called ultimate goal variable like full employment as a guide to policy is impractical for several reasons. In trying to determine how rapidly to expand the money supply in the case of a downturn (or how rapidly to contract it in the case of inflation), the monetary authorities cannot base their decision on the behavior of a variable like the unemployment percentage, which is importantly affected by various forces other than monetary policy. In other words, using the unemployment percentage as the guide for pumping into the system whatever amount of additional money is needed to correct the unemployment problem

could produce serious inflation without even then fully correcting the unemployment problem.

Furthermore, the ultimate goal variables are affected not only by forces other than monetary policy but also by monetary policy only with some lag. According to some economists like Friedman, this lag is, on the average, not only long but quite variable from one case to the next. Consequently, even if variables like output, employment, and prices were completely determined by monetary policy—which is not at all the case—they would still not be a satisfactory guide. They would always be indicating the results of monetary policy pursued some time earlier. What is needed as a guide is a variable that promptly responds to monetary policy so that the authorities can determine from it the direction in which their most recent policy decisions have been carrying them.

One more difficulty of this kind is that changes in the overall position of the economy that are reflected by changes in the unemployment percentage, price indexes, and growth rates are observable only after some time. If the monetary authorities await clear signs that a downturn is under way before they adjust policy to meet the problem, the problem will be more difficult to handle than if it had been attacked sooner. However, if they move to an expansionary policy at the first sign of a downturn, they may create a problem where none existed before. If the first sign was false, then expansionary policy will not check a downturn, because that is not occurring; it will produce undesirable inflationary pressures that would not have existed otherwise.

Yet another problem, of a different nature, that is faced in trying to use the ultimate goals as guides is the incompatibility that exists among some of them—for example, between full employment and price stability. Which way should monetary policy turn if it bases policy on these ultimate goals but finds itself faced with a rising unemployment percentage and a rising rate of inflation, an extreme case of which was faced in 1974?

Because of these various difficulties, the variable that the monetary authorities choose as a guide must be much more closely tied to monetary policy in the sense that changes in its value are substantially determined by changes in monetary policy and promptly follow them. Such a variable provides the authorities with an indicator of the direction in which and speed with which they are moving. It is also, of course, indispensable that this variable be related to the ultimate goal variables. That is, changes in it must be expected to lead to changes in these goal variables. The authorities can then operate to produce changes in the chosen variable with some assurance that these changes will work through the system to produce changes in those ultimate variables the control of which is the end goal of monetary policy.[18]

Monetary Aggregates Versus Credit Conditions as Guides

Which variables meet these requirements? As a rule, a variable that comes closer to meeting one requirement falls farther short of meeting the other one. Consider the following illustrations. The amount of U.S. government securities held by the Federal Reserve Banks changes only because of actions taken by the Federal Reserve authorities. However, this variable is not at all closely related to the ultimate goal variables, because short-run changes in the Reserve Banks' security holdings may not cause changes in member bank reserves or the public's currency holdings and thereby may not cause changes in the money supply. And it is through changes in the money supply, either directly or via interest rates, that the monetary authorities are able to influence the ultimate goal variables.

From this example we could conclude that the monetary authorities should choose the money supply as their guide variable. Although monetarists argue that the money supply shows a relatively close and stable relationship with the ultimate goal variables, changes in this variable cannot promptly and accurately indicate to the monetary authorities the impact of the actual actions taken by them, because short-run changes in the money supply are not completely determined by Federal Reserve actions. Various other factors such as changes in the public's currency-to-deposit ratio or in the commercial banks' excess reserves-to-deposit ratio affect this. Consequently, a rising money supply does not necessarily indicate that actions of the Federal Reserve authorities on balance have been expansionary. The money supply may be rising in spite of actions taken by the Federal Reserve authorities, not because of them. If the authorities evaluate the direction and speed with which they are moving by the changes that occur in the money supply, the evaluation of their policy stance may at times involve sizable error.

A possible alternative guide variable is the amount of reserves held by the commercial banking system. Changes in this variable are almost completely under Federal Reserve control, so they reflect changes in Federal Reserve actions more closely than do changes in the money supply. However, because changes in the amount of reserves do not mean proportional changes in the money supply, they are less closely related to the ultimate goal variables.

The nature of the problem may be apparent from these illustrations. Without undue elaboration, we may see that a number of related variables—such as commercial bank reserves, the monetary base, the money supply, or total commercial bank credit—are possible guides to monetary policy, but none ideally meets both the requirements noted. In the present context, this class of variables is usually referred to as **monetary aggregates**.

---

[18]For a full discussion of the various aspects of this complicated area of guides, targets, indicators, and goals of monetary policy, see the various papers in K. Brunner, ed., *Targets and Indicators of Monetary Policy*, Chandler, 1969, and T.R. Saving, "Monetary-Policy Targets and Indicators," in *Journal of Political Economy*, Aug. 1967, Part II, pp. 446–65. See also B.M. Friedman, "Targets, Instruments, and Indicators of Monetary Policy," in *Journal of Monetary Economics*, Oct. 1975, pp. 443–73.

A quite different class of variables that can serve as guides are those that reflect conditions in credit markets. Credit conditions are measured by variables such as the amount of member bank borrowing from the Federal Reserve Banks, the free reserve position of the member banks, the Treasury bill rate, the federal funds rate, other interest rates, and the intangible known as the "tone and feel" of the market. Among these variables, interest rates receive the most attention.

Do interest rates meet the requirements previously set forth for a guide to monetary policy? Whatever the extent of their control over a monetary aggregate such as the money supply, the Federal Reserve authorities have less control over interest rates. However, they can cause short-run marginal changes in interest rates, which is the significant issue here. But because interest rates do not change solely in response to actions taken by the Federal Reserve authorities, it is not possible for them to accurately evaluate what their policy has been by observing the movement of interest rates. Falling interest rates do not necessarily indicate to the authorities that their actions on balance have been expansionary; interest rates may be falling not because of actions taken by the authorities, but in spite of them. The margin for error here is greater than in the use of the money supply as a guide, because changes in the money supply are more closely tied to changes in Federal Reserve actions than changes in interest rates are. With regard to the requirement that changes in the variable chosen as a guide should lead to changes in the ultimate goal variables, economists who believe that monetary policy affects those ultimate goal variables by causing changes in interest rates obviously have great confidence in interest rates as a guide.

Determining what guide should be followed by the monetary authorities essentially involves choosing between a monetary aggregate such as total reserves or the total money supply and a measure of credit conditions such as interest rates. Until 1970, the Federal Reserve authorities

had been guided in policy making almost completely by credit conditions, especially as reflected by interest rates. Starting in 1970, they began to pay for more attention to the money supply and other aggregates than they had before, and this has continued over the following years.

A Criterion for the Choice of a Guide The Federal Reserve, of course, chooses between guides in the belief that its choice will contribute more to the stability of the economy than an alternative. However, under one set of conditions, the choice of interest rates as a guide may do more to stabilize the economy, whereas under another set of conditions, the choice of the money supply may do more in that direction. The issue here may be seen most clearly through the *IS* and *LM* curves in Figure 26-1.[19]

In all of our previous work with *IS* and *LM* curves, we never specifically noted that, in practice, the positions of both the *IS* and *LM* curves are never known with certainty. This is relevant here because it is the relative uncertainty as to the position of the two curves that helps us determine whether interest rates or the money supply will be the better guide.

Consider Part A of Figure 26-1 first. This, the most unrealistic case, assumes that the positions of both the *IS* and *LM* curves are known with certainty. Knowing that *IS* and *LM* are positioned as shown, the Federal Reserve can achieve the full employment income level, Y_f, by using either the money supply or the interest rate as a guide. In either case, the Federal Reserve will adjust the money stock or the interest rate so that the resulting *LM* curve intersects the *IS* curve at the full

---

[19]The following analysis is based on W. Poole, "Optimal Choice of Monetary Policy Instruments in a Simple Stochastic Macro Model," *Quarterly Journal of Economics,* May 1970, pp. 197–216. See also his "Rules-of-Thumb for Guiding Monetary Policy," in *Open Market Policies and Operating Procedures—Staff Studies,* Board of Governors of the Federal Reserve System, 1971, pp. 135–89, reprinted in part in R.L. Teigen, ed., *Readings in Money, National Income, and Stabilization Policy,* 4th ed., Irwin, 1978, pp. 327–33.

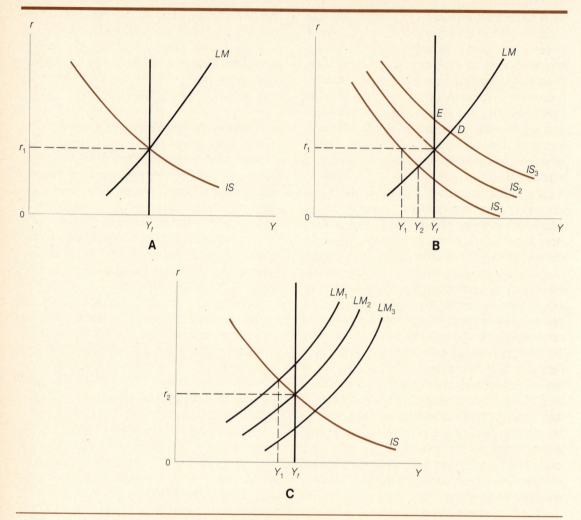

FIGURE 26-1
Income Instability under an Interest Rate Guide
and a Money Supply Guide

employment income level. To simplify another part of the argument here, we assume that there is price stability as long as the *IS–LM* intersection is at or below the full employment income level.

Part B drops the assumption that the *IS* curve is known with certainty. All that is now known is that this curve lies somewhere between *IS*₁ and

*IS*₃, including *IS*₂ as a possibility. The assumption that *LM* is known with certainty is retained; accordingly, with the given money supply, *LM* is positioned as shown. In this situation, if the interest rate of r_1 is used as a guide, the range of instability in real income will be Y_1 to Y_f or the range set by the *IS*₁ and *IS*₂ curves. If the *IS* curve were positioned between IS_2 and IS_3, inflation would result and continue as long as the Federal Reserve persisted in expanding the money supply in its effort to maintain the r_1 interest rate. What if the money supply is used as a guide in this case? The range of income instability will then be Y_2 to Y_f. Assuming that the IS curve were positioned at the lower limit of its range, IS_1, the economy would hit the bottom of the income range at a higher level of income with the money supply as a guide than with the interest rate as a guide. With the money supply guide, market forces are permitted to force down the interest rate; a lower interest rate means a higher level of income with any given downward sloping IS curve. If the IS curve were positioned between IS_2 and IS_3, say at IS_3, inflation would result, but it would be self-correcting because the inflation-induced decrease in the real money supply causes the LM curve to shift to the left from its intersection with IS_3 at D to its intersection at E, the full employment income level. From Part B of Figure 26-1, therefore, we may conclude that the real income level shows a greater range of instability with an interest rate guide than with a money supply guide, Y_1 to Y_f compared with Y_2 to Y_f. The interest rate guide will also expose the economy to the possibility of an inflation that continues as long as that guide is adhered to; in contrast, any inflation that occurs with a money supply guide will be self-correcting.

Part C reverses the assumptions of Part B. Now the assumptions are that the position of the IS curve is known with certainty, but the position of the LM curve corresponding to a given money supply may be anywhere between LM_1 and LM_3, including LM_2 as a possibility. In this situation, if the Federal Reserve uses the money supply as a guide, the range of instability in real income will be Y_1 to Y_f, the range set by the LM_1 and LM_2 curves. If LM actually lies between LM_2 and LM_3, there will be inflation, but the inflation will be self-correcting as the inflation-induced reduction in the real money supply shifts the LM curve upward to the LM_2 position. Given the conditions in Part C, what if the interest rate is used as a guide?

Here the interest rate guide enables the Federal Reserve to achieve the full employment income level (and also to avoid inflation, given the assumption that prices are stable up to the full employment income level). If the position of the IS curve is known for certain, all that is needed is that the Federal Reserve pick as its guide that interest rate at which the IS curve intersects the vertical line at Y_f and then vary the money supply as required to obtain that interest rate.

The analysis in Parts B and C of Figure 26-1 leads us to conclude that the interest rate guide will result in less income stability than the money supply guide in a world in which the position of the IS curve is more uncertain and that the interest rate guide will result in greater income stability in a world in which the position of the LM curve is more uncertain. In general, monetarists believe that the position of the LM curve corresponding to any given money supply is relatively stable; therefore, its position is subject to less uncertainty than the position of the IS curve. This leads to the conclusion that the money supply is the better guide to monetary policy. In general, Keynesians argue that the opposite is the case; they conclude that the interest rate is the better guide to monetary policy.

Although the analysis in Figure 26-1 has the advantage of laying out basic differences by portraying two polar cases, it obviously oversimplifies the problems of actual policy making. At any time, there is considerable uncertainty as to the positions of both the IS and LM curves; moreover, there is no way of knowing with any assurance whether upward pressure on the interest rate at any time is due to an upward shift of the IS or the LM curve. On the one hand, if it were known that the upward pressure on the interest rate was the result of a temporary or irregular change in the demand for money (an upward shift in the LM curve), that change could properly be met by an increase in the money supply that maintains the interest rate unchanged and prevents the decrease in real income that would follow from a rise in the interest rate. On the other hand, if it were known that the upward pressure on the interest rate was due to a surge in aggregate spending (an upward shift in the *IS* curve), that pressure should not be automatically resisted in an economy operating near full employment. The interest rate should be allowed to rise, because in this case, by choking off excess spending, the rise contributes to overall economic stability.

The Federal Reserve's Leaning Toward the Interest Rate as a Guide   There is a long-standing complaint among some economists that the Federal Reserve, because of its traditional concern with the stability of financial markets and its attachment to an interest rate guide, has often moved to prevent interest rates from changing when it should have permitted them to change. This has typically been followed by an overreaction to its earlier error with the net result of large changes in the rate of growth of the money supply. One of many illustrations occurred at the time of the escalation of the Vietnam War in 1965 when rapidly rising military expenditures added to an already vigorously expanding economy. Under the circumstances, the Federal Reserve authorities might have been expected to adopt a policy of slowing the rate of expansion of the money supply, but they actually did the opposite. The policy they followed reflected their concern over the fact that interest rates were rising quite rapidly during the year. It was not until December that they recognized that the pressures on interest rates were not temporary. Their reaction was to reverse policy in 1966, which replaced the rapid rate of money growth with a rate approaching and, during part of the year, actually reaching zero. Interest rates in 1966 then showed one of the largest jumps then on record. There was much disorder in financial markets, culminating in a "credit crunch" by late summer of 1966. A few months later, the Federal Reserve once again reversed policy.

Critics of the Federal Reserve argue that the emphasis the authorities place on interest rate stability results in errors in both the timing and the scope of action. Using the 1965–66 episode

as an example, Friedman wrote as follows in 1968:

> Too late and too much has been the general practice. For example, in early 1966, it was the right policy for the Federal Reserve to move in a less expansionary direction—though it should have done so at least a year earlier. But when it moved, it went too far, producing the sharpest change in the rate of monetary growth of the postwar era. Again, having gone too far, it was the right policy for the Fed to reverse course at the end of 1966. But again it went too far, not only restoring but exceeding the earlier excessive rate of monetary growth. And this episode is no exception. Time and again this has been the course followed—as in 1919 and 1920, in 1937 and 1938, in 1953 and 1954, in 1959 and 1960.[20]

This statement, if written twelve years later, would have extended the list to include episodes in 1969–70, 1974–75, and 1979–80.

The objective of policy in 1969 was to slow the booming economy, the hope being a reduction in the rate of inflation without a recession. The growth of the money supply was cut back in the last half of 1969 to a 1.2 percent annual rate, an action similar to that in 1966 but not as drastic. The result was a "credit squeeze" and a sharp rise in interest rates. Then, according to the critics, came the usual policy reversal in 1970 as the money supply growth rate increased to 5.2 percent.

The critics point to a similar experience in 1974–75. The growth of the money supply was reduced in 1973, then reduced even more sharply in the latter half of 1974. From mid-1974 to early 1975, it grew by less than 2 percent. Federal Reserve policy in 1974 was apparently primarily directed at meeting an interest rate target; to do this called for a severe restriction in the rate of growth of the money supply. According to the critics, this restrictive money supply

---

[20]M. Friedman, "The Role of Monetary Policy," in *American Economic Review,* March 1968, p. 16.

growth and the record high interest rates at least deepened or perhaps even caused the drastic business downturn that started at the end of 1973 and ran to early 1975. The rate of monetary growth accelerated in early 1975; from then to early 1976 the money supply increased about 6 percent.

The most recent episode of this kind occurred during 1979–80. Later we will review the operating procedure adopted by the Federal Reserve on October 6, 1979, which tolerated much greater variation in interest rates than formerly. Note here, though, that the actual record over the year following October 6, 1979, shows extremely large gyrations in interest rates and in the growth rate of the money supply. From October 1979 to March 1980, the money supply grew at an acceptable 5.3 percent rate, a rate below the upper limit of the range within which the Federal Reserve then sought to hold monetary expansion. Although interest rates had already shown a pronounced increase from October 1979 to year end, albeit with a pause at year end, they soared to record high levels by March–April 1980. The three-month Treasury bill rate reached 15.5 percent and the six-month commercial paper rate hit 16.5 percent. The prime rate rose to 20 percent. These soaring short-term interest rates reflected the spurt in the inflation rate that averaged about 18 percent for the first quarter of 1980, this in turn being partly the result of the doubling of OPEC oil prices in 1979.

To help reduce the inflationary pressures, in March 1980 the Federal Reserve announced a credit restraint program, including restrictions on consumer credit. This and other Federal Reserve actions not only stopped the growth of the money supply, but brought about an actual decrease during March, April, and May of 1980. While this was occurring, there was evidence that earlier in 1980 the economy may have entered into the seventh post-World War II recession, which had been widely expected to start in the preceding year. The Federal Reserve then sharply reversed: From May to September of 1980, the money sup-

ply grew at a 17 percent annual rate following the negative rate of the previous three months. Monetarists and others were appalled by this drastic swing; at the time, Friedman called it "disgraceful." This swing was then followed by a slowing in the growth rate of the money supply to 6.2 percent from September 1980 to March 1981.

The critics who argue that such swings in Federal Reserve policy have so often been destabilizing rather than stabilizing find the Federal Reserve reliance on interest rates as a guide to policy to be a major cause of its errors. Although there was less reliance on interest rates in recent years than in earlier years, the experience in early 1980—when the rise in interest rates was so large and rapid as to threaten a collapse of the long-term bond market and an end of fixed-rate mortgage lending—could not be altogether ignored by the Federal Reserve. So extreme a rise in rates called for some corrective action. Starting in May, the Federal Reserve acted by rapidly expanding the money supply. Interest rates fell as dramatically as they had risen earlier in the year. Then, after reaching a low in July–August, a new upsurge began, which by the end of the year had carried some interest rates above the level reached during the preceding spring. The prime rate, which had peaked at 20 percent in the spring, rose to 21.5 percent at year-end. This rise occurred despite the fact that the money supply rose at approximately an 11 percent rate over the last few months of the year. The Federal Reserve showed no inclination to try to meet this surge with a more rapid rate of money supply growth. It appeared that the Federal Reserve deemed it appropriate to act against the sharp rise in interest rates that occurred in the spring, but not against the sharp rise that occurred in the final months of the year.

According to Friedman and some other monetarists, the issue of whether the Federal Reserve should resist or accept particular changes in interest rates in the effort to provide greater overall stability in the economy would not arise, were it not for the fact that the Federal

Reserve acts in a way to produce large variations in the growth rate of the money supply. They maintain that the instability of interest rates is typically the result of such instability in the growth rate of the money supply and is not an alternative to it. Instability in the growth rate of the money supply results in instability of prices and price expectations; these in turn cause instability in the size of the inflation premium that is part of the interest rate.[21] In other words, in the monetarist view, a stable growth rate of the money supply will not mean that interest rates will be subject to larger fluctuations than otherwise. As the monetarists view the workings of the economy, the case is clear that monetary policy should have as its guide the growth rate of the money supply.

Regulating the Money Supply by Rule

If the Federal Reserve should use the growth rate of the money supply as its guide, what is the appropriate growth rate for the money supply? How do we regulate the growth rate of the money supply so as to make monetary policy exert a counter-cyclical effect and contribute to economic stabilization rather than to the destabilization that some maintain will occur with regularity under an interest rate guide?

The Lag in the Impact of Monetary Policy

Friedman and those monetarists who support his position answer this question by simply saying that no attempt should be made to use monetary policy in a counter-cyclical fashion. The lag between the time that action is taken by the monetary authorities and the time the effects of that action are felt on the income level is believed to

be both long and variable.[22] Monetary policy can be used counter-cyclically only if the monetary authorities know the length of the lag between the execution of any policy and the impact of that policy on aggregate demand and income.[23] Then it will be at least potentially possible to conduct an effective counter-cyclical policy by basing policy actions on a forecast of what conditions will be when the action taken today takes hold. However, in the present state of knowledge, forecasts are frequently far off the mark and the danger of such error increases with the length of the forecast. If the lag in monetary policy is long, this then is a compelling argument against trying to pursue a counter-cyclical monetary policy.

An additional consideration is the variability of the lag. Even if accurate forecasting of future economic conditions were possible, simply knowing what the average lag has been in the

---

[21] On this subject, see, for example, W.E. Gibson, "Price-Expectations Effects on Interest Rates," in *Journal of Finance,* March 1970, pp. 19–34, and "Interest Rates and Inflationary Expectations: New Evidence," in *American Economic Review,* Dec. 1972, pp. 854–65. See also E. Shapiro, "The Monetary Growth Rate and the Interest Rate: A Diagrammatic Presentation," in *Nebraska Journal of Economics and Business,* Spring 1976, pp. 3–17.

[22] In comparing turning points in the cycles of the rate of growth of the money stock with the turning points in business cycles as dated by the National Bureau of Economic Research, Friedman and Schwartz found that the peak in the business cycle was reached, on the average, 17.6 months after the peak in the growth rate of the money stock; the trough in the cycle was reached 12.0 months after the trough in the growth rate of the money stock. The variability of the lags as measured by the standard deviation was found to be 6.9 months at peaks and 5.7 months at troughs. "Money and Business Cycles," *Review of Economics and Statistics,* Supplement, Feb. 1963, p. 38.

[23] This is formally known as the "outside" lag. The full process of determining and carrying out policy involves three lags, the first of which is the "inside" lag between the moment at which there is a need for a change of policy and the moment at which the central bank acts. Inside lag is sometimes divided into "recognition" lag and "action" lag, but the time between recognition of the need for action and the taking of action is so short, relatively speaking, that the inside lag in effect becomes the recognition lag. The second lag is the "intermediate" lag between the moment at which action is taken and the moment at which the economy is faced with changed money supply and interest rates. The third lag is the "outside" lag between a change in the cost and availability of credit and the effect thereof on aggregate spending, income, and output. (See T. Mayer, *Monetary Policy in the United States,* Random House, 1968, Ch. 6, and the references given there for further reading.)

past is not sufficient information on which to base today's policy, if there has been considerable variability around that average. If the lag may vary from a few months to a few years, the fact that there is no way to predict the length of the lag in any particular case means that an effective counter-cyclical monetary policy is simply beyond reach. This has long been the position of Friedman and some others. However, monetary economists differ considerably as to the length of the lag and its variability; consequently, their judgments differ as to whether or not an effective counter-cyclical monetary policy is possible.[24]

Although everyone recognizes that some lag exists and that the lags will not always be the same length, many argue that the lag is neither so long nor so variable that a policy in which the Federal Reserve at least "leans against the wind" will not be better than one in which it stands straight up whichever way the wind is blowing. In reply, Friedman has written:

> We seldom in fact know which way the economic wind is blowing until several months after the event, yet to be effective, we need to know which way the wind is going to be blowing when the measures we take now will be effective, itself a variable date that may be a half-year or a year or two years from now. Leaning against next year's wind is hardly an easy task in the present state of meteorology.[25]

To Friedman, these uncertainties rule out any possibility of a successful counter-cyclical monetary policy. He would have the Federal Reserve abandon its attempts to employ monetary policy in this way and instead follow a rule of expanding the money supply at a fixed rate of about 4 per-

cent per year in line with the long-run rate of growth of the economy, no matter which way the wind was blowing in any particular year. In his judgment, any other action is more likely to contribute to instability than to help in achieving stability.[26]

Between a rigid monetary rule that remains unchanged no matter what happens in the economy and complete discretion by the Federal Reserve is the possibility of a monetary rule that includes formula flexibility in a way similar to the use of formula flexibility in fiscal policy. (See pp. 579–80.) For example, instead of rigidly holding to, say, a 4 percent annual growth rate of the money supply, permit that rate to vary in response to changes in the unemployment rate. Accordingly, the formula might be something like this:

$$\Delta M/M = 4.0 + 1.5(U - 6.0)$$

The growth rate of the money supply, $\Delta M/M$, would be 4 percent as long as the unemployment rate, U, was 6 percent. For a 1 percentage point increase in U, $\Delta M/M$ would rise by 1.5 percentage points. This would still be regulating the money supply by rule—the monetary authorities would have no discretion—but it would automatically adjust the money supply to changes in the economy evidenced by changes in the unemployment rate.

Toward a More Stable Rate of Growth in the Money Supply Either because the Federal Reserve independently came to accept the

---

[24]See T. Mayer, *Monetary Policy in the United States,* Ch. 6, for a discussion of this subject and p. 183 for a listing of pertinent literature. See also M.J. Hamburger, "The Lag in the Effect of Monetary Policy: A Survey of Recent Literature," in *Monthly Review,* Federal Reserve Bank of New York, Dec. 1971, pp. 289–98.

[25]M. Friedman, *A Program for Monetary Stability,* Fordham University Press, 1960, p.93.

[26]There have been attempts to measure the results that would have followed if a rule had been adhered to instead of the discretion actually exercised by the Federal Reserve authorities. See L.R. McPheters and M.B. Redman, "Rule, Semi-Rule, and Discretion during Two Decades of Monetary Policy," in *Quarterly Review of Economics and Business,* Spring 1975, pp. 53–64; F. Modigliani, "Some Empirical Tests of Monetary Management and of Rules vs. Discretion," in *Journal of Political Economy,* April 1964, pp. 211–45; M. Bronfenbrenner, "Statistical Tests of Rival Monetary Rules," in *Journal of Political Economy,* Feb. 1961, pp. 1–14; and J.A. Richardson, "Monetary Rules and Optimal Monetary Policy," in *Nebraska Journal of Economics and Business,* Autumn 1975, pp. 45–63.

advisability of more closely limiting the variation in the growth rate of the money supply or because Congress directed the Federal Reserve to take steps in this direction, the variations in the growth rate of the money supply have been *relatively* smaller in the last few years than in earlier years. (The *absolute* growth rate of the money supply has been much higher than in earlier years—for example, 1958–64—of very low inflation rates.) However, there still have been some large variations in the last few years on a quarter-to-quarter basis, but these are at least partially the results of the Federal Reserve's inability to exercise very close control over the growth rate during a time period of that duration. For example, there was the earlier noted, extraordinary short-run change from a negative rate of growth in March, April, and May of 1980 to the 17 percent rate of growth from May to September of that year. However, for the full year from December 1979 to December 1980, the growth rate averaged a not unreasonable 6.5 percent. In earlier years, there were cases in which a relatively rapid growth rate would persist for six months or longer and then be followed by a relatively slow rate for a similar time span. The money supply increased at an annual rate of 5.5 percent from June 1973 to June 1974, at a 1.4 percent rate from June 1974 to January 1975, and then at an 8.9 percent rate from January 1975 to July 1975. Much greater swings in the growth rate occurred during 1971–72. From January to July of 1971, the money supply grew at an 11.6 percent annual rate and then from July to December of 1971 at only an 0.8 percent rate. Over the following year—December 1971 to December 1972—the rate was 8.3 percent.

During the second quarter of 1980, while the money supply was not only not growing but actually contracting, interest rates reached record highs. Although the rise was more than anybody had expected, a very substantial rise was acceptable to the Federal Reserve at that time as an unavoidable consequence of its policy of restricting monetary expansion and reducing the inflation rate. In earlier cases, the Federal

Reserve had been much more sensitive to a sharp rise in interest rates or even to the expectation of such a rise. For example, the rapid growth rate of the money supply in early 1971 resulted from the Federal Reserve's fear that "sharp increases in long term rates at this juncture might have adverse consequences for spending. . . . and might thus pose a threat to the economic recovery under way." The attitude of the Federal Reserve toward higher interest rates in 1980 stands in contrast to its attitude ten years earlier, although the difference is explained to some degree by the difference between the moderate inflation rate of 1971 and the double-digit rate of 1980.

This suggests that by the beginning of the 1980s Federal Reserve Policy had moved some distance from its earlier emphasis on stabilizing interest rates and allowing the wide swings in the growth rate of the money supply needed to do so, but it does not by any means imply that policy had moved in the other direction all the way to accepting a monetary rule and permitting interest rates to move to whatever extent a rule would demand. The Federal Reserve continues a policy of varying the growth rate of the money supply in a way that "leans against the wind," even though this produces swings in the growth rate of the money supply. However, it does so to a lesser degree than it did in the past. This is probably due in some part to the fact that its ability to do so has been somewhat restricted by law, as we will see in the following section.

Target Growth Ranges for Monetary Aggregates

Through the late 1960s and into the 1970s, more and more members of the U.S. Congress became convinced of the wisdom of a policy of limiting the swings in the monetary growth rate; in 1975 Congress took direct but very limited action on the subject. From the time Congress created the Federal Reserve System in 1913, it had introduced various changes in the structure and the scope of operations of the system, but it had left the formulation of monetary policy completely to the discretion of the Federal Reserve authorities. However, in 1975 it adopted a "sense of Congress" resolution (House Concurrent Resolution 133), which amounted to a first small step away from a complete "hands off" position. Among other things, this resolution requested the monetary authorities—the Board of Governors and the Federal Open Market Committee—"to maintain long-run growth of the monetary and credit aggregates commensurate with the economy's long-run potential to increase production so as to promote effectively the goals of maximum employment, stable prices, and moderate long-term interest rates."[27] In accordance with this resolution, the Federal Reserve authorities began the practice of publicly specifying each quarter target growth ranges for the year ahead for several monetary aggregates. Also, in accordance with another part of the resolution, the Chairman of the Board of Governors was requested to report on those targets to the Congress each quarter. These reports became a requirement with the Federal Reserve Reform Act of 1977.[28] Finally, with the passage of the Full Employment and Balanced Growth Act of 1978, better known as the Humphrey–Hawkins Act, the format of the target growth ranges was changed in a way that gave the Federal Reserve less flexibility in this area than it had over the period from 1975 to 1978. Through these actions, Congress has imposed some restriction on the Federal Reserve's freedom in monetary policy decisions and has provided for surveillance of these decisions.

When it began publicly specifying annual target growth ranges in 1975, the Federal Reserve followed a policy of announcing annual ranges each quarter. For example, in April 1978, it adopted ranges that applied to the period from the first quarter of 1978 to the first quarter of 1979; in July 1978, it adopted ranges that applied to the period from the second quarter of 1978 to the second quarter of 1979. Accordingly, it could and at times did change the annual target growth ranges for the monetary aggregates every three months. The Humphrey–Hawkins Act required that the Federal Reserve establish calendar year growth ranges in February of each year. The Federal Reserve may reconsider these ranges at any time and it must review them at mid-year. However, it may not change the period to which the one-year ranges apply. Unlike the earlier arrangements in which the base period of the target growth ranges changed every three months, the base period now changes once a year.[29] The next steps along this path, which may or may not be taken by the Congress in the future, would be to limit the width of the target ranges or even to eliminate the ranges and demand that the Federal Reserve commit itself to hitting specific annual growth rate targets for the various aggregates. This would be what is usually meant by the concept of a monetary rule discussed in the preceding section.

Under the present arrangement, the requirements are those of the Humphrey–Hawkins Act. Under those requirements, the target growth ranges announced by the Federal Reserve in February 1980 for the year from the fourth quarter of 1979 to the fourth quarter of 1980 were as follows: M-1A, 3.5–6 percent; M-1B, 4–6.5 percent; M-2, 6–9 percent; and M-3, 6.5–9.5 percent. The pair of black lines in each of the four parts of Figure 26-2 shows the range of dollar amounts that is consistent with the target growth range for each of the aggregates. The ranges set

---

[27]See *First Report on the Conduct of Monetary Policy,* Senate Committee on Banking, Housing, and Urban Affairs, U.S. Congress, June 25, 1975, p. 3. Earlier actions of this nature had not gotten beyond the committee level. See *Standards for Guiding Monetary Action,* Joint Economic Committee. U.S. Congress, June 1968.

[28]See *Federal Reserve Bulletin,* Dec. 1977, p. 1076.

[29]With the base period changing every three months, a problem called "base drift" arose. This led to the allegation that the Federal Reserve implicitly employed a "forgiveness principle" by adopting ranges in successive quarters that forgave it for not achieving its earlier target growth ranges. See, for example, R.W. Lang, "The FOMC in 1979: Introducing Reserve Targeting," *Review,* Federal Reserve Bank of St. Louis, March 1980, pp. 2–17.

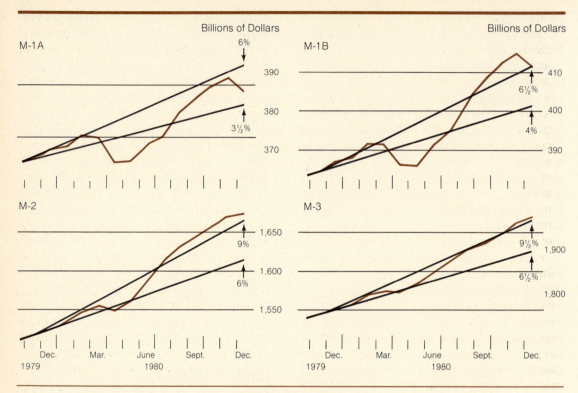

FIGURE 26-2
Target Growth Ranges and Actual Monetary Growth
(billions of dollars)

SOURCE: *Federal Reserve Bulletin*, April 1981.

by the Federal Reserve in February 1980 indicated that the Federal Reserve at the time intended to seek an appreciable slowing in the growth rate of the narrower monetary aggregates. The mid-point of the M-1A range was 4.75 percent for 1980; the actual growth rate of M-1A in 1979 (fourth quarter of 1978 to fourth quarter of 1979) was 5.5 percent. For M-1B the comparable figures were 5.5 and 7.3 percent. At its mid-year review of the growth ranges selected in February, the Federal Reserve decided to maintain these ranges unchanged for the remainder of 1980.

How did the actual growth of the monetary aggregates in 1980 compare with the target growth ranges set by the Federal Reserve? The color lines in each part of Figure 26-2 show that, except for M-1A, at the end of the year the aggregates were above the upper limit of the range set by the Federal Reserve in February. Not only did three of the aggregates end the year outside the target range, but over the course of the year the growth of the narrower monetary aggregates showed extraordinarily large variations. On a quarterly basis, the growth rate of M-1A varied from 4.6 to −4.4 to 11.5 to 8.1 percent, and M-

1B from 5.8 to − 2.6 to 14.6 to 10.8 percent.[30] In the spring quarter, M-1A and M-1B were well below the bottom of the range; in the summer quarter, they were within the range; and in the fall quarter, M-1B rose well above the top of its range. The variability in monetary growth rates in 1980 was greater than it had been over any of the preceding ten years. In part this was due to unusual circumstances in 1980 like the extreme decline in economic activity—real GNP fell at a 9.9 percent annual rate from the first to the second quarter—and the disruptive effect of the Carter administration's sudden imposition of a credit control program and its removal a few months later.

In February 1981, the Federal Reserve reported to Congress its target growth ranges for 1981: M-1A, 3–5.5 percent; M-1B, 3.5–6 percent; M-2, 6–9 percent; and M-3, 6.5–9.5 percent.[31] In comparison with the 1980 targets, there is no narrowing of the ranges but a reduction of 0.5 percentage point in the upper and lower limits of the range for M-1A and M-1B and no change at all in the range for M-2 and M-3. The reduction in the M-1A and M-1B target ranges is another small step in what the Federal Reserve believes must be a slow drawn-out process of reducing the growth rate of the aggregates to noninflationary levels. How close the Federal Reserve will come to its 1981 targets, of course, will not be known until early 1982.

As this was written in early 1981, the record book shows results for the years from 1975, when the Federal Reserve first publicly announced money supply targets, to 1980. Over this period, in some years the Federal Reserve did much better in this regard than it did in 1980. How well the Federal Reserve has done overall so far is not a question that lends itself to a short or noncontroversial answer. Evaluation of how good or bad the Federal Reserve's record has been overall varies with the evaluator of that record. However, it is clear that, unlike the earlier situation, the Federal Reserve has at least given increasing attention to controlling the monetary aggregates. Before the 1970s, the guide was almost entirely interest rates, so from a long-term perspective the past decade brought a major change in Federal Reserve policy on this matter.

Controlling the Monetary Aggregates: Federal Funds Targeting and Reserve Targeting

From the time the Federal Reserve began to pay particular attention to the monetary aggregates in the early 1970s, it had tried to maintain control over the aggregates through an operating procedure now referred to as *targeting the federal funds rate.* Then, in a major change on October 6, 1979, the Federal Reserve announced a switch to what is called *targeting reserves.* The purpose of this switch was to achieve a better control over the growth of the monetary aggregates than had been realized with federal funds targeting. At the time of this writing, the new procedure had been in effect for a year and a half, and the experts did not agree as to whether the Federal Reserve would more closely achieve its growth targets for the aggregates with the new procedure of reserve targeting than it would with federal funds targeting.[32]

Before reviewing the nature of these alternative operating procedures, we must put this into perspective by recalling our earlier discussion of the money supply versus interest rates as

---

[30]See *Federal Reserve Bulletin,* March 1981, p. A3.
[31]*Ibid.,* p. 205.

[32]A large number of Federal Reserve staff papers on this question were prepared by economists within the Federal Reserve System. These papers are summarized in S.H. Axilrod, "New Monetary Control Procedure: Findings and Evaluation from a Federal Reserve Study," *Federal Reserve Bulletin,* April 1981, pp. 277–290. See also N.G. Berkman, "Bank Reserves, Money, and Some Problems for the New Monetary Policy," *New England Economic Review,* July–Aug. 1980, pp. 52–64; and C. Sivesind and K. Hurly, "Choosing an Operating Target for Monetary Policy," *Quarterly Journal of Economics,* Feb. 1980, pp. 199–204.

guides to Federal Reserve actions aimed ultimately at achieving the goals of price stability,
full employment, and the like. As we have seen,
the Federal Reserve has moved toward the
money supply or, more generally, toward monetary aggregates as a guide since the early 1970s.
The several steps Congress took in recent years
have directed the Federal Reserve to move in this
direction. However, given that the monetary
aggregates are chosen as a guide, the next issue
is the best operating procedure to achieve
selected growth ranges for the monetary aggregates. In practice, this is quite a complicated
task. The operating procedure that was used by
the Federal Reserve from the early 1970s until
October 1979 was federal funds targeting.

Federal funds are simply funds that banks
have on deposit at the Federal Reserve Banks.
At times, some banks have more or less than the
amount needed to meet legal reserve requirements. Banks that have more than they need lend
(or sell) that amount; banks that have less than
they need borrow (or buy) that amount. The interest rate on such loans—ordinarily of a one day
maturity and in large units, usually $1 million—is
known as the federal funds rate. The Federal
Reserve has closer control over the federal funds
rate than any other interest rate, because it can
raise or lower the rate in short order by increasing
or decreasing the total reserves of the banks by
an appropriate amount through open market
operations.

The link between the federal funds rate and
the growth of the money supply is found in the
demand for money. As was considered in a general framework in Chapter 11, the demand for
money is primarily a function of the dollar volume
of transactions and the interest rate. Because
data on transactions are available only with a lag,
the Federal Reserve must, in effect, "forecast"
the volume of current transactions. On the basis
of econometric estimates of the way in which the
amount of money demanded varies with transactions volume and the interest rate, given its
forecast of current transactions volume, the Federal Reserve can estimate the amount of money

that will be currently demanded at each interest
rate. Because its objective is to achieve a target
growth rate for the money supply, the final step
is to find that interest rate at which the demand
for money will be equal to the supply of money
called for by the target growth rate for money.
The interest rate determined in this way is the rate
the Federal Reserve selects as its target. The
Federal Reserve adds to or reduces the total
amount of reserves held by the banks in the
amount needed to make the actual interest rate
equal to the target rate. Because the analysis is
carried out in terms of the Federal funds rate, the
interest rate determined in this way becomes the
federal funds rate target. To the degree that
everything works out, the supply of and demand
for money will be in balance at this Federal funds
rate. Therefore, the supply of money at which this
balance exists will be that which was called for
by the money supply growth target.

As we noted earlier, the Federal Reserve
does not aim at a single-valued target for the
growth rate of any monetary aggregate, but at a
range of rates. In targeting the federal funds rate,
a range is also adopted. However, over the years
when the federal funds rate served as the target,
the Federal Reserve sought to keep the funds rate
within a relatively narrow range and to change it
slowly by small amounts in the absence of almost
incontrovertible evidence that stronger action
was appropriate. During the years just preceding
the October 6, 1979, switch in operating procedure, the Federal Reserve usually set a target
range for the funds rate no wider than 0.75 percentage points. For example, during most of the
first half of 1979, that range was 9.75 to 10.5 percent. Furthermore, with rare exceptions, the Federal Reserve kept the actual funds rate within the
designated narrow range, whereas the actual
growth rate of the monetary aggregates was
more frequently outside their growth ranges.

Whatever the degree of success the Federal
Reserve achieved through this operating procedure in earlier years, it was much less in the several years preceding October 1979. The Federal
Reserve found the growth rates of the aggre-

gates repeatedly exceeding its objectives. Because people in the financial markets had come to pay considerable attention to the Federal funds rate, the Federal Reserve felt restrained from effecting significant changes in that rate over any short period of time. Typically, adjustments in the Federal funds rate were made in steps of .25 percentage point or less from one week to the next and only occasionally as large as 1 percentage point during a month. Such stability in the Federal funds rate caused a similar degree of stability in other short-term interest rates. Under these circumstances, people in the financial markets came to believe that credit would be available continuously at an interest rate close to the prevailing rate. To the extent that the procedure of targeting the Federal funds rate gave rise to such belief, that procedure in itself could contribute to growth in the monetary aggregates in excess of what the Federal Reserve sought.

Reacting in part to monetary growth rates persistently and significantly above its target ranges through the spring and summer of 1979, the Federal Reserve announced its new operating procedure on October 6. This was one of several actions then taken to "assure better control over the expansion of money and bank credit, help curb speculative excesses in financial, foreign exchange, and commodity markets, and thereby serve to dampen inflationary forces."[33] In particular, the Federal Reserve announced the change in operating targets in the following words:

> This action involves placing greater emphasis in day-to-day operations on the supply of bank reserves and less emphasis on containing short-term fluctuations in the federal funds rate.[34]

Under the new operating procedure, the Federal Reserve permitted the federal funds rate to vary over a much wider range than before and adjusted the target range itself more promptly

than before. Deviations in the growth rates of the monetary aggregates from the targeted ranges now called forth more quickly the responses in money market conditions needed to restrain the growth of bank reserves to amounts in line with the desired growth rates of the monetary aggregates. Over the first year and a quarter following the adoption of the new operating procedure, interest rates displayed an unprecedented volatility, not all of which, however, can be attributed to the Federal Reserve's moving away from federal funds rate targeting. The federal funds rate rose from about 12 percent at the time the new procedure was announced to over 19 percent in April 1980, fell below 9 percent in July, and rose again to over 19 percent in January 1981. Accompanying these movements of the federal funds rate were very large swings in other short-term interest rates.

Greater volatility of interest rates is an inevitable consequence of the switch from federal funds targeting to reserve targeting. However, in the Federal Reserve's view, the resulting variability has not imposed appreciable costs in the form of reduced efficiency of financial markets or increased costs of capital. More of the very real strain in financial markets during 1980 could probably be attributed to the influence of a higher inflation rate and heightened inflationary expectations in raising the level of interest rates than to the Federal Reserve's new operating procedure. Whatever success or failure the new operating procedure may demonstrate after a few years, the decision to switch from federal funds targeting to reserve targeting represented a major change in the way the Federal Reserve seeks to achieve its objectives and stands as one of the principal developments in recent U.S. monetary policy.

A Concluding Note

The first page of this book began with the observation that, in an area that changes as fast as economics, anything that persists for more than

[33] *Federal Reserve Bulletin,* Oct. 1979, p. 830.
[34] *Ibid.*

a decade qualifies as "traditional." What we have done in the last chapters of this book is to consider some of the "traditional" body of thought found under the heading of macroeconomic policy. A key proposition in that body of thought is that activist fiscal and monetary policies will produce a better record of output and employment over time than will result if government stands by passively. As we have seen, there has been no shortage of dissenters to this proposition.

Foremost among these have been Milton Friedman and some other monetarists whose record of dissent can be traced back to the 1950s. In their view, there is no question that increasing or decreasing the growth rate of the money supply will have definite effects in the short run on the level of real economic activity; the issue is the inability of the Federal Reserve to use monetary policy to obtain stabilizing rather than destabilizing effects. More recent is the appearance of that school of dissenters known as the rational expectationists who maintain that the issue is not that policy actions may be destabilizing or stabilizing, but that the policy actions—unless they come as a surprise to the public—cannot affect real economic activity in the first place. There is still another school of dissenters who, unlike the rational expectationists and some monetarists, do not deny that activist monetary and fiscal policies can be typically successful, but they maintain that such policies will be unsuccessful if applied to problems which are beyond their capacity. Economists like Henry Wallich, Sidney Weintraub, and the late Arthur Okun have advanced incomes policies, specifically various types of tax-based incomes policies (TIPs), as the only practical means of dealing with the ongoing inflation problem and restoring stability to the economy. Currently, the question of whether or not there is a role for counter-cyclical policies receives altogether different answers from some of our foremost economists.

Years ago, there was almost an equal difference in the answer to the question of whether government could more closely achieve its sta-

bilization goals through fiscal or monetary policy. At the two extremes were those who believed that the economy typically operated virtually under "liquidity trap" conditions (horizontal *LM* curve) so that only fiscal policy could affect the level of output and employment and those who believed that the economy typically operated under "classical" conditions (vertical *LM* curve) so that only monetary policy could affect the level of output and employment.

Although the differences of opinion on this issue have been largely resolved, it is unlikely that the larger issue of whether or not there is a role for activist fiscal and monetary policies will be settled in the foreseeable future. During the 1950s and 1960s, the economics profession, with a few notable exceptions, accepted with little question that there is a role for stabilization policy. Since that time, more doubters have appeared, not only because more people question whether economists so far have the expertise to devise policies that will be stabilizing in effect, but also because the problem over the past decade or so has gone a good distance beyond economics into politics. Fiscal and monetary policy decisions have never been completely free of political influence, but there is reason to believe that policy decisions since the election year of 1972 have been appreciably different in election years and in years preceding election years from what they would have been in the absence of the elections.

An incumbent president and members of the controlling party in Congress will have a much better chance of winning reelection if the unemployment rate is declining and the growth rate of real GNP is rising over the months preceding an election. It is, therefore, understandable that they may strongly favor tax cuts and increased government spending before an election. Although the Federal Reserve authorities are supposed to be above political influence, the president and certain congressmen can exert considerable pressure on these people to effect the expansionary monetary policy that will improve their reelection prospects. It is not very realistic to believe that the monetary authorities are unmoved by these pressures.

If the result of the politically-induced expansionary policies were not only to raise GNP and lower unemployment but also to worsen inflation, the policies might well turn out to have been politically disadvantageous. A worsening of inflation may be as dangerous to politicians' health as a worsening of unemployment. However, the impact of expansionary policy will more likely be first on output and employment and only later on prices. If the effect on prices does not appear until after the first Tuesday in November, the expansionary policy clearly turns out to have been politically beneficial. However, if that policy later raises the inflation rate and perhaps leads to vigorous anti-inflationary policy that in turn

brings on a recession, that earlier expansionary policy turns out to have been socially harmful. The economy may end up with a political business cycle in which ups and downs in economic activity are political in origin. This is a possible phenomenon that has been much discussed since the 1972 election. To the degree that activist monetary and fiscal policies are sometimes determined not on the basis of what appears most likely to help stabilize the economy but on the basis of what seems most likely to help incumbent politicians stay in office, the chances that activist policies will be economically successful are that much diminished and the number of people who question such policies is that much enlarged. We apparently are not there yet, but the doubters may eventually be more numerous than the believers.

Index